Microsoft® Office Administrator's Desk Reference

Bill Camarda, et al.

Microsoft® Office Administrator's Desk Reference

International Standard Book Number: 0-7897-1718-2

Library of Congress Catalog Card Number: 98-85160

Printed in the United States of America

First Printing: September, 1998

00 99 98 4 3 2 1

Trademarks

All terms mentioned in this book that are known to be trademarks or service marks have been appropriately capitalized. Que Corporation cannot attest to the accuracy of this information. Use of a term in this book should not be regarded as affecting the validity of any trademark or service mark.

Warning and Disclaimer

Every effort has been made to make this book as complete and as accurate as possible, but no warranty or fitness is implied. The information provided is on an "as is" basis. The authors and the publisher shall have neither liability nor responsibility to any person or entity with respect to any loss or damages arising from the information contained in this book or from the use of the CD or programs accompanying it.

Credits

Executive Editor
Karen Reinisch

Acquisitions Editor
Don Essig

Development Editors
Heidi Steele (lead developer)
Deborah Craig

Managing Editor
Thomas F. Hayes

Project Editor
Heather E. Talbot

Copy Editors
Jill Bond
Malinda McCain

Indexer
Chris Wilcox

Technical Editor
Bill Bruns

Software Development Specialist
Andrea Duvall

Interior Designer
Ruth C. Lewis

Cover Designer
Dan Armstrong

Production
Brad Lenser
Paul Wilson

Contents at a Glance

Table of Contents

About the Author

Bill Camarda's most recent computer books include *Special Edition Using Word 97 Bestseller Edition* (Que), *The Cheapskate's Guide to Bargain Computing* (Prentice Hall PTR), *Windows Sources Word 97 for Windows SuperGuide* (Ziff-Davis Press), *Upgrading & Repairing Networks for Dummies* (IDG Press), and *Inside 1-2-3 Release 5* (New Riders Publishing). He has more than 15 years experience writing about technology for users at all levels of expertise, and for corporate clients such as IBM, AT&T, MCI, Bell Atlantic, Philips, and many others.

Dedication

To my wife, Barbara, and my son, Matthew. For all the love, all the support, and all the fun. For being who you are. For, hopefully, making me just a little bit better. For blessing my life in ways I never imagined possible.

Acknowledgments

Thanks to *everyone* at and around Que who made this book possible. That's gotta start with my hard-working, long-suffering acquisitions editor, Don Essig. (Don—we'll try to make it easier next time!) Thanks to my extremely talented, extremely supportive development editors, Heidi Steele and Deborah Craig—and my top-notch technical editors, Bill Bruns and Doug Klippert. Thanks as always to the talented copy editors, Jill Bond and Malinda McCain; project editor, Heather Talbot; and indexer, Chris Wilcox, who've worked tirelessly to make this book as accurate, readable, and convenient as possible. Thanks to some great contributing authors—without them, no book!

Thanks to the marketing, public relations, and sales teams that partner with editorial to make Que #1—and are going to sell lots of copies of this book <grin>! Thanks, big time, to my agent, Lisa Swayne!

Most important, thanks to **you** for choosing this book. I sincerely hope it'll make your life as an Office administrator easier for years to come!

Tell Us What You Think!

As the reader of this book, *you* are our most important critic and commentator. We value your opinion and want to know what we're doing right, what we could do better, what areas you'd like to see us publish in, and any other words of wisdom you're willing to pass our way.

Fax: [317-817-7070]

Mail: Macmillan Computer Publishing
201 West 103rd Street
Indianapolis, IN 46290 USA

Introduction

There are plenty of books for the casual Office user. But what about a comprehensive, independent reference for people who are responsible for *managing* Office? People whose livelihoods depend on Office working the way it's supposed to? People, in short, like *you?*

There's only one book like that, and you're holding it.

Que's *Microsoft Office Administrator's Desk Reference* is the objective guide to all the critical Office management issues you care about:

- Getting Office installed and configured as cost effectively as possible
- Integrating Office in a real-world environment that probably isn't 100% Microsoft-based
- Customizing Office so that it supports your business goals—instead of shoehorning your business into Office's default limitations
- Helping your colleagues use Office to create documents that are consistent, accurate, professional, and reflect your organization's image
- Leveraging Office's powerful workgroup capabilities to support today's fast-moving virtual teams
- Mastering the management tools, enhancements, and third-party solutions that can make Office more valuable to you
- Making sure your colleagues know how to use Office as effectively as possible—and showing them where to get fast answers when they don't
- Troubleshooting those tough Microsoft Office problems your users can't solve—or the ones they create for themselves

If you're like most people who manage Office, no two days are alike. Monday, you're troubleshooting damaged Normal.dot templates in Word. Tuesday, you're testing third-party Excel add-ins. Wednesday, you're figuring out how to use Access data on your intranet. To be successful, you need a wide range of information, much of which can't be pigeonholed into traditional "computer book" topics.

Accordingly, this 1,000-page book covers a lot of territory—bringing together a lot of information that's never been brought together before (if it even existed).

From customizing your Office installation across the network, to exporting Word files into desktop publishing programs, you'll find it here. You'll discover strategies for managing the development and review of large documents and presentations by multiple authors. You'll learn how to use Microsoft's Excel plug-ins to access worksheets on your intranet—even if you've standardized on Netscape Communicator instead of Internet Explorer.

It's an eclectic mix, but you've got an eclectic job!

Who Should Read This Book?

This book is for you, if

- You're a system administrator or other technology professional responsible for managing Office on a network or in a mobile environment
- You're an office manager or other business professional who is responsible for making sure your colleagues can work with Microsoft Office effectively

- You're responsible for providing Office support or training, either formally (through a Help Desk or training department) or informally
- You're responsible for a publishing organization or other production environment that uses Word and Office to produce large documents, and may use Office together with desktop publishing software
- You're in a cross-platform organization with users working on both Windows and Macintosh systems
- You're a Web professional who wants to use Office documents on your Web or intranet site
- You're an Office "power user" who often finds yourself helping other Office users throughout your company or organization
- You're an Office Visual Basic for Applications (VBA) developer who needs information on deploying your custom applications effectively

How This Book Is Organized

Microsoft Office Administrator's Desk Reference is organized in seven parts.

Part I: Managing Installation and Deployment

The book begins with a close look at what it takes to install and configure Office so that it best meets the needs of your organization. You'll walk through the planning process and review your options for streamlining installation—including scripted installations across the network, and automating installations with Microsoft's System Management Server.

In Part I, you'll also learn about recent Service Releases and other upgrades Microsoft has made available to resolve known bugs—and revamp a few of Office 97's less practical features. You'll walk through network installations of both Microsoft Office 97 for Windows and Microsoft Office 98 for the Macintosh. Finally, you'll learn practical techniques for troubleshooting failed installations.

Part II: Customizing Office to Your Organization's Needs

In Part II, you'll learn specific ways to customize each of Office's major applications to your organization's needs: Word, Excel, PowerPoint, Access, and Outlook. You'll learn how to customize user interfaces and toolsets to make important features more accessible and eliminate features you don't want to support.

You'll learn how to customize Office applications at startup via Autoexec macros, and how to deploy productivity options such as custom dictionaries and AutoText lists. Finally, you'll take a close look at Outlook, arguably the most malleable personal information manager ever created—and understand your options for customizing Outlook (with and without Microsoft Exchange).

Part III: Using Office to Support Teams and Workgroups

Nowadays, few documents, worksheets, or presentations are created solely by a single individual. In Part III, you'll learn all you need to help Office users work together as teams. You'll learn how to organize and streamline the work of creating and reviewing documents, worksheets, presentations, and databases; and how to share schedules and corporate address books built with Microsoft Outlook.

Part IV: Integrating Office in Your Heterogeneous Environment

Notwithstanding the hype, few organizations use 100% Microsoft technology. And even those organizations often face the challenge of managing multiple versions of Office applications—with their multiple file formats. Part IV shows how to integrate Office into your real-world environment.

Whether you're introducing Word into a law office that has used WordPerfect 5.1 for DOS since Ronald Reagan was President of the United States; trying to figure out why RTF files suddenly don't import into PageMaker properly; managing mixed Windows/Macintosh environments; or using Excel worksheets with Lotus Notes, you'll find practical solutions here. You'll also learn about Microsoft ValuePack add-ons and third-party products that can help you solve problems Office won't solve by itself.

Part V: Office, the Internet, and Intranets

More than ever before, organizations distribute the bulk of their information electronically—internally, via intranets, and externally via Web sites. Much (if not most) of that information is originally created in Microsoft Office. In Part V, you'll walk through your company's extensive options for getting Office-based information onto the Web—from saving Office documents as HTML to running live Internet presentations with NetShow and PowerPoint. You'll also look at Outlook from another perspective: as Microsoft's latest "preferred" Internet email and news client.

Part VI: Superior Techniques for Managing Office

Microsoft Office doesn't exist in a vacuum: It exists in real organizations with real challenges, opportunities, risks, schedules, and budgets. In Part VI, you'll learn techniques that can make Office a better "citizen" of the organization. You'll learn how to lower the cost of operating Office; make Office more secure; resist macro virus infections; raise productivity by providing better support without spending more; support your increasingly mobile base of Office users; and manage Office in international, even global organizations. Last but not least, you'll consider Office Y2K compliance issues, determine whether you're at risk, and learn how to address any problems that may exist.

Part VII: Troubleshoot and Optimize Office

Finally, Part VII brings together detailed, up-to-date troubleshooting information for each major Office application. You'll find just enough "theory" to help you understand how each Office application is designed and structured—so you can "reason out" solutions to the problems that aren't covered here. The book wraps up with a detailed look at additional resources—Microsoft and otherwise—that can help you identify and troubleshoot even more problems.

Part VIII: Appendixes

To enhance this book, you receive three supplementary appendixes. The first appendix lists what you'll find on the CD-ROM, including several types of software and the vendors from whom you can obtain the software. Appendix A also describes the four Que books you'll find on the CD-ROM. Appendix B provides an Office 97 file list and reference table, and Appendix C provides the updated Office 98 file list and reference table.

How This Book Is Designed

Que works hard to make sure its books deliver the quickest possible access to the most relevant information—and this book is no exception. In addition to the table of contents at the front of the book, each chapter begins with its own summary table of contents, helping you target the precise information you're looking for. At the back of the book, you'll find an exceptionally detailed index. And throughout the book, you'll find icons flagging several types of information designed to add value:

Tips point out shortcuts, ideas, and techniques for managing Office that you might not discover on your own.

NOTE Notes offer a closer look at some Office features or issues you may want to know more about—without distracting you from the fast answers you're looking for.

CAUTION

Cautions help you avoid Microsoft Office management and feature pitfalls that can cost your organization both time and money.

ON THE WEB

On the Web references point you to Web addresses with more specific information you may find valuable. For instance, **http://www.microsoft.com/Office/Office97/documents/isvs/** connects you with a list of third-party "Microsoft Office Compatible" products that look and work like Office. (Incidentally, you can learn more about several of these products in Chapter 27.)

What's on the CD-ROM

Bound into the inside back cover of this book, you'll find the *Microsoft Office Administrator's Desk Reference* CD-ROM—an extraordinary resource whether or not you support or use Office.

If you're running Office 97 and you aren't running Microsoft's Service Release patch, you'll find it here, courtesy of Microsoft. In addition, you'll find an extensive library of converters and other utilities to enhance Office 97 (and Office 95) and make them easier to manage.

Better yet, you'll also find four complete, best-selling, easy-to-search Que best-sellers on the CD-ROM:

- *Migrating to Office 95 and Office 97: A Corporate User's Quick Reference,* by Laura Monsen—a great task-oriented reference that can help you ease your users' migration to the latest versions of Office.
- *Windows 95 and NT 4.0 Registry & Customization Handbook,* by Jerry Honeycutt, Bernard Farrell, Rich Kennelly, and Jerry Millsaps—not just a detailed reference to Windows Registry keys, but a thorough guide to Registry security, with practical explanations of the System Policy Editor, Registry Editor, and even Registry programming with Microsoft C++ and Visual Basic.
- *Sams Teach Yourself Project 98 in 24 Hours,* by Tim Pyron—the quickest way to learn Project. If you're getting ready to deploy Office 97, this book is the fastest way to master Project, and take advantage of Microsoft's free Project-based deployment planning files.
- *Sams Teach Yourself Publisher 98 in 24 Hours,* by Ned Snell—provides basic product features and general desktop publishing and design techniques that help the reader use and customize templates for a variety of publications.

If you were to buy these books separately, you'd pay nearly twice the price of this book alone—but they're yours, free, with the Microsoft Office Administrator's Desk Reference.

Conventions Used in This Book

Que *Desk Reference* and *Special Edition* books share typographical conventions that make them easy to understand—once you've read one, you're right at home with all the others.

For example, you may read about key combinations such as Ctrl+Y, Office's standard shortcut for repeating the last command. Ctrl+Y means hold down the Control key, press Y, and then release both keys.

Also, when you're instructed to select a menu item, you'll find the menu name and item have one letter underlined. For example, to display Word's Print dialog box, select File, Print.

Here is some other formatted text you may run across:

- Internet addresses are specified in boldface, for example, **www.microsoft.com**. If a Web address must continue on the following line due to page width restrictions, the address will be divided at the backslash. This indicates that the same Web address continues on the following line due to page width restrictions, but that you should treat it as one line of text, without pressing Enter or entering spaces. You can see this in the following example:

  http://www.yahoo.com/headlines/970803/business/stories/ups_6.html
- Terms introduced and defined for the first time are formatted in *italic*, as in the following example:

  A *toolbar* is a set of buttons that perform related tasks.

- Text formatted in boldface may also represent type that should be entered verbatim, as in the following example:

  Or if you prefer, you can tell users to run Setup using a command line such as:

  setup.exe /q1 /b1.

- Finally, text formatted in "typewriter" type represents code listings, such as Visual Basic for Applications program listings, as in the following example:

```
Sub Macro7()
'
' Macro7 Macro
' Macro recorded 07/10/98 by Bill Camarda
'
  Selection.Font.Bold = wdToggle
End Sub
```

As an Office professional, you're responsible for the software tools your colleagues depend on most. You have unique leverage within your organization: You can dramatically improve everyone's productivity by managing Office more effectively. This book will show you how. ●

PART I

Managing Installation and Deployment

CHAPTER 1

Planning Your Office Installation

If you're responsible for deploying Microsoft Office 97 for Windows, Office 98 for the Macintosh, or the versions of Office that follow, your success depends in large part on your initial planning.

In this chapter, you walk through the planning steps that you consider prior to implementing Office in your organization, and identify resources you can use to streamline the process.

Understanding Your Goals for Office

In determining how (and whether) to deploy the latest versions of Office, begin by considering what you hope to achieve by the upgrade. Potential reasons to upgrade include the following:

- *Improved productivity.* May result from Office 97/98's new automated features, increased intuitiveness, and the new Outlook personal information manager
- *Lower support costs.* This is due to Office 97/98's improved help system, including the Office Assistant and natural language help
- *Lower cost of ownership.* May result through centralized user profiles and system policies, and support for the Zero Administration Kit
- *Better team support.* Results through Office 97/98's new workgroup features, such as Excel workbook sharing, and (in Windows) PowerPoint presentation conferencing over the Web
- *Better integration with your intranet, Web site, and extranets.* This is possible via new HTML authoring tools, Excel Web form wizards, and other new features
- *Better support for 32-bit custom development.* This is possible through the integrated Visual Basic for Applications development environment, newly extended to Word, PowerPoint, and Outlook

As you might expect, Microsoft has done an excellent job of quickly marshalling the arguments for upgrading. At **www.microsoft.com/office/tco** the following tools and resources are collected:

- *The TCO & ROI Desktop Advisor.* A set of Excel worksheets that enable you to calculate the potential savings associated with upgrading to Office 97 from 16-bit Office 4.x applications (see Figure 1.1).
- A study by The Giga Group, a consulting firm, on the costs and benefits of migrating to Office 97 at 14 large organizations that migrated shortly after Office 97 was introduced.

  In this study, funded by Microsoft, The Giga Group found that Office 97 reduced training time from 13.1 to 8.8 hours and reduced help desk costs by 22 percent in the first few months, with a potential total reduction of 30 percent. Giga also found that the Office Assistant help tool was responding successfully to 75 percent of user inquiries, a number that seems a little on the high side. Finally, Giga found that upgrading to Office 97 required a hardware upgrade of approximately 20 percent of all systems intende to run it (typically, to add memory).
- An International Data Corporation White Paper presenting case studies showing how Office 97's new workgroup and intranet collaboration tools can make companies more competitive and drive down costs through easier access to information on intranets, replacement of email gateways with the Outlook/Microsoft Exchange combination, and support for streamlining many business processes.

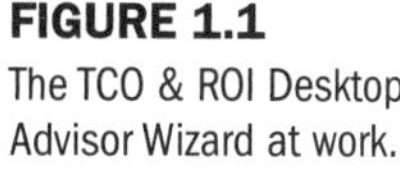

FIGURE 1.1
The TCO & ROI Desktop Advisor Wizard at work.

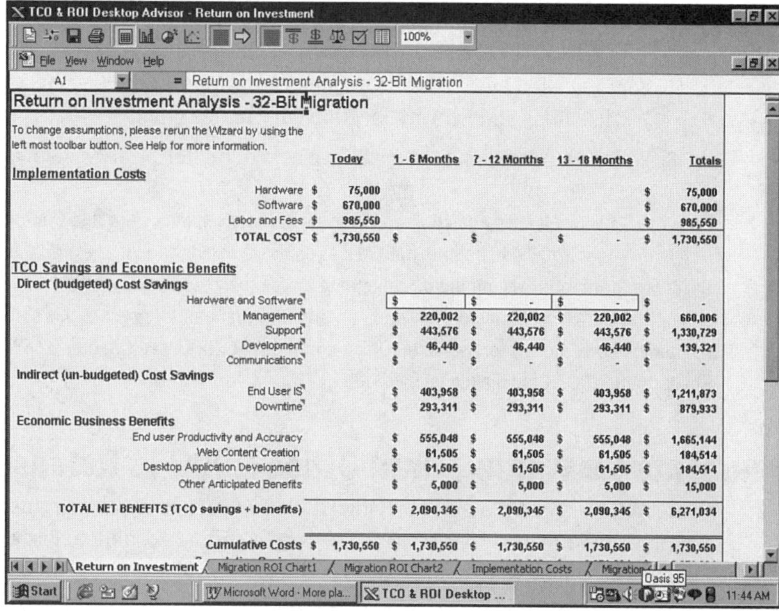

	Today	1 - 6 Months	7 - 12 Months	13 - 18 Months	Totals
Implementation Costs					
Hardware	$ 75,000				$ 75,000
Software	$ 670,000				$ 670,000
Labor and Fees	$ 985,550				$ 985,550
TOTAL COST	$ 1,730,550	$ -	$ -	$ -	$ 1,730,550
TCO Savings and Economic Benefits					
Direct (budgeted) Cost Savings					
Hardware and Software		$ -	$ -	$ -	$ -
Management		$ 220,002	$ 220,002	$ 220,002	$ 660,006
Support		$ 443,576	$ 443,576	$ 443,576	$ 1,330,729
Development		$ 46,440	$ 46,440	$ 46,440	$ 139,321
Communications		$ -	$ -	$ -	$ -
Indirect (un-budgeted) Cost Savings					
End User IS		$ 403,958	$ 403,958	$ 403,958	$ 1,211,873
Downtime		$ 293,311	$ 293,311	$ 293,311	$ 879,933
Economic Business Benefits					
End user Productivity and Accuracy		$ 555,048	$ 555,048	$ 555,048	$ 1,665,144
Web Content Creation		$ 61,505	$ 61,505	$ 61,505	$ 184,514
Desktop Application Development		$ 61,505	$ 61,505	$ 61,505	$ 184,514
Other Anticipated Benefits		$ 5,000	$ 5,000	$ 5,000	$ 15,000
TOTAL NET BENEFITS (TCO savings + benefits)		$ 2,090,345	$ 2,090,345	$ 2,090,345	$ 6,271,034
Cumulative Costs	$ 1,730,550	$ 1,730,550	$ 1,730,550	$ 1,730,550	$ 1,730,550

- A help desk study by Technology Business Research indicating that 60 percent of users are likely to use the Office 97 help system and that the help system solves their problems 51 percent of the time. The study also shows that Office 97 leads to a reduction in technician site visits of 5–11 percent, netting out to a support savings of approximately $58 per user per year in a large organization.
- A study by the Kelly Services temporary employee company showing that users were 32 percent faster at completing tasks accurately with Office 97 than with Office 4.3, and that the percentage of users who could complete tasks accurately increased by 36 percent with Office 97.

Arguments Against Upgrading Office

It is conceivable that none of the arguments described in the previous section are compelling reasons to upgrade from Office 4.2 or 4.3. Your organization may be reluctant to upgrade if any of the following situations apply to you:

- Your users have barely scratched the surface of the features available in their current version of Office (the 32-bit Office 95 suite or the 16-bit Office 4.x suite).
- You handle Web or intranet publishing through a specialized group of employees; you do not need or want to provide HTML publishing tools to all your users.
- You are still running Windows 3.x on many of your workstations, and you have an extensive base of 16-bit custom applications that you're not prepared to upgrade.

- You've established a long-term direction away from Windows PCs and toward Java-based network computers.
- Your installed base of hardware does not support Office 97/98 (see the "Inventorying Workstations and Servers" section later in this chapter).
- Your organization has other IT projects of higher priority, such as Y2K upgrades.

NOTE Microsoft Office has its own Y2K issues. Older versions Word and PowerPoint are not strictly Year 2000 compatible, but unless you make extensive use of WordBasic macros, you're unlikely to have too many problems continuing to use these packages past the year 2000. You need to carefully evaluate Excel macros, however, on an individual basis. Access 2.0 is simply not Y2K compatible. (For more information on Office and the Year 2000, see Chapter 37, "Managing Office-Related Year 2000 Compliance Issues.")

Arguments for Waiting Until Office 2000 Is Released

Some of the arguments for deploying Office 97/98 now are also arguments for postponing an upgrade until the next version of Office is released. According to early published reports, Office 2000 will be released late in 1998 or early in 1999, and will include these improvements:

- A componentized architecture that gives the Office administrator unprecedented flexibility over what can be installed where
- Significantly improved Web/intranet integration, including XML support
- Further improvements in the natural language help system to reduce users' dependence on help desks
- Stronger integration with BackOffice applications, such as Systems Management Server and Microsoft Exchange

The internal business requirements that drive your upgrade schedule may well drive it past the introduction of Office 2000. For example, if you work in a manufacturing organization, it's unlikely that you'll plan a major Office upgrade at the same time you're retooling your plant for a new product. If you support the IT needs of an accounting firm, it's unlikely that you'll upgrade Office during tax season. By the time your business is ready to upgrade, Office 97/98 may have been replaced.

Coordinating with the rest of your IT strategy could also lead to a delay. For example, some organizations will roll out Office 2000 and Windows NT Workstation 5.0 (expected in mid-1999) concurrently, thereby lowering the cost of deployment by performing only a single rollout. You may also want to time your upgrade to correlate with new hardware purchases or leases so that you can deploy Office at the same time that you deploy your hardware. This also gives you the option of deploying Office first on the hardware most capable of running it well.

Evaluating the Costs of Deploying Office

If, after considering these issues, deploying Office 97 appears to offer financial or competitive benefits, your next step is to evaluate the costs associated with deployment. These include the following:

- *Office software*. Take into account participation in corporate volume discount programs such as Microsoft Open License Program, which is available for companies purchasing software for 25 or more desktops; or Microsoft Select, which offers tiered, volume discounts based on your organization's total two-year forecast of acquisitions within a category of products.
- *Third-party software that must also be updated*. Includes foreign language dictionaries and vertical market add-in products
- *Costs for planning and deployment*. Includes costs of setting up a test lab, trial rollouts, and managing the rollout process
- *Additional hardware requirements*. For example, memory or processor upgrades and the cost of visiting the desktop to perform those upgrades
- *Costs associated with updating custom software*. These are a factor especially if you are upgrading from 16-bit applications
- *Additional server and bandwidth capacity if Office 97 is to be run from the network*. Includes the costs of deploying these (over and above network enhancements you would have made anyway)
- *Costs of training and support*. Includes in-person training, computer-based training, Microsoft and third-party books and videos, retraining of help desk personnel, and communication with users

For more information about supporting Microsoft Office, see Chapter 34, "Supporting Office."

After you've compared costs and benefits, you can make the decision to deploy or not, based on these questions:

- Based on your comparison of costs and benefits, how quickly will Office 97 pay for itself?
- How does that payoff compare with the other IT projects competing for your limited time and resources?
- Actually install Office 97 and get yourself familiar with it. What do your instincts tell you? Which of these features do you envision your users working with? Are other features impractical for your organization? What do your best help desk people think about it?
- Finally, what (if any) are the costs of not upgrading—costs in lost productivity and potential competitive disadvantage?

The Deployment Planning Process

If, after you've performed the cost/benefit analysis described in the previous section, you've concluded that deploying Office 97 (or Office 98 for the Macintosh) makes sense, the next step is to plan the deployment.

Microsoft uses the acronym SMART to describe the goals of planning. Your plan should be specific, measurable, achievable, results-based (with realistic outcomes), and time-oriented (with realistic schedules and milestones). Your plan should also:

- Reflect a risk assessment that identifies potential obstacles, the likelihood of these obstacles causing problems, and contingency/fallback plans.
- Specify which resources will be available to handle each step.
- Be thoroughly documented, with feedback mechanisms in place to improve future rollouts. The documentation should be in a form that can be used to support future rollouts as well—for instance, a Systems Management Server equipment database that can also be leveraged in operating systems upgrades.

Gathering Resources for Planning

Microsoft has published a number of documents that can help you avoid reinventing the wheel as you plan your Office 97/98 rollout.

The Microsoft Office Deployment Planner, at **www.microsoft.com/office/ork/appa/appa.htm#dex51**, includes predefined steps, timetables, and schedules in both Microsoft Project and Microsoft Excel, as shown in Figure 1.2.

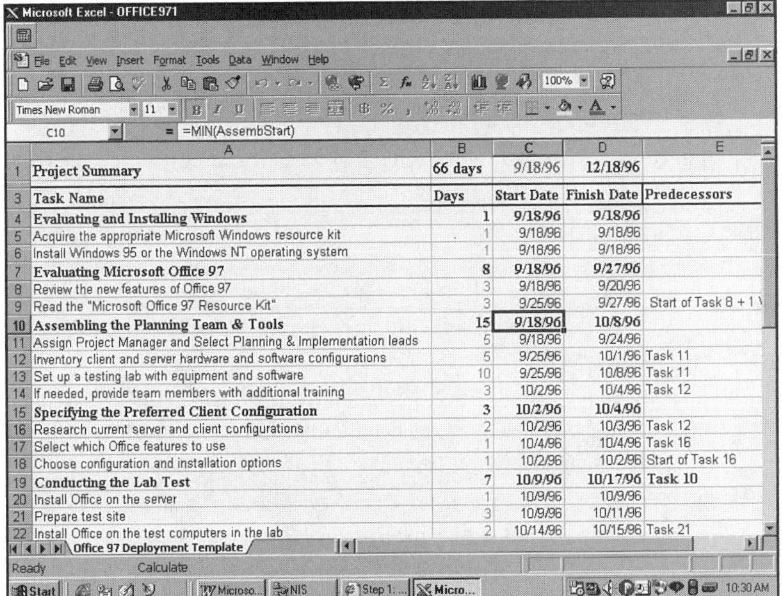

	A	B	C	D	E
1	Project Summary	66 days	9/18/96	12/18/96	
3	Task Name	Days	Start Date	Finish Date	Predecessors
4	Evaluating and Installing Windows	1	9/18/96	9/18/96	
5	Acquire the appropriate Microsoft Windows resource kit	1	9/18/96	9/18/96	
6	Install Windows 95 or the Windows NT operating system	1	9/18/96	9/18/96	
7	Evaluating Microsoft Office 97	8	9/18/96	9/27/96	
8	Review the new features of Office 97	3	9/18/96	9/20/96	
9	Read the "Microsoft Office 97 Resource Kit"	3	9/25/96	9/27/96	Start of Task 8 + 1 \
10	Assembling the Planning Team & Tools	15	9/18/96	10/8/96	
11	Assign Project Manager and Select Planning & Implementation leads	5	9/18/96	9/24/96	
12	Inventory client and server hardware and software configurations	5	9/25/96	10/1/96	Task 11
13	Set up a testing lab with equipment and software	10	9/25/96	10/8/96	Task 11
14	If needed, provide team members with additional training	3	10/2/96	10/4/96	Task 12
15	Specifying the Preferred Client Configuration	3	10/2/96	10/4/96	
16	Research current server and client configurations	2	10/2/96	10/3/96	Task 12
17	Select which Office features to use	1	10/4/96	10/4/96	Task 16
18	Choose configuration and installation options	1	10/2/96	10/2/96	Start of Task 16
19	Conducting the Lab Test	7	10/9/96	10/17/96	Task 10
20	Install Office on the server	1	10/9/96	10/9/96	
21	Prepare test site	3	10/9/96	10/11/96	
22	Install Office on the test computers in the lab	2	10/14/96	10/15/96	Task 21

FIGURE 1.2
The Microsoft Office Deployment Planner, running in Microsoft Excel.

The *Deploying Microsoft Office 97 Service Guide* presents a Microsoft framework for assessing your needs, building planning, development, and deployment teams; identifying dependencies, avoiding risks, producing complete plans; addressing technical and business issues; and planning for maintainability, supportability, and reliability. Designed primarily for Office rollouts of 10,000 users or more, this service guide is also valuable to smaller companies. The service guide is available from Microsoft at 800-255-8414 for $49.95 plus shipping and handling.

You can find additional Microsoft resources from the Enterprise Desktop Information Center, Implementing Microsoft Office Page at **www.microsoft.com/office/org/implement**.

Creating an Office Deployment Team

In a sizable organization, you need to establish a team with clear individual responsibilities, led by a project manager with clear authority and the support of management. This team should include most or all of the following:

- IT experts familiar with the organization's enterprise computing architecture
- Microsoft Office and Microsoft operating system platform specialists
- Members of user organizations
- Support and training specialists
- Network administrators
- Security specialists
- Internal custom software developers

Don't neglect to provide any up-front training that your team members need in order to be effective participants in Office planning and implementation.

Inventorying Workstations and Servers

When your team is in place, begin the process of inventorying the workstations and servers you expect to run Office 97. Are they powerful enough? Do some need to be upgraded with more memory? Do some have to be upgraded from Windows 3.1? Do other systems need to be replaced? Establish a testing lab with representative computers and software, and begin evaluating the performance you can actually expect.

Consider using the Office 97 or NT 5.0 rollout as an opportunity to standardize hardware, limiting the number of vendors and technologies your IT organization must support.

Table 1.1 presents Microsoft's stated system requirements for Windows, along with a more realistic view of what you need to achieve decent performance with Office. Of course, these estimates are only a starting point. Take into account issues that are specific to your organization, such as:

- The complexity of work your users do
- Any custom applications that must integrate with Office
- Your network's performance, especially if you are planning to deploy some or all of Office on network servers instead of client workstations

Table 1.1 Office 97 for Windows System Requirements

Requirement	Minimum	Realistic
Processor	Any 486	486/100, Pentium 60
Operating System	Win95/NT 3.51 with SP-5	Win95/NT 4.0 with SP-2 (for SR-1)
Memory (Win95)	8MB; 12MB to run Access	24MB; 32MB to run Access
Memory (WinNT)	16MB	32–64MB
Hard Disk Space	92–210MB	92–210MB Needed for Office 97 files
CD-ROM Drive	Yes	Can run from network without CD-ROM drive
Video	VGA; SVGA	SVGA recommended

Table 1.2 presents Microsoft's stated minimum and practical system requirements for Office 98 Macintosh Edition. Microsoft's estimates seem fairly realistic, except that some early users have noted that individual Office applications seem to run better with more memory assigned to them than these estimates might permit, especially when creating large, complex documents, worksheets, or presentations.

Table 1.2 Office 98 for Macintosh System Requirements

Requirement	Minimum	Realistic
Processor	Any PowerPC	PowerPC 120 MHz
Operating System	MacOS 7.5	MacOS 7.5.5 preferably MacOS 8.1
Memory	16MB	32MB
Hard Disk Space	49–120MB	100–120MB
CD-ROM Drive	Yes (or install from network)	Yes (or install from network)
Monitor	16 grays or 256 colors, 640 x 400	16 grays or 256 colors, 640 x 400

Specifying Client Configurations

At this stage, you can begin to identify the appropriate version of Office 97/98 for each workgroup or constituency in your organization. Currently six versions of Office are targeted to a variety of audiences, from small business to developers. Table 1.3 lists the products included in each edition.

Table 1.3 Versions of Office and Their Components

Component	Prof. Edition	Standard Edition	Small Bus. Edition	Devel. Edition	Macintosh Edition	Macintosh Gold Edition (Retail Only)
Access	X			X		
Bookshelf						X
Bookshelf Basics	*					
Development Tools				X		
Encarta 98 Deluxe						X
Excel	X	X	X	X	X	X
FrontPage						X
Outlook	X	X	X	X		
Outlook Express					X	X
PowerPoint	X	X		X	X	X
Publisher			X			
Small Business Financial Manager			X			
Streets 98			X			
Visual SourceSafe				X		
Word	X	X	X	X	X	X

**Optional*

Keep in mind opportunities to reduce costs. For instance, in many organizations, relatively few users need access to Microsoft Access databases; these companies may save money by purchasing more Standard Edition licenses and fewer Professional Edition licenses.

Beyond specifying the correct version of Office, you can also make preliminary choices about the features your users do and do not need. For example, consider which of the following features (or subsets of features) can be included or removed from the default installation:

- Web authoring tools
- Database querying tools and drivers
- File import and export filters (as well as default file formats to be used by Office 97 users)
- ValuPack applications, such as Microsoft Photo Editor and Microsoft Camcorder
- Document templates (and custom templates you may create)
- Help system components, such as help for writing Visual Basic for Applications programs

Choosing the Best Approach to Installation

Office 97 provides a variety of installation options, including the following:

- Local installation on each client workstation, from CD-ROM, disks, or removable media
- Installation to local client workstations across the network, either automatically or with varying amounts of user intervention
- Network installations that require users to have access to a server in order to use some or all of Office's features
- Customized installations via scripts built with the Network Installation Wizard
- Installation with System Policies that customize and limit how users can work with Office applications
- Installation with Microsoft Systems Management Server or another desktop management tool

At this stage, your team should decide which of these options are the most cost-efficient, the least disruptive, and the easiest to use, given the technical and financial resources available to you. (For more information about customized network installation scripts and installing with Systems Management Server, see Chapter 2, "Scripting and Automating Office Installations.")

Testing Office in the Lab

Now that you have a pretty good idea of how you'd like to deploy Office to your users, put your plan to the test in the lab before you try it out on real users:

- Test the installation process on both servers and representative client workstations
- Write and debug any installation scripts you need
- Test the uninstall process on representative workstations
- Test existing macros and add-ins (now might also be a good time to test for Y2K compliance in custom macros and VBA code, as discussed in Chapter 37)
- Test workstation and server performance working with representative files

Planning and Running a Pilot Rollout

At this point, you're ready to pilot your Office 97 rollout. Working with your user representatives, identify a workgroup or department that

- Is at least moderately receptive to new technology
- Is not facing an unusually challenging business deadline
- Has management willing to support the pilot rollout

NOTE Some organizations run prepilot rollouts with even smaller groups.

Before installing Office 97 on pilot systems, do the following:

- Communicate clearly and specifically with the users who will be affected.
- Develop plans for training the users and providing help desk support. (Unfortunately, many companies neglect this step until the enterprise-wide rollout—causing many more problems during the pilot process than are necessary.)
- Determine who will be responsible for each aspect of the pilot rollout.
- Schedule the pilot rollout to minimize business disruption.

After the rollout, carefully evaluate the results, asking the following:

- Did your systems for automated installation work? In other words, did Office install properly, with the proper features, at the correct times?
- Did your systems for support and training work? Did you get more (or fewer) support calls than you expected?
- How did the time and cost of the pilot rollout compare with what you expected?
- What did your users like (and dislike) about the rollout process?
- What do they like (and dislike) about Office 97 now that they're running it?

Learning Lessons for Organization-Wide Rollout

Based on the answers to these questions, adjust your plans for your enterprise-wide rollout as follows:

- Revise your budgets and staffing to reflect what you now know about schedules, support, and rollout costs.
- Revise network installation scripts and other key customization.
- Finalize your enterprise communications plans so that users will know exactly what to expect.
- Establish a final phased deployment plan for the business units that you intend to upgrade, based on business constraints, receptiveness to technology, and other issues—who should be upgraded first, next, last, or not at all?

- Update your policies and procedures guidelines to reflect the forthcoming rollout.
- Make arrangements to purchase and take delivery of the software and hardware you need.
- Prepare and communicate a detailed schedule with milestones and timelines that take into account contingencies and holidays.
- Get final management approvals, as needed.

Rolling Out Office 97 Enterprise-Wide

Finally, you're ready to roll out Office 97 enterprise-wide. Start by running administrative installations on each of your servers, as explained in detail in Chapter 2.

Next, communicate with users, telling them the following:

- What to expect
- Where to get more information if they need it
- When the upgrade will happen, and what impact it may have on them
- Whether there are steps that the users need to perform, such as logging on to a server and running the installation from the desktop

If individual workstations must be upgraded, or if incompatible software must be removed from them, do so—either centrally, through Systems Management Server or another desktop management package, or locally at each client workstation. Check to make sure that all network permissions are in place. Finally, install Office using whichever techniques you've chosen and tested.

Of course, rolling out Office 97 doesn't end the process; you need to closely monitor its impact, both to improve future phases of the rollout and to enhance user support and productivity. Check the following:

- Is your feedback process working to ensure that users and managers can communicate problems and opportunities for improvement? Similarly, do you have a way to replicate successes with Office throughout the enterprise?
- With which features are users having trouble? Can more computer-based (or other) training be provided to support these features?
- Are there features, such as workgroup features, where you expected more widespread usage than you're seeing? If so, what communications methods are available to evangelize these features?
- What additional templates and sample documents can you provide?
- Can you improve coordination with departmental and workgroup managers in later phases of the rollout, or later rollouts?
- Finally, have you documented your own successes and failures in terms of automating rollout processes with system policies, user profiles, installation scripts, and Systems Management Server?

CHAPTER 2

Scripting and Automating Office Installations

Now that you've done the high-level planning associated with deploying Microsoft Office 97, you're ready to plan and run the installation process itself.

You can choose from several approaches to installing Office. In choosing the right alternative for your organization, you will need to balance "empowering" your users with greater autonomy (and possibly higher performance) against the potential lower support costs associated with central control.

For instance, if you specify in advance exactly which Office components are to be installed on every workstation, you can largely avoid worrying about supporting components that are not installed. (As an example, if none of your users needs photo-editing capabilities, you can avoid installing the optional Microsoft Photo Editor.) However, if your users are called upon to perform a wide variety of tasks that you cannot always predict in advance, installing Office this way may actually cause more support problems: you may be repeatedly called upon to add components piece by piece. In such an environment, it may make more sense to allow users to customize their own Office installations.

Similarly, as will be covered later in this chapter, you can install Office locally at individual workstations; or centrally, to be run from a server (trading performance for manageability).

In the following sections, you will walk through the key choices you make as you install Microsoft Office 97. Reading these sections will help you determine the type of installation you want to use and the features and characteristics you want your Office 97 systems to have.

Choosing Installation Types

At the outset, the Microsoft Office 97 setup program presents you with a key, high-level decision about how you will install and run Office. You can choose from four types of installations: Typical, Custom, Run from CD-ROM, and (if you are installing across a network) Run from Network Server.

Here are the types of installations in greater detail:

- **Typical**—This option installs the applications and components that Microsoft believes most users will need. If you make this choice, you will not be asked to select specific components.
- **Custom**—This option gives you the most control, allowing you to select the specific components you want to install. Unless you intend to have users run their own installations, you will almost certainly want to choose this option and define, in advance, the components you want to install.
- **Run from CD-ROM**—This option allows users to install a relatively small number of files on their hard drives (to save space) and access the remaining files as needed from the original CD-ROM. Because this option assumes each user will have access to an Office CD-ROM, and because it results in relatively poor application performance, it is rarely a reasonable choice in the corporate environment. This option is not available for installations from a network server.
- **Run from Network Server**—In this option, crucial files are installed on the user's individual workstation, but less crucial (or commonly used) files are installed on the network server, with pointers to those files added where necessary. This approach can give the network administrator a great deal more control over how Office is deployed and upgraded. As always, however, there are tradeoffs. Table 2.1 presents the advantages and disadvantages of running Office from a network server.

Table 2.1 Installing Locally Versus Sharing Microsoft Office Over the Network

Issues to Consider	Locally Installed	Shared on the Network
Disk space	Takes up space on the users' computer.	Requires increased disk space on the server.
Maintenance and support	When installing updates, the change would have to be made at all the computers individually.	When installing updates, the change can be made at one location. This saves a considerable amount of time.

Issues to Consider	Locally Installed	Shared on the Network
Network offline	If the network is offline, users can continue to run programs installed on their computers.	If the network is offline, users would not be able to run programs that they share over the network.
Performance	Users typically would be able to run Office applications faster.	Typically, Office applications will run slower over a network.

The option Run from CD-ROM uses predefined settings that list which components will be installed on a user's local hard disk and which will not.

NOTE According to Microsoft's published white papers, the forthcoming Office 2000 will offer much more control to the network administrator.

For example, administrators will be able to choose whether each individual component will reside on a local hard drive or server. The administrator will even be able to specify that a component be "Installed on Demand"–in other words, installed from the server the first time a user tries to invoke it.

Choosing Installation Methods

Now that you've decided how Office 97 will run, you must decide how you will handle the installation process itself. You have three options:

- You can run the installation from each machine individually using the CD-ROM. Because this method assumes that you or a colleague will be physically present at each computer, it is rarely efficient in large organizations.
- You can install from the network, creating a customized script that defines the user's installation options. The user still chooses when to upgrade, but the administrator can decide whether to give the user any flexibility in *how* to upgrade. This is called a "pull" installation because the user pulls the software from the network server onto his or her workstation.
- You can install from the network with no user involvement at all via a "push" installation. Typically, you edit each user's logon script to run the Office setup program when the user next logs on to the computer. The installation can happen in the background (in "quiet mode"), giving the user no input. You may also use desktop management software such as Microsoft's Systems Management Server to perform push installations on a predefined schedule—preferably at night, or on the weekend, when there will be less disruption.

> **CAUTION**
>
> If you choose to run Office installations from users' network logon scripts, be careful to stagger the installations so as not to degrade network performance. Remember that morning and afternoon are typically times of high activity on the network. If every logon also triggers a 200-300MB Office installation on the same morning, network performance may rapidly deteriorate to an unacceptable level.

Uninstalling Previous Versions of Office Applications

Prior to installing Microsoft Office 97, some network administrators choose to remove older versions of Microsoft Office, thereby minimizing conflicts.

The Microsoft Office 97 CD-ROM contains a tool—the Microsoft Office Upgrade Wizard (Offcln97.exe)—designed for this purpose. The Upgrade Wizard can remove not only old Office files, but also old Office-related registry entries, Windows 3.x INI file entries, Start menu items, and Program Manager items. It can identify files from Microsoft Office versions 4.x and 95; Project 4.0 and 95; Publisher 2.0, 3.0, and 4.0; and Team Manager 97.

You can find the wizard in the \Valupack\Offclean folder. When you run it, the wizard presents you with three alternatives (see Figure 2.1). No matter which option you choose, the Wizard will show you a list of files it intends to delete, and it will allow you to remove any files you want to preserve. No files are actually deleted until you choose Finish to complete the Wizard.

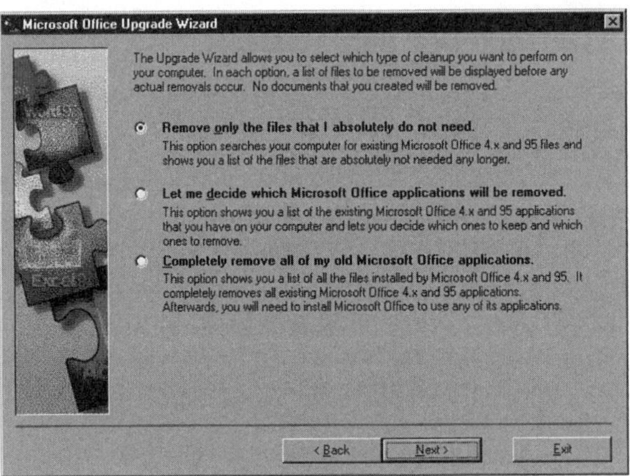

FIGURE 2.1
The Microsoft Office Upgrade Wizard allows you to choose how aggressively you want to search for old Office files.

Here are the three options for upgrading Office, in greater detail:

- **Remove only the files that I absolutely do not need.** If you choose this option, the wizard searches for files that no other program needs, such as .DLL files associated with versions of Office that have already been removed from the computer. This option is very cautious: it will not remove files associated with any application currently installed in Windows 95, 98, or NT, nor any shared applications such as the Office spellchecker or clip art files.

- **Let me decide which Microsoft Office applications will be removed.** If you choose this option, the Upgrade Wizard will first list the Office-related applications it finds on your computer, as shown in Figure 2.2. You can then specify which ones you want removed. The Wizard finds all files related to those applications, as well as the obsolete files it searches for if you choose this option.
- **Completely remove all of my old Office applications.** If you select this option, the Upgrade Wizard will work in "aggressive mode," searching for any file related to any Office application it can recognize, as well as shared files such as proofing tools. If Office 97 is installed on your computer, it will remove many of these files as well.

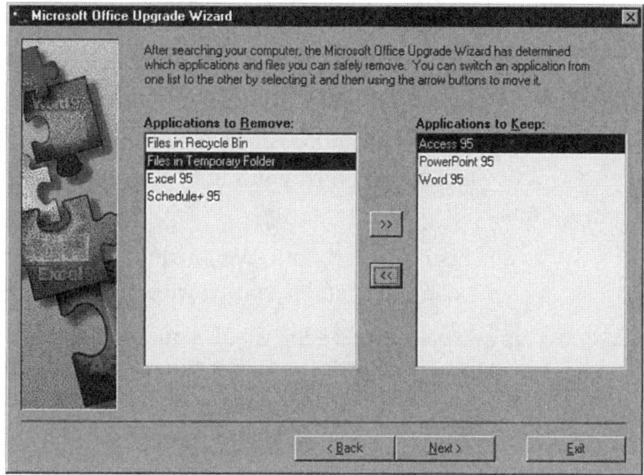

FIGURE 2.2
Choosing which Office applications and related files you want to remove.

You may at some point want to remove Office 97 from a workstation. As you probably know, this is normally done from the Windows Add/Remove Programs control panel applet. However, if you cannot successfully remove Office 97 through the Control Panel (perhaps because the Office 97 Setup program is missing), Microsoft has made available a utility to help you: the Office 97 File and Registry Eraser Utility (Eraser97.exe). This utility is available from the Microsoft Software Library. For more information on this utility, visit **support.microsoft.com/support/kb/articles/q158/6/58.asp**.

Performing the Uninstalling Process at All Computers with a Batch File

Needless to say, it is impractical to run the Microsoft Office Upgrade Wizard individually on hundreds or thousands of computers. However, you can automate the process by creating a batch file that can be used to run Offcln97.exe with your detailed specifications at each user's computer as part of a logon sequence. Follow these steps:

1. Copy the Offcln97.exe file to the MSOffice folder on the server.
2. Open a new Notepad document.
3. You will build your command line depending on how you want the cleaning process to be executed. The first part of your command line will tell the wizard to open the Office Clean application (drive:\ MSOffice\offcln97.exe).
4. Add switches from this table depending on what you want accomplished:

/s	Chooses the Let Me Decide Which Microsoft Office Applications Will Be Removed option. However, the user is not given an opportunity to remove files from the list of files to be deleted after that list is created.
/a	Chooses the Completely Remove All of My Old Office Applications option (aggressive mode). Again, the user is not given an opportunity to remove files from the list of files to be deleted after that list is created.
/q	Runs the Upgrade Wizard without prompting the user for information or displaying informational messages (quiet mode). You must first choose /s or /a to specify how you want the Upgrade Wizard to behave when it runs.
/r	If /q is also selected, this switch can be used to automatically shut down a user's computer and restart it without prompting the user.
/l*logfile*	This switch creates a log file. If you don't include a name after the /l, the log file is saved in the same folder as the Upgrade Wizard program, using the default name Pclogout.txt.

NOTE Do *not* put a space between the /l and the name of the log file.

/l!*logfile*	If you use this switch along with others, the Upgrade Wizard will simulate the deletion of files. This creates a log file listing the files that would have been deleted if you hadn't specified this switch. In other words, you can use this switch to see what the Upgrade Wizard plans to delete before actually letting it delete those files.

If you want to control the behavior of the Upgrade Wizard even more precisely, you can create an OPC file—a special text file containing definitions and commands that the Upgrade Wizard can use in place of directions from a user. Place the OPC file in the same folder as the Upgrade Wizard. Then run the Upgrade Wizard from a command line (or batch file) that specifies the OPC file, as in the following command:

```
Offcln97.exe /a /q /r batchfl.opc
```

To learn how to create an OPC file, review the default OPC file that comes with the Upgrade Wizard (Offcln97.opc) and the instructions in Chapter 9 of Microsoft's online Office Resource Kit, available at **www.microsoft.com/office/ork/009/009.htm**.

Installing Office 97

So far, you've planned how you want your installation to run (locally or from a network server). You've also planned how you want Office to run (from a local hard drive, a CD-ROM, or a network server). Now we'll walk through a standalone Office 97 Professional Edition installation. (Office 97 is quite similar, except that it does not include options for installing Microsoft Access and Bookshelf Basics components.)

The same component choices are available in a network installation. However, in a network installation, you will first create an *administrative installation point* on your network server and then install Office on individual workstations from the network server. Creating the administrative installation point is covered later in this chapter, in the section titled "Streamlining Server-Based Installations with the Network Installation Wizard."

NOTE If you are running a dual-boot system using Windows NT 4.x and Windows 95 or 98, you will need to install Office 97 twice—once in each environment. ■

To proceed with the installation, follow these steps:

1. Insert the Office 97 CD-ROM disk into the disk drive.
2. Click on Start, Run, and then type `drive:\setup.exe` and click on OK. (*Drive* represents your CD-ROM drive.)
3. A dialog box is displayed, warning you to close all other applications before proceeding. Do so, and choose Continue.
4. Type your name and the name of your organization. Click on OK to proceed. A confirmation dialog box appears to confirm what you entered in the previous wizard dialog box.
5. If the information is correct, click on OK. If you need to revise the information, click on Change.
6. Enter your Product ID number located on the Office 97 Certificate of Authenticity or the back of the CD-ROM case, and click on OK. A confirmation dialog box appears to confirm the Product ID number and to inform you that if you call for technical support, you will have to provide this number. After installation, this number can be found by choosing Help, About from any Microsoft Office application.
7. Click on OK again. The Setup program searches for installed components. You're then asked to specify a folder where Microsoft Office will be installed; the default folder is C:\Program Files\Microsoft Office.
8. If you approve of this destination, choose OK. Otherwise, choose Change Folder and specify where you want Office 97 installed.
9. After you've selected a folder, click on OK twice to proceed.

   Earlier in this section you determined the method of installation that you want to use: Typical, Custom, or Run from CD-ROM. (If a user is installing from an administrative installation point, another option—Run from Network Server—is available.) Now click on the option you prefer.

If you choose Typical, proceed to step 10.

If you choose Custom, skip to step 13.

If you choose Run From CD-ROM, the Setup program immediately installs the necessary files and reports that it has completed successfully. Click on OK to finish the installation.

10. If you selected a Typical installation, the setup program makes most of the choices about what will be installed, but you still have a few options to choose from, as shown in Figure 2.3. These options are described briefly here:

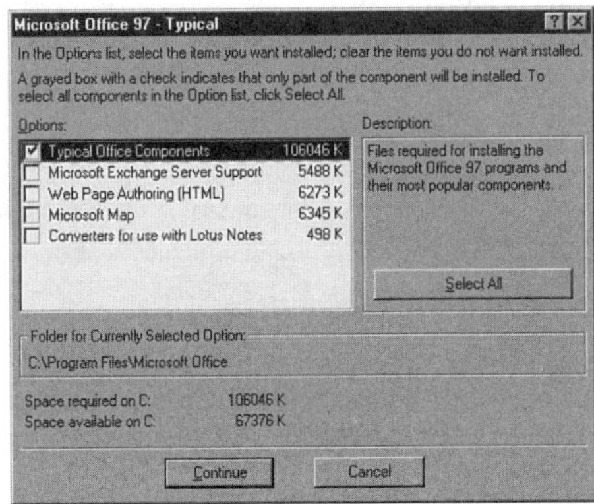

FIGURE 2.3
Specifying options in a Typical installation.

- **Microsoft Exchange Server Support:** Enables Microsoft Outlook to connect to a Microsoft Exchange Server and use Exchange-shared folders. These components are useful only if you've installed Exchange.
- **Web Page Authoring (HTML):** Enables Web page creation and editing features in Excel, PowerPoint, and Word, including Form features. If you are installing from an original set of Office 97 CD-ROM disks, be aware that a more recent version of Microsoft's Word Web authoring tools is available at **www.microsoft.com/office/enhword.asp**.
- **Microsoft Map:** This is an applet that works from within Excel and PowerPoint, enabling you to incorporate maps (and map-related data) into your worksheets and presentations.
- **Northwind Database:** This is a sample database for use with Microsoft Access (available only in Microsoft Office Professional Edition).
- **Converters for use with Lotus Notes:** These converters make Word 97 and Excel 97 files readable by users of Lotus Notes 3.x and 4.x. Note, however, that Word 97 links with Notes 4.x can still be troublesome; see the Lotus Technote "'Object Request Has Not Completed Because the Object Is Not Available' Activating MS Word Link," available through **support.lotus.com**.

After you have chosen the options that you want installed, click on Continue. The Setup program will check for disk space and then start copying files, keeping you informed of its progress.

If you are upgrading Office from a previous version, you may be offered an opportunity to delete older Office files that still remain on your system; choose Yes if you want to do so.

11. You may be asked if you want to make Microsoft Word the default HTML editor. If you already have an editor such as FrontPage, or if you do not want this workstation to have Web-editing capabilities, choose No. Otherwise, click Yes.
12. If all files are copied successfully, the Setup program will report this. Click on OK to complete the installation process.
13. If you chose a Custom installation in step 9, the window shown in Figure 2.4 will appear. Unless you have customized a setup script, the components checked in this window will correspond to those included in a Typical Office installation. (Check boxes marked in gray correspond to elements containing some components that are selected and others that are not.) However, Custom setup enables you to add or remove components, as discussed next.

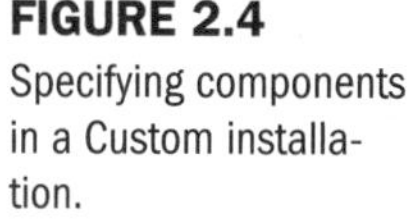

FIGURE 2.4
Specifying components in a Custom installation.

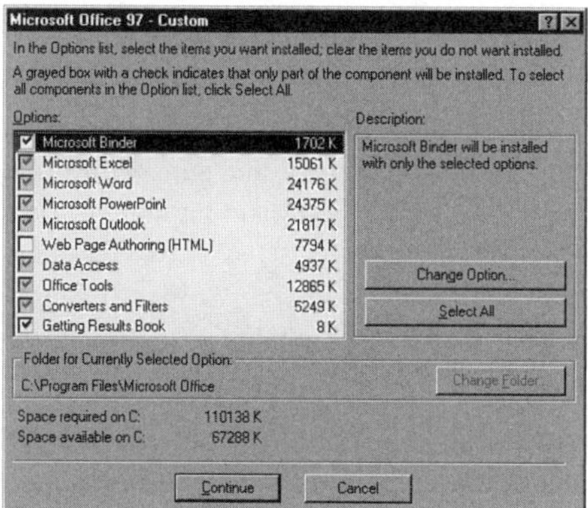

14. To customize how a part of Office is installed, select it and click on Change Option; the individual components will be displayed. Figure 2.5 shows the options available for installing Excel.

A more-detailed list of options appears in the next section.

After you are finished selecting the options that you want installed, click on Continue. Setup will check for disk space and start copying files, as described in steps 11 and 12 above. If all files are copied successfully, Setup will report this; click on OK to complete installation.

Office 97 Component Options

This section briefly describes the components available in a custom installation of Microsoft Office.

FIGURE 2.5
Options available for installing Excel.

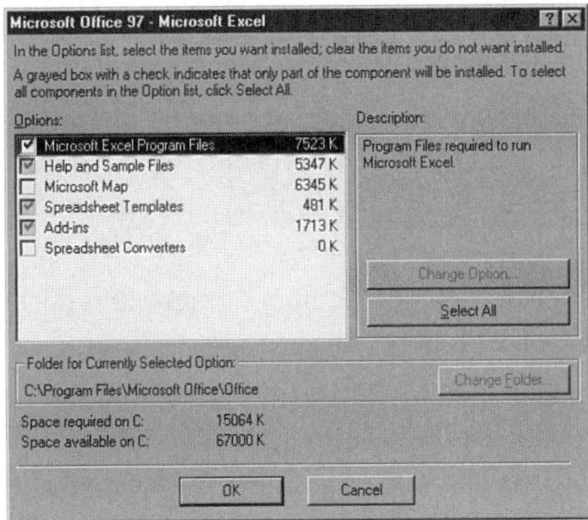

Microsoft Binder

- **Microsoft Binder Program Files:** Program files associated with the Binder applet, which allows users to create Binders containing files from multiple Office applications.
- **Microsoft Binder Help:** The Binder8.hlp help file associated with Binder.
- **Microsoft Binder Template:** A sample Report Binder containing a preformatted boilerplate cover letter, executive summary, and supporting analysis Word documents; a PowerPoint slide show; and an Excel worksheet for supporting data.

Microsoft Excel

- **Microsoft Excel Program Files:** Files needed for Excel to run.
- **Help and Sample Files**, including the following:
  - **Help for Microsoft Excel:** Several Excel help files, including Xlmain8.hlp (the primary Help file); Xlnew8.hlp (focusing on new features); Xltip8.hlp (tips for using Excel), and Xltmpl8.hlp (tips for customizing built-in Excel templates).
  - **Help for Visual Basic:** Help for using the Visual Basic for Applications macro language from within Microsoft Excel.
  - **Sample Files:** Sample worksheets that demonstrate Excel features to users and can be adapted to their own needs.
- **Microsoft Map:** An applet and accompanying data that can be used to insert maps into worksheets and presentations.
- **Spreadsheet Templates:** These include the following Excel templates (.XLT files):
  - **Expense Report Template:** For tracking and logging expenses.
  - **Invoice Template:** For billing and invoicing.
  - **Purchase Order Template:** For providing purchase orders to vendors.

- **Add-ins:** Optional Excel features likely to be valuable to only selected users. These components include the following:
    - **AccessLinks:** Enables users to edit and analyze Access reports and forms from within a Microsoft Excel data table.
    - **Analysis ToolPak:** Contains advanced statistical and engineering analysis tools.
    - **AutoSave:** Enables Excel to save worksheets automatically at specified intervals.
    - **File Conversion Wizard:** Helps Excel quickly import files from text and custom formats.
    - **Lookup Wizard:** Helps users create formulas that look up data in list.
    - **Report Manager:** Helps users print reports containing sets of views and scenarios.
    - **Conditional Sum Wizard:** Helps users sum up selected data in a list.
    - **Solver:** Provides features for equation solving and optimization. (See the "Improving Excel's Decision Analysis Capabilities" section of Chapter 27 for a look at more powerful third-party alternatives.)
    - **Template Wizard with Data Tracking:** This option will allow users to set up a Microsoft Excel document that will automatically copy data entered into fields of a workbook into a database for tracking and analysis.
    - **Spreadsheet Converters:** Includes optional converters for importing Quattro Pro (1.0 through 5.0) worksheets.

Microsoft Word

- **Microsoft Word Program Files:** Files needed for Word to run.
- **Help:** Includes the following Help options:
    - **Help for Microsoft Word:** Several Word help files, including Wdmain8.hlp (the primary Help file); Wdnew8.hlp (focusing on new features); and Wdtip8.hlp (tips for using Word).
    - **Help for WordPerfect Users:** Help and examples for users transitioning from WordPerfect 5.x for DOS.
    - **Help for WordPerfect Users:** Help and demonstrations for WordPerfect users.
    - **Help for Visual Basic:** Help for using the Visual Basic for Applications macro language from within Microsoft Word.
- **Wizards and Templates:** Includes the following options:
    - **Faxes:** Templates for creating contemporary, elegant, or professional faxes.
    - **Memos:** Templates for creating contemporary, elegant, or professional memos.

- **Reports:** Templates for creating contemporary, elegant, or professional reports.
- **More Wizards:** Templates for creating newsletters and legal pleadings.
- **Resumes:** Templates for creating contemporary, elegant, or professional resumes.
- **Letters:** Templates for creating contemporary, elegant, or professional letters.
- **Macro Templates:** Templates that contain utility macros.

- **Proofing Tools:** Proofing options include the following:
  - **Grammar:** Checks Word documents for possible grammar and syntax errors.
  - **Hyphenation:** Checks Word documents for correct hyphenation and inserts hyphenation when requested to do so.
  - **Thesaurus:** Provides alternative words with the same or similar meanings; also includes some antonyms.
- **Address Book:** Helps Word users access names from Outlook and Microsoft Exchange Personal Address Book.
- **WordMail in Exchange:** Enables users to use Word as their email editor, thereby benefiting from Word's formatting and proofreading capabilities. Do not use this option if you are installing Office on relatively low-powered computers, or if you limit users to text-only email messages.
- **Text Converters:** Includes the Text with Layout Converter, which allows Word to convert documents created in other word processing, spreadsheet, and database software, "faking" their layouts by adding empty spaces as needed.

Microsoft PowerPoint

- **Microsoft PowerPoint Program Files:** Files needed for PowerPoint to run.
- **Content Templates:** Includes the following templates for creating presentations that already contain structure and some text, as well as a visual theme:
  - **Typical Content Templates:** Includes a wide variety of standard business presentations, including presentations for meeting leaders, organization overviews, speaker introductions, and several more.
  - **Additional Content Templates:** Includes presentation templates for business plans, corporate home pages, and progress presentations.
  - **Design Templates:** Provides 17 standard, consistent color schemes and design elements for presenters to work from.
- **Help:** Includes the following Help options:
  - **Help for Microsoft PowerPoint:** Several PowerPoint help files, including Ppmain8.hlp (the primary Help file); Ppnew8.hlp (focusing on new features); and Pptip8.hlp (tips for using PowerPoint).

- Online Help for Visual Basic: Help for using the Visual Basic for Applications macro language from within Microsoft PowerPoint.

- **Animation Effects Sounds:** Installs animation and sound effects for use in PowerPoint presentations.
- **Presentation Translators:** Includes the following import filter options:
    - **Lotus Freelance 4.0 for DOS:** Allows PowerPoint to open presentations created in Lotus Freelance 4.0 for DOS.
    - **Harvard Graphics 3.0 for DOS:** Allows PowerPoint to open presentations created in Harvard Graphics 3.0 for DOS.
    - **Harvard Graphics 2.3 for DOS:** Allows PowerPoint to open presentations created in Harvard Graphics 2.3 for DOS.
    - **Lotus Freelance 1.0 – 2.1 for Windows:** Allows PowerPoint to open presentations created in Freelance 1.0 – 2.1 for Windows.
- **Genigraphics Wizard & GraphicsLink:** Allows users to send a Microsoft PowerPoint presentation to Genigraphics devices or service providers, and to create 35 mm slides, color overheads, posters, and other high-resolution output.

Microsoft Access

- **Microsoft Access Program Files:** Files needed for Access to run.
- **Help Topics:** Includes the following Help options:
    - **Product Help:** Help for using Microsoft Access product features.
    - **Programming Help:** Help for using the Visual Basic for Applications macro language from within Microsoft Access.
- **Wizards:** Access programs that guide users through the steps of creating forms and reports.
- **Advanced Wizards:** Sophisticated wizards for charting, resolving conflicts, and splitting databases; and for converting older Access macros to VBA.
- **Sample Databases:** Databases designed to help users master Access features, including the following:
    - **Northwind Database:** A sample company database for novice users, demonstrating how Access can be used to create a wide variety of useful reports.
    - **Order Database:** For moderately experienced users and power users who want to see how a live order database can be built with Access.
    - **Developer Solution Database:** For power users and application developers; shows the most efficient methods to use in solving common Access development problems.
- **Microsoft Briefcase Replication:** Helps users and companies keep databases synchronized, even when copies must be stored on a notebook PC. Works with the Briefcase feature built into Windows 95 and 98.

- **Calendar Control:** To view the options, select Calendar Control, then choose Change Options:
    - **Calendar Control:** An ActiveX control that allows users to insert programmable calendars in their forms and reports.
    - **Calendar Control Help:** Help for using the Calendar Control.

Microsoft Outlook

- **Microsoft Outlook Program Files:** Files needed for Microsoft Outlook to run.
- **Microsoft Exchange Server Support:** Files needed for Outlook to connect with a Microsoft Exchange Server.
- **Visuals for Forms Design:** Files needed for designing new forms.
- **Holidays and Forms:** Files needed to add worldwide holidays to Outlook calendars.
- **Lotus Organizer Converters:** Files needed to import Lotus Organizer 1.1 and 2.1 files for use in Outlook.
- **Microsoft Outlook Help:** Help files explaining Outlook product features.
- **Schedule+ Support Files:** Files that allow users to import files from Schedule+ and work with others still using it.

Web Page Authoring (HTML)

- Installs components that enable Excel, PowerPoint, and Word to create HTML files for use on the Internet or your corporate intranet.

Microsoft Bookshelf Basics

- Installs the Bookshelf Basics reference books (dictionary, thesaurus, and book of quotations) and makes them accessible from within Word, Excel, and PowerPoint.

Data Access

- **Database Drivers:** Includes the following options for accessing data:
    - **Microsoft Access Driver:** Enables users to import data from Microsoft Access databases.
    - **dBASE and Microsoft FoxPro Drivers:** Enables users to import data from dBASE and Microsoft FoxPro databases.
    - **Microsoft Excel Driver:** Enables users to import database data from Microsoft Excel workbooks.
    - **Microsoft SQL Server Driver:** Enables users to import data from Microsoft SQL Server database.
    - **Text and HTML Driver:** Enables users to import data from text files.
- **Microsoft Query:** Enables users to access external data sources for use in Excel or Word.
- **Data Access Objects for Visual Basic:** Installs objects used by custom Visual Basic applications to access external data. It includes ODBCDirect functionality.

Office Tools

- **Microsoft Office Shortcut Bar:** Files needed for the Microsoft Office Shortcut Bar to operate, providing one-click access to Office applications from the desktop.
- **Office Assistant:** Provides animated characters that offer help suggestions and context-sensitive access to the Office Help system.
- **Spelling Checker:** Includes the spellchecking files used by all Office software.
- **Organizational Chart:** An applet for creating organizational charts that can be used in any Office program (see the "Using Microsoft Organization Chart 2.0" section of Chapter 26 for more information about this applet).
- **Microsoft Graph:** An applet for building graphs from data in Word, Excel, PowerPoint, or Access.
- **Microsoft Graph Help:** Help for using Microsoft Graph.
- **Equation Editor:** An applet for incorporating mathematical symbols and equations into a document (see the "Using Microsoft Equation Editor" section of Chapter 26 for more information about this applet).
- **Microsoft Photo Editor:** An applet for scanning, converting, and modifying photos and other images (see the "Using Microsoft Photo Editor" section of Chapter 26 for more information about this applet).
- **MS Info:** A troubleshooting tool that gathers extensive system configuration information (see the "Using Microsoft System Information" section of Chapter 26 for more information about this applet).
- **Popular Clipart:** A small collection of clip art for use in any Office document.
- **Clip Gallery:** An applet that can index, display thumbnails, and provide quick access to all clip art, pictures, sound, and movies on a PC or available across the network (see the "Using Microsoft Clip Gallery" section of Chapter 26 for more information about this applet).
- **Fast Find:** An applet that indexes documents on a PC, helping users find them more quickly from within the Open dialog box. Find Fast works in the background, which means it can impact performance on slower workstations.
- **Microsoft TrueType Fonts:** Includes the following fonts: Arial Narrow, Arial Black, Bookman Old Style, Garamond, and Impact.
- **Lotus VIM Mail Support:** Provides support for Lotus messaging applications such as Lotus Notes 3.x–4.x and cc:Mail 2.x, enabling users to access these applications from within Office.
- **Find All Word Forms:** An optional capability used by features such as Find/Replace and AutoSummarize, this installs information Word can use to find related forms of a word. (For example, if you search for "provide" with Find All Word Forms installed and turned on, Office can also locate "providing.")

- **Converters and Filters**
  - **Text Converters:** Office includes the following text converters:
    - **Word for Windows 2.0 Converter (Import/Export):** Not needed to simply open Word for Windows 2.0 documents.
    - **Word for Macintosh 4.0-5.1 Converter (Import/Export):** Not needed to simply open Word 4.0-5.1 for the Macintosh documents.
    - **Microsoft Excel Converter:** Converts Excel 2.x, 3.0, 4.0, 5.0, 95, and 97 worksheets to Word 97 format. It can open Excel documents in Word, but it cannot resave in these older Excel formats.
    - **Word 6.0/95 for Windows/Macintosh:** Converts documents from Word 6.0/95 for Windows/Macintosh formats. (See the discussion of Word 6.0/95 compatibility in Chapter 20, in the section titled "Step 1: Preparing Office 97 for the Conversion.")
    - **Word 97 for Windows/Macintosh:** Used with Word 5.1 for the Macintosh or Word 6.0 for either Windows or the Macintosh. It enables these older versions of Word to open Word 97/98 documents. Even if you include this converter in your installation, you will still have to install it into the older version of Word afterward.
    - **Word 6.0/95 Export Converter:** Not needed for simply opening Word 6.0 documents.
    - **WordPerfect 6.x Converter:** Converts documents from WordPerfect 6.0 for DOS and WordPerfect 6.0 and 6.1 for Windows.
    - **WordPerfect 5.x Converter:** Converts documents to and from WordPerfect for Windows and WordPerfect 5.0 and 5.1 for DOS.
    - **Lotus 1-2-3 Converter:** Imports documents created in Lotus 1-2-3 versions 2.x, 3.x, and 4.0.
    - **Works for Windows 3.0.**
    - **Works for Windows 4.0.**
    - **Recover Text Converter:** Helps users recover at least some text from nearly any file containing text.
    - **HTML Converter:** Converts documents to and from Hypertext Markup Language.
    - **Converters for Use with Lotus Notes:** Enables Lotus Notes 3.x and 4.x to read files created in Word 97 and Excel 97.
  - **Graphic Filters:** Includes the following filter options:
    - **Tag Image File Format (TIFF) Import**
    - **Encapsulated PostScript (EPS) Import**

- **Windows Bitmap (BMP) Import:** (This filter will not import OS/2 BMP files.)
- **Enhanced Metafile (EMF) Import.**
- **Truevision Targa (TGA) Import.**
- **AutoCAD DXF Import:** (May also import CAD files from compatible software such as Visio IntelliCAD.)
- **Micrografx Designer/Draw (DRW) Import.**
- **CorelDRAW (CDR) Import:** (Imports files created in CorelDRAW! 3.0 through 6.0.)
- **Computer Graphics Metafile (CGM) Import.**
- **PC Paintbrush PCX Import.**
- **WordPerfect Graphic (WPG) Import.**
- **WordPerfect Graphic (WPG) Export:** Can be used only with the WordPerfect document export converter.
- **Macintosh PICT Import.**
- **Windows Metafile (WMF) Import.**
- **GIF (Graphics Interchange Format) Import:** Essential for anyone who will use Web graphics.
- **Kodak Photo CD (PCD) Import.**
- **JPEG File Interchange Format Import:** Also essential for anyone who will use Web graphics.
- **Portable Network Graphic (PNG) File Format Import.**

- **Getting Results Book:** The Getting Results Book is an online introductory guide for Office beginners.

Streamlining Server-Based Installations with the Network Installation Wizard

In the previous sections, you walked through a standalone installation of Office. The choices and decisions you made will also be relevant in a network installation; but if you want to distribute Office 97 across a network, you will have to take a few additional steps. These include

- Preparing the network server
- Creating an administrative installation point
- Running the Network Installation Wizard

Preparing the Network Server

To distribute Office across the network, you must first install it on your network server in a special folder you create called an *administrative installation point.* Before doing so, follow these steps:

- Make sure any Office folders that may be on your network server are empty.
- Log all users off the network. (As mentioned earlier, it makes sense to prepare your network server at night or on a weekend.)
- Prevent network users from accessing the folders during installation.
- Temporarily disable any virus-detection software on the network server.
- Create a folder on the network server where you will install Office (your administrative installation point).
- Share that folder, providing Read sharing and security permissions for all users who will install Office from here. (If you are installing Office Professional Edition with the Run from Network Server option, you will have to provide Change permissions to the Workdir folder Office will create, so that users can work with Microsoft Access Wizards.)

Creating an Administrative Installation Point

To install Office 97 on the network server, follow these steps:

1. Insert the Office 97 CD-ROM into a CD-ROM drive on a workstation connected to your network server.
2. From the taskbar, choose Start, Run to display the Run dialog box.
3. Enter ***drive:*\setup /a** (where *drive*: represents your CD-ROM drive name); click on OK. Office Setup starts.
4. Type the name of your organization and choose OK twice. Office will use this name in every client installation.
5. Enter your product key from the back of your Office 97 CD-ROM case and choose OK twice.
6. Click on Change Folder; then browse to and select the folder you created as your administrative installation point. Choose OK twice.
7. Specify a folder for shared applications; the default is \MSAPPS. Choose OK.
8. The Network Server Confirmation dialog box will appear (see Figure 2.6). In the Server text box, enter the server name you have used for the Shared Applications folder. In the Path text box, type the precise network path that users will need to type when they access these files.
9. If your network is set up to provide access to the server via a drive letter, click on the Drive Letter button and choose the letter from the Drive drop-down box. If your network is set up to use Universal Naming Convention (UNC) paths, click on the Server Name button instead.

10. Choose Continue. The dialog box in Figure 2.7 appears. You're now asked how you want users to run shared applications: from the Server, or on their Local Hard Drives. A third option, User's Choice, leaves it up to the individual user.
11. Choose Continue. You're asked which paper format and language you want Office to use as a default. Make your selection (in the U.S., the default is US Letter, US English dictionaries).
12. Choose OK. The Setup program checks to make sure that you have enough disk space, and then it copies all Office files to the administrative installation point, reporting when it has succeeded.

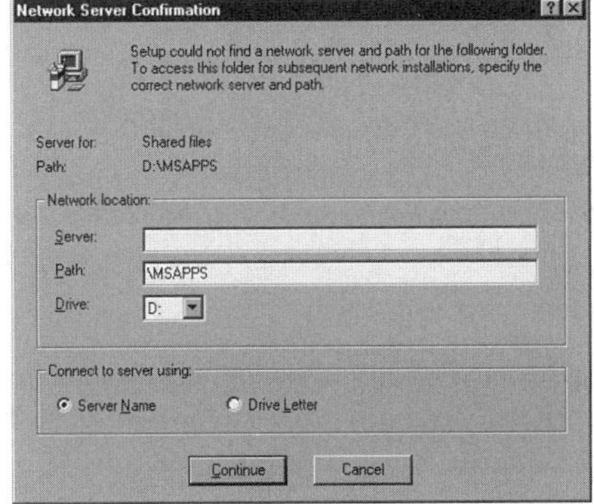

FIGURE 2.6
The Network Server Confirmation dialog box.

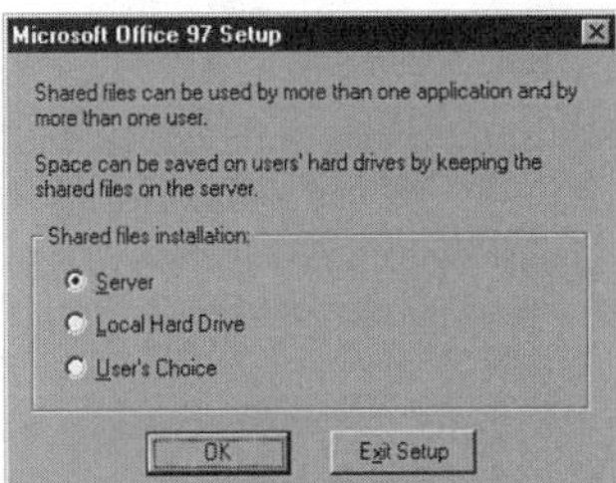

FIGURE 2.7
Specifying where users should run shared applications from.

Running the Network Installation Wizard

Now that you have created an administrative installation point, users can install Office by accessing it and running Setup the way they normally would. In some cases, this is all you need to do. If, however, you want to take more control over how Office is installed on each client workstation, you need to take another step. You must run the Network Installation Wizard to create modified STF and INF files used by the Setup program to control the Office installation process.

NOTE The latest Network Installation Wizard is downloadable from Microsoft's online Office Resource Kit at **www.microsoft.com/office/ork/appa/appa.htm#ORKappaC1**. It can also be found in the Tools\Niw folder in the printed Microsoft Office Resource Kit.

The Network Installation Wizard asks you for information it needs to compile customized files for your network installation, including

- Primary location for Microsoft Office files on the server
- Where shared files will be installed
- The network location of shared files
- Whether you want to create an installation log
- Whether you want users to use Typical, Custom, or Run from Network Server installations
- Which component options to install
- Whether to answer Yes or No to the questions Setup asks during an install (for example, whether to delete old Office files)
- Which icons and Start menu items to install

Your responses are used to create an STF file, which in turn also creates a matching INF file. Once you have run the Network Installation Wizard and created these files, you need to determine which method you want to use to install Microsoft Office.

You can choose an interactive process, in which users are prompted for information. If you prefer, you can specify a batch installation, in which a batch file that you create is run and the user has no involvement.

You may also decide to use a push installation method, in which you place a customized setup command line that you created into the user's system logon script. When the user logs on, the logon script installs Microsoft Office using the settings you specified in the Network Installation Wizard.

After you've made your choice, you can write your script or create a "job" using Microsoft's System Management Server.

Overview of System Management Server (SMS)

Microsoft System Management Server (SMS) is a Microsoft BackOffice product that runs on Windows NT Server and enables network administrators to manage the installation of Microsoft Office on client workstations across the network.

SMS gives the network administrator the ability to automatically distribute the software through the use of packages. The network administrator creates these packages with information about the software and how to install it. With this software, Microsoft Office can be installed either with the push method or the pull method.

The SMS creates and uses Package Definition Files (PDFs) to perform network distribution of Office 97. PDF files for standard Office installations are downloadable from Microsoft's online Office Resource Kit at **www.microsoft.com/office/ork/appa/appa.htm#ORKappaC1**. They can also be found in the Tools\PDF folder in the printed Microsoft Office Resource Kit. The accompanying Readme.doc file contains a valuable explanation of how to use these PDF files. Consult this document before using SMS to install Office 97.

NOTE Don't confuse these PDF files with the Portable Document Format files created by Adobe Acrobat.

Installing Office 97 Using SMS

To install Office 97, you need to first create or import the PDF and then set it up as a Run on Workstation job. To do this, perform the following steps:

1. Start the Systems Management Server Administrator and switch to the Packages window. Click File, New, and then in the Package Properties dialog box click on Import.
2. Browse to and select your PDF file of choice, usually either Off97std.pdf for Office 97 Standard edition or Off97pro.pdf for Office 97 Professional Edition.
3. In the Package Properties dialog box, click on Workstations.
4. In the Source Directory, name the network administrative point (typically a folder used by all users for finding the batch files for downloading software).
5. In the Workstation Command Lines box, select the type of installation you want to perform.
6. Now switch to the Jobs window of the SMS. Click on File, then New.
7. In the Job Properties box, open Details. In the Package box, click on the PDF file you selected in step 2.
8. Under Run Phase, select the Run Workstation Command check box. Click on OK.

SMS will now distribute the Office components to the appropriate servers and command them to download the run-time components to the workstations. Each user can then run the setup script from his or her workstation to finish the installation process.

Making Changes to the Existing Installation

After installation, you or another user may determine that a previously omitted option is required. To add this option, follow these steps:

1. Insert the Microsoft Office 97 CD-ROM into the computer of the user who needs this option.
2. Choose Start, Run, type in ***drive:* setup**, and click on the OK button (*drive* represents your CD-ROM drive).

3. Click on the Add/Remove button.
4. Select the options that you want to install.
5. Click on Continue.
6. Microsoft Office informs you that it is updating your system.
7. Microsoft Office then informs you that it has successfully installed your new options.
8. Click on OK to complete the additional installation.

CHAPTER 3

Installing Service Releases and Updates

Since the release of Microsoft Office 97, there have been two service releases, each designed to fix a set of bugs that Microsoft and its customers discovered after release.

NOTE In order to install the second service release (SR-2), you must have already installed the first service release (SR-1).

Separate from SR-1 and SR-2, Microsoft has also released updates to Office that improve its capabilities as a Web development and drawing tool.

In this chapter, you'll learn about these updates to Office 97—what problems they solve, where to get them, and how to install them.

Understanding SR-1

Microsoft's first Office 97 service release, SR-1, comes in the following two versions:

- SR-1 Enterprise Update
- SR-1 Patch

SR-1 Patch is a downloadable file available at Microsoft's Web site (**www.microsoft.com/office/office/enhancements/sr1off97.asp**). The SR-1 Patch contains most, but not quite all, of the bug fixes that Microsoft had identified by July 1997. For example, the SR-1 Enterprise Update fixes a bug that sometimes generates incorrect dates for Thanksgiving and the Lunar New Year but is not fixed in the SR-1 Patch.

NOTE You can also use the SR-1 Patch to update Microsoft Office 97 Small Business Edition. It contains updates for Word, Excel, and Outlook, but not for Internet Explorer, Expedia Streets, Microsoft Publisher, or Microsoft Small Business Manager.

The SR-1 Enterprise Update is a complete Office 97 CD-ROM that contains all the bug fixes provided in the SR-1 Patch, as well as several additional ones. To get a copy in the United States, you must contact Microsoft Customer Service. If you received it packaged with a computer, you must contact the manufacturer of your computer. Depending on when you purchased Microsoft Office 97, you may already be running SR-1 Enterprise Update.

NOTE To find out whether you are running SR-1, choose Help, About in any major Office application. If you are running SR-1, this will be reported alongside the program name (as shown in Figure 3.1).

Installing either version of SR-1 lets you install the more recent SR-2. Given an option, your best choice is typically to fully remove Office 97 and reinstall the Office 97 SR-1 Enterprise Update from scratch. After installing the SR-1 Patch, a relatively small number of users have reported system instabilities that do not appear to exist after installing the SR-1 Enterprise Update. Moreover, if you use the patch and you must remove and reinstall Office 97 for any reason later, you will first have to reinstall the original version and then install the patch over it again.

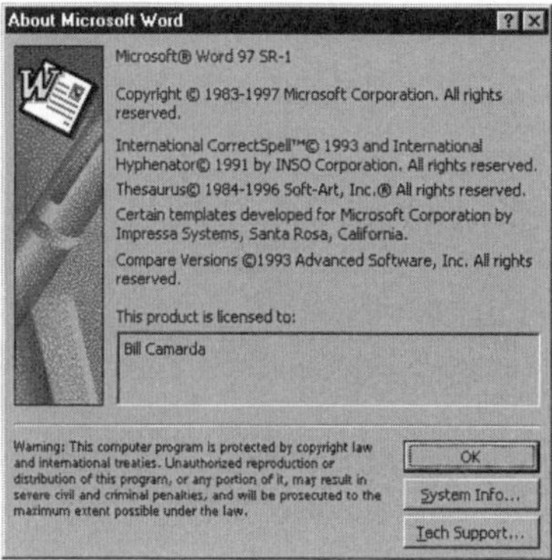

FIGURE 3.1
Checking whether you are running SR-1 (either Enterprise Update or Patch).

You may not have the option of installing the Enterprise Update, however, if any of the following applies:

- If you purchased Office 97 as part of a new computer bundle, Microsoft will refer you to your Original Equipment Manufacturer (OEM)—the company that manufactured your computer. Different companies have different policies about providing the SR-1 Enterprise Update.
- In some international markets, Microsoft's local offices have reportedly been reluctant to provide the SR-1 Enterprise Update.

According to some third-party reports, Microsoft has been more responsive to requests for the Enterprise Update from licensed users who report that they run Office 97 from CD-ROM, and therefore have no alternative for upgrading their software other than a new disk.

Installing the SR-1 Enterprise Update

You install the SR-1 Enterprise Update the same way you installed Office 97. It gives you the same network and automated installation options you had when you installed Office 97 originally. (Refer to Chapter 2, "Scripting and Automating Office Installations," for more information about installing Office 97 across a network.)

If you install over a current Office 97 installation, however, Microsoft says you must use the exact same settings as in the original installation, with the same setup options. (To be precise, you can add setup options but you cannot delete any.)

Rather than taking any chances, many Office administrators prefer to completely remove the original installation of Office 97 and then install SR-1 Enterprise Update as a fresh installation.

Installing the SR-1 Patch

To install the SR-1 Patch, first make sure your computer is running one of the following operating systems:

- Windows 95 or 98 (no service pack required)
- Windows NT Workstation 4.0 (SR-1 requires Service Pack 2 or later, and SR-2 requires Service Pack 3 or later)
- Windows NT Workstation 3.51 (Service Pack 5)

You need 32MB of disk space to run the SR-1 Patch from your hard disk, and the patch increases the size of your Microsoft Office installation by 8MB.

After you copy the patch file to your hard drive, you can simply double-click on the patch file to install it. Several optional switches are available to customize the way the patch is installed (see Table 3.1). You can include the switches in a command you run from the Start, Run dialog box, as shown in Figure 3.2.

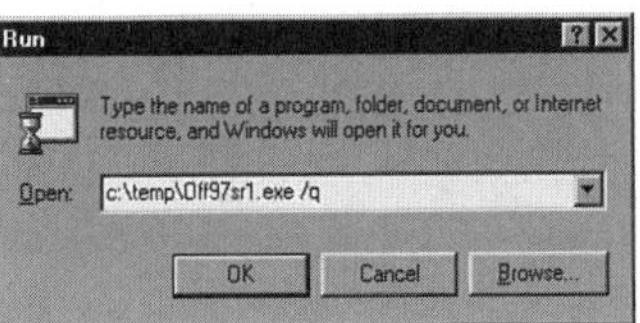

FIGURE 3.2
Running the SR-1 Patch with switches, via the Run dialog box.

Table 3.1 Switches Available in SR-1 Patch Installation

Switch	What It Does
/q	Quiet mode installation; no user prompts. You must restart Windows manually afterward.
/t:path	Specifies a folder other than the system's Temp folder for storing temporary files during the installation process
/c	Used with /t:path to extract patch files to a folder of your choice. Using this switch does not actually install the patch; it only places copies of the patch files on your hard disk.

CAUTION

On occasion, installing the SR-1 Patch fails, and you may not get an error message. To check whether all SR-1 files have been updated properly, open the SR-1 Patch Log File, 97sr1_0.txt, and look for error messages there. If you've installed SR-1 more than once, there will be more than one log file. The newer files will end in numbers higher than 0.

One common problem that can interfere with SR-1 installation is trying to install from a folder with a filename containing extended non-English characters with acute or grave accents, umlauts, tildes, cedillas, or circumflexes. To solve the problem, rename the folder before you install the SR-1 patch.

Checking Which SR-1 Patch You're Using

If you've already installed the SR-1 Patch, you may want to know that Microsoft has released two versions of this patch. The first, Sr1off97.exe, was dated 7/11/97. On some systems, it has caused problems with Word 97 file saves. The second version, which uses the same filename and is dated 8/21/97, fixes this problem.

If you have the original patch file, it's easy to tell which version of the patch is installed—simply check the file date in Windows Explorer: The most recent SR-1 patch is dated 8/21/97. Earlier versions had a file date of 7/11/97.

Of course, there's not much point in worrying about this unless your users are having trouble with Word file saves.

What's Included in SR-1?

Both the SR-1 Enterprise Update and SR-1 Patch fix a number of troublesome problems throughout Microsoft Office. The following sections describe the fixes built into SR-1 Patch, as well as the additional fixes built into SR-1 Enterprise Update.

NOTE To learn exactly which Office files are updated in SR-1, see Microsoft Knowledge Base article Q172387, available by searching for the article number at **support.microsoft.com/support**.

SR-1 Office-Wide Fixes

The SR-1 Patch contains the following two key fixes that affect multiple Office programs:

- Fixes bugs that led to corrupted AutoCorrect (ACL) files, which in some cases prevented Office applications from starting properly
- Provides updated Open Database Connectivity (ODBC) 3.0 files, which Microsoft says improve the security of database queries

The SR-1 Enterprise Update also contains the following Office-wide fixes:

- Corrects an installation problem that occasionally generates the error message: `Bdrintl.dll Was Unable to Register Itself.`
- Installs the Office Shortcut Bar (OSB) by default in a Typical installation. This does not happen in the original version of Office 97.
- Includes revised Help (HLP) and (TXT) files.

SR-1 Word Fixes

The SR-1 Patch provides the following several improvements to Microsoft Word that you will not want to be without:

- Provides a Word 6.0/95 filter that actually creates Word 6.0 files, not RTF files with .doc extensions that can cause problems both within Word and for programs that need to import Word documents. (For more information, see Chapter 20, "Integrating Office Documents with Desktop Publishing Systems.")
- Fixes a limitation that prevented Office 97 users from working with permanently mapped network drives.
- Allows Office 97 users to open Word for the Macintosh files and preserve Encapsulated PostScript images for printing to a PostScript printer.
- It changes the way inserted graphics behave; they now default to inline graphics rather than floating over text (this is a response to a common user complaint).
- Fixes bugs that led some graphics to be displayed as blank boxes containing a red letter X.
- Fixes bugs that previously caused inserted pictures to lose sizing information after they were resized.
- Fixes bugs that occasionally caused document corruption in documents containing heavily edited headers or footers.
- Stores correct language defaults when running under international versions of Windows.
- Prints graphics properly when using printers with unusual nonsymmetrical resolutions.

The SR-1 Enterprise Update also fixes the following problems:

- Improves the compatibility of the Avery Wizard third-party add-on
- Fixes a bug that caused an error message when running the SuperDocStatistics macro stored in Macros8.dot

SR-1 Excel Fixes

As in Word, SR-1 fixes the following several Excel problems, most of which affected relatively few users, but caused significant problems to the users they did affect:

- Fixes recalculation problems that existed in ROW and COLUMN worksheet functions after new rows or columns were inserted into worksheets
- Fixes problems with views and reports created in previous versions of Excel
- Fixes invalid characters in module names when you save a workbook in Excel 97 XLS format
- Supports cutting and pasting of cells containing data used in PivotTables
- Fixes the bug that prevents you from printing titles using a medium-width bottom border
- Allows worksheet database functions to refer to ranges larger than 32,768 rows
- Allows the Excel HTML Wizard to be controlled from a VBA macro
- Allows sheet names to include characters outside the ANSI character set

The Enterprise Update adds a new Excel 97 Viewer for Windows 95/98/NT, enabling users to view Excel 97 worksheets without having a copy of Excel 97 installed.

CAUTION

Four significant recalculation problems in Excel 97 are *not* fixed in SR-1. To fix these, you must also install SR-2. If you depend on complex worksheets, install as quickly as possible, if you haven't already.

SR-1 PowerPoint Fixes

In PowerPoint, the SR-1 Patch fixes the following three problems:

- As in Word, it fixes bugs that led some graphics to be displayed as blank boxes containing a red letter X.
- It includes a significantly improved Freelance Graphics 2.1 import filter.
- In saving PowerPoint 97 presentations to PowerPoint 95 (7.0) format, it also saves Graph 97 objects to Graph 95 (7.0) format. Previously, these were retained as Graph 97 objects that were not readable on systems that only contained Graph 95.

The Enterprise Update adds a new PowerPoint 97 viewer for Windows 95/98/NT users who do not have PowerPoint 97. It also includes an import filter PowerPoint 4.0 users can use to open PowerPoint 97 files.

SR-1 Access Fixes

In Access, SR-1 adds a significant new feature: Microsoft Access Snapshot Creator. This feature allows you to save a snapshot of data in a specific table, and provide it to your colleagues. Microsoft Access Snapshot Creator lets you share information with users who don't have their own copy of Access. It also gives you an easy way of sharing limited information—without sharing your entire database.

The Enterprise Update also contains an Access 97 Snapshot Viewer for viewing and printing these snapshots under Windows 95/98/NT. This Snapshot Viewer is downloadable from Microsoft's Web site at **www.microsoft.com/access**.

Both the SR-1 patch and Enterprise Update also fix an Access bug that impacted reporting updates to the LinkChildFields and LinkMasterFields properties.

SR-1 Outlook 97 Fixes

SR-1 contains the Internet Mail Enhancement Patch for Outlook (IMEP), which makes Outlook 97 and Microsoft Exchange Server more reliable in sending and receiving Internet Mail via Exchange's Internet Mail Transport Service. SR-1 also improves the reliability of Outlook's MAPI email spooler.

According to Microsoft, SR-1 Enterprise Update also includes the following fixes:

- More complete support for Exchange Server 5.*x* features
- Better performance when switching between the Exchange client and Outlook while using forms

- A new Send Security Keys security feature
- Support for forms larger than 32K
- Correct handling of Thanksgiving and Lunar New Year holidays
- Accurate updating of appointments when using the Daylight Savings Time option
- No extraneous characters when importing Lotus cc:Mail messages that contain Greek characters
- Support for inheriting Microsoft Schedule+ permissions
- Correct display of the Delegate with Permissions option

NOTE Neither SR-1 nor the SR-2 patch includes the free update to Outlook 98 available at Microsoft's Web site. This update is discussed later in the chapter.

Understanding SR-2

After SR-1 was released, Microsoft and its customers found some additional bugs, including four significant calculation problems that can affect the results in Excel workbooks. In the summer of 1998, Microsoft released Service Release 2 (SR-2), which includes the Excel fixes and several additional fixes as well. Among the more significant is a new filter that exports PowerPoint 97 files to PowerPoint 4.0 format, using Year 2000 compatible dates.

SR-2 will install on any Office 97 system that already contains either the SR-1 Patch or Enterprise Update, including recent "out-of-the-box" Office 97 installations that already reflect the SR-1 fixes. (These include installations of the latest version of Office 97 Small Business Edition.)

Registered Office 97 users can download SR-2 or order it free of charge from Microsoft. Microsoft Select customers who have purchased Office 97 should receive it automatically.

CAUTION

If you downloaded Excel 97 recalculation patches prior to April 22, 1998, you may not have all of them. Either download a new set, or upgrade to the complete SR-2.

Outlook 98

Since the release of Office 97, Microsoft has delivered a significant upgrade to Outlook, called *Outlook 98*. This new version is available at no cost to registered Office users on the Web at **www.microsoft.com/outlook/outlook98/default.htm**. (See Figure 3.3.)

Outlook 98 includes the improvements contained in the SR-1 Patch and Enterprise Update, as well as the following sizable changes:

- According to Microsoft, better performance in many common tasks
- Faster exiting on most systems
- Revised, easier to understand menus, dialog boxes, and toolbars
- An Organize button for bringing order to folders
- A Rules Wizard for discarding junk e-mail. (Be cautious—some users report that Outlook 98's default settings can be too aggressive about throwing away messages)
- Tighter integration with Internet Explorer 4.0, Exchange Server, and Office 97
- Synchronization of offline folders in the background

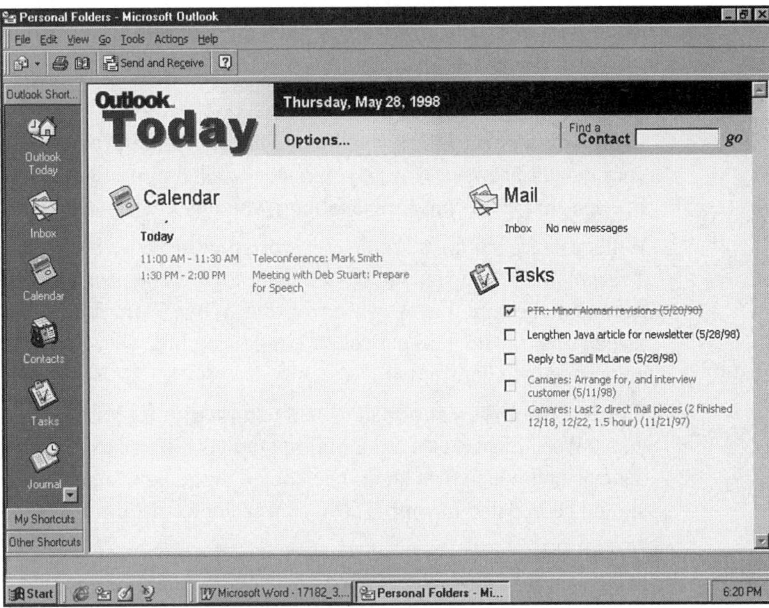

FIGURE 3.3
The Outlook Today window brings together all your activities for the day.

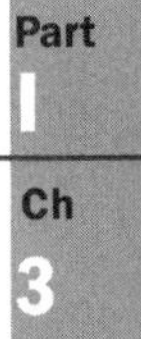

Draw 98

The original Office 97 came with enhanced drawing tools with one enormous limitation—they could not be exported to graphics formats usable outside of Word, especially on the Web. Microsoft offered a downloadable applet, Microsoft Draw 97 (recently updated to Draw 98), which allows users to create text effects, AutoShapes, connectors, diagrams, and other types of drawings, and save them in GIF format for use on the Web.

Draw 98 works with any OLE-compliant application, including Word, Excel, Outlook, and Publisher, but you must have an Office 97 program installed on your system before you can install Draw 98. You can download draw98.e XE at **www.microsoft.com/office/office/enhancements/draw98.asp**, and double-click on it to install the program. Once installed, you can use

Draw 98 by choosing Insert, Object, Microsoft Draw 98 Drawing from within any Office 97 program.

Web Authoring Tools Update

Word 97 comes with the Web page authoring environment, which contains many tools for authoring new Web pages or converting existing documents into Web pages. The tools that shipped with Word 97, however, have significant limitations. For example, there's no easy way to preview your pages in more than one browser or to check for broken hyperlinks—two critical elements of the Web site testing process.

Microsoft has made available a free upgrade, the Web Authoring Tools Update, which addresses these problems and strengthens the Web page authoring environment in other ways as well. The improvements include the following:

- In the original Word 97, if you chose File, Web Page Preview, Word automatically opened your default browser. Now, if you have installed more than one browser, the Web Page Preview dialog box appears, enabling you to select the browser that you want to use.
- While you are editing a Web page, Word now provides a Check Links command in the Tools menu. When you run Check Links, Word checks all the hyperlinks on the current page to make sure that they are working. When Word finds a link that does not work, it displays the Check Links: Broken Link dialog box where you can edit the link or choose a new one (see Figure 3.4).
- Word can now preserve links even if you save an HTML file to a new location. When you do so, Word displays the Link Fixing Options dialog box, which gives you detailed control over which files should be copied to the new folder, and which links (if any) should be updated in your HTML source code.

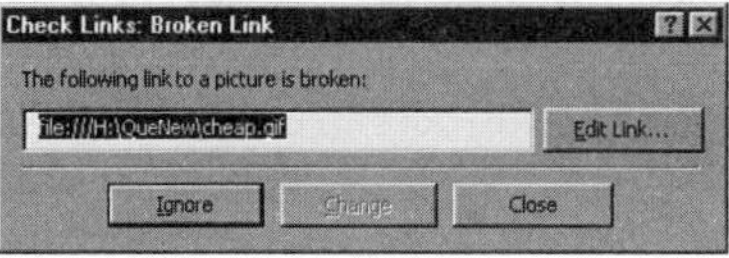

FIGURE 3.4
When you run Check Links, Word can help you update broken links.

The Web Authoring Tools Update also makes the following minor improvements:

- Adds a new online resume option to the Web Page Wizard
- Provides several new backgrounds, notably jade, papyrus, and rattan
- Enhances the Web Publishing Wizard, which streamlines the process of uploading files to a Web server. You can see the changes by choosing File, Publish to Web.

The Web Authoring Tools Update, Wd97au.exe, can be downloaded at **www.microsoft.com/word/enhancements/wd97au.asp**. It is not included in either SR-1 or SR-2; you have to retrieve it separately. After you download the file, double-click on it in Windows Explorer to install it. After the installation is complete, restart Windows. ●

CHAPTER 4

Managing Macintosh Installations and Deployments

Microsoft Office 98 represents one of the more important fruits of a new working relationship between Microsoft Corporation and Apple Computer. Instead of porting the Windows version of the Office applications directly to the MacOS, Office 98 for Macintosh was written independently of the Windows version and actually sports several unique features. This is especially evident in the installation procedures for Microsoft Office 98 for Macintosh. At the same time, great care was taken to enable the MacOS and Windows versions of the Office 98 applications to coexist peacefully. You notice that the two sets of applications have the same look and feel and can even exchange Office documents.

Human-Related Issues

With Windows as a *de facto* standard in many corporate environments, many users are naturally wary of interacting with Macintosh computers. Office 98 for Macintosh, however, has been designed to have the same appearance and functionality as the Windows version, thereby eliminating many of the obstacles when transferring documents between platforms.

Many Macintosh users have complained about the poor performance of the applications in previous versions of Office. For example, Word 6.0 was seen as excessively slow and cumbersome until it was quickly updated to version 6.1. The reason was that, until recently, Microsoft did a straight port of the Windows version to the MacOS without much customization for the Macintosh. In contrast, the applications in Office 98 for the Macintosh were written directly for the MacOS as a separate incarnation from the Windows version. The Office code was written to take advantage of the PowerPC processor found in the Macintosh computer, enabling much faster and more efficient operation.

Macintosh Hardware Requirements

Along with the sophistication of the Office applications, the hardware requirements for the system have grown. Before you install Office 98 on your system, be sure that your computer has the following capabilities:

- *Processor.* Any Macintosh or Macintosh-compatible system that uses a PowerPC chip can run Office 98, but Microsoft recommends that your computer CPU have a clock speed of at least 120 MHz.
- *RAM.* You need at least 16MB of RAM to run any of the Office applications separately. Because it's often advantageous to run several Office applications simultaneously, you may need more than 16MB of RAM. Microsoft recommends 32MB of RAM if you run the Office applications simultaneously.
- *Hard Drive.* Set aside 50MB to 120MB of your hard disk for your Office installation. Later in this chapter, you learn how you can customize your installation to include as many or as few of the Office accessories you want.
- *MacOS Version.* You need MacOS 7.5 or later, but System 7.5.5 is recommended.
- *Monitor.* Your monitor should display 16 levels of gray or 256 colors with a resolution of at least 650 × 400 pixels.
- *Peripherals.* You need a CD-ROM drive to install the software; in an office environment, you may need a network connection to install the software from an office LAN. Microsoft also recommends that you have some sort of connection to the Internet that you have to

provide separately. Such a connection enables you to make use of some of the Internet functionality within Office as well as access to conversion filters and updates on the Microsoft Web site.

Upgrade Issues

Microsoft goes to great pains to maintain backward compatibility in the Office applications. This means that you can open Excel 5.0 files with this latest version of Excel. You can probably open files that were written with even older versions of Excel; however, you can't easily open Excel 98 files in older versions of Excel. Being the first one in the office with Office 98 can be a difficult experience as none of your coworkers are able to read your files.

Microsoft does provide converters, however, for various versions of the Office applications. Some of these converters are on the Microsoft Web site and some are included in the Value Pack on the installation CD. Some of these converters can be used with older versions of the Office applications to read Office 98 documents. Most of the converters on the installation CD enable you to save your Office 98 files to older versions of Office.

Cross-Platform Issues

Many Windows users are under the impression that it is difficult to get information in and out of Macintosh computers mostly because of the difference in operating systems. Actually, it is quite simple to exchange data and files between the two platforms. The MacOS can use many of the same networking protocols as Windows, meaning that Macintoshes and Windows computers can exchange information within the same network. This is usually done with through file servers, or even simple email.

TIP The Macintosh can even read and write to DOS-formatted floppy disks. You can exchange information between the two types of computers just by using floppy disks.

With previous versions of Office, the file conversion between the two platforms had been less than optimal. Office 98 for the Macintosh, however, can easily read files written by the Windows version.

Overview of Macintosh Installation

Installing Office 98 for Macintosh is somewhat different from installing its Windows counterpart. In this section, you learn some of the mechanics of the installation process as well as some of the tools provided in the installation.

The Office 98 CD

Open the CD containing Office 98 and you see the folders displayed in Figure 4.1. Note that four main folders are visible containing the following items:

- *Microsoft Office 98 for Macintosh files.* In conventional Macintosh or Windows installations, the applications are stored in compressed formats. Even on the Windows version of Office, the application files don't look anything like they will in a final version on the hard drive. In the Macintosh install, however, the files are uncompressed and appear much as they will on your hard drive.
- *Value Pack.* Small tools and accessories that complement the Office applications.
- *Microsoft Internet.* Contains the Internet Explorer Web browser and the Outlook Express email client.
- *Office Custom Install.* Contains the conventional installation files familiar to Macintosh users.

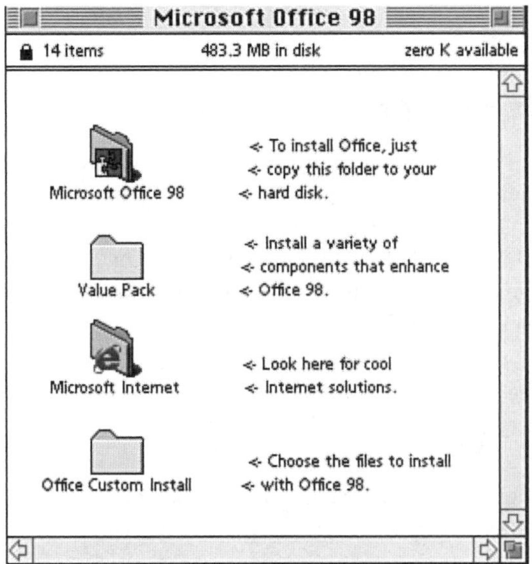

FIGURE 4.1
This CD contains all the files required to install Microsoft Office 98.

In the next sections, you learn how to install the Office 98 applications as well as some of the tools that add functionality to the package.

Using Drag-and-Drop Installation

If you open the folders entitled Microsoft Office 98, shown in Figure 4.1, you see the files and folders shown in Figure 4.2. The novel feature of Office 98 for Macintosh is that you can install the software via drag-and-drop. From the CD shown in Figure 4.1, you can simply drag the Microsoft Office 98 folder over to your hard drive and install Office 98 the easy way. This is much simpler and more direct than using an Installer program, which is the way Office 98 for Windows is installed.

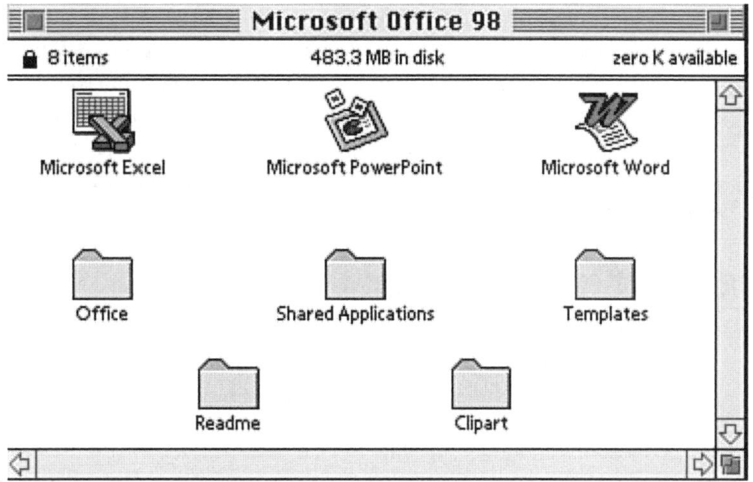

FIGURE 4.2
The Microsoft Office folder on the installation CD looks a lot like it will look on your hard drive.

Dropping the Microsoft Office 98 folder on your hard drive icon installs a slightly scaled-down version of Office 98 that enables you to perform most of your work. You can also install a complete version of Office 98. The size difference between the complete and scaled-down versions is about 14MB; the smaller version does not include some of the Value Pack applications and the Outlook Express email client. To install the full version of Office 98, go into the Office Custom Install folder on the CD, select the Microsoft Office 98 folder, and drag that folder to your hard drive.

Table 4.1 summarizes your drag-and-drop installation options:

Table 4.1 Installing Office 98 by Using Drag-and-Drop

To Get This...	Drag This to Your Hard Drive
Easy Install	The Microsoft Office 98 folder at the CD root directory
Full Install	The Microsoft Office 98 folder in the Custom Install folder

Many MacOS applications use additional files called extensions or preferences. These files reside in the System Folder on your local hard drive and are essential to running your applications. Office 98 for Macintosh makes extensive use of these types of files; however, extensions and preference files are not installed directly during the drag-and-drop installation. When you start the software for the first time after a drag-and-drop installation, Office 98 transfers the necessary system extensions and other pertinent files into Macintosh's System Folder. This process, referred to as First Run Installation (FRI), delays the startup of the Office applications as these files are copied into their necessary locations. This startup delay only occurs the first time that you use Office 98 after a drag-and-drop installation.

One useful feature of the drag-and-drop installation is that the First Run Installation (FRI) checks your System Folder for any files that might be needed but are not present, such as

QuickTime or any other software libraries. Also, FRI protects against inadvertent removal of any important files from the System Folder. If you accidentally delete a relevant extension, FRI senses that the next time you launch an Office application and replaces that file. Furthermore, FRI is beneficial when you upgrade to newer versions of the MacOS. The operating system upgrades require that you remove many files from your System Folder. By doing a clean system install, you can clear out your System Folder and have FRI reinstall the required files upon launching one of the Office applications.

Using the Office 98 Installer Program

Instead of using the drag-and-drop method to install Office 98 on your Macintosh, you can use the conventional installer program, which is similar to installation programs you have probably used in the past. Although the Office Installer takes longer than the drag-and-drop method, it has several advantages. The installation program enables you to customize, to a great degree, the applications and tools you want to load onto your local hard drive. The Installer enables you to selectively step through the different programs and add-on tools available in the installation. With drag-and-drop, in contrast, you can only drag two different folders of Office to your hard drive. Also, the Installer removes previous copies of Office from your hard drive, including old extensions and preference files. When installing via drag-and-drop, you have to manually sort through the old applications to drag them to the Trash.

To use the conventional installer program, follow these steps:

1. Open the Office Custom Install folder on your CD.
2. Launch the Installer application by double-clicking the Installer icon. If the Installer detects earlier versions of Microsoft Office applications, it asks whether you want to remove those applications.

If you have the space on your hard drive, keep your earlier version of Office intact while installing Office 98. Although Office 98 can read and write earlier versions of the software, you can eliminate any possible conversion problems by keeping your old software around until you're ready to delete it.

3. Following that, you're prompted with the dialog box you see in Figure 4.3. This third-party installer program is used for several large MacOS applications, so you are probably familiar with how it works. As you can see in the figure, you can pick and choose which elements of the various applications you want to include in your Office 98 installation. For example, help files take a lot of hard disk space. If you are an experienced Excel user, you may not want to include Excel's help files in the installation, and can simply uncheck the box next to the Help button.

Clicking the buttons in the right column provides information on that item.

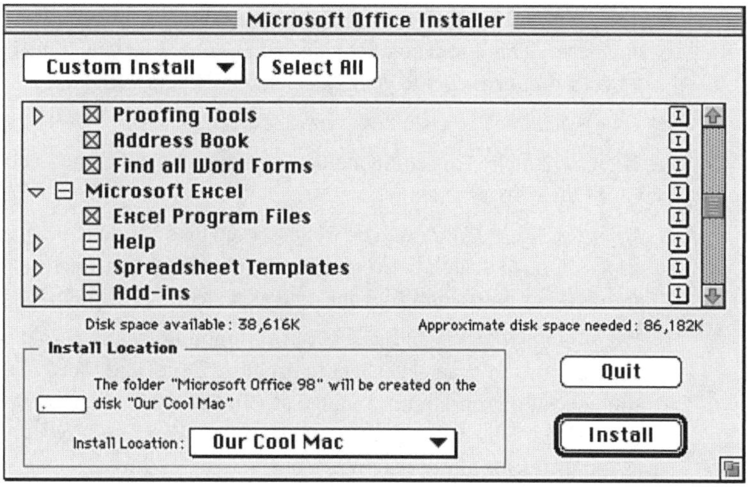

FIGURE 4.3
The Office 98 Installer enables you to pick and choose which capabilities to include in your Office 98 applications.

4. After clicking the Office tools to include in the installation, click the Install button. You're prompted for your name and organization, which are used to personalize your Office applications. Then your installation begins.

Choosing Value Pack Components

Along with your Office 98 applications, the installation CD contains a variety of complementary applications. You can drag and drop some of these components from the Value Pack folder on the CD; you need to install other components using the Value Pack Installer, an installer program that works very much like the Office Installer discussed earlier. To install the Value Pack components onto your hard drive, you must have already installed a copy of Microsoft Office.

The Value Pack components are as follows:

- *Assistants*. Office 98 enables you to have several different types of assistants—online aids that offer help with Office applications. You can load these assistants into any Office program.
- *Bookshelf Integration*. Microsoft Bookshelf is a separate multimedia reference application that you can use to perform research. You can search Bookshelf for a variety of types of information. When you have Bookshelf, Office 98, and the Bookshelf Integration component on the same computer, you can search Bookshelf from the various Office applications. Special commands are added to the PowerPoint and Word menus so that you can perform searches in Bookshelf without having to leave Office.
- *Business Templates*. A variety of templates are available for business applications that you can apply towards your Word, Excel, and PowerPoint files.
- *Clipart*. What PowerPoint presentation is complete without a jazzy QuickTime movie or background texture? The Clipart component contains dozens of PICT files, movies, graphics, and textures for use in your Word and PowerPoint documents.

- *Data Access.* Microsoft Query is a database access tool you can use to access external databases. This component enables you to use Query to connect to databases and download information to your Excel spreadsheets.
- *TrueType Fonts.* You can never have too many fonts.
- *Microsoft Movie.* This component enables you to embed a QuickTime movie into one of your Office documents.
- *Microsoft Office Manager.* The Manager enables you to launch the different Office applications or switch between active applications by using the keyboard. This tool shows up as both a control panel and as an icon in the menu bar.
- *Programmability.* Visual Basic is a programming language that you can use to build small applications. You can also use it to program Excel and Word macros. You can build sophisticated programming aids to streamline work involved in constructing your documents. This component contains sample Word and Excel macros that you can use as templates for future macros.
- *Proofing Tools.* This component enables you to install hyphenation, dictionary, and thesaurus files for a variety of languages.
- *Templates.* This component contains a large number of templates for your PowerPoint, Word, and Excel documents. You can get a head start on a crisp memo or presentation using one of the intricate templates included in this component.
- *Text Converters.* The text converters in this component enable you to import files from previous versions of Word for Windows, WordPerfect, Word for Macintosh, and other formats into your Office 98 documents.
- *Unbinder.* Microsoft Binder for Windows is an application that enables you to combine PowerPoint, Excel, and Word documents into a single file. Unfortunately, you cannot work on files while they're in a binder. This component unbinds these documents so that you can work on the elements of the bound files separately.
- *Word Speak.* This component enables Office to speak the contents of your Word documents out loud.

The following components are installed with the full Office Installation. If you perform an Easy option, however, either by using the Installer or drag-and-drop, you need to add these components separately. You can do this with the Value Pack Installer.

- *More Help.* Get more help on Visual Basic for your macro programming needs.
- *Wizards.* Wizards guide you step-by-step through sophisticated document creation.
- *Microsoft Excel Add-ins.* These files are a collection of macros and wizards that add functionality to your Excel application. Such capabilities include auto-saving and file-conversion as well as statistical and analytical tools.
- *Genigraphics Wizard and GraphicsLink.* These files are useful for printing PowerPoint documents.
- *Equation Editor.* This component enables you to incorporate sophisticated equations into your Word and PowerPoint documents.

Running Office 98 from a CD or a Network Drive

You can run Office 98 from the installation CD or a remote network drive rather than installing it on your local hard drive. Each time you run Office 98 from either a CD or a network drive, however, there is a performance hit as the MacOS loads the shared libraries into memory. This same process occurs when Office is on your hard drive, but information travels much more slowly over a network or CD-ROM drive than from a local hard drive.

As in the drag-and-drop installation, FRI runs the first time you activate an Office application from a CD or network drive, at which time you incur a startup delay. Successive launches do not have the FRI delay.

Installing from a Macintosh Server

If you are managing multiple Macintosh computers, you're faced with the problem of tediously installing Office 98 on every local hard drive. If your computers are networked via a central file server—either AppleShare, Novell NetWare, or Microsoft NT—you have the option of installing Office via a network. Several options are at your disposal.

NOTE If you do not want to purchase a copy of Office 98 for each user on your network, you can purchase a License Pak for each user. This is cheaper than buying a CD and documentation for each user and gives you the right to make a copy of Office for each user. This License Pak option is available through your favorite software retailer. ■

Your deployment strategy is similar to the installation process described in the section "Using the Office 98 Installer Program" except that you are installing the software onto a network hard drive. You need to begin this procedure by working on a computer that has write privileges to your network hard drive. Your strategy consists of the following:

- Launch the Office Installer program and select a desired location on the remote hard drive.
- Using the Installer sequence described earlier, select the Office capabilities and Value Pack components that you want to include in the installation. Complete the selection process and allow the installation to occur.
- Use the Value Pack Installer to add a desired set of components.
- Add any custom templates you may have to the appropriate Templates folders in the Office 98 folder on the remote hard drive.
- Optionally, clear the name and organization information from the installation point by copying the Microsoft Office 98 file over to the new Office 98 folder on the remote hard drive.
- Transfer the Microsoft Office folder to each hard drive.
- Optionally, initiate FRI to save users time and headaches when they first install the new software.

Let's cover these steps in more detail.

Installing Office 98 on a Remote Hard Drive In the Office Custom Install folder on the installation CD, run the Installer program and select an appropriate place on the network hard drive. This process works the same as the installer process described earlier in the section "Using the Office 98 Installer Program."

Selecting Desired Accessories Using the installation process described earlier, add the various accessories to your Office installation. These should include Help files and assistants to aid users new to Office 98. Click the Install button and complete the installation.

Adding Value Pack Components Using the Value Pack Installer, install the desired Value Pack Components. Remember that your users may have widely varying experience levels with Office 98 so that you may opt for a full Component installation.

Customizing Your Network Office 98 Folder You may want to include custom templates for use within your organization. Place these templates in the Templates folder in the Microsoft Office 98 folder on the network hard drive. You can add Excel Add-ins to the Microsoft Office 98:Office:Excel Add-ins folder. You can even insert documents you wanted displayed at each user startup by inserting these documents in the Microsoft Office 98:Office:Startup folder.

Clearing the Personalization Information When you installed the software on the network hard drive, the Installer prompted you for your name and organization. If you do nothing about it, your users see your name and organization every time they launch their Office applications. To let users customize their own Office applications, you can remove this personalization information. To do this, go to the following folder on the installation CD:

Office Custom Install:Microsoft Office 98:Office

From this folder, drag the file Microsoft Office 98 from the CD into the Microsoft Office 98:Office folder on the network drive. When your users launch an Office application for the first time, they're prompted for their name and organization.

Transferring the Office 98 Folder to Local Hard Drives You can transfer the new Office 98 folder on the network hard drive to your users' hard drives in two ways. You can push the folder to the local hard drive. This assumes that you have write access to your users' hard drives. If so, you can drag the Microsoft Office 98 folder to your users' hard drives using plain old File Sharing. You may have access to a network management tool, however, which can facilitate access to your client computers. If so, you can automate this process instead of pushing the folders computer by computer.

NOTE *Network Management Tools.* If you are running an AppleShare server, you can use some of the AppleShare tools to push the Office 98 folders to your users' hard drives. Microsoft lists such third-party tools as File Wave Enterprise Edition from Wave Research, Net Octopus from Dr. Solomon's Software, and Systems Management Server from Microsoft.

Another option besides manually pushing the data to your users' computers is to install a script—using either Frontier, AppleScript, or some other scripting language—that launches the Installer on the network hard drive. Create the script so that the Microsoft Office 98 folder is copied from the remote hard drive down to the local hard drive. If inserted in the users' System Folder:Startup Items folder, the script launches when the users restart their computers.

Probably the most work-intensive option is for you to manually pull the folder off the network hard drive onto each local hard drive. This may seem tedious but it may be your only choice if your users turn their computers off during off-hours or if your network privileges prohibit you from writing to local hard drives.

Internet Explorer and Outlook Express

Also included in the Office Installation CD are two very popular Microsoft applications: Internet Explorer and Outlook Express. Internet Explorer (IE) is the popular Web browser developed by Microsoft. Like Microsoft Office, the version of IE on this CD was written specifically for the MacOS and as a result is sizzlingly quick at formatting the images and text during Web downloads.

Similarly, Outlook Express is the freeware version of Microsoft's Outlook communication package. Outlook Express enables you to communicate with other users via email and newsgroups. Both Outlook Express and Internet Explorer work in concert with the Microsoft Office applications. These programs, however, are configured in more detail than the Office applications and should be installed separately from your Office installations.

Installing Internet Explorer In the Microsoft Internet folder on the CD, you find two installation programs (shown in Figure 4.4). To install Microsoft Internet Explorer, double-click the Internet Explorer 4.0 Installer icon. You're prompted with the usual legal disclaimer; click the Accept button to continue. You then see a dialog box similar to the one shown in Figure 4.5. If you want to complete a full installation of Internet Explorer and its associated applications, click the Install button. Internet Explorer and all the supplementary fonts and applications, including Java, are then installed in the appropriate places.

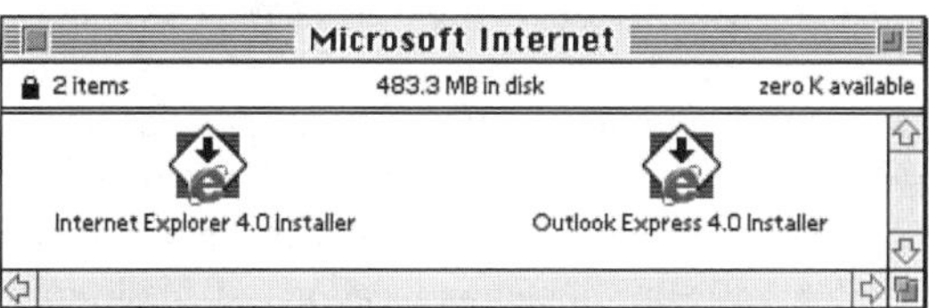

FIGURE 4.4
Internet Explorer and Outlook Express have separate installer programs.

You may not need all the fonts and supplementary applications in the full IE installation. For example, you may already have the fonts included in the installer; furthermore, newer copies of MacOS 8 come with Java included. You may already have Java installed on your Macintosh. For this reason, you may want to customize the installation.

In the pop-up window in the upper-left corner of the dialog box (shown in Figure 4.5), select Easy Install. You see a series of check boxes (shown in Figure 4.6). Note that you can install Outlook Express using the IE installer. Outlook Express and IE work interchangeably, so it is useful to have them both installed.

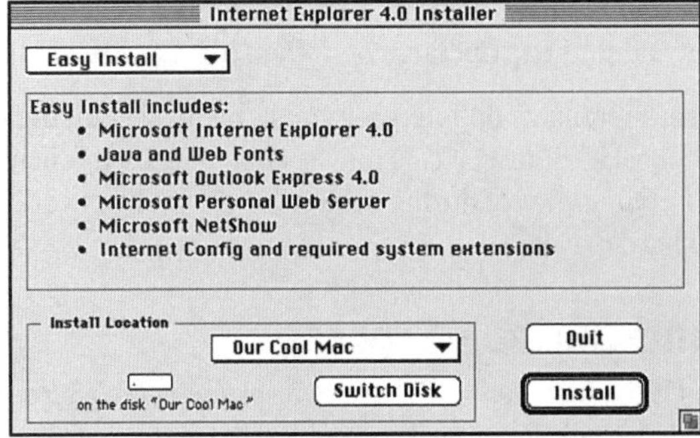

FIGURE 4.5
You can take the easy way out and complete a full installation of the Internet Explorer program and associated applications.

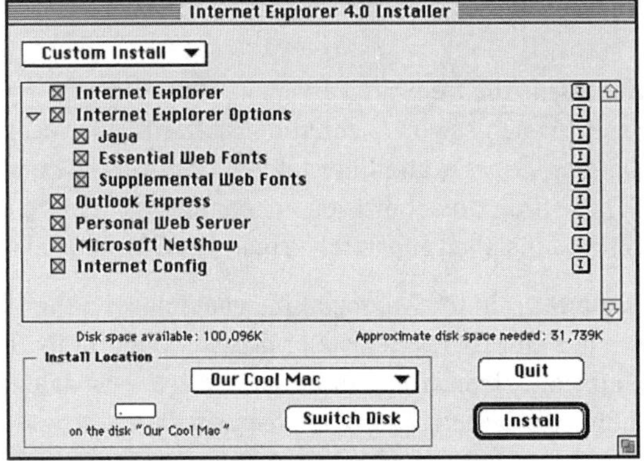

FIGURE 4.6
You can pick and choose which Internet Explorer options you want to include in your installation.

Microsoft NetShow is an application that enables you to play NetShow movies on the Web. It works much like RealNetworks' RealPlayer. Personal Web Server, from Apple Computer, enables you to set up your computer to host Web pages over a local network, or even over the Internet. This application is not powerful enough for you to serve large numbers of users, but it can enable you to serve small amounts of information to various users. Internet Config enables you to configure several of your Internet applications with a common database of information. In the early days of the Web, you had to specify the same information, such as your email address, your signature files, and your helper applications, all in different Internet applications. Using Internet Config, your email program, your Web browsers, and your Usenet newsreader all have the same helper applications and incorporate other pieces of personalized information.

NOTE As with Office 98, you can install Internet Explorer for large numbers of users. It is beyond the scope of this book, however, to explain how to do so. You can download a copy of the Microsoft Internet Explorer Administration Kit at **www.microsoft.com/ie/ieak/**.

Select the desired options and click the Install button to complete your customized installation of Internet Explorer.

Installing Outlook Express Installing Outlook Express is much simpler than installing IE because fewer supplementary applications are required. Double-click the Outlook Express 4.0 Installer button in the Microsoft Internet folder on the CD. The familiar installation process commences. If you accept the disclaimer, you're prompted for a full install of Outlook Express. Of course, you can also select Custom Install in the upper-left pop-up box, which gives you the options of installing Outlook Express and Internet Config. If you already have Internet Config, you can deselect this option before you click the Install button. ●

CHAPTER 5

Troubleshooting Office Installations

In an ideal world, all software installations would proceed smoothly and would not result in problems; however, this chapter is about reality. Whenever you introduce a new software package to a company, a high potential exists for problems. This chapter looks at how to prevent these problems and how to cope with the ones you fail to prevent.

The Importance of Prevention

The best way to troubleshoot a problem is to not experience it in the first place. Chapter 1 emphasized the importance of planning and testing the rollout of Office 97. Chapter 2 outlined the installation options that enable you to add features to the basic Office 97 package. These two chapters helped you think through the form and function you want available to Office 97 users.

No matter how carefully you plan your Office rollout, however, you can't avoid playing a resources game. Office 97 is a huge collection of software. The applications are large, and the resources used are significant. Each time you decide to add another interesting feature to Office 97, you are using up another bit of your total system's resources. The result is a balancing act for the administrator; you must select your installation options wisely.

The following are some steps to take to ensure a smooth and fairly trouble-free installation.

- *Get the Office 97 Resource Kit.* This book contains many important tips for installing and using Office 97. It also includes the Tools and Utilities CD-ROM with wizards, utilities, and templates that ease the installation process.
- *Get all the RAM you can into workstations and servers.* Office 97 is a major memory hog. We recommend nothing less than 64MB of RAM in a machine using Office 97. Machines with 128MB run even better.
- *Use fast disks.* The faster the hard drive, the better. Office 97 makes extensive use of hard drives. The faster the drive works, the smoother the applications operate. On servers, you need fast SCSI drives.
- *Have a clean running network available.* Before installing Office 97 on a local area network, be sure all workstations are communicating as intended with the servers. Any problem with access or communication between machines will only be magnified when you install Office 97 on top of the situation.
- *Install operating system upgrades long before Office 97.* If your company also plans to upgrade from Windows 95 to Windows NT, complete the upgrade and test it thoroughly before installing Office 97. Windows NT uses a different type of file allocation for hard drives and several other security features that are hard to reset after Office 97 is in place.
- *Use the Installation Wizard for network installation and scripting.* The Tool and Utility CD that comes with the *Office 97 Resource Kit* includes a wizard for installing Office 97 to a network. For scripting and batch processing, this wizard helps you avoid many problems.
- *Watch out for other programs stealing your resources.* Some older programs used a nondynamic method of flagging RAM. Take the example of older versions of WordPerfect—if loaded first, WordPerfect would take all the available RAM it could find. The memory flags it left behind were not always readable by other applications; thus, RAM sat empty and unused. The lesson here is to load Office 97 first, and then other applications.

- *Run Office 97 locally where possible.* If your network is already burdened with traffic (that is, greater than 50% bandwidth used during an average hour), run Office 97 locally. The accessing of several applications by many people will quickly bring your network to its knees.

Prototyping

Chapter 1 discussed how to pilot-test Office 97 before rollout. Another approach is to prototype the installation. In a *prototype* situation, you use an independent computer to test various types of installations. To prototype a network installation, you hook one to three computers to a server.

The entire prototype system should be independent of the local area network and should use your normal operating systems. In this way, you can test the success of push and pull installations. After you load Office 97 onto the target machines, you can evaluate whether your scripting instructions have executed as expected, whether the applications are functioning properly, and whether various access settings interfere with the installation process.

NOTE A *push installation* occurs when you set the network to force the installation of Office 97 to the workstations as users log on. A *pull installation* occurs when each user goes to a common administration point on the server and downloads the installation script.

The reason for prototyping is to uncover problems that might occur in an actual installation. Users won't be pleased if they have to sit by while MIS spends hours trying to fix an installation glitch. Remember, one of the first steps in upgrading from Office 95 to 97 is to remove older applications. This could potentially leave groups of users with no applications to run until the installation problem is reduced or fixed.

Standalone Office Installation Problems

A large portion of the problems that can occur when installing Office 97 on a standalone system stem from obsolete files still on your system. These files can be earlier versions of Office or, if you're reinstalling Office 97, they might be Office 97 files that shouldn't still be on the system.

To get rid of earlier versions of Office on your system, run Offcln97.exe, located in the \ValuPack\Offclean folder on the Office 97 CD-ROM.

To remove Office 97 before reinstalling it, start the setup program on your Office 97 CD-ROM and click on Remove All. This program removes Office 97 files so you can reinstall the whole program.

NOTE When you run the setup program, intending to install Office 97, you might discover you aren't given the option of choosing Typical, Custom, or Run from CD-ROM/Server. If so, setup has found an earlier version of Office and thinks you just want to add or remove components rather than installing from scratch. To remedy the situation, uninstall Office 97 and then reinstall the whole program.

Networked Office Installation Problems

Network installations can give rise to a host of problems. Networks come in many different flavors, and you need to install Office 97 with the peculiarities of your network in mind. You might also need to cope with multiple operating systems. A company could be running both Novell and AppleTalk networks with workstations using Apple System 7, Windows for Workgroups, Windows 95, and Windows NT.

Given these complexities, your first step toward a successful network installation is to make sure the network is running cleanly and efficiently. Then get as many workstations as possible running the same operating system, preferably Windows 95 or NT.

Because so many types of networks can be used, a discussion of the problems associated with each one is beyond the scope of this book. Instead, this chapter uses examples from the most popular network, Novell, to illustrate some of the difficulties you might experience and how to fix them.

Network Bogs Down When Running Office 97

Running Office 97 as a shared application can bog down some networks. If your Novell network has more than a handful of users or has to handle other large bandwidth operations, the wiser course is to run Office 97 locally. Set up shared and common files on the network server, and make sure each user links to these.

Applications Fail to Share or Collaborate

The real power of Office 97 lies in its capability to share information with other users on a network. However, you might occasionally encounter "you do not have access" or "system error" messages, such as the one shown in Figure 5.1.

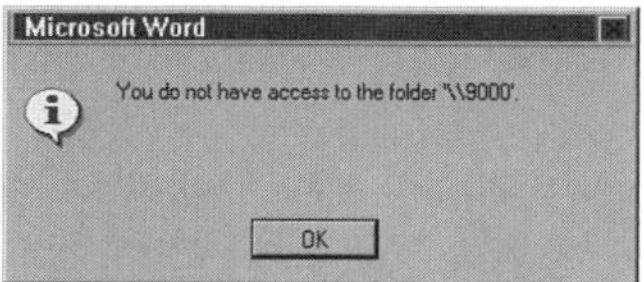

FIGURE 5.1
A "you do not have access" error message.

You might also find that when you try to open a data file from another part of the network, you are greeted with a password challenge such as the one shown in Figure 5.2. When you enter your password, you continue to receive the challenge, and reaching the data file seems impossible, even though the folder is shared.

FIGURE 5.2
A password challenge error message.

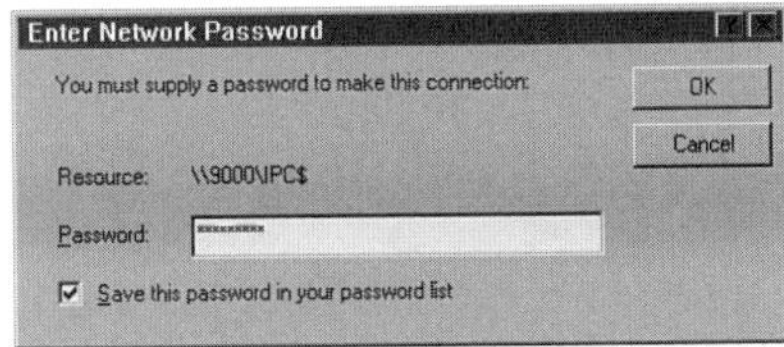

A few solutions are available for problems that generate error messages such as these.

When installing Office 97, make sure Novell's security and access settings match those of your operating system (most likely Windows 95 or NT). Mismatches can shut some users out of what should be an open area of the server.

Applications might also fail to share or collaborate if you haven't granted full read and write permissions to the subfolders Office 97 uses. Under Windows NT, you should leave these subfolders open to read/write:

C:\
C:\Temp
C:\Winnt
C:\Winnt\Forms
C:\Winnt\System32
C:\Program Files\Microsoft Office
C:\Program Files\Microsoft Office\Office
C:\Program Files\Microsoft Office\Xlstart
C:\Program Files\Microsoft Office\Templates

To check the permission status of these drives and folders, right-click on an item, choose Properties, and click on the Permissions button on the General tab. The Security tab allows you to set permissions for which accounts can access the drive or folder.

In addition, you need to examine the following files to make sure none are set to read-only:

C:\Ffastun.ffa
C:\Ffastun.ffl
C:\Ffastun.ffo
C:\Ffastun.ffx
C:\Winnt\Artgalry.cag
C:\Winnt\LogonID.acl
C:\Winnt\LogonID8.xlb
C:\Winnt\LogonID.fav
C:\Winnt\Mso97.acl
C:\Winnt\Msoprefs.232
C:\Winnt\Outlook.fav
C:\Winnt\Outlook.prf
C:\Winnt\Outlook.prt
C:\Winnt\Forms\Frmcache.dat

C:\Winnt\System32\Ffastlog.txt
C:\Winnt\System32\Msforms.twd

Under Windows 95, these sharing problems are far less likely to occur. The folders to check for permissions are:

C:\
C:\MSOffice or C:\Microsoft Office

To check the permission status of these folders, right-click on the folder or drive in Windows 95 Explorer. Choose Sharing from the shortcut menu and check the sharing characteristics set up for these objects. You should allow full read and write permissions.

If fixing these permissions doesn't clear up the problem, consult the list of files for network installations to see if one of the critical components of your network is missing or is located in a folder without proper sharing properties. This file list is located on the Tools and Utilities CD-ROM included with the *Office 97 Resource Kit*; look in the Lists subfolder for a file called Network.xls.

Runtime Applications Won't Work from the Server

You have loaded a runtime application on a server, but it doesn't work when users request the application. One likely cause of this problem is that you installed Office 97 as an upgrade after the runtime was created for an earlier version of Access. To fix the problem, reinstall Office 97 and then reinstall the runtime application.

Other possible causes of a nonfunctioning runtime application include the following:

- You have a sharing violation, such as those described in the previous section.
- A utility called up by the application does not exist on the target machine.
- The runtime data file is corrupted.

Microsoft Data Map Error Message

Users might encounter this error message when they attempt to run Office 97 from a Novell server. The problem occurs when the registry for Office is pointing to the wrong location for the administration point. This often happens when a computer originally had a local copy of Office 97 installed and then someone reinstalled Office to run from the network.

To avoid this problem, you should always remove existing Office components before performing network installations. You could go into the registry and edit pointers to the correct locations, but just wiping out the existing installation and reinstalling as a Run from Network Server installation is usually easier.

Open Database Connectivity Doesn't Work with Web Pages

This is a somewhat common problem with Windows NT machines that were already running Office 97 when Novell's Web server or the Microsoft Internet Information Server was loaded.

To prevent this problem, make sure all Web servers are installed and running before Office 97 is installed. Otherwise, you need to reinstall Office 97.

General Network Troubleshooting

If fixes described in the previous sections haven't fixed your network problem, or if you are experiencing a different problem than the ones described here, take the following steps:

1. Run the Novell NetWare diagnostic tools to determine if the problem is in Office 97, NetWare, or somewhere else, and be sure to call the appropriate technical support people. Microsoft will not fix Novell problems.
2. Check for the problem on other computers in the network. Patterns of where the problem occurs can give you strong clues about its cause. A system- or workgroup-wide problem indicates the trouble is probably in the server.
3. Always search for the root cause. Just because a fix seemed to clear up a problem doesn't mean it will stay that way. Double-check your network to see if the same problem-causing conditions are located in other parts of the system.

Other Problems

You can encounter plenty of miscellaneous problems during installation. For example, Office 97 doesn't always get along with other major applications, such as high-end CAD packages. This section discusses some other installation-related problems you might have to grapple with.

Setup Has Encountered a Problem Updating Your System Registry (Setup Error 168)

When this problem occurs, you receive another message informing you that Microsoft Office 97 setup was unsuccessful. This problem happens when you have done one of the following three things:

- The account you used to log on to a computer running Microsoft Windows NT 3.51 or 4.0 is a member of the Users group but is not a member of the Administrators group.
- When installing Office 97, you chose the Custom install.
- During installation, you changed the folder used by Excel, Word, PowerPoint, or Access to a folder other than the default folder.

To remedy this situation, do one of the following:

- Exit Windows NT and log in again, using an account that is a member of the Administrators group. Then run Office 97 setup again.
- Run Office 97 setup again and do not change the default folders.

Error Message: Disk Is Full

This situation occurs if you have inadequate disk space or if there is a problem with your compressed drive. You might receive a Disk is Full error message even though setup reports that you have enough disk space to install Microsoft Office 97. The amount of available disk space depends on the types of files on your compressed drive and how effectively the various data types can be compressed.

For both situations, free up more disk space and run setup again.

Setup for Microsoft Office Cannot Locate the Program Files Folder

This problem occurs when the Office setup program doesn't correctly identify where the Program Files folder is located on your computer or network. When this happens, setup usually attempts to install the Office components in another folder.

To correct this problem, use the Registry Editor to make sure the correct path is entered in the registry. Look for the Path command under HKEY_LOCAL_MACHINE, and change it if it isn't correct.

> **CAUTION**
>
> Changing anything in the registry can cause problems that might result in your having to reinstall your operating system. When working in the Registry Editor, pay special attention to what you are changing so you can avoid making serious mistakes. You should also make backup copies of the registry files (System.dat and User.dat). These files are located in the Windows folder and are hidden files. If you don't see them, choose View, Options in the Explorer or a folder window, click on the View tab, and mark Show All Files.

To correct a problem in the registry, follow these steps:

1. Start the Registry Editor (Regedt32.exe) and navigate to the following key (see Figure 5.3): HKEY_LOCAL_MACHINE\SOFTWARE\Microsoft\Windows\CurrentVersion.

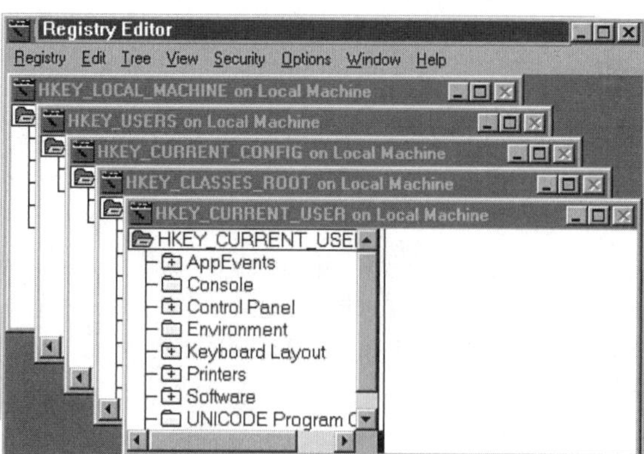

FIGURE 5.3
The Registry Editor shows you the areas available for editing.

2. Double-click on ProgramFilesDir in the right pane of the Registry Editor to display the Edit String dialog box (see Figure 5.4).

FIGURE 5.4
Your target for editing is the ProgramFilesDir portion of the registry.

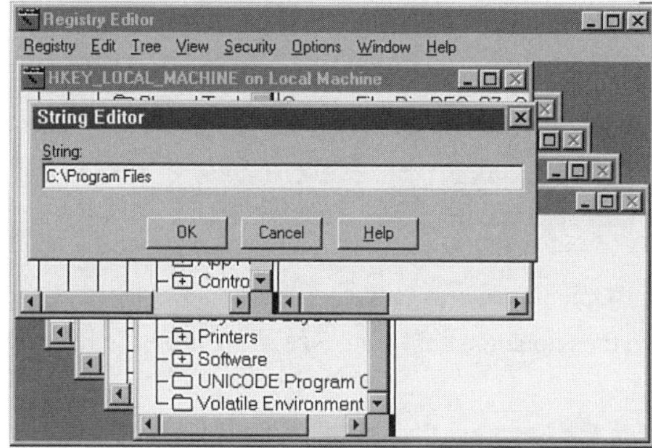

3. Check the path to the Program Files folder in the Value Data field, correct it if necessary, and click on OK.
4. Double-click on CommonFilesDir in the right pane of the Registry Editor to display the Edit String dialog box.
5. In the Value Data field, type the correct path to the Common Files folder, and click on OK.
6. Close the Registry Editor.

Receive Error Message When Reading from CD-ROM Drive

Before making any changes to the CD-ROM drive setup, inspect and clean the disk. Wipe it with a soft cloth in a straight line from the center, working your way out to the edge. If the disk has any scratches on it, call the Microsoft Order Desk at 800-360-7561 and request a replacement disk.

If the disk is scratch free, proceed with the corrective actions described in the next two sections.

Option 1—Disable the CD-ROM Drive Cache Occasionally a problem occurs with the CD-ROM drive cache on Windows 95 computers (not usually on Windows NT machines) that requires you to disable the cache before using the Office CD-ROM. Even though the drive cache makes the drive more reliable, it reduces performance. To disable the cache, follow these steps:

1. Choose Start, Settings, Control Panel.
2. Run the System applet and click on the Performance tab.
3. Click on the File System button to display the File System Properties dialog box, and click on the CD-ROM tab (see Figure 5.5).

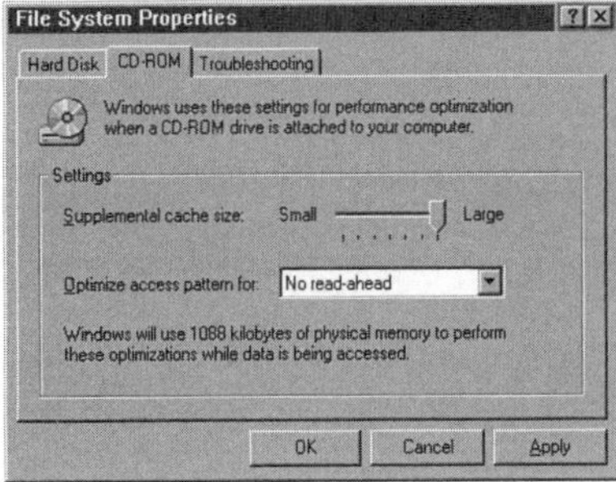

FIGURE 5.5
You can reset your CD-ROM settings to disable read-ahead.

4. Display the Optimize Access Pattern For drop-down list, and choose No Read-Ahead.
5. Make sure the Supplemental Cache Size slider is positioned to the far left, and click on OK.

Option 2—Disable the Compact Disk AutoPlay Feature in Windows 95 AutoPlay continuously checks your CD-ROM drive to determine if there is a CD-ROM in the drive. If a disk is present and it has an Autorun.inf file, Windows 95 runs the file listed on the *open=* line in Autorun.inf.

To disable AutoPlay, complete the following steps:

1. Choose Start, Settings, Control Panel.
2. Run the System applet and click on the Device Manager tab.
3. Expand the CD-ROM branch and double-click on the entry for your CD-ROM drive to display its Properties dialog box (see Figure 5.6).

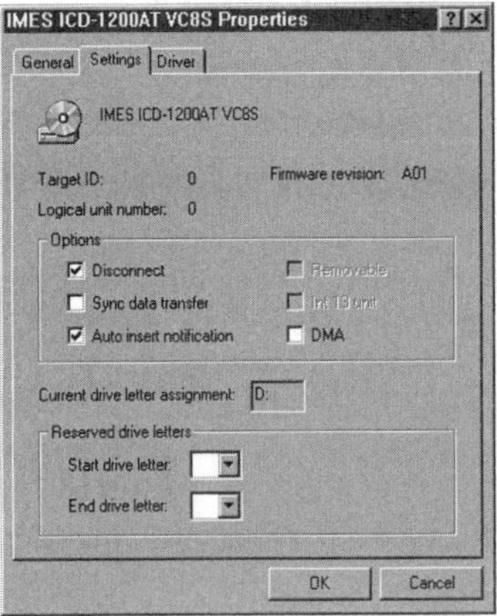

FIGURE 5.6
Use the Properties dialog box for the CD-ROM to improve or change its performance.

4. Click on the Settings tab, clear the Auto Insert Notification check box, and click on OK.
5. Click on OK in the System Properties dialog box, and restart your computer when you are prompted to do so.

Reinstalling Microsoft Office

Occasionally the changes necessary for fixing a particular problem will require you to totally reinstall Office. Even though this is a time-consuming activity, it will ensure that you install the correct files. Follow these steps to do a completely new installation:

1. Insert the Office 97 CD-ROM in your CD-ROM drive.
2. Choose Start, Run, type **`D:\setup`** (replacing D: with the appropriate drive letter), and click on OK.
3. When the Microsoft Office 97 Setup dialog box appears, click on Remove All.
4. After the uninstall process is complete, reinstall Office 97.

Contacting Microsoft for Assistance

Before calling Microsoft for assistance, first visit its Web site (support.microsoft.com/support) and investigate the sections on troubleshooting.

In the online support area, you can enter search phrases for your particular problem and see postings related to your inquiry. For example, if you are having problems accessing the Remote Access Service (RAS) from Outlook on your Windows NT machine, you might enter a search string such as **`RAS problems with Outlook 97`**.

Be careful how you word your search strings. The string *RAS* brings up a different set of hits than *Remote Access Service*. To make your searches more precise, use the Boolean statements OR, AND, and NOT in your strings.

When the list of articles appears, read through the titles and click on the ones that seem to address your problem. Keep a running log of what you are reading, and check the end of the articles for links to related postings not on your original results list. By cross-checking with your log, you can make sure you are not missing an important posting.

Use the word *patch*, *updates*, or *fixes* in your search string to find downloadable files for fixing undocumented problems.

If you need to call Microsoft, you should have a few pieces of information ready for the tech support person: the error code you received, the build number, your product ID number, and the version of Office 97 you're using, as well as the version of the operating system under which it's running. ●

PART II

Customizing Office to Your Organization's Needs

CHAPTER 6

Customizing Word to Your Organization's Needs

Microsoft may have created Word, but you can *re*-create it as a word processor designed specifically to serve the needs of your organization. A relatively small investment of time in customizing Word can significantly improve the productivity of your entire workgroup or company. And, as you'll see, if you're prepared to invest somewhat more time, you can have an even greater impact.

This chapter gets you to the heart of customizing Word, showing you how to turn nearly any task your users perform into a one-step process accessible from a toolbar, menu, or the keyboard.

CAUTION

Some customizations, such as changing existing keystroke commands or moving existing menu items, may confuse users who are relying on standard books and training materials, and generally should be avoided.

Other customizations should at least be briefly explained to your users, so they will not be surprised by differences between the customized version of Word they are using and the one they may be familiar with from home, previous jobs, books, or training materials.

A Closer Look at Microsoft Word Templates

Templates are critical to customizing Word, so it's critical that you understand them. Chances are, you already know one role that Word templates play: they can include "patterns" of text, formatting, and graphics that form the basis of new documents. This aspect of working with templates is covered in detail in Chapter 11. In this chapter, you'll focus on a less familiar role of templates: *as storage locations for Word's customizations.*

Word templates can store a wide range of document settings and customizations, including the following:

- Custom styles
- AutoText entries (boilerplate text, graphics, and other document elements)
- Macro procedures (whether recorded using Word's Macro Recorder or written from scratch in Visual Basic for Applications)
- Custom toolbars and buttons added to any toolbar
- Custom menus and commands added to any menu
- Custom keyboard shortcuts

In Word 97, for the first time, styles, macros, and custom toolbars can also be stored in documents. However, AutoText boilerplate text entries—an important component of many Word customizations—are still stored only in templates.

Unless you have a specific requirement to provide customizations along with an individual document (for example, you're sending a customized document to a recipient who can't be relied upon to install a separate Word template properly), it still makes sense to maintain all your customizations in templates. For one reason, templates are typically stored only in assigned templates folders, whereas documents can be stored anywhere—making customizations in documents potentially much harder to track.

Later in this chapter, you'll learn how to add these elements to a template. First, however, you'll take a closer look at how templates work in Word, so you can plan a strategy for using them most effectively.

The Normal Template: Word's Most Important Template

Whenever you open a Word document, you're already using at least one template: the Normal template. In Windows, this template is stored as Normal.dot in your Templates folder, typically C:\Program Files\Microsoft Office\Templates, the folder that stores all of Office's templates. On the Macintosh, it is typically stored at Microsoft Office 98:Office:Templates:Normal.

All Word's default styles (heading styles, text styles, and so on) are collected in the Normal template. So are Word 97's built-in AutoText entries for letters and business documents. Whenever a user clicks the New button on the Standard toolbar, or chooses Blank Document in the File, New dialog box, he or she is creating a document based on the Normal template.

What's more, the styles and other settings stored in the Normal template are always available to *all* Word documents, so any changes made to a user's Normal template can affect new documents created with it later. When users customize their own systems with new AutoText entries or macros, these are typically stored in the Normal template as well (although, as you'll see later, this can be changed). Out of the box, the Normal template is 27K, but in the hands of an active user, it can balloon to several hundred kilobytes or more.

NOTE If you delete or rename the Normal template, intentionally or inadvertently, Word restores it to the original settings it had when you first installed Word. This means that deleting or renaming the Normal template is a last resort for salvaging it if you have hopelessly damaged it.

After you delete or rename the Normal template and restart Word, Word looks for the Normal template in the locations where it would typically be found: in the Templates folder, the Workgroup Templates folder if you've set one, or in a different User Templates folder you may have specified in the User Information tab of the Tools, Options dialog box.

When Word cannot find the Normal template in these locations, it assumes the file is not present, and creates a new one with standard Word settings. Of course, this restored Normal template does not have any of the customizations contained in the previous Normal template—either customizations you provided, or customizations your user added afterwards.

How Word Works with Additional Templates

Beyond the Normal template, Word also allows you to create and use additional templates—both templates built into Word, and those you create yourself.

If you choose File, New, click the Report tab, and double-click on Contemporary Report, for example, Word creates a new report document based on its built-in Contemporary Report template. Although the Normal template is still available and open, the styles contained in this document are based on the styles contained in the Contemporary Report document. Similarly, any user interface settings that might be stored in the Contemporary Report template (as it happens, there aren't any) will also be available for use.

Attaching a New Template to a Document Assuming that you stay with consistent style names, *especially those that Word's built-in styles use,* you can change the look and feel of a document instantly, by attaching a different template to it. This works best if you select a new template that contains style names similar to the ones in the currently attached template. If you are working with a document based on the Contemporary Report template, for example, you could quickly change the document's look by attaching the Professional Report template instead. To attach a new template to your document, follow these steps:

1. Choose Tools, Templates and Add-Ins to display the Templates and Add-ins dialog box (see Figure 6.1).
2. Click Attach.
3. In the Attach Template dialog box, browse to the template you want to use, and click OK.
4. In the Templates and Add-ins dialog box, mark the Automatically Update Document Styles check box.
5. Click OK.

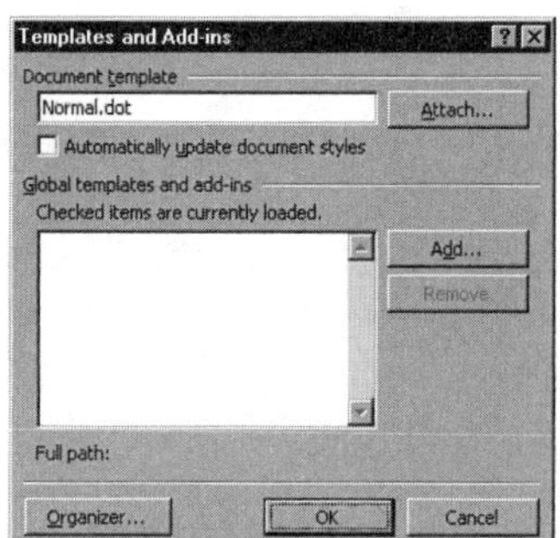

FIGURE 6.1
You can change the template attached to a document through the Templates and Add-ins dialog box.

If you've been careful about structuring your templates, this makes it extremely easy to update all your corporate documents in the wake of a company merger or graphic redesign. Create and deploy a new template with revised styles, and then attach it to your documents. Or, better yet, copy the updated version of the template *over* the previous version. If Automatically Update Document Styles is checked, then the documents will update themselves automatically.

Loading Global Templates You can open as many templates as you need at any given time, although loading a large number of templates will slow down Word's performance. Follow these steps to open a template as a *global template,* and thereby make its settings available to all Word documents:

1. Choose Tools, Templates and Add-Ins.
2. Click Add.
3. In the Add Template dialog box, browse to the template you want to use, and click OK.
4. The template appears in the Global Templates and Add-ins box, with a check mark next to it.
5. Click OK.

The template is now "globally" available to all documents in the current session. If a user exits Word and restarts it again, however, the template will not be available unless the user displays this dialog box and rechecks the check box associated with the template.

While a global template's user interface settings and AutoText entries are available for use in any Word document, its styles are not. Even after you open a global template, each document continues to use the styles in the template to which it is attached.

If you want a template to load as a global template automatically every time Word starts, copy it into Word's startup folder. In Windows, this is typically C:\Program Files\Microsoft Office\Office\Startup. On the Macintosh, it is typically Microsoft Office 98:Office:Startup:Word. Word's startup folder is covered in the section "Customizing Word's Own Startup Folder" at the end of this chapter.

Setting a Strategy for Customizing Templates

Until now, you've been reviewing Word's basic techniques for loading and working with templates that already exist. Now, briefly consider how you might approach using customized templates to improve productivity in your organization.

If you are deploying Word 97 for the first time, or if you are confident that your users have not already personalized their Normal templates with AutoText entries or other changes, consider replacing Word's built-in Normal template with one adapted to your company's needs. Your company's Normal template can include all the customizations that the majority of your users will benefit from, as in the following examples:

- Suppose that your department routinely publishes long documents with Word. You might create a special Long Document toolbar with shortcuts for indexing, cross-referencing, building tables of contents, and so on.
- Suppose that you have a series of forms that all your people use—vacation request forms, requisition forms, and so on. You might create a Company menu with commands that load these forms from specialized templates (or, possibly, commands that run Internet Explorer and display an intranet page containing the appropriate form).

In addition to these company-wide templates, you can also build specialized templates that address the needs of subsets of your users: specific workgroups, or users in many different departments who perform the same tasks. For example:

- Suppose that you're called upon to support the needs of a sales department. You might create a Sales template with toolbar buttons and macros that run your custom mail-merge routine for sales letters; and provide access to AutoText boilerplate text for proposal documents.
- Suppose that you support clerical staff who use Word exclusively to prepare pre-designed letters, memos, and reports. You could create a Clerical Support template that displays a dialog box at startup that allows the user to choose which kind of document to create.

If you support sophisticated users who have already customized their own Normal templates extensively, you can place your company-wide customizations in a second template (perhaps Normal2), and copy it to each user's Word startup folder. Now, Word loads two templates at startup: the Normal template each user has customized, and the Normal2 template that includes your company-wide customizations.

NOTE Many users do customize their own systems, but *not* in ways that affect the Normal template. For example, they may add words to their custom spelling dictionaries. These dictionaries are separate DIC files, which are available to all Office applications on a specific computer.

Similarly, new text-only AutoCorrect entries are stored in ACL files available to all Office applications. If Word users create formatted AutoCorrect entries, or entries that contain graphics, however, these are stored in the Normal template, and would be eliminated if you replace the user's Normal template with your own. ■

Creating a New Template for Customization

If you want to store your custom settings in the Normal template, all you have to do is open a document based on the Normal template and start creating your settings. If you want to create a new template for customization, however, follow these steps:

1. Choose File, New.
2. Select Blank Document in the General tab, if it is not already selected.
3. Click Template in the Create New area.
4. Click OK.

You now have a new template where you can store customized text and graphics, styles, AutoText entries, custom toolbar and menu settings, macros, and other elements.

Changing Styles in a Custom Template A key element of many templates is a set of consistent, distinctive styles that helps users build consistently formatted, attractive documents. For more information about building templates with consistent styles, see Chapter 11.

When you create a new template, it contains the styles that appeared in the template you based it on. Word provides several ways to change these styles. Following are two approaches that are especially worth discussing:

- With Style by Example, you can format text manually and transform that formatted text into a style. Style by Example is extremely easy to use, and allows you to see exactly how your text will be formatted. The styles you modify are stored in the document you have open—in this case, the new template you've just created. Also, you cannot change the Normal style using this feature.
- Through Word's Style dialog box (accessible through Format, Style), you can create all your styles, optionally basing one style on another to ensure consistency. The Style dialog box is less intuitive, but it is more systematic, enabling you to see all the style options available to you.

Each approach is covered in the following sets of steps. You can choose the one that's most convenient, or use them both together.

To create a new style using Style by Example, perform the following steps:

1. Enter a paragraph of text in the template you've created. This is dummy text you can use to simply give you something to format. Any amount of text is sufficient, as long as you end it with a paragraph mark.
2. Format the paragraph the way you want it.
3. Select the paragraph.
4. In the Style box at the left end of the Formatting toolbar, type the style name you want to use. If you use a style name that already exists, the Modify Style dialog box opens, as shown in Figure 6.2. Word asks whether you want to reformat the style, or reformat the text using the existing style. Choose to reformat the style.
5. Click OK.

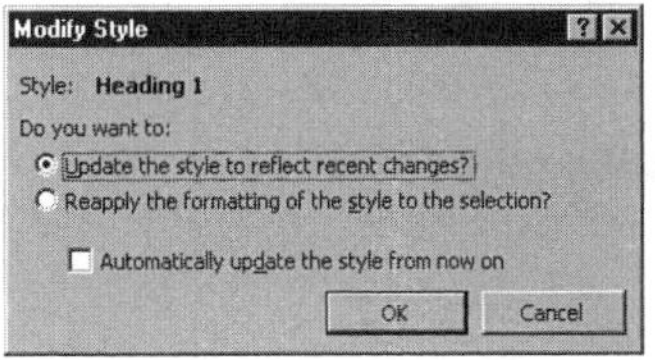

FIGURE 6.2
The Modify Style dialog box asks whether you want to change the style or reformat the text using the existing style.

To create a new style using the Style dialog box, perform the following steps:

1. Choose Format, Style.
2. In the Styles scroll box, choose Normal, if it isn't already selected (see Figure 6.3).
3. Click New. The New Style box appears.
4. Enter a new style name in the Name text box.

Because you chose Normal in step 2, your new style is based on the Normal style, which means that it will contain all of the Normal style's attributes, except where you override them. As you build a set of styles, you may find it convenient to base some of these new styles on each other. If you want all your newsletter headlines to use the same font, for example, create a basic Headline style, and then create additional styles based on it—changing font size, and adding italics, boldface, or effects as desired.

5. Click Format to display a list of formatting categories, as shown in Figure 6.4. When you choose one of these categories, its standard dialog box appears. If you choose Font, for example, the Font dialog box appears.
6. When you finish changing the formats in a formatting dialog box, click OK to return to the New Style dialog box.

7. Repeat steps 5 and 6 to add all the desired formatting to the style.
8. Mark the Add to Template check box, and click OK in the New Style dialog box.
9. Click Close in the Style dialog box.

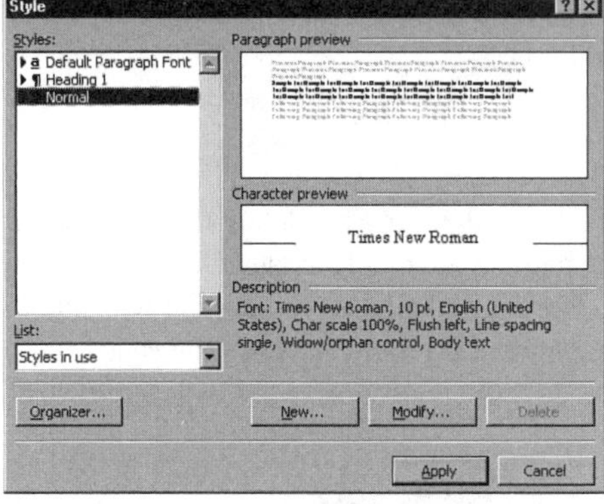

FIGURE 6.3
In the Style dialog box, choose Normal as the style you want to modify.

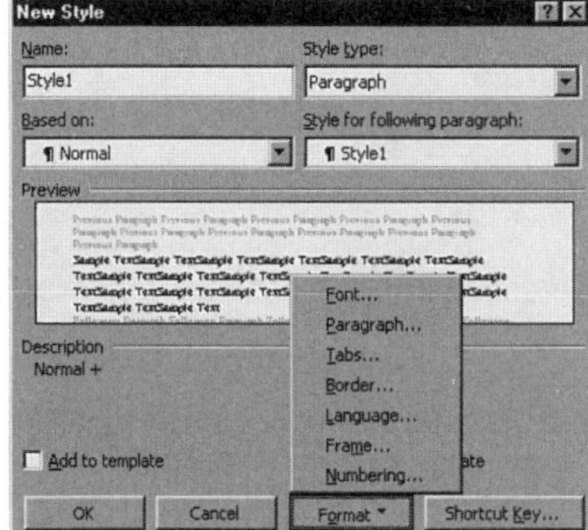

FIGURE 6.4
Click Format to choose the category of formatting you want to change.

CAUTION

If you want to stay in control of the styles you create, you may want to turn off Word's automatic style creation feature, which creates new styles as you format text, even if you don't ask it to do so. To turn this feature off, perform the following steps:

1. Choose Tools, AutoCorrect.
2. Click the AutoFormat As You Type tab.
3. Clear the Define Styles Based on Your Formatting check box.
4. Click OK.

Adding AutoText Entries to a Custom Template AutoText entries, covered in detail in Chapter 11, are blocks of boilerplate text (and other document elements) that you can insert into any document by typing a few characters of the entry's name, and pressing Enter as soon as a ScreenTip appears, offering to replace text you've typed with the corresponding AutoText entry.

To incorporate an AutoText entry into a custom template, making it available to all documents based on that template, perform the following steps:

1. Open the custom template or a document based on it.
2. Select the material that you want to incorporate into an AutoText entry.
3. Choose Insert, AutoText, AutoText. The AutoText tab of the AutoCorrect dialog box opens.
4. In the Enter AutoText Entries Here text box, edit the name of your AutoText entry.
5. In the Look In box, choose the name of your custom template, instead of Normal (the default setting).
6. Click OK.

Recording Macros for Inclusion in a Custom Template Visual Basic macros, covered in more detail in Chapter 16, are a key element of many custom Word templates. You can record or write VBA macros that automate complex procedures, and then perform the following tasks:

- Attach those macros to toolbar buttons, menu commands, and/or keyboard shortcuts, giving users fast access to them
- Run macros automatically at specific times, without any user intervention

All the macros stored in the Normal template are available to all the documents a user creates. All the macros stored in other templates loaded as global templates are available to all documents, as long as those templates are still loaded as global templates. In addition, macros stored in a custom template are available to any document attached to that template.

NOTE In Word 97, Microsoft has changed the way macros are stored. This is discussed later in this chapter, in the "Choosing the Templates or Documents You Want to Organize" section.

By default, when you record a new macro, it is stored in the Normal template. To store a macro in another template when you record it, however, perform the following steps:

1. Choose Tools, Macro, Record New Macro.
2. Enter a name and description for the macro in the Macro Name and Description text boxes.
3. In the Store Macro In drop-down box, choose the custom template where you want to store the macro. (The template must already be loaded.)
4. Click OK.
5. Record the macro.
6. Click the Stop Recording button on the Stop Recording toolbar when you're finished.

NOTE For a comprehensive guide to writing Visual Basic for Applications macros, get *Special Edition Using Visual Basic for Applications 5* by Paul Sanna, Que, ISBN: 0-7897-0959-7.

Defining Macros to Run Automatically As listed in Table 6.1, Word reserves five macro names for automatic macros intended to run at specific times during a Word session. Word looks for macros using these names, and runs them automatically, without user intervention.

Table 6.1 Automatic Macros Available in Word

Macro Name	What It Does
AutoExec	If stored in the Normal template, runs when Word starts. If stored in another global template, loads whenever that global template is loaded.
AutoExit	Runs when Word exits.
AutoNew	Runs whenever you create a new document based on the template containing the AutoNew macro.
AutoOpen	Runs whenever you open a document based on the template containing the AutoOpen macro.
AutoClose	Runs whenever you close a document based on the template containing the AutoClose macro.

You can use the following automatic macros in a wide variety of ways:

- You might use an AutoExec macro to automatically open a specific document, such as a tracking sheet, or to open the last document the user was working on.
- You could use an AutoNew macro to display a dialog box giving the user choices about what should be entered in a document, and then inserting text into the document based on the user's selections. Some companies use AutoNew to display the Summary tab of the File, Properties dialog box, encouraging the user to enter information that can be used later to track documents.
- You could write an AutoOpen macro to check whether the document being opened was written by the individual opening it. If not, it might ask if the reader wants to turn on the Track Changes feature to mark revisions.
- You might use an AutoClose macro to automatically create a backup copy of the file in a different folder or location on the network.
- You could create an AutoExit macro to restore Word's user interface to the settings it had when the session began.

If you're careful, you can store multiple AutoNew, AutoClose, AutoExec, or AutoOpen macros on the same computer, as long as they are stored in different templates. This can come in handy. For example, it enables you to define a set of actions that should occur whenever a run-of-the-mill document is created, but a different set of actions that take place when a *specialized* document is created using a custom template.

Customizing Word's Interface

Thus far, you've focused on customizations that add new capabilities to Word, but do little to change its appearance. You can also customize Word's appearance in a many ways, both simple and complex.

In this section, you'll focus on changing toolbars and menus. You can store these changes in templates, which enables to you customize Word's appearance for all your users (via the Normal template or another global template), or only for specific users creating specific kinds of documents (via custom templates attached to specific documents).

NOTE Later in this chapter, you'll learn about additional customizations that you can make in the Tools, Options dialog box, which are stored in the registry.

An Overview of Customizing Toolbars and Menus

In Word 97, you can create your own toolbars and menus, and add virtually anything to a toolbar or menu whether you created it or not. For example, you can create toolbar buttons or menu items corresponding to the following:

- Any of the hundreds of Word buttons already assigned to specific tasks. (Many of these already appear on one or another of Word's toolbars, but quite a few don't.)
- Any individual Visual Basic for Applications command corresponding to an individual task Word can perform. These commands include every Word menu item, most Word formatting options, and even obscure commands such as GoToNextFootnote or DrawInsertMoon (which switches you into Page Layout view and transforms your mouse pointer into a moon-shaped drawing tool).
- Any macro you've recorded or written in Visual Basic for Applications.
- Any font available on your computer. (In other words, you can create a button that reformats text in whatever font you specify.)
- Any AutoText entry you've created. (In other words, when a user clicks your customized toolbar button, Word inserts the text, graphics, or field codes associated with the entry.)
- Any style you've created, or any built-in Word style.

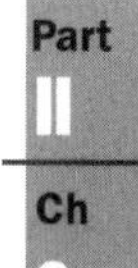

You can add customized menus, toolbars, and keyboard shortcuts to the Normal template—in which case, all documents will have access to these shortcuts unless you specify otherwise. Or you can customize a specific template, creating different working environments for different situations. Imagine that the following three people share a computer:

- Joe has poor eyesight. Joe's template automatically displays enlarged toolbar buttons and text magnified to 150 percent.

- Diane is the part-time office manager; Diane's template includes toolbar buttons for sending email, creating purchase orders, and completing quarterly reports on office activity.
- Kevin is a salesperson who's on the road most of the time. Kevin's template duplicates the customized template in his notebook PC, providing the tools he needs to build customized sales documents fast.

You could write an AutoNew macro to display a dialog box asking who is using the computer (or checking who most recently logged onto Windows). Based on this information, the macro would automatically load the appropriate template, thereby customizing Word to the needs of the specific user.

Customizing Toolbars To control the contents of a toolbar, or to create a new one, choose Tools, Customize. The dialog box shown in Figure 6.5 appears.

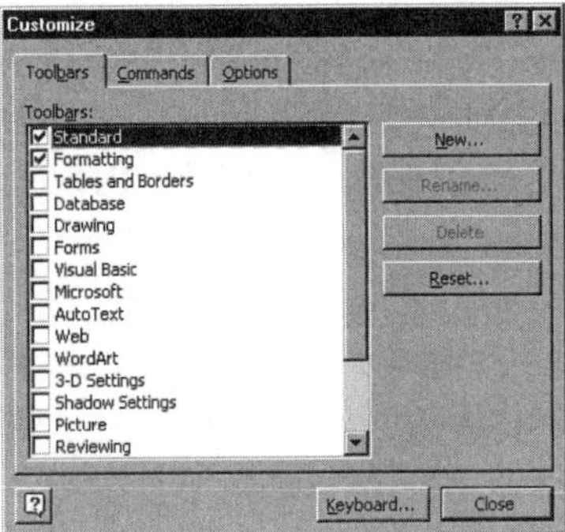

FIGURE 6.5
From the Customize dialog box, you can customize toolbars, menus, and keyboard commands.

Toolbars that are already open are marked with check boxes; you can display any other toolbar for customization by marking its check box.

Creating a New Toolbar To create a new toolbar, follow these steps:

1. Click the Toolbars tab in the Customize dialog box if necessary, and then click New; the New Toolbar dialog box opens (see Figure 6.6).
2. In the Toolbar Name text box, enter a brief descriptive name for your toolbar.
3. In the Make Toolbar Available To drop-down box, choose the template where you want to store your new toolbar. The template must already be open.
4. Click OK. A small toolbar containing no buttons appears onscreen. You may want to move it out of the way by dragging its title bar.

Adding a Command to a Toolbar Now that you have displayed the toolbars you want to customize, click the Commands tab in the Customize dialog box (see Figure 6.7).

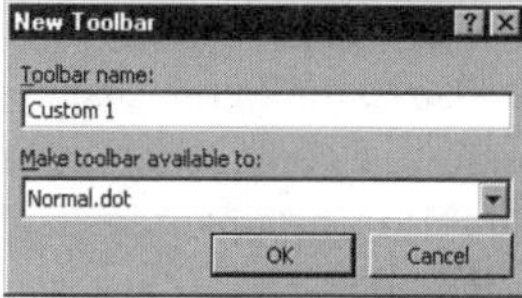

FIGURE 6.6
Enter the name of the new toolbar and the open template where you want to store it.

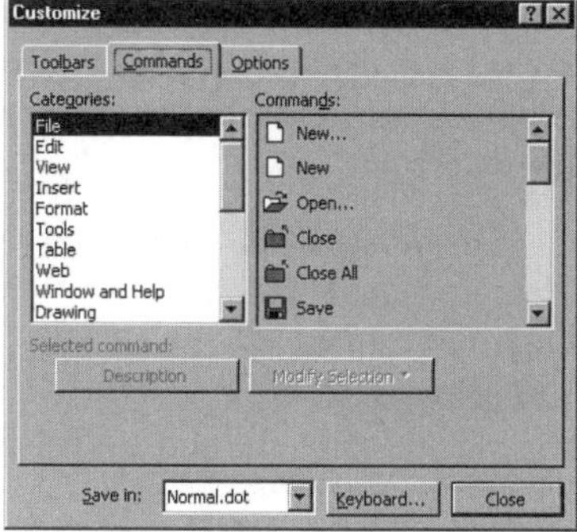

FIGURE 6.7
The Commands tab of the Customize dialog box.

Word displays the commands available to be added to a toolbar, organized into the following categories:

- The *File, Edit, View, Insert, Format, Tools, Table,* and *Window and Help* categories correspond to the commands on each Word menu, with many additions. The File menu, for example, contains commands such as Close All and Save All.
- The *Web, Drawing, AutoShapes, Borders, Mail Merge, Forms,* and *Control Toolbox* categories correspond to commands available on specialized Word toolbars—again, with many additions. The Drawing category, for example, contains specialized tools such as Shadow On/Off and Disassemble Picture, which aren't included on the standard Drawing toolbar.
- *All Commands* lists the methods available to Visual Basic for Applications—in other words, virtually anything you can do to anything in Word is here—over 1,200 commands in all.
- *Macros* lists all of the recorded macros currently available to Word—in other words, in global templates that are currently loaded.
- *Fonts* lists all fonts installed on the computer.
- *AutoText* lists all AutoText entries currently available to Word.
- *Styles* lists all styles in use in the document that is currently open (but not necessarily all styles available to Word).

- *Built-in Menus* includes copies of each menu built into Word. Note that you can add menus not only to Word's menu bar but also to toolbars. Also note that the Work and Font menus are included here. This means you can customize Word for Windows to include all the menus contained in Word 98 for the Macintosh—simplifying the transition for Macintosh users who are moving to Windows.
- Finally, *New Menu* allows you to add a new menu to either the menu bar or any toolbar.

To add a button to a toolbar, select it from the Commands scroll box, and drag it to the position on the toolbar where you want it. As you move the button onto a toolbar, a thick cross-hatch marking appears to help you see where your mouse pointer is. When you release the mouse button, the new button appears on the toolbar.

Changing a Button's Text or Image In many cases, the commands you add to toolbars already have ready-made icons attached to them. This will not always be the case, however. If you drag a custom macro to a toolbar, for example, Word inserts the entire macro name, including its project name (for example, Normal.NewMacros.NameOfMacro). This takes up a lot of real estate. To solve the problem, right-click on the button to display the Customize shortcut menu.

If you can abbreviate the macro's name to a reasonable length (3 to 5 characters, for example), edit it in the Name text box. If not, click Change Button Image; Word displays 42 generic buttons available for you to use (see Figure 6.8).

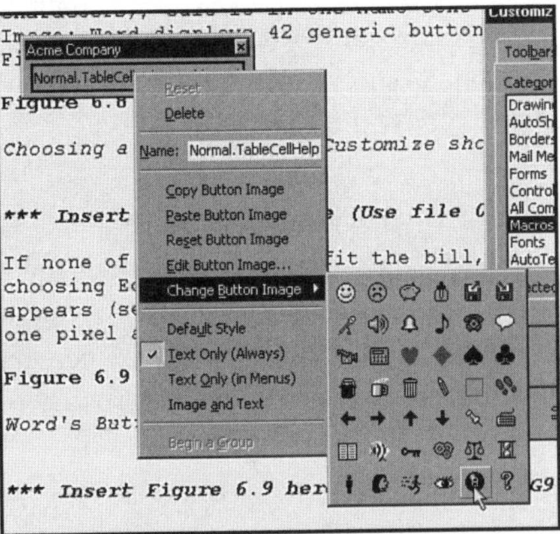

FIGURE 6.8
Choosing a button in the Customize shortcut menu.

If none of these buttons fits the bill, you can create your own button by choosing Edit Button Image from the shortcut menu. Word's Button Editor appears (see Figure 6.9). In this dialog box, you can edit your button one pixel at a time—an excruciatingly slow task.

Unless you're an artist blessed with patience, you might find that creating your own button image from scratch with the Button Editor is difficult—to put it charitably. You do have an alternative: you can import an image from a clip art library or graphics program.

FIGURE 6.9
Word's Button Editor.

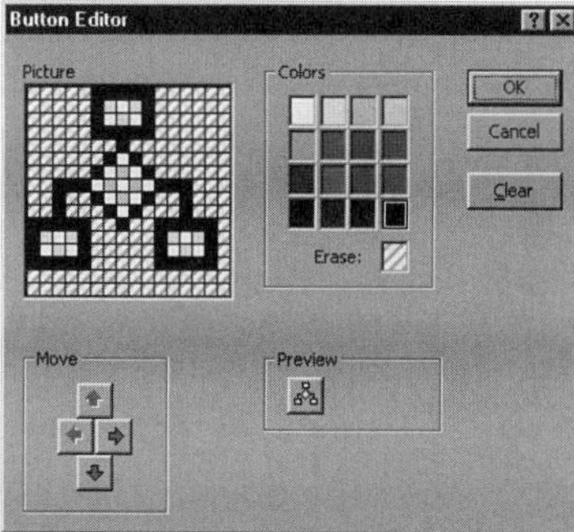

Unfortunately, relatively few clip art images, including Word's, were designed to be clear at 1/4-inch square. But if you want to try to import art, follow these steps:

1. Open the application containing the artwork.
2. Copy the artwork into the Clipboard. If you have a choice, copy it as a bitmap.
3. Switch back to Word.
4. Make sure the toolbar button you want to change is visible.
5. Choose Tools, Customize.
6. With the dialog box open, right-click on the button you want to change to display the Customize shortcut menu.
7. Choose Paste Button Image.

Removing a Command from a Toolbar To remove a button from a toolbar, make sure the Customize dialog box is open, and then drag the button off the toolbar. You can drag buttons off any toolbar, including Word's Standard and Formatting toolbars. You can also drag buttons from one toolbar to another. By making these types of changes, you can create a version of Word that is elegant in its simplicity, putting buttons where they are most convenient and hiding those that your users will never need.

NOTE If the Customize dialog box is closed, you can remove a button by pressing and holding down the Alt key as you drag the button off the toolbar.

Resetting Toolbars to Their Original Settings If you decide you've gone too far in changing a toolbar, you can restore it to its original settings by performing the following steps:

1. Choose Tools, Customize.
2. In the Toolbars scroll box, select the toolbar you want to reset.
3. Click Reset.
4. Click Close.

Making Toolbars Easier to Work With The Options tab of the Customize dialog box contains three options that can make Word toolbars a bit easier for users to work with (see Figure 6.10).

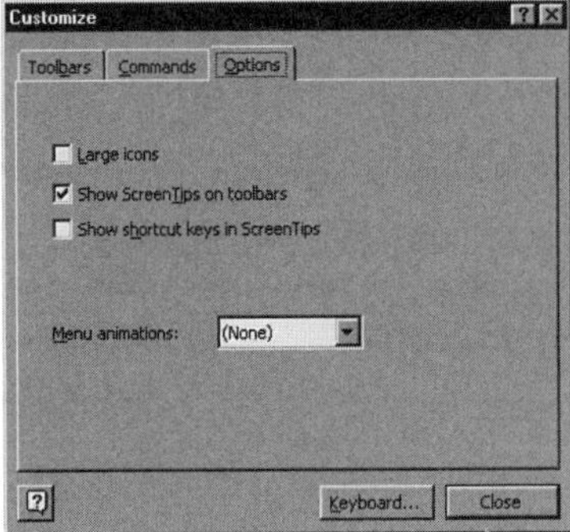

FIGURE 6.10
The Options tab of the Customize dialog box.

One of these options, Show ScreenTips on toolbars, is turned on by default. With this option turned on, when a user hovers the mouse pointer over a toolbar button, Word displays the button's title. You can help users learn hard-to-remember keyboard shortcuts by turning on a complementary option: Show Shortcut Keys in ScreenTips. With this option checked, Word displays the keyboard shortcut that is equivalent to the toolbar button, along with the button's name.

As the resolution of computer monitors has increased to 800×600 and beyond, Word's toolbar buttons have grown increasingly tiny. You can compensate by checking the Large Icons option. As you can see in Figure 6.11, these icons are *very* large.

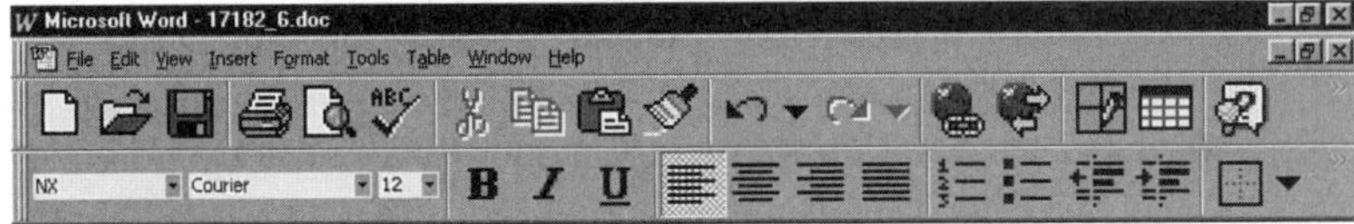

FIGURE 6.11
A toolbar with the Large Icons setting turned on.

Customizing Menus You can also create or customize menus from the Customize dialog box. To create a new menu, perform the following steps:

1. Choose Tools, Customize.
2. Click on the Commands tab.
3. In the Categories scroll box, select New Menu.
4. Click New Menu in the Commands scroll box.
5. Drag New Menu from the Commands scroll box to the menu bar, dropping it where you want the new menu to appear. You now have a new menu named *New Menu*.
6. Right-click on New Menu in the menu bar; the Customize shortcut menu appears.
7. In the Name text box, enter the name that you want to use for your new menu.

To specify a keyboard shortcut, place the "&" (ampersand) symbol before the letter to use as the shortcut. Don't use the following letters, which are already shortcuts for other menus: F, E, V, I, O, T, A, W, or H.

8. Press Enter. The edited menu name appears on your menu bar.

Adding a Command to a Menu Whether you want to add a command to a built-in menu or a new menu, the procedure is the same. With the Commands tab of the Customize dialog box displayed, perform the following steps:

1. Select the category of commands you want.
2. Select the specific command from the Commands scroll box.
3. Drag the command to the desired menu, which may be located on the menu bar or on a toolbar.
4. With the mouse button still pressed, drag down the menu to the location where you want to place the new command.
5. Release the mouse button. The new menu item remains displayed and selected.
6. If you want to edit the command—either to shorten it or to change the keyboard shortcut associated with it—right-click on it, and click inside the Name text box on the Customize shortcut menu.
7. Edit the command name and press Enter.

Removing a Command from a Menu To remove a command from a menu, display the Customize dialog box, select the command from the menu, and drag it off the menu. You can drag commands off any menu, including Word's built-in menus. You can also drag entire menus off the menu bar.

Using Word's Organizer to Copy Elements Among Templates

You've now walked through creating a custom template, and adding styles, AutoText entries, macros, toolbars, and menus to that template. But what happens if one of your colleagues has built a macro you'd like to incorporate in a custom template for wider use? Or what if you need to reorganize your library of AutoText entries, combining entries stored in multiple templates? Or how about if you want to copy customizations into a specific document, for use by a colleague who wouldn't want to bother with installing templates?

When you need to copy elements among templates (or between templates and documents), use the Organizer. To display the Organizer, perform the following steps:

1. Choose Tools, Templates and Add-Ins.
2. Click on the Organizer button. The Organizer appears (see Figure 6.12).

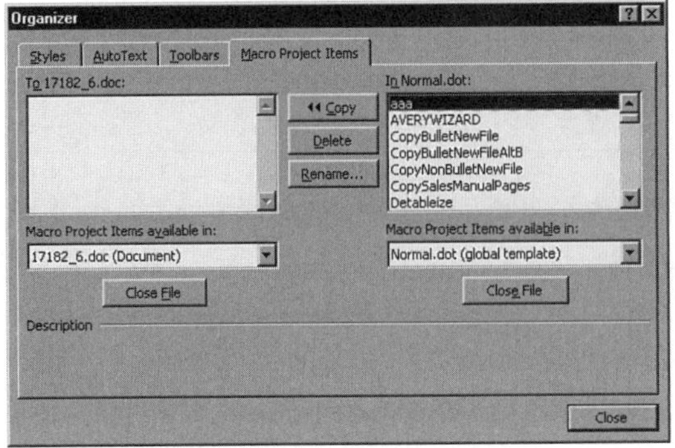

FIGURE 6.12
In the Organizer, you can copy styles, toolbars, and macro project items among templates and documents; and copy AutoText entries between templates.

By default, the Organizer displays the elements stored in your current document in the left-hand pane, and elements stored in the Normal template in the right-hand pane. If you want to change which two templates (or documents) are displayed, see the next section. You can copy elements in either direction, as follows:

1. Click the tab containing the element that you want to copy. (Because you can't store AutoText entries in a document, if you click the AutoText tab, Word displays the template to which your document is attached.)
2. In either the left-hand or right-hand pane, click the element that you want to copy.
3. Click Copy.

You can delete a template element by selecting it, clicking Delete, and clicking Yes to confirm. You can rename a template element by selecting it, clicking Rename, entering a new name in the Rename dialog box, and clicking OK.

Choosing the Templates or Documents You Want to Organize

As discussed earlier, much of the time you will want to copy elements between templates—and not necessarily the templates the Organizer displays by default. To select a different template, perform the following steps:

1. Click Close File on either side of the Organizer dialog box. The template or document's elements disappear, and the name of the button you clicked changes to Open File.
2. Click Open File.
3. Browse to and select the template (or document) you want to open.
4. If necessary, repeat the process in the opposite pane, so the Organizer displays both of the templates (or documents) you want to work with.

If you are creating a custom template, be careful to copy all the elements into it that you will need. In particular, if you create a toolbar with buttons that run macros, make sure you also copy the macros.

In Word 6.0 and Word 95, the Organizer copied individual macros, and Word 97 still copies individual macros that have been converted from older WordBasic versions. For macros created in Word 97, for example, the Organizer moves only *macro project items*, in other words, modules that may contain multiple individual macros all stored together within a specific template. As a result, you may not see the names of the VBA macros you expect to see.

If this happens, choose Tools, Macro, Visual Basic Editor to open the Visual Basic Editor, and then browse the Project window to identify the module containing the macros you need. (If you've recorded the macro as part of the Normal template, for example, you'll find it in Normal\Modules\NewMacros.) Then use the Organizer to move that module.

Keep in mind that the Visual Basic Editor displays only modules contained in templates that are currently in use, so you may have to open additional templates in Word before you find the macro you're looking for.

Providing Custom Spelling Tools

Word's spell checker is a blessing—except when it identifies hundreds (or thousands) of words as possible errors when you know better—perhaps those words are really product names or names of your company's senior executives.

In Chapter 11, you learn how to customize AutoCorrect to fix some of these errors automatically; and in Chapter 27 you learn where to get supplemental dictionaries with additional legal, business and medical terms, or foreign language spellings. But what if you want to include a custom dictionary specific to your organization? It's easy, just perform the following steps:

1. Open a new document.
2. Enter all the words you want to include, one on each line. If you're adding names, consider importing the last name field from an Outlook or Access database, and then eliminating the duplications by hand or with a macro.
3. Save the file as Text Only, using the .dic extension.
4. Copy the file to the folder containing Microsoft Office's dictionaries (typically C:\Program Files\Common Files\Microsoft Shared\Proof in Windows; Microsoft:Custom Dictionary on the Macintosh).
5. Choose Tools, Options.
6. Click the Spelling & Grammar tab.
7. Click Dictionaries. The Custom Dictionaries dialog box opens, listing all dictionaries stored in that folder (see Figure 6.13).

NOTE Typically, this dialog box already lists Custom.dic, the file where Word stores all the words that users add to the spelling dictionary.

8. Mark the check box next to the dictionary you just created.
9. Click OK.

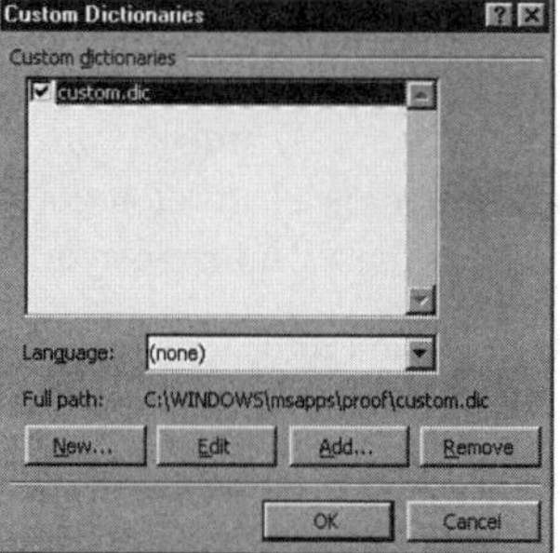

FIGURE 6.13
Adding a custom dictionary.

Customizing Options Stored in the Registry

Word includes a variety of customization settings that are not stored in templates, but rather in the Windows registry. Users can control most of these settings via tabs in the Options dialog box. However, you can also control many of these centrally—either by setting them during the installation process (see Chapter 2) or later, via System Policies (see Chapter 33). Options settings fall into ten categories: View, General, Edit, Print, Save, Spelling & Grammar, Track Changes, User Information, Compatibility, and File Locations. Eight of these categories are discussed in the following section. The remaining two, Track Changes and Compatibility, are discussed in Chapter 12 and Chapter 24, respectively.

Controlling View Options

View options control the document elements Word displays onscreen, including non-printing elements (see Figure 6.14). View Options also controls whether the status bar and scrollbar display. Following are some ideas for using View Options to optimize Word:

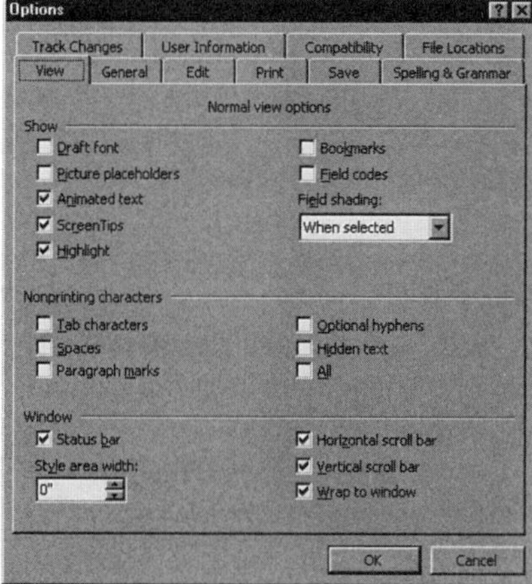

FIGURE 6.14
The View tab of the Options dialog box.

Running on a slow computer where heavy formatting isn't a concern (for example, running Office 97 on a Windows terminal using Microsoft Terminal Server). Speed Word up by marking Draft Font and Picture Placeholders.

Need to get a quick look at the styles in your document? Set Style Area Width to 1 inch, and style names will appear on the left edge of the document window. (This setting isn't available in Page Layout view.)

Need to see all the text in a document, from the left to right margin—without making the text smaller onscreen, and therefore harder to read? Check Wrap to Window (also not available in Page Layout view).

Controlling General Options

General options control settings that don't fit anywhere else (see Figure 6.15) . Be especially aware of the following:

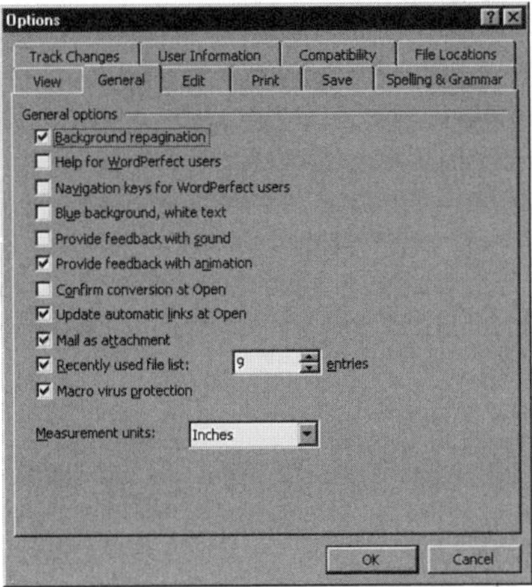

FIGURE 6.15
The General tab of the Options dialog box.

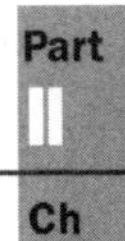

Marking the Help for WordPerfect Users, Navigation Keys for WordPerfect Users, and Blue Background, White Text check boxes can simplify the transition for users experienced with WordPerfect for DOS.

The Recently Used File List spinner box specifies how many recently used files to display on the File menu. The default setting is four. Many users with high-resolution monitors prefer to list the maximum number, nine.

Macro Virus Protection specifies that Word warn users when opening a document containing a macro. In general, you'll want to leave this turned on. However, consider turning it off if you have *reliable* third-party virus protection and sophisticated users who regularly work with macros and find the warning message disruptive.

Finally, the Measurement Units drop-down box allows you to customize Word's dialog boxes to display centimeters, points, or picas in place of inches.

Controlling Editing Options

Editing options control settings that are likely to be especially useful for users migrating from older word processing software (see Figure 6.16). They give you a way to turn off Word shortcuts, such as Drag-and-Drop Text Editing and Use Smart Cut and Paste, which most users have come to appreciate (or tolerate), but others cannot abide.

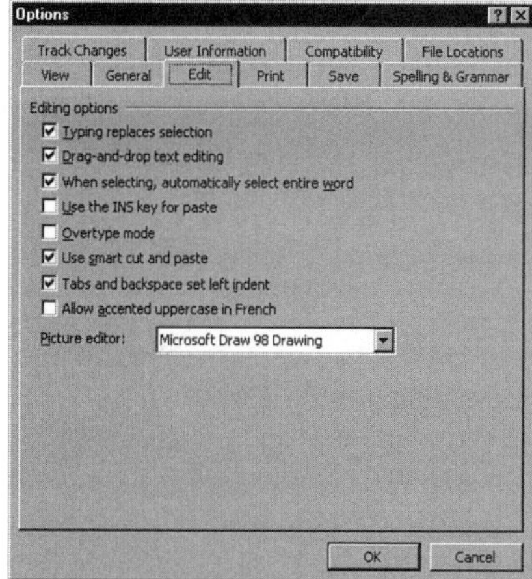

FIGURE 6.16
The Edit tab of the Options dialog box.

One additional setting, Picture Editor, allows you to control which installed graphics program (or Word's own graphics tools) will be used by default to edit Word images.

Controlling Print Options

Print options control the elements that are included in a printed document, and how Word should go about printing (see Figure 6.17). Among the more useful options to know about are the following:

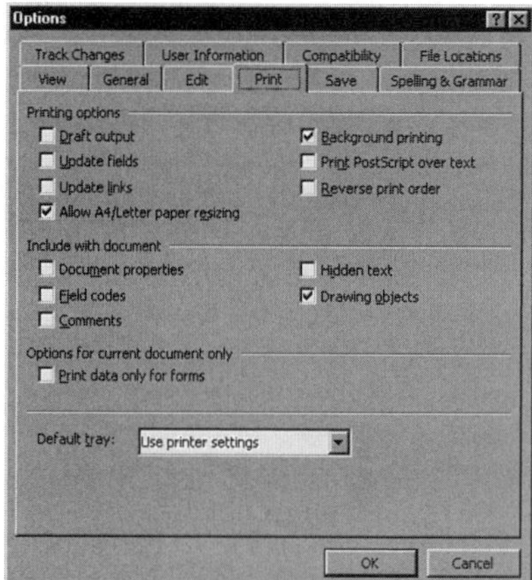

FIGURE 6.17
The Print tab of the Options dialog box.

The Update Fields and Update Links check boxes let you control whether information in your document is automatically updated before printing.

Allow A4/Letter Paper Resizing, checked by default, allows Word to stretch or squeeze a document to fit the European A4 or U.S. 8 1/2" × 11" standard letter size.

Print PostScript Over Text allows Word for Windows to print Word for Macintosh documents containing watermarks that can be created only through the use of raw PostScript code.

Finally, Default Tray allows you to override your printer driver and specify a different paper input bin or manual feed for your print jobs.

Controlling Save Options

Save options control how Word saves files (see Figure 6.18). Several of these options are significant.

FIGURE 6.18
The Save tab of the Options dialog box.

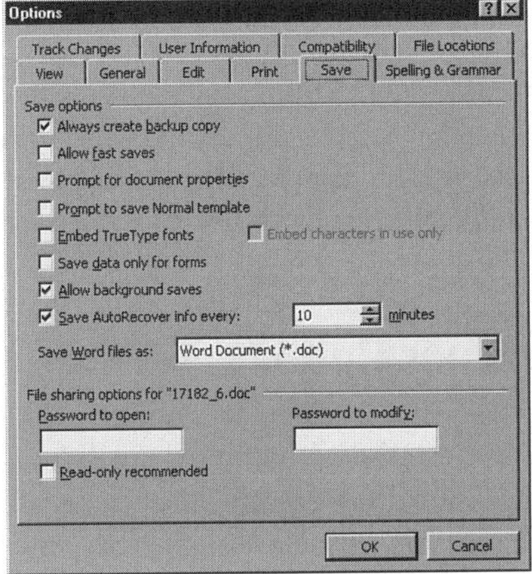

Always Create Backup Copy tells Word to create a copy of the *previous* version of the file with a .wbk extension every time it saves a file. Note, however, that because the backup is stored in the same folder as the original, you still won't have a copy of your file if your hard drive crashes.

Allow Fast Saves permits Word to save only the changes in a document, rather than the entire document. With Fast Saves turned on, Word doesn't actually place the changes in the correct locations within the document. Instead, it creates a list of changes that aren't integrated until the next time you save normally. If you plan to export files, turn off the Fast Save option since the files may be read by software that doesn't know how to recognize Fast Save information.

NOTE Even if you're using Fast Saves, Word occasionally performs a normal save to take care of all the housekeeping that accumulates.

Word can store a wide variety of information about a document along with that document, including keywords, comments, subject matter, and many other types of data. Much of this is inserted automatically by Word, but not all. To help make sure that users include relevant information in the Properties dialog box instead of ignoring it, mark the Prompt for Document Properties check box. If you do, Word displays the Properties dialog box whenever a file is saved for the first time.

The Embedding TrueType Fonts option allows you to include TrueType fonts as part of your document file, enabling others to view and print your file as it's supposed to look, even if they don't have the fonts you used. As you can imagine, embedding fonts can significantly enlarge the size of your file. Therefore, Word 97 has added a new option, Embed Characters in Use Only. If you mark this check box, and Word finds that you've used 32 or fewer characters in a font, Word will embed only those characters. This is especially useful for headlines. Don't mark this option if you expect a recipient to edit it, however. If the recipient adds characters that you haven't embedded, Word may not be able to display the new characters properly.

You can use Word to create online forms that can be filled in by many people throughout your organization. When it comes time to compile the information stored in these forms, you may want to "throw away" the form's text and formatting, and keep only the information entered by a user. Checking Save Data Only for Forms saves the data in your forms as a single, tab-delimited record in text-only format, making it easy to import that information into the database of your choice. (For information about using the password settings available through the Save tab, see Chapter 34.)

Controlling Spelling & Grammar Options

Spelling & Grammar options control settings related to Word proofing (see Figure 6.19). This tab gives you the opportunity to turn off Word's "on-the-fly" spell-checking and/or grammar-checking, or to keep them running but not display potential errors with wavy underlines. Because the errors are still tracked, they are available for immediate review whenever a user chooses.

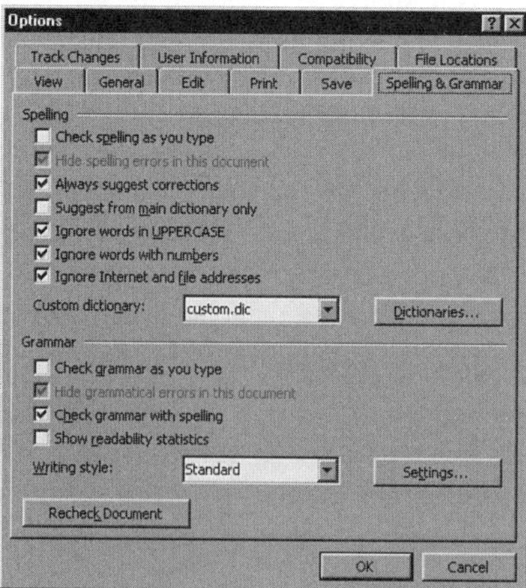

FIGURE 6.19
The Spelling & Grammar tab of the Options dialog box.

You can also click Settings to control how the grammar checker works. While most users find Word's default grammar settings a bit overbearing, you can adjust them in the Grammar Settings dialog box to catch only really obvious problems (clichés, for example), or to enforce company document standards (whether to include a comma before the last item in a list, how many spaces between sentences should be used, and so forth) (see Figure 6.20).

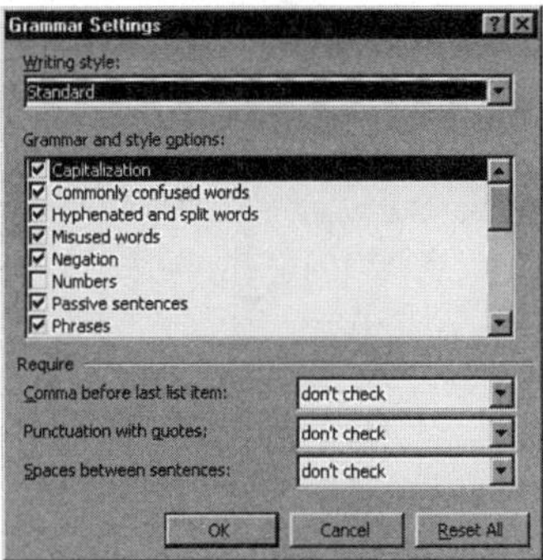

FIGURE 6.20
The Grammar Settings dialog box.

Controlling User Information Options

User Information options include text boxes for the user's name, initials and mailing address (see Figure 6.21). Changes to these settings take effect as soon as the Options dialog box is closed.

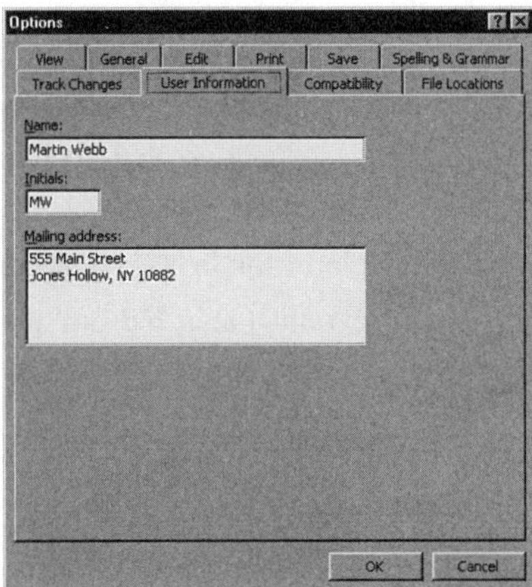

FIGURE 6.21
The User Information tab of the Options dialog box.

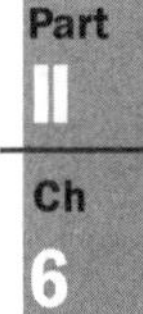

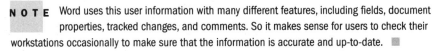

NOTE Word uses this user information with many different features, including fields, document properties, tracked changes, and comments. So it makes sense for users to check their workstations occasionally to make sure that the information is accurate and up-to-date. ■

Controlling File Locations Options

File Location options control where Word looks for documents, clip art pictures, user and workgroup templates, user options, AutoRecover files, and tools, as well as the location of Word's startup folder (see Figure 6.22). To set or change any of these, display the File Locations tab, click Modify, browse to the folder you want, and click OK.

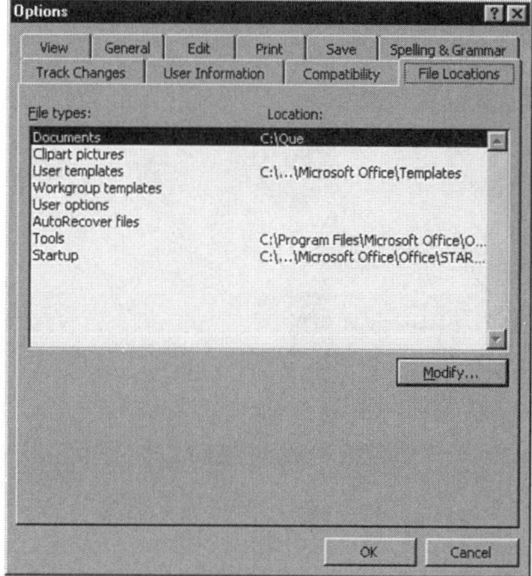

FIGURE 6.22
The File Locations tab of the Options dialog box.

Customizing How Word Starts in Windows

You have extensive control over how Word starts up—including control over *when* it starts up. If your users nearly always work with Word, you can set Windows 95, 98, or NT to run Word automatically at startup. To do so, copy a shortcut to Word into your computer's startup folder. Assuming that you haven't customized your system, or created system profiles that point to a startup folder on a network server, follow these steps:

1. Choose Start, Programs, Windows Explorer (or, in NT, Windows NT Explorer).
2. Browse to C:\Windows\Start Menu\Programs (or, in NT, C:\Winnt\Start Menu\Programs).

NOTE If a user has a roaming profile on an Windows NT domain, the Start menu items will be on a server in that domain, and on the local Windows NT Workstation in a folder named c:\winnt\profiles*username*\start menu\programs. Because roaming profiles are synched on the workstation from the server upon login, you should edit them at the server. In Windows 98, they might be stored locally in a folder named c:\windows\profiles*username*\start menu\programs.

3. In the right-hand pane, right-click on the Microsoft Word shortcut, and choose Copy from the shortcut menu.
4. In the left-hand pane, click StartUp to display the contents of your computer's startup folder.

5. Right-click inside the right-hand pane, and choose Paste from the shortcut menu.
6. Shut down and restart Windows. Word will start automatically.

The Properties dialog box for a Windows shortcut (accessible by right-clicking the shortcut and choosing Properties) contains a command corresponding to the shortcut's target (a program, folder, or file). This command is displayed in the Target text box of the Shortcut tab. Typically, the command for a shortcut to Word is the following:

```
"C:\Program Files\Microsoft Office\Office\WINWORD.EXE"
```

If you want, you can edit this command to include a Word startup switch, or to follow Winword.exe with the path and name of a document or template you always want to load. (Make sure to add text within the quotation marks only.)

Table 6.2 lists some of Word's startup switches.

Table 6.2 Commonly Used Word Startup Switches

Switch	What It Does
/a	Prevents add-ins and global templates from loading. Also prevents Word settings from being read or modified (this setting is commonly used in troubleshooting).
/l	Starts Word and loads a specific add-in (include the add-in's path and filename after the switch).
/m	Runs Word without running any AutoExec macros (see "Defining Macros to Run Automatically" earlier in this chapter). /m followed by the name of a macro starts Word and runs that macro.
/n	Starts Word without opening a document.
/t	Follow with the name of a document. Starts Word and opens the document *as a template.*

You can use these startup switches in the Start, Run dialog box to specify how Word runs at any time, not just at startup. You can also create a separate shortcut that loads Word with specific switches and copy it to the Desktop alongside a standard Word shortcut. This way, users can choose which way they want to start Word in any given session.

On the Macintosh, you can make an alias and copy it into the Startup folder, as follows:

1. Click to select the Microsoft Word program icon (typically in the Microsoft Office 98 folder).
2. Choose File, Make Alias.
3. Drag the alias into the Startup Items folder within the System Folder.
4. Choose Special, Restart to restart the Macintosh. Word will start automatically.

Customizing Word's Own Startup Folder

Like Windows, Word also has a startup folder. In Windows, Word's startup folder is typically C:\Program Files\Microsoft Office\Office\Startup. (The typical Macintosh location is Microsoft Office 98:Office:Startup:Word.)

Anything placed in this startup folder—documents, templates, or (in Windows) WLL add-ins—is loaded when Word starts. You can even place shortcuts in Word's startup folder; the files they point to will be loaded into Word.

A template placed into Word's startup folder loads as a global template. This means that the macros, AutoText entries (boilerplate text), toolbars, menus, and keyboard shortcuts contained in it are available to all documents, no matter which template is attached to those documents. ●

CHAPTER 7

Customizing Excel to Your Organization's Needs

Excel is sufficiently flexible to meet the needs of your organization for many situations. In some cases, however, it is beneficial to customize Excel to enable users with different skill levels to work more efficiently. Whereas a new user may want Excel's built-in toolbars and help menu, an advanced user may want keyboard shortcuts, customized toolbars, and macros. This chapter looks at how you can customize Excel to meet the needs of different users within your organization.

Customizing the Interface

Understanding Excel's interface can help you take advantage of its features and customize those features to each user's skill level. This section explores how the various interface components of Excel work together, and how the application handles changes that users make to those components.

Options

The Options dialog box (Tools, Options) enables you to adjust settings that control how you view and work with Excel files (see Figure 7.1). These settings are saved to the Windows registry and are read when Excel starts. When two or more users open a shared workbook or template, each user's individual settings are applied to the file.

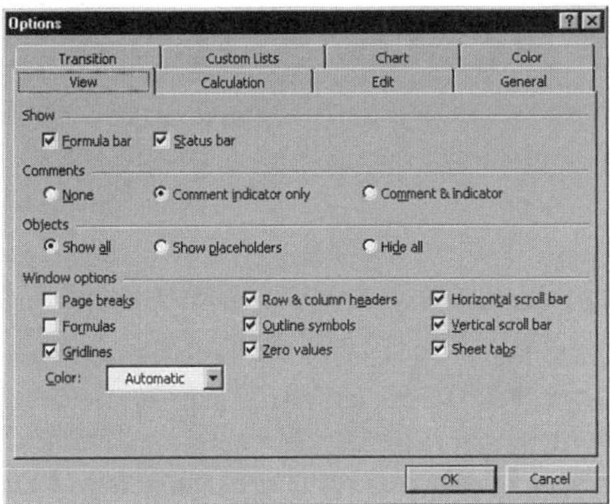

FIGURE 7.1
Customizing individual settings with the Options box.

The following is a description of the settings that you can change in the eight tabs in the Options dialog box:

- *View.* These options control how Excel worksheets look. Color, comments, column and row headings, gridlines and sheet tabs are just a few of the settings that you can individualize from this tab.
- *Calculation.* By default, Excel automatically calculates values for formulas entered into cells. Sometimes, however, you don't want this. For example, you may have a workbook that queries an external database for quarterly sales data. Depending on the time it takes to perform the query, you may want to manually control cell calculation at a time when network traffic is minimal. You can also control how efficiently Goal Seek and Solver functions arrive at solutions from this tab. The higher the number of iterations and the smaller the change between calculation results, the more time Excel needs to calculate a worksheet.
- *Edit.* This tab enables you to control cell drag and drop, Excel's AutoComplete feature, and other data entry and editing processes.
- *General.* Here you can specify the working and alternate startup folder locations, a user name, a cell reference style, and other settings.

- *Transition.* The options in this tab make it easy for users of Lotus 1-2-3 to switch to Excel. You can enable Lotus 1-2-3 help and select a default file format in which to save your Excel files. You can even change the way data is entered and manipulated so that users can enter formulas and navigate much as they did in 1-2-3.
- *Custom Lists.* These enable you to quickly fill in a series of cells with presorted data. Excel comes with standard lists, such as days of the week and months of the year. You can, however, create and maintain custom lists from this tab if you find yourself continually entering the same data in the same sequence.
- *Chart.* This tab enables you to specify settings for chart tips and enables you to customize how zero values are plotted.
- *Color.* Here you can customize color palettes and specify chart line and fill colors.

The Startup and Alternate Startup Folders

The startup folder and alternate startup folder contain workspace files, templates, and charts that you want opened automatically when Excel starts. When you install Excel, the startup folder is created and named Microsoft Office\Office\Xlstart. By default, an alternate startup folder is not created.

The alternate startup folder is handy if you want to share templates with others in a workgroup. To create an alternate startup folder, specify its drive and path in the Alternate Startup File Location text box in the General tab of the Tools, Options dialog box.

NOTE If you specify an alternate startup folder, Excel attempts to open every file in that folder. Make sure that the alternate startup folder you specify contains only files that Excel can open. ■

Default Workbook and Worksheet Templates

Excel opens a new, unsaved workbook if you do not specify a default workbook. This new workbook is based on built-in program settings with a reserved filename, Book.xlt. When Excel starts, it looks for this file in the startup or alternate startup folder. If the template Book.xlt does not exist, Excel uses its built-in defaults. To create a new default workbook template, do the following:

1. Create or open a template with the formatting options you want.
2. Choose File, Save As.
3. In the Save In box, locate your startup or alternate startup folder.
4. In the Save As Type drop-down box, select Template.
5. In the File Name text box, type **Book.**
6. Click Save.

The process that Excel uses when you add a new worksheet to a workbook is similar to the process of locating a default workbook template. For worksheets, Excel checks the startup and alternate startup folders for the presence of Sheet.xlt. If the worksheet template does not exist, Excel uses its built-in defaults. To create a new default worksheet template, do the following:

1. Create a workbook with one worksheet that includes the formatting and other information that you want to appear on all new worksheets.
2. Choose File, Save As.
3. In the Save In box, locate your startup or alternate startup folder.
4. In the Save As Type drop-down box, select Template.
5. In the File Name text box, type **Sheet**.
6. Click Save.

Custom Workbook Templates

Templates stored in the Xlstart folder or the alternate startup folder are available on the General tab of the New dialog box (File, New). Built-in templates appear on the Spreadsheet Solutions tab. To include custom templates in the New dialog box, follow these steps:

1. Create or open a template with the formatting options you want.
2. Choose File, Save As.
3. In the Save In box, locate the Microsoft Office\Templates folder. To group your custom templates on a separate tab of the New dialog box, create a subfolder in the Templates folder. The name you give this folder will appear on the tab.
4. In the Save As Type drop-down box, select Template.
5. In the File Name text box, type a valid filename.
6. Click Save.

To display a picture of the first page of a custom template in the Preview area of the New dialog box, open the template, choose File, Properties, click the Summary tab, and mark the Save Preview Picture check box.

Figure 7.2 shows an example of a New dialog box that contains an additional tab for a custom template. To create this tab, a folder named Data Analysis was created in the Microsoft Office/Templates folder. A template named Mortgage Calculator was then created and saved to this folder.

Excel Startup Switches

Excel startup switches contain parameters that are passed to the application when you start Excel, customizing how you want the application to start. To use startup switches, do the following:

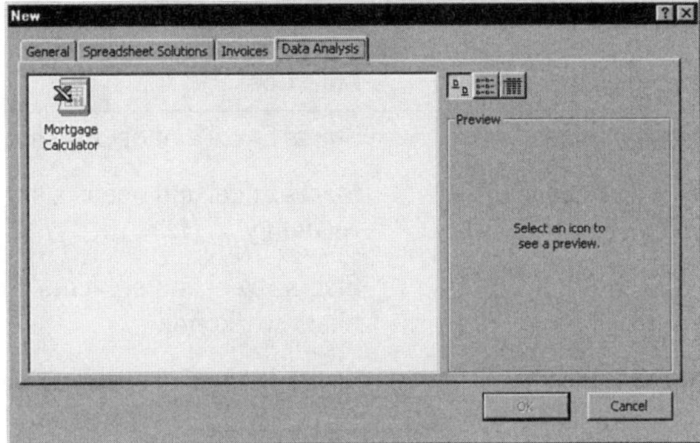

FIGURE 7.2
Creating and grouping custom templates.

1. Right-click the Start button and select Open in the shortcut menu.
2. If you used the default location to install Excel, double-click the Programs icon.
3. Locate the Excel shortcut icon.
4. Right-click the Excel shortcut icon and select Properties in the shortcut menu to display the Microsoft Excel Properties dialog box.
5. Click the Shortcut tab, as shown in Figure 7.3.

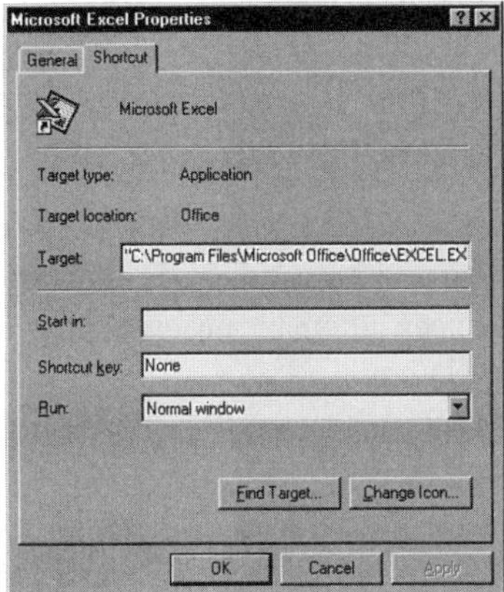

FIGURE 7.3
Controlling how Excel starts using startup switches.

6. In the Target text box, type a space after the path to the Excel program, and then type one of the switches listed in Table 7.1.

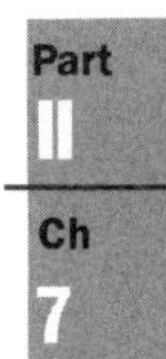

Table 7.1 Excel Startup Switches

Switch	Function
`"workbook path\filename"`	Starts Excel and opens a specific workbook
`/r "workbook path\filename"`	Starts Excel and opens a specific workbook as read-only
`/e`	Starts Excel and prevents the display of a new blank workbook
`/p "folder path\folder name"`	Starts Excel and specifies the working folder

NOTE If you specify a working folder using `/p`, this overrides any folder specified in the Default File Location box on the General tab of the Tools, Options dialog box.

Workspace Files

If you find yourself frequently keeping the same group of workbooks open at once, you may want to create a workspace file so that Excel can handle the task of opening the files and arranging them on screen for you. A workspace file contains information on which workbooks you want to open, the location of each file, and the size and position of each workbook in the Excel window. To create a workspace file, follow these steps:

1. Open the workbooks that you want to include. If the workspace file will be shared, make sure the workbooks are located on a network drive or in a shared folder.
2. Position and size the workbooks.
3. Choose File, Save Workspace.
4. If you want the workspace file to open automatically each time you start Excel, specify Excel's startup folder in the Save In box.
5. Give the workspace file a name, and click Save.

The drive and path information for each workbook is saved in the workspace file. If you move the workbook files, Excel is not able to find them when you open the workspace file. To avoid possible problems, save the workspace file in the same folder as the workbook files.

Customizing the Toolset

Excel contains a variety of tools that make working with spreadsheets easier. Toolbars enable you to organize and group commands so that they're convenient and easy to use. Add-in programs are supplemental tools that enhance the functionality of Excel and extend its capabilities.

Displaying and Hiding Toolbars

To display additional built-in Excel toolbars, right-click any toolbar and select the toolbar you want to show from the shortcut menu. The shortcut menu lists the most commonly used toolbars. If you do not see the toolbar you want on the shortcut menu, do the following:

1. Right-click any toolbar and select Customize from the shortcut menu to display the Customize dialog box.
2. Click the Toolbars tab (shown in Figure 7.4).

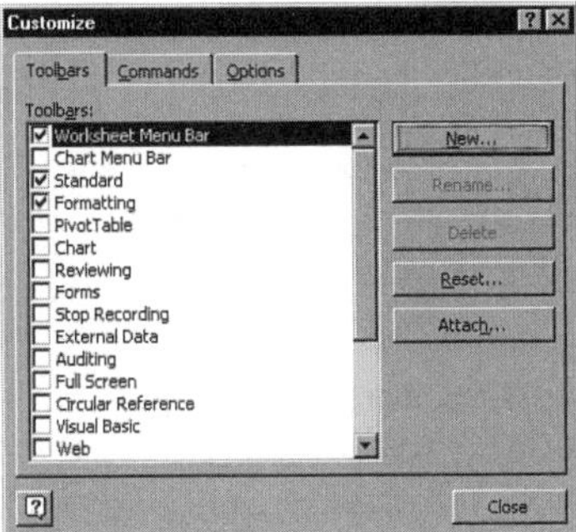

FIGURE 7.4
Displaying additional built-in Excel toolbars.

3. Mark the check box for the toolbar you want to display.

To hide a floating toolbar, click the Close button (X) on the toolbar. To hide a docked toolbar, right-click it and click the toolbar in the shortcut menu that appears. (See the next section for more information about floating versus docked toolbars.)

Moving and Resizing Toolbars

By default, Excel displays the Standard toolbar and the Formatting toolbar docked (attached) at the top of the program window, just below the title bar. You can dock any toolbar at the top of the program window or at the left, right, or bottom edges of the window.

A toolbar that is not docked is a *floating* toolbar. You can easily resize and move floating toolbars around the program window as you work on your spreadsheet. Figure 7.5 shows the difference between a docked and floating toolbar.

To move a floating toolbar, simply click the title bar and drag the toolbar to a new location. If you want to dock a floating toolbar, drag the toolbar to the top, left, right, or bottom edge of the program window. When you drag the toolbar to the edge of the program window, you notice that the toolbar outline snaps into place. Figure 7.6 shows the Forms toolbar, which was floating in Figure 7.5, now docked on the left side of the program window.

Notice that the docked Forms toolbar now has two small lines at the top of the toolbar. This is the move handle. To create a floating toolbar out of a docked toolbar, simply click the move handle and drag the toolbar out over your spreadsheet. To dock a toolbar in another location, click the move handle and drag the toolbar to a different edge of the program window.

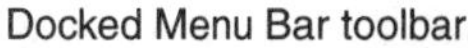

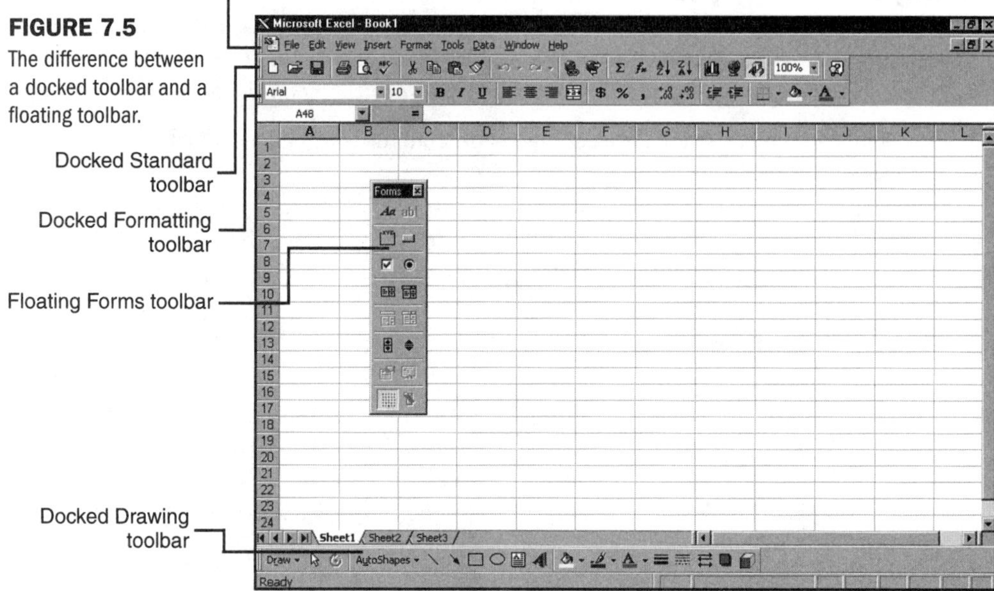

FIGURE 7.5
The difference between a docked toolbar and a floating toolbar.

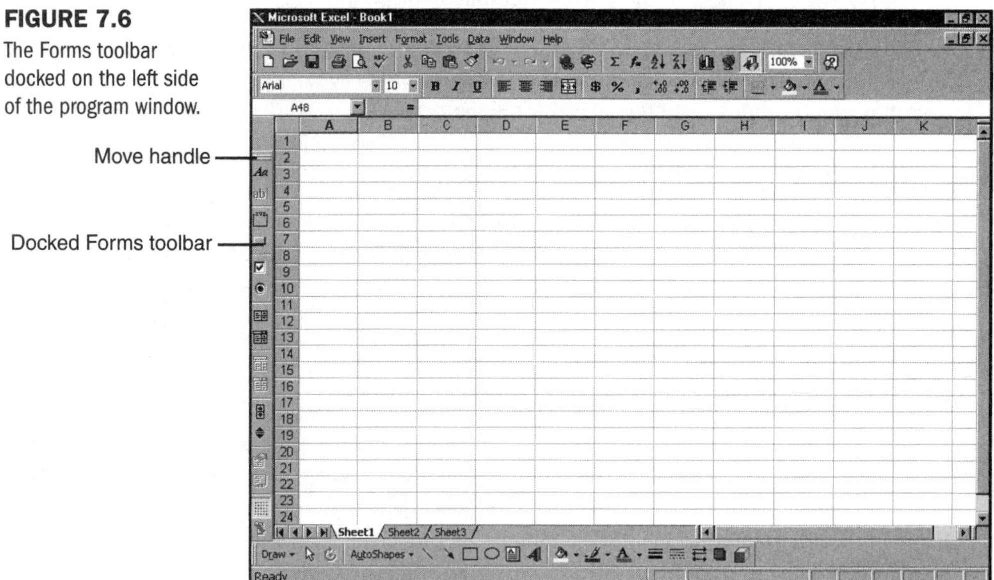

FIGURE 7.6
The Forms toolbar docked on the left side of the program window.

After a toolbar is docked it cannot be resized. You need to undock it first and create a floating toolbar. To resize a floating toolbar, position the mouse pointer over any edge until it changes to a double-headed arrow and then drag the edge of the toolbar.

Customizing Toolbars

Commands accessible from toolbars can either be command buttons or menus. Command buttons contain a picture that represents an action, such as the familiar floppy disk that represents the command to save your file. Menus contain a drop-down list of related commands. In Excel, you can create, add, delete, and edit toolbars to fit the needs of your workgroup.

Creating a Custom Toolbar When you make changes to the toolbars, these changes as well as the toolbars currently displayed are saved to a toolbar settings file in your Windows folder. Each time you start Excel, it reads these settings and displays the appropriate toolbars. If you find yourself using a few commands from several of the built-in Excel toolbars, you may want to edit the built-in toolbars or create a custom toolbar with only those commands and menus that you use frequently.

To create a custom toolbar, follow these steps:

1. Choose Tools, Customize to display the Customize dialog box, and click the Toolbars tab (shown earlier in Figure 7.4).
2. Click the New button.
3. In the Toolbar Name text box, type the name of your new toolbar and click OK. Excel displays a blank toolbar with the name you entered in the title bar.
4. To add a button to the toolbar, click the Commands tab of the Customize dialog box (see Figure 7.7). Select a category for the command in the Categories box. Drag the command button you want from the Commands box to your new toolbar. If you make a mistake, drag the button off the toolbar and it disappears.

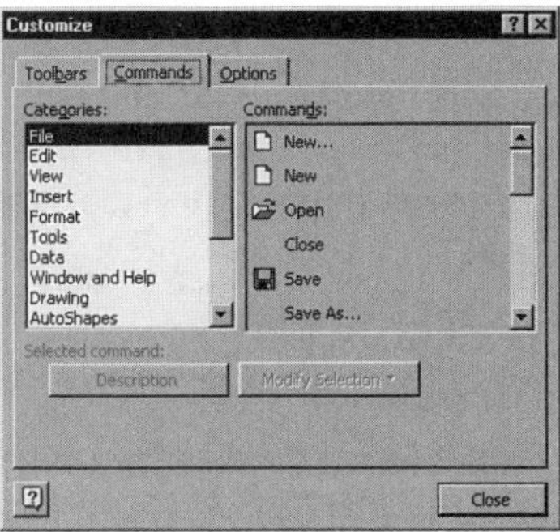

FIGURE 7.7
Adding commands to a custom toolbar by selecting command categories.

5. To add a built-in menu to the toolbar, click the Commands tab of the Customize dialog box. Select Built-in Menus from the Categories box. Drag the built-in menu you want from the Commands box to your new toolbar.
6. When you're finished adding command buttons and menus, click Close. Figure 7.8 shows a custom toolbar named Frequently Used, which was created with command buttons from the Standard and Formatting toolbars, and the Track Changes command from the Tools menu.

FIGURE 7.8
A custom toolbar named Frequently Used.

Attaching a Toolbar After you've created a custom toolbar, you need to attach it to the workbook so that it is always available with that workbook. To attach a toolbar, do the following:

1. Create a custom toolbar using the steps in the previous section.
2. Open the workbook to which you want to attach the toolbar.
3. Choose Tools, Customize and click the Toolbars tab.
4. Click the Attach button to display the Attach Toolbars dialog box shown in Figure 7.9.

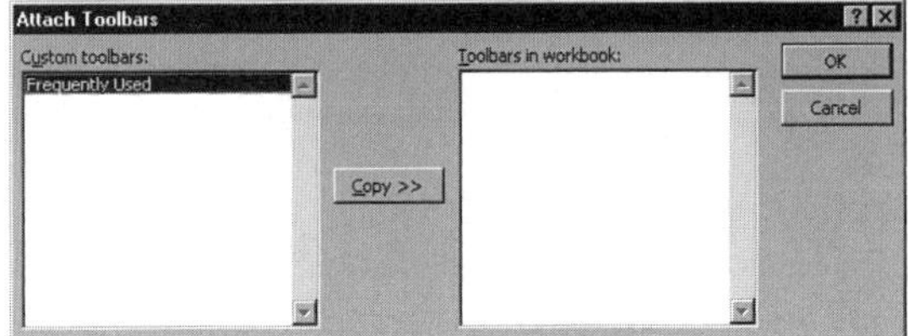

FIGURE 7.9
Attaching a custom toolbar to a workbook.

5. In the Custom Toolbars box, select the toolbar you want to attach and click the Copy button.
6. The toolbar appears in the Toolbars in Workbook box. Click OK.

NOTE Be sure to save your workbook after you attach your custom toolbar.

Adding a Custom Menu to a Toolbar Sometimes you may not want all the commands on a built-in Excel menu. In this case, you can add a custom menu to a toolbar with only those menu items you need. Follow these steps to add a custom menu to a toolbar:

1. Display the toolbar to which you want to add a custom menu.
2. Choose Tools, Customize and click the Commands tab.
3. In the Categories box, select New Menu.
4. Drag New Menu from the Commands box to the displayed toolbar.
5. Right-click the New Menu on the toolbar and enter a name in the Name text box on the shortcut menu. If you use a combination of Alt and a letter to choose menu commands, include an ampersand (&) before the letter that you want to use to choose the command. The letter will be underlined on the menu. Make sure to select a letter that is not already used by another command on the same menu. Press Enter.
6. To add a command to your custom menu, click the newly named custom menu on the toolbar to display an empty box. In Figure 7.10, the custom toolbar that you saw in Figure 7.7 has a newly added (and currently empty) Shortcuts menu. Select a category for the command in the Categories box. Drag the command button you want from the Commands box to the empty box in your custom menu.

FIGURE 7.10
Creating a custom menu on a toolbar.

7. After you've added all your commands, click Close in the Customize dialog box. In Figure 7.11, the Open, Close, and Save commands have been added to the Shortcuts menu.

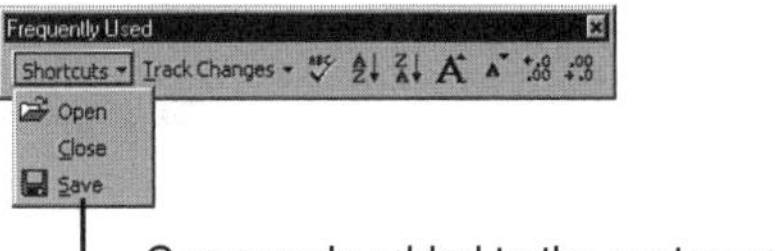

FIGURE 7.11
Open, Close, and Save commands have been added to the Shortcuts menu.

Modifying Toolbar Commands After you have added commands to a toolbar, you can always modify them. Follow these steps to modify a toolbar command:

1. Display the toolbar containing the command you want to modify.
2. Choose Tools, Customize and click the Commands tab.
3. Right-click the toolbar menu or command you want to modify to display a shortcut menu that enables you to do the following:
   - Reset the command
   - Delete the command
   - Manipulate a command button image
   - Change the way the command is displayed
   - Group related commands
   - Assign a macro

Deleting a Toolbar Command To delete a toolbar command, you can either choose Delete after clicking the Modify Selection button described in the previous section, or do the following:

1. Display the toolbar containing the button you want to delete.
2. Hold down the Alt key and drag the button off the toolbar.

NOTE If you delete a built-in toolbar button, it remains available for placement on other toolbars in the Customize dialog box. If, however, you delete a button whose name or image that you have modified, your changes are lost. To save custom buttons, create a toolbar to store the buttons and move the buttons to the toolbar.

Working with Add-Ins

An add-in is a hidden, read-only file in which Visual Basic, XLM, or C code has been compiled to provide supplemental and specialized functionality to Excel workbooks. By default, Excel installs these files in the Microsoft Office\Office\Library folder or one of its subfolders. You can recognize add-in programs by the common file extensions of .dll, .xll, or .xla. The following are descriptions of the add-ins that are available with Excel 97:

- The Access Links Add-In enables you to import Excel 97 data into Access 97 and use Access forms and reports. You must have Access 97 installed to use this add-in.
- The Analysis ToolPak adds financial, statistical, and engineering analysis functions.
- AutoSave automatically saves workbooks at specified intervals.
- Use the Conditional Sum Wizard to create a formula that sums data according to specified criteria.
- Use the Lookup Wizard to create a formula to lookup data in a list based on a known value in the list.
- The File Conversion Wizard converts a group of files to Excel 97.
- The ODBC Add-In connects to ODBC external data sources.
- The Report Manager enables you to quickly create reports based on different print areas, custom views, and scenarios within a workbook.
- The Excel Internet Assistant converts worksheet data and charts to HTML.
- Use the Solver Add-In to calculate what-if scenarios based on adjustable variables and constraints.
- The MS Query Add-In for MS Excel 5.0 converts external data ranges in Excel 97 to Excel 5.0/95 format.
- The Template Utilities add-in provides utilities used by Excel's built-in templates.
- Use the Template Wizard with Data Tracking to create a template that enters worksheet data into a database and tracks changes.
- The Update Add-In Links converts add-ins from previous versions of Excel to built-in features of Excel 97.
- The Web Form Wizard assists you in setting up a Web form.

To load any of the Excel add-ins or a third-party add-in, do the following:

1. Choose Tools, Add-Ins to display the Add-Ins dialog box shown in Figure 7.12.
2. If you want to use an Excel add-in, mark the check box in the Add-Ins Available box. To install a third-party add-in, click the Browse button and locate the add-in program on your hard disk.
3. Click OK.

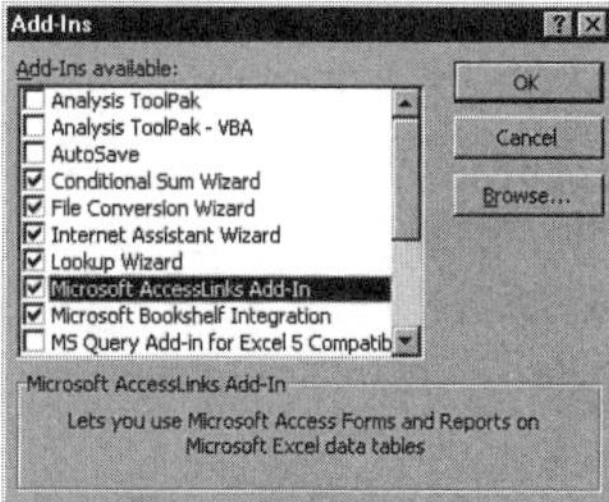

FIGURE 7.12
Loading Excel add-in programs.

After the add-in is loaded, associated commands are available through the appropriate menu. Typically, specialized functions appear as menu items on the Tools menu, or the add-in is available in the Tools, Wizard menu. To conserve memory, you should unload add-ins that you don't use. Unloading an add-in removes its features and commands from Excel, but does not remove it from your computer. To unload an add-in, do the following:

1. Choose Tools, Add-Ins to display the Add-Ins dialog box.
2. In the Add-Ins Available box, clear the check box next to the add-in you want to unload.

Improving Productivity with VBA Macros

Macros enable you to automate tasks that you perform repeatedly. They consist of a series of commands contained in a Visual Basic (VB) module. The VB module is attached to the workbook and available to users who have access to the workbook.

Macros can be as simple or as complex as you need. For example, you can create a macro that simply bolds and left justifies text in a selected cell. A more complex macro may query an external data source and run a report every time a workbook is opened. If you're considering using macros to improve your productivity, it's a good idea to plan the steps and commands that you want the macro to perform prior to creating a macro. Keep in mind, however, that the more complex a macro, the more familiar you need to be with the Visual Basic programming language.

Creating a Macro

You can create a macro in two ways. The first method is to record a macro. This method is the easiest because it requires less knowledge of Visual Basic. The second method involves writing and editing Visual Basic commands in the Visual Basic Editor. With the second method, you gain additional functionality and access to Visual Basic commands that cannot be recorded. Of course, you can always record a macro and edit it later.

Recording a Macro Recording a macro is similar to recording an audio cassette, except in this case you're recording mouse movements, menu commands, formatting, and so on. When you run the macro, you simply playback the actions that you recorded earlier. To record a macro, take these steps:

1. Choose Tools, Macro, Record New Macro to display the Record Macro dialog box shown in Figure 7.13.

FIGURE 7.13
Using the Macro Recorder to create a macro.

2. In the Macro Name box, type a name for your macro. The first character of the macro name must be a letter. Other valid characters are letters, numbers, and the underscore character (_). Spaces are not allowed in a macro name, so you may want to use the underscore character to separate words.
3. If you want to run the macro by pressing a keyboard shortcut key, enter a letter (A–Z) in the Shortcut Key text box. Excel distinguishes between lowercase keyboard shortcuts (Ctrl+letter) and uppercase shortcuts (Ctrl+Shift+letter), so there are 52 possible keyboard shortcuts available. Keep in mind, however, that the shortcut key you specify overrides any default Excel shortcut keys—such as Ctrl+P to print or Ctrl+S to save—while the workbook containing the macro is open.
4. In the Store Macro In drop-down box, select a location where you want to store the macro. The Personal Macro Workbook is a workbook located in the XLStart folder. This workbook is started each time you use Excel, so the macro is always available.
5. Include a description of the macro in the Description text box, and click OK.
6. Excel displays the Stop Recording toolbar (shown in Figure 7.14). The Relative Reference button enables you to toggle cell selection between absolute and relative cell references. By default, Excel records cell selections with absolute cell references (the Relative Reference button is not pushed in). An absolute cell reference selects the same cells regardless of which cell is selected first, because it references cells using an exact address (A1, B16, C8, and so on). Relative cell references take into account the cell that was first selected and contain references to other cells relative to the first cell. If your macro needs to select cells two columns to the right and three rows down, then you need to push the Relative Reference button in during macro recording.

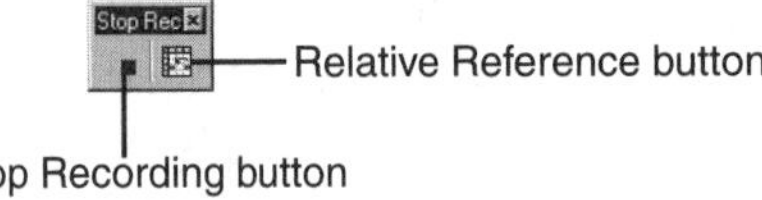

FIGURE 7.14
The Stop Recording toolbar.

7. Carry out the actions you want to record.
8. When you're finished, click the Stop Recording button.

The Visual Basic Editor Before you edit a macro, you should be familiar with the Visual Basic Editor. The Visual Basic Editor is used to write and edit macros attached to Excel workbooks. If you're unfamiliar with Visual Basic, the easiest way to get started is to record a macro to generate the code you need. After you generate the code, you can modify it to do exactly what you want.

A detailed look at the Visual Basic Editor is beyond the scope of this chapter. Figure 7.15, however, shows you how the default editor looks and gives you an overview of each of the windows.

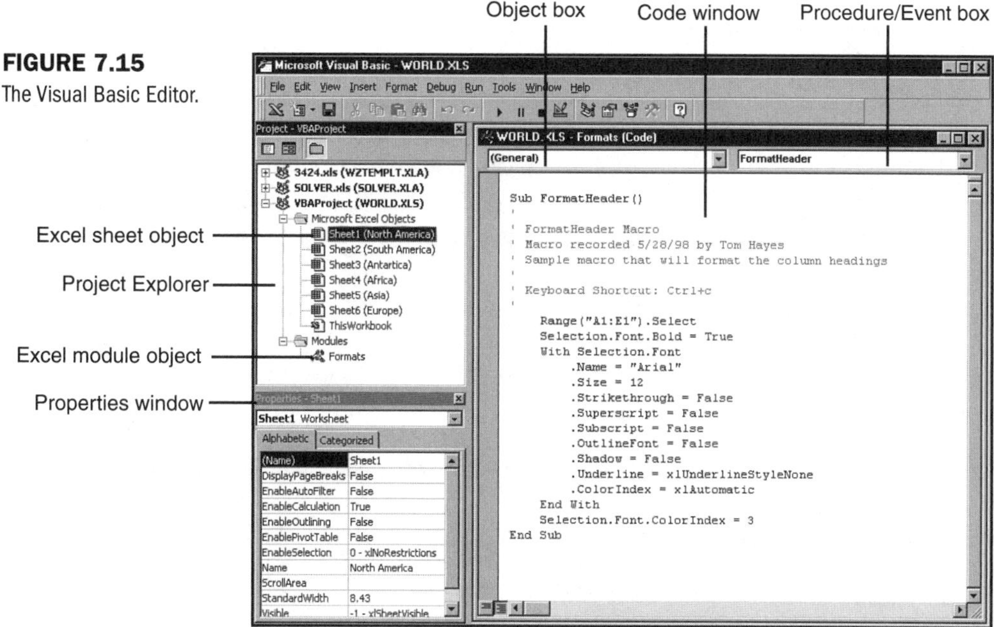

FIGURE 7.15
The Visual Basic Editor.

- *Project Explorer.* The Project Explorer displays a hierarchical list of the projects and all the items contained in and referenced by each of the projects. Objects displayed in the Project Explorer can take the form of Documents (Excel workbooks and worksheets), UserForms, Modules, Class Modules, and References (links to other projects).
- *Properties window.* The Properties window lists the design-time properties for selected objects and their current settings. In Figure 7.15, the properties for Sheet1, which is selected in the Project Explorer, are displayed. When you select multiple controls, the Properties window contains a list of the properties common to all the selected controls.
- *Code window.* You use the Code window to write, display, and edit Visual Basic code. You can open as many Code windows as you have modules, so you can easily view the code in different forms or modules, and copy and paste between them. The Object box

displays a list of all objects associated with the form. The Procedure/Event box lists events associated with a control or procedures in a module. All events associated with a control or procedures in a module appear in a list that is sorted alphabetically by name. Selecting a procedure using the drop-down list moves the insertion point to the first line of code in the procedure you select.

In addition to these windows, the Visual Basic Editor contains windows that help you debug your procedures and design dialog boxes for user input.

- *Immediate window.* The Immediate window is available from the View menu and enables you to type or paste a line of code and press Enter to run it. After you've corrected any syntax errors, you can copy and paste the code from the Immediate window into the Code window.
- *Locals window.* The Locals window is available from the View menu and displays all the declared variables in the current procedure and their values. It is automatically updated every time you break or pause the execution of the current procedure.
- *Watch window.* The Watch window appears automatically when watch expressions are defined in the project. A watch expression pauses or breaks the procedure execution if a variable reaches a certain value or if an event is triggered.
- *UserForm window.* The UserForm window appears when you highlight a form in the Project Explorer and choose View, Object. This window enables you to create the forms and dialog boxes in your project by drawing controls on a form.

Editing a Macro To edit a macro, do the following:

1. Choose Tools, Macro, Macros to display the Macro dialog box shown in Figure 7.16.

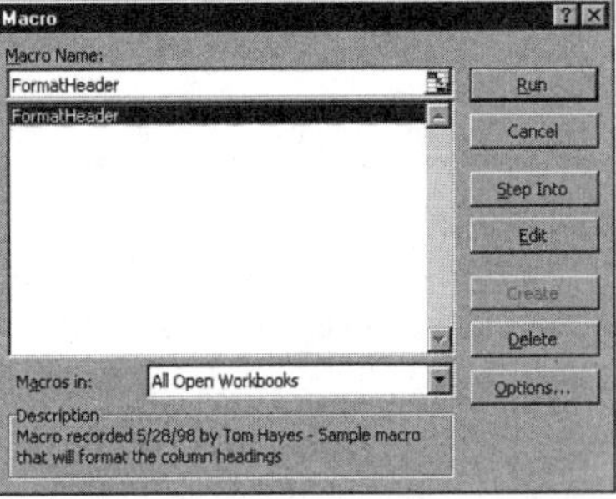

FIGURE 7.16
Use the Macro dialog box to edit and manage workbook macros.

2. In the Macro Name box, select the macro name.
3. Click Edit to display the Visual Basic Editor (refer to Figure 7.15).

By creating and editing macros in the Visual Basic Editor, you gain additional functionality and access to Visual Basic commands that cannot be recorded. For example, the following code illustrates a recorded macro that increases the point size and changes the color of text in the selected cells:

```
Sub Recorded_Macro()
    With Selection.Font
        .ColorIndex = 3
        .Size = 12
    End With
End Sub
```

The recorded macro works, but in a very limited way. The user always has to select the cells to be formatted prior to running the macro. Moreover, if you wanted the formatting applied only to cells that meet a certain criteria—a value greater than 20, for example—there is no way to record this criteria. You have to either create the macro in the Visual Basic Editor, or record it and then edit it. The following code shows the recorded macro edited with a For...Next loop that checks the value of each cell and applies special formatting only to those cells with a value greater than 20:

```
Sub Modified_Macro()
For Each Cell_In_Loop In Range("A1:A100")
  If Cell_In_Loop.Value > 20 Then
    With Cell_In_Loop.Offset(0, 1).Font
        .ColorIndex = 3
        .Size = 12
    End With
  End If
Next
End Sub
```

Running a Macro

After you've created your macros, running the macro and repeating the commands is easy. Fortunately, Excel gives you a variety of ways to do this. You can run a macro from Excel or the Visual Basic Editor. You can also assign a macro to run when a user clicks a toolbar button or a hot spot on a graphic. Finally, macros can run when an event such as opening a workbook or recalculating the worksheet occurs.

Running a Macro from Excel To run a macro from Excel, use the keyboard shortcut for the macro (if you assigned one) or do the following:

1. Choose Tools, Macro, Macros to display the Macro dialog box.
2. In the Macro Name box, select the macro name.
3. To modify the keyboard shortcut or description assigned to the macro, click the Options button and make your changes.
4. Click Run.

Running a Macro from the Visual Basic Editor To run a macro from the Visual Basic Editor, follow these steps:

1. Open the workbook that contains the macro you want to run.
2. Choose Tools, Macro, Macros to display the Macro dialog box.
3. In the Macro Name box, select the name of the macro you want to run.

4. Click the Edit button to display the Visual Basic Editor.
5. Click the Run Macro toolbar button.

If you want to run a different macro while you're in the Visual Basic Editor, choose Tools, Macros to display the Macros dialog box. Select the name of the macro you want to run and click Run.

Running a Macro from a Toolbar Button You can assign a macro to a button on a built-in toolbar or a custom toolbar. Each time you click the button, the macro runs. To assign a macro to a toolbar button, do the following:

1. Display the toolbar you want to modify.
2. Choose Tools, Customize and click the Commands tab.
3. Choose Macros in the Categories box and then drag Custom Menu Item or Custom Button from the Commands box to the toolbar. Right-click your new menu item or command button and choose Assign Macro from the shortcut menu to display the Assign Macro dialog box (shown in Figure 7.17).

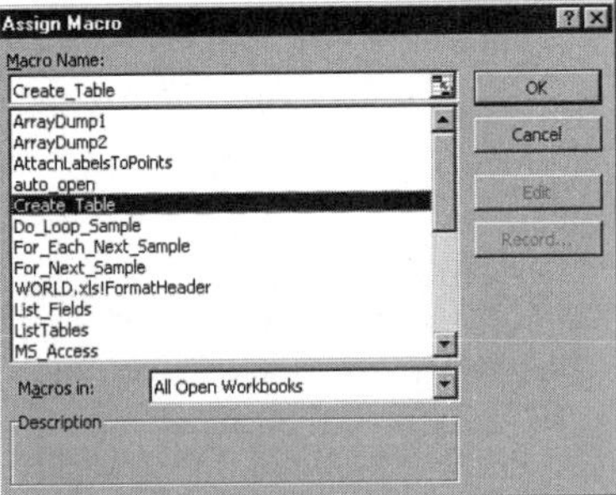

FIGURE 7.17
Assigning a macro to a toolbar button.

4. Select the macro to assign from the list, and click OK.

Running a Macro from a Hot Spot on a Graphic Object A hot spot is similar to an image map used on Web pages. When a user clicks a certain area of the image, a different Web page is displayed or a procedure is run. In Excel, yocu can define a hot spot and assign a macro to run when the user clicks the hot spot. Follow these steps to create a hot spot:

1. Create or insert a graphic object. In Figure 7.18, a clip art image is inserted in an Excel worksheet by choosing Insert, Picture, Clip Art.
2. Draw another graphic object over the first object in the place where you want the hot spot. The easiest way to do this is to display the Drawing toolbar and use one of Excel's AutoShapes. In Figure 7.19, a circle was drawn over the original graphic and will become the hot spot.

FIGURE 7.18
Inserting a graphic.

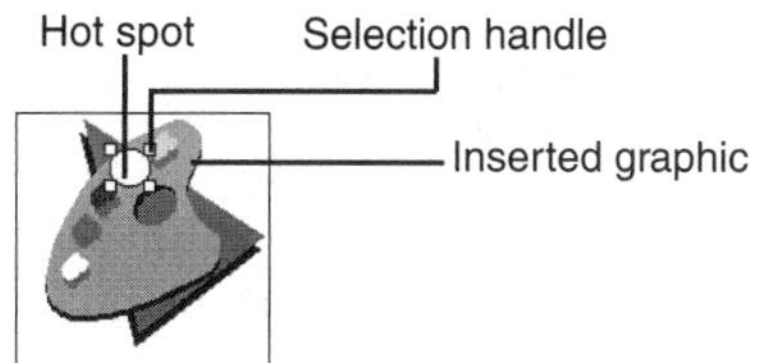

FIGURE 7.19
Defining a circle as the hot spot on the graphic.

3. With the second graphic object still selected, right-click a selection handle of the graphic object to display the shortcut menu.
4. From shortcut menu, click Assign Macro to display the Assign Macro dialog box. To assign an existing macro, select the macro from the list and click OK. To record a new macro, click Record.
5. With the second graphic object still selected, right-click a selection handle of the graphic object to display the shortcut menu again.
6. From the shortcut menu, select Format AutoShape to display the Format AutoShape dialog box and then click the Colors and Lines tab (shown in Figure 7.20).

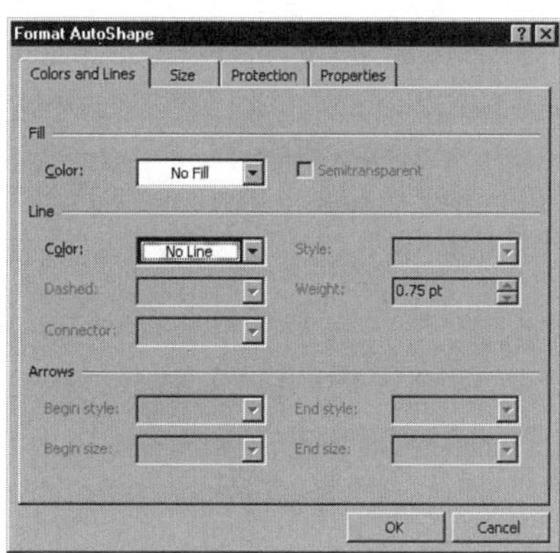

FIGURE 7.20
Using the Format AutoShape dialog box to select no fill and no line for the hot spot.

7. Under Fill, select No Fill from the Color drop-down box. Under Line, select No Line from the Color drop-down list box.
8. Repeat steps 2 through 7 for each hot spot you want to create. Make sure, however, that your hot spots do not overlap.

When you're finished, the mouse pointer changes to a hand every time it's positioned above a hot spot, and clicking a hot spot runs the macro that you assigned to it.

Running a Macro When an Event Occurs To further automate repetitive tasks, you can run your macro when an event occurs. Because event-triggered macros cannot be recorded, you have to be familiar with Visual Basic and the Visual Basic Editor to take full advantage of this feature. (Table 7.2 lists Excel methods and properties and the related event that can be used to cause a macro to run.)

Table 7.2 Events That Cause Procedures to Run

Methods or Property	Event
OnAction Property	Clicking a control or a graphic object, clicking a menu command, or clicking a toolbar button
OnCalculate Property	Recalculating a worksheet
OnData Property	The arrival of data from another application through OLE or a DDE channel
OnDoubleClick Property	Double-clicking anywhere on a chart sheet, dialog sheet, module, or worksheet
OnEntry Property	Entering data using the formula bar or editing data in a cell
OnKey Method	Pressing a particular key or key combination
OnRepeat Method	Clicking Repeat on the Edit Menu
OnSave Property	Using the Save or Save As command
OnSheetActivate Property	Activating a chart sheet, dialog sheet, module, worksheet, workbook, or Excel itself
OnSheetDeactivate Property	Deactivating a chart sheet, dialog sheet, module, worksheet, workbook, or Excel itself
OnTime Method	Waiting until a specific time arrives, or waiting for a specified time delay
OnUndo Method	Selecting the Edit, Undo menu
OnWindow Property	Activating a window

CHAPTER 8

Customizing PowerPoint to Your Organization's Needs

PowerPoint is a powerful, yet flexible program that can be used for everything from slide presentations to printed flyers and other desktop publishing. To create the most effective set of tools for your users and to make frequently used features quick and easy to find, you can customize the PowerPoint interface and toolbars. Through the use of Visual Basic for Applications (VBA) macros, you can also automate the execution of frequently performed tasks.

Microsoft PowerPoint is a presentation application, and a long-time member of the Microsoft Office suite. Enhanced in small ways through most of the Office upgrades, PowerPoint has seen two major enhancements in recent releases. The integration of Microsoft Organization Chart with version 4.0 gave users the ability to create organization charts without having to draw boxes and connecting lines manually.

The next major upgrade was found in the release of Office 97. PowerPoint's new and improved tools for adding animation and sound provide the user with a greater ability to design true multimedia presentations. In addition, as seen in all the Office 97 applications, PowerPoint is now strongly connected to the powers of the Internet through the Web Publishing Wizard and the ability to save presentation files as HTML.

Designed for creating electronic presentations, PowerPoint gives users the ability to create slides that can be printed on paper, transparencies, or 35mm slides. To take full advantage of PowerPoint's capabilities, however, a slideshow run onscreen or projected directly from the computer is the most effective presentation medium. PowerPoint's contribution to the user's software arsenal is considerable:

- *Training presentations.* From new hire orientations to informative presentations on how the company's new phone system works, PowerPoint can be a major part of an organization's effective training plan.
- *Sales presentations.* Exciting, polished presentations can be given in a one-on-one meeting shown on a laptop, or displayed to a large seminar audience through an LCD panel or other projection device.
- *Desktop publishing.* For simple one-page pieces such as flyers, announcements, and signs, PowerPoint gives you the ability to place text and graphics on a page with complete freedom to move, resize, and manipulate the appearance of both.
- *Web publishing.* Users can save a presentation as HTML and create a Web page directly, or post a PowerPoint presentation on a website for visitors to view remotely.
- *Graphic resource.* Graphic text, clip art, and drawn objects created in PowerPoint (where it is often much easier to do so) can be pasted or linked to Word or Excel documents.

Regardless of your organization's use of PowerPoint, this already friendly program can be made more so through the manipulation of software defaults and options.

Customizing the Interface

PowerPoint's user interface offers users flexible options at each stage of a presentation's development. Starting with the first dialog box that appears after the program is opened, the user is offered a variety of wizards and templates from which to begin working. This interface can be manipulated to reduce the decision-making process for users who have very specific and consistent needs within PowerPoint.

Establishing a Default Presentation

One of PowerPoint's strengths is that it offers so many options for the process of building a presentation. These options are supported by defaults, some of which can be changed to increase productivity and consistency.

PowerPoint's first dialog box is shown in Figure 8.1. This dialog box asks the user to choose how they'll begin using PowerPoint:

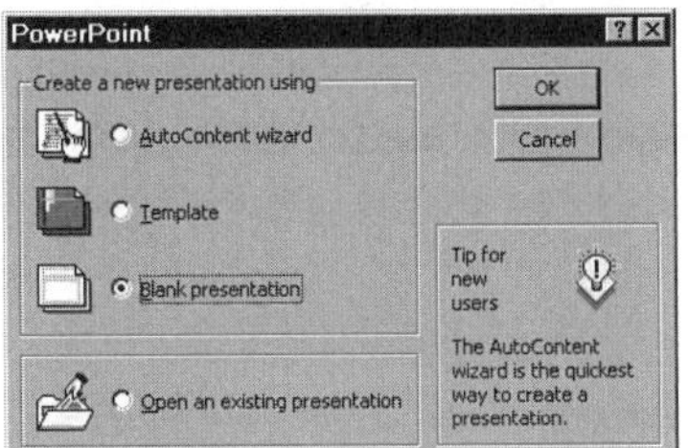

FIGURE 8.1
From a great deal of help for new users to very little intervention for the seasoned designer, PowerPoint offers a flexible starting point.

- **AutoContent Wizard.** A time-consuming process, the wizard asks the user what the presentation should accomplish, what the general topic is, and how long the presentation is expected to be. A skeletal presentation, including sample text that instructs users how and where to insert their own content is built based on users' answers to the wizard's questions.
- **Template.** To speed the process of building a colorful presentation, PowerPoint offers a variety of Presentation Designs. In most companies, and often within specific departments, a specific template is selected, giving presentations given by that group a consistent look.
- **Blank Presentation**. Not truly blank, this template merely has no background color or any graphics on it. The user can leave the white background and use the default black text, or apply a template to the presentation later. This option is normally selected by people who will be printing in black and white, or by those who find the background distracting while they're building their content.
- **Open an Existing Presentation.** In lieu of choosing File, Open, this option takes users to the Open dialog box, from which they open their presentation-in-progress.

Certainly, agreeing upon a specific template for the entire company or for specific departments within it is a good idea, but PowerPoint provides no structure to assure that this selected template is used. Many of the template filenames are quite similar, and the margin for error and confusion is great.

To provide a structured procedure for starting each presentation with the same template, use either of these methods:

- Rename the selected template to Blank Presentation.pot. Before renaming it, rename the real blank to Blank Presentation.pxx to preserve it should you want to restore it later.

After your selected template is set up as the Blank, it will be the template that appears whenever you select Blank Presentation from the first dialog box.

- Combine a simple procedure with a macro. Establish a procedure wherein all users start with the Blank Presentation (the original Blank), and as soon as the presentation opens, run a macro that applies a particular template to the presentation.

Renaming the Blank Presentation template is somewhat risky. If the real Blank presentation is lost or if you forget to rename it before renaming your selected template, you may have to reinstall the software to reestablish a true Blank Presentation template. Also, any users who want a real Blank will not be able to use it, unless your new name retains the .pot extension and you move it to the Presentation Designs folder. In either case, you've removed some of PowerPoint's flexibility. Depending on your situation, this could be a positive feature of this approach.

To rename the Blank Presentation template, follow these steps:

1. Open the Windows Explorer.
2. Navigate to the Templates folder under Microsoft Office, as shown in Figure 8.2.

FIGURE 8.2
In Word, Excel, and PowerPoint, templates stored in the Templates folder appear on the General tab in the New dialog box.

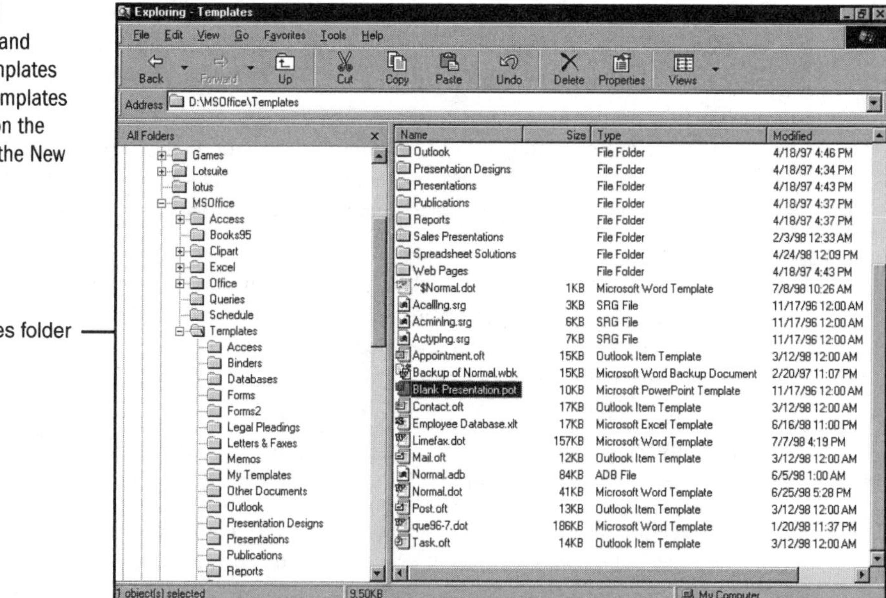

3. Click once on the Blank Presentation.pot file.

TIP You can also right-click the file and choose Rename from the shortcut menu.

4. Choose File, Rename.
5. Decide whether you want this to be available under another name, such as Blank2.pot (retaining the .pot extension), or if you want to rename it in such a way that it cannot be accidentally used, such as Blank Presentation.pxx.

The extension change to .pxx (or something similar) keeps this file from appearing in the New dialog box as a template or in the Open dialog box unless the All Files format is selected in the Files of Type list box.

6. Navigate to the Presentation Designs folder, and find the file for your preferred presentation template.
7. Copy the file to the Templates folder.
8. Rename the copy in the Templates folder Blank Presentation.pot. Be very careful to spell it correctly.
9. Close or minimize the Explorer.

Using a macro to launch a specific presentation is probably preferable to renaming the Blank Presentation file, depending on your staff's ability to consistently perform a specific procedure. If they're willing to consistently choose to start a presentation with the blank presentation and then run the macro, this approach will be useful and easy to change should your firm's preference in templates change. To find out more about creating a macro, read "Improving Productivity with VBA Macros" later in this chapter.

Customizing Application Defaults

To make your users' efforts with PowerPoint more productive, it should be simple to use and meet their needs without much interaction from them. By using PowerPoint's Options dialog box, you can change the defaults in up to seven areas. To access the following defaults, choose Tools, Options.

- **View.** The View tab offers options for what features appear onscreen (see Figure 8.3). Among the items listed in the Show section, the Startup dialog and New slide dialog options can be turned off if you decide to automate the startup process with macros.
- **General.** Click this tab (as shown in Figure 8.4) to increase or decrease the number of Recently used files listed in the users' File menu. Leave Macro Virus Protection on, and opt to leave Link Sounds with file size greater than 100Kb on. You can adjust this minimum file size to whatever is appropriate for your goals. This setting reduces your PowerPoint file sizes by not making large sound files part of the presentation file. This is important because large presentation files can cause PowerPoint to run slowly and in some cases, cause the program to crash.

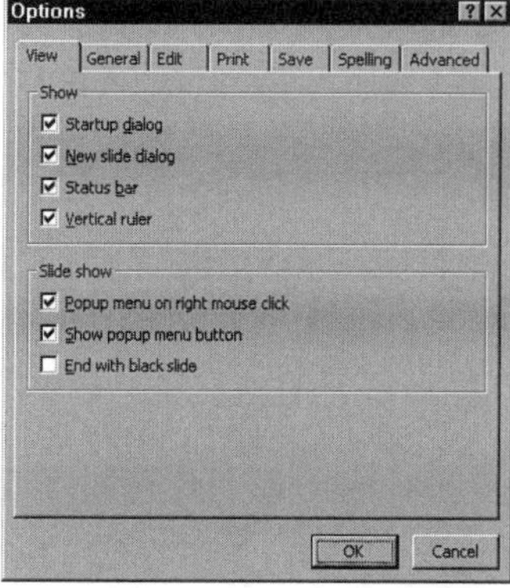

FIGURE 8.3
Choose your onscreen elements during the development and slideshow phases of your presentation.

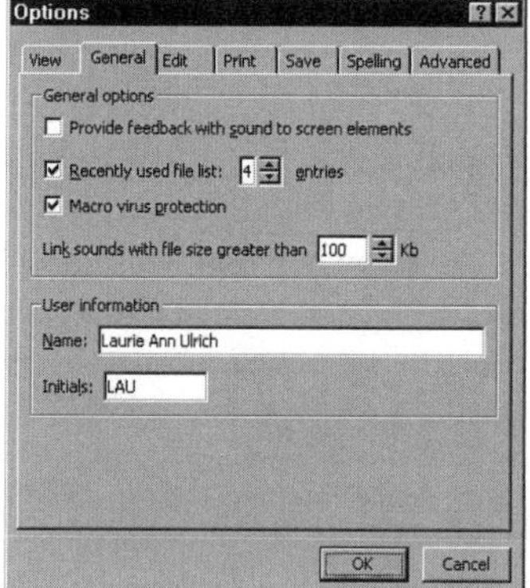

FIGURE 8.4
Use the General tab to control file size and file access.

- **Edit.** Click this tab to give the user more control over PowerPoint's text editing tools (see Figure 8.5). Many users find Automatic word selection to be counter-productive, as it makes it impossible to select an individual letter within a word. Smart cut and paste is a great feature, inserting appropriate spaces before or after pasted text. Whatever edits (or other actions) have been performed, a maximum of 150 Undo levels gives the users plenty of room to change their minds.
- **Print.** Of primary interest is the Print TrueType fonts as graphics option, as shown in Figure 8.6. This option can eliminate the need to download TrueType fonts to your printer. If your printer doesn't have a lot of memory and often fails to print complex PowerPoint presentations, turn this option on. If it is dimmed, your printer is not compatible with the option.
- **Save.** It's easy to forget that a remote office has an earlier version of PowerPoint. If your users are often sending files to users of older versions of PowerPoint, choosing the appropriate default file format in the Save PowerPoint Files as list box can be helpful, but should be performed with caution, as some features of the newer release of PowerPoint can be lost when the file is saved to an older version. Figure 8.7 shows the list of formats.

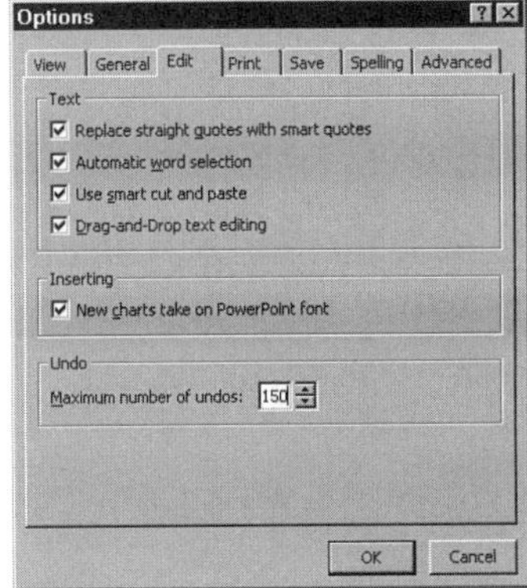

FIGURE 8.5
Control of the mouse and the Clipboard can be found in the Edit tab.

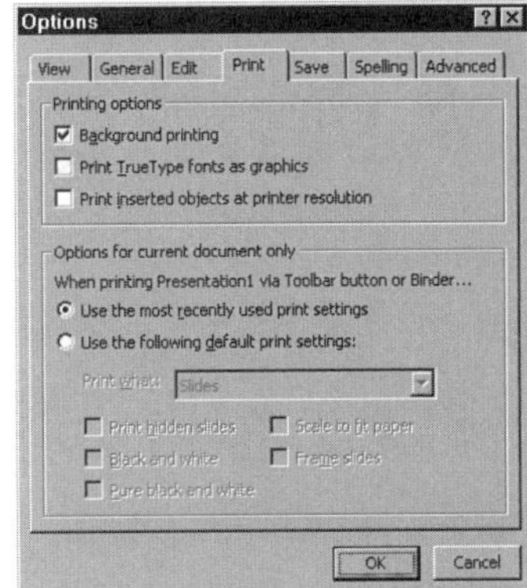

FIGURE 8.6
Save resources while performing a print job by printing TrueType fonts as graphics.

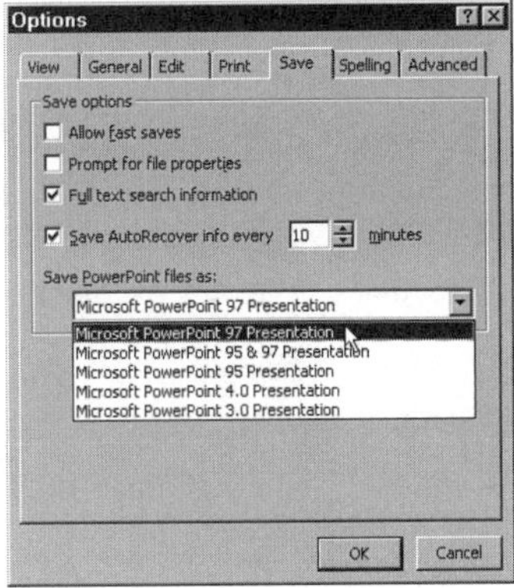

FIGURE 8.7
Backward compatibility is built in, but watch out for features that will be lost if you save to an older version that doesn't support them, such as animation and sound.

- **Advanced.** The most useful feature here isn't all that advanced. As shown in Figure 8.8, the Advanced tab enables you to set a default location for all saved files, such as a network folder to which all users have access. Type a path into the Default File Location text box.

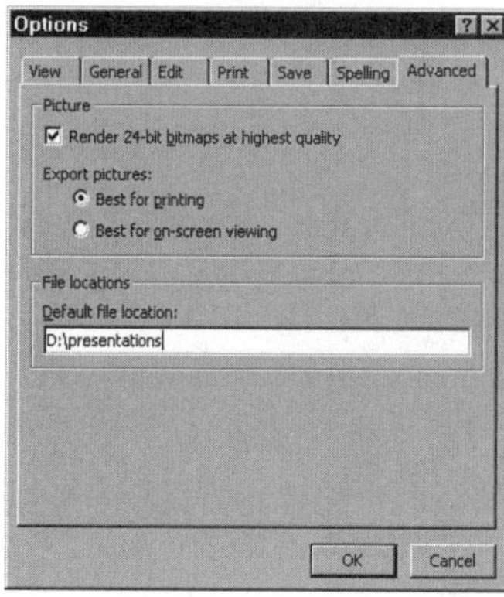

FIGURE 8.8
Eliminate the bottleneck of lost or missing files. Choose a default file location for PowerPoint presentations.

Customizing the Toolset

PowerPoint opens and displays the Standard, Formatting, and Drawing toolbars by default. Users can choose to add any of the 13 PowerPoint toolbars they want by right-clicking one of the displayed toolbars and choosing a toolbar from the menu (see Figure 8.9).

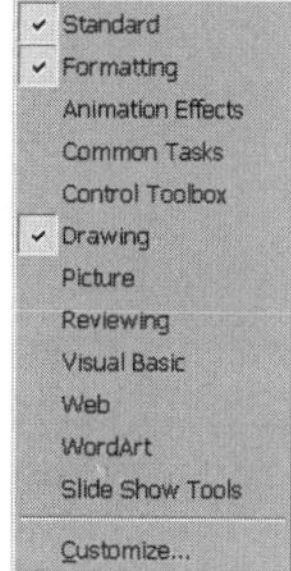

FIGURE 8.9
The Standard, Formatting, and Drawing toolbars are onscreen by default. Choose to view one or more of an additional ten toolbars.

Having too many toolbars open at once, however, limits the visible workspace, and the sheer number of buttons can be intimidating to any user. Instead of opening many toolbars to gain access to a variety of tools, you can customize the user's workspace by adding particular tools to the Standard, Formatting, or Drawing toolbars, or create your own toolbar with its own set of toolbar buttons.

To edit a PowerPoint toolbar, follow these steps:

1. With the target toolbar displayed, choose Tools, Customize.
2. Click the Commands tab in the Customize dialog box (see Figure 8.10).
3. Scroll through the Categories, and for each one view the Commands. When you see a command you want on the toolbar, drag it out of the dialog box and up to the toolbar, releasing it where you want the button inserted. Figure 8.11 shows a toolbar button for the Close command being added to the toolbar.

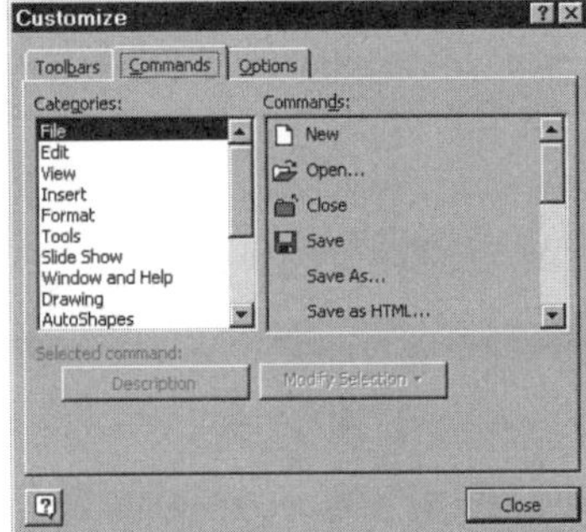

FIGURE 8.10
View a list of menus, macros, and all commands that PowerPoint has to offer.

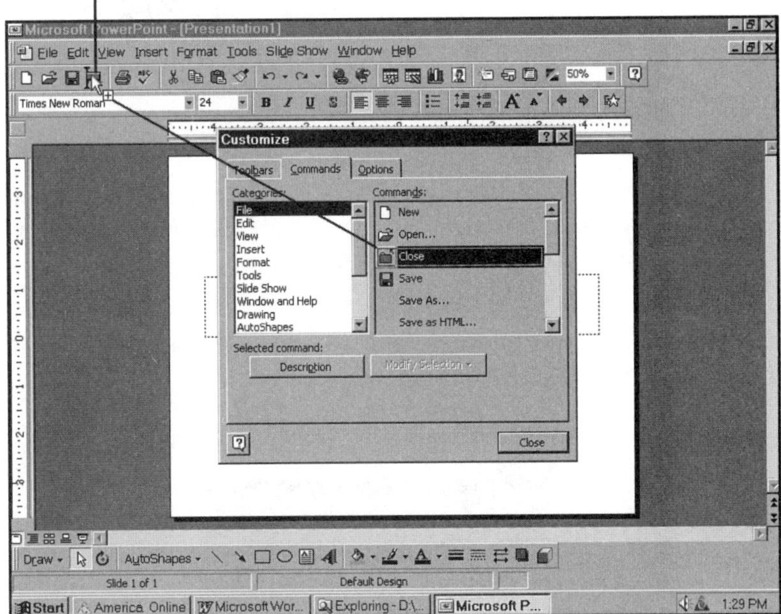

FIGURE 8.11
Drag PowerPoint commands up to the toolbar, instantly converting them to toolbar buttons.

4. Continue to add buttons as needed, dragging them to any of the displayed toolbars. Existing buttons can be rearranged while the Customize dialog box is open.

When rearranging toolbar buttons, use your mouse to drag the button you want to relocate, moving it left or right within the current toolbar, or up or down onto other displayed toolbars.

5. To delete a button from the toolbar, drag it down and off the toolbar. Be sure not to remove any of the original buttons from any toolbar, as this can be confusing to your users and reduce the effectiveness of any documentation that is based on your toolbar's original settings.

6. If you want to change a button face, click the Modify button. From the menu, choose Change Button Image. A palette of button graphics appears (see Figure 8.12). Click one to apply it to the selected button.

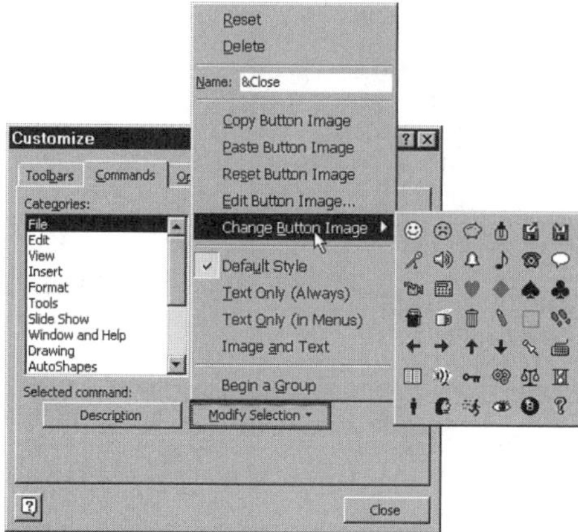

FIGURE 8.12
If possible, choose a button face that will be easy to remember and associate with the command it represents.

7. If your button has text on it (normally the name of the command or macro represented by the button), you can remove the text and leave the graphic image. Click the Modify button and choose Text Only (in Menus).
8. Click the Close button to close the dialog box.

Further toolbar customization can be performed by creating new toolbars—personalized sets of tools from a variety of command categories.

1. Choose Tools, Customize, and click the Toolbars tab, as shown in Figure 8.13.

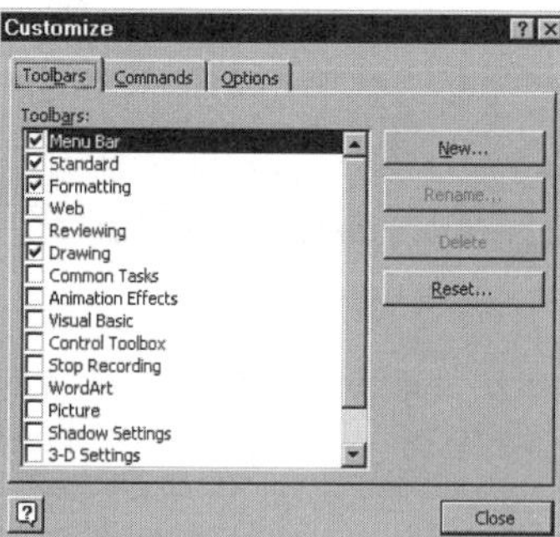

FIGURE 8.13
Add your own custom toolbar to the list.

2. Click the New button, which opens the New Toolbar dialog box. Type a short and illustrative name for your toolbar. If possible, the name should indicate the type of tools to be found on it, so users who have turned the toolbar off can find it and redisplay it as needed.

3. After naming the toolbar, click OK.
4. Your new toolbar (see Figure 8.14) appears as a floating toolbar on top of your Customize dialog box. The name of the toolbar is truncated until the number of toolbar buttons you add makes the bar wide enough to display the entire name.

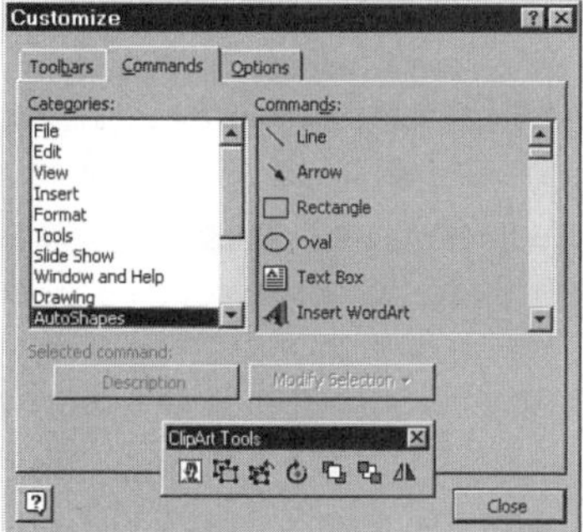

FIGURE 8.14
Drag commands from the Customize dialog box onto your new toolbar.

5. Click the Commands tab, and select your categories and the commands within them that you want to add to your toolbar. Drag the commands onto the floating toolbar.
6. You can rearrange the new buttons as needed and drag any from the toolbar that you decide you don't want.
7. When the toolbar is complete, click the Close button in the Customize dialog box.

Your floating toolbar remains onscreen, and it can be dragged to the top or bottom of your application window to join your currently displayed toolbars, or placed on either the left or right side of the application window.

Improving Productivity with VBA Macros

Macros are programs that you create by recording a series of frequently performed steps. VBA (Visual Basic for Applications) is the programming language that Office uses to create these macros, although the user need not know VBA to create a macro—the code is inserted by Office as people record their steps. The user can execute the program at any time, thus automating the steps contained in the macro. Macros can be written for just about any activity you perform in PowerPoint. Although many tasks that previously required macros are now automated directly through the software itself—such as AutoCorrect or inserting Word Tables—there are still several processes that can be automated to save time and support consistency:

- *Starting a presentation.* Build a macro that will open a new presentation, choose a particular template, select a specific layout, and leave the user at their first blank slide, after having only clicked a toolbar button. The macro could also include the creation of a title slide, should your title slides have consistent content.

- *Opening toolbars.* Create a macro that opens specific toolbars for specific tasks, such as opening the Drawing and Picture toolbars when a piece of clip art is inserted. By creating a macro that inserts a particular piece of clip art and then opens the desired toolbars, three tasks are converted to one simple keystroke or button-click.
- *Formatting changes.* A macro that opens the Slide Master in PowerPoint and inserts, moves, and resizes your company logo on the slide can save a lot of steps and assure consistent placement of your logo on any presentation template. Of course, if a specific presentation template has been chosen for everyone to use and a macro created to apply it, the master should have already been set up for that template.
- *Printing.* If every presentation created must be printed in a particular format for hardcopy storage, create a macro that initiates the print job, selects the output format, and prints the file. By making a macro for this task, you can be assured that all your presentation hardcopies are, for example, three-slide per page handouts, and that two sets are made.
- *Running a slideshow.* Create a macro that selects a particular slide show, starts on a particular slide, and runs the show. This saves the audience from having to see the file selected and the Slide Show command invoked. If timings and a recorded narration are part of the show, the macro becomes even more powerful by invoking built-in automation.

Recording a VBA macro is simple, and doesn't require knowledge of VBA (Visual Basic for Applications). If, however, you are familiar with VBA, the editing and enhancement of macros will be much easier for you.

To record a PowerPoint macro, follow these steps:

1. Before recording, be sure that you have set the stage so that the macro begins at the point users will be when they invoke it later. For example, if users will already have the presentation open when the macro is invoked, have the presentation open when you begin to build the macro.
2. Choose Tools, Macro, Record New Macro. The Record Macro dialog box opens, as shown in Figure 8.15.
3. Give the macro a name (no spaces) and choose which presentation the macro will be stored in (and thus available to). Type a description, if needed.

NOTE If you store a macro in the active presentation, it is only available from within that presentation. If, however, you store it in a presentation created purely for the use of macros, you have access to the macro whenever that presentation is open. You can store all your general-use macros in a macro presentation (call it Macro.ppt, for example). To access these macros, your users can open that presentation, and then invoke any macro they want. If the macro presentation is empty (of any text or graphic content), it will be a small file and not create any problems in terms of system resources if you have it open while working on other presentations.

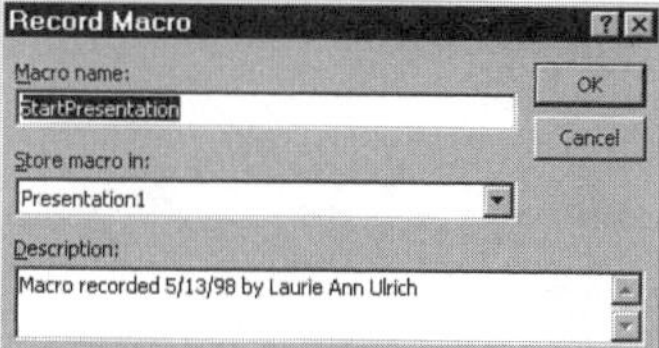

FIGURE 8.15
Give your macro a name that indicates the function that the macro performs. Keep it short, and use no spaces.

4. Click OK to close the Record Macro dialog box. Your macro is now recording, signified by a small floating toolbar onscreen with a Stop button on it (see Figure 8.16).

FIGURE 8.16
Have a written list of steps in front of you to help you perform your macro's steps seamlessly.

5. Record your macro. Perform each step in the exact order you want it performed each time the macro is run.
6. When your steps are completed, click the Stop button.

After you've created your macro, you can use the Tools, Customize command to assign it to a toolbar button. To invoke a macro, click the button assigned to it. If the macros you create will be helpful to other users, you can distribute a copy of the Normal.dot template from the computer where the macros were recorded, thus making the macros available to other users. In many cases, however, it's a better idea to simply rerecord the macros on the other users' computers, so their Normal templates need not be replaced. Replacing the Normal template can also replace (and eliminate) AutoCorrect and AutoText entries that a user may have accumulated.

In most cases, PowerPoint macros are rather simple, even if they encompass several steps and take a few minutes to record. You'll find that if they don't work, it's easier to rerecord them than to try to edit them, even if you are familiar with VBA. ●

CHAPTER 9

Customizing Access to Your Organization's Needs

Microsoft Access is a powerful tool when you use it to customize a database for your needs. You might, for example, customize a database for an inventory system, a data entry model, or an employee file. If you use the wizards Access provides and have some familiarity with database structure, you will find customizing fairly easy to do. This chapter demonstrates three aspects of customizing a database: how to customize the interface, how to customize the toolset, and how to improve productivity with VBA macros.

Customizing the Interface

The first step in customizing a database is to customize the interface. The interface determines how the database is displayed and what options are available to the end user. You can customize the interface by changing settings in the Options dialog box, by creating a switchboard, and by modifying startup settings.

Changing Settings in the Options Dialog Box

The default settings in the Options dialog box work fine for a simple database, but when you are creating a customized interface, you need to change many of these settings.

To display the Options dialog box shown in Figure 9.1, choose Tools, Options.

FIGURE 9.1
The Options dialog box contains ten tabs in which you can change default settings.

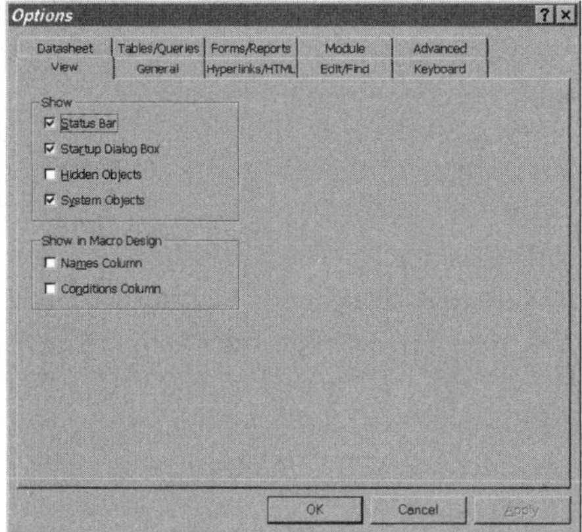

The next ten sections describe the options available in each of the Options dialog box tabs.

View The View tab contains four check boxes you can use to specify which objects are shown or hidden in the Access interface. The Status Bar check box, which is marked by default, displays the status bar at the bottom of the Access window. The Startup Dialog Box check box, also marked by default, displays the Startup dialog box on startup, giving you the options to create a blank database, create a database using the Database Wizard, or open an existing database. If you want to open an existing database, you can choose from among the four databases you've most recently used, or browse to another one. With the two remaining check boxes, you can show or hide hidden and system objects. These check boxes are not marked by default.

You can also mark the Names Column and Conditions Column check boxes in the View tab to display the Names and Conditions columns when you are creating or modifying a macro. By default, Access only displays macro commands and comments; if you mark these check boxes, the user can also view the conditions for the macro and the name fields of other macros. Even if you choose not to mark these check boxes, you can display the Names and Conditions columns in Macro Design view by choosing View, Macro Names or View, Conditions.

General The General tab enables you to set different print margins. The default is one inch. If you are going to have several reports with different margins, set your default for the one you will use the most. You can change the other reports' margins in the Design view for the report.

From the General tab, you can also choose the location to which Access will default when creating a new database. If you do not specify a path, Access defaults to C:\My Documents.

The default sort order specifies the alphabetic sort order to be used when creating a new database. The default of General is used for English, French, German, Italian, Portuguese, and Modern Spanish. If you change the alphabetic sort order of an existing database, you must compact the database before the changes are applied.

This tab also contains an option box for accompanying sound with feedback. If this box is checked, feedback such as error alerts provide sound along with the message. Choosing this option also affects feedback in Excel, Word, and PowerPoint.

Hyperlinks/HTML This tab enables you to format hyperlink colors and styles, define an HTML template, and set data source information. If no template location is listed, Access looks in the \Program Files\Microsoft Office\Templates\Access folder. Access can output database objects, such as forms and reports, to an Internet application. To do this, it merges the HTML template file with the output files.

Edit/Find The Edit/Find tab contains options for setting search types, confirmation settings, and filter-by-form defaults.

You can perform three types of searches. No matter what search type you choose as the default, you can change the criteria in the Find In Field dialog box.

You can select when confirmation messages will appear. Depending on what you have selected, Access asks for confirmation when deleting documents, changing records, and performing action queries. The default is for all three check boxes to be marked.

Keyboard Under the Keyboard tab, you can choose keyboard actions such as arrow key behavior, where the focus goes after you press Enter, and the behavior when entering data in a field.

Datasheet This is the tab where you select the formatting of the datasheet. The Datasheet view displays data in a row-and-column format and is available in queries, forms, and tables. The attributes you can change are colors, fonts, font size, gridline effects, cell effects, and column width. You can also make datasheet formatting changes by opening the object in Datasheet view and choosing Format, Font.

Tables/Queries You can set default field sizes and types for tables in the Tables/Queries tab. (If you want to override the defaults for a particular table, you can do so in Table Design view.)

The Tables/Queries tab also enables you to change a few options for queries. For example, you might want your queries to display table names. This option is handy if your queries contain multiple tables, because it readily shows you which table each field comes from. (You can also change this option for an individual query in that query's Design view.)

In addition, you can choose whether Access automatically outputs all fields or whether this is specified within the query. This option applies only to new queries, not existing ones.

If you select the AutoJoin option, Access creates an inner join between two tables. AutoJoin only works if there are fields with the same name and data type in both tables and one is a primary key.

Access defaults to use the user's permissions. You change this setting to use the owner's permissions instead, which only affects new queries. Having owner permission might allow users to run and view queries they were not able to access with user permission. Be careful when choosing to use user permissions—this allows all users to view or run the query, although the owner is still the only one who can save changes to the query.

Forms/Reports The Forms/Reports tab enables you to specify a default form or report template other than the Normal template. Access then uses the specified template when you create a form or report without using the wizard. The template defines the sections in the form or report. Changing the template does not change existing forms or reports.

NOTE Changes to templates are stored in the workgroup information file (System.mdw), not in the database. Therefore, this change applies to any database that is opened or created. ■

Module The Module tab contains options you can use when writing code. These options include code colors, font type and size, coding options, and window settings. Unless you are doing an extensive amount of coding, the default options will work appropriately.

Advanced The Advanced tab includes settings for record locking, DDE operations, open mode, arguments, and error trapping. The most important of these is the open mode. Databases are designed for a multiuser environment. If you choose the Exclusive option button, only one person at a time will be able to open the database.

Designing a Switchboard Form

One way to customize a database is to create a switchboard to help users navigate through the database. The user can click on buttons on the switchboard to perform such tasks as opening forms and reports, opening other switchboards, running macros, or quitting the application. Access provides a Switchboard Wizard to help you set up the switchboard, which you can then customize to suit your preferences. The Switchboard Manager makes it easy to maintain the switchboard after you have it up and running.

A switchboard consists of a switchboard form and switchboard pages. The *switchboard form* is the actual form the end user sees. This form contains buttons and text and any other objects you put on it. The buttons on the form perform actions you define on the *switchboard pages*. The pages and action items are stored in a table called Switchboard Items.

Creating a Switchboard by Using the Switchboard Wizard Follow these steps to create a switchboard by using the Switchboard Wizard.

1. Choose Tools, Add-Ins, Switchboard Manager.

NOTE If you are creating a new switchboard, Access prompts you, saying it was unable to find a valid switchboard and asking if you would like to create one. Click on Yes. After you set up your switchboard, you will use this same command to make changes to the switchboard items.

2. Access displays the Switchboard Manager, which contains a list of switchboard pages. The main switchboard is the default unless you change it later. Click on the Edit button to display the Edit Switchboard Page dialog box.
3. If there are not any current items on the switchboard, the only active button is New. If you have set up items already, you can also choose Edit, Delete, Move Up, or Move Down (you'll learn about these options later). Click on New to display the Edit Switchboard Item dialog box.
4. The text you enter in the Text field appears on the switchboard form, next to the button for the item on the switchboard.

   The Command field provides a drop-down list of available commands, as shown in Figure 9.2.

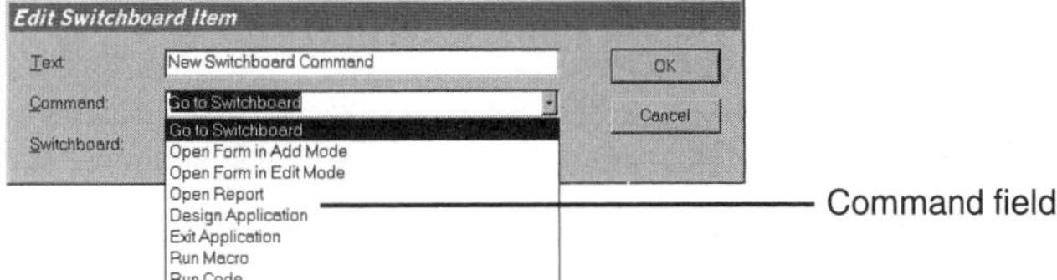

FIGURE 9.2
You can choose from among eight commands in the Command field of the Edit Switchboard Item dialog box.

   The third field is dynamic; its name changes depending on the command you choose in the Command field. For example, if you select Go to Switchboard in the Command field, the third field becomes the Switchboard field to let you specify the switchboard you want to go to. If you choose Open Report in the Command field, the third field becomes the Report field to let you specify the report to open. Two commands do not produce a third field: Design Application and Exit Application.
5. After you fill out all three fields, click on OK to add the item and return to the Edit Switchboard Page dialog box. You can now modify the item or move it up or down on the list. The order in which the items appear in the Switchboard Manager dialog box is the order in which they will appear on the actual form.
6. Click on Close to return to the Switchboard Manager, and click on Close again to exit the Switchboard Manager.

You will set up a switchboard that has a Main switchboard with these items:

- Customer Information (This will open another switchboard.)
- Exit Database

The Customer Information switchboard will contain these switchboard items:

- Add/Edit Customers (This will open a form for entering customer information.)
- Customer Address Report (This will open a report of customers and their addresses.)
- Return to Main Switchboard

To create a new switchboard page, follow these steps:

1. Choose Tools, Add-Ins, Switchboard Manager.
2. Click on the New button to create the Customer Information switchboard.
3. Enter the new switchboard name `Customer Information`, and click on OK. The Customer Information switchboard is added to the list.

You can now add items to either switchboard or add more switchboards, if needed.

Creating the Items on the Main Switchboard To create items on the switchboard page, follow these steps:

1. Select the Main switchboard in the list of switchboards in the Switchboard Manager dialog box, and click on Edit.
2. Click on New.
3. In the Text field, type `Customer Information Switchboard`.
4. In the Command field, choose Go To Switchboard.
5. In the Switchboard field, choose Customer Information. Click on OK.
6. Click on New.
7. In the Text field, type `Exit Database`.
8. In the Command field, choose Exit Application. Click on OK.

You now have two items on the Main Switchboard (see Figure 9.3). At any time, you can edit, delete, or add new items. Clicking the Move Up and Move Down buttons reorders the items.

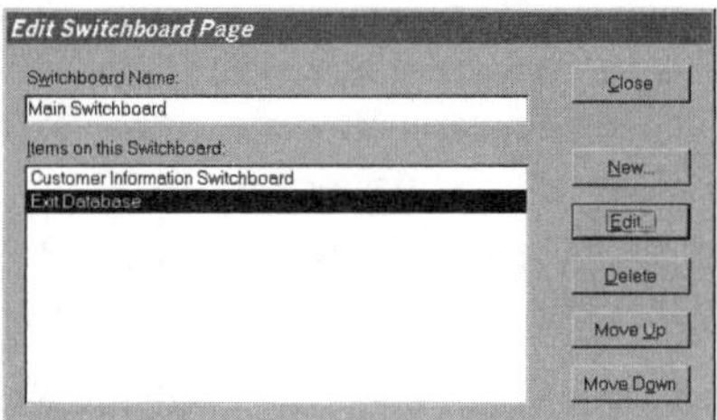

FIGURE 9.3
The Main Switchboard page has two items: Customer Information Switchboard and Exit Database.

Creating Items on the Customer Information Switchboard To add items to the Customer Information Switchboard page, follow these steps:

1. Go back to the Switchboard Manager dialog box, where the switchboard pages are listed. Select Customer Information Switchboard, and click on Edit.

2. Click on New.
3. In the Text field, type **Go To Main Switchboard**.
4. In the Command field, select Go To Switchboard.
5. In the Switchboard field, select Main Switchboard, and click on OK to return to the Edit Switchboard Page dialog box.
6. Click on New.
7. In the Text field, type **Add/Edit Customers**.
8. In the Command field, select Open Form in Edit Mode.

NOTE You can open forms in two modes, Add and Edit. The Add mode displays a blank form for data entry without showing the existing records. The Edit mode displays all records, but you can add new ones.

9. Select the form to be opened, and click on OK.

NOTE You must define forms, reports, macros, and so on before you can create items for them on a switchboard, so creating switchboard items is one of the last things you do in the database design process.

10. Click on New.
11. In the Text field, type **Customer Address Report**.
12. In the Command field, choose Open Report.
13. Select the report to be opened in the Report field, and click on OK. Figure 9.4 shows how the items in the Customer Information switchboard should look now.

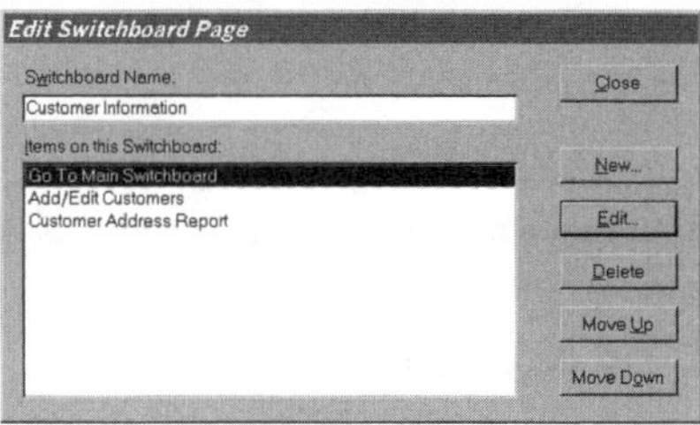

FIGURE 9.4
The Edit Switchboard Page dialog box contains three items: Go To Main Switchboard, Add/Edit Customers, and Customer Address Report.

You probably want the item that returns users to the Main switchboard to be last on the list. To make this change, follow these steps:

1. Select Go To Main Switchboard.
2. Click on Move Down until the item is at the bottom of the list.
3. Click on Close until you are back at the database window.

The items you just created are stored in the Switchboard Items table, as shown in Figure 9.5.

FIGURE 9.5
The Switchboard Items table stores information corresponding to actions you defined in the Switchboard Manager.

Switchboard Items : Table

SwitchboardID	ItemNumber	ItemText	Command	Argument
1	0	Main Switchboard	0	Default
1	1	Customer Information Switc	1	2
1	2	Exit Database	6	
2	0	Customer Information	0	
2	1	Add/Edit Customers	3	Switchboard
2	2	Customer Address Report	1	2
2	3	Go To Main Switchboard	1	1
0	0		0	

The Switchboard Items table contains five fields: SwitchboardID, ItemNumber, ItemText, Command, and Argument. You can modify your switchboard in this table, but a better way is to make changes through the Switchboard Manager. When Access creates the Switchboard Items table, it assigns predefined command numbers to the items you create. These command numbers correspond with the choices you make when creating or modifying the switchboard pages. Using the Switchboard Manager to modify your switchboard is convenient because it updates the command numbers for you—you don't have to know what they are.

The form is stored as Switchboard. Figure 9.6 displays what the default form looks like before any formatting or customization.

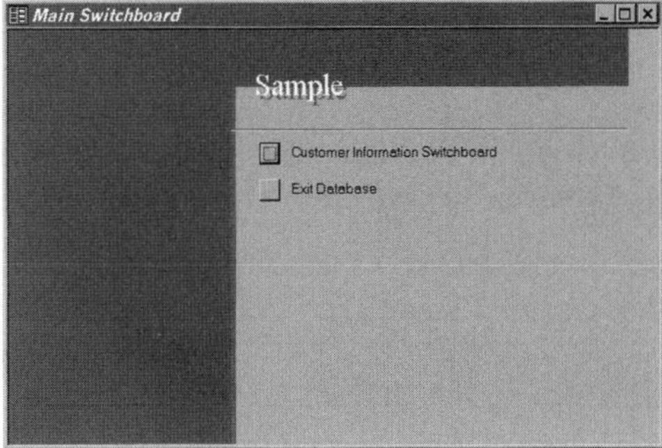

FIGURE 9.6
The default switchboard form setup.

Formatting a Switchboard Form You can customize the switchboard form by rearranging the buttons, changing fonts, changing colors, adding logos, and so on.

Go to the Design view of the form, as shown in Figure 9.7.

Notice that your text is not shown next to the buttons; the form pulls the information from the Switchboard Items table instead. You can make formatting changes in the Properties box.

NOTE Even though the Design view shows several buttons, the form only shows the buttons in Datasheet view that have items assigned to them.

The form has colored boxes, which you can move, resize, or delete. You can also move the labels.

FIGURE 9.7
The switchboard form in Design view.

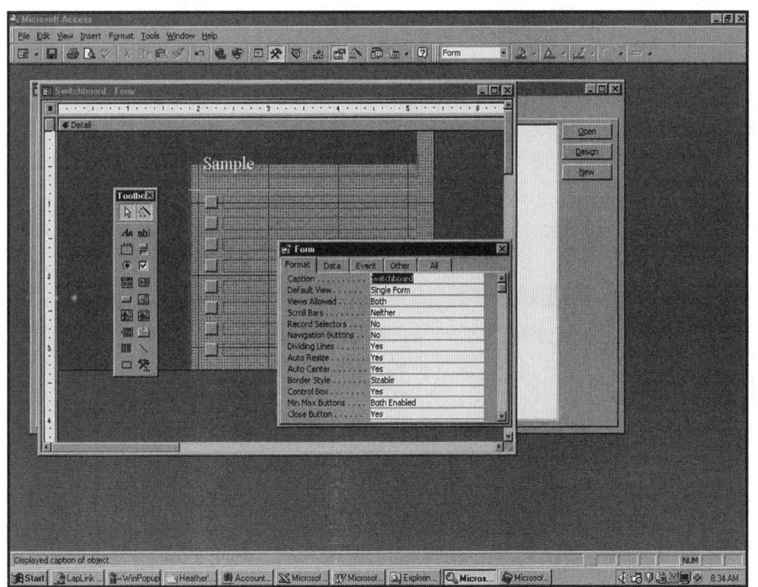

You can insert a picture or logo by clicking on the Unbound Object Frame button, Bound Object Frame button, or Image button in the toolbox, or by selecting Insert, Object or Insert, Picture. A picture can be either embedded or linked. An embedded picture is stored within the database file. If the picture is linked, Access stores pointer information to where the picture is located.

You can change the picture properties in the Properties box when the picture is selected in Design view. If you select Embedded as the picture type, the file size of the database increases, depending on the size of the picture. The file size of the database does not increase if you link the picture, but you have to reestablish the link if the picture is moved. If a linked picture is deleted, you must choose another location for the picture, or the form displays an error.

A picture can have three size modes: Clip, Stretch, and Zoom. You can also change this property in the object's Properties box in Design view. *Clip* displays the picture at actual size. The image is cut off if it is larger than the control area. *Stretch* sizes the picture to fit in the control area, but sometimes distorts the picture. *Zoom* displays the picture entirely after sizing to fit either the height or width of the control area. This mode does not distort the image.

Creating a Switchboard Form from Scratch If you decide the switchboard needs to be extensively changed and formatted, it might be better to develop a form from scratch, name it *switchboard*, and set it as the startup form. Assigning startup forms is discussed in the next section, "Modifying Startup Settings."

When creating your own switchboard form, select Insert, Form. Choose Design View, and click on OK. You can add images and text to your form by using the toolbox. For the switchboard, you need to insert buttons that perform the desired actions.

To add a button that opens a report, follow these steps:

1. Select the Command Button icon from the toolbox and drag over to the form. The Command Button Wizard appears. If you are just opening a report, you can use the wizard to assign your commands. You can also design a more complex button command by canceling out of the wizard and assigning code to the button.
2. Several categories and actions appear in the Command Button Wizard. Choose the Report Operations category and the Preview Report action (see Figure 9.8).

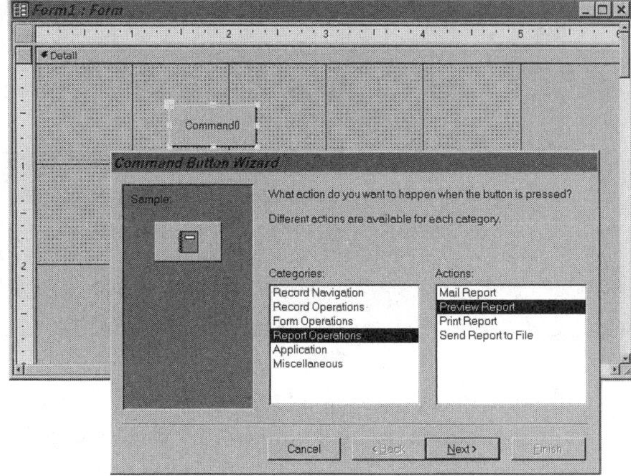

FIGURE 9.8
The Command Button Wizard contains several categories and actions you can choose.

3. Click on Next. Reports that have been previously created are listed. Choose the report you would like this command button to open, and click on Next.
4. You can have the button display text or a picture. Choose the option you prefer, and click on Next.
5. Assign a name to your button. The defaults are command1, command2, and so on, but if you name your button something more descriptive, referencing the button later will be easier. Click on Finish to close the Command Button Wizard and return to the form in Design view.

You can add other buttons, rearrange the buttons, and resize them to get the appearance you want. Figure 9.9 shows a sample switchboard created from scratch instead of by using the Switchboard Wizard.

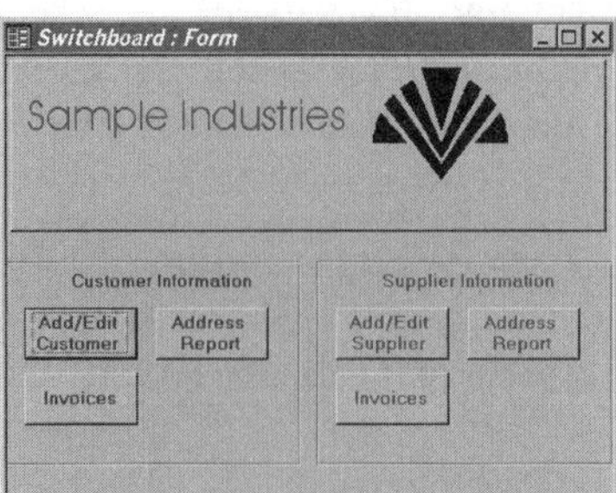

FIGURE 9.9
You can design a form to act as a switchboard.

Modifying Startup Settings

You can specify options to be applied when the database is opened. Select Tools, Startup to open the Startup dialog box, in which you can set several options for the startup of the database.

The Application Title appears in the upper-left corner of the Access window, next to the key icon. If no application title is specified, the title bar displays the name Microsoft Access. You can also specify a different icon to be displayed instead of the Access key. Enter the full path of the icon in the Application Icon field, or click on the button labeled with an ellipsis (...) to browse for icons.

You can specify what menu bar appears on startup. You can also create custom menu bars, as discussed in the next section, "Customizing the Toolset." If you do not create any other menu bars, the default bar is shown. This is true with the shortcut menus as well. The shortcut menus are displayed when you right-click on items, with commands that vary depending on where you right-click. You can customize a shortcut menu if you like, and use it on startup.

If you would like a form such as a switchboard to appear on startup, choose the form in the Display Form field. You can display other forms as well as switchboards on startup, but a switchboard is particularly appropriate because its purpose is to provide an easy way to navigate through the database.

The database window can be hidden. If you clear the Display Database Window check box, the window containing the tables, queries, reports, and so on becomes hidden. After the database is open, choosing Window, Unhide displays the database window again.

To open a database without enabling the startup options, hold down the Shift key while the database is opening.

Customizing the Toolset

The toolbar displayed in the Access window by default is the Database toolbar. Access comes with several other toolbars you can use as well. If you like, you can tweak these toolbars by adding buttons and menus, or you can create your own custom toolbars.

Select View, Toolbars, Customize. The Customize dialog box appears, with three tabs: Toolbars, Commands, and Options.

Toolbars

This tab lists all the available toolbars. If you created new toolbars, they are listed at the bottom. To see the properties of any toolbar, highlight it and click on Properties. The Properties dialog box enables you to change the toolbar name, type, and options regarding moving and showing the toolbar. You can only modify the name and type of user-defined toolbars, not predefined ones.

You can create three types of toolbars: menu bar, toolbar, and pop-up. Menu bars are drop-down menus, toolbars contain command buttons, and pop-ups are text commands on shortcut and drop-down menus. If your toolbar is going to be the startup toolbar, select Menu Bar in the Type drop-down list.

Commands

The Commands tab lists the various command buttons and descriptions. Categories are listed on the left, with the commands in each category on the right. You can select a command and then click on Description to see what each button does (see Figure 9.10). Besides just listing the command buttons and what they do, you can drag a command button from the dialog box out onto a toolbar. After you add a button to a toolbar, you can right-click on it to modify its settings.

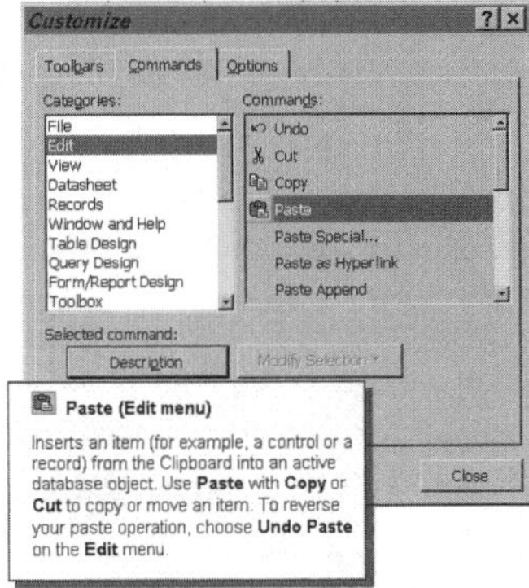

FIGURE 9.10
The Commands tab contains icon categories, commands, and descriptions.

Options

On the Options tab are check boxes for displaying large icons, showing ScreenTips on toolbars, and listing shortcut keys in ScreenTips. If you mark Show ScreenTips On Toolbars, a description of each toolbar button appears when you rest the mouse pointer over the button. If you mark Show Shortcut Keys In ScreenTips, the ScreenTips include any shortcut keys assigned to the command. For example, if the Show Shortcut Keys In ScreenTips check box is cleared and you point to the Copy button, the ScreenTip displays the word Copy. If the check box is marked, the ScreenTip says Copy (Ctrl+C). You can also choose an option for menu animation on this tab. Menu animations change the way a menu is displayed when it's selected.

Creating a New Toolbar

To create a new toolbar, follow these steps:

1. Choose View, Toolbars, Customize, and click on New on the Toolbars tab.
2. Type the name for the new toolbar and click on OK.
3. A small gray box with an X in the corner appears. This is your new (empty as of yet) toolbar, onto which you can drag and drop command buttons or menus.

4. On the Commands tab, find the buttons or menus you would like on your new toolbar and drag them over to the blank bar.
5. While the Customize dialog box is open, you can right-click on the items on your new toolbar to modify them. For example, you can change the button image, copy the image, or delete the button. Figure 9.11 shows the available options for modifying a toolbar item.

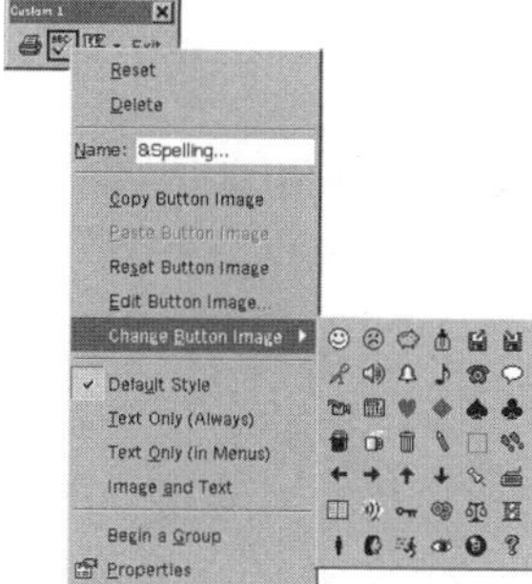

FIGURE 9.11
You can modify several options for each button.

6. You can move and resize the new toolbar as needed. If you want to hide the toolbar, either click on the X in its upper-right corner or choose View, Toolbars and click on the toolbar to clear the check mark next to its name.

One reason for creating a customized toolbar is so that not all users have access to all commands. For example, you might want to create a toolbar that only has buttons for printing, running a spell check, outputting to other Office products, and quitting the application. You could specify this toolbar in the Startup dialog box (Tools, Startup) and designate your switchboard as the opening form. Clear the Display Database Window check box. Now you have an interface a user can navigate through, but with limited options and no way to manipulate the data. This form of security is much easier to maintain than user-level access. Figure 9.12 shows this type of startup window.

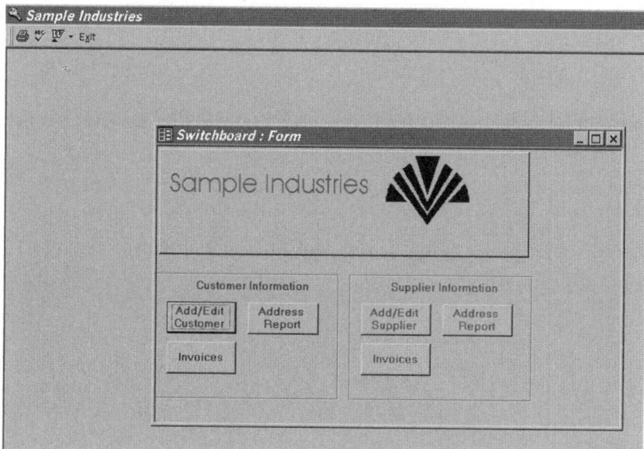

FIGURE 9.12
The startup options are set to display the switchboard form, hide the database window, and display the custom toolbar.

Remember to hold down the Shift key if you want to open the database without the startup options.

Improving Productivity with VBA Macros

Macros can automate tasks that otherwise would have to be done individually. A macro contains a list of actions and arguments. Macros are listed in the Macros tab of the database window.

To create a new macro, click on the New button in the Macros tab. The default view shows actions and comments. You can also choose to view macro names and conditions by choosing View, Macro Names and View, Conditions or by marking the Names Column and Conditions Column check boxes in the View tab of the Options dialog box (see the "View" section earlier in this chapter).

In the Actions field, you can select actions ranging from opening a report to transferring an entire database. After you choose the action, you must enter the action arguments in the appropriate fields.

If you want macros to run only if a certain condition is met, display the conditions. Then, in the Condition field, type the condition that must be met. If the condition is not met, the action will not be performed and the macro will step to the next action. If that action has a condition also, it will once again check for validity before performing the action.

One way to troubleshoot a macro is to have the macro single-step through the actions, showing each action and its results. After each action, you have the option to Step, Halt, or Continue.

After you create your macro, you have to save it before you can run it. To modify a macro, select it in the Macros tab of the database window, and click on the Design button.

Macros increase productivity because they can be assigned to buttons on forms. Earlier in the chapter, you saw how to create a button that opened a report. You could also create a macro that runs a query, opens the report, and displays a message box. If you assign this macro to the button, the button performs three actions instead of only one. (You can increase the speed of a macro by converting it to a Visual Basic module; see Chapter 41 for more information.)

To create a macro that runs a query, opens a report, and displays a message box, follow these steps:

1. Click on New in the Macro tab of the database window.
2. Display the drop-down list under the Action column heading in the Macro window, and select OpenQuery.

3. The fields that appear at the bottom of the Macro window are dynamic; they change depending on the action you select. When you select OpenQuery, you get three fields: Query Name, View, and Data Mode. Select the query to run in the Query Name field.
4. Select the desired View option—Datasheet, Design, or Print Preview. *Datasheet* runs the query and displays the results in a datasheet. *Design* opens the query in Design view. *Print Preview* displays a preview of the query results as they will appear when printed.
5. Select the desired Data Mode option—Add, Edit, or Read Only. *Add* allows users to add new records. *Edit* allows users to modify existing records or add records. *Read Only* does not allow any modifications, additions, or deletions of records.
6. Optionally type a comment about the OpenQuery action in the Comment field to the right of the action.
7. Under the OpenQuery action, add the OpenReport action. This action displays four fields at the bottom of the Macro window: Report Name, View, Filter Name, and Where Condition.
8. Choose the name of the report to open in the Report Name field.
9. In the View field, select Print, Design, or Print Preview. *Print* opens the report and prints it. *Design* opens the report in Design view. *Print Preview* opens the report in Print Preview.
10. Optionally specify a filter in the Filter Name field to restrict or sort the records used in the report.
11. Optionally specify a Where condition in the Where Condition field. A Where condition is similar to a filter; it is an SQL statement that determines which records are selected from the underlying tables or queries.
12. Optionally type a comment in the Comment field for the OpenReport action.
13. Under the OpenReport action, add the MsgBox action. This action displays four fields at the bottom of the Macro window: Message, Beep, Type, and Title.
14. Type the message to be displayed in the Message field. The message can be a maximum of 255 characters.
15. Choose Yes or No in the Beep field to specify whether you want the computer to beep when the message box is displayed.
16. In the Type field, select which type of icon you want displayed in the message box. Your choices are None, Critical, Warning?, Warning!, and Information.
17. In the Title field, type the text you want to appear in the title bar of the message box.
18. Optionally type a comment next to the MsgBox action.
19. The macro is now complete (see Figure 9.13). Save it and close the Macro window.

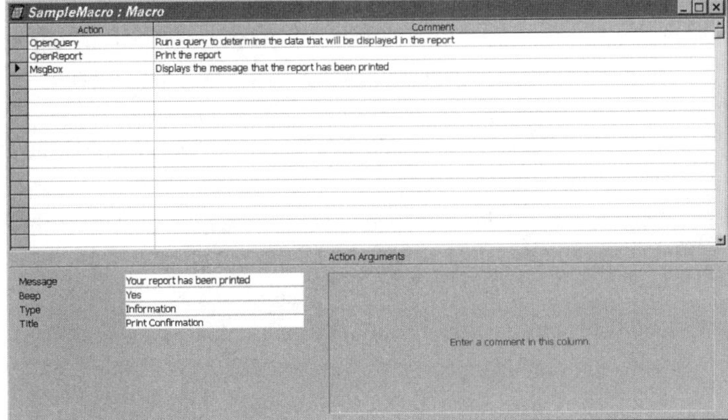

FIGURE 9.13
The Design view of this macro shows the actions and comments.

You can't run a macro before saving it. If you make changes to a macro, you also have to save it before running it again.

CHAPTER 10

Customizing Outlook to Your Organization's Needs

Microsoft introduced Outlook, the messaging and collaboration client of Microsoft Office, as a new application in Office 97. As follows, Outlook combines several areas of functionality into one program, replacing multiple individual applications for many users:

- **Email**. Outlook provides the tools necessary to create and send email messages, and to read and respond to email messages. As an email *client*, Outlook doesn't actually provide the delivery system for email messages, but works together with existing email systems such as Microsoft Exchange, Microsoft Mail, or an Internet service provider (ISP).
- **Contact management**. Outlook keeps track of the names, addresses, and phone and fax information for your business and personal contacts.
- **Calendar**. Outlook helps you manage your schedule, keeping track of meetings and appointments.
- **Journal**. Outlook can keep a diary of your activities, from phone calls and client contacts, to the history of editing a word-processing document.
- **Tasks**. You can keep a list of the things you have to do, with or without deadlines. Outlook can provide automatic reminders and track the status and completion of tasks.
- **Notes**. This feature is for all the little bits of information that otherwise end up as pieces of paper taped to your computer, desk, or refrigerator. Outlook enables you to keep them electronically.

Many of the features in Outlook were previously only available in separate programs. In general, these programs are referred to as Personal Information Managers (PIMs). Many users in the past used one program for managing contacts, another for scheduling, and yet another for email. While these programs were often excellent, it was difficult to share information between them, which made it hard to take full advantage of their functionality.

By combining all these functions into an integrated application, Outlook improves on the individual applications. With Outlook, you can search through your contacts for an email address, and then automatically send a message to that person. If you want to plan a meeting with several colleagues, you can use Outlook's shared calendar capabilities to search for a time when everyone is available, and then send invitations out and keep track of the responses.

While Outlook contains several areas of functionality, it is important to remember that Outlook is essentially a messaging, or email, application. As such, its data is stored in the message storage files provided by the email system. If you are using Outlook as a client to Microsoft Exchange on a network, your Outlook data, including email messages, contact data, calendar items, and so on, is typically stored in the Exchange message store on your organization's Microsoft Exchange Server. This has the advantage of centralizing the data, making it available for regular backups by the Exchange administrator or network administrator. If you are using Outlook on a standalone computer or notebook computer, your data may be stored in a personal storage file (PST) or offline storage file (OST).

What Is Outlook 98?

First introduced as Outlook 97, Outlook was upgraded separately from the rest of Office 97 in early 1998. Outlook 98 retains the functionality of Outlook 97, adding improvements in the user interface, along with new features for messaging and collaboration. The features that are covered in this chapter refer to both Outlook 97 and Outlook 98, unless specific differences in the versions are pointed out.

Following are some of the most significant new features of Outlook 98:

- Support for a wide variety of Internet standards, including POP3/SMTP, IMAP4, LDAP, and NNTP.
- Support for HTML and Multipurpose Internet Mail Extensions (MIME). This feature enables you to send messages that are formatted as Web pages, including images and links to Internet sites. Messages sent as HTML can be read by HTML-based browsers and email clients, as well as by Outlook 98.
- Security for email messages is supported through Secure Multipurpose Internet Mail Extensions (S/MIME). Digital signing enables you to send secure messages to users with other browsers that support S/MIME.
- vCard and vCalendar are standards that enable you to exchange business information over the Internet. vCards contain personal information such as names, addresses, phone numbers, and email addresses. vCalendars contain meeting and appointment information.
- Options available as add-ins in Outlook 97, such as a preview pane for viewing email messages and the Rules Wizard for automating the processing of messages, are now built in. The Rules Wizard is also supplemented with tools for filtering junk and adult-content messages.
- *Net folders* enable users to share message folders over the Internet. With net folders, you can share information with clients and partners as a series of email messages.

Outlook 98's Installation Options

Outlook 98 can be installed in the following three modes, depending on a user's requirements:

- **Corporate or Workgroup.** This is the primary configuration for corporate users. Outlook works as a client to an email system such as Microsoft Exchange Server, Microsoft Mail, cc:Mail, or another server.
- **Internet Mail Only (IMO).** Your Internet service provider provides email support, which might be a local company, or a national provider such as America Online (AOL) or CompuServe. You can work offline, and connect to your ISP via modem when you are ready to send or receive mail.
- **No Email Support.** In this mode, Outlook's contact, calendar, journal, task, and other features are available, but there is no email support.

When you install Outlook 98 on a computer that has a previous version of Outlook installed, the setup program asks whether you are upgrading from a previous version.

If you answer Yes, Outlook examines your current configuration to determine which mode to set up for you. If you answer No, the setup program checks your computer for evidence of other email programs.

If it finds a program, such as Netscape Communicator, Outlook Express, or Internet Mail and News, the setup program asks you which program you want to upgrade from. If you select one of the programs, Outlook is installed in IMO mode.

If you answer None of the Above, you have the choice of installing Outlook in any one of the three modes.

Outlook's Relationship to Other Microsoft Email Clients and Internet Products

Because email is one of the key strategic features of Outlook, it is important to understand the role that Outlook plays within Microsoft's family of email clients and messaging services. Microsoft provides the following programs that you can use as email clients and to work with the Internet.

- **Microsoft Exchange client**. This email client, also known as *Windows Messaging*, is automatically installed on most Windows 95 and Windows NT computers. Outlook is designed as an upgrade to the Exchange client. When you install Outlook 98, the Exchange client is removed from the Desktop.
- **Outlook 97**. This is the initial version of Outlook that was distributed with Office 97. Outlook 97 is also included with recent releases of Microsoft Exchange Server, so that it can function in its role as a client to Exchange.
- **Outlook 98**. This is the updated version of Outlook that was released independently from the rest of Office 97, in early 1998. Both Outlook 97 and Outlook 98 run on 32-bit Windows (Windows NT, Windows 95, and Windows 98).
- **Outlook 16-bit Windows and Macintosh**. These versions of Outlook are designed to provide a consistent messaging platform for organizations that must support Windows 3.*x* and Macintosh platforms along with 32-bit Windows.
- **Outlook Express**. This is the email client that is included as part of Microsoft Internet Explorer 4.0 and 4.01. Despite its similar name, it is a completely separate product from Outlook, and is not, strictly speaking, a subset of Outlook. In fact, Outlook Express contains support for working with Internet newsgroups, an important feature that is missing from both Outlook 97 and Outlook 98. If you need a newsgroup client, you should install Outlook Express or a third-party newsgroup reader.
- **Internet Explorer**. While Internet Explorer is not an email client, it provides some features for working with Internet messages that are required by Outlook 98. Therefore, when you install Outlook 98, Internet Explorer 4.01 is automatically installed.
- **Outlook Web Access**. Available to users of Microsoft Exchange 5.5 or later, Outlook Web Access enables users to gain secure access to their email, calendar, group scheduling, and Exchange public folder information using a Web browser such as Internet Explorer. This enables mobile users to get their messages and other information even if they are working on another platform, such as UNIX.

The corporate user who is connected to a network and a mail service would typically use Outlook for its messaging and information-management features, and use Internet Explorer to browse the Internet. To participate in Internet newsgroups, he or she might use Outlook Express, unless the Exchange administrator has set up newsgroup support in Exchange public folders. In this case, Outlook can be used for reading and contributing to the newsgroups.

An independent user who has the IMO configuration of Outlook 98 would also use Outlook Express for working with newsgroups, and use Internet Explorer for browsing the Internet. He or she would use Outlook's information-management features as well.

A user who doesn't use email or Internet newsgroups can use Outlook for its information-management features. This user would not need Outlook Express or Internet Explorer.

A user who requires fast and reliable Internet email and newsgroup functionality, but who doesn't need any of the information-management features of Outlook, can choose to use Outlook Express and Internet Explorer instead. This is a good solution for many home and small business users, and for Office for Macintosh users.

Outlook's Relationship to Microsoft Exchange

Of all the ways you can use Outlook, one of its key strategic roles is as a client to Microsoft Exchange. Exchange is a client/server messaging system that is built around Microsoft Exchange Server, a powerful application that runs on a Windows NT server on an organization's network. Individual users on the network run client software to create, edit, send, and read messages, while Exchange Server provides the centralized storage, delivery, and collaboration services for the network.

Many users in an Exchange Server environment work at computers that are physically connected to the Exchange Server through a Windows NT network. When you log on to the NT network, you gain access to the resources of the network, including your Exchange Server account, which is secured by your network login and password.

Exchange can also be used by remote users, who connect to the Exchange Server using a dial-up connection and a modem, or via the Internet.

Each user has one or more *email profiles*, which determine his or her email options while using Windows. Each profile can contain one or more *services*, which allow you to communicate with different email systems, such as Microsoft Exchange Server, Microsoft Mail, or Lotus cc:Mail. By customizing your profile, you can select the mail services you will use.

You can configure your Windows email profile by using the Mail applet in the Control Panel, or by issuing commands in Outlook. If you have Outlook installed, but you are not configured to use your organization's Exchange Server with Outlook, follow these steps to add the Exchange Server service to your profile.

1. In Outlook, choose Tools, Services to display the Services dialog box, shown in Figure 10.1. Any services that are already installed are listed.

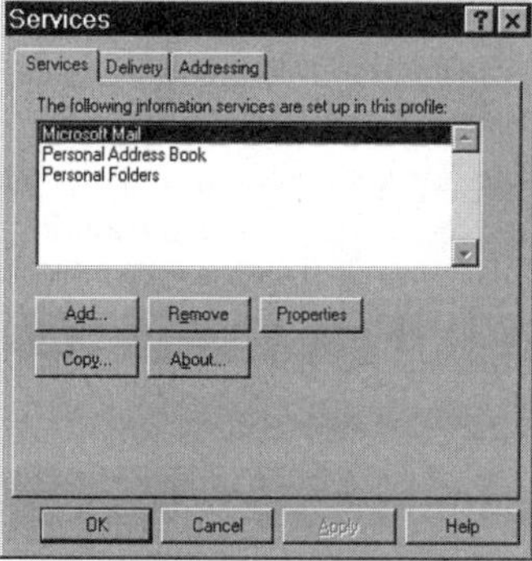

FIGURE 10.1
Use the Services dialog box to install additional services in your mail profile.

2. Click Add to display the Add Service to Profile dialog box, as shown in Figure 10.2.

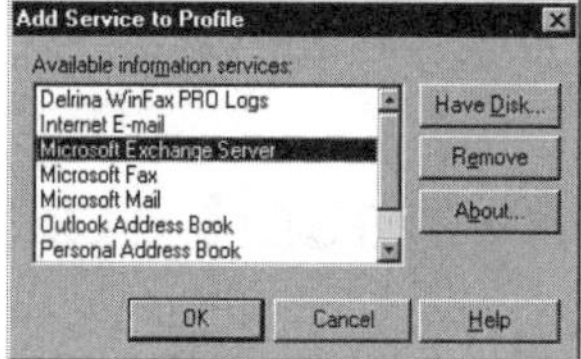

FIGURE 10.2
Select the service that you want to add to your mail profile.

3. Select Microsoft Exchange Server, and click OK to configure the service.
4. The Microsoft Exchange Server dialog box appears. Use the options in the General tab, shown in Figure 10.3, to identify your Exchange Server and your Exchange mailbox. Enter the name of your Exchange Server and your mailbox name. If you will be connected to the Exchange Server each time you use Outlook, mark the Automatically Detect Connection State option button. If you will be working remotely, choose the connection state option that best matches your working patterns.

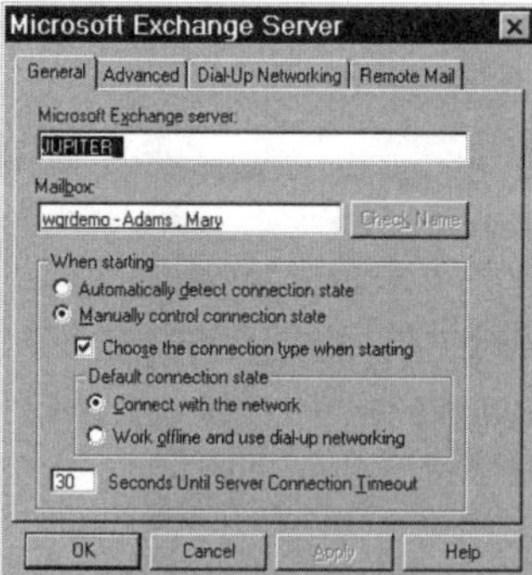

FIGURE 10.3
Use the General tab to enter your Exchange Server account information.

5. Use the options in the Advanced tab, shown in Figure 10.4, to select additional mailboxes to open when you start Outlook, and to enable offline use. You can only open the

mailboxes of users who have given you the appropriate permissions. You can also choose to encrypt your messages, providing extra security while working offline, as well as when you are logged onto your network.

FIGURE 10.4
Use the Advanced tab to select additional mailboxes to open and set security options.

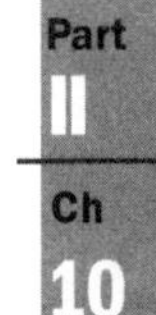

6. To set up offline folder files, click the Offline Folder File Settings button, to display the dialog box shown in Figure 10.5. (If you will be using your computer remotely, and connecting to Exchange Server using a modem, Outlook will store a copy of your messages in the offline folders, while keeping the originals in your online folders on the Exchange Server.) Select or type the name of the file that you will use to store your offline messages, and select the encryption settings that you want to use. You can't change the encryption settings after you have created the offline folders. Click Compact Now to recover unused space from the offline folder file. Click Disable Offline Use if you will no longer be working offline.

FIGURE 10.5
Use the Offline Folder File Settings dialog box to identify your offline folder file, and to select the encryption setting for the file.

7. Use the options in the Dial-Up Networking tab, shown in Figure 10.6, to select or configure a Dial-Up Networking connection for working over a modem. You can select an existing connection from the drop-down list, or click New to create a new Dial-Up Networking connection. Enter your user name, password, and domain name to log onto your network with the dial-up connection.
8. Use the options in the Remote Mail tab, shown in Figure 10.7, to configure your computer for working remotely. When working remotely, you can choose to mark the messages individually that you want to download, or you can apply a filter to control

which messages are downloaded. You might, for example, want to download all messages from a specific author, or all message that contain certain text in the subject line. You can also schedule connections on a periodic schedule, such as every hour.

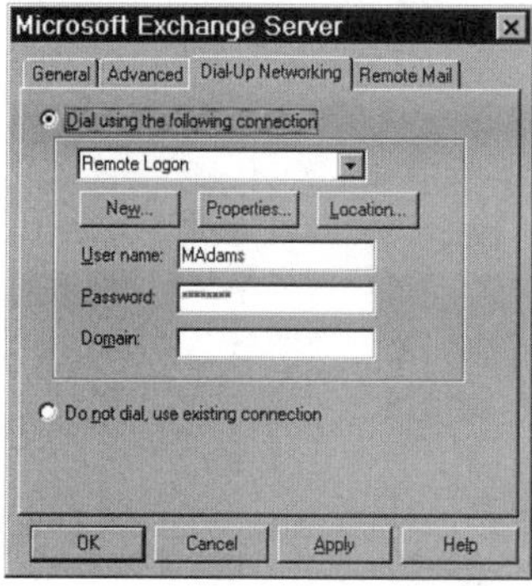

FIGURE 10.6
Select an existing Dial-Up Networking connection, or create a new one.

FIGURE 10.7
Use the Remote Mail tab to select your options for working remotely with Microsoft Exchange, and to schedule periodic connections.

9. Click OK to complete your changes and close the Microsoft Exchange Server dialog box.

Customizing the Outlook Interface

Outlook provides a flexible user interface, which users can customize to meet their preferences and requirements.

Using Outlook Today in Outlook 98

In Outlook 98, you can display the Outlook Today screen (see Figure 10.8) to summarize your activity in Outlook. Outlook Today enables you to see at one time whether you have any new email messages, any items on your calendar, or any outstanding tasks.

FIGURE 10.8
The Outlook Today screen shows you the current activity in your Outlook session.

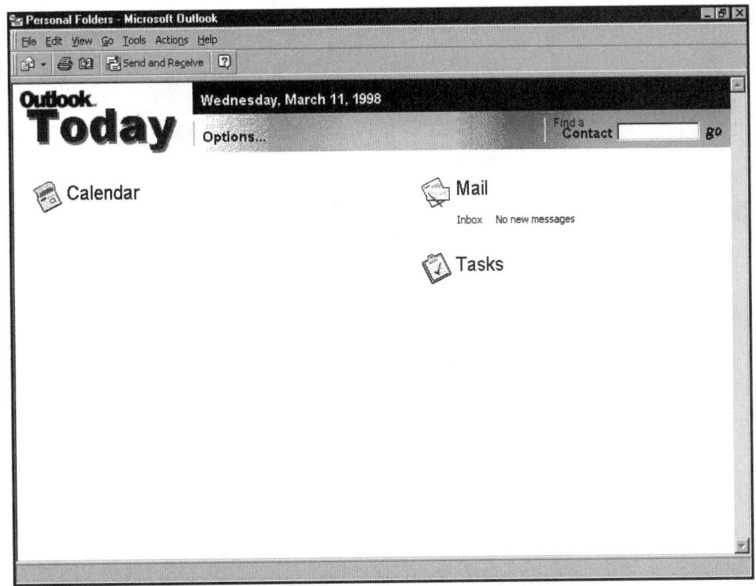

To display the Outlook Today screen, Choose Go, Outlook Today.

Click the Options link in the Outlook Today screen to control whether to go directly to Outlook Today each time you start Outlook, and to customize the display of the Calendar and Task lists.

Using AutoPreview

Outlook, like most email programs, displays the headers of incoming messages in a message window, as shown in Figure 10.9. The message window shows you who each message is from, the subject of the message, and the date and time the message was received. Click the column heading that you want to use to sort the messages in the message window. For example, Click the From heading to display the messages alphabetically by the sender's name, or click the Received heading to sort the messages by the date they were received. Use the toolbar at the top of the message window to print, reply to, and forward messages, and so on.

If you prefer to read an email message in a separate window, double-click its message header.

While the message window is useful, it can be time consuming to open your messages and read them one at a time, especially if you receive a high volume of messages.

Activating the AutoPreview feature, as shown in Figure 10.10, displays the first three lines of each message. This makes it easier to select which messages you want to read first. In the case of short messages, you might even see the entire message in the AutoPreview display.

To activate AutoPreview, select the Inbox folder or any other folder that contains messages. Then choose View, AutoPreview. To turn off the AutoPreview feature, select the same command.

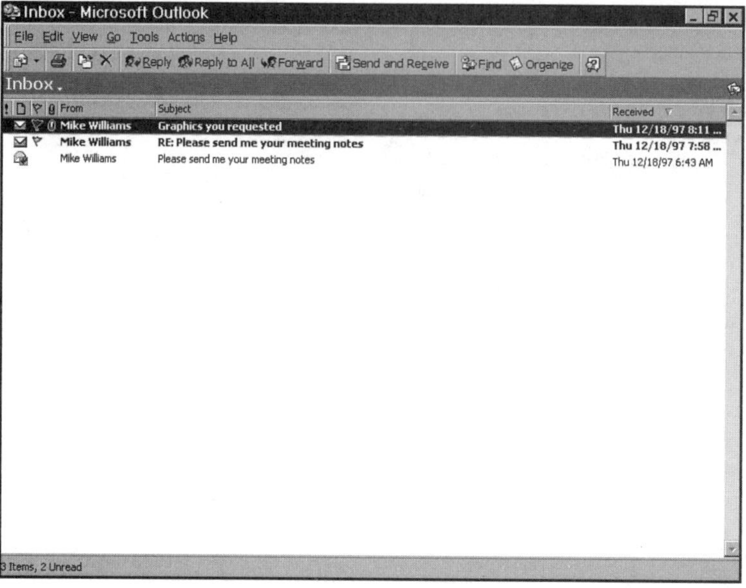

FIGURE 10.9
The message window shows the headers of the email messages that you have received.

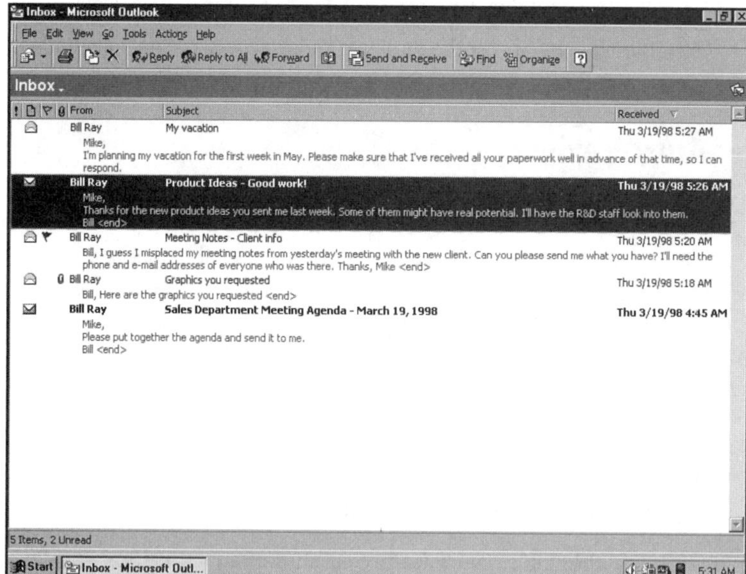

FIGURE 10.10
The AutoPreview feature shows up to three lines of each message in your Inbox.

Using the Preview Pane in Outlook 98

Outlook 98 adds an enhancement that goes a step further than the AutoPreview feature. The Preview Pane enables you to display the contents of a message in a resizable pane that takes up as much of the screen as you want. Figure 10.11 shows a message whose contents are displayed in the Preview Pane. This enables you to see much more of the message than you would see if you used AutoPreview. The Preview Header (the gray bar at the top of the Preview Pane) lists the sender, the subject, and the addresses to which the message was sent. You can resize the Preview Pane by dragging the border separating it from the message window.

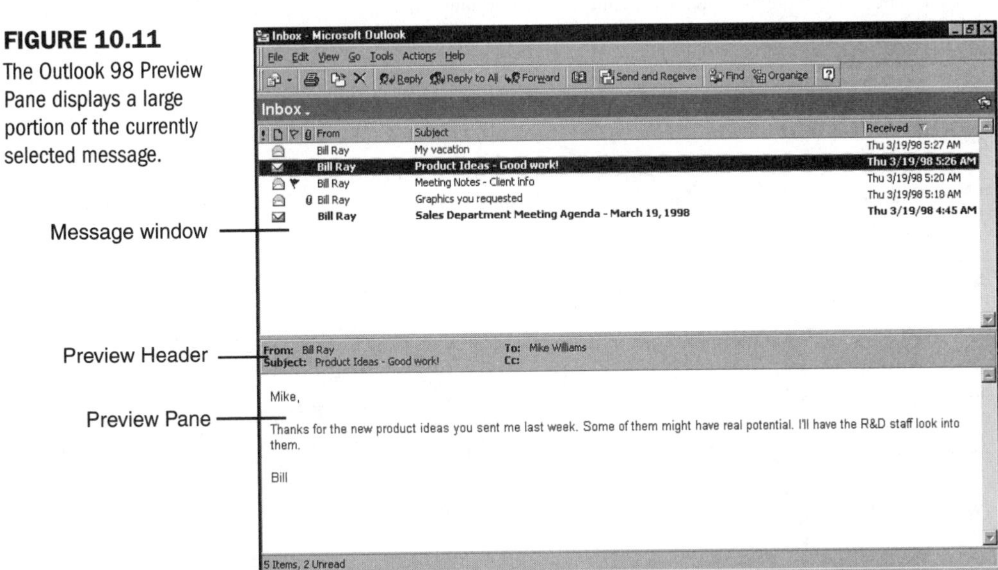

FIGURE 10.11
The Outlook 98 Preview Pane displays a large portion of the currently selected message.

To display the Preview Pane, activate a folder that contains messages, and choose View, Preview Pane. To close the Preview Pane, select the same command.

You can control the appearance and behavior of the Preview Pane with the Preview Pane dialog box, as shown in Figure 10.12. To display the dialog box, right-click the Preview Pane header, and then select Preview Pane Options from the shortcut menu that appears.

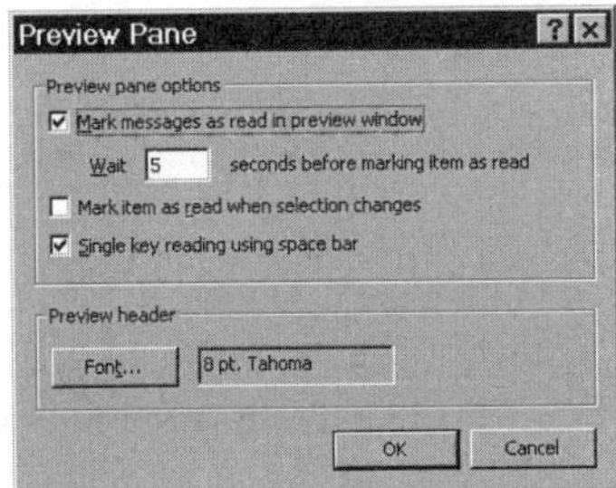

FIGURE 10.12
Use the Preview Pane dialog box to control how the Preview Pane appears and functions.

If you check Mark Messages As Read in Preview Window, Outlook considers a message as having been read once it has been displayed in the Preview Pane for the number of seconds listed in the Wait *x* Seconds Before Marking Item As Read box. You can also choose to mark an item as read when you move away from it by selecting another message or folder. If you check

Single Key Reading Using Space Bar, you can move from message to message by pressing the Spacebar.

Click Font to select the font that is used in the Preview Header.

Using the Outlook Bar and Folder List

The Outlook Bar and Folder List, shown in Figure 10.13, provide two easy methods for navigating among your Outlook folders. You can display either window, neither, or both, according to your preferences.

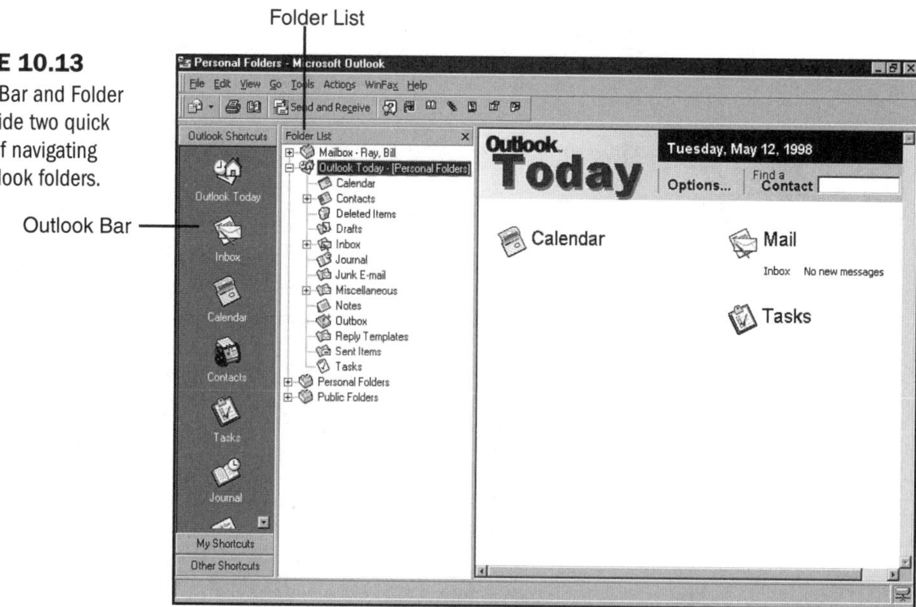

FIGURE 10.13
Outlook Bar and Folder List provide two quick means of navigating your Outlook folders.

The Outlook Bar contains icons representing the different folders and functions of Outlook. You can activate a feature, such as the Contacts folder, by clicking its icon in the Outlook Bar.

The Folder List window displays all your Outlook and Exchange folders in an Explorer-style tree. You can navigate the folder list quickly by clicking on the folders. To expand/collapse a branch of the list, double-click it. The Folder List generally displays more folders in the same amount of space as the Outlook Bar.

To display the Outlook Bar, choose View, Outlook Bar. Select the same command to hide the Outlook Bar.

To activate the Folder List, choose View, Folder List. To hide the Folder List, select the same command, or click the Close button in the upper-right corner of the Folder List.

Customizing the Outlook Options

Outlook has many customizable options, which you can control through the Options dialog box. To display the Options dialog box, choose Tools, Options. Then click the tab that contains the options that you want to customize.

NOTE The options described in this section reflect the features of Outlook 98. Outlook 97 has a similar, but smaller set of options that you can set.

The Preferences tab, shown in Figure 10.14, enables you to control the default reminder time for new Calendar and Task items. By clicking on any of the Options buttons, you can select from a wide variety of additional options for the major areas of Outlook.

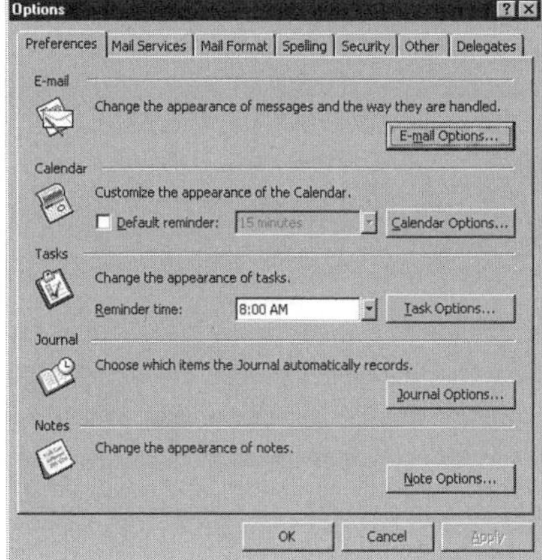

FIGURE 10.14
The Preferences tab of the Options dialog box leads to more detailed options for each of Outlook's major functions.

The E-mail Options dialog box (see Figure 10.15) enables you to control how messages are saved, and how the message window operates as you send messages. It also controls the layout of replies and forwarded messages.

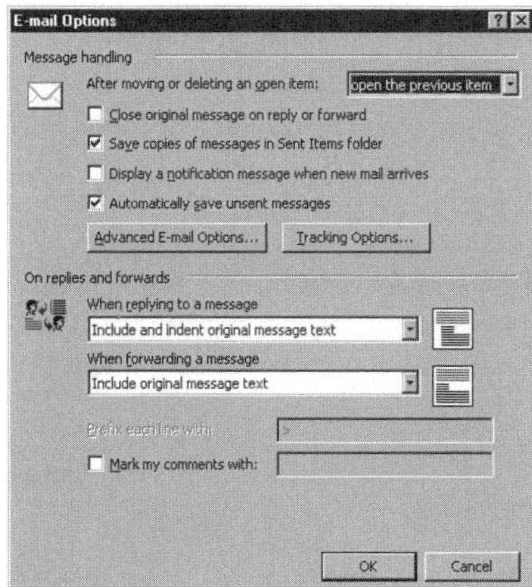

FIGURE 10.15
The E-mail Options dialog box enables you to choose options for sending and receiving messages.

Clicking Advanced E-mail Options or Tracking Options leads to more detailed dialog boxes.

Use the Advanced E-mail Options dialog box (see Figure 10.16) to specify how messages are sent and received in more detail. The Save Messages section controls how Outlook saves copies of the messages you send.

FIGURE 10.16
The Advanced E-mail Options dialog box enables you to control the details of sending and retrieving messages.

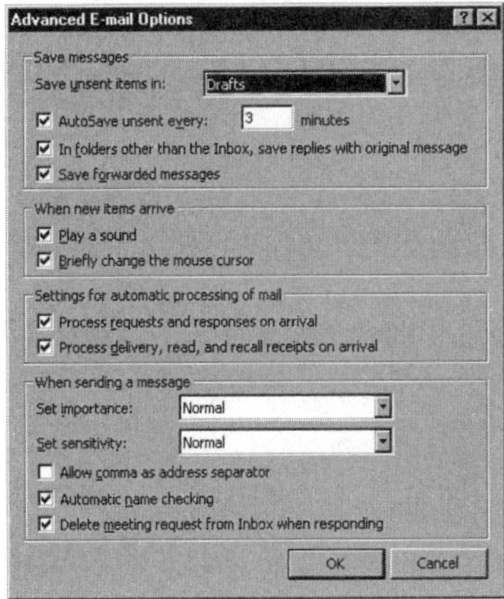

NOTE Outlook 98 provides a Drafts folder to save messages in progress. If you close a message before you are ready to send it, it is saved in the Drafts folder, so that you can finish the message and send it later. In Outlook 97, you need to choose File, Save to save a message that you are not ready to send. Your message is saved in the Inbox by default. Later you can open it, and send it as usual when it is ready.

You can also specify when and how incoming messages are received, and the default importance and sensitivity for each new message.

Use the Tracking Options dialog box to set the default method that Outlook uses to track the messages you send (see Figure 10.17). (You can change the tracking for an individual message using the Options toolbar button while you are creating the message.) Check Tell Me When All Messages Have Been Delivered to be notified when messages have been successfully transferred to the recipient's email address. Check Tell Me When All Messages Have Been Read to be notified when each addressee has actually opened his or her message. Check Delete Receipts and Blank Responses After Processing if you don't want to keep the notices that are returned by the system once you have read them.

You can use the Calendar Options dialog box, shown in Figure 10.18, to specify the days in your workweek, and the starting and ending time of the working day. You can also use this dialog box to set your time zone, national holidays, and options for processing scheduling requests.

The Task Options dialog box, shown in Figure 10.19, controls the display color of overdue and completed tasks.

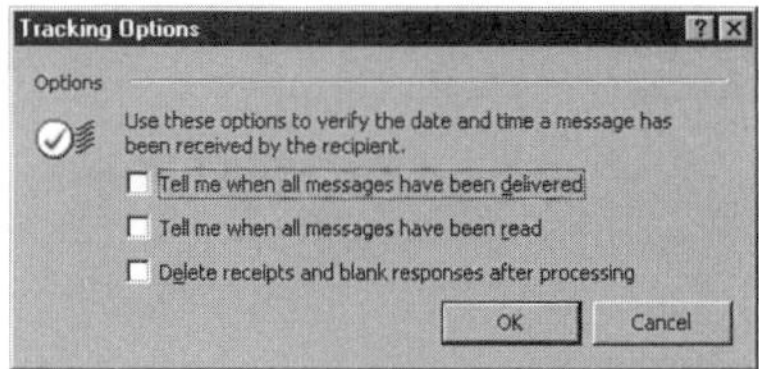

FIGURE 10.17
Use the Tracking Options dialog box to set the default tracking for all future messages.

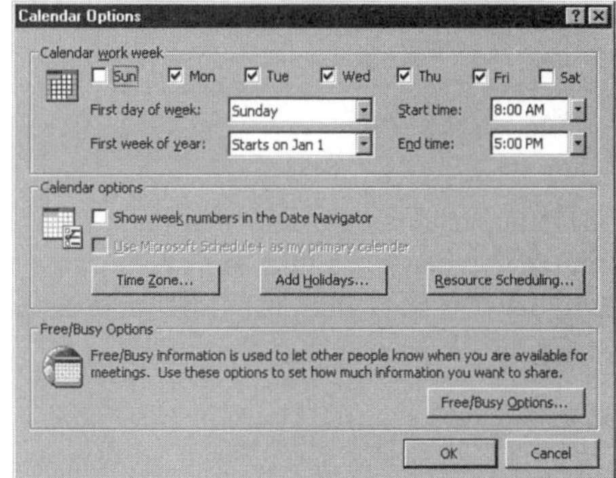

FIGURE 10.18
Use the Calendar Options dialog box to control the display of the Calendar window.

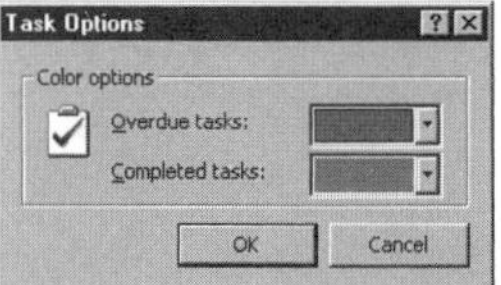

FIGURE 10.19
Use the Task Options dialog box to control the color of overdue and completed tasks.

The Journal Options dialog box, shown in Figure 10.20, enables you to control what items you want Outlook to automatically add to the Journal. Check the boxes next to the items that you want to be recorded in the journal. Click next to the name of a contact to record all items that you either sent to or received from that contact. Select one or more Office 97 applications to record the history of your work with any documents from those applications.

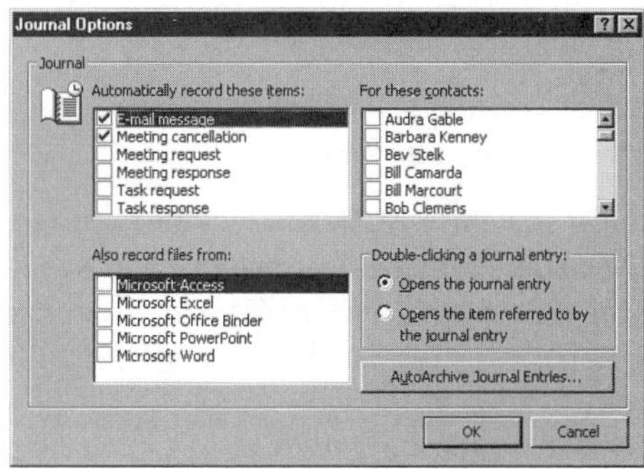

FIGURE 10.20
Use the Journal Options dialog box to select the Outlook items you want Outlook to record, including correspondence or documents that you have exchanged with specific email contacts.

Use the AutoArchive Journal Entries button to determine how often you want to copy items from the Journal folder to an archive file.

Use the Notes Options dialog box, shown in Figure 10.21, to customize the default color, size, and font for new notes.

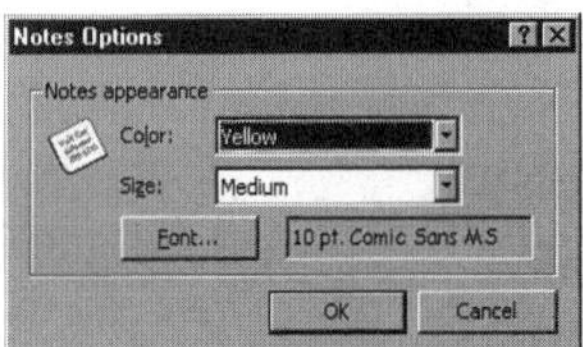

FIGURE 10.21
Use the Notes Options dialog box to control the appearance of Notes.

The Mail Services tab of the Options dialog box, shown in Figure 10.22, controls how Outlook selects a mail profile at startup. If you use more than one profile, you can have Outlook prompt you for the profile to use each time you start Outlook. Otherwise, select the profile that you want Outlook to use as a default.

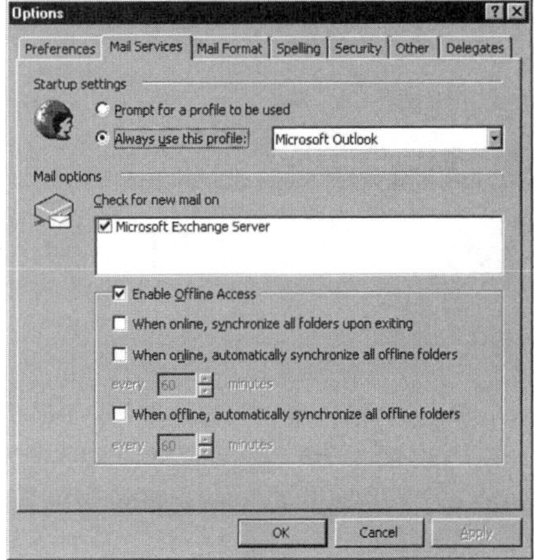

FIGURE 10.22
Use the Mail Services tab to select your startup profile, and to control how Outlook checks for mail.

Select one or more mail services to check for mail on. All mail services that you have installed in the profile are displayed in the Check for New Mail On list.

Finally, use this tab to determine whether you will allow offline access in this profile, and how folders will be synchronized when working offline.

Use the Mail Format tab, shown in Figure 10.23, to select the message format—HTML, Outlook Rich Text, Plain Text, Microsoft Word, and so on—that you want to use for new messages. You can also select your default font, stationery for HTML messages, and a signature that is automatically added to your new messages. Use the Signature Picker button to select from existing signatures or to create new ones.

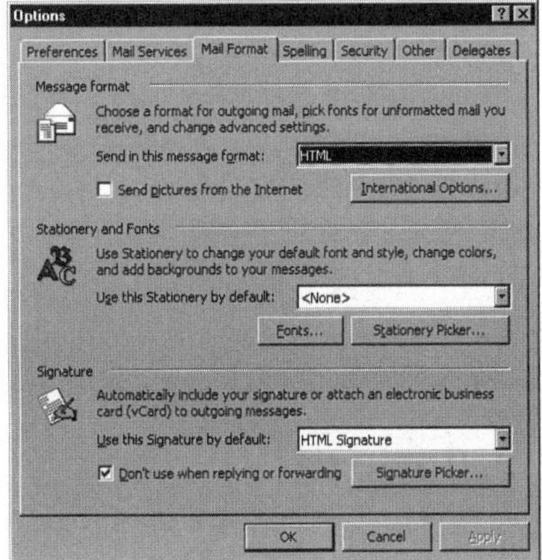

FIGURE 10.23
The Mail Format tab lets you select the message format, appearance, and a default signature for the messages you create.

Use the Spelling tab, shown in Figure 10.24, to set preferences for spell checking your messages, including the special cases that you want the spell checker to ignore. You can also use this tab to edit the contents of your custom dictionary, and to select a dictionary if you have installed a dictionary in more than one language.

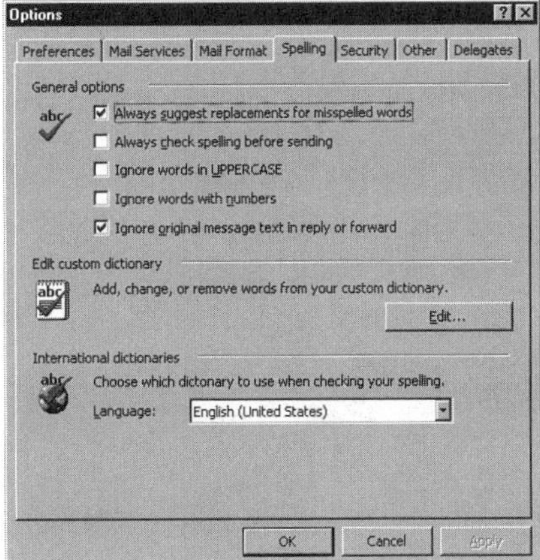

FIGURE 10.24
Use the Spelling tab to select your preferences for the spelling checker and to manage your spelling dictionaries.

The Security tab lets you modify your settings for secure email. As shown in Figure 10.25, these options are unavailable unless your email administrator has enabled security features at the server level.

You can also use this tab to customize the security settings for the Internet, your intranet, restricted sites, and trusted sites. Adjusting these settings can protect you from potentially dangerous viruses and unwanted programs or scripts that might be included with messages that you receive.

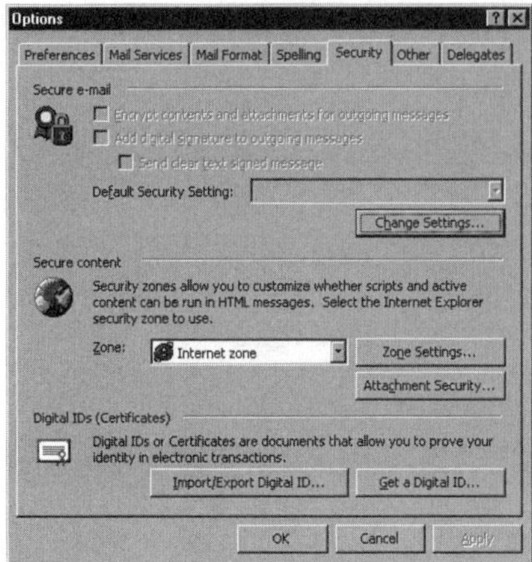

FIGURE 10.25
Use the Security tab to select secure email options and to control the execution of scripts in messages you receive.

The Other tab (see Figure 10.26) enables you to specify whether you want to automatically empty your Deleted Items folder when you exit Outlook. If you check this box, you will not be able to recover items that were in your Deleted Items folder at the time you exited Outlook.

You can also use this tab to set more advanced options, or to customize the AutoArchive and Preview Pane features.

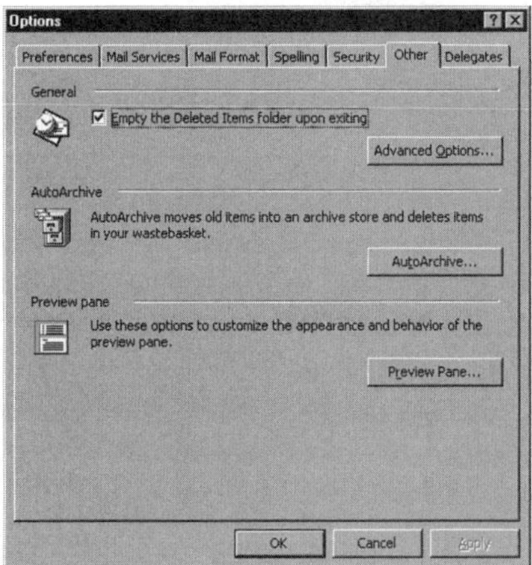

FIGURE 10.26
The Other tab of the Options dialog box leads to more advanced options as well as to AutoArchive and Preview Pane settings.

Clicking the Advanced Options button in the Other tab displays the Advance Options dialog box (see Figure 10.27). You can use this dialog box to set the folder that should be active when you start Outlook. If you check Warn Before Permanently Deleting Items, Outlook asks for confirmation before completely deleting items, including the automatic deletion of items in your Deleted Items folder. The Appearance Options section controls the display in the Calendar and Notes folders. Additional buttons give you more detailed control over reminders and tasks. The Add-In Manager button enables you to install, configure, or remove add-in components that are available from Microsoft and third-party suppliers. The Custom Forms button enables you to manage forms, copying them among private and public forms libraries.

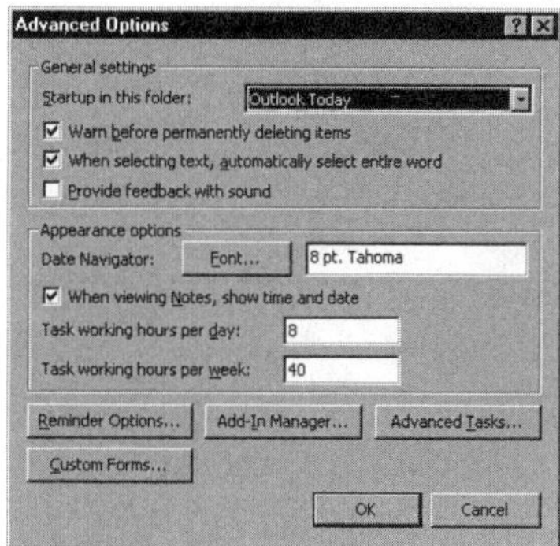

FIGURE 10.27
The Advanced Options dialog box enables you to control several details of Outlook operation.

Click the AutoArchive button in the Other tab to display the AutoArchive dialog box (see Figure 10.28). This dialog box enables you to control the frequency of the AutoArchive process, which periodically moves older items to a separate storage file so that your primary storage file doesn't get too large.

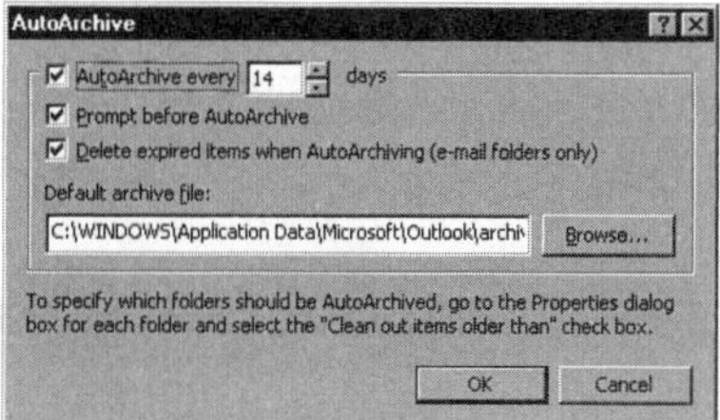

FIGURE 10.28
The AutoArchive dialog box controls the schedule and behavior of AutoArchive operations.

In Outlook 98, the AutoArchive process executes in the background, so you can continue working while the archive is executed. In Outlook 97, you can't do other work in Outlook while the folders are being archived.

Click the Preview Pane button in the Other tab to bring up the Preview Pane dialog box. See the section "Using the Preview Pane in Outlook 98" earlier in this chapter for a description of this dialog box.

The Delegates tab, shown in Figure 10.29, enables you to select other users who are authorized to act on your behalf. You must be logged on to your Exchange Server to use this feature. After adding users to the delegates list, you can set individual permissions, such as which of your folders the users can see and open, and whether they can create new items or just read existing ones.

After making changes to any of the tabs in the Options dialog box, click Apply if you want to activate the changes while leaving the dialog box open. To close the dialog box, click OK.

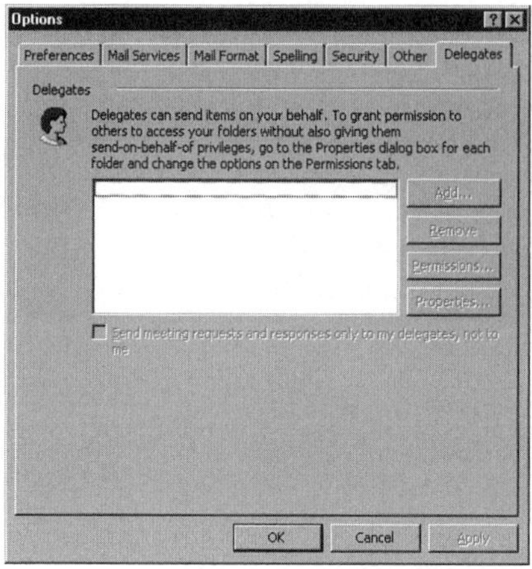

FIGURE 10.29
The Delegates tab enables you to select other users whom you want to allow to send Outlook items on your behalf.

Creating Custom Views

When you are looking at the items in one of Outlook's folders, such as the Inbox, Calendar, or Contacts folder, you are seeing the items as the result of a *view*. Outlook installs a variety of views by default, giving you different ways of organizing and working with data.

For example, the Messages view of the Inbox folder shows the message headers, while the Messages with AutoPreview view activates the AutoPreview feature to show the first three lines of each message. The Last Seven Days view shows only those messages received in the last week, while the By Sender view groups the messages according to who sent you the message.

You can select the active view by choosing View, Current View, and selecting the view you want from the submenu that appears.

NOTE In Outlook 97, the Standard toolbar contains a list of the currently available views for each folder, and the quickest way to switch between views is to select a view from the list.

In Outlook 98, the Current View list moved from the Standard toolbar to the Advanced toolbar. To display the Advanced toolbar, choose View, Toolbars, Advanced.

You can change the settings for a view, or create your own custom views in Outlook. To edit the view that you currently have open, choose View, Current View, Customize Current View. The View Summary dialog box appears, as shown in Figure 10.30. This dialog box shows the following settings for the current view in six categories:

- **Fields**. Select which fields for the item should appear in the view.
- **Group By**. Select an optional grouping expression. For example, grouping your email messages by the From field puts all the message for each sender together.

- **Sort**. Select one or more fields to use to determine the order in which the items are displayed. For example, you might want a view of the Contacts folder to be sorted alphabetically by last name, or by zip code.
- **Filter**. Select a condition that limits which items should appear. You might want to show only the Calendar items with a certain keyword in the Categories field, or only those that are more than one day in duration.
- **Other Settings**. Change display attributes such as fonts, shading, border lines, and whether the Preview Pane is displayed.
- **Automatic Formatting**. Define rules for automatic formatting, such as using red text for high-priority items, or a different font for completed tasks.

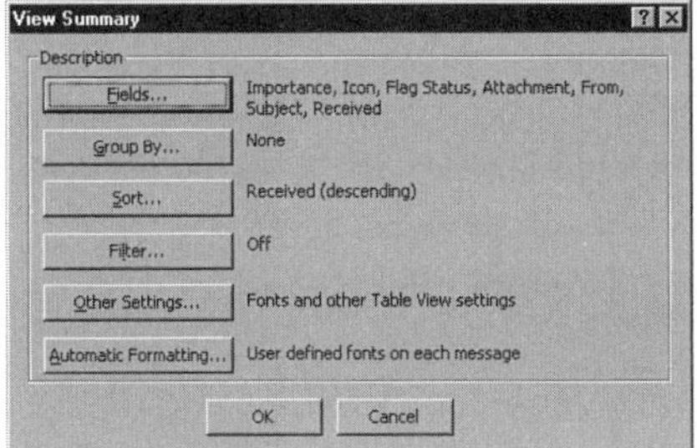

FIGURE 10.30
Use the View Summary dialog box to display a description of the current view, and to change its attributes.

To change any of these attributes for the current view, click the appropriate button and use the dialog box that appears to customize your settings.

To create new views, or to make a copy of a view, choose View, Current View, Define Views. The Define Views dialog box for the folder appears, as shown in Figure 10.31.

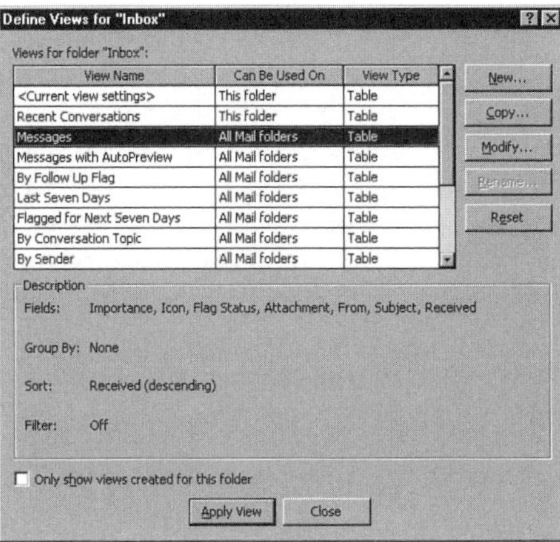

FIGURE 10.31
Use the Define Views dialog box to select a view to modify, or to create a new view.

Click New to create and name a new view for the current folder. To make a copy of an existing view, select the view in the list, and then click Copy.

After you create a view or copy an existing one, you can modify the new view's properties to meet your requirements. ●

PART III

Using Office to Support Teams and Workgroups

CHAPTER 11

Standardizing Document Production with Word and Excel

Even the most traditional companies are increasingly becoming "virtual": their most important work done by cross-functional teams that may include not just members of different departments, but also freelancers, outsourcers, suppliers, and even customers.

With the walls of the corporation growing so permeable, it can be a challenge to present your company as a single integrated entity, capable of serving customers and making decisions. Of course, the challenge goes beyond appearances: how can you actually be a coherent entity under these circumstances?

If you manage Microsoft Office well, you can make a significant contribution toward maintaining a coherent corporate image, and even toward grounding that image in reality. Conversely, if you fail to manage Microsoft Office, you can easily find yourself publishing documents that look as if they came from different planets, not just different companies. Worse yet, you can find yourself making decisions based on inconsistent information and assumptions.

In this chapter, you learn practical techniques and Office features that can help you standardize and organize your document production company-wide, while at the same time improving productivity. In particular, you learn about the following:

- How to deploy templates that allow users to share the latest styles and shortcuts for building consistent documents
- How to set up and standardize AutoCorrect lists that make it easier for your users to create accurate documents
- How to use AutoText boilerplate entries to streamline document production and make it more consistent
- How to create standardized charts and graphs that present the same image in all your documents

The first step, as always, is planning. What ought to be standardized first? Next? What's worth the effort, and what isn't? Who should be involved? This chapter begins by addressing these key planning issues.

Planning to Standardize Your Company's Documents

As a starting point, it's worth considering which types of documents—and which aspects of those documents—ought to be standardized.

Deciding Where to Focus Your Attention First

In most organizations, common sense dictates that you focus attention on the documents that accomplish the following:

- Represent you to your customers
- Offer the greatest potential gain in quality and/or productivity
- Are created most often

Although organizations differ, you may want to use Table 11.1 as a starting point.

Table 11.1 Identifying Documents for Standardization

Type	Priority	Role	Program
Customer presentations	High	External	PowerPoint
Estimates	High	Internal	Excel/Access
Expense reports	Middle	Internal	Word
Fax covers	Middle	Internal	Word
Forms	High	Internal	Word
Internal presentations	Low	Internal	PowerPoint

Type	Priority	Role	Program
Letters	High	Int./Ext.	Word
Manuals	Middle	Internal	Word
Memos	Low	Internal	Word
P&Ls	High	Internal	Excel
Product sheets	High	External	Word
Proposals	High	External	Word
Purchase orders	Middle	Internal	Word
Reports	Middle	Internal	Word/Access

Later in this chapter, you find some tips that can help you extend customization beyond these standard types of documents, to other documents such as Intranet pages, product catalogs, and meeting agendas.

Understanding What You Can Standardize

Within documents such as these, the following elements are ripe for standardization:

- Fonts, typically to match corporate standards
- Graphics, especially logos
- Color schemes, again to match corporate standards
- Charts
- Design layouts
- Formulas, to ensure accuracy and consistency
- Fields (in Word), to automate documents without requiring all users to understand complex Word features
- Links among documents, again to ensure accuracy and consistency
- Form elements, for example, drop-down boxes and list boxes

In pursuing document standardization, consider the following issues:

- Your organization may already have graphic design standards that cover some of the documents you intend to standardize. Ask your corporate communications or marketing department, if your company has one. If graphics standards do exist, make sure your organization's computers have the fonts needed to implement them. Deploying a specialized font company-wide can be expensive; you may want to work with your designers to come up with a reasonable alternative that users already have installed on their systems.
- Be aware of production constraints. For example, in designing a letter, make sure it accommodates your corporate stationery. Before deploying a customized color scheme

for slides, make sure the colors reproduce well in both 35 mm and overhead formats if necessary.

- There may be legal constraints you should be aware of. If you want to standardize product sheets, for example, you may need to include standard disclaimers or trademark language. Ask your legal department, if you have one.
- Most important, involve the people who will be using the documents you develop—ideally, from start to finish. Use whatever resources are available, including sample documents that already exist.

Templates: Office's Most Powerful Tool for Standardization

With these management basics in mind, let's look at some of the tools Office provides for standardizing your documents. Office's most powerful tool for standardization is the template, available in Word, Excel, and PowerPoint. Templates let you pre-define and standardize virtually any content, formatting, or elements that can appear in an Office document. For example, Office templates can contain the following:

- **Boilerplate text.**
- **Manual text formatting.** Boldface, italics, font size, and so on.
- **Paragraph formatting (in Word).** Indentation, spacing before and after paragraphs, line spacing, tab settings, and so on.
- **Document formatting.** Margins, page breaks, backgrounds, and so on.
- **Styles.** For headings, headers, footers, tables of contents, and so on.
- **Images.** Logos, photographs, clip art, and so on.
- **Tables (in Word and PowerPoint).**
- **Multiple worksheets (in Excel).**
- **Protected/hidden areas of worksheets (in Excel).**
- **Slide show settings and Notes pages (in PowerPoint).**
- **Formulas and functions.** These can perform calculations, insert current dates, build tables of contents (in Word), or automate links to other Office data anywhere on your network, such as current information stored in an Excel worksheet.
- **Form controls.** For creating electronic forms that users can fill out online (in Word, these are called form fields).

Word and Excel templates also enable you to build specialized tools into your documents—including custom macros, toolbars, menus, keyboard shortcuts, and (in Word) AutoText entries—that are relevant only to a specific type of document. Techniques for doing so are covered at length in Chapter 6.

If you choose to customize your templates this way, be sure to educate your users, who might otherwise find it disconcerting that tools "appear" and "disappear" depending on the document they are working on.

By providing templates to your users, you make it much easier for them to create standardized documents. In effect, you've done most of the formatting work for them in advance—and in many cases, you've done much of the work of structuring documents for them as well. Of course, your custom templates also significantly improve productivity: users no longer have to "reinvent the wheel" each time they create a document; they can instead focus more of their efforts on the added-value thinking associated with their work.

While templates work slightly differently in each Office program, the same four-step process applies: you create the template, save it, test it, and deploy it.

NOTE Outlook also provides a feature called an Outlook Item Template, which is essentially a pad of electronic forms that you can use to track contacts, send email, or perform other personal information management tasks. This feature is covered in Chapter 10.

This chapter focuses primarily on Word and Excel templates; you take a closer look at PowerPoint templates in Chapter 13.

Creating Boilerplate Documents to Use As Templates

Your first step in creating a template is to create a boilerplate document that looks and behaves the way you want it to, including all the components that can reasonably be standardized. You do this using the same editing and formatting tools that Word, Excel, and PowerPoint make available for creating any document.

As already mentioned, it's best to involve the individuals who will be using the documents. You may be able to use their existing documents as a starting point; you may also have professionally designed materials that can serve as a starting point.

Prior to saving your template, spell-check it—and if it is a Word document, consider running Word's grammar tools on it. Even though the grammar tools flag many sentences that are perfectly acceptable, they also flag some errors you may not have realized were there.

In Word and Excel, you can also record or write VBA macros for storage within your templates. Macros are discussed in several places throughout this book, including later in this chapter. (In PowerPoint, macros are stored within individual presentations.)

Saving Templates

After you edit your document to include all the contents you need, save it as a template by performing the following steps:

1. Choose File, Save As.
2. Type the name of the template in the File Name text box.

3. In the Save As Type drop-down box, specify that you want to save the file as a template. In Word 97, choose Document Template; in Excel 97, choose Template (.xlt); in PowerPoint 97, choose Presentation Template (*.pot).
4. Click Save.

Testing Templates

After you save your document as a template, open a new document based on that template. Now, make sure the document looks and works the way you intended. If possible, test the template on a representative sample of the systems that will run it, not just your own computer.

A template-testing checklist appears in Table 11.2.

Table 11.2 Template-Testing Checklist

Category	Tasks
Accuracy	Do the documents created by your template *look* the way they're supposed to? Have any spelling or grammatical errors crept in? Are calculations consistently accurate when a wide variety of values are plugged in? In Word, do fields, especially date and time fields, report accurate results that are formatted appropriately?
Availability	Does the template have access to all the resources it needs, no matter where you run it from? For example, does it depend on fonts that are unavailable on some computers? Does it link to documents that some users will not have rights to access?
Usability	Is the template easy to use and understand? Does it contain the features users need most? Does it accommodate the needs of users? For example, does a fax cover sheet template include sufficient room for users to enter notes? Does a form's drop-down box contain the options users are most likely to need? Will the document look good in print as well as onscreen?
Macro Correctness	Do macros run properly on all systems, or do they report error messages users will find confusing? If you are deploying in a cross-platform environment, have you tested them on Macintosh and Windows systems? Have you added help to your macro where appropriate? Has the template been checked for macro viruses with an up-to-date virus scanner before even a test deployment?

Involving Your Team in the Testing Process

While you're developing a complex Word or Excel template such as a proposal document or an estimate worksheet, you may receive extensive feedback on content, both your boilerplate text and the assumptions you've built into your calculations. To streamline testing, use Office's tools for tracking changes.

Invite each of your testers to create a new document based on the template, turn on Word's or Excel's Track Changes tool (Tools, Track Changes, Highlight Changes), and make their recommended changes.

Then use Word's Merge Documents feature (Tools, Merge Documents) or Excel's Share Workbook feature (Tools, Share Workbook) to combine all of the reviewers' changes into a single document. After you resolve all the issues, you can resave the revised file as a template again. (For more information about Track Changes and Merge Documents, see Chapter 12.)

Deploying Your Templates

After you create and test your templates, the next step is to deploy them so that all users have access to them. You have two decisions to make: *where* to deploy them, and *how* to deploy them.

Choosing Where to Install Custom Templates

You can deploy your custom templates *locally*, or *centrally*.

You can place a copy of each custom template on each workstation where Word, Excel, and/or PowerPoint is installed. With this option, the templates are available even if the network is not. Updating the templates, however, can be challenging.

In small, informal organizations, copying templates to individual workstations is often sufficient. For mobile users whose primary systems are notebook PCs that aren't always connected to the network, this may be the only option.

Given a choice, most Office administrators prefer to store custom templates centrally, on a network server, typically in a read-only folder that only they have rights to change. When the time comes to update your templates—as it certainly will—you only have to do it once, on the server.

CAUTION

Whichever method you choose, make sure to keep a separate backup of your custom templates in the event of a server crash or macro virus infection.

Installing Custom Templates on Each Workstation To copy templates to individual workstations, it's helpful to understand the folder structure Office uses to display templates. Office stores all local templates in the \Program Files\Microsoft Office\Templates folder, or in a subfolder within that folder.

Templates stored in the \Program Files\Microsoft Office\Templates folder appear in the General tab of the New dialog box whenever a user chooses File, New. In addition, the New dialog box displays a separate tab for every folder within the Templates folder that contains at least one template or wizard usable by the application you are working in. By default, following are the folders:

- Binders (Office Binder program)
- Legal Pleadings (Word)
- Letters & Faxes (Word)
- Memos (Word)
- Other Documents (Word)
- Outlook (Outlook Item Templates)
- Presentation Designs (PowerPoint)
- Presentations (PowerPoint)
- Publications (Word)
- Reports (Word)
- Spreadsheet Solutions (Excel)
- Web Pages (Word)

If you have installed Office 97 over Office 95, you will also have a folder named Office 95 Templates, containing many older templates not included in the Office 97 installation.

NOTE The folders displayed in the New dialog box are nothing more than ordinary subfolders you can create in Windows Explorer. Therefore, you can easily create your own subfolders, for specialized categories of documents, such as proposals, estimates, or reports. To do so, perform the following steps:

1. Choose Start, Programs, Windows Explorer.
2. Browse to and select the \Program Files\Microsoft Office\Templates folder (or wherever else you've stored your Office templates).
3. Choose File, New, Folder. A new folder appears.
4. Type the name of the folder as you want it to appear on a tab in the New dialog box.
5. Press Enter.

Except for the Outlook folder, all the folders are available when a user opens a new Office document from the Desktop by choosing Start, New Office Document.

Whenever you copy a template into any of these folders—via the Windows Explorer, from the command line, or via any other technique—the template appears the next time a user opens the New dialog box on that workstation.

Deploying Word 97 Templates on Word 98 for the Macintosh If you create Word templates on a Word 97 system and deploy them in a cross-platform environment, you need to perform a few extra steps to make your Windows-based templates work with Word 98 for the Macintosh.

NOTE The following procedure also applies to moving templates from Word 6 or Word 95 on a Windows platform to Word 6 on the Macintosh.

1. Copy the file to the Macintosh, either across the network or by opening it from a DOS-formatted floppy disk. (You need to have Apple File Exchange installed on your Macintosh to read DOS disks.)
2. On the Macintosh, rename the file, removing the .dot file name extension.
3. Open Word 98 for the Macintosh.
4. Choose File, Open.
5. In the Open dialog box, browse to wherever you copied the template, and select it.
6. Click Open. The template opens.
7. Choose File, Save. Word saves the template with a Macintosh file Resource Fork, enabling the file to be recognized as a Word for the Macintosh template.
8. Close the template.
9. Quit Word.
10. Move your template into the Microsoft Office 98\Templates folder.
11. Run Word again. The template should now work properly.

TIP For more information about using Word templates and documents in cross-platform environments, see Chapter 24.

Customizing Office 97's Template Folder Structure You have nearly complete flexibility in how you customize Office's template folders and the template files they contain. For example, you might not want to give users access to *any* of Word's standard templates, especially if you've provided carefully customized alternatives. In that case, you can use Windows Explorer to delete these templates, as well as the folders containing them.

Deploying Custom Templates Along With Office If you are deploying custom templates to individual workstations at the same time you are installing Office on them, you can build the custom templates into the Office installation process.

Office 98 for the Macintosh makes this quite easy. A detailed explanation appears in Chapter 4, but the basic steps are quite simple:

1. Run a custom installation on a network drive. (Issue the command to set up a network installation point, as discussed in Chapter 4.)
2. Copy your custom templates to folders within the Microsoft Office 98\Templates folder.
3. Drag the entire Microsoft Office 98 folder to each workstation you want to install. The custom templates are installed along with the rest of Office.

With Office 97 for Windows, including the templates in the installation process is a bit more challenging. You'll need to customize an installation script using the Network Installation Wizard. This process is described in detail in Chapter 2.

Deploying Custom Templates After Office Is Installed

Even if you've had the time to create custom templates prior to rolling out Office, it's still likely you'll want to add more later. When the time comes, if you've chosen to deploy templates to individual workstations, you can deploy additional templates in one of the following ways:

- By copying the files to one workstation at a time through Windows Explorer (each connected PC is listed under the Network Neighborhood icon)
- Through a maintenance install of Office that simply adds the templates to the individual workstation folders that already exist, as discussed in Chapter 2
- By setting up a new job in Microsoft Systems Management Server (also discussed in Chapter 2) or another network software distribution program, such as Attachmate NetWizard

On large networks, each of these methods can be a bit of a hassle. At this point, it's worth taking a closer look at the alternative to distributing templates on every workstation: centralizing templates on a network server.

Centralizing Templates on a Network Server

To centralize templates on a network server, begin by creating a folder and ensuring that users have full read rights to the folder but no rights to make changes. In Windows NT Server, you can do this by providing a network share. Follow these steps after you create the folder in Windows NT Explorer:

1. Right-click on the folder to display the shortcut menu.
2. Choose Sharing. The folder's Properties dialog box appears (see Figure 11.1).
3. Click Shared As. The Share Name text box becomes active. You can edit it or leave the default name that Windows NT provides, which matches the name of the folder (or the last part of the folder name if it contains multiple words). While share names can include blanks and be up to 12 characters, limiting them to 8 characters with no blanks helps you avoid potential problems, especially if you're providing access to non-Windows systems.
4. Click the Permissions button. The Access Through Share Permissions dialog box appears (see Figure 11.2).
5. In the Type of Access drop-down box, choose Read.
6. Click OK twice.

Sharing a folder, as described here, is the simplest method of providing access on a Windows NT Server network. If you have formatted your network drive using the NTFS file system, however, you can get finer control by using NT folder and file permissions. These enable you to specify which users and groups of users can access a folder, or even a specific file (in this case, a template).

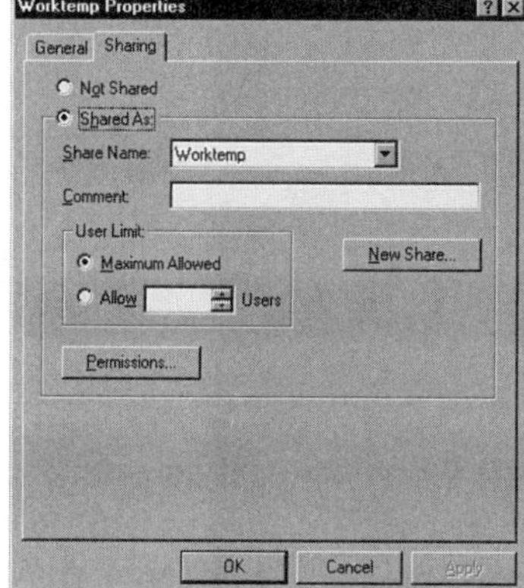

FIGURE 11.1
Establishing a network share for a folder in Windows NT Server.

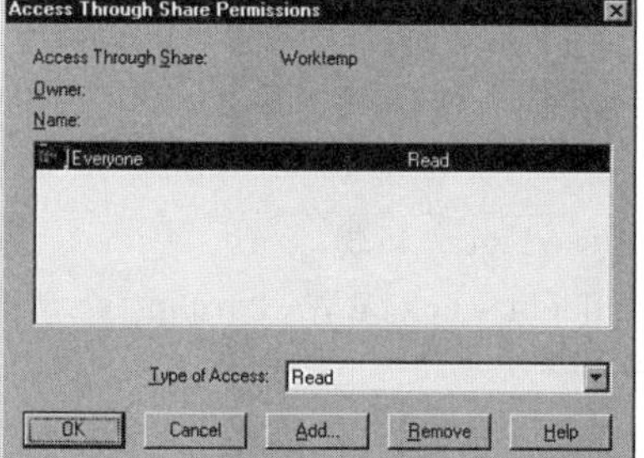

FIGURE 11.2
Setting the shared folder as read only.

Permissions are available through the Security tab of the Properties dialog box associated with each folder or file—but only if the drive is formatted with NTFS. You can use them together with folder sharing to "layer" on additional security where it's needed. For example, you can share the entire Templates folder (which automatically shares all subfolders within it). Then, you can restrict individual subfolders. For example, if only your Sales department should have access to proposal templates, first create a Proposals subfolder and store the templates there. Next, create a Sales group of users with NT Server's User Manager for Domains utility, and limit access to the Proposals subfolder to members of the Sales group. Now that the folder has been shared, and you've restricted access as needed, you need to instruct your Office applications to look for templates there.

In the next section, you'll learn how to establish a location for Word workgroup templates from within Word. In the section after that, you'll learn how to specify a network location for all Office workgroup templates when you install Office.

You can also use System Policies to define a common Office-wide location for workgroup templates at any time.

See Chapter 32 for an extensive discussion of how to establish Microsoft Office System Policies, which enable you to centrally define a workgroup template for all the users on your Windows NT network every time they log onto the network.

Follow the detailed instructions in Chapter 32 for establishing a System Policy using the System Policy Editor. You will find the setting for Workgroup Templates in the System Policy Editor, under the following heading: Default User\Office 97\Common.

Setting a Workgroup Template for Word From Individual Workstations In Word, a feature called Workgroup Templates makes this easy. You can set up Word to look in a networked Workgroup Template folder at the same time it looks in the local template folder on the user's workstation—in other words, whenever the user chooses File, New. Then, if it finds any templates in the workgroup folder, it displays them in the General tab of the New dialog box alongside templates stored locally.

To specify a Word Workgroup Template folder on a single workstation, do the following:

1. Choose Tools, Options.
2. Click the File Locations tab (see Figure 11.3).
3. In the File Types scroll box, double-click on Workgroup Templates. The Modify Location dialog box opens (see Figure 11.4).
4. Click on the Look In drop-down box, and choose Network Neighborhood.
5. Browse to the computer and folder you've set up for the purpose.
6. Click OK twice.

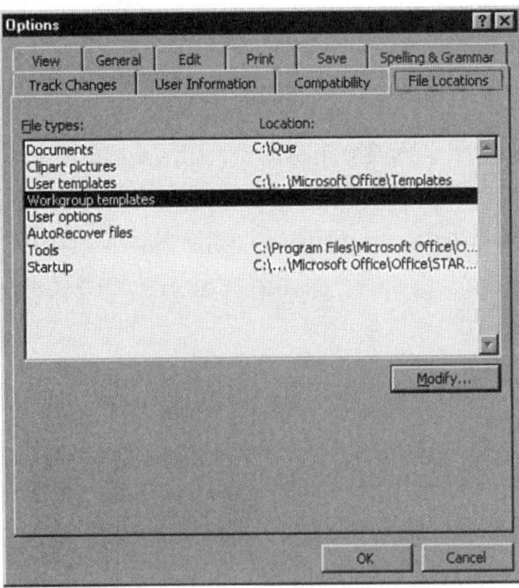

FIGURE 11.3
The File Locations tab tells you where your workgroup templates are, if they've been set.

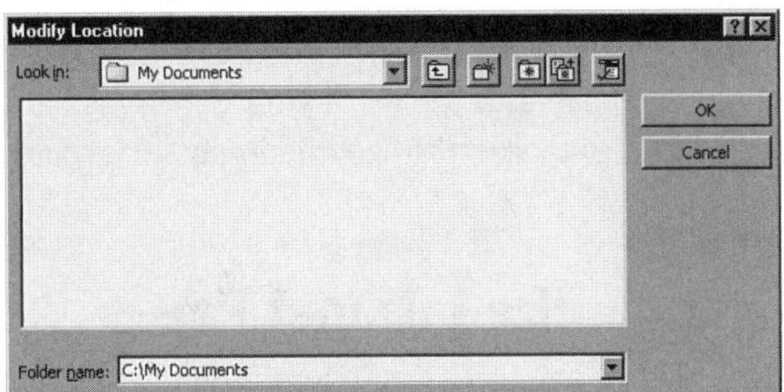

FIGURE 11.4
In the Modify Location dialog box, you can browse to the shared folder you want to use for your workgroup templates.

If you prefer not to set Workgroup Templates or System Policies on each computer, you do have an alternative. You can store the template centrally, create a shortcut to it, and copy the shortcut into each user's Templates folder. When the user chooses the shortcut, Word will find the original template on your server (assuming the server is available). To do this, follow these steps:

1. In Windows Explorer (or Windows NT Explorer), right-click on the file and choose Create Shortcut from the shortcut menu. A shortcut to the template appears.
2. Press Ctrl+C to copy the shortcut file.
3. Using Network Neighborhood, paste the shortcut into the Office 97 Templates folder on each computer on which you want to use it. (Typically, this folder is C:\Program Files\Microsoft Office\Templates.)

Setting an Office Shared Workgroup Template During Installation If you haven't yet deployed Office 97, you can customize a network installation script to incorporate a workgroup template location of your choice for all Office applications on all workstations, all at the same time. Run the Network Installation Wizard, as described in detail in Chapter 2. Then, when you arrive at the Add Registry window, add the following two registry keys:

```
1.
Root: HKEY_Local_Machine
Data type: SZ
Key: Software\Microsoft\Office\8.0\New User
Settings\Common\FileNew\SharedTemplates
Value name: SharedTemplates
Value data: Enter the name of your shared workgroup template folder here
2.
Root: HKEY_Current_User
Data type: SZ
Key: Software\Microsoft\Office\8.0\Common\FileNew\SharedTemplates
Value name: SharedTemplates
Value data: Enter the name of your shared workgroup template folder here
```

Standardizing More Types of Documents with Word 97

As you become increasingly familiar with the work your colleagues are doing, you may be able to identify additional opportunities to standardize documents. Here are a few quick tips to make the job easier.

Using Templates to Standardize Intranet Pages

In Word, you can save any HTML page as a document template. As you'll see, there are significant limitations to this feature. But it does give you a relatively easy way to let your people publish simple, standardized pages on your corporate Intranet, such as the following:

- Internal resumes for your company skills database
- Project updates and information
- Simple product sheets

To create a document template from a Word Web document, perform the following steps:

1. Create the Web page using Word's authoring tools.
2. Choose File, Save As.
3. Choose Document Template in the Save As Type drop-down box.
4. If you want to store your Web page template with Word's other Web page templates, double-click on the Web Pages folder.
5. Click Save.

What's the problem with this procedure? When the template is reopened, any graphics that appeared in the original Web page are missing, replaced by empty boxes. There are three possible solutions:

- Avoid the use of graphics; these are, after all, intended to be simple Intranet pages.
- Ignore the absent graphics for the time being, and plan to publish the pages in a Web site folder that contains the graphics.
- Copy the missing graphics to the same folder where users save the new file, so the graphics will be visible as users edit the page.

One other point: the new documents created with a template need to be saved as HTML files (with File, Save as HTML). Otherwise, Word will assume they are standard documents.

Using ValuPack Templates to Create Additional Custom Documents

As mentioned earlier in this chapter, if you have installed Office 97 over Office 95, a set of Office 95 Word wizards and templates will appear in the Office 95 Templates tab of the New dialog box; they can also be copied from the ValuPack folder of the Office 97 CD-ROM, or retrieved from Microsoft's Web site at `www.microsoft.com/OfficeFreeStuff/Word`. (If you are still running Office 95, you already have access to these wizards and templates. In fact, many of them were available as far back as Office 4.2 and Word 6.)

Several of these wizards represent a great starting point for customizing other types of documents, beyond the basic ones discussed earlier in this chapter. Consider running the wizard to create a document based on the settings your colleagues will use most. Then customize the styles and appearance of the resulting document, and resave it as a new template. You may find the following wizards to be especially valuable:

- The Agenda Wizard
- The Award Wizard
- The Brochure Wizard
- The Calendar Wizard
- The Weekly Time Sheet Template

Using Custom AutoCorrect Lists to Enforce Consistent Spelling

Are your users often called upon to accurately spell unusual names of people or products? Do they find it difficult to get the spellings correct? Then it may be worth your time to modify Office so that it automatically fixes these spelling mistakes before you're embarrassed any further.

To do so, you need to understand the AutoCorrect feature built into Office 97. With AutoCorrect set to Replace Text As You Type, all the major Office programs except Outlook can automatically fix errors based on a database of mistakes and corrections that Office creates the first time you run any of these programs. This database of AutoCorrect revisions is stored in the following two locations:

- Formatted text and graphics are stored in each user's Normal.dot template (and are only accessible to Microsoft Word)
- Other text corrections are stored in an .acl file accessible to all major Office applications except Outlook. This is typically located in the main Windows folder (typically C:\Windows, or in Windows NT, C:\Winnt). The file is typically named with the user's initials (for example, bc.acl).

To create a standardized .acl file, manually add all the custom entries you want, following this procedure:

1. In Word, Excel, PowerPoint, or Access, choose Tools, AutoCorrect. The AutoCorrect dialog box opens (see Figure 11.5).
2. Enter an incorrect usage in the Replace text box.
3. Enter a correct usage in the With text box.
4. Click Add.
5. Repeat the process until you're finished.

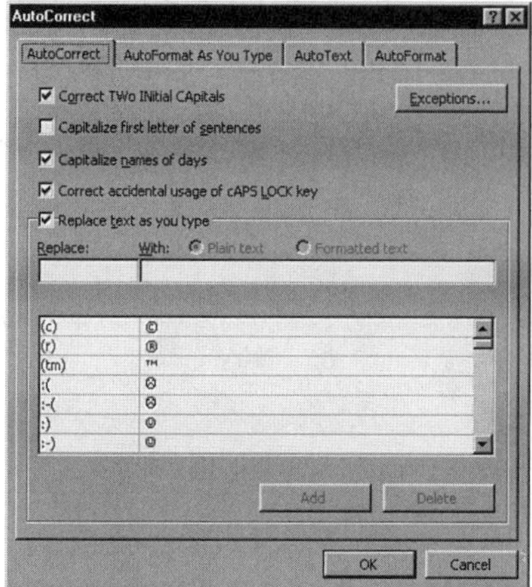

FIGURE 11.5
You can create a standardized AutoCorrect file by adding entries in the AutoCorrect dialog box.

Earlier, you learned that in Word, users can store not just corrections but also blocks of formatted text and graphics as AutoCorrect entries. This gives your sophisticated users a great way to quickly get repeated images (such as manual icons) and formatted text blocks into their documents.

To create a Word AutoCorrect entry that includes a graphic or formatted text, first select a block of copy that includes the text and image. (You can't simply select an image; there must be surrounding text or a table as well.) Then select the block of text and graphics, and choose Tools, AutoCorrect. Enter the text shortcut of your choice in the Replace box, and click Add.

While you're editing your AutoCorrect file, you may also want to *subtract* a few AutoCorrect entries from your customized Office .acl file. In particular, if you often create documents with manual subheadings such as , you may want to remove the entry that automatically replaces with the copyright symbol ©. Similarly, Word 97 automatically replaces three dots (...) with an ellipsis (…) which is slightly more attractive but cannot be understood by much email software and does not convert properly when transferred to non-Windows PCs.

To remove an entry, select it in the AutoCorrect window, and click Delete.

Now that you have a standardized AutoCorrect file, copy it to the Windows folder on each computer where you want to use it. Now you have two options for activating it.

First, you can rename the existing .acl file; then rename the file you've just copied there, giving it the name the original .acl file had.

CAUTION

Never rename an .acl file named mso97.acl. This is the default AutoCorrect file that Office uses to create new .acl files from.

Second, you can leave the filenames unchanged, but edit the Registry so that it uses your customized .acl file instead of the original. To do so, perform the following steps:

1. Run Regedit.exe. The Registry Editor opens (see Figure 11.6).

2. Navigate to the following key: HK_CURRENT_USER\Software\Microsoft\Office\8.0\Common\AutoCorrect.
3. In the right-hand pane of the Registry Editor, double-click Path in the Name column.
4. In the Edit String dialog box (see Figure 11.7), edit the Value data text box to reflect the name and location of the .acl file you want to use.
5. Click OK.
6. Close the Registry Editor.

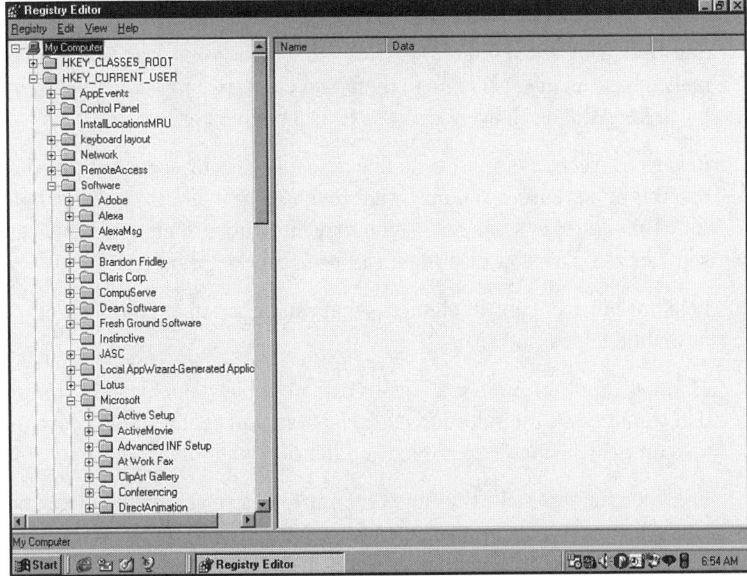

FIGURE 11.6
Choosing a registry key in Regedit.exe.

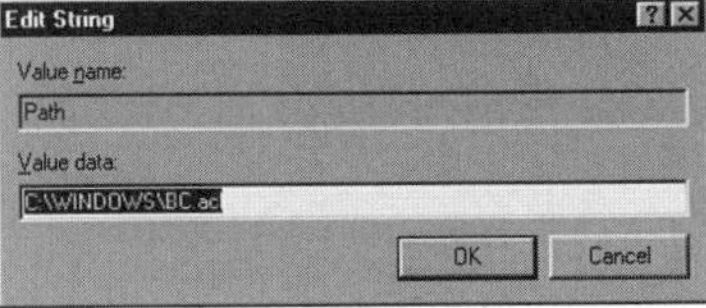

FIGURE 11.7
Editing the path and filename of the AutoCorrect file.

CAUTION

AutoCorrect, AutoText, and most of Word's other automatic features (such as Check Spelling As You Type, Check Grammar As You Type, AutoFormat As You Type and AutoComplete) may significantly reduce the performance of voice dictation systems such as Dragon's Naturally Speaking and IBM's ViaVoice families of software products.

AutoCorrect can also trigger unexpected events in Microsoft Access form controls (for more information, see Knowledge Base Q165480, available at `support.microsoft.com/support/kb/articles/q165/4/80.asp`). You can either turn off AutoCorrect completely, or set the individual form control's Allow AutoCorrect property to No.

Using Custom AutoText Entries to Provide Standard Copy Blocks

Word's AutoText feature is designed to help users manage and quickly insert boilerplate text. As an Office administrator, you can use it to build a boilerplate library and make it available to all the users on your network at once. These AutoText libraries can be so useful, it's worth a little time to plan them carefully.

Planning Your AutoText Library

Start by giving some thought to how you'll name your AutoText entries. Make sure your entry names have an internal logic to them and can be easily remembered by your colleagues. Also try to keep them relatively short so they'll be quicker to enter.

Review a selection of representative documents your organization creates to look for language that might be reused. You may want to edit your existing language before storing it as an AutoText entry. In some cases, you may find entire documents that can be reused and saved as separate templates, as discussed earlier in this chapter.

Look for other document elements that can be saved as AutoText entries: logos, signatures, formatted tables, and so on.

Think about other AutoText entries that would be valuable to have, such as proposal language that would assist the sales force; disclaimers and certifications; corporate capabilities language; the company history, experience and mission statement; and so on.

Consider ways to make the AutoText entries more accessible to inexperienced users. For example, you might create a custom toolbar or menu that contains the AutoText entries your colleagues are likely to use most (refer to Chapter 6).

Give people hard copy listings of all the AutoText entries you're providing them. To print a list of AutoText entries, perform the following steps:

1. Create or open a new document based on the template containing the entries you want to print.
2. Choose File, Print.
3. In the Print What drop-down box, choose AutoText entries.
4. Click OK.

Creating Your AutoText Library

After you know which AutoText entries you want to create, you can begin the process of creating them. All AutoText entries are stored in templates, so create a new, empty template where you can store yours by performing the following steps:

1. Choose File, New.
2. Select Blank Document, and click the Template option button in the Create New area.

3. Click OK. You now have a new template file.
4. Choose File, Save As.
5. Enter a name for your template in the File Name box.
6. Click Save. Word saves the template in your Templates folder.

Now create a document based on that template by performing the following steps:

1. Choose File, New.
2. Select the template you just created.
3. Click OK.

Next, you have to tell Word to store the entries in the new template, not Normal.dot (where it would normally store them). This is important: if you copy your Normal.dot template into other users' Templates folder, you'll overwrite all of their custom settings. To tell Word to store AutoText settings in the template you've just created, instead of Normal.dot, follow these steps:

1. Choose Insert, AutoText, AutoText. The AutoText tab of the AutoCorrect dialog box opens (see Figure 11.8).
2. In the Look In box, choose the name of the template you just created. (This option doesn't just tell Word where to look for AutoText entries, it also tells Word where to place new ones.)
3. Click OK.

FIGURE 11.8

Specifying which template your AutoText entries will go into.

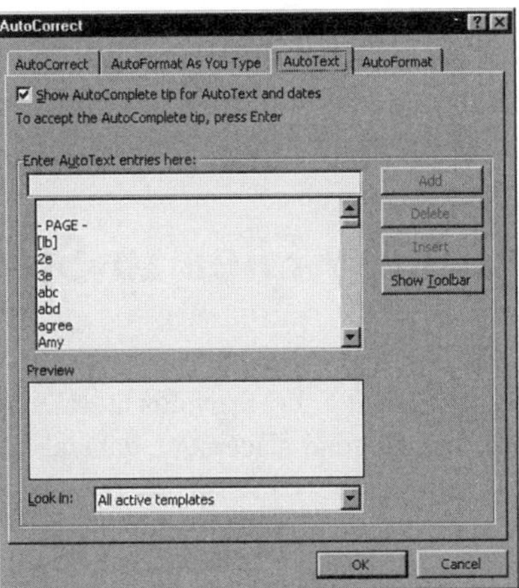

You're finally ready to start adding custom AutoText entries of your own. To add an AutoText entry, perform the following steps:

1. Type the text into your document (or if you prefer, copy it there from another document).
2. Select the text.
3. Choose Insert, AutoText, New. The Create AutoText dialog box opens (see Figure 11.9).

4. In the Please Name Your AutoText Entry box, type the abbreviation users will use to invoke the AutoText entry.
5. Click OK.
6. Repeat the process for each new entry.

FIGURE 11.9
Creating a new AutoText entry.

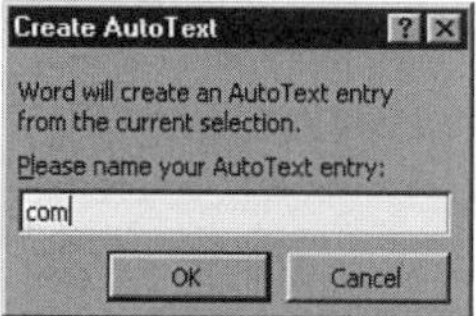

Now, all that's left to do is make your AutoText-filled template available to all the users in your workgroup. There are several ways to do so; here's one of the best.

1. Store the template on your server in a location that is accessible to all your users.
2. In Windows Explorer (or Windows NT Explorer), right-click on the file and choose Create Shortcut from the shortcut menu. A shortcut to the template appears.
3. Press Ctrl+C to copy the shortcut file.
4. Using Network Neighborhood, paste the shortcut into the Office 97 Startup folder on every computer on which you want to use it. (Typically, this folder is C:\Program Files\Microsoft Office\Office\Startup. Don't confuse it with the Windows 95 or NT Startup folder.)

After you do this, Word will search for the template and load it at startup along with Normal.dot, making all your custom AutoText entries available to users. Because the template itself is still stored on your server, however, it's easy to update.

Using Custom Chart Gallery Files to Standardize Charts

When it comes to creating charts, Microsoft Excel provides literally millions of different combinations of chart type, colors, titles, axes, legend placement, data labels, gridlines, backgrounds and so forth. That's great. But all this flexibility can make it very challenging to get all your charts looking like they came from the same organization. You may not care much about variations in internal documents, as long as your users generate charts that are readable, accurate, and not misleading. Charts created for customers are another story, however. Here, it's important to make sure all your charts are consistent—and of consistently high quality.

Excel 97 (and Excel 98 for the Macintosh) enables you to do this with a feature called **User-Defined Chart Gallery**. With this feature, you create one or more charts with the exact settings you want to be reflected in all of your users' charts. You might, for example, define "official" pie charts, bar charts, line charts and area charts. Once you've perfected your charts, you can store them as custom chart types, and distribute them to all the users in your workgroup.

Here's how it works.

First, create the chart.

1. In an Excel worksheet, select sample data you want to build your chart with.
2. Choose Insert, Chart to display the Chart Wizard (see Figure 11.10).
3. Select the chart type and sub-type you want to create, and click Next.
4. Walk through the remaining screens of the Chart Wizard, creating settings for data ranges, series, titles, axes, gridlines, legends, data labels, data tables, and other chart elements. (The elements will vary depending on the type of chart you're working with.)
5. Click Finish; the chart appears.
6. Now refine the chart to more precisely reflect the design you want to use. You can edit individual elements of your chart by right-clicking on them and choosing the Format command from the top of the shortcut menu. For example, to change the way individual data series are formatted, right-click on one data point and choose Format Data Series. You can now control a wide variety of settings associated with this data series, including color, patterns, and borders; whether each data point is labeled with a name or value; the order in which data series are presented; and much more.
7. After you finish, right-click on the edge of the chart to select the entire chart (not a specific chart element).
8. Choose Chart Type from the shortcut menu.
9. Click the Custom Types tab. An approximate sample of your chart appears in the Sample window (see Figure 11.11).
10. Click User-Defined in the Select From area.
11. Click Add. The Add Custom Chart Type dialog box appears (see Figure 11.12).
12. In the Name text box, enter a text name for your new custom chart type.
13. If you want, describe your custom chart in the Description text box.
14. Click OK twice. Your custom chart now appears as a user-defined chart type in the Custom Types tab of the Chart Types dialog box.

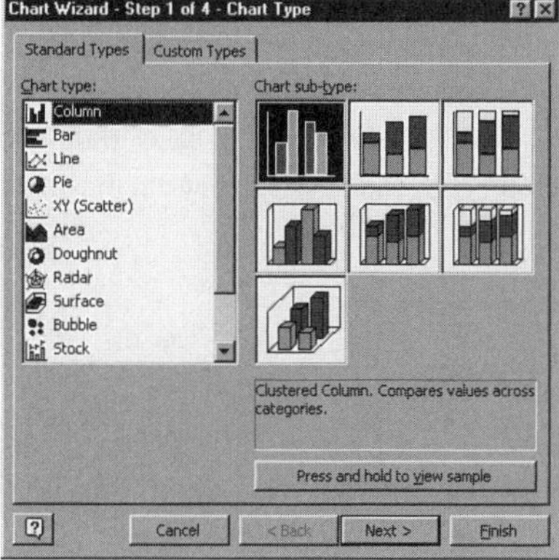

FIGURE 11.10
Use the Excel Chart Wizard to start building a custom chart.

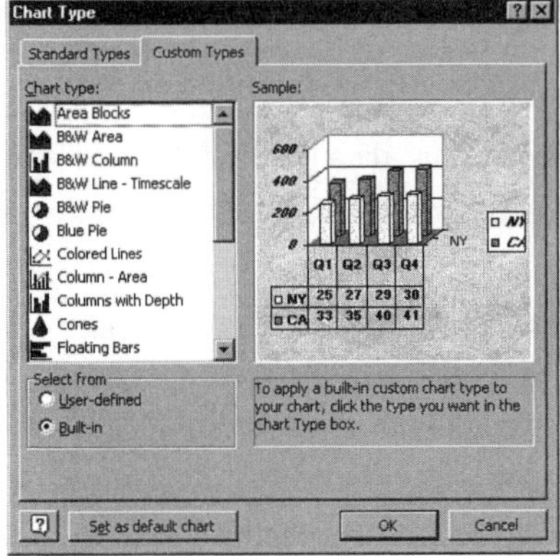

FIGURE 11.11
View a rough preview of your custom chart; note that fonts may not be correct.

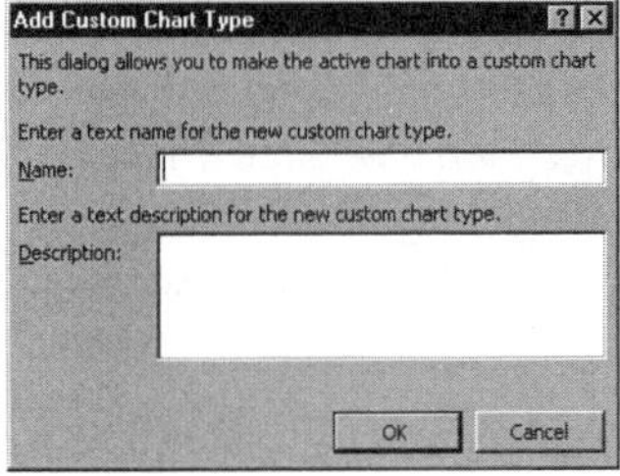

FIGURE 11.12
Name and describe your custom chart in the Add Custom Chart Type dialog box.

All the custom chart types you create are stored in a separate Excel file that can be distributed or shared. In Excel 97 for Windows, the file is called Xlusrgal.xls, and is normally found in C:\Program Files\Microsoft Office\Office. In Excel 98 for the Macintosh, the file is called Excel Chart User Gallery, and is found in System Folder:Preferences. You have two options for distributing this file:

- You can copy it to the appropriate folder on each workstation.
- You can store the file on a network server, and use the System Policy Editor to define where Excel should look for it. Using the System Policy Editor is discussed at length in Chapter 32. You will find the setting for User-Defined Chart Galleries under the following heading: Default User\Excel 97\Miscellaneous\Chart Gallery.

NOTE The custom chart types are only available from within Excel; however, you can create a chart within Excel using a custom chart type, and paste it (or link to it) in Word or PowerPoint.

CHAPTER 12

Managing Workgroup Revisions and Approvals with Office

Office has extensive features that make it easier for teams and workgroups to share documents, review them, organize and resolve everyone's comments, gain approval, and take action.

Very few users start working with these features on their own, however: most need training, coordination, encouragement, and guidance. As your organization's Office administrator, it falls to you to provide this assistance—and if you do so, you can make your organization substantially more productive. That's what this chapter is about: helping you understand Word and Excel's most widely used workgroup features so that you can help your colleagues make the most of them.

For more information about Outlook's workgroup features, see Chapter 14, "Workgroup Scheduling and Contact Management with Outlook 98." To learn about Access' features for sharing databases, see Chapter 15, "Sharing Database Resources with Access 97." For a discussion of PowerPoint's workgroup features, see Chapter 13, "Enhancing PowerPoint's Value in Team Settings."

Using Word's Revision Tools

Word 97 contains several powerful tools for managing the revisions process.

The Comments feature, formerly called Annotations, enables you and other reviewers to mark a document with comments that don't appear when the document is printed. Because it's easy to find and read comments, this feature makes it easy to respond to the comments of reviewers.

The Track Changes feature, formerly called Revisions, enables you to propose specific changes in a document's text (and in some cases, formatting), which can then be accepted or rejected. (You can also use a closely related feature, Compare Documents, to check changes made between two versions of a document, so that you can determine where a problem arose, or whether a change requested by a team member was disregarded when a new draft was created.

Highlighting is the electronic equivalent of that transparent yellow pen you may have used in high school: a simple way to mark questionable text in color.

Finally, Word 97 introduces Versioning, which allows you to save multiple documents in the same file. That means no more worrying about finding multiple files to compare or keeping track of changes that mysteriously disappear.

In Word 97, Word's revision tools have been brought together on a single Reviewing toolbar (see Figure 12.1). To display the Reviewing toolbar (or any other toolbar), choose View, Toolbars and select it from the list. Although there are other ways to access these tools, your colleagues will usually find it most convenient to work with them from the toolbar.

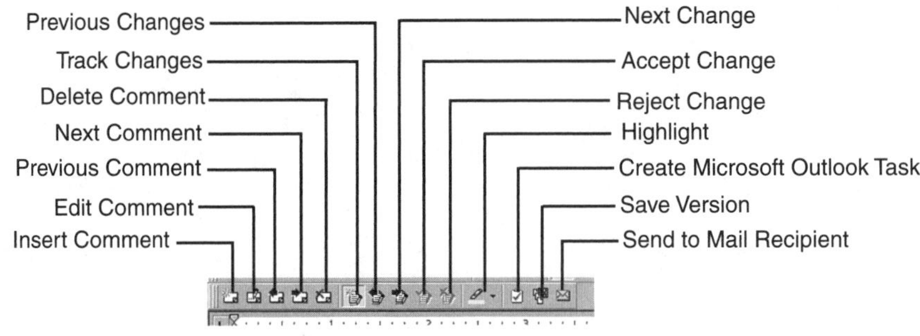

FIGURE 12.1
Word's reviewing tools are now all accessible from the Reviewing toolbar.

Using Word's Comments Tool

How can users make comments on each others' documents without adding text that will need to be deleted manually at some point? How do they make comments throughout an entire document in a way that makes those comments easy to manage and resolve? The solution is Word's Comments feature.

Inserting a comment places a comment mark in the document and opens a separate Comments pane where users can type responses, and others can read them (see Figure 12.2).

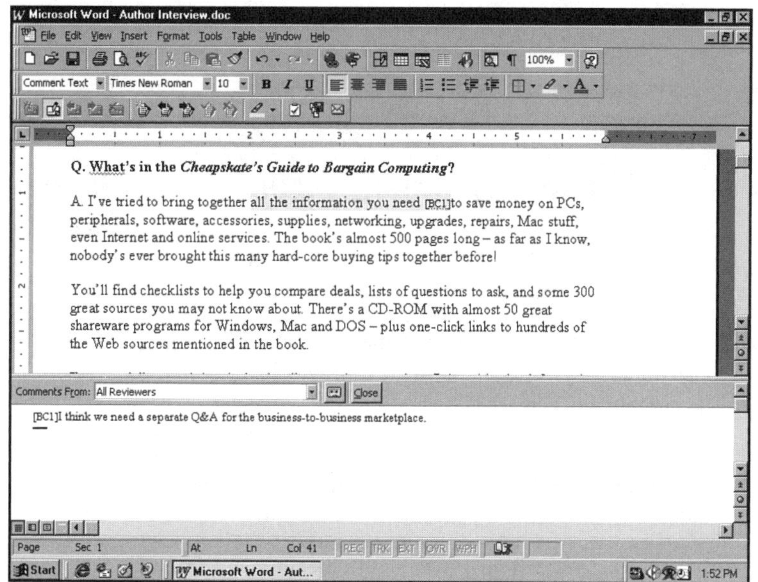

FIGURE 12.2
The Comments pane, with comments displayed.

To insert a comment, perform the following steps:

1. Place the insertion point where you want the comment to appear, or select the text you want to comment upon.
2. Click the Insert Comment button on the Reviewing Toolbar, or choose Insert, Comment. Your initials and the comment number appear in the document as hidden text. At the same time, the Comments pane opens.

NOTE Word uses the user's initials as stored in the registry. These initials are typically set when Office is installed, and can be changed in the User Information tab of the Tools, Options dialog box.

3. Type and format your comments in the Comments pane.

4. To close the Comments pane, click on Close or press Alt+Shift+C. To create another comment, click in the editing pane, place your insertion point where you want the next comment, and repeat steps 1 through 3.

Users can enter just about anything in a Comments pane, including graphics, sound annotations, and most fields (with a few exceptions, such as table of contents and index entries). They can also copy text or graphics from the editing window to the Comments pane, and vice versa.

The comment number that appears in the document reflects the sequence in which comments appear in the document. Word does not number each individual's comments separately. When comments are inserted, moved, copied, or deleted, all other comments are automatically renumbered as needed.

Numbered comment marks are visible in the editing pane whenever the Show/Hide button (the ¶ symbol on the Standard toolbar) is toggled on.

Reviewing Comments Already Inserted in a Document

Word uses pale yellow highlighting to mark text in a document that has comments associated with it. In Word 97, you can see the contents of a comment instantly by positioning your mouse pointer above text that has been highlighted. The comment appears as a ScreenTip.

To edit a comment, or to review many comments at once, open the Comments pane by double-clicking on any comment in the document. The Comments pane shows all the comments in a document; you can scroll through them. When you position your insertion point on a comment in the Comments pane, Word scrolls the document to the matching position.

The easiest way to move between comments is to click the Next Comment or Previous Comment buttons on the Reviewing Toolbar.

If you want to review only the comments made by a specific reviewer, press F5 to open the Go To dialog box. Then select Comment in the Go to What box. You can then choose the name of the reviewer from the Enter Reviewer's Name drop-down box. To move to the next comment, click Next; to move to the previous comment, click Previous.

Deleting Comments from Your Document

After you respond to a comment in your document, you may want to delete it. To delete a comment, select the entire comment mark in your document (but don't include the highlighted text associated with it). Then click the Delete Comment button on the Reviewing toolbar or delete the comment mark as you would any other text in your document.

Limiting Reviewers to Only Making Comments

The Comments feature gives reviewers a way to comment about a document without actually changing the text. That way, the author or editor maintains control over what actually makes it into the document. You can go one step further and prevent reviewers from making any changes to a document except for comments. Follow these steps to protect the document for comment:

1. Choose Tools, Protect Document. The Protect Document dialog box opens (see Figure 12.3).

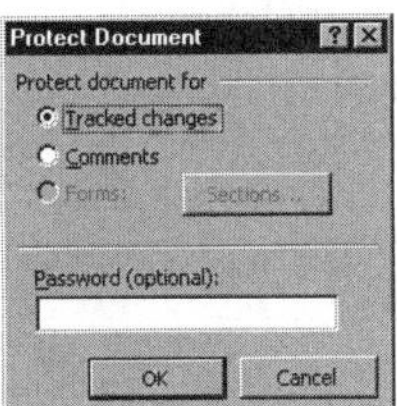

FIGURE 12.3
In the Protect Document dialog box, you can prevent reviewers from making changes, except as comments.

2. Choose Comments.
3. Type a password in the Password text box, and click OK.
4. The Confirm Password dialog box opens; retype the password and click OK. (As always, remember to store your password in a secure location.)

Inserting Audio Comments

With audio and voice recognition becoming more widespread in business PCs, more of your users may be comfortable speaking to their PCs via microphone. If so, they may want to use Word's Comments feature to insert spoken comments, as follows:

1. Click where you want to insert the spoken comment.
2. Click the Insert Comment button on the Reviewing toolbar (or choose Insert, Comment).
3. Click the Insert Sound Object icon at the top of the Comments pane (it looks like a cassette tape). A cassette tape icon appears next to the comment mark in the Comments pane.
4. The Windows Sound Recorder opens, as shown in Figure 12.4. Click the Record button and record the comment.

FIGURE 12.4
Recording a comment using the Windows Sound Recorder.

5. If you're asked to update the object, do so.
6. Close the Comments pane.

Because you're using the standard Windows Sound Recorder, you have access to all of its features. For example, you can choose Insert File from the Sound Recorder's Edit menu and include a sound file you've already recorded or stored elsewhere. You might use this feature to provide access to a sound clip copied from your intranet or a recent speech by one of your company's executives.

After a comment is inserted in a document, you can listen to it as follows:

1. Choose View, Comments to display the Comments pane.
2. Double-click on the microphone icon that appears next to the comment that you want to hear.
3. Close the Comments pane after you finish.

CAUTION

Be aware that the routine use of voice comments can dramatically enlarge document files and increase the strain on your network. If hard drive space or network bandwidth are at a premium, you may want to discourage the use of voice comments.

Printing Comments

Often, you may find it convenient to print the comments in a document. There are two ways to do so. First, you can print the document with its comments. This method prints the comment marks in the text, so you can see the locations that correspond to each comment. (Because comment marks are hidden text, this means other hidden text also appears.) The comments appear on a separate page. To print the document with comments, perform the following steps:

1. Choose File, Print.
2. Click Options.
3. Mark the Comments check box. The Hidden Text check box is automatically marked as well.
4. Click OK.
5. Select any other print settings you want in the Print dialog box and click OK.

Or you can print only the comments by performing the following steps:

1. Choose File, Print.
2. Select Comments in the Print What drop-down box.
3. Click OK.

Working with Word's Track Changes Feature

Comments are well-suited for observations about a document, but less well-suited for specific corrections. For this, Word offers another feature: Track Changes.

With Track Changes, you can propose inserted text, which will appear underlined; all of your proposed insertions will appear in the same color. You can also propose deletions. The text that you delete does not disappear, but rather appears in color with strikethrough formatting. These underlined insertions and deletions marked as strikethrough are collectively known as *change marks*. If several users suggest revisions, each user's changes are automatically marked in a different color. After all changes have been proposed, the original author can decide whether to accept or reject them—one at a time, or all at once.

To turn on the Track Changes feature, double-click TRK in the status bar. The letters TRK become darkened, and now all the changes you make will be marked as revisions. (You can also turn on Track Changes by clicking the Track Changes button on the Reviewing toolbar.) You can turn off Track Changes whenever you want; either by double-clicking the TRK box in the status bar, or by clicking the Track Changes button in the Reviewing toolbar again to toggle it off.

CAUTION

If you reorganize your document by cutting and pasting large blocks of text, these will appear as large deletions and insertions. Within the blocks of pasted (inserted) text, you won't have any way to tell whether additional copy edits were made.

NOTE With Track Changes turned on, you may occasionally be surprised to see change marks showing up where no new text has been entered. These change marks may be updated fields. Here's a common example: If you enter a date in a document using Insert, Date and Time, and leave the Update Automatically check box marked in the Date and Time dialog box, the new date will be marked as a text change when you update the fields in your document. This was a deliberate design decision (the alternative was to ignore that any change occurred)—but many users will find it disconcerting.

Viewing and Hiding Revisions within a Document

Figure 12.5 shows a sample document with revisions marked. To the far left, vertical lines, called *revision bars*, appear next to each line that has revisions. This makes it easier to tell where revisions have been made.

Many editors and writers find it distracting to watch all the colored text, underlines, and strikethroughs pile up as they revise a document. You can have Word track revisions without showing them onscreen. By doing so, you can work with the document as if track changes weren't turned on. However, because Word is still invisibly tracking your changes, you or your colleagues can accept or reject them later. To track changes without displaying them onscreen, perform the following steps:

1. Right-click on the TRK button in the status bar and choose Highlight Changes from the shortcut menu. (Or, if you prefer, choose Tools, Track Changes, Highlight Changes.) The Highlight Changes dialog box appears (see Figure 12.6).

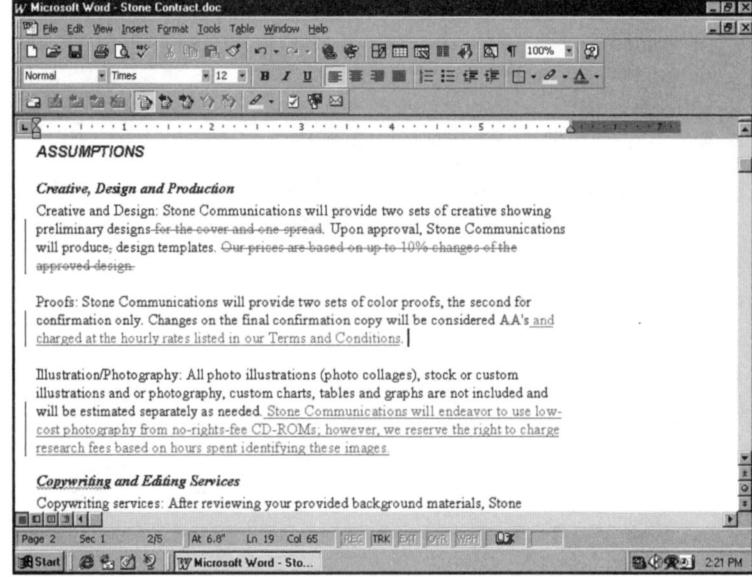

FIGURE 12.5
A sample document, including revision marks.

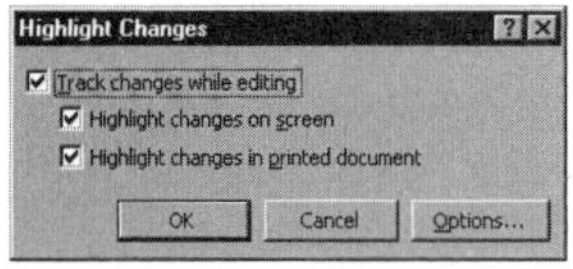

FIGURE 12.6
The Highlight Changes dialog box controls whether tracked changes appear onscreen or in print.

2. Clear the Highlight Changes on Screen check box.
3. Click OK.

Hiding Revision Marks When You Print

By default, the changes you enter in a document are shown in any printouts you make. If those changes are highlighted onscreen, Change Marks appear as well. You might not want that. For example, perhaps you're proposing revisions, but it hasn't been decided whether to accept them. If you want Word to print the original unrevised copy, do the following:

1. Right-click on the TRK button in the status bar and choose Highlight Changes from the shortcut menu (or, if you prefer, choose Tools, Track Changes, Highlight Changes)
2. Clear the Highlight Changes in Printed Document check box.
3. Click OK.

Options for Controlling the Way Track Changes Works

Word 97 gives you nearly complete control over how Track Changes behaves. For example, as you've learned, text that you insert while Track Changes is turned on appears in your document with an underline; text that you delete appears in strikethrough. As mentioned earlier, Word automatically assigns a color to each document reviewer. Word also marks lines that have been changed with vertical bars on the outside border of each page—in other words, on the left margin of even-numbered pages, and on the right margin of odd-numbered pages. You can change these behaviors, and others as well. To do so, right-click on TRK in the status bar, and choose Options from the shortcut menu. (You can also reach the same dialog box by choosing Tools, Options, Track Changes.) The Track Changes dialog box appears, as shown in Figure 12.7.

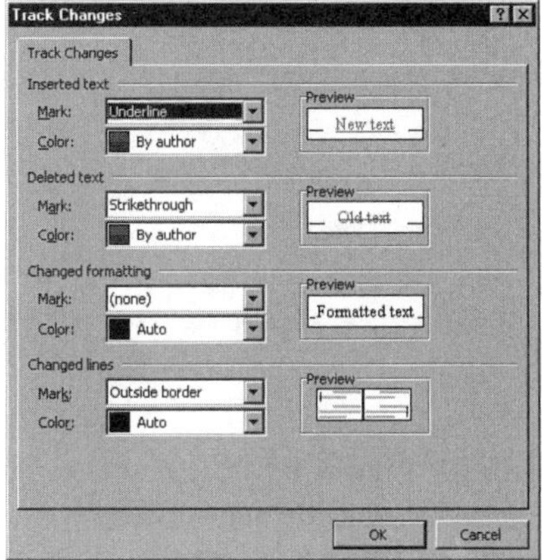

FIGURE 12.7
The Track Changes dialog box controls how changes appear in your documents.

To change the way inserted text is marked, choose Underline, Bold, Italic, Double Underline, or (none) in the Mark drop-down box, located in the Inserted Text area. Whenever you make a change, its effects are displayed in the Preview box to the right of the drop-down box you've changed.

You can control the way deleted text appears in the same way: In the Deleted Text area of the dialog box, choose an option from the Mark drop-down box.

Controlling How Word Assigns Colors to Reviewers

In most organizations, it's common for several people to review one document. Whenever a reviewer turns on Track Changes, Word searches Word's Tools, Options, User Information registry settings to identify the reviewer. If this reviewer hasn't worked on the document before, his or her revisions appear in a different color.

Word has fifteen colors available in its color drop-down box, but it only automatically assigns colors to the first eight reviewers. If a document has more than eight reviewers, the revisions can still be tracked separately, but some reviewers will have to share a color. If you prefer that all revisions appear in the same color, choose the color yourself in each Color drop-down box.

NOTE You don't get quite as much control over colors as you might like. For example, if you specify a color for inserted text or deleted text, every reviewer's changes will appear in that color. You *cannot*, for example, set aside a specific color for each individual or each job task (blue for copy editor, red for legal reviewer, and so on).

If you review a document twice, you may want to display each reviewing "pass" in a different color. To do so, before you review the document for the second time, change the name stored in the User Information tab of the Options dialog box (accessible through Tools, Options, User Information). If you're named John Doe, for example, you might change the name to *John Doe 2nd Review* or something equally descriptive.

CAUTION

Before you start using Track Changes (or adding comments with the Comments feature), make sure that your correct name and initials appear in the User Information tab of the Tools, Options dialog box. If your company frequently reassigns PCs, it's common for this dialog box to store the name of a previous user.

Controlling How Changed Lines Appear

As you've learned, Word flags changes in a document by displaying vertical lines along the outside border of the page, on every line containing a change. In the Changed Lines area of the Track Changes dialog box, you can control where these lines appear and how they look.

In the Mark drop-down box, you can specify that they always print along the left border, the right border, or not at all. By default, the color of these lines is Auto, which is typically black; you can specify a color manually as well.

NOTE If you encounter anomalies where changed lines appear in Word 97, see Microsoft Knowledge Base article Q160112.

Controlling How Formatting Changes Are Marked

In previous versions of Word, there was no way to track formatting changes. If you changed formatting while Word was tracking revisions, the change would not be marked in any way.

Word 97 now tracks formatting changes. By default, however, formatting changes are not marked in your document, even though vertical lines do appear in the margins next to them. This can be very confusing: When you review a document that includes tracked formatting changes, you'll see that changes have been made, but you'll have no idea what those changes were.

The Track Changes dialog box allows you to specify a mark for changed formatting: Bold, Italic, Underline, or Double Underline. (You'll probably want to use a mark that isn't used for a different kind of tracked change. If you haven't customized your other settings, Double Underline may be your best bet.)

Limiting Reviewers to Only Making Tracked Changes

Earlier in this chapter you learned how to protect a document for comments, which prevents reviewers from making any changes to the document except for adding comments. You can do the same thing with Tracked Changes. With Protect Document for Tracked Changes turned on, no editing is allowed unless it is made with Track Changes turned on, unless the reviewer enters the correct password. To protect your document for Tracked Changes, perform the following steps:

1. Choose Tools, Protect Document. The Protect Document dialog box opens, as shown earlier in Figure 12.3.
2. Choose Tracked Changes.
3. Type a password in the Password text box and click OK.
4. The Confirm Password dialog box opens; retype the password and click OK.

Marking Tracked Changes Automatically with Compare Documents

Many people don't know Word well, and even more people don't follow directions well. Imagine you've given a colleague a lengthy document for review, and he or she has neglected to use Word's Track Changes feature as you requested. Back comes the document, full of changes—but what has actually been changed? How can the changes be evaluated?

Or perhaps you have two drafts of a document, and you need to know which specific changes were made between them, perhaps to help you determine which version is newer? (File date stamps aren't always conclusive in this respect.)

Using Word's Compare Documents feature, you can automatically compare the two files and use Tracked Changes to mark all the differences between them. To do so, perform the following steps:

1. Open the document where you want the change marks to be placed—commonly, the most recent version.
2. Choose Tools, Track Changes, Compare Documents. The Select File to Compare with Current Document dialog box appears.
3. Browse to and select the file that you want to compare to the file that's already open.
4. Click Open.

Word moves through the document, adding change marks wherever additions or deletions were made in the document. In a long document, this can take some time. In the status bar, Word tells you what percentage of the document has been compared. When Word finishes, you can work with these change marks the same way you would if you had created them using the Track Changes feature.

In a long document with many changes, using Track Changes can slow down Word. Instead of using Track Changes, you might deliberately choose to use Compare Documents, marking all your changes at once after you've edited the document.

Note that this shortcut can lead to a few minor discrepancies. For example, Compare Documents cannot mark some changed field results with change marks, if the field results are longer than 750 characters.

Merging Revisions from Multiple Reviewers

If you've been handed revisions from several reviewers, each of whom has saved his or her file separately, you can merge these separate files into a single document, where you can then decide how to resolve all their concerns at once. Follow these steps:

1. Open the file where you want all your colleagues' changes to be placed.
2. Choose Tools, Merge Documents.
3. The Select File to Merge Into Current Document dialog box appears.
4. Browse to and select the file that you want to merge into your current file.
5. Click OK.

One by one, you can repeat this process with each set of revisions; all revisions will then display in the same document, with each reviewer's changes appearing in a different color.

Resolving Proposed Changes to a Document

Now that you (and your colleagues) have marked up a document with change marks, the next step is to resolve the changes.

To walk through a document containing Tracked Changes, first open the document, and then display the Reviewing toolbar. Click the Next Change button; Word selects the first change in your document. To accept the change, click Accept Change. To reject it, click Reject Change; the change will disappear from the document, and the original text will be restored. (Of course, you always have the option of accepting or rejecting a change and then editing the text to reflect the reviewer's concerns in your own way.)

You may often want to see who made a change: For example, you might have to pay more attention if the change came from the CEO than if it came from someone in the next cubicle. Place your mouse pointer over the change; Word displays a ScreenTip showing who made the change, when the person made it, and what kind of a change he or she made.

It's not essential to resolve all changes at the same time; you can simply leave the change marks that you cannot yet resolve. When there are no more changes in the document, clicking Next Change displays a dialog box saying that Word found no tracked changes.

Controlling How You View the Document

As you review changes, you might want to see what the document would look like if *all* changes were accepted, or what it looked like before *any* changes were made. If so, right-click on the TRK icon on the status bar and choose Accept or Reject Changes from the shortcut menu. The Accept or Reject Changes dialog box appears, as shown in Figure 12.8.

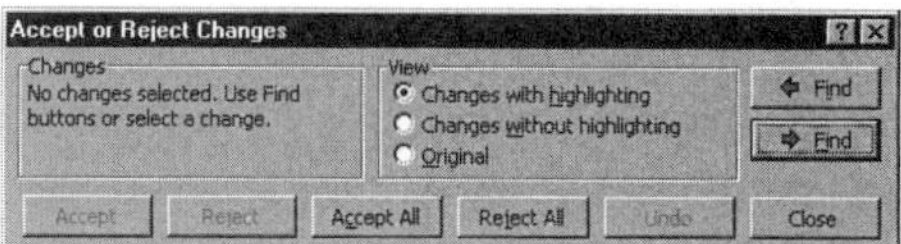

FIGURE 12.8
The Accept or Reject Changes dialog box.

To view changes with Word's underline, strikethrough, or other markings, mark the Changes with Highlighting option button. To view the document as it would look if all changes had been accepted, mark the Changes without Highlighting option button. To view the document as it would look if all changes were rejected, mark Original. If you like, you can keep working with this dialog box open, toggling back and forth to see how the document would look "before and after" potential changes were made.

Accepting or Rejecting All Changes at Once

Occasionally, you might want to accept or reject all of a reviewer's changes at the same time, rather than reviewing them individually. To do so, perform the following steps:

1. Choose Tools, Track Changes, Accept or Reject Changes. The Accept or Reject Changes dialog box opens.
2. To accept all changes, click Accept All. (To reject all changes, click Reject All.)
3. A confirming dialog box appears; click OK.

If you change your mind immediately, you can reverse your decision by clicking Undo within the Accept or Reject Changes dialog box, or use the Undo button on the Standard toolbar afterward. All the change marks reappear in your document, and you have the opportunity to review them one at a time again.

The Highlighter: Low-Tech Revisions

A low-tech substitute for Track Changes and Comments is Word's Highlighter tool, which allows users to mark text in yellow (or any of 15 other colors), just as they may have done in their high school textbooks.

To use the Highlighter in Word or Excel, just select a block of text and click the Highlight button in the Standard toolbar; the text now appears in color. Or, in Word, click the Highlight button and then drag across the text that you want to highlight.

Because the Highlighter is extremely easy to use, many people use it in place of other revisions tools. From a management standpoint, however, the Highlighter leaves something to be desired.

It's clumsy to move among highlights in a document (although this can be done from within the Find and Replace dialog box). Since there's no easy way to annotate highlighted text without adding it to the document, many users simply highlight text without explaining the concern they have with it. Finally, few users know a quick way to get rid of all the highlights in a document once they're there—as a result, stray highlights are often left in a document after they're no longer necessary.

There is a shortcut for eliminating all highlighting, if you know where to look:

1. Choose Ctrl+A to select the entire document.
2. Click the drop-down arrow next to the Highlight button on the Standard toolbar; choose None.

Using Word's Versioning Feature

In business environments, you're commonly faced with the challenge of locating an old version of a document, tracking the process by which a document was changed, or discovering who was responsible for a specific change. As the Office administrator, you may be called upon to come up with a solution that simplifies the process. Word 97's new Versioning feature may be what you need.

With Versioning, Word can store all versions of a document together, in the same file. Because Word only stores the changes among versions, the file sizes remain smaller than they would if you had saved separate files.

To use Versioning, click the Save Version button on the Reviewing toolbar. The Save Version dialog box opens, as shown in Figure 12.9. You're asked to make comments about the version you're saving; for example, why the draft was created, or whose input it reflects. Word automatically records the date and time the draft was created, and who created it.

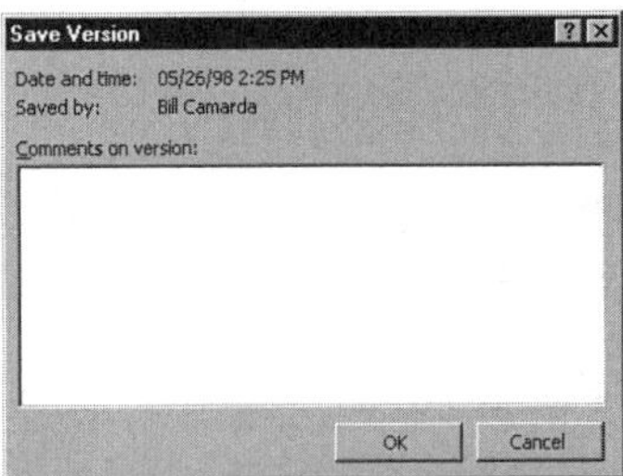

FIGURE 12.9
The Save Version dialog box.

If you want more control, choose File, Versions. The Versions dialog box opens, as shown in Figure 12.10. You have several options. You can choose Save Now to save a separate version immediately. If you do, the Save Versions dialog box will open, and you'll be invited to make a comment that will accompany the saved version.

FIGURE 12.10
The Versions dialog box.

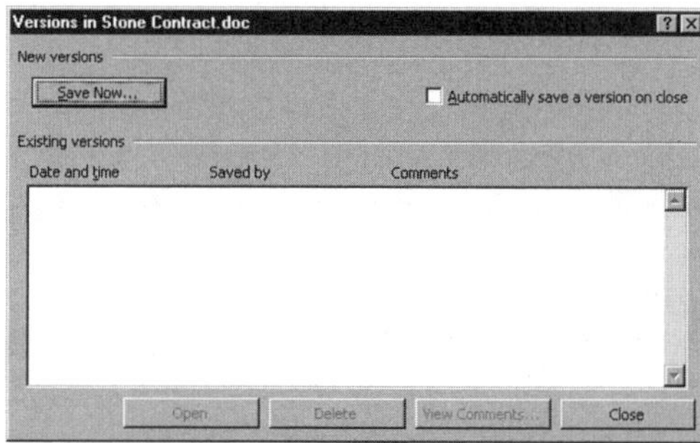

If you don't want to worry about saving versions manually, you can tell Word to save a new version whenever you save the file after making changes. In the Versions dialog box, mark the Automatically Save a Version on Close check box. Word inserts the comment *Automatic version* whenever you save a version using this automatic save feature.

NOTE If you choose to close a file and then ask Word to save the changes, these are likewise saved in a new version when the Automatically Save Version on Close check box is checked. This option does *not* automatically save a new version when you close a file after leaving it unchanged. (In other words, the feature is incorrectly named: it automatically saves *changes* in a new version, regardless of whether the file is closed or not.)

Displaying an Older Version of a File

By default, Word assumes you want to work with the most recent version of your file, preventing you from inadvertently editing older versions. Sometimes you'll want to view an older version—perhaps to retrieve some language that had been deleted, but is now useful again. To view an older version of a file:

1. Choose File, Versions.
2. Choose the version from the Existing Versions window.
3. Click Open.

Word opens the second version in a separate window, tiling both windows, as shown in Figure 12.11. In the title bar of the window containing the older version of the file, Word displays the date and time that version was saved.

You can only open additional versions while you're working in the window containing your most current version. Word can open several versions at once, but it only displays two in the editing window. You can reorganize the screen so all versions are visible by choosing Arrange All from the Window menu.

Viewing Comments About a Version

If you've stored comments about a version, the first few words of those comments are visible in the Versions dialog box. If you need to read a comment that's longer than the space available, however, click the View Comments button. The View Comments dialog box opens, as shown in Figure 12.12. Notice that comments on older drafts can only be read—not edited. This is a security precaution to help prevent your colleagues from "rewriting history." It's less than airtight, however; someone who is determined to do so could export each version to a separate Word file and create a new file containing all the versions, along with the comments of their choice.

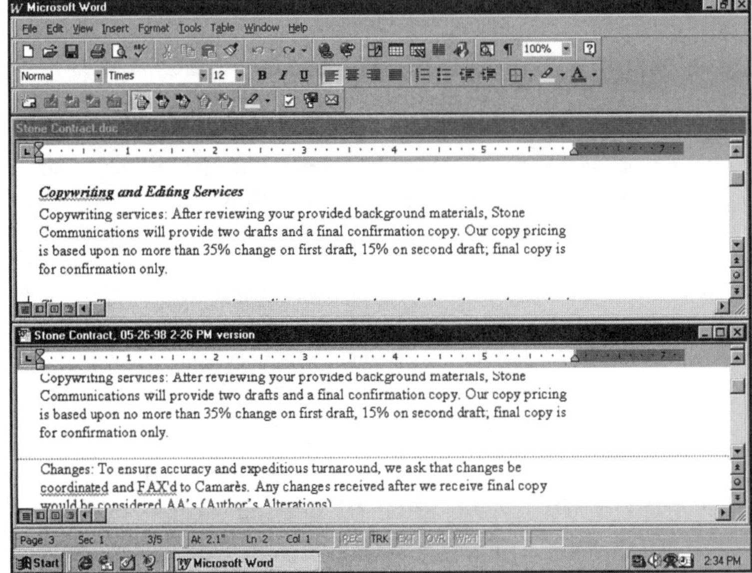

FIGURE 12.11
Displaying a current and older version of a file at the same time.

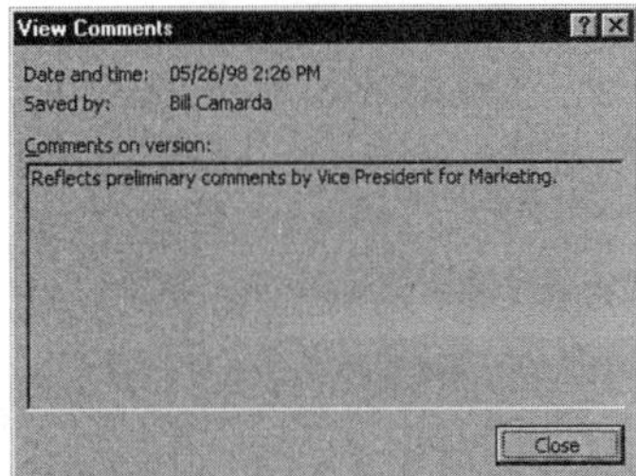

FIGURE 12.12
The View Comments dialog box.

CAUTION

Be cautious about using Versioning in an environment where multiple versions of Word are in use. Saving a Word 97 file to an earlier version of Word eliminates all older versions.

Keep an eye out for potential problems with Versioning in using Word 97 files with desktop publishing software. It remains to be seen how well Word 97 import filters will understand files containing multiple versions.

Using Word's Master Documents Feature

As Office administrator, you may be asked to coordinate team efforts to build large documents with many chapters or other document elements. You can streamline the process with master documents.

A master document is a container that holds hyperlinked pointers to individual documents that are called *subdocuments*. (A master document can also contain anything else a regular document can, including text, graphics, and formatting.)

Master documents closely resemble Word outlines, except that the material being organized and integrated can come from many different documents and locations. Master documents help you do the following:

- Quickly see where elements appear in a large document
- Reorganize a large document, even though its components are in different files
- Make sure that all parts of your document are formatted consistently, even if they're in different files
- Create cross-references, tables of contents, and other tables that encompass multiple documents
- Send one command that prints the entire document, even though the document is split into several files
- Create pagination and headers and footers that work across subdocuments, making it easier to build consistent large documents

Master documents also can speed up Word, because extremely large individual documents tend to be cumbersome to work with.

CAUTION

If you are working with a version of Word prior to Word 97, think twice about depending heavily on master documents. In previous versions of Word, they were not consistently reliable enough for production use. But master document reliability is much improved in Word 97 and 98. Keep in mind the following constraints:

The total size of a master document and its subdocuments together cannot exceed 32MB. On Word 98 for the Macintosh, the size of a master document and its subdocuments is limited by free memory available between the system memory and the applications (and can be reduced by misbehaving Macintosh applications that do not load where they're supposed to).

You can create a master document in two ways: from the ground up or by merging existing documents into a master document, which transforms the existing documents into subdocuments. When edited within the context of a master document, subdocuments behave much like Word document sections. They can have their own headers, footers, margins, page size, page orientation, and page numbers. But you can also override differences in sectional formatting by editing and printing from the master document, where the formatting follows a single consistent template.

Creating New Master Documents

To create a new master document, choose View, Master Document. Word displays the Outlining toolbar on the left (this toolbar is also displayed when you choose View, Outline) and the Master Document toolbar on the right (see Figure 12.13). Table 12.1 describes the buttons in the Master Document toolbar.

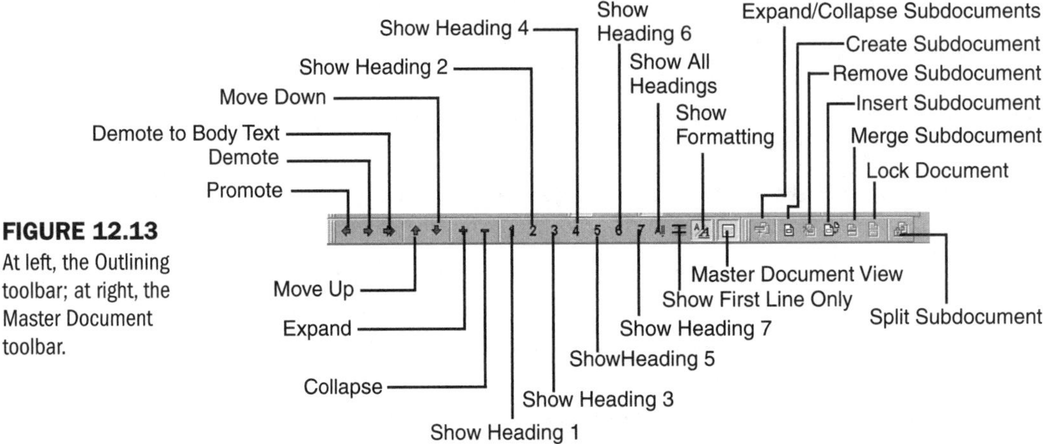

FIGURE 12.13
At left, the Outlining toolbar; at right, the Master Document toolbar.

Table 12.1 Word's Master Document Toolbar

Button	What It Does
Expand/Collapse Subdocuments	Toggles the display of subdocuments on and off
Create Subdocument	Turns selected outline items into individual subdocuments
Remove Subdocument	Removes a subdocument from a master document
Insert Subdocument	Opens a subdocument and inserts it in the current master document
Merge Subdocument	Combines two or more adjacent subdocuments into one subdocument
Split Subdocument	Splits one subdocument into two
Lock Document	Locks master document or subdocument so that it cannot be edited

Most experienced Word users prefer to begin creating master documents using Word's outlining tools, finishing the outline for the entire large document—and getting it approved, if necessary—before breaking the outline into subdocuments. Whether you choose this route or not, it makes sense to use consistent heading styles (Heading 1, Heading 2, and so on) throughout your document before you break it into subdocuments.

Creating a Subdocument

After you outline (or otherwise organize your document), your next step is to specify which text should be placed in subdocuments.

To transform a portion of a large document into a subdocument select it and click the Create Subdocument button. A small document icon appears in the upper-left corner of the area you select, and a light gray box appears around the text (see Figure 12.14).

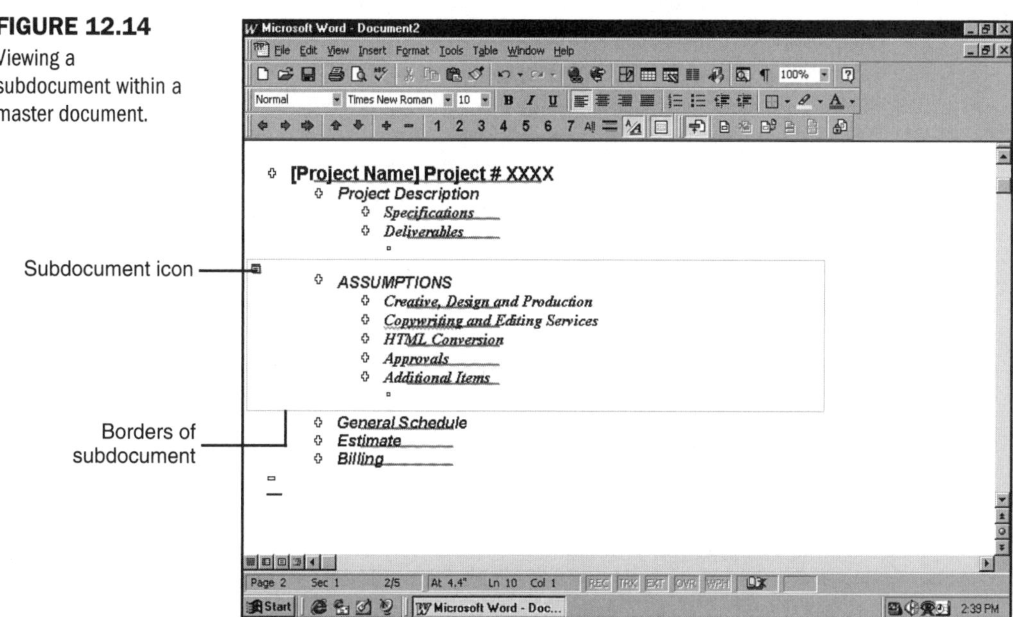

FIGURE 12.14
Viewing a subdocument within a master document.

If you've used Word's heading styles (or, in Word 97, the new Outline Level feature), you can create many subdocuments at once by displaying the Word outline level where you want the headings to break. For example, follow these steps if you have a large document and want to break it into subdocuments that begin at each second-level heading:

1. Click the 2 icon on the Outlining toolbar to display only first- and second-level headings.
2. Press Ctrl+A to select the entire document.
3. Click the Create Subdocument button.

Word creates a separate subdocument that starts at each second-level heading and contains all the text beneath that heading.

Transforming an Existing Document into a Master Document

If you already have a large document that you want to transform into a master document, it's easy to do so, as long as you've used Word's built-in heading styles (or in Word 97, the Outline Levels available in the Paragraph dialog box). Failing that, depending on how your document was formatted, it may be worth the time to add styles, by using one or more of the following techniques:

- Searching for manual formatting that corresponds to document headings, and replacing that formatting with Word's built-in heading styles, such as Heading 1, Heading 2, and so on
- Carefully using the AutoFormat feature to make these style changes for you
- Using Word 97's new Outline Levels feature to connect custom styles (which do not use the built-in heading style names) with outline levels, which Word can use as the top-level elements in subdocuments

NOTE Regarding this last method, in previous versions of Word, the only way to assign outline levels for use in automatic numbering or in master documents was to use Word's heading styles (Heading 1, Heading 2, and so on). This is no longer the case. Now, when you create a style, you can also specify an outline level from 1 to 9.

So, for example, you could create a style called Main Heading that included an outline level of 1. Then, in outlines and master documents, and when AutoFormatting, Word will treat paragraphs formatted with this style exactly as it would treat paragraphs formatted with the built-in Heading 1 style.

Do the following to create custom styles for your headings that include outline levels:

1. Format a paragraph of text (typically, one of your headings) the way you want that heading level to appear.
2. Make sure that the insertion point is in the paragraph and choose Format, Paragraph. The Paragraph dialog box opens.
3. In the Indents and Spacing tab, choose an outline level from the Outline Level drop-down box.
4. Click OK.
5. Click in the Style box on the Formatting toolbar.
6. Type the name of your new style and press Enter.
7. Repeat these steps to create styles for the remaining heading levels in your document, including the appropriate outline level in each style. ■

Saving a Master Document

When you save a master document, Word also saves all of its individual subdocuments. If these subdocuments don't have names yet, Word assigns names to them based on the first letters contained in them—adding numbers if the filenames would otherwise be identical—for example, Chapter1.doc, Chapter2.doc, Chapter3.doc, and so on.

After you save a subdocument, its text is contained in that subdocument, not in the master document. This has two important implications. First, you can edit subdocuments individually, as if they were regular documents. In fact, you can even use them in other master documents. Second, if you delete a subdocument or move it, its text disappears from the master document.

If you want to edit a subdocument in a way that affects the master document, open the subdocument from within the master document. To add elements that will reference the contents of other subdocuments, such as fields, a table of contents, or an index, for example, edit your subdocument from within the master document. Unless the master document is open, the subdocument will not have access to the other files it needs, and error messages are likely to be displayed in place of the information you want.

You can rename or move a subdocument—even to another workstation or server—as long as you open it from within the master document by double-clicking on its subdocument icon, and as long as the master document is still open when you resave it with its new name or location.

Opening a Subdocument

You can edit subdocuments in three ways. First, you can edit them within the master document. Second, from within the master document, you can double-click on the subdocument icon to display a file that contains only the subdocument. Third—and usually least desirable—you can open the subdocument without opening the master document and edit it the same way that you edit any other document.

A Word About Styles in Master Documents and Subdocuments

If you open a subdocument from within the master document, it will use the master document's styles. If you open the subdocument separately using Word's File, Open command, it will use any styles associated with the subdocument.

Some users are surprised at changes in a subdocument's formatting from one editing session to the next—this is usually the explanation. In general, it makes the most sense to work on your subdocuments from within the master document whenever that's practical, and maintain consistent formatting and styles that are all managed from the master document rather than individual documents.

Printing Master Documents and Subdocuments

To print all the contents of a master document, switch to Normal view and print from there. To print only selected contents, or an outline at only specified levels, use Word's Outline view tools. You also can print individual subdocuments by double-clicking on them and then printing them as you would any other document.

NOTE If you print from Normal view, Word places a section break between subdocuments. By default, this is a next page section break, meaning that it functions as a section break and a page break combined.

If you want the next subdocument to start printing on the same page as the previous one, delete the next page section break and use the Insert, Break dialog box to insert a continuous section break instead.

Adding an Existing Document to a Master Document

Sometimes you may be creating a master document largely from scratch, but you have one existing document you would like to incorporate into it. Follow these steps to incorporate an existing document as a subdocument in a master document:

1. Open the master document. The Outlining and Master Document toolbars appear.
2. Place the insertion point where you want to insert the new document.
3. Click the Insert Subdocument button. The Insert Subdocument dialog box appears.
4. Find and select the document you want to insert. Click on OK. The document appears in a box in your master document.
5. To open the subdocument you've inserted, double-click on its subdocument icon.

When Word saves a file that has been turned into a subdocument, the file retains its original name. If you import a subdocument that uses a different template from the master document, the master document's template applies if you open or print the subdocument from within the master document. If you open your document without using the master document, the individual file's template takes effect.

Adding an Index, Table of Contents, or Other Table

Master documents make it possible to build indexes, tables of contents, figures, or authorities that encompass multiple documents. To do so, perform the following steps:

1. Open the master document. (Make sure that all subdocuments are present and accounted for.)
2. Switch to Normal view.
3. Place the insertion point where you want the index or table.
4. Choose Index and Tables from the Insert menu, and follow the same steps you normally would to create indexes or tables of contents.

Working with Others on the Same Master Document

Because master documents are likely to be used by many people—each responsible for a component—Word makes special provisions for sharing them.

When you open a master document, you can edit any subdocument that you created in the first place. You can read the ones that someone else created, but you can't edit them without unlocking them first.

To unlock a subdocument, place the insertion point inside it and click on the Unlock Document toolbar button. You cannot retrieve and edit a file that someone else is currently editing.

To determine who created a file, Word checks the Author text box in the Summary tab of the file's Properties dialog box (File, Properties). If you change that information, you can change the subdocument's read-write behavior.

Managing Read-Write Privileges

Normally, you can't write to a document if someone else is using it—even if he or she is viewing it as read-only. If you have to be able to edit a file at all times, you can reserve read-write privileges by setting a password. You can accomplish this by performing the following steps:

1. Open the master document or subdocument and save it by choosing File, Save As.
2. Click Options. The Save tab of the Options dialog box opens.
3. If you want to prevent others from writing changes to the file, type a password in the Write Reservation Password text box. Type the password again to confirm it. (And, as always, store the password in a secure place where you can gain access to it.)
4. Press Enter. Word will ask you to confirm any passwords you've added.
5. Type the password again and click OK.

If you want to discourage, but not prevent, changes by others, you can check Read-Only Recommended. When the file is opened, Word encourages users to open the file as read-only, but doesn't require them to do so.

Reorganizing Your Master Document

All of Word's outlining tools work in master documents as well, once you click the Expand Subdocuments toolbar button to see your detailed document outline. You can move body text or headings within a subdocument or between subdocuments. You can promote or demote headings. You can select and move large blocks of copy by displaying only high-level headings and cutting and pasting those.

You can also move all the contents of a subdocument. To do so, first click its subdocument icon to select it, and then drag it wherever you want.

Merging and Splitting Subdocuments

You can combine two subdocuments into one. Or, perhaps you would rather split one subdocument into two when it gets too big or when you want to delegate parts of it to another author. To combine two subdocuments, perform the following steps:

1. Move both subdocuments next to each other in the master document.
2. Select both subdocuments.
3. Click the Merge Subdocument button.
4. Save the master document. When Word saves the merged subdocument, it uses the name of the first subdocument contained in it.

NOTE You can also select several subdocuments that are not adjacent. Click the first subdocument icon, hold down the Shift key, and click the icons of each other subdocument that you want to select.

To split one subdocument into two, follow these steps:

1. Place the insertion point where you want the subdocument to split.
2. Click the Split Subdocument toolbar button.
3. Save the master document.

Removing a Subdocument

To remove a subdocument but retain its text in the master document, click on the subdocument icon, and click the Remove Subdocument toolbar button.

To remove the subdocument and also remove its text, click its subdocument icon and press Delete. The document file remains on the disk, but it is no longer attached in any way to the master document.

Troubleshooting Master Documents

Because master documents are typically used on large projects that involve quite a bit of effort, when they run into problems there's a lot at stake.

If Word reports that a master document may be corrupt, select all the contents of your master document (including subdocument contents) and copy them to a new document. You may have to copy the contents of subdocuments individually, or you can create a new master document that incorporates the existing subdocuments, which are rarely, if ever, damaged.

If Word won't save a master document, it may be out of memory. Try this:

1. Cancel the save, close other programs and files, and try again.
2. If this fails, convert some subdocuments into text within the master document by selecting them and clicking the Remove Subdocuments toolbar button. Then try saving again.

Also make sure that the version of Word 97 you're using has been updated at least to SR-1, which contains some master document bug fixes.

If you're still having problems saving a large master document, consider the following alternatives:

- Use Word's Insert, File feature, which enables you to insert the entire contents of a file into your document. This is just like pasting the text into your document, and creates no links with the source file.

- Use the {INCLUDETEXT} field, which incorporates an entire Word document or a bookmarked selection from one. By default, {INCLUDETEXT} allows you to edit the text in your new document and save changes back to the source document by pressing Ctrl+Shift+F7.
- Use Office 97 Binder, which allows you to group many documents together for printing and distribution, but doesn't offer the editing or management capabilities of Word's master documents.

Using Excel's Workgroup Tools

Thus far, you've learned about Word's features for organizing a document in a workgroup. But in many organizations, the key workgroup tool for organizing and planning is Excel. Excel 97 and 98 also include the following several powerful features for workgroups:

- The Comments feature, much like Word's, which allows one or more reviewers to comment on individual cells
- The Share Workbook feature, which allows more than one individual to work in an Excel workbook at the same time
- The Merge Workbook feature, which allows you to integrate and reconcile data from differing versions of the same workbook

NOTE Another feature, not covered in this chapter, is Data Consolidation, which allows you to compile repetitive, highly-structured data from many worksheets into one summary worksheet, or from many workbooks into a summary workbook.

Using Excel's Comments Feature

Often, you may want to make a comment on a value (or other element) of a cell in an Excel worksheet. To do so, select the cell you want to comment on and choose Insert, Comment. A yellow "sticky tag" appears pointing to the cell; you can enter your comment beneath your name.

If you plan to make several comments at once, choose View, Toolbars, Reviewing to display Excel's Reviewing toolbar (see Figure 12.15). From there, you can click the New Comment button each time you want to make a comment.

To systematically review comments in a workbook, display the Reviewing Toolbar, and click Next Comment. Read the comment, make any necessary changes to the workbook, and then (if you want) click Delete Comment to eliminate the comment.

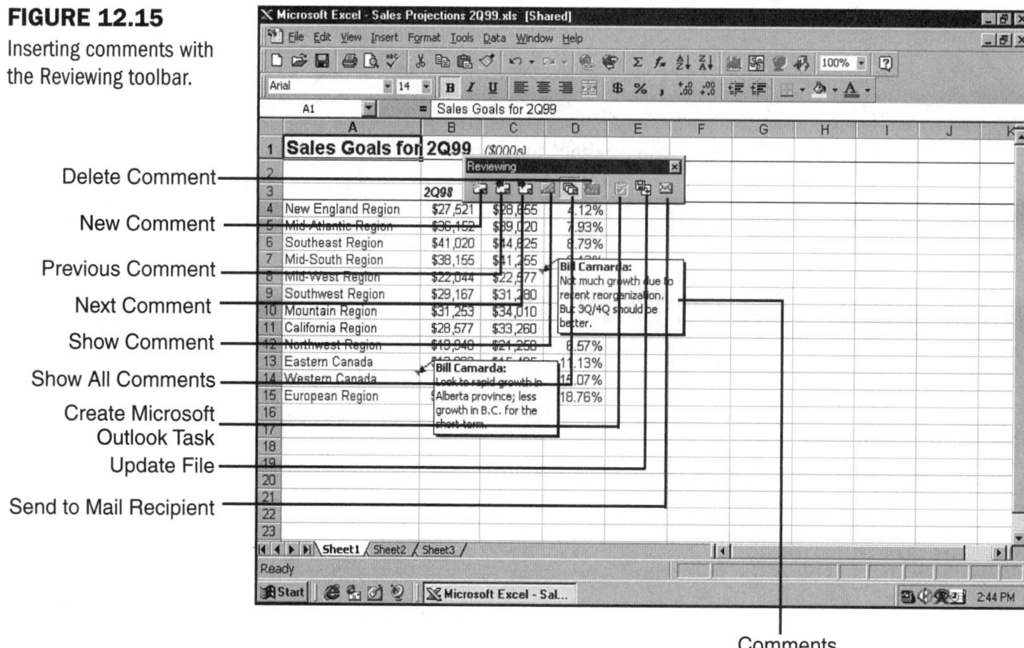

FIGURE 12.15
Inserting comments with the Reviewing toolbar.

Using Excel's Share Workbook Feature

Using shared workbooks, several members of a workgroup can edit the same Excel 97 or 98 workbook at the same time. Excel tracks the changes each user makes, and provides a mechanism for reconciling potential conflicts they may introduce.

Shared workbooks have many applications. You can use them to provide information that many salespeople or telephone representatives need at the same time, while storing and updating it centrally. Or you might allow individual managers to update worksheets in their areas of responsibility, while maintaining control over a summary worksheet that shows how the company as a whole is doing.

To set up a workbook for sharing, perform the following steps:

1. Choose Tools, Share Workbook. The Share Workbook dialog box opens, showing who currently has the workbook open (see Figure 12.16).
2. Mark the Allow Changes by More Than One User check box.
3. Click OK.

CAUTION

Sharing a workbook opens it to any user who can reach it—in other words, any user who has rights to access the file on the network. Use Excel's separate password features, covered in Chapter 34, "Supporting Office," to determine who can open or modify your shared workbooks.

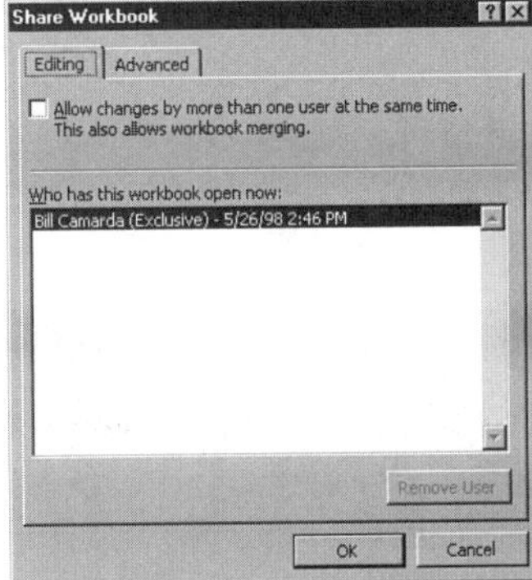

FIGURE 12.16
In the Share Workbook dialog box, you can set up a workbook to be shared throughout your workgroup.

> **CAUTION**
> Excel 97 may crash with an invalid page fault if you use shared workbooks containing more than 98 worksheets, or slightly fewer than 98 worksheets if they contain an unusually large amount of data.

Updating Workbooks to Reflect Your Colleagues' Changes

Changes that others make to a workbook are not instantly reflected in the workbook. By default, you only see them when you save the workbook. If this is insufficient, you can force regular updates as follows:

1. Choose Tools, Share Workbook. The Share Workbook dialog box opens.
2. Make sure the workbook is already shared, and click the Advanced tab (see Figure 12.17).

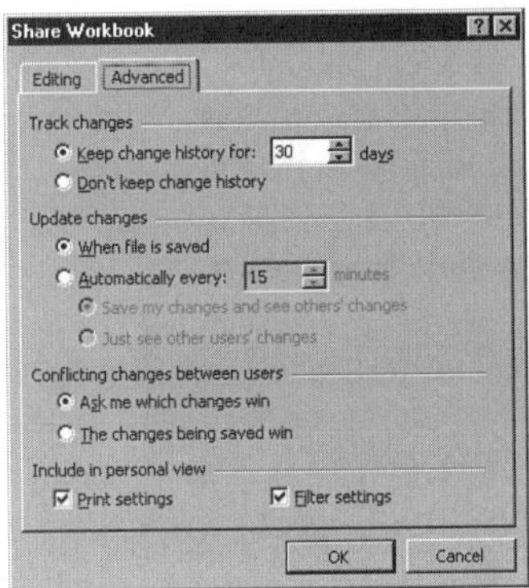

FIGURE 12.17
In the Advanced tab, you can control how Excel manages the shared workbook.

3. Mark the Automatically Every option button, and use the scroll box to specify how frequently you want the changes updated. The default setting is 15 minutes. By default, Excel saves your file whenever it displays new changes; if you prefer not to save at each update, mark the Just See Other Users' Changes option button.

4. Click OK.

When you save a shared workbook in which one of your colleagues has made a change, Excel notifies you that a change has been made and marks the cell. If you select the cell (or hover the mouse pointer over it), Excel displays a ScreenTip showing who made the change, and which change he or she made (see Figure 12.18).

FIGURE 12.18
When you select a cell that a colleague has changed, Excel tells you the details.

Sales Goals for 2Q99	(000s)		
	2Q98	2Q99	Year over Year Change
New England Region	$27,521	$28,655	4.12%
Mid-Atlantic Region	$36,152	$39,020	7.93%
Southeast Region	$41,020	$44,625	8.79%
Mid-South Region	$38,155	$41,255	8.12%
Mid-West Region	$22,044	$22,577	2.42%
Southwest Region	$29,167	$31,280	7.24%
Mountain Region	$31,253	$34,010	
California Region	$28,577	$31,255	
Northwest Region	$19,940	$21,2[illegible]	
Eastern Canada	$13,862	$15,405	
Western Canada	$9,755	$11,225	
European Region	$10,114	$12,011	18.76%

Bill Camarda, 5/26/98 2:48 PM:
Changed cell C11 from '$33,260.00' to '$31,255.00'.

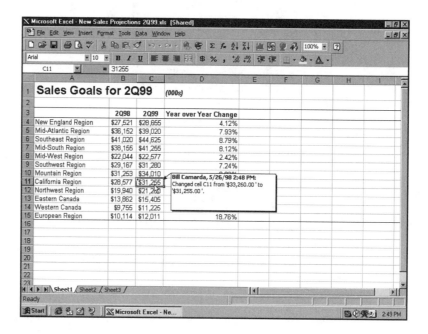

Resolving Conflicts Between Changes

What if you enter a value in a shared workbook, and a few minutes later a colleague enters a conflicting value in the same cell? By default, Excel displays a dialog box showing the conflict, as shown in Figure 12.19. You can then choose which value to accept, yours or someone else's.

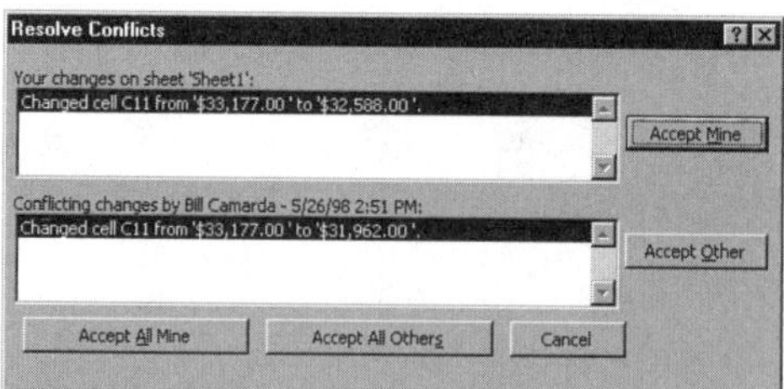

FIGURE 12.19
In the Resolve Conflicts dialog box, you can choose between your value and conflicting values set by one or more colleagues.

If you don't even want to review a colleague's conflicting changes, you can set Excel to disregard them by performing the following steps:

1. Choose Tools, Share Workbook. The Share Workbook dialog box opens.

2. Make sure the workbook is already shared, and click the Advanced tab.
3. Mark the The Changes Being Saved Win option button.
4. Click OK.

Now, whenever you save, Excel saves your changes and discards anyone else's conflicting changes without ever displaying the Resolve Changes dialog box.

NOTE As Office administrator, you may be called upon to make sure that only authorized individuals set Excel to disregard conflicting changes without even reviewing them.

Systematically Reviewing Changes

By default, you only see your colleagues' changes marked in your workbook until the next time you save them, but you can view all the changes that have made since the workbook was shared, and systematically review them, accepting or rejecting them one at a time. To change the way you view colleagues' revisions in a shared workbook, follow these steps:

1. Choose Tools, Track Changes, Highlight Changes. The Highlight Changes dialog box opens (see Figure 12.20).

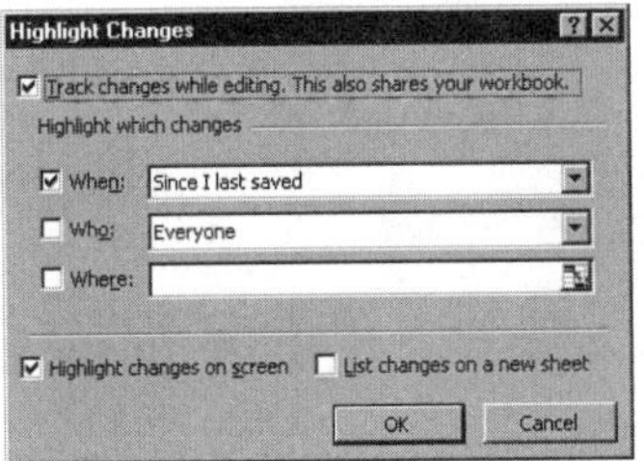

FIGURE 12.20
In the Highlight Changes dialog box you can control which changes you want to view.

2. In the When drop-down box, choose which changes you want to view: changes made since you last saved; changes you haven't reviewed; changes since a specific date; or all changes.
3. If you want to review changes made by a specific individual, mark the Who check box and choose the individual whose changes you want to review. Another alternative, Everyone But Me, allows you to ignore the changes you made in the workbook to focus on the changes made by your colleagues.
4. If you want to view changes to a specific range of cells, mark the Where check box. Then click in the worksheet and drag the mouse pointer to select a range of cells you want to review.
5. By default, Excel highlights all changes on the screen. You can also have the changes summarized on a separate new sheet in your workbook. If this sounds helpful, mark the List Changes on a New Sheet check box.
6. Click OK.

Beyond viewing changes, someone in your workgroup will be called upon to resolve them. Here's how it's done:

1. Choose Tools, Track Changes, Accept or Reject Changes. The Select Changes to Accept or Reject dialog box opens (see Figure 12.21).

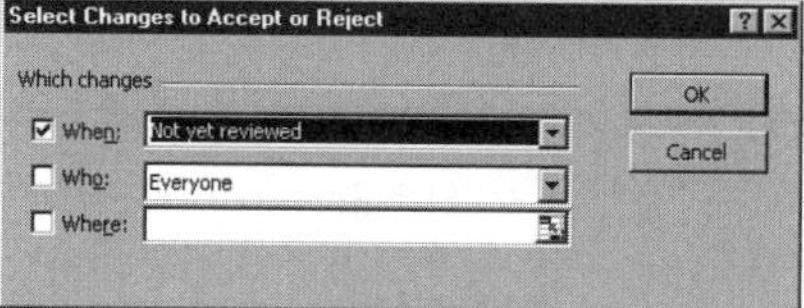

FIGURE 12.21
Specifying which tracked changes you want to resolve.

2. Using the When, Who, and Where boxes, specify which changes you want to resolve, as described in the previous steps.
3. Click OK. Excel selects the first change in your workbook and offers you the chance to accept or reject it (see Figure 12.22). At this stage, you can also choose Accept All or Reject All to accept or reject all of the changes at once.

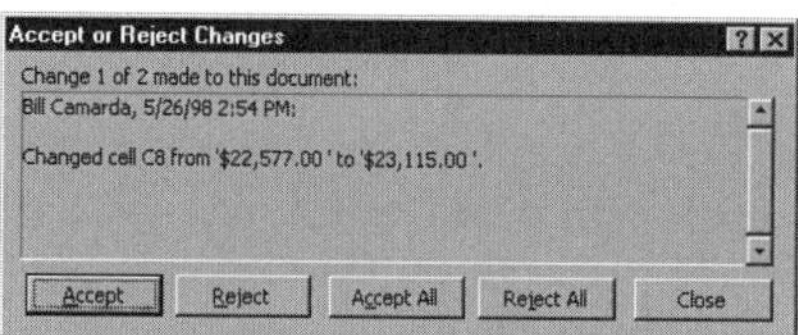

FIGURE 12.22
Excel tells you about the tracked change and gives you the opportunity to accept or reject it.

If you choose to accept or reject the changes one at a time, Excel will continue through the workbook, flagging proposed changes one at a time. You can stop at any time by clicking Close.

Tracking the History of a Shared Workbook

By default, Excel tracks all the changes made to a shared workbook for 30 days. You can adjust this setting—or stop Excel from tracking changes—in the Advanced tab of the Share Workbook dialog box (as shown earlier in Figure 12.17). If you want to track *all* changes made to your workbook—even at the risk of slowing down Excel a bit—you can reset the value as high as 32,767 days—nearly 90 years.

CAUTION

As soon as you stop sharing a workbook, all shared workbook histories disappear. If you want to archive the decision-making process that went into a workbook, make a backup copy before you turn off workbook sharing.

Limitations of Shared Workbooks

Several of Excel's features are off-limits in a shared workbook. You cannot do the following:

- Assign, change, or remove passwords
- Delete worksheets
- Insert or delete blocks of cells (although you may insert or delete rows and columns)
- Insert or revise charts, pictures, objects, hyperlinks, or drawings that use Excel's drawing tools
- Merge cells
- Create or apply conditional formats
- Set up or change data validation
- View, change, or save scenarios
- Group or outline data
- Insert automatic subtotals
- Create data tables
- Create PivotTables or change their layout
- Change dialog boxes or menus
- Create, edit, or assign macros within the shared workbook (although you can record a macro and save it to a workbook that isn't shared)

Protecting a Workgroup for Sharing with Track Changes

Earlier in this chapter, you saw how to protect a Word document so that no edits could be made without Track Changes turned on. You can do the same thing in Excel with a shared workbook.

To protect a shared workbook so that all changes are tracked and nobody can turn off tracking without a password, follow these steps *before* you share the workbook:

1. Choose Tools, Protection, Protect and Share Workbook. The Protect Shared Workbook dialog box opens (see Figure 12.23).

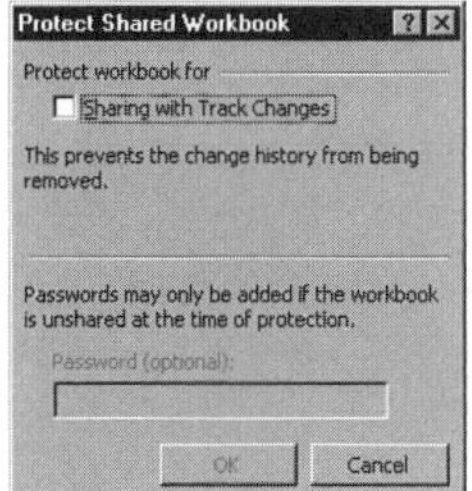

FIGURE 12.23
The Protect Shared Workbook dialog box.

2. Mark the Sharing with Track Changes check box.
3. Enter a password and click OK. The Confirm Password dialog box opens.
4. Enter the password again and click OK.

Using Excel's Merge Workbooks Feature

In some cases, your team members will need to create separate copies of the same shared workbook as they work. For example, one of your team members may need to work on a notebook PC while traveling; she may use File, Save As to save a copy of the workbook you've been sharing. You can merge multiple copies of the same workbook together, resulting in a workbook that looks the same as it would have if all changes were made to the same shared workbook.

CAUTION

For the Merge Workbooks feature to work, you must first do the following *before* you make copies of the workbook.

1. Share the workbook.
2. Make sure the Track Changes (history) feature is turned on.

You must also merge the workbooks within the time period you specified in Track Changes.

To merge multiple copies of a workbook, perform the following steps:

1. Open the shared workbook that you want to import changes into.
2. Choose Tools, Merge Workbooks. (This menu item is only available if you have a shared workbook open.) The Select Files to Merge Into Current Workbook dialog box appears.
3. Browse to and select the workbook (or workbooks) that you want to incorporate. (You can merge several workbooks at the same time, using Shift+click—assuming each of these files began life together as the same shared workbook.)
4. Click OK.

CHAPTER 13

Enhancing PowerPoint's Value in Team Settings

You can streamline your office's use of PowerPoint through the development and implementation of presentation standards—a standard template, approved graphics and animation files, and an overall look for all of your company's presentations. PowerPoint's Presentation Designs make it simple to create consistency without limiting creativity; you can build your own templates and control user access to them. You also can make presentation development a team effort with PowerPoint tools such as Meeting Minder and presentation conferencing.

Standardizing on Custom Presentation Formats

PowerPoint offers more than 20 Presentation Design templates to help you create presentations, signs, and flyers, as shown in Figure 13.1. Within any company, division, or department, it is often desirable for presentations to have a standard look and feel.

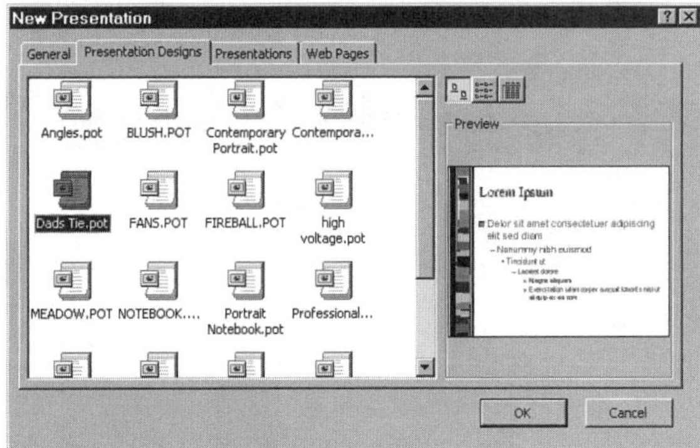

FIGURE 13.1
PowerPoint's Presentation Designs folder contains 21 installed templates, plus any that users have created and saved in a template format.

Although too much standardization can stifle creativity, setting some basics—background colors, text formats, and so on—often enhances productivity, and may even free your designers to be more creative. They can turn their attention to more powerful features, such as graphics, photographs, video, sound, and animation effects.

Choosing Standardization Levels

When standardizing a presentation format, it's best to decide the level of standardization you want to impose, as in the following:

- **Complete control.** Standardize the template, fonts, number of bullets per slide, colors for charts, acceptable clip art images, and the level of multimedia to be used, if appropriate for your output methods.
- **General control**. Choose a template, select font styles and colors, but otherwise let users add presentation content and extra elements as they see fit.
- **Bare minimum**. Choose a template, but beyond that take a hands-off approach to presentation content.

The more control you impose, the more consistent your presentations will be. At the same time, too much consistency can be boring. At a long meeting with many presentations, the audience is likely to lose interest if all the presentations look exactly alike.

Taking a hands-off approach encourages creativity. Presentations from different departments and divisions will have a lot more variety—in the choices of fonts, colors, and the use of animation and sound. Too much variation, however, may prove distracting. In addition, this strategy may highlight the varying skill levels in different departments—one department may give a sharp, high-tech presentation, while another gives a more simplistic show because they're less familiar with PowerPoint's "bells and whistles."

Implementing Standardization

Regardless of the level of control you seek, imposing that control is the next step, as in the following:

- To control the entire look of a presentation, you must fine tune your presentation template and save it to the Presentation Designs folder with all fonts, colors, layouts, and Master elements setup.
- If you only want to control a few features, make sure these attributes are set and saved as part of the Presentation Design file. Although the presentation will contain default fonts and colors, your developers will have the freedom to change them.

To ensure that your staff uses these approved presentation templates, you can take one of the following actions:

- Create a macro that users are instructed to invoke as soon as they open a new presentation. The macro can close the existing presentation and open a new one, using the standardized template. Another macro approach might be to record the process of applying the standardized presentation template to the open presentation, thus overriding the open presentation's formats. This latter approach does not control anything more than the content of a template—colors, fonts, and any graphics inserted on the Master.
- For ultimate control, remove all the other Presentation Design templates from the Presentation Designs folder, moving them to a folder not within the Templates folder. Although they will still be on the system if anyone wants to use them, they're not there in plain sight to tempt anyone. Your users will have no choice but to use either the blank presentation or the standardized presentation template.

Customizing Presentations

When creating your standardized template, remember the following PowerPoint features that are at your disposal for customizing a presentation:

- You can place items on the Master to have them appear on every slide in the presentation. Any formatting applied to the Master will be applied to all slides based upon that Master. You might do this with your company logo or an approved graphic. You open the Master by choosing View, Master, Slide Master (or Title Master). Figure 13.2 shows the slide master for the Dad's Tie.pot template. If the presentation is saved as a template (.pot extension), the Master content will apply to all presentations started using the template.

- You can create your own presentation design templates to be used as the basis for new presentations. To create an entire presentation—titles and most text included—choose File, Save As, and use the Save As Type option to create a Presentation Template (.pot). Figure 13.3 shows the Save As dialog box with the presentation file format selected.

FIGURE 13.2
Format text and insert graphics on the Master to control the content of all the slides in the presentation.

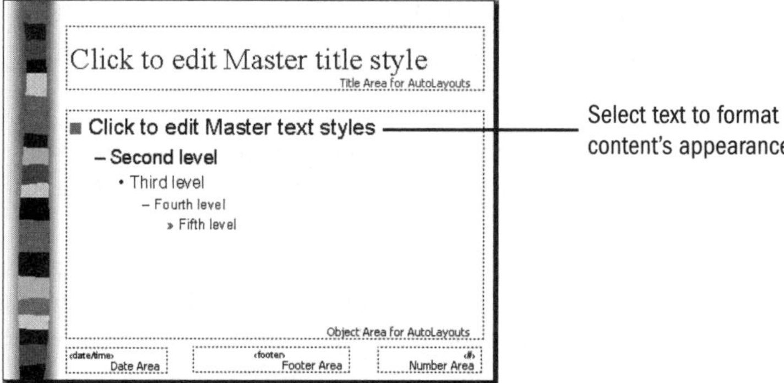

FIGURE 13.3
To create a custom template, choose the Presentation Template format and save the file to the Presentation Designs folder.

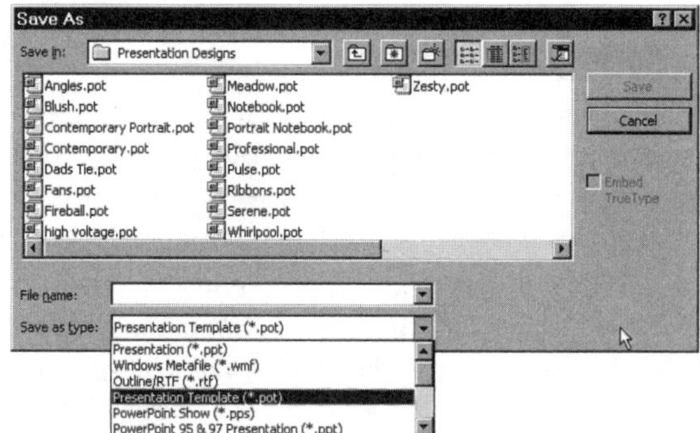

- You can choose Tools, Options to work with PowerPoint's defaults to control the way the software works. Figure 13.4 shows the Options dialog box with the Advanced tab on top. For more information on standardizing the user interface, including Options dialog box settings, see Chapter 8, "Customizing PowerPoint to Your Organization's Needs."

FIGURE 13.4
Choose a default directory for all saved presentations in the Options dialog box.

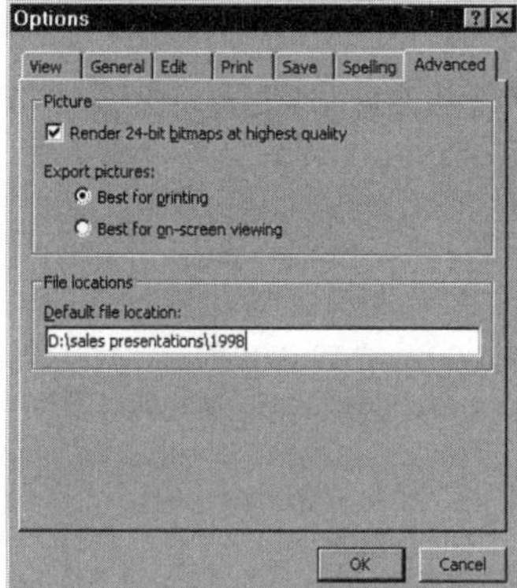

Using Workgroup Features

PowerPoint includes two significant features that make presentation building a true team effort. Both tools enable two or more users to watch, work on, and comment on a presentation in progress. This process is completely interactive—all members of the group can see the other members' comments and view the show simultaneously.

Using Presentation Conferencing

Presentation Conferencing is a tool, set up with a wizard, that enables two or more users on a network to watch a presentation. One member of the group must act as Stage Manager and control the progress of the show. The other members of the team watch the show and make their own annotations for the whole group to see. As the show progresses, the Stage Manager can tweak the show in terms of timing per slide, and add notes for improvements.

Before starting the Presentation Conference Wizard, it's a good idea to perform some of the following advance work:

- Decide who will be the Stage Manager. Like a banker in Monopoly, this person should be someone whom everyone trusts—in this case to take notes, be objective, and pay attention as the team works together to watch and make suggestions for the improvement of the presentation.
- Determine your connection method. If you're on a network in your office, write a list of every team members' computer name/number as they're seen on the network. If you'll be connecting over the Internet, get a list of their Internet addresses.
- Decide which slides you're going to see—the whole slide show or just a section of it. Set this up by choosing Set Up Show from the Slide Show menu. Enter the From and To slide numbers and click OK.

To set up and run a Presentation Conference, perform the following steps:

1. Start the Presentation Conference Wizard by choosing Presentation Conference from the Tools menu. The Wizard opens with a dialog box that describes the steps involved in setting up the conference (see Figure 13.5).
2. Click Next to begin the first step. To go back at any point, click Back.

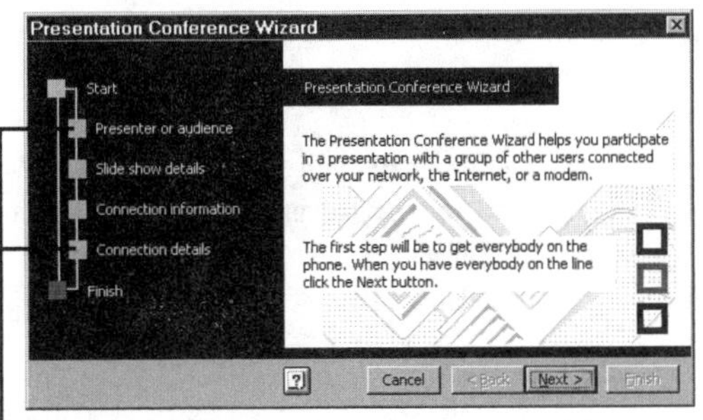

FIGURE 13.5
The first page of the wizard shows the general steps involved. If you click on a particular step, you'll see what information or decisions it requires.

Click these step boxes to view the dialog box for the corresponding step

3. In the next dialog box, select the role you will play. As mentioned, you should decide ahead of time who will be the Presenter. All others must choose the Audience option (see Figure 13.6). Click Next to proceed.

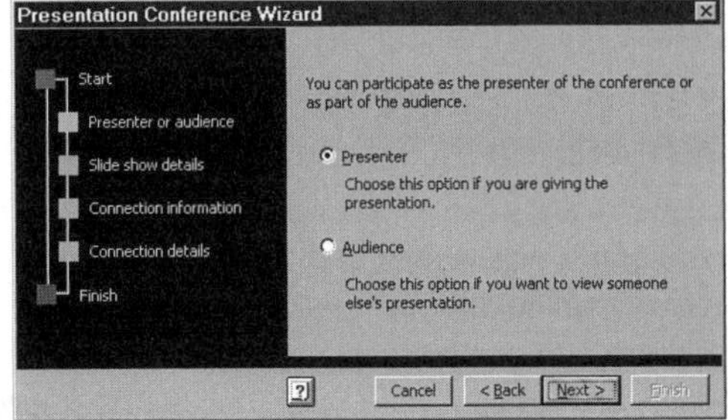

FIGURE 13.6
Choose the role of Presenter or Audience. You should decide who will do which job before starting the wizard.

4. Show All Slides is the default; click Next to accept it. To change the slides that will be shown, click Cancel and choose Set Up Show from the Slide Show menu.
5. In the Connection Information dialog box, follow the instructions for a Network connection or an Internet connection. (Remember, you should have made this decision in advance.) Click Next when you're ready to move on.
6. Enter the network addresses or Internet addresses (depending on your connection method) for each member of the audience. Click Add after typing each one. If this is a group you'll be working with again, click the Save List button. Click Next to go to the Finish dialog box.
7. Click Finish to begin the Presentation Conference.

After the conference begins, the team members will watch the show as the Stage Manager controls it. Any team member can annotate slides that appear onscreen merely by clicking on them. The mouse pointer will turn into a pen, and team member can write on the slide. The rest of the team can see the annotations, and make their own responding annotations as necessary.

The Stage Manager controls the show. He or she makes notes by right-clicking the screen and choosing Speaker's Notes from the shortcut menu. The Manager also reviews the timing of the slides and the ongoing annotations of the audience. If an idea or problem comes up that requires action, the Manager can invoke the Meeting Minder by right-clicking the screen and choosing Meeting Minder from the shortcut menu.

NOTE If you and a coworker want to review a presentation together, connect your two computers with a null modem cable (available at most computer stores or office supply superstores). Choose View on Two Screens from the Slide Show menu. Your screen and that of the connected computer will show the presentation simultaneously.

Using the Meeting Minder

The Meeting Minder is a task-assignment tool that you can use in conjunction with the Presentation Conference tool or on its own during a discussion or formal meeting. To use the Meeting Minder to assign tasks to the team, perform the following steps:

1. Invoke the Meeting Minder during a conference by right-clicking the active slide and choosing Meeting Minder from the shortcut menu. To invoke it on its own (not during a conference), choose Meeting Minder from the Tools menu. A two-tabbed dialog box appears (see Figure 13.7).

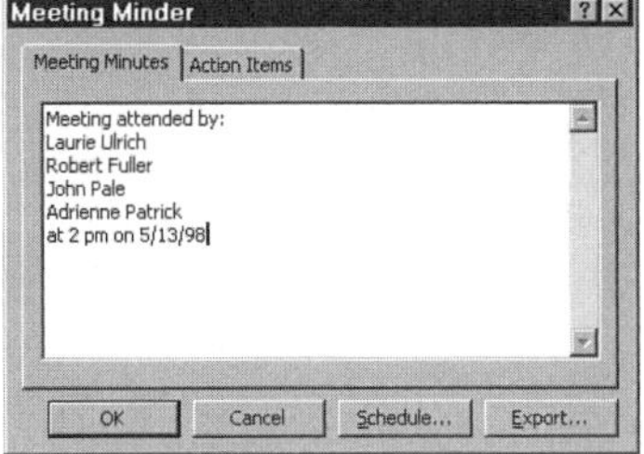

FIGURE 13.7
The Meeting Minder enables you to take meeting notes and/or set up tasks and assign them to members of your presentation team.

- **Meeting Minutes**. Simply type notes, comments, or thoughts into this box during the meeting. The box will hold over 50 lines of text, and word wrap is in effect. If you want to use your notes in a printable (and more editable) Word document, click Export. Click Schedule to open Outlook and enter an appointment or task related to the meeting minutes.
- **Action Items**. As the presenter in a conference, or in a managerial role in a meeting, you can assign tasks to different members of the team. Click this tab to enter a task description, assign the task to someone, and enter a completion date. Click Add to add it to the list of tasks (see Figure 13.8). Click Export to send the task list to Word for printing/editing or to Outlook for scheduling.

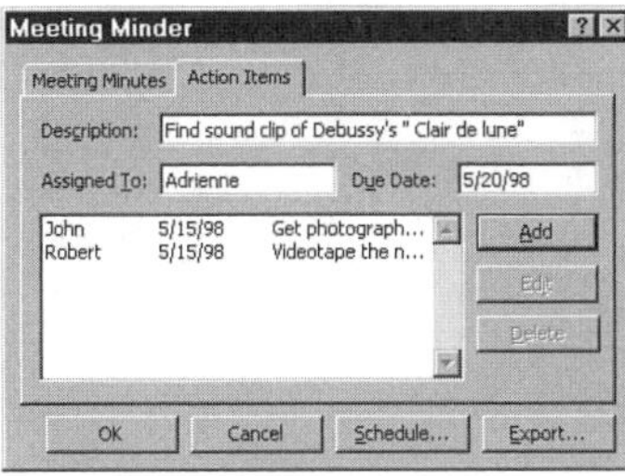

FIGURE 13.8
Set up tasks and assign them to a team member. Click Add to build the list of tasks.

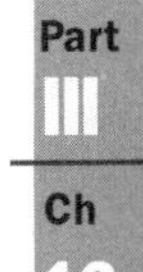

2. Make your entries into one or both of the tabs, and click OK. This will save your entries and close the dialog box.

Your Meeting Minder notes and tasks will accrue for this presentation. When you choose Meeting Minder again (during a subsequent conference or in another meeting) with this particular presentation open, the previous meetings' notes and tasks will appear and you can add to them. To save separate meeting notes and/or tasks, click the Export button (in either tab) to send the content to Word and save them as a document. You can do this for each meeting, generating a separate Word document in each case. It's a good idea to save these files with a name that reflects the meeting date—this will make specific documents easier to track down later. ●

CHAPTER 14

Workgroup Scheduling and Contact Management with Outlook 98

In this chapter, you learn about Microsoft Outlook's collaborative features for planning and scheduling meetings, which include the capability to find available time on other people's calendars. You also find out how Outlook users who use Microsoft Exchange Server can create and use public folders to share information. Finally, you learn to customize Outlook's forms, changing the ways Outlook looks and feels while you work with Outlook items.

Using Group Scheduling

Microsoft Outlook uses your organization's email system together with Outlook's Calendar and Contact features to enable you to schedule meetings and manage contacts within your organization. In this chapter, you go beyond tracking your own calendar and contacts and learn how to share this information with members of your workgroup.

Sending a Meeting Request

Suppose you need to schedule a meeting with several members of your organization. Traditionally, you might call each person to inquire about availability, or even send each person an email message. Comparing everyone's obligations and free time to find the best opportunity for a meeting is quite a chore.

Outlook makes the scheduling process faster and more reliable, taking advantage of both the Outlook Calendar and email. As long as everyone in your organization is diligent in keeping an up-to-date calendar, you're able to find out quickly when people are available and then send them invitations to your meeting.

Later in this chapter, you learn how to check for available times on other people's schedules before you send them a meeting request. If you can't rely on the accuracy of other people's calendars, you might prefer to just send them the meeting request and wait for their responses.

To send a meeting request to someone, follow these steps:

1. Open your calendar in any view.
2. Choose Actions, New Meeting Request to display the Meeting form (shown in Figure 14.1).

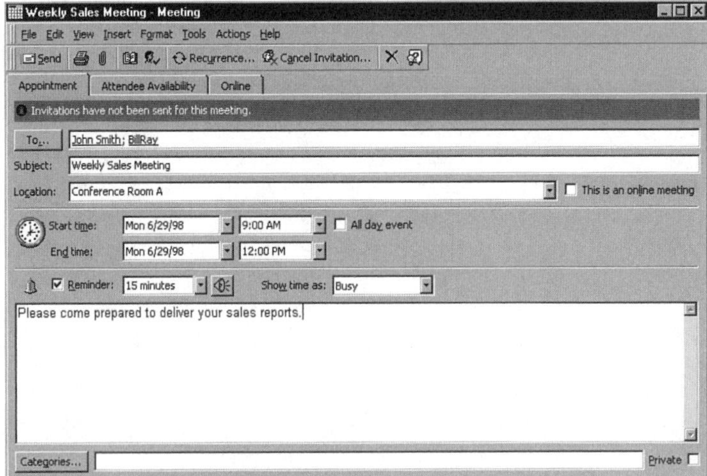

FIGURE 14.1
Use the Meeting form to schedule a meeting with your colleagues.

Outlook uses the term form to refer to a window, such as the one shown in Figure 14.1, that you use to work with items in an Outlook folder. For more information, see "Customizing Forms in Outlook" later in this chapter.

3. Click the To button to display the Select Attendees and Resources dialog box (shown in Figure 14.2). If you have more than one address book, select the address book you want to use with the Show Names From The drop-down box.

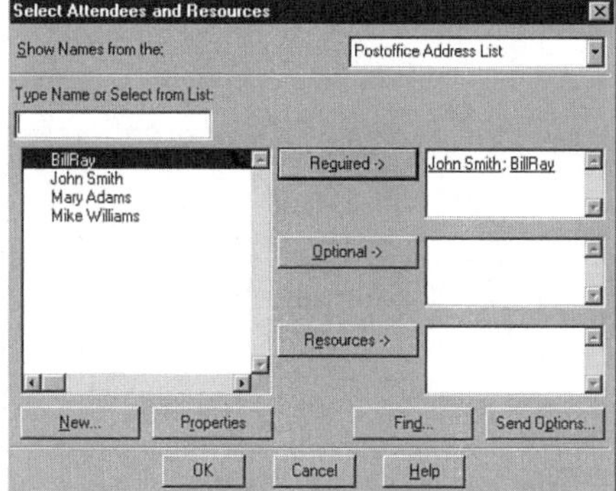

FIGURE 14.2
Select the people whom you want to invite to the meeting and the resources you want to reserve.

4. Select the name of a person (or a resource) you want to invite to the meeting from the list box. Click Required or Optional to invite a person, or Resources to reserve a resource such as a conference room or some video equipment. Click OK when you have made all your selections.
5. Fill the remaining fields in the Meeting form, including the date and time of the meeting, and any comments you want to send in the message.
6. Click Send to send the meeting request to each person or resource via email.

Outlook marks the meeting on your calendar and sends the meeting request to each person or resource you selected. You can double-click on the meeting item in your calendar to check the responses from the people you have invited.

Receiving a Meeting Request

If you have been invited to a meeting, a message appears in your Inbox, as shown in Figure 14.3. Double-click on the message to open it in its own window, as shown in Figure 14.4.

You can respond to the meeting request by clicking Accept, Tentative, or Decline. After you click one of these buttons, Outlook presents the response options shown in Figure 14.5.

FIGURE 14.3
A new meeting request has arrived in the Inbox.

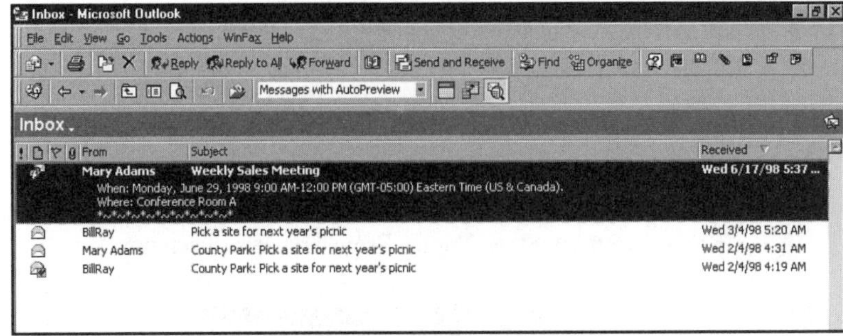

FIGURE 14.4
The Meeting window shows the details of the proposed meeting.

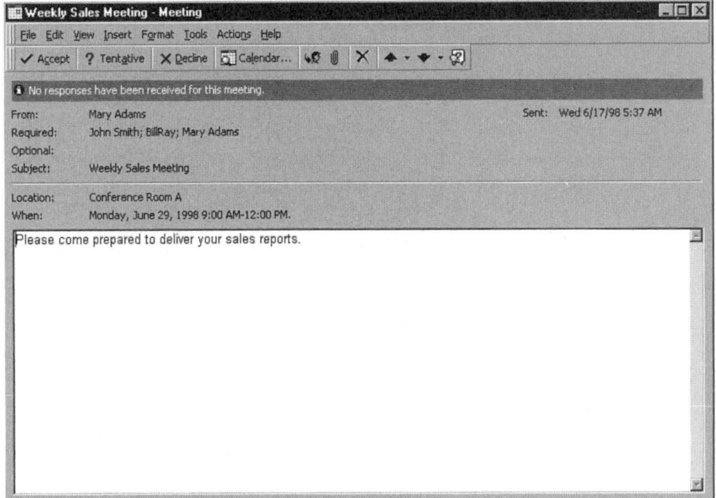

FIGURE 14.5
Use this dialog box to determine how to respond to a meeting request.

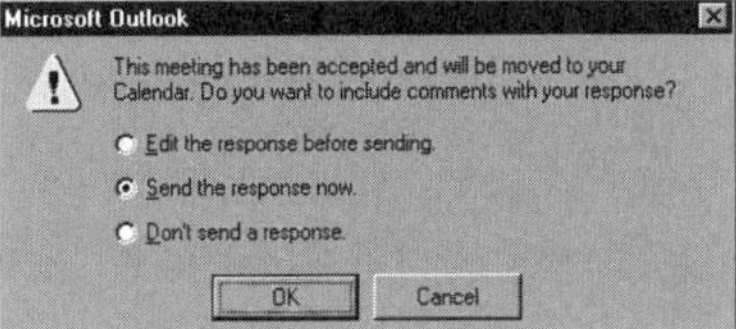

- If you select Edit the Response Before Sending, Outlook displays a message window to enable you to type additional comments to go with your response.
- If you select Send the Response Now, Outlook immediately sends a message to the person who invited you to the meeting, informing him or her of your decision.
- If you select Don't Send a Response, Outlook doesn't send a message in response to the request.

Receiving Responses to a Meeting Request

As people respond to your meeting request, Outlook sends you email messages, as shown in Figure 14.6. You can double-click a message to read it in more detail.

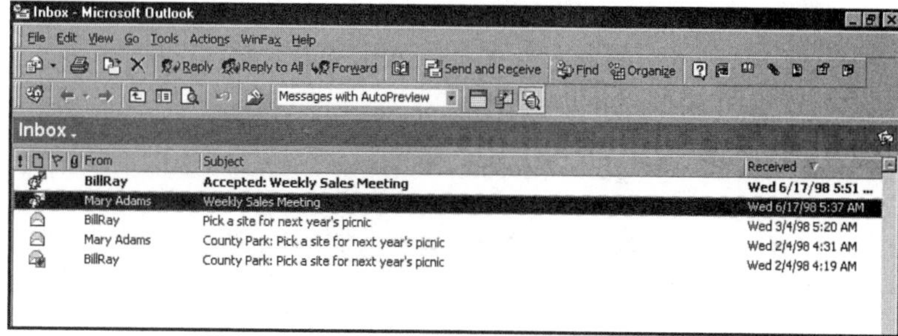

FIGURE 14.6
Replies to the meeting request appear in your Inbox.

As shown in Figure 14.7, the message window for a meeting response gives you information about how many people have accepted or declined your invitation.

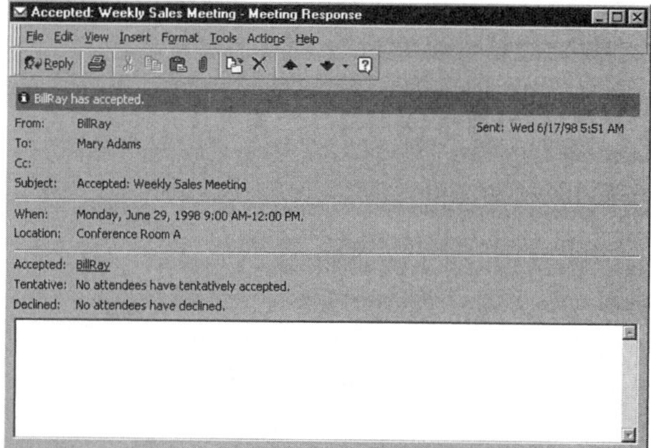

FIGURE 14.7
The meeting response includes details about the replies that you have received.

Updating a Meeting's Information

After you have planned a meeting, you might need to send additional information, such as changes in the meeting time or location, to those who will be attending. To send updated information to all attendees, double-click the meeting on your calendar to display its Meeting form. Edit the details of the Meeting form, and click Send Update. The updated meeting item is sent to each person.

If you change the date or time of a previously scheduled meeting and you save the changes to the meeting, Outlook automatically asks you whether you want to send an update to each of the attendees.

If you just want to send a message to each of the attendees, without changing the information about the meeting itself, choose Actions, New Message to Attendees while the Meeting form is open. Outlook displays a standard message window with the attendees already entered in the To text box. Fill out and send the message just as you would normally create an email message.

Canceling a Meeting

To cancel a meeting, double-click the meeting on your calendar to open its Meeting form. Choose Actions, Cancel Meeting. Outlook displays the message box shown in Figure 14.8.

FIGURE 14.8
Outlook offers to notify the attendees when you cancel a meeting.

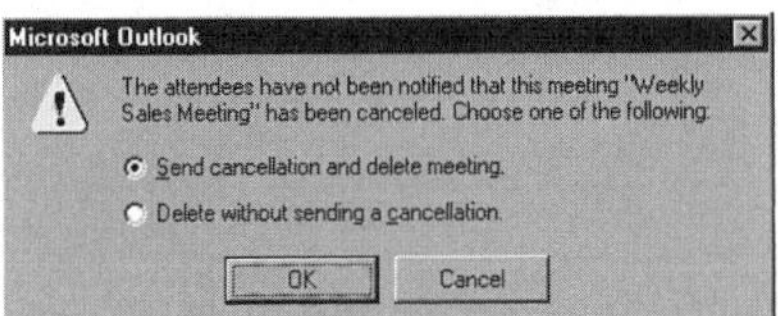

Choose Send Cancellation and Delete Meeting to send a message to each attendee, and to remove the meeting from your calendar. After each attendee opens your cancellation message, Outlook deletes the meeting from his or her calendar.

Choose Delete Without Sending a Cancellation to delete the message from your calendar without sending a message to the attendees.

Using Recurring Meetings

Many organizations have meetings that occur on a regularly scheduled basis. You might have a weekly staff meeting or a quarterly budget review. Outlook can automatically schedule recurring meetings.

Take these steps to enable Outlook to automatically schedule recurring meetings:

1. Open your calendar in any view.
2. Choose Actions, New Recurring Meeting to display the Appointment Recurrence dialog box (shown in Figure 14.9). Fill out the fields in the dialog box to define the recurrence schedule of the meeting, and click OK.
3. Select the attendees and fill out the rest of the meeting details.
4. Click Send to send the meeting request.

You can also convert a single meeting that you have scheduled into a recurring meeting. Double-click the meeting item on your calendar to open the Meeting form, and click the Recurrence toolbar button. Fill out the Appointment Recurrence dialog box, and then send the meeting request as usual.

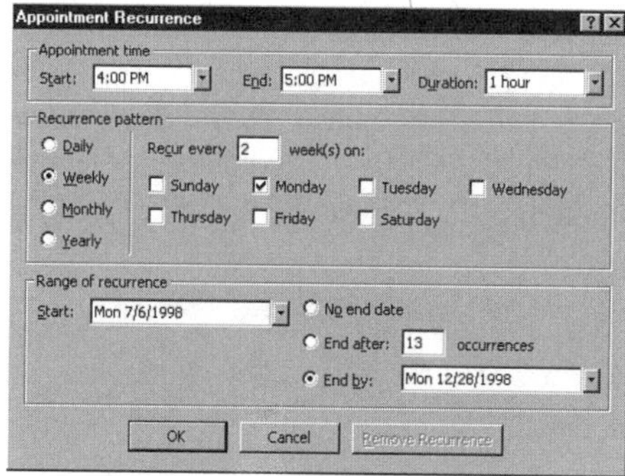

FIGURE 14.9
Use the Appointment Recurrence dialog box to define how often a meeting should occur.

Finding Time for a Meeting

The problem with sending meeting requests is that you have no guarantee that the attendees have the time available on their schedules. Fortunately, Outlook enables you to plan a meeting by finding available time on everyone's schedule. Of course, for this system to work, everyone has to maintain his or her schedule in Outlook on a regular basis.

To schedule a meeting when people are available, follow these steps:

1. Open your calendar, and select the date on which you want to schedule the meeting.
2. Choose Actions, Plan a Meeting. The Plan a Meeting form appears.
3. Choose Invite Others to select the names of the people and resources that you want to attend the meeting. After you have made your selections, click OK to return to the Plan a Meeting form.
4. The form is updated to show the busy times on each person's schedule, as shown in Figure 14.10. Notice in this figure that Bill Ray is busy on the selected date. The form shows color-coded information for busy, tentative, and out-of-office commitments.

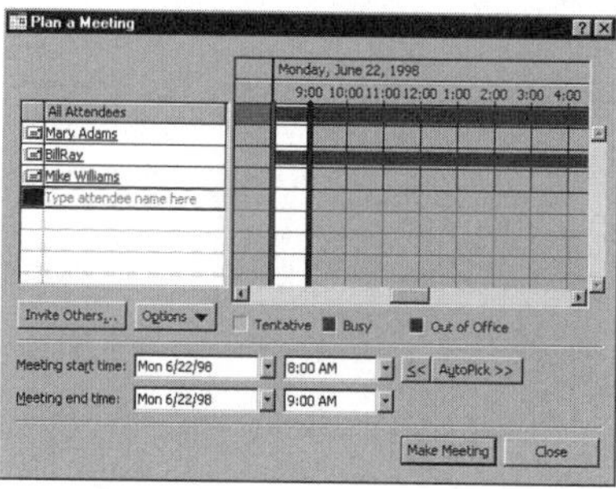

FIGURE 14.10
The Plan a Meeting form shows conflicts for the proposed meeting time.

5. To enable Outlook to find the first available time for the meeting, enter a proposed start and finish time for the meeting, and then click AutoPick. Outlook searches for the first available block of time when all the people you have invited are available. In Figure 14.11, Outlook has selected the day following the original proposed meeting time to accommodate Bill's previous commitment.

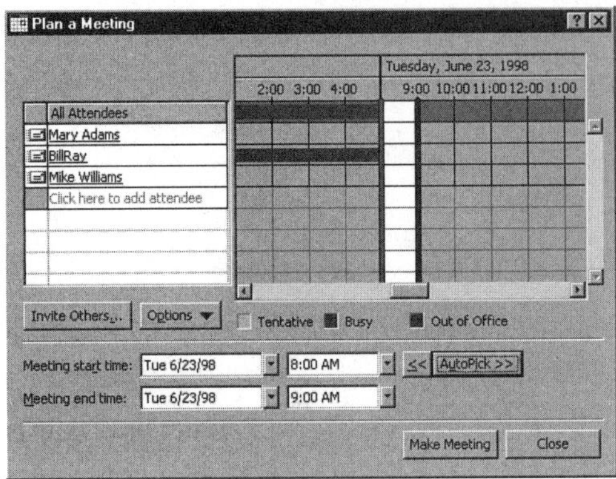

FIGURE 14.11
Outlook's AutoPick has found the first available time for a meeting.

6. Click Make Meeting to accept the proposed time for the meeting. Fill out the rest of the fields in the Meeting form and send it as usual.

Using Outlook with Exchange Public Folders

If you are using Outlook together with Microsoft Exchange Server, you can use *public folders* to share messages and other Outlook items with other people in your organization. Public folders are stored on your organization's Exchange Server, where they can be made available to all the users on the network. They can function as an electronic bulletin board for the exchange of ideas and announcements, official company documents, and other common information. Storing shared information in public folders is more efficient than sending individual messages to each user, and it makes the information easy to find and to use.

Because public folders is a feature of Microsoft Exchange Server, you can't use them if you don't use Exchange Server as one of your messaging services. (You can, however, use Outlook 98's Net Folders add-in to share information with other users over the Internet.)

What Is in a Public Folder?

Public folders can contain Outlook items, such as email messages, contacts, appointments, and notes. Public folders can also contain other files, such as Word documents, Excel spreadsheets, PowerPoint presentations, or multimedia files.

The owner of a public folder can restrict the type of items that can be placed in a particular folder. For example, if you have access to a folder that contains the company's client list, you may be allowed to put only contact items in the folder. Most public folders are created to store email messages. You can use Outlook to read the messages in a public folder, to respond to those messages, and to create, or post, new messages.

Accessing Information in Public Folders

Reading an item in a public folder is similar to reading an item in your personal folders.

1. Using the Outlook Bar, click the Other group bar, as shown in Figure 14.12, and click the Public Folders shortcut in this group.

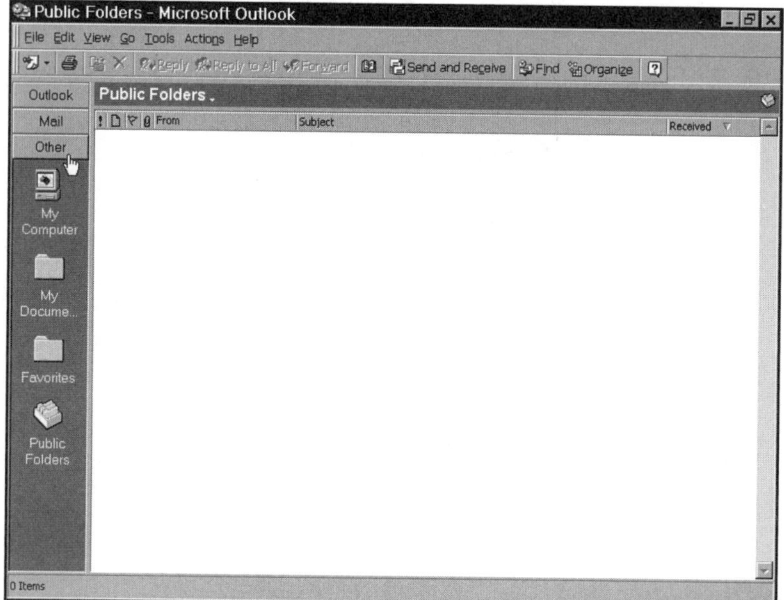

FIGURE 14.12
The Public Folders shortcut is in the Other section of the Outlook Bar.

2. Click the Folder List, and expand the folder tree to display the folder that you want to work with, as shown in Figure 14.13.
3. Select an item in the folder, and double-click it to open it. The item is opened with the default form for the selected folder.

Public folders work very much like your Inbox and other personal folders. The following list shows that you can use many of the same Outlook features for viewing public folders as you would use with your other folders:

- Choose View, AutoPreview to activate the automatic preview of unread messages in a public folder.
- Choose View, Preview Pane to open the Preview pane, displaying a larger amount of the content of each message in the folder.
- Choose View, Current View to select a view from the list of available views.

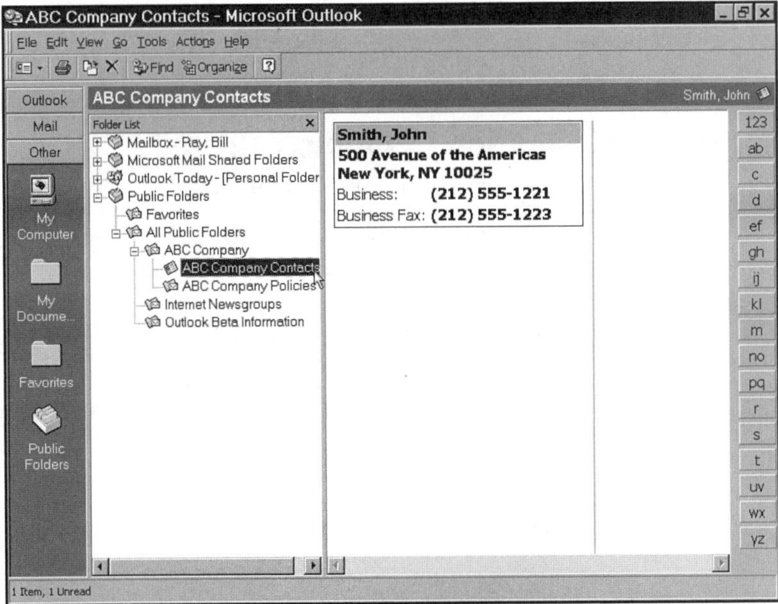

FIGURE 14.13
The ABC Company Contacts folder in this example is used to store information about ABC Company's customers.

Sometimes you might find an item in a public folder that you want to copy to your own folders. For example, you might want to copy an event from the company's calendar to your personal calendar. This enables you to add your own comments or notes to the calendar item without sharing them on the public folder.

To copy an item from a public folder, select the item you want to copy, and choose Edit, Copy to Folder. Select the destination folder in the dialog box that appears, and click OK.

Posting Information on Public Folders

If you have permission to create items in a public folder, you can post information to the folder. Posting an item is much like sending an email message, but the item's destination is the public folder, not an email recipient.

The person who created the folder, the folder's owner, can grant a variety of permissions to other users of that folder. You might have permission to post items in some folders, but not in others. For example, someone from your company's personnel department might have created a folder for posting job openings within the company. You would probably have the right to read these messages, but not to post your own messages.

Your company might have folders for posting product ideas, special events, complaints, or other information that might come from anyone in the organization. In this case, you have probably been granted the permissions to create messages, as well as to read them.

Beginning a New Conversation

Users can respond to the messages that others have posted, creating a public discussion group (also known as a conversation).

To begin a conversation by posting a message in a public folder, follow these steps:

1. Select the public folder in which you want to post an item.
2. Click the New Post in This Folder toolbar button. The default form for this folder appears for editing.
3. Fill in the subject and the text of the message, as shown in Figure 14.14. The Post To and Conversation lines are filled in automatically with the name of the folder and the name of the discussion.

FIGURE 14.14
The form for posting information to a public folder is just like an email form, except for the Post button on the toolbar.

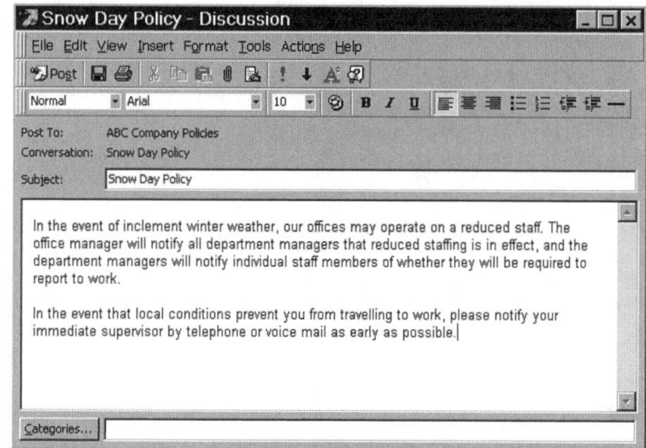

4. Click the Post button to close the form and save the message to the selected public folder.

Posting a Response to a Conversation

After you read a message in a public folder conversation, you can post a response to the message for others to read.

1. Double-click a message in a public folder to read it.
2. Click the Post Reply toolbar button. The default form for this folder appears for editing.
3. Fill in the subject and the text of the reply. The Post To and Conversation lines are filled in automatically with the name of the folder and the name of the discussion.
4. Click the Post button to close the form and post the new message in the discussion.

Viewing Messages by Conversation

A public folder can contain messages from many conversations. As with any other folder, you can select from a variety of Outlook views for displaying the contents of the folder. The most useful view for reading messages in a conversation is the By Conversation Topic view. Choose View, Current View, By Conversation Topic. Figure 14.15 shows the appearance of the public folders when viewed by conversation topic. By clicking the plus sign to the left of a conversation heading, you can expand the conversation to see all its messages, as shown in Figure 14.16.

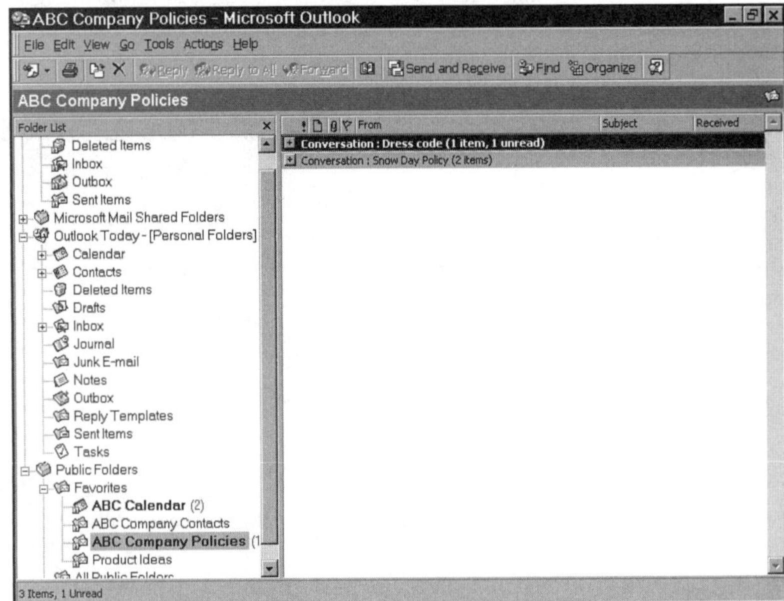

FIGURE 14.15
This public folder contains two conversations whose individual messages are collapsed.

Sending an Email Response to a Discussion

Sometimes you might want to send a response directly to the person who posted a message in a public folder, without posting a message for everyone to see. Additionally, you might want to forward or copy a message to another user, even someone who doesn't have access to the public folders.

To reply to the person who posted the message, simply click the Reply button while you are reading the message. Outlook creates a new message addressed to the sender of the original message. As with any email message, you can select additional To, Cc, and Bcc addresses.

To forward the message to another user without replying to the sender, click the Forward button while reading the message. Outlook creates a new message for you to forward. In this case, you have to fill in the To address before sending the message.

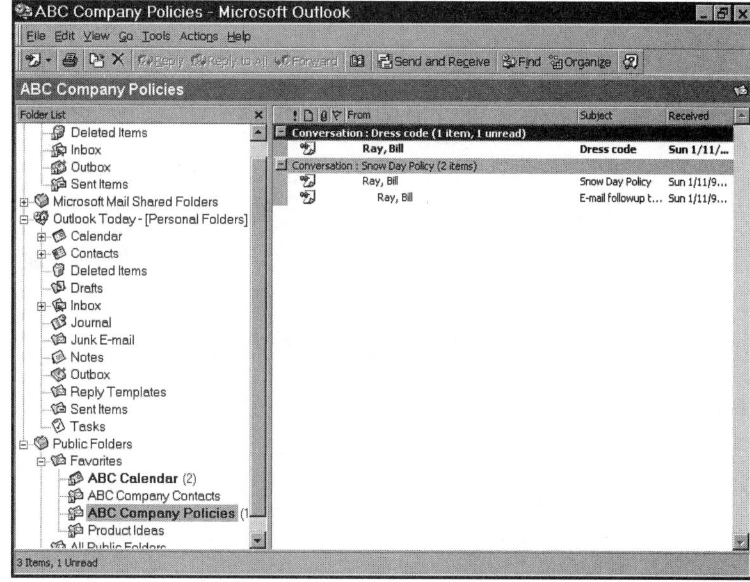

FIGURE 14.16
The conversations have been expanded to reveal the individual messages.

Creating a Public Folder

If your Exchange administrator has given you the right to create a public folder, you can use Outlook to create a public folder just as you would any other folder. Once you create the folder, you are automatically the owner; you have the capability to designate the permissions of other users to view the folder, and to read, create, edit, and delete items in the folder.

Just like personal folders, public folders can contain subfolders, so the steps for creating a public folder start with selecting its parent folder. To do so, follow these steps:

1. Select the parent folder of the new public folder.
2. Right-click on that folder to display the shortcut menu.
3. Choose New Folder to create the folder.
4. Type the name for the new folder and press Enter.

About Forms and Public Folders

When you create a new public folder, you and the other users on your network can use the same forms for viewing, editing, and creating items in the folders as you would use in your personal folders. For example, if a public folder is designed to hold email items, you can use the usual forms for creating and reading email messages. By default, a new public folder can contain email messages, but the folder's owner can change the default item type for the folder.

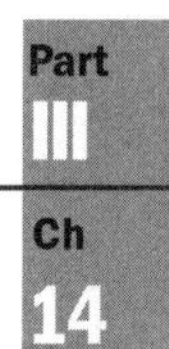

Because public folders are often used for special purposes within an organization—such as a discussion of product ideas or information about company policies—you might want to use custom forms for working with items in a public folder. Outlook enables you to associate one or more forms with a folder, and to designate a default form for a folder.

To view and modify the forms associations for a public folder, follow these steps:

1. Display the Folder List, if it is not already visible.
2. Right-click the folder name whose properties you want to modify, and choose Properties in the shortcut menu.
3. Select the Forms tab in the Properties dialog box (see Figure 14.17).
4. In the Allow These Forms in This Folder area, select your preference for which forms are available to this folder. In the example in Figure 14.17, the folder has been restricted to allow the use of only the form named ABC Client Form.

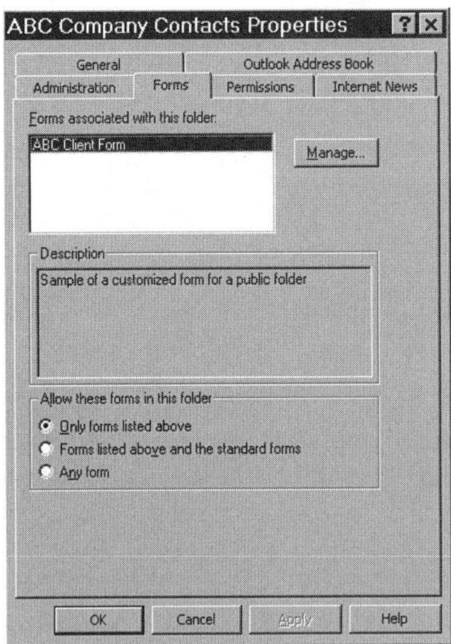

FIGURE 14.17
The Forms tab of the Properties dialog box for a folder shows which custom forms you can use with the folder.

5. Click Apply to apply your changes, and OK to close the dialog box.

In this example, all items created in this folder are edited using the custom form that you selected.

Making a Public Folder Available Offline

Normally, public folders are available only when you are connected to your Exchange Server. If, however, you have users who must read from or post messages to public folders while working remotely, you can make a public folder available offline. Right-click the folder, and choose Properties in the shortcut menu. Select the Synchronization tab in the Properties dialog box, as shown in Figure 14.18. Under This Folder Is Available, select When Offline or Online to make the folder available for offline use.

Users can now add this folder to their Favorites folder so that it is synchronized along with other folders when the user connects to the Exchange Server after working offline.

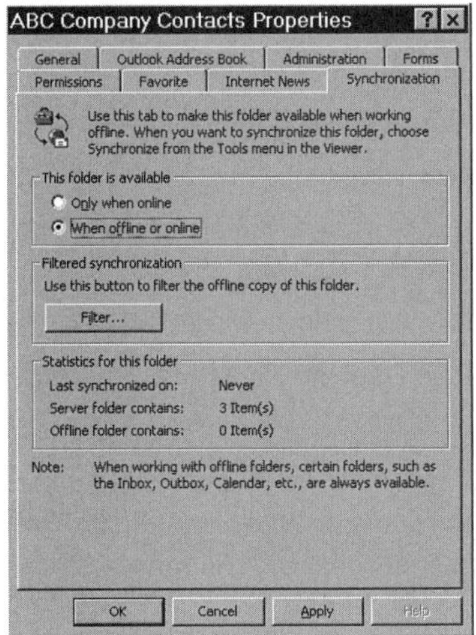

FIGURE 14.18
Use the Synchronization tab of a public folder to make the folder available for offline use.

Customizing Forms in Outlook

Outlook uses forms as a way of displaying the different types of items that are stored in Outlook folders. When you create a new item, such as an email message, or open an existing item for editing, you are using a form to view the information. A form is a window in Outlook that contains controls such as text boxes, check boxes, lists, and buttons.

Outlook's built-in forms provide an easy and convenient method for entering and editing data. A well-designed form enables you to see many fields on the screen at one time. The Table view, in contrast, can be difficult to use, because you often can see only a few fields at a time.

You can customize the forms that come with Outlook to create forms that are personalized, or that perform specific functions within an organization. In the next section, you review the forms that come with Outlook, and then learn how to customize forms for your own use.

Reviewing Outlook's Standard Forms

Outlook comes with a standard set of forms for creating, reading, and editing the items in the different Outlook folders. You usually don't even have to think very much about using forms. When you double-click on an item, such as a contact, Outlook automatically opens the item using the default form for the active folder. Many users simply use the default forms that come with Outlook, and don't have any need to create custom forms.

You might want to customize a form in Outlook simply to make cosmetic changes, such as modifying the form's background color, font, or the arrangement of the controls. (Controls are the items on the form that enable you interact with the form, such as text boxes, check boxes, buttons, and list boxes.) Maybe you have created one or more custom fields. If so, you can display those fields on a built-in form if you customize it.

You can also modify a blank page of an existing form, as though you were creating a form from scratch. This is an especially attractive solution if you have designed a custom application in a public folder in which you're using many custom fields.

To build a form in Outlook, you begin by modifying an existing form. Therefore, it's a good idea to start by reviewing the following built-in Outlook forms:

- The Message form is used to create and edit email messages.
- The Contact form is used to work with contact items.
- The Appointment form is used to work with appointments and meetings in the Calendar folder.
- The Journal Entry form is used for creating journal entries.
- The Meeting Request form is used to send a meeting request to another person via email.
- The Note form is used for creating and editing notes.
- The Post form is used for posting messages to a folder. This form is most commonly used for posting messages in a public folder, although you can use it to post a message in one of your personal folders as well.
- The Task form is used to create a task in your Task folder.
- The Task Request form is used to send an email message to someone requesting that he or she perform a task.

Outlook includes the following two additional special-purpose forms:

- The Standard Default form is used by Outlook when it is unable to load the default form for a message or folder.
- The Security Key Exchange form is used for sending secure message keys to another user, so you can send encrypted messages to one another. This form is only available if your Exchange administrator has enabled advanced security for you.

You can also use Microsoft Office documents as templates for items to be posted to an Outlook folder. If you choose File, New, Office Document, the New Office Document dialog box is displayed. Select the Office application that you want to use, and click OK. You can either post the document to a folder, or send the document as an email message.

Understanding a Form's Anatomy

To create and modify forms, you need to know a little about the structure of a form. Two concepts that are essential to understanding a form are tabs and controls. By customizing these two elements, you can create a unique and distinctive form for any purpose.

Tabs Many of the standard forms in Outlook have several pages. Each of these pages is identified by a tab, a button at the top of the page that identifies it. Within a form, each page must have a unique name, which should be descriptive of the function of that page. Some forms, such as the Notes form and the Journal Entry form, have only one page, and therefore have no tabs.

Controls Outlook has a wide variety of controls that you can use on your forms, including text boxes, list and combo boxes, check boxes, and command buttons. You can move the controls around on a form, change the text that appears on a label, and change the font for a control. You can also add new controls to a form and delete controls that you don't need.

Creating New or Modified Forms

To create a new form or to modify an existing one, you work with the form in Design view. Outlook's Design view provides a set of tools for adding and modifying controls to a form and for modifying the properties of the form. These design tools are similar to the tools that are available in Visual Basic for Applications (VBA), which is used to create automated applications in the Office 97 versions of Word, Excel, PowerPoint, and Access. Because Outlook doesn't use VBA, it has its own set of design tools. Outlook uses Visual Basic, Scripting Edition, commonly known as VBScript, for creating automated applications. VBScript is a simpler version of Visual Basic than VBA.

To edit an existing form, open the form as usual, either by opening an existing item using that form, or by creating a new item with the form. For example, to edit the Contacts form, you could begin by creating a new contact.

After you have the form open, switch into Design view by choosing Tools, Forms, Design This Form if you have Outlook 98, or Tools, Design This Form if you have Outlook 97. Outlook displays the form in Design view, as shown in Figure 14.19.

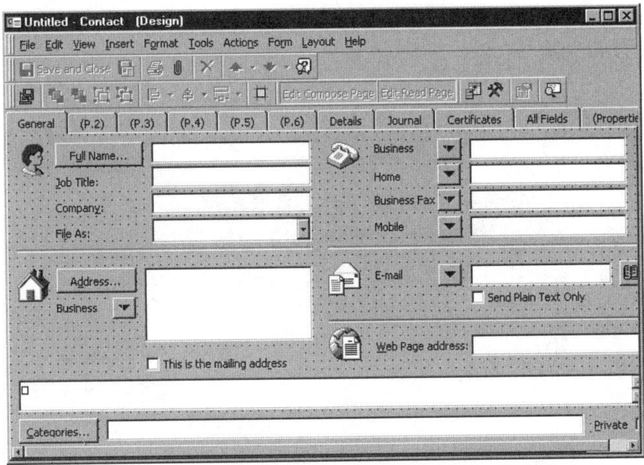

FIGURE 14.19
Design view displays the Design toolbar.

To create a new form, open any item. Then choose Tools, Forms, Design a Form. The Design Form dialog box appears (shown in Figure 14.20). Select the form that you want to use as a model for your new form, and click Open. The form is opened in Design view.

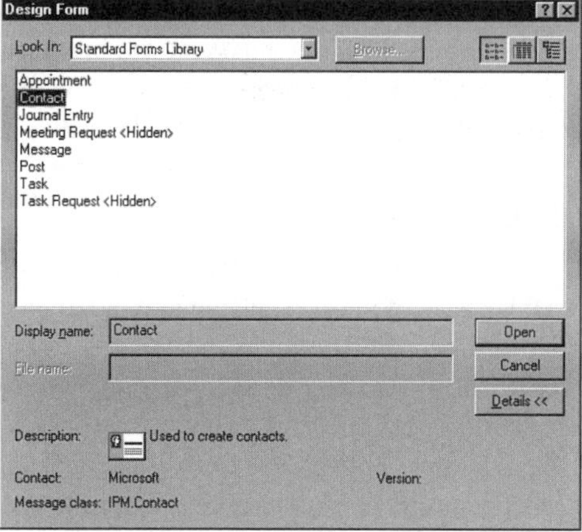

FIGURE 14.20
The Design Form dialog box enables you to select a form to use as a starting point for a new form.

Saving and Publishing Forms

After you make changes to a form's design, you want to save your changes. If you opened an existing form for modification and you want to save your changes and update the form, choose File, Save or press Ctrl+S.

To save the form as a new form, you need to publish the form. Publishing a form saves it in a folder or a forms library. Publishing a form in a folder makes that form available in that folder. Publishing a form in a forms library makes the form available to be opened at a later time, or to be shared with other users.

To publish a form, click the Publish Form toolbar button, or choose Tools, Forms, Publish Form. The Publish Form As dialog box appears (shown in Figure 14.21).

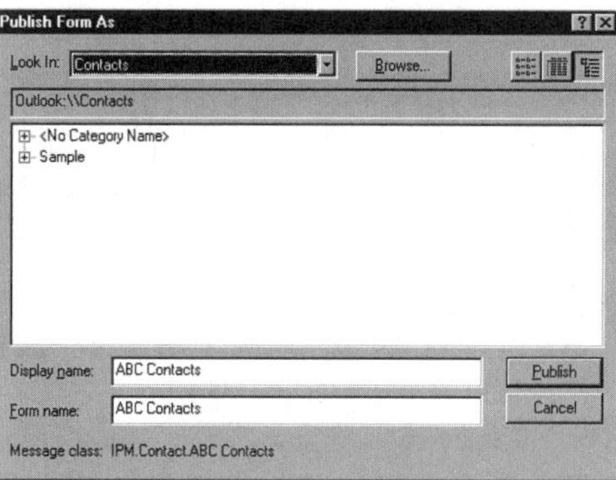

FIGURE 14.21
The Publish Form As dialog box enables you to publish a form to a folder or a form library.

Type a name in the Display Name text box. Outlook automatically uses this name as the form name. If you want to use a different name for the form, type it in the Form Name text box.

The Look In list determines where the form will be saved. If you select an individual folder, the form will be saved in that folder, and will be available for use in that folder. If you select Outlook Folders, the form will be available in any of your Outlook folders. If you want to use this form in a variety of other folders, select Personal Forms Library. Later, you can copy the form from the library to any folder. You can also select the Organizational Forms Library to make forms available to anyone in your organization.

Click Publish to close the dialog box and publish the form.

Setting a Default Form for a Folder

If you have published a form, you can select it as the default form for a folder. Then any new items you create in the folder are created using the custom form.

In the Folder List, right-click the folder that you want to customize, and choose Properties from the shortcut menu. The Contacts Properties dialog box appears (shown in Figure 14.22). Select the form that you want to use from the When Posting to This Folder, Use drop-down box. If you published the form to this folder, its name appears in the list.

FIGURE 14.22
You can use the Contacts Properties dialog box to set the default form for a folder.

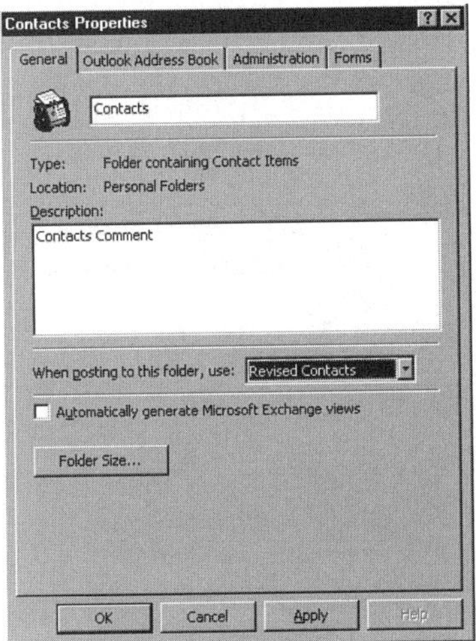

If the form you want to use is not on the list, click Forms to display the Choose Form dialog box (shown in Figure 14.23). In the Look In drop-down box, select Personal Forms Library to find any forms you have published in your personal library. To use one of Outlook's standard forms, select Standard Forms Library. Select the form you want to use, and click Open.

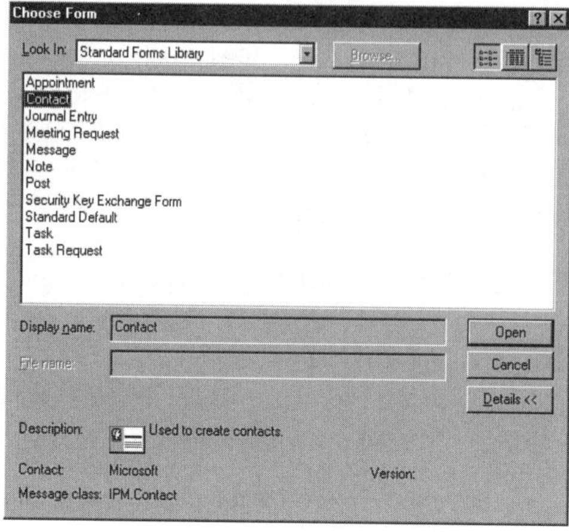

FIGURE 14.23
The Choose Form dialog box enables you to select a form from the Standard Forms Library.

Using a Forms Library

You can use a forms library to store forms that you want to reuse in many different folders. Click the Forms tab of the Properties dialog box, and click Manage Forms. The Forms Manager dialog box appears (shown in Figure 14.24). You can use the Forms Manager to copy a form from a library (such as your Personal Forms Library) to a folder.

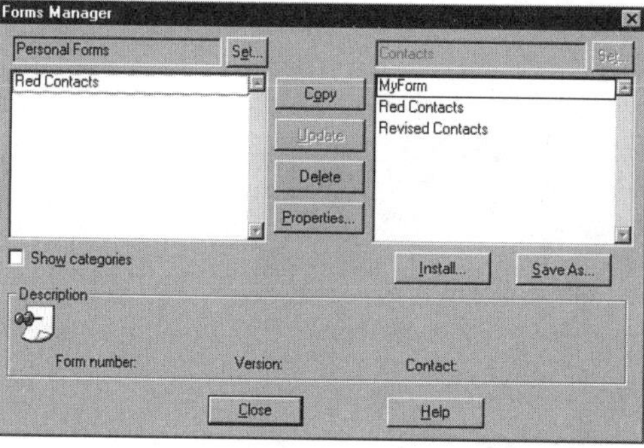

FIGURE 14.24
Use the Forms Manager to copy forms from a library to a folder.

To select a library, click the Set button. The Set Library To dialog box appears (shown in Figure 14.25). To use a form from your Personal Forms Library, select Personal Forms in the Forms Library drop-down box, and click OK. When you return to the Forms Manager, any forms in your Personal Forms Library are displayed. To copy a form from the library to the current folder, select the form you want to copy, and click the Copy button. Click Close when you are finished managing your forms.

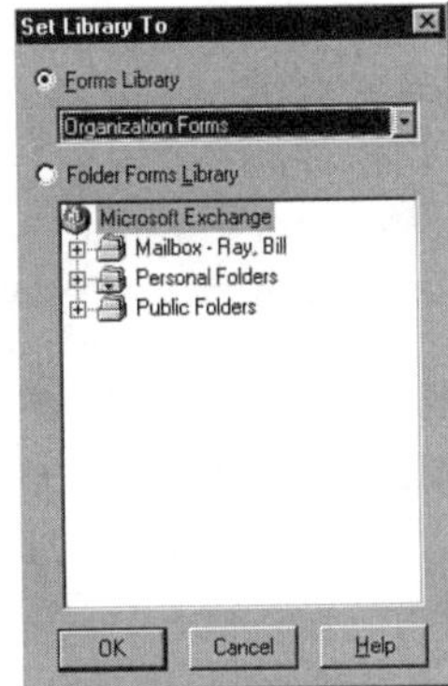

FIGURE 14.25
Use the Set Library To dialog box to choose the forms library with which you want to work.

Adding and Removing Controls

You can add controls to a form by using the toolbox. The toolbox (shown in Figure 14.26) is only available when you are in Design view. You can show or hide it by clicking the Control Toolbox toolbar button, or by choosing Form, Control Toolbox.

FIGURE 14.26
Use the toolbox to add controls to a form.

The toolbox has the following buttons for each of the standard controls that you can use on a form:

- *Label control.* Used to display text on a form. The user can't edit the text, so labels are commonly used for instructions, or to identify the different areas of a form.
- *TextBox control.* Provides a box that the user can type text in. Text boxes can be a single line, such as the Subject box on many forms, or multiline, such as the Notes area of most forms.
- *ComboBox and ListBox controls.* Enable you to display lists of information on a form. Listboxes take up a set amount of space on the form, while combo boxes can be set up as drop-down lists, which only display their lists when the user clicks on them.
- *Checkbox control.* Commonly used for true/false or yes/no questions. The user can easily change the value of the check box by clicking it.
- *OptionButton control.* Enables a user to select one option out of a short list. When you have a group of option buttons working together, selecting one option button automatically turns the other options buttons off.

- *ToggleButton control.* Looks like a push button, but has two states, or values. Clicking the button once leaves it pushed in, which represents true, or on. Clicking it again makes the button appear raised, representing false, or off.
- *Frame control.* Used as a container for other controls. In addition to using it to draw a border and add a label to a form, you can use it to group a set of controls within the frame. If you place two or more option buttons within a frame, they are automatically treated as a group so that only one button in the group can be selected at a time.
- *CommandButton control.* Creates a push button on the form. Clicking the button causes some event to occur. Command buttons are commonly used by programmers as a way to run their VBScript programs.
- *Image control.* Can be used to add images to your form. You can insert the contents of an image file in several different formats, including Windows bitmaps (BMP), Windows metafiles (WMF), enhanced metafiles (EMF), icons (ICO or CUR), GIF, and JPEG (JPG).
- *Tabstrip and Multipage controls.* Enables you to create the dynamic effect of multiple pages or multiple sets of controls within a form. VBScript programming is required to make effective use of these controls.
- *Scrollbar and SpinButton controls.* Provide graphical controls that the user can click to set or change numeric values. VBScript programming is used to transfer these values to other controls.
- *Select Objects button.* This is not a control, but just a button that enables you to select controls on the form by clicking on them.

Adding a Control

To place a control on a form, click the button on the toolbox that represents the control you want to use. Then click the location on the form where you want the control to appear. The control is placed with its upper-left corner at the location that you clicked. If you prefer, instead of just clicking the location of the corner, you can click and drag a rectangle to set the initial size of the control.

Selecting Controls

Many operations on controls require you to select one or more controls first. You can select a control by clicking it. A group of white buttons, called selection handles, appears around the selected control.

You can select more than one control at a time so that you can reposition the controls as a group, or edit the properties of the controls as a group. After selecting one control, Ctrl+click the additional controls that you want to select. The most recently selected control shows white selection handles, while the previously selected controls show black selection handles.

Another method for selecting multiple controls is to drag a rectangle around the controls. Begin by clicking a location on the background of the form where there are no controls. Drag a rectangle from that point to surround or touch any controls that you want to select.

If you have several controls selected, and you want to reduce the selection to just one control, click on a control that is not selected to remove the current selection. Then you can select the control you want.

Deleting Controls

To delete a control, select the control, and then press the Delete key, or click the Delete toolbar button. Be careful that you have not selected more controls than you want to delete. If you accidentally delete too much, use Edit, Undo to restore the controls.

Adding Fields

Many of the controls that you place on a form are used to work with the fields for items in Outlook folders. For example, a Contacts form usually has controls to edit the name, title, and phone numbers of the contact, as well as many others.

Not every available field is displayed on the standard Outlook forms. (To include all of them would result in some very crowded forms.) You might want to add one of these standard fields (or a user-defined field) to a built-in or custom form.

To display the list of available fields, click the Field Chooser toolbar button. The Field Chooser window appears (shown in Figure 14.27). To add a field to the form, drag the desired field from the Field Chooser onto the form. A control that represents the field appears on the form. You can drag the control to a new location if you don't like its position on the form.

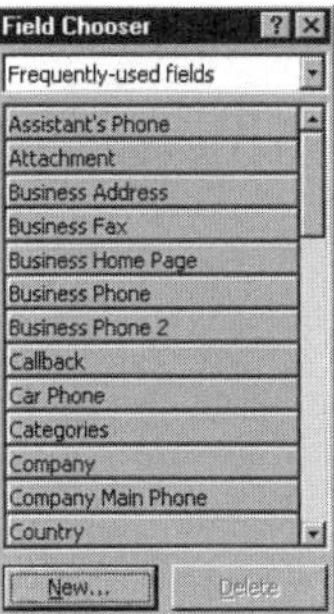

FIGURE 14.27
Use the Field Chooser to add standard and user-defined fields to a form.

Controlling a Form's Appearance

Outlook forms, and the controls on the forms, are designed as objects. This is most important to VBScript programmers because VBScript is designed to work with the methods and properties of objects. Objects are used throughout Office 97 to represent elements such as documents, workbooks, database tables, and many other items.

To control an object's appearance, you can modify the properties of the object using VBScript programming, or by using the Properties toolbar button, as you learn in this section.

When you are designing an Outlook form, you can work with the properties of the form and the controls on the form. Properties are attributes that describe the appearance and functionality of the form or control. Some properties are very simple. For example, a form has ForeColor and BackColor properties, which control the foreground and background color. Label controls have a Font property, which controls the appearance of the text of the label, and a Caption property, which defines the text that appears on the label.

There are many properties, and in most cases, you can leave the properties unchanged from their original values. Sometimes, however, you might need to change the properties of a control or form.

To view the properties of a control, select the control, and then click the Properties toolbar button. The Properties dialog box appears (shown in Figure 14.28). You can use the Display tab to change the name of the control as well as its appearance properties. The Value tab (shown in Figure 14.29) enables you to connect the control to one of the fields for the items you will be editing with the form. The Validation tab (shown in Figure 14.30) enables you to declare that a field is required for this item and set a validation rule guaranteeing that appropriate data is entered in the control.

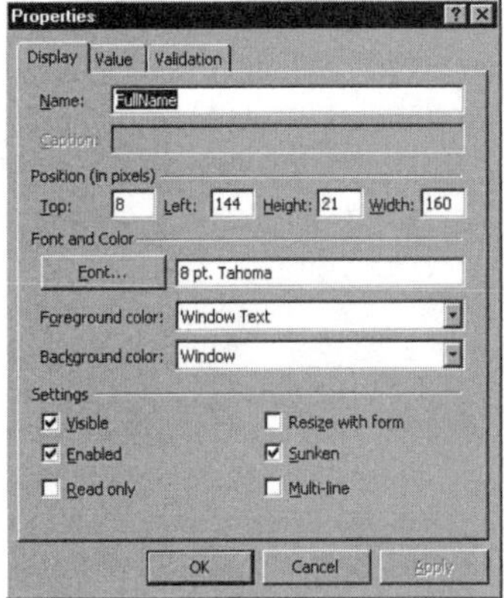

FIGURE 14.28
The Display tab of the Properties dialog box shows the name and other attributes of a control.

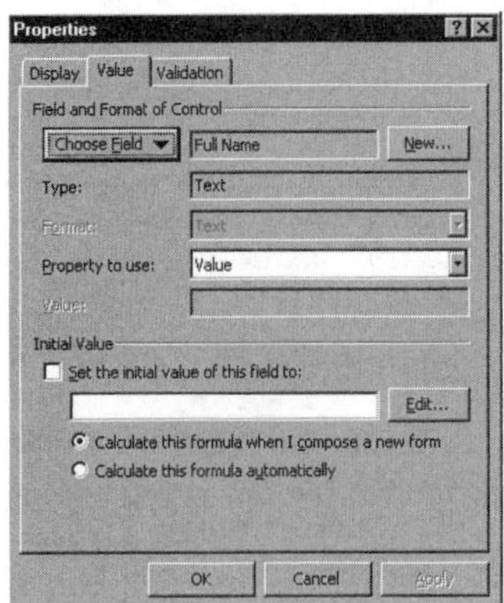

FIGURE 14.29
The Value tab of the Properties dialog box shows how the control gets its value.

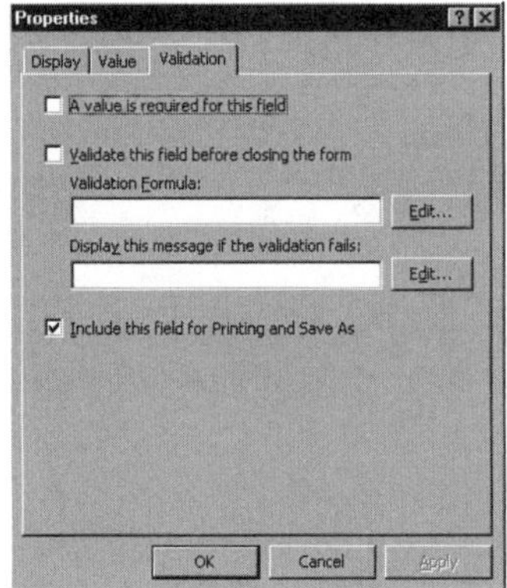

FIGURE 14.30
The Validation tab of the Properties dialog box enables you to create a validation rule, insuring accurate data entry.

There are even more properties than those you can see in the Properties dialog box. If you want to see all the available properties for a control, select the control, and then choose Form, Advanced Properties. The Properties window that appears shows all the properties of the selected object (see Figure 14.31). You can scroll through the list of properties, and edit the value of any available property. You can leave the Properties window open as you move from one control to another, and the window updates to display the properties of the currently selected control.

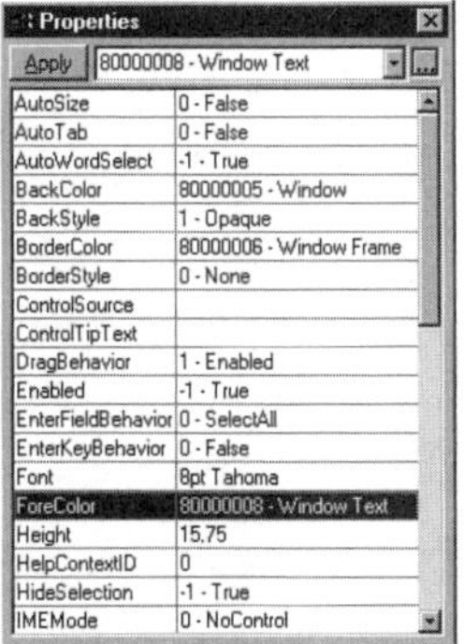

FIGURE 14.31
The Properties window shows all the available properties of a control.

CHAPTER 15

Sharing Database Resources with Access 97

Databases enable multiple users to enter and retrieve data simultaneously. This chapter focuses on ways to facilitate data entry by multiple users and explains the multiuser environment in general.

Using Access Features to Streamline Data Entry

Forms in Microsoft Access make data entry more user friendly. In a form you can add or delete records, search for records, modify records, and print records. Each of these functions can be customized for your business solution. For example, you can make adding records quicker and easier by adding pull-down menus to the form, automatically populating certain fields, or prompting the user for specific data. You can also customize a search engine to facilitate locating records. You can accomplish all of these things by customizing a data entry form. This section focuses on how to set up a form by using the Form Wizard, make changes to that form, create a form from scratch, form options such as the ones mentioned above, and add other form enhancements.

This chapter focuses on forms for data entry; however, forms can be used for other purposes, such as a database switchboard (covered in Chapter 9, "Customizing Access to Your Organization's Needs"), an input box for criteria for reports or queries, or a subform. This chapter explains how to use subforms in a data entry environment.

A form can have an underlying data source from which it pulls and in which it stores data. Because these forms will be used for data entry, you will want to have a table as your data source. (You can also use queries as data sources for forms, but queries don't let you modify or add new records, which defeats the purpose of using forms for data entry.) You should create the table before starting the form. Then you can modify the table if you need more fields as the form is created.

Creating a Data Entry Form by Using the Form Wizard

You will create a form for entering new customers. This form can also be used to view existing customers and modify the records. You will need a Customer Information table as your underlying control source (data source). You will have a table called Customer Information with the following fields: Cust_ID, Customer_Name, Address, City, State, Zip, Telephone, Fax, Contact_Name, and Position. Figure 15.1 shows such a table in Design view.

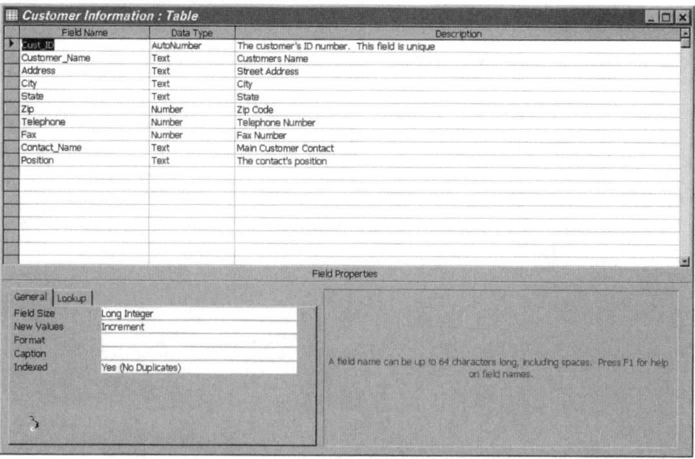

FIGURE 15.1
The Design view of the Customer Information table shows the field names and field data types.

On the Forms tab, click on New. Select Form Wizard and choose Customer Information as the table from which the object's data comes. You will now see a series of steps by which you can choose options for your form. The first screen lists all available fields so you can choose the fields you want on the form. If you click on the double-arrow button, all fields are moved to the list to be included on your form (see Figure 15.2).

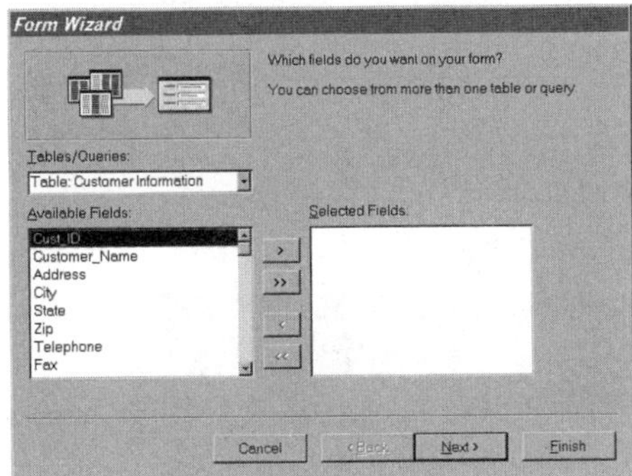

FIGURE 15.2
The Form Wizard gives you a choice of which fields from tables or queries will make up the control source.

You can also include fields from another table in your form. For you to do this, a primary key, a field or fields containing unique records must link the tables. The uniqueness of the field or combination of fields makes it possible to link data in multiple tables. The example in this chapter includes two tables: the Customer Information table and a Customer History table with the fields Cust_ID, Customer_Name, Credit_Limit, and Outstanding_Balance. Cust_ID will link these two tables. When you choose your fields, choose all of the fields in the Customer Information table and the Credit_Limit field from the Customer History table. Because you are using two tables, you are next given the choice of how you want to represent the data from two tables; if you had chosen data from only one table, you wouldn't see this screen.

The data from different tables can be represented on a form in any of three ways. The first is through a subform (see Figure 15.3). The form shows the fields from the first table, with the fields from the second table in a subform. Check the option button for Form With Subforms if this is how you want to display your data. An alternative to a subform is to have the data pop up when a button is pushed. This is called a *linked* or *pop-up form* (see Figure 15.4). Check the option button for Linked Forms if this is how you want to display the data. If you want all of the data displayed in a single form, choose to view by the second table, which in this example is the option By Customer History (see Figure 15.5).

For this example, choose to display all of the data in a single form. After you click on Next, the Form Wizard dialog box prompts you to choose a layout for your format—Columnar, Tabular, Datasheet, or Justified. Columnar displays the data in columns, Tabular displays the data in a row format, Datasheet displays it in a spreadsheet format, and Justified sizes the fields so they fit into a rectangular format. Choose Justified. In the next box you choose the style, which sets the background colors, font colors, and label and text box styles. Choose Colorful 2. Finally, you can title your form and choose to open it in Design view or Form view.

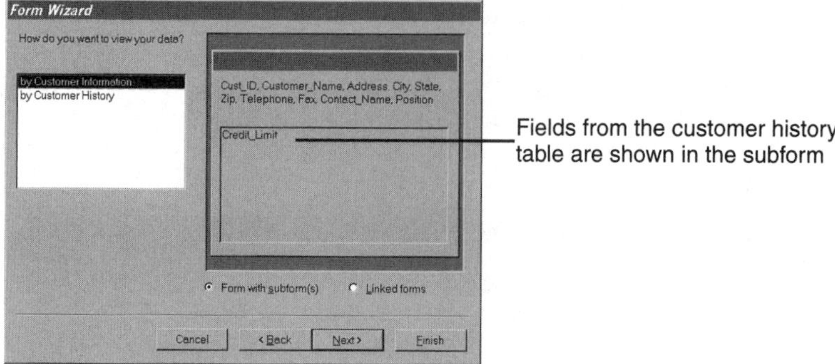

FIGURE 15.3
One choice for representing multiple tables on a form is by using a subform.

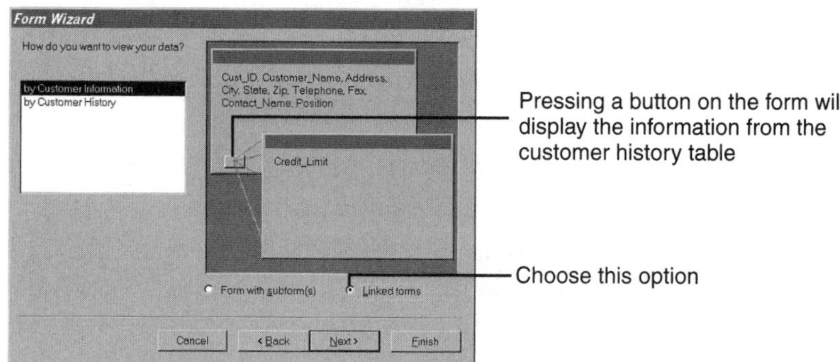

FIGURE 15.4
Another choice for representing multiple tables on a form is by using linked forms.

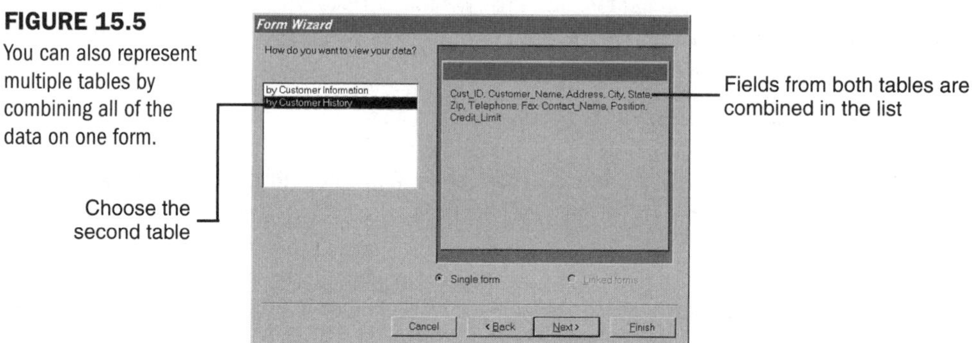

FIGURE 15.5
You can also represent multiple tables by combining all of the data on one form.

Open the form in Form view to see if you like what you created. Figure 15.6 shows the finished form.

You can modify your form by going to Design view and moving fields, changing text boxes, expanding or shrinking field sizes, changing colors, and more. You can also add more items, such as buttons, subforms, pictures, and boxes. If you find you are doing an extensive amount of customizing after you use the wizard to create your initial form, it might be best to just build your form from scratch.

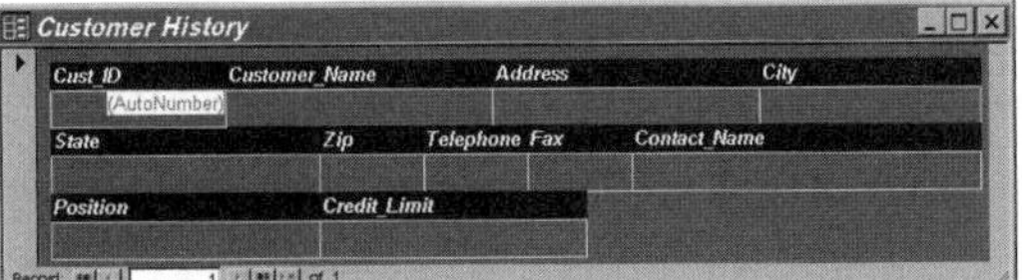

FIGURE 15.6
The selected fields are displayed in the form created by the Form Wizard.

Creating a Form Without Using the Form Wizard

On the Form tab in the database window, choose New. Choose Design view and choose Customer Information as the source for the object's information. Design view shows the blank form, the properties box, and the toolbar. The default view is for the detail section of the form, but if you want to add a form header and footer, choose View, Form Header/Footer to create a form header on which you will add buttons for form navigation. Items on the form header and footer are static, but data displayed on the objects in the main part of the form changes as the user navigates through the records. For example, you can place buttons on the header and footer so they are always visible, no matter what records are displayed.

Modifying Form Properties Clicking on the Form Selector box in the left corner of the form displays the properties for the form. Here you can change the caption, choose the views allowed, decide what should be shown, assign macros for the form, change the data source, and change the formatting. Right now, just change the caption—which will be displayed at the top of the form—by typing `Customer Information`. You will change the other options as the last step in creating the form.

Adding Fields Choose View, Field List to display a list box with all of the available fields from your table. Drag and drop the fields you want onto the form. You can then move them around, resize them, and change the labels or the text boxes.

The form is now in a basic form for data entry, as you can see in Figure 15.7. You could have generated a form like this with the Form Wizard, so your next job is to add some features not offered by the Form Wizard.

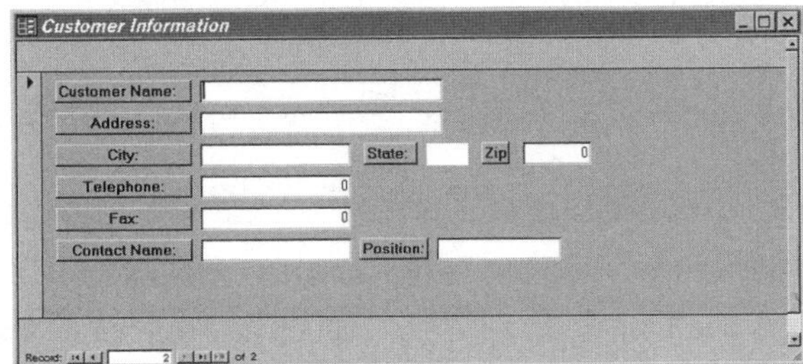

FIGURE 15.7
The chosen fields are displayed on the created form.

Adding Subforms Now add a subform that will contain the customer history information. Click on the subform/subreport icon on the toolbox. Drag the box onto the form and size it appropriately. A Subform Wizard appears to help add the form. You can either choose another form that is already created or you can add a table or query. Because you do not have an existing form that contains the data you want to show, choose Table/Query. If you use an existing form, that form should be in Datasheet view.

A button for control wizards is in the upper-right corner of the Form Design toolbox. If this button is selected, Access provides wizard help for the controls, such as buttons, subforms, combo boxes, and list boxes. If this button is not selected, you need to set all parameters and options in the properties box for the control. Using the control wizards saves you time and trouble.

Choose the table and the fields you want on the subform. Select Customer History and the Credit_Limit and Outstanding_Balance fields. Also add Cust_ID to create a common field between the two tables.

Next you must choose how the subform will be linked, so the form knows which fields to pull from the other table. The wizard guesses the link, or you can define your own link. When you define your own, choose the fields in each table that need to be identical. For this example, choose the Cust_ID field on each form. Select a name for the form and click on Finish.

The Forms tab of the database window should now show the subform you created. You can go to Design view and make any changes to that subform, or you can double-click on the subform in Design view of the main form to make changes.

NOTE You can see the linked fields by looking at the Data tab on the property sheet. The parent link is the main table, and the child link is the field from the subform data source. You can also change other properties for the subform on the subform property sheet (see Figure 15.8).

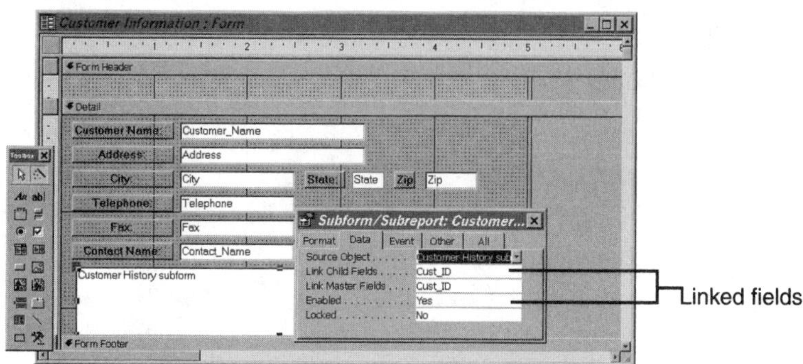

FIGURE 15.8
The source object and linked fields can be changed on the subform property sheet.

Adding List Boxes and Combo Boxes You can add list boxes or combo boxes to a form to provide users with a list of data from which to choose. A list box displays the list at all times, and the user can only choose from the list items. A combo box displays only one item at a time from the list, taking up less space on the form because not all items are displayed, and can also enable users to enter values not on the list. Suppose your company is focused in a tri-state area—Indiana, Kentucky, and Ohio—but you have a few customers in other states. You can set up your State field as a combo box with the choices IN, KY, and OH and also let users enter other state prefixes.

Because you are going to replace the current State field with a combo box, first delete the existing State field. Then click on the combo box icon on the toolbox and draw the combo box where you want it on the form. You can move and size the box later. The Combo Box Wizard asks you where the box should get its values (see Figure 15.9). The values can come from an existing table, you can type in the values, or you can find a value on the form based on the combo box value. The last option (find a value on the form based on the combo box value) is useful for searches. This option creates a combo box containing data from the data source. The form displays the corresponding record, based on the selection in the combo box. For example, if the combo box contains the Cust_ID entries, the record shown will match the chosen Cust_ID entry. For this example, you'll go to the next screen and type in the values.

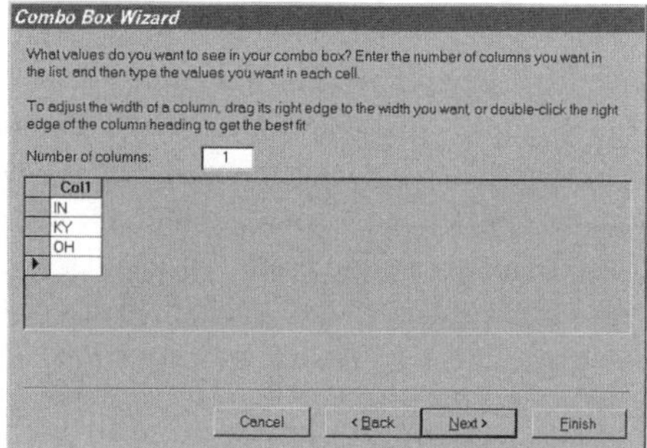

FIGURE 15.9
Type in the values you want displayed in your combo box.

Click on Next and indicate that you want one column. Type `IN`, `KY`, and `OH` in the boxes and click on Next.

You can also size columns on this screen by placing your cursor at the end of a column and expanding or shrinking the column to the desired width. You can shrink this column because the state abbreviations are small. You can either assign a value for later use or store the selection in a field. Storing a value for later use stores the value with that field name but only until the form is closed; the value is not permanently stored as it would be in a table. In this example, you want to store the value in the State field of the table. The final step is to choose a label for the field. Your label will be State. Now click on Finish.

By default, combo boxes accept values that are not on the list. You can change this behavior by setting the Limit to List field in the properties to No; this way users will only be able to enter IN, KY, or OH. You can also set the AutoExpand feature to choose values based on one or two characters entered. In the example, if someone types `I`, it automatically expands to IN.

Adding Option Groups Another control useful on a data entry form is the option group—a box that contains a list of items from which users can check the appropriate value. Suppose your customer contacts are usually Account Managers, Sales Reps, or Purchasing Agents. You can set up an option group with these three options, plus Other.

Once again, delete your current position field before creating the option group. Then select the Option Group icon on the toolbox and drag it where you want the group on your form. The

Option Group Wizard appears (see Figure 15.10). First list the option labels—in this example, Account Manager, Sales Rep, Purchasing Agent, and Other. (You can choose a default value, but there's no need to do so now.) Click on Next.

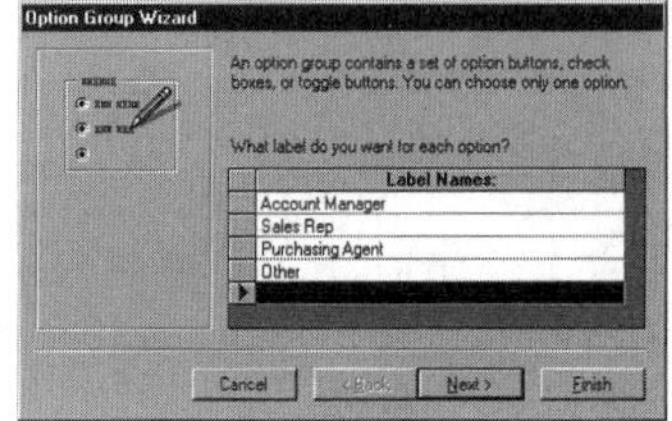

FIGURE 15.10
Type in the values that will be displayed in the option group.

The next step is to assign a value to the options. The default is incremental numbers beginning with 1, which will work for the example. Next you can select whether to store this value in a field or for later use; choose to store it in a field. The next screen is where you can format the box. You can have option buttons, check boxes, or toggle buttons, and the box can be etched, flat, shadowed, sunken, or raised. Choose option boxes with a raised style. The final step is to add a label to the box. Type `Position` and click on Finish; then size and place the box on the form. Check that the control source in the properties box is for Position. Figure 15.11 shows how the form should look now.

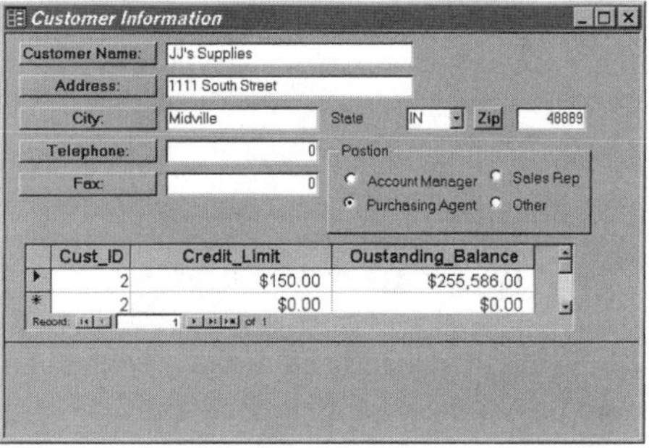

FIGURE 15.11
The form now has fields, an option group, a combo box, and a subform.

NOTE Look at the Customer History table now. Instead of text appearing in the position field, you should now see a number between 1 and 4, which coincides with the option group choice.

Tab Order and Record Navigation Because you have added, deleted, and moved fields around, you will want to check the *tab order* of your form (the order in which the focus goes from field to field as the user presses the Tab key). In data entry, the tab order needs to make sense. To view the current tab order, choose View, Tab Order. To change the order, select the field to change and drag it to the new location. When you have the fields in the order you'd like, click on OK.

Forms have built-in navigation buttons on the bottom, but people not familiar with Access might not know how they work. You can create larger navigation buttons to facilitate the data entry. In the example, you will place these buttons in the form header.

Drag the Command Button icon on the toolbox over to the form header portion of the form. The Command Button Wizard appears. First you'll create a button for going to the previous record. Select the Record Navigation category and the Previous Record action. You can either put text on the button or select a picture. For this example, choose the picture of a hand pointing left. Then choose a name and click on Finish. You can add other buttons in the same way for going to the next record, deleting records, adding records, and exiting from the database.

Because you have added buttons for navigation on the form header, you can conceal the default navigation buttons. You can also hide the scrollbars or the Minimize and Maximize buttons. All these options are found in the properties box for the form. Set Scroll Bars to Neither, Record Selectors to No, and Navigation Buttons to No. Figure 15.12 shows the finished form.

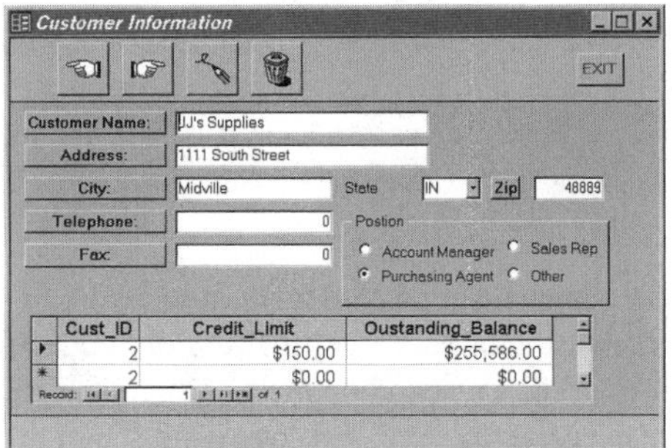

FIGURE 15.12
The form shown in Figure 15.11 now has navigation buttons.

Control Options You do not have to just choose options from the Command Button Wizard. You can potentially assign your own macro, expression, or code to every control on the form, with commands that execute on enter, on exit, on lost focus, on got focus, on click, on double-click, on mouse up, on mouse down, on mouse move, on key down, on key up, on key press, after update, and before update.

Select any of the controls on the form in Design view. Choose the Data tab in the properties box to view all the possibilities. In each of these fields, you can choose to assign a macro, build an expression, or develop code. For example, on the sample form, suppose you want the Delete button to verify whether the user really wants to delete the record. Select the Delete Record button created earlier. On the Data tab, you will see [Event Procedure] for the `onclick` event. Click on the ellipses (...) to view the code. The Command Button Wizard created the current code. You can modify the code to prompt the user with an input box and only perform the other action if the response is yes. Here is the code:

```
Private Sub Command33_Click()
Dim Message, Title, Result, buttons
Message = "Are you sure you want to delete this record?"
Title = "Delete Check" ' Set title.
buttons = vbYesNo 'Sets the buttons that will appear
Result = MsgBox(Message, buttons, Title)
If Result = 6 Then '6 is the value assigned to yes
  DoCmd.DoMenuItem acFormBar, acEditMenu, 8, , acMenuVer70
```

```
  DoCmd.DoMenuItem acFormBar, acEditMenu, 6, , acMenuVer70
ElseIf Result = 7 Then
  MsgBox ("The record was not deleted")
End If
End Sub
```

NOTE You can have as many events for controls as you like. You can have fields populate when focus is lost on a field, reports run on the click of a button, forms open on the double-click of a button, and so on. Just choose the control that will run the action, choose the command (such as on click or on focus), and assign a macro or code. ■

Using Message Boxes Records are added when you move to the next record unless otherwise specified. One way to ensure the data is stored is to display a message box when the last field loses focus. To do this, create a new macro with the macro action MsgBox that displays the message "Your record has been added." Save your macro and name it `messagebox`. In Design view, select the last field to have data entered. On the Data tab, click on the On Lost Focus field and choose the Macro Messagebox. Now when the user moves from that field, the message box will appear.

Form Modes Forms can be opened in two modes. In the Add mode, the user does not see the other records but only a blank form for data entry. In the Edit mode, the user sees all entries and can also add and modify records. Depending on the situation, you can have the form open in the mode that suits your needs. If this form is to be opened from the switchboard, you can assign the mode in which the form will open. (A switchboard is Access's database navigation device. Switchboards are covered in detail in Chapter 9.)

Using Access in Multiuser Environments

The purpose of a database is to store related information in one location. Unlike Excel, Word, or PowerPoint, Access allows several users to access the same database simultaneously and make changes. In other words, Access is a *multiuser environment.*

The advantage of a multiuser environment is that many users can maintain one consistent set of data, and different users can retrieve and update the data from different locations. One problem with a multiuser environment is that other users are locked out when one user is applying updates.

Understanding Record Locking

With several people updating the same record, locking can occur, causing data to be lost or corrupted. Because others could be using the same record as you, you can protect records by choosing a record-locking strategy. Record-locking gives one user exclusive rights to the record she is editing. Three record-locking strategies are available:

- *No Locks.* As the name implies, no locks occur on the records. If two or more people are editing a record at the same time, Access informs them that another person has changed the record. You can then choose to overwrite the other user's changes, copy your changes to the Clipboard, or ignore your changes.

- *Edited Records*. This strategy locks the record being edited, preventing others from making changes to it.
- *All Records*. This strategy locks all records in the table or tables you are editing until you close the table or tables. Avoid this strategy unless you are the only person who will update records. If many people will be updating records, this strategy is unproductive, because users will often have to wait for records to be unlocked. Users might find themselves wasting time attempting to update records that cannot be updated.

To set the strategy, choose Tools, Options and click on the Advanced tab.

If you use a record-locking strategy other than No Locks, Access provides symbols to help users know the record status. The symbols are displayed in the current record selector. A forward arrow indicates that the current record has not been edited. A pencil indicates you have edited but not saved the record; when this symbol is displayed, others cannot edit the record or view your changes. As soon as the record is saved, other users will see the changes. A circle with a line through it appears if another person locked the record. If you try to edit this record, you'll see a message indicating that the record is locked and who has it locked.

The Advanced tab in the Options dialog box provides four settings that help prevent locking conflicts:

- *Refresh Interval*. The number of seconds for which records are updated. You can choose a value between 0 and 32,766 seconds, with the default being 60 seconds. If you are doing extensive data entry and others need to see the data quickly, decrease this interval.
- *Update Retry Interval*. The number of milliseconds for which Access retries to save a locked record. You can choose values between 0 and 1,000; the default is 250.
- *Number of Update Retries*. The number of times Access retries to save the locked record. The default is 2, but you can choose values between 0 and 10.
- *ODBC Refresh Interval*. If you are using ODBC, this sets the interval for refresh. As with the Refresh Interval option, you can choose anywhere between 0 and 32,766 seconds. The default is 1,500 seconds.

Because Access is a multiuser environment, you should open the database exclusively if you are going to make extensive changes to the database. This helps eliminate conflict errors and avoids confusing other users. Opening a database exclusively means only you can make changes; all other users will be opening the database in read-only mode.

TIP When updating objects, you should also update all dependent objects. If all dependent objects are not updated, discrepancies can result in the objects and data.

NOTE If you make changes to an object another person has open, he will have to close that object before seeing the modifications.

Understanding Front-End/Back-End Database Applications

A front-end/back-end application contains two databases: One stores all the tables and the other contains the queries, forms, reports, macros, and modules. The back-end database, which stores the tables, is usually located on a network, and the front-end database is on individual systems. The tables on the front-end database are linked to the back-end database.

Here are some of the reasons for having a front-end/back end application:

- *Size*. Having two databases decreases the size of the files, which reduces the chance of data corruption.
- *Manageability*. If you have all the tables on the network, they can be backed up frequently, which wards off data loss.
- *Customization*. If several users want the same underlying information but want to do different things with it, they can have different front-end applications.
- *Security*. Linked tables cannot be modified; the records can be changed, but the design cannot. This prohibits front-end users from manipulating the design of the tables.

If the front-end application is the same for everyone, this method might not be the best choice. If you change any objects other than the tables, you will have to update all the front-end databases individually. In such a case, you should use database replication, which is covered in the next section.

To create a front-end/back-end application, you can either create two different databases or use the database splitter to convert an existing database.

Creating a New Front-End/Back-End Application To create a new front-end/back-end application, first create a new database with the tables that will be used for the front-end application. Then create another new database, but link the tables from the first database. To link tables, choose File, Get External Data, Link Tables. Choose the database you just created and all available tables appear. Choose one, multiple, or all of the tables to link. You can now create queries, forms, reports, macros, and modules in the front-end database. You can create several front-end databases that all link to the same back-end database. Make sure you always link to the back-end database, because you cannot link to a linked table.

Creating a Front-End/Back-End Application from an Existing Database You can convert an existing database to a front-end/back-end application by using the database splitter. Choose Tools, Add-ins, Database Splitter. The Database Splitter Wizard appears.

CAUTION

Always back up your database before performing a split.

The wizard explains that this process can take a while and asks if you would like to continue. The wizard then asks for the location and name of the back-end database. Access recommends naming the databases the same except adding _be for back-ends. After you choose the location and name for the back-end database and click on OK, you'll see a message box indicating that the database has been split. The name of your existing database remains the same but you will notice that the tables are now linked.

Managing Database Replication

Another way to take advantage of a multiuser environment is through replication. Database replication consists of a design master database and replica database(s). If not everyone can get to the main database, you can create replica sets of the master database. When you synchronize, changes between the master and replica sets are applied to all databases.

A few changes occur to a database when it is replicated. Three additional fields are added to each table:

- s_GUID is a unique identifier for each record.
- s_Lineage is a binary field that stores information about changes to each record.
- s_Generation stores information about groups of changes.

Several tables might also be added to the database. If a conflict occurs during replication, MsysSidetables is added, containing information regarding the conflicts. MsysErrors contains information regarding where and why errors occurred during synchronization. It identifies the table, record, and replica affected and states the last change to the record, the type of operation that failed, and the reason for the failure. MsysSchemaProb is created if an error occurs while updating the design of a replica. MsysExchangeLog stores information about the sychronizations.

These tables are system tables, which do not have to be viewable. To change whether the tables are viewable, choose Tools, Options and use the Show System Objects option on the View tab.

Changes occur to any AutoNumber fields in a replicated database. AutoNumber fields in existing records do not change, but AutoNumber values for inserted records are random. If you have any applications that rely on incremental numbering, change the AutoNumber field to a Date/Time field before replicating.

You can use Briefcase replication, replication from the Tools menu, or the Microsoft Replication Manager. The Microsoft Replication Manager is only available if you have Office 97, Developer Edition.

Briefcase replication involves dragging a database from a shared folder onto My Briefcase in Windows Explorer. When you do this, the database is converted to a design master and a replica is created in My Briefcase. You're most likely to use Briefcase replication when you are moving between a laptop and a desktop computer. You can have the same database in both places, can make changes to both, and can synchronize these changes. To synchronize the databases, click on the My Briefcase icon and then click on the database file. Select Update Selection and then Update.

NOTE If you do not have Briefcase installed, click on the Windows Start button and choose Settings. Click on Control Panel, click on Add/Remove Programs, and double-click on Accessories on the Windows Setup tab. To install Briefcase replication, run the Access Setup program.

Replication tools are located under Tools, Replication. To create a replica, choose Tools, Replication, Create Replica. If you have the database open, Access tells you it is going to close the database and convert it to the design master. It also prompts you to make a backup copy of the database before replicating. This is recommended—if you do not like what the replication does to your database, you can delete it and use the backup copy. The next dialog box prompts you for a location for the new replica. Choose a location and name and click on OK. All of the objects in the design master database now show they are replicated, as you can see in Figure 15.13. The circle icons (the ones containing two arrows) next to the objects indicate replicated objects.

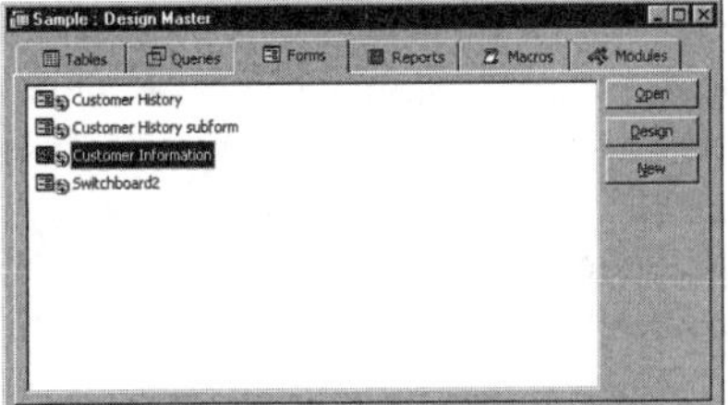

FIGURE 15.13
An icon with bidirectional arrows notes replicated objects.

Changes to the design can only be made to the design master, but changes to the records in tables can be made to the replicas and the design master. For changes to be applied to all databases, you must synchronize the databases.

To synchronize, choose Tools, Replication, Synchronize Now. Access asks you which database to synchronize with. If you have several replicas, you will have to repeat this step for each one. On this screen you can also choose to switch the design master. If there are no conflicts, you get a message box indicating the synchronization is complete. If there are conflicts, a message indicates that you need to resolve the conflicts. You can choose to do so now or later. If you do not resolve the conflicts, this message will occur every time any of the databases is opened. When you resolve the conflicts, a list appears with the conflicting records of each table so you can choose which table's record to accept.

If you have Microsoft Access Developer's Edition, you can use the Replication Manager. This gives a visual interface for making changes to the replication set as well as scheduling synchronization.

Any objects you add to the design master can be local or replicable. If you do not want the objects to replicate to other databases, make them local. By choosing View, Properties on an object, you can choose whether the object is replicable.

If the design master becomes damaged or deleted, you can make a new design master from one of the replicas. Open the replica you want to use for the design master and choose Tools, Replication, Synchronize Now. Select the replica in the list and click on OK. Repeat this process for each remaining replica in the set. Then choose Tools, Replication, Recover Design Master.

You can remove a replica by deleting it in Windows Explorer.

Customizing Views for Each User

You can specify which views a user can have. As mentioned, you can have a form open in either Add or Edit mode. You can also limit whether a user can switch between Datasheet, Design, and Form views. Limiting views is useful when you want users to be able to only see certain forms or enter data on certain forms.

Choosing which views are allowed can be done in several places. One is on the property sheet of a form. If you are opening a form by using a macro, you can specify in the macro the view in which the form is opened. Through Visual Basic commands, you can use the ViewsAllowed command.

Another way to customize views is by using the Workgroup Administrator. If users belong to a workgroup, you can set permissions for each user. Users' permissions will not determine the views they can see but will limit the type of changes they can make. User and Group accounts and permissions are found under Tools, Security.

You can use Visual Basic along with permissions to change views for users. The code looks at users to determine which group they belong to. You can then use Case…Select statements or If…Then statements to determine how a form is opened. This code can be assigned to a button on the switchboard so pressing the button opens the form in a predetermined view. ●

CHAPTER 16

Managing VBA and Other Macros

The applications that make up Microsoft Office have long been powerful development tools, as well as end-user applications. Word and Excel, for example, have both contained powerful macro languages since the products were first introduced in Windows versions. As the features of the applications have grown and evolved, the macro languages and other development tools have grown as well.

A *macro* is a program written in a programming language that is built in to an Office application. Macros automate the process of everyday operations of the programs, making your work faster and more reliable. When a user runs a macro, he or she doesn't even have to understand all the individual commands that the macro is using, so he or she can get productive work accomplished more quickly and with less training.

The primary macro language for Office 97 is Visual Basic for Applications, or VBA. VBA shares the same syntax, or programming rules, as Visual Basic for Windows, which you can use to develop standalone Windows applications. The inclusion of VBA in Word, Excel, PowerPoint, and Access gives programmers a consistent language and programming environment for customizing Office applications.

Office applications include some other programming tools as well:

- Visual Basic, Scripting Edition, or VBScript, is used as the programming language of Outlook 97 and Outlook 98. VBScript is a simplified version of Visual Basic, and is also used by some other Microsoft products, such as Microsoft Internet Explorer.
- Access includes a simplified macro language, in addition to VBA. Database designers who don't want to get into the complexity of programming in VBA use access macros. These macros, however, lack many of the advanced features of VBA, such as error checking and calling Windows API functions.
- Excel contains support for its old function-style macros, which are now referred to as *Excel 4 macros*. These macros are sometimes called *XLM macros*, since they were once stored in files with the .xlm extension. Since VBA was first introduced to Excel in version 5, this older macro language has been included for compatibility. However, it's best to develop all new macros in VBA.
- Word 97 contains support for WordBasic, the previous macro language for all versions of Word for Windows. This support is embedded into Word's VBA object model, so that old WordBasic macros can be automatically translated into VBA macros, using the WordBasic object. Any new macros you create in Word 97 should be created as VBA code.

The Role of Object Models in Office VBA

VBA is an *object-based* programming environment. This means that most of the actions in VBA are performed by working with *objects* in the individual applications. There are many examples of objects in Office:

- An *Application* object represents one of the Office programs.
- A *Document* object in Word represents any open document.
- A *Cell* object in Excel represents any cell on an Excel worksheet.
- A *QueryDef* object in Access represents a query definition that has been saved in the database.
- An *Item* object in Outlook represents an email message, contact, calendar, or other item that you can store in an Outlook folder.

These are but a few of the hundreds of objects that are available for control by VBA and VBScript. These objects are not actually defined in the VBA language. Instead, each application provides a type library, which is installed along with the applications themselves. The type library contains a definition of that program's *object model*, which defines the functionality of the application that you want to control.

The object model helps both the programmer and VBA itself. Because VBA doesn't know anything about an object's models, it uses the object model to interpret the individual lines of code as it executes them. For the programmer, the object model defines the extensions to VBA that are provided by each application.

As an example of how objects work, consider the code required to perform a simple operation, such as creating a new document in Word. In WordBasic, which is a traditional procedural language, you could have written the following statement:


```
FileNew
```

In VBA the following statement performs the same task:

```
Documents.Add
```

This statement instructs VBA to add one object to the collection of document objects in Word. The statement has three components:

- `Documents` is an object (in this case a *collection* of objects) representing some content or feature of the application.
- The dot (.) is an operator that joins the parts of a statement together.
- `Add` is a method, which is an instruction to carry out some type of action; in this case adding a new document.

Look at one more example of how VBA uses objects. In Excel VBA, you might use the following statement:

```
ActiveCell.Formula = "Bill Ray"
```

This statement assigns a text value to the cell, effectively typing the text into the cell. Breaking the statement down into its parts, we get the following:

- `ActiveCell` is an object, referring to the active worksheet cell.
- The dot (.) operator is used to join the parts of the statement together.
- `Formula` is a property, which is an attribute, or value, associated with an object.
- The equal sign (=) is an *assignment operator*, indicating that you want to assign a value to a property or a variable.
- The text between the quotation marks is a *literal value*, representing data that you want to assign to the `Formula` property.

These two simple examples give you a glimpse into VBA's capability to work with objects. In most VBA code, the vast majority of statements in your macros work with the objects of the Office application you are using. Becoming familiar with the object model of each Office application is one of the major steps to gaining skill as a VBA developer.

One of the best ways to learn about VBA objects is to record macros. Word, Excel, and PowerPoint can record VBA macros, which you then can view and edit in the VBA Editor that is integrated into Office. Unfortunately, you can't record Access VBA or Outlook VBScript code.

Organizing and Storing Macros

While VBA is designed to bring a much greater degree of consistency to macro development than previous development tools, there are still some inconsistencies in Office VBA. One of the most obvious is the way in which each of the Office applications store VBA code.

VBA code is organized into three levels of detail. Each Office application must store VBA code in procedures, modules, and projects. Before learning how each program stores these objects, you need to understand what they are.

- A *procedure* is a collection of VBA statements, organized together to perform a task. Procedures can range from just a few lines of VBA code, to hundreds of lines of code. There are two types of procedures:
  - *Sub procedures* perform a series of VBA actions. Most VBA procedures, and all recorded macros, are subprocedures.
  - *Function procedures* can also perform actions, but also return a result. Function procedures are often used for custom calculations.
- A *module* is a collection of procedures, functions, and declarations. Some modules are defined automatically. For example, each VBA form contains a module, and each Word document contains a module. Every procedure must be stored in a module.
- A *project* is a collection of modules. Generally, a project is contained in a single file, so opening the file that contains the project makes the modules and procedures of the project available for execution.

Each Office application has its own system for organizing and storing project files. Understanding how and when projects are loaded will help you decide where to store VBA code to get the best performance and flexibility.

Storing Macros in Word

In Word, projects are stored in templates and in documents. It is most common to store VBA code in templates, and prior to Office 97, WordBasic macro code could only be stored in templates. Starting with Word 97, you can also store VBA code in individual documents.

Because a template typically is used as a model for a specific type of document, such as a letter, memo, fax, report, or some other document you use, you can store the macros related to that type of document in the associated template. For example, you might create a macro that prompts the user for the information you want to display in a memo. You then can store this macro in the memo template. If you do, the macro will only be available when the memo template is open, or when a document based upon the template is open.

Word provides three locations for storing templates. You can designate separate folders for each of these locations by choosing Tools, Options, and clicking the File Locations tab (see Figure 16.1). To change the folder for any of the file locations, click on the location you want to change, click Modify to display the Modify Location dialog box (shown in Figure 16.2), and select the desired location.

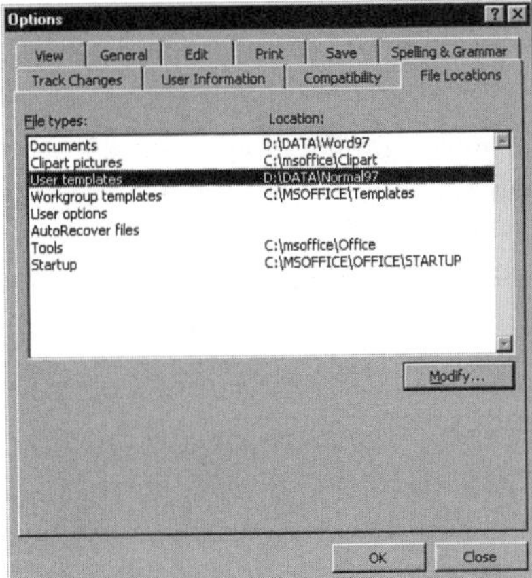

FIGURE 16.1
Use the File Locations tab of Word's Options dialog box to control where Word saves different types of files.

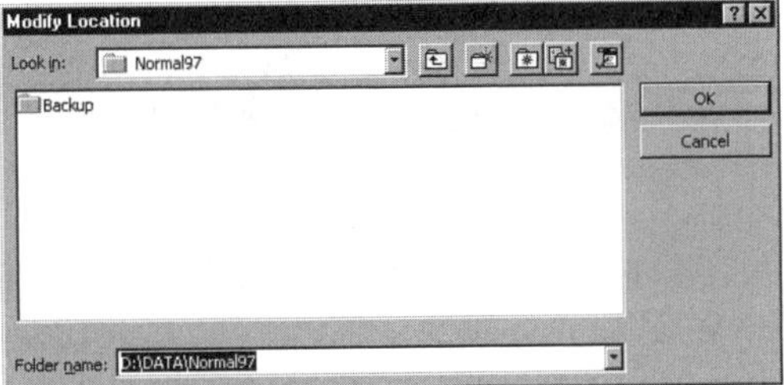

FIGURE 16.2
Use the Modify Location dialog box to change the folder of one of the file locations.

These three file locations are used to store templates, which in turn can store VBA projects:

- **User templates**. This is the folder where the user's Normal.dot template is stored, and where a user can store additional templates that he or she creates. Each user must have write access to this folder, so it should either be on the local hard drive, or in the user's personal storage area on the network. It is not recommended that you attempt to share this folder, or that you share a Normal.dot file among users.
- **Workgroup templates**. This is the best place to store shared templates, such as those for creating your organization's standard documents (letters, memos, fax covers, and so on). For users on a network, you might want to share this folder, and make it read-only for them. This will prevent the users from accidentally modifying these key templates.
- **Startup**. Use this folder to store global templates that are loaded automatically when Word starts. This folder is for templates not used as document templates, but simply as storage locations for global macros and other customizations, such as menu, toolbar, and shortcut key customizations. Any templates that are in the startup folder are opened as read-only and are hidden to the user, but the macros and other customizations are available. The templates remain open as long as the user is running Word. On a network, you can make this a shared, read-only folder to prevent any accidental modifications of these templates.

Beginning in Word 97, you can also store macros in a document. This enables you to distribute a document electronically—and distribute the macros for working on that document along with it—without distributing a separate template file. This is a good approach for single-document solutions, but it is less efficient for applications in which many documents share the same macros, because the same code is duplicated in each document.

NOTE If you send a document to users who have Word's macro virus protection feature enabled, they will get the warning message when they open your document. If they weren't expecting to find macros in the document they received, they might choose to disable the macros before opening the document. (See "Macro Viruses and Office 97's Macro Virus Protection" later in this chapter for more information about macro viruses.)

Word supports the following two additional types of files that can help you create automated solutions:

- *Wizards* are templates that have been saved with the .wiz extension, and that contain VBA macros. Wizards are typically used to create documents automatically, using a standard interface that was designed by Microsoft. If you have created a wizard, you'll probably want to store it in the workgroup templates folder.
- *Add-ins* are special program files written in the C programming language. They can perform similar activities as VBA programs, but the source code is completely protected from modification since it is not stored in the distributed add-in file. Add-ins are most commonly used by commercial developers who want to distribute a solution widely. Add-in files must be loaded globally, so they should be stored in the startup folder.

The Role of Normal.dot in Word

The Normal.dot file, often referred to as the *global template*, is one of the most important files to understand in Word. As with any template, the Normal template can be used to store VBA macros, styles, page layout, AutoText entries, and boilerplate text. The initial document that appears when you start Word is based upon the Normal template.

Each user must have his own copy of the global template, stored in the location indicated by the user templates folder. In other words, the template is "global" only to that user, not to be shared among users. Any time the user records a macro, creates a custom style, or saves an AutoText entry, it can be saved in that user's Normal template, without affecting the environment of other users. If you want to distribute solutions among many users, you should create one or more templates that will be stored in the workgroup or startup folders.

When Word starts, it loads the Normal template into memory and keeps it loaded for the rest of the working session. If it doesn't find the Normal template in the user templates folder, Word searches other folders, such as the Word program folder, to find a copy of Normal.dot. Once it finds a Normal template, it loads that template, and doesn't look any further for matching template names. If it can't find a Normal.dot file, Word automatically generates a new one in memory, and uses it for the rest of the working session. This template is based upon Word's "factory default" settings for margins, fonts, and so on, and contains no customizations. At the end of your working session, Word saves the new global template in the default location for user templates.

When each user exits Word, the program checks to see whether any changes have been made to the Normal template, and whether those changes should be saved. Word can either save the changes automatically, or it can ask the user whether he or she wants to save the changes, depending upon the following option setting: Choose Tools, Options, and then click the Save tab. If you check the box labeled Prompt to Save Normal Template, Word will ask for confirmation before saving changes upon exiting. If you leave this box unchecked, Work will automatically save the changes, without asking for confirmation. Many users prefer the automatic saving method, which speeds the process of exiting Word.

The actual location for storing the user's Normal.dot file is determined by the Tools, Options, File Locations command. The User Templates setting should contain the name of the folder where you want Word to save the user's Normal.dot file, as well as any custom templates that he or she creates. Make sure that the folder indicated here is either on the user's hard drive or is a private folder on the network.

In order to prevent confusion regarding Normal templates, you should make sure that there are no stray copies of Normal.dot floating around the network. I have seen Word go out of its way to find these copies and load them into memory, preventing the proper loading of the user's Normal.dot. The most common problem seems to occur when a copy of Normal.dot exists in the shared program folder in a networked installation. This template may get loaded, and because the folder is usually read-only for users, they are not able to save any changes they want to make. Be careful to remove any such copies of Normal.dot, and make sure that all users' file locations are set properly to match your installation strategy.

Storing Macros in Excel

In Excel, projects are stored in workbooks and add-ins. Opening a workbook makes the VBA code in that workbook available for execution. When you record a macro, you have an opportunity to select the location for the macro.

Choose Tools, Macro, Record New Macro. The Record Macro dialog box appears, as shown in Figure 16.3. Notice that the Store Macro In list is displayed in this figure to show the options for storing a new macro. Select This Workbook to store the recorded macro in the active workbook. To run the macro in the future, that workbook will have to be open. Select New Workbook if you want Excel to create a new workbook in which to store the new macro. Once again, you will have to open this new workbook to run the macro. Select Personal Macro Workbook to store the macro in a workbook named Personal.xls, which is stored in your Excel startup folder. Macros stored in Personal.xls are available to all workbooks, because this file is automatically loaded as a hidden workbook every time Excel starts.

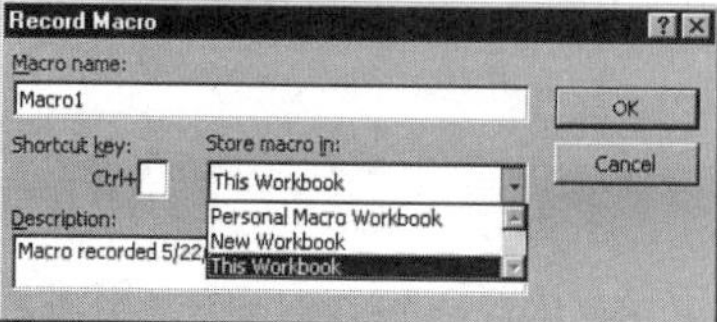

FIGURE 16.3
Excel's Record Macro dialog box enables you to specify where to store your macros.

Excel's Startup Folders

Excel has a startup folder that works much like the startup folder in Word. Any files in your startup folder, such as workbooks and add-ins, are opened automatically when Excel starts, but are invisible to the user. This make the macros in these workbooks available for execution.

Excel's default startup folder is named XLStart, and it is an immediate subfolder of Excel's program folder. This folder is automatically created by Excel's setup program. If you are running Excel as a shared network installation, the XLStart folder should be read-only, and it is a good place to distribute macros that everyone in your group can use.

Excel lets you designate an alternate startup folder as well, so that individual users can have their own startup folders in addition to the shared startup folder. To specify an alternate startup folder, choose Tools, Options, and click the General tab. Enter the alternate startup folder in the Alternate Startup File Location text box.

Using Add-Ins in Excel

Excel add-in files provide a way to distribute finished Excel applications. After a workbook has been saved as an add-in, it can't be edited. It's important, therefore, to keep a copy of the original workbook, in case you need to make changes to the application.

To create an add-in file in Excel 97, open the workbook that you want to convert to an add-in. Choose File, Save As. In the Save As dialog box, shown in Figure 16.4, enter a name for the file you are creating, and select Microsoft Excel Add-In in the Save as Type list.

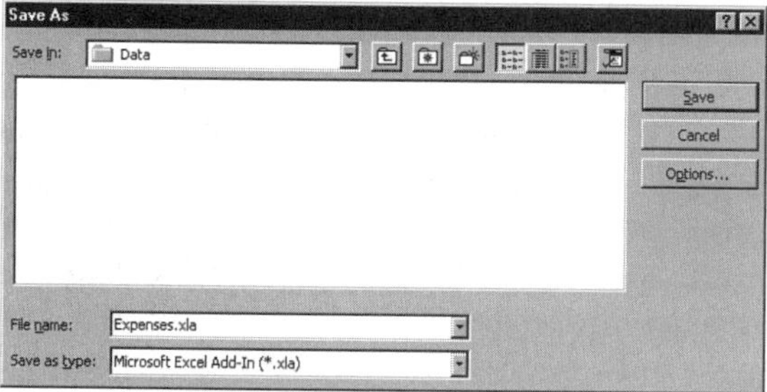

FIGURE 16.4
Use the Save As dialog box to select the Microsoft Excel Add-In type when you want to save a workbook as an add-in.

Several add-ins are provided with Excel. These add-in files provide added features such as an Analysis ToolPak, an AutoSave feature, and a File Conversion Wizard. Commercial developers may develop all or part of their solutions as add-ins. You can also use the C programming language to develop add-ins.

You can load an add-in file into memory in the following three ways:

- Open the add-in file directly using the File, Open command. Once the add-in file is open, its macros are available for use, as though they were built-in commands.
- Place the add-in file in your Excel startup folder. If you do this, the add-in opens automatically each time Excel starts and remains loaded as long as you are in Excel.
- Use the Add-In Manager to load and unload add-ins.

To use the Add-In Manager, choose Tools, Add-Ins. The Add-Ins dialog box, shown in Figure 16.5, appears. You can use the Add-In Manager in the following ways:

- To load an add-in, mark the check box next to its name.
- To unload an add-in, clear the check box.
- If you don't see the add-in you are looking for in the list, click the Browse button to search your drives and folders for the add-in file.

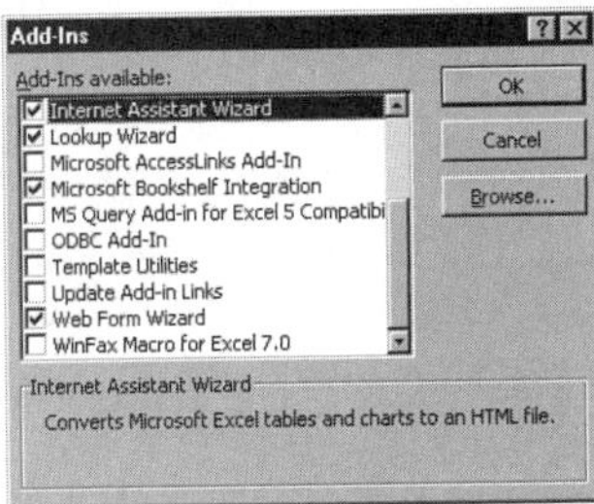

FIGURE 16.5
Use the Add-Ins dialog box to load and unload Excel add-ins.

After you have loaded an add-in using the Add-In Manager, the add-in will be loaded each time you start Excel, until you uncheck it in the Add-In Manager.

Of course, if you don't expect to need the features of an add-in on a regular basis, it's a good idea not to have it loaded automatically every time you run Excel.

Storing Macros in PowerPoint 97

In PowerPoint 97, VBA projects are stored in the presentation files you create, or in presentation templates. You can also create add-ins to further customize the PowerPoint environment.

When you record or create a macro in PowerPoint, the macro is saved in the active presentation file. If you later save the presentation as a template, the macros are copied to the template. When you create a new presentation based upon a template, the macros are not copied from the template to the new presentation.

You can also save a presentation as an add-in, using the File, Save As command. You can use add-ins that contain VBA code to customize the PowerPoint environment by adding custom toolbars or menu commands. You can also write PowerPoint add-ins in the C programming language. Commercial developers might distribute their custom solutions as add-ins.

After you create an add-in, you can load it using the Add-In Manager. Choose Tools, Add-Ins to display the Add-Ins dialog box, as shown in Figure 16.6. The add-ins that have previously been loaded are listed in the dialog box. If there is an X next to an add-in's name, it is currently loaded.

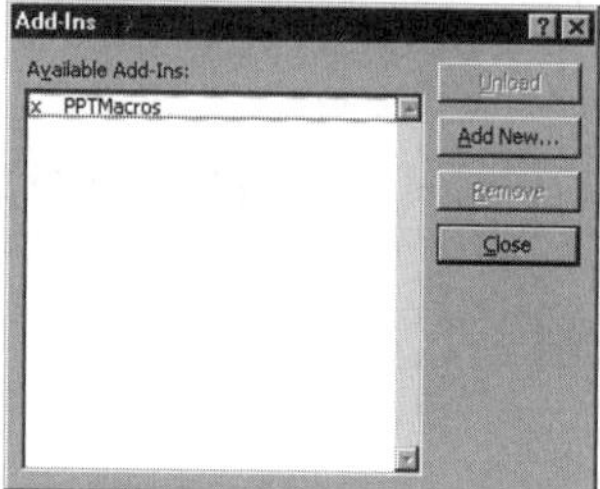

FIGURE 16.6
You can use PowerPoint's Add-Ins dialog box to add, load, unload, and remove add-ins.

You can use this dialog box in the following several ways:

- To unload an add-in and leave its name on the list, select the add-in and click the Unload button. The button label changes to *Load*.
- To load an add-in that is on the list but not checked, select the add-in and click Load.
- To add an add-in to the list, click Add New to browse your drives and folders for add-in files.
- To remove an add-in from the list, select the add-in, and then click Remove.

Storing VBA and Macros in Access 97

In Access, each database file contains its own project. Within an Access database, you can create three kinds of VBA modules:

- Each *form* contains a module to hold the event code associated with the form. The code executes in response to such events as opening or closing the form, clicking on a button, moving from record to record, or changing the data that is displayed on a form. Because many Access applications are primarily form-driven, it is not uncommon to find most of the VBA code for a database in its form modules.
- Each *report* contains a module to hold the event code for the report. Report modules are useful for handling dynamic operations such as conditional formatting based on specified data values at print time.
- General purpose modules in the *modules* container of a database are used to store VBA code that is not specific to an individual form or report. This is a good place to store common procedures and functions that you use throughout an application, or code that you want to reuse in other databases. By copying the module to another database, you can make the same functionality available without reentering the code.

In addition to VBA, Access has a separate macro facility. The Access macro language lets you automate most of the operations in Access by selecting macro actions from drop-down lists.

For beginning developers, using the macro language is quite a bit easier than writing VBA code; however, Access macros don't have the integrated debugging and error checking features of VBA, and they don't have the capability to call Windows API functions. For the most reliable, secure, and high-performance Access applications, most developers prefer to use VBA.

Access does not have the capability to record either VBA code or macros, although there are several wizards built into Access that generate significant amounts of VBA code, especially associated with form events.

Storing VBScript Code in Outlook

In Outlook, you can create VBScript code that is associated with the event procedures of a form. VBScript is a simplified version of the Visual Basic language that doesn't support all the features of VBA. It does, however, let you control Outlook's object model, which enables you to automate the operation of Outlook.

The only place to enter VBScript code in Outlook is in a form, using the Form Designer. You have to start with an existing form and either save changes to it or publish it as a new form.

In Outlook 97, open the form that you want to modify, and then choose Tools, Form Designer to activate the form design tools.

In Outlook 98, open the form that you want to modify, and then choose Tools, Forms, Design This Form. Figure 16.7 shows an Outlook 98 Contact form open in Design view.

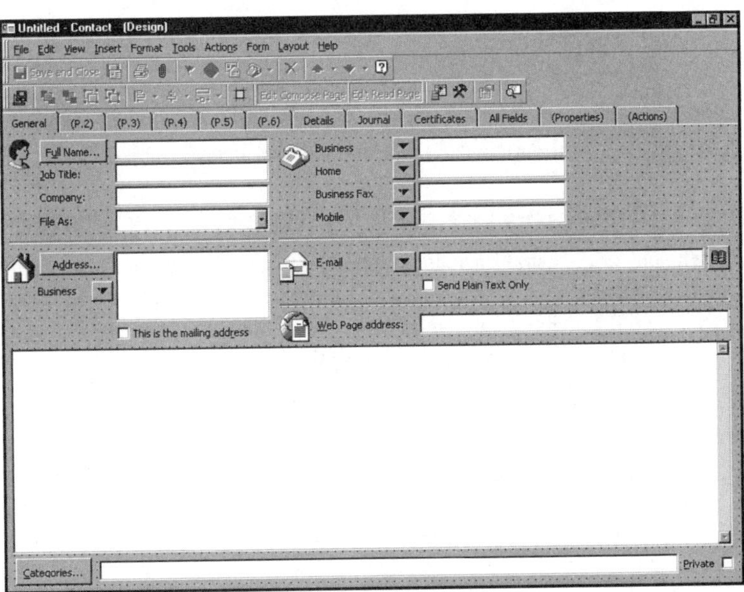

FIGURE 16.7
This Outlook 98 Contact form has been opened in Design view so that it can be modified.

To enter VBScript code, choose Form, View Code. The Script Editor appears, as shown in Figure 16.8.

FIGURE 16.8
Use the Script Editor to enter VBScript code for an Outlook form.

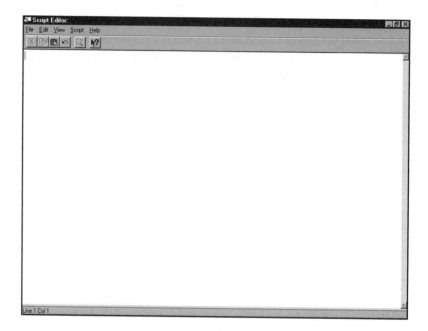

NOTE The Script Editor does not have the integrated debugging and other advanced tools of the Visual Basic Editor that the other Office applications use for working with VBA code.

When you are done entering your VBScript code, choose File, Close. Your VBScript code will be saved with the form when you publish the form.

Macro Viruses and Office 97's Macro Virus Protection

The power of Visual Basic for Applications has, unfortunately, presented an opportunity for those who develop macro viruses. A *macro virus* is simply a macro that performs some sort of unwanted activity when you open an Office document and spreads itself from document to document, usually through the application's templates.

One of the mechanisms of macro viruses is the use of automatically executing macros. Word, Excel, and PowerPoint can execute macros automatically based upon certain events, such as opening a file, closing a file, or creating a new file based upon a template. This automatic-execution capability is a great way to automate processes such as document production, but, unfortunately, it also is a gateway for macro viruses. Because the viruses are often written to run automatically when a document is opened, the user might not even notice the macro until is has already copied itself to a global template or to other open documents.

While there is no completely foolproof method for avoiding macro viruses, Office 97 provides a built-in feature for Word, Excel, and PowerPoint to identify documents that might contain macros. If you have turned on the macro virus protection in all of these applications, each time you open a Word document, Excel workbook, or PowerPoint presentation, Office checks to see whether the file contains any macros, toolbar customizations, menu customizations, or custom keyboard shortcuts. You can choose to turn macro virus protection on or off for each of these three applications independently.

To turn on macro virus protection in Word, Excel, or PowerPoint, choose Tools, Options, click the General tab, and mark the Macro Virus Protection check box.

If you have macro virus protection enabled and any macros or other customizations are found when you open a document, the warning message shown in Figure 16.9 is displayed.

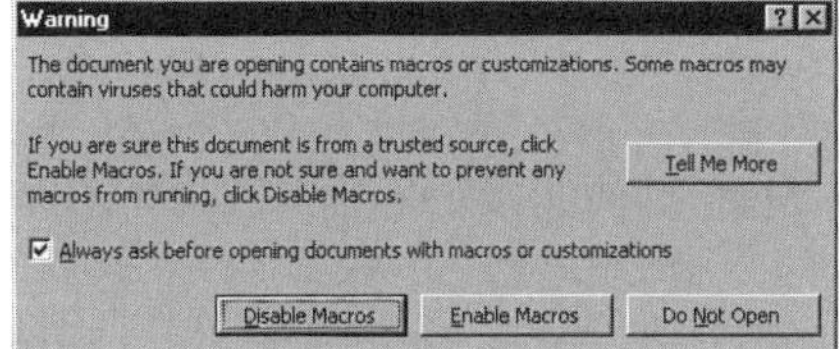

FIGURE 16.9
The Warning dialog box informs you that the document you are opening might contain viruses, but it doesn't make any attempt to remove the viruses.

If the Warning dialog box appears, you have several choices:

- Click Disable Macros to open the file but disable all of the macros and customizations in the document. If you have any doubts about the origin of the file, and you didn't expect any macros or customizations, select this option.
- Click Enable Macros to open the file as normal, with all of the macros and customizations available. Select this option if you trust the origin of the file and know that the macros are not viruses.
- Click Do Not Open if you are unsure about the origin of the file, and you don't want to take any chances with unexpected macros.
- To see a help file with more information about macro viruses, click Tell Me More.
- To disable macro virus protection in the application, clear the Always Ask Before Opening Documents with Macros or Customizations check box. Clearing this check box disables any detection of potential macro viruses.

It is important to understand the limitations of the macro virus protection tool. All it does is identify that there are macros or other customizations in the document. The tool does not make any attempt to distinguish between good and bad macros. Neither does it provide any mechanism for cleaning or removing macros or virus from the templates. It is up to you either to check and remove the macros manually, or to use another utility to check the document.

Several popular commercial tools are available for detecting macro viruses, as well as other viruses that might infect your computer. It is highly recommended that you install such a utility on your computer and your network.

Migrating Legacy Macros

If you have a library of existing macros in any of the Office applications, and you are upgrading to a newer version of Office, you need to understand how macros and other program code are converted automatically, and what additional modifications you are likely to have to make. Because of the variety of different versions of applications and different macro languages, it is necessary to look at each application individually.

Because PowerPoint did not include macro features before Office 97, there is no facility for converting macros from earlier versions.

Upgrading from Word 6.0 or Word 95 to Word 97

Prior to the release of Word 97, the macro language for Word was WordBasic. WordBasic was a dialect of earlier versions of the Basic programming language, customized for the features of Word. New statements were added to Word Basic as each new version of Word added new features to the product. Virtually everything that you could do with the Word user interface could be automated with WordBasic. Listing 16.1 shows how you could write a macro to create a new document and type the headings for a memo directly into the new document.

Listing 16.1 This WordBasic Macro Creates a New Document and Types the Headings for a Memo

```
Sub MAIN
' NewMemo - a macro to create a new memo document

  FileNew
  FilePageSetup   .LeftMargin = "1 in", .RightMargin = "1 in"
  FormatTabs .Position = "1 in", .Align = 0, .Set
  Bold 1
  Insert "To:"
  Bold 0
  Insert Chr$(9)
  FormatParagraph .After = "12 pt"
  InsertPara
  Bold 1
  Insert "From:"
  Bold 0
  Insert Chr$(9)
  InsertPara
  Bold 1
  Insert "Date:"
  Bold 0
  Insert Chr$(9)
  InsertDateTime .DateTimePic = "M/d/yy", .InsertAsField = 0
  InsertPara
  Bold 1
  Insert "Subject:"
```

```
    Bold 0
    Insert Chr$(9)
    InsertPara
End Sub
```

When you open a Word 2.0, Word 6.0 or Word 95 template in Word 97, Word automatically converts the existing macros to VBA, using the WordBasic object of the Word 97 object model. For example, the NewMemo macro would be converted as shown in Listing 16.2. Notice that the code is copied line for line, and is preceded by a reference to the WordBasic object. This means that each line of code is translated from the original WordBasic source at the time it is executed.

Listing 16.2 The NewMemo Macro Has Been Converted to VBA Using the WordBasic Object

```
Public Sub MAIN()
WordBasic.FileNew
WordBasic.FilePageSetup LeftMargin:="1 in", RightMargin:="1 in"
WordBasic.FormatTabs Position:="1 in", Align:=0, Set:=1
WordBasic.Bold 1
WordBasic.Insert "To:"
WordBasic.Bold 0
WordBasic.Insert Chr(9)
WordBasic.FormatParagraph After:="12 pt"
WordBasic.InsertPara
WordBasic.Bold 1
WordBasic.Insert "From:"
WordBasic.Bold 0
WordBasic.Insert Chr(9)
WordBasic.InsertPara
WordBasic.Bold 1
WordBasic.Insert "Date:"
WordBasic.Bold 0
WordBasic.Insert Chr(9)
WordBasic.InsertDateTime DateTimePic:="M/d/yy", InsertAsField:=0
WordBasic.InsertPara
WordBasic.Bold 1
WordBasic.Insert "Subject:"
WordBasic.Bold 0
WordBasic.Insert Chr(9)
WordBasic.InsertPara
End Sub
```

As an alternative to accepting the automatic translation, you might choose to re-create the macro from scratch in VBA, either by using the macro recorder, or by typing the code into the Visual Basic Editor. Listing 16.3 shows the equivalent VBA macro as it might be created by recording and editing the recorded code in Word 97.

Listing 16.3 This Version of the NewMemo Macro Is Written in VBA, Using the Word 97 Object Model

```
Sub NewMemo()
'
' NewMemo Macro
' Macro created 05/19/98 by Bill Ray
'
    Documents.Add
    With ActiveDocument.PageSetup
        .LeftMargin = InchesToPoints(1)
        .RightMargin = InchesToPoints(1)
    End With
    Selection.ParagraphFormat.TabStops.Add Position:=InchesToPoints(1), _
        Alignment:=wdAlignTabLeft, Leader:=wdTabLeaderSpaces
    Selection.Font.Bold = True
    Selection.TypeText Text:="To:"
    Selection.Font.Bold = False
    Selection.TypeText Text:=vbTab
    Selection.ParagraphFormat.SpaceAfter = 12
    Selection.TypeParagraph
    Selection.Font.Bold = True
    Selection.TypeText Text:="From:"
    Selection.Font.Bold = False
    Selection.TypeText Text:=vbTab
    Selection.TypeParagraph
    Selection.Font.Bold = True
    Selection.TypeText Text:="Date:"
    Selection.Font.Bold = False
    Selection.TypeText Text:=vbTab
    Selection.InsertDateTime DateTimeFormat:="M/d/yy", InsertAsField:=False
    Selection.TypeParagraph
    Selection.Font.Bold = True
    Selection.TypeText Text:="Subject:"
    Selection.Font.Bold = False
    Selection.TypeText Text:=vbTab
    Selection.TypeParagraph
End Sub
```

In the simple example shown in this section, the automatically converted macro works effectively, and little is gained by re-creating the macro in VBA. You should consider re-creating your WordBasic macro in VBA code if any of the following conditions are true:

- Your macros are very large. VBA code executes much faster in Word 97 if it doesn't have to translate through the WordBasic object. Furthermore, as you learn to take better advantage of the VBA object model, you might be able to create additional performance improvements.
- You use complex dialog boxes. The VBA forms development environment is much more flexible than the dialog box development tools in WordBasic. In many cases, you can provide similar functionality in VBA with much less programming code than was necessary in WordBasic. VBA also lets you add ActiveX controls to your forms, giving you much more functionality than was available in WordBasic.

- You expect to make extensive changes to your macros. It will be much easier to add functionality to your macros by using VBA and its object model than to add WordBasic object model statements to your macros.
- You expect to use the macros for a long time. There is no guarantee that the WordBasic object will be supported in future versions of Word. If you expect to use the macros for years to come, it's probably worth translating them to VBA as soon as you can.

Upgrading from Excel 5.0 or Excel 95 to Excel 97

Excel was the first Office application to support VBA, beginning in version 5.0. Therefore, upgrading your macros from Excel 5.0 or Excel 95 to Excel 97 is a relatively simple process. The most obvious difference is how the macros and forms are stored and edited.

In Excel 5.0 and Excel 95, VBA macros were stored in special sheets in the workbook, called *module sheets*. You could type your VBA code directly into a module sheet or record a macro, which would be stored in a module sheet. You could store all the macros for a workbook in a single module sheet, or spread them among several module sheets. The main advantage to splitting your macros into multiple sheets was that you could easily copy a sheet from one workbook to another.

Dialog boxes were also stored on sheets, known as *dialog sheets*, in Excel 5.0 and Excel 95. Only one dialog box could be stored on a dialog sheet. When a dialog sheet was active, you could use a control toolbox, similar to the one included in the Office 97 Visual Basic Editor, to place controls on the dialog box.

When you open an Excel 5.0 or Excel 95 workbook that contains macros in Excel 97, Excel displays the message box shown in Figure 16.10. This is simply a reminder that the Visual Basic modules are still stored in the workbook, but are now edited in the Visual Basic Editor. After you are familiar with this process, you might choose to mark the Do Not Show This Dialog Again check box so that the message will no longer appear.

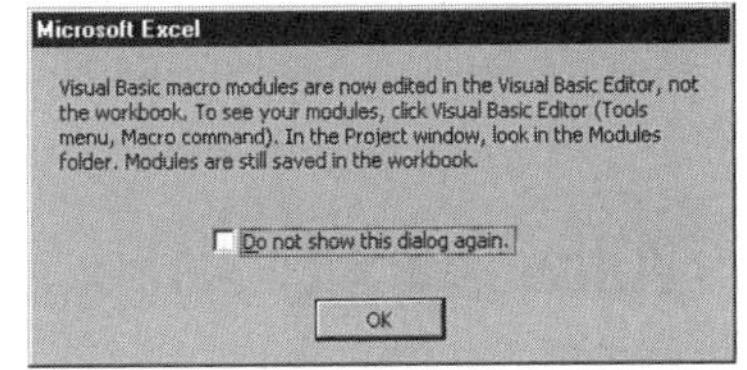

FIGURE 16.10
When you open an Excel 5.0 or Excel 95 workbook in Excel 97, Excel 97 notifies you that the modules in the workbook are now edited in the Visual Basic Editor.

Existing dialog sheets are retained when the workbook is opened in Excel 97. You can continue to use the existing dialog sheets after converting the workbook to Excel 97, or you can re-create them as forms in the Visual Basic Editor.

Upgrading from Excel 4.0 to Excel 97

Prior to Excel 5.0, Excel used a function-based macro language that was unique to Excel, and was not at all similar to Visual Basic. While it was a very powerful language, the fact that this macro language was unique to Excel made it difficult for programmers to create applications that worked with the other Office applications. Listing 16.4 shows an Excel 4.0 macro that types some text and a date stamp into the active spreadsheet.

Listing 16.4 This Excel 4.0 Macro Types Headings and a Date Stamp into an Excel Spreadsheet

```
=FORMULA("Name:")
=SELECT("R[1]C")
=FORMULA("Date:")
=SELECT("RC[1]")
=FORMULA("=NOW()")
=SELECT("R[1]C")
=COLUMN.WIDTH(,"C",,3)
=SELECT("R[-1]C")
=FORMAT.NUMBER("m/d/yy")
=SELECT("R[1]C[-1]")
=FORMULA("Subject:")
=SELECT("R[1]C")
=RETURN()
```

In Excel 5.0 and Excel 95, when you recorded a macro, you had the option of recording it as a VBA macro or as an Excel 4.0 macro.

For compatibility with existing applications, Excel 97 retains existing Excel 4.0 macro sheets, and even allows you to add new Excel 4.0 macro sheets to a workbook. Excel 97 no longer allows you to record macros as Excel 4.0 macros, but you can enter Excel 4.0 macro code directly into an Excel 4.0 macro sheet. If you have extensive and complex Excel 4.0 macros, you might find that it is not practical to convert these macros to VBA, because there is no automatic conversion in Excel 97. In most circumstances, you should develop new macros in Excel VBA.

Upgrading from Access 2.0 or Access 95 to Access 97

When you open a database in Access 97 that was created in Access 2.0 or Access 95, the Convert/Open Database dialog box is displayed, as shown in Figure 16.11. If you choose to open the database without converting it, the existing AccessBasic or VBA code and Access macros can be executed in Access 97, but it can't be modified in Access 97. Select this option if you need to continue to use this database in the earlier version of Access.

If you choose to convert the database, it is saved as a new database file in Access 97 format, and the existing code is converted to Access 97 VBA. Existing Access macros are also converted to run in Access 97.

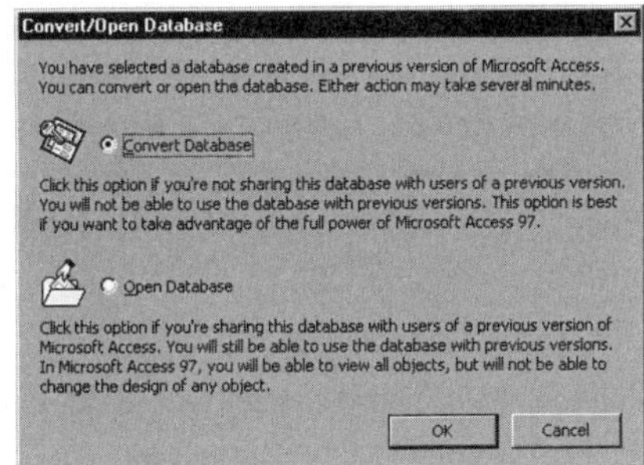

FIGURE 16.11
When you open a database in Access 97 from an earlier version, you can convert the database to Access 97 format.

If you choose to open the database without converting it, Access 97 can still execute the module and macro code from the previous version, in most cases.

Database Conversion Issues for Access

If you want to convert an Access 2.0 or Access 95 database to Access 97, you need to do three things first:

- Fully compile your Access database. In Access 2.0, open each module in the database, and choose Run, Compile Loaded Modules. In Access 95, open any module in the database, and choose Run, Compile All Modules.
- Create a backup copy of the database, and make sure that no other user on the network has the database open.
- Eliminate from your existing Access 95 VBA code any words you used as identifiers that are now keywords in Access 97 VBA. These words are: `AddressOf`, `Assert`, `Decimal`, `DefDec`, `Enum`, `Event`, `Friend`, `Implements`, `RaiseEvent`, and `WithEvents`.

When you convert Access 2.0 modules from AccessBasic to VBA, you need to be aware of the following several items:

- The `Category` property of forms, reports, and controls is no longer supported.
- 16-bit OLE controls on Access 2.0 forms and reports may not be automatically converted to 32-bit equivalents. Make sure that you have 32-bit ActiveX controls installed on your system to replace any custom OLE controls.
- Event procedure calls that pass arguments to ActiveX controls may require the addition of the `ByVal` keyword.
- The `CurDir` function in Access 97 always returns the current path. Changing folders in Windows 95 does not affect the path in Access.
- In AccessBasic, you used `DBEngine(0)(0)` to refer to the current database. It is now recommended that you use the `CurrentDB` function to refer to the current database. The previous syntax is still supported, but Microsoft recommends the change in syntax.
- Any calls to 16-bit DLL functions, including the Windows API, must be replaced by 32-bit calls.

Custom toolbars, menus, and shortcut menus have been redesigned to be more consistent with the Office 97 features. Custom menus created using the Menu Builder in previous Access versions still work, but are not converted to the new style. You can convert existing macros that create custom menus into Access 97 format by selecting the macro group in the database window, and choosing Tools, Macro, Create Menu from Macro. The new menus you create still depend upon the macros you created in the previous version of Access, so don't delete the macros.

Access macros generally convert successfully from earlier versions to Access 97. You need to be aware of several issues, however, when you convert macros:

- The `SendKeys` action may need to be recoded to reflect the changed structure of the Access 97 menus. Wherever possible, replace `SendKeys` statements with equivalent macro actions or VBA methods.
- VBA used the `DoCmd` object and its methods to execute macro actions in a VBA procedure. Access automatically converts existing `DoCmd` statements in AccessBasic to the `DoCmd` *object.method* notation.
- The `TransferSpreadSheet` macro action no longer supports Microsoft Excel version 2.0 or Lotus 1-2-3 version 1.0 spreadsheets. Convert these spreadsheets to a later version of the corresponding application before importing them into Access 97.

Converting 16-Bit Solutions for 32-Bit Windows

In addition to the specific macro-conversion issues for each Office application, there some general issues that affect conversions from 16-bit versions of Office applications to 32-bit versions. Applications that were originally designed to run in Windows 3.*x* and earlier are 16-bit applications.

These Office applications are 16-bit applications:

- Word 6.0 and earlier
- Excel 5.0 and earlier
- Access 2.0 and earlier
- PowerPoint 4.0 and earlier

All later versions of Office applications, including all versions of Outlook, are 32-bit applications, and they require Windows 95, Windows NT, or later operating systems. As noted in the previous sections, most Office macros are converted automatically. You must address a few issues, however, by manually recoding for the 32-bit environment.

The most common issue that developers must address in upgrading to 32-bit Windows is the use of function calls using dynamic link libraries (DLLs), including the Windows Application Programming Interface (API). DLLs are created in the C programming language or another programming language, providing a library of functions that programmers can call at runtime, extending the functionality of VBA. 32-bit programs can't call DLL's that were written for 16-bit Windows, nor can 16-bit programs call 32-bit DLLs.

If you use any third-party DLLs, you must replace them with 32-bit versions before converting your custom applications to 32-bit VBA. In most cases, you'll have to change the declarations and calling code in your modules as well. Check the documentation for the DLL for more detailed instructions.

The same principle applies to using Windows API functions. The 32-bit API in Windows 95 and Windows NT requires new declarations and calling conventions. The Microsoft Office 97 Developer's Edition Tools provide a Win32 API Viewer to assist in this conversion.

Office Developer's Edition Tools

Anyone who spends extensive time developing custom solutions for Office 97 might consider purchasing Microsoft Office 97, Developer's Edition, known as the ODE. The ODE is a full version of Office 97 Professional, and it also provides a variety of tools to extend the development environment for custom applications in Office 97.

Creating Automated Setups with the Setup Wizard

The Setup Wizard included in the ODE enables you to create Office-style setup routines for your custom solutions. This allows you to distribute your solutions via diskette to clients or remote offices, without worrying about installation problems.

Runtime Support for Access 97 and Graph 5.0

With the ODE, you can create custom solutions using Microsoft Access 97 and Graph 5.0, and distribute those applications to users who don't have Access installed on their systems. A runtime Access application does not allow the user to open a database window, but only to interact with your custom application through its forms, reports, menus, and toolbars. Applications may be distributed free of any royalties.

If your application uses any third-party controls or code libraries, make sure you comply with any licensing or royalty requirements of those tools.

Replicating Access 97 Databases

Database replication lets you make two or more copies of a database so that data and objects can be updated among the databases. Replication is particularly useful when remote or mobile users, who are not directly connected to a network, must use a database. You can also use replication to share data among distant offices, to update an application, or to back up data.

While there are replication commands built into Access 97, Microsoft Replication Manager version 3.5, included in the ODE, provides a visual interface to make replication easier to manage. Replication Manager includes tools that enable you to convert databases, create replica sets, view the properties of replicas, and manage the relationships between replicas.

With Replication Manager, you can distribute replicas over the Internet or your corporate intranet. You can also create scheduled synchronization, so the replicas can be updated automatically at a specific time.

Source Code Control for Access

The ODE provides software that allows Access to work with source-code control software, such as Microsoft Visual SourceSafe. This type of software is useful for teams of programmers who are working together to build complex applications.

ActiveX Controls in the Office Developer Edition

ActiveX controls enable you to extend the power of your applications by adding graphical controls to the forms and reports in Office 97 applications. You can also place ActiveX controls directly on a Word document, an Excel spreadsheet, or a PowerPoint presentation.

Many ActiveX controls are available from third-party developers. The cost of these controls varies, and some require royalties or licensing fees if you distribute applications using the controls.

The ODE includes a variety of ActiveX controls that you can use to extend the features of Office 97 and to add Internet-related features to your applications.

- The CommonDialog control lets you add commonly used Windows dialog boxes, such as File Open, Print Setup, and Fonts, to your applications.
- The ImageList control lets you store a collection of images that can be used by other image controls.
- The Internet Transfer control allows you to connect to the Internet via Hypertext Transfer Protocol (HTTP) and File Transfer Protocol (FTP). You can use this control to retrieve HTML documents and to upload and download files from FTP servers. You can also use the UserName and Password properties to log onto secure servers.
- The ListView control lets you display lists of items in several different views, including small and large icon views.
- The ProgressBar control enables you to indicate the progress of long processes by displaying a rectangle that is filled from left to right as the process executes.
- The RichTextBox control lets you display and enter formatted text in a VBA form. Unlike the standard TextBox control, the RichTextBox control lets you apply formatting to individual parts of the text within the control. Support is included for loading and saving files into the RichTextBox control.
- The Slider control enables users to easily adjust a numeric value by clicking the control to move a slider through a range. The keyboard can also control the control.
- The StatusBar control enables you to add a status bar to the bottom of a window, usually a form. The status bar can be divided into as many as 16 different areas, known as *panels*, to display different types of information.
- The TabStrip control provides a notebook-style set of tabs for controlling an area of a window or dialog box.
- The Toolbar control is a collection of buttons that you can use to control your application.

- The TreeView control provides an Explorer-like tree structure that you can use to represent data in your application. This control is especially useful for representing hierarchically organized data.
- The UpDown control has a pair of buttons with arrows that the user can click to increase or decrease a value. This control is a handy alternative to typing numbers in a numeric control.
- The Winsock control provides access to TCP and UDP network services for Access, Visual Basic, Visual C++, and Visual FoxPro applications. The control is not visible to the user. The control lets you connect to a remote computer and exchange data in both directions.

Creating Help Files with Microsoft Help Workshop

You can use the Microsoft Help Workshop in the ODE to create Windows help files (.hlp files). Help Workshop includes tools to create help projects, combining source text, bitmaps, topic files, and other source material into a single help project that can be viewed with the Windows Help program.

The Win32 API Viewer

The Win32 API viewer enables you to view the Visual Basic code for declaring API functions, constants, and types. You can copy the examples from the API Viewer into your VBA source code, speeding the development process and reducing the number of errors in entering API code.

ODE includes two files of API help information. Win32api.txt includes the information for the main body of functions in the Windows API. Mapi32.txt includes information about the Windows Messaging API, which is used for interacting with MAPI-compliant email systems.

Figure 16.12 shows the Win32 API Viewer with the declaration information for the API function `GetCurrentDirectory` displayed.

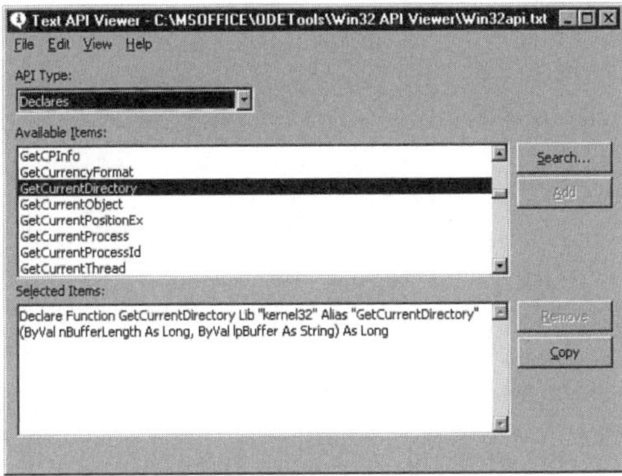

FIGURE 16.12
Use the Win32 API Viewer to find the correct syntax for declarations, types, and constants.

PART IV

Integrating Office in Your Heterogeneous Environment

CHAPTER 17

Migrating from or Coexisting with Legacy Applications

Most companies' first experience with computer applications is not with Office 97. Typically, companies are now upgrading from other applications to take advantage of the increased speed, flexibility, and features of Office 97. When companies upgrade from Office 95, the migration is a fairly smooth process. This chapter is not for those companies.

Instead, this chapter is for those who are migrating from or coexisting with non-Microsoft applications such as WordPerfect, dBase, and Lotus 1-2-3. Both migration and coexistence can be more difficult than you might think.

All Office 97 applications have a File, Open command that lets you open a file in a format other than the one used in Office 97. In many cases, this command works just fine and allows you to bring in data from other applications. Also, the cut and paste features under Windows allow sections of data to be transported between different applications.

This chapter emphasizes two specific circumstances:

- You have existing collections of databases, documents, spreadsheets, and the like that have to be converted into a form Office 97 can use so that the original work spent on this data is not lost.
- You plan to continue using non-Microsoft applications along with Office 97, and you need the two sets of programs to cooperate in exchanging data files back and forth.

The first situation is called *migration* because you leave your original application behind and the data created moves to Office 97. The second situation is called *coexistence* because both your original applications and Office 97 are used in your company for the foreseeable future. This chapter discusses specific examples of each.

The Importance of Planning

Earlier in this book you learned the importance of proper planning before introducing Office 97 into your company. The importance of such planning is doubly important in migration and coexistence situations. If you can foresee potential problems during the change-over, you can prevent many difficult situations.

This planning process should include the following steps:

1. Evaluate your hardware and software versus system resources to ensure that the migration or coexistence will not overwhelm any of your computers.
2. Identify the data files that will be converted to new formats or must coexist with Office 97. Make copies of these files to be used for testing.
3. Load Office 97 into a test machine along with your older applications. Test the capability of Office 97 to successfully convert these files. Test the capability of Office 97 files to be converted into a form the older applications can use. Test links between data files.
4. Determine the locations where conversions were difficult or unsuccessful. Find alternative means of making the conversions or rethink your software system setup.
5. Create work instructions on the proper way to exchange data. Distribute these to the people involved and give them training based on the type of work they will actually perform.

In this way you can ensure that the conversion and exchange of information will proceed smoothly and effectively. By training people to do it right the first time, you will prevent many problems.

Moving from WordPerfect to Word

WordPerfect has existed in many versions and has been owned by many companies. At one time, WordPerfect ruled the word processing field and was the standard by which other programs were measured. However, Word now holds that distinction, and it is very common for offices to update from WordPerfect to Word.

Much of the discussion about the conversion from WordPerfect to Word also applies to other legacy word processing programs, such as AmiPro and WordStar. The migration path is usually fairly easy and straightforward. Most problems come with documents with elaborate formatting or from rare versions of word processing programs.

There are two basic paths a company can take to migrate from a legacy word processing program to Word:

- Old word processing files are transferred directly into Word and saved as Word documents.
- Old word processing files are converted into a format Word can deal with, or they are sent through the conversion filters provided with your Office 97 software.

WordPerfect is an excellent illustration of how this migration is accomplished. WordPerfect format 5.1/5.2 is a standard formatting scheme that most word processors possess or can use. Therefore, it provides a fixed, known format to fall back on if any problems arise during the migration process.

Bringing Legacy Documents into Word

For single documents created on legacy word processors, the easiest method of migration is to open Word and then open the target file. Choose File, Open; the Open dialog box that activates contains a drop-down list of file formats (see Figure 17.1).

If you used a common extension for your legacy files (for example, .doc) the drop-down list of files will limit what is seen in the open file window; this makes file selection easier.

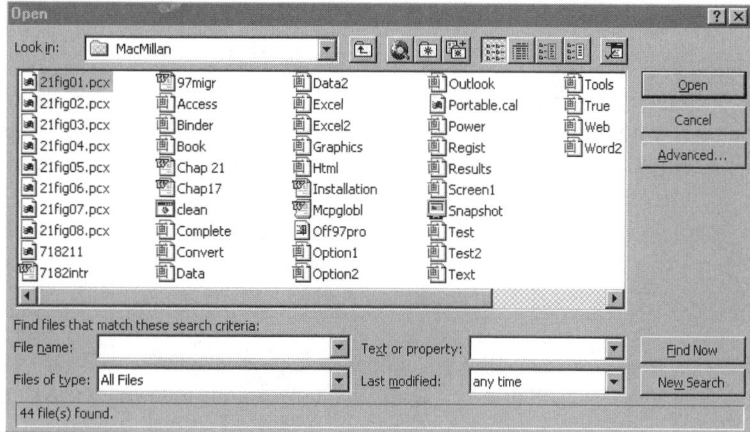

FIGURE 17.1
In the Open dialog box you can select the type of file formats to import and the conversions to maintain or change.

Let's use a specific example of how this is done. Assume that a doctor's office used WordPerfect 6.0 to create correspondence. One of the most widely used documents was a form letter sent to patients to alert them of an upcoming appointment. The letter stressed the importance of keeping appointments and mentioned whom to call if a rescheduling was necessary.

Into this document was placed information on the patient's name, date, and time of the appointment, along with which doctor would be seen. This information used to come from a dBASE IV database. However, that has been migrated to an Access database, and the office administrator would also like to migrate the letter to Word to re-create the same mail-merged document.

To open the WordPerfect document from within Word, the administrator would perform the following steps:

1. Choose File, Open.
2. Set the file format to WordPerfect 6.x if the .doc extension was used so that the list of files that appears is shorter and easier to work with.

3. Highlight the target file.
4. Name a destination file in the common folder to be used in Office. Click on OK, and the file is automatically converted in Word.

In most cases, this is all you need to do to make the transition. If the document fails to transfer, you can open it in WordPerfect and save it as a 5.1/5.2 file. This file can then be opened in Word. Often you don't even have to specify the original file format; Word figures that out by itself.

Either way, the original merge fields will have to be replaced with the new links to the Access database to complete this project. One possible method would be to create a form letter in Word using the text of the converted letter, and then go to the Tools menu and click Mail Merge. Following the steps in the window, you would connect to the target Access database and place the new fields into your letter.

Adding Conversion Packages to Word

Word comes with a nice selection of conversion utilities for word processing documents. However, your legacy applications may not be in the standard list of file formats supported by Word. Office 97 software comes with additional conversion packages that you can load to expand the capabilities of Word to cope with different word processing formats.

You should add additional conversion capabilities to a computer only when needed. Each addition will take more resources from your system.

Conversion packages can be found in both your installation software and the Office Resource Kit. When you perform a typical install of Word, the following formats are supported:

- Older versions of Word
- Document templates
- Rich Text Format (RTF)
- Text files
- Unicode text files
- Personal address book
- Outlook address book
- Schedule+ contacts
- Excel worksheet
- Word 4.0 to 5.1 for Macintosh
- Works 3.0 and 4.0 for Windows
- Recovered text from any file
- WordPerfect 5.x and 6.x

The Office Resource Kit CD-ROM comes with utilities for the following additional formats:

- Windows Write 3.0 and 3.1
- RFT-DCA
- Lotus AmiPro 3.x
- WordStar 1.0 to 95

In some situations you may want to remove several of the conversion options that will never be used by your system to conserve resources and reduce confusion for users.

If you need these types of conversions you should purchase the Office Resource Kit. Note that Word comes with an extensive array of graphics conversion filters as well.

Batch Conversion of Documents into Word

You can also convert batches of legacy word processing files using Word's Conversion Wizard. This approach works best when you have a large number of files to convert. If you have only a few files to convert, you can open them all at the same time and have them converted. To do this, follow these steps:

1. Place all files for conversion into a single folder.
2. Choose File, Open and then select the file type you wish to convert—for example, WordPerfect 5.1.
3. When the list of available files appears use Shift+click or Control+click to highlight several files for conversion.

The files are then converted and opened in Word. You can also select conversion options to control how the documents are converted (see Figure 17.2).

When you convert a legacy word processing file, be sure it has a file extension that matches the format for the application. For example, WordPerfect 5.1 files should end with .doc.

At the time of installation you had the option to load a conversion wizard for Word. Most companies do not notice this option under the Custom Install and thus do not know it exists. The file is called Convert8.exe; it can be copied from the CD-ROM or run from the disk.

If you installed the wizard, you can activate the batch conversion wizard from inside Word by choosing File, Open and then working your way down to the following:

```
Program Files\Microsoft Office\Office\Macros
```

Otherwise, you navigate to your CD-ROM and highlight the program there under the following:

```
Microsoft Office\Office\Macros
```

Click on A Batch Conversion of Files and follow the instructions (see Figure 17.3).

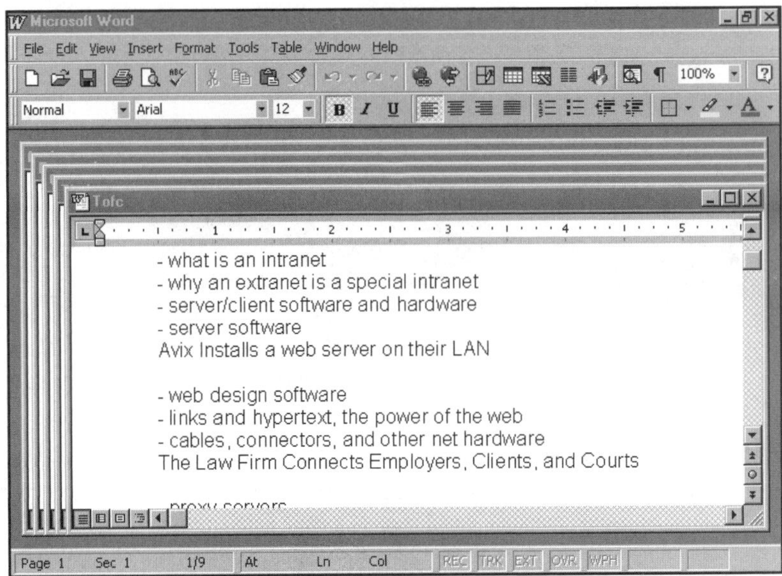

FIGURE 17.2
Using the Open File command and highlighting several files opens the files in Word.

When searching for program files from inside Word, be sure to set your file-format choice to All Files.

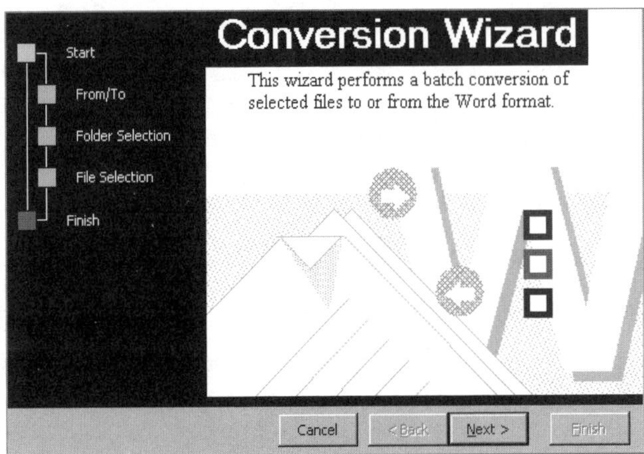

FIGURE 17.3
The Batch Conversion Wizard can speed the transfer of many files with one pass.

The following steps are used to make the conversion:

1. Select the batch processing option from the opening screen.
2. Select the file format you want to translate either from or to Word.
3. Set the source and destination folders.
4. Highlight the files you want to convert and click on Next.

Coexisting with Legacy Word Processors

In a few cases a company may want to maintain the legacy word processing programs while using Word. For example, a publishing company may use Word exclusively within its offices. However, the hundreds of contracted authors may tend to use WordPerfect and a handful of other word processing programs to create content for submission.

Because the editors at the publishing house want to send the same file format back and forth during the editing phase of production, the authors' word processors must coexist with Word. This is best accomplished by finding a file format that supports the formatting of the documents and the equipment being used.

One possible solution is to have all the authors update their packages so that they can create Word 95 or 6.0 file formats. This should preserve many of the features of Word as the files are passed back and forth.

Another option is to use the Rich Text Format (RTF). Where older word processors remain in use, files could be converted to RTF before being sent. This tends to be a stable and reliable way to preserve the format of documents between platforms. Practically all Windows-based word processors support the RTF format, which is a nonproprietary standard.

Another Example: Law Firms Many types of corporations migrate to Office 97. One of the situations where special software has been developed to support Office 97 migrations occurs in the practice of law.

The American Bar Association has a strong technology section that studies the integration of popular software packages into law offices. Office 97 is one of the most popular choices. The most common migration path for law firms recently has been from WordPerfect, the former preferred package for law work, to Word and Office 97.

Also, a variety of third-party software companies produce templates, macros, and other support packages for Office 97 to increase its ability to cope with the work demands of a law office. For example, Lawtech produces programs such as WinDraft and LawOffice.

The LawOffice 97 Document Management add-in is used under Windows NT on the server to assist Microsoft Word. When a new document is saved, the user is prompted for information on the following items:

- Name of the client
- Matter being handled
- Author of the document
- Case type involved
- Type of document being saved

Using this information, the program makes a copy of the file both on the server and locally. It also finds the appropriate file on the network in which to store the document. This information also permits an indexing system to be established for rapid document retrieval. In fact, you can use Boolean logic and proximity locators to find the documents you need.

Moving from 1-2-3 to Excel

The migration from older spreadsheets to Excel is an easy process and rarely causes major headaches. Only when people have created very large spreadsheets or complex formulas do they encounter any difficulty. Here you will find out how to work around these types of issues.

To begin with, most spreadsheets from legacy applications can be easily imported into Excel. For example, you can lift a spreadsheet from the Macintosh version of ClarisWorks and import it directly into Excel. The following example uses Lotus 1-2-3 spreadsheets to illustrate how to migrate to Excel.

To import a 1-2-3 worksheet into Excel, you do the following:

1. Open a new workbook or worksheet in Excel.
2. Choose Open from the File menu, select one of the compatible 1-2-3 worksheet formats, and then highlight the legacy file you have targeted for conversion.
3. Click on Open, and the legacy spreadsheet is loaded into Excel (see Figure 17.4).

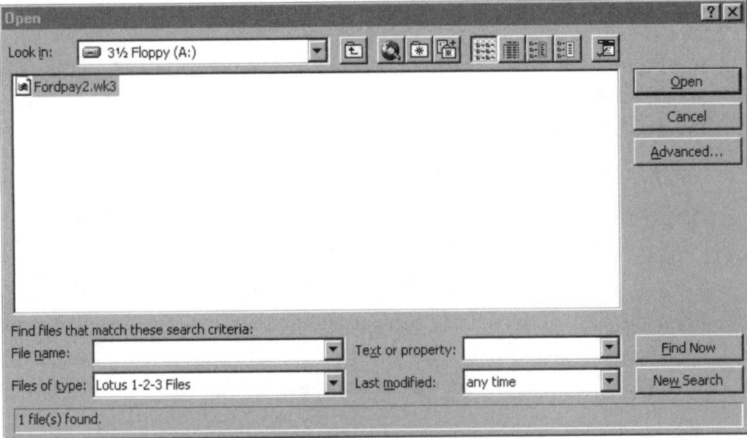

FIGURE 17.4
The main power of conversion to Excel lies within the Open dialog box.

That's it. Typically, the spreadsheet is loaded starting from the A1 cell position. If you need to position it in some other location, load the 1-2-3 spreadsheet first into a blank worksheet. From there you can cut and paste it to the desired position on the final Excel spreadsheet.

The file formats that can be imported using this method include

- Text files
- Older Excel file formats (including Excel 4.0 macros)
- 1-2-3 files (WK1, WK3, and so on)
- Quattro Pro
- Works 2.0

- dBase
- SYLK (.slk)
- Data Interchange Format (.dif)
- HTML documents

You can also coexist with legacy spreadsheet programs using this method. Only if it is impossible to import using this method should you consider translating the legacy spreadsheets to a different format before migrating to Excel. If you need to exchange spreadsheets back and forth with a legacy application, you should try to stay in the legacy's format.

Two of the most effective alternative formats to try when all else fails are .slk and .dif. Legacy spreadsheets saved in these formats can also be opened in Excel. However, you will likely suffer interesting effects—such as cell font sizes being too small to read—and you may experience errors in reading the cell contents.

Migrating from Nonspreadsheet Legacy Programs to Excel

In some cases, the features and ease of use of Excel make it a candidate for migration from legacy programs that are not spreadsheet programs. For example, you may have originally performed invoicing on a word processor because you sent out only two or three invoices a week. The information may have also been copied to 1-2-3 to track delinquent accounts.

Let's say that you want to put the invoice into Excel and have it print the invoice and track the accounts, all on one spreadsheet. This requires the original invoice to be stored as a text file (.txt). Select the text-file format when opening the invoice for the first time in Excel. The text-file wizard will pop up and walk you through the process (see Figure 17.5).

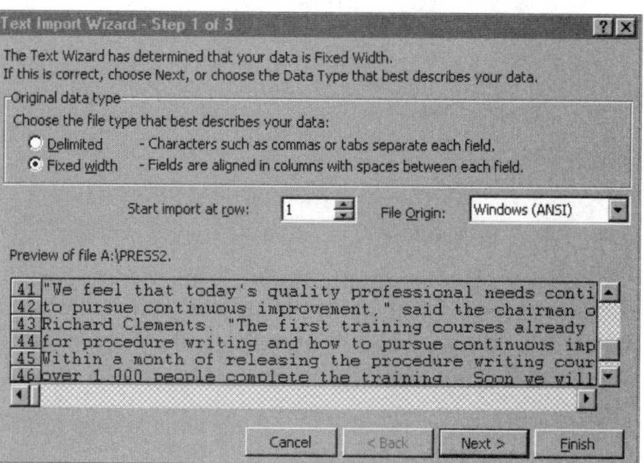

FIGURE 17.5
When importing a text-based file you are automatically presented with the Text Import Wizard screen. Be sure to identify all text characteristics before proceeding with the file importation.

After the file is imported into the Excel worksheet, add the formulas and cell formats to create the invoice appearance and function you desire. Then save it in Excel format.

Another situation in which migration from a nonspreadsheet program may be useful arises if your office has small, flat databases. These can be imported into Access (this will be described in a moment). However, if the use of the database is light and you want convenience, you can import them into Excel and skip elaborate database procedures.

To do this, first see if you can import the database directly into Excel without losing the structure of your data. If you cannot, then translate the legacy database into a .dif file and attempt to open that file. This will always load the cells from the original database into the Excel worksheet starting from the A1 position.

Another Way to Migrate from 1-2-3

A handy Excel feature is the capability to reprogram keystroke functions to match those used in 1-2-3. This allows you to set Excel to behave like 1-2-3, thus making the transition easier for the users.

To activate this option, choose Tools, Options, and then select the Transition tab (see Figure 17.6).

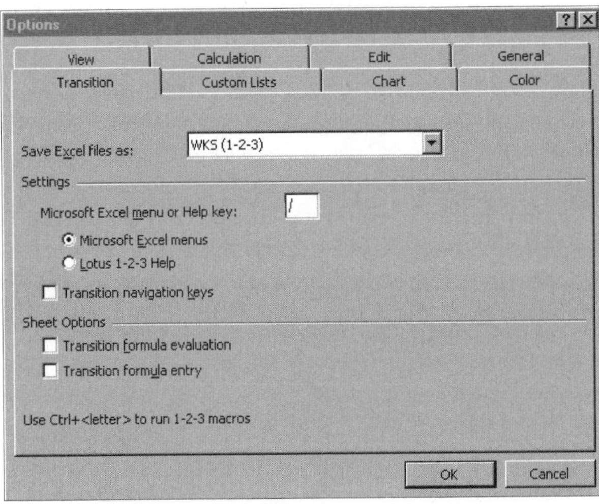

FIGURE 17.6
The Transition tab can be used to make Excel behave like 1-2-3 in many respects.

On the transition screen you can identify the keystrokes and other effects from 1-2-3 you want to preserve in Excel. This can reduce the training and transition time for the users. However, you must consider this option carefully.

If you want all users to become familiar with Excel and to eventually abandon 1-2-3, preserving its keystrokes may not be a good idea. It is usually better to have the users make the transition in one step and never turn back. However, if you need to ease users into the transition or expect some of the users to go back and forth between 1-2-3 and Excel, this option makes a lot of sense; users need to remember only one set of keystroke commands and protocols.

Moving Old Database Files into Access

The migration to or the coexistence with another database is one of the great nightmares for software administrators. Despite the best intentions of the software designers of both products, it seems that something always goes wrong. However, you do not need to be discouraged.

In fact, the failure of most database conversions is a result of not quite getting a series of decisions right on the first attempt. In almost every case, there is a successful path for the conversion or exchange of data. As you have learned with Word and Excel, the process is simple and usually successful.

Database applications such as Access are different because there are so many formats used in databases that a longer series of decisions are required. One wrong decision—such as indicating that your files are comma-delimited when they actually are not—can cause a lot of problems. This section explains how to avoid these types of problems.

First, the good news: Access accepts the file formats of a lot of popular database programs, including the following:

- dBase III, III+, IV, and 5.0
- FoxPro 2.x and 3.0
- Paradox 3.x, 4.x, 5.0
- Text-based data files, both delimited and fixed-width fields
- Lotus 1-2-3 worksheets
- Excel worksheets
- HTML documents and Open Database Connectivity files
- Outlook and Exchange data

With databases you may find that you have to work in stages. Start with a small and commonly used database. Attempt your conversions and see what happens. To make sure the conversion was successful you should examine the resulting Access database and make sure that the following steps were actually completed:

- All records were transferred.
- Information ended up in the correct fields.
- All information is present; nothing was clipped and no extraneous characters were added.
- Relations in relational databases were preserved.
- Created tables are searchable.
- Report formats are intact.

The actual sampling plan and testing methods should be noted in a work instruction; the database specialists can use this to confirm the success of your conversions.

When converting an existing database to Access, use the field names from your legacy database for the new receiving database in Access. Conversions are much more successful when field names are preserved between the two databases.

Another important step to take before attempting conversions and exchanges is to know exactly how the data is used and what is planned for the new database. A couple of examples can illustrate how this can be beneficial.

Example of a One-Step Conversion Take the example of a company that sells and fulfills magazine subscriptions. Its database has been kept in dBase IV format. The database has the subscriber's name, address, phone number, and email address. To this is added the magazines purchased, the date of payment, the date the subscription ends, the amount of money still owed, and so on.

This database is very large, but it is in a simple, flat format. The company wants to convert this to Access so that it can eventually be linked to Excel for fast reports on cash flow.

With this information you would know that the existing database must be converted, the existing data would continue to be manipulated and edited in Access, and new subscribers would be added after conversion. Therefore, you need a rapid conversion during the night so that subscription-data-entry people are ready to use the new database the next day. You cannot move in stages because all the information has to stay together.

Therefore, you would attempt a full conversion with a copy of the database to work out any problems before the official conversion. This would include testing how well data entry people can cope with Access and the new database.

Example of Conversion in Stages In a second example, a company has been using Approach to create a multilevel relational database to track all operations. This includes order entry, customer complaints, quality-assurance inspections, production planning, and so on. In this situation different parts of the database will be linked to the new Access database in stages. In other words, conversion will take place one department at a time.

One of the major problems will be the lack of a conversion utility for Approach. Therefore, the Approach file will be translated to a format Access can accept. Then the separate data tables will be linked and new relationships defined within Access. This will involve a lot of planning and work to carry off successfully.

We should note here that Access can bring in sets of data in two different methods:

- **Importing.** The data file and many of its characteristics are directly converted to Access format.
- **Linking.** The old data file can be linked as a table inside an Access database.

Importing tends to be used when you want to convert a database to Access format without really changing the size, scope, or function of the database. Linking is used in cases when you are building a coalition of databases. Linking is also used when you want to continue to use the legacy database program. Linking leaves the data in its original format and allows Access users to access the data fields.

Linked tables in Access can accept queries without any problem.

How to Import a Legacy Database into Access

This example involves importing a very simple dBase III database into Access. The extremely small database helps illustrate what happens during conversions.

Let's assume that the database contains the following fields:

First Name:

Last Name:

Address:

The First Name field is text, fixed at 40 characters in length. The Last Name field is the same. The Address field is text fixed at 80 characters in length. There are 100 records to convert. The name of the legacy file is Contact.dbf.

Use the following steps to import the database into Access:

1. Begin by setting up the database to receive the legacy data. Open Access and click on New Database. Click on the Database tab and choose the Address Book template. Save this as Address Test. This is your test database to see if the conversion works.
2. Follow the Database Wizard that appears and design Address Test to have the same field names as Contact.dbf (see Figure 17.7).

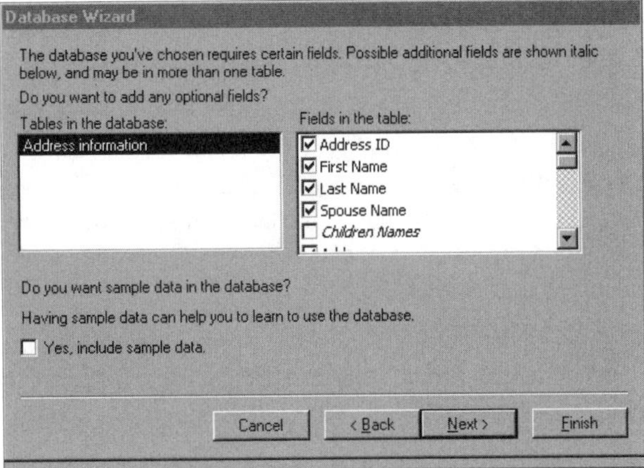

FIGURE 17.7
The Database Wizard will perform most translations from one database format into Access format.

3. Be sure to set indexes and relationships that also match your legacy database. This will smooth the conversion process considerably.
4. After the new, empty database is created, click on the Access switchboard to enter data (see Figure 17.8).

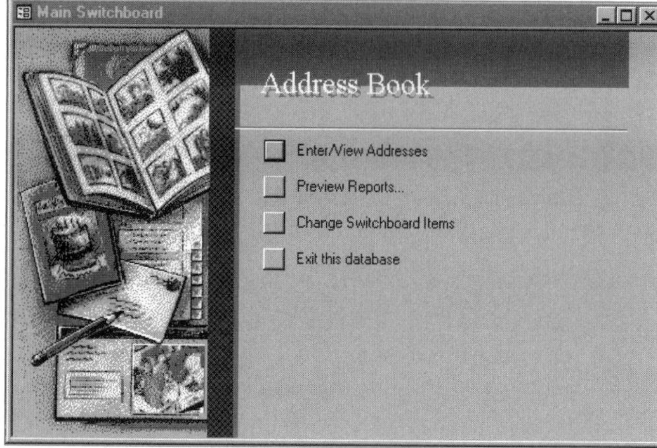

FIGURE 17.8
In the example you created an Address database in Access.

5. Choose File, Get External Data, Import.
6. In the list box that appears, select the legacy database file and be sure the file format is set to the appropriate database format (in this example, dBASE III). Click on Import.
7. The information should transfer successfully into the new database and be ready for use (see Figure 17.9). Test the new database for accuracy and querying.

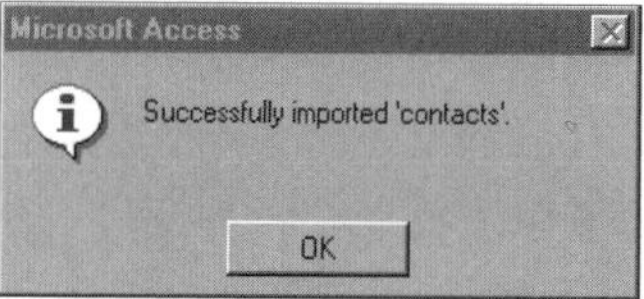

FIGURE 17.9
This dialog box confirms that the data was successfully imported.

If you first had to convert the legacy database to delimited-text format, there would be a few additional steps. After step 6, you would see the Import Text Wizard (see Figure 17.10). This would present you with a series of decisions—such as how the data fields are delimited, the widths of columns, the original format of the data, and so forth. Answering these questions correctly will ensure a successful conversion. If you experience problems, try other answers in the wizard and retest your results.

Examining the finished database in Figure 17.11 reveals an almost-successful conversion. The field names matched and all format settings were checked; however, the address data landed in the wrong field.

FIGURE 17.10
The Import Text Wizard appears when you are trying to import text-based databases, such as those with comma-delimited data.

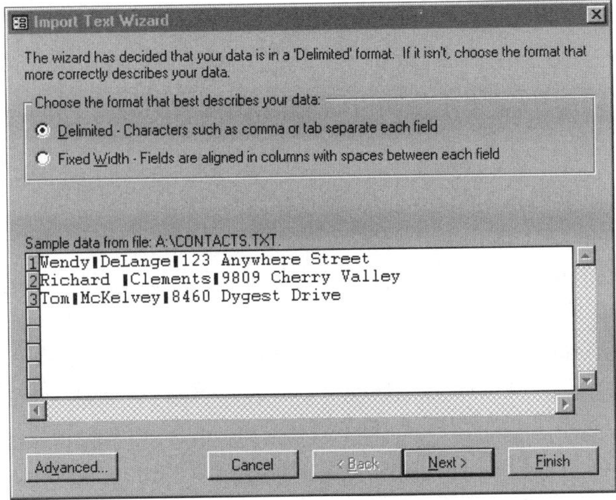

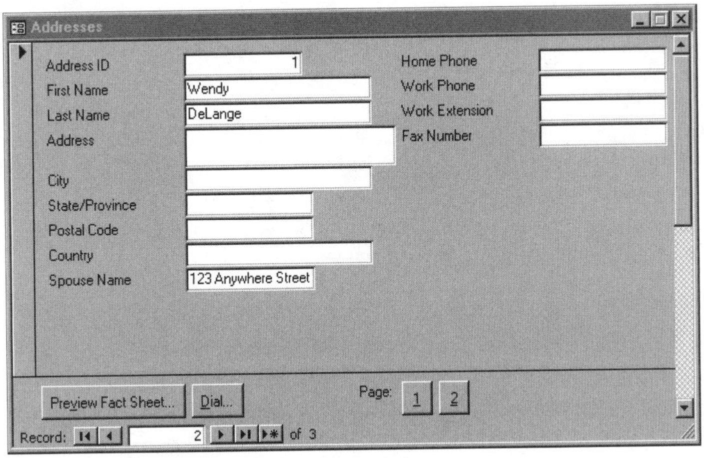

FIGURE 17.11
Here is the Address database in Access after importation of legacy data. Note that the wizard has mistakenly placed the address field data in the field for spouse's name.

In cases like this you need to go back and double-check the field settings, indexes, and relations of the original database versus the new Access database. You need to correct and repeat the process until you have a successful conversion. It is not unusual to have to do this several times.

However, if it takes longer than several tries, you should consider an alternative—such as looking for third-party conversion tools or translating your legacy data into a different format before testing again.

Example of Linking a Legacy Database into an Existing Access Database Staying with the sample legacy database (Contact.dbf), let's now assume that a company wants to incorporate this information into an existing Access database. This existing database has multiple tables of information. In this case you want to link your legacy data to the Access database using the following process:

1. With the Access database open, choose Insert, Table.
2. Highlight Link Table and click on OK.
3. Now find the legacy database to link, highlight it, be sure the correct database format is set, and click on OK.
4. After a delay, you should get a message that the link was successful. You can either close the linking window or continue to make links to other legacy databases.

For text-based databases, you see the Link Text Wizard. Again you make a series of choices on how the original data was formatted. In general, the wizard tends to make the correct choices; so if you are not certain, try the recommended settings first (see Figure 17.12).

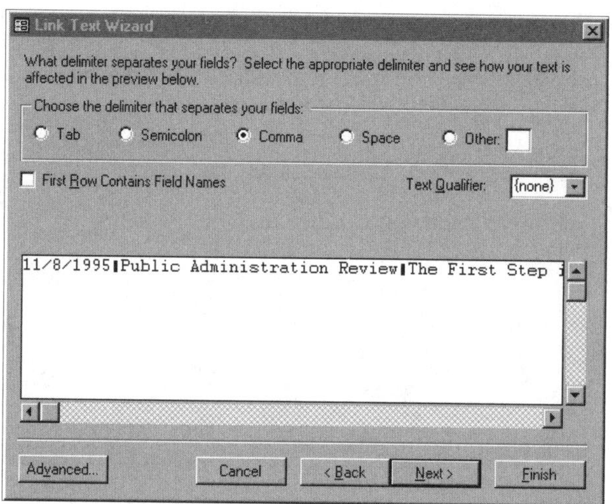

FIGURE 17.12
The Link Text Wizard is available whenever you attempt to link legacy data to a new or existing Access database.

Old PIM Files and Outlook

The addition of Outlook to the Office 97 package lets you accumulate different scheduling programs into a common format and coordinate between different personal information managers (PIMs). Thus, migration to Outlook is fairly easy and opens up several new opportunities to migrate outward from Outlook.

The outward migration is possible because of the introduction of a new generation of personal digital assistants (PDAs) driven by Windows CE. Many of these new devices include either smaller versions of Outlook or Outlook-compatible software. Thus, your office staff can call in from the field using the modems on their pocket-sized devices. By having common schedule folders on your server, people can coordinate schedules with their office machines, set up meetings, and perform other related tasks.

However, this assumes that you first migrated all existing PIMs to Outlook and then established a standard for your company on which software and file formats can be used with Outlook.

The type of formats supported by Outlook for importation are

- dBase
- Lotus Organizer
- Access
- Excel
- Exchange Personal Address Book
- FoxPro
- Schedule+ 1.0, 4.0, and 95
- NetManage ECCO Pro 3.x
- Starfish Sidekick
- Symantec Act! 2.0

When you need to export, the choices are fewer. The best bet is to use Comma Separated Values. Most PIMs and databases can cope easily with this format.

How to Migrate from SideKick to Outlook

The ValuPack comes with many filters for importing information from many types of PIMs, including SideKick from Starfish.

Sidekick is a PIM that was given away in many software bundles over the past several years. It was one of the first organizers for computers and thus makes an excellent example of what you will encounter when you try to migrate to Outlook.

The import/export converter for Sidekick is in the ValuPack on your Office 97 CD-ROM at the following location:

```
ValuPack\Convert\Outlook\Outcvt.exe
```

This can be added to the converters already in Outlook. To import the schedule and contact information from a SideKick file (.skcard), perform the following steps:

1. In Outlook, choose File, Import and Export. This brings up the Import and Export Wizard (see Figure 17.13).

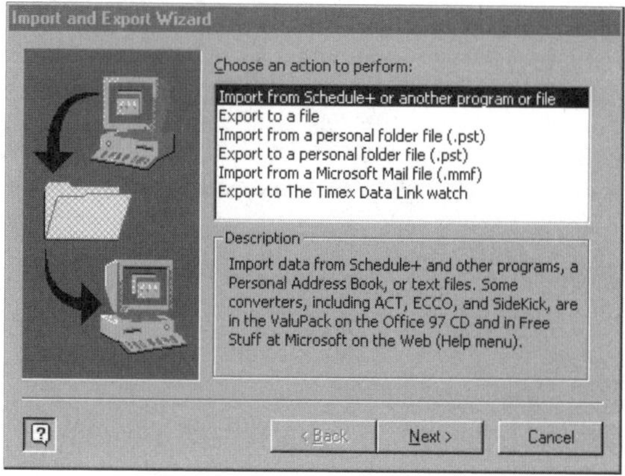

FIGURE 17.13
Outlook has an Import and Export Wizard to help you load legacy data.

2. Click on Import from Schedule+ or Another Program or File.
3. Follow the instructions given by the wizard. First select the file type (SideKick) and browse until you locate and highlight the target file. At this point you also have to decide whether to create duplicate data. If you are importing into an existing Outlook file that already has some of the information you are importing, don't duplicate.
4. If you are asked, enter the password for the file. If your SideKick file was password-protected, or if you get a network challenge, enter the correct password.
5. Map out the fields to be transferred between the two programs. This is the only way to ensure the correct transfer of information.

The wizard will now complete the importation. Naturally, you should double-check the imported data to make sure the transfer was successful and the data landed in the correct fields.

Not all PIMs are fully compatible with Outlook. That means the wizard will ask you questions on how to handle specific pieces of information in your legacy PIM database.

For example, in SideKick the following situations occur:

- The contact log in SideKick is treated as an extended Notes field in Outlook.
- Recurring appointments become individual appointments in Outlook, and you will need to restore the recurring feature manually.
- SideKick tasks, calls, and goals are all converted to tasks in Outlook.
- The field names in the contact, task, and appointment fields have different names in many cases, and these need to be mapped manually in the wizard.

As you can see, the migration to Outlook from a legacy application is nearly as difficult as the database transitions described earlier. Again, the same advice applies: you should plan your migration, train people to use Outlook using their actual data, and then make the transition.

How to Migrate and Coexist with Schedule+

Previous users of Windows for Workgroups had Schedule+ 1.0; previous Windows 95 users had either Schedule+ 4.0 or 95. If you use these previous applications, you will want to migrate to Outlook to gain several advantages.

However, this means that as an administrator you have to migrate and possibly coexist with Schedule+. The migration from Schedule+ to Outlook is fairly simple because this is the most-expected migration. As such, Outlook has the Import from Schedule+ option listed first in the Import and Export command on the File menu.

The chief difficulty comes from exporting Outlook information back to Schedule+. In rare cases, there may be members of the staff or contracted employees that will not be upgrading to Outlook in the near future. Therefore, if you need to send them, say, your calendar for the next six months, you will need to export the data.

Outlook's export function does not allow you to directly export data to Schedule+. However, you can convert the desired data into a comma-separated file, which can be imported by Schedule+ and many other applications.

Additional Filters from Microsoft

As mentioned, Microsoft provides a wider array of conversion filters for its programs than the ones automatically loaded with the applications in Office 97. There are basically three primary sources for these filters:

- In the ValuPack included with your Office 97 software, look in these directories:

  `ValuPack\Convert\`

  `Office\Convert\Macros`

  `Office\Convert\Xlators`

  The Office 97 Resource Kit also details how to locate and load these additional filters.
- You can go to the Microsoft Web page for Office 97 (`www.microsoft.com/office`) and download additional filters as they become available. You can also consult the Microsoft technical support area (`www.microsoft.com/support`) and search for patches and filters for a particular situation.
- The CD-ROM included with the Microsoft Office 97 Resource Kit also includes some of the filters you may need. The book indicates their locations on the disc.

Third-Party Sources for Filters

When your company handles many types of file formats on a regular basis, you may need to turn to third-party filters for importing and transferring files. Also, if you have unusual file formats to deal with that Office 97 doesn't cover, you will need third-party filters.

You can locate sources of such third-party filters by searching the Internet. Typically, you would conduct a search on one of the larger search engines, such as

- `www.yahoo.com`
- `www.altavista.digital.com`
- `www.hotbot.com`

The search string you use is important because it is easy to stray into a list of companies that perform conversions. Instead, you want just the software for performing the conversions. This method of searching helps you find the most recent options because translation and conversion utilities are constantly being introduced or removed from the market. Some of the conversion packages are even free.

Recommended search strings include the following:

"Office 97" + conversion software

"Office 97" + spreadsheet transfer software

"Office 97" + database migration

"Microsoft Word" + software migration

"Microsoft Excel" + filters

"Microsoft Access" + conversion software

Not only will this uncover conversion utilities, but it will yield other benefits. This will include conversions from other operating systems such as AS 400. It will also include articles on how other companies handled their migration to Office 97 components.

Sample Utility: Quick View Plus 4.5

One of the most-well-known file conversion utilities is Quick View; the newest version is Quick View Plus 4.5. This utility can work with over 200 file formats. Not only does it cover almost every DOS, Windows, and Macintosh format, it also works without the need for you to possess the original application. Therefore, if you used 1-2-3 years ago, changed to Excel 4.0, and now use Excel 97, you can still migrate the spreadsheets even though the original copy of 1-2-3 is long gone.

Quick View also integrates with your email and browser systems to allow people to send and convert files using the corporate Intranet or Internet. This includes additional utilities that allow your users to view fully formatted documents. That permits your users to scan a document to see how it should look before and after conversion.

Capabilities such as these not only support the migration from legacy applications, they also allow you to increase collaboration between users on your network. In short, it expands the capabilities of Office 97. To learn more about this particular utility visit the Inso Web site at `www.inso.com/products/corporate`.

Other Conversion Packages

One of the weaknesses of Excel is that it converts only one file at a time. Missing is a batch conversion utility. Luckily there is a free utility to perform this function. Excel File Conversion Wizard is distributed by *PC World* at its Web site:

`www.pcworld.com/software_lib/data/articles/business/3825.html.`

This conversion utility will batch convert Lotus 1-2-3 and Quattro Pro worksheets into Excel. The file is called fileconv.xla, and it requires only 141KB of disk space.

Advanced Computer Innovations, Inc. produces a utility called WordPort that can convert to and from many different word processing programs. Its strength lies in its ability to preserve advanced formatting features. It can be run in batch mode for translating up to thousands of files in one pass. The ACI Web site can be found at `www.acii.com/conv.htm`.

ACI also offers R-Doc/X for the conversion of very old (in computer years) word processors, such as Spellbinder, PeachText, Leading Edge WP, and Word Marc.

Also available is ListPort, which will convert flat data between most database programs. This includes options to reorder the data, break up data fields, combine fields, and others that can be quite helpful in migrating to Access.

And, finally, there is HiJaak Pro for the capture and conversion of graphic files—a migration question that has not yet been addressed. Many of the applications in Office 97 allow you to incorporate graphics into forms, documents, spreadsheets, and so on. Often, however, corporations forget that they have a collection of logos, illustrations, drawings, and photos that also have to migrate into Office 97.

For the older formats or for Macintosh-to-PC conversions, a third-party utility such as HiJaak Pro is necessary. HiJaak is produced by QuarterDeck (`www.quarterdeck.com`).

In summary, a wide variety of third-party options is available. As with any software program, you should first test their capabilities with actual sets of your data to ensure that they work properly. ●

CHAPTER 18

Managing Multiple Versions of Office

With software manufacturers releasing updates packed with new timesaving features on an annual basis, it is difficult for an office administrator to keep track of the various applications and versions of applications on everyone's workstation. Inevitably, a situation arises in which a few users have an older version of an application. The question then becomes how can these users still share information with others in the office. This chapter examines some of the decisions facing office administrators as they attempt to manage file format changes in the various Office 97 applications.

Managing Changes in Word File Formats

If your office is using a combination of Word 97, Word 95, and Word 6.0, you can exchange documents and templates among these versions by using one of these methods:

- Convert files to Word 97 format.
- Save Word 97 documents in Word 6.0/95 format.
- Install the Word 97 file format converter and open Word 97 documents directly in Word 95 or Word 6.0.

Converting Files to Word 97 Format

To convert most types of files saved in another format, simply open the file in Word 97. If Word recognizes the format, it automatically converts the document and opens it. Then you can save the file as a Word 97 document. If Word does not recognize the format, open the document in the application it was created in and save it to a compatible format. Table 18.1 lists the file converters supplied with Word 97 and indicates whether you can open or save a document in each format. If you used a Typical setup when you installed Word, not all of the converters listed in Table 18.1 are available.

To install an additional converter, run the Word setup program:

1. Insert the Office 97 CD-ROM.
2. Click the Windows Start button, point to Settings, and click Control Panel.
3. Double-click the Add/Remove Programs icon and select the Install/Uninstall tab.
4. Select Microsoft Office from the list of programs and click the Add/Remove button.
5. Click the Add/Remove button in the Microsoft Office 97 Setup dialog box. The Maintenance dialog box appears (see Figure 18.1). Select Microsoft Word and click the Change Option button to display a list of available items under the Microsoft Word category. Mark the Text Converters check box and click OK.

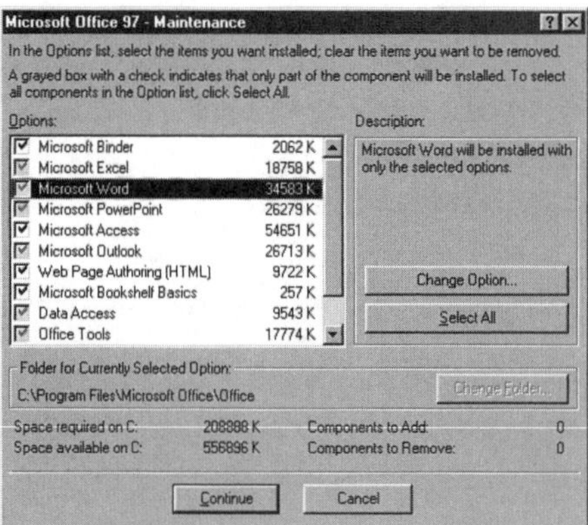

FIGURE 18.1
Installing additional Word 97 file converters through the Office 97 setup program.

6. From the Maintenance dialog box, select Converters and Filters and click the Change Option button to display a list of available items under the Converters and Filters category. Mark the Text Converters check box and click OK.

Table 18.1 File Format Converters Supplied with Word 97

File Format	Version	Open	Save
HTML	2.0	Yes	Yes
WordPerfect (DOS)	5.*x*	Yes	Yes
WordPerfect (DOS)	6.0	Yes	No
WordPerfect (Windows)	5.*x*	Yes	Yes
WordPerfect (Windows)	6.0	Yes	No
Microsoft Word (Windows)	2.x	Yes	Yes
Microsoft Word (Windows 95)	6.0/95	Yes	Yes
Microsoft Word (Macintosh)	4.*x*,5.*x*	Yes	Yes
Microsoft Works (Windows)	3.0	Yes	Yes
Microsoft Works (Windows 95)	4.0	Yes	Yes
Lotus 1-2-3	2.*x*,3.*x*,4.0	Yes	No
Microsoft Excel	2.*x*–97	Yes	No
Rich Text Format (RTF)	NA	Yes	Yes
MS-DOS text with layout	NA	Yes	Yes
MS-DOS text with line breaks	NA	Yes	Yes
MS-DOS text only	NA	Yes	Yes
Text only	NA	Yes	Yes

The Word Conversion Wizard Converting a large number of documents would be a tedious process if you had to open each one and save it as a Word 97 document. Fortunately, Word 97 comes with a Conversion Wizard that enables you to convert a large number of documents to and from Word 97 format.

To start the Conversion Wizard, follow these steps:

1. Place all of the documents you want to convert in a single folder.
2. Choose File, Open.
3. In the Files Of Type box, select All Files.

4. Locate the Conversion Wizard in the \Microsoft Office\Office\Macros folder.
5. Double-click Convert8.wiz.
6. If a Warning dialog box appears notifying you of possible viruses associated with macros, click the Enable Macros button.
7. In the Conversion Wizard dialog box, click A Batch Conversion Of Files to display the Conversion Wizard shown in Figure 18.2.

FIGURE 18.2
With the Word 97 Conversion Wizard, you can convert a large number of files simultaneously.

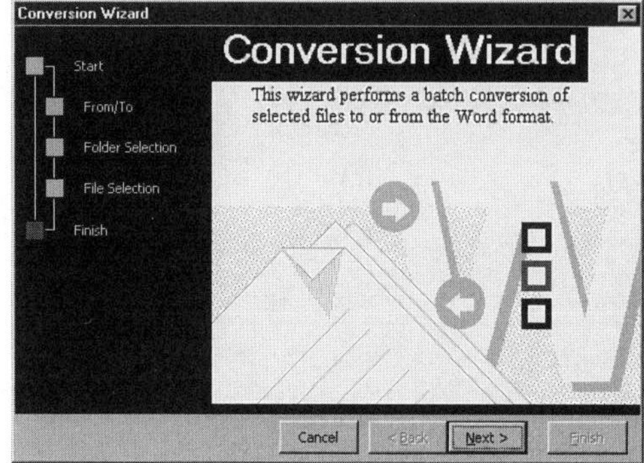

8. Follow the directions in the wizard.

NOTE If you do not have the Convert8.wiz file on your computer, run the Word 97 setup program to install this wizard. After you mark the Wizards, Templates, And Letters check box, mark the Macro Template check box.

Saving Word 97 Documents in Word 6.0/95 Format

If you have a large number of coworkers who are using Word 95 or Word 6.0, you can share files by saving your Word 97 documents and templates to the Word 6.0/95 format. To save to this dual format, follow these steps:

1. Choose File, Save As.
2. In the Save As Type box, select Word 6.0/95 from the list and then click OK.

CAUTION

Because not all Word 97 features are supported in Word 95 and Word 6.0, you might lose data and formatting when you save your document to Word 6.0/95 format. This is especially true if your document relies heavily on VBA macros. See Table 18.2 for a list of Word 97 features and their corresponding levels of support.

Table 18.2 Features Lost When Saving a Word 97 Document to Word 6.0 95 Format

Word 97 Feature	Word 6.0/95 Support Level	Result of Conversion
Embedded fonts	None	Embedded fonts are lost. The closest font available is assigned.
Multilevel bullets	None	Multilevel bullets are converted to regular text and retain their appearance.
Page borders	None	Page borders are lost.
Character shading, borders, engraving, and embossing	None	Text remains, but all special formatting is lost.
Paragraph borders	None	Paragraph borders are lost.
Animated text	None	Text remains but is not animated.
Floating graphics with text wrap	None	Graphics are converted to a WMF (Windows Metafile) with a frame.
Floating OLE objects	None	Floating OLE objects are converted to text boxes.
Highlighting	Partial	Highlighting is preserved in Word 95 but lost in Word 6.0.
Tracked changes for properties, paragraph numbers, and display fields	Partial	Tracked changes for these items are lost, but other tracked changes are saved.
Document protection	None	All document password protection is lost.
Protection for tracked changes, comments, and forms	None	All document protection is lost.
ActiveX form controls	Partial	ActiveX controls can be used but not modified.
Unicode characters	Partial	Foreign characters are converted to the corresponding ANSI equivalent or a question mark. Conversion could result in potential data loss.
Visual Basic macros	None	Word 97 VBA macros are lost.

NOTE When you save a Word 97 file in a Word 6.0/95 format, the document is actually saved in RTF (Rich Text Format), but it still has the Word file extension (.doc).

If you find yourself continually saving Word 97 documents to a different file format, you can specify a default file format for saving documents. To do so, follow these simple steps:

1. Choose Tools, Options to display the Options dialog box shown in Figure 18.3. Click the Save tab.
2. In the Save Word Files As box, select the file format you want, and then click OK.

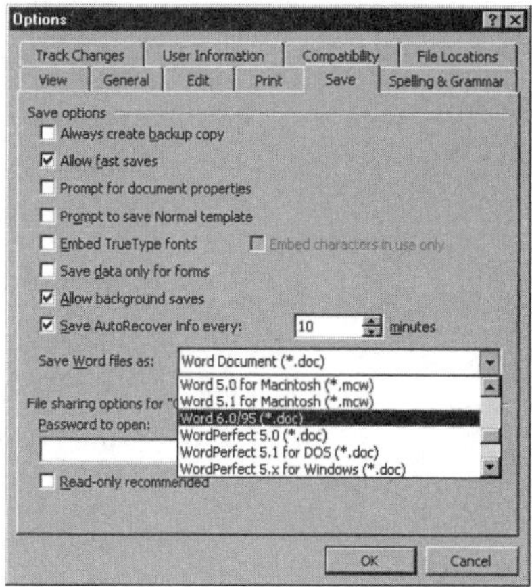

FIGURE 18.3
Changing the default file format for saving Word 97 documents.

Installing the Word 97 File Format Converter

Another way to share documents with coworkers is to use the Word 97 file format converter. With this installed, users who have Word 95 or Word 6.0 can open and work with Word 97 documents; however, features of the converted Word 97 document are still subject to the limitations outlined in Table 18.2. Because each Word 6.0 and Word 95 workstation must have the file format converter installed, this method of sharing documents might not be practical if you need to share documents with a large number of users.

If you have access to the Office 97 CD-ROM, install the Word 97 file format converter by double-clicking the VALUPACK\WRD97CNV\Wrd97cnv.exe file. When you see the confirmation message box shown in Figure 18.4, click Yes to install either Mswrd832.cnv (the 32-bit version for users of Word 95) or Msword8.cnv (the 16-bit version for users of Word 6.0) and update the necessary registry entries. The converter also installs a readme file named Wrd97cnv.doc, which contains additional information.

With the file format converter installed, you can open a Word 97 document in Word 95 or Word 6.0. To do so, follow these steps:

FIGURE 18.4
Installing the Word 97 file format converter.

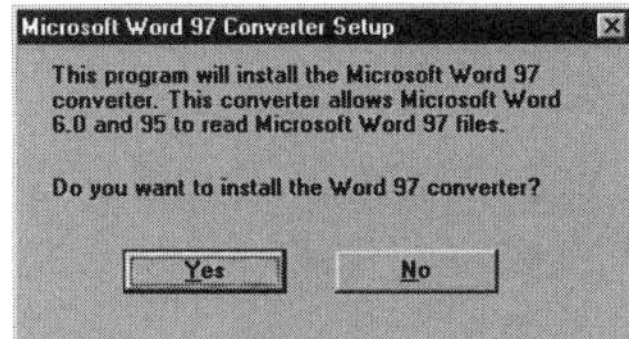

1. In Word 95 or Word 6.0, choose File, Open.
2. Select the Word 97 document you want, and then click Open.
3. If the Confirm Conversions At Open check box is selected on the General tab of the Tools, Options dialog box, select the Word 97 option when the confirmation dialog box appears. Otherwise, the document opens automatically.

NOTE If you do not have access to the Office 97 CD-ROM, you can download the Word 97 file format converter from Microsoft's Web site: `www.microsoft.com/word/freestuff/converters/wrd97cnv.htm`. ■

Managing Changes in Excel File Formats

By default, Excel 97 saves workbooks in Excel 97 format. If you want users with an earlier version of Excel to open your Excel 97 workbooks, you have two options:

- Convert Excel 5.0/95 files to Excel 97 format.
- Save Excel 97 files in Excel 5.0/95 format.

Converting Files to Excel 97 Format

Microsoft Excel 97 contains most of the file converters you need. To convert a file, simply open the document and save it as an Excel 97 workbook. If you do not see the file format you want in the Files Of Type drop-down box in the File, Open dialog box, you can install the appropriate converter by running the Excel setup program. To do the installation, follow these steps:

1. Insert the Office 97 CD-ROM.
2. Click the Windows Start button, point to Settings, and click Control Panel.
3. Double-click the Add/Remove Programs icon and select the Install/Uninstall tab.
4. Select Microsoft Office from the list of programs and click the Add/Remove button.
5. Click the Add/Remove button in the Microsoft Office 97 Setup dialog box. The Maintenance dialog box appears (shown in Figure 18.5). Select Data Access and click the Change Option button to display a list of available items under the Data Access category. Click the Select All button.

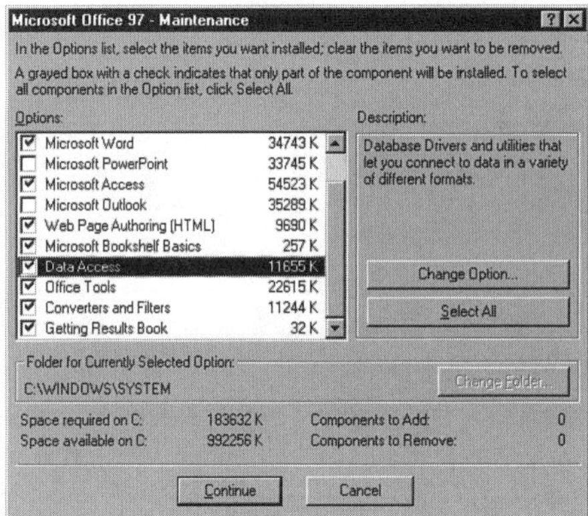

FIGURE 18.5
Installing additional database drivers through the Office 97 setup program.

The Excel Conversion Wizard Excel 97 also comes with a Conversion Wizard that enables you to convert a large number of files. Unlike the Word Conversion Wizard, however, the Excel Conversion Wizard runs as an add-in (a supplemental program that extends the capabilities of Excel by adding custom commands and specialized features). Before you begin, choose Tools, Add-Ins and make sure the File Conversion Wizard check box is selected.

To convert a large number of files, follow the next few steps:

1. Place all the files you want to convert in a single folder.
2. Choose Tools, Wizard, File Conversion to display the first dialog box of the Excel Conversion Wizard shown in Figure 18.6.
3. Follow the directions in the wizard.

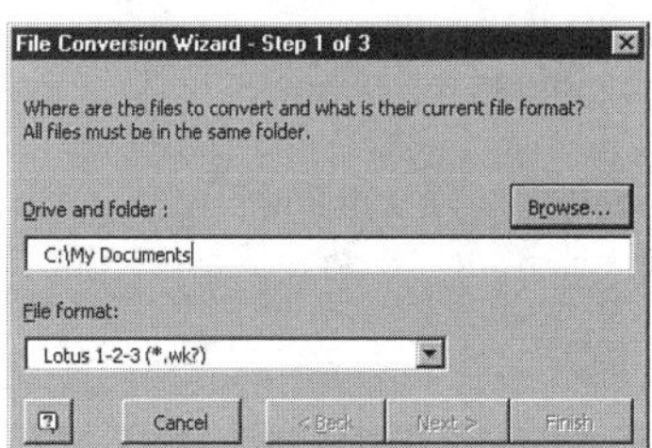

FIGURE 18.6
With the Excel Conversion Wizard, you can convert a large number of files simultaneously.

Saving Excel 97 Documents in Excel 5.0/95 Format If you do not wish to convert all of your documents to Excel 97 format, you can save your Excel 97 workbooks to Excel 5.0/95 format. However, if you save an Excel 97 workbook in a different file format, features unique to Excel 97 will be lost. Table 18.3 outlines features that are lost when saving an Excel 97 workbook to Excel 5.0/95 format.

Excel 97 also comes with a special dual-file format that will save your document in Excel 97 format and 5.0/95 format. Although the resulting file is larger than it would be otherwise, you might want to choose this option if hard disk capacity is not an issue and you have Excel 97 and Excel 5.0/95 users who need access to your document.

If you save your document in this dual format, users with Excel 5.0 or 95 who open this document will be given a warning that they should use this file in a read-only state. If they ignore this warning and save the file, features and formatting only available in Excel 97 will be lost.

To save a document in the dual format, do the following:

1. Choose File, Save As.
2. In the Save As Type box, select Microsoft Excel 97 and Excel 5.0/95 Workbook.
3. To prevent Excel 5.0 and 95 users from modifying your file, click the Options button and specify a password in the Password To Modify box.

Table 18.3 Features Lost When Saving an Excel 97 Workbook to Excel 5.0 95 Format

Excel 97 Feature	Excel 5.0/95 Support Level	Result of Conversion
65,536 rows per worksheet	None	Rows after 16,384 are deleted.
32,000 characters per cell	None	Characters after 255 are deleted.
Custom views	None	Custom views are not saved.
Attached toolbars	None	Attached toolbars are lost.
Shrink-to-fit text	None	Text is retained at the original point size.
Rotated text	Partial	Text rotated at angles other than 90 or –90 degrees is oriented horizontally.
Indentation in cells	Partial	Indentation is removed and cells are left-aligned.
Merged cells	Partial	Merged cells are split to their original configuration.
Conditional formatting	Partial	Cells are formatted with the Normal style.
Sheet backgrounds	None	Sheet backgrounds are lost.
New border styles	None	Border styles are converted to the closest available style.
Data tables in charts	None	Data tables are lost.
Text rotated on axis	Partial	Saved as horizontally oriented text.
Gradient fills/patterns	None	Saved as the closest available solid color.
Surface chart shading	None	Shading is not saved.

continues

Table 18.3 Continued

Excel 97 Feature	Excel 5.0/95 Support Level	Result of Conversion
Series/points shadows	None	Shadows are not saved.
Sizable line/data markers	None	Default size saved.
Special data label placement	None	Default placement saved.
Map objects	Full	Map objects saved.
Comments	Partial	Comments saved as cell notes.
Hyperlinks	None	Hyperlinks are not saved.
Change tracking	None	Change history is lost.
Cell data validation	None	Data validation is lost.
ActiveX controls	None	ActiveX controls appear but cannot be used.
Dialog box controls	None	Dialog box controls are not saved.

NOTE Additional features such as OLE objects, Visual Basic modules, and data access and analysis functions might be limited when saving an Excel 97 workbook to an Excel 5.0/95 format. See the Excel 97 Help file for more information. ■

If you find yourself frequently saving Excel 97 documents to a different file format, you can specify a default file format for saving documents. To do so, follow these simple steps:

1. Choose Tools, Options, to display the Options dialog box and click the Transition tab.
2. In the Save Excel Files As box, select the file format you want, and then click OK.

Managing Changes in PowerPoint File Formats

If you want to share presentations among coworkers, you have three options:

- Convert files to PowerPoint 97.
- Save PowerPoint 97 presentations in PowerPoint 95 format.
- Install a PowerPoint 97 converter.

Converting Presentations to PowerPoint 97

To convert a presentation from an earlier version of PowerPoint to PowerPoint 97, simply open the presentation. The presentation opens as a read-only file. When you save the presentation with a new name in PowerPoint 97, the conversion is complete. The following file formats are resident in PowerPoint, and you can import and export them directly:

- Outline format (including text formats such as .rtf and .txt)
- Windows Metafile (.wmf)

- Macintosh PICT (.pct)
- Presentation for PowerPoint 97
- Presentation Template
- PowerPoint Show
- PowerPoint Add–in
- PowerPoint versions 3.0–95

You can also open Harvard Graphics presentations (versions 2.3 or 3.0 for DOS) and Freelance presentations (versions 1.0–2.1 for Windows and version 4.0 for DOS) directly in PowerPoint 97 with the appropriate converters. If you have a later version of Harvard Graphics or Freelance, save the presentation to a compatible format before attempting to open the presentation in PowerPoint 97.

If you want to convert a presentation from a program for which there is no converter, you can import the graphics into PowerPoint 97 if the program you're converting from can export the presentation to a Windows Metafile (.wmf) or Macintosh PICT (.pct) format.

Saving PowerPoint 97 Presentations in PowerPoint 95 Format

If you save a PowerPoint 97 presentation in a different file format, features unique to PowerPoint 97 will be lost. Table 18.4 outlines features that are lost when saving a PowerPoint 97 presentation to PowerPoint 95 format.

Like Excel, PowerPoint has a dual-file format that enables you to save presentations in PowerPoint 95 and 97 format. The problem with this format is that the file can become quite large with lengthy presentations, and the additional file size means the file takes longer to load.

To save a presentation in this dual format, do the following:

1. Choose File, Save As.
2. In the Save As Type box, select PowerPoint 95 And 97 Presentation.
3. To prevent PowerPoint 95 users from modifying your file, click the Options button and specify a password in the Password To Modify box.

Table 18.4 Features Lost When Saving a PowerPoint 97 Presentation to PowerPoint 95 Format

PowerPoint 97 Feature	PowerPoint 95 Support Level	Result of Conversion
Animated chart elements	None	Appear as static chart objects.
Custom shows	None	Slides appear in presentation.
Elevator effects	None	Converted to Wipe Up.

continues

Table 18.4 Continued

PowerPoint 97 Feature	PowerPoint 95 Support Level	Result of Conversion
Resident format movies and sounds	None	Converted to media player objects.
3-D effects	None	Converted to pictures.
Curves	None	Converted to connected line segments.
Gradient fills	Partial	Semitransparency is lost.
Embedded/linked objects	Partial	Brightness, contrast, and color transformation settings are lost.
Picture fills	None	Converted to picture objects.
Engraved shadows	None	Converted to embossed shadows.
Perspective shadows	None	Converted to shapes or pictures.
Text effects	None	Converted to pictures.
Thick compound lines	None	Converted to picture objects.
Comments	Partial	Converted to Rich Text. Hidden comments are displayed.
Object-embedded hyperlinks	None	Hyperlinks are lost.
Unicode characters	Partial	Foreign characters are converted to the corresponding ANSI equivalent or a question mark. Conversion could result in data loss.
PowerPoint macros	None	PowerPoint macros are lost.

To specify a default file format other than PowerPoint 97 for saving presentations, follow these steps:

1. Choose Tools, Options to display the Options dialog box and click the Save tab.
2. In the Save PowerPoint Files As box, select the file format you want, and then click OK.

Installing the PowerPoint 97 Converters

With the PowerPoint 97 Converters, a PowerPoint 95 or PowerPoint 4.0 user can open and work with PowerPoint 97 presentations; however, features of the converted PowerPoint 97 presentations are subject to the limitations outlined in Table 18.4. This might include such features as 3-D effects, WordArt, texture and picture fills, and some drawing objects.

To install the Microsoft PowerPoint 97 Converter for PowerPoint 95, do the following:

1. Download Pp8to7.exe from `www.microsoft.com/powerpoint/enhancements/pp8to7.asp`.
2. Double-click the file to begin the converter installation.
3. Follow the directions onscreen.
4. If prompted, restart your computer to complete the installation.

NOTE You can download the Translator for PowerPoint 4.0 from `www.microsoft.com/powerpoint/enhancements/pp8trans.asp` and install it by using the above steps. The file is named Pp8trans.exe.

Managing Changes in Access File Formats

The format of Access tables is the same in Access 97 as in Access 95. In most cases, you'll want to convert Access 95 databases to Access 97; however, after you do so, you can't open the database in the version of Access it was created in, and you can't convert it back.

On the other hand, if you're in a multiuser environment where all the users cannot upgrade to Access 97, you can share the database in Access 97 and maintain the original format so users of previous versions of Access can continue to use the database. If you share a database in Access 97 without converting it, you can neither change the design of objects in that database with Access 97 nor take advantage of the new features in Access 97 until you convert the database.

Depending on your situation, you'll be faced with one of two options:

- Convert a database from a previous version of Access.
- Share a database with several versions of Access.

Converting an Access 1.x or 2.0 Database to Access 97

Before you convert your Access database, make sure each linked table in your database is in a valid folder. A linked table is a data source outside of the open database, such as a FoxPro or dBase file, from which Microsoft Access can access records. Converting an Access database with linked tables does not convert the linked tables. If you want to move the location of a linked table, do so after the conversion and re-link the table by using the Linked Table Manager located in the Tools, Add-Ins dialog box. If Access cannot find a table linked to a database that's being converted, you won't be able to use the converted database.

To convert your database, follow these steps:

1. Make a backup copy of the database.
2. Close the database. If you're in a multiuser environment or the database is in a shared folder, make sure no other users have it open.

3. Choose Tools, Database Utilities, Convert Database to display the Database To Convert From dialog box shown in Figure 18.7.

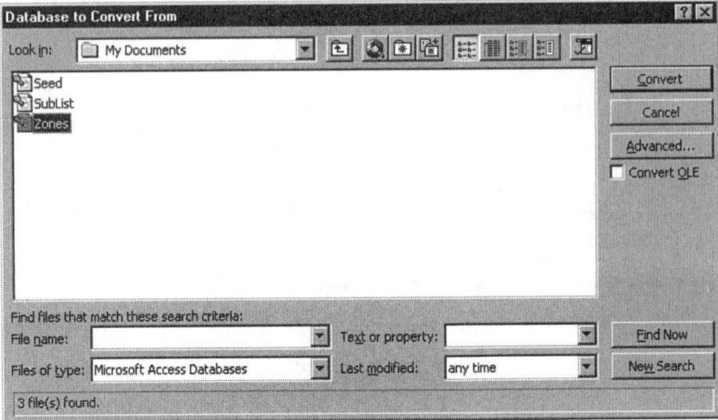

FIGURE 18.7
Converting an Access database.

4. Select the database you want to convert and click the Convert button to display the Database To Convert Into dialog box.
5. Type a new name for the database (without the .mdb extension), or enter the same name but select a different folder.
6. Click Save.

Here are a few of the common problems associated with converting an Access database, with some possible solutions:

- During the conversion process, Access 97 appends an underscore to the converted database or project name if the database you are converting has a database name or project name that uses a reserved word. Check to make sure any references to renamed projects are correct so that your application runs properly.
- If your Access 1.*x* forms have controls that include a right bracket in the name, you must rename the control without using a right bracket if you want to modify the control in Access 97. If you do not plan on modifying the control, it will function the same as it did in the Access 1.*x* database.
- If an object name in an Access 1.*x* database includes a backquote character (‘), you won’t be able to convert the database to an Access 97 format. To work around this problem, rename the object in Access 1.*x* prior to conversion. If you have to rename an object, make sure you change any references to that object in your queries, forms, reports, macros, and modules. To see if you have any objects with this invalid character, choose Tools, Analyze, Documenter.
- Access 97 converts Access Basic code to Visual Basic. If your code won’t compile in the converted database, open a module in Design view and choose Debug, Compile All Modules. As Access compiles, it stops at any line of code that contains an error to help you locate the source of the problem.

- In Access 2.0, you could set some margins to 0. After the conversion, this value is set to the minimum margin allowable for the default printer. If your reports have different margins, you need to adjust the column width, column spacing, or number of columns so the width of the columns plus the width of the default margins is less than the width of your paper.

Sharing an Access 97 Database with Previous Versions of Access

The strategy for sharing an Access database with several versions of Access is to create a front-end/back-end application. A front-end/back-end application consists of two database files: a back-end database that contains the tables and a front-end database that contains the queries, forms, reports, macros, and modules. Typically, the back-end database resides on a network server or in a shared folder, and copies of the front-end database are distributed on individual workstations. As long as the back-end database remains in the earliest version of Access, users with different versions of Access will be able to access the data in the tables.

To share an Access 97 database, follow these steps:

1. Convert your database to Access 97, using the steps in the previous section, "Converting an Access 1.x or 2.0 Database to Access 97." Make sure you specify a new name.
2. Open the converted database and choose Tools, Add-Ins, Database Splitter to display the Database Splitter Wizard shown in Figure 18.8. Follow the directions in the wizard to split your database into two files.

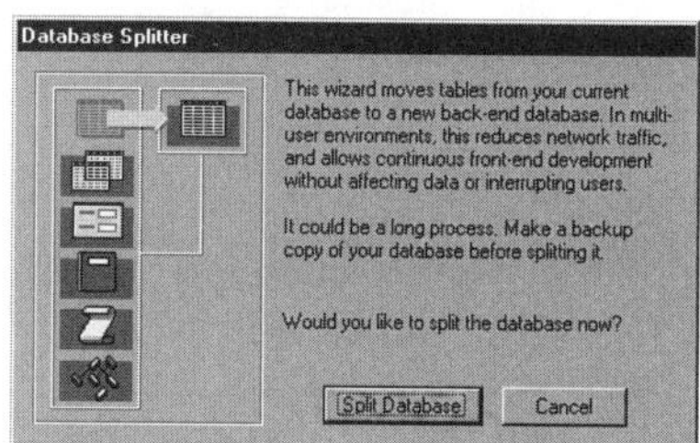

FIGURE 18.8
Using the Database Splitter Wizard to share a database with several versions of Access.

3. After the database has been split, delete the converted back-end database.
4. Choose Tools, Add-Ins, Linked Table Manager to link your converted front-end database to the tables in the back-end database in the previous version of Access.

If you're already using a front-end/back-end application, the process is basically the same; however, you won't need to split the database because it's already split. You only need to convert your front-end database to Access 97 and run the Linked Table Manager to access the back-end database.

Managing Outlook, Schedule+, and Personal Address Book Formats

You can import address book contacts and email messages from a variety of popular Internet email programs, such as Symantec's ACT!, Netscape's Communicator and Navigator, and Microsoft's Personal Address Book. Table 18.5 outlines the file format converters supplied with Outlook. If you do not see your program listed, a converter might be available from a third-party vendor. If you cannot locate an appropriate converter, you can export your contact information from the original application to a comma-separated text file (.csv) and import it to Outlook using that option.

Table 18.5 File Format Converters Supplied with Outlook

File Format	File Extension	Import	Export
Comma Separated Values	.cxv,.txt	Yes	Yes
Tab Separated Values	.txt	Yes	Yes
FoxPro, dBase	.dbf	Yes	Yes
Lotus Organizer 1.0, 1.1, 2.1	.org,.or2	Yes	No
Microsoft Access	.mdb	Yes	Yes
Microsoft Excel	.xls	Yes	Yes
Microsoft Exchange Personal Address Book	.pab	Yes	Yes
Microsoft Schedule+ 1.0, 95	.cal,.scd	Yes	No
NetManage ECCO Pro 3.0, 3.01, 3.02	.eco	Yes	No
Starfish Sidekick	.skcard	Yes	No
Symantec ACT! 2.0	.dbf	Yes	No

NOTE Converting data from ACT! 2.0, ECCO Pro, or Starfish Sidekick requires the use of an appropriate converter that must be installed separately. Converters for these programs can be found on the Office 97 CD-ROM (double-click the Valupack\Convert\Outlook\outcvt.exe file) or downloaded from Microsoft's Web site at the following address:

`www.microsoft.com/office/outlook/enhancements/outcvt.asp`.

DataViz, Inc, developed these converters. For information on additional converters, visit the DataViz Web site at `www.dataviz.com`.

To import an address book or email message store, follow these steps:

1. Choose File, Import, and click Address Book or Messages, depending on what you want to import.
2. Click the address book or file type you want to import, and then click Import.
3. Outlook attempts to automatically locate the file on your hard disk. If it cannot find the file, a message box appears asking if you want to manually locate the file. Click Yes.
4. Locate the file on your hard disk and click Import.

CHAPTER 19

Integrating Office Applications More Effectively

For many companies and individual computer users, Microsoft Office 97 is the software suite of choice. When utilized to the fullest potential, MS Office 97 synchronizes its suite of professional applications: Word, Excel, Access, and PowerPoint.

This allows users to collaborate on projects using your network. We have discussed this in earlier chapters. In this chapter we look at the most popular feature of Office 97, its capability to share data freely between applications. This goes beyond cutting and pasting data between programs. In Office 97 you can integrate applications to link, share, and import data between applications.

To enable independence and self-sufficiency in the workplace, the challenge for Office administrators is to fully understand Office 97 functionality while minimizing any potential trouble spots.

This chapter gets right to the source issues and problem solving so that your system is up and running with Microsoft Office quickly and efficiently. Topics to be covered include the following:

- How to share files among Office applications
- How to integrate Word documents and Excel worksheets
- How to integrate Word documents and PowerPoint presentations
- How to publish Word documents with Access data
- How to use Excel as a database front-end
- How to track Office files and tasks with the Outlook Journal
- How to track documents with Find Fast, Web Find Fast, and Document Properties

Sharing Files Among Office Applications

One of the most powerful features of Office 97 is its capability to move entire files between applications. You can place Excel data in Access, PowerPoint, or Word. You can put Word data into Excel and then move it to Outlook. You can also share selected parts of files. It is this flexibility that makes a group of software applications a suite.

Sharing Data Between Applications

There are three ways that Windows is able to move files among applications: pasting, linking, and embedding. To paste data from one Office application to another use the following steps:

1. Select your data in the source program, and choose Cut or Copy from the Edit menu.
2. Switch to the receiving program and place the insertion point in the document where you want the pasted information to appear.
3. Choose Paste Special from the Edit menu (see Figure 19.1).

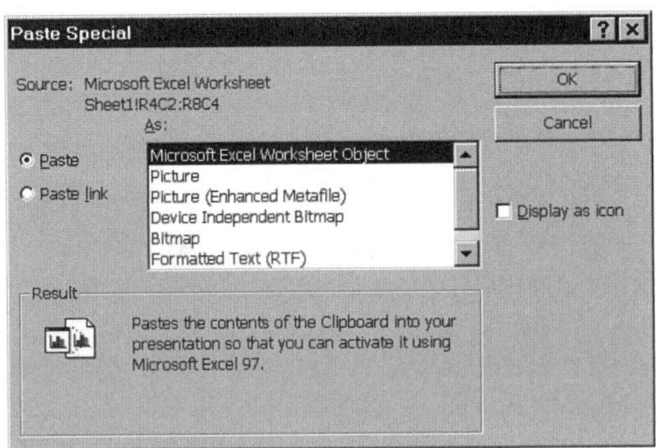

FIGURE 19.1
Selecting the Display as Icon box inserts an icon in place of the actual data. Notice the Result box at the bottom of the window.

4. Select the Paste option.
5. Select the data format from the As: list. (Selecting OK inserts the data into the document.)
6. Check the Result box for a description of each formatting choice. The format above shows in the Result box.

Object Linking and Embedding

Another way to move files among Office applications is object linking and embedding (OLE). To understand OLE, the following definitions are necessary:

- *Object.* Data that is linked or embedded in another document. An object can be any size, from one word to a large Excel worksheet. Examples of objects are logos, sound clips, Excel fields, or Word documents.

- *Destination document.* The document you are copying the data into. It contains the links to other Windows programs.
- *Source file.* A document containing the object you are linking.
- *Client applications.* The Office applications in which you assemble the destination documents.
- *Server applications.* The Windows application that created an object linked to a destination file. If you create an object in PowerPoint and embed it in Word, PowerPoint is the client application and Word is the server application.
- *Linked.* The files that are changed or updated in server applications are automatically updated in the destination file.
- *Embedded.* An object inserted into a document. There are no links to the source file for updating. However, you may make modifications to the information as it appears.

There are two ways to create an OLE link. One way is to use the Paste Special command, and the other is to use the Insert Object command.

The following steps show how to create an OLE link using the Paste Special command (see "Using the Insert Object Command" later in this chapter):

1. Copy the desired object to the Clipboard. One way to do this is to select the object and then select Edit, Copy.
2. From the client application, select Edit, Paste Special. The Paste Special dialog window appears from which you make your selections. (See the following bullet points for more information on your options.)
3. Click OK to accept your link. You see the data inserted into your document.

   The options available in the Paste Special dialog box include the following:

   - *Source.* This shows the original name and location of the object in the Clipboard.
   - *Paste (Embed).* This puts contents of the Clipboard into a document at an insertion point. A link is not maintained, but you can double-click pasted material to edit. (This is also called embedding.)
   - *Paste Link.* This is available only if the Clipboard content can be linked to a destination document.
   - *The As: list box.* Displays various ways the Clipboard object may be formatted and pasted. The formats vary for different objects. For example, when pasting a part of a Word document into an Excel document you are given the following options: Microsoft Word Document Object, Picture (Enhanced Metafile), Unicode Text, Text, and Hyperlink.
   - *Result.* This describes the outcome of a particular option selected in the dialog box.

Part IV Ch 19

NOTE If you have not saved the source file, the Paste Link Option is not available.

NOTE If Paste Link is unavailable, or the source program does not support linking, the data in the Clipboard cannot be linked.

Using the Display as an Icon box allows the pasted object to show up as an icon in the destination folder. This is only available with Paste Link, and is especially useful for sounds and media clips to be played at a later time.

When the document is printed, only the icon is printed. In a Word document, linking types of data in a certain format allows the Float Over Text option. If selected, the data is in a box outside the normal flow of text. You can now position it anywhere on the page.

The type of linking, embedding, or pasting that is done depends on your choice of Paste or Paste Link and your choice of formats in the As list. Figure 19.2 shows the final document with the linked Excel worksheet within the Word document. Notice the white boxes around the data. You can stretch or shorten the room taken up by this information. You can also move the data anywhere in your document.

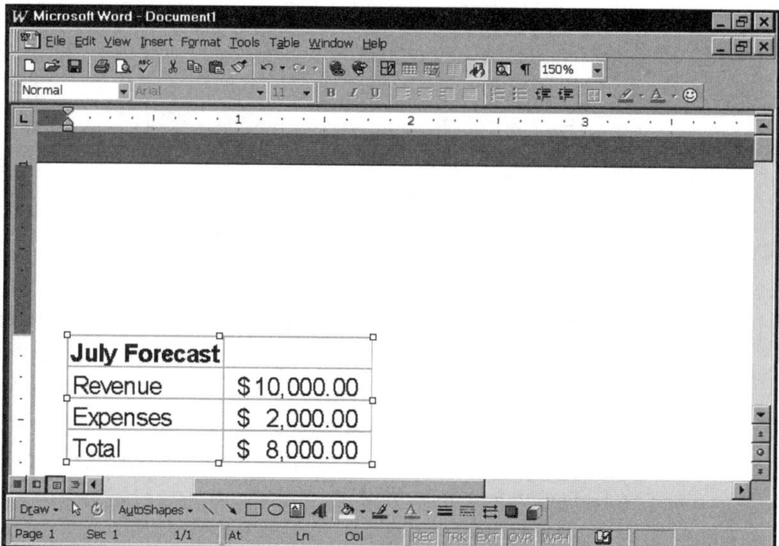

FIGURE 19.2
Final document with linked Excel sheet within a Word document.

Using the Insert Object Command

Using the Insert Object command is useful if you have not yet created the object in the source application. It's also helpful if you want to insert an entire document as your object.

You can use Insert Object to link only an entire file. You cannot use Insert Object to link a portion of a file.

To create the link, go to the Insert menu, click Object and choose either Create New or Create from File depending on what you are inserting.

To create a new object, follow these steps:

1. Under Object, select the Create New tab.
2. Select Create from File under Objects.
3. The display box enables the user to type the filename that is to be linked or embedded.

To create a new object from a file, select the OLE-compatible application that you want to create from the Object Type list.

Editing OLE Links

MS Office 97 enables you to edit from either the source or the destination file.

Use the following steps to edit a linked object from the source file:

1. Start the server application and open the source file that contains the object to edit.
2. Edit the object as necessary.
3. Save the document and close the server application.
4. Start the client application and open the destination file. Changes are automatically updated.

To edit a linked object from the destination file, use the following steps:

1. Open the destination file and double-click the linked object. This opens the server application and displays the source file.
2. Edit the object.
3. Choose File, Save in the server application.
4. Choose File, Exit in the server application. You are back in the destination file.

Updating OLE Links

Updates to your object are automatic by default. In other words, when you modify the source document, the client document automatically changes. If you decide to limit updates or want to do them manually, access the Edit menu, choose Links, and select the link that you want. Choose Manual, Update Now, OK, File, Save.

If the links are set to be updated manually, remember to update them each time you want the client file to be updated.

Links may be locked to protect files from being changed or updated. To lock (or unlock) a document with a linked object, first choose the Edit menu, click Links and select a link to lock (or unlock), click OK. (See Figure 19.3.)

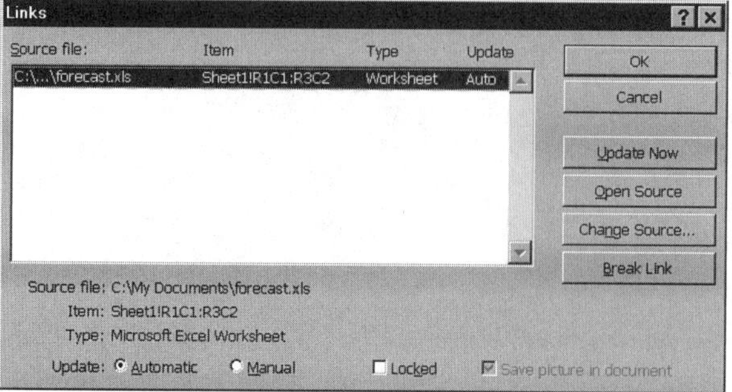

FIGURE 19.3
This is the Links dialog box, which enables you to modify the source (discussed later) and lock your link(s).

A locked link is updated until it is unlocked.

Breaking and Changing Links

You may want to break a link for a document when the source file has been deleted or if you no longer want to have the client document updated by the source document. Breaking links does not change or delete the object. It only removes the ties between that object and the source file. To break a link choose Edit, click Links and select Break Link.

If you move a file or rename a file, it is necessary to update or change the source of a link. Follow these steps to update your link:

1. Open the client file.
2. Choose Edit, Links.
3. Select the link you want to update.
4. Click Change Source. The Change source dialog box appears (see Figure 19.4), showing the location of the linked object.

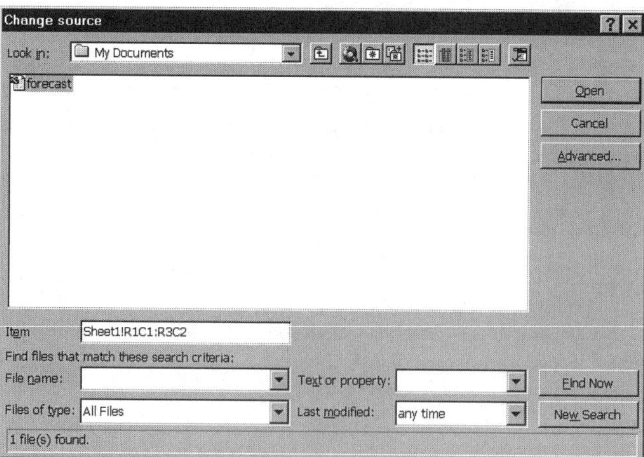

FIGURE 19.4
The Change source dialog box. Notice that you may change the range or the filename from this dialog box.

5. Choose a different filename/location to show the new name/location of the source file.
6. Click Open.

Embedding Objects

Embedding an object is similar to linking but the connection between source and destination is different. The data is placed in the destination file, but there is no link between that data and the source file. The advantage of embedding over linking is the ease of editing parts of the destination file.

Table 19.1 shows the two ways to embed an object into a document.

Table 19.1 Embedding Objects in Documents

Insert Object	Paste Special
Start at the destination file and choose Insert, Object. This launches the server application, creates the object, and embeds it into the destination file.	Create the object in the server application and embed it in the destination file using Paste Special. This is best when embedding only parts of a document.
1. To create a new object, start the client application and open the destination document.	1. Start the server application and create or open the object to embed.
2. Select Insert, and then Object.	2. Select the object to be embedded.
3. Choose the server application you want to use, and click OK.	3. Choose Edit, then Copy (it copies to the Clipboard).
4. Create the object using the server's tools and commands.	4. Switch to the client application and open or create the destination document.
5. After you have created the object, click the destination window. The server closes and the object appears in the destination document.	5. Place the insertion point where you want the object to be.

continues

Table 19.1 Continued

Insert Object	Paste Special
6. Save the destination document.	6. Select Edit, Paste Special.
	7. Select the Object data type of your choice.
	8. Click OK.
	9. Save the destination document.

To edit an embedded object, simply double-click the object. The source application starts and you can edit. If updating is not a primary concern, embedding (instead of linking) makes it easier to edit.

Integrating Word Documents and Excel Worksheets

There are two main scenarios when integrating Word and Excel. The first is if you need to add data to your Word document, and the second is if you need to link that data from Excel to Word.

Linking a Worksheet

If you are working on a report and need to input numbers or charts, you may need to link your data from an Excel worksheet to a Word document.

Follow these steps to link an Excel worksheet into Word:

1. Select and copy the cells in Excel that you want to place in the document.
2. In the Word document, place the cursor where the data is to be placed.
3. Click the Edit menu and Paste Special menu item.
4. Select one of the following options:
    - **Paste Link.** Select this option if you plan to make changes to the Excel worksheet and want the changes to be reflected in the document.
    - **Paste.** Select this option if you are not going to make changes to the Excel worksheet. This is a static paste.

Using just the Paste option significantly increases the size of your document because the data is actually embedded in the document, causing the size to increase.

Embedding a Worksheet

Embedded data is different from linked data in that it is placed statically in the document. You cannot change the data from the source and expect it to change in the embedded data.

To embed an entire spreadsheet into a Word document, follow these steps:

1. Position your cursor where the spreadsheet is to be placed.
2. From Excel, select Insert, Object (see Figure 19.5).

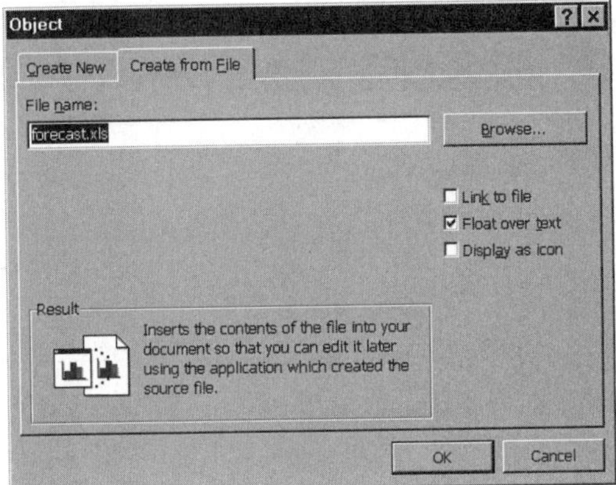

FIGURE 19.5
Note the three options in the Object dialog box: Link to File, Float Over Text and Display as Icon.

3. From the Object dialog box, click the Create from File tab.
4. Type or browse for the filename and make sure the Link to File option is not selected.
5. Click the OK button to embed the data into this document.

TIP You can modify a linked spreadsheet from Word by double-clicking the spreadsheet.

Integrating Word Documents and PowerPoint Presentations

Word documents can be embedded in a PowerPoint presentation as an icon. During the PowerPoint presentation, when the icon is clicked, data pops up from another source. This process is known as drilling down. This can be effective when providing supporting assumptions, additional information, listing sources, or bibliographies during a presentation. During the slideshow, you click the icon to display the information in its original form. Word documents or Excel spreadsheets can be embedded. (A graph may be drilled down to its raw data, for example.)

To create a drill-down document, you first must embed the existing object.

1. Choose Insert, Object, Create from File.
2. Then click Browse. Select the file you want to embed.
3. Click OK.

The object you choose appears on the current slide as an icon (see Figure 19.6).

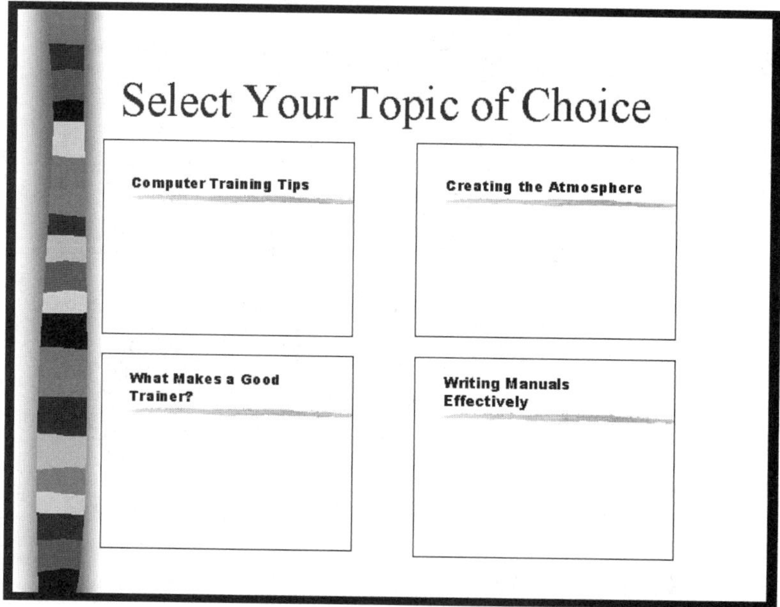

FIGURE 19.6
When you double-click the icon, the application opens its own window.

PowerPoint Presentations and Branching

When you embed a drill-down object into a PowerPoint presentation, you can branch (or connect) to that presentation or document from inside another slideshow (see Figure 19.7).

To embed a PowerPoint presentation, follow the procedure in the preceding section. Choose "PowerPoint Presentation" as the object you want to embed. This branching allows interactive training and information exchange. The viewer is able to select the drill down. They can double-click the topic preferred and each drill-down choice starts a different slideshow.

Creating Batch Files to Play a Series of Slideshows

Using Microsoft Word as a text editor, you can create a batch file to play a series of slideshows automatically.

To create the batch file, include the command to start the PowerPoint presentation, the /s switch for slideshow view and the full pathname for each PowerPoint presentation included in the final show.

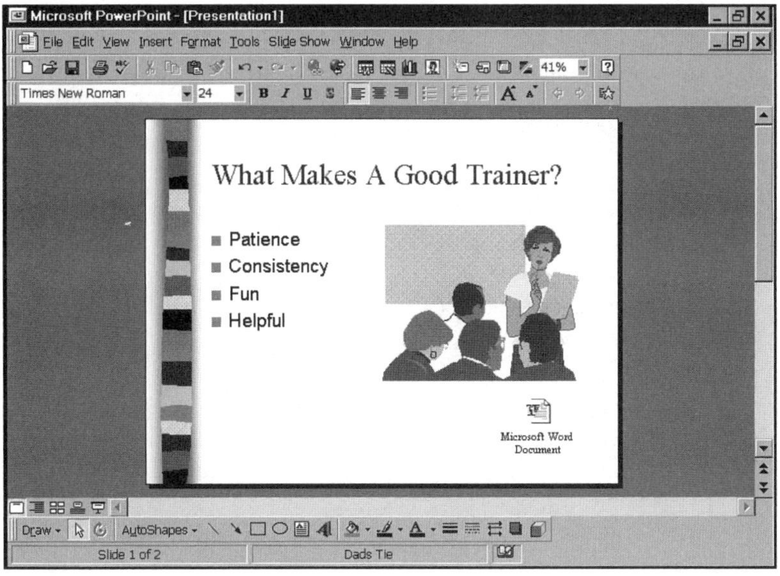

FIGURE 19.7
Double-clicking the Word document icon branches to that document while in another presentation.

The following is a sample command line:

```
    start PowerPoint/s c:\slideshow\"name of first
➥slideshow".ppt\c:\slideshow\"name of secondslideshow".ppt\c:\slideshow\"name
➥of third slideshow".ppt\
```

To run the preceding command, invoke it from the Windows Run command line.

NOTE When you run the batch file, the slideshows play in the order that they appear in the command line.

Publishing Word Documents with Access Data

Sharing data between Access and Word can be done by importing or exporting information or object linking and embedding using OLE object field.

To share data between Access and Word using OLE, follow these steps:

1. Open the Access table that is storing the data you want to share and insert OLE object data in a field.
2. Display the data sheet and click a record in OLE Object Field. Select Insert, Object. Access displays the Insert Object dialog box.
3. Perform one of the procedures shown in Table 19.2.

Table 19.2 Inserting OLE Objects

A New OLE Object	An Existing OLE Object
1. Select File, and choose Create New option.	1. Select File, Create.
2. Select the object type from Object Type list. Click OK. Access loads the correct application automatically, so you can create the object.	2. Enter the filename.
3. When done, select File, Close and return to "Table" (is the current Access Table).	3. If you desire a linked file, check link box, or access, insert file as embedded object.

NOTE Whether as a new or existing object, you can use the Display as Icon box to insert the object as an icon. The icon is seen if you display the table in a form.

Performing Mail Merge with Office

Mail Merge involves combining two applications to produce personalized form letters, envelopes, catalogs, or labels.

When creating documents for Mail Merge, you must have a main document and a data source. A main document contains the text and other items that remain the same in each letter. A data source contains the information that changes in each letter, such as the name and address of each recipient. A merge field, which you insert into the main document, instructs Word where to put information from the data source.

When you merge the documents, Word replaces merge fields with information from the data source. Each row of information from the data source produces a unique version of the form letter.

1. First, a main document must be created. Open the document that you want to use as the main document. You can open an existing letter or use a new, blank window for your letter. (Make sure that the data source is not your active document.)
2. Select Tools, Mail Merge. The Mail Merge Helper dialog box appears (see Figure 19.8).

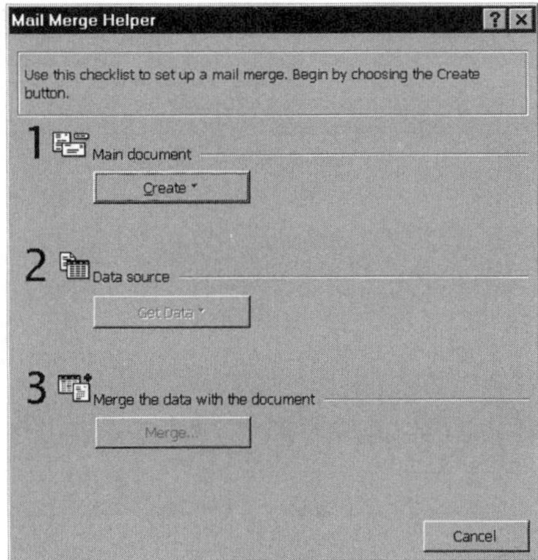

FIGURE 19.8
Notice that there are no options selected in the Mail Merge Helper dialog box.

3. Under the Main Document section, click Create and choose from form letters, mailing labels, envelopes, and catalogs.
4. When the dialog box appears (see Figure 19.9), click Active Window.

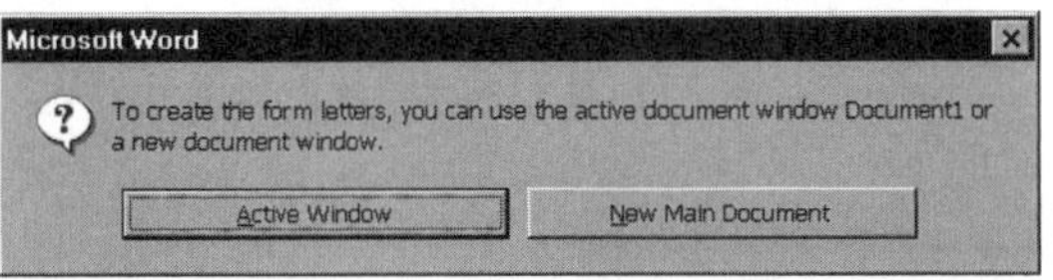

FIGURE 19.9
This dialog box asks you to select between creating a new document or using an existing document.

5. Now you need to supply the data (such as names, addresses, or other information) to merge with the main document. From the Mail Merge Helper dialog box, click the Get Data button and then choose Open Data Source. The Open Data Source dialog box appears (see Figure 19.10).

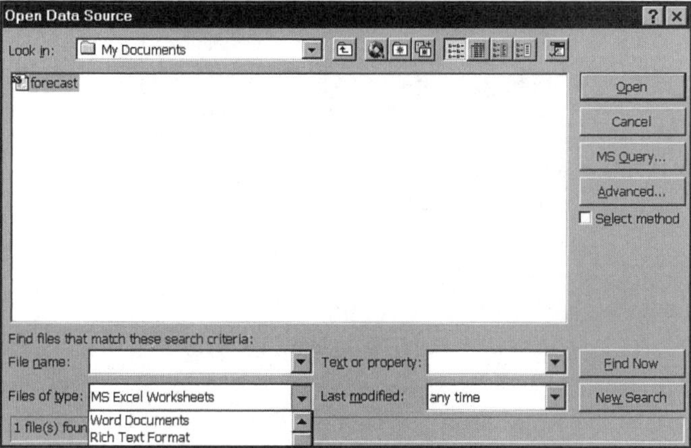

FIGURE 19.10
Select your data source in the Open Data Source dialog box.

6. Select the data source you want. The data source can be an Excel spreadsheet or Access database. You can also choose queries, dBASE databases, other Word files, ASCII delimited files, and named ranges from Excel as your data source.
7. Click OK. The Confirm Data Source dialog box appears. Select the correct type of data source (normally the correct type is highlighted).
8. Click OK. Another dialog box appears asking you to select the correct sheet (Excel) or correct table (database). (See Figure 19.11.)

FIGURE 19.11
From here you can select the named range, sheet or table.

9. Click OK. Another dialog box appears warning you that Word found no merge fields in the document (see Figure 19.12).

FIGURE 19.12
When you see this dialog box, you need to place your fields in the document.

10. To add the fields, select the Edit Main Document button. Notice, now, that there are two buttons below your toolbar that say Insert Merge Field and Insert Word Field. You will be working with Insert Merge Field to insert your fields into the document.
11. Place the fields in the appropriate places. If you need to have spaces, commas, or other delimiters in your document, make sure you place them as they should be in the final document.
12. After you add the fields, save the document by clicking the Save button or select File, Save.
13. After saving the document, start the mail merge by clicking the Merge to New Document button.

Now your main document is merged with your data source and a new document is created. You do not need to save your new merged document because you can re-create it any time.

Using Excel as a Database Front-End

A popular use for two applications is to use a spreadsheet as the front-end of a database. This occurs in situations where you want data for the database loaded into a spreadsheet before it is transferred to a central database.

Take the example of a company that sells products through a catalog. The database would have the name, address, and other related information about each customer. The company has several dozen people working in accounts receivable. They receive payments from customers and post this information to the database.

By giving the accounts receivable people a shared spreadsheet to use to enter payment information you can accomplish several things. Following are two of the largest benefits:

- The central database isn't being held open by many people, thus saving network resources
- The spreadsheet can be used to validate and filter the data before it is used by the database

The actual connection between the spreadsheet and the database can be made by linking the two. Then as data is edited on either application, the other is automatically updated. Thus, everyone is using a current copy of the data and can operate in a dynamic environment.

The following discussion explains your options when using Excel and Access together.

Importing or Linking Data from Excel to Access

The data that is entered into the spreadsheet can be used in Access using a linked table rather than importing the data. The main and most important difference between linking and importing is that importing creates a copy of the data in a new table whereas linking enables you to read, access, and update the data live. The original data source may also be used, because the format is not changed. So you can have a spreadsheet for data entry and use that same spreadsheet in Access for a completely different application.

To link your Excel data with the Access database, follow these steps:

1. Open your Access database.
2. Select File, Get External Data, Link Tables.
3. From the Link dialog box, change your files to Microsoft Excel and select your spreadsheet from the list.
4. Click the Link button to create the link between your spreadsheet and the Access database (see Figure 19.13).

NOTE If you are linking from Microsoft Excel version 5.0 or greater, you can select a worksheet from the workbook. With all other versions, you must first save the spreadsheets as separate files and then link. ■

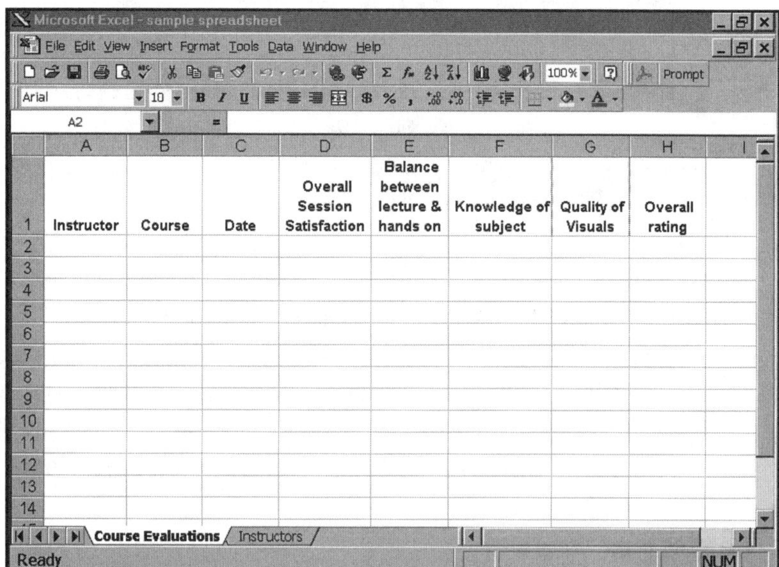

FIGURE 19.13
Sample simple list for course evaluation.

Creating a Simple List in Excel

Excel has a number of automatic features that make it easy to manage and analyze data in a list. To take full advantage of these features, enter rows and columns in a list according to the following steps:

1. Open a new workbook or a new sheet in an existing workbook.
2. Create your column heading from each column in the list.

The following are some guidelines you should follow when creating lists in Excel:

- Avoid having more than one list on a worksheet, because some list management features, such as filtering, can be used on only one list at a time on a worksheet.
- Leave at least one blank column and one blank row between your list and other data on the worksheet. This helps Excel automatically select your list when you sort, filter, or insert automatic subtotals.
- Do not include any blank rows or columns within your list.

The following are some guidelines for creating column labels in Excel:

- Create column labels in the first row of your list. Excel uses these labels to create reports and find and organize data.
- Use a font, data type, alignment, format, pattern, border, or capitalization style for column labels that is different from the format you assign to the data in your list.
- Use cell borders to insert lines below the labels, if you want to separate the labels from the data. Do not use blank rows or dashed lines.
- Column labels, like other cells, can contain a maximum of 255 characters.

3. Format the cells for the data (such as number format, alignment, and any other formats).
4. Add your data.

The following are some guidelines for formatting rows and columns:

- Design your list so that all the rows have similar items in the same column.
- Do not insert extra spaces at the beginning of a cell. Extra spaces affect sorting and searching.
- Use the same format for all the cells in a column.

You can use either uppercase or lowercase characters when you type data in a list. Excel distinguishes between uppercase and lowercase characters only when you sort, and then only when you select the Case Sensitive sort option.

Using Forms to Enter and Validate Data

After you create a simple list, if you want to pass on the task of editing data to staff and do not want the layout rearranged, use a form. The user can then easily add, delete, and search data in the list. To create a form, select Data from the menu and then the Form command. The form automatically appears with your column headings and date. By default, the first item in the list is displayed.

If you are having someone else enter data, it will be important that the information be accurate and precise. For example, you may require that only January 1997–December 1997 data be entered or sales between $100 and $10,000. To enforce data validation, follow these steps:

1. Select the range you want to protect. This should include current and future data cells.
2. From the Data menu select Validation. The Data Validation dialog box appears (see Figure 19.14).

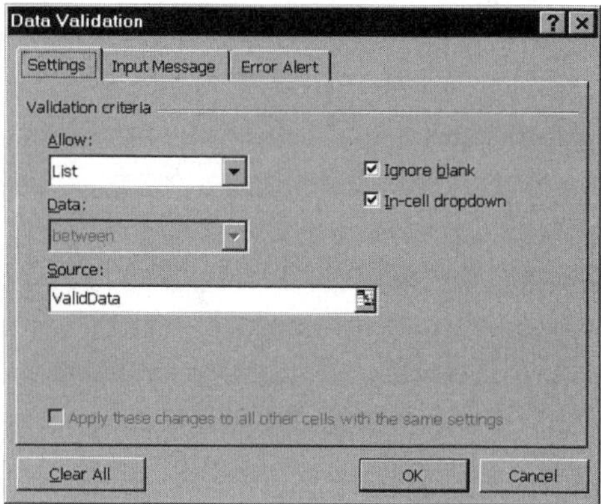

FIGURE 19.14
Protect your data in the Data Validation dialog box.

3. In the option boxes, you can enter values, cell references, or formulas. These are described in Table 19.3.

Table 19.3 Data Validation Operators

Operator	Options
between	Values are greater than or equal to the entry
not between	Values are less than the entry
equal to	Values match the entry
not equal to	Values do not match the entry
greater than	Values exceed the entry
less than	Values are below the entry
greater than or equal to	Values match or exceed the entry
less than or equal to	Values match or are below the entry

4. Click the Settings tab in the Data Validation dialog box.
   - In the Allow drop-down menu, select either the whole number, decimal, list, date, time, text length, or custom. (Use any value to remove existing date validation.)
   - In the Data drop-down menu, select one of the data validation operators (see Table 19.3).
   - In the Source box, enter the restricted values.

If the list of valid entries is short, you can type them in the Source box instead of typing the entries on a worksheet, separated by the Windows list separator character (commas by default). For example, you could type **Low, Average, High** in the Source box instead of entering the three words on a worksheet.

If the list of valid entries might change, name the list range, and then enter the name in the Source box. When the named range grows or shrinks because of changes you make to the list on the worksheet, the list of valid entries for the cell automatically reflects the changes.

If the list of valid entries is in another worksheet or workbook, define a name for the external data to the active worksheet in the Source box. You can then refer to the name on the same worksheet. For example, if the data you want to use in a formula is in cells A6:A12 on the first worksheet in a workbook named evaluation.xls, you could define the name ValidData on the active worksheet to be =(evaluation.xls)Sheet1!$A$6:$A$12 and then enter =ValidData in the Source box.

5. If you want to notify the person entering data that an error has occurred, then click the Error Alert tab and select the Show Error Alert After Invalid Data Is Entered box (see Figure 19.15).

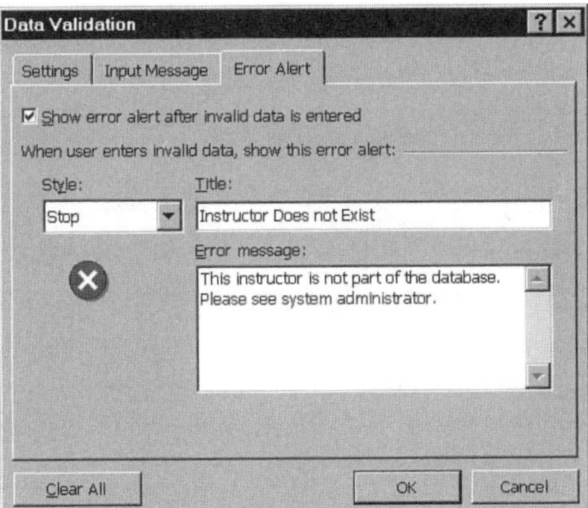

FIGURE 19.15
Enter error messages on the Error Alert tab.

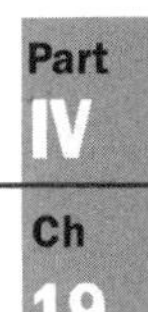

6. Type the words you want the user to see in the Error Message text box and click OK.

- If users copy or fill data in restricted cells, error messages don't appear, and incorrect data may be placed in the cells.
- If manual recalculation is in effect, uncalculated cells may prevent data from being validated properly. To turn off manual recalculation, select Tools, Options and click the Calculation tab. Select Automatic under Calculation.
- Data restriction will not work for formulas that have errors, such as #REF or #DIV/0.
- If you restrict the valid data for a cell that contains a formula and then change a cell referenced by the formula so that calculation of the formula results in incorrect data, the error message for the cell is not displayed.

Sorting Data in Excel

There are three main types of sorting: simple, multi-columns, and custom. To do a simple or multicolumn sort, follow these steps:

1. From the Data menu select Sort. All records are selected.
2. From the Sort dialog box (see Figure 19.16), select the columns to sort but make sure that Header Row is selected. Click OK.

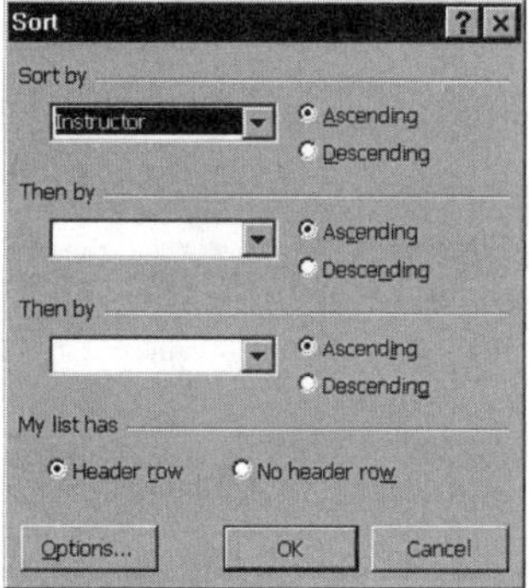

FIGURE 19.16
Select the columns to sort in the Sort dialog box.

You can quickly sort one column by clicking in that column and clicking the Sort Ascending or Sort Descending button. You can only sort by three levels.

If your lists are not to be sorted in alphanumeric or date order but rather by your own process, you can create a custom sort. Follow these steps:

1. Select Tools, Options, and click the Custom Lists tab (see Figure 19.17).

FIGURE 19.17
The Custom Lists tab.

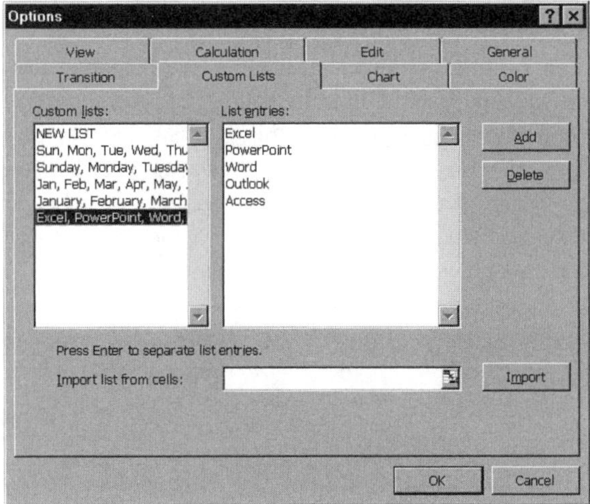

2. Click the New List item from the Custom Lists box, and then type the list in the List Entries box. Click the Add button and then the OK button when done.

TIP You can put commas between the values to sort or put each item on a separate line.

Figure 19.18 shows an example of using the custom sort list you just created in the Sort dialog box.

FIGURE 19.18
Course Evaluation List completed with data and custom sort applied.

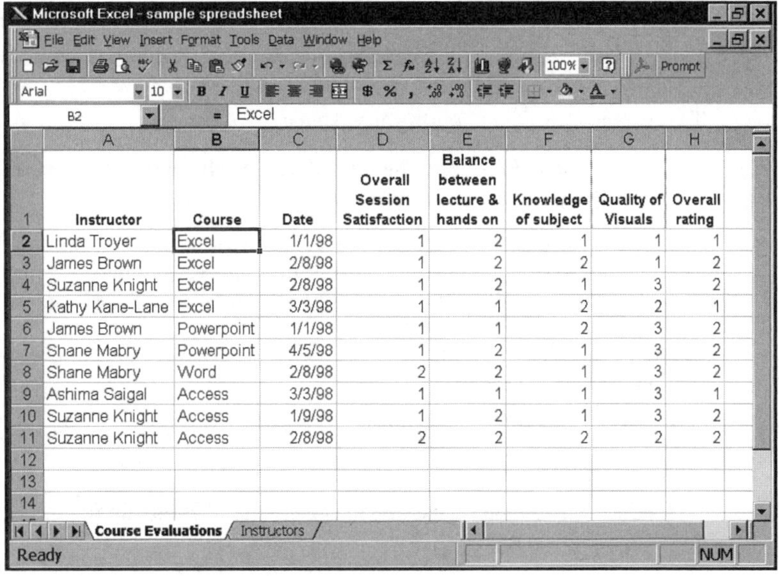

	A	B	C	D	E	F	G	H
1	Instructor	Course	Date	Overall Session Satisfaction	Balance between lecture & hands on	Knowledge of subject	Quality of Visuals	Overall rating
2	Linda Troyer	Excel	1/1/98	1	2	1	1	1
3	James Brown	Excel	2/8/98	1	2	2	1	2
4	Suzanne Knight	Excel	2/8/98	1	2	1	3	2
5	Kathy Kane-Lane	Excel	3/3/98	1	1	2	2	1
6	James Brown	Powerpoint	1/1/98	1	1	2	3	2
7	Shane Mabry	Powerpoint	4/5/98	1	2	1	3	2
8	Shane Mabry	Word	2/8/98	2	2	1	3	2
9	Ashima Saigal	Access	3/3/98	1	1	1	3	1
10	Suzanne Knight	Access	1/9/98	1	2	1	3	2
11	Suzanne Knight	Access	2/8/98	2	2	2	2	2
12								
13								
14								

Part IV Ch 19

Filtering Data in Excel

When a spreadsheet becomes large and difficult to sort (which can be time-consuming in a long spreadsheet) you may want to filter the data to hide rows that do not meet certain criteria. The AutoFilter command enables you to do this. It is found under the Data menu. This places a drop-down list box at the top of each column you select in your list (see Figure 19.19). For example, you may want to show only Linda's training results for January 1, 1998. So from the drop-down list boxes you would select Linda as the employee; January 1, 1998 for the day; and the data that did not match would be hidden (see Figure 19.20).

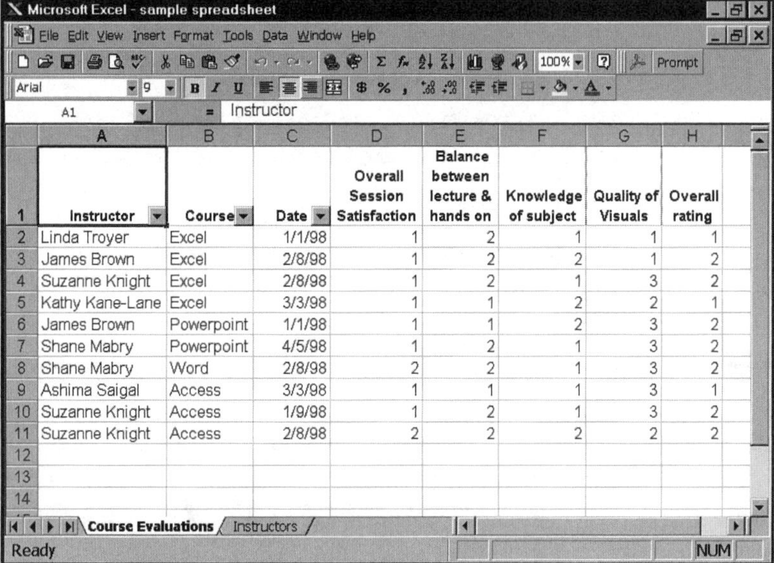

	Instructor	Course	Date	Overall Session Satisfaction	Balance between lecture & hands on	Knowledge of subject	Quality of Visuals	Overall rating
2	Linda Troyer	Excel	1/1/98	1	2	1	1	1
3	James Brown	Excel	2/8/98	1	2	2	1	2
4	Suzanne Knight	Excel	2/8/98	1	2	1	3	2
5	Kathy Kane-Lane	Excel	3/3/98	1	1	2	2	1
6	James Brown	Powerpoint	1/1/98	1	1	2	3	2
7	Shane Mabry	Powerpoint	4/5/98	1	2	1	3	2
8	Shane Mabry	Word	2/8/98	2	2	1	3	2
9	Ashima Saigal	Access	3/3/98	1	1	1	3	1
10	Suzanne Knight	Access	1/9/98	1	2	1	3	2
11	Suzanne Knight	Access	2/8/98	2	2	2	2	2

FIGURE 19.19
Same spreadsheet as Figure 19.18 with filters on the Instructor, Course and Date fields.

To create an AutoFilter, follow these steps:

1. Select Data, Filter, and then AutoFilter. Each column now has a down arrow allowing you to filter the information.
2. Click the down arrow next to the heading you want to filter. If you want selected columns, highlight them first and then select AutoFilter. If your column has one or more blank cells, you see (blanks) and (nonblanks) options.

Custom filters, like custom sorts, can also be created. To create a column filter with an existing filtered list, follow these steps:

1. Click the drop-down box at the top of the column you want to filter.
2. Select Custom from the list.
3. Click the Operation list box to specify the relationship (equal, >, <, >=, <=).
4. Then select the value.

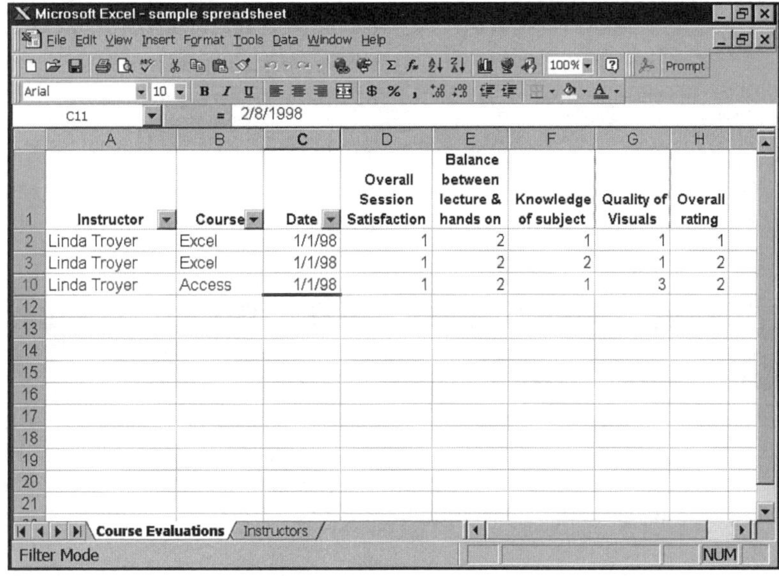

FIGURE 19.20
The same spreadsheet as Figure 19.19 and 19.18 filtered by instructor. Note, only Linda Troyer information is showing, including her overall rating.

5. You may also want to have a secondary criteria (that is, sales that are greater than $500.00 but less than $2,000).

Tracking Office Files and Tasks with the Outlook Journal

Microsoft Outlook provides various tools such as a calendar, email, contact list, and much more. The Journal is a tool that allows you to track activities. With the Journal, you can track files and tasks to help you manage your time and projects effectively.

To add a file to your journal, follow these steps:

1. Select File, New, Journal Entry. The Journal Entry dialog box appears.
2. Select the type of journal entry. Then choose Insert, File.
3. Select your file from the Insert File dialog box.
4. Click Save and Close.

To automatically open the attached file, follow these steps:

1. Click Tools, Options.
2. Click the Journal tab.
3. Check the Opens the Referred to By the Journal Entry option.

Now when you double-click the journal entry that has a file attached, that file opens automatically.

Recording Activities Automatically with the Journal

You can also enable the Journal to record certain activities. It is important to be selective or else your journal can get quite long.

You select activities from Tools, Option. Make sure the Journal tab is selected.

Every time you modify a file, send or receive email or a request, or cancel an entry or task, a journal entry can be created. Remember, be careful what you ask for!

Tracking Documents with Find Fast, Web Find Fast, and Document Properties

The greatest integration tools in all Office applications are the Find Fast utilities and Document properties. These enable you to keep track of documents and make their retrieval much faster for each user. The Find Fast features can index documents once and be ready for use in any of the applications within Office 97.

Document Properties

To access the document's Summary properties, select File, Properties (see Figure 19.21). The Author and Title lines are automatically filled in. Author is based on information from the setup. You may delete and make changes if this information is incorrect. Title is based on the first line of text. Change this information if necessary. The Subject, Manager, and Company lines may be filled in as appropriate.

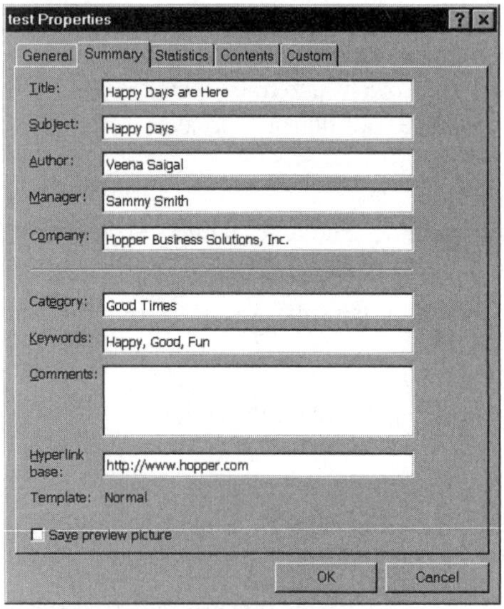

FIGURE 19.21
The test Properties dialog box showing the Summary tab.

The more information given, the easier it is to find files with Find Fast.

NOTE New to properties in MS Office 97 is the Hyperlink Base address box. It can be used to go to corresponding sites in your document, another file, or on the World Wide Web.

Custom Properties enables the user to use track documents in an individualized format. If you need to customize the tracking system, click the Custom tab. Microsoft allows you to choose a predefined name from the drop-down list, or supply your own. The value type may be selected from the Type box (see Figure 19.22). Value types include Text, Date, Number, and Yes/No.

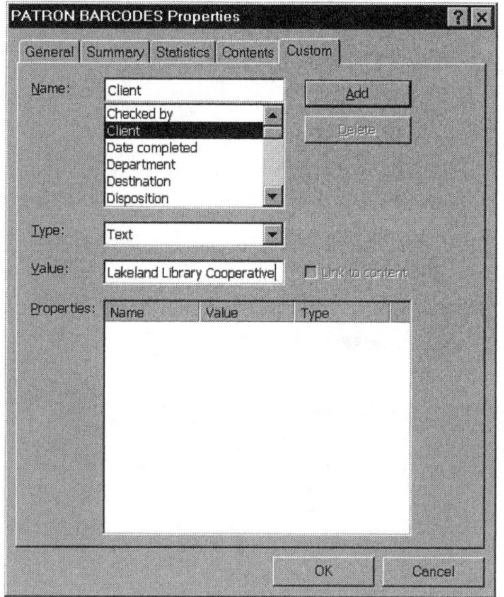

FIGURE 19.22
Adding a new property and value helps the client to find the document later.

For example, you may want to track a document with a due date for a specific time. You could create a custom property for a date completed and make it a Yes/No value. Then you could do a search for all documents that were done by that specific date.

You have the option to be prompted automatically for the document properties when the document is saved the first time. To activate this feature use the following steps:

1. Select Tools, Options.
2. Click the Save tab.
3. Select Prompt for document properties.

Find Fast

Find Fast runs automatically in the background, if it is installed. To determine whether it has been installed, do the following:

1. Check the startup folder under Windows Explorer.
   `c:\windows\startmenu\programs\startup.`
2. If you can't find it, install Find Fast from Run MS Office SetUp, select Add/Remove, highlight Office Tools, and check Change Buttons for Fast Find.

CAUTION

Do not install Fast Find NT *and* the Fast Find Single User that comes with MS Office on the same computer. Delete the single user from Start Up.

NOTE Find Fast used inside MS Office is not related to the Find function from Windows 95 Start button.

Find Fast creates hidden .ff* files in the root directory. The specified default is an indexed file at the root directory of each hard drive. Using Find Fast from the Control Panel, you see each of the directories that are being indexed (see Figure 19.23).

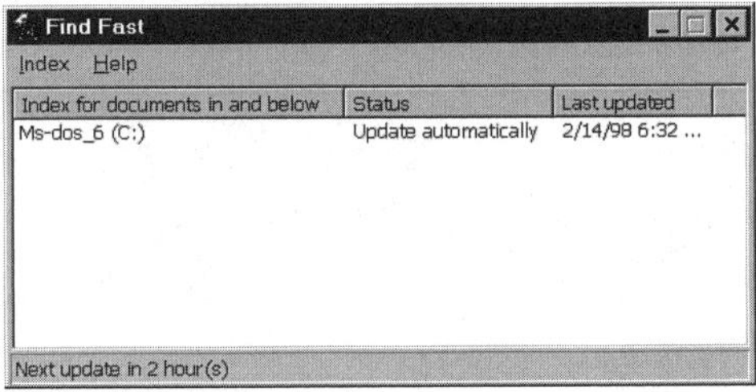

FIGURE 19.23
The Find Fast dialog box shows each directory that is indexed.

NOTE It is inefficient to have Find Fast search each directory when it performs updates. If you save all your documents to a specific directory, you can instruct Find Fast to index in and below that directory only. It includes all subdirectories.

Web Find Fast

The best way to understand Web Find Fast is to distinguish it from Find Fast. Web Find Fast also performs indexing of documents on your system, but it can select unrelated folders and subdirectories. Its best application is on your intranet.

Take the example of a company using the ISO 9000 model of management with strict document control. The Web Find Fast can be instructed to index the common folders on several servers that have procedures and work instructions. The created index file can be used to track the location of the copies of documents or to assist users in quickly locating the procedure or work instruction they need to find.

In addition, Web Find Fast (see Figure 19.24) can only be used on Windows NT machines that are running Web servers. The search screen is actually an HTML page shown on a Web browser.

FIGURE 19.24
Web Find Fast setup shown as an HTML page.

You can install Web Find Fast from the Office Setup CD by following these steps:

1. Place the CD in the CD-ROM drive. Use Windows NT Explorer to go to \Srvpack\Setup and double-click the setup program.
2. You are given three options in setup. You must choose to index and at least one other option. Do not load the indexer alone.
3. Enter a logon account that gives the indexer the authority to index the target locations. For example, with the administrative account it can go anywhere.

Running Web Find Fast

After loaded, the Web Find Fast becomes another application under the IIS administration area. You must run the application to start and continue indexing operations.

1. From the Start button on your Windows NT machine, select Programs and then Find Fast from the Web Find Fast area.
2. After the Web Find Fast screen is open you can start, stop, create, and monitor indexing of your Web content.

3. To perform a search, you either embed the search screen into your Web site or create a shortcut to the search page. There are two types of search pages provided—basic and advanced. Following are the locations of the search pages:

```
Program Files\Microsoft Office\Office\Webffast\query.htm
Program Files\Microsoft Office\Office\Webffast\queryadv.htm
```

CAUTION

Be careful when the password for the administration account is changed. This stops Web Find Fast. You must manually restart the indexing under the new password.

CHAPTER 20

Integrating Office Documents with Desktop Publishing Systems

While Microsoft Office has come a long way in enhancing its publishing capabilities, many organizations still find it necessary to integrate Office documents with specialized desktop publishing (DTP) software. This raises unique challenges for both Office users and publishing professionals, who must come up with solutions through trial and—all too often—error.

In this chapter, you'll explore the key issues that arise at the interface between Microsoft Office and the graphic arts department:

- Which documents should be "published" within Office, and which ones should be migrated into desktop publishing software?
- What are the best ways to convert Office files for use by the leading desktop publishing software packages?
- When does it make sense to use other alternatives, such as using Adobe's Acrobat Exchange or Acrobat Distiller software to create platform-independent PDF files for electronic distribution and viewing with the free Acrobat Reader?

The goal of this chapter is simple—to offer you the hard-to-find guidance you need to achieve the best possible results at the lowest cost.

NOTE In many organizations, document preparation is performed on Windows PCs, but desktop publishing is handled on the Macintosh. For additional information about managing key cross-platform issues, such as font substitutions, graphics formats, and file name incompatibilities, see Chapter 24.

Integrating Office with DTP Systems: High-Level Guidelines

At all too many companies, crucial decisions about publishing workflows are made by individuals familiar only with Office, or familiar with specific desktop publishing and graphics software, but not with both. Often, the result is that documents take longer to produce—and cost more—than they should.

The solution is to objectively understand the advantages, disadvantages, and integration issues associated with Office and today's publishing software prior to taking on a large project or organizing your department's workflow. In this section, you'll consider key issues that can make or break your next major publishing project.

Avoiding Multi-Program Workflows Wherever Possible

It's a fact of life in print publishing: today's leading "industrial-strength" desktop publishing and graphics design tools, such as QuarkXPress, Adobe PageMaker, and Adobe Photoshop, are published by software companies other than Microsoft. While more designers use PCs nowadays, these packages are still more likely to run on Macintosh rather than Windows platforms.

For the Office administrator, therefore, delivering Office documents to desktop publishing professionals usually means working in a cross-platform environment. In such an environment, Microsoft support—inconsistent as it can be—is largely absent. You may find yourself struggling with import file filters that are less than state-of-the-art, and staffers unfamiliar with the foibles of Office (who may be unforgiving of anything or anybody Microsoft-related).

Given these realities, the Office administrator will benefit from a clear understanding of when it is really necessary to move Office documents into a desktop publishing/graphics design environment—and when this can be avoided.

Documents That Do—and Don't—Require Professional-Level Desktop Publishing It's still necessary to work with desktop publishing professionals and use professional-level software for documents that do the following:

- Will be printed in full color—in other words, 4-color or more—such as product and corporate brochures, and most catalogs
- Must reflect the highest possible design values, such as advertisements and annual reports, which require superb typography and state-of-the-art graphics
- Include high-quality photography that has to be "tweaked" to look as good as possible

- Require very complex multi-column layouts (while Word is much better at this than it used to be, it is still not a full-fledged desktop publishing program)
- Call for specialized printing techniques such as die-cuts, duotones, or washes

Having said all this, for most organizations, the "meat-and-potatoes" of document production lie elsewhere, in the following:

- Newsletters, fliers, and data sheets that are either one-color or utilize a single additional "spot" color
- Most manuals, directories, and long-form documents

Many, if not most, of these documents can now be handled at least as effectively in Word and Office as in professional desktop publishing software, typically at lower cost.

Moreover, print publishing is increasingly shifting toward a "print-on-demand" model. In such a model, print runs are extremely short, and can be customized to the needs of very narrow audiences, even audiences of one. Business software such as Word and Access lends itself to producing documents like these more effectively than most traditional desktop publishing and graphics software.

Strategies for Keeping More Documents in Office Depending on how your company's workflow is organized, it may be a reasonable strategy to increase the percentage of documents that remain in Word and Office from conception through printing. This has the additional advantage of minimizing the number of hands that touch each document, potentially reducing cost and the likelihood of error. If this makes sense in your organization, take the following steps:

- Build relationships with printers who are willing to work with Microsoft Office files, especially printers using new on-demand reproduction systems such as Xerox Docutech high-volume printers, which integrate high-speed xerography with inputs from Windows or Macintosh computer files.
- Become proficient at creating PostScript files from Office documents. These PostScript files can be used to create film for traditional printing, whereas native Office files typically cannot. (See "Creating PostScript Files from Office Documents" later in this chapter.)
- Hire or identify freelance graphics professionals who are willing to work in Word and Office when necessary; alternatively, offer basic training in Office to the design professionals already on staff.

- As discussed in Chapter 11, invest in well-designed Office document templates that "typical business people" can use to build attractive documents with less involvement from professional designers.
- Consider using Microsoft Publisher for low-end publication projects. Publisher 98, available as a standalone product or as part of Microsoft Office 97 Small Business Edition, integrates exceptionally well with Word 97. For example, not only can Word 97 files be imported into Publisher, once imported they can still be edited by Word—simply select the text box you want to edit, and choose Edit, Edit Story in Microsoft Word. (For more information about Microsoft Publisher, see the "Managing Microsoft Publisher 98" section of Chapter 25.)

Goals for the Conversion Process

In the previous section, you learned ways to keep documents within Office as long as possible—minimizing the need to worry about complex conversions and other problems. But often this is not possible. Then the question becomes: how can you make the conversion process as simple and cost-effective as possible? Your goals in managing the interface between Office and desktop publishing/graphic design software should be:

- To retain as much of the intelligence you have built into your Office documents as possible. That means trying to preserve formatting, linkages, automated fields, and so on. It means attempting to minimize the amount of work that must be done twice, because it was lost in the conversion process.
- To maximize accuracy by reducing the number of opportunities for error. This goal is closely related to the first. The more rework is needed, the more errors will creep in—especially since few graphic design professionals are expert typists.
- To transition documents from Office to desktop publishing software at the most cost-effective time possible—typically, as late in the process as possible, after all content revisions have been made.
- To ensure that the individuals preparing documents in Office understand the software, production, and scheduling constraints that graphic designers face in transforming their "raw documents" into effective printed materials, and know how to provide Office documents that are "designer-ready."
- Conversely, to ensure that the graphic designers understand the issues faced by other business professionals, including the messages they are trying to communicate, the occasional difficulty getting timely signoffs, and the need to find ways to accommodate text or design elements that may not import smoothly from Microsoft Office.

  Quite reasonably, most graphic designers are much more concerned with what "goes out the back end," in other words, the finished printed or electronic product, than they are with what "comes in the front end" from the business people and others who provide source material and copy. So it falls to you, the Office administrator to be concerned about those issues—if you don't, chances are nobody will!

With these high-level goals in mind, the next section begins addressing the nuts and bolts of document conversion between Office and three leading desktop publishing software packages, QuarkXPress, Adobe PageMaker, and Adobe FrameMaker.

Using Word Documents with QuarkXPress

Among professional graphics designers, QuarkXPress is the market leader in desktop publishing software. The long-awaited latest version, QuarkXPress 4.0, adds some new tools, including some high-end illustration capabilities, new long-document features such as indexing and tables of contents, and better color management. Many of the improvements in QuarkXPress 4.0, however, are incremental, so some design professionals have chosen to continue using the "tried-and-true" QuarkXPress 3.32.

Because QuarkXPress is so popular, it's likely that you'll be called upon to deliver Word documents to designers who use it. Therefore, this section contains detailed coverage on how to make QuarkXPress work better with Word documents. It also focuses primarily on the Macintosh version of QuarkXPress, which has by far the largest installed base.

NOTE In reading the following detailed discussion of importing Word files, you may wonder why linking and embedding Word documents is not discussed. While QuarkXPress supports OLE 2.0 for Windows as well as the Macintosh equivalent, Publish and Subscribe, it does so only for image and graphics editing programs, not for word processing software.

In some organizations, the advantages of maintaining live links between your word processing documents and desktop publishing files may be compelling. If you need this capability, consider using Quark's leading competitor, Adobe PageMaker, as discussed later in this chapter in the section "Using Word Documents with Adobe PageMaker." ■

As installed "out of the box," neither version of QuarkXPress can import any Office 97 files directly. QuarkXPress 4.0 ships with version 3.2 of Quark's Word filter, which recognizes Word documents in the following formats:

- Word 3.0 through Word 5.1 for the Macintosh
- Word 6.0/7.0 for Windows, and Word 6.0 for the Macintosh

If your publishing professionals are using QuarkXPress 3.32, chances are they are using Quark's Word filter 3.1, which can work with the same Word versions.

An early beta of a Word 97 filter has recently been posted on the QuarkXPress Web site (www.quark.com/ftp008.htm). If your documents make extensive use of Word 97 features, you may want to give it a try. Otherwise, stick with the Word 6.0 filters.

Next, you'll walk through converting a Word 97 document for use in QuarkXPress.

Step 1: Preparing Office 97 for the Conversion

Unless you're prepared to try the untested Word 97 filter (or Quark has finalized the filter by the time you read this), you'll want to save a copy of your Word document to Word 6.0/95 format before you import it into QuarkXPress. This presents no problem if you are using Word 98 for the Macintosh or either service release of Office 97—or, of course, if you are using Word 6.0 or Word 95. (For information about the service releases of Office 97, refer to Chapter 3.)

If you are using the original release of Office 97, however, it's a different story. In that release, saving a Word 97 file to Word 6.0/95 format actually creates a Rich Text Format (RTF) file with a .doc extension. In other words, it *looks* like a Word file to the naked eye, but it can't be read by Quark's Word import filter. In late 1997 and early 1998, this caused enormous problems for Word and Quark users everywhere.

To make matters even worse, Microsoft also slightly changed the RTF file format, making it difficult even for software with RTF import filters to use these files.

Microsoft eventually posted a new Word 6.0/95 export filter on the World Wide Web at (`www.microsoft.com/word/enhancements/wrd6ex32.asp`). This new filter, which is also included in Office 97 Service Release 1, actually saves files in native Word 6.0/95 format when you ask it to. If you haven't upgraded, now would be a great time to do so.

In the meantime, try saving your files in Word 5.1 for Macintosh format. You'll probably lose even more features in the translation, but you will maintain the file's basic text formatting and styles—which is a whole lot better than working from ASCII text.

If you're converting many files at once, use Word's batch converter. To learn how, see the "Using Word's Batch Conversion Tool" section in Chapter 17.

Step 2: Preparing Your Word Document for Conversion

The next step is to take stock of the document you want to convert. If your document is very simple, you can skip most of what follows. If your document contains elements such as styles, fields, indexes, tables, or bullets, however, it will be worth your time to read this.

NOTE While this discussion is presented in the context of importing to QuarkXPress, much of this information will be helpful in preparing documents for importation to Adobe PageMaker or Adobe FrameMaker as well.

Preparing Styles for Conversion Your QuarkXPress (or PageMaker) designer can import Word styles, converting them automatically to reflect the formatting he or she chooses to use. Give your designer the opportunity to do so. Many designers claim the only reliable way to import a Word file is as ASCII text. *This is not true!*

Your Word styles can save your designer so much time, it's worth making sure all your long documents contain them. If you have a document that doesn't contain styles, but rather uses manual formatting for headings and other document elements, consider running AutoFormat to transform much of this manual formatting into styles your designer can use.

AutoFormat's default settings may make changes you won't want, and some of the changes it makes will be undone by Quark's import filter. The following steps show you how to limit AutoFormat to converting the elements that will be of value to your QuarkXPress designer:

1. In Word, choose Format, AutoFormat. The AutoFormat dialog box opens.
2. Click the Options button to display the AutoFormat tab of the AutoCorrect dialog box.
3. Mark the following check boxes:

   Headings

   Other Paragraphs

   Ordinals (1st) with superscript

   Bold and _underline_ with real formatting

   Styles (marking this check box ensures that you preserve any styles that may already be in your document)
4. Make sure all other check boxes are cleared.
5. Click OK.
6. In the AutoFormat dialog box, make sure AutoFormat Now is selected, and click OK. (If you prefer to review every change individually, select AutoFormat and Review Each Change instead.)

Preparing Fields for Conversion The QuarkXPress import filter can't handle fields properly. It inserts the raw field codes into its documents *instead*, or in some cases *alongside* the field results you would prefer to see displayed. As a result, QuarkXPress designers may see obscure text like this scattered throughout their imported documents:

```
SUBJECT \* MERGEFORMAT
TIME \@ "M/d/yy h:mm:ss am/pm
```

If your document contains any of the following, you have field codes that you need to deal with before you import the document into QuarkXPress:

- Automated times and dates
- Index entries or indexes
- Tables of contents
- Cross-references
- Bookmarks
- Formulas
- Hyperlinks
- Mail Merge Codes

You may want to make a backup copy of the document before you delete the fields, so you still have access to all the interactivity your fields provide, in the event you're called upon to rework the document in Word later. Then, delete the fields as follows:

1. If the Show/Hide button (it shows a ¶ symbol) in the Standard toolbar is not selected, click it to display all the hidden text in your document. Doing this lets you easily locate and delete fields such as index entries that are hard to delete while they are invisible.
2. Press Ctrl+A to select the entire document.
3. Press F9 to update all the fields in your document that can be updated, including fields such as date/time fields and cross-references.
4. Make sure the entire document is still selected, and press Ctrl+Shift+9. This unlinks all the fields you've just updated, replacing the field codes with their current results. At this point, you've removed most types of fields, but some—such as index entry fields—remain. You'll need to get rid of these using Word's Find and Replace feature, as follows:
5. Choose Edit, Replace.
6. In the Find What text box, type **^d** (Word's shortcut for finding fields).
7. Make sure the Replace With text box is blank.
8. Click Replace All.
9. Click Close.
10. Save the document.

Preparing Indexes for Conversion As mentioned in the previous section, QuarkXPress cannot understand Word index entries, which are fields. The procedure described in the previous section deletes index entries along with other fields, so they do not appear as stray text in your designer's QuarkXPress file.

If someone has done all the hard work of building an index in Word, however, it seems a shame to start all over again in QuarkXPress. Moreover, Word contains some indexing automation features not available in QuarkXPress, such as the capability to index every appearance of a word or phrase at the same time, or build an index from a list of words you provide (available by choosing Insert, Index and Tables, AutoMark). It's common for Word's automated features to handle as much as half of a large document's index automatically, often more. You'd hate to waste all of these productivity features simply because the QuarkXPress Word filter isn't all it could be.

By using the following procedure, you can at least *view and edit* your Word index entries in QuarkXPress, making it significantly easier to rebuild your index. This procedure is tedious. But if the alternative is to recreate a large document's index entirely from scratch, it will save you a significant amount of time.

NOTE Only QuarkXPress 4.0 has built-in indexing capabilities, although add-on Quark XTensions are available to add indexing to Quark 3.3x.

To make sure QuarkXPress 4.0's indexing feature is available and working, choose Utilities, XTension Manager, and make sure a check mark appears next to the Index XTension (see Figure 20.1). If not, click to the left of the word *Index*, click OK, quit the program, and start it again. ■

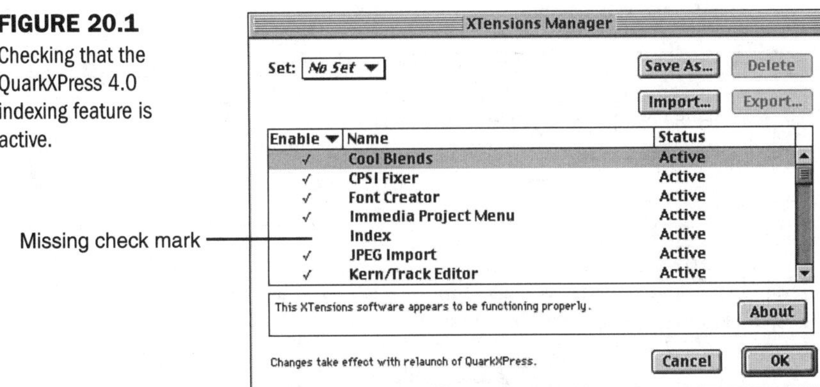

FIGURE 20.1
Checking that the QuarkXPress 4.0 indexing feature is active.

First, delete all the fields in your document *except* for the invisible fields. Follow the procedure discussed in the previous section, with one exception. In step 1, do *not* display invisible text by clicking the Show/Hide button. In fact, if the Show/Hide button is toggled on, click it to *hide* the invisible text in your document.

Later, after you've opened the file in QuarkXPress 4.0 (as you'll learn how to do shortly), you'll see the index entries appearing in your document as text like the following:

```
XE "Microsoft"
```

The text within the quotation marks is the index entry you had specified to appear in Word. Wherever you (or your designer) encounter an `XE` entry, you can manually replace it with an QuarkXPress index entry. To do so, follow this procedure in QuarkXPress:

1. Choose Edit, Find Change to display the QuarkXPress Find/Change dialog box.
2. Mark the Document check box to tell QuarkXPress to search the entire document.
3. Type **`XE "`** in the Find What text box.
4. Click Find Next.
5. When QuarkXPress finds the first index entry, choose View, Show Index to display the Index dialog box.
6. Click in the document, and cut the text within the quotation marks.
7. Paste the text into the Text field in the Entry area of the Index dialog box.
8. Click Add. QuarkXPress places a small red (nonprinting) square where the index entry will appear.
9. Click inside the Find/Change dialog box to activate it if necessary, and click Find Next. QuarkXPress finds the next index entry. Repeat steps 6–8.

Figure 20.2 shows how QuarkXPress will look while you're working on transforming Word index entries into QuarkXPress index entries.

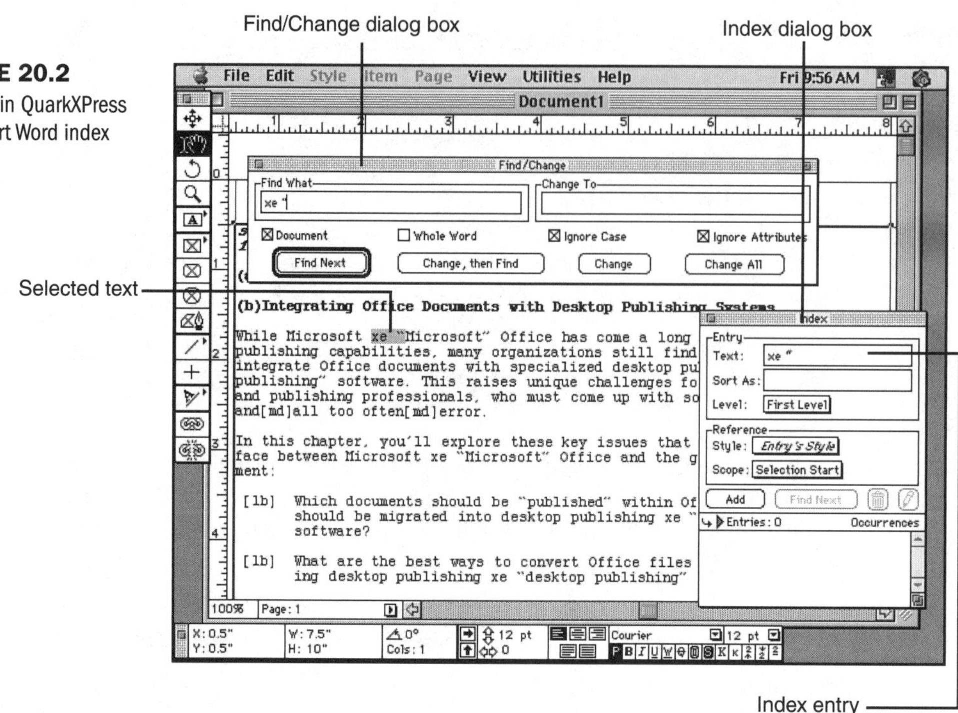

FIGURE 20.2
Working in QuarkXPress to convert Word index entries.

After you finish all the entries, you can get rid of all the remaining stray text from Word's index fields, while leaving the index entries intact by performing the following steps:

1. Choose Edit, Select All.
2. Return to the Find/Change dialog box, and type **XE "** in the Find What text box.
3. Make sure nothing is entered in the Change To text box.
4. Click Change All to delete all instances of *XE* and the opening quotation mark.
5. In the Find What text box, enter a quotation mark, and then another space.
6. Click Change All to remove the closing quotation marks.
7. Double-check your document to make sure that you haven't removed any close quotation marks you need to keep.

If you have access to expertise in the UserLand Frontier cross-platform scripting language, or AppleScript for the Macintosh, you may be able to automate this part of the conversion process.

Preparing Bullets and Numbering for Conversion Word's automatic numbers and bullets don't import into QuarkXPress, so you'll have to decide where it will be easier to replace them with manual bullets and numbering—in Word, or in QuarkXPress. While there's little difference in the work involved, adding them in Word reduces the chance that they'll be overlooked later. On the other hand, if you're moving from Word for Windows to QuarkXPress on the Macintosh, the manual symbols you insert (using Insert, Symbol) may not translate across platforms properly. For more information about which symbols will translate properly and which ones won't, see the "Managing Font and Character Set Issues" section of Chapter 24.

Preparing Tables for Conversion QuarkXPress' Word import filters have never been very good at importing Word tables. At best, you'll get tab-delimited text, which may or may not line up accurately. QuarkXPress may also insert several lines of formatting, or ignore your table altogether, and in some cases, ignore all the text that follows it. In any case, you'll get none of the table formatting that Word can provide.

There are two solutions, neither of them ideal. The first one preserves font formatting and approximate layout, but sacrifices table formatting. The second option, available only on the Macintosh, preserves every bit of formatting and design, but sacrifices print quality and prevents designers from making text changes to the table.

Option 1: Preserving Table Text and Font Formatting To retain the contents of your table, along with its font formatting (boldface, italics, and so on), perform the following steps:

1. Select the table.
2. Choose Table, Convert Table to Text.
3. In the Convert Table to Text box, make sure Tabs is selected.
4. Click OK.

QuarkXPress imports your table as blocks of text separated by tabs. You'll lose table formatting such as borders, gridlines, and backgrounds.

If your document has many tables, you can move among them quickly using Word 97's Browse by Table feature:

1. Click the Select Browse Object button (see Figure 20.3).

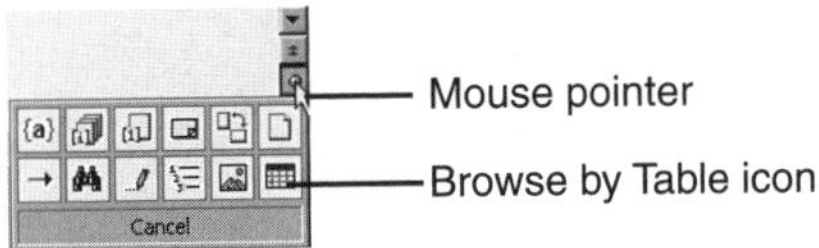

FIGURE 20.3
Setting Select Browse Object to browse from one table to the next.

2. Click the Browse by Table icon in the grid that appears (the rightmost icon in the second row).
3. Click the blue double-down-arrow to move to the next table (see Figure 20.4).

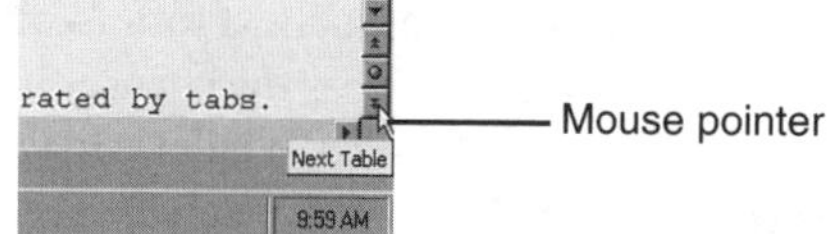

FIGURE 20.4
Browsing to the next table.

Option 2 (Macintosh-Only): Copying the Table As a Graphic If you're running Word on the Macintosh, there's a second workaround that retains all of the formatting in your table, but may sacrifice some print quality. This procedure transforms your table into a PICT graphic and places it in a QuarkXPress document:

1. In any version of Word since 5.0, create and format the table.
2. Select the table by clicking inside it and choosing Table, Select Table.
3. Press Command+Option+D. Word copies the text to the clipboard in Macintosh's PICT format.
4. Open or switch to QuarkXPress and display the document where you want to insert the table.
5. Click the Rectangle Picture Box tool on the Tool Palette, and drag the mouse pointer to create a new picture box.
6. Choose Edit, Paste. QuarkXPress pastes the table into the picture box.

You could simulate this in Windows by using a screen-capture program to capture a picture of the table, opening it in a graphics program, copying it to the Clipboard, and pasting it into QuarkXPress.

Clearing Password Protection Prior to Conversion When you password-protect a file in Word, it is encrypted—and therefore, no other program can read it properly. If you're working with a password-protected file, perform the following steps prior to importing it into *any* desktop publishing system:

1. Choose File, Open.
2. Browse to and select the password-protected file.
3. Click Open. The Password dialog box appears.
4. Enter the document's password. Passwords are case sensitive.
5. Click OK.
6. Choose Tools, Options.
7. Click the Save tab.
8. Clear the asterisks in the Password to Open text box. If there are asterisks in the Password to Modify text box, clear those, too.
9. Click OK.
10. Save the file.

This removes the encryption so that the file can be read by desktop publishing software.

Resaving with Fast Saves Turned Off Word contains a shortcut, Fast Saves, which speeds up file saves by storing all changes at the end of the file instead of integrating them within the document where they belong. Occasionally, when you save a file, Word will take care of the "housekeeping" it deferred, but most of the time, your Fast Saved files contain text and other elements that aren't in the right order.

QuarkXPress (and other DTP) import filters may have trouble with Fast Saved files. (One symptom: Inexplicably, a file appears not to reflect the most recent set of changes you made, even though you know you saved them.)

Prior to saving a file for use in any desktop publishing program, do the following:

1. Choose Tools, Options.
2. Click the Save tab.
3. Clear the Allow Fast Saves check box.
4. Click OK.
5. Resave the file.

You've now gone a very long way towards getting your files ready for QuarkXPress. (Your designer owes you dinner at the finest restaurant in town!)

Step 3: Preparing QuarkXPress to Accept Your Files

Now it's time to make sure QuarkXPress is ready for your files. First, make sure you have the most recent Word file converters installed. On the Macintosh, look in QuarkXPress 4.00 Folder:Xtension. There should be a file called MS-Word Filter.

Select the file, and choose File, Get Info. The MS-Word Filter Info window appears, displaying the date the file was created. In Windows, you can get the same information by checking the modified date for MS-Word Filter.xnt in the XTension folder in Windows Explorer.

Visit Quark on the Web (`www.quark.com/ftp008.htm`) to see if newer filters are available. For example, the original Word filter released with QuarkXPress 4.0 for the Macintosh is dated 9/12/97, but it has already been updated at least once (at press time, the newest version was named Beta 2 and dated 2/27/98).

Next, run QuarkXPress. Choose Utilities, XTensions Manager and make sure a check mark appears next to MS-Word filter. If not, add a check mark. Click Save As to create a new set of XTensions that includes MS-Word Filter. Name the set, and click OK. If you've had to add the Word filter to your set of loaded XTensions, quit QuarkXPress and start it again.

Step 4: Importing Your Word File into QuarkXPress

Finally, you're ready to import the file. In QuarkXPress, do the following:

1. Choose File, New, Document to open a new document in XPress. The New Document dialog box appears.
2. Make sure Automatic Text Box is checked, and click OK. QuarkXPress displays an empty page.

3. Click inside the page.
4. Choose File, Get Text. The Get Text dialog box opens (see Figure 20.5).

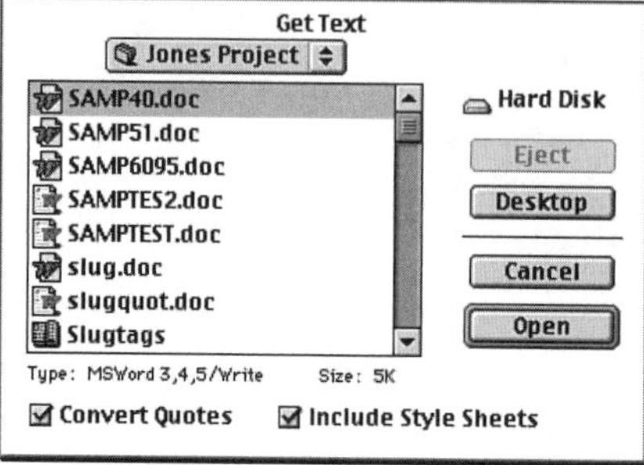

FIGURE 20.5
The QuarkXPress 4.0 Get Text dialog box.

5. Make sure that the Include Style Sheets check box is marked, or else Quark XPress will disregard your Word styles.
6. Browse to the Word file you want, and click Open.
7. QuarkXPress may ask you how to resolve conflicts between your style names and the ones it already contains. For example, both Quark XPress and Word contain a Normal style. If you want to use the style already available in QuarkXPress, choose Use Existing Style. If you want to rename your styles so that their formatting specifications remain available to you, choose Rename New Style.
8. Quark imports the document.

If you've transferred your file from Word for Windows, and Quark XPress for the Macintosh cannot find it, try one of the following:

1. If you are using QuarkXPress on the Macintosh, make sure you have Microsoft's OLE Extensions installed in your Macintosh system folder. If the computer isn't running any Microsoft software–and many designers' systems do not–you may have to download these files from the Quark Web site.
2. Reopen and resave the file in Word 6.0 for the Macintosh, if you have the program available.
3. Or, download and run the PC-Macintosh MS Word Script available at Quark's Web site (www.quark.com/ftp006.htm).

Exporting Files from QuarkXPress to Word

While text that finds its way into QuarkXPress tends to stay there, occasionally you may want to export text back to Word. You have four options for doing so:

- **ASCII Text.** This can be read in any editor, from Windows Notepad to Word 97.
- **MS Word 4.0.** The best available option if you plan to do extensive editing in Word, this option preserves a good deal of formatting—though far from all of it.

- **MS Word 3.0/MS Write**. An option you're unlikely ever to need.
- **XPress Tags**. This is the best option if you only expect to do very light editing and don't want to force your designer to totally rework all of his or her pages. It saves an ASCII text file, tagged with formatting codes in much the same way that HTML and RTF files are. If you use Word to edit the text file and then resave it in Text Only format, your designer can reimport it to QuarkXPress with design instructions relatively intact.

To export the text in a QuarkXPress document, perform the following steps:

1. Choose File, Save Text. The Save Text dialog box opens (see Figure 20.6).

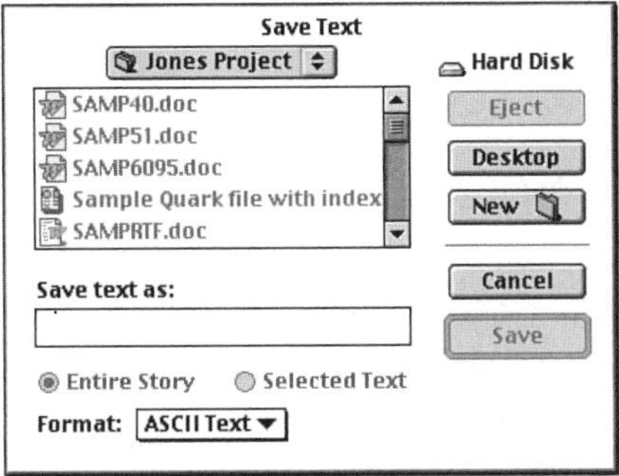

FIGURE 20.6
Exporting text to Word from QuarkXPress.

2. Enter a filename in the Save Text As text box. If the file will be used in Windows, enter an 8.3 file name with an extension that Word can easily recognize, such as .doc for Word files, or .txt for ASCII files.
3. In the Format drop-down box, choose the format that you want to save the text in: ASCII Text (the default setting), XPress Tags, MSWord 3.0/Write, or MSWord 4.0).
4. Click Save.

Using Word Documents with Adobe PageMaker

PageMaker is the software that invented desktop publishing, but it rapidly fell behind QuarkXPress in winning the hearts and minds of designers. Recently, Adobe has worked hard to soup up PageMaker and make it competitive again.

Among the areas Adobe has worked hardest at is improving integration with Microsoft Office. In PageMaker 6.5, the most current version, you have remarkable flexibility in integrating Word—and other Office documents—into desktop publishing documents. For example, you can perform the following tasks:

- Place a document in PageMaker so that it can either be edited in PageMaker or edited in Word and automatically updated in PageMaker
- Link or embed tables and spreadsheets up to 40 columns wide, as well as charts and other images

- Integrate database information from Microsoft Access or other applications, via the separate PageMaker Open Database Connectivity (ODBC) plug-in filter

If you're going to work with PageMaker and Office together, spend a few minutes with Chapter 11 of the PageMaker 6.5 manual, which contains admirably detailed coverage of PageMaker's many options for importing Office (and other) documents and graphics.

Advantages and Limitations of PageMaker's Word 97 Filter

While PageMaker's infrastructure for integrating with Microsoft Office is stronger than that of QuarkXPress, like Quark it relies on a filter that translates Word documents into information it can use. And that filter has many limitations. It will not, for example, import the following:

- Audio and video clips and other OLE objects
- Automatic bullets and numbering
- Backgrounds, borders and shading
- Bookmarks
- Comments (In Word 6.0/95, called Annotations)
- Emboss, engrave, or double-strikethrough character formatting
- Endnotes (footnotes do import)
- Equations built with older versions of Equation Editor (1.0 or 2.0)
- Form fields
- Graphics created with Word's Drawing toolbar
- Headers and footers
- Hidden text
- Hyperlinks (import as colored, unlinked text)
- Hyphenation, justification, character spacing (called letter spacing in most desktop publishing software), and kerning (PageMaker wants to do its own, and so will your designer)
- Page breaks
- Subdocuments in a master document (prior to importing, merge all subdocuments into a single document)
- Table formatting (except for tab-delimited text and character formatting, much like QuarkXPress)
- Vertical text
- WordArt images

Note that there are some elements that you *can* import in PageMaker, which you cannot import automatically in QuarkXPress and could make a *big* difference in your productivity:

- Index entry fields for building an index
- Table of contents entry fields for building a table of contents

Where to Get Updated PageMaker Word Filters

As with QuarkXPress, it's likely that you can find a more effective filter on the Web than in the shrink-wrapped CD-ROM you paid for. In particular, while PageMaker 6.5 does not currently ship with a Word 97 filter, you can get one on the Internet at the following locations:

`ftp://ftp.adobe.com/pub/adobe/pagemaker/`

or

`www.adobe.com/supportservice/custsupport/download.html`

At its Web site, Adobe also provides detailed instructions for installing these filters.

At press time, the most recent version of the Office 97 filter is release 1.4, which fixes some nagging problems in previous versions. In particular, it does the following:

- Imports graphics stored in Word documents as Portable Network Graphic (PNG) files, if the free PNG filter is also installed. This is how Word stores both clip art graphics and WordArt images; however, WordArt images still do not import properly.
- Also imports inline graphics in five other formats—JPEG, EMF, WMF, PICT, and BMP—once again, assuming PageMaker's graphics filters are also installed.
- Imports text in Word text boxes, placing that text at the beginning of the PageMaker story.

If you need to import a file into PageMaker before you are able to retrieve a Word 97 filter from the Internet, you can save it to one of the following formats first:

- Word 6.0/95 format (but only if you have updated Word 97 to save true Word 6.0/95 files, as discussed in the section "Step 1: Preparing Office 97 for the Conversion" earlier in this chapter)
- RTF files with .rtf extensions (not .doc extensions)
- WordPerfect 6.0 files

Getting Your Word Document Ready for PageMaker

Because PageMaker's filter has many of the same limitations as Quark's, you may want to follow some of the same steps for preparing your document as were discussed in the "Preparing Your Word Document for Conversion" section earlier in this chapter:

- Make sure your document uses styles consistently and as much as possible
- Unlink fields in your document, except hidden index entry fields and table of contents entry fields (PageMaker will take care of many common fields, such as date and time fields)
- Give consideration to the best way to handle tables, bullets, and numbering
- Clear password protection from your document, if necessary
- Save, with Fast Saves turned off, in a format compatible with your installed PageMaker filters

Importing Your Document into PageMaker

In this section, you'll walk through importing a Word 97 document into PageMaker for the Macintosh; the steps to follow in Windows are extremely similar. With PageMaker already open, do the following:

1. Choose File, New. The Document Setup dialog box opens.
2. Click OK.
3. Choose File, Place. The Place Document dialog box appears (see Figure 20.7).

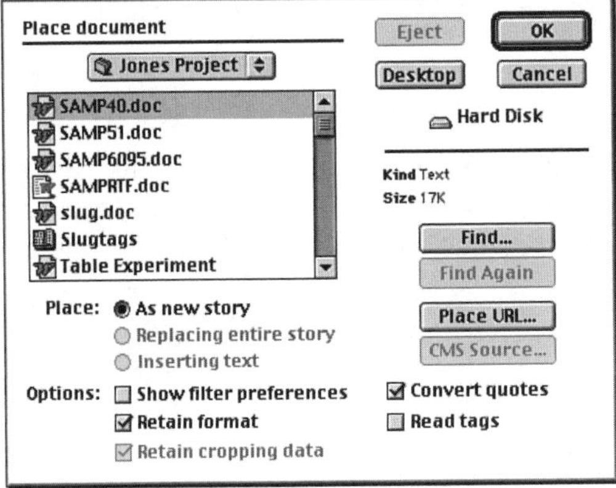

FIGURE 20.7
Choosing a document to place in PageMaker 6.5 for the Macintosh.

4. Browse to the document that you want to place in your PageMaker document.
5. Mark the Show Filter Preferences check box.
6. Click OK. The Import Filter dialog box appears (see Figure 20.8).

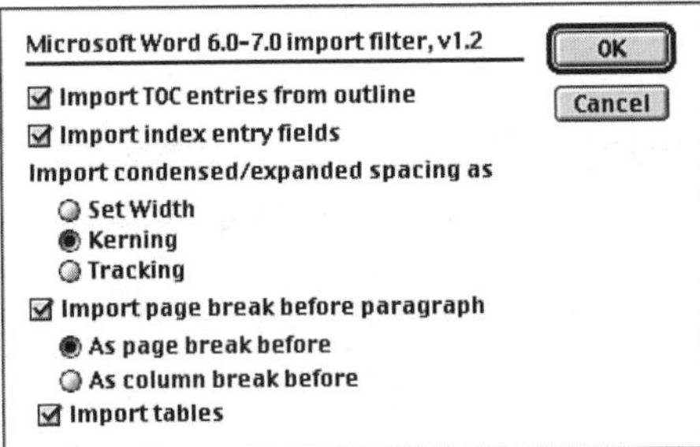

FIGURE 20.8
Controlling which elements of your Word document are imported into PageMaker.

7. Make sure the settings are as you want them. To use Word's index entries, for example, make sure that Import Index Entry Fields is checked.
8. Click OK. The imported text appears in your document with PageMaker's text icon.
9. Click on the page where you want the text to be inserted.

If PageMaker cannot recognize a Word file saved with Word 97 or Word 98, try saving it to Word 6.0 format, reopening it in Word 6.0 for the Macintosh, and resaving it.

Using Word Documents with Adobe FrameMaker

In many technical organizations, as well as other organizations where extremely large documents are routinely created, you may be asked to export Word documents to the publishing program Adobe FrameMaker.

The differences between FrameMaker's long document capabilities and Word's have narrowed dramatically in recent years. Many documents that once required FrameMaker can now stay within Word, at least from a technical standpoint. Moreover, for relative novices, Word is a much easier, more intuitive program to learn.

Having said that, established workflows and procedures may dictate that your organization continue to use FrameMaker. You may, for example, have a staff of publishing and editorial professionals with long experience in FrameMaker and a preference for it. You may have a large library of documents formatted with FrameMaker. And FrameMaker does represent more than a legacy solution: it offers the following advantages over Word even today:

- A convenient one-step authoring environment for interactive Adobe PDF electronic documents
- A cross-platform solution that encompasses not only Windows and Macintosh, but also a variety of UNIX workstation platforms
- Precise, capable tools for publishing in Japanese
- Conditional text that allows you to switch easily between multiple versions of the same document—in essence, a more elegant, capable version of Word 97's Versions feature
- Superior equation editing
- An optional version, FrameMaker+SGML 5.5, that supports the Standardized General Markup Language (SGML), a powerful tool for organizing and repurposing large documents

NOTE SGML is a complex language that makes it possible to build structure and intelligence into documents by tagging them with codes similar to those of HTML, and writing Document Type Definitions (DTDs) that interact with these codes to present information in any number of ways. HTML, the language of World Wide Web documents, was derived from SGML.

SGML has traditionally been most widely used in high-volume production publishing organizations serving military and other government customers, where manuals run in the thousands of pages.

The idea at the heart of SGML, however, is a very powerful one with broad applicability. *If you separate content from formatting, and tag documents based on their structure, you make it possible to automate and streamline the reuse of information in virtually any format.*

Recently, a streamlined version of SGML, the Extensible Markup Language (XML), has emerged. XML eliminates some of SGML's complexity while maintaining its advantages, and many observers believe it will become a key delivery mechanism for electronic documents on the World Wide Web and intranets—supplanting HTML in many applications.

For the Office administrator interested in SGML or XML, the following alternatives exist:

1. Export Word and other documents to a program designed to handle them, such as FrameMaker+SGML
2. Purchase Microsoft's SGML Author for Word, version 1.2, a set of templates that add SGML capabilities to Word (at $595 per copy)
3. Wait for Microsoft Office 99, which is expected to include significant (but as yet unspecified) XML support

Understanding the FrameMaker Import Filter for Word

As with QuarkXPress and PageMaker, FrameMaker comes with an import filter designed to accept Word files in the following formats:

- Word for Windows 1.*x*, 2.*x*, 6.0 and 95
- Word for the Macintosh 3.0, 4.0, 5.0, 5.1, 6.0
- RTF

Like the other filters discussed in this chapter, FrameMaker's filter does quite a good job of importing manual character formatting and paragraph styles, but does not handle embedded graphics well. Unlike QuarkXPress and PageMaker, it also can import Word tables intact. It does preserve some important long-document features, notably index entries.

Importing a Word Document into FrameMaker

To import a Word document into FrameMaker, follow these steps:

1. First, create a new document in FrameMaker. Choose File, New. FrameMaker's New dialog box opens (see Figure 20.9).

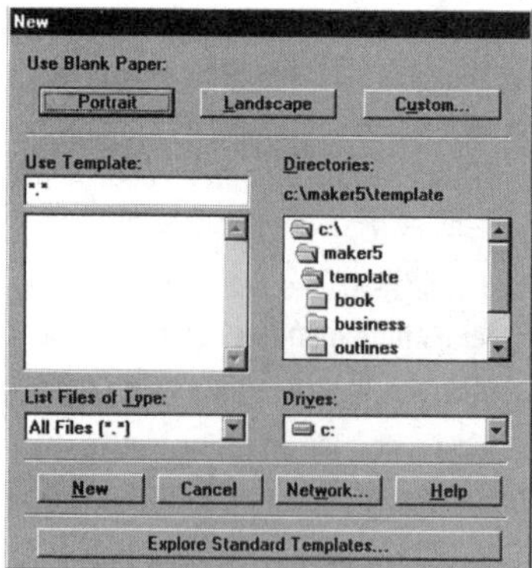

FIGURE 20.9
Creating a new document in FrameMaker.

2. Browse to select a template corresponding to the type of document you want to create.
3. Click New. The document opens.
4. Choose File, Import, File.
5. Mark the Copy Into Document check box to copy the Word document's text into your FrameMaker document.
6. Browse to select the Word document you want to import.
7. Click Import.
8. If FrameMaker displays the Unknown File Type dialog box, choose Microsoft Word in the Convert From list, and click Convert.
9. Click Import.

Creating PostScript Files from Office Documents

If you are planning to have your Office documents printed professionally, you may be called upon to create a PostScript file that your printer can use to make film for printing. To do so, perform the following steps:

1. Install the Apple LaserWriter II NT printer driver from your Windows or MacOS disks. (This is the basic no-frills PostScript driver that virtually every printer can use—but check to see whether your printer prefers you to use a different driver.)
2. When you're ready to create a PostScript file, choose File, Print. The Print dialog box opens.
3. In the Name drop-down box, choose Apple LaserWriter II NT.
4. Mark the Print to File check box.
5. Click OK.
6. The Print to File dialog box opens. Specify a name for your PostScript file. (Windows uses the .prn extension by default; some printers like to use the .ps extension.) Limit your file name to eight characters, in case your printer is outputting from a Macintosh that does not recognize Windows long file names.
7. Click OK.

In some cases, PostScript works better when your documents use PostScript fonts rather than the TrueType fonts that come with Windows and the Macintosh. Discuss this with your printer in advance.

Using Adobe's Portable Document Format (PDF) to Publish Office Documents Electronically

Until now, this chapter has focused solely on print production with Office and desktop publishing systems. Increasingly, Office document professionals face the challenge of finding cost-effective ways to publish formatted documents electronically. Chapter 28 covers a variety of Web publishing solutions. However, one option for publishing Office documents electronically is important to mention here: Adobe Acrobat.

With Acrobat, you can create compact PDF files containing all images and formats, and distribute them electronically to anyone who has the free Acrobat Reader software. According to Adobe, more than 20 million copies of Acrobat Reader have been downloaded; you can be reasonably sure that any audience with Web access will have access to it. After the file is opened in Acrobat Reader, it can be printed or read onscreen, and text from the file can be selected and copied into other documents. Acrobat PDF files can be searched, and can contain internal links and tables of contents that make them quite convenient to use. (One drawback of PDF files: text can be a little blurry onscreen, even though it prints exceptionally well.)

While using Acrobat PDF files does nothing to improve the quality of your graphics design, it can streamline the production process from whatever software you work with. For example, you can create electronic documents that your recipients can print themselves on a color or black-and-white printer, rather than hassling with conventional print production. Where conventional printing is still required, PDF files can be used by printers to double-check PostScript files you send, and streamline prepress work.

To use Acrobat with Word, first install Acrobat, and then download and install the new PDFMaker macro for Word 97, available at `ftp://ftp.adobe.com/pub/adobe/acrobat/win/3.x/pdfmaker.exe`. This adds the Create Adobe PDF command to Word's File menu; choosing File, Create Adobe PDF transforms a Word 97 file into PDF format.

As you can see in Table 20.1, PDFMaker does quite a good job of maintaining the interactivity you build into your Word documents.

Table 20.1 How PDFWriter Converts Word Features

Word Feature	PDF Feature
Headings	PDF bookmarks
URLs	PDF Weblinks
Cross-references	PDF links
Page numbers	Links to destinations
Links to other documents	PDF links
Footnote/endnote citations	Links to the notes
Comments/annotations	PDF text notes
Text boxes	PDF article threads
Document properties	PDF document information

While there are no "one-button macros" for creating PDF files from other Office applications, doing so is easy. Like fax software, PDF behaves like a printer driver, showing up in the list of printers in your Print dialog box. You simply choose PDFWriter in the Name drop-down list instead of your current printer:

1. Choose File, Print.
2. Choose PDF Writer in the Name drop-down box in the Printer area.
3. Click OK.
4. Windows prepares to create the PDF file. You're asked to enter a filename for the PDF file and a location where it will be stored.
5. Click OK; the PDF file is created and stored in the location you specified.

CHAPTER 21

Using Office with Windows NT

Office 97 operates either under Windows 95/98 or NT. As mentioned in Chapter 2, if your company is planning to upgrade to Windows NT as part of the installation of Office 97, then the change to NT should occur first.

This chapter focuses on the use of Office 97 with Windows NT. We begin with a general description of Windows NT that emphasizes the differences from Windows 95 and the special problems and opportunities with Windows NT.

Windows NT is specially designed to operate in a networking environment. Both Windows NT Workstation and Server work with a wide variety of network operating systems (NOS). As such, you must have a properly installed and functioning local area network before Office 97 can be used to its full potential.

NOTE Much of the technical literature available for Office 97 that mentions Windows NT notes the difference between version–3.5.1 and 4.0. To avoid many problems and for greater efficiency, make sure your company is upgraded to at least version 4.0 or a newer version if it is available. This chapter assumes that you are using version 4.0 or higher, and all procedures used here work for 4.0 and newer versions of Windows NT.

What Makes Windows NT Special

In a local area network, a file server presents files to the clients. Windows NT is designed to take full advantage of client-server architecture and comes in two components:

- Windows NT Server provides file server capabilities and other domain controlling functions.
- Windows NT Workstation serves as the operating system for client machines in the network.

In a typical network installation, a file server is loaded with Windows NT Server and each client computer using the network uses Windows NT Workstation as its operating system. As we shall see, you can also mix and match operating systems and perform dual boots under Windows NT.

Windows NT has several advantages over Windows 95. These advantages also create some challenges for you when using Office 97 under NT. These advantages are:

- Full 32-bit operation of programs with true multitasking for maximum speed
- Optimized for several different platforms so that you can use microprocessors from Intel, Digital, DEC, and other manufacturers
- A high level of security available from file storage level up to group accounts
- Capability to support multiple domains on a network and to form trust relationships with other file servers (Windows NT Server)
- Built-in Internet Information Server (Windows NT Server only) to facilitate the creation of an intranet or to provide Internet connectivity
- Greater protection against your software programs crashing through increased fault-tolerance
- Support for the TCP/IP addressing system to send packets over networks
- Support for multiple processors on one machine (2 for Workstation, 32 for Server)
- Ease of administration through the use of policy statements within the operating system
- Integration with BackOffice products
- Large number of sources for help information

On the surface this makes NT appear to be the operating system of choice for network applications such as Office 97. Windows NT, Office 97, and Microsoft BackOffice were designed to run together. BackOffice is the server side; NT is the client; and Office 97 provides the applications to run under this system. Indeed, the workgroup functions within Office 97 are well supported by Windows NT; however, it takes planning and strict attention to detail to get Office 97 to work successfully under Windows NT.

Because of its improved capabilities and because it is designed to run under networking, Windows NT needs a lot of RAM. Make sure your workstations have at least 64MB of RAM if you plan to use both Windows NT Workstation and Office 97.

In particular, you must have a clear picture of how your network operates, its current account and security settings, and the way you want Office 97 to be used. You also have to consider who has access to your computers. If your office has Internet connections or an intranet, additional security considerations come into play.

Issues Related to NT Workstation

A host of issues are related to the use of Windows NT Workstation, especially when used as the operating system supporting Office 97. In this section, we explore the most important of these issues to help you prevent problems and successfully use Office 97. Specifically, the following issues are addressed:

- File structure
- Network security
- Access on the network

Windows NT uses a file structure different from Windows 95 and other earlier operating systems. This file structure is called NT File System or NTFS.

NTFS is unique because it is designed for very rapid recovery of data from very large hard drives. This includes mass storage devices such as RAID arrays. NTFS includes robust security measures at the most basic hard disk formatting levels and built-in attributes to support security and access control. In short, it is superior to the File Allocation Table (FAT) system used by Windows 95.

At least part of your hard drive, however, must be formatted to NTFS before Windows NT can be loaded and used to its full potential. Consequently, if you are going to change operating systems, complete and test an upgrade to Windows NT before considering loading Office 97.

You can use Windows 95 and NT on the same machine. Windows NT enables you to format any portion of your hard disk space to NTFS and the rest to FAT. Formatting in this way enables you to preserve, for example, an old copy of Office 95 and Windows 95 and still use Windows NT Workstation. Windows 95, however, must reside in the primary partition of your hard drive (C:\) and that partition must be formatted as FAT, because Windows 95 cannot read an NTFS partition.

NOTE When a hard disk has both FAT and NTFS installed, possible leaks are opened to the security system. Although the security under Windows NT is robust, a person can log in and access the FAT area of a disk to go around some security measures. ■

During the installation of Windows NT, a message indicates how many hard drives (both real and virtual) you have on your computer. You are then given the option of formatting parts or all of them into NTFS format. Doing so destroys the data stored on the targeted area; therefore, take the following steps before loading Windows NT Workstation onto a particular computer:

- First determine whether you want to preserve the previous operating system. If you do, then you may want to create a virtual hard drive (such as D:\) with your unused disk space and format that to NTFS. Be sure to defragment the hard drive first. If you don't want to preserve your previous operating system, then back up the entire disk and reformat the drive during installation.
- Next, determine whether you want to preserve the original application programs that Office 97 is replacing or upgrading. Do not overwrite these with the NTFS format. Backup all files on a computer before installing Windows NT Workstation.
- Where you have both NT Workstation and another operating system on one machine, you are greeted at bootup with a message asking which system to install. This is called a dual boot. Boot to the non-NT system only when you want to run previous versions of application programs.
- If you already have a computer with NT Workstation installed, install Office 97, and do not set security or sharing levels until you have established the account settings for your network connection during installation. The user name, group name, and password at the time of installation should be set for the administrator.

Network Security Issues for Windows NT

The advanced security features of Windows NT can really help to keep your network under control. You can, however, run into a situation in which, for example, a user in Sales wants to coordinate schedules with a user in the Legal Department. Both users are running Office 97 and have set the pointer in Outlook toward each other and given permission to share their schedules stored in the common file on the network. Unfortunately, the first user is greeted with a message saying that access is denied. Although everything is set correctly in Office 97, the collaboration doesn't work because Windows NT is also working correctly. If the user accounts in Windows NT Workstation or IP packet filtering on Windows NT Server are set to keep causal users out of the Legal Department, then the collaboration can be blocked.

You need to be aware, therefore, of how security operates on Windows NT. When users first boot up Windows NT Workstation they receive a message asking them to log in. The usernames they use determine what levels of access they have within the system. Thus, a single person could possess several different levels of access through multiple login identities. The workgroup identified by the user triggers a search for access permissions for members of this group.

Windows NT Workstation is designed to support the workgroup model in which a user shares files and resources with a local group of computers, usually off of one file server. For example, the production team for a corporation's Training Department might be made up of seven people who create training material for the company intranet. In Windows NT Workstation, you give the seven computers used by these people the same workgroup name.

To share files, you open the Windows NT Explorer program, highlight the subdirectories of interest, right-click, and set sharing on for your workgroup (see Figures 21.1 and 21.2). This allows the users to freely access each other's work.

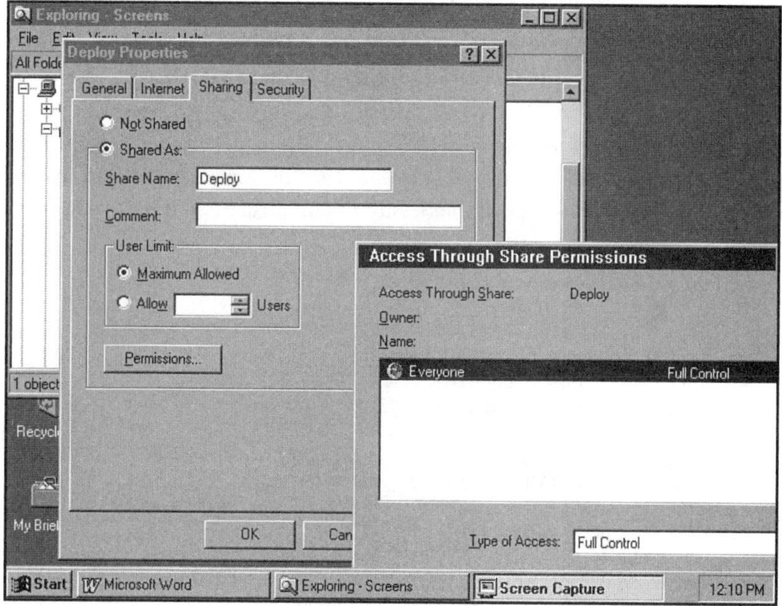

FIGURE 21.1
Note the rich sharing environment under Windows NT in which you can set group permissions for a subdirectory.

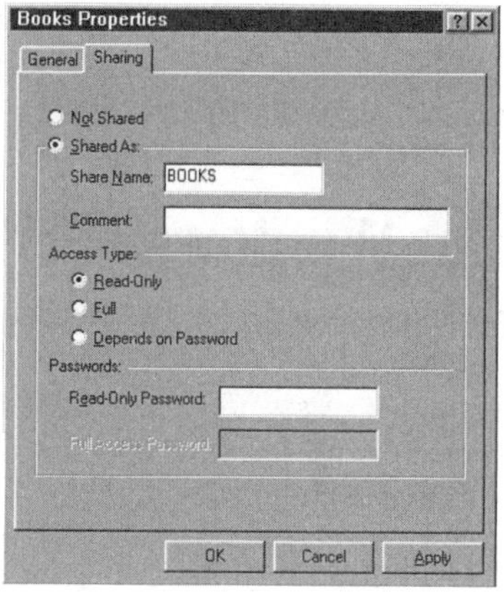

Books Properties
General | Sharing
Not Shared
Shared As:
Share Name: BOOKS
Comment:
Access Type:
Read-Only
Full
Depends on Password
Passwords:
Read-Only Password:
Full Access Password:
OK | Cancel | Apply

FIGURE 21.2
To appreciate the strength of Windows NT, compare Figure 21.1 with the sharing screen from Windows 95 shown here.

In Office 97 collaboration work can occur several ways; however, your operating systems have to have been set to read and write from common and shared file areas. You need to make sure, therefore, that sharing is open between users.

To do this, the following directories had to be set to read and write privileges during installation of Office 97:

```
C:\
      C:\Temp
      C:\Winnt
      C:\Winnt\Forms
      C:\Winnt\System32
      C:\Program Files\Microsoft Office
      C:\Program Files\Microsoft Office\Office
      C:\Program Files\Microsoft Office\Xlstart
      C:\Program Files\Microsoft Office\Templates
```

To do this, open Windows NT Explorer, right-click the subdirectory of interest, and choose Sharing. This is where you set your read and write permissions. In addition, you need to examine the following files to make sure that none are set to read only:

```
C:\Ffastun.ffa
C:\Ffastun.ffl
C:\Ffastun.ffo
C:\Ffastun.ffx
C:\Winnt\Artgalry.cag
C:\Winnt\<LogonID>.acl
C:\Winnt\<LogonID>8.xlb
C:\Winnt\<LogonID>.fav
C:\Winnt\Mso97.acl
C:\Winnt\Msoprefs.232
C:\Winnt\Outlook.fav
C:\Winnt\Outlook.prf
C:\Winnt\Outlook.prt
C:\Winnt\Forms\Frmcache.dat
C:\Winnt\System32\Ffastlog.txt
C:\Winnt\System32\Msforms.twd
```

The other network model used by Windows NT is based on domains. In this arrangement, a logical group of servers and their accompanying users are grouped together. You do this by sharing the information on each server in the domain with the other domain servers.

Network Access Issues for Windows NT Workstation

Inside each of the Windows NT Workstation computers is the information that identifies its domain, workgroup, and so on. The servers contain a Security Accounts Manager, which handles and stores information on usernames, passwords, and levels of access available. A user that has logged onto the network is provided with security identifiers that are used to indicate which rights and permissions are associated with this user.

It is up to the network administrator to determine the rights and permissions granted to each user. The advantage of the Windows NT system over Windows 95 is that a greater level of user access can be established. For example, a Guest account can be granted from a single administrative site to allow any user access to the corporate intranet site for general company information.

Access, however, is a double-edge sword. If you fail to grant access permissions to a user to reach a shared Office 97 file, then collaboration is prevented. Also, Windows NT comes with a lot of different ways to restrict access. These all have to be coordinated to keep the flow of information moving smoothly.

At the same time, you have to enforce and maintain internal security and access. Later in this chapter we talk about this in greater detail when we look closer at Windows NT Server. For right now, you have to design each Windows NT Workstation setup to accept a limited number of user accounts.

As an administrator you need to decide whether your users will have the capability to make changes to user accounts or create new accounts. This decision is based on the level of control you want the users to have. In most cases you establish a single user account with all the account modification privileges revoked to prevent users from manipulating their network status.

Take the case in which you want to place Office 97 on your workgroup's file server for migration to each workstation. You need to create a single set of access permissions that allow the users full read/write access to the server. You give such a set of permissions a name, such as Marketing. When you establish individual user accounts, you can then bind them to the permissions under the Marketing access policy.

Administration for Windows NT Workstation

When users of Windows 95 boot up Windows NT for the first time, they tend to be surprised by how much the two operating systems look alike. In fact, looks are deceiving. Although the look and feel is similar, the functionality is different. For example, under Windows NT Workstation, new hardware is not automatically detected and installed. Instead, you have to go to the Control Panel and activate the Add New Hardware program, which gives you full manual control of how the new equipment is installed and run.

Users quickly discover that greater control means a greater need for knowledge. Moreover, as an administrator you find that Windows NT Workstation requires you to be more actively involved with your users.

Setting Up Remote Access for Windows NT Workstation

Under Windows 95, users can load in a favorite modem program or configure Dial-Up Networking to gain remote access to other computers outside their network. With Windows NT Workgroup, you can also use the Remote Access Service (RAS) to enable users to connect to their desktop machines from home or on the road. This enables Office 97 users to log on to their own computers to coordinate schedules in Outlook, download Excel files, upload a new Word template, and so on.

To use the RAS, click the Dial-up Networking icon from the Control Panel and fill out the information used to make connections from your modem. Typically, this is the information for an Internet connection over the phone line, not the network. Some of the information stored in Dial-Up Networking is used to configure RAS.

RAS is installed into Windows NT Workstation by performing the following:

1. Open Control Panel and double-click the Network icon.
2. Select the Services tab and then choose Add.
3. From the pop-up list select Remote Access Service.
4. List the source of your Windows NT files for installation.
5. Indicate the current installed modem in the machine.
6. At the Remote Access Setup box establish the TCP/IP service and set the RAS to accept incoming calls (see Figure 21.3).

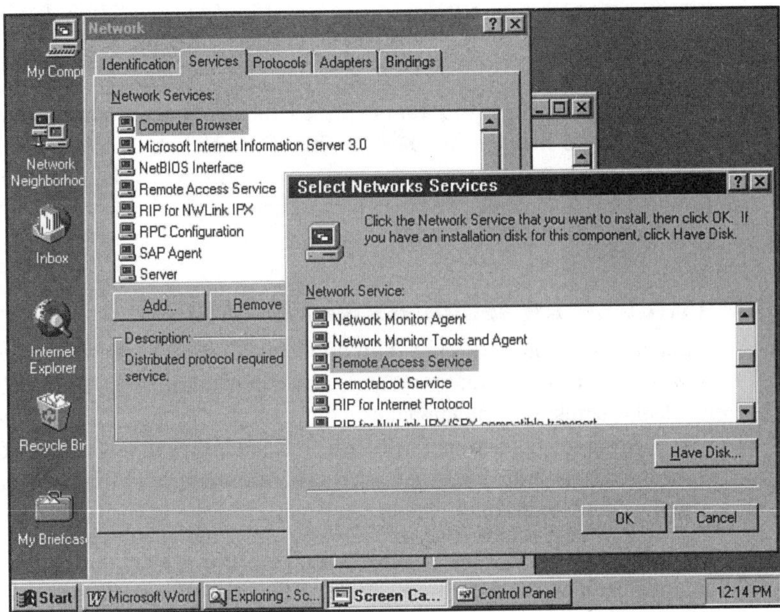

FIGURE 21.3
To install RAS you open the Network icon in the Control Panel, select the Services tab, and highlight RAS.

TIP Provide RAS with a static pool of just a few IP addresses it accepts. This limits the number of computers that can make the connection. It also provides addresses for your network firewalls to use to prevent unauthorized users from reaching many parts of your network.

Use the call-back feature and other security measures for home based workers and mobile workers to make sure that only authorized people are gaining access to your computers. A stolen laptop with stored passwords and a copy of RAS can be used to quickly gain access into your company's network.

Issues Related to Dual Boot Installation

As mentioned earlier in this chapter, it is possible to have a single computer run both Windows 95 and Windows NT Workstation. If your existing computer is running Windows 95, you can install Windows NT by following the procedures that come with the software. Then each time you boot the computer, the Windows NT boot loader appears and gives you the choice of proceeding with either Windows 95 or Windows NT.

For smooth operation of two operating systems on the same machine, load Windows 95 into the primary partition of the C drive and Windows NT into a separate and virtual drive (for example d:).

Keep in mind that Windows NT does not accept the range of devices that Windows 95 does. You need to make sure, therefore, that the list of acceptable devices is checked very closely for each target machine to make sure that compatibility problems do not result. Otherwise, you find that a device that doesn't run under Windows NT works just fine when Windows 95 is in use.

If you install Windows NT Workstation on a computer with Windows 95, you also have to reinstall your Windows applications to have them function properly when running Windows NT.

How to Install Windows NT Workstation on a Computer Already Running Windows 95

If you have computers running Windows 95 in your office and you want to upgrade them to Windows NT Workstation, follow these steps:

1. Back up your full system, and erase data from the hard drive.
2. Install Windows NT Workstation to the recommended folder.
3. During installation, select one portion of your hard drive and make it a virtual drive. Format this portion to NTFS and proceed with installation. Leave your primary partition a FAT sector.
4. Copy your backup to the FAT area and new software to the NTFS area.
5. Store the NT version of a program in a folder different from Windows 95 program folders and reinstall it in the NTFS area.

One easy way to remember to keep program versions separate is to create different names for folders on two different drives. For example, the existing Windows 95 applications might be in `c:\Program Files` while the new Windows NT based applications can be stored in `d:\NT Program Files`.

The D drive is formatted to NTFS so that the programs and the operating system are on the same drive. Doing so also enables faster speed and greater security of NTFS for your applications.

How to Add Windows 95 to an Existing NT Machine

If you find that you are running Windows NT machines and need to add Windows 95, things become a little more complicated. To load Windows 95 in this situation, you must follow these steps:

1. Create or obtain your current Emergency Repair Disk for Windows NT. You can run rdisk.exe to ensure that your NT Emergency Repair Disk is current.
2. Install Windows 95.
3. Reboot to MS-DOS from the NT boot menu, not a floppy disk based boot disk.
4. Select MS-DOS from the NT boot menu.
5. Type the `WIN` command to start Windows if it does not automatically start.

Make sure you do not store the Windows 95 operating system in the Winnt subdirectory. Windows NT and Windows 95 cannot function if they are on the same partition formatted by Windows 95, let alone the same directory.

If the Windows NT boot menu does not appear when you reboot, take the following steps:

1. Insert your Windows NT disk and start setup with the repair option.
2. Of the repair options that appear, deselect all but Inspect Boot Sector. Click Continue.
3. Insert the Emergency Repair Disk when prompted.
4. Remove Emergency Repair Disk when prompted and reboot the computer.

This should restore the Windows NT boot menu at startup. If not, you need to contact technical support.

Issues Related to NT Server and Office 97

The Windows NT Server is an operating system that is typically installed on a computer used for file or Web page serving. It uses the look and feel of the Windows NT Workstation; however, Windows NT Server has a powerful suite of applications and features of particular importance to the administrator of a network, in addition to the features for NT Workstation.

Windows NT includes these capabilities to help you support Office 97:

- The capability to establish domains
- Group access permission setting
- Web server supported by Office 97
- SMS integration

How to Set Up Domains

Windows NT enables the use of domain models on networks. Domains are groups of file servers grouped together to share information. This is usually done along logical lines of corporate structure. For example, the file, email, and Web servers at a regional headquarters of a corporation might be grouped together into a single domain.

Windows NT Server can be configured during installation to be the master domain server, a backup server, or a stand-alone server.

- As a master domain server, it stores all the information about the domain in its databases. It is the server that the other servers look to for information on whether particular people have permission to carry out a specific operation. In this way, several workgroups can collaborate by having all the workgroup file servers use a master domain server to control access and security.
- A backup server configuration is used for all the cooperating file servers in a domain, except the master domain server. During installation you indicate where the master domain information is stored on the network. Periodically the backup domain server consults the primary domain server's database to ensure that the backup server has the most current information on users.
- Stand-alone servers are used where you want to isolate a file server from your normal network traffic. Typically, this is your Internet Web server. You want the world to have access to your Internet site, but not the rest of the network.

Domains can then form trust relationships with other domains. Such relationships enable a user in one domain to gain access into another domain. So, as you can see, Windows NT Server is designed for power and flexibility. You need to carefully plan the access and security for both Office 97 users and the network together, however, to ensure that people wanting to collaborate, communicate, and share files across your network are not impeded.

How to Set Up Domain Level Access

You can use the User Manager for Domains to create domain level access and security. This saves you both time and effort by enabling you to work on groups of people at a time instead of entering information for each individual (see Figure 21.4).

To create domain level access and security using the User Manager for Domains, take these steps:

1. Open the User Manager for Domains from the Administration Program group.
2. From the list of domains that are shown, select the one you want to modify.
3. Choose Policy, Account.
4. In the Account Policies dialog box you can fill out the levels of access and security measures you desire for your domain (see Figure 21.5).

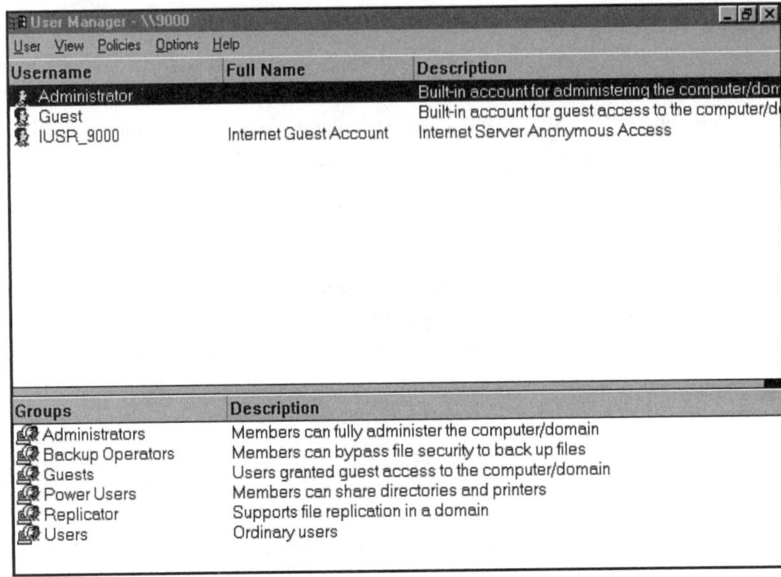

FIGURE 21.4
The User Manager is called up to establish user accounts and to set access and security policies.

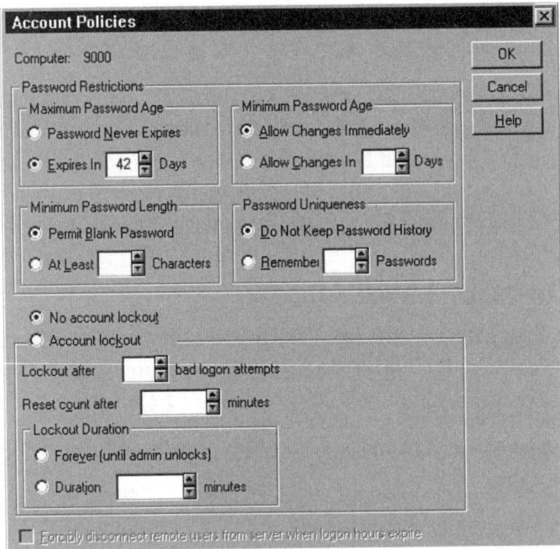

FIGURE 21.5
The Account Policies screen within the User Manager sets important information such as how long passwords can be used, password histories, and types of passwords allowed.

5. Now you can choose User, New Global Group to set up account information for use over your entire domain. (You choose User, New Local Group to go beyond your own domain.)
6. Give the global group a name and select the users that can belong to this new group.

Domain level access and security gives you the capability to set a common set of access, rights, and permissions for your domain or for portions of your domain. You can also add and subtract people from this global setting whenever you want. This enables you to follow the dynamic flow of work teams as they form, change, and disband. Such flexibility enables you to keep security and access up to speed with the needs of your workgroups and domains from a single location within Windows NT Server.

Using the Internet Information Server

Within Windows NT Server is the Internet Information Server (IIS), which enables you to set up one or more Internet/intranet sites on your server. IIS is a powerful Web site server that can integrate smoothly with Office 97. In fact, your Office 97 users can create Web content and directly publish these to the IIS Web server.

The RAS can also be used under Windows NT Server to allow simultaneous access to a Web server over a direct dedicated phone line for up to 256 users. This gives you the capability to use IIS for intranet applications or for creating Web servers off of the Internet.

A good document control practice is disallowing Office 97 users direct access to the Web site for publishing. Instead, proposed documentation is first copied to an administrator's shared folder for approval. After formal review and approval the administrator publishes the new material to the Web site. This prevents mistakes, poor spelling, incorrect information, and the like from being seen on the Internet or intranet.

IIS has within it a Service Manager that can determine access to the Web site. If you are using Office 97 to create Web content, then you also have to set the accounts in the IIS service manager correctly for the transfer of material from your users to the Web server. The good news is that IIS service manager can read the account rights and permissions set by Windows NT.

In the IIS Service Manager window (see Figure 21.6), you select the user accounts set up by Windows NT that can have access to the Web site. This includes the capability to read and write to the site. Users responsible for maintaining Web sites with programs such as FrontPage need to have read and write permission to do their jobs.

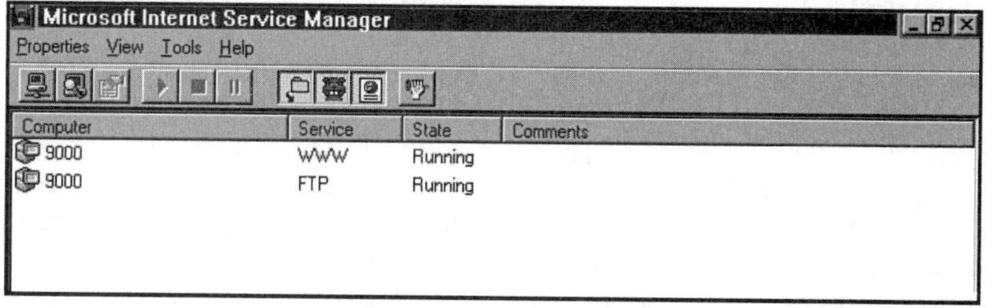

FIGURE 21.6
The Internet Service Manager starts up Internet services such as FTP and Gopher. It also sets the properties for these services, such as who is allowed access.

This enables you to do the following:

- Set login requirements for remote clients
- Set logins for network based clients
- Set access and security levels for all clients
- Create home directories and virtual directories for Web publishing
- Install and distribute encryption technologies
- Set audit and logging options
- Monitor Web site activities

Using the Systems Management Server with Windows NT and Office 97

The Systems Management Server (SMS) is a BackOffice product intended to work with Windows NT Servers to give you the capability of performing the following tasks for your entire network from one site:

- Collect hardware and software inventories from your network
- Manage the running of applications, such as Office 97, from servers to clients
- Distribute software from servers to clients
- Remotely monitor and troubleshoot a client computer

Because Office 97 can either be installed to client machines from a server or run from a server, SMS is an option for keeping close control of this process. For example, you can set up the SMS machine to distribute copies of Office 97 to all servers in your organization so that they can, in turn, distribute it to client computers. This enables you to set the installation options for the organization just once.

Setting up the SMS machine to distribute copies of Office 97 to all servers in your organization is an option that requires expert skill and experience to carry off successfully. If you feel that you are up to this task, then refer to the instructions that come with SMS.

Integrating Office 97 with Microsoft Exchange

Microsoft offers a powerful email server for use with Windows NT and other network operating systems. Called Microsoft Exchange Server, this software package can handle extremely heavy loads of traffic on networks, intranets, or the Internet.

Despite the power of Exchange, when anything more than light email traffic exists in your system, put the Exchange Server on a dedicated machine with plenty of memory and disk space. Email serving can quickly eat up computer resources or bog down another server running on the same machine.

When you load Windows NT Workstation, you are giving your computer the capability of working with Exchange. When you load Office 97, you get an Exchange client as part of your package. This enables you to use programs such as Outlook to access your email and other Exchange functions.

Troubleshooting Office on Windows NT

Because Windows NT Workstation brings many new features and options to your system, it also introduces more opportunities for problems. To be fair, however, the NTFS and internal fault-tolerance of Windows NT Workstation go a long way towards preventing problems.

How to Troubleshoot as an Administrator

As the administrator of Office 97, be aware of a couple of concepts used by professional managers to troubleshoot computer problems. These concepts are root cause, corrective action, and preventive action.

A root cause is the fundamental cause of a failure within Office 97 or Windows NT. When you receive error messages or a program fails to operate correctly, several causes are possible. When identified and fixed, however, the problem is prevented from occurring again.

Take our earlier example of two users finding that they cannot collaborate using Office 97 on your network. You many find that the read/write permissions were not set correctly on the shared file. Correcting this might start the collaboration but not fully solve the problem. Looking deeper into the situation you might also find that the Legal department's server filters out the IP address of the other user's computer. Thus when logged onto a different computer, collaboration proceeds, but when at his own desk collaboration fails. By removing the root cause, you eliminate the problem.

The next concept is corrective action. In this case, you take steps to solve a problem. When you do so, investigate how long this problem has been going on and how many people are affected. You might find that several unreported problems are associated with your root cause. Preventive action, however, is what this book emphasizes—planning and carefully testing your network system and the Office 97 setups to ensure that many problems are avoided.

Using the Diagnostic Tool

Windows NT Workstation comes with a built in diagnostic tool that can be used as a starting point for tracing the root cause of your problems experienced with Office 97 (see Figure 21.7).

Access the diagnostic tool by clicking the Start button on your desktop, and choosing Programs, Administrative Tools, Windows NT Diagnostics.

What comes up is a set of tabbed pages, each containing information about your system, the software that is running, and the status of various settings (see Figure 21.8).

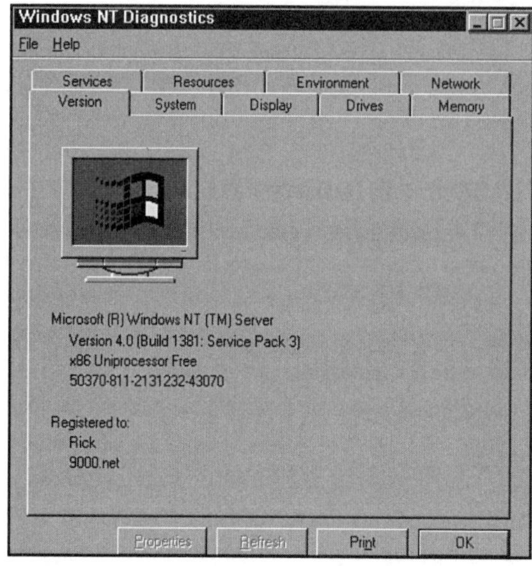

FIGURE 21.7
The diagnostic tool screen presents several tabs, each of which describes current conditions on your computer and in the software.

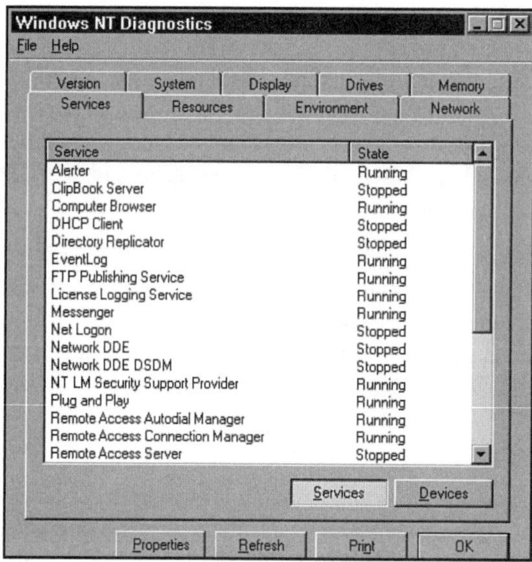

FIGURE 21.8
This is an illustration of the type of information given by the diagnostic tool—in this case, the Services currently running on the system. Note that RAS is shown at the bottom of the list as stopped.

This provides you with the basic information you need to start your troubleshooting process. As you make changes to your system and software, either turn the diagnostic tool off and re-launch after each change or refresh the page being viewed to see the results of your efforts.

A key planning point in any organization is to decide how much control users have over their own computers. Some companies distribute Reaction Plans that tell users the first steps to take before calling technical support or the help desk. Opening the diagnostic tool is usually one of the steps.

Write down the Windows NT version information, including the build number, before you call a help desk or technical support service. Because so many variations of NT exist, these numbers help pinpoint potential problems and known patches.

Next you need to evaluate the problem and consult the appropriate page.

- For problems related to slow software execution or failures to complete operations, consult the Memory and Resources tabs.
- For problems with accessing Windows NT support programs such as the Remote Access Service, check the Services tab. Typically you find that a needed service of NT wasn't started. This tab enables you to attempt forcing the start of a service.
- Problems with the monitor can be addressed in the Display tab. If you lose monitor functionality, try rebooting to the Windows NT Workstation VGA mode. This restores the monitor to a simple VGA setting so that you can adjust normal video card settings.
- Problems with modems, mice, and other port devices can be checked on the Resources tab, which shows the current system interrupts being used. Look for conflicts.
- Network related problems can be handled in the Networks tab as a starting point for detecting obvious conflicts or missing services.
- Difficulties with reading and writing data to a local drive using Office 97 can be checked on the Drives tab. Additional disk utility programs, however, are recommended.

In short, the diagnostic tool is very good at detecting the obvious and quick-to-fix problems. If the problem seems to be severe or hidden, then other programs or technical support should be used. The diagnostic tool is still kept open so that you can read off the current setup of the computer to a technical support person.

When to Use Internet-Based Support

For preventive action, the Internet provides a wide variety of free technical information sources. These sources can be consulted to keep you up to date with the latest discoveries made by other Office 97 users under Windows NT.

Naturally, Microsoft's support site on the Net is an important place to check on a regular basis. The one service you want to use is the free email newsletter that Microsoft distributes from its technical support area, which can be found at **www.microsoft.com/support.**

You also want to find the discussion groups for both Office 97 and Windows NT. The two best search engines for these types of searches are the Yahoo! (**www.yahoo.com**) and Alta Vista (**www.altavista.digital.com**) sites and HotBot at Wired Magazine's site (**www.hotbot.com**).

The problem you encounter when accessing these search engines is deriving a proper search string. Whenever you use Office 97 or Windows NT as part of a search string, you retrieve large numbers of retailers that sell these products. We therefore recommend the following strings be tested:

"Discussion Group" AND "Office 97"

"Discussion Group" AND "Windows NT"

"Troubleshooting Office 97" AND "Windows NT"

Currently, these are three good sites to visit:

Windows NT Tip of the Day at **www.tipworld.com**

Boston Windows User Group at **www.bwug.org**

Shareware at **mitec.softseek.com**

When to Use Microsoft Support

After you have exhausted your internal technical support and Internet resources, you typically turn to Microsoft technical support using the support contract terms you have established at your company. This type of technical support comes in two basic forms—static and interactive.

Static resources are publications and databases of known problems that you can use at your company, including the TechNet series of CD-ROMs. You receive two CD-ROMs every month on a subscription basis. These contain information about product features, troubleshooting tips, resources kits, patches, and the like. By loading these into a file server in your network, you can make this information available to all users and internal technical support people.

Microsoft also publishes a wide variety of guides and resource kits for their products. It is highly recommended that you obtain the Resource Kits for both Office 97 and Windows NT if you use these two products together. The cost is about $60 each, and they come with CD-ROMs filled with programs to assist you. For example, the Office 97 Resource Kit comes with a wizard for network installation. (Microsoft also produces similar guides for each of the application programs within Office 97.)

Interactive support is back-and-forth communication with a person or a database. These services include:

- Phone support for Office 97—206-635-7041
- Priority support—900-555-2020 or 800-936-5500
- Text Telephone support—800-668-7975
- Fast Tips—800-936-4100
- Web sites
  www.microsoft.com/office
  www.microsoft.com/nt
  www.microsoft.com/support

- Knowledge base—**www.microsoft.com/kb**
- Download service (via modem)—206-936-6735

You can also call Microsoft at (800) 765-7768 or consult the Internet for a list of Microsoft Solution Providers. (More information is available at **www.microsoft.com/msp/**.) Authorized Support Centers, frequently listed in your local yellow pages, are also available. (You can call [800] 936-3500 to learn more about this option.) Also check [800] 426-9400 to learn about Microsoft Consulting Services in your area.

Continuous Improvement is making small improvements to your system each day to eventually reach larger goals. This concept should always be kept in the back of your mind when administering Office 97.

Finally, you can always seek help from independent third-party consultants, however, investigate and test these consultants before using them to alter the setup of your system.

CHAPTER 22

Using Office with Novell Application Launcher

In the old days, you could copy an application's executable file to a network file server (such as NetWare) and all your users could run it from the network without a hitch. Today complex applications such as Microsoft Office 97 require completely new tools for efficiently distributing software.

If your company supports Novell Directory Services (NDS), Novell NetWare, or IntraNetWare servers, the Novell Application Launcher (NAL) (a component of Z.E.N.works) is an excellent way to distribute and manage Microsoft Office 97 (or any other software) across the enterprise.

The Novell Application Launcher provides tools for creating an exact image of an application on a workstation, storing that application in an NDS tree on a NetWare server as an application object, and distributing it on demand to any user with proper rights to that application.

By distributing a working image of an application, your users get not only the software but also any preference changes or different configurations of the package you create. To the user, the NAL-deployed application looks like a local application in the NAL window or standard Windows Explorer window. NAL also lets you automatically add icons for the application to the user's Desktop, Start menu, or system tray.

NOTE NAL was once a separate add-on to NetWare 4.11. Novell has recently repackaged the NAL as part of Z.E.N.works and simply calls it the Application Launcher (dropping the N). See the "Z.E.N.works Software" section later in this chapter for a complete description of what is in Z.E.N.works.

To take advantage of NAL—which is part of the free Z.E.N.works Starter Pack delivered on the CD-ROM that comes with this book—your organization must have its workstations connected to a NetWare server (4.11 or higher) that supports NDS. From that server, you can distribute Microsoft Office or other applications to Windows 95, Windows 98, Windows NT, and Windows 3.x client machines.

NOTE The version of Microsoft Office that you distribute must run on the target workstation. For example, because Microsoft Office 97 (a 32-bit application) doesn't run on Windows 3.x systems, it makes no sense to distribute it to your 3.x workstations.

This chapter describes the following:

- Requirements for installing Microsoft Office using the Novell Application Launcher
- How NAL works
- How to install Microsoft Office using the NAL
- How users can access Microsoft Office using the NAL

You also learn about the features of Novell's Z.E.N.works for supporting the entire process of managing software and hardware across your organization.

Understanding How NAL Works

Using the Novell Application Launcher feature of Z.E.N.works, you can distribute and manage applications so that they are available to every workstation in your enterprise. Applications can be specifically packaged and tuned to the way you want them to look and behave on every user's workstation. When you change or update a software package, those changes are automatically picked up by the user's workstation.

There are four basic components to the NAL: two components are used by the administrator and two are specific to the user workstations. Administrative components include snAppShot (for creating the application template) and a NAL snap-in component that works with NWAdmn32 (for creating the application object and setting its properties on the NetWare server). User components include the NAL window (for viewing and running distributed applications) and NAL Explorer (for having the NAL applications appear in the Windows Explorer window).

In addition to the NAL components, you need a good understanding of NetWare 4.11, Novell Directory Services, and how Z.E.N.works fits together with them.

NAL Administrative Components

As an administrator, you use snAppShot to create an application template on a clean workstation. Then you run NWAdmn32 to create the application object on the NetWare server. The next two sections describe what the two components do.

Using snAppShot The snAppShot program creates the application template you use to create the application object. Run snAppShot from a clean computer and install the software you want to distribute.

Then snAppShot gathers any file, registry entry, or other component that has changed on your computer since the time before the installation and creates the application template from the differences. During snAppShot, you can also automatically install the application template directly to the NetWare server from which it will be distributed to users.

Using NetWare Administrator NAL Snap-In The NAL NWAdmn32 snap-in adds features to the basic NetWare Administrator command so that it can be used to manage application objects. Using NWAdmn32, you create the application object from the template of the application. Then you can identify many properties for the application object, including the application's executable, the types of systems it runs on, how it is distributed, and other information.

NAL User Components

To the user whose workstation is properly configured to use NAL, applications that are ready to be distributed from the NetWare server simply look like application icons that are ready to run. Those icons can appear in the NAL Window or in the Windows Explorer window. As administrator, you can also add these icons to the Desktop, Start menu, or system tray.

Using the NAL Window The NAL window shows you the applications that are available to the user from the NDS tree on the NetWare server. The users open application folders from the NDS tree, and then they select icons for the applications they want to run. If the application has not been installed yet, it is installed and then launched on the workstation. If it has been installed, it is simply launched.

Using Windows Explorer Because many people use the Windows 95 Explorer window to navigate their computers, NAL adds features that enable users to launch NAL applications from Explorer. An entry called Application Explorer appears in the Windows Explorer window.

NOTE The Application Launcher does not yet integrate with Microsoft Internet Explorer. You must use Windows Explorer with Windows 98.

The NDS tree containing the applications appears under the Application Explorer folder. Users can select NAL applications from this folder as they would from the NAL window.

Installing Microsoft Office Using the NAL

Z.E.N.works stands for Zero Effort Networks. The "Zero Effort" part, however, applies to the end user and not the administrator. As an administrator, you have to do a bit more setup to get Microsoft Office ready for installation using NAL. The time and effort you save later, however, will quickly make up for your initial groundwork as the application is deployed throughout your enterprise.

As noted earlier, NAL requires a NetWare and Novell Directory Services infrastructure to be in place already. (Those prerequisites are detailed in the sections that follow.) After everything is in place, however, deploying and installing Microsoft Office using NAL can be broken down into the following major steps:

- *Creating the Microsoft Office application template.* Run the snAppShot program from a clean workstation (the same kind that will eventually use the application). The snAppShot program discovers all the components on your workstation's disk, asks you to install the application (Microsoft Office), and then rechecks all components.

  The differences between the two discoveries becomes the application template (consisting of the files, registry entries, and other information that make up an installed Office application suite). You then copy the application template to a NetWare server (either as part of the snAppShot process or manually at a later time).
- *Creating the Microsoft Office application objects.* Run the NWAdmn32 program from the NetWare server. This will let you create application objects from the application template you created for Microsoft Office and set properties for those objects.
- *Distributing Microsoft Office to the workstations.* Set up each workstation to have access to the application objects you created for Office. The user simply opens the icons representing the application objects; this installs the application and launches the program. The next time the user opens the icon, it simply runs from the installed copy on the local hard disk. This can be repeated for hundreds or thousands of workstations.

Figure 22.1 illustrates how the NAL works to deploy Microsoft Office to the workstations in your enterprise.

CAUTION

You are about to create and distribute a replica of an installed application. This method of software distribution does not limit the number of workstations on which you can install the application. It is up to you to make sure that your company has obtained the proper number of licenses to use the application.

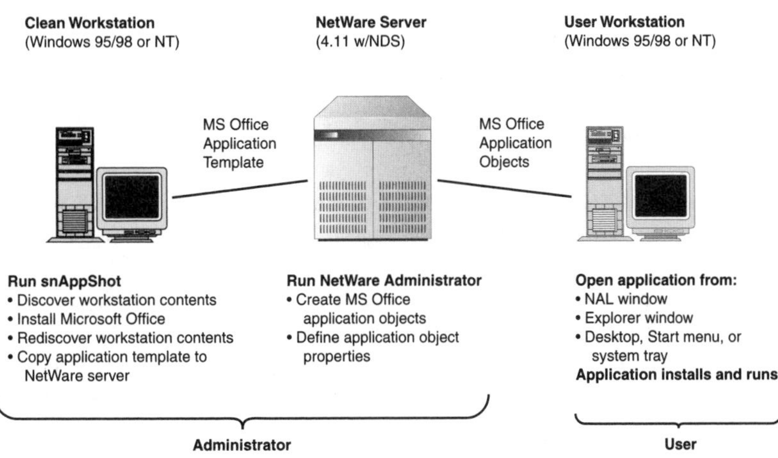

FIGURE 22.1
Use NAL to deploy Microsoft Office to user workstations.

Prerequisites for Installing Office 97 with NAL

The more copies of an application you need to install in your organization, the more efficient it is to use NAL. If you have to install Microsoft Office on only one or two workstations, you probably don't want to go into the overhead associated with NAL. If you must set up many users with Office, however, you will save tremendous time using NAL to distribute software.

Before you can begin distributing applications with NAL, you need to have a NetWare infrastructure in place. That infrastructure includes having workstations connected to a NetWare network that has the correct type of server and NDS configured. You also need to install the NAL (which is part of the Z.E.N.works Starter Pack that comes on the CD-ROM with this book). The next four sections further describe what you need.

NetWare Server Because NAL needs a recent version of NDS, your network must have access to a NetWare 4.11 (or more recent) server. An NDS tree must be configured so that you can associate the application objects with particular User, Group, Organization, or Organizational Units in the NDS tree.

NOTE For a complete description of NetWare servers, NDS, and other issues relating to setting up a NetWare network, refer to one of the many books available that describe NetWare. In particular, we recommend Que's *Special Edition Using NetWare 4.1*.

The NetWare 4.11 server must have at least 70MB of available memory and 205MB of free disk space for Z.E.N.works. As the administrator of NAL, you must have Supervisor rights to the NetWare server and to the NDS container in which NAL will be installed. You also need the rights to change the schema on the NDS tree.

The workstations to be used for the installation of applications using the NAL must have access to the NetWare server. This requires a physical network connection to the server as well as the correct rights configured for the workstations' users.

Client Workstations The workstations (the ones that ultimately run the application) that can be supported by NAL include those that use the following operating systems: Windows 95, Windows 98, Windows NT, and Windows 3.x. When you deploy an application to different types of workstations, each type typically requires that you create a different application object.

NOTE Although there is not yet a Windows 98 client with the Z.E.N.works Starter Pack, you can install the Windows 95 client on a Windows 98 machine and it should work fine.

When you configure the properties for an application object, you will identify the object as an application compatible with Windows 95, NT, or 3.x when it is deployed. (Windows 95 application objects appear to Windows 98 computers.) A user at a NAL-enabled workstation won't even see an application that isn't noted as compatible with its operating system. (For example, a Microsoft Office 97 application object does not appear to a Windows 3.x or Windows NT version released before 3.51.)

NOTE With a few minor modifications, the same application object can be deployed to both Windows 95 and Windows NT workstations. A procedure for doing this will soon be available from the Z.E.N.works site (**www.zenworks.com**). Check for links to this procedure in the Tip of the Week section of this Web site.

To the end user at the workstation, the application's icon appears in the locations defined by the administrator (such as the NAL window, Explorer window, Start menu, Desktop, or system tray). The first time the user opens the icon, the software is automatically installed to the user's workstation and the application is launched. After that, opening the icon simply launches the application locally. Software will be installed again only if the administrator changes the application object.

Clean Administrative Workstations A Microsoft Office application object that is distributed by NAL consists of the complete set of files, registry entries, and other components that result from installing Office. That application object is created by the following:

1. Discovering all components on the entire drive (or several drives) of a workstation
2. Installing Microsoft Office
3. Rediscovering the contents of the drive
4. Creating an application template from the differences between the first and second discoveries

The template and the new files, registry entries, and so on that make up the application are copied to a NetWare server. Using the NWAdmn32 command, you can then turn the template into an application object and set a variety of properties for it.

Novell highly recommends starting this process with a clean workstation—one with little more than the operating system installed and the network properly configured. The cleaner the computer is, the faster the drive can be scanned.

The workstation for creating the application object needs to match the workstation that will use the application. So you might need clean Windows 95, Windows 98, Windows NT, and Windows 3.x workstations if you support all these configurations.

To start with a clean computer each time you create an application object, you can use disk image software to copy and restore a working image of your disk. Two products you might want to look into are PowerQuest Drive Image (**www.powerquest.com**) and Ghost (**www.ghost.com**).

Z.E.N.works Software Although NAL began as a free add-on product for NetWare 4, it is now officially part of the Z.E.N.works product from Novell. To get you started, the Z.E.N.works Starter Pack (which includes all NAL software) is contained on the CD that comes with this book. To get the full Z.E.N.works product, you have to purchase it.

The Z.E.N.works Starter Pack contains these two components:

- **Novell Application Launcher (NAL).** NAL is used to deploy and manage applications across the enterprise. Information about how NAL works and how to use it to install Microsoft Office is described in the rest of this chapter.
- **Novell Workstation Manager.** This component lets you gather information about the workstations in your enterprise.

The complete Z.E.N.works product contains three additional major features:

- **Remote Control.** This component lets you remotely manage your company's workstations based on information stored in NDS.
- **Help Requester.** This application provides utilities that help end users resolve their workstation problems and allow them to troubleshoot their own problems on the network. It also helps create a database of contacts so that users can more easily determine whom to contact for their particular problem.
- **Hardware Inventory.** This utility allows you to associate actions with workstation objects that you gather in the NDS. For example, you can remotely determine which workstations need more memory, require changes to printer settings, or have an outdated BIOS. Often you will be able to correct the problem remotely.

Z.E.N.works is rich in administrative features and extremely flexible. For more information about Z.E.N.works, see the Z.E.N.works Cool Solutions page (**www.novell.com/coolsolutions/zenworks**). Select the article titled "The Basics" for a description of what you need to know to use Z.E.N.works.

Before you can use NAL, you must install the following components from the Z.E.N.works Starter Pack:

- **Server software.** This includes the tools that are installed on the NetWare server. (The install screen button is labeled "Install Z.E.N.works.")
- **Client software.** This includes the tools that are installed on the client workstations that will ultimately use the application object. There are different installation paths for Windows 95, Windows NT, and Windows 3.x clients. (The install screen buttons are labeled "Windows 95 Client," "Windows NT Client," and "Windows 3.x Client." Use Windows 95 client for Windows 98 computers.)

To install Z.E.N.works server software, you must be logged in to the NDS tree as Admin from a Windows 95, Windows 98, or Windows NT workstation. After the software is installed, you can add a nwadmn32.exe icon to each administrative workstation from sys:public\win32 on the NetWare server.

More-detailed instructions for setting up Z.E.N.works can be found in the help file that comes with Z.E.N.works. Look for dmpolicy.hlp in the zenworks\public\nls\english directory. Also, for information about how to design an NDS tree that can be used with Z.E.N.works, look for the zendsgn.htm document that comes with the Z.E.N.works Starter Pack.

Creating the Microsoft Office Application Template

If the prerequisites have been fulfilled (the NetWare server is accessible and Z.E.N.works has been installed), you are ready to create the application template for Microsoft Office. Start from the clean computer (running Windows 95, Windows 98, Windows NT, or Windows 3.x) and have your Microsoft Office CD-ROM ready for installation.

NOTE Remember that the workstation you use here must be the same as the type of workstation that will run the application later. For example, you cannot create an application template to run on Windows 3.1 from a Windows 95 workstation.

When you follow the procedure to create your Microsoft Office application template, the following components are installed on a NetWare server directory:

- All the files that make up an installed Microsoft Office application. These files will appear as numbered files with a .fil extension.
- A filedef.txt file that identifies where all the files should be placed on the target system. This is a text file that you can read if you are curious.
- An Application Template file (binary version), given the name of the application and an .aot extension.
- An Application Template file (text version), given the name of the application and an .axt extension.

The AOT and AXT files contain identical information. Both contain the data needed to re-create the application on the user's workstation, including registry entries, INI identifiers, and file changes. However, you can read the AXT file with a text editor; and AOT is about half the size and runs faster when you build the application object.

Later, when you use NWAdmn32 to create the application object from the application template, you will be asked whether to use the AXT or AOT file. Use the AXT file only if you need to make some manual changes to it. (Manual editing is not recommended, however, because it can cause errors.)

Following is the procedure to create a Microsoft Office application template:

1. Start snAppShot (from products\zenworks\public\snapshot\snapshot.exe on the NetWare server). The snAppShot dialog box appears, as shown in Figure 22.2.

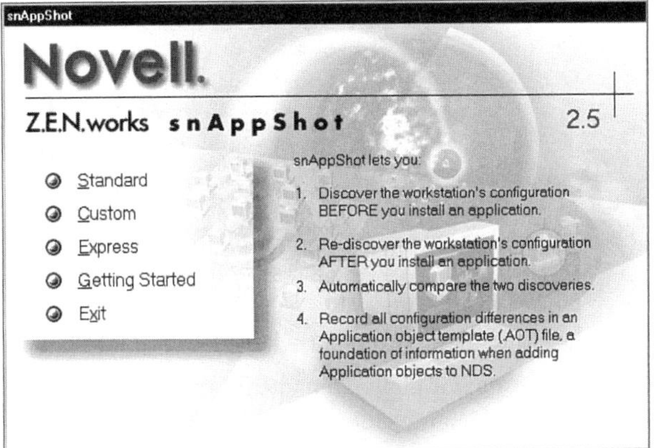

FIGURE 22.2
Create an application template from snAppShot.

2. Choose either Standard, Custom, or Express to discover the contents of your workstation. (This procedure assumes the Standard option.) Following are the descriptions of each choice:
   - Standard uses default settings to discover the contents of the disk.
   - Custom lets you specifically choose the files and folders, INI files, system configuration files, Windows shortcuts, and registry hives to include or exclude during discovery.
   - Express relies on a snAppShot Preferences file (created during a previous discovery) to use for comparison.

   After you make your choice, a dialog box appears, asking you to name the application object and the title on the application's icon.

3. Type the name of the application object and a name to use on the application icon and click on Next. ("MS Office" will be used for both names in this example. Later, application names will be changed to match each executable: Word, Excel, and so on.) A dialog box asks where to install the application files and NAL application template files that are distributed by snAppShot.
4. Browse for or enter the name of a folder to hold the files that will make up the application object, and then click on Next. (I strongly recommend putting the files on the NetWare server where the application object will eventually be installed. Otherwise, you will have to copy them there later manually.) Figure 22.3 identifies the location for the application template files as the "sys\Snapshot\MS Office" directory on a server named "madlad."

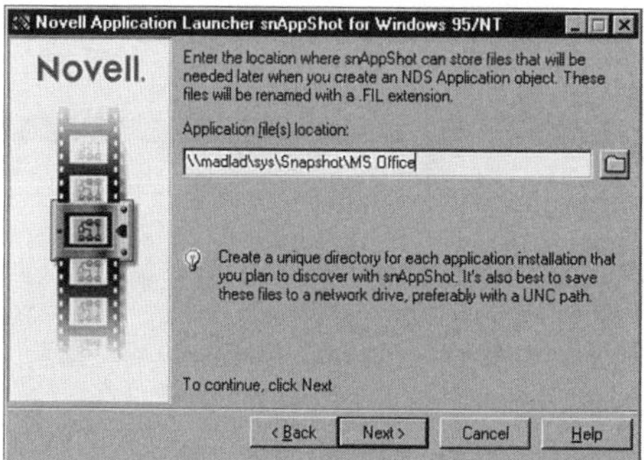

FIGURE 22.3
Copy application template files to the server or hard disk.

A dialog box asks you to name and provide a location for the application template file.

5. Type or browse for the location and name for the application and click on Next. (You should use the same location entered in the previous step. In this example I entered `\\madlad\sys\Snapshot\MS Office\MS Office.AOT`.) A dialog box asks which drives you want to scan.
6. Enter the drive you want to scan and click on Next. (Typically you will simply enter `C:`. However, you need to enter any drive that the application will be installed on.) A dialog box appears, showing you a summary of the settings you just entered.
7. Scroll through the settings, then click on Next. (You can also click on Save Preferences to save the settings you just entered to use on another scan.) At this point, snAppShot scans your drive to determine the current state of the components on your computer. When the scan is done, snAppShot asks you to install the application.

CAUTION

Don't change any files or settings on your computer from this point on except for those files that relate to the installation and configuration of the application (in this case, Microsoft Office). Files or settings you add or change before the entire snAppShot completes will end up as part of the application object that is distributed.

8. Leave the snAppShot application alone for the moment (minimize it or move it aside, but don't close it) and install Microsoft Office as you would on the local computer.
9. After Microsoft Office is installed, change any settings to suit your preferences. For example, you might want to remove icons or change preferences for any of the Office applications.
10. When Microsoft Office is configured exactly as you like it, go back to the snAppShot dialog box (it may have changed to a Waiting for Application Installation to Finish dialog box), and click on Next. A dialog box appears, asking for the location of the application's install directory.
11. Type the location of the Microsoft Office install directory. (For example, you might have used `C:\Program Files`.) Your computer is rescanned to gather the results from the installation of Microsoft Office, and then it generates the application template. When the template is complete, the snAppShot Completion Summary dialog box appears.

NOTE The rescan after installing Microsoft Office will take a while (possibly several hours). Several hundred files need to be gathered and more than 15,000 changed registry entries must be stored. Be patient. ■

12. Scroll through the Completion Summary dialog box to review where files are located and what the next steps are. You should click on the Print button to print out this information.
13. Click on Finish to complete the snAppShot process.

At this point, you should have all the application files (FIL) and template files (AOT and AXT) you need to create the application stored in a directory on the server. If for some reason you distributed these files to the local hard disk, you should go ahead now and copy them to a directory on the NetWare server from which the application object will be created.

If you want to create an application object that can be used in either a Windows 95 or Windows NT workstation, some special modifications have to be made.

Now you are ready to create application objects for each of the applications in the Microsoft Office suite (Word, Excel, and so on) on the server.

Creating the Microsoft Office Application Objects

Using the NetWare Administrator (NWAdmn32) command with enhancements that were added when you installed Z.E.N.works, you can make application objects out of the files and template you created for Microsoft Office using snAppShot. Because Microsoft Office consists of several applications, you should create one application object for each of the following applications:

- Microsoft Word
- Microsoft Excel
- Microsoft PowerPoint
- Microsoft Outlook
- Microsoft Binder

To store these application objects, you must create application folders on the NetWare server. Rights to access these folders must be assigned. (Later, each user who is granted access to an application through NAL can have the application appear in his or her NAL window, Explorer window, Start menu, Desktop, or system tray, as you define.)

Each application object will also have its own set of properties. The properties define such things as which workstation types it can run on, when the application is available, and the rights associated with the application (in other words, who can use it). Although most of the properties will be the same for the Microsoft Office application objects you create (for Word, Excel, and so on), you will at least need to set a different icon name, icon, and executable file for each application object.

When all the Microsoft Office application objects are complete, all these application objects need to be grouped under one Global Unique Identifier (GUID). This way, after a user has installed any Office application, running any of the other applications will not also run the installation of the entire Microsoft Office again from the server.

The following procedure assumes you have already created an application template (using snAppShot) for Microsoft Office and that the files associated with that template are available on your NetWare server.

Follow these steps to create the Microsoft Office application objects:

1. Run NWAdmn32. The NetWare Administrator window appears.
2. Create an application folder to contain the Microsoft Office application objects as follows:
    - Right-click on the object (such as an Organization Unit or Country) that you want to contain the new application folder.
    - Click on Create, Application Folder, and OK.
    - Type a name for the folder, choose Define Additional Properties, and click on OK.
    - Click on the Folders button.
    - Click on Add, Folder and type a name for the folder (such as MS Office 97).
    - Add subfolders if you like.
3. Create an application object for the first Microsoft Office application as follows:
    - Click on the application folder you just created.
    - Click on Object, then Create, then Application.

    A Create Application Object dialog box appears, as shown in Figure 22.4.
4. Select Create an Application Object with an .aot/.axt File (as shown in the figure) and click on Next. A dialog box asks you for the path to the AOT or AXT file. Figure 22.5 shows this dialog box with the location of the AOT file on the NetWare server used in an earlier procedure.

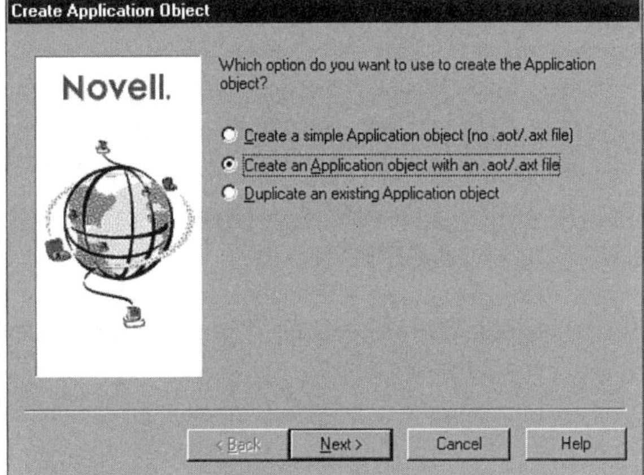

FIGURE 22.4
Create a Microsoft Office application template from NetWare Administrator.

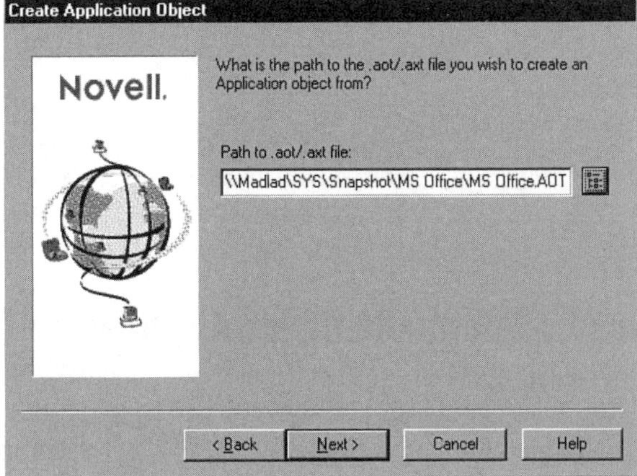

FIGURE 22.5
Identify the location of the application template files you created.

5. Type the full path to the AOT file (or AXT file) that is on the NetWare server and click on Next. (Remember that the server name should be preceded by two backslashes.) A dialog box asks you to add customize information to the new application object.
6. Add the following customized information:
   - **Object Name.** This name identifies the object in the folder. You should change this name to match the first application object you create, such as "MS Office Word."
   - **SOURCE_PATH.** Type the location of the FIL files that were created with the application template. (This is probably the same folder that contains the AOT file.)
   - **TARGET_PATH.** Enter the directory on the client workstation where the programs will appear. (You can probably accept the default of %*WinSysDisk% \Program Files.)

After this information is added, click on Next. A review of the application object information you created appears.

7. After you have reviewed the information, click on Create Another Application Object After This One, and then select Finish. The new application object is created, and then a dialog box appears asking you how to create the next application object.
8. Click on Duplicate an Existing Application Object, and then click on Next. A dialog box asks you the name of the application you want to duplicate.
9. Type (or browse for) the name of the application object you just created. (For example, you might have called it "Microsoft Office Word.") A dialog box appears, asking you to customize the new application object.
10. Return to step 6, but this time type the object name for the next application (For example, you might want to call this new application "Microsoft Office Excel.")

CAUTION

Make sure you type a new object name! Problems can occur if you have two applications in the same folder with the same name. The source path and target path will probably be the same as they were for the previous application object.

11. Repeat the remaining steps until you are finished with all the application objects (one for each of the five Microsoft Office applications). For the last application object, just click Finish without creating another application object.

Adding Properties to Microsoft Office Application Objects

After you have created an application object for each program in the Microsoft Office suite, you need to change the properties of each of those objects. The application object properties define who has access to the object, what executable is run, what types of workstations can run the object, and a variety of other features.

The following procedure assumes you have already created an application object (using the NetWare Administrator) for each application in the Microsoft Office suite and you are now ready to set each object's properties.

Run NWAdmn32 to display the NetWare Administrator window, and then follow these steps to modify the properties pages of your application objects:

1. Find the first Microsoft Office application object you created (for example, MS Office Word), right-click on it, then select Details. This is illustrated in Figure 22.6.

   The Identification properties page appears, as shown in Figure 22.7.
2. On the Identification properties page, you must set unique values for Application Icon Title, Path to Executable File, and Application Icon. Here are examples of what you can use for applications in the Microsoft Office 97 suite.

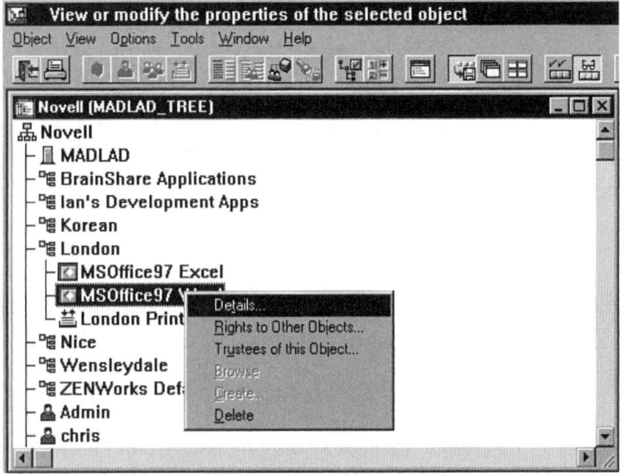

FIGURE 22.6
Open the properties for an MS Office application object.

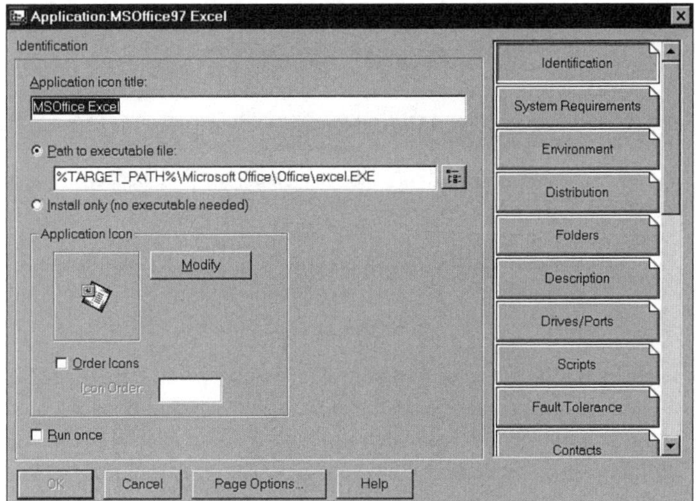

FIGURE 22.7
Set the icon title, executable, and icon values on the Identification properties page.

Table 22.1 Applications in Microsoft Office 97

Application	Application Icon Title	Path to Executable File
Binder	MSOffice97 Binder	%TARGET_PATH%\Microsoft Office\Office\binder.exe
Excel	MSOffice97 Excel	%TARGET_PATH%\Microsoft Office\Office\excel.exe
Outlook	MSOffice97 Outlook	%TARGET_PATH%\Microsoft Office\Office\outlook.exe

continues

Table 22.1 Continued

Application	Application Icon Title	Path to Executable File
PowerPoint	MSOffice97 PowerPoint	%TARGET_PATH%\Microsoft Office\Office\powerpnt.exe
Word	MSOffice97 Word	%TARGET_PATH%\Microsoft Office\Office\winword.exe

3. Click on the System Requirements button to set the properties associated with the types of workstations that will be able to use the application object. Here is what you can change:
   - **Operating System.** Select Windows 3.x, Windows 95, or Windows NT. The application object will appear only on workstations that are running the selected operating systems. (Use Windows 95 for Windows 98 computers.) You can also indicate that a particular major and minor version of the system is able to use the application.

CAUTION

An application object created on a Windows 3.x workstation can only be used on other Windows 3.x systems. Windows 95 and Windows NT applications can be shared between those two systems, but only if some modifications are made to the application template, as noted earlier in this chapter.

   - **Display applications on machines that have at least....** You can require that an application be made available to only those workstations that have at least a certain amount of RAM and free disk space.
4. Click on the Environment button to set properties that change how the application is run. Typically, changes to these properties are not needed. You may, however, want to add command-line parameters to the executable, change the application to run as minimized or maximized (instead of normal), or define a file to enable error logging. Clean Up Network Resources is particularly important if an application remaps drives or captures ports that must be released when all applications that use the resource exit.
5. Click on the Distribution button to set properties relating to how the application is distributed. You should mark Show Distribution Progress and Prompt Before Distribution, and Prompt User for Reboot Always. These settings keep the application from taking over the user's computer without asking first. For example, if a user casually opens an application icon and Prompt Before Distribution is not selected, the user gets no chance to prevent what might be an hour-long application distribution to his or her workstation.
6. Click on the Folders button to set folder properties for the application object. This dialog box identifies the folder containing the application object and lets you add the application object to additional folders.

7. Click on the Description button to add or change a description of the application object. This lets the administrator keep track of the services provided by the application object.
8. Click on the Drives/Ports button to add or modify drives that need to be mapped or ports that need to be captured for the application object. (If you map drives or capture ports, make sure that Clean Up Network Resources is selected on the Environment properties page so the resources will be released when the application exits.)
9. Click on the Scripts button to add any scripts that should be run before launching or after terminating the application.
10. Click on the Fault Tolerance button to add information to help make sure the application is always accessible, even when the server is not available. Add load-balancing objects to ensure that, if the application object is not available, another application object chosen randomly from the objects you enter can be delivered. Add fault-tolerance objects if you would like an application object that is not available to be replaced by objects in a specific order.
11. Click on the Contacts button to add information on whom end users can contact if they have problems with this application object.
12. Click on the Associations button to indicate which objects (such as an organizational unit, organization, country, user, or group) can use this application object. Click on Add, and then browse for the object to be associated with the application object. (Although all applications are displayed to the user by default in either the NAL window or Explorer window, setting an association lets you add icons later to the user's Start menu, Desktop, or system tray.)
13. Click on the Administrator Notes button to add notes about the application object that are only available to the administrator of the object. This is a way to track changes to the application object or add reminders of tasks you need to do with the object.
14. Click on the Macros button to add macros that can help simplify items used in the creation of the application object, such as long pathnames. For example, this page will always include a definition of the SOURCE_PATH and TARGET_PATH macros to define where the application's source files and output files are placed, respectively. You can easily change all references to a macro value at once by changing it on the Macros properties page. To reference a macro, you need to surround it with percent signs (for example, %SOURCE_PATH%).
15. Click on the Registry Settings button to view all the registry settings that are modified by the application object. You can also make changes to or create additional registry changes for the application object using this page. Figure 22.8 shows an example of an application object's registry settings.
16. Click on the INI Settings button to display and modify any INI file changes associated with the application object.
17. Click on the Application Files button to display, add, modify, or delete files that make up the application object.

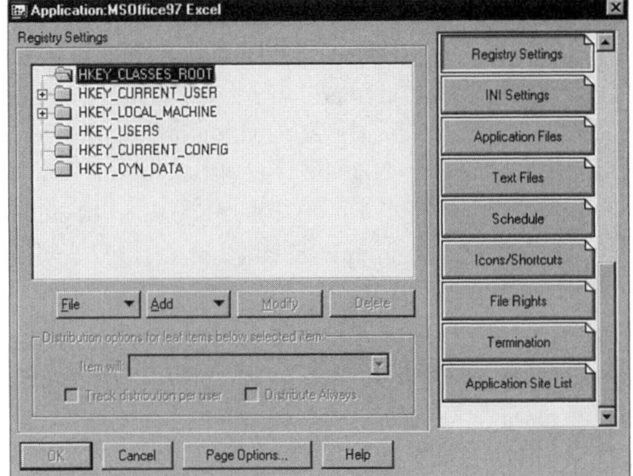

FIGURE 22.8
Display and change Windows registry settings for an application object.

18. Click on the Text Files button to add, modify, or delete additional text files to go with the application object. For example, you could import additional text files created with snAppShot into this page so that the new files can be distributed with the application object.
19. Click on the Schedule button to schedule the application to be available only at particular times. Typically, you would want the application to be available to your users all the time. However, you can change the schedule to have the application only available during a range of days (such as Monday through Friday) or only at certain times (for example, making games available to run only after work hours).
20. Click on the Icons/Shortcuts button to view, add, modify, or delete the icons and shortcuts that are associated with the application object.
21. Click on the File Rights button to add rights to volume objects and paths that are associated with the application object. You can assign supervisor, read, write, create, erase, modify, file-scan, and access-control rights to the volume.
22. Click on the Termination button if you want to define behavior that will occur when the administrator needs to terminate the application on the users' workstations. You can send messages of your choosing at set intervals and then terminate the application after the time expires.
23. Click on the Application Site List button to associate the application with different locations. The advantage of using this feature is that if a user travels to different offices in the company, the application object might be deployed more efficiently from the location the user is currently visiting.
24. When you are satisfied with the properties changes you have made, click on OK.
25. Repeat this procedure for each of the Microsoft Office application objects you have created.

To prevent the entire Microsoft Office suite from being installed each time an application is run, you need to synchronize the application objects. To do this, you must have all the objects assigned to a single Global Unique Identifier (GUID).

After you sync the GUIDs, the whole Office distribution will be installed the first time a user executes any one of the synced Office application objects. When a user later opens any of the other application objects, that application just runs without any additional installation.

Following is how you sync the GUIDs:

1. From the NetWare Administrator window, highlight all the application objects in the Microsoft Office distribution.
2. Click on Tools, Application Launcher Tools, Sync Distribution GUIDs. The application objects are immediately synced together.

The final steps in making Microsoft Office available to your users from NAL involves defining where the icons for the application objects appear. By selecting the User, Group, Organization, or Organizational Unit object associated with the application objects, you can define where on the users' workstations the icons for each application appear.

Following is how to assign launch options:

1. From the NetWare Administrator window, open the User, Group, Organization, or Organizational Unit object associated with the Microsoft Office application objects.
2. Click on the Applications button. A dialog box listing the applications associated with the object is displayed, as shown in Figure 22.9. (This example shows an organization called Novell and the application objects assigned to it.)

FIGURE 22.9
Assign application objects to appear on user workstations.

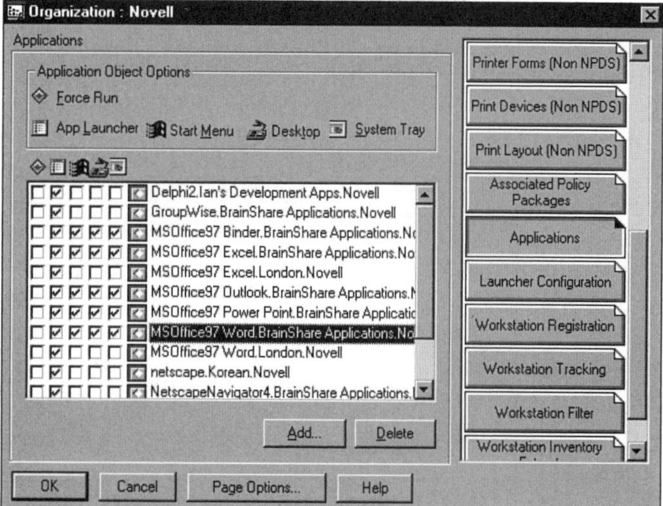

3. Scroll to find the application objects you created for Microsoft Office.
4. Select any of the following to turn on icons on the workstations of members of this object:
   - Novell Application Launcher Window
   - Windows Start Menu
   - Windows Desktop
   - Windows System Tray
5. Click on OK.

The icons are now available to appear in the selected location on the users' workstations.

Distributing Microsoft Office to the Workstations

After you have completed the administrative procedures for preparing the Microsoft Office application objects for deployment with NAL, users can immediately use the applications from their workstations. For the user, it is easy.

As noted earlier, the users who are set up to use NAL will automatically see the application icons in one of several locations on their workstations (depending on how you defined it). From Windows Explorer, the NAL window, the Start menu, the Desktop, or the system tray, a user can open the NAL-delivered application—and it will be installed on the local workstation (if necessary) and then run.

Launching Applications from Windows Explorer In the standard Windows Explorer window (accessible by clicking on Start, Applications, and Windows Explorer), an Application Explorer folder will appear. In that folder, the user will see the NDS tree that includes the application folders and application objects that are delivered by NAL.

Figure 22.10 shows an Explorer window with the MS Office 97 folder displaying the application objects that you have created. A user simply double-clicks on the icon to use the application.

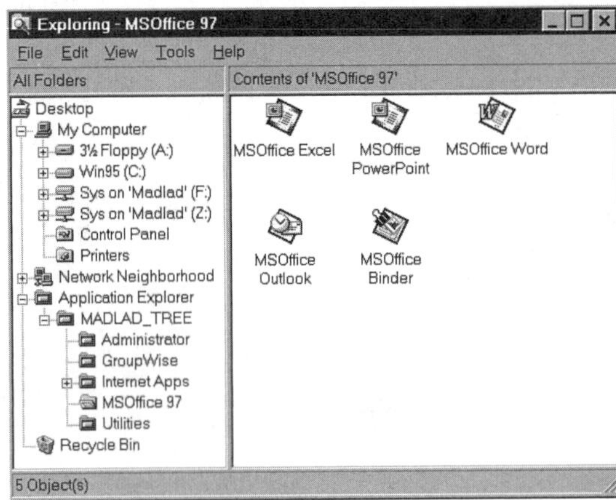

FIGURE 22.10
View and launch NAL application from Windows Explorer.

CAUTION

The feature for adding NAL applications to Windows Explorer is not available in Windows 3.x operating systems. In those cases, users must run NAL applications from the NAL window.

To make the NAL features of Windows Explorer available to a user's workstation, you can add the following text to the user's login script:

```
if platform = "w95" then
        @\\server\sys\public\nalexpld.exe
    end
    if platform = "wnt" then
        if os_version = "v4.00" then
             @\\server\sys\public\nalexpld.exe
        end
end
```

Here *server* is replaced by the name of the NetWare server that contains the nalexpld.exe command.

Launching Applications from the NAL Window The Novell Application Launcher window is another way a user can view the applications that are made available from NAL.

Figure 22.11 shows the NAL window with the MS Office 97 folder open and displaying the installed Microsoft Office application objects you have created. Notice that the window also contains an item labeled Start Menu. This item contains all the items in the workstation's local Start menu. This allows the user to maximize the NAL window and have all network-deployed and local applications available from one window.

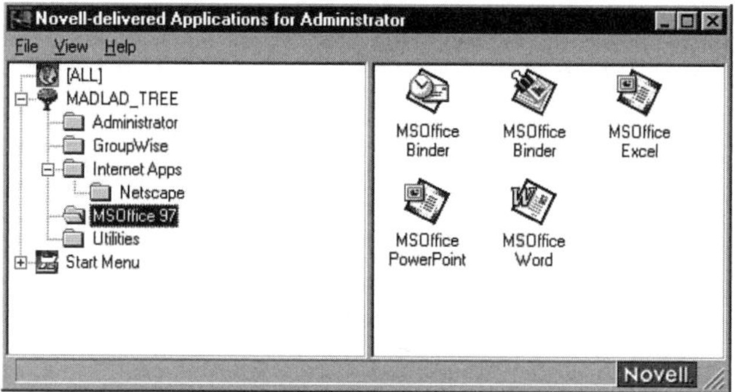

FIGURE 22.11
Users can display Novell-delivered applications from the NAL window.

NOTE A change to NAL applications, such as adding an application icon, may not immediately appear on a user's workstation. For a user to receive the changes, have the user choose View, Refresh in the NAL window.

You can start the NAL window from sys:public\nal.exe on the server. However, the preferred way is to run nal.exe from a user login script. You can do this by adding one of the following lines to the user's login script:

```
#\\server\sys\public\nal.exe
```

or

```
@\\ server \sys\public\nal.exe
```

Here *server* is replaced by the name of the NetWare server that contains the nal.exe command. ●

CHAPTER 23

Using Office with Lotus Groupware and Mail Systems

What's a chapter on a Lotus product doing in a book on Microsoft Office? Aren't Lotus and Microsoft as diametrically opposed in the marketplace as they are on opposite sides of the country (Cambridge, Massachusetts versus Redmond, Washington)? As an administrator responsible for Microsoft Office applications, why should you care about Lotus Notes? To put it simply, with the sheer volume of Notes licenses in the marketplace, you are bound to encounter Notes at some point in your career. Believe it or not, Lotus and Microsoft do work together, as you'll see in this chapter.

What Is Groupware?

At the heart of the information age is knowledge. A business lives and dies by its capability to utilize, manage, and share information—turning raw data into knowledge. The term *groupware* (group information management software) is a loosely defined concept that refers to a type of application that lets groups of people collaborate to create, share, and use information more effectively. Since the inception and ensuing popularity of Lotus Notes, groupware has really caught on. Groupware promotes working together in teams. This fits in well with today's business climate, where teams are encouraged and heavily emphasized in almost every sector of business. These concepts have made their way into Microsoft Office as well—Microsoft has added version control, security, document routing, and so forth to Office applications to enable collaboration among team members.

What Is Lotus Notes?

Lotus Development Corporation introduced Lotus Notes in 1989. By the time Release 3 was introduced in 1994, there were approximately one million users. Today, Lotus has around 25 million licenses in the market place, and Notes is the premier groupware application. Lotus has concentrated heavily on enabling Notes to work within almost any environment, including Microsoft Office applications. It is a client/server application—meaning that it uses a server, called the Domino server, to provide services to clients. To cite a few services, the Domino server hosts database applications, calendaring and scheduling, and mail. Clients can be Web browsers or Lotus Notes clients. Clients and servers are available for many different platforms, from the PC to the AS/400, and even for the mainframe.

It is impossible to adequately describe Notes in a single chapter. Fortunately, Notes has extensive help and reference databases that are installed with the product. There are also a number of very good books on Notes that you can turn to for more information, including *Que's Special Edition Using Lotus Notes and Domino 4.6* by Cate Richards and *Lotus Notes and Domino Server 4.6 Unleashed* by Randy Tamura, et al.

NOTE The terms Notes and Domino can be somewhat confusing. Notes generally refers to the client, and Domino refers to the server. However, Notes is frequently used to refer to both the client and the server. ■

What Is a Notes Database?

A Notes database (or Domino database) is not quite like other databases that you may be familiar with, such as FoxPro, SQL Server, or Sybase. While some database applications in Notes may consist of more than one database, a database itself is self-contained: the file has all the code as well as the data for the application. A Notes client and server can support many, many database applications. Servers can host one thousand or more mail files, and at the same time host many discussion and other database applications.

Databases are represented on the Notes workspace by an icon, a small rectangular area that contains a graphic and the title of the database. The icon for your mail file, for example, displays your name and an image of an envelope. Because the Notes client contains the "front end" of the application—the menus for printing, viewing, editing, and so on—the database files are relatively small. They contain only the code necessary for the functionality specific to that database application. Some applications involve more than one database. In order to address your email, the mail database looks up information in two other databases, the Public Address Book and your Personal Address Book.

In other databases, such as FoxPro or SQL Server, only the data resides in the database file. The application programs are completely separate files, and must be built from the ground up. For example, you have to create a menu system specifically for the application and program all the actions. As a consequence, these applications are generally made up of many files, and can be quite large in comparison to Notes databases.

Notes databases contain documents, which are roughly analogous to records in other database systems. Documents are presented to users in views and folders. While Notes is similar to other database systems, it is not a relational database. Notes is unstructured, meaning that unlike a record in an relational database table, a document does not have a fixed length or a fixed set of fields.

Notes comes with quite a few database templates, which you can use to create fully functional applications. Notes databases have the file extension .nsf (Notes Storage Facility) and templates have the extension .ntf (Notes Template Facility). These templates are an excellent way to put Notes into production quickly. The most commonly used templates are the Discussion and Document Library templates. As a Notes database administrator or developer, you simply base the design of a new database on a template, and you have a fully functional application! The section "Using the Microsoft Office Document Library Database," later in this chapter, discusses a database built using one of these templates.

Using Office with Notes Mail

Notes Mail is really just a specialized Notes database application on the Domino server. Like Lotus cc:Mail, Microsoft Outlook, and Netscape Communicator, Notes Mail supports rich text. In other words, you can use different font faces, font sizes, and font colors in your messages. You can also embed files and images in the body of a mail message.

This chapter discusses the standard Notes client. However, depending on the release of your Notes server, and what your Notes administrator is running on the server, you may be able to access Notes Mail using other clients as well.

Figure 23.1 shows the Notes Mail interface. The Navigator pane in the upper-left corner of the window allows you to move through the various folders in your mail database. The View pane on the far right lists your message headers. The Preview pane at the bottom of the window displays the contents of your messages. You can turn the Preview pane on and off. When it's on, it displays the top portion of the current message. When it's off, the Navigator and View panes occupy the entire window. You can also open a message into a separate window by double-clicking its header in the View pane.

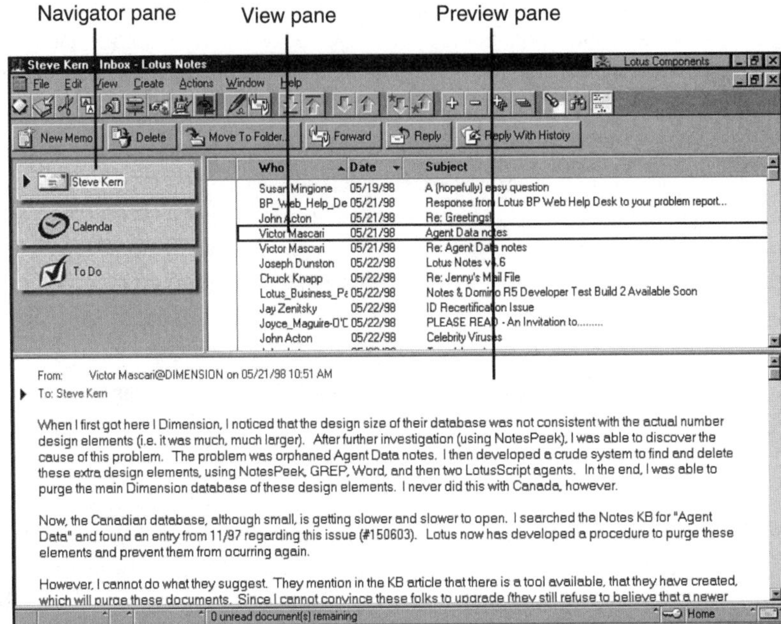

FIGURE 23.1
You can use the Preview pane to view your messages.

You can use Office with Notes Mail in two principal ways: you can use Word as an alternate mail editor, and you can route Office documents via Notes Mail.

Using Word as Your Mail Editor

With Notes Release 4.6, the option of using another mail editor became available. The Notes 4.6 client is a 32-bit application that is only available on the Win32 platforms: Windows 95/98 and Windows NT. Because it is 32-bit, Notes 4.6 can use Windows ActiveDoc technology to work with other mail editors. The mail editors that are currently certified are Lotus Word Pro 97, Microsoft Word 95, and Microsoft Word 97. To enable Microsoft Word as your mail editor, take these steps:

1. Open the Notes client.
2. Choose File, Tools, User Preferences.
3. Click the Mail icon in the User Preferences dialog box.
4. Select Microsoft Word in the Document Memo Editor drop-down box (see Figure 23.2).
5. Click OK.

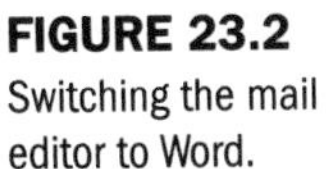

FIGURE 23.2
Switching the mail editor to Word.

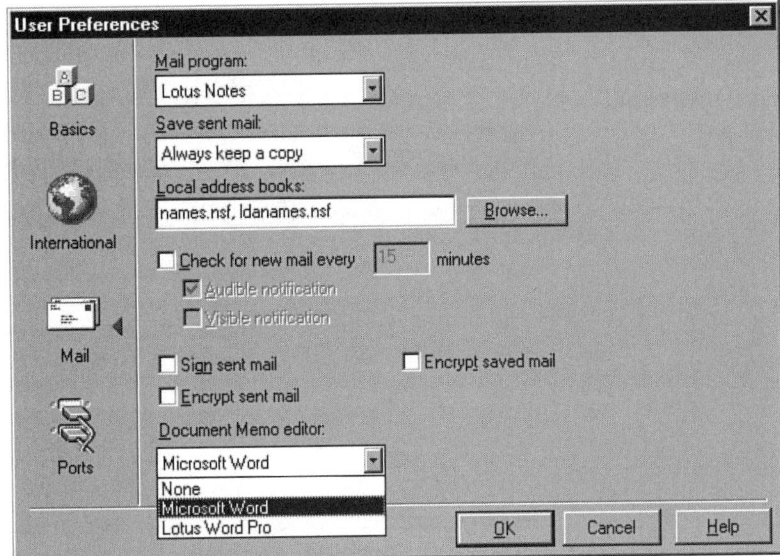

NOTE You must have a supported version of Word (or Word Pro) installed on your computer for this to work! ■

After you complete these steps, you can create a mail message using Word as your editor by opening your mail database and choosing Create, Word Memo.

If you are familiar with the standard Notes mail editor, you will definitely notice some changes! As shown in Figure 23.3, the standard Notes toolbar is replaced with the Word toolbars. There is a new Action button labeled Envelope. The address area is gone, replaced by a dialog box from which you choose recipients for your new memo. The memo itself is a blank Word document with rulers. (The rulers are there by default; you can hide them by choosing View, Ruler.)

Using Word as an alternate mail editor lets you prepare your memos in an application that you may be more familiar with. While the standard Notes editor is sufficient for most email messages, Word gives you more options for presenting your material because it is a full-featured word processor.

Routing Office Documents through Notes Mail

You can send any type of file through Notes Mail by attaching the file to a mail memo. You can also copy a file, such as a Word document, Excel spreadsheet, or graphic image to the Clipboard, and then paste it into the body of a Notes memo. You then address the memo and send it.

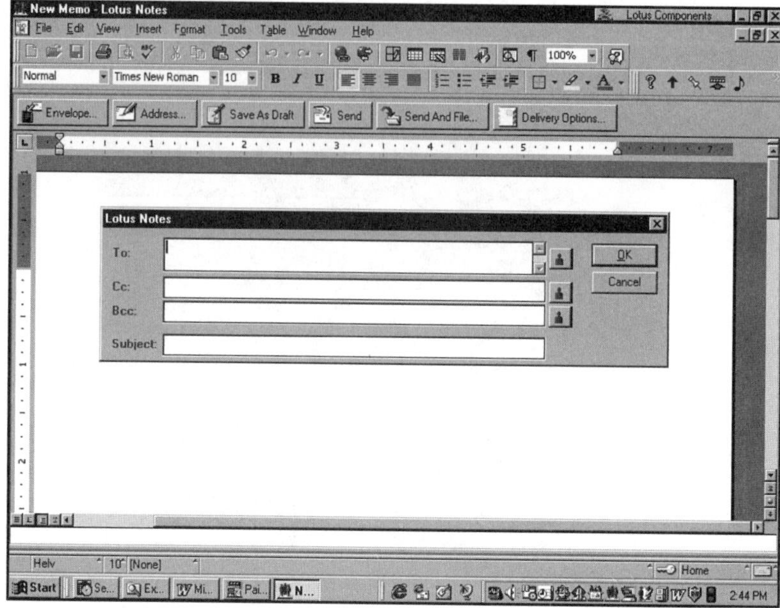

FIGURE 23.3
A mail memo composed using Word. Note the addressing dialog box.

Sending File Attachments To attach a file to a Notes mail memo, take these steps:

1. Open your mail database.
2. Click the New Memo button.
3. Address the memo, and enter a subject.
4. Choose File, Attach, and in the Create Attachment(s) dialog box, choose the file(s) you want to attach (see Figure 23.4).
5. Click the Create button.

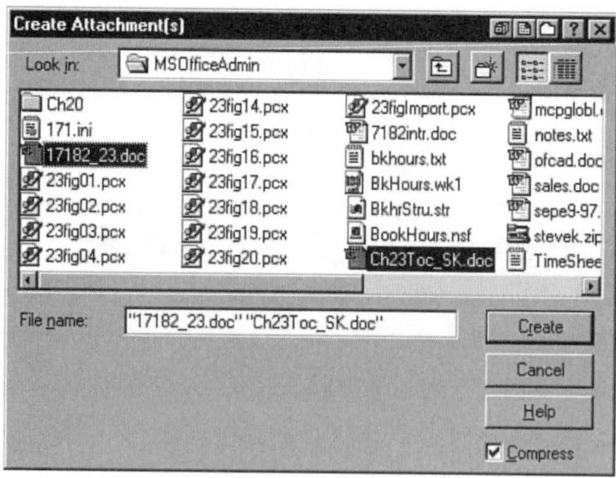

FIGURE 23.4
You can select more than one file in the Create Attachment(s) dialog box.

The file or files are now attached to your mail memo. Each attachment is represented by an icon in the body field (see Figure 23.5). If Notes recognizes the file type, it displays the appropriate icon.

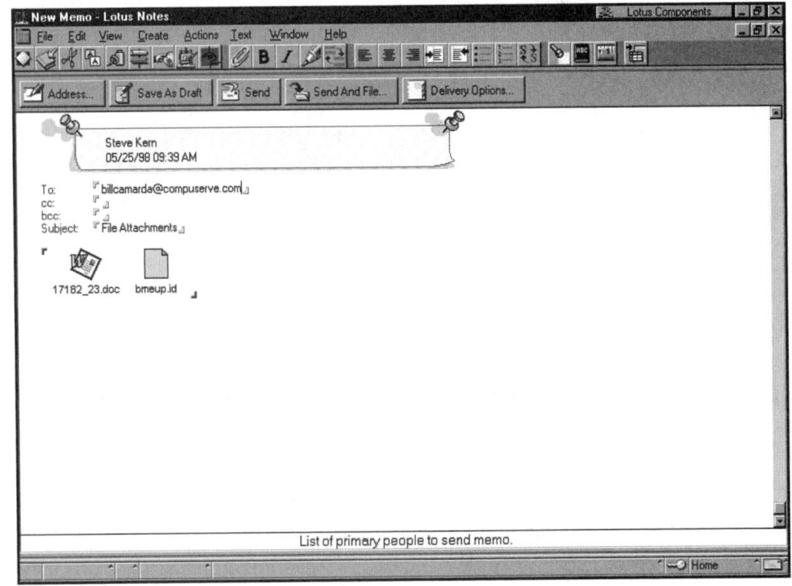

FIGURE 23.5
The familiar Word icon represents an attached Word document. The icon for an attachment of an unregistered file type is a gray page.

CAUTION

If the File, Attach command isn't available, it is probably because the insertion point is not in the body of the mail memo. You can only embed file attachments in a rich text field, which in a mail memo is the body field. The body field is not labeled, but it is immediately below the Subject field and is surrounded by red angle brackets (refer to Figure 23.5).

Working with File Attachments To open a file attachment, simply double-click the file icon. The Properties InfoBox appears with three buttons: View, Launch, and Detach. Clicking View launches a universal viewer that is capable of viewing most, but not all file types you are likely to encounter. Clicking Launch opens the attachment in the appropriate application. For example, clicking on the Word icon in Figure 23.5 and then clicking Launch opens the attached document in Word. The Launch button only works if the file type of the attachment is registered and you have a copy of the source application on your machine. Clicking Detach lets you copy the attached file to a local or network drive.

Pasting and Importing into a Mail Memo Pasting an image or part of a Word document or Excel spreadsheet into a mail memo is very straightforward. Simply select the image, text, or range, and then copy it to the Clipboard. Switch to the Notes memo, click in the body field, and paste the contents of the Clipboard into the memo. You can also link a document to a mail memo using OLE (Object Linking and Embedding), OLE 2 (the most recent version of OLE), or DDE (Dynamic Data Exchange). See "Attaching and Embedding Office Documents in Notes Databases" later in this chapter for further discussion.

You can also import certain file types directly into the body field of the memo. For more information, see "Importing Office Documents and Data into Lotus Notes" later in this chapter.

Tools for Integrating Office with Notes

The techniques that you use to integrate Office applications with Notes Mail are the same as those you use to integrate Office applications in other areas of Lotus Notes. For example, because Notes Mail is just a specialized database application, the technique for attaching files to a Notes mail memo is exactly the same as the one you use to attach a file to a discussion database or document library. You will learn about embedding, linking, importing and exporting. You also will read about a special Notes database that is dedicated to the Microsoft Office suite, the Microsoft Office Document Library.

Attaching and Embedding Office Documents in Notes Databases

OLE and OLE 2 are technologies that let applications share information. OLE is available on Windows and Macintosh operating systems. OLE 2 is available on 32-bit Windows platforms: Windows 95, 98, and NT. OLE clients can exchange information with OLE servers. Notes can act as an OLE client, and Excel and Word can act as an OLE server. OLE objects can be Word documents, Excel spreadsheets, or OLE custom controls (OCXs). (An OCX is also referred to as an *applet*. These applets are small modules that can interact with the underlying document and are based on OLE 2.) To create an OLE object in a Notes document, you must have the document open in Edit mode and the insertion point must be in a rich text field. Objects can be linked or embedded.

Linking Notes Documents to Office Documents You can link a Notes document to a source file, such as a Word document. When you do this, Notes stores a pointer to the source file, and when the source file changes, Notes updates the view of it in the Notes document. The drawback to this use of OLE is that each user who needs to edit the linked object must be able to run the application (Word, for example). Furthermore, users must have access to the physical file. If the file is stored on a file server, the drive mappings must be identical, or else OLE will fail. When the source file is moved or deleted, the link will again fail.

To create an OLE link, follow these steps:

1. Open the source document, and copy what you want to appear in Notes to the Clipboard.
2. Go to Notes, and open a document in Edit mode. Click in a rich text field.
3. Choose Edit, Paste Special.
4. In the Paste Special dialog box, select Paste Link to Source (see Figure 23.6).
5. Mark the Display As Icon check box, if you want.
6. Click OK, and save the document.

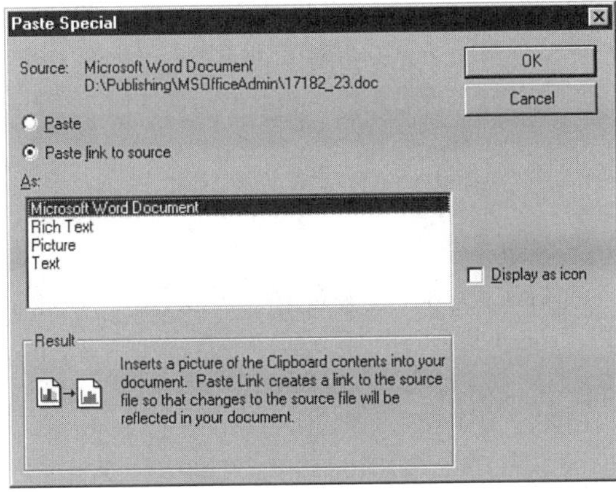

FIGURE 23.6
The Result area at the bottom of the dialog box changes with your selections.

Whenever you open the document, Notes prompts you to refresh the linked document, as shown in Figure 23.7.

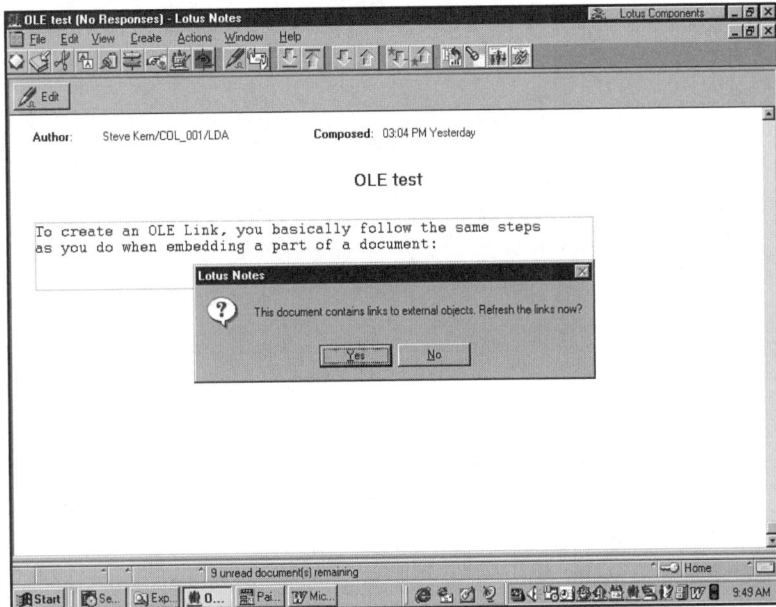

FIGURE 23.7
Notes offers to refresh the document link when you open it.

Embedding Office Documents in Notes *Embedding* files gets around some of the limitations of linking because a copy of the source file is stored in the Notes document. If the source file is changed, however, the embedded file will not reflect the change. The user still has to be able to run the source file's application to edit the embedded object. Embedding a file is useful when you want to share a file with another Notes user who may not have access to the file server, or who may be working remotely via dial-up access to the Notes server. This is slightly different than attaching a file, because you can use the source document's application to edit the object in Notes. You can embed all or part of a file inside a Notes document.

Follow these steps to embed an entire file:

1. Open a Notes document in Edit mode, and place the insertion point in a rich text field.
2. Choose Create, Object.
3. In the Create Object dialog box, choose Create an Object from a File (see Figure 23.8).
4. Enter the path and filename, or click the Browse button and browse to the file.
5. Mark the Display As Icon check box if desired.
6. Click OK.

The object is now embedded in your Notes document.

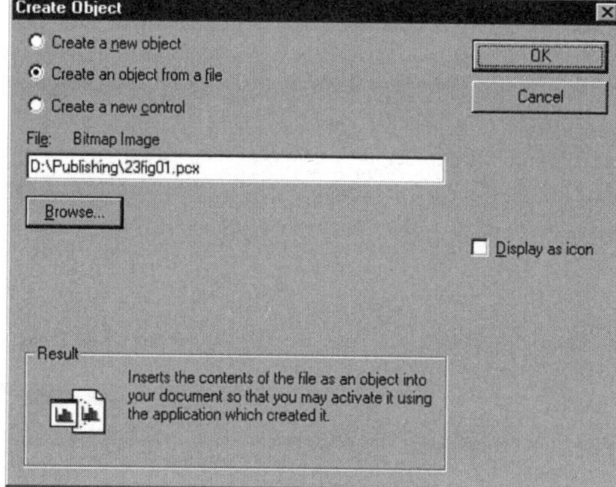

FIGURE 23.8
Embedding an object in a Notes document is simple.

Follow these steps to embed part of a file:

1. Copy the part of the file that you want to embed to the Clipboard.
2. Open the Notes document in Edit mode and place the insertion point in a rich text field.
3. Choose Edit, Paste Special.
4. Mark the Paste option button if necessary, and mark the Display As Icon check box if desired.
5. Click OK.

NOTE DDE, Dynamic Data Exchange, is an older but similar technology that is also available on OS2. It is more restrictive because both the server application (such as Word) and Notes must be open for it to work.

Importing Office Documents and Data into Lotus Notes

You can import information from applications external to Notes into two areas: documents and views. To import into a document, you must be in Edit mode, and the insertion point must be in a rich text field. You can import many different file types, from images (.bmp, .pcx, and so on) to Word documents (see Listing 23.1). When you import into a view, the range of choices is limited to Structured Text, Tabular Text, and Lotus 1-2-3 Worksheet. You typically import into a view when you want to create multiple documents; for example, if you have a spreadsheet of timesheet information, after importing it into a view, all the rows become documents.

Listing 23.1 File Types for Importing and Exporting to and from Notes Documents

Windows and OS/2
Ami Pro
ANSI Metafile
ASCII Text
Binary with Text
BMP Image
Excel 4.0/5.0
GIF Image
JPEG Image
Lotus PIC
Lotus 1-2-3 Worksheet
Microsoft Word RTF
PCX Image
TIFF 5.0 Image
WordPerfect 5*x*/6*x*
Word for Windows 6.0
Macintosh
ANSI Metafile
ASCII Text
Lotus 1-2-3 Worksheet
Microsoft Word RTF
TIFF 5.0 Image

To import a file into a document, follow this general procedure:

1. Make sure the document is in Edit mode, and that your insertion point is in a rich text field.
2. Choose File, Import.
3. Choose a file type to import, and select the file you want to import (see Figure 23.9).
4. Click Import.

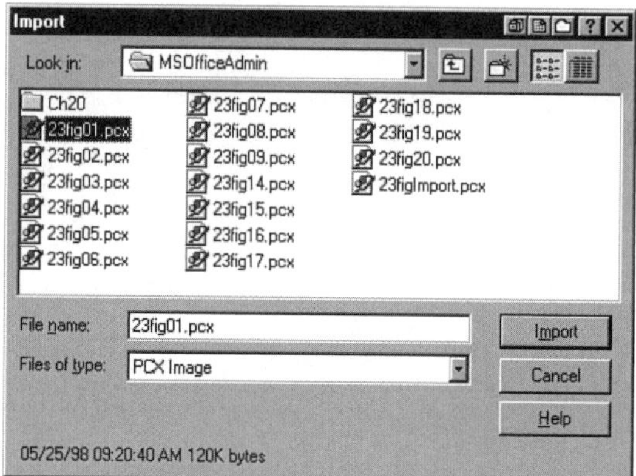

FIGURE 23.9
Select the file type from the drop-down list and then select the file.

Importing data into a view is more complicated. You can import structured text, tabular text, or worksheet (.wk1) files. You can also create a column descriptor (.col) file to massage the data while it is being imported. Column descriptor files can only be used with tabular text or worksheet files. They contain a list of column definitions followed by formulas (in the Notes Formula language) that define how the data is added to Notes—they are essentially field maps. Developers often create COL files to import existing data into Notes. Extensive discussion of this technique is beyond the scope of this chapter, but it is adequately documented in the Notes Help database, Help4.nsf.

To import data into Notes views, you must have a form for the documents and a view. Each import option—tabular text, structured text, and worksheet—has a different dialog box, but the basic procedure is very similar (see Figure 23.10). It is often easiest to use a WK1 file, so if you want to import an Excel workbook, you will have to save it as a WK1 file.

The basic steps to import a spreadsheet into a Notes view are as follows:

1. Open the database to the view you want to use.
2. Choose File, Import.
3. Optionally choose Lotus 1-2-3 Worksheet in the Files of Type drop-down list to display only WK1 files in the dialog box. Then select the file and click the Import button.
4. Select the form that you want to use. In Figure 23.10, the form is called Timesheet.
5. Choose the desired option under Column Defined. See the Notes documentation for a full description of these choices.

6. Click Import.

When the import is complete , the rows of the spreadsheet become rows in the view (see Figure 23.11). Each row in the view represents a document in Notes.

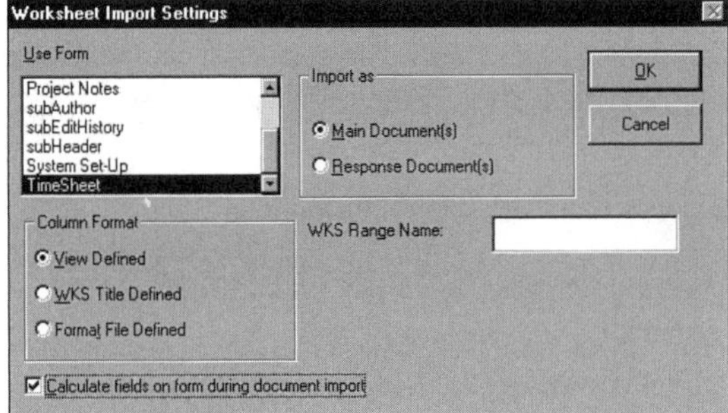

FIGURE 23.10
The Worksheet Import Settings dialog box. Note that the TimeSheet form has been selected.

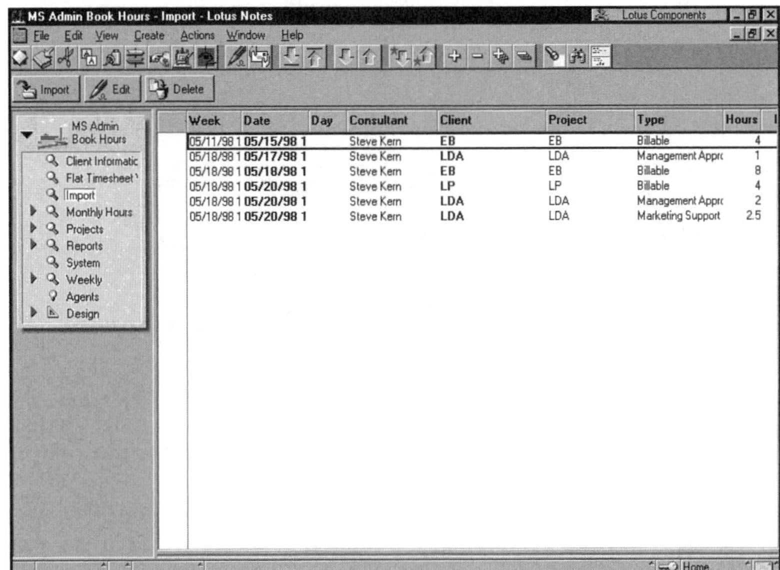

FIGURE 23.11
The view after the import is complete displays the Notes documents that used to be rows in the spreadsheet.

Exporting Data from Lotus Notes to Office

Exporting data is essentially the reverse of importing it. The dialog boxes you use are the same, and the choices for exporting documents and views are the same as those for importing. In other words, you can export documents from a view to the same three file types that you can import from structured text, tabular text and worksheets.

To export some, but not all, documents from a Notes view, click in the view selection margin to the left of the documents that you want to export. A check mark will appear next to each document name. When you export, mark Selected Documents.

Exporting data from Notes views is an important technique because Notes has a fairly limited reporting facility. Outside of views, there is no built-in method to display Notes data, either printed or onscreen. This is discussed further in "Using Excel to Present Notes Data" later in this chapter.

To export data from a view to a worksheet, follow these steps :

1. Optionally select the documents that you want to export.
2. Choose File, Export.
3. Choose Lotus 1-2-3 Worksheet as the file type, and supply a name.
4. Click Export.
5. Choose Selected Documents (or All Documents if you want to export the entire view), and mark Include View Titles if you want the titles of the view to show as column headers in the spreadsheet (see Figure 23.12).
6. Click OK.

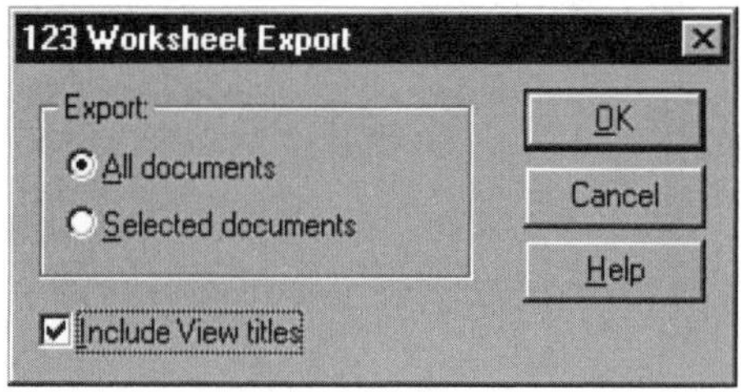

FIGURE 23.12
Click Include View Titles to convert the titles to column headers in the new spreadsheet.

The file is created according to the choices you made. You can then open the file in Excel and use it in whatever way you want.

Using the Microsoft Office Document Library Database

To create a new database using the Microsoft Office Document Library template, you must have a Domino Designer license. If you want to place this database on a server, you must have the appropriate access level to the server. Take the following steps:

1. Choose File, Database, New.
2. Leave the server set to Local to create the new database on your local hard drive.
3. In the New Database dialog box, enter a filename and database title (see Figure 23.13).
4. From the templates list box, choose Microsoft Office Library (R4.6).
5. Click OK.

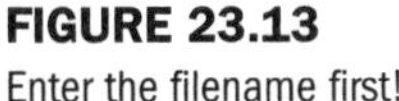

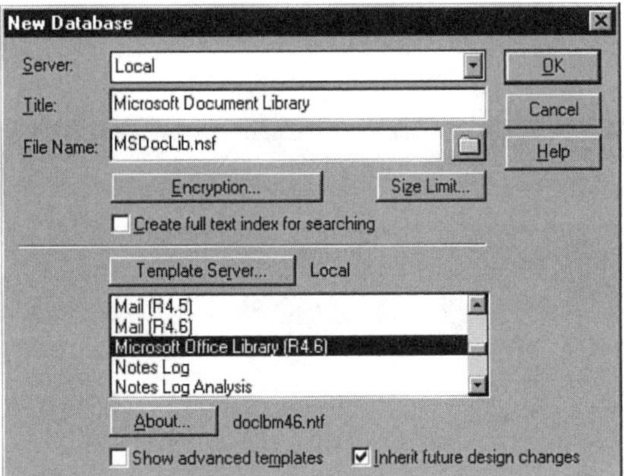

FIGURE 23.13
Enter the filename first!

CAUTION

If you enter the title first, the database title becomes the filename. Any spaces in the database title are transferred to the database filename. Therefore, it is good practice to enter the filename first so that you can control how your new database is identified to the operating system. Bear in mind that some systems do not support long filenames, so you may want to consider using the standard 8.3 naming convention.

When creation of the new database is complete, which usually takes just a few moments, you will see a document describing the purpose of the database. This document is called the "About" document, and is always available from the Help menu when the database is selected or opened. To see the document at a later date, choose Help, About This Database. Additional information about this database is available by choosing Help, Using this Database.

This database features a built-in capability to embed documents based on Office applications using OLE and ActiveX. When you create a document based on an Office application, the server application takes over the interface. This is similar to what happens when you switch the mail editor to Word. Supported Office document types are: Excel Workbook, Paintbrush Picture, PowerPoint Presentation, and Word Document. To create a document based on an object from one of these OLE server applications, choose Create, MS Office (see Figure 23.14). This allows you to edit these documents in-place without leaving Notes.

The document in Figure 23.14 was created in the Lotus Notes Microsoft Office Document Library database. You can see the Word menus and toolbars, as well as buttons from the Notes Action bar. The Action bar allows you to interact with Notes—you can click Save and Close, Mark Private, and Setup Review Cycle. Clicking Properties allows you to specify a document title and category.

This database takes advantage of the powerful workflow capabilities built into Notes. You can set up review cycles for your documents, either serial or parallel. You can also maintain version control of the document so that the original remains intact. This database has many other capabilities as well, such as archiving and flagging documents as private (which locks the document and prevents others from reading it). This means that you can create documents, spreadsheets, and so forth in the familiar Office applications, and use Notes features to route them to other users for review.

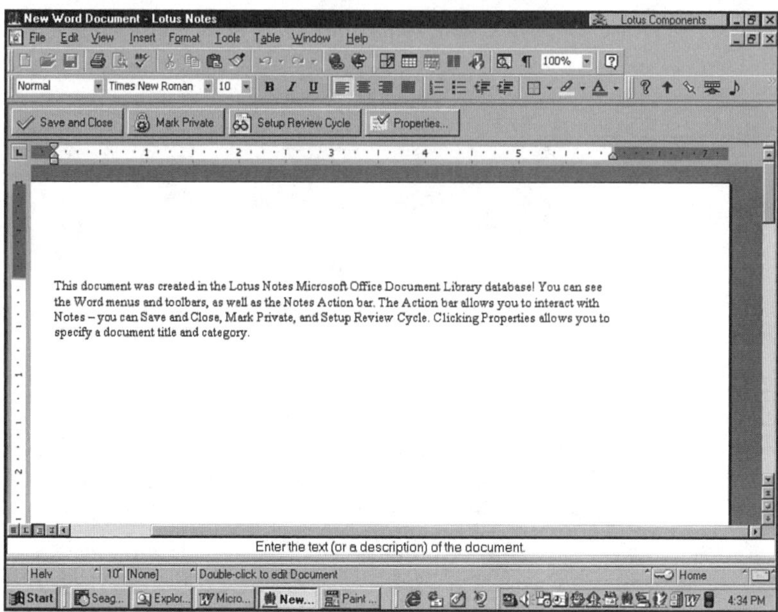

FIGURE 23.14
A Word document created in the Microsoft Office Library looks like Word, but has an additional set of buttons.

Reporting on Notes Data with Office Applications

Notes has no real reporting facility other than views to present documents in summary format. Views are quite powerful in their own right; you can create multiple lines per row, and add summary columns, average columns, percent columns, and group documents in nested categories. You can even create headers and footers when you print out the data in a view. However, many users, especially at the executive level, prefer a more polished report. Lotus does provide solutions to this in its own Lotus SmartSuite and in the Notes Reporter. Lotus Approach (a component of SmartSuite) is similar to Microsoft Access in its scope and use. The Notes Reporter is basically the reporting functions taken out of Approach. As an Office administrator, however, you'll be most interested in learning how to prepare reports using Access and Excel.

A typical view in a database that keeps track of hours is shown in Figure 23.15.

As you can see, views can be a very sophisticated means of presenting Notes data. You can click the twisties (small cyan triangles) beside each category to expand and collapse the category. This is great for onscreen display because it lets you drill right down to the level of detail you want to see. You can select the categories and documents you want to print, and choose File, Print. When you click Print View, only the selected documents and categories will print.

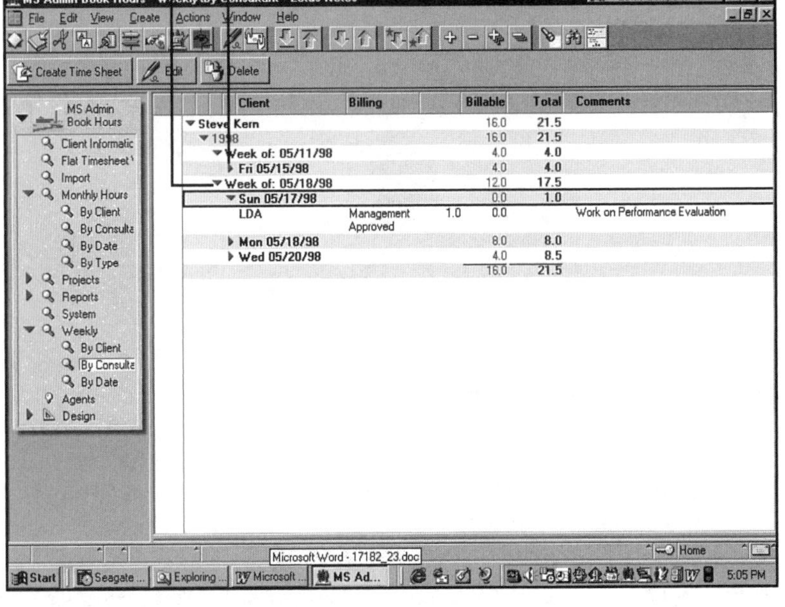

FIGURE 23.15
Note the summary columns and the nested categories in this view.

Nonetheless, you may need to resort to another reporting tool to present data. You may want to sort the data differently, or total some columns that are not totaled in a view, or perform some sophisticated ad-hoc calculations. There are a couple of options in Office that work. The first and simplest option is to export Notes data to a 1-2-3 Worksheet, as described in the section "Exporting Data from Lotus Notes to Office" earlier in this chapter. You can then open the WK1 file in Excel. The other option is to use Access to open Notes data.

Using Excel to Present Notes Data

Two methods of getting data into Excel work quite well. One is to export to a 1-2-3 Worksheet file, and the other is to export to a tabular text file. When the export is complete (see "Exporting Data from Lotus Notes to Office"), you can open the file in Excel. Opening a WK1 file is very straightforward, but opening a tabular text file is a little more complex.

Excel has a very nice method of working with tabular text files: the Text Import Wizard enables you to choose which columns to import and set the data type (see Figure 23.16). If you've got a view that has six columns you want, and four you don't need, now is the time to get rid of those extraneous columns. When you open a tabular text file in Excel, Excel detects it, and launches the Text Import Wizard.

The Text Import Wizard is a three-step process. In the first step, you determine the row to start the import. Excel detects whether the file is fixed width or delimited; a tabular text file is fixed width. In the second step, you adjust the field widths. The third step lets you determine the type of data in each column, and whether or not to skip the column (see Figure 23.16). You can move back and forth between the three steps, and when you are satisfied, click Finish.

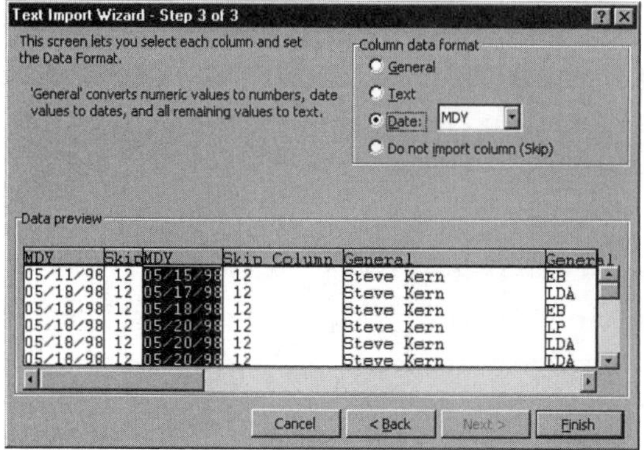

FIGURE 23.16
Using Excel's Text Import Wizard: columns 1 and 3 are set to a date format, and columns 2 and 4 are set to be skipped.

After you have the data in Excel, you can work with the cell borders, fonts, background colors, and so forth. You can also use Excel's sophisticated formula capabilities to present data. If you have a report that you prepare frequently, you might consider writing a macro in Excel to automate the spreadsheet. You can store this macro in your Personal.xls file, which will make it available to any spreadsheet. Figure 23.17 shows a very simple application of cell formatting to present timesheet data.

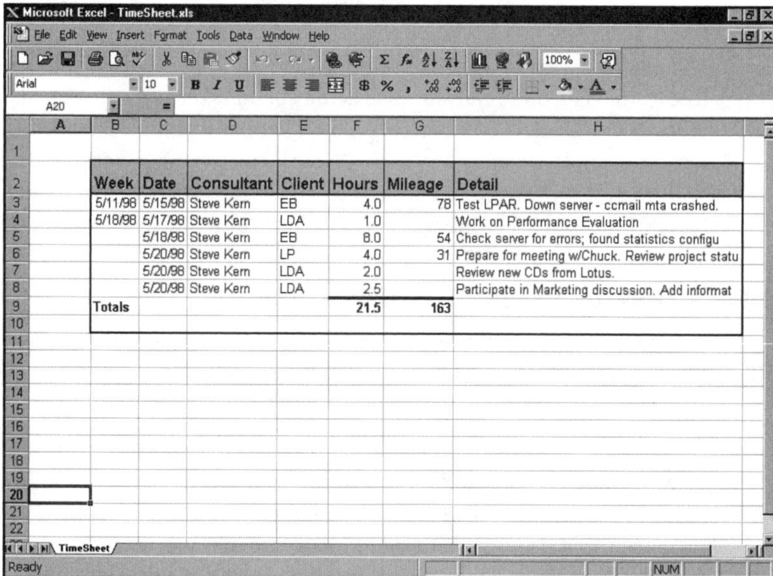

Week	Date	Consultant	Client	Hours	Mileage	Detail
5/11/98	5/15/98	Steve Kern	EB	4.0	78	Test LPAR. Down server - ccmail mta crashed.
5/18/98	5/17/98	Steve Kern	LDA	1.0		Work on Performance Evaluation
	5/18/98	Steve Kern	EB	8.0	54	Check server for errors; found statistics configu
	5/20/98	Steve Kern	LP	4.0	31	Prepare for meeting w/Chuck. Review project statu
	5/20/98	Steve Kern	LDA	2.0		Review new CDs from Lotus.
	5/20/98	Steve Kern	LDA	2.5		Participate in Marketing discussion. Add informat
Totals				21.5	163	

FIGURE 23.17
Spicing up Notes data with an Excel spreadsheet is easy!

Using Access to Query Notes Data

Access, as its name implies, is often used to query data from other database applications. These other databases are often relational, such as Microsoft's SQL Server, Sybase, or Oracle. The database system is referred to as a *source* and there is usually some setup involved to configure your PC so that Access can open the database tables. The tools that allow you to get to these database sources are referred to as *drivers*. Access also supports opening any data source that is ODBC-compliant. ODBC (Open Database Connectivity) is a widely used standard. You must set up an ODBC driver to get to an ODBC data source.

Notes is no exception to this, and Lotus provides its own driver, NotesSQL. NotesSQL allows you to get at Notes data using SQL statements. Despite this capability, don't forget that Notes is not a relational database! In fact, Notes is really just one large table.

Setting Up ODBC with NotesSQL Setting up NotesSQL is pretty straightforward. You can find NotesSQL on Lotus' Web site at `www.lotus.com`. After you download it, place the file (Nsqlw32.exe) in its own folder, and run it to extract the setup files. Next, run Setup.exe in the folder you've created for NotesSQL. Answer the Install Shield prompts, choosing Typical or Custom. When completed, you have to configure a data source for NotesSQL. To do so, follow these steps:

1. Choose Start, Settings, Control Panel.
2. Open the 32bit ODBC manager.
3. Click the System DSN tab, and click the Add button.
4. Click Lotus Notes SQL 2.0 (32-bit) ODBC Driver (.nsf), as shown in Figure 23.18.
5. Click Finish, and fill in the fields in the Lotus Notes ODBC 2.0 Setup dialog box (see Figure 23.19).
6. Specify a name for the data source, the server (local is best!), and the filename including the path. Leave the rest of the settings alone for now.
7. Click OK to return to the System DSN tab.
8. Click OK to close the ODBC manager.

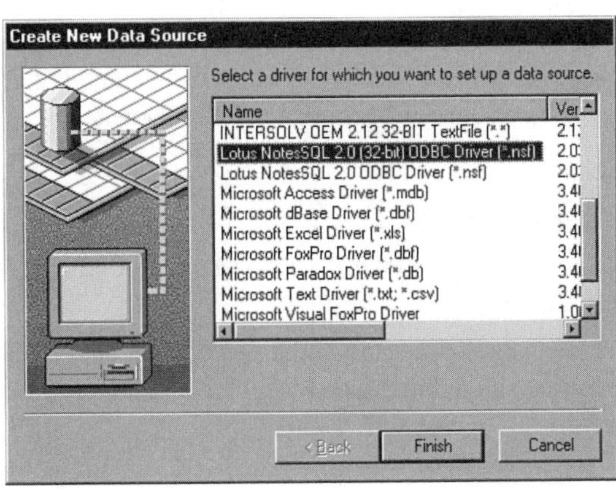

FIGURE 23.18
It is usually best to configure a System DSN, especially if you are working on a network.

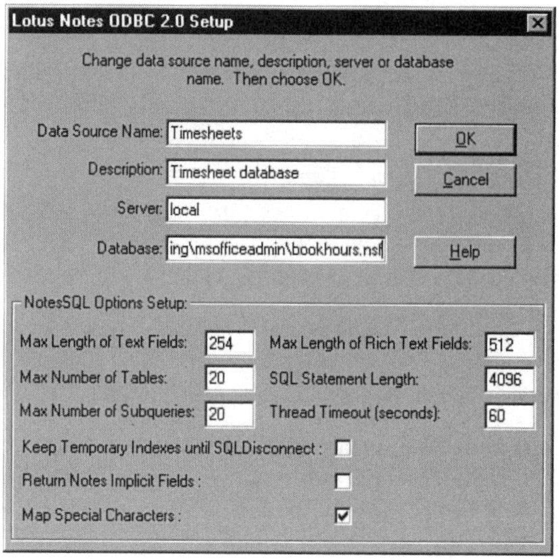

FIGURE 23.19
Leaving the server field blank means that you must have a copy (called a *local Replica*) of the database on your hard drive.

Now that you have a data source set up, you can open it with Access.

> **CAUTION**
>
> The ODBC driver treats all Notes fields as text, regardless of how Notes itself registers them. Furthermore, in some cases, all fields will be the width that you specified in the Lotus Notes ODBC 2.0 Setup dialog box, which defaults to 254. If you are having difficulty with your queries, open the this dialog box and change the default from 254 to a smaller value. You must keep this in mind when working with numbers because you will have to convert them from text in order to perform calculations.

Querying Notes Data with SQL When you open your data source in Access, it will not look much like the relational databases that you are used to. Design elements such as forms and views are treated as tables. It is often best to use a view, but this means that the information you want to report on must be in a view column.

When you open an external data source in Access, you can either import the data or link to the tables. If you are going to report on Notes data that will be changing, it is a good idea to use the link option. To open the data source in Access, you take these steps:

1. Create a new blank database in Access.
2. Choose File, Get External Data, Link Tables.
3. In the Link dialog box, choose ODBC Databases () from the Files of Type drop-down box (see Figure 23.20).
4. Click the Machine Data Sources tab in the Select Data Source dialog box, and choose the Notes ODBC source you defined (see Figure 23.21).
5. Click OK.

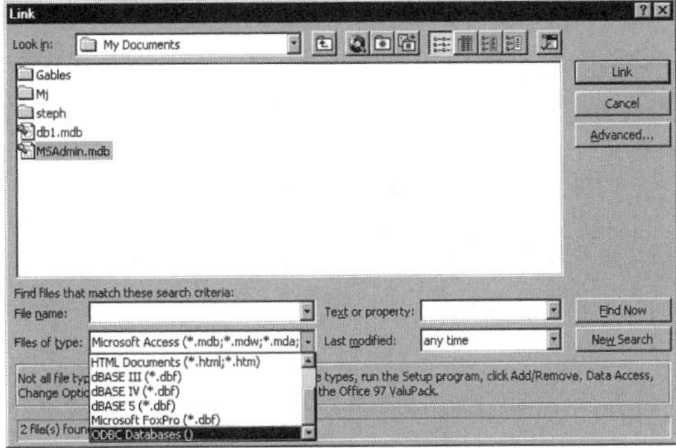

FIGURE 23.20
The Link dialog box allows you to specify the file type as ODBC.

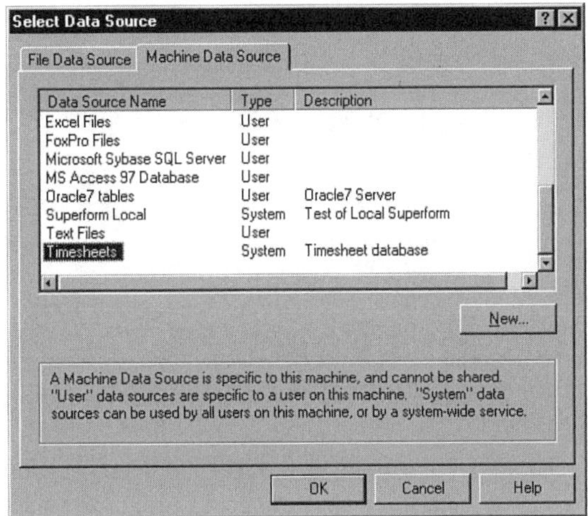

FIGURE 23.21
Click the Machine Data Source tab to select your Notes ODBC data source.

After you choose the Notes ODBC data source, the Link Tables dialog box appears with what may be a bewildering array of elements (see Figure 23.22). Here you must have some knowledge of the internal design of the database in order to determine which element to choose.

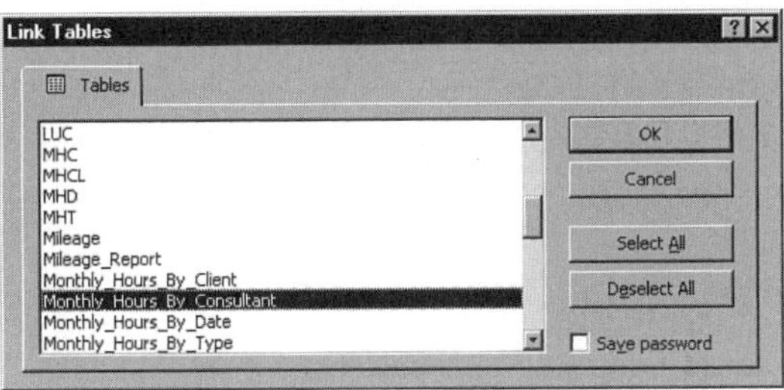

FIGURE 23.22
Knowledge of the database's design will help you choose the correct design element for your report.

After you choose an element, Access prompts you to choose a field or fields to uniquely describe each record—again, you need to have some knowledge of the design of the Notes database. After this is completed, you can query the "table." See Figure 23.23.

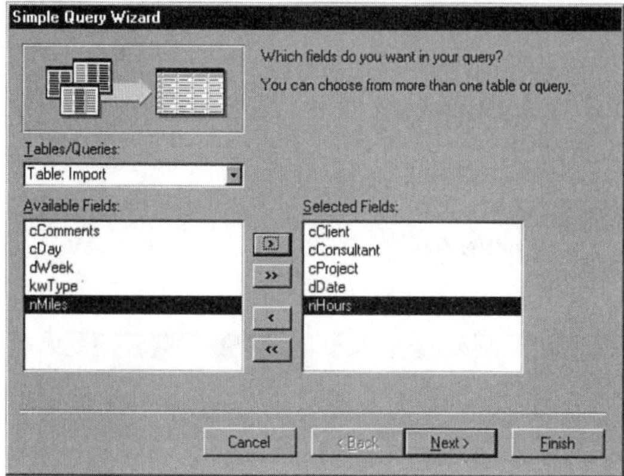

FIGURE 23.23
The Simple Query Wizard after several fields have been selected.

Now that you have a query, you can apply the selection criteria you need, and you can use any of the sophisticated reporting tools available in Access to present a polished report.

Using Office with Lotus Notes/FX

Lotus Notes/FX, or Field Exchange, is based on OLE technology, and enables Notes to exchange field-level information with other applications. Not all the Office applications or all versions are FX-enabled. For example, none of the Office 95 applications will work with Notes 4. Office 97 has three applications that support Notes/FX: Excel, PowerPoint, and Word. Access does not support Notes/FX.

Information can be exchanged in one direction, or in both directions, between a Notes document and an OLE server application. Notes/FX has to be set up by a Notes developer because the forms and/or actions are part of the database design.

NOTE For both Notes/FX and NotesFlow (discussed in the section "Enabling Workflow with NotesFlow" later in this chapter) to work, the OLE Server application must be launched from within Notes. A Notes developer sets a property on the NotesFlow enabled form to automatically launch the application.

Exchanging Fields

All the OLE server applications that support Notes/FX provide help. For example, you can search Word 97 help for Notes FX and find several documents, including a table of fields. These fields are described as file properties and are available in each FX-enabled Office application. Some fields are the same throughout each FX-enabled application, and some are specific to the application. For example, common properties include items such as Title, Subject, Author, and Date Created; Multimedia Clips is a property in PowerPoint, but not in Word. For

Notes/FX to function, there must be corresponding fields in the OLE server application and in the Notes form. The tables in the server application list the names that the fields must have in Notes in order to function with Notes/FX. See Table 23.1 for a list of Notes/FX fields in Word.

Table 23.1 Notes/FX Fields in Word 97

Property Field	Notes Field Name	Notes Data Type
Title	Title	Text
Subject	Subject	Text
Author	Author	Text
Keywords	Keywords	Text
Comments	Comments	Text
Template	Template	Text
Manager	ManagerText	Text
Company	Company	Text
Category	Category	Text
Created	DateCreated	Time
Modified	LastSavedDate	Time
Last Saved By	LastSavedBy	Text
Size	NumberOfBytes	Text
Revision Number	NumberOfRevisions	Number
Total Editing Time	TotalEditingTime	Number
Printed	LastPrintedDate	Time
Pages	NumberOfPages	Number
Slides	NumberOfSlides	Number
Words	NumberOfWords	Number
Characters	NumberOfCharacters	Number
Characters (with spaces)	NumberOfCharacters WithSpaces	Number
Paragraphs	NumberOfParagraphs	Number
Lines	NumberOfLines	Number
Security	Security	Number
Document Class	DocumentClass	Text
Name of Application	NameOfApplication	Text

Enabling Workflow with NotesFlow

Application developers in Lotus Notes can use special settings in Notes forms to publish a *NotesFlow action* to an OLE server application. An *action* is a scripted event attached to a form. For example, there may be an action titled ***Submit for Review*** that sends the document to others in your team for review. In Office, Word, Excel, and PowerPoint all recognize NotesFlow actions. NotesFlow actions appear in a special Action menu to the left of the Window menu. This corresponds to a similarly named menu in Notes. NotesFlow is only available in Release 4 or later of Notes. Figure 23.24 shows an Action menu in a Word document.

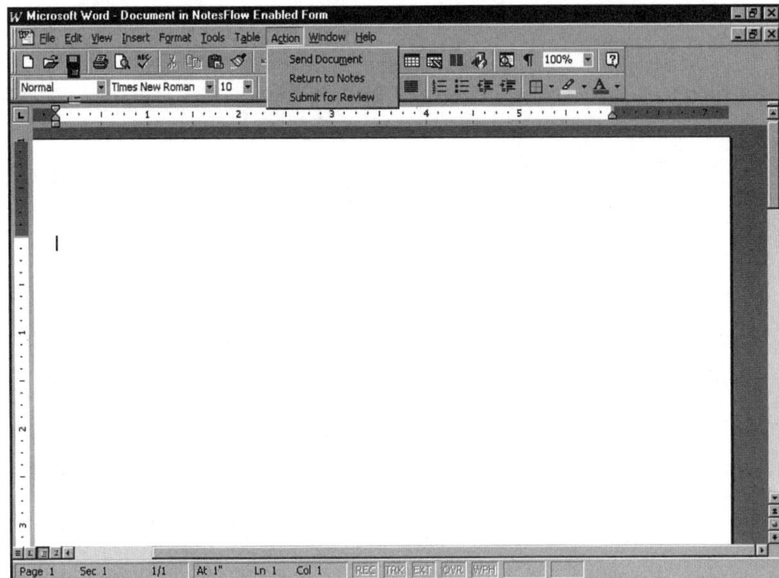

FIGURE 23.24
Clicking the Action menu in Word shows the published actions.

CHAPTER 24

Managing Mixed Macintosh/Windows Office Environments

Microsoft Office is a cross-platform product, available on both Microsoft Windows and Apple Macintosh platforms. Managing Office in both environments at once, however, brings its own challenges. Some of these challenges relate to differences in Office's features and behavior on each platform; others relate to connectivity; and still others relate to differences in the way the platforms themselves handle key tasks such as fonts and printing.

In this chapter, you walk through the basics of managing Office in a cross-platform environment, identifying techniques and products that can make the process significantly easier.

Major Elements of Office for Windows Are Missing from Office for the Macintosh

Although Office 98 is a full-featured suite of productivity applications, it is missing some elements that exist on the Windows platform. If your custom solutions or business processes depend on these elements, you have to adjust them accordingly. What's missing follows:

- *Microsoft Access.* There is no Macintosh version of Access; however, you can deliver database data to Macintosh users in at least four ways. You can build intranet-based applications with browser front ends. You can query Access (or other Windows databases) using ODBC drivers built into Office on both platforms. You can export static reports to Excel, RTF, HTML, tab, or comma-delimited formats. Finally, you can build a cross-platform Microsoft FoxPro database, and front-end it with FoxPro on the Macintosh, and Access 97 on Windows PCs. (This last option is by far the most complex.)
- *Microsoft Outlook.* Outlook Express, a more limited Internet email and news client, is provided instead.
- *User profiles and System Policies.* The Macintosh does not support logon scripts, and Microsoft has not provided user profiles and System Policies. These limitations make it difficult to enforce restrictions on Macintosh Office users through the network, as you can do in Windows.
- *The Office Binder.* This feature enables users to pull together several Word, Excel, or PowerPoint files in a single file called a *binder.* In order for Office 98 users to work with the contents of an Office 97 binder, they must run the Unbind Utility in the Office 98 ValuPack.
- *The Find Fast and Web Find Fast (for Windows NT) features.* In Windows, these features streamline searching for documents on a local computer or corporate intranet.
- *The Excel Web Form Wizard.* In Windows, this feature simplifies the creation of intranet-based data entry forms from within Excel.
- *WordMail.* This feature enables Word to be used as the email editor for Microsoft Exchange clients.
- *Posting to public Microsoft Exchange folders.* In Office 97, Outlook enables users to post Office documents to public Microsoft Exchange folders for easy company-wide access. The Outlook Express email client does not provide this capability.
- *PowerPoint Web-based presentation conferencing.* In Windows, PowerPoint works with Microsoft's NetMeeting software to enable conferencing over the Web; this feature is not present on the Macintosh.
- *Other advanced PowerPoint features.* Features missing in Office 98 include Speaker Notes, AutoClipArt, and support for integration of Lotus Notes custom workflow (Lotus NotesFlow) commands.

- *Microsoft Photo Editor.* This image-editing applet is missing from Office 98 for the Macintosh. Microsoft may have assumed that most Macintosh users already have access to an image-editing program, such as PhotoShop.
- *Microsoft Camcorder.* In Windows, Camcorder enables Office administrators to record AVI movies of onscreen actions and procedures for training purposes. The Camcorder applet is absent on the Macintosh, which supports the QuickTime video format instead of AVI.

Conversely, Office 98 for the Macintosh contains features not available on Office 97 for Windows:

- Balloon help
- Support for Apple Publish and Subscribe, Apple's method of integrating information across documents (Object Linking and Embedding is supported on both platforms)
- Support for Macintosh Drag and Drop
- QuickTime movie and QuickTime VR panorama support
- Optional Word 5.1 for the Macintosh menus, designed to simplify migration for Word 5.1/Macintosh users
- Word Speak, a Word add-in that works with MacInTalk to convert text to speech

Other differences between the platforms include the following:

- ValuPack components are significantly different on each platform.
- Web access works differently from within Office 98 applications. Rather than opening a Web browser from within Word, for example, Word opens a separate copy of Internet Explorer.
- Microsoft provides different software for enabling one-click access to Office applications. In Office 98, Microsoft Office Manager is provided, whereas Office 97 for Windows includes the Office Shortcut Bar instead.
- Minor command differences exist in Visual Basic for Applications, to reflect the slightly different command set available on Windows and the Macintosh.

Word 98/Word 97 Windows Feature and Interface Differences

Some years ago, when Microsoft introduced Office 4.2 for Windows, and later on Office 4.2 for the Macintosh, Microsoft sought to make the Macintosh versions of Word, Excel, and PowerPoint mimic the Windows versions in virtually every detail. The goal was to simplify cross-platform management of Word and Office.

The experiment failed: Macintosh users rebelled against the Windows-like look and feel of these Office programs, and many also objected to slow performance on these ported applications. As a result, many Macintosh users are still working with the ancient Word 5.1.

With Word 98 and Office 98 for the Macintosh, Microsoft learned its lesson, carefully restoring most aspects of the Macintosh look-and-feel, along with many of the interface features Word 5.1 users are accustomed to. Although Macintosh users generally seem pleased with the result, Office administrators face platform differences that did not exist previously. Most of these differences are relatively minor and easy to manage, when you understand them.

For example, in Word 98 for the Macintosh (see Figure 24.1), two additional menus appear: the Font menu, which enables users to easily format selected text in any font installed on the system; and the Work menu, which enables them to list the current file so that it is more easily accessible in future sessions. (To learn how to add Font and Work menus to Word for Windows, see Chapter 6.)

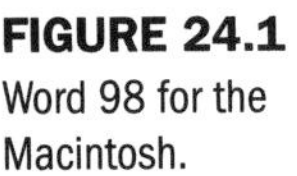

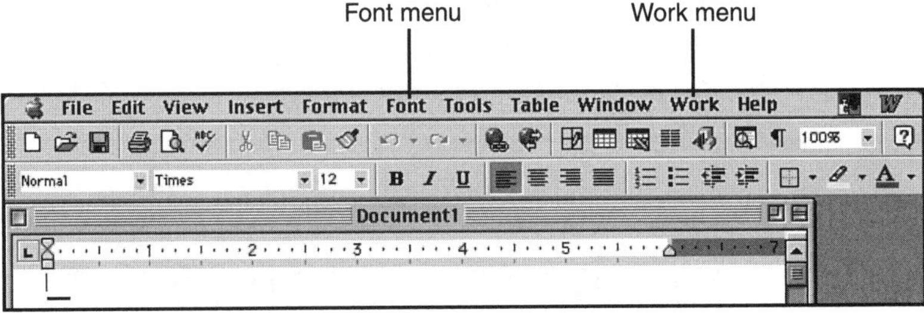

FIGURE 24.1
Word 98 for the Macintosh.

Options for Sharing Office Files

A number of issues are associated with sharing Microsoft Office files between Macintosh and Windows computers. These issues fall into the following two major categories:

- Can the file be read at all? (Cross-platform networking and removable media issues)
- Can the file be recognized for what it is? (Long filename, extension, and Macintosh application/file type issues)

The good news is that file sharing has become significantly easier than it once was, especially if you are running the latest version of the MacOS (currently, MacOS 8.1).

Reading Windows Office Files on the Macintosh

If you are running MacOS 8.1 or higher with the PC Exchange extension loaded, your Macintosh recognizes both Windows 95 long filenames and Office file extensions such as .doc for Word documents and .xls for Excel workbooks. The Macintosh then automatically assigns the appropriate Macintosh application and document types, which Macintosh applications use to recognize and open files.

Windows 95/98 long filenames can be as long as 255 characters; Macintosh filenames can only be as long as 32 characters. As a result, a very long filename in Windows 95 may be truncated when opened on the Macintosh. You can usually recognize a truncated filename by the presence of the pound (#) symbol.

If you are running MacOS 7.5x, 7.6x, or 8.0x, PC Exchange still recognizes DOS three-character extensions and assigns correct Macintosh application and file types. These versions of PC Exchange cannot recognize Windows long filenames, however. Instead, it uses the corresponding 8.3 character alias (short) filename that Windows also generates.

If you are running an older version of the MacOS, consider purchasing DOS Mounter95 from Software Architects, which also offers strong support for Windows long filenames on the Macintosh. A time-limited demo version is available at **www.softarch.com/us/demofiles/dm95_demo_form.html.**

Ensuring That Macintosh Document Types Are Correct

As mentioned earlier, the Macintosh relies on application type and file type information stored in the resource fork of every file—not file extension names—in order to open a file in the correct program. If, for some reason, filenames are being associated with incorrect applications or document types, you can make adjustments through the PC Exchange control panel (see Figure 24.2).

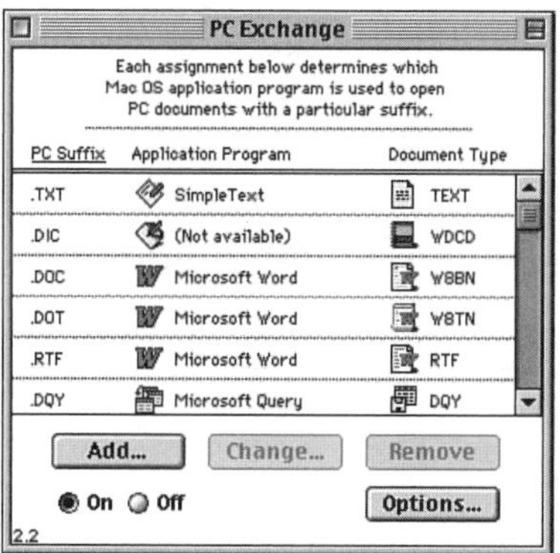

FIGURE 24.2
The PC Exchange control panel.

The most common problem with document types in Office for the Macintosh occurs when multiple versions of Office are installed on the same computer. If you install an older version of Office after you install Office 98, you may find that double-clicking a Word, Excel, or PowerPoint 97 document created in Office 97 for Windows incorrectly opens the older Office program on the Macintosh, such as Word 6, Excel 5, or PowerPoint 4. This is especially troublesome because of the changes in file formats between versions of Office. A Word 97 file cannot be read in Word 6 unless you download and install a special filter, and even then, Word 97 features embedded in the document can easily be lost.

To solve the problem, associate the PC file suffix with the correct application program and document type, as follows:

1. Choose PC Exchange from the list of Control Panels in the Apple menu.
2. Select a file extension (PC suffix) you want to change.
3. Click Change. A new dialog box opens (see Figure 24.3).

4. In the list of files and folders at the bottom, browse to and select the Office application that you want to assign to the extension you chose. For example, if you want to assign the extension DOC to Word 98, select Microsoft Word in the Microsoft Office 98 folder.
5. Click on the current document type and choose a new document type from the list that displays. For example, if you want DOC files to open into Word 98 as documents (rather than as templates, for instance), choose W8BN. (Table 24.1 lists the most common Office 98 document types.)
6. Close the PC Exchange control panel.

FIGURE 24.3
Changing the Document Type associated with a DOC file extension (suffix).

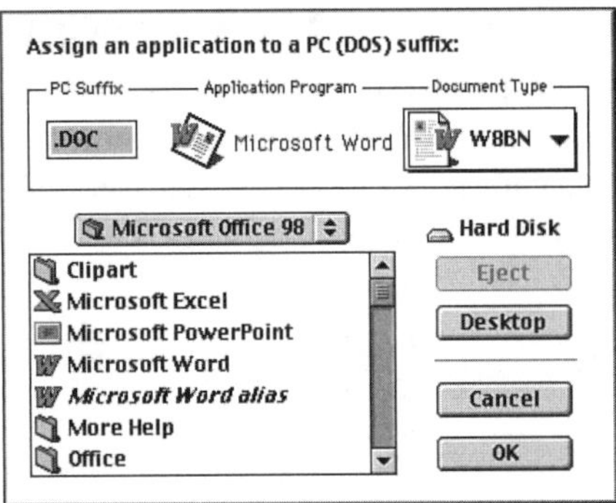

Table 24.1 Office 97 PC Extensions and Office 98 Macintosh Document Types

PC Extension (Suffix)	Macintosh Document Type
DIC (Dictionary file)	WDCD
DOC (Word document)	W8BN
DOT (Word template)	W8TN
RTF (Word Rich Text Format)	RTF
DQY (Microsoft Query file)	DQY
XLS (Excel Workbook)	XLS8
XLT (Excel Template)	sLS8
XLW (Excel Workspace)	XLW8
XLC (Excel Chart)	XLC
XLA (Excel Add-In)	XLA8
PPT (PowerPoint Presentation)	PPT
PPA (PowerPoint Add-In)	PPPA
PPS (PowerPoint Slide Show)	PPSS
POT (PowerPoint Template)	PPOT

Reading MacOS Office Files on Windows Computers

Windows machines cannot read disks formatted in the MacOS format, so if you need to read disks created on the Macintosh, you have two options: You can format the disks in PC format, either on the Macintosh or on the PC. Alternatively, you can install a third-party program that enables PC floppy disk drives to read MacOS formatted disks. Software options include the following:

- MacOpener 3.0 from DataViz (**www.dataviz.com**)
- MacDrive 95 from Media4 Productions (**www.media4.com**)
- Here & Now from Software Architects (**www.softarch.com**)

Note that of these products, MacOpener 3.0 is currently the only one that runs under Windows NT 4.0 (and it also happens to be the least expensive).

Although MacOS 8.1 can now store long filenames (up to 32 characters) on PC-formatted disks in a form that can be recognized by Windows, keep in mind that Office and other Macintosh applications typically do not automatically assign extensions to files. This means that Windows systems do not automatically know which programs are associated with a given Macintosh file. You have two options for dealing with this:

- Open the Office (or other application program) first. Display All Files in the application's File, Open dialog box so that all files appear whether they have the correct extension or not. Choose the file to be opened, and click Open.
- Require Macintosh users to add DOS/Windows compatible extensions (as listed in Table 24.1 previously in this chapter) to all their document files. If you are running MacOS 8.1 or higher, you can permit long filenames up to 32 characters; otherwise, you should require old-fashioned DOS-style 8.3 filenames.

Windows 95 to Macintosh Peer-to-Peer Solutions

Many small, peer-to-peer Ethernet networks are comprised of several PCs with one or a few Macintoshes, or several Macintoshes with one or a few PCs. Most of these networks can benefit from simple file sharing solutions that enable users to share Office files across platforms. Several options exist.

If your network is primarily made up of Macintoshes with just one or a few PCs, consider PC MacLAN from Miramar Systems (**www.miramarsys.com**). With this Windows software, which enables your PC to speak the AppleTalk networking protocol, Windows PCs can act as file or print servers for Macintoshes, and vice versa.

If you have one or a few PCs that must access a Macintosh network but it isn't important for the Macintoshes to be able to retrieve information stored on those PCs, or print to printers stored on those PCs, consider COPSTalk 2.5 for Windows, from Cooperative Printing Solutions (**www.copstalk.com**). After COPSTalk is installed on a Windows PC, Macintosh computers on the Ethernet appear as part of an Isolated AppleTalk Network that appears in the Network Neighborhood (shown in Windows Explorer in Figure 24.4). Note that even with COPSTalk, some characters in Macintosh computer names do not translate accurately in Windows (as in the example shown in the figure).

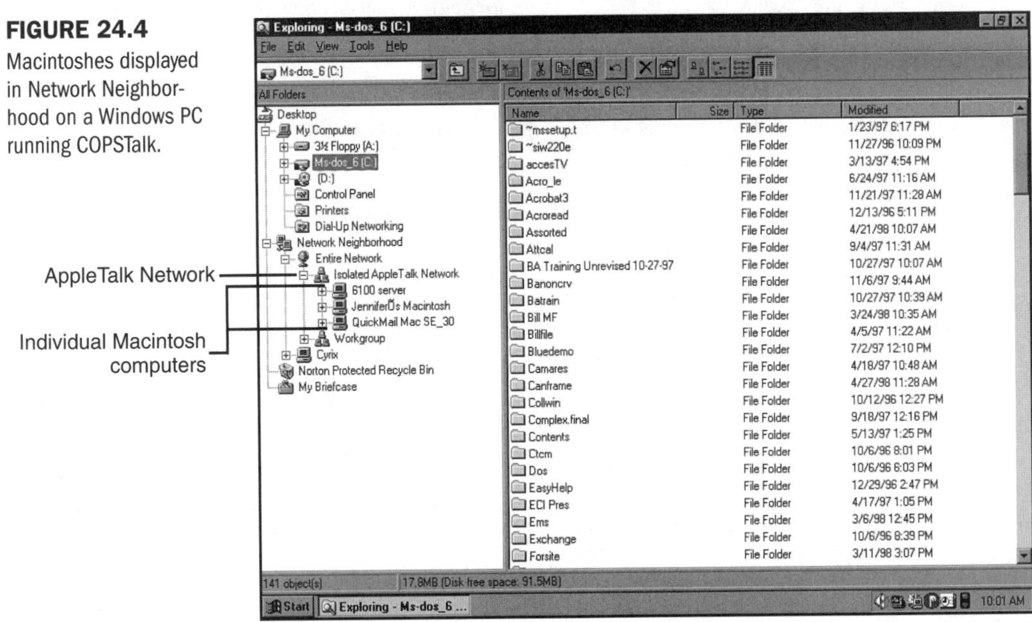

FIGURE 24.4
Macintoshes displayed in Network Neighborhood on a Windows PC running COPSTalk.

COPSTalk also supports TCP/IP, which means that you can connect your PC to an intranet hosted on a Macintosh server, if you've chosen to run TCP/IP alongside of (or instead of) the traditional Macintosh AppleTalk protocol.

If your network is primarily made up of PCs, but you have one or two Macintoshes, consider Dave 2.0 from Thursby Software Systems (**www.thursby.com**). This software installs on a Macintosh, using Mac TCP/IP or Windows NetBIOS to connect with Windows 95, 98, NT, or Windows 3.1 PCs. Dave 2.0 enables Macintosh users to see PC drives through the Macintosh Chooser and PC users to see Macintosh drives and printers through the Windows Network Neighborhood.

One final option for integrating Macintoshes and Windows PCs is Timbuktu Pro from Netopia (**www.netopia.com/software/tb2/**), a remote access program that enables Macintoshes to control Windows PCs (and run Windows software in a window on the Macintosh), or vice versa.

Supporting Macintoshes on NT Server Networks

Windows NT Server 4.0 has built-in support for Macintosh clients, making it a natural server solution for cross-platform environments. After you get it running right, NT Server looks like just another Macintosh to the Macintosh client workstations. This section presents a high-level look at what's involved in enabling Macintosh support on NT Server networks. (For a more detailed discussion of connecting Macintosh clients to an NT Server network, see *Using Windows NT Server 4* by Roger Jennings, published by Que Corporation, ISBN: 0-7897-0251-7.)

Start by making sure that Ethernet is installed and working on all the Macintoshes you want to connect. If you're not sure, you can check in the AppleTalk control panel in MacOS 7.6 or higher (see Figure 24.5).

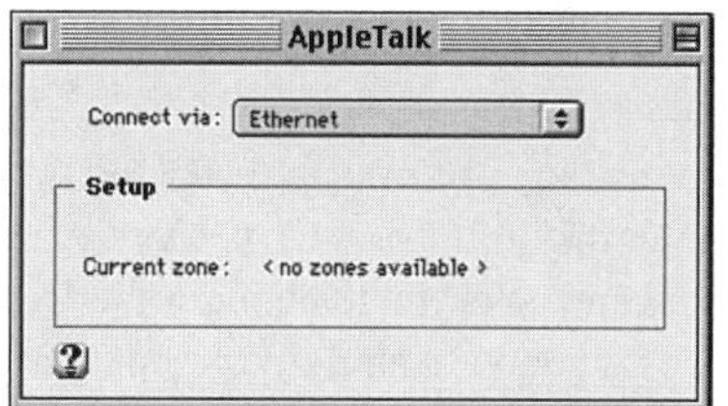

FIGURE 24.5
The MacOS 7.6 AppleTalk control panel, showing an Ethernet connection.

Of course, make sure the Macintoshes are physically connected to the NT Server system you want to use. Finally—and this shouldn't be a problem—make sure that all your Macintoshes are running at least System 6.07 or higher. (Very few business Macintoshes nowadays are running MacOS versions older than 7.5x.)

NOTE Years ago, it was common for low-speed Apple-compatible LocalTalk cards to be installed in PC servers, enabling them to connect with the Macintosh's built-in LocalTalk network connections. However, Ethernet is now virtually universal on Macintoshes in business, making this unnecessary.

Occasionally, you may encounter a Laserwriter NTX or a lone Macintosh SE using its LocalTalk port to connect to the Ethernet through a GatorBox, an older product from Cayman Systems (**www.cayman.com**) that is no longer sold. ■

Next, make sure your NT Server system is up and running properly. It should be updated to the latest NT Service Pack, and it should have at least one partition formatted with NTFS, NT's more sophisticated file system. (In NT Server, NTFS can host Macintosh-accessible volumes. Old-fashioned FAT partitions cannot.) Using NT's User Manager for Domains utility, create user accounts for the Macintosh users with whom you are working.

Now, install Services for Macintosh on the NT Server system, if they are not already installed. On NT Server, choose Start, Settings, Control Panel, and double-click on the Network applet. Click the Services tab, and click Add. The Select Network Service dialog box appears (see Figure 24.6). Choose Services for Macintosh, and click OK.

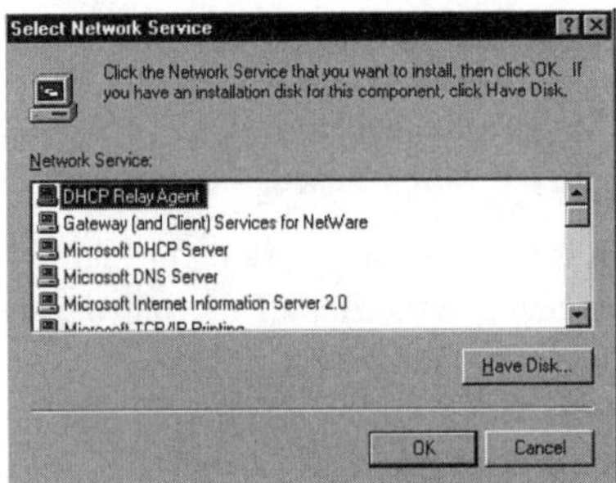

FIGURE 24.6
Beginning the installation of Services for Macintosh on NT Server 4.0.

Windows NT Setup opens and you're asked to browse to the CD-ROM or network location where you have the original NT Server disk or files. After you've copied the files, Windows NT starts the AppleTalk network protocol and asks you to configure it. Depending on the size of your network and whether an AppleTalk router is already present, you may or may not have to enable AppleTalk routing.

When you're finished configuring AppleTalk Protocol Properties, you are prompted to restart NT Server. Do so. When NT Server restarts, two new services are listed in the Services control panel applet: File Server for Macintosh and Print Server for Macintosh. In Windows NT Explorer, you also see a new folder installed on your NTFS drive named Microsoft UAM Volume. This contains the authentication and password encryption software Macintoshes need to operate securely on an NT network. Later, you install this software on each Macintosh on your network.

Still on the server, you need to create Macintosh-accessible volumes—shared folders that support Macintosh resource and data forks, and the other elements of a typical Macintosh file system. To do so, create and share a new folder using Windows NT Explorer. Next, open NT's Server Manager administration utility; choose the server you're working on; and click MacFile, Volumes, Create Volume. In the Volume Name text box, enter the name of the folder you just created and shared. From this dialog box, you can also set security, user limits, and permissions.

After you've done all this, it's time to head back to the Macintosh client workstations. In the Macintosh Chooser, click AppleShare to see the network resources available to you. You should see one corresponding to the NT Server system you just set up. Choose that one and click OK. Log on with your name and password, and browse the available volumes to find Microsoft UAM Volume. Choose OK. Close the Chooser. A Microsoft UAM Volume icon is now on the Macintosh desktop. Drag it into the System folder. Shut down and restart the Macintosh. Finally, log on again as a Registered User, and choose the Mac-accessible volume you want to use.

Sending Compressed Files Across Platforms

With the explosion of email, more and more files are transmitted over the Internet—and in many cases, users compress these files first. Macintosh and Windows compression standards are different. Most Macintosh users work with one of the StuffIt family of products from Aladdin Systems (**www.aladdinsys.com**). Most Windows users use the ZIP format originated by PKZIP (**www.pkzip.com**) and now most commonly generated by WinZip from Nico Mak Computing (**www.winzip.com**).

Aladdin Systems makes available a free utility, StuffIt Expander, for both the Macintosh and Windows. This utility is capable of decompressing StuffIt (SIT) files, as well as MacBinary (BIN), BinHex (HQX), ZIP (ZIP), Uuencoded (UUE), and other compressed files. If you need to create ZIP files on a Macintosh, consider the shareware package ZipIt 1.38, available from Tom Brown at **www.awa.com/softlock/zipit/**.

Managing Font and Character Set Issues

In moving documents between Windows and the Macintosh, Office administrators need to be aware of issues related to both fonts and character sets.

First, Windows and the Macintosh do not use identical character sets, so a character you type on Windows may not be represented as the same character on the Macintosh, or vice versa. This can especially become a problem if you're creating documents for electronic publishing on the Web or your corporate intranet, where different browsers can interpret the same character differently, even within the same platform. (Figure 24.7 shows the characters available in the standard Windows character set. Figure 24.8 shows a document containing the same characters as displayed by the Macintosh.)

FIGURE 24.7
The Windows character set.

!	"	#	$	%	&	'	(	)	*	+	,	-	.	/	0	1	2	3	4	5	6	7	8	9	:	;	<
=	>	?	@	A	B	C	D	E	F	G	H	I	J	K	L	M	N	O	P	Q	R	S	T	U	V	W	X
Y	Z	[	\	]	^	_	`	a	b	c	d	e	f	g	h	i	j	k	l	m	n	o	p	q	r	s	t
u	v	w	x	y	z	{	|	}	~	¡	¢	£	¤	¥	¦	§	¨	©	ª	«	¬	-	®	¯	°	±	²
³	´	µ	¶	·	¸	¹	°	»	¼	½	¾	¿	À	Á	Â	Ã	Ä	Å	Æ	Ç	È	É	Ê	Ë	Ì	Í	Î
Ï	Ð	Ñ	Ò	Ó	Ô	Õ	Ö	×	Ø	Ù	Ú	Û	Ü	Ý	Þ	ß	à	á	â	ã	ä	å	æ	ç	è	é	ê
ë	ì	í	î	ï	ð	ñ	ò	ó	ô	õ	ö	÷	ø	ù	ú	û	ü	ý	þ	ÿ	Œ	œ	Š	š	Ÿ	ƒ	ˆ
˜	–	—	‘	’	‚	“	”	„	†	‡	•	…	‰	‹	›	™	·										

The best solution is to avoid special characters in cross-platform documents wherever possible. One tip: turn off the Fractions with Fraction Character check box in the AutoFormat As You Type tab of the AutoCorrect Options dialog box (accessible by choosing Format, AutoFormat, Options).

Other special characters used by Office applications are formatted in the Wingdings TrueType font. Although this font is available on both Windows and Macintosh platforms, many Macintosh users prefer to use the Zapf Dingbats PostScript font instead, especially for documents that are printed professionally. Be aware that Wingdings and Zapf Dingbats are different, though a few of the more common characters (such as round bullets) are consistent.

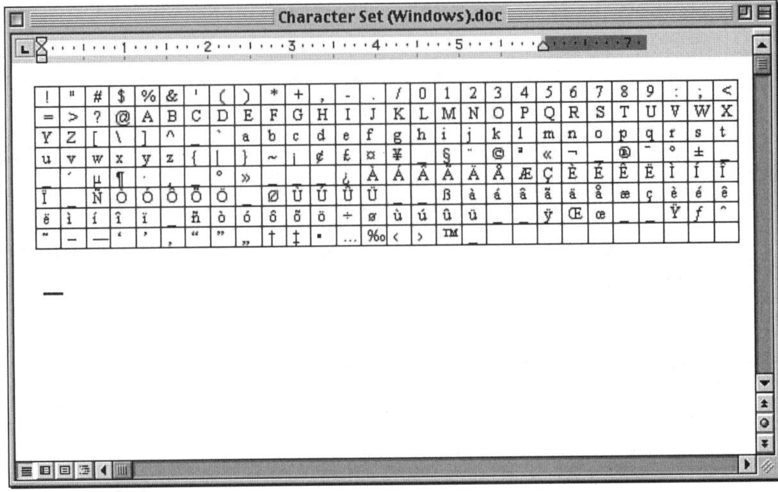

FIGURE 24.8
The characters in the Windows character set, in a document displayed on the Macintosh.

Although Microsoft installs the same TrueType fonts along with both Windows and the Macintosh, other fonts may not be identical across platforms, even if they share the same or similar names. These differences can cause problems in finished documents. If the precise typography of a cross-platform document matters, purchase the identical font from the identical font vendor.

You can find an excellent discussion of differences between the Windows and Macintosh character sets, and their impact on Web pages, at **www.hit.net/~bobbau/platforms/specialchars/**.

Controlling Font Substitutions Across Platforms

If you move a document across platforms and a font available on one platform is not available on the other, Word may substitute another font, commonly Times New Roman or Arial. You may have another font installed that more closely reflects the appearance you want to display, or uses widths similar to the original font (and therefore does not enlarge or shrink your document as much).

Word enables you to manually control font substitutions in any file where a font substitution has been made. To do so, follow these steps:

1. Choose Tools, Options, and click the Compatibility tab.
2. Click Font Substitution. (If this option is grayed out, no fonts are substituted in your current document.) The Font Substitution dialog box opens (as shown in Figure 24.9).
3. Under Missing Document Font, select the missing font for which you want to assign a different substitute.
4. Select the substituted font you prefer to use in the Substituted Font drop-down box.
5. Click OK.

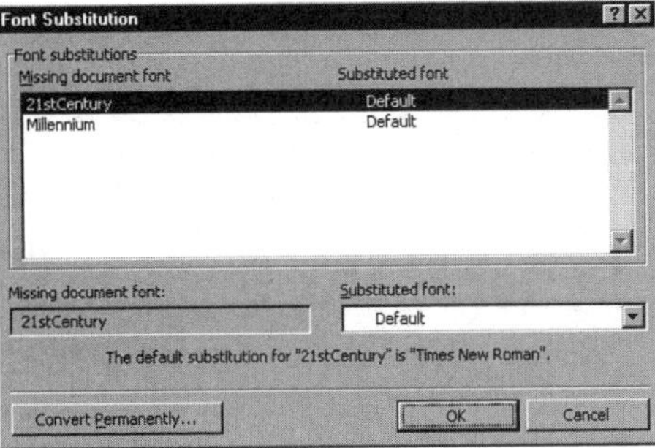

FIGURE 24.9
The Font Substitution dialog box.

Although the original font name is preserved (in case you move the file back to a computer that contains that font), the document instead displays the substituted font you choose.

If you never expect to move the document back to its original computer, you can click Convert Permanently in the Font Substitution dialog box, and Word reformats any text in the document to use the fonts you have substituted. The original font names are no longer present.

Managing Differences in the Windows and Macintosh Color Palette

If you are using Office applications such as Microsoft Photo Editor for Windows to create images that are used in cross-platform environments, you need to be aware of differences in the color palettes used by each platform. This is especially an issue for intranet and Web work, but it can crop up in any application where you must see accurate colors onscreen in a cross-platform environment.

Only 216 colors are shared in common between Windows and the Macintosh. If you use other colors, they are dithered, looking different from what you intended, and often much worse. None of the Office applications are capable of designing around this 216-color palette. If you use Office applications to generate images for the Web or your corporate intranet and you expect your audience to use both Windows and Macintosh systems, at minimum, check your images in both environments before deploying them.

For a detailed look at the issue of browser-safe Web color palettes, visit **www.microsoft.com/workshop/design/color/safety.asp**.

If you're serious about color on the Web, consider the shareware package ColorSafe, from BoxTopSoft (**www.boxtopsoft.com**), which maps images using millions of hybrid colors formed by combining four pixels of two different colors that are common to both the Macintosh and Windows platforms.

ColorSafe, available for both the Macintosh and Windows, works as a filter plug-in to Adobe PhotoShop and a wide variety of image-editing applications that support PhotoShop 2.5 plug-ins. These include the low-cost Paint Shop Pro shareware package from Jasc (**www.jasc.com**), as well as Microsoft Image Composer 1.5, a free add-on included with Microsoft FrontPage 98.

Controlling Subtle Differences Between Word 97/98 and Word 5.1 for the Macintosh

Over the years, Microsoft has made a number of subtle changes to Word's behavior, which may not be obvious to even the expert user. Some of these changes may cause documents to behave in unexpected ways. For instance, in Word 5.1 for the Macintosh, small caps appear larger than they do in newer versions of Word.

If you have carefully designed a document in an older version of Word, such as Word 5.1 for the Macintosh, and move it to a newer version, such as Word 97 for Windows, you may not want these settings to change. Word enables you to preserve settings such as these through the Compatibility tab of the Tools, Options dialog box (see Figure 24.10).

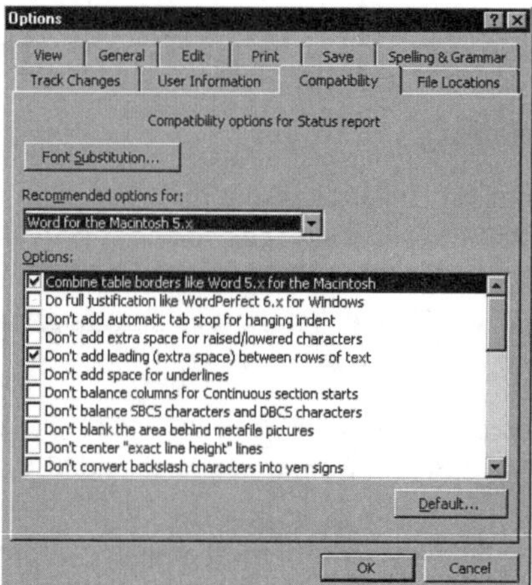

FIGURE 24.10
The Compatibility tab of the Options dialog box.

In the Recommended Options For drop-down box, choose the version of Word with which you want to remain compatible. Word displays the setting changes it makes. You can clear any of the marked check boxes. Click OK, and Word reformats the document to reflect these changes.

NOTE This is not purely a cross-platform feature—you can adjust Word 97 for Windows documents to reflect Word 2 for Windows formatting just as easily as Word 5.x for the Macintosh. Given the widespread use of Word 5.x for the Macintosh for nearly a decade, however, and the great popularity of Office 97 for Windows, this feature is likely to prove especially helpful to cross-platform Office administrators.

CHAPTER 25

Managing Microsoft Office 97 Small Business Edition

For many smaller companies, and companies of all sizes that rarely make presentations, Microsoft Office 97 Small Business Edition may be an attractive alternative to the Standard Edition of Microsoft Office. In place of Microsoft PowerPoint, the latest version of Microsoft Office 97 Small Business Edition substitutes the following three powerful programs:

- Microsoft Publisher—A desktop publishing program designed specifically for business users rather than graphic design professionals
- Microsoft Expedia Streets—A nationwide database of street information that can be used to plan both local and long-distance business trips throughout the United States
- Microsoft Small Business Financial Manager—A set of integrated worksheets that load into Microsoft Excel, import data from several leading PC accounting programs, and support a wide range of financial analysis

Small Business Edition Installation Issues

One significant *disadvantage* to Office 97 Small Business Edition is that it does not come with a unified installation routine, as do Office 97 Standard and Professional Editions. When you insert Disk 1 of the three CD-ROMs that come with this version of Office, Windows displays a window that enables you to choose separate installations of each program component, one at a time, as shown in Figure 25.1.

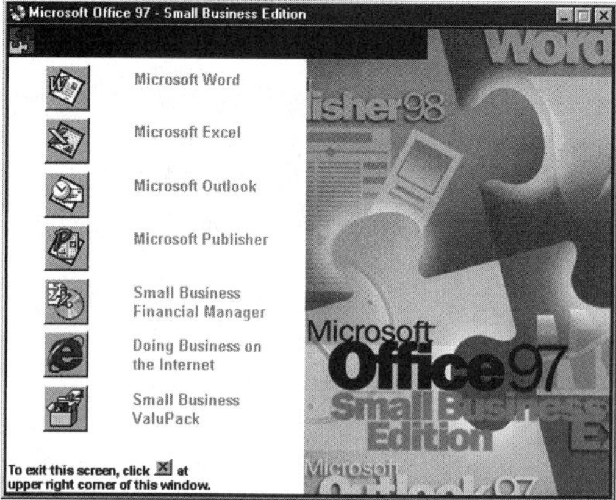

FIGURE 25.1
You can install Microsoft Office 97 Small Business Edition one program at a time from this window.

NOTE If this window does not appear, you may be one of many users who have turned off Windows' AutoPlay feature, you may have a CD-ROM drive incompatible with AutoPlay, or you may be running Windows NT Workstation 3.51, which does not support AutoPlay. Whatever the reason, you can install programs individually by finding their setup programs, which are located in the following folders (on Disk 1 unless specified otherwise):

- Word: \Word\Setup.exe
- Excel: \Excel\Setup.exe
- Outlook: \Outlook\Setup.exe
- Publisher (Disk 2): \Pub\Setup.exe
- Small Business Financial Manager: \Sbfm\Setup.exe

- Doing Business on the Internet (installs Internet Explorer 4.01, Direct Mail Manager, and other Internet resources; requires a Web browser to already be installed): \ValuPack\Internet\default.htm
- ValuPack Help file (provides information about each ValuPack component, which you then can install separately): \ValuPack\Valupk8.hlp
- Expedia Streets 98 (Disk 3): \Setup.exe

If you choose, you can customize a network installation of each individual application. To do so, follow the steps described in Chapter 2 and use the .stf and .inf files that appear in each program's folder. You can also automate the installation of Microsoft Office 97 Small Business Edition with Microsoft Systems Management Server, using the .pdf (Package Definition File) files provided in the Excel, Outlook, and Word (but not Publisher) folders.

Managing Microsoft Publisher 98

Microsoft Publisher 98 offers tremendous desktop publishing power to mere mortals. It includes built-in wizards for creating newsletters, brochures, flyers, business stationery and forms, awards, certificates and many other types of publications. Using these wizards, you and your colleagues can create publications in an extraordinary range of styles and formats, doing the "design work" in a matter of minutes. You can even "repurpose" your print publications as hyperlinked Web pages.

Publisher 98 even comes with "design sets" that make it easy to create consistent, matching publications to meet the needs of your entire organization.

As truly remarkable as Publisher 98 is, it also has the following significant limitations that you should be aware of as an Office administrator:

- Although it's very likely that Publisher's wizards can create publications that will meet your needs, if they cannot, Publisher's "from-scratch" design tools are more limited than those of high-end desktop publishing software.
- As a Web publishing tool, Microsoft Publisher 98 provides no way to view HTML source code and make the minor changes that are often necessary (although you can open source code in another editor, such as Notepad). In addition, Publisher's Web Forms feature—while very seductive to users—requires you or your Internet Service Provider to install and customize special script files from Microsoft's Web site. This is a significant hassle, and one you may not want to bother with.
- As discussed later, in the "Commercial Printing with Microsoft Publisher" section of this chapter, it can be very difficult to find a commercial printer willing to work with Microsoft Publisher files.

- Finally, a minor quibble: while Publisher 98's tools are extremely easy compared to "professional" desktop publishing software, the workspace can get very cramped. Publisher is much more convenient to use with a large, high-resolution monitor.

The following sections are designed to give you the tools you need to manage Publisher. You'll learn how to do the following:

- Install Publisher for use on a network
- Create a basic publication with Publisher
- Create a custom template that you can provide to all your colleagues, thereby helping to standardize your publications company-wide
- Use Publisher 98 and Microsoft Word 97 together
- Prepare Publisher publications for a commercial service bureau or printer

Installing Publisher 98 for Use on a Network

You've already learned that you can install the Publisher component of Microsoft Office 97 Small Business Edition by running the setup program in the \Pub folder on Disk 2 of the CD-ROM set. To streamline the installation process, you can also run an administrative installation on your network server, and allow users to install from there.

To create the administrative installation point, load the CD-ROM and enter the command `D:\Pub\Setup.exe /a` (use your CD-ROM's drive name in place of D:). Using the setup wizard, install Publisher with the options you prefer. Make sure your users have read rights to the administrative installation point folder.

After you've done all this, users can browse to the folder and run a standard setup (with no switches or parameters). You can mandate (or allow users to choose between) the following:

- **Workstation installation**. Running the program files from the network server (still requires 75MB local hard disk space, excluding clip art resources)
- **Complete installation**. Installing the software completely on the local workstation (requires 119MB local hard disk space, excluding clip art resources)
- **Custom installation**.The user can select components to be installed

If your network performance is especially good, or your workstation disk space is especially limited, consider running more of Publisher across the network from your network server. Running Publisher across a network also makes it simpler to create a shared template folder containing publication designs that you want everyone to use. This is covered later in the "Creating Shared Publishing Templates with Publisher 98" section of this chapter.

NOTE Running software from the server typically requires more RAM than running it from the local hard drive.

CAUTION

Most of Microsoft Publisher's wizards assume the presence of TrueType fonts included as part of the Publisher installation. If these are not present, the wizards default to Times New Roman or Arial, which may cause subtle problems with text flow in text frames and tables. To avoid these problems, make sure the fonts are installed locally.

If you have network software capable of metering software licenses, Microsoft permits you to purchase concurrent Microsoft Publisher 98 licenses for use on your network. If most of your users require only occasional access to Publisher, or if you need Office 97 Standard Edition but also need access to Publisher, this may be a cost-effective approach.

Creating a Basic Publication with Publisher 98

After you complete the installation, it is extremely easy to create the framework for a publication with Publisher 98. The following procedure shows you how to construct the framework of a newsletter:

1. Open Publisher. Publisher's catalog of publications appears (see Figure 25.2).

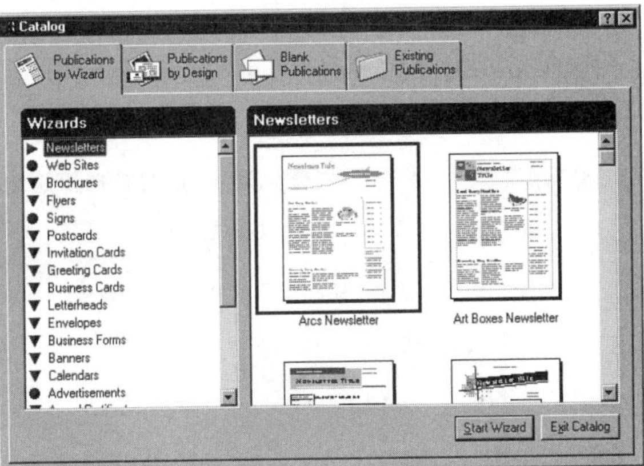

FIGURE 25.2
Microsoft Publisher 98 opens by providing an extensive choice of publication wizards to streamline production.

2. In the Wizards scroll box, choose Newsletters (if it is not already chosen).
3. Scroll through the Newsletters box, and click on the newsletter you want to use as your model (Publisher offers 28 options). Click the Start Wizard button to begin the process of customizing your layout.
4. Publisher creates a default newsletter (see Figure 25.3). As you walk through the wizard, Publisher adjusts the newsletter on-the-fly to show you the changes you're making.

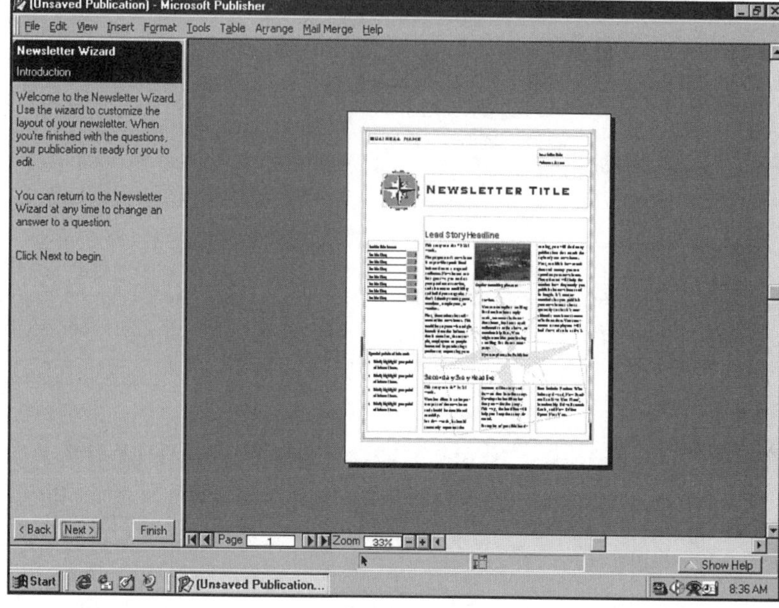

FIGURE 25.3
The Newsletter Wizard starts, enabling you to customize the newsletter layout that appears in the preview window.

5. Click Next.
6. The wizard asks you to select a color scheme—a set of colors that is guaranteed to harmonize well—from the 62 available schemes, as shown in Figure 25.4. Choose a color scheme and click Next.

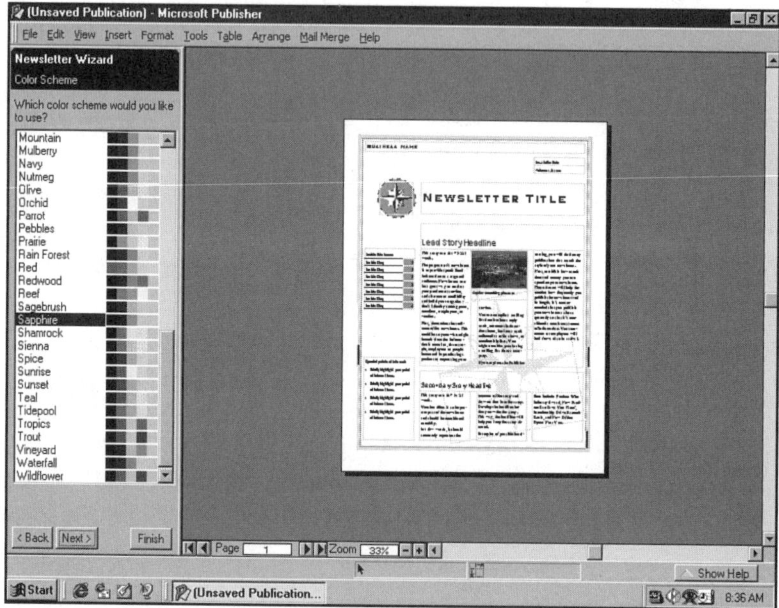

FIGURE 25.4
In this window, you can choose a color scheme from 62 sets of colors that Publisher makes available.

7. The wizard asks you to specify how many columns your newsletter will be: one, two, or three. Choose the number of columns and click Next.
8. The wizard asks whether you want a placeholder for the customer's address—in other words, whether you want to make space on the back of your newsletter for a mailing label. Choose Yes or No, and click Next.
9. The wizard asks whether you will print on one side or both sides of the paper; choose Single-sided or Double-sided, and click Finish. The wizard finishes making changes to your layout and displays the finished layout in the Workspace window.

After the framework for your newsletter is in place, you can edit the publication, replacing default graphics and text with your own.

Notice that Publisher has already placed newsletter titles, volume and issue numbers, tables of contents, captions, callouts, and other copy elements. Before you print the final publication, double-check that you've replaced them all with "real" copy, and deleted any leftovers.

Replacing a Boilerplate Graphic with a New Graphic It's easy to select any of the "boilerplate" images Publisher places in your publication and replace it with one of your own—just complete the following steps:

1. Right-click on an image; the shortcut menu appears.
2. Choose Change Picture, Picture, From File. The Insert Picture File dialog box opens.
3. Browse to the file that you want to insert, and click OK.

If your new picture is a different size from the one that was there before, Publisher automatically reflows text to accommodate it.

Replacing Boilerplate Text with New Text Similarly, it's easy to replace Publisher's boilerplate text with your own newsletter copy. To do so, perform the following steps:

1. Click inside any *frame* (section of text) to select all the boilerplate text.
2. Choose Insert, Text File. The Insert Text File dialog box appears.
3. Browse to the file that you want to insert, and click OK.

If your file is longer than the space available, Publisher offers to AutoFlow it into other text frames, or even create new pages as needed.

The boilerplate text in each large text frame tells you how many words will fit there, making it easier to adjust your copy to fit. If you have time to read the boilerplate text, you'll find useful tips on creating your publication.

Publisher can import text in a wide variety of formats, including Word 97/98, Word 6.0/95, RTF, Word 4.0 through 5.1 for the Macintosh, Windows Write, Microsoft Works 3.0 or 4.0 for Windows, WordPerfect 5.*x*/6.*x*, WordStar, Microsoft Excel, Lotus 1-2-3, and, of course, other Publisher publications.

Linking and Embedding Material from Other Office Applications

You can use Object Linking and Embedding (OLE) to insert part or all of a Word document, Excel worksheet, PowerPoint presentation, or other OLE-compatible document into Publisher. To do this, perform the following steps.

1. In the source application, select what you want to include.
2. Press Ctrl+C to copy it to the Clipboard.
3. Click on Microsoft Publisher in the taskbar (or load Publisher if it isn't already running).
4. In Publisher, click on the frame where you want to paste the item.
5. Choose Edit, Paste Special. The Paste Special dialog box appears (see Figure 25.5). To *embed* the Clipboard contents so they cannot change if the source document changes, click the Paste button and click OK. (You also may get to choose into which form you want the materials embedded in.) If you prefer to *link* with the Clipboard contents so that your Publisher publication *does* reflect changes made to the source document in the future, click Paste Link and click OK.

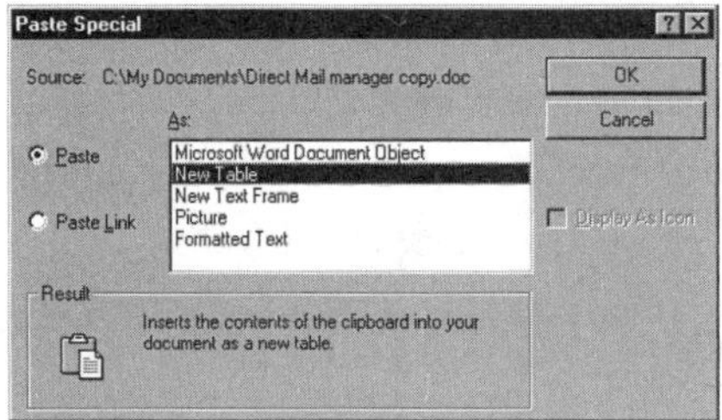

FIGURE 25.5
Linking or embedding material from another Office application.

Using Word and Publisher Together

Microsoft Word and Microsoft Publisher are tightly linked. In "Replacing Boilerplate Text with New Text" earlier in this chapter, you learned that you can import documents from several versions of Word into Publisher using the Insert, Text File command. When you do so, Word's styles and most of its font formatting remain intact.

> **CAUTION**
>
> Not all Word formatting survives. For example, headers and footers are lost, as are the animation effects available through the Animation tab of Word's Font dialog box.

Conversely, after you import text into Publisher, you may want to edit it with Word—a program truly designed for editing. To do so, follow these steps:

1. Right-click on the text frame. The shortcut menu appears.
2. Choose Change Text, Edit Story in Microsoft Word. Word opens with the contents of the text frame displayed.

3. Edit the text as you wish.
4. When you're finished editing, choose File, Close & Return. Word closes, and your edits are reflected in your Publisher publication.

Creating Web Pages from Your Publisher Publication

When your publication is ready to go, you can convert it to a set of hyperlinked Web pages. The quickest way to do so is with the Web Site Wizard:

1. Choose File, Create Web Site from Current Publication. Publisher creates Web pages and links based on your print document; for example, each entry in a newsletter's table of contents is transformed into a live hyperlink. It may also replace some standard graphics with animated GIFs that display brief animations when users browse to your page.
2. Make any manual adjustments to your Web pages that you believe necessary, using Publisher's editing and formatting tools.
3. Choose Tools, Design Checker. Publisher runs the Design Checker, which steps through your Web site a page at a time, identifying potential improvements to your layout (see Figure 25.6) and, if you want, pages that may load too slowly in users' browsers.

Design Checker works with both text and electronic documents.

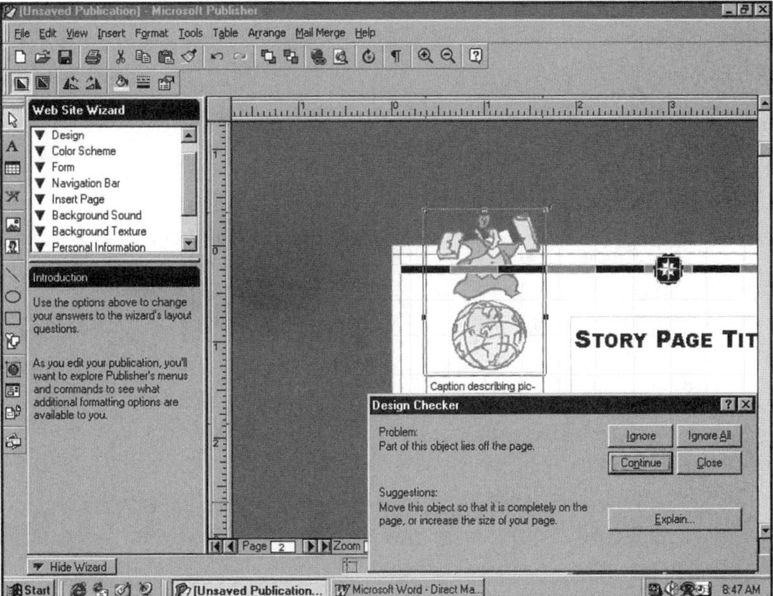

FIGURE 25.6
The Design Checker flags possible problems with your design; Click the Explain button for a detailed explanation.

4. Choose File, Web Properties to enter information about your site and individual Web pages.

   For example, on the Site tab (see Figure 25.7), you can specify keywords and descriptions that will appear as hidden *metatags.* Web search engines can use these metatags to accurately index your site. You can also specify whether to target your site to people with newer browsers (HTML 4.0+ browsers) or a wide range of new and old browsers (HTML 2.0+ browsers).

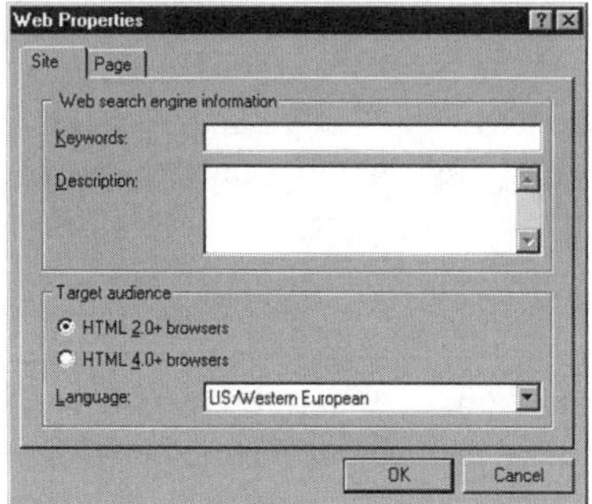

FIGURE 25.7
Specifying properties for your entire site, such as metatags.

   On the Page tab (see Figure 25.8), you can specify file names and extensions for each page, as well as the titles that will appear in users' browsers when they visit the page. All these site and page settings become part of the HTML code that Publisher creates.

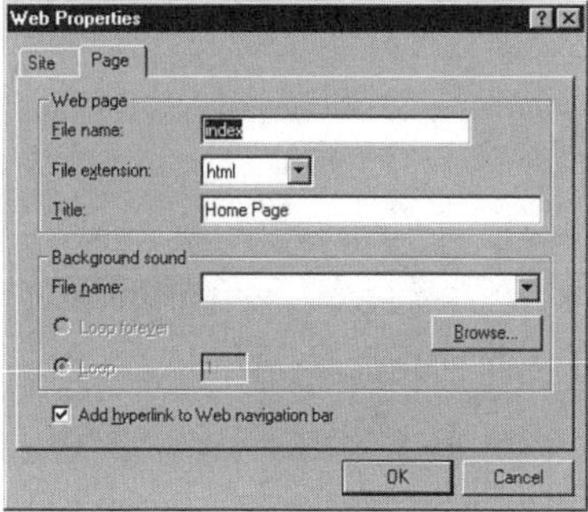

FIGURE 25.8
Specifying properties for individual pages, such as titles and filenames.

5. Choose File, Web Site Preview to display your pages in Microsoft Internet Explorer (see Figure 25.9). You can choose to view an individual page or your entire site with all links working.
6. When you've finished perfecting your Web pages, choose File, Publish to Web (see Figure 25.10) to walk through actually copying your pages to a Web server for "publication."

FIGURE 25.9
Previewing your pages in Internet Explorer 4.01.

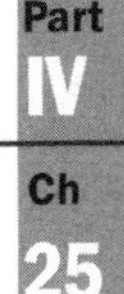

FIGURE 25.10
Running the Web Publishing Wizard.

Creating Shared Publishing Templates with Publisher 98

Whether you are creating print publications or Web pages with Publisher, you may want to standardize them so that it's easy for your colleagues to build documents with a consistent look. In Chapter 11, "Standardizing Document Production with Word and Excel," you learned how to create Word templates that made publications more consistent while also streamlining the process of creating them. You can do much the same thing with Publisher.

Start by creating your publication—most likely by using one of Publisher's many wizards. Add any custom elements that you expect to need regularly. For example, if all your newsletters include a "Letter from the President," set up a page that includes his or her photo, an appropriate headline and byline, and a blank space corresponding to the size of his or her monthly column.

Replace the generic components of the wizard's publication with your own; for example, insert your own newsletter title and corporate logo. Make any design adjustments you want; for example, use your company colors and typefaces in the document. Discard boilerplate text that you know you'll never need, but leave boilerplate headlines in place to help give the publication its shape.

When you've finished all this, choose File, Save As. In the Save As dialog box, check the Template box, and click Save. Publisher saves the file as a template.

To open a new document based on the template, perform the following steps:

1. Choose File, New.
2. Click the Existing Publications tab.
3. Click Templates. The Open Template dialog box opens, listing all of the templates stored in the Publications folder.
4. Double-click the template that you want. Publisher opens a new publication based on that template.

If you want to make available shared templates for everyone on your network to use, install Publisher so that the main application files are run across the network. Then copy the template files you want to share into the \Mspub\Template folder on the network server.

Even if you have installed all of Publisher's application files on individual workstations, you can edit the registry to point to a networked folder as the default folder for templates and other publications. To do so, perform the following steps:

1. Run the Registry Editor (regedit.exe).
2. Navigate to this registry key: `HKEY_CURRENT_USER\Software\Microsoft\Office\8.0\Publisher.`
3. In the right-hand pane of the Registry Editor, double-click on Default Path.
4. In the Edit String dialog box, enter the complete path to the network folder that you want to use.
5. Click OK.
6. Exit the Registry Editor.

CAUTION

As always, be extremely careful when editing the registry, and back up your System.dat and User.dat files before you begin.

CAUTION

Publisher 98 is very sensitive to lost network connections. If you open a publication from a network drive, and the network connection is lost, you may be prevented from saving the file, ***even if the connection is restored.*** At that point, the only way to save your file is to run a new Publisher session and copy changed pages one at a time from the first instance of Publisher to the second.

Commercial Printing with Microsoft Publisher

If you want to prepare a publication for commercial printing, Publisher 98 contains extensive tools to assist you. Before you begin, however, your absolute first step is to consult with your printer—the earlier, the better.

Unfortunately, as easy as it is to create publications with Microsoft Publisher, it can be equally challenging to find a professional service bureau or printer who will work with them. Many Macintosh-oriented service bureaus and printers refuse to work with Publisher files, primarily because the files are unfamiliar, but also because they can sometimes be troublesome. If you find that no service bureau in your area will work with you, the following resources may help:

- Victor Printing Service Bureau, Sharon, PA (`http://www.victorptg.com/service.html`, 800-443-2845)
- Newburyport Press Service Bureau, Newburyport, MA (`http://www.newburyportpress.com/homey.html`, 800-491-4700)
- RAM Offset, White City, Oregon (`http://www.ramoffset.com`, 800-352-6888)
- Megaprint (for oversized graphics only), Holderness, NH (`http://www.megaprint.com`, 800-590-7850)

The national printing chain Sir Speedy (`http://www.sirspeedy.com`) has many franchisees who work with Publisher files. Two other companies, Printovation (`http://www.printovation.com`) and Delu XE (`http://www.deluxe.com`) also print Publisher files with one major limitation: you must use their predefined templates. The special Printovation software and templates are included as part of the Microsoft Office 97 Small Business Edition ValuPack. Finally, in British Columbia, Canada, Mike Bailey (`http://www3.bc.sympatico.ca/mikeb/Mikeb.htm`) runs a business that specializes in creating reliable PostScript files from Microsoft Publisher documents.

A detailed guide to preparing Publisher files that will output to film well is located at `http://www.ramoffset.com//mspub.htm`.

Assuming that you've found a printer that will work with you, or a service bureau that will create film you can deliver to any printer, your next steps are as follows:

1. Consult with your printer on how he or she wants to have the files delivered, and on any special issues associated with graphics, fonts, or printer drivers. Make sure you

understand the process and workflow that will be used to get your document ready for printing—and the costs.

Microsoft Publisher provides a Printing Service Checklist you should use when you have this conversation. To print a copy, choose File, Prepare File for Printing Service, Print Publication Information, Printing Service Checklist.

2. Review the Publisher Help section named *Avoid common PostScript printing problems*, and make sure that your document reflects its recommendations.
3. Install the Windows PostScript printer driver that your printer wants you to use. This may be a Linotronic 330 printer driver, an Apple LaserWriter NT II printer driver, or a printer driver associated with a specific imagesetter—in which case, your service bureau or printer may provide it. After you've installed the printer driver, select it. You may need to make adjustments in your publication to reflect the slight (or not-so-slight) changes in layout this can cause.
4. Choose File, Prepare File for Printing Service, Set Up Publication, and follow the steps the wizard provides (see Figure 25.11).
5. In most cases, your printer will want you to deliver your publication in the form of a PostScript file. If so, choose File, Prepare File for Printing Service, Create PostScript File (see Figure 25.12). Make sure the right printer driver is selected, and click OK.

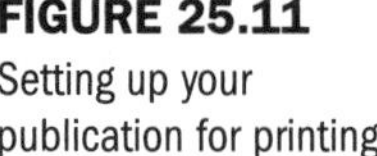

FIGURE 25.11
Setting up your publication for printing.

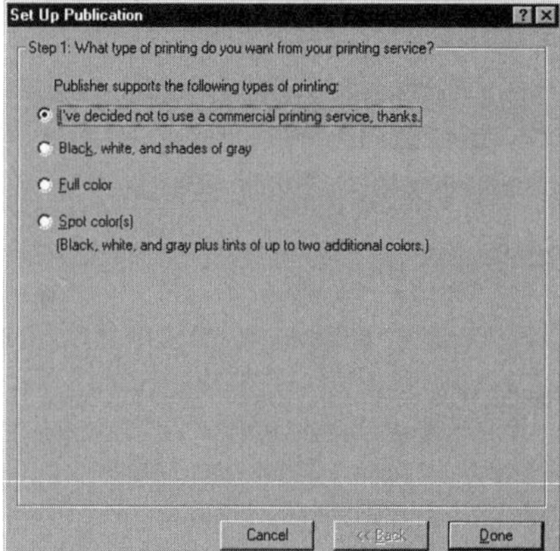

CAUTION

After you create a PostScript file, you cannot make changes to your document's contents, so be sure the document is correct before you take this step.

6. In the Print to File dialog box, browse to the location where you want to save the file, enter a file name, and click OK. Note that some printers prefer the file extension .ps (for PostScript) instead of Publisher's default extension .prn.

FIGURE 25.12
Printing your publication to a PostScript file.

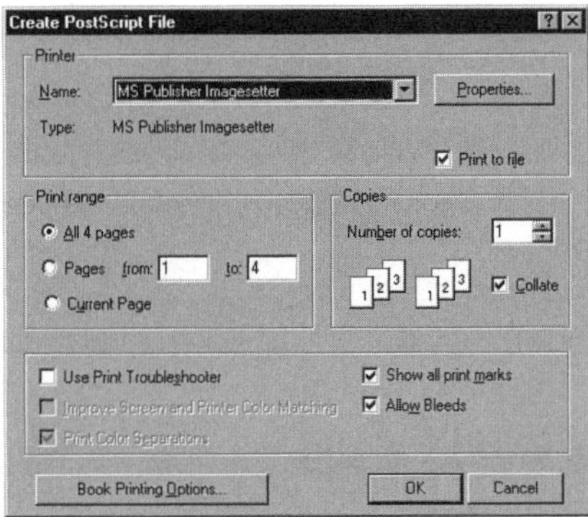

7. Publisher displays a dialog box recommending that you print a final proof and an "InfoSheet" (collection of information for your printer). Click Yes to print the document.

   Note that the document will print on your normal printer. If this is not a PostScript printer (and most business printers are not), there could be discrepancies. Ask your printer to see a proof created on a PostScript printer before you approve a job to be printed. If you happen to have a PostScript printer available on your network, use it if possible throughout the publication process.

8. Deliver your PostScript file to your printer, either on disk or via modem. (PostScript files tend to be large: you may need a Zip drive or some similar device in order to deliver them. Make sure your printer has a compatible drive.)

Managing Expedia Streets

Microsoft Expedia Streets (see Figure 25.13) enables you to locate and map street addresses and locations throughout the United States; personalize and print maps; get expert Zagat Survey restaurant recommendations; even choose a hotel and book it on Microsoft's Expedia travel Web site. While originally designed as a "home" product, Expedia Streets is useful for several business applications, including:

- Planning local and long-distance business trips—especially when you have the opportunity to make multiple visits within a small geographical area
- Choosing hotels that fit your business budget, and making reservations efficiently at Microsoft's Expedia travel site (`http://www.expedia.com`)
- Mapping your customer base to identify trends and opportunities for reaching new customers
- Creating maps for use by your sales force

> **CAUTION**
>
> You can copy maps from Expedia Streets to other applications through the Windows Clipboard. Remember, however, that these maps are not licensed for use in commercial publications such as newsletters, magazines, or Web sites.

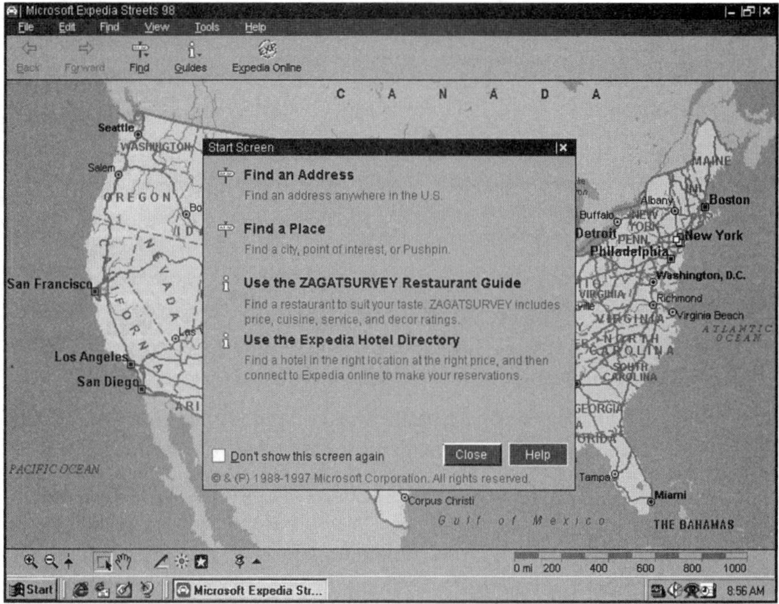

FIGURE 25.13
Expedia Streets opens with options to find an address, place, restaurant, or hotel.

Microsoft Expedia Streets fills the third CD-ROM of the Microsoft Office 97 Small Business Edition, and installs separately from the other applications. Note that Streets' Web connectivity features assume the presence of Internet Explorer 3.02 or higher. (Version 3.02 is included on the Expedia Streets CD-ROM, even though Internet Explorer 4.01 is also included on Disk 1 of the Microsoft Office 97 Small Business Edition CD-ROM set. If you've already installed IE 4.01, don't bother to install the older version.)

While you can install Expedia Streets on a network to provide convenient access for all your users, Microsoft's license requires you to purchase a separate license for every user. Of course, if you've purchased a copy of Microsoft Office 97 Small Business Edition for each user, you already have the license, but you cannot purchase just one copy of Microsoft Office 97 Small Business Edition and share the license concurrently with multiple users.

If you or your colleagues use Windows CE hand-held computers, you can now use Streets 98 to create custom maps that run on your Windows CE device. To do so, download Microsoft's Free Expedia Pocket Streets 98 and City Maps software at `http://www.microsoft.com/expedia/streets/pocket.htm`. Fourteen city maps are currently available at no charge: Atlanta, Boston, Chicago, Houston, Las Vegas, Los Angeles, Miami, New York, Philadelphia, Phoenix, San Diego, San Francisco, Seattle, and Washington, D.C. If the city you need isn't listed, Streets 98 has an export feature you can use to create your own city map.

Marking a Location with Expedia Streets

To find and mark a location with Expedia Streets, follow these steps:

1. If the Start Screen is displayed, click Find an Address. If not, choose An Address from the Find menu.
2. Enter the address in the Find Address dialog box (Figure 25.14), using as much detail as possible.

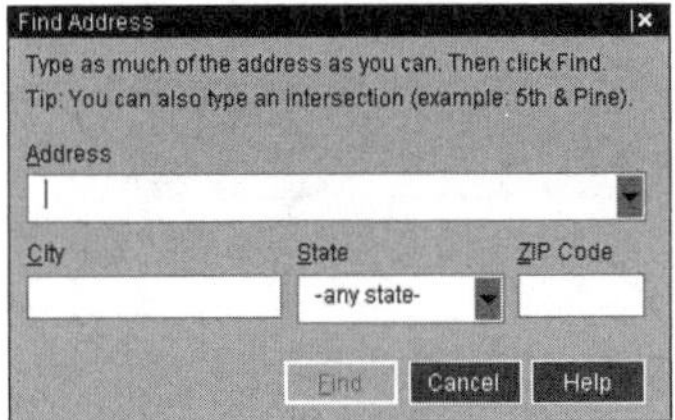

FIGURE 25.14
Enter the address in the Find Address dialog box, in as much detail as you can.

3. Expedia Streets reports the address (or multiple possible addresses) it has found. Choose the one you want, and click OK.
4. Expedia Streets displays a map of the area, with the address marked with a Pushpin.
5. If you want, you can edit the text on the Pushpin label. For example, you might want to include a company name in the first line, as shown in Figure 25.15.

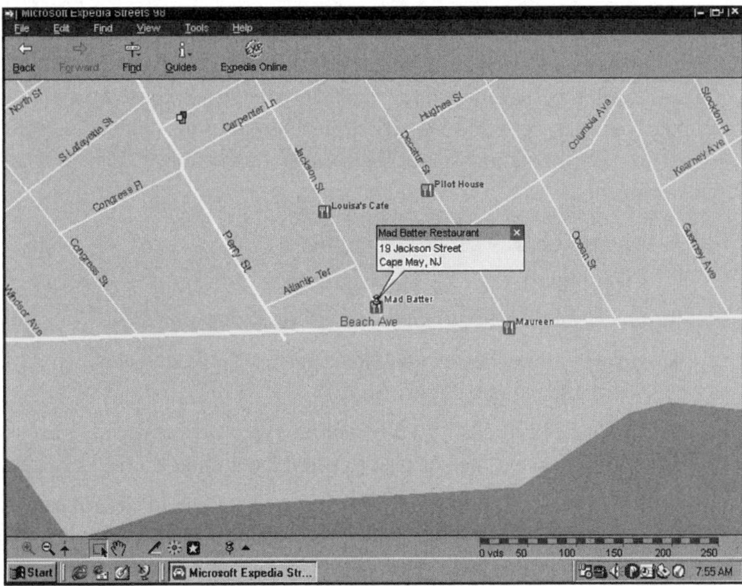

FIGURE 25.15
You can edit the Pushpin label to add a company name on the first line.

Later, if you want to find the address quickly, you can do so by choosing Tools, Pushpin Explorer; the first line of the Pushpin label appears in the Found Addresses folder (see Figure 25.16).

FIGURE 25.16
You can go back to a map quickly by choosing it in Pushpin Explorer.

Importing Multiple Names in a Pushpin Set

Finding locations one at a time is all well and good, but your organization may have hundreds, or even thousands of contacts. Fortunately, you can import address lists of up to roughly 14,000 names into Streets, which will apply Pushpins automatically. After you've done that, you can see at a glance how many contacts you have in a specific area; identify geographical trends in your business; and potentially discover new opportunities.

If you need to import more than 14,000 names, you can do so by splitting your address database into smaller files of 14,000 or less. You can import several database files into the same set of Pushpins.

To prepare an address file for import, save it as a comma-delimited (CSV) or tab-delimited text file. (Excel, Access, and Outlook can all create files in these formats.) Use the following data fields: Name, Street Address, City, State and Zip Code. Optionally, you can add an Additional Text field for annotations about the company or location. Then, in Expedia Streets, perform the following steps:

1. Choose Tools, Pushpin Explorer.
2. Click Import.
3. Select All Files in the Files of Type drop-down box.
4. Browse to the file you want to import, select it, and click Open. The Text File Import Wizard starts (see Figure 25.17).
5. Choose Text Balloon as the Pushpin type. (If you already have extensive text in the Additional Text field or plan to add it later, choose Full-Sized Attachment instead.)
6. If you want, click on the Symbol drop-down box to choose a custom symbol that will be associated with only the Pushpins in your new set of Pushpins. (For example, if you're importing sales leads, you might want a different icon than the one you used for current customers.)
7. Click New Set. The New Set dialog box opens.
8. Enter a name for this new set of Pushpins and click OK.

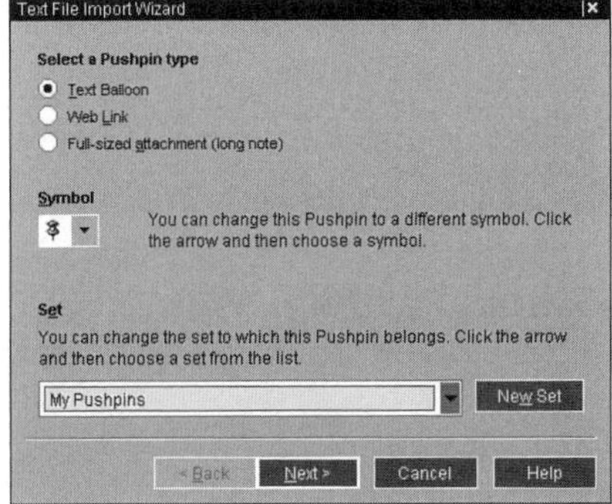

FIGURE 25.17
In the Text File Import Wizard, you can begin the process of importing an address file into Expedia Streets.

9. In the Text File Import Wizard window, click Next.
10. The wizard guesses which separator character you've used, Comma, Tab, Semicolon, or Other. Usually, it's right—but if not, fix the setting.
11. If the first row of your imported text contains column headings, check the First Row Contains Column Headings check box. Expedia Streets grays out that row, indicating that it won't be imported as a Pushpin.
12. Click Next.
13. In each Data Preview drop-down box, choose a field name corresponding to the contents of each column.
14. Click Next.
15. Review how Expedia Streets plans to create your notes and handle errors or ambiguous geographical information (see Figure 25.18), and make changes if necessary.

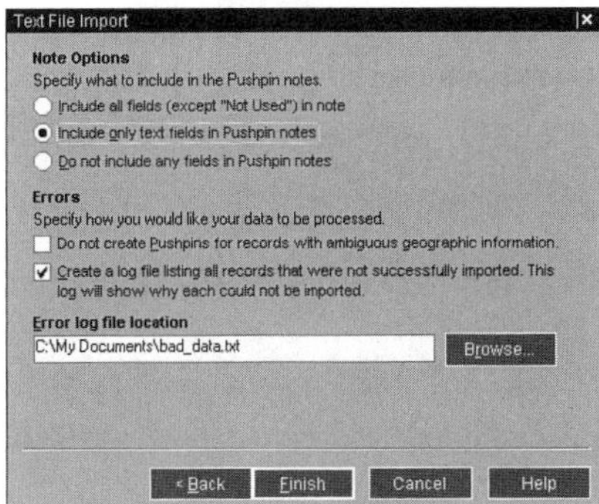

FIGURE 25.18
You have control over how Expedia Streets creates notes and handles ambiguous or incorrect addresses.

16. Click Finish. Streets imports the data, stopping for clarification whenever it encounters an ambiguous address. When it finishes, the new Pushpins are listed in Pushpin Explorer.

After you've created a set of Pushpins, you can provide it to another Expedia Streets user by exporting it. To do this, perform the following steps:

1. Choose File, Export Pushpins.
2. In the Export Pushpins dialog box, select the Pushpin set that you want to export, and click OK.
3. In the Export File dialog box, click Save. You now have an .spp file that other Expedia Streets users can easily import by using the File, Import Pushpins, From Pushpin File command.

Managing Small Business Financial Manager

Small Business Financial Manager (see Figure 25.19) imports the financial data you've created in any of several leading desktop PC accounting packages, adding powerful analysis capabilities that give you a clearer sense of where your business stands. Small Business Financial Manager 97 can import data from the following accounting packages:

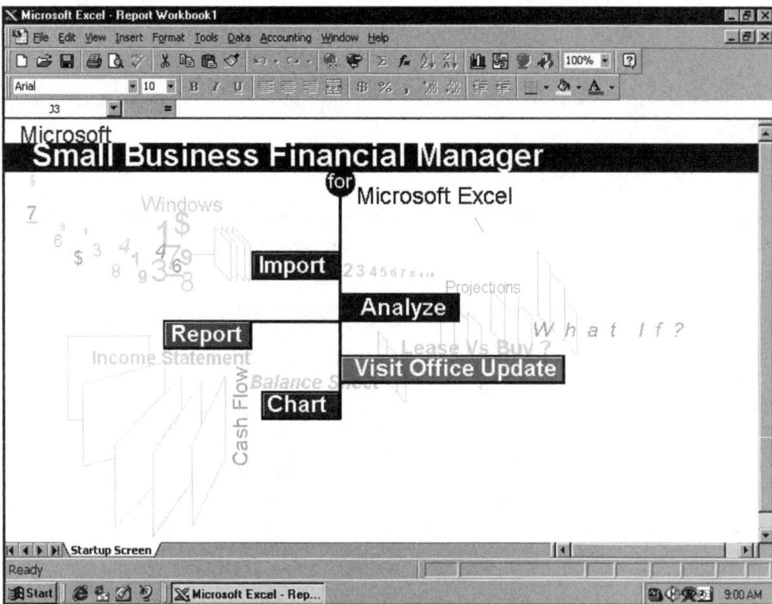

FIGURE 25.19
Small Business Financial Manager.

- ACCPAC Plus Account 6.1a (DOS)
- BusinessWorks for Windows 9.0 (Windows)
- DacEasy Accounting 5.0 (DOS)
- Great Plains Accounting 8.0, 8.1, 8.2 (DOS)
- MAS 90 Evolution/2 1.51 (DOS)

- One-Write Plus 4.03 (DOS)
- Peachtree Complete Accounting for DOS 8.0 (DOS)
- Peachtree for Windows 3.0, 3.5, 4.0, 5.0 (Windows)
- Platinum Series for DOS and Windows 4.1, 4.4 (DOS/Windows)
- QuickBooks 3.1, 4.0, Pro 4.0, 5.0 (Windows)
- Simply Accounting 3.0, 4.0, 5.0 (Windows)

Small Business Financial Manager 97 isn't a standalone program; rather, it is an add-in to Microsoft Excel 97. The results it generates make extensive use of Excel 97 pivot tables, so anyone who plans to use the program should become familiar with this feature first.

During the installation process, you're asked to choose the import filter that matches your accounting software, and whether you need a U.S. or Canadian version of the package. Once installed, you can either double-click on its icon to run it, or run Excel and choose its components from the Accounting menu that is added to Excel.

CAUTION

Keep in mind that the information Small Business Financial Manager provides may be sensitive to tax, legal, and accounting changes the software has no way of knowing about. Before you make major decisions based on the analysis you perform here, check it against common sense and/or consult a professional advisor.

To import your existing financial data into Small Business Financial Manager, first run the program. If you're warned that macros are about to run, choose Enable Macros. After the program is running, follow these steps:

1. Click Import. The first dialog box of the Import Your Accounting Data Wizard opens.
2. Make sure the Import option button is selected, and click Next. Screen 2 opens.
3. Either browse to your accounting files or allow the program to find them for you; click Next. Screen 3 opens.
4. Select the file you want to open, and click Next.
5. You're warned that the import process may take a few minutes. Choose Yes to continue. Screen 4 opens.
6. You now have the following three choices:
    - **Remap your accounting data.** This gives you a chance to double-check that your data has imported properly. It usually makes sense to choose this option first. After you've done so, move on to one of the other options.
    - **Create a financial report.** This enables you to choose among several key reports: balance sheets, cash flow, income statements, ratios, sales analysis, changes in stockholder equity, and trial balance reports.
    - **Perform a what-if analysis.** This enables you to project the impact of changes in sales revenue, costs, prices, inventory levels, rent or other individual expenses, and new or alternative methods of financing.

Depending on which choice you make, new step-by-step wizards appear to walk you through the rest of the process.

NOTE If you want to import data from QuickBooks, one of the most popular PC accounting packages, there are several important issues you should be aware of.

First, a registered copy of QuickBooks must be running on the same computer as Small Business Financial Manager.

Second, you must temporarily clear password protection from the file you want to import. Remember to restore password protection after you import the data.

Next, in QuickBooks, enter any "memorized transactions" that should be reflected in your analysis. To do so, first see if any memorized transactions exist by choosing Lists, Memorized Transactions. In the Memorized Transaction List dialog box, choose a transaction and click Enter Transaction.

Next, make QuickBooks Reminders unavailable. Choose File, Preferences. Click Reminders in the left-hand window, and for each option in the Reminders dialog box, click Don't Remind Me.

Finally, make sure no transactions dated more than 12 months ago are still open. (Most accounting software won't permit this, but QuickBooks does.) Choose File, Passwords. In the Transaction Password area, note the date through which books are closed: this date should not be more than 12 months prior to the current date. If it is, Small Business Financial Manager will hang while trying to import your data.

CAUTION

Small Business Financial Manager does not automatically password protect your financial data. If you're concerned about security, you should add a password yourself, as follows:

1. Choose File, Save As.
2. Click the Options button.
3. In the Password to Open text box, enter a password and click OK.
4. In the Confirm Password dialog box, retype the password and click OK.
5. Click Save.

Using Direct Mail Manager

Microsoft provides several "minor" components with Microsoft Office 97 Small Business Edition that you may find extremely valuable. One of the most useful is Direct Mail Manager (see Figure 25.20)—a great tool for streamlining and enhancing mailings of up to 3,500.

Using a simple, wizard-like interface, it starts by importing names and addresses you may already have stored in Outlook address books, Excel worksheets, Access databases, or Word tables. If you don't have the addresses you need, the software contains hyperlinks to leading Web-based list vendors, where you can purchase and download the names immediately.

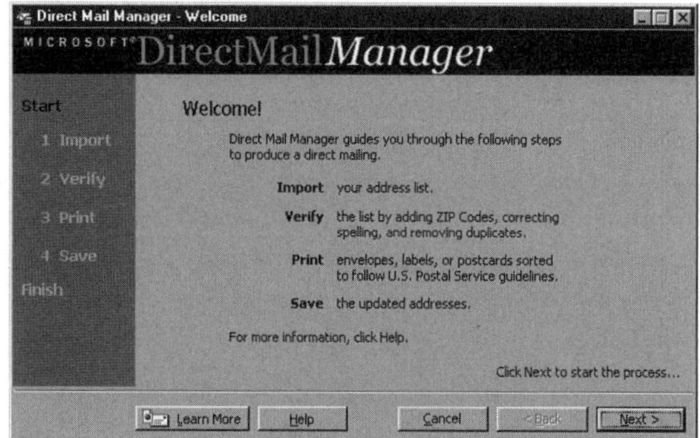

FIGURE 25.20
Direct Mail Manager for Office 97 Small Business Edition.

Assuming that you do have your own list, Direct Mail Manager gives you a chance to verify your names. Next, it connects to the Internet and compares each name in your database against the U.S. Postal Service's national zip+4 database, inserting the correct zip+4 zip code and correcting common addressing errors. In many cases, this can make your mailing eligible for significant postage discounts. Running on a 33.6 modem, it processes a little more than one address per second, which translates to roughly 15 minutes per 1,000 names.

After it's done all this, you get another chance to fill in holes, and Direct Mail Manager flags possible duplicate names, helping you save money by mailing fewer pieces. It then creates a data file that you can use to merge and print envelopes and documents created in Microsoft Word or Microsoft Publisher. Working with Word and Publisher's envelope and mail-merge features, Direct Mail Manager can even print envelopes with the correct postal bar codes for mailing.

For more complex mailings, you may want to upgrade to DAZzle Express, the enhanced version of Direct Mail Manager from Envelope Manager Software (`http://www.EnvelopeManager.com`, 800-576-3279). Unlike the version bundled with Office 97 Small Business Edition, the enhanced version can handle the following tasks:

- Mailings over 3,500 pieces
- Discount first-class mail-automation letters and cards (mailings exceeding 500 pieces)
- Enhanced Carrier Route Sorted Standard Mail (A) Automation Letters
- Nonprofit mailings

CHAPTER 26

Leveraging Office's Free "Mini-Applications"

Microsoft Office 97 comes with a suite of "mini-applications" that few Office users or administrators ever fully explore. In this chapter, you'll walk through the following five applications, learn what each of them can do for your business, and discover how to make the most of them:

- Microsoft Clip Gallery
- Microsoft Photo Editor
- Microsoft Equation Editor
- Microsoft System Information
- Microsoft Organization Chart

You may be surprised at how much power is hidden away on the Office CD-ROM in Office's so-called "minor" applications.

Using Microsoft Clip Gallery

Documents increasingly contain images and multimedia components. Microsoft Office contains a program for managing all the graphics and multimedia resources available to Office users: Microsoft Clip Gallery. (Office 97 SR-1 comes with Clip Gallery 4.0; Office 98 and the original shipping version of Office 97 come with Clip Gallery 3.0.)

To run Clip Gallery from either Office 97 or Office 98, choose Insert, Picture, Clip Art from whatever Office application you have open. After you open Clip Gallery, you can select an image (or other clip media), and click on Insert to insert it in your Office document.

Figure 26.1 shows Microsoft Clip Gallery 4.0 for Windows; Figure 26.2 shows Microsoft Clip Gallery 3.0 for the Macintosh. The most significant difference between the two versions is that Clip Gallery for Windows can import additional clip art directly from Microsoft's Web site; as the Office administrator, you may or may not want to permit this.

FIGURE 26.1
Microsoft Clip Gallery 4.0 for Windows.

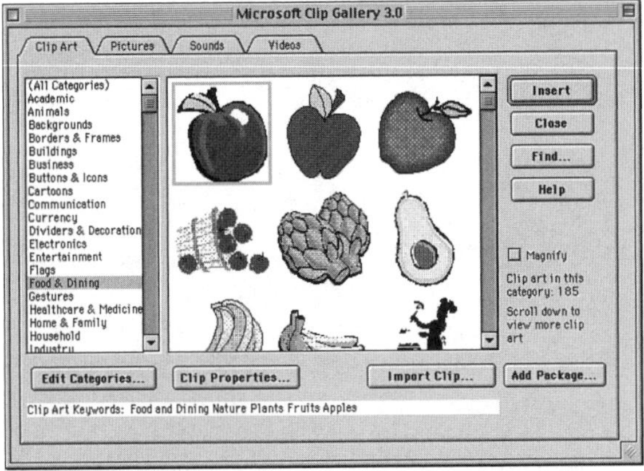

FIGURE 26.2
Microsoft Clip Gallery 3.0 for the Macintosh.

In Clip Gallery, media resources are organized into the following four categories:

- **Clip Art**. Includes Windows metafiles in Office 97 or PICT files in Office 98, as well as any other vector graphics you import into Clip Gallery.
- **Images**. Include bitmap graphics such as photographs, in formats such as BMP and JPG.
- **Sounds**. Includes Windows WAV and cross-platform MIDI or Apple QuickTime files.
- **Motion Clips**. May include Windows AVI files, Apple QuickTime files, and animated GIFs that can be used on Web or intranet sites.

Clip Gallery doesn't actually contain all the clips. Rather, it contains a database that stores thumbnail previews, category names, and keywords describing the clips. When you add clip art or change categories, as discussed next, you are actually updating this database. In Windows, the default database is a file called Artgal40.cag, which is typically stored in the Windows folder. On the Macintosh, it is called Clip Gallery User Database and is stored in System Folder:Preferences.

Importing Additional Clips Into Clip Gallery

Whether you have a new third-party package with 100,000 clip art images, or a half-dozen logos and product photos that are specific to your company, you can easily allow your users to access them through Clip Gallery. To add new images to the Clip Gallery database—and create new clip art categories if you choose—follow these steps:

1. Choose Insert, Picture, Clip Art to open the Clip Gallery.
2. Choose Import Clips.
3. In the Add Clips to Clip Gallery dialog box, browse to and select the clips you want (see Figure 26.3). You can select several consecutive files in a folder by holding down the Shift key while clicking to select the first and last files. You can select individual files by holding down the Ctrl key while you choose each image.
4. Click on Open. The Clip Properties dialog box opens (see Figure 26.4).
5. If you want to create a new category for your clips, click on New Category, enter a name in the New category name box, and click on OK. Otherwise, choose a category from the Categories scroll box.

You might want to force a category to appear first in the list of Categories—for example, to make sure users know there are company-specific clip files available to them. To do so, add an asterisk before the name of your new category.

6. In the Keywords text box, add any keywords that can help your users find the clip when they search for it.
7. If you want to give all your new files the same keywords and categories, check the Add All Clips to the Selected Categories check box.
8. Click OK.

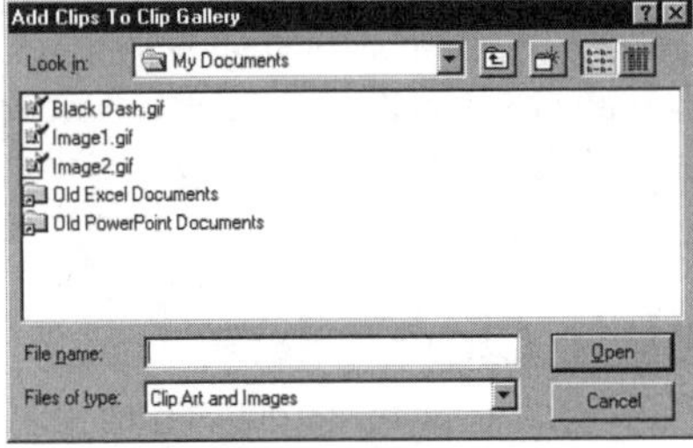

FIGURE 26.3
Here, you can select one or more clips to add to your Clip Gallery database.

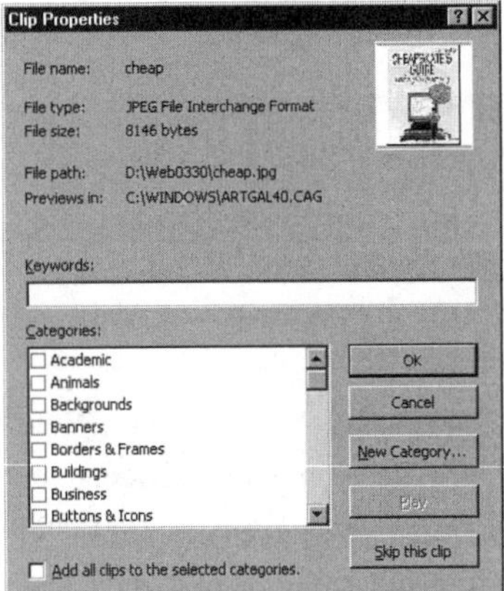

FIGURE 26.4
In the Clip Properties dialog box, you can specify information that makes media files easier to find.

Managing Microsoft Clip Gallery Centrally

You can install nearly 80MB of clip art and media as part of the Office 97 installation routine, and even more is available on the Office 97 Value Pack. If you happen to be running Office 97 Small Business Edition with Microsoft Publisher, there's an additional 254MB of clip art available, and that doesn't count any third-party clip art packages you may own.

For the Office administrator, the key question is how to make all this clip art available to your users without installing it all on every hard drive. This section shows you how.

Giving workstation users access to a centralized Clip Gallery database is a two-step process, and works virtually the same whether you are using Windows or Macintosh servers and workstations. First, you prepare the server. Second, you prepare the user workstations.

Preparing the Server First, copy all your clip media files to a folder on a network server to which your users will have access. If you're planning to use a shared CD-ROM drive (or a multi-CD mini-server or dedicated CD-ROM server) to store your clip art images, insert the CD-ROM or CD-ROMs now.

If Office 97 and Clip Gallery are installed on your network server, you already have a Clip Gallery database available on your server. You can use this database or you can make a copy of it with a different name that will serve as your network database. Some Office administrators like to place the database and the clip art images in the same folder, but this isn't necessary: every database entry contains the complete network path of the associated clip. Of course, if you're maintaining the clip files on read-only CD-ROMs, you couldn't store the database and the clips together even if you wanted to.

Next, on the network server, open an Office application and run Clip Gallery. As described earlier, customize the categories you want to use in your shared database, and import all the images you want to provide access to. This may take a little while, especially if you're importing images from a multi-CD clip art package with many folders on each CD-ROM.

CAUTION

Be aware of license restrictions that may prevent you from legally networking some CD-ROM graphics packages.

After you finish, close Clip Gallery. To prevent users from changing your clip art database without authorization, set it to read-only. (To do so in Windows NT, set the permissions for the database on the server to read-only for all users (the Everyone group). On the Macintosh, click once on the file; choose File, Get Info; and check the Locked check box.)

Preparing Workstations Now that your server is ready to deliver information from the shared Clip Gallery database, you need to set up each workstation to do so as well. Usually, you need to do this from the individual workstation. Typically, the most convenient method is as follows:

Ask each user to open Clip Gallery, click on Import Clips, browse to the new Clip Gallery database you've just created, select it, and click on Open. After a user does this once, Clip Gallery will always look for that database when it opens.

NOTE If you are working with Office 97 for Windows, and have an automated desktop management tool such as Microsoft Systems Management Server, you have another option. You can create a REG file and run it remotely on each of the systems you want to update.

Detailed directions for creating the .EG file appear in the Clip Gallery Help file, under *Information for network administrators*, in the section *Create a shared Clip Gallery database and configure users' computers.*

Using Microsoft Photo Editor

Microsoft Photo Editor, available for Windows only, is a basic photo editing program with the following capabilities:

- Cropping, resizing, rotating, and color-balancing images (the available choices in the Image menu).
- Basic special effects, such as sharpening, embossing, posterizing and adding textures (the available choices in the Effects menu).
- The capability to run any TWAIN-compatible scanner (File, Scan Image). TWAIN is a widely accepted interface standard for scanners.

Microsoft Photo Editor can open and save bitmapped files in the following formats: JPG, GIF, BMP, TIF, PNG, PCX, and Targa. (It can also open, but not save, files in Photo CD format. Other formats, such as WMF, can be copied in through the Windows Clipboard.) Because Photo Editor can work with JPG and GIF files, one of its most common applications is as a quick and easy way to create and enhance graphics for intranet and Web sites.

Note that Microsoft Photo Editor is not automatically installed with Office 97; you must check the Microsoft Photo Editor box in the Office Tools category of Office Setup in order to install it. If Microsoft Photo Editor is not installed, run a maintenance setup to add it.

If you own Microsoft FrontPage 98, also take a close look at the free, extremely powerful Microsoft Image Composer 1.5 software that comes with FrontPage (see Figure 26.5). Unlike Microsoft Photo Editor, it was designed from the ground up to create images for the Web, such as backgrounds, collages, GIF animations and more. It even contains a wizard that can help you create well-designed Web buttons in just a few moments.

To run Microsoft Photo Editor from within another Office program, or any program that supports OLE, perform the following steps:

1. Choose Insert, Object.
2. Choose Microsoft Photo Editor 3.0 Photo.
3. In the New dialog box, choose how you want to get your picture: you can acquire it through a scanner, create a blank picture, or open an existing picture (see Figure 26.6).
4. If you choose Blank Picture, specify the dimensions of your picture in the Blank Picture dialog box.
5. Click on OK.

You can also run Microsoft Photo Editor as a standalone application. Depending on how it was installed, it may appear as an item in the Programs list in the Start menu. Failing that, you can browse for the Microsoft Photo Editor Windows shortcut, which typically appears in C:\Program Files\Microsoft Office folder. Figure 26.7 shows Microsoft Photo Editor with an image displayed.

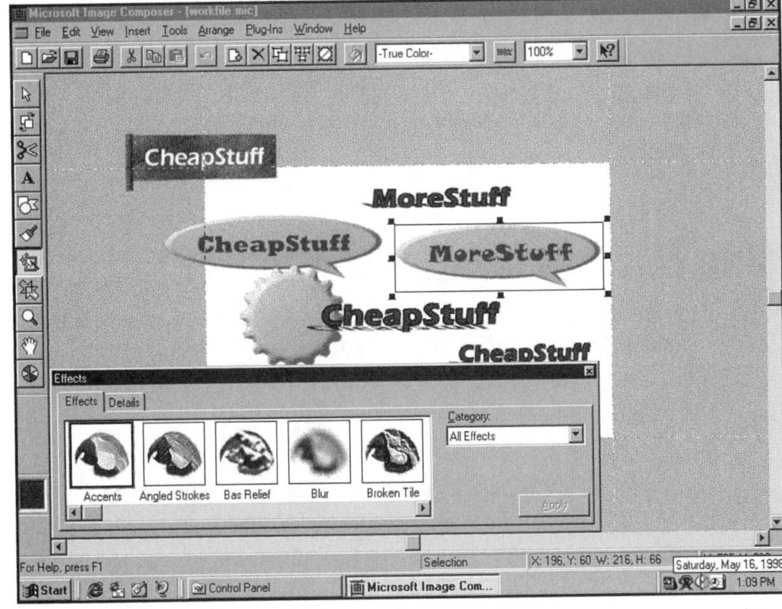

FIGURE 26.5
Microsoft Image Composer 1.5, a free add-on for Microsoft FrontPage.

FIGURE 26.6
Deciding whether to open, create, or scan an image.

Part IV
Ch 26

FIGURE 26.7
Editing an image with Microsoft Photo Editor.

If you (or your colleagues) create images in Microsoft Photo Editor that must be reviewed by others on the network, choose File, Send. Assuming that you're connected to a network and using Mail Application Programming Interface (MAPI) compatible email, Microsoft Photo Editor will open your email client software with the current image already attached. MAPI is Microsoft's widely accepted standard for sharing email messages across Windows applications.

Using Microsoft Equation Editor

If you are producing documents in a technical environment, you may need to create specialized equations. Office 97 and Office 98 come with a capable program to do the job: Equation Editor 3.0. These programs are not part of the default Office installation, but can be installed by checking the Equation Editor 3.0 box in the Office Tools category during the Office installation process.

To run Equation Editor 3.0 from any Office 97 or Office 98 application, choose Insert, Object, and select Microsoft Equation 3.0. A blank equation is inserted in your document and the Equation toolbar appears, as shown in Figure 26.8.

FIGURE 26.8
Equation Editor starts by presenting a blank equation and the Equation toolbar.

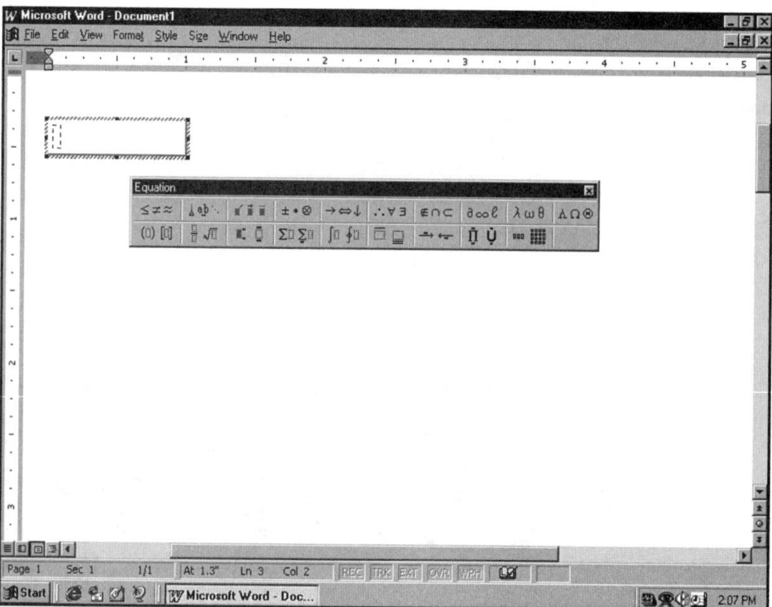

When you need to type standard numbers, variables, or standard mathematical operators (for example, plus, minus, or equal signs), do it from the keyboard. When you need a specialized mathematical symbol, click on the toolbar button that relates most closely, and then click on the symbol that appears. In Figure 26.9, for example, a Greek uppercase letter is being selected from a list of all Greek uppercase letters.

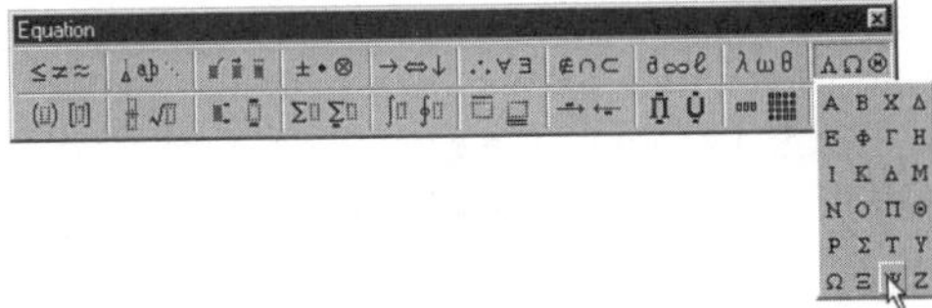

FIGURE 26.9
Choosing an item from an Equation Editor toolbar list.

To make an element in a formula superscript, press Ctrl+H; to make it subscript, press Ctrl+L. To more closely adjust the spacing of a formula, choose Format, Spacing, and work in the Spacing dialog box (see Figure 26.10).

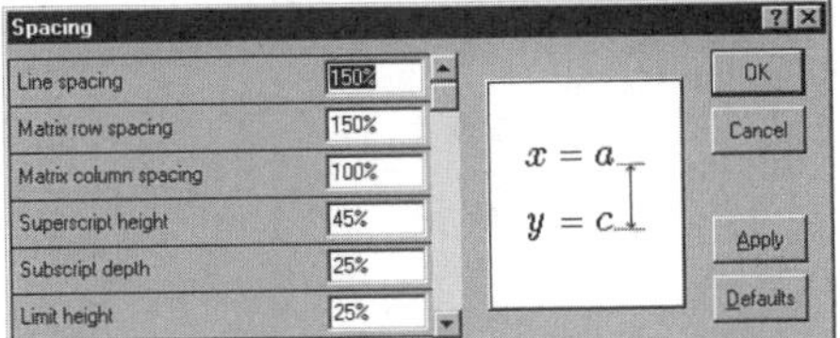

FIGURE 26.10
The Spacing dialog box offers precise control over the spacing in an equation.

Troubleshooting Differences Between Equation Editor 2.0 and 3.0

Equations created with earlier versions of Microsoft Equation Editor may be spaced differently after they are opened with Equation Editor 3.0. Occasionally, such equations may be widened beyond Equation Editor 3.0's capability to display them. In this case, you may receive the following error message:

```
This equation is the maximum size allowed. Please save the equation immediately.
If you want to continue, you must divide it into smaller pieces.
```

Disregard the message, and keep clicking on OK until it goes away. Then perform the following steps:

1. Double-click on the equation to select it for editing.
2. Choose Format, Spacing.
3. Scroll to the item marked Spacing Adjustment, and click inside the text box.
4. Change the 100% setting to 50%.
5. Click on OK.
6. Click *outside* the equation.
7. Press Ctrl+A and then F9. This updates all the fields in your document, including the equations.

Font Issues in Equation Editor

Equation Editor 3.0 depends on the presence of three TrueType Fonts: Symbol and Times New Roman, which are installed with Windows; and MT Extra, which is installed when Equation Editor is installed. If you copy documents containing equations to a computer where these fonts are not installed, the equations will not display or print properly.

The challenge arises when you need to output equations on a PostScript printer, and you do not want to use TrueType fonts. If you only have a few equations in your document, one possible solution is to convert the equations to metafile graphics before sending them into production. Note that line spacing may have to be adjusted after equations are converted into graphics.

CAUTION

Be sure to keep a copy of the document that contains the original equations (not converted into metafile graphics), in case you need to edit them later.

The following Visual Basic for Applications program will search your document for the next equation, and convert it to a metafile:

```
Sub FixEqs()
'
' FixEqs Macro
'
    Selection.GoTo What:=wdGoToEquation, Which:=wdGoToNext, Count:=1, Name:=""
    Selection.MoveRight Unit:=wdCharacter, Count:=1, Extend:=wdExtend
    Selection.Copy
    Selection.PasteSpecial Link:=False, DataType:=wdPasteMetafilePicture, _
        Placement:=wdFloatOverText, DisplayAsIcon:=False
End Sub
```

If you're publishing equations as part of a Web page, choose File, Save as HTML, and Word will automatically convert all your equations to GIF files.

If you're planning to use the same equation repeatedly, save it as an AutoText entry. If your colleagues are going to all use the same equations, build a library of AutoText entries and make it available to all of them. Equations inserted via AutoText work—and can be edited—no differently than equations you create manually in Equation Editor 3.0.For more information read up on AutoText entries in Chapter 11.

If You Need More Equation Capabilities

Equation Editor **3.0** is a stripped-down version of MathType, equation software published by Design Science, Inc. (telephone 800-827-0685 in the U.S. and Canada; 310-433-0685 elsewhere; **www.mathtype.com**). One especially useful feature that MathType offers is the capability to export equations to TeX, a widely used language for technical publishing.

Using Microsoft System Information (MS Info)

Microsoft System Information (MS Info), available in Office 97 for both Windows and Macintosh platforms, is a remarkably under-appreciated tool for system tracking and trouble-shooting. To access Microsoft System Information, choose Help, About Microsoft Word from within Word (or Help, About... from within any other Office application). Next, in the About Microsoft Word dialog box, click on System Info. The Microsoft System Information application opens.

TIP Microsoft System Information can also be run as a standalone program. It's typically located in C:\Program Files\Common Files\Microsoft Shared\Msinfo\Msinfo32.exe.

Figure 26.11 shows Microsoft System Information for Office 97 running in Windows 95; Figure 26.12 shows it running in Microsoft Office 98 for the Macintosh under MacOS 8.1.

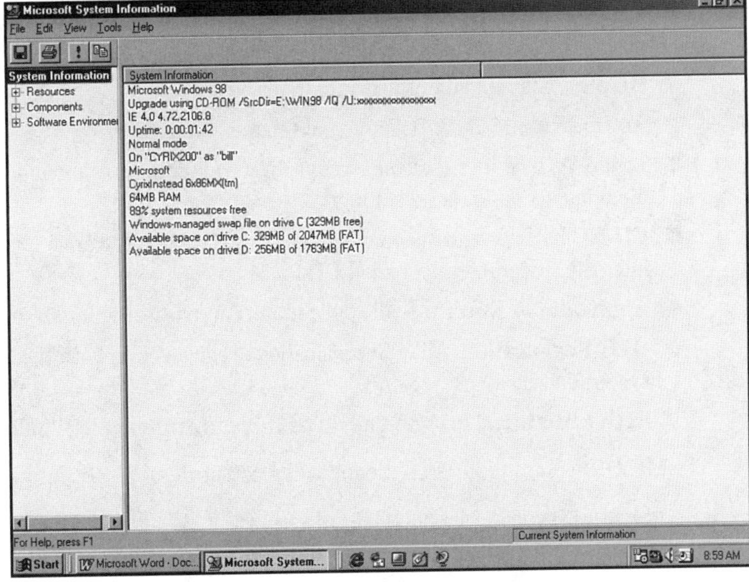

FIGURE 26.11
Microsoft System Information for Office 97, running under Windows 95.

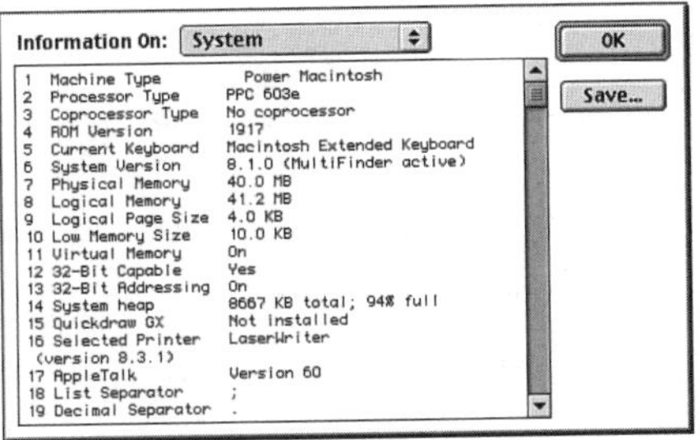

FIGURE 26.12
Microsoft System Information for Office 98, running under MacOS 8.1.

Microsoft System Information reports on virtually every aspect of a computer relevant to the operation of Microsoft Office (and most other Windows applications, too). In Windows, it provides detailed information in all the following categories:

- **Windows System Information**. The version of Windows running on the computer, swap files and available disk space, USER and GDI memory in use, printer drivers, and running DLLs

- **Fonts**. Lists of font substitution settings (for example, Helv to MS Sans Serif), presence of third-party font managers such as Adobe Type Manager
- **Proofing**. Registry settings, INI settings (if any), and custom files related to Office proofing tools
- **Graphics Filters**. Lists of all import and export filters available to Office, with file sizes, version dates and associated file extensions
- **Text Filters**. Lists of all import and export filters available to Office, with file sizes, version dates, and associated file extensions
- **Display**. Current video card and driver
- **Audio**. WAV, MIDI, CD-Audio and related settings
- **Video**. AVI, codecs (software or hardware for compressing and decompressing video files) in use, and related settings
- **CD-ROM**. Type and speed of system CD-ROM drive, transfer rates, data transfer integrity, and currently loaded CD-ROM
- **Applications Running**. All applications currently running in the system
- **OLE Registration**. All OLE applications registered in both the Windows registry and system INI files
- **Active Modules**. Program modules currently running in Windows

The MacOS version reports on the following categories:

- **System**. Type of Macintosh, hardware, OS and finder versions, memory usage, system heap, selected printer, AppleTalk version, video output, and more
- **Disk storage**. Available hard drives, file system, date initialized, free space, number of files and folders
- **Fonts**. Lists all installed fonts and whether they are TrueType fonts
- **System Extensions**. Lists all loaded system extensions, with creation dates, size, and version numbers
- **Application**. Lists the Office application running, with version information
- **Converters**. Lists text and graphics import and export filters
- **Proofing Tools**. Lists proofing files, custom dictionaries, and installed languages

In the Windows version of Microsoft System Information, you can print a copy of your system's current settings by clicking on the Print icon. You can also click on Save to compile a tab-delimited listing of all the same settings. Either way, it may take Microsoft System Information a few minutes to gather all the information it needs. If you choose to save the file, it is stored in C:\Windows\MSinfo32.txt. On the Macintosh, the default filename is MSInfo Output, and the default storage location is the Microsoft Office 98 folder.

If you don't have a formal desktop management and remote troubleshooting system in place, consider compiling copies of MSinfo32.txt for all the systems you install Office on.

Using Microsoft System Information as a Supplementary Control Panel

You can use the Windows version of Microsoft System Information as a supplementary "Control Panel" for managing your PCs. For example, if you choose File, Run, Microsoft System Information displays the Run Application dialog box, which gives you one-click access to nearly all the programs you might need to reconfigure a system that's causing trouble (see Figure 26.13).

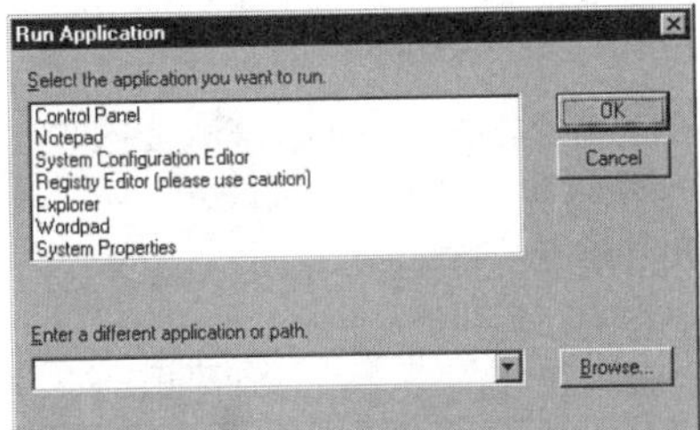

FIGURE 26.13
The Run Application dialog box.

You can also test and reconfigure a system's multimedia settings from inside Microsoft System Information—a feature that might come in handy if, for example, one of your colleagues is having trouble with the soundtrack to a PowerPoint presentation.

To test whether audio is working, perform the following steps:

1. Click on the Audio category in the main Microsoft System Information window.
2. Click on the type of audio you want to test—for example, WAV or MIDI file.
3. Choose Test, Test Media Driver. Microsoft System Information will locate and attempt to play an audio clip in the format you've selected. (If the program can't find a clip, it will ask you to browse for one.)
4. After the clip is played, Microsoft System Information asks whether you heard it. If so, click on Yes; the program enters Yes in the Tested OK? category. If not, click on No.
5. To check your multimedia settings, choose Tools, Configure Multimedia, and the Multimedia Properties dialog box appears, from where you can configure all Windows multimedia devices and settings.

By default, Microsoft System Information's System category does not show available space on network drives, but if you have Office components or data stored on network drives you might want this information. When you click on System to display available drive space, also hold down the Shift key, and the program will list space on available network drives.

Using Microsoft Organization Chart 2.0

You probably won't want to create the master organization chart for a Fortune 500 company using Microsoft Organization Chart 2.0. For that, you'd want a full-fledged organization chart program like Broderbund Org Plus.

Having said that, Microsoft Organization Chart 2.0 *is* a valuable tool for the quick-and-dirty org charts needed by departments, workgroups, and on-the-fly "virtual teams." It's also quite useful for planning the structure of small intranets.

To open Microsoft Organization Chart 2.0, perform the following steps:

1. Choose Insert, Object.
2. In the Object Type list box, choose MS Organization Chart 2.0, and click on OK. (In Office 98 for the Macintosh, choose Microsoft Organization Chart 2.0.)

From inside Excel or PowerPoint, choose Insert, Picture, Organization Chart. Whichever method you choose, Microsoft Organization Chart 2.0 appears, with a sample organization chart already in place, as shown in Figure 26.14.

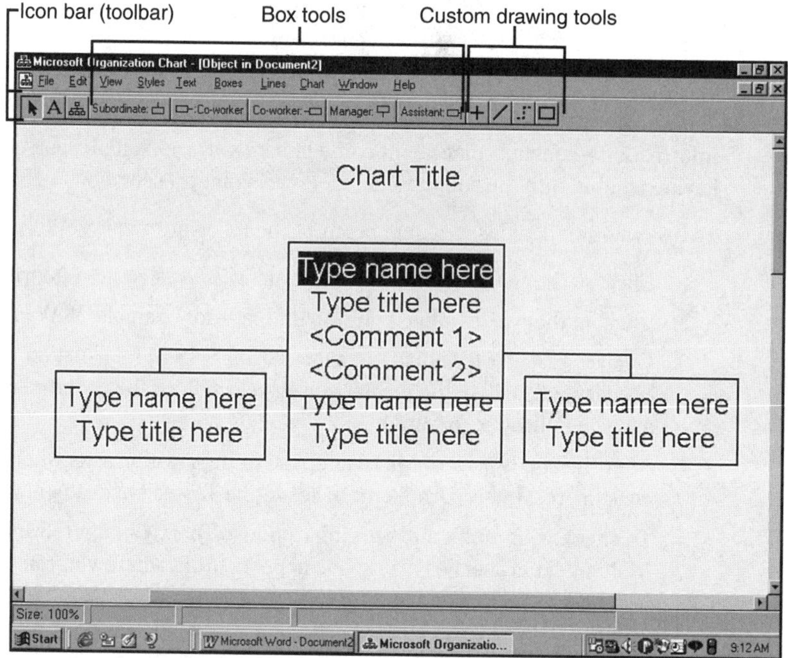

FIGURE 26.14
Microsoft Organization Chart 2.0 opens with a chart containing a supervisor and three subordinates.

Editing Organization Charts

After your organization chart is open, you can click on any existing text (for example, *Type name here*, *Type title here*, and two comment lines) and enter information about any individual.

You can easily add new individuals to your organization chart. On the icon bar (toolbar), click on the box tool corresponding to the type of employee you want to add: subordinate, coworker, manager, or assistant. Then, click on the existing box with which the new employee has the relationship. If you're adding a manager, for example, click on the box of someone the manager will manage. Organization Chart adds a blank box for your manager; you can now enter his or her name, title, and two comment lines.

You can change relationships by dragging individual boxes to reflect the new relationships, or by adding lines using the Custom Drawing Tools for creating new horizontal, vertical, and diagonal lines, and rectangles. (If the custom drawing Tools aren't visible on the toolbar, choose View, Show Draw Tools.) You can even downsize someone by selecting his or her box, and pressing the Delete key.

Microsoft Organization Chart 2.0 also offers moderate control over formatting. To reformat a box, first select it. If you want to reformat more than one box, hold down the Shift key while you select them all, or drag the arrow pointer across all the boxes that you want to select. Another approach is to right-click on the organization chart's background and select the categories of boxes you want to format—for example, All Managers or All Assistants (see Figure 26.15).

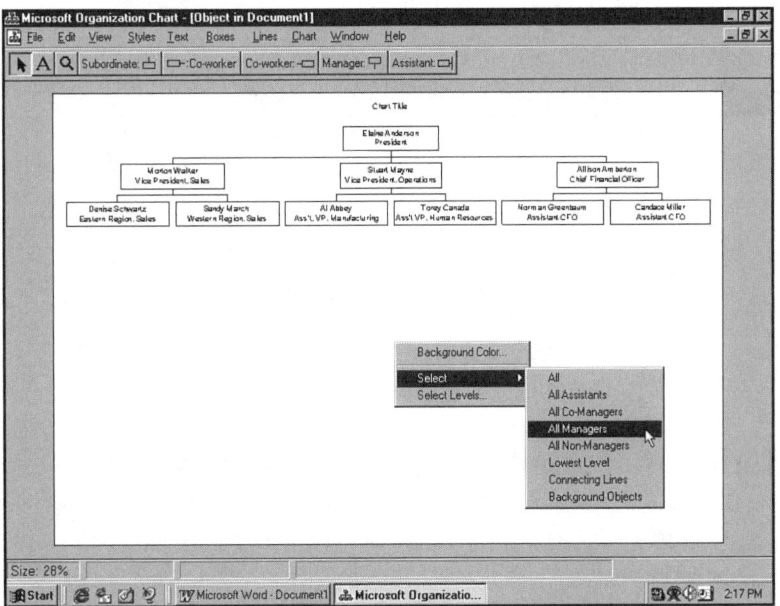

FIGURE 26.15
Choosing to reformat only boxes containing Managers.

After you select the boxes, lines, or objects you want to format, you can perform the following tasks:

- Format groups of employees from the Styles menu
- Format text in boxes from the Font menu
- Format box borders and fills from the Boxes menu
- Format line thickness, style, and color from the Lines menu
- Format the chart's background color from the Chart menu

NOTE One limitation to Microsoft Organization Chart formatting: organization charts have a way of getting very wide quickly. The only way to limit the size of individual boxes is to reduce the size of text inside them.

Incorporating Your Company Logo in Your Org Charts

Using Microsoft Organization Chart 2.0, you can place your company's logo (or any other bitmapped image) in the background of your organization charts.

To place an image in your org chart, open Microsoft Organization Chart 2.0 and follow these steps:

1. Open a bitmapped version of your corporate logo, such as a BMP, PCX, TIF, GIF, or JPG file. (Depending on the format, you can use Microsoft Paint, Microsoft Photo Editor, or another graphics program.)

If you only have "vector art," such as a CorelDRAW file, you may be able to open it in a program such as Paint Shop Pro, and copy it to the Clipboard from there.

2. In your graphics software, select the image (or part of it).
3. Choose Edit, Copy.
4. Switch to Microsoft Organization Chart 2.0.
5. Click on the background of your organization chart (don't click on a box within the chart).
6. Choose Edit, Paste. The image will appear in your organization chart.
7. Drag the image to the location where you want it to appear.

Storing an Image for Use on Your Intranet

Today, one of the most common uses for organization charts is on corporate intranets. Not surprisingly, the native OPX format for organization charts isn't readable on the Web. It's easy to save an organization chart in Web-readable format, however, with the help of Microsoft Photo Editor (discussed earlier in this chapter).

To save an organization chart in a form that's readable on the Web, perform the following steps:

1. In Microsoft Organization Chart 2.0, choose Edit, Select, All (or press Ctrl+A) to select all the boxes in your org chart. (The title is not selected.)
2. Choose Edit, Copy.
3. Open Microsoft Photo Editor. (If you've installed this program, you can typically open it by choosing Start, Programs, Microsoft Photo Editor.)
4. Click on the New toolbar button. The Blank Picture dialog box appears.
5. If your organization chart contains colors, make sure Palette or 256 Color is selected in the Image Type drop-down box.
6. If your organization chart is especially wide, create a wider image by setting Width to 10". You may also have to adjust the Height setting.
7. Click on OK. Photo Editor creates a new, empty image.
8. Choose Edit, Paste. The organization chart appears.
9. To crop the image, click on the Select toolbar button, drag the mouse pointer to select only the area of the image you need, and choose Edit, Copy. Then choose Edit, Paste as New Image.
10. Choose File, Save.
11. Select CompuServe GIF in the Save As Type drop-down box.
12. Click on Save.

In general, organization charts saved as GIF files look much better than those saved as JPGs. If you save a document, worksheet, or presentation containing an organization chart as an HTML Web page, Office will automatically convert the organization chart to GIF format.

Integrating Microsoft Organization Chart 2.0 with Org Plus for Windows

Microsoft Organization Chart 2.0 is actually a stripped-down version of Broderbund's Org Plus for Windows, and can open OPX chart files created by the following versions of Org Plus for Windows:

- Version 3.1
- Advanced Versions 4.0, 5.0, 6.0, and 6.01
- Org Plus for Windows Versions 1.0 and 2.0

Org Plus features that do not exist in Microsoft Organization Chart 2.0 will be lost once the file is saved again, so it makes sense to save the file under a new name.

If you save a chart in OPX format, you'll be able to open it in Org Plus for Windows.

Advanced Features Not Available in Microsoft Organization Chart 2.0

If you need any of the following capabilities, you may want to upgrade to Org Plus for Windows:

- The capability to create bigger charts and squeeze bigger charts into less space
- More control over how individual boxes (or groups of boxes) appear
- Hidden boxes and hidden information
- Images in boxes, such as photos of individuals
- Additional text fields for each individual
- Automatically updateable date stamps and Amount fields
- Find/Replace information in org chart boxes
- Style sheets for standardizing chart appearance
- Calculations and employee counting features
- The capability to import org chart information from databases and other software
- More extensive graphics file import/export capabilities

TIP For information about one additional Office applet, the Microsoft Chart Wizard, see Chapter 11.

CHAPTER 27

Enhancing Office with Third-Party Add-Ins and Products

Office is remarkably malleable: it can be extended in many ways, including templates, recorded macros, Visual Basic programs, and Word add-ins, to name a few. This gives software developers significant opportunities to build on Office, delivering features that Microsoft left out, or specialized capabilities unlikely to be made part of a general-purpose office software suite. Often these supplementary products give the Office administrator important options for solving business problems or improving productivity. In this chapter, you'll learn about the following important categories of products for extending Microsoft Office:

- Supplemental proofing tools
- Third-party Excel worksheets and add-ins
- Enhancements to Microsoft Word
- Voice recognition software
- Vertical market software
- Tools for publishing help files

In reading this chapter, you may discover that a third-party developer has already streamlined tasks you thought were impossible or impractical with Office, and built them into a product you can purchase off the shelf.

Comprehensive Proofing Tools from Alki Software

Office 97 and Word 97 for Windows ship with Microsoft's standard English-language proofing tools, including a 137,000-word dictionary based on the *American Heritage Dictionary.* You may, however, want to extend Office's proofing capabilities by adding specialized dictionaries available from Alki Software, 206-286-2600, **www.alki.com**.

Alki's Comprehensive Spelling Dictionary for Office 97 replaces Word's built-in dictionary, adding 75,000 specialized medical, legal, and business terms, such as *bailee, immunodeficiency, glycemia, conveyancing, interpleader,* and *unamortized*—all terms unrecognized by the standard dictionary.

NOTE In the U.S., Alki Software also markets foreign language proofing tools, which are discussed in detail in the "Adding International Proofing Tools" section of Chapter 37.

Third-Party Excel Worksheets

Several companies are in the business of developing pre-built Excel worksheets that simplify the preparation of a wide variety of financial statements and documents.

Village Software (**www.villagesoft.com**) offers two lines of business products. Its FastPlans products are designed to streamline the processes of creating business and marketing plans, preparing proposals, organizing meetings, and tracking reports. The company's FastAnswers products provide in-depth analysis for tasks such as the following:

- Preparing financial plans for investors (Fast-Cast for Ventures)
- Analyzing key financial ratios (Ratio Evaluator FastAnswer)
- Leasing versus purchasing (Lease vs. Purchase FastAnswer)
- Troubleshooting key areas of operating and financial risk (Business Troubleshooter FastAnswer)

KMT Software, Inc., (**www.kmt.com**) offers the Office In Color—Platinum Template Collection; a set of attractively designed Excel templates for company finance, business forms, and planning (with matching Word and PowerPoint templates for creating sets of matching documents wherever appropriate). KMT's Winning Business Plans In Color includes a Business Plan Wizard that simplifies business plan development in Excel, and also includes matching Word and PowerPoint templates for professional presentation.

Power Utility Pak for Excel 97 (PUP 97) from JWalk & Associates (**www.j-walk.com**) adds more than 40 functions to Excel, including useful functions like CREDITCARD, which returns the card type of a credit card number, or returns 'Invalid' if the number is not valid. PUP 97 also adds more than 30 utilities for editing text, formatting, managing worksheets, workbooks, charts, batch printing, and exporting range selections as graphics or separate files. Figure 27.1 shows PUP 97's dialog box for converting units of measurement between the metric and English systems.

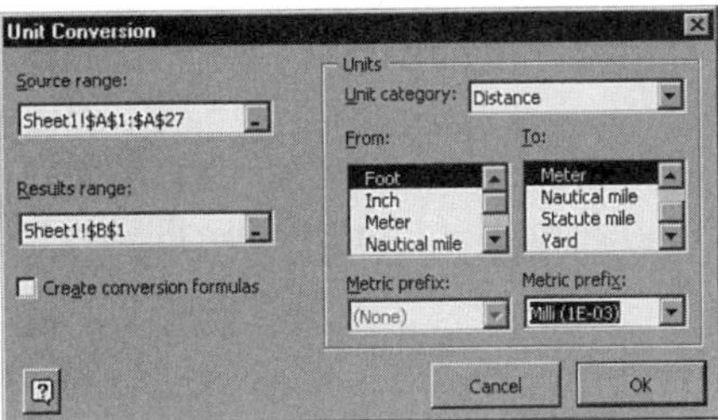

FIGURE 27.1
PUP 97's Unit Conversion dialog box.

Baarns Consulting (**www.baarns.com**) has made several of its Excel worksheets available at no charge at **www.baarns.com/Publish**. Some of these products were created for earlier versions of Excel but should continue to work in Excel 97 (although no technical support is available). The no-cost worksheets include the following:

- **Cost Estimating Form.** For estimating job costs, based on unit material costs and/or labor hours. This worksheet is shown in Figure 27.2.
- **Employee Database.** For tracking employees records
- **Inventory Tracker.** For tracking inventory levels and reordering information
- **Scheduler.** A simple way to track scheduling of a project without project management software
- **Time Billing Log and Invoice.** For tracking hours, preparing statements, and creating invoices

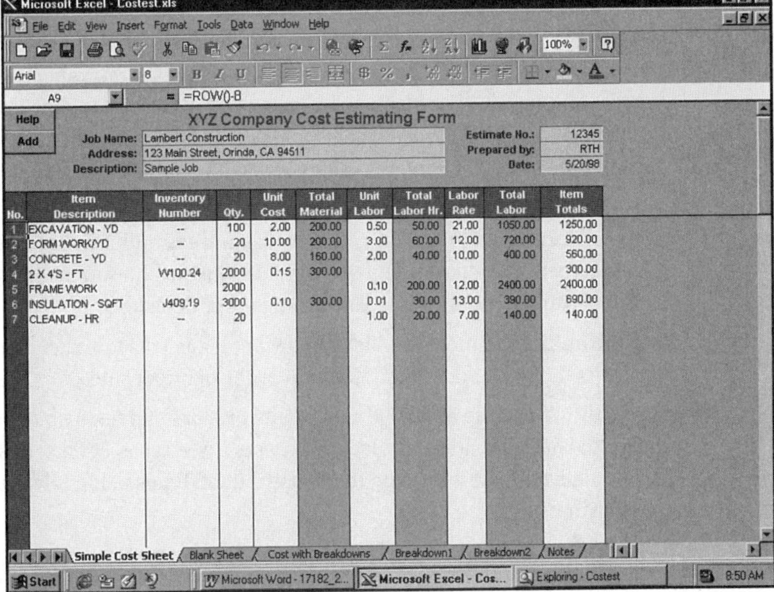

FIGURE 27.2
Baarns Consulting's free Estimating worksheet.

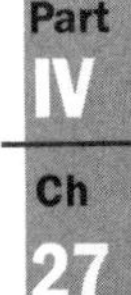

Improving Excel's Decision Analysis Capabilities

Excel 97 comes with a variety of analysis tools, including Solver, Goal Seek, and Scenario Manager. But for many sophisticated worksheet users, especially enterprise planners and decision-makers, these tools may be insufficient. Third parties have filled in the gap with a variety of tools, which are discussed next.

Premium Solver Plus: Replacing Excel's Solver

Excel 97's Solver feature is designed to help you identify the best solutions to a problem given a certain set of facts and assumptions. Some sophisticated users may find that the built-in Solver feature does not provide adequate speed or power. (In particular, the standard Solver limits users to 200 decision variables.)

For these users, you may want to consider Premium Solver Plus, from Frontline Systems, Inc. (**www.frontsys.com**, 702-831-0300). This is an upwardly compatible Solver extension built by the company that helped create the Solver included in Excel. It is designed to solve much larger problems, at speeds from three to several hundred times faster than the standard Solver.

After you install Premium Solver, it appears in place of the standard Solver when you choose Tools, Solver. It provides similar dialog boxes with additional features, and can work with existing Solver models, macros, and custom VBA procedures your users have already developed.

Risk Assessment Tools

DecisionTools Suite from Palisade Corporation (`www.palisade.com`, 800-432-7475) adds an Excel toolbar providing integrated access to the five following advanced analysis products:

- **@RISK.** Adds Monte Carlo simulation to worksheet models. Monte Carlo simulation works like this: REPLACE uncertain values in your worksheet with @RISK functions representing ranges of values. Select one or more bottom-line cells as outputs, and start a simulation. @RISK recalculates your spreadsheet hundreds or thousands of times, each time selecting random values based on your @RISK functions. You learn not only what could happen in a given situation, but how likely it is to happen.
- **PrecisionTree.** Helps you create decision trees and influence diagrams in your worksheets to better let you see the relationships between components of a problem, model sequences of events, and make better decisions.
- **TopRank.** Adds more sophisticated what-if analysis to Excel, showing which cells affect results the most and linking them in order of importance.
- **BestFit.** Takes up to 30,000 data points or pairs and tests up to 26 distribution types to find the one that fits best. BestFit accepts three types of data: sample, density, and cumulative. BestFit tests up to 26 distribution types using advanced optimization algorithms.
- **RiskView.** A companion program for viewing, assessing, and creating probability distributions.

A competing product, Crystal Ball Pro from Decisioneering (**www.decisioneering.com**, 1-800-289-2550), also works as an Excel add-in and provides sophisticated Monte Carlo simulation.

With Crystal Ball Pro's OptQuest component, Excel can automatically search for an optimal set of decision variables within a simulation model based on the goal you're trying to achieve. Although none of today's decision analysis tools are easy to use, OptQuest provides wizards that simplify things a good deal. Crystal Ball Pro also comes with Extenders that can help you refine your analysis and display the results in Tornado charts that make it easy to see the impact of individual variables on your target outcome.

General Word Enhancements

Thanks to Visual Basic for Applications (VBA)—and its predecessor, WordBasic—you can now extend Word with a wide variety of new features.

Woody Leonhard's Pinecliffe International (`www.wopr.com`) specializes in such enhancements, and WOPR (Woody's Office Power Pack) 97 is the latest release. WOPR 97 has literally dozens of components, but as an Office administrator, you may especially appreciate using (or providing to your colleagues) the following:

- **WOPR Enveloper.** A more powerful envelope printing utility that simplifies the management of multiple custom envelopes
- **Word 2x4.** Allows users to easily print documents in duplex, 2-up, 4-up, trifold, booklet, and thumbnail formats
- **WOPR Rebuild File.** Can reconstruct many corrupted Word documents or templates
- **WOPR Normal Quotes.** Converts "smart quotes" to normal quotes for export to software that can't understand smart quotes

One good source of inexpensive Word and Office add-ons is SoftSeek (**softseek.com/Business_and_Productivity/Microsoft_Office/**).

Integrating Voice Recognition into Word and Office

Slowly but surely, voice recognition software is coming of age. The newest generation of voice recognition products is the first to support continuous voice recognition, which means users can speak naturally, without inserting artificial pauses between every word. Several of these new packages offer some level of integration with Microsoft Word, enabling automated dictation and control of many Word features.

It's unlikely that you'll implement voice recognition company-wide any time soon—especially if you use an open office layout that routinely gets noisy. You may, however, want to provide this software for the following:

- Executives and others with private offices who do extensive dictating
- Employees who do not type or need their hands free
- Physically challenged employees

Be aware of the following two crucial limitations to today's voice recognition systems:

- Hardware requirements are stiff. Typically 166 MHz MMX Pentiums are a bare minimum, and the systems need large chunks of hard disk space. You also need high-quality microphones and a highly SoundBlaster-compatible sound card. In some cases, the audio built into your business PCs may not be sufficiently compatible.
- Where users invest time in "training" the system to recognize a specific voice, voice recognition accuracy rates may be as high as 95 percent—but that still means one correction every twenty words. Moreover, because voice recognition software "types" only real words, the remaining errors are largely immune to spell-checking (although grammar checking may help somewhat). Even small differences in performance can make a large difference in the ultimate productivity gains that voice recognition delivers.

Following are three product families are market leaders in the voice recognition business:

- Dragon Systems' NaturallySpeaking products
- IBM's ViaVoice products
- Lernout & Hauspie's Voice Xpress products

Each will be covered next.

Dragon NaturallySpeaking

Dragon NaturallySpeaking Preferred and NaturallySpeaking Deluxe are widely acknowledged to offer very strong performance. NaturallySpeaking Deluxe adds macro capabilities, multiple topics (enabling users who dictate on several subjects to improve performance by telling the software which topic they're about to discuss), and access to a larger active dictionary—a dictionary that is immediately available while the user is dictating.

Each of these products integrate with Word 97, but not quite as smoothly as they might. Currently, you must download a free add-on, Dragon NaturalWord, from Dragon Systems' Web site (`www.dragonsystems.com`). Note that a lower cost product, NaturallySpeaking Personal, offers the same speech recognition engine but requires users to dictate into Dragon's own stripped-down word processor.

Dragon Systems also offers specialized legal and medical voice recognition systems, which are typically configured and sold by resellers.

IBM ViaVoice Products

IBM's ViaVoice Gold offers reasonable-quality voice recognition, the capability to dictate into Microsoft Word 97, and limited capability to control Word 97 menus and formatting commands by voice. (A lower-cost product, ViaVoice, allows for dictation into Word but no voice control of Word.)

Lernout & Hauspie's Voice Xpress Plus

L&H Voice Xpress Plus enables users to dictate into Word 97 and control the software's menus and formatting commands by voice. In early reports, L&H Voice Xpress Plus' Natural Language Technology appears to be delivering high-quality results. Voice Xpress Plus supports macros—that is, you can define a short phrase that corresponds to a large block of text that the software will automatically insert, much like an AutoText entry. It also contains speaker profiles that may improve accuracy for men, women, teenagers, and children.

The software also supports Microsoft's new Speech Application Programming Interface (SAPI), which could lead to easier integration of voice recognition with future applications. It's worth mentioning that Lernout & Hauspie has made strategic agreements with Microsoft that could eventually result in its base voice recognition technology becoming part of the Windows operating system.

Word Text-to-Speech Solutions

In some cases, you may get more productivity benefits from having computers talk to users, rather than the other way around. Several programs provide "text-to-speech" capabilities—either for all Windows 98/95 applications or in selected contexts.

For example, many SoundBlaster-equipped computers ship with Monologue, a basic text-to-speech application. Text-to-speech applications designed specifically to improve accessibility for those who cannot easily use visual information include the following:

- ASAP for Windows, from Microtalk (**www.screenaccess.com**, 903-792-4150)
- Hal 95 for Windows 95, from Dolphin Systems (**www.dolphinaccess.com/products/brochure/hal95.html**, UK phone: +44-1905-754577)
- JAWS for Windows, from Henter-Joyce, (**www.hj.com**, 800-336-5658)
- outSPOKEN for Windows, from ALVA Access Group (**aagi.com**, 510-883-6280)
- Protalk32, Biolink Computer R&D Ltd., (**biz.bctel.net/biolink**, 604-984-4099)
- ScreenPower for Windows 95 from Telesensory Corp. (**www.telesensory.com**, 415-969-9064)
- SLIMWARE Window Bridge from Syntha-voice Computers (**www.synthavoice.on.ca**, 800-263-4540)

Most of these applications will work within any Windows 95 application.

You may have specialized applications for text-to-speech. Sound-Proof by JWalk & Associates (**www.j-walk.com**), for example, is specifically designed to read back Excel cell contents, making it easier for you and your colleagues to proofread data entry in worksheets. SoundProof can read cell content back using natural language. For example, 213.26 is read as "Two hundred thirteen point two six." Dates and times are read as actual dates and times: "May twelfth, nineteen ninety-nine, ten twelve AM."

Vertical Market Tools

There are specialized tools for Office users in a wide variety of industries. This section presents just a few examples.

Real Estate

Real Estate Investment Analysis, Version 10.0, from RealData (**www.realdata.com**, 203-838-2670) is a comprehensive income-property investment analysis tool for residential or commercial real estate, in the form of an Excel workbook. Each linked module corresponds to a page in the workbook, giving users the flexibility to perform simple or complex analysis.

Finance

CMO Analyst from Intex Solutions, Inc., (**www.intex.com**, 781-449-6222) provides add-in spreadsheet functions, descriptive data, and price/yield forecasts for underwriting and investing in Collateralized Mortgage Obligations.

Corporate Video

For your corporate video department, Indelible, Ink.'s ScriptWright (**www.kois.com/ink/info.html**, 212-255-1956, ext. 301) transforms Word into a dedicated screenplay word processor, with the styles, keyboard, menu, and toolbar customizations and tools that streamline all the mechanics of writing and editing a screenplay. ScriptWright enables you to format your screenplay in three ways: Draft, Master, and Shooting. A stripped-down, free demo version is available at **www.kois.com/ink/**.

Help File Publishing Tools

Many organizations create manuals and other long documents, and for some, Microsoft Word's built-in tools aren't enough. Even more to the point, what if you want to turn Word files into electronic help files? Two third-party packages can help.

Doc-to-Help 3.0 from WexTech Systems, Inc.

Doc-To-Help 3.0 from WexTech Systems, Inc. (**www.wextech.com**, 914-741-9700) installs into Microsoft Word and adds features that enable you to build documentation, interactive and Web-based help systems at the same time, from a single source file.

Doc-to-Help also contains professional, customizable templates that handle virtually all layout details, including headers/footers, tables, crop marks, sideheads, even and odd pages, gutters, page numbering, margin notes, and a good part of the work involved in building glossaries and indexes.

After you build your source file, you can create help in virtually any format you want, including print and the following electronic formats:

- Windows 95/NT Help (standard 32-bit Windows help files)
- Windows 3.0 and/or 3.1 Help (standard 16-bit Windows Help files)
- HTML Help (Microsoft's new, HTML-based Help files)
- Doc-to-Help (will create compiled, ActiveX-enabled or Java-enabled HTML Help)
- Standard HTML (for posting on intranets or Web sites)

EasyHelp/Web from Eon Solutions, Ltd.

Doc-to-Help is by far the market leader and most comprehensive solution available. Organizations that want a less expensive, simpler solution may be interested in EasyHelp/Web 3.0 from Eon Solutions, Ltd. (**www.eon-solutions.com**, UK phone: +44 1625 827 037).

EasyHelp/Web creates Windows help files and traditional HTML files (though not compiled HTML Help). For those who view creating Windows help files as an arcane, complex process, it's worth a moment to show EasyHelp/Web at work.

Installing EasyHelp/Web adds a set of templates, macros, and toolbars to Microsoft Word. If you've built a Word document with heading styles, you can use EasyHelp/Web's AutoTopic feature to transform those headings into pages in your help file. To add a hyperlink, select the text you want to make into a hyperlink and click on AutoLink. After you finish adding headings and hyperlinks, click on Process on the EasyHelp toolbar, and EasyHelp/Web goes to work. In a couple of minutes, EasyHelp/Web reports that it's finished. You now can click on Build and EasyHelp/Web creates and displays your help file.

Other Office-Compatible Software

Microsoft has established a program of certification for vendors who want to create "Office-compatible" software, and several vendors have built a good business in this marketplace, notably Visio and Software Publishing Corporation. Office-compatible products must share nearly identical menu structures, toolbars, shortcut keys, and shortcut menus with Microsoft Office, and provide strong data exchange capabilities with Microsoft Office. In many cases, these applications install toolbar buttons within Microsoft Office applications, providing one-click access to the application.

Visio 5.0 from Visio Corporation

Visio 5.0 provides comprehensive business drawing tools based on libraries of templates and shapes that eliminate the need for users to create their own graphics from scratch. Visio also works with the Microsoft Office Binder, making it possible to create files that combine Visio pages with text from Word and worksheets from Excel.

Visio 5.0 includes extensive flowcharting shapes for total quality management, audit, and data flow diagrams; easier ways to publish diagrams on the Web; new marketing shapes; importing and exporting of diagrams from Microsoft Project; and support for the Visual Basic for Applications macro programming language. And if you choose, Visio 5.0 can install a toolbar button on the Standard toolbar in either Word or Excel, making it especially easy to access from within Office.

ActiveOffice from Software Publishing Corporation

ActiveOffice from Software Publishing Corporation (**www.spco.com**, 973-808-1992) is an add-in for Office 97 and Office 95 that streamlines the process of creating attractive graphics in Word, Excel, and PowerPoint documents. ActiveOffice installs as a toolbar button within Word, Excel, and PowerPoint, and displays as a bar along the right-hand side of the screen (see Figure 27.3).

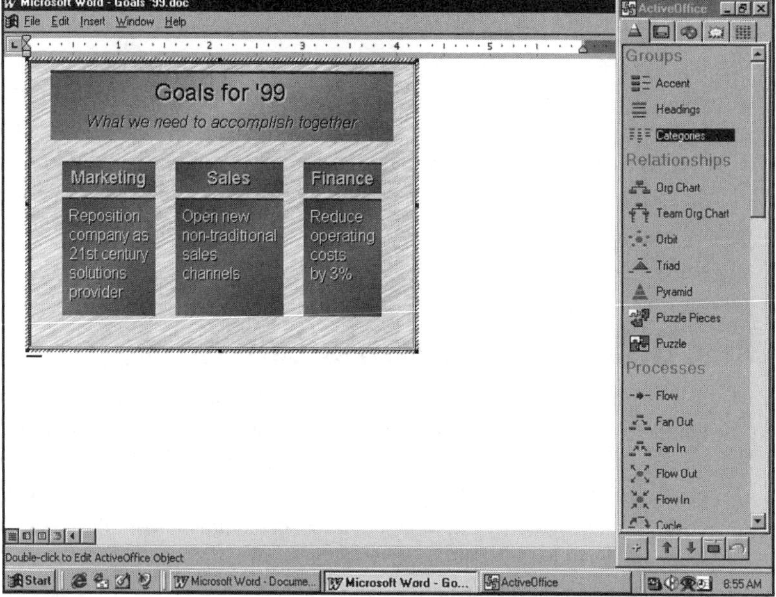

FIGURE 27.3
ActiveOffice runs from a bar across the right-hand side of the screen.

ActivePresenter from Software Publishing Corporation

An increasing number of presentations are done across the Internet. ActivePresenter from Software Publishing Corporation can significantly simplify the process of creating and delivering Web presentations. In the core ActivePresenter module, you can either create your own presentation using SPC's speedy Intelligent Formatting technology, or incorporate a Microsoft PowerPoint presentation. When your presentation is complete, you publish it to the Internet with SPC's free WebShow 2.0, via FTP—either for immediate, live presentation or for playback later, on-demand.

WebShow also sends a configured Web page to everyone who will view your presentation; each user loads that URL and connects to your presentation, which can be password-protected if you wish. Users need the free WebShow ActiveX control for Microsoft Internet Explorer or plug-in for Netscape Navigator to view the presentation. ●

PART V

Office, the Internet, and Intranets

CHAPTER 28

Using Office Documents on Your Intranet or Web Site

The Internet—and particularly the Web—has become an invaluable means of exchanging information with people around the world, including employees, consultants, partners, vendors, and customers. Using the Web's powerful publishing capabilities, businesses can disseminate information to the outside world much more easily and rapidly than ever before.

This model for publishing and exchanging information translates well to a company's internal network. Based on Internet protocols and technologies, intranets have become the most efficient means of information exchange among coworkers within the company.

Recognizing these trends, Microsoft integrated its suite of Office 97 applications with Internet and intranet technologies, including HTML-browsing capabilities. But because information often needs to be presented in many different ways, Office 97 document support was also integrated into Web-browsing software, so that users had a choice of publishing formats and were no longer limited to HTML alone.

This chapter describes how Office documents *and* applications work with the intranet and the Web. You'll learn how to complete the following tasks:

- Determine when to publish HTML documents and when to publish Office documents on the intranet
- View Office documents with a Web browser
- View HTML documents with Office applications

The most powerful intranets provide a rich web of information, combining HTML and office documents. This chapter shows how users can access such an intranet seamlessly, no matter what tools they choose.

Choosing Between Office File Types and HTML

An effective intranet should not be limited to one publishing format. Rather, the document type is chosen to best fit user needs and the purpose of the information being published. When publishing to the intranet, the question often becomes: when is it most useful to leave documents in their native Office formats, and when it is more expedient to translate them to HTML? Table 28.1 outlines some general guidelines to help you make this decision.

Table 28.1 Guidelines to Determining Whether to Publish Intranet Documents in HTML Format or in Office Document Formats

HTML	Office Formats
Simple content	Rich content
Static information	Frequently changing information
Documents requiring extensive navigation	Documents requiring analysis, editing, and collaboration
Documents requiring widespread distribution across multiple platforms	Documents requiring distribution in multiple media types (printed, slide show, online)

Office document formats are the best choice for heavily formatted information, such as budgets, review contracts, and presentations. When group collaboration and workflow are required, Office formats offer more flexibility than HTML. Using the comments, versioning, and tracking features, several members of a team can work on one document across the intranet and keep track of who has made updates. When completed, the document can be published to the intranet as-is—no conversion to special formats is required.

Office document formats are also optimized for ad hoc analysis of data. For example, a user requests a quarterly sales report from the intranet and then realizes that monthly figures are needed instead. If the report were published in HTML, the user would have to request and download another view. If the report were published using PivotTables in Excel, however, the user could simply pivot the information for the monthly data, getting the necessary figures within seconds.

When collaboration and analysis aren't as important, or when the information being presented lends itself better to the navigational features of HTML, Office applications can be used to convert existing documents and create new ones in HTML format. Established, static information, such as company policy manuals, directories, and product information, are more easily and uniformly distributed across multiple platforms in HTML format. An extensive set of documents may benefit from the use of hyperlinking to create an easy-to-use navigational scheme or to cross-reference the document to related sources of information elsewhere on the intranet or out on the Internet.

NOTE To learn how to use Office applications to publish in HTML format, see Chapter 29.

Viewing Office Documents on the Intranet and Web

Regardless of which format information is published in, users need to be able to access it all with a single tool. Web browsers are commonly used to navigate intranets—they're easy to get, they're easy to learn, and they're the best tools for presenting information in HTML format. Web browsers also support seamless connections between the intranet and external Web sites.

Microsoft's ActiveX document technology enables Office document viewing inside the Web browser. Not only is the document shown with its original formatting intact, but it can also be manipulated, edited, and saved from within the browser window, using all the tools and functionality of the parent application (as long as the application or an appropriate viewer is installed on the user's computer). Because many popular Web browsers can support ActiveX document technology (either natively or via an add-in), the browser remains an effective tool for navigating the intranet, no matter what document type is being accessed.

Office Document Support in Internet Explorer

Because Microsoft Internet Explorer (version 3.0 or later) natively supports ActiveX document technology, it can open and display Office documents seamlessly, requiring no add-ins or additional steps on the part of the user. This integration enables the user to navigate Office documents and HTML files on the intranet or Web site seamlessly, as one integrated whole.

When the user clicks on a hyperlink or opens a URL to an Office document using Internet Explorer, the document displays inside the browser window with all its original formatting intact. The Tools button that appears in Internet Explorer's toolbar enables users to show and hide the toolbars of the original application and access application functions. Figure 28.1 depicts an Excel workbook open inside Internet Explorer; simply click on the Tools button to turn off Excel's toolbars and show more of the workbook.

Office Document Support in Netscape Navigator

Many users will prefer Netscape Navigator (or Communicator, which includes the Navigator Web browser) as their primary intranet and Internet client. Unlike Internet Explorer, Navigator does not natively support ActiveX document technology. This support is provided by a *plug-in* called DocActive, an add-in component that enables Navigator users to view Office documents inside the browser window, as long as the user has the appropriate Office application or viewer installed on his or her computer.

DocActive simply adds ActiveX document support to Navigator. After the plug-in is installed, users can navigate to, open, manipulate, and edit Office documents from inside the browser, in much the same way they can with Internet Explorer. Figure 28.2 shows a Word document that was opened inside the Navigator window with the help of DocActive. Notice that editing tools are accessible via the standard Word toolbars; a drop-down menu (called Menu) provides access to Word's menu functions.

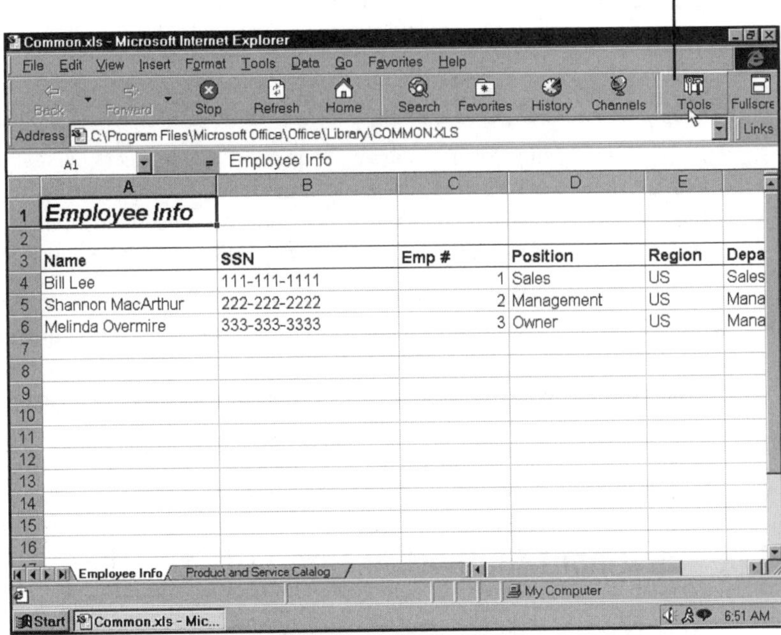

FIGURE 28.1
Internet Explorer's native ActiveX support enables seamless viewing and manipulation of all Office document formats from inside the browser.

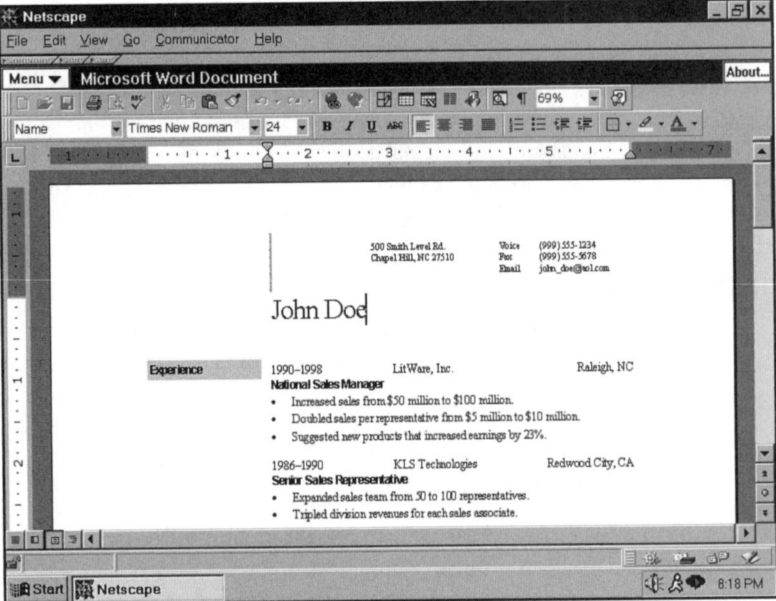

FIGURE 28.2
Using the DocActive plug-in, Navigator users can view Office documents on the Web or intranet.

DocActive requires the following software and hardware:

- Netscape Navigator or Netscape Communicator, version 3.*x* or version 4.*x*
- Office 95 or later or compatible Office viewers
- Windows 95 or Windows NT 4.0 or later
- 8MB RAM
- 486 DX33 PC
- 14.4Kbps or faster Internet connection

DocActive is provided by its developer, NCompass Labs Inc., for commercial licensing. Get more information and download a 30-day trial version for testing from NCompass Labs' Web site at **www.ncompasslabs.com/DocActive/index.htm**.

NOTE To get the evaluation copy of DocActive, you must download the ScriptActive plug-in (both plug-ins are included in the same package). ScriptActive enables Navigator to run ActiveX controls and scripts. To install the plug-ins, simply download the package to a temporary directory, double-click on the downloaded file to expand the setup files, and follow the instructions in the setup wizard. Once installed correctly, ScriptActive and DocActive should be listed in Navigator's About Plug-ins page (select Help, About Plug-ins).

Using Office Programs as Helper Applications

You may not want to invest in the DocActive plug-in. In that case, Navigator users can still access Office documents on the Web or intranet via the browser's support for helper applications. However, users must wait for a separate application to open and display the document, rather than viewing the document inside the browser window as if it were a seamless part of the Web site or intranet.

When you try to open a file that isn't supported by a plug-in, Navigator accesses the computer's file types registry to determine which application to launch as a helper for the file type. If the appropriate Office application is locally installed, Navigator downloads the file and launches its parent application. To see which applications are configured as helpers for each Office document file type, choose Edit, Preferences, expand the Navigator category, and click on Applications. Then, scroll down the large window until you find the file type you want to check, such as Microsoft PowerPoint or Microsoft Word. The File type details area lists which application is configured to open files of that type when Navigator encounters them. Click on Edit if you want to designate a different helper application to handle the file type (such as the smaller Word Viewer rather than the full-featured Word application, which takes longer to open and uses more resources). Use caution, however; changing the helper applications also changes the file registry, which can cause unexpected results when attempting to open files from Windows Explorer.

Office Document Viewers

To take advantage of the Office document-viewing capabilities of Internet Explorer or Navigator and DocActive, the user must have the Office suite installed locally. Otherwise, the browser is unable to display the document with full functionality and editing capabilities.

For many of your users, this will not be a problem. However, others with access to your intranet or Web site—such as partners, vendors, and consultants—may not have the application or the appropriate version of the application to view crucial documents.

To make it easy for all users to share Office documents, Microsoft provides freely distributable viewers for Word, Excel, and PowerPoint. You can place these viewers on your intranet or Web site so that anyone who needs them can download and install them. The installation process automatically configures the viewers as helper applications for both Navigator and Internet Explorer, thus enabling the user to view documents as they were meant to be seen, without having to purchase and install the full application.

All three viewers enable users to open and print Office documents from within the browser. They also support certain application features, such as Word's document views or Excel's AutoFilter feature; however, they do not provide full editing capabilities. Table 28.2 lists the locations at Microsoft's Web site where these viewers may be freely downloaded.

Table 28.2 Download Locations of Office Document Viewers

Viewer	URL
Excel 97 Viewer	**www.microsoft.com/excel/internet/viewer/**
PowerPoint 97 Viewer	**www.microsoft.com/powerpoint/internet/viewer/**
Word 97 Viewer	**www.microsoft.com/word/internet/viewer/viewer97/**

Using Office Applications to View Web Documents

Using ActiveX document technology, Web browsers can navigate seamlessly among HTML files and Office documents on the Web site or intranet. This tight integration of Office and Web technology is also available in all of the Office applications, enabling users to navigate among and view HTML files from within the application. This lets users choose an intranet client that meets their needs at the time: the Web browser or the Office application.

Web-Browsing Features in Office

Office builds on the Web metaphors that users are already familiar with to make viewing HTML files within Office applications intuitive. Hyperlink support and a Web toolbar that resembles the toolbars of many Web browsers enable users to easily access HTML files from within the Office application.

Following are three ways to access HTML files on the intranet, Internet, or local disk from within an Office application:

- Open the file directly using the File, Open command; enter the file's address in URL format in the File Name box
- Click on a hyperlink embedded in an Office document that links to an HTML file
- Select a navigational feature from the Web toolbar

Hyperlinks Hyperlinks are the power behind the Web, enabling the reader to quickly jump to context-related information elsewhere on the Web. Office applications also support viewing, navigating, and embedding of hyperlinks within HTML files and Office documents, as shown in Figure 28.3. These hyperlinks can go anywhere—to other Office documents, to HTML files on the intranet, or to any file on the Internet with a recognized URL, such as a Web page or FTP file. Simply click on the underlined, blue text to follow the hyperlink.

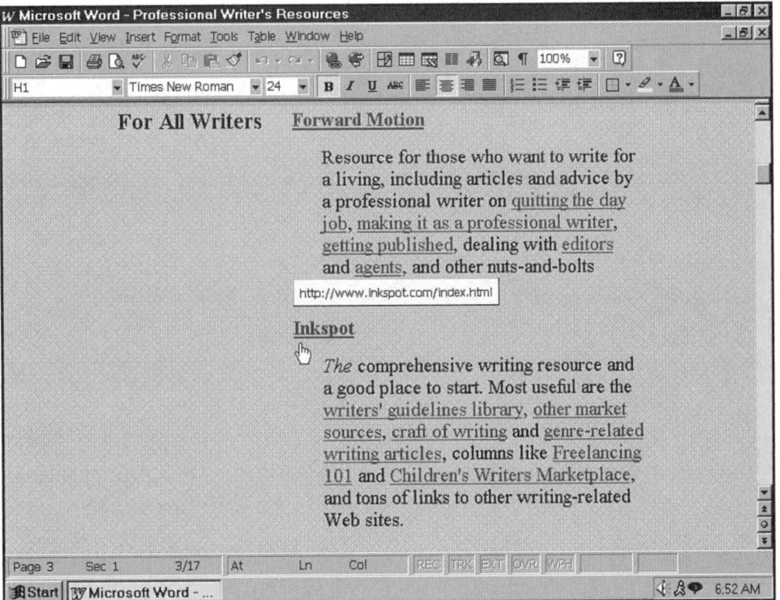

FIGURE 28.3
Word displaying an HTML file with hyperlinks.

Sometimes you may encounter an error message after clicking on a hyperlink inside an Office document or HTML file. This could indicate any of the following, depending on the type of hyperlink the user is trying to access:

- If the linked page is on the Web, the Internet connection may be down or the Web server being accessed may be busy. Try reconnecting, or wait until later to access the site.
- If the linked page is on the intranet, the network server may not be running; check the network connection. The user may also not have access to that location of the intranet.

- On the Internet or intranet, the URL of the referenced file may have changed. Try searching for the new URL or asking the owner of the page for its new location.
- If the linked page is on the local drive, the path to the hyperlink may have been identified by its full address (for example, C:\My Documents\Sales.html) and then the file was moved to another location on the hard drive. Try browsing to the file instead.

The Web Toolbar Word, Excel, PowerPoint, and Access all share a common toolbar for browsing the Web. This Web toolbar borrows most of its features from the toolbars of popular Web browsers. For example, navigational buttons enable users to move back and forth among a set of Web pages and to jump to a "home" page. Users are presented with a unified navigational metaphor, no matter whether they're using a Web browser or an Office application as the Web or intranet client.

Open the Web toolbar in one of the following ways:

- Click on an embedded hyperlink; the Web toolbar automatically opens within the HTML document.
- Choose View, Toolbars and Web.
- Click on the Web Toolbar button in the standard toolbar (Word, Excel, and PowerPoint only).

Table 28.3 describes the functions of the Web toolbar, which are also pointed out in Figure 28.4.

Table 28.3 The Functions of Office's Web Toolbar

Tool	Function
Back button	Moves back to the last page in the history list
Forward button	Moves forward to the next page in the history list
Stop Current Jump button	Stops loading the page (available only when loading Internet and intranet files)
Refresh Current Page button	Reloads the page from the server, showing any updates
Start Page button	Opens the designated home page
Search the Web button	Opens the designated Web or intranet search engine page
Favorites menu	Lists favorite pages
Go menu	Displays the history list and duplicate navigational tools
Show Only Web Toolbar button	Hides the other application toolbars to display more of the open HTML file
Address box	Type in the URL or file location in URL format of an HTML file to open it inside the application's window

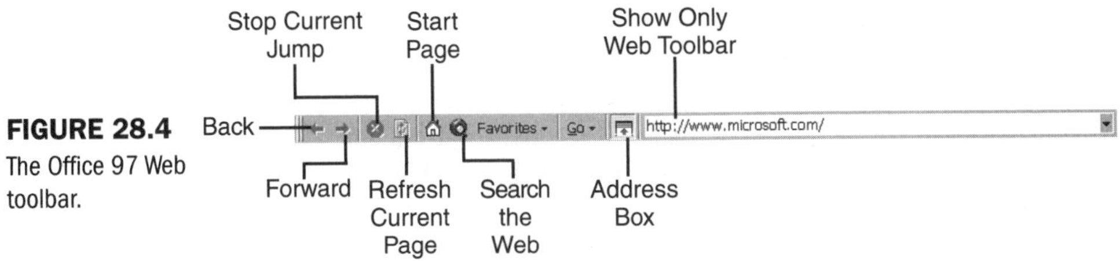

FIGURE 28.4
The Office 97 Web toolbar.

Note that the favorites, history list, start page, search, and other Web-browsing preferences that are accessible from the Web toolbar are shared across all Office applications and Internet Explorer. The last ten Web pages that were accessed make up the history list in all applications, regardless of which application the page was opened in. By the same token, pages added to the Favorites list in Internet Explorer appear in the Favorites menu on Office's Web toolbar, and vice versa.

TIP Click on the arrow to the right of the Address box in the Web toolbar to open a menu of recently opened URLs. Then, you can select one of these URLs to load its associated Web page.

Therefore, the start page and search page referenced on the Web toolbar are the same as the home page and search page specified in Internet Explorer. You can change these defaults from within Office, as well as from Internet Explorer. To do so, open the page that you want to designate as the new default. Then, click on the Go menu in the Web toolbar, and select either Set Start Page or Set Search Page to set the open page as the default in every Office application *and* in Internet Explorer.

Office employs the navigational and searching metaphors of the Web to enable users to quickly search the full text of both HTML and Office documents on the intranet. This capability is provided by the Web Find Fast indexing software, included with the Office Server Pack of utilities. Web Find Fast includes an HTML-formatted search engine page that is similar to Web-based search engines like Lycos and AltaVista. (When using Web Find Fast, it's a good idea to have users configure this page as the default search page for all Office applications and Internet Explorer.) From the Web Find Fast search page, users can search and index the full content of all HTML and Office documents stored on the intranet. Search results display as an HTML file listing document properties and providing hyperlinks to each found document that matches the search criteria.

Opening Web Pages in Outlook

Outlook is the only Office application that doesn't share the Web toolbar; however, you can still access the Web or the intranet from within Outlook in the following ways:

- Open a contact's Web page—Outlook's Contacts item enables you to store an associated URL for the contact in the Web Page Address field (see Figure 28.5). From the contact, click on the hyperlink in this field to open the contact's associated Web page in the default Web client (choosing Actions, Explore Web Page or clicking on the Explore Web Page button in the Advanced toolbar does the same thing).

- Search for intranet files—Use the Web Find Fast search page to locate HTML files stored on the company intranet.
- Access favorite Web sites—Access designated favorite Web pages from within Outlook. These favorites are stored in the Favorites folder; click on Other Shortcuts in the Outlook Bar, and then click on Favorites. Double-clicking on a favorite Web page opens the page in the default Web client.

FIGURE 28.5
Store and access contacts' Web pages in Outlook's Contacts module.

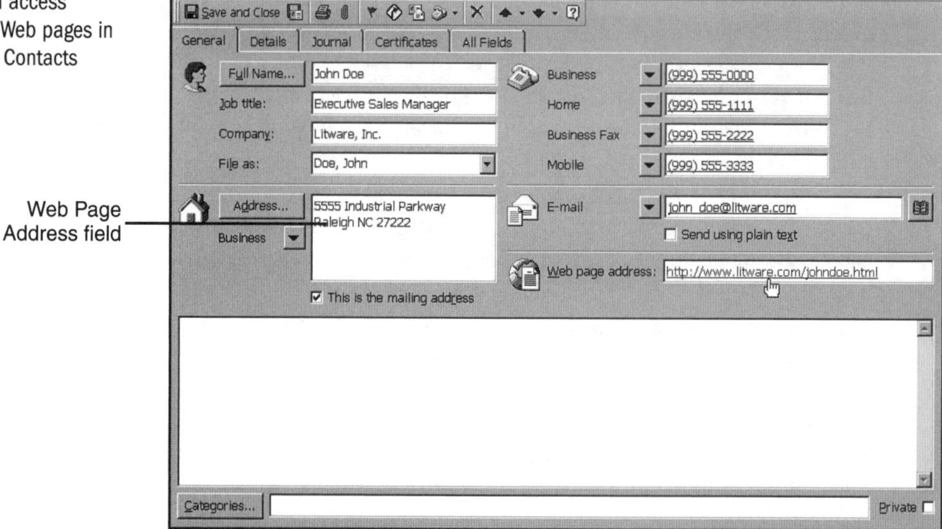

TIP Accessing the Favorites folder in Outlook is an easy way to organize and set properties for your favorites outside Internet Explorer. Right-click on a file (or choose File, Properties) to edit the favorite's properties. You can change the favorite's URL, create a shortcut key, or subscribe to the page as a channel. You can also create custom views to better organize Web pages and folders inside the Favorites folder. For example, you might want to create a table view that shows customized text fields listing the Web page's owner, URL, and subject.

CHAPTER 29

Using Office Tools for Web/Intranet Publishing

The Internet has invaded the business world and is here to stay. From an Office 97 perspective, the major question is: How can I integrate or use my existing Office documents and applications in an Internet environment? Can I do Web publishing with Office 97?

Web publishing is the process of generating a series of related documents and making them available via HTTP services from a Web server. Web publishing requires

- A computer with Web server software
- Some type of TCP/IP network connection, either internally with the company network and/or externally with the Internet
- Software to create and manage Web files

Office 97 is the first incarnation of Microsoft Office to include significant native Web publishing capability. In this chapter you learn about Web publishing with Office 97, including

- How to incorporate hyperlinks into native Office documents (DOC files, XLS files, and so on)
- How to use Word as a basic HTML editor
- How to convert Office documents to HTML in Excel, Word, PowerPoint, Access, and Publisher
- How to use Web queries from Excel
- How to query an Access database from a browser
- How to build an entire Web site using Microsoft Publisher

Understanding Office Web Publishing Capabilities

The most common Web publishing scenario is to create HTML files, acquire and modify image files (or other multimedia), add hyperlinks, and then place (or publish) these files onto a Web server. Browser requests for these files are met via HTTP services by the Web server.

Office 97 enables you to add Office files in their native formats to a typical Web site. The first Web capability added to an Office product was the Internet Assistant add-in for version 2 of Word. Later, with Office 95, Microsoft introduced more and somewhat better Internet Assistant add-in modules. Word's Internet Assistant enabled it to read HTML documents and convert existing Word documents to HTML. The Excel and PowerPoint Internet Assistants let you convert existing documents in earlier versions of Office to HTML. Now, all the major applications in Office 97 (Word, Excel, PowerPoint, Access, and Publisher) include a variety of Web capabilities including

- The ability to embed active hyperlinks into Office native files
- Forward, Back, and Stop buttons in a Web toolbar, just like Web browsers
- An address bar for entering URLs
- A favorites list of Web sites
- The ability to read HTML files
- The ability to write HTML files or convert existing documents to HTML

NOTE Access 97, due to its nature as a database, does not have any browsing capability. You can, however, add hyperlinks to forms and reports. ■

The preceding capabilities give the user more flexibility in integrating Office documents into the modern, Web-oriented workplace. Some possibilities include

- Linking Office documents with hyperlinks
- Creating HTML documents using Office applications
- Linking to live information on the Internet
- Converting Office files to HTML for use with any browser
- Dynamically serving up-to-the-minute data from a Web site

Building Hyperlinks into Office Documents

Why put hyperlinks into native Office documents? Consider the following possibilities:

- A sales report with hyperlinks to more detailed financial reports in Excel, a related PowerPoint presentation, and the latest corporate status report from the CEO in Word
- Financial reports with real-time links to stock quotes
- A technical report with links to other relevant information on the Internet or company Intranet

All these hyperlinks would be live from within their respective Office applications; you don't even need to crack open a browser. In putting together any report, you do not have to collect and integrate the disparate documents into a single report. You can just link to the necessary documents from within your report summary. If you email your report, you are emailing a much shorter package, reducing network traffic and the load on the email server.

You do not need to learn HTML to build hyperlinks into Office documents. With a consistent interface for inserting hyperlinks across all the Office applications, you need to provide only a URL. The URL can be in the form of a TCP/IP address, a network address (UNC, for Universal Naming Convention), or a file location on your local hard drive. The following are examples of these three types of locations:

- **TCP/IP address:**
  http://www.microsoft.com or **http://207.68.156.49**
- **Network UNC:**
  \\myserver\somefolder\afile.html
- **Local hard drive file:**
  file:\\c:\somefolder\afile.html or even just c:\somefolder\afile.html

Adding a Hyperlink in Word, Excel, and PowerPoint

The dialog box for entering hyperlinks to documents is identical in Word, Excel, and PowerPoint. In any document, spreadsheet, or presentation, either select the words you want to hyperlink or place the insertion point where you want the link to appear. If you don't select any words, the hyperlink displays the address of the link. Choose Insert, Hyperlink (or press

Ctrl+K or click the Insert Hyperlink button in the Standard toolbar) to display the Insert Hyperlink dialog box (see Figure 29.1).

FIGURE 29.1
Inserting a hyperlink into Word 97, Excel 97, or PowerPoint 97.

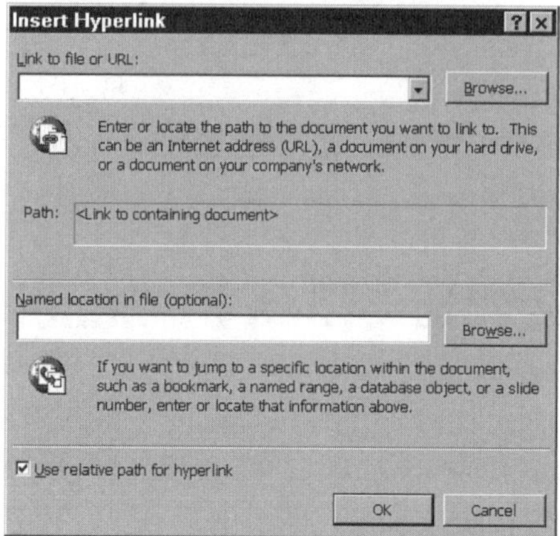

Enter the address of the hyperlink target in the Link to File or URL text box. You can type it in the text box, or click the Browse button to display the Link to File dialog box. If the target is on your local network or hard drive, browse to it in the dialog box. If the target is on the Internet and you have added it to your favorites list, click the Look in Favorites button at the top of the dialog box and then select the address from the list. You can also click the Search the Web button at the top of the dialog box to launch your browser and search for the site on the Web from Microsoft's search Web page.

The address in the Link to File or URL text box in the Insert Hyperlink dialog box should change dynamically as you surf the Web with your browser. However, it may not behave this way. If the contents of the text box don't update, delete the existing contents before you browse to each new Web page. Also, you can browse to the Internet address with your browser and copy and paste the URL from the browser's address box into the Link to File or URL text box.

NOTE You can also link to a file on an FTP site. If you know the base address of an FTP site containing the file you want to link to (**ftp.microsoft.com**, for instance) you can select the Add/Modify FTP Locations option at the bottom of the Look In list in the Link to File dialog box.

In the Add/Modify FTP Locations dialog box, type the base address of the site in the Name of FTP Site text box. Specify how you want to log on (Anonymous or User) and enter a password if one is required (use your email address for the password if you're logging on anonymously). Click Add, and then click OK to return to the Link to File dialog box. Next, select the FTP site and click Open to display the contents of the site. Finally, browse the folders to select the file that you want to link to and click OK.

The complete FTP address now appears in the Link to File or URL text box in the Insert Hyperlink dialog box. This will not work with addresses starting with HTTP.

Keep in mind that you can use relative or absolute addresses in a hyperlink. An absolute address is the full URL, UNC, or file path. A relative address describes only the path from the current working document. For instance, if you are inserting the hyperlink in a Word document named sales.doc, you could use a relative address in any of these formats:

- The address **clients.xls** would link to a document in the same folder as the one containing sales.doc.
- The address **WordDocs\clients.xls** would link to a folder one level below the one containing sales.doc.
- The address **WordDocs\Word97\clients.xls** would link to a folder two levels below the one containing sales.doc.
- The address **..\clients.xls** would link to a folder one level above the one containing sales.doc.
- The address **..\..\clients.xls** would link to a folder two levels above the one containing sales.doc.

It is best to use relative references whenever possible when building hyperlinks to Web pages within your own site or intranet. This enables your code to be more portable if you ever have to move your files to another server. Otherwise, you might spend a lot of time fixing broken links. For hyperlinks to addresses outside of your Web server or to files that you do not control, it is best to use absolute references in your hyperlinks.

The Named Location in File text box in the Insert Hyperlink dialog box asks for a named location within a document. This can be any of the following:

- A bookmark (Word or HTML)
- A specific database object (table, report, query, or form) within the same or another Access database
- A specific worksheet or named ranges in an Excel workbook
- A specific slide in a PowerPoint presentation

You can click the Browse button to display any bookmarks (or named ranges, objects, slides, and so on) available in the file listed in the Link to File or URL text box. Click the appropriate bookmark and click OK to enter the bookmark name in the Named Location in File text box. Click OK again to close the Insert Hyperlink dialog box. An active hyperlink appears in your document.

If you begin to build many hyperlinks in Office documents, take advantage of this feature's ability to target a specific location within a Web page or Office document. Your users will no longer have to scroll through pages of text, multiple worksheets, or piles of slides to get to one piece of information they want. One click of a hyperlink can take them there.

You can also add hyperlinks to graphic images in Word, Excel, or PowerPoint. After you've inserted your graphic or created it using WordArt or tools from the Drawing toolbar, make sure the graphic is selected (it will be surrounded by selection handles). Then choose Insert Hyperlink and fill in the dialog box as described in this section.

Editing or Removing Hyperlinks from Word, Excel, and PowerPoint

Someone moves or deletes a file that's targeted in a hyperlink, and all of a sudden the hyperlink doesn't work. To edit a hyperlink to change the target location, right-click the hyperlink to display a shortcut menu, and choose Edit Hyperlink to display the Insert Hyperlink dialog box. Change the address (or named location) as needed and click OK.

To delete a hyperlink (but not the document or graphic to which it points), right-click the hyperlink, click the Remove Link button in the lower-left corner of the Insert Hyperlink dialog box, and click OK.

You can change the font color and font style for hyperlinks and followed hyperlinks. Choose Format, Style to display the Style dialog box, select Hyperlink from the Styles list on the left side of the dialog box (if you don't see it in the list, choose All Styles in the List drop-down box), and modify its formatting as you would any other style.

Increasing Productivity Using Hyperlinks in Word 97

Word is often used as the basis for business documents, including letters, memos, invoices, and so on. Using hyperlinks can increase the scope and ease of use of these documents in common business practice. Here are some suggestions for how you might use hyperlinks in Word 97:

- Build a table of contents based on logic rather than file location. If you have many related files on many network or Web servers, you can build a Word document that contains links to these files based on their content, such as all the files related to a particular project or department. Users have to load only a single Word document with the table of contents and click hyperlinks to access all the remaining files.
- Use hyperlinks as a primitive versioning system. Rather than constantly redistributing updated files and having people worry about whether they have the latest version of any given file, just distribute one Word document with hyperlinks to the files. Then you only need to update a single set of files. If people wonder whether they have seen the most recent data, they can click the hyperlinks in Word to jump to the latest and greatest file versions.
- Distribute links, not files. Is your email system clogged with too many Office documents or other files being passed around? Send a simple Word document with hyperlinks to files. This can greatly ease bandwidth congestion on your network and reduce the load on your mail server.
- Hyperlink to detail. If you send an invoice in Word to a customer, for example, you can include hyperlinks that point to more in-depth explanations of particular parts of the invoice. Maybe your customers can't remember what they bought based on the brief

product name listed on the invoice. The product name could be a hyperlink to a description and picture of the product on your Web server. With proper security and database connectivity, you can even enable customers to link to their account history at your business. Adding detail via hyperlinks can save an immense amount of phone time answering questions from customers.

- Add your email address as an alternative or in addition to your phone number. If you use a `mailto:` URL in your hyperlinks, you can give your recipient the power to instantly reply via email to your document. Tired of phone tag?
- You can point readers to relevant newsgroups by using `news:` URLs in your hyperlinks. Your Word document becomes a window to a larger discussion about topics of interest to your recipient.

Using Hyperlinks in Excel 97 as Navigational Tools

You can use hyperlinks in Excel 97 to jump to a specific cell. For instance, you may have a Sales workbook containing a Summary sheet that is linked to four Regional sheets. You want to closely monitor sales for NewProduct in the Western region from your Summary sheet. You can create a hyperlink on the Summary sheet that jumps to the NewProduct data on the Western Region sheet.

To do this, type the word `NewProduct` in a cell on the Summary page, keep the cell selected, and display the Insert Hyperlink dialog box. Click the Browse button next to the Named Location in File text box to display the Browse Excel Workbook dialog box. Either mark the Sheet Name option button and specify the cell address and sheet containing the NewProduct data, or, if you've named the range that contains the NewProduct data, mark the Defined Name option button and select the name from the list. Then click OK and OK again.

Now when you are in the Summary sheet, clicking the NewProduct hyperlink takes you immediately to that data in the Western Region sheet. If you're organized, you'll also have a Back to Summary hyperlink near the NewProduct data to return you to the Summary sheet.

Excel also contains a `HYPERLINK` function. You can use this function to build macros that respond to user input. It is also a great way to transform lists of URLs into active links without retyping them.

This is the syntax for the `HYPERLINK` function:

```
HYPERLINK(Link_location,Friendly_name)
```

Link_location is the hyperlink address and *Friendly_name* is some descriptive text used to describe the link. Here are three ways that you can use this function:

- `HYPERLINK("http://yahoo.com","Yahoo!")` displays the text `Yahoo!` in the cell and jumps to `http://yahoo.com` when clicked.
- `HYPERLINK("[http://www.irs.ustreas.gov/Tax_worksheet.xls] Sheet1!C3",G4)` displays the contents of G4 in the cell and jumps to cell C3 in Sheet 1 on the IRS Internet site. (Note that this URL is only an example.)

- `HYPERLINK(A5,C5)` displays the contents of cell C5 (the text `Microsoft`, for example) and jumps to the address referenced in cell A5 (for instance, **http://www.microsoft.com**).

You could use this last method to build a series of active hyperlinks in an Excel worksheet. For instance, if you have a strictly text-only series of URLs, you could import them into a column in an Excel worksheet and type descriptions for them in an adjacent column. Use the `HYPERLINK` function in a third column to build active hyperlinks from these two columns.

Action Buttons and Slide Master Hyperlinking in PowerPoint

Three hyperlinking capabilities are unique to PowerPoint: Action buttons, Slide Master hyperlinking, and Action Settings. Action buttons are a set of pre-drawn buttons—you'll find them under Slide Show, Action Buttons—that allow for a variety of actions, including hyperlinking, within a presentation. Adding hyperlinks to the master slide using the standard technique enables you to propagate the same hyperlink throughout your entire presentation. This is useful for building a navigation menu or for providing access to online help at all times. To work with Action Settings, select an object or word in any slide and choose Slide Show, Action Settings. You can then build a hyperlink to any other slide show, URL, PowerPoint presentation, or file. You can set up the hyperlink to be triggered by a traditional mouse click or by passing the mouse over it.

Hyperlinks and Access 97

You can add hyperlinks to text and graphics within forms and reports in Access 97 using the same techniques you use to add hyperlinks in Word, Excel, and PowerPoint. You can't hyperlink text in tables due to database constraints.

Access 97 has, however, introduced a new Hyperlink data type, which has three parts to it:

```
displaytext#address#subaddress
```

Each part of the data type is separated by the pound sign (#). Following are descriptions of the parts:

- The *`displaytext`* is the descriptive text for the hyperlink.
- The *`address`* is the URL or UNC.
- The *`subaddress`* is the bookmark in an HTML file or Word document. Within Excel, Access, and PowerPoint files, the subaddress is the worksheet/cell address, data object, or slide, respectively.

You can build Hyperlink records as the Hyperlink data type by using any of the following methods:

- Type the information manually using the *`displaytext#address#subaddress`* syntax.
- Use the Insert Hyperlink dialog box.
- Paste hyperlinks from other Office documents.

The Insert, Hyperlink command becomes active only when you are in a Hyperlink data type field. Type the `displaytext` first, then choose Insert, Hyperlink, and fill out the Insert Hyperlink dialog box.

Hyperlinks and Microsoft Publisher

Publisher 98 uses wizards to build a wide variety of document types. One of these is the Web Site Wizard. The Web Site Wizard lets you build a group of Web pages using selected templates and stores all these files in a single Publisher file. Hyperlinking is active only within the Web Site Wizard or a file built with this wizard. You cannot add hyperlinks to other Publisher document types. To build a hyperlink on a Web page from within the Web Site Wizard, select the descriptive text or graphic and choose Insert, Hyperlink. The Hyperlink dialog box that appears is different from the dialog box in other Office 97 applications (see Figure 29.2).

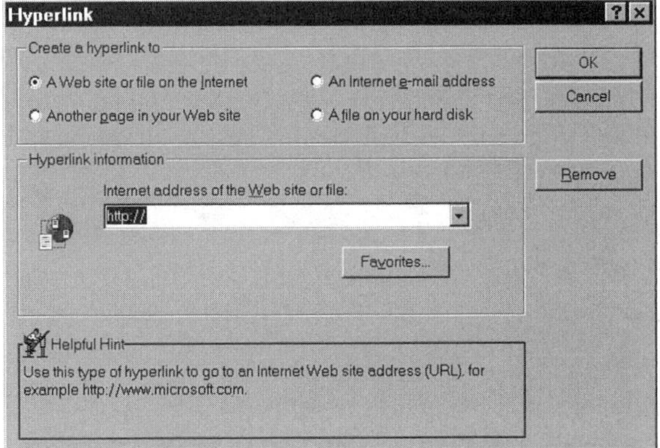

FIGURE 29.2
Inserting hyperlinks into a Publisher 98 Web site.

The name of the text box in the middle of the Hyperlink dialog box changes depending on which of the four option buttons you marked under Create a Hyperlink To. After you've entered the address, click OK to turn your text or graphic into a hyperlink.

Publisher also enables you to add hot spots to graphic objects. An imagemap is HTML code that describes different hot spots on an image, each hyperlinked to a different document or location. For instance, you might have a graphical map of the United States that is divided into four regions. You can create hot spots over each region that link to information specific to that region. To do this, select the graphic, and click the Hot Spot button on the Objects toolbar. Drag around one of the regions to outline it. When you release the mouse button, the Hyperlink dialog box appears (shown earlier in Figure 29.2) to let you specify the target of the hot spot. Repeat this process to create hot spots over the remaining three regions. The HTML code defining the hot spot within the imagemap is automatically generated by Publisher.

Word also can build imagemaps when you use it to create HTML documents (see "Simple Web Publishing with Word" later in this chapter). PowerPoint exports slides as imagemaps when you save a presentation in HTML format.

Pasting As Hyperlink

You can also create text hyperlinks between Office documents via the Clipboard. First, select a phrase in one document and copy it to the Clipboard (Ctrl+C or Edit, Copy). Select a second Office document and choose Edit, Paste As Hyperlink. This pastes the Clipboard text with a link back to your original document. With this method, there are no dialog boxes to fill.

NOTE The hyperlinks built with Paste As Hyperlink use absolute references only. Relative references are not available using this technique. ■

Simple Web Publishing with Word

You can use Word 97 as a basic HTML editor to create or edit HTML documents. Word 97 is not a full-featured HTML editor like FrontPage. However, it does support the following common HTML features:

- Background colors and textures
- Fonts and font properties, including color, size, bold, italics, underline, superscript, and subscript
- Paragraphs and indents
- Text and sentence justification
- Hyperlinks
- Imagemaps
- Bulleted and numbered lists
- Tables
- Multimedia elements, including images, clip art, sound, video, and animated GIFs
- A scrolling marquee (supported only by Internet Explorer browsers)
- Charts, equations, and OLE objects as images
- ActiveX controls

Word 97 does not support more advanced HTML authoring techniques such as frames, Java applets, or cascading style sheets. Word 97 is useful for authoring simpler documents or touching up Word documents after conversion to HTML.

Before beginning to use Word to edit or create HTML files, you need to make sure that the library required to perform HTML operations has been installed. It is not installed by default. The easiest way to check in Word is to choose File, New, and look for a Web Pages tab in the New dialog box that contains some templates and at least one wizard. If you don't see it, you need to rerun Office setup, click the Add/Remove button, and make sure that the Web Page Authoring (HTML) check box is marked.

The simplest way to put Word into HTML-authoring mode is to open an existing HTML file or choose File, New, click the Web Page tab, and open a blank Web page, template, or the Web

Page Wizard. The Web Page Wizard enables you to choose a basic style (table of contents, calendar, and so on) and theme (background texture with matching graphics) for your page. All you need to add is the content.

Before starting, you may also want to check whether you have the latest Web enhancements to Word 97. Make sure you're connected to the Internet and in HTML-authoring mode, and choose Tools, AutoUpdate. After a confirmatory dialog box, Word checks for any updates, downloads them, and installs them without any intervention from you.

In HTML-authoring mode, the Word 97 toolbars appear very similar to the standard Word toolbars (Standard, Formatting, and Web toolbars from the top down) as shown in Figure 29.3.

FIGURE 29.3
Word 97 in HTML-authoring mode.

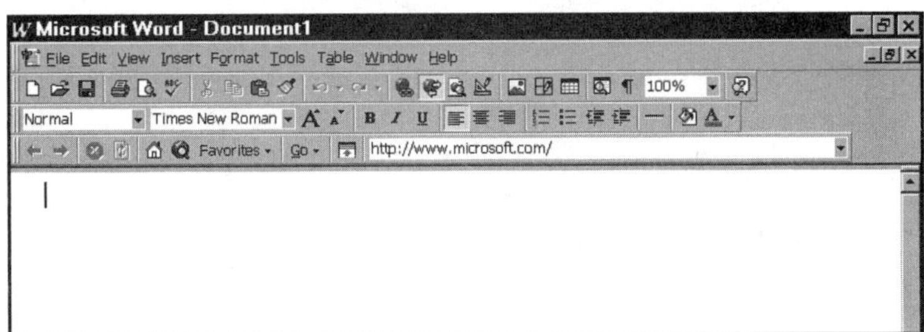

To create your HTML page, enter text just as you would for any word processor, choosing fonts and relative font sizes. HTML does not support exact font sizes for cross-platform compatibility, but only larger and smaller. You insert graphics using the Insert, Picture command. Note that you are not restricted to the GIF or JPG (or the newer PNG format supported by version 4 or higher of the major browsers) graphical file formats supported by HTML. Other formats you can use include WPG, WMF, EMF, BMP, TIF, PCX, EPS, DXF, CGM, CDR, PCD, and PCT. Word automatically converts these formats to GIF when you save your HTML file. You can also add video and sound to your Web page.

NOTE After you start building your own Web pages, you need an image editor. Microsoft Photo Editor comes with Office 97 (although it is not part of the default installation); it is not available in Office 98 for the Macintosh. You can use Photo Editor to resize, crop, and display images. To install it, rerun Office setup, click the Add/Remove button, and highlight Office Tools. Click the Change Option button and mark the Microsoft Photo Editor check box. Click OK and OK again to install Photo Editor.

You may find it helpful to include tables in your HTML documents. You can not only use them to present data in a spreadsheet style format, but also to lay out text and graphics on a Web page. Before cascading style sheets, many Web publishers used tables to mimic columns and other standard desktop publishing techniques. The table can span the entire Web page, and you can use each cell for a separate area of the page. This gives you more control over the appearance of the page and the position of text blocks and graphics.

If you know HTML, you may want to view the HTML source or edit it directly by choosing View, HTML Source from the menu. AutoUpdate also has added a Preview mode (File, Web Page Preview) to see how your page looks in any browser you have installed on your PC. Note that the HTML page title (what is displayed in the title bar of the browser) is hidden away under File, Properties. In addition, AutoUpdate has the added capability to verify hyperlinks (Tools, Check Links). Broken hyperlinks are an extremely common problem on Web pages. AutoUpdate may add even more Web capabilities for Word in the future.

NOTE The complete art of publishing Web pages for multiple browsers, Web site management, bandwidth issues, navigation systems, and interface usability is beyond the scope of this chapter. If you are doing a great deal of Web page authoring, you might want to explore the numerous free tutorials and in-depth information on the Web. The HTML Writers Guild (**www.hwg.org**) is a good place to start.

If you want to train users in Web publishing using Office applications, you may want to use my beginner's tutorial, *Sams Teach Yourself Web Publishing with Office 97 in a Week* (Sams.net Publishing, ISBN 1-57521-232-3). Your users follow a series of exercises to learn how to build an Office-integrated Web site using Office 97.

Saving your HTML document converts all graphics to GIF or JPG and places the converted files in the same folder as the HTML file. If you want to keep your multimedia files in separate folders from your HTML files, you need to edit the HTML source manually or move to a full-fledged HTML editor.

CAUTION

Windows-based Web servers are not case sensitive for filenames; UNIX-based Web servers are. Under UNIX, graphic.jpg and graphic.JPG are two different files. Make sure the filenames in the HTML file exactly match the actual filenames. If they don't, your graphics may not display, and your hyperlinks may not work. The easiest way to prevent this type of problem is to make all your filenames lowercase.

Using Word's HTML Conversion Tools

If your shop is like most businesses, you have a great deal of information built in to many Word documents on your company Web site that you would now like to share with the world. Or maybe you want to standardize on HTML and convert all your Word documents, often from several different Word formats, to HTML. Word 97 not only allows you to edit and build HTML pages, it also enables you to convert existing Word documents to HTML as well.

The easiest way to convert a Word document to HTML is to load it into Word, and then choose File, Save As and select the HTML format. After conversion, make sure that you load the HTML file into a browser to see if it looks okay. Also note that hyperlinks contained in native Word documents will be retained during the conversion to HTML.

Word has many powerful formatting and document properties that simply have no equivalent in HTML. The following are issues that you have to contend with when you save Word documents to HTML:

- Some fonts might be lost. There are numerous initiatives out now that would allow an HTML document to maintain its fonts regardless of the platform. None has been standardized as of this writing. Currently, the translation to HTML maintains the basic nature of the font (monospaced or proportional), but the actual font used may vary across platforms.
- Point sizes are not supported in HTML, only relative sizes. The font size of certain portions of your document may need to be increased or decreased after translation to maintain the same document look.
- Text-formatting effects—such as emboss, shadow, small caps, and so on—are lost. The text itself is retained.
- WordArt and drawing objects in the Word document are lost. If you want to retain these objects, you need to load the converted HTML file, copy the graphics into it via the Clipboard, and resave it.
- Animations are lost. You must use other multimedia effects (marquee effects or animated GIFs) to duplicate these.
- Page numbers and margins are lost.
- Drop caps are lost. You can replace them with graphical elements, if desired.
- Tabs are retained through the use of a special HTML code, but you may want to use a table in place of tabs to organize text.
- Highlighting is not retained.
- Page borders and borders or lines around text do not translate to HTML.
- Headers, footers, end notes, footnotes, and comments are all lost in the conversion. After the conversion, you must manually transfer them, adjust their font sizes and styles, and set their alignment.
- Columns do not transfer. You can use tables to mimic newspaper-style columns.
- The portions of styles that are supported by HTML (such as boldface and italic) will transfer. Portions with no HTML equivalents will not.
- Tracked changes are not supported.

These shortcomings will be addressed in upcoming versions of Microsoft Office, which will support a more flexible, enhanced Web language called XML (Extensible Markup Language). XML should allow all Word's powerful capabilities to translate intact.

Loading, saving, and checking the Word files that you want to convert to HTML one at a time is simply not feasible when you want to convert tens of thousands of documents. Again, AutoUpdate now includes the Conversion Wizard (File, New, Web Pages tab). This wizard enables you to select a source folder and a destination folder for all files that you want to convert. The wizard also enables you to convert to and from other formats besides HTML and Word, including WordPerfect, Text, RTF, and Works.

Converting Excel Worksheets to HTML

The rows and columns that make up a typical spreadsheet are a natural for conversion to HTML tables, and charts make compelling graphic images in HTML pages.

The Internet Assistant Wizard, which starts when you choose File, Save As HTML, helps you convert spreadsheets to HTML (see Figure 29.4). The wizard converts cell ranges in any open worksheet or workbook to tables in new HTML pages or inserts tables into existing HTML pages.

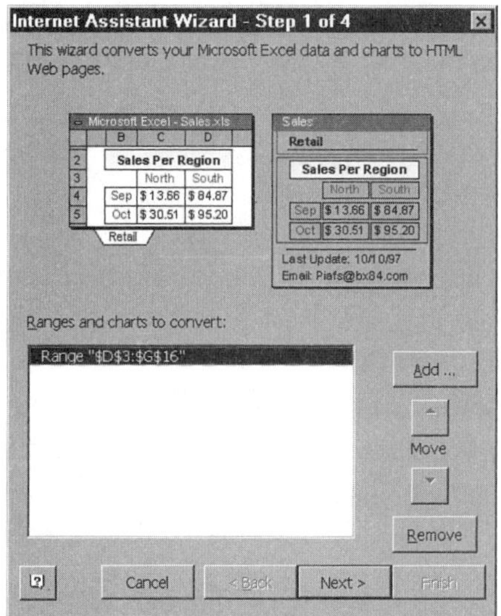

FIGURE 29.4
Beginning the conversion of spreadsheets to HTML using Excel's Internet Assistant Wizard.

Make sure all the worksheets and workbooks that contain the data you want to use are open before you invoke the wizard. When the wizard is running, you need to use the keyboard shortcut Ctrl+F6 to move between workbooks because the Window command is not accessible.

If you choose to add an HTML table to an existing HTML file, you need to add a placeholder in the HTML file before starting the wizard. The placeholder text is

```
<!--##Table##-->
```

This text will be replaced by the table contents in the HTML file. The easiest way to insert this placeholder is to open your HTML file in a pure text editor, such as Notepad, and type it in.

The wizard guesses which range of cells you want to convert and displays that range in the Ranges and Charts to Convert box. If you want to specify a particular range, select it first before invoking the wizard. You can use the Add and Remove buttons to modify the list. Clicking the Add button displays a dialog box requesting a cell range. You can type the range address or select the range in the worksheet with your mouse. If you use this second method, the range displayed in the text box dynamically updates as you drag over cells in the worksheet. After the list of cell ranges in the Internet Assistant Wizard is correct, use the Move arrows to put them in the desired order. The order in this list is the order in which the tables will be published.

NOTE A separate HTML table will be generated for each cell range in the list. If you want a single HTML table output, you will need to place your data ranges together into a single worksheet before invoking the wizard. ■

Next, move on to indicate to the wizard whether to make a new HTML page with the table or insert the table into an existing HTML file. If you choose to create a new HTML file, the wizard prompts you to fill in some basic information, as shown in Figure 29.5.

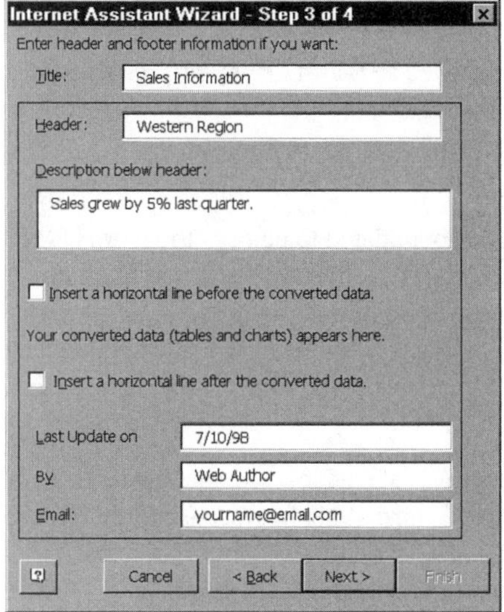

FIGURE 29.5
Filling in new HTML page information in Excel's Internet Assistant Wizard.

The final step of the wizard enables you to specify a name and location for the HTML file or save the file to a FrontPage Web. If you choose FrontPage Web, the FrontPage Explorer asks you to select the Web to which you want to add the page. Click Finish to save the HTML file.

Due to the limitations of HTML, certain elements from Excel spreadsheets do not translate well or at all into HTML tables. The following are some of the results of saving Excel data as an HTML table:

- Table border thickness and style formatting is lost. HTML supports borders of varying thicknesses, styles, and colors, so you can add these formatting options using Word 97 or an HTML editor.

- Only formula results are translated. HTML does not support dynamic formulas. You cannot change the value in an HTML table cell and see new results "ripple" through the table. HTML tables are strictly static data tables.
- Images, drawing objects, and WordArt objects are lost. HTML does, however, let you place an image in a table. One workaround is to copy your images from your Excel worksheet to the Clipboard, paste them into the appropriate cell of the translated HTML table in Word 97, and then resave the table.
- Cell patterns are lost. Cell background colors are, however, retained. Excel page backgrounds are lost.
- Special text alignment such as angled text or vertical text is not translated.
- Word wrapping for a specific row may or may not be translated because, by default, all cell contents in HTML have the capability to wrap (that cross-platform compatibility thing again).
- Row heights in HTML are scaled to fit the font size. You can set row heights higher in the HTML table by enlarging the CELLPADDING attribute, which places space between an HTML element and its cell border. Changing row height in Excel has no impact on row height in the HTML table.
- Cell indenting is not translated to HTML. However, HTML supports this attribute, so you can add it from within Word 97.
- Hyperlinks attached to images are lost. You need to edit the HTML file in Word 97 to restore these links.
- Hyperlink references are not updated to point to the new HTML table. If a hyperlink in an Excel worksheet references another worksheet or another cell within the worksheet, this hyperlink continues to point to the original Excel worksheet or cell and not to the translated HTML table or cell. You need to manually update these hyperlinks if you want them to point to the appropriate HTML tables, or remove them entirely if they are no longer appropriate.

If you want to create an attractive HTML table—one that uses colors, borders, and graphics extensively—it is easiest to do this formatting in Word 97 or another HTML editor. Use Excel strictly to provide the data and basic structure of the HTML table, and then format it later.

You can also use Excel's Internet Assistant Wizard to export charts as static GIF images. This is similar to taking a snapshot of your chart. If your chart changes, you need to re-export the image and update your HTML page, if required. All the text and structure of the chart will be faithfully reproduced in the GIF image.

The process for exporting charts as images is identical to making HTML tables. If you open a worksheet that contains charts and then launch the Internet Assistant Wizard, the charts appear in the first wizard dialog box (refer to Figure 29.4). Again, you have the option to publish the graphic to a new HTML file or to an existing one. (Use the same placeholder, `<!--##Table##-->`, if you export it to an existing HTML file.) The wizard places charts into the HTML file one below the other. You can change their positions using Word 97 or another HTML editor.

The best way to control the size of the output GIF image is to resize the chart in Excel before starting the wizard. Resizing the output GIF image later in an image editing program usually results in significant quality degradation, reducing the readability of text.

CAUTION

Any free-floating clip art in your Excel chart will not translate to the GIF image. If these graphics are key to your chart, it may be easier to do a screen dump of your Excel chart and use an image editor to edit, size, and convert it to a GIF or JPG image.

Querying Web-Based Data Sources from Excel

Excel 97 has a unique ability to dynamically query HTML files or Web search engines or other data compendia and pull that information into a cell in a spreadsheet. This feature is handy for pulling stock quotes off the Internet. You query Web-based data by creating a Web query. A Web query is a very simple text file that gives Excel the following information:

- Where to go on the Internet or local network
- Which file to access
- How to access the file or which parameters to send to a Web server or search engine

You can create two types of Web queries: static Web queries and parameter or dynamic Web queries. A static Web query requests the same file over and over. A dynamic Web query includes text that opens a dialog box in which the user enters data, which is then passed on to the Web server.

To make sure you have the Web query capability, choose Data, Get External Data, Create New Query. An error message will pop up with installation instructions if you don't have the capability installed. If this happens, run the Office 97 setup program, click the Add/Remove button, select Data Access, click the Change Option button, and mark the Microsoft Query check box.

You must manually create a Web query in a text editor before you can run it from Excel. Save the text file with the extension for Web queries, .iqy.

A typical static Web query contains three lines:

```
WEB
1
http://anyURL.com/anypage.html
```

The first line, `WEB`, is the type of query. (There is only one type at this time.) The second line is the query version number. Again, only version 1 is currently in use. The third line is the URL or network address of the file that you want to access.

An optional fourth line adds required `POST` parameters if the query addresses a Web server that uses `POST` rather than `GET`. You will only rarely use this fourth line.

The following example is a typical dynamic query. It prompts a user for a keyword to search AltaVista:

```
WEB
1
http://www.altavista.digital.com/cgi-bin/query?
➥pg=q&what=web&fmt=.&q=["q","Enter a keyword for search."]
```

Whatever the user types in the dialog box generated by this parameter query will be passed as part of the "q" variable to the AltaVista Web server.

After you have built a query (or chosen to use one of the prebuilt queries that comes with Office 97) and set it to point to an HTML page (data imports best if it comes from an HTML table), the next step is to run the query. Connect to the Internet, open a blank worksheet in Excel, and choose Data, Get External Data, Run Web Query. Then select the query by name (some predefined Web queries that come with Office 97 are also listed) and click the Get Data button. The Returning External Data to Microsoft Excel dialog box appears to let you specify the beginning Excel cell address into which you want to place the results of the query (see Figure 29.6).

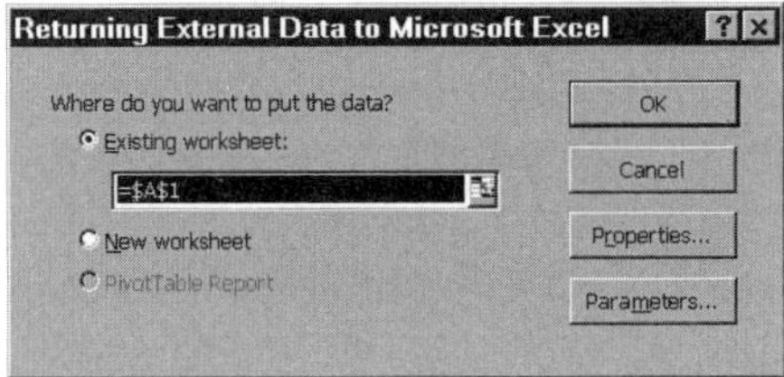

FIGURE 29.6
Choosing the Excel worksheet and beginning cell for returning data from a Web query.

Clicking the Properties button brings up the External Data Range Properties dialog box, shown in Figure 29.7, which enables you to fine tune your query in the following ways:

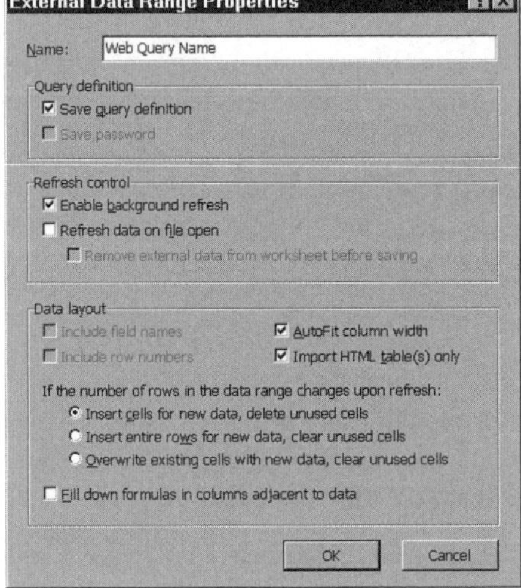

FIGURE 29.7
Customizing the results of a Web query in the External Data Range Properties dialog box.

- Make sure the Save Query Definition check box is marked to save the query to the worksheet. This gives you the option of refreshing the data at a later time.
- The Enable Background Refresh check box enables the query to run in the background, so you can continue to work in Excel while you're waiting for the results.
- The Refresh Data on File Open check box reruns the query whenever you open the worksheet.
- There are four check boxes under Data Layout, but two will probably be grayed out. The AutoFit Column Width is self-explanatory. If Import HTML Table(s) Only is not marked, you import the entire HTML file rather than just the table portion.
- Below the Data Layout area are three option buttons that let you choose what to do if the data table you bring in is larger or smaller than previous query results. Choose whichever option is appropriate.
- The Fill Down Formulas in Columns Adjacent to Data check box controls the use of formulas that are in cells to the right of the data imported via the query. If this check box is marked, Excel automatically eliminates or adds formulas as the number of rows of imported data shrinks or grows.

After you've made your selections in the External Data Range Properties dialog box, click OK to return to the Returning External Data to Microsoft Excel dialog box. If you are running a parameter query, you can enter the parameters for your query by clicking the Parameters button. The Parameters dialog box, shown in Figure 29.8, gives you three options:

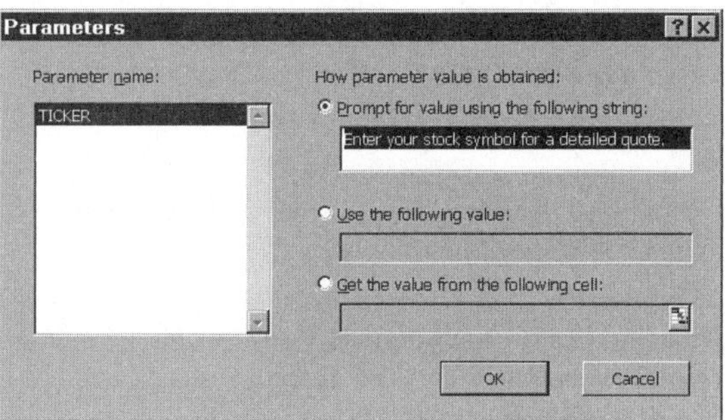

FIGURE 29.8
Choosing Excel Web query parameter options in the Parameters dialog box.

- Edit the text used to prompt the user for data entry
- Enter the parameter(s) directly
- Enter a cell address where Excel can find the parameter value

After making any changes here and clicking OK, run the query by clicking OK in the Returning External Data to Microsoft Excel dialog box. A small, green, rotating globe shows up on the status line of the Excel window as Excel retrieves the data. The query is complete when your Excel worksheet is filled with results (see Figure 29.9).

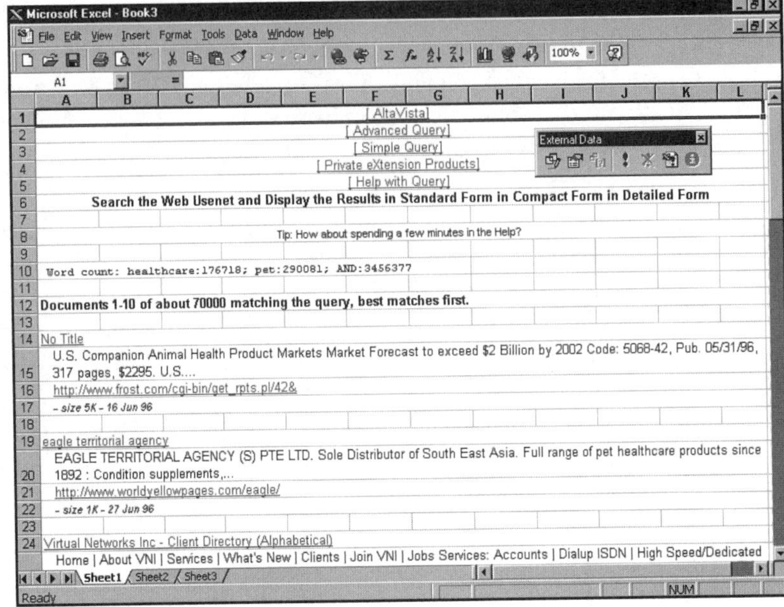

FIGURE 29.9
The results of running a Web query against the AltaVista search engine.

Parameter queries can take multiple entries, as shown in the following AltaVista Web query:

```
WEB
1
http://www.altavista.digital.com/cgi-bin/query?
➥pg=q&what=web&fmt=.&q=["q","Enter the first keyword."]+
➥["q1","Enter the second keyword."]+["q2","Enter the third keyword."]+
➥["q3","Enter the final keyword."]
```

This query prompts you for four separate keywords and passes the results to the AltaVista Web server within the appropriate "q" variable.

You can often obtain Web server syntax to use in a Web query by reading the help files at the search engine site. Also, you can perform a search and then dissect the string passed on to the Web server as it appears in your browser's Address box.

Saving PowerPoint Presentations as HTML Slide Shows

You spent hours putting together a great, whiz-bang presentation in PowerPoint. It all paid off with kudos from the department head. There's only one problem: he wants you to put it on the company Web site for immediate companywide distribution, and many other company locations do not have Office 97. How do you make sure everyone can read your presentation? PowerPoint 97 gives you three options for solving this problem:

- Post your presentation in its native format.
- Convert your presentation to HTML.
- Save your presentation as a PowerPoint animation (.ppz extension) that can be read by browsers with the proper plug-in or ActiveX controls.

Posting your presentation in its native PPT format works well if your audience is using Windows. There are viewers available at the Microsoft site (**www.microsoft.com/msoffice/office/viewers.asp**) that enable users with earlier versions of PowerPoint to view your presentation. This option guarantees that what you generated is exactly what everyone will see. However, it isn't workable if any user is dialing in from a computer with a non-Windows operating system because the viewers are all Windows-based.

Converting the presentation to HTML guarantees that anyone anywhere can view your presentation using almost any browser. PowerPoint uses a similar approach to other Office 97 applications in using the Save As HTML Wizard to help you customize your HTML files. To start the wizard, choose File, Save As HTML. The opening dialog box, shown in Figure 29.10, outlines the choices you can make to ensure that your presentation is converted optimally.

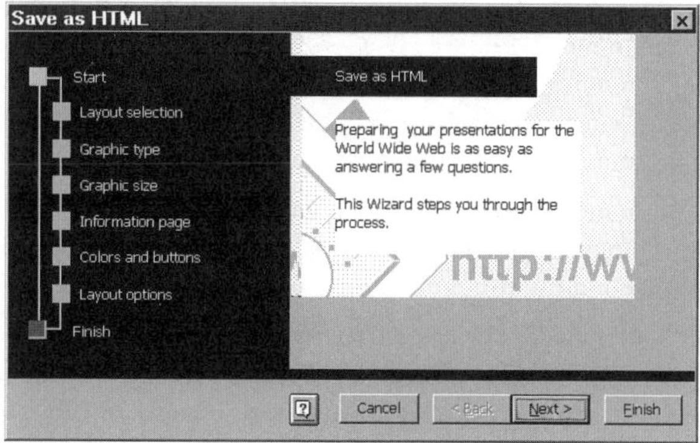

FIGURE 29.10
Beginning conversion of PowerPoint slides to HTML.

Follow these steps to complete the Save As HTML Wizard:

1. Choose Next in the first dialog box of the wizard. In the following dialog box, choose an existing layout or a new layout. (A layout is a collection of your answers to the questions presented by the Save As HTML Wizard. If you use the same settings repetitively, save your answers as a layout at the end of the interview process so that you can reuse them in the future.) Click Next. (If you select an existing layout, you will jump to the last wizard dialog box.)
2. Choose a page style—either a full-window browser display or frames. Frames allow the users more flexibility in navigating through the presentation. Some older browsers do not support frames, although this is less of a problem now that sophisticated browsers are available for free. Click Next.
3. Choose which graphical file type to use: GIF, JPG, or PPZ. Choose GIF if your presentation contains only a few colors. If your presentation contains many color gradients or is

photographic, the JPG format gives you smaller files. The JPG format is lossy, which means that choosing less than 100 percent compression discards information from your images. The most notable degradation is in text readability, which you'll normally see if you go below 80 percent. Choose the PPZ format for a PowerPoint animation. Click Next.

4. Specify the size of your graphic (your choices are based on monitor resolutions from 640×480 up to 1280×1024 pixels) and indicate how much of the screen you want to fill, from 1/4 width to full width. Choosing higher resolutions and greater screen widths can often result in huge graphics, thus extending download times for modem users. Conversely, choosing a low resolution and smaller screen width can make the text in your presentation unreadable. A good place to start is 640×480 with full-screen width. Click Next.
5. Add an optional email address, home page address, and comments on every page of your presentation. Mark the Download Original Presentation check box if you want the wizard to build a link to your original PPT file. Mark the Internet Explorer Download Button check box to add a link that lets users download the latest version of the Internet Explorer browser. Click Next.
6. Select the colors that you want to use for HTML text, hyperlinks, visited hyperlinks, and the page background. Mark the Transparent Buttons check box if you want the background colors to show through the navigation buttons. Click Next.
7. Select the style for your navigation buttons. You can choose among three graphical styles and one text-only style. Click Next.
8. Specify the side of the slides on which you want the navigation buttons to appear. If you have any slide notes with your presentation, you also have the option to include this text with the slides. Click Next.
9. Enter the folder in which you want to save the HTML files. Click Finish. The wizard displays the Save As HTML dialog box to let you name your layout settings if you want to save them, as mentioned in step 1. Either type a name and click Save, or click Don't Save.

The wizard performs the conversion and then presents a message box stating that the presentation was successfully saved. It is a good idea to preview the presentation (it begins with index.html) in a browser. Make sure all the text is readable. You may need to rerun the wizard with a different resolution or graphics file type. Note that the wizard also generates text-only HTML files, which are handy for browsers such as Lynx that do not support images.

NOTE If, in step 5 of the wizard, you chose to include a link to your PPT file, you'll notice that the PPT file saved with the HTML files is probably a good deal smaller than your original PPT file. The wizard compresses the PPT file for Internet use; otherwise, it works identically to the original file. Even if you don't want to use the HTML files, you can still run the wizard to obtain a smaller PPT file.

As with Excel and Word, HTML does not have equivalents for many of the options available in PowerPoint. As a result, certain things will not survive the translation to HTML:

- Hyperlinks to images in the Slide Master are lost. Hyperlinks to free-floating images are, however, maintained.
- PowerPoint graphic animations and their associated sounds do not appear in any form.
- Text animations and their associated sounds are lost.
- Animated charts don't make it through; they convert as static chart images.
- Background MIDI music added to slides is lost. You can easily remedy this by adding background sound to the HTML page.
- No slide transitions survive.
- Embedded movies show up only as a static image of their first frame.

You can add video and sound in Word 97. If you want to include text and chart animations, you have to laboriously recreate them as animated GIFs or video files. If these effects are important to your presentation, consider using the animation format, PPZ.

The PPZ format is a compromise between the HTML translation and the original PowerPoint format. It retains many more of PowerPoint's elements and can still be played in a browser.

If, when you run the Save As HTML Wizard, you choose the option to create a PPZ file, the resulting index.html file contains a link to the Microsoft ActiveX PowerPoint Animation Player and a link to start the animation. Links to text-only slides are also available from this page. The PPZ file is similar in size to your original PPT file. After you have clicked the link to install the ActiveX control and clicked the link to start the animation, the animation will not begin until the entire animation file has loaded. (This is not streaming media.) You advance slides in the animation by clicking them. Right-clicking lets you back up to the previous slide.

Right-clicking a slide and choosing Full Screen enables you to play the animation at your full screen resolution. If you place a note on index.html indicating to users to use this feature, you no longer need to worry about which monitor resolution to select to improve the readability of small text in the Save As HTML Wizard. If you choose to tell your users about this Full Screen option, you may want to output your presentation at a monitor resolution of 640×480 and set the graphics width at full screen for optimal viewing.

Of course, using the PPZ format requires a few compromises:

- Hyperlinked images in the Slide Master are no longer clickable.
- Hyperlinks, whether attached to free-floating clip art, WordArt, or photographs, are also lost.
- PowerPoint chart animations only show the final chart.
- Background MIDI music is lost.
- Any objects embedded into a slide are no longer active. However, if they display information (such as an embedded spreadsheet), the information is still visible.
- None of the action buttons work.

For optimal compatibility, you may want to publish your presentation in all three PowerPoint formats (PPT, PPZ, and HTML) and let users choose what works best for them. It's so easy with the Save As HTML Wizard.

Publishing Microsoft Access Data on the Internet

Making database information directly available from a Web server causes shivers of dismay for most database administrators. Security nightmares, visions of database corruption, and the thought of generating endless HTML pages after every database change haunt many dreams at night. Fortunately, Access 97 gives you several options for publishing database information to a Web site:

- You can use the Publish to the Web Wizard to convert database objects to HTML tables. This wizard also enables you to use custom HTML template files.
- You can do a simple export of tables, reports, or forms to HTML.
- The Publish to the Web Wizard also lets you build files for sending dynamic queries to the database from a browser.
- Access can link to or import HTML tables or lists.

Access 97 has a very sophisticated Publish to the Web Wizard that enables both static and dynamic database publishing. Static publishing mostly converts database objects (tables, reports, forms, and queries) into HTML tables. Dynamic publishing enables users to directly query the database via ODBC (open database connectivity) drivers and pass results on as browser-readable HTML through a Web server. Two technologies are used to perform dynamic queries:

- IDC/HTX file pairs (internet data connectivity paired with HTML template files, HTX)
- ASP files (active server pages)

IDC/HTX is an older and simpler technology and is giving way to the much more powerful and flexible ASP technology.

Publishing a Static Database with the Publish to the Web Wizard

First, let's look at the static capabilities of the Publish to the Web Wizard. To start the wizard, choose File, Save As HTML command. Then follow these steps to create HTML pages and tables:

1. The first wizard dialog box lets you choose from a list of Web publication profiles, which are saved responses from previous uses of the wizard. These are the same as the layouts that you can select in PowerPoint's Save As HTML Wizard. Click Next.
2. The wizard displays a miniature tabbed representation of all tables, queries, reports, and forms contained in your database, as shown in Figure 29.11. Each item has a check box next to it. To publish any or all database objects, mark the desired check boxes. Click Next.

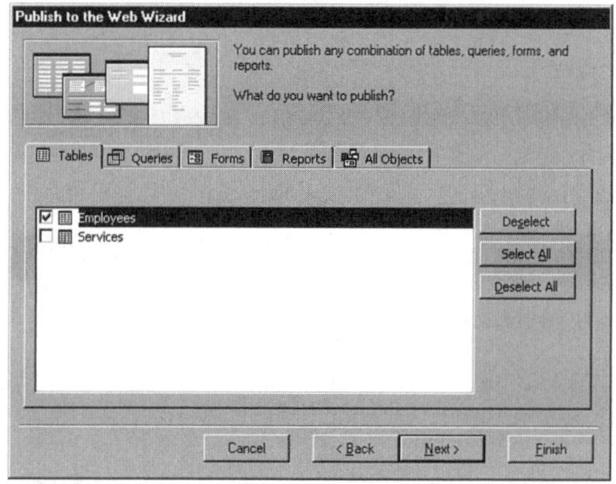

FIGURE 29.11
Choose the database objects to publish as HTML tables from the Access Publish to the Web Wizard.

3. Choose an HTML template in which the output will be placed. You can use the same template for all objects or different templates for different objects. Leave this dialog box blank if you don't want to use a template. The templates use placeholders to tell the wizard where to place the title (the Access object name), the table, and navigation links (if you don't want to use the Access-generated default navigation system). Before starting the wizard, use a text editor to add the placeholders into your HTML template file. The title placeholder is usually placed between the title tags (`<title>` and `</title>`). You can place the table and optional navigational placeholders anywhere in the body of the HTML document (between the `<body>` and `</body>` tags). Figure 29.12 shows a sample HTML template file containing all the placeholders. The placeholder nomenclature is as follows:

```
<!--AccessTemplate_Title-->
<!--AccessTemplate_Table-->
<!--AccessTemplate_FirstPage-->
<!--AccessTemplate_PreviousPage-->
<!--AccessTemplate_NextPage-->
<!--AccessTemplate_LastPagev>
<!--AccessTemplate_PageNumber-->
```

4. After dealing with templates, click Next. You now have the option of choosing static or dynamic output. The Static HTML option produces HTML table output for your database objects. The two Dynamic options generate the files needed for IDC/HTX or ASP. The dynamic files are discussed in greater detail in the section "Using IDC/HTX Files with Access" later in this chapter. (If you want to publish certain objects as static and others as dynamic, mark the check box labeled "I want to select different format types for some of the selected objects." A dialog box appears that lets you choose static or dynamic for each object.) Choose Static HTML, and click Next.
5. Specify a location for saving your file locally, or choose the option to use the Web Publishing Wizard (a standalone application discussed later in this chapter in "The Web Publishing Wizard"). You can either choose to set up a path to a new Web server or, if

you've used the Web Publishing Wizard before, choose the "friendly name" of an existing Web server. Click Next.

6. The wizard now asks if you want to create a home page. The home page is an index page (also called the Switchboard from within Access) with links to all your published pages. This is usually a good idea if you're publishing more than one or two objects. Click Next.
7. The last wizard dialog box gives you the option of saving your answers to the wizard's questions in a Web publication profile. Enter an optional name for the profile to save it, and click Finish to generate the HTML files.

Each object is published as a table in a separate HTML file. Multipage Access reports are split across multiple HTML pages with navigation links between pages.

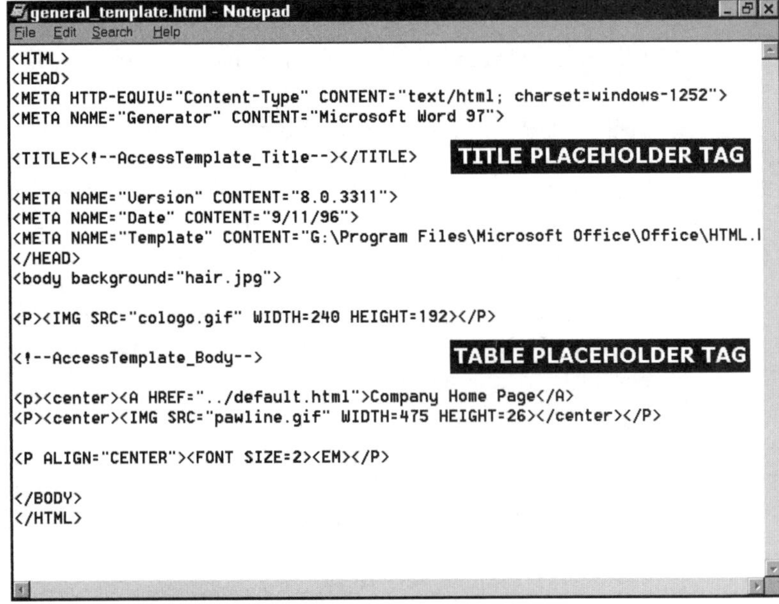


```
<HTML>
<HEAD>
<META HTTP-EQUIV="Content-Type" CONTENT="text/html; charset=windows-1252">
<META NAME="Generator" CONTENT="Microsoft Word 97">

<TITLE><!--AccessTemplate_Title--></TITLE>

<META NAME="Version" CONTENT="8.0.3311">
<META NAME="Date" CONTENT="9/11/96">
<META NAME="Template" CONTENT="G:\Program Files\Microsoft Office\Office\HTML.I
</HEAD>
<body background="hair.jpg">

<P><IMG SRC="cologo.gif" WIDTH=240 HEIGHT=192></P>

<!--AccessTemplate_Body-->

<p><center><A HREF="../default.html">Company Home Page</A>
<P><center><IMG SRC="pawline.gif" WIDTH=475 HEIGHT=26></center></P>

<P ALIGN="CENTER"><FONT SIZE=2><EM></P>

</BODY>
</HTML>
```

FIGURE 29.12
A sample HTML template file demonstrating the use of Access placeholder tags.

NOTE Make sure to include navigational placeholders in the HTML template files used for the output of multipage reports. Without them, only the first page of the report will be accessible from the home page. ■

Database Objects and Information That Translate Well to Static HTML Tables

The following database objects and information translate well using the Access Publish to the Web Wizard:

- The text of all the records
- Database field names

- Header and footer text from reports
- The basic table structure of the object
- Information in any field of the Hyperlink data type (comes across as active hyperlinks in the output HTML table)
- Font colors, types, and styles used in reports and forms

Database Objects and Information That Do Not Translate Well to Static HTML Tables

A few things do not translate to HTML through the wizard:

- Special Access backgrounds used in forms or reports
- Separation lines between form and report sections
- Images used in report headers or footers
- Unbound hyperlinks in form headers or footers
- OLE objects, either inside or outside of data controls
- Report subforms

Exporting Access Objects to HTML

If you have only a single report, form, table, or query to export, you can bypass the Publish to the Web Wizard. To do this, first select the object in Access that you want to export. Then choose File, Save As/Export, mark the To an External File or Database option button, and click OK. This displays the dialog box shown in Figure 29.13.

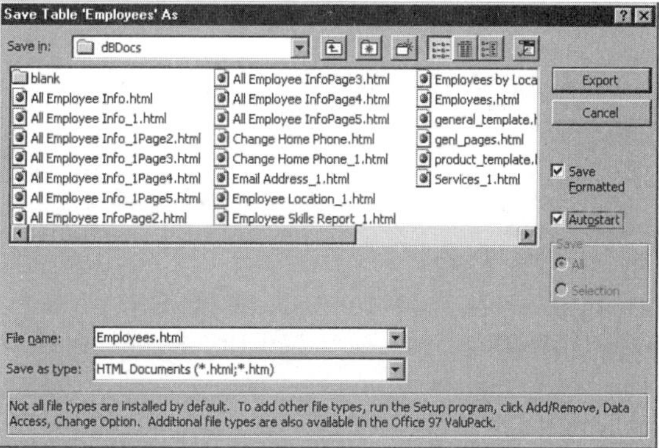

FIGURE 29.13
Exporting a single Access object to HTML.

Choose the HTML Documents file type in the Save As Type drop-down box. The Save Formatted check box becomes active. Mark this check box if you want to use an HTML template file. Marking the Save Formatted check box activates the Autostart check box. Mark this check box if you want to immediately load the exported HTML file into a browser for preview. After you've selected the folder to save your HTML file in, click the Export button to generate your

HTML table. This method is much quicker and simpler than using the Publish to the Web Wizard, but you can only export one database object at a time.

Connecting an Access Database to the Web

Exporting data to an HTML table from an Access database gives you only a snapshot of the database contents at the moment it was exported. If your databases are constantly being updated, your static tables can quickly become outdated, even seconds after you generate an HTML table. Traditionally, database applications give users access to up-to-the-minute information from the database. This is great inside corporate walls, but not feasible if you want to share all or some portion of your database information in a Web environment.

It is possible to send a query from any Web browser through a Microsoft Web server (currently called the Internet Information Server, or IIS) into Access and return the results of the real-time query to the browser as formatted HTML using the pathway shown in Figure 29.14. Note that this process will not work using other Web servers, such as those from Netscape or the Apache Web server. This capability is currently unique to IIS.

FIGURE 29.14
Querying from a Web browser to Access and returning the results as HTML.

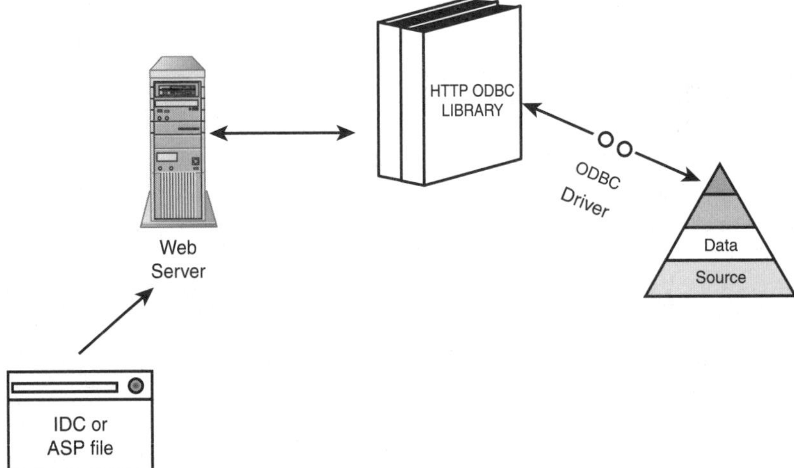

For this process to work, Access and IIS must be tied together. You can do this by registering the database with the ODBC library using the ODBC applet in the Control Panel (called 32-bit ODBC in Windows 95/98). Make sure you have an ODBC driver installed on the machine containing the Web server.

It is not necessary for the Access database to reside on the same PC as the IIS Web server. In fact, this improves security because you can use a non-TCP/IP network to connect the Web server with the database machine. It also improves performance because the Web server and the database are using separate CPUs. The network connection between the two machines should, however, only carry requests between the Web server and database. Other network traffic should not be carried on this line or the performance gained by using multiple CPUs will be negated.

Double-click the ODBC applet in the Control Panel. Register the Access database using the System DSN tab, and browse to the location of the database. It is a good idea to keep the data source name simple because you will need to refer to the database by this name from within IDC/HTX or ASP files.

Now you need to set up the Web server. The only Web server that will work with IDC/HTX or ASP is IIS, also called Personal Web Server (PWS). The server will run under Windows 95 (and, presumably, Windows 98), and Windows NT Workstation or NT Server. I recommend using Windows NT Server for enhanced security and better integration with the operating system. Windows NT Server also gives you more sophisticated Web server administration tools.

Under NT 4.0, IIS is included in the NT Option Pack, available for free from Microsoft. Installation is straightforward, and the Web server installs itself as several NT services, including HTTP, FTP, and Gopher. For the purposes of this chapter, you just need to make sure the Web server is running by double-clicking the Services applet in the Control Panel. The Web server should appear in the list of NT services. It will be listed as World Wide Web Publishing Services and should say "Started" next to it. You will find more information about installing and administering IIS or PWS in Chapter 31, "Using Office with Microsoft Web Software."

Now that the Web server is up and can communicate with the Access database, it is time to start getting database information dynamically.

NOTE When I refer to getting data dynamically from a database and outputting it to a browser, I am not referring to dynamic HTML. Dynamic HTML uses various features in HTML 4.0 and has no relationship with IDC/HTX or ASP files.

Using IDC/HTX with Access

IDC/HTX is a very basic form and forerunner of ASP. It is still useful in situations where only basic queries are needed, and it is extremely easy to use. Figure 29.15 shows a basic IDC and HTX file pair. The figure only shows the part of the HTX file related to the query in the BODY portion of the HTX file. The remainder of the HTX file is in standard HTML.

As you can see, the IDC file is extremely simple. It contains only the following elements:

- *Datasource.* This is the name that you gave the Access database when you registered it with ODBC.
- *Template.* This is the name of the HTX template file.
- *SQLStatement.* This is the actual SQL query.

You can add an optional username and password data to the IDC file.

In the HTX file, the active area of the file begins with `<%begindetail%>` and ends with `<%enddetail%>`. Each field name is formatted similarly, as `<%Field_name%>`. You can include with the field names any kind of HTML code to obtain the formatting you need. You can even make hyperlinks from the field data.

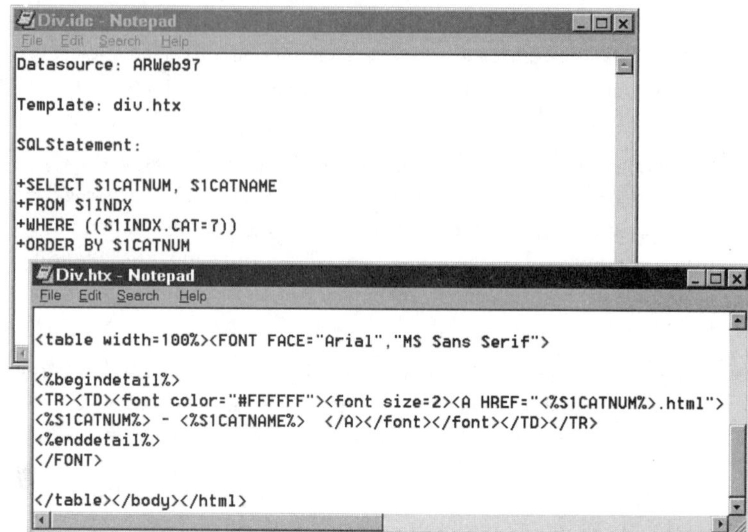

FIGURE 29.15
A sample IDC query and HTX template file.

You can write IDC files in a text editor, pasting in the SQL statement directly from Access, or use the Publish to the Web Wizard in Access. After you've selected your query in the second wizard dialog box and skipped the option to choose an HTML template file, the next dialog box enables you to choose Dynamic HTX/IDC. Choose this option and click Next to display the dialog box shown in Figure 29.16. This dialog box requires you to fill out some information for the IDC file.

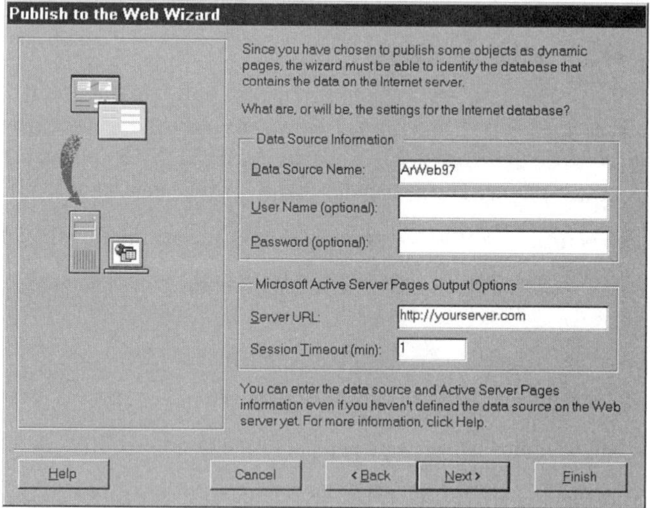

FIGURE 29.16
Filling out information for an IDC query from the Access Publish to the Web Wizard.

Make sure to specify the complete URL (including http://) for your Web server. Click Next, and then choose where to save your files. Choose the Scripts folder off the root of your Web. This is very important because whatever folder the IDC/HTX files reside in must have Execute privileges under the Web server, and the Scripts folder has those rights by default. After you click the Finish button in the wizard, your IDC/HTX file pair (named after the query they came from) shows up in the Scripts folder. The HTX file will be very generic, and you may want to edit it in Word 97 or another HTML editor. Test that the query works properly before going live on the Internet.

> **CAUTION**
>
> When you test your IDC file (or ASP file), you must load the file using its full URL, such as ***YourWebServer/Scripts/Some.idc***. If you try to double-click the file in Windows Explorer or drag and drop the file into Internet Explorer, Internet Explorer will only see a text file and display it as such, without executing the query.

You can also make IDC/HTX file pairs using the File, Save As/Export command. Just select Microsoft IIS 1-2 (*.htx; *.idc) from the Save As Type drop-down box after choosing the query you want to export.

One significant way that you can use IDC is to combine it with HTML forms to put together a page of preselected queries. After you've generated the IDC/HTX file pairs, you can include them in hyperlinks or as part of drop-down boxes, or even allow users to type keywords. Figure 29.17 shows an HTML form with the HTML code in bold required to execute each form element using IDC files.

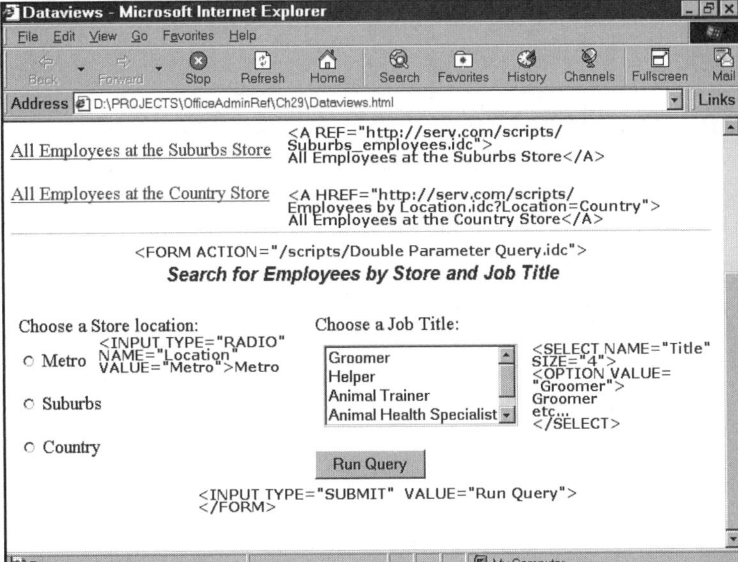

FIGURE 29.17
An HTML form and the IDC queries used to query Access from a browser.

The technology behind IDC/HTX has been expanded to form the basis of the more powerful Active Server Pages.

What are Active Server Pages?

An active server page file (.asp extension) contains both the query for the database and the HTML tags required to pass the results back to the browser. With IDC/HTX, the IDC file contains the query plus the information to connect to ODBC, and the HTX file is the HTML template file for passing the results back. ASP also adds significant programming enhancements, allowing the use of scripting (usually VBScript or JScript) and ActiveX controls. Making and using more complex ASP files is very much a job for a programmer. The Web server and ODBC setup required for IDC/HTX works fine for ASP; you don't need to make any changes to it.

Again, you can use the Access Publish to the Web Wizard to build basic ASP files from your queries. In the wizard, instead of choosing Static HTML or Dynamic HTX/IDC, choose Dynamic ASP (Microsoft Active Server Pages). This displays the dialog box shown earlier in Figure 29.16. Again, choose to save your file in the Scripts folder of your Web root. If you examine an ASP file generated by the wizard in a text editor, you will find it to be much more sophisticated than the IDC/HTX files. Because the intricacies of ASP programming are beyond the scope of this chapter, you may want to buy a book dealing strictly with that topic or check out several online resources for more information on ASPs. Here are some good places to start:

www.microsoft.com/iis/
www.aspdeveloper.net
www.genusa.com/asp/
www.activeserverpages.com

You can associate ASP files with hyperlinks and HTML forms in the same manner as IDC/HTX files (refer to Figure 29.17).

Linking to or Importing HTML Files into Access

You can incorporate HTML lists and tables into Access databases by linking to them or directly importing them into Access tables. Note that if an HTML page does not contain a table or list, linking or importing will not work.

To link to an HTML page, begin by choosing File, Get External Data, Link Tables. In the Link dialog box, choose HTML Documents in the Files of Type drop-down box and type the complete URL in the File Name text box. As soon as you click Link, the Link HTML Wizard opens with the results of the link. The wizard includes each list and table that it finds in the HTML file as a line, as shown in Figure 29.18.

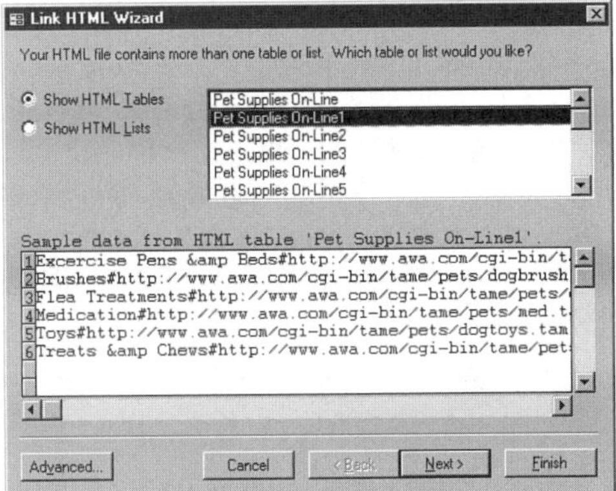

FIGURE 29.18
All the lists and tables from an HTML file parsed into the Access Link HTML Wizard.

To easily find which line contains the information you want, display the HTML page in a browser while the Link HTML Wizard is still open. Using the browser helps you select the table of information you want, especially if the page contains numerous tables. You will only be able to link to one table or list at a time. Moving through the Link HTML Wizard enables you to do the following:

- Define delimiting characters
- Specify numerical formats (decimals, date fields, and so on)
- Type headers if the tables or lists have none
- Choose to skip various columns of information

After completing the wizard, the linked table or list shows up in the Tables tab in your Access database.

If you will be linking many external tables into your Access database, you may want to use the Link Table Manager on the Tools, Add-Ins menu. This add-in provides more options for refreshing and managing linked data.

If you want to import information from an HTML table or list, use the Import HTML Wizard, which starts when you choose File, Get External Data, Import. This wizard is the same as the Link HTML Wizard, except that you end up with a table of data rather than a link. You will likely need to clean up the table before you can use it in any Access operations.

Using Microsoft Publisher to Build a Web Site

Microsoft Publisher 98 enables you to create desktop publishing documents, such as newsletters or flyers, without the steep learning curve of a professional page layout package. That same ease of use is now extended to making Publisher documents available at a Web site, or even creating an entire Web site using Publisher templates.

Publisher 98 opens with a Catalog dialog box, which enables you to choose from a wide variety of publication wizards. One of these is the Web Site Wizard. This wizard lets you build a single page or an entire Web site based on one of the many templates offered by the wizard. The major advantage of using a Web Site template is that you can easily change the basic elements of all your Web site pages at the same time with the click of a single button. You can experiment with new color schemes or even change the entire theme of your Web site. This ease of use makes it easy for a novice to get an immediate professional look and allows Web designers to prototype very large Web sites.

The wizard takes you through a number of steps to build your Web site. You can change most of these options later as you customize the site:

1. After choosing the Web Site Wizard, select one of the many Web site designs or styles. Then click the Start Wizard button to begin the interview process for building the Web site.
2. Click Next in the first wizard dialog box to move to the Color Theme selection. On the left, more than 60 different themes are displayed. On the right is the home page of your Web site. As you select each theme, it is immediately reflected in your Web page.
3. After you've managed to settle on a color theme (or create your own custom theme), click Next. The wizard now lets you create any of the following six pages:
   - Story
   - Calendar (uses the current month and year)
   - Event
   - Special offer
   - Price list
   - Related links

   Each page has a distinctive style. All the pages that you add will be included in a graphical navigation system. You will have the opportunity to add more pages later, including blank pages. Click Next.
4. You can now choose forms pages, including an order form, response form, and sign-up form. Click Next.
5. Continue moving through the remaining wizard dialog boxes. The wizard asks you for the following information:
   - Where to place your navigation bars
   - Whether to place a background sound on the home page
   - Whether you want a background texture

Click Finish to build all the pages that you selected. You can keep the default content of the pages or replace it with your own. You may want to preview your entire site in a browser using File, Web Site Preview. This builds the navigation hyperlinks between all the pages. You may also want to save your work at this time. Note that you must save your file as a Publisher (.pub) file to reload and edit it later. If you save it as HTML, you will not be able to re-edit your now separate HTML pages in Publisher.

Publisher also provides other HTML editing features. You can add your own HTML code to individual pages with the Insert, HTML Code Fragment command. The File, Web Properties command gives you access to the following settings:

- The page title
- The filename
- The file extension, .htm or .html
- Document descriptions and keywords required for indexing by Web search engines
- Choice of your target audience, either version 2.0 browsers or 4.0 browsers.

NOTE A rule of thumb is to publish to the lowest common browser denominator (version 2.0) for Web pages going on the Internet and to 4.0 browsers in more controlled settings (a company Intranet, for instance) where you know what the browser population is. Publisher uses cascading style sheets (CSS) for page layout if you target version 4.0 browsers. Earlier browser versions cannot read CSS, and your page layout may look disastrous.

If you like drop caps (Format, Drop Cap), they are a cinch to add in Publisher and difficult to add using regular HTML editors. Another difficult feat to accomplish easily in browsers or HTML editors is converting Web pages to a form that can be printed. A Convert to Print option in Publisher makes this task simple and lets you convert your Web site to a brochure or a newsletter.

The Web Publishing Wizard

Automatically publish your Web files to a Web server using the Web Publishing Wizard, free from Microsoft. You can invoke this wizard from either Access or Publisher or use it as a standalone application. The primary advantage of using this wizard is that it transfers an entire set of files (folders and subfolders) to your Web server without intervention.

Before you start the wizard

- Make sure that you have write access to the Web server.
- Make sure that you have a user account on the Web server.
- Confirm that you know the complete URL destination for transferring your files.
- Make sure that you are connected to the Internet.

The wizard begins with helping you build a profile. The dialog boxes it presents will help you do the following:

- Select the folder you want to upload from.
- Give a descriptive name to the Web server.
- Type the URL of the Web server where your files will be stored. This is usually in the form of **http://yourwebserver.com**.

The Web Publishing Wizard then connects to your Web site and requests user authentication. Enter your Web server user ID and password. After authentication, the wizard asks how you want to transfer files. The following are your options:

- FTP
- HTTP Post
- FrontPage Extended Web
- Microsoft Content Replication System

Select the means that suits your Web server (FTP is the most common), enter any additional addressing information (such as the address to your FTP server), and the wizard does the rest.

Unfortunately, there are no switches in the Web Publishing Wizard that enable you to send only newer or changed files, so it can't double as a "Web Update Wizard." Nonetheless, it is still very useful for publishing to your Web server the first time. ●

CHAPTER 30

Using Outlook as an Internet Mail and News Client

Electronic mail has proved itself as a means of communication that's as indispensable in business today as the phone and fax. Email's low cost, speed, and capability to transmit not only plain-text messages, but also formatted documents and even programs, ensures that it is here to stay.

Another powerful, Internet-based, communications network is the newsgroup. Modeled on a bulletin board metaphor, in which users exchange messages by "posting" them in a public area, newsgroups are useful forums for disseminating information to a wide group of people, finding an expert who can answer a question, and exchanging news on any topic.

To take advantage of the Internet's power to enable global communication, users need an email and news client that helps them manage large volumes of messages, keep track of contacts' email addresses, and send messages in a variety of formats. Outlook 98 supports all these capabilities and more. This chapter shows how to configure Internet mail and news access using Outlook in a variety of computing environments. You'll learn how to do the following:

- Set up Outlook to receive and send email via the Internet
- Set up Outlook's newsreader component to access Internet- and Intranet-based newsgroups
- Configure Outlook Express for the Macintosh

Configuring Outlook to Send and Receive Internet Mail

Outlook makes email management easy with features like message flagging, rules for processing incoming messages, and junk mail filters. Outlook's Internet mail functionality is fully integrated with its other modules. For example, you can track email messages in the Journal or easily address an email message to a contact. Outlook's integration with other Office programs applies to its email capabilities as well, enabling users to designate WordMail as their email editor. Because of its organizational and integration capabilities, Outlook is a good choice for any user who frequently sends and receives email across the Internet.

Microsoft Exchange Environments

Outlook can send and receive Internet email via Exchange Server if Exchange Server is configured with a gateway to the Internet via the Internet Mail Service connector. As with email messages received from within the system, Internet email messages are funneled to the user's Inbox, located on a central Exchange Server computer. The user can then access and download these messages along with internal mail. Similarly, all messages the user sends to the Internet are routed to the central Exchange Server and then sent out through the gateway configured on the server. Therefore, for Outlook to access Internet mail in an Exchange environment, you only need to configure an Internet E-mail information service that downloads email from the user's Inbox and sends email to the Internet Mail Server gateway. For more information about using Outlook in Exchange environments, see Chapter 10.

Installing Outlook as an Exchange Server Client Outlook 98 must be installed in Corporate or Workgroup (CW) mode to connect to Exchange Server via the Internet E-mail information service. If Outlook is primarily used as an Exchange Server client—to access internal mail, public folders, and group scheduling capabilities—then it's already in CW mode and ready for connecting to the Internet via Exchange Server. If not, you need to add the CW component.

Determine which mode Outlook is running in by choosing Help, About Microsoft Outlook. The mode is listed under "Microsoft Outlook 98."

To add the CW component, just follow these steps:

1. Quit Outlook if it is running (also quit any other open programs).
2. Choose Settings, Control Panel from the Start menu.
3. Double-click on Add/Remove Programs.
4. On the Install/Uninstall tab, scroll down until you find Microsoft Outlook 98 and select it.
5. Click on Add/Remove.
6. Click on Add New Components (see Figure 30.1).

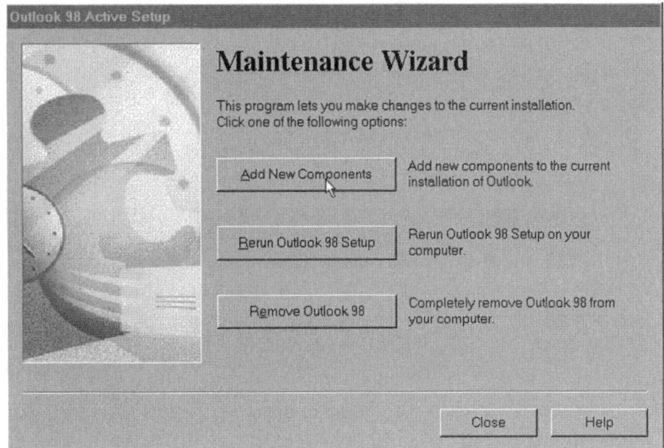

FIGURE 30.1
Using Active Setup to add new components to Outlook 98.

7. If you originally installed Outlook from a CD, insert it in the CD-ROM drive and click on Install from CD; otherwise, click on Install from Web.

CAUTION

Make sure that Internet Explorer is not in offline mode (Work Offline is *not* selected on the File menu).

8. Click on Yes; Active Setup determines which components are installed.
9. Under Mail Components, select the Corporate or Workgroup E-mail Service check box (see Figure 30.2).
10. Click on Next.
11. If installing from the Web, select the nearest download site from the drop-down menu.
12. Click on Install.
13. After the installation is finished, restart your computer.

FIGURE 30.2
Select the Corporate or Workgroup E-mail Service component to upgrade to CW mode.

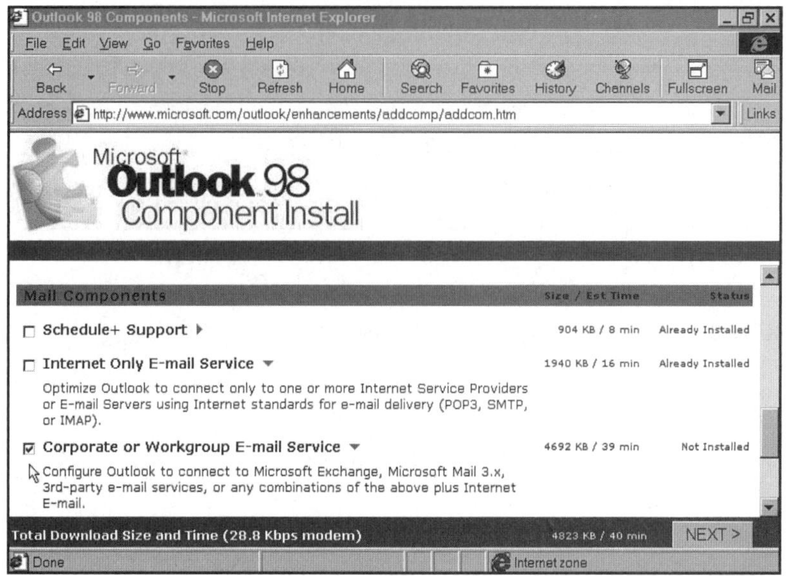

Because Exchange Server can also function as an IMAP or POP3 mail server, you don't necessarily have to upgrade to CW mode to use Outlook as an Internet mail client with Exchange Server. Instead, configure Outlook to connect to Exchange Server in the same way as any other mail server (see the upcoming section "Non-Microsoft Exchange Environments"). POP3 or IMAP support must be enabled on the Exchange Server computer, however. Also, this method doesn't allow Outlook to access other Exchange features, such as group scheduling, groupware, and in POP3 mode, public folders.

Configuring the Internet E-mail Information Service Once Outlook is running in CW mode, set up the Internet E-mail information service to connect to Exchange Server by performing the following steps:

1. Choose Tools, Services.
2. Select the Internet E-mail information service on the Services tab. (If it's not listed, click on Add, select Internet E-mail, and click on OK.)
3. Click on Properties.
4. In the Mail Account field on the General tab, enter a name for the Internet E-mail information service (see Figure 30.3).
5. Enter the user's full name in the Name field.
6. Enter the company name in the Organization field (optional).
7. Enter the user's Internet email address in the E-mail Address field; the email address is usually provided by the Exchange Server administrator and takes the form of `alias_name@organization_name.com`.

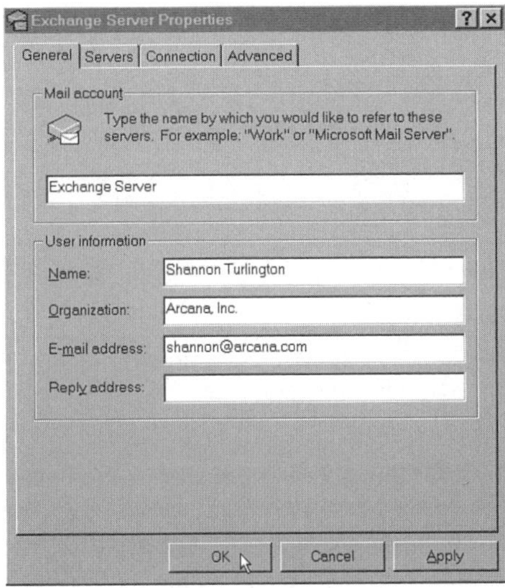

FIGURE 30.3
Configuring general properties for the Internet E-mail information service.

8. If desired, enter a different email address in the ReplyAddress field where all replies should be sent.
9. Click on the Servers tab (see Figure 30.4).

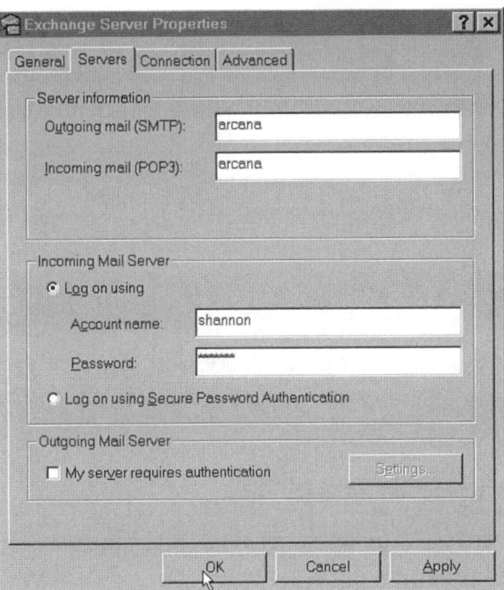

FIGURE 30.4
Configuring mail server properties for the Internet E-mail information service.

10. In the Outgoing Mail (SMTP) field, enter the name of the Exchange Server computer running the Internet Mail Service.
11. In the Incoming Mail field, enter the name of the Exchange Server computer that hosts the user's Inbox.

12. Select the Log on Using button.

CAUTION

Do not select the Log on Using Secure Password Authentication option, unless directed to by the Exchange Server administrator; otherwise, you'll be unable to make the connection.

13. Enter the user's Exchange Server Inbox alias name in the Account Name field.
14. Enter the user's Inbox password in the Password field.
15. If the outgoing mail server also requires logon via a username and password, select the My Server Requires Authentication check box, click on Settings, set the username and password as before, and click on OK.
16. Click on the Connection tab and choose the appropriate connection type—generally Connect Using My Local Area Network (LAN) in Exchange environments. If the user connects via remote access, however, choose Connect Using My Phone Line and select the appropriate connection from the Use the Following Dial-Up Networking Connection drop-down menu. If the connection is not listed, get the necessary settings from the Exchange Server administrator and click on Add to create the new connection.
17. Click on OK.

Non-Microsoft Exchange Environments

Outlook 98 can connect to and download email messages from any Internet mail server that supports Internet Message Access Protocol (IMAP) or Post Office Protocol 3 (POP3). The user may set up an email account with a commercial Internet service provider (ISP), or the user may receive email via a mail server running on the company intranet.

NOTE POP3 and IMAP are standard protocols for transferring email over the Internet. POP3 is the most commonly used protocol. Unlike IMAP, POP3 doesn't permit messages to be stored and managed in folders on the mail server; rather, messages are downloaded to the user's computer and stored on the hard drive. This makes IMAP a better choice for users who access email from multiple computers or who have limited storage space. However, because IMAP stores messages on the mail server, IMAP servers are more vulnerable to unauthorized access by anyone with access to the server.

What You Need Before You Begin If Outlook is not operating in an Exchange environment, it should have been set up in Internet Only mode. This mode supports connections to an ISP or to an Internet-standard mail server in the enterprise.

If you selected No Email mode when you installed Outlook, you can still set up an Internet email account and switch to Internet Only mode by following the steps to set up an Internet mail account.

You will also need to determine the following (generally provided by the ISP or network administrator):

- Email account information: username, password, and email address
- Type of incoming mail server: POP3 or IMAP
- Incoming (POP3/IMAP) and outgoing (SMTP) mail server domain names or IP addresses
- Type of connection: LAN, Windows dial-up networking, or another dialing program

Setting Up an Email Account Follow these steps to configure the IMAP or POP3 account:

1. Choose Tools, Accounts.
2. On the Mail tab, select Add and Mail (see Figure 30.5).

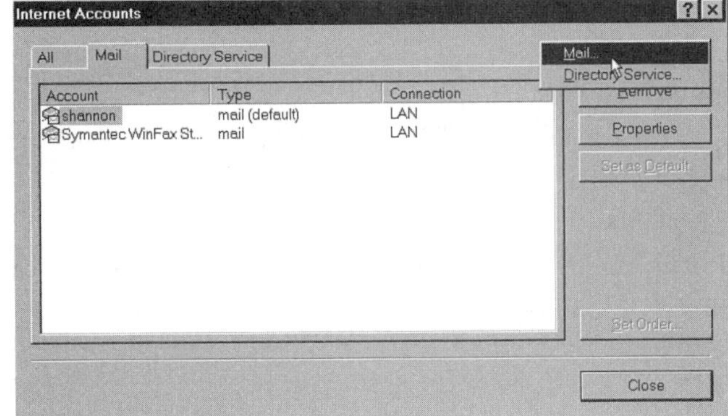

FIGURE 30.5
Creating a new Internet mail account.

3. Enter the name that will appear on sent messages in the Display Name field and click on Next.
4. Enter the user's Internet email address in the E-mail Address field and click on Next.
5. Select POP3 or IMAP next to My Incoming Mail Server Is A (see Figure 30.6).

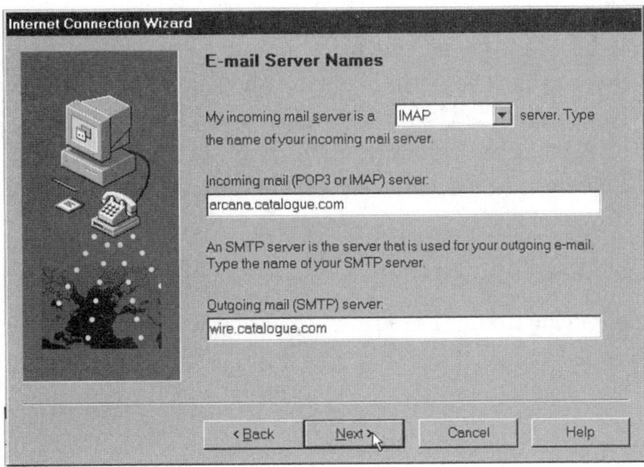

FIGURE 30.6
Configuring servers for the Internet mail account.

6. Enter the IP address or domain name of the IMAP or POP3 server in the Incoming Mail (POP3 or IMAP) Server field.
7. Enter the IP address or domain name of the SMTP server in the Outgoing Mail (SMTP) Server field (often, the incoming and outgoing mail servers are the same).
8. Click on Next.
9. Select Log on Using, type the email account's username in the POP3/IMAP Account Name field, and type the account's password in the Password field.

CAUTION

Some ISPs require users to log on using Secure Password Authentication (SPA). If your ISP requires this, select the Log on Using Secure Password Authentication (SPA) button; you'll be prompted to enter your email account name and password each time you log on. If your ISP doesn't require SPA, make sure the option is *not* selected; otherwise, you'll be unable to make the connection.

10. Click on Next.
11. Type a name in the Internet Mail Account Name field to identify the new account; this is useful for distinguishing between multiple accounts.
12. Click on Next.
13. Select the connection type: Connect Using My Phone Line, if using Windows dial-up networking; Connect Using My Local Area Network (LAN), if connecting through a network; or I Will Establish my Internet Connection Manually, if using a third-party dialer.
14. Click on Next.
15. Depending on the connection type you chose, complete the setup with the following steps:
    - If connecting via a LAN or manually, click on Finish.
    - If connecting via a phone line and the connection has already been set up in Dial-Up Networking, click on Use an existing dial-up connection and select the appropriate connection. Then, click on Next and Finish.
    - If the dial-up connection has not been set up, select Create a new dial-up connection and click on Next. Fill in the phone number for the connection and click on Next. Enter the User name and Password for the Internet access account and click on Next. Select No (unless otherwise specified by your ISP) and click on Next. Enter a name for the connection in the Connection name field, click on Next, and click on Finish.
16. Click on Close.

If you're experiencing trouble establishing a connection or sending and receiving Internet mail messages, turn to Chapter 42.

Configuring Outlook to Retrieve Internet News

A news-only version of Outlook Express functions as a newsreader for Outlook 98. Newsreaders enable reading and posting of messages to various kinds of newsgroups, including the Usenet network on the Internet and company newsgroups on an intranet. To access the Outlook 98 newsreader, choose News from Outlook's Go menu or choose Microsoft Outlook Newsreader from the Start, Programs menu.

If you're using Outlook in conjunction with an Exchange Server that's hosting newsgroups, you can access them in the same way as any other public folder.

Installing the Outlook Newsreader

If you're not finding the Outlook newsreader, you may not have installed the newsreader component with Outlook 98. You can add the component using Active Setup by performing the following steps:

1. Determine which Outlook components are missing (see the "Installing Outlook as an Exchange Server Client" section in this chapter).
2. Under Extra Components, select the Microsoft Outlook Newsreader check box.
3. Click on Next.
4. If installing from the Web, select the nearest download site from the drop-down menu.
5. Click on Install.
6. After the installation is finished, restart the computer.

Configuring the Outlook Newsreader

Before configuring the Outlook newsreader, ask your ISP or network administrator for the domain name or IP address of the news server hosting the user's connection. The news server may also require logon via a username and password. Then, follow these steps to set up the connection:

1. Open the Outlook newsreader.
2. Choose Tools, Accounts.
3. Click on Add and News.
4. Enter the name to appear on newsgroup postings in the Display Name field and click on Next.
5. Enter the user's Internet email address in the E-mail Address field and click on Next.
6. Enter the domain name or IP address of the news server in the News (NNTP) Server field (see Figure 30.7); if logon with an account name and password is required, select the My News Server Requires Me to Log On check box.
7. Click on Next.

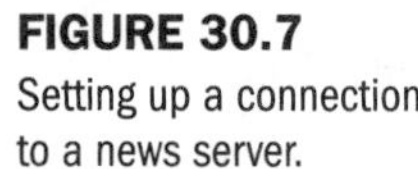

FIGURE 30.7
Setting up a connection to a news server.

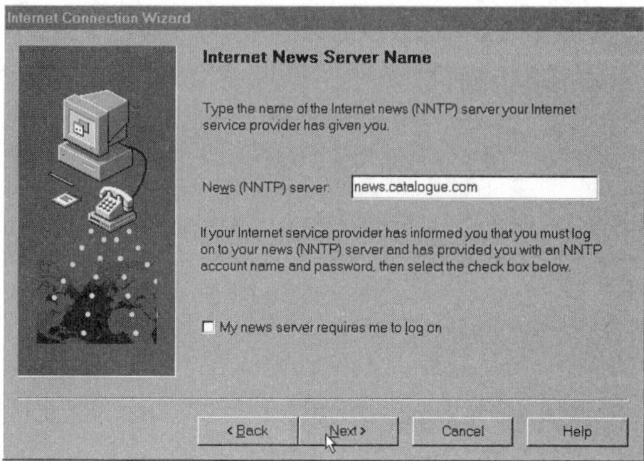

8. Enter a name for the account in the Internet News Account Name field; this is helpful for managing multiple accounts.
9. Click on Next.
10. Select the connection type as for an Internet mail account and click on Next (see "Setting Up an Email Account," steps 13–15).
11. Click on Finish.
12. Click on Close.

Now the user can download newsgroups from the news server, choose which groups to subscribe to, and begin reading and posting messages.

If you cannot view any newsgroups or get a news connection error message, double-check the news account's properties against the settings provided by the ISP or network administrator—choose Tools, Accounts, select the news account, and click on Properties. In particular, make sure that the Server Name field on the Server tab matches the NNTP server name provided by the ISP, and find out if a logon is required. On the Advanced tab, check that the port number in the News (NNTP) field matches the one provided by the ISP (most news servers use port 119). Finally, try setting Server Timeouts to Long, because some news servers take more than a minute to establish a connection. If you're still experiencing problems, check with the ISP that the settings are correct and that the news server is up and running.

Configuring Outlook Express for the Macintosh

Although Outlook 98 is not available for the Macintosh, Outlook Express is—it's installed with the Office 98 suite and with Internet Explorer 4.*x*. Outlook Express is a scaled-down version of Outlook. It doesn't have the contact, schedule, and task management capabilities, but it does enable management of Internet mail and news accounts.

What You Need Before You Begin

You need the following to set up an Internet mail or news account via Outlook Express:

- Access to the Internet through an ISP or LAN
- MacTCP *or* the TCP/IP control panel with Open Transport 1.08 or later
- Config PPP or similar PPP connection software (dial-up users)
- Account information: username, password, email address, type of mail server, and domain names or IP addresses of the incoming mail server, outgoing mail server, and news server

Configuring Internet Mail Support

Follow these steps to set up an Internet mail account in Outlook Express:

1. Click the Preferences button.
2. Click New Account.
3. Enter a name to identify the account in the Account name field.
4. Under Account type, select POP or IMAP; this is the protocol supported by the incoming mail server.

If you want to access an Exchange Server email account, the Exchange Server must support POP3 or IMAP access. Set up the account in the same way as for any other mail server.

5. Click OK.
6. Enter the name to appear in sent messages in the Full Name field.
7. Enter the user's Internet email address in the E-mail Address field.
8. Enter a company name in the Organization field (optional).
9. Enter the domain name or IP address of the outgoing mail server in the SMTP Server field.
10. Enter the username for the email account in the Account ID field.
11. Enter the domain name or IP address of the incoming mail server in the POP/IMAP Server field (often the same as the outgoing mail server).
12. Enter the password for the email account in the Save Password field.

CAUTION

Selecting the Save Password check box means that you won't have to enter a password every time you download email. However, this poses a security risk, as anyone with access to your computer can read your email and send messages in your name. In most office settings, it's best *not* to save your password.

13. If this is the default email account, click on Make Default.
14. Click on OK.

Configuring Internet News Support

Follow these steps to set up an Internet news account on Outlook Express for the Macintosh:

1. Click on the Preferences button.
2. Click on News under Accounts.
3. Click on New Server.
4. Type a name in the Account name field to identify the account in the folder list.
5. Click on OK.
6. Enter the domain name or IP address of the news server to connect to.
7. Select the Display this News Server in the Folder List check box.
8. If the news server requires logon via a username and password, select the This Server Requires Authentication check box and type the username and password in the appropriate fields.
9. To make this account the default news account, click on Make Default.
10. Click on Advanced only if you need to set specific properties, such as change the default NNTP server port, specify additional header information, or set up a secure connection. Otherwise, click on OK.

CHAPTER 31

Using Office with Microsoft Web Software

Office 97 applications enable you to add hyperlinks to native Office files, convert Office files to HTML, and, in the case of Word, edit or create Web pages. But if you're serious about creating many Web pages, managing and building entire Web sites, or using a Web server to do more than serve up HTML pages, you'll quickly need supplements to Office 97. Microsoft offers solutions for both dedicated Web creators/managers and for Webmasters. From very simple pages to complex corporate or e-commerce Web sites, the widely popular FrontPage lets you both create Web pages and manage entire Web sites. And if you're a Webmaster, you may appreciate the Internet Information Server (IIS), Microsoft's complete, free Web server solution.

Using Office Documents with FrontPage

FrontPage is a full-fledged HTML editor and Web site management package, both features required by modern, large and/or complex Web sites. Typically when you build a Web site, you think only of HTML pages with their associated files, such as graphics, sounds, other multimedia, or scripts. However, given that Office 97 applications can convert existing Office documents to HTML, you can also add content from Office documents to your Web site. Furthermore, you can consider using Office documents in their native file formats on your Web site, especially if your site is the company Intranet. Because Office 97 files support hyperlinks, you can connect them to other files on the Web. FrontPage enables you to use native Office 97 files in your Web site almost as easily as HTML files.

Importing Office Files to Your Web with FrontPage Explorer

FrontPage treats Office documents no differently than HTML documents when you place them in your FrontPage Web. Use the FrontPage Explorer to select the Web in which you want to place Office documents. Choose File, Import to display the Import File to FrontPage Web dialog box, as shown in Figure 31.1.

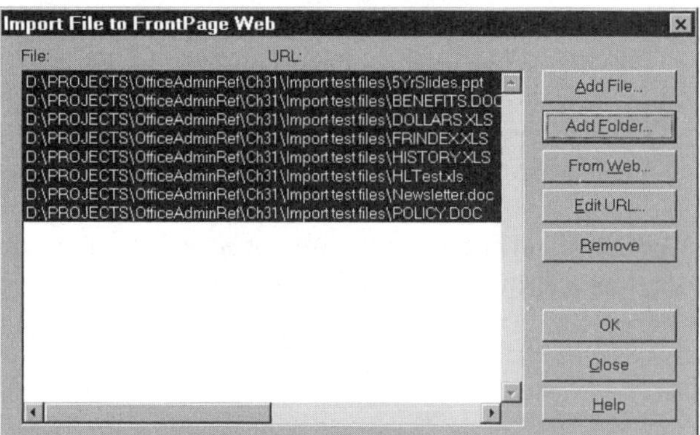

FIGURE 31.1
Importing Office files into a FrontPage Web.

You can add individual files or entire folders containing Office documents. Note that if you choose the Add Folder option, both the folder and the files in it are imported to your Web. In other words, the folder shows up as a subfolder under the root of your Web. You can select individual files, or you can select a group of files using the standard Shift+Ctrl key methods. The files that you have selected appear in the box in the middle of the Import File to FrontPage Web dialog box. To import them, click OK. If you click Close, FrontPage Explorer retains your file list until you close Explorer, but the files will not be imported to your Web.

You can also import files from the Import File to FrontPage Web dialog box by clicking the From Web button. This starts the Import Web Wizard that enables you to get files from a Web (or folder) on your local drive or from the Internet. If you choose to add files from a local drive, the next wizard dialog box lists all the files and lets you exclude any that you don't want in your Web. Clicking Finish in the next wizard dialog box completes the import process.

If you choose to get files from an Internet Web site, the next wizard dialog box, shown in Figure 31.2, requests information as to how deep and how much of the Web site (in kilobytes) you want to import.

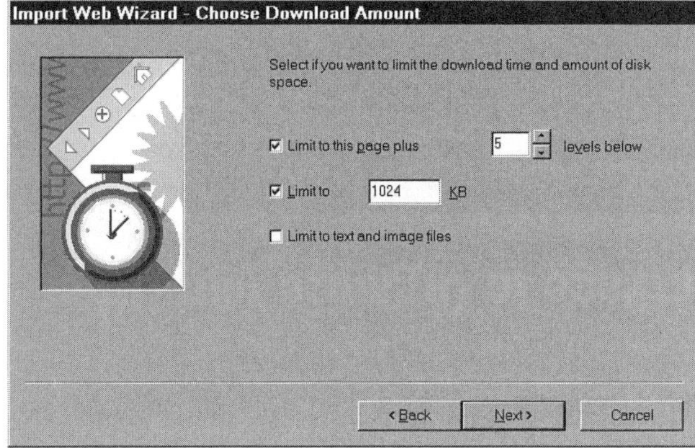

FIGURE 31.2
Determining how much of a Web site to import into FrontPage.

In this dialog box, you have to decide:

- The number of levels down in the Web site to look for files (up to 100)
- Whether to set a disk space limit in kilobytes at which to stop downloading
- Whether to limit your file types to just images and text

After making these choices, click the Finish button in the last wizard dialog box to begin the import process from the Web site. The Import Web Progress dialog box displays each file as it is downloaded (see Figure 31.3).

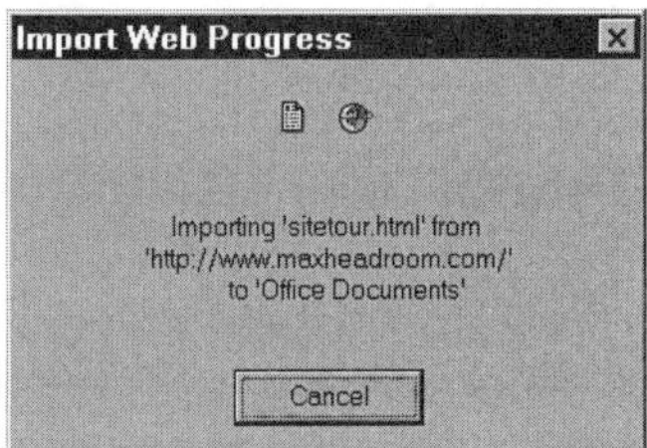

FIGURE 31.3
FrontPage lets you watch the progress of importing from an Internet Web site.

After the wizard has completed the import, hyperlinks within the files are updated to reflect their new home on your FrontPage Web.

After the files have been imported from their various locations, you can use the views within FrontPage Explorer to observe the relationships between the Office documents and other files in your Web. The Hyperlinks view (View, Hyperlinks) is especially useful. FrontPage Explorer can "see" and display the hyperlinks in native Office documents, as shown in Figure 31.4.

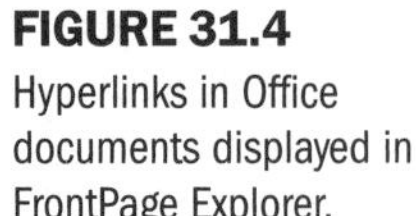

FIGURE 31.4
Hyperlinks in Office documents displayed in FrontPage Explorer.

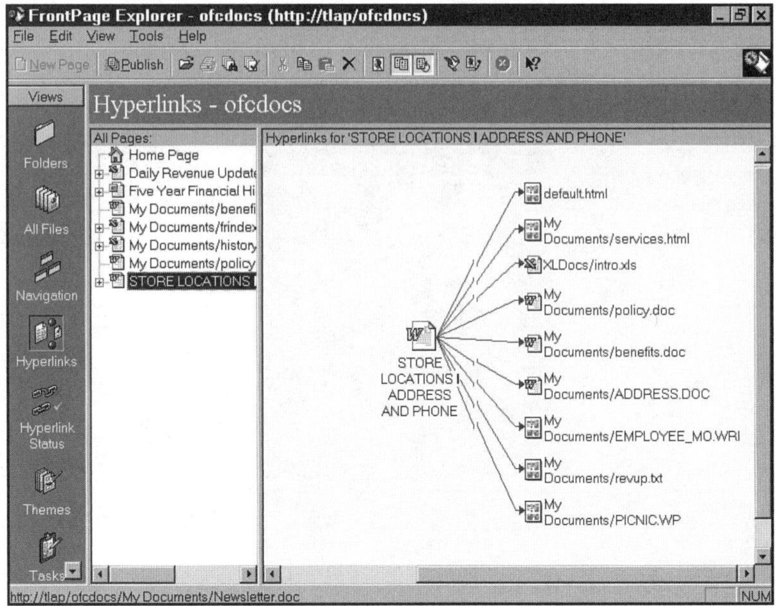

Office documents can be both the source and target of links, just like HTML files. This enables you to tightly integrate Office documents into any existing Web.

The decision to use Office documents in their native format must be based on whether your audience can view them. If you know your audience has Office 97, go ahead and use Office 97 files. If your users are on multiple platforms or are using earlier versions of Office, however, you need to give them a way to view the Office files. If much of your audience is on non-Windows platforms, you may want to consider converting Office documents to HTML for your Web site.

Using the FrontPage Editor to Open Office Documents

In addition to importing and using Office documents in their native format on your FrontPage Web, you can also bring Office documents into the FrontPage Editor, edit them if desired, and save them as HTML documents to your FrontPage Web. You can do this directly with only Word and Excel documents. With PowerPoint and Access, it is probably easier to save the information as HTML before bringing it into the Editor. Access also enables you to use the Database Region Wizard, as described later in this section.

NOTE You can bring other file types into the FrontPage Editor as well, including text files, several versions of Word, WordPerfect files, preprocessed HTML files (HTX and ASP), and several versions of Microsoft Works. You can also attempt to recover text from any other file format.

To bring a Word or Excel document into the Editor, first open a blank new page (File, New [Ctrl+N], or the New toolbar button). Choose Insert, File, and browse to the file location. After selecting the file, you may be asked how you want to open the file—as RTF (Rich Text Format), HTML, or text. If you are inserting a Word document, use the RTF format to retain most of the formatting. Excel worksheets insert as HTML tables. Hyperlinks are maintained in both Word and Excel. Any charts or graphics in Excel (and their underlying hyperlinks, if any) are lost. You have to transfer these to the Editor via the Clipboard as described later in this section. Graphics (as pictures) are maintained from Word documents. WordArt or drawing objects are lost unless you convert them to pictures in the Word document first, or you insert them later via the Clipboard.

After you've inserted the Word or Excel document, you can edit it as any other HTML file, and it will be saved as an HTML file to your Web.

You can also insert information from Office documents (or from many other types of documents for that matter) into existing HTML documents using the Windows Clipboard. From within an Office document, copy the information to the Clipboard. In FrontPage Editor, place your insertion point where you want the information to appear, and issue the Paste command. FrontPage does its best to retain as much formatting as HTML allows. This technique is especially handy for getting Word, Excel, or Access tables translated to HTML tables in your HTML document. It also makes for a cheap graphics file-format converter. For instance, let's say you have an image document on disk that's not GIF or JPG (say, the company logo), but you want to include it in an HTML document and don't have an image program handy to do the conversion. Just open Word, insert the image as a picture in a blank document (or open a document that already has the company logo), select the image, copy it to the Clipboard, and paste it into your FrontPage document. When you next save your HTML document, the Save Embedded Files dialog box appears and lists your file with a default name such as defaul1.jpg or defaul2.gif (see Figure 31.5).

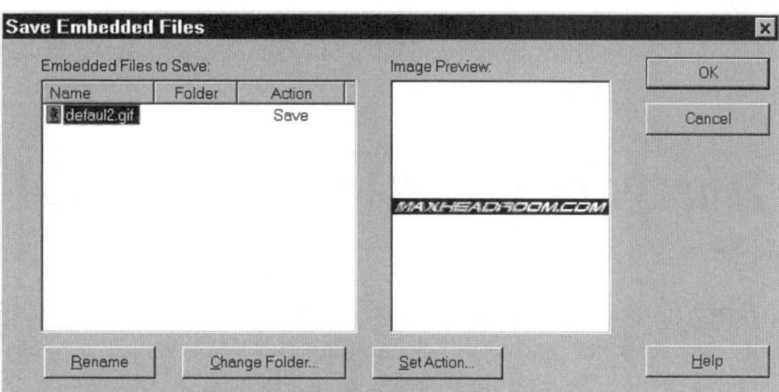

FIGURE 31.5
Saving images from the Clipboard to a FrontPage Web page.

You can rename the file if you like, and you can save the file to your FrontPage Web.

CAUTION

If you click the Set Action button in the Save Embedded Files dialog box, do not choose the Don't Save option when using the Clipboard to transfer image files to your HTML documents in FrontPage Editor. Choosing this option builds a path to the image file in a temp folder on your hard drive. You may lose the image when the temp folder is cleaned out. And, of course, this path will "break" if you transfer your Web to another machine or Web server. Always make sure to save images transferred via the Clipboard to your FrontPage Web.

One additional means of adding database information to an open page in the FrontPage Editor is to use the Database Region Wizard. You can directly issue an SQL query to a database associated with a Web server via ODBC, and the results of the query are returned as a table directly into the open FrontPage document.

NOTE For a thorough explanation of how to register a database via ODBC with a Web server turn to the section "Connecting an Access Database to the Web" in Chapter 29.

It is much easier to build, execute, and then export as HTML the results of a query from within Access rather than using the Database Region Wizard in the FrontPage Editor. This wizard is most useful if you are conversant in SQL and have a thorough knowledge of the database you are querying. ■

To invoke the Database Region Wizard, choose Insert, Database, Database Region Wizard. The first wizard dialog box requests the OBDC data source name of the registered database. This is the name given the database when it was registered with ODBC on the Web server. Options are available to enter username and password information also. Next, you enter the SQL query. You can type the query directly or obtain the SQL code from an existing query in the Access database. You can view the SQL string inside Access by opening a query in Design view and then choosing View, View SQL. The wizard then requests the database field names required by the query and gives you the option of returning the results in a table. After you have added the field names, click Finish to execute the query and place the table into the open HTML page in FrontPage Editor.

Using FrontPage to Organize Your Office-Based Intranet

A modern intranet is a hodge-podge of file formats, including HTML files and associated multimedia files, text files, and Office documents of varying versions. Managing these files can be a time-consuming, administrative headache without the right tools. With FrontPage, you can do the following:

- Look at the relationships between all the files on your Web from a variety of views
- Change file locations
- Use standardized templates and themes

- Import existing Webs into FrontPage Webs
- Double-click files in Explorer view to edit them in their appropriate applications
- Use shared borders to generate consistent navigation throughout your Web site
- Use a built-in spell checker
- Control access privileges
- Control the structure of your Web
- Use a To-Do list to manage tasks for multiple authors
- Automatically generate a table of contents
- Build an index of all the text on your site
- Publish your entire Web to a Web server
- Edit or remove hyperlinks
- Verify all hyperlinks, including those in Office documents

It is beyond the scope of this chapter to discuss all these features in-depth, but you learn about several of the key management features in FrontPage Explorer, including editing and checking hyperlinks, generating a table of contents, and controlling the structure of and access to your Web site.

Editing and Checking Office 97 Hyperlinks Using FrontPage

FrontPage Explorer enables you to change, edit, or remove hyperlinks from within Office documents. These changes are reflected and updated in your FrontPage Explorer views. Links to and from Office documents are shown in the same manner as typical hyperlinks between HTML documents. The hyperlink checker (Tools, Verify Hyperlinks) in FrontPage Explorer checks, displays, and enables you to edit hyperlinks in Office documents just as it does hyperlinks in HTML pages. After you've verified hyperlinks in your Web, the hyperlink checker displays a list of any broken hyperlinks it found. To fix a broken link, double-click it. The Edit Hyperlink dialog box appears, as shown in Figure 31.6.

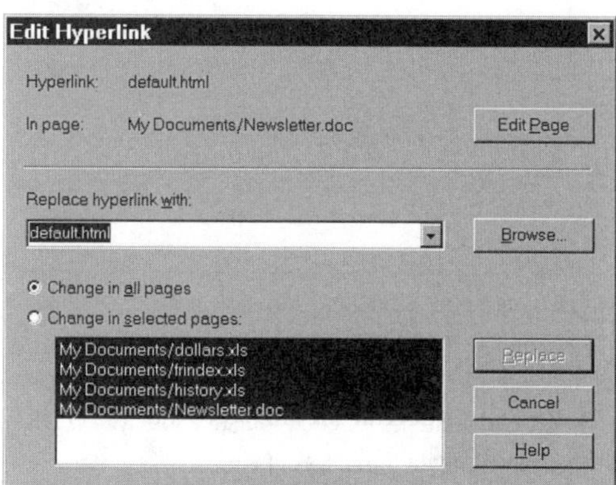

FIGURE 31.6
Editing choices in FrontPage Explorer for fixing broken hyperlinks in Office documents.

You can use this dialog box to fix broken hyperlinks in Office documents in two ways:

- Click the Edit Page button to launch the appropriate Office application (for instance, Word launches if you're editing a DOC file) and load the document. You can then use tools from within the Office application (described in Chapter 29) to edit or remove the hyperlink, and then save the file and return to FrontPage Explorer.
- Use the Replace Hyperlink With text box. This is the most convenient method of fixing broken hyperlinks in Office documents. If you know the correct location for the broken hyperlink, type it in this text box (or use the Browse button to go to the correct location) and click the Replace button. The hyperlink(s) within the Office document will be quickly modified and updated without opening any Office applications, and the modified file will be saved in its native Office format.

Generating a Table of Contents Using FrontPage

One of the most common complaints of visitors to any Web site is that they can't easily or quickly find certain information. This is a chronic problem on very large Web sites and can become an issue as your own Web site grows. Many Webmasters respond to this need by building a site map or site index page listing every page or every major feature of the Web site for visitors. Managing this index can become a full-time job on a large or dynamically changing site. The Table of Contents feature in FrontPage automatically generates a hyperlinked list of all the pages in your FrontPage Web. This table of contents automatically updates as pages are added or deleted during the normal operation of your Web site.

You add a table of contents to a page from within FrontPage Editor. After opening the page you want to use for the table of contents, choose Insert, Table of Contents. The Table of Contents Properties dialog box, shown in Figure 31.7, requests the starting file for building the table of contents. The default page is your Web site home page.

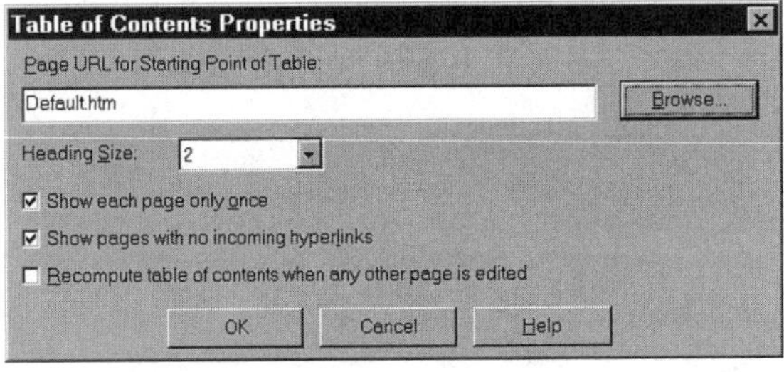

FIGURE 31.7
Building a table of contents for your Web site in FrontPage Editor.

You may want to layer your table of contents for a large Web site. Instead of building a mega-list of every page from the home page, identify the key topical pages under your home page. Build a table of contents from each of these topical pages. Then, build a top-level table of contents page from your home page leading only to the table of contents for each topical subpage. Do this in as many layers as necessary to enable people to easily navigate through your site.

After choosing the starting or topmost file for your table of contents, you need to make several other decisions about your table of contents properties:

- The header size for the *Table of Contents* header text
- Whether to show each page only once
- Whether to show pages with no hyperlinks from other pages in your Web
- Whether to automatically rebuild the table of contents if any of the pages are edited

If your Web site is large, you may want to clear the Recompute Table of Contents When Any Other Page Is Edited check box. You can manually rebuild the table of contents at any time by opening and resaving the file containing the table of contents.

After you've made your choices, click OK to generate the table of contents page. Unfortunately, any Office documents included on your Web will not be automatically built in to the table of contents; only HTML pages get links in the table of contents page. The hyperlinks use the title of the page linked to as the text for the hyperlink. Multiple layers are indented as the list goes deeper into the structure of your Web site. If you want to add Office documents to the table of contents, you have to do so by manually building the hyperlinks.

Managing Web Site Structure and Access Privileges

Web site structure can be divided into two types—physical and navigational. The physical structure is the actual file folder structure and location of associated files such as ODBC-compliant databases, which may not even physically reside on the Web server. Physical structure usually revolves around some type of logic, such as placing all images in one folder, sounds in another, and scripts in a third, because the scripts folder must have Execute privileges. When FrontPage builds a Web, it automatically adds specialty folders, including a number of hidden folders that cannot be accessed by Web browsers, as well as an images folder. You can add any number of additional folders, public or private, to your Web site as needed.

All hidden folders by default begin with the underscore character–the _private folder, for example–and you can make any folder hidden simply by using an underscore as the first character in its name. You might want to do this if the folder will contain files that you don't want visitors to directly access, such as a database.

Navigational structure is, by far, the most important element to organizing your Web site. If your navigation is logical and clear, visitors will come away with a positive feeling. Illogical or inconsistent navigation can lead to frustration and even drive visitors away, no matter how superb your content. FrontPage offers a number of features to ease the burden of designing, building, and maintaining a navigational system, including the different views in FrontPage Explorer, especially Navigation view, and shared borders and the navigation bar.

An Overview of the Explorer Views FrontPage Explorer gives you a number of different ways to view your site, which are summarized in Figure 31.8.

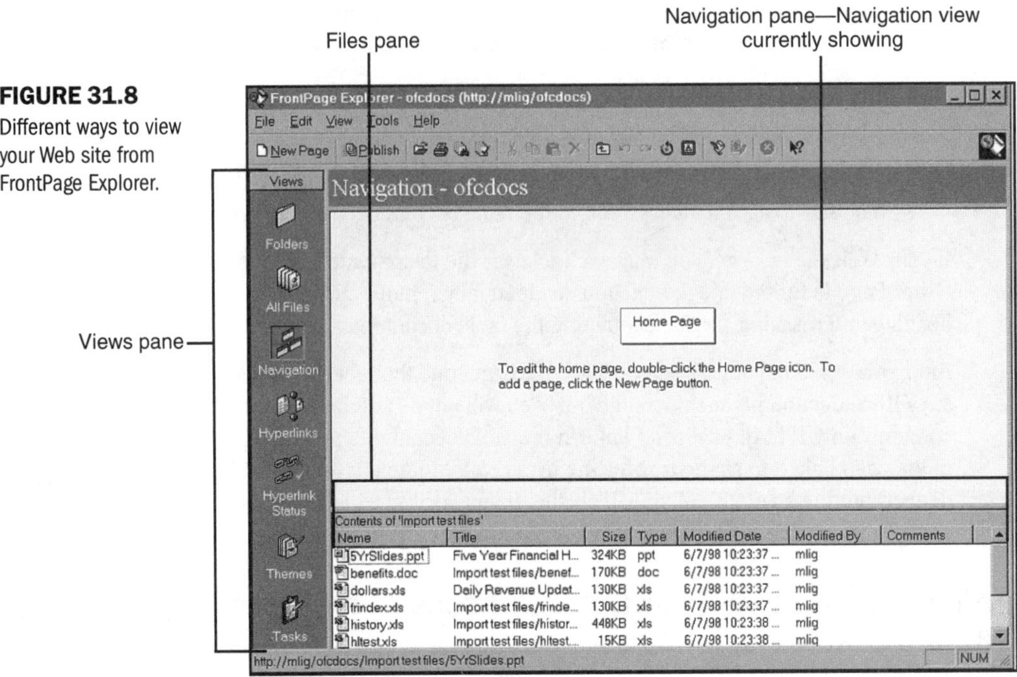

FIGURE 31.8
Different ways to view your Web site from FrontPage Explorer.

Most of these Web site views are self-explanatory, but here is a brief description of what they show:

- **Folders view.** This view shows the actual physical structure of folders and files.
- **All Files view.** This view shows the Web site as a single list of files, very similar to Windows Explorer.
- **Navigation view.** This view is the most useful for designing or changing the navigational structure of your site. (See the following section.)
- **Hyperlinks view.** This view shows relationships between files based on their hyperlinks. Broken hyperlinks are shown as broken arrows.
- **Hyperlinks Status view.** This view displays a list of broken hyperlinks and lets you fix them.
- **Themes view.** If you used a theme as the basis for your Web site, this view enables you to apply a different theme to your entire site and preview the results.
- **Tasks view.** This view shows the contents of the prioritized To Do list, along with responsible parties and dates.

An In-Depth Look at Navigation View Navigation view (refer to Figure 31.8) gives you an easy way to change the relationship between the files on your Web site. You can change your viewpoint by choosing various buttons on the toolbar including Rotate, which offsets your home page up and to one side, and Size to Fit, which displays your entire site onscreen. You can create a new folder by selecting the parent folder or clicking anywhere in the Files pane to create a new folder on the same level as the parent folder and choosing File, New Folder. You can drag a file from the Files pane onto a file in the Navigation pane to associate the two files. When you associate files via drag-and-drop, FrontPage builds a hyperlink into the upper-level (parent) file that targets the lower-level (child) file.

Using the Navigation Bar and Shared Borders Navigation view also makes it easy to add a navigational structure to your Web site. The first time you add a new page, a dialog box appears asking whether you want to add a navigation bar to all your Web pages. The navigation bar is a set of text hyperlinks to other pages on your Web site contained in a common content area in each Web page called shared borders. FrontPage automatically generates this bar, adds it to each page, and updates the bar as you add or remove pages. You can change the location of the navigation bar on any HTML page by choosing Tools, Shared Borders in FrontPage Editor. Navigation bars are not added to Office documents, but links to Office documents are built and updated in the navigation bars. Also, you cannot associate one Office document with another by using drag-and-drop in Navigation view. You can only associate HTML documents with Office documents. The text of the hyperlinks built in to navigational bars is the page title for HTML files; for Office documents, it is the file and folder name.

You can set up your Web site hierarchy and build an almost complete navigation system (totally complete if you don't use Office documents) simply by importing files, adding navigation bars to your pages, and using drag-and-drop in FrontPage Explorer's Navigation view.

Pre-Flighting Your Web or Intranet Site with Personal Web Server

It is essential to tweak and test all corners of a modern Web site before releasing it into the unforgiving land of the Internet or into the hands of users on your company intranet. You will probably want to test your Web site offline, that is, on a Web server that cannot be accessed from the Internet or intranet. You can do this easily with Personal Web Server (PWS), which you can download from Microsoft's Web site at **www.microsoft.com/windows/downloads**. This basic Web server installs on Windows 95/98 or NT Workstation. If you are using Windows NT Server, I recommend installing the much more sophisticated Internet Information Server (IIS), which is also free. (See the section "Publishing Your Web or Intranet Site with Microsoft Internet Information Server" later in this chapter.)

Installing the Personal Web Server

Installation for PWS versions for Windows 95, Windows 98, and NT Workstation is identical. You cannot install PWS for Windows 98 on a Windows 95 machine unless you have also installed Winsock 2 on your Windows machine (setup will do this for you). PWS for Windows 98 is on the Windows 98 CD-ROM. If you download PWS from the Internet, it is currently part of the Windows NT Option Pack 4.0. You can use this version for Windows 95 or NT Workstation.

The Select Components step in the PWS installation process is shown in Figure 31.9.

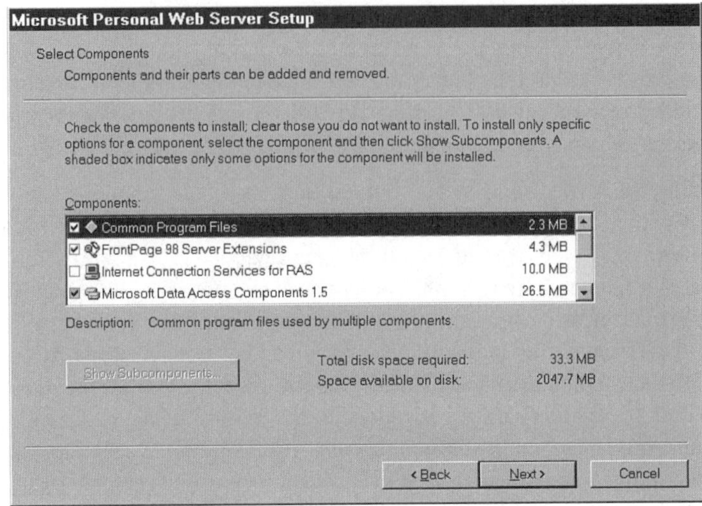

FIGURE 31.9
You have to choose which components to install when setting up Personal Web Server.

Here is some advice about whether to install the various components of PWS:

- *FrontPage 98 Server Extensions.* You won't need these if you don't plan to use FrontPage with PWS.
- *Microsoft Data Access Components.* I recommend leaving the defaults. This will install ODBC drivers (essential if you are using Active Server Pages or IDC/HTX), ActiveX Data Objects (ADO, another means, more extensible than ODBC, of accessing data), or Remote Data Service (RDS, a Web technology for making database publishing capabilities available to Web applications).
- *Microsoft Message Queue (MSMQ).* Not installed by default. You won't need this unless you require Web applications to notify one another regarding transactions.
- *Personal Web Server.* All the documentation, management tools, and the Web server. You need this one.
- *Transaction Server.* This environment is for Web application development, enabling you to deploy Internet applications. You really don't need this unless you are developing applications.
- *Visual InterDev RAD Remote Deployment Support.* This installs the capability to support the remote deployment of applications to your Web server from within Visual InterDev. This option is also intended for application developers and is not needed otherwise.

After selecting where to install the Transaction Server files (assuming you elected to install the Transaction Server earlier), setup installs the components you selected and you are asked to reboot your machine. When you do, the Web server will be running. You can test it by typing either of the following URLs into a browser address box:

http://*YourMachineName*
http://*localhost*

In the first URL, replace ***YourMachineName*** with the name of the machine on which the Web server is installed. If you don't know the machine name, you can also use ***//localhost***, as shown in the second URL. You should now see the default page for your local Web site in your browser.

NOTE If you're not sure what your machine name is, open Control Panel, open the Network applet, and click the Identification tab. Your computer name and workgroup are both listed here.

So where are these local files located? If you have FrontPage installed on your machine, they should be in the root Web, which you defined when you installed FrontPage. If you don't have FrontPage, you can usually find them under the WWWRoot subfolder of the WebShare folder on the same drive in which Windows or NT Workstation is installed. It is important to know where your local root Web is so that you can use this location to start from when you test your Web site.

Administering the Personal Web Server

To administer the Personal Web Server, you use the Personal Web Manager, shown in Figure 31.10. If you used the default folders, you can start the Personal Web Manager by choosing Start, Programs, Microsoft Personal Web Server, Personal Web Manager. You can also start the Personal Web Manager by double-clicking the Personal Web Server icon in the system tray.

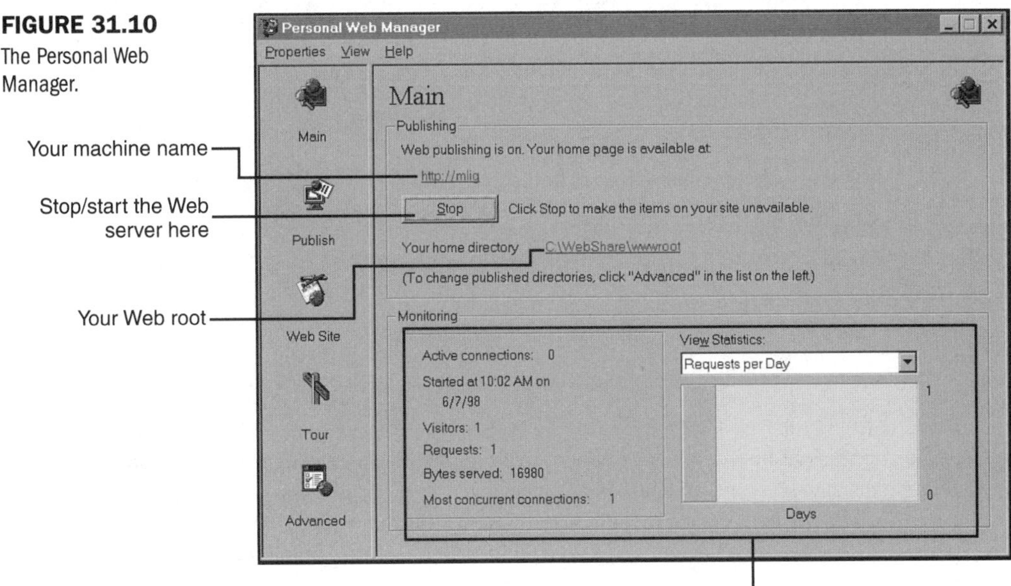

FIGURE 31.10
The Personal Web Manager.

The opening Main page of the Personal Web Manager gives the URL for your local machine and the location of your Web root directory, both as hyperlinks. Clicking the URL link opens the default page in Internet Explorer (**default.htm**); clicking the home directory link opens Windows Explorer at your root directory. You can also stop and start the Web server using the same button (whose name toggles between Stop and Start). The lower half of the window shows some monitoring statistics, including the following items:

- Number of active connections
- Time the Web server was started
- Number of unique visitors to your site up to a total of 50 unique addresses
- Requests made to the Web server, also commonly known as hits
- Bytes served to browser requests since the Web server was last started
- The most concurrent connections since the Web server was last started

The lower-right corner of the Main page also shows a graphic representation of any one of these statistics:

- Requests per day
- Requests per hour
- Visitors per day
- Visitors per hour

If this is the first time you've used PWS, the next step is to click Web Site on the left side of the Personal Web Manager window and run the Home Page Wizard. Even if you aren't interested in making a home page for your local machine, you need to run this wizard before you can run the Publishing Wizard. The Home Page Wizard lets you enter the following information via a series of buttons and text boxes:

- Choose a basic template for your home page
- Add a drop box and/or guest book
- Add links
- Enter a page title
- Enter some personal information about yourself
- Enter some subtitles and text paragraphs for whatever content you want to add

Clicking the Enter New Changes button builds your home page based on your input and loads it into your default browser. Note that your new home page is now displayed as default.asp. The ASP file displays the time and date in addition to any text or links you added from the Home Page Wizard. You can replace this file with the default.htm file that is also installed in this root when the Personal Web Server is installed, although you won't be able to edit default.htm with the Home Page Wizard.

NOTE The PWS recommends using Internet Explorer 4.0 or later for viewing locally generated pages. It builds your home page using cascading style sheets, which are not supported by earlier browser versions. You can also use Navigator 4.0 or later to view pages containing cascading style sheets.

Choosing files to add to the Webpub folder off the root Web on your local machine is also easy from within the Personal Web Manager. The Webpub folder is the folder accessible to visitors to your Web site; they cannot see the remainder of your Web site under WWWRoot. Click Publish on the left side of the Personal Web Manager window to launch the Publishing Wizard, and move past the opening wizard dialog box. The next dialog box enables you to build a list of files to place in the Webpub folder. Click the Browse button to display the Server File System window, shown in Figure 31.11.

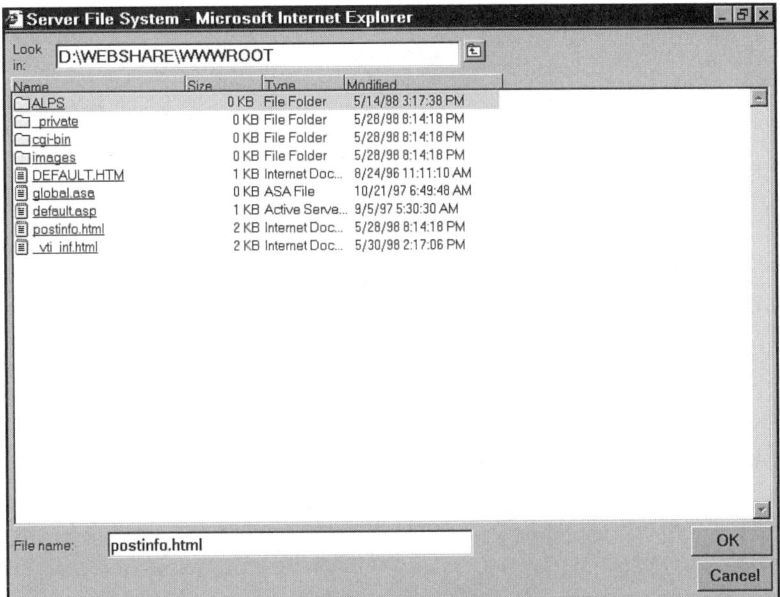

FIGURE 31.11
Selecting files to publish from the Personal Web Manager.

You probably need to maximize this window to use it. Go to your Web root directory. Double-click the subfolder that contains the file you want to add, and select the file. The folder name appears in the Look In box, and the filename appears in the File Name text box at the bottom of the window. Click OK. This takes you back to the Publishing Wizard, as shown in Figure 31.12. Add a description for the file and click the Add button to add the file to the list of files to publish. Note that the entire file path is not shown in the file list, only the filename and file description.

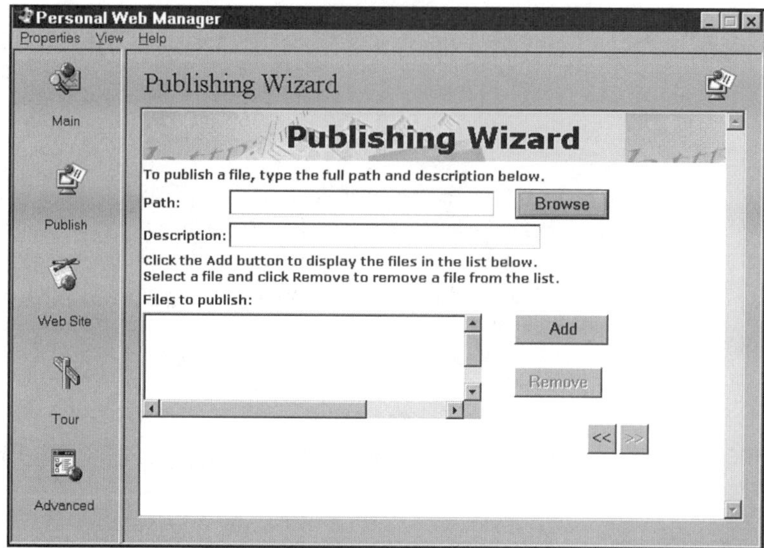

FIGURE 31.12
Building a file list to publish in Personal Web Manager.

You have to go through this process for every file you want to publish to the Webpub folder. You cannot add the contents of an entire folder using this wizard. After you have your list of files, click Finish to copy the files to the Webpub folder.

If you want to take a tour of Personal Web Manager's features, click Tour on the left side of the window. The tour is very basic, giving only an overview of Personal Web Server.

The Advanced button in the Personal Web Manager gives you the heart of the Web server. From this page, shown in Figure 31.13, you can customize the operation of PWS.

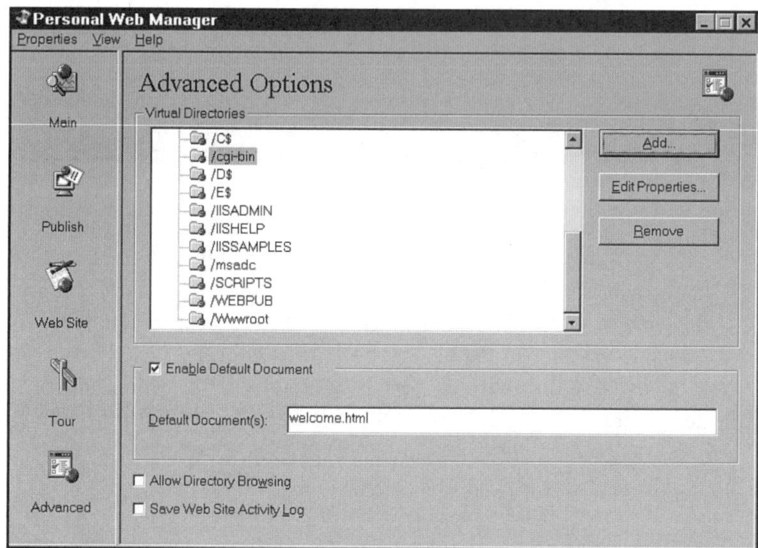

FIGURE 31.13
Customizing the Personal Web Server.

The directory listing begins at the Web server root directory and lists all actual and virtual directories. A virtual directory is a folder that has been assigned an alias so that it appears to be a part of the Web but actually may be on an entirely different drive. Adding a new virtual directory is as easy as clicking the Add button, browsing to the file folder, choosing an alias, and selecting the access rights. You generally assign access rights to virtual directories as follows:

- *Read rights.* Allows visitors to read any files in the folder. You usually set this level of access for HTML files and other files served up by the Web server. Make sure that you don't give Read rights for folders containing executable scripts (CGI, ASP, IDC, and so on).
- *Script rights.* Should only be granted for folders where a script engine needs to run—IDC or ASP, for instance.
- *Execute rights.* These are reserved for running programs from the Web server. Generally, you need to assign both Script and Execute rights to folders that contain scripts for the scripts to operate properly.

You can modify access rights at any time by selecting the folder and clicking the Edit Properties button.

You may notice that the root directories of many of the drives on your system are listed under virtual directories. For security, especially if you are putting your Web server up publicly, you should remove the entries pointing to the root directories of the hard drives on your system, unless, of course, you want them to be accessible. You will still be allowed, though, to create virtual directories that point to specific files on these drives.

Three more check boxes in the Advanced Options page add additional functionality to your Web server:

- **Enable Default Document.** Lets you specify which files are default. Disabling this feature sends an error message to a browser that doesn't specifically list the filename in its URL, unless Allow Directory Browsing is enabled.
- **Allow Directory Browsing.** Serves up a directory list of files if a visitor specifies a folder and the folder does not contain a default file (default.htm). It is clear by default. This feature is handy if you want to give users access to a group of files to download without having to build or update a list of hyperlinks.
- **Save Web Site Activity Log.** Writes the log to the \System\LogFile\W3spc1 directory under Windows. A new log in NSCA format is started each month.

Testing Your Web Site with Personal Web Server

After you have PWS up and running, you can test almost all aspects of your Web site before going live on the Internet or your intranet.

First, if you didn't build your Web site in the Web root directory of PWS, you need to point to the topmost folder of your Web site by giving your site an alias in a virtual directory. Your Web site must be on a local drive; you cannot map a network drive to a virtual directory. Also, make sure the default document information for your virtual directory is correct. For instance, some Web sites use welcome.html or index.html as their default page. Check that your Web server can find your Web site properly by typing the following into a browser:

http://*localhost/YourAlias/*

The home page for your Web site should come up. If it doesn't, check your alias information and make sure that PWS is running. After you've demonstrated that PWS is working properly and serving up your Web site, you can begin to test out your site. Here are some of the items that you can check:

1. Check if all your images are showing. Blank boxes and icons are easy to spot.
2. Test your hyperlinks. Make sure you are connected to the Internet before testing if your URLs point to Internet locations.

HTML editors such as FrontPage have hyperlink checking modules, which make the job of testing large numbers of hyperlinks systematic and bearable. You may not need to try all hyperlinks manually if you've validated your hyperlinks already.

3. Test your scripts (CGI, ASP, IDC, ISAPI, and so on). Troubleshoot any scripts that don't act properly.
4. Test HTML forms by entering dummy information and making sure you get the proper actions.
5. Test your search engine(s), if present.
6. Confirm that your multimedia plays as expected, including animated GIFs, sounds, videos, streaming media, and any specialty items such as Macromedia Flash or Shockwave animations that require plug-ins. Also make sure you have the necessary links and instructions for getting plug-ins.
7. Check out your Web site with at least the major Netscape and Microsoft browsers to make sure no HTML tags act improperly or are browser-specific. See how your site looks with images turned off in the browsers. Also check how your site looks with earlier versions of the major browsers (Internet Explorer and Netscape Navigator) because many people do not regularly upgrade their browsers.
8. If you are using VBScript or JavaScript in your pages, make sure to test all possible conditions, again using multiple browsers.

After you've tweaked and fixed everything to your satisfaction, you're now ready to publish your files to the Internet or intranet Web server. Alternately, you can use PWS to host your Web site. Note, however, that Windows 95 and 98 do not have the sophisticated security of Windows NT Server or Unix servers. Unless PWS is on a nonnetworked (internally) machine with noncritical material on it, I do not recommend using PWS to host a Web site.

Using the Macintosh Personal Web Server

A minimum Macintosh platform for PWS is a 68030 or 68040 Power Macintosh, or comparable MacOS-compatible computer with a minimum of 8MB RAM and 1.2MB of RAM available. You also need MacOS System 7.1 or later, an Internet connection, and MacTCP. If your MacOS is less than System 7.5 on a 68K Macintosh, you need Thread Manager 2.0. This is automatically placed into the Extensions folder in your System folder during installation.

PWS for the Macintosh contains much of the same functionality as PWS for Windows. This includes the following:

- Supports many Active Server Page features, including VBScript
- Supports AppleEvents, CGIs (Common Gateway Interface scripts), and MacOS plug-ins
- Saves a server activity log
- Enables you to build a basic home page
- Supports image maps
- Provides FTP support
- Encodes BinHex files for proper transmission over the Internet
- Provides user-access control

The Macintosh PWS also runs in the background, and you can use it to pre-flight your Web site locally.

Publishing Your Web or Intranet Site with Microsoft Internet Information Server

The Microsoft Internet Information Server (IIS) version 4.0 is an enterprise-level Web server with all the sophisticated features required for the demanding needs of a modern Web site, including many security options and support for Web commerce sites. IIS is designed to run under Windows NT Server, version 4.0 or later, as an NT service. It currently does not run under any other operating system or platform. IIS is free from the Microsoft Web site (**www.microsoft.com/iis**) and is currently part of the NT Option Pack. IIS comes with Windows NT Server as well.

A number of modules in this comprehensive Web server package are new and/or not present in PWS. Among them:

- *Certificate Server.* This server application manages all aspects of digital certificates. Digital certificates are used for authentication (both server and client) under Secure Sockets Layer (SSL), secure email, and Secure Electronic Transactions (SET). Certificates are produced in the standard X.509 format.
- *Internet Connection Services for Remote Access Service (RAS).* This collection of applications is designed to help developers set up and use Virtual Private Networks (VPN), secure networks between groups over the Internet.

- *Transaction Server.* A developer's environment, Microsoft Transaction Server (MTS) is used for creating customized server applications using standard programming tools such as C++ or Visual Basic. MTS provides a runtime environment, a graphical user interface, and application programming interfaces for producing enterprise applications.
- *Index Server 2.0.* This is a text-indexing engine, similar to what Internet search engine spiders use to index Web sites. It produces an index searchable from a Web page.
- *Microsoft Management Console (MMC).* You use this stand-alone application to manage IIS. MMC enables you to access and administer all parts of the Web server.
- *Site Server Express.* This is a basic site log analysis tool. It is made up of three components: Content Analyzer for managing hyperlinks and site structure, Usage Import and Report Writer for generating Web site usage reports, and Posting Acceptor for managing access by multiple locations to post files to a Web server. This last component also works with PWS.
- *Windows Scripting Host.* You can use this as a scripting alternative to DOS batch files. You can run scripts from the desktop and use them to automate administrative and routine scheduled tasks.
- *NNTP newsgroup server and SMTP mail server.* These two components are also a part of this complete IIS package.

As you can see, IIS is a very large package of applications and capabilities. It is beyond the scope of this chapter to investigate the entire package in detail. Rather, the remaining sections in this chapter teach you how to install the server and how to do some basic server administration and management. They also discuss security, explain how to monitor Web site usage, and teach you how to tune and monitor Web server performance. You should be able to determine from this discussion whether IIS can possibly meet your particular needs for a Web server.

Installing Internet Information Server

The IIS Web server and its associated applications are all contained in the NT 4.0 Option Pack, which you can download for free from the Microsoft Web site or buy on CD-ROM for a nominal price. It is very likely that the next version of IIS will be included as part of the NT 5.0 CD-ROM. Before installing this package, make sure you have decided which applications you want to install and that TCP/IP is properly set up on your NT Server. The recommended configuration for a Web server running IIS is a 90MHz Pentium with 64MB of RAM. A 6X CD-ROM and 200MB of hard drive space are also recommended. A minimum configuration is a 486 running at 66 MHz and 32MB of RAM. If you are expecting heavy traffic or will be running a great number of Web applications through your server, more RAM and a faster CPU will be required. You also *must* have the latest NT Service Pack installed (Service Pack 3 at this time) before proceeding with IIS installation.

After you've met the software and hardware requirements, you can begin IIS installation. Choosing the Custom option during setup gives you the most flexibility in choosing applications. Figure 31.14 shows the installation window where you will make most of your decisions about which components and subcomponents to install. Make sure to closely examine the subcomponent windows also.

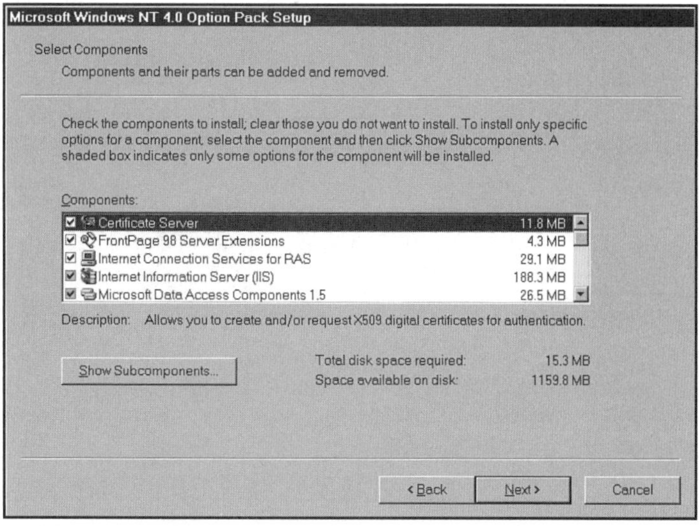

FIGURE 31.14
Installing the Internet Information Server and related components.

After making your choices, click Next, choose where you want your Web site root to be (WWWroot is default), and finish the installation. You need to reboot when all is completed.

After rebooting, you need to test the installation of the Web server. If you are uncertain if the Web server services are running, check that the World Wide Web Publishing Service is started in Services in the Control Panel. Next, open a browser and type either of the following URLs:

http://*localhost*
http://*YourWebServerName*

If either (or both) of these is successful, you should see an introductory page for IIS similar to Figure 31.15.

IIS has extensive online documentation for all its segments. Included are tutorials, audio and video walk-throughs, sample code, entire sample Web sites demonstrating key features, and tons of online help. You can search online help through a keyword index or by using a flexible search engine. The documentation is accessible as a separate item from the Windows Start button and runs best from within Internet Explorer 4.0 or later.

Setting Up the Microsoft Management Console

You administer the majority of the IIS components using the Microsoft Management Console (MMC), shown in Figure 31.16.

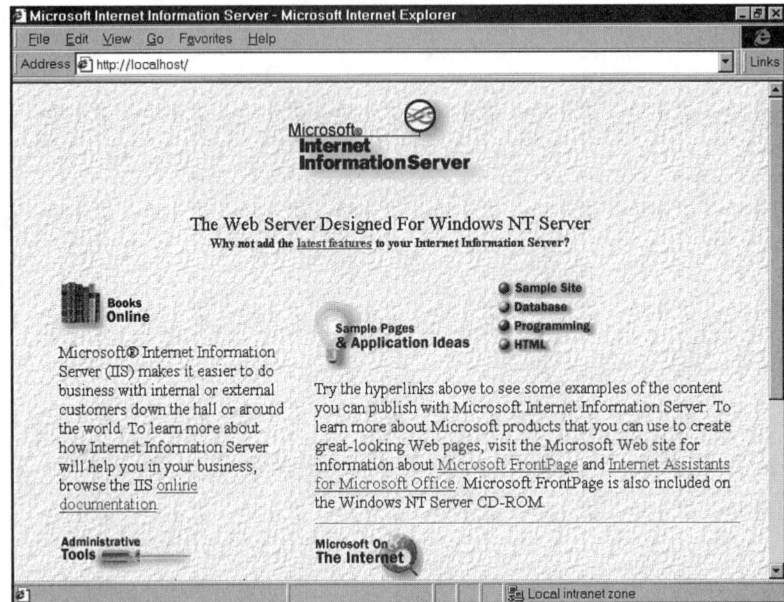

FIGURE 31.15
Testing the Internet Information Server after installation.

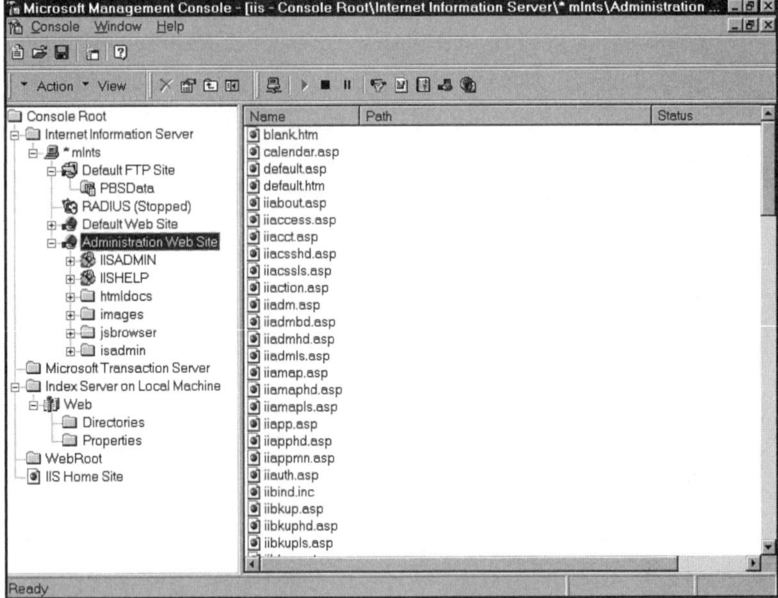

FIGURE 31.16
Managing Internet Information Server through the Microsoft Management Console (MMC).

The MMC uses the concept of a snap-in. A snap-in is an individual component that can be added to the console. For instance, the Index Server is a snap-in complete with all the functionality required to manage the Index Server. This means that you can customize the console and also make and save as many console configurations as you want. Adding future extensions with new capabilities to the console is, well, a snap. Think of the MMC simply as a terminal or console to a modular computer.

Customizing the MMC by adding or deleting components is easy. Choose Console, Add/Remove Snap-in (or press Ctrl+K). This displays the list of installed snap-ins. Choosing a snap-in and clicking the Remove button eliminates the snap-in from the console. Clicking the Add button displays a list of all available snap-ins. You may need to provide some simple information during the addition process depending on the snap-in you select. Each snap-in you add shows up in the left pane (also called the namespace) of the MMC.

You can administer the MMC remotely from a browser either as a Windows NT Administrator or as a Web site operator. Type the URL for the Web server followed by **/iisadmin/** to bring up the Internet Service Manager, as shown in Figure 31.17.

FIGURE 31.17
Using the Internet Service Manager for remote Web site administration.

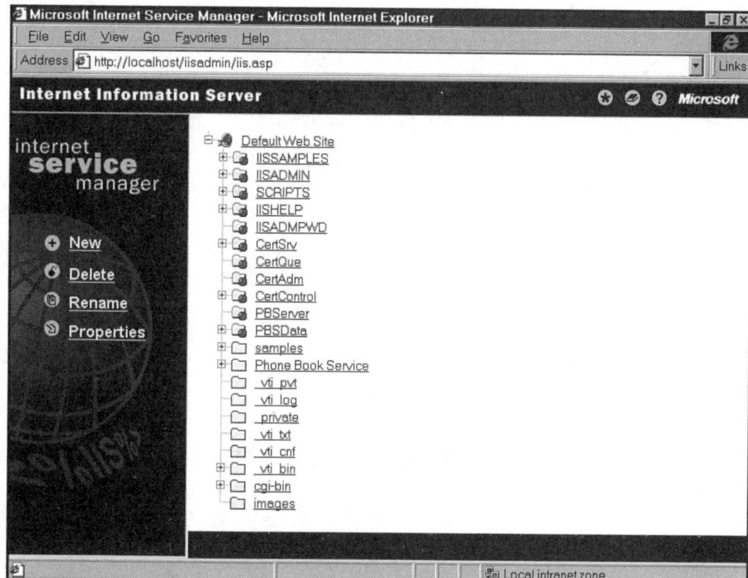

From this page, you can add, delete, start, or stop Web or FTP sites. You can also edit many of the Web server properties described in the following section.

Administering Internet Information Server

You have to set up and administer the IIS Web server through the MMC. You can begin basic administration by expanding the Internet Information Server snap-in to display the Web server(s). Right-click the Web server and choose Properties (or click the Properties button on the MMC toolbar) to display the Properties dialog box, as shown in Figure 31.18.

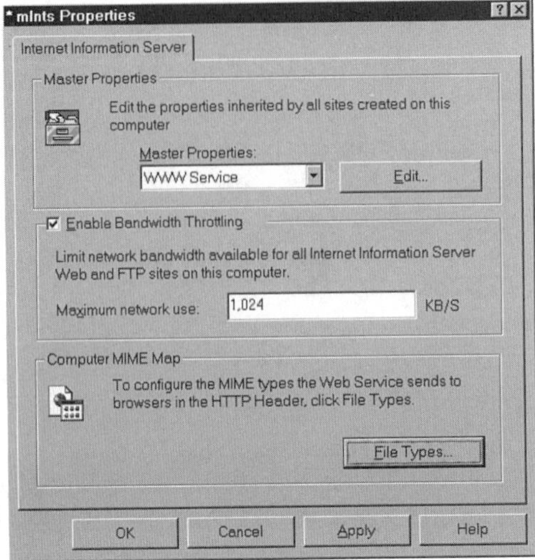

FIGURE 31.18
Internet Information Server properties available for editing.

From this dialog box, you can do the following:

- Edit the WWW Service or FTP Service to control all aspects of these services
- Select the Enable Bandwidth Throttling option if you don't want to make the entire network bandwidth available to this Web server
- Configure MIME mapping by adding, editing, or removing MIME file types

If you click the Edit button with WWW Service displayed in the Master Properties drop-down box, a tabbed WWW Service Master Properties dialog box for the selected Web server appears, as shown in Figure 31.19.

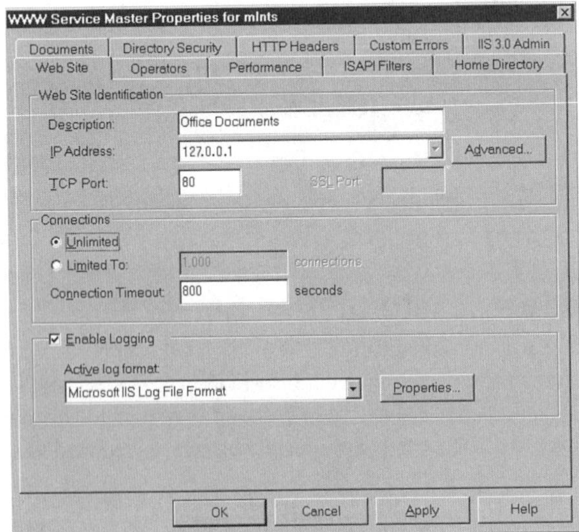

FIGURE 31.19
Administering Web server properties.

Here is a brief overview of the features that you can control in each of the tabs:

- **Web Site.** This tab enables to you review your IP address information, assign a TCP port (if the default of 80 is not suitable), limit the number of connections to the server as well as the connection timeout, and enable/disable Web server logging and choose your log format.
- **Operators.** You can grant Web site operator privileges based on the same Windows NT User Accounts used to grant access privileges to NT server. An operator can set server access permissions, change default Web pages, and edit content expiration and ratings.
- **Performance.** You can set performance tuning based on expected daily hits to the Web server at <10,000, <100,000, or >100,000. You can also enable/disable HTTP Keep-Alives, which maintains established connections as enabled under the newer HTTP 1.1 protocol.
- **ISAPI Filters.** You can install/remove applications (such as FrontPage Server Extensions) loaded by the Web server at startup. You can also edit and prioritize each filter.
- **Home Directory.** This tab enables you to alter the access rights (Read, Write, Execute, and so on) or even change the location of your Web server root Web site directory. You can designate your home directory as an application (define it as the starting point for all virtual directories involved in a particular application), meaning that all these directories can be involved in items such as Active Server Pages or secure operations.
- **Documents.** This tab enables you to enable/disable the default document, name the file (usually default.htm), and add more than one file. Alternately, you can reassign the default document to a different folder.
- **Directory Security.** Here you can control anonymous access and authentication to the Web server, define secure communications using the Key Manager, and restrict access by IP address or domain.
- **HTTP Headers.** You can use this tab to enable content expiration to prevent browsers from loading cached pages after a period of time. You can also enable your server to send custom HTTP headers, disable, enable, or define the content rating for your site, and, once again, edit MIME mappings.
- **Custom Errors.** You can customize the error page sent to a browser when a Web server error is encountered. Each error condition and the location of the HTML error page are listed for easy editing.
- **IIS 3.0 Admin.** One last administrative detail is backward compatibility with IIS 3.0. For applications that install files to the IIS directory, you need to set the installation location as the Default Web root or the Administrative Web.

Security and Internet Information Server

The public nature of most Web servers, whether internal Web servers used for intranets or Web servers on the Internet, demands the highest possible security. Information on your Web server needs to be protected from alteration, and access to other parts of your network has to be restricted to prevent criminal activity.

Security starts with the NT operating system. You can use the Server Manager and the User Manager to restrict access to various folders and drives to certain individuals or groups. Placing the Web server on a volume supporting the NT File System (NTFS) gives you additional control over user access rights through the User Manager.

IIS enables you to control some Web server security and rights access. You can enable Web server authentication by turning off anonymous access within IIS. If you do this, the Web server defaults to NT user access rights (basic authentication). This option requires a valid NT user account. You can also use Windows NT Challenge/Response to restrict access, but this option only works with Internet Explorer browsers. Finally, you can establish additional authentication using Secure Sockets Layer (SSL) Client Certification supported by IIS. SSL determines the validity of encrypted digital certificates during user login.

Security auditing features under Windows NT track logon attempts and attempts to access restricted areas of the NT server. You can set the items to monitor via auditing in the NT User Manager, and you can set up responses to intrusions (including shutting down the server). Your auditing policy should balance user needs with your server security requirements.

Monitoring Web Site Usage

After your Web server is online and serving information, you will probably want to monitor that information flow. This requires enabling Web server logging and then using Site Server (or any other commercially available log analysis package) to monitor the flow of users and information through your site. Some of the Web server usage information available from a log includes the following:

- Number of hits per day
- Number of unique and repeat visitors based on IP addresses
- Total bandwidth used, that is, total MB files served up
- Number of accesses to any given file
- Accesses by file type (HTM, ASP, GIF, WAV, and so on)
- Times and dates a file is viewed
- Browser and platform from which requests were made
- Referring sites, that is, where a visitor was immediately before he/she visited your site
- Server error conditions and broken hyperlinks

You can use this information for marketing (which areas are visited most? where are visitors coming from?), server hardware/software/network bandwidth upgrades (how many hits do I get per day?), fixing hyperlinks, and deciding which Web server applications to use (which platforms are visitors using the most?).

The Usage Import program, part of Site Server Express, can apply a variety of filters to a Web server log (see Figure 31.20).

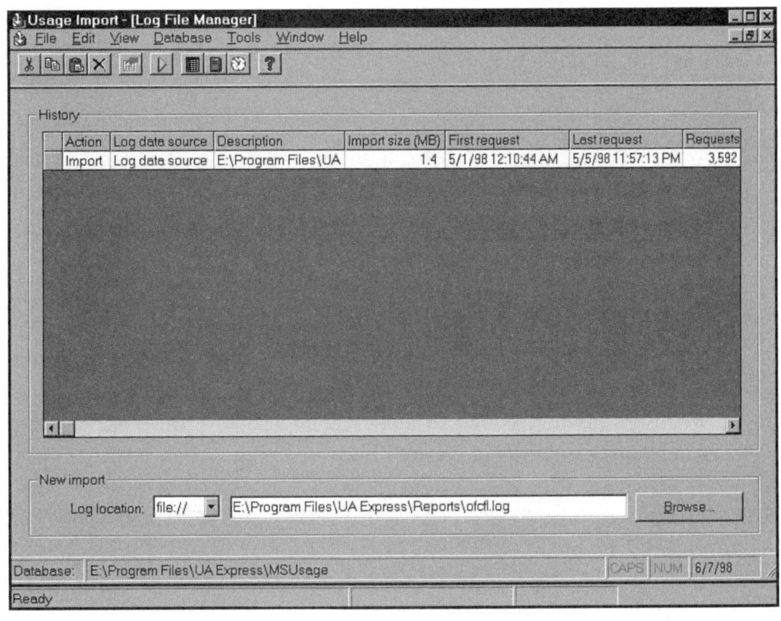

FIGURE 31.20
Usage Import in Site Server Express processes and condenses Web server logs.

After you have imported server logs via Usage Import, you can use Report Writer to answer many questions about Web site usage through a series of customizable reports. You can output reports as HTML pages, Microsoft Word documents, or Excel workbooks. A portion of a sample Executive Summary report (Visits by organization type) in HTML is displayed in Figure 31.21.

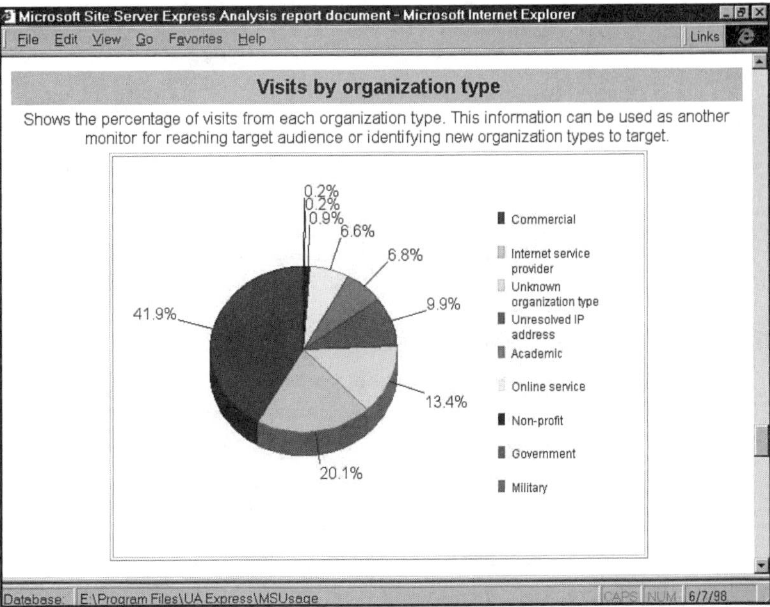

FIGURE 31.21
A portion of a sample Executive Summary report from a Web server log created with Report Writer.

Other portions of the Executive Summary report include the following:

- Daily visit trends
- Daily usage summary
- Usage by day of week
- Usage by hour of the day
- Top 20 requests
- Top 20 organizations
- Top 20 countries

Content Analyzer, another part of Site Server Express, contains a number of Web management tools, similar to those found in FrontPage. These include site mapping and visualization (called Webmaps), remote administration, and hyperlink verification. An example of the site visualization features is shown in Figure 31.22.

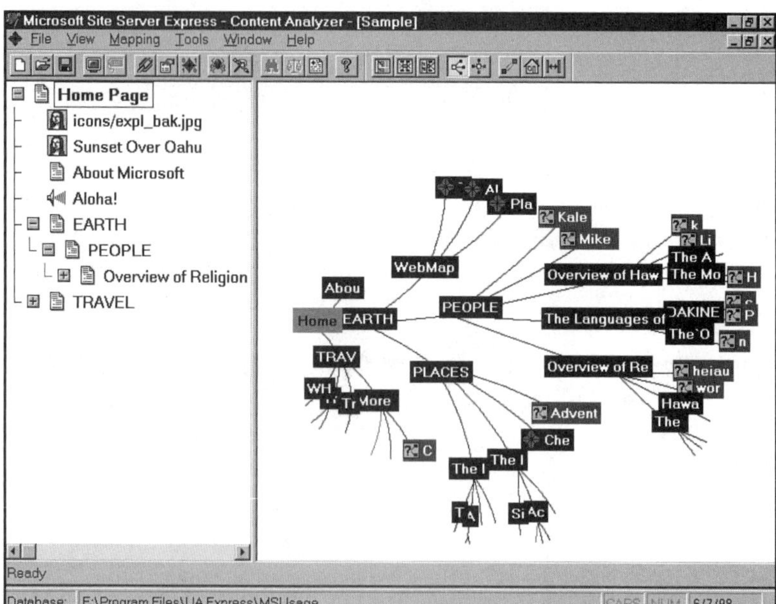

FIGURE 31.22
A sample Webmap using the Content Analyzer tool from Site Server Express.

Web Server Performance Tuning and Monitoring

The idea behind performance tuning is to maximize the performance of the Web server within the hardware/software/network constraints of your particular server and Web site. There are several ways you need to tune Web server performance.

You must determine your bandwidth needs. If your Web server is the only requirement on your leased T-1 line, then letting the Web server have the entire bandwidth is a no-brainer. But what if you have a mail server? A news server? How about reserving some bandwidth for uploading new files on a daily basis? Are you constantly serving large video or compressed program file archives? You need to monitor the bandwidth required by everything and adjust the amount consumed by the Web server. Generally, if you are exceeding 50 percent of your total bandwidth for most of any given day, you should consider obtaining more bandwidth.

You have to decide whether to limit the number of simultaneous connections. If you set a limit, then any requests above that limit will not be serviced. Yet if you allow unlimited connections, at some point the Web server will be unable to meet all the connections, resulting in an agonizingly slow HTML page load time.

You need to decide how much memory to allot to the Web server. Generally, the more memory given to the Web server, the better your response will be. Again, this depends upon what other applications are running on the Web server (such as ASP, CGI scripts, databases, and so on), how many hits your Web server is taking per day, and how much memory the NT operating system needs for optimal performance. For example, allocating more RAM to the Web server may reduce your disk cache performance or size and actually cause a net reduction in performance.

You have to determine what speed and how many CPUs are optimal. Generally, faster is better. Windows NT also can use more than one CPU. Note that at a certain point your bus speed may become a limiting factor regardless of how many CPUs you put in.

You have to use the right type of network card and network connection. If you have a large amount of bandwidth available, but a slow network card, the speed of your Web server is limited by the network card speed. Also, you should investigate your network connection to the Internet. Some areas of the Internet experience heavy congestion, and if your Web server is near one of these areas, your apparent Web site performance may decline dramatically.

Obviously, to make decisions related to Web server performance tuning, you need data, data, and more data. You can obtain this data only through consistent and planned monitoring. Some possible monitoring directions might include the following:

- Using Performance Monitor under NT Server to monitor RAM usage, CPU usage, processes running on NT (iissrv is the Web server process), and many of the Web Service items, too numerous to list here
- Using the Event Viewer, an NT administration utility, to check out error conditions
- Monitoring the size and content of the Web server logs, processing the logs regularly, and especially tracking total bandwidth/day and looking at peak bandwidth times to determine when to add more network capacity
- Using NetStat and Network Monitor, both administration applications under NT server, to follow the network traffic to and from your Web server computer; be sure to monitor traffic between computers if other key Web components, such as a database, reside on computers other than the Web server computer

PART VI

Superior Techniques for Managing Office

CHAPTER 32

Reducing Total Cost of Ownership

In the wake of independent studies from the Gartner Group and others, which estimated the total cost of owning, managing, and maintaining PCs at $15,000 or more per machine per year, business customers have become increasingly worried about the total costs of desktop computing. These costs take many forms, including the cost of hardware and software, training and help desk services, and custom software development, to name a few.

Microsoft is taking a number of approaches to reduce the total cost of ownership (TCO) of Windows PCs. Some of these approaches, such as the Zero Administration Kit for Windows, are already available for implementation with Office 97 running on Windows 95, 98, or NT 4.0. Other technologies, such as componentized "Installation on Demand," are promised for Office 2000. Technologies such as IntelliMirror are promised for Windows NT, due in 1999. Still other approaches require additional Microsoft products, such as Microsoft Windows NT 4.0, Terminal Server Edition.

In this chapter, you'll learn about your options for lowering the total cost of owning Microsoft Office, now and in the future.

Using System Policies with Office 97

System Policies are at the heart of many of Microsoft's efforts at lowering Microsoft Office management costs. First introduced in Windows 95 and available in Windows NT 4.0, System Policies are files that control aspects of a program's behavior by changing entries in the Windows registry.

You can deploy System Policies on a server and run them at login from individual Windows 95/98 or NT Workstation 4.0 workstations. (They are not available for Macintosh computers, even those running on NT Server networks.)

System Policies give the Office administrator a way to control the behavior of Office for the following:

- Individual workstations
- Individual users sharing a workstation
- Groups of users
- Every user at once

You can implement System Policies at any time, although if you're planning to impose highly restrictive policies, it's usually best to do so at the same time you deploy Office 97, or else face the challenge of users who want to know why restrictions are suddenly necessary.

NOTE System Policies run at login only if you choose the correct primary network login for each workstation. In NT Server networks, you must use Client for Microsoft Networks, and define an appropriate Windows NT domain on each workstation.

In NetWare networks, System Policies are easiest to implement if you use Microsoft Client for NetWare, specifying a preferred server for login. If you prefer to use Novell's client software, you must manually download System Polices from a mapped drive on each computer. For detailed directions on doing this, see Chapter 15 of the Windows 95 Resource Kit. ■

As you'll see, Office administrators can edit system policies using the System Policy Editor. Windows 95 came with a version of the System Policy Editor stored in the \Admin\Apptools\Poledit folder. You can install this version as an optional Windows system component using Windows 95's Add/Remove Programs applet. Installing the System Policy Editor this way adds an entry to the Startup folder, making the program conveniently available. It also places the Grouppol.dll file in the Windows system folder and updates the registry to recognize its presence. This step is essential if you want to use System Policies that affect groups, not just individuals.

After you do this, however, you'll want to upgrade your copy of System Policy Editor to the latest version. The Office 97 Resource Kit utilities include a version of System Policy Editor that you can use on both platforms.

To get the new System Policy Editor, point your Web browser to **www.microsoft.com/office/ork/appa/appa.htm** and download SetupPol.exe. After you download this file, double-click on it in Windows Explorer to extract and install the new System Policy Editor. Double-clicking SetupPol.exe also extracts Microsoft's basic Office 97 Policy templates for both Windows 95 and NT.

NOTE Microsoft provides separate templates for Office 97 depending on whether you are running Windows 95 or Windows NT 4.0. On Windows 95 systems, use Off97w95.adm; on NT systems, use Off97nt4.adm.

Separate Policy templates for Microsoft Access 97 (Access97.adm), Outlook 97 (Outlk97.adm), and Microsoft Query (Query97.adm) *do* work on both NT 4.0 and Windows 95. Note, however, that in order to create a policy file for Windows 95, you must be running System Policy Editor on a Windows 95 computer. To create a policy file for Windows NT Workstation, you must run System Policy Editor on an NT Workstation system. ■

The 100+ individual System Policies Microsoft provides for Office 97 do not control every aspect of Office's behavior, or even every Office-related element stored in the Windows registry. However, they do control many of the behaviors Office administrators will be most concerned with.

Some of them allow you to tighten your control of Office (and presumably reduce your cost of ownership). Others are primarily intended to give you more flexibility in deploying Office to users throughout your network. Many correspond to settings that users would otherwise set individually in the Tools, Options dialog boxes of individual Office applications.

Outside Office, you can use other Policy templates to place restrictions on the rest of the Windows environment. For example, you can use the Windows 95 admin.adm System Policy template, available on the Windows 95 CD-ROM, to limit individual users to running specific applications, such as Word. (The setting to do this is Default User\System\Restrictions\Only Run Allowed Windows Applications.)

CAUTION

If you're planning to use the Windows 95 policy Only Run Allowed Windows Applications, make sure to include Poledit.exe (System Policy Editor) as one of those applications, or you may not be able to change the settings later!

NOTE Understanding System Policies also lays the groundwork for understanding the Zero Administration Kit, which can provide tighter control (see the section "Using the Zero Administration Kit (ZAK) for Windows" later in this chapter). ■

Running System Policy Editor

After you install System Policy Editor, you can run it as follows:

1. Choose Start, Programs, Accessories, System Tools, System Policy Editor. The System Policy Editor opens (see Figure 32.1). If System Policy Editor is not listed as an option in the System Tools menu, you can run Poledit.exe from the Ork97\Policy folder.

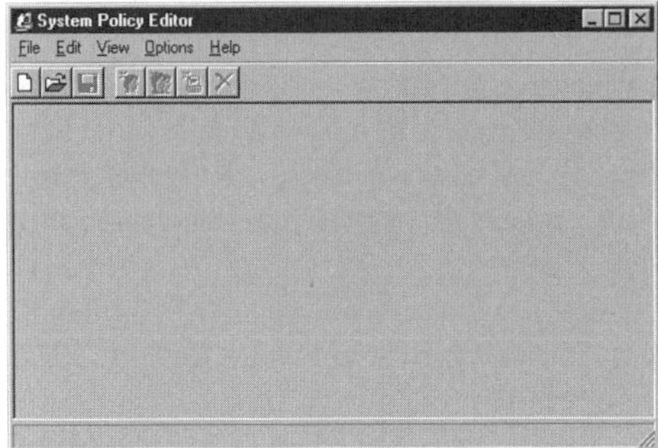

FIGURE 32.1
The System Policy Editor window.

2. Choose Options, Policy Template. The Policy Template Options dialog box opens, listing any current Policy templates already installed. If no Policy templates are installed, click Add to display the Open Template File dialog box. This lists the Policy templates available (but not installed) in the Policy folder. Choose Off97w95.adm (or Off97nt4.adm if you are running Windows NT 4.0). If you want to set policies for Access, Outlook, or Microsoft Query, add their templates as well. Then click OK. (Figure 32.2 shows this dialog box with several standard Policy templates listed.)

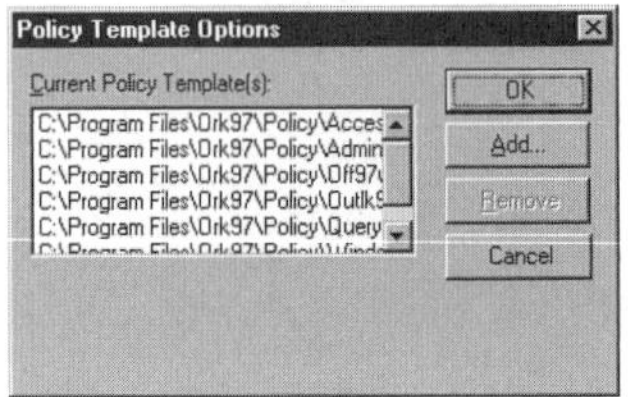

FIGURE 32.2
The Policy Template Options dialog box lists currently installed policy templates.

NOTE When a Policy template is listed in the Policy Template Options dialog box, the settings contained within it are available for customization (see steps 5 and 6). If a Policy template is not listed in this dialog box, its settings are not available. So, for example, if you want to control general Windows 95 settings, you need to find and install the admin.adm template file, which contains them.

3. Click OK again. The blank System Policy Editor window returns.

4. Click the New button or choose File, New Policy. As shown in Figure 32.3, the System Policy Editor window now displays two icons: Default Computer, which controls System Policies related to an entire computer (or computers); and Default User, which displays System Policies associated with a specific user (or group of users).

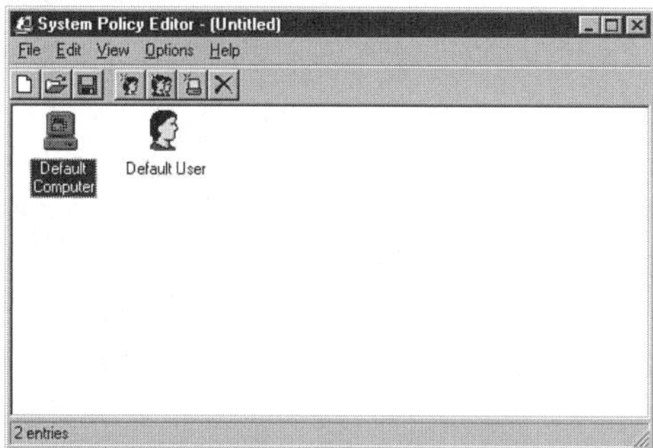

FIGURE 32.3
The System Policy Editor window after you've chosen a template to work from.

NOTE Some Office 97 System Policies affect all users on a specific computer; these are accessible through Default Computer. Others can be attached to individual users, even if multiple users share the same computer. These are accessible through Default User.

In order to set policies for individual users, you must first enable User Profiles on their workstations. To do this in Windows 95, start the Passwords applet in the Control Panel, click the User Profiles tab, and mark the option button labeled Users Can Customize Their Preferences and Desktop Settings.

5. Click the icon associated with the System Policies that you want to work with (Default User or Default Computer). The Default User Properties or Default Computer Properties dialog box will appear, listing the categories of System Policies available for editing (see Figure 32.4).

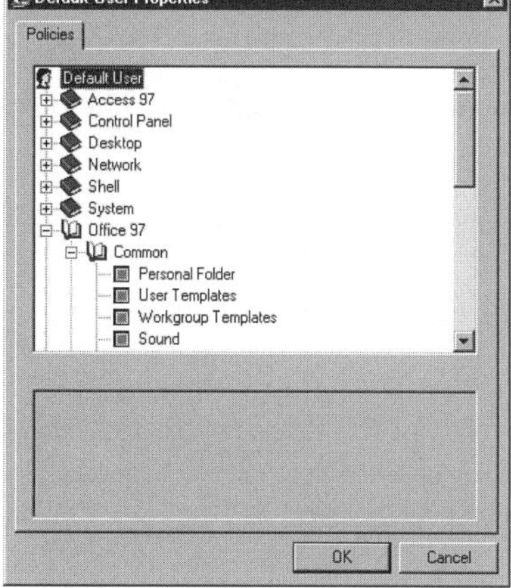

FIGURE 32.4
The Default User Properties dialog box, with some of Office 97's suite-wide settings displayed.

6. Scroll down to the policy you want to change, and make the selection you want. For each policy, you have three choices:
   - *Checked.* The policy always goes into effect as soon as the user logs onto the network, and cannot be changed by the user.
   - *Cleared.* The policy is never in effect; again, a user cannot override this setting.
   - *Grayed.* The system policy leaves local settings alone; the user can decide what setting to use.
7. When you finish changing settings, click OK. You return to the System Policy Editor window with its Default Computer and Default User icons; if you want to make changes to a category of settings you haven't worked with yet, click its icon and repeat steps 5 and 6.
8. When you finish, click the Save button or choose File, Save. The Save As dialog box appears.
9. Enter a name for your policy—Ntconfig.pol if you're setting a policy for NT Workstation systems, or Config.pol for Windows 95 systems.
10. Browse the network to the NetLogon folder on the Primary Domain Controller that controls your user logons, and click Save. The new Policy is saved with the .pol extension. (If your users log onto a NetWare network, instead save the POL file to the Sys\Public folder on their preferred server.)

Specifying Policies for Individuals or Groups

When you create System Policies for the Default User, those System Policies affect all users except those for whom you have created separate policies. Similarly, when you create System Policies for Default Computer, those affect all computers which do not have System Policies to the contrary.

The real benefits of System Policies come when you customize them to the needs of specific groups within your organization. You might, for example, have a roomful of computers that are used by account executives during the day and telemarketers at night. You might provide your account executives access to Excel to help them prepare high-level proposals, but limit your telemarketers to the software they need to take orders and check on order status.

To create System Policies for a specific group, first open the System Policy Editor, and then follow these steps:

1. If you already have a system policy file (Config.pol or Ntconfig.pol), choose File, Open to open it. If not, choose File, New to create a new system policy file.
2. Choose Edit, Add Group. The Add Group dialog box appears. Enter the name of the group that you want to add.

NOTE The groups you add in System Policy Editor should correspond to groups recognized by your network server. If you are running on an NT Server network, for example, use the group names you have established in User Manager for Domains.

3. Click OK. The new group appears as a separate icon next to Default Computer and Default User.

4. Double-click on the new icon to display the policies available for editing.
5. Make your edits, click OK, and save your policy file.

A Closer Look at Selected Office 97 System Policies

As mentioned earlier, the Office 97 Policy templates contain more than 100 System Policies that are available for customization. (A complete listing of Office 97's available System Policies appears as Appendix C to the Office 97 Resource Kit; you can read or download it from **www.microsoft.com/office/ork/appc/AppC.htm**.) The next two sections focus on some of the entries that you might want to pay special attention to in your role as Office administrator.

Commonly Changed Office 97 Default Computer Policies The following settings help control the way Office 97 runs for all users on a specific computer:

- **Office 97\Default Save.** When you mark this check box, if users try to save a file in a format other than the one you have specified, they receive a message from the Office Assistant telling them which format to use instead if the file is going to be shared. Marking this check box works only if the Office Assistant is running, and it works only for Office programs where you have specified a default save format in the Default User policies.
- **Office 97\Uninstall.** By default, if you need to uninstall or change an Office installation, the Office 97 setup program looks for the Off97pro.stf (Professional Edition) or Off97std.stf (Standard Edition) setup file. If you've moved the setup file—perhaps in connection with deploying a new server—uninstall will fail. Using this System Policy, you can point setup to a new location.
- **Excel 97\Microsoft Map\Map Data.** This setting allows you to specify a folder where map data is stored for use with Microsoft Map. Another setting, Search Paths, allows you to specify one or more folders where shared map data is stored for use by the entire workgroup.
- **Outlook 97\Use Schedule+.** Setting this policy instructs Outlook to use Microsoft Schedule+ 95 for all calendar operations instead of Outlook's built-in calendar feature. You may want to use this if you recently standardized on Schedule+ 95 and are not prepared to update all your users to the Outlook calendar.

NOTE This policy setting is available only if you have Outlk97.adm listed as a Current Policy Template in the Policy Template Options dialog box (accessible by choosing Options, Policy Template).

- **Word 97\Spelling Advanced\Default AutoCorrect File.** In Chapter 11, you learned that Word allows you to create a custom AutoCorrect file with names and other words that you want Word to fix automatically. The best way to automatically provide a custom AutoCorrect (.acl) file to new users is to create it, place it on a network server, and use this setting to point to it. The user's computer will then locate and copy the custom ACL file, storing the copy locally under a different name.

- **Clip Gallery 3.0\Concurrent Database #1.** This setting, along with Concurrent Database #2 and Concurrent Database #3, allows you to specify additional locations where the Microsoft Clip Gallery can find image databases.

Commonly Changed Office 97 Default User Policies The following settings help control the way Office 97 runs for individual users:

- **Office 97\Common\Personal Folder.** Specifies where an individual user's files are stored by default; if this is not set, Office uses the C:\My Documents folder.
- **Office 97\Common\User Templates.** Specifies an additional location, typically on a network server, where a user can store additional Word, Excel, and/or PowerPoint templates beyond those installed locally.
- **Office 97\Common\Workgroup Templates.** Specifies where a workgroup's shared templates are stored, typically on a network server.
- **Office\97\Assistant\Options Tab.** Contains several settings that control how the Microsoft Office Assistant behaves.
- **Office\Internet\FTP Sites\Add FTP Sites.** By default, if you choose File, Open in any Office application and browse to Internet Locations (FTP), no FTP sites are listed. This policy allows you to specify up to 10 FTP site addresses that will appear. It's a useful shortcut if you use FTP to distribute information over an intranet or Web site, or if you commonly need access to FTP sites provided by your customers or suppliers.
- **Office\Internet\Help_Microsoft on the Web\Disable Submenu.** By default, Office 97 installs with a set of Help, Microsoft on the Web submenu items that encourage users to visit Microsoft's Web site and download additional resources or get additional help. Some Office administrators prefer to eliminate this menu, thereby reducing unnecessary "Web surfing" and Microsoft advertising on their desktops, and helping to avoid the introduction of unauthorized add-ons that require support. Alternatively, you can set the Customize Submenu policy to limit the Microsoft resources listed, without getting rid of them altogether.

You can also use Customize Submenu to provide links to any other Web, intranet page, or network location you like. This is a very convenient way of providing quick access to shared custom Help or other resources.

- **Excel 97\Tools_Options\General\Alternate Startup Folder.** Enables you to specify an alternative startup folder for default workbook or worksheet templates.
- **Excel 97\Tools_Options\Transition\Default Save.** Enables you to specify whether Excel workbooks are saved in Excel 97 format or a different format. Choose a different format if most of the users you share files with do not use Excel 97 yet.

NOTE Similar Default User policies are available for Word and PowerPoint.

- **PowerPoint 97\Tools_Options\General\Macro Virus Protection.** Enabling this setting requires PowerPoint's built-in macro virus protection to be turned on. A similar policy is available in Word.
- **PowerPoint 97\Tools_Options\Edit\Replace Straight Quotes with Smart Quotes.** You may want to check this if all of your presentations stay within the Windows environment, where Smart Quotes can always be understood properly. You may want to clear this if your users work across platforms and you want to avoid characters that cannot be read properly on the Macintosh.
- **PowerPoint 97\Miscellaneous\Multimedia Directory.** Use this to point to a standard folder where PowerPoint should look for audio and video clips. The folder you choose is the one that will appear when the user chooses Insert, Movies and Sounds, Movie from File (or Sound from File). You can use a similar setting, Picture Directory, to store image files. The folder you choose is one that will appear when the user chooses Insert, Picture, From File.
- **Word 97\Tools_Options\General\Help for WordPerfect Users.** If you are migrating from WordPerfect for DOS, you can specify that certain users' machines display certain help targeted for WordPerfect users. You can also specify that Word substitute WordPerfect's keyboard shortcuts for its own, perhaps during a temporary transition period.
- **Word 97\Tools_Options\Spelling & Grammar\Background Spelling (and Background Grammar).** By default, Word checks spelling as you work, flagging potential errors with a red wavy line. It also checks grammar, flagging potential errors with a green wavy line. If you are running Office 97 on relatively slow PCs, or if you have provided voice recognition software to your users, you may want to clear these check boxes to disable these features.
- **Word 97\Tools_Options\File Locations\Startup.** By default, Word looks to a local startup folder for templates, add-ins, and files to run at startup. If all your users will work with the same startup resources, you might use this policy to place the startup folder on a network server.
- **Access 97\Tools_Options\Datasheet.** Contains a variety of policy settings that help you define a standard look and feel for your Access datasheets.
- **Access 97\Tools_Options\Keyboard.** Contains a variety of settings that customize the way data entry works, and can be used to make Access work more like previous systems your data entry staff may have experience with.
- **Outlook 97\Tools_Options\Calendar.** Can be used to customize Outlook's calendar in a variety of ways, including specifying working hours, work weeks, the beginning of the week, and whether to show week numbers.
- **Query 97\File_New\Data Source Folders.** Allows you to specify a path to where your Query 97 queries can typically find their data.

Using the Zero Administration Kit (ZAK) for Windows

The Zero Administration Kit (ZAK) for Windows builds on System Policies and User Profiles, enabling you to establish tightly controlled, centrally managed workstations where both Office 97 (and/or other programs) are stored on a network server running Windows NT Server, using the local hard disk as a cache to improve performance.

The local computer may run Windows 95, Windows 98, or Windows NT 4.0 Workstation. Whichever client workstation you choose, users cannot install unauthorized applications or gain access to local settings.

The Zero Administration Kit is free, and available at **www.microsoft.com/windows/zak**. At the same site, Microsoft also provides documentation and free self-paced training that walks you step by step through deploying ZAK with Microsoft Office 97. You should download and read these carefully before proceeding with ZAK.

Microsoft's Zero Administration Kit includes two predefined "user modes." *AppStation* mode gives users access to a limited number of applications, and enables them to switch among these applications using the taskbar or the Alt+Tab keyboard shortcut. You can see the typical AppStation taskbar in Figure 32.5.

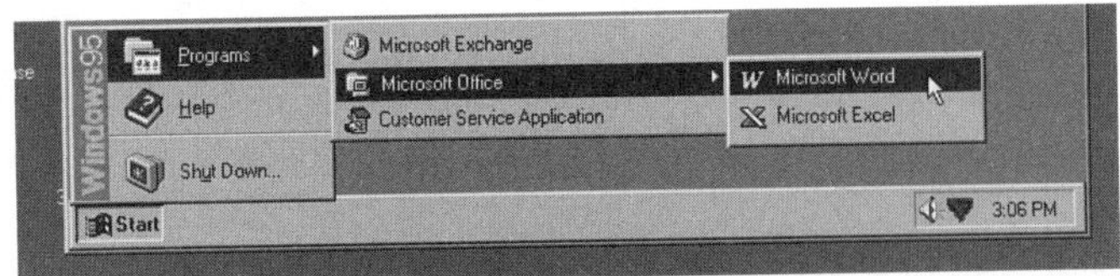

FIGURE 32.5
The typical AppStation taskbar.

TaskStation mode is even more limited: it automatically loads to a single application, typically a custom application (which nowadays might be deployed through a Web browser). There is no taskbar or Start button because there's no need to load or switch programs: the user gets only one program, which loads at startup. Office administrators are likely to find only AppStation mode interesting, so the procedures discussed in the next section focus on this mode.

Microsoft positions these two modes as "intended for a pilot network…only examples of what you can do with the Zero Administration Kit." In fact, many early users of ZAK have found that AppStation mode requires some tweaking in order to provide access to all the files that users require, even if they are working with only one or a few Office applications. Even in the best of circumstances, ZAK is fairly complex, and it takes time to plan.

In some respects, ZAK is a stop-gap measure—a quick response to users' concerns about total cost of ownership that will eventually be supplanted by improved management capabilities built into the operating system (particularly NT 5.0). Having said all this, if you need what ZAK offers, and you can't wait until mid-'99 or later, it's worth serious consideration.

The Basic ZAK Installation Process

ZAK is designed to set up both your network and individual workstations to work together in providing carefully circumscribed access to individual users. ZAK requires a server based on Windows NT 4.0 Server (with at least Service Pack 3 installed), and workstations that can run any of the following:

- Windows 95 (with Service Pack 1 installed, or OSR2)
- Windows 98
- Windows NT 4.0 Workstation (with Service Pack 3 installed)

ZAK installs the Windows operating system on client workstations, so you should start with new systems or existing workstations with newly formatted hard drives. If you start with new workstations, you may want to configure them with network cards that are compatible with NT Server 4.0's Network Client Administration Tool. This streamlines the process of creating the boot disks that will be needed for each workstation.

The process described below installs ZAK client software on Windows 95 workstations, but the process for building Windows 98 or NT 4.0 Workstation systems is similar.

NOTE The standard ZAK procedure discussed here involves an across-the-wire installation of Windows and Office via the network, but ZAK can also be installed on client workstations locally via devices such as Jaz drives. ■

Step 1: Gathering the Components The first step is to pull together all the components you need to install the Zero Administration Kit:

- The Zero Administration Kit for Windows 95 or the Zero Administration Kit for Windows NT, depending on the client workstations you intend to use (before you go on to the next step, extract the ZAK files onto your hard disk)
- If you're working with Windows 95, the complete CD-ROM—the Windows 95 upgrade edition cannot be used to install ZAK on a new system
- If you're working with Windows 95, the Windows 95 Service Pack 1, downloadable at **www.microsoft.com/windows95/info/service-packs.htm**
- The Microsoft Office 97 CD-ROM
- A CD-ROM containing Microsoft Internet Explorer (ZAK was originally designed to work with Internet Explorer 3.0*x*; by the time you read this, it may have been updated to support a more recent version)

Step 2: Preparing Your Network Next, you have to get your network ready. Set up a Windows NT Server Primary Domain Controller (PDC), which will be used to manage the AppStations on your network. Make sure that the network account you use has the permissions it needs: it must be a member of the Domain Admins global group with write access to the \NetLogon shared folder on the PDC you use.

NOTE In order to copy files to the NetLogon share, the folder's share name must be given read-write access. It isn't enough to log on as a network administrator and use the network administrator's rights to the folder. After you've finished installing ZAK, you'll want to reset the folder share to read-only.

Step 3: Running the ZAK Wizard Now you need to run the Zero Administration Kit Wizard, shown in Figure 32.6. First, insert your Windows 95 CD-ROM into your CD-ROM drive. Next, double-click Zaksetup.exe. You'll walk step-by-step through a lengthy wizard that helps you create a network distribution point for both Windows 95 and Microsoft Office, specify domains, workgroups, network share locations, printers, client folders, and if you want to provide email access, Microsoft Exchange server information. If you're running ZAK on NT Server 4.0, you can also build a network boot disk for your client machines.

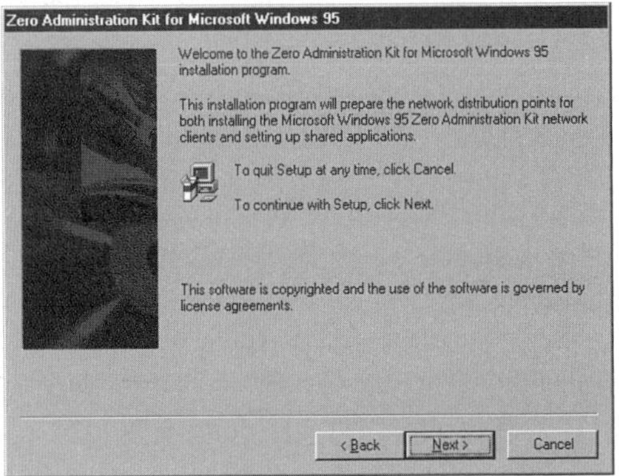

FIGURE 32.6
The Windows 95 Zero Administration Kit Wizard.

After you enter all this information, the wizard prompts you to insert each of the CD-ROMs you need; typically, the Windows 95 CD-ROM, the Windows 95 Service Pack 1 CD-ROM, Microsoft Office 97, and Microsoft Internet Explorer. At this stage, the wizard also provides information for configuring your Office 97 distribution point. Write it down; you'll need it to configure your Office 97 distribution point. Click Next, and the wizard prompts you for the Office 97 CD-ROM so that it can copy additional files.

You've now completed the automated component of ZAK setup. The remaining steps are manual, and you must perform them carefully in order for ZAK setup to succeed.

Step 4: Preparing the Server Distribution Point To prepare the server distribution point, you need to accomplish these tasks:

- Share two of the folders you just created in the ZAK distribution point: \Setup and \NetApps. For \Setup, provide read-only permissions to the Everyone global group. For \NetApps, give Change permission to the same global group.
- Create an AppUser global group on your Windows NT Server 4.0 PDC, using the User Manager for Domains utility.

- Create a Users folder on your network server, and assign to the Everyone global group Full Control permissions to this folder. This will be the shared folder where your AppStation users store their data.
- Create user accounts for each individual, using NT Server's User Manager for Domains utility. Assign each AppStation account to the AppUser group, and specify the Applogon.bat login script. This script is provided as part of the Zero Administration Kit; you'll edit it a bit later in the process.
- Create a Zaksetup user account for yourself to manage the AppStations from. This user account should be part of the Domain Admins global group and use the Zaksetup.bat login script (which is also included in the ZAK package and will require editing).

Step 5: Editing Scripts You have to edit three scripts that are needed to make ZAK work properly. These scripts contain generic values that must be adapted to specify your company name, product IDs, and other key information. As usual with editing scripts, use a text editor such as Notepad, or if you prefer to use Word or WordPad, make sure to save the script as Text Only with absolutely no formatting. You can find these scripts in the \Zak\Scripts folder. Before you edit them, you have to clear their read-only attributes.

- In Msbatch.inf, the script used to custom-configure Windows 95 workstations, change the generic information included for ProductID, ComputerName, Name, and Org. Also check to ensure that the ZAK Wizard has correctly incorporated the network, workgroup, and other locations you specified in Step 3. (Msbatch.inf isn't used if you're installing ZAK on NT 4.0 Workstation systems.)

CAUTION

The generic script includes asterisks surrounding these entries. The asterisks are simply there to call your attention to them; they should be deleted before you run the script.

- In Applogon.bat, the login script that will be used by AppStations, replace the following two values with your network's server and share names: <\\office application server\share> and \\<dist-server>\<user share>. (These values are contained in NET USE commands.) After you finish, copy Applogon.bat to the NetLogon share folder on your PDC.
- In Zaksetup.bat, the login script you will use in managing AppStations, edit the `net use o:` and `net use s:` commands to reflect your server name and the Netapps and Setup folders you've created. For example, if your server name is HEADQUARTERS, the statements would normally read

```
net use o: \\HEADQUARTERS\NETAPPS
net use s: \\HEADQUARTERS\SETUP
```

  Then, copy ZAKSETUP.BAT to the NetLogon share folder on your PDC.

Step 6: Building Your First ZAK Client PC Now you're ready to build your first ZAK client PC. You can also follow these instructions to build additional ZAK clients once you're satisfied with how everything is working.

1. Create a network boot disk that will start the client workstation and connect it to your PDC. If you have network cards compatible with the Windows NT Server 4.0 Network Client Administration Tool, this step will have been performed automatically through the ZAK Wizard. Otherwise, you'll have to make the disk manually, including the correct real-mode driver files for your Ethernet card (see the card's documentation).
2. Log onto your NT Server Network as a member of the Domain Admins global group; this should run the ZAksetup.bat logon script you installed in Step 5.
3. Browse to the S:\Win95 folder. (Zaksetup.bat maps the S:\ drive to the \Setup folder.)
4. Run setup to install Windows, using the Msbatch.inf file you edited earlier. Microsoft suggests streamlining the process with the following command:

   ```
   SETUP /iw /is /id MSBATCH.INF
   ```
5. On the final reboot in the Windows 95 installation process, log onto the network again as the same Domain Admins user. At this point, Msbatch.inf runs the Internet Explorer and Windows 95 Service Release setup programs.
6. The Windows 95 installation has placed Start menu shortcuts on the local desktop, but you want AppStation users to access shortcuts from the network. Therefore, you must copy the shortcuts from the local C:\Windows\Start Menu folder to identically named folders on the network server's \NetApps share, which is mapped to the O:\ drive on the client workstation.

This completes the installation of ZAK on a Windows 95 workstation; at this point, a user should be able to log in and see the restricted AppStation desktop. In reality, you'll have some tweaking and troubleshooting to do before you get this working exactly as you want. Basic ZAK troubleshooting is covered in Appendix A of the ZAK Administrator's Guide.

NOTE In particular, you may want to edit your System Policy files (Config.pol for Windows 95; Ntconfig.pol for NT 4.0) to get Office working exactly the way you want it to. To do so, you'll need access to multiple Policy templates, which means you will have to update the copy of System Policy Editor that may have been installed with Windows 95. You can either copy the version provided with NT Server onto a Windows 95 workstation, or upgrade to the version provided with the Office 97 Resource Kit. ■

Windows NT Terminal Server and Office 97

Windows NT Terminal Server adapts Windows NT Server 4.0 with a multiuser core that can host multiple, simultaneous 32-bit Windows client sessions running on Windows 3.1, Windows 95, Windows NT, and new *Windows Terminals*. Using an add-on product, pICAsso from Citrix, even non-Windows systems such as Macintosh computers and X Windows terminals can be used to deliver 32-bit Windows applications to users.

Windows NT Terminal Server uses the Remote Desktop Protocol, a proprietary extension of the industry-standard T.Share/T.120 protocol, to communicate between workstation and server. T.120 is the same protocol that is used in Microsoft's NetMeeting Internet-conferencing software and a wide variety of third-party products. For security, T.120 transmissions may be encrypted.

At the workstation, Windows NT Terminal Server installs client software capable of booting, connecting to the server, and presenting or displaying the Windows user interface—but little else. Application processing and operating system functions are handled at the server, as you would expect in a traditional "terminal-to-host" architecture. In the Windows world, this is the thinnest client Microsoft has ever introduced.

For organizations discouraged by the complexity of new Windows rollouts, updates, and upgrades, Windows NT Terminal Server offers the potential for major TCO benefits: with the exception of one piece of client software, all application and operating system upgrades are handled at the server. Windows NT Terminal Server also provides access to Microsoft Office 97 and other 32-bit Windows applications on devices that could not otherwise run them effectively, potentially extending the life of older PCs and Macintosh computers. It may also use scarce network bandwidth more effectively than running server-based applications on networked workstations.

Having said all this, there are some drawbacks to Windows NT Terminal Server for Office administrators considering it as a solution for deploying Office 97.

First, licensing fees for Terminal Server are substantial. Second, Microsoft has structured its Office 97 licensing arrangements to prevent you from using Terminal Server as a way of saving money on Office 97 licenses. For example, if you have 100 Windows terminals that use Office at least once in awhile, but only 50 of them use Office at any given time, you still must purchase 100 Office licenses.

Second, application installation may not be 100 percent seamless. For example, Windows applications assume they are installing in single-user mode, and Microsoft-provided compatibility scripts must be executed at runtime to ensure that installations work properly. Microsoft is providing scripts for Office 97, but you need to make sure that they are available for any other applications you plan to run.

Third, with all processing offloaded to the server, you will need far more powerful servers than you may be accustomed to purchasing—and, quite likely, more of them as well. You'll also have to worry about implementing load balancing and scalable multiprocessor servers to maximize the performance of all your servers—a fairly complex task. In early tests of Terminal Server, each CPU and 128MB of RAM could handle a maximum of 15 users.

For all this, application performance typically won't rival that of today's mainstream PCs. These performance and customization limitations mean that Windows NT Terminal Server will probably be most popular in task-oriented environments that have only moderate requirements for access to industrial-strength applications such as Word and Excel.

Finally, as important as server reliability is already, it will be much more important in a Terminal Server environment. With PCs, if the server fails, people can still run applications locally. With Terminal Server, if the server goes down, no work gets done. You'll have to decide for yourself whether NT Server 4.0 is up to this stringent challenge. At minimum, expect to invest more money and time in ensuring reliability through fault-tolerant hardware and other means.

Looking to Future Versions of Office and Windows

Although Office 2000 and Windows NT 5.0 Server have not yet been released, Microsoft has publicly offered some insights into these products that will be valuable in your planning efforts.

According to Microsoft, Office 2000 will be "componentized," meaning that

- Office administrators will have more flexibility and control over which components are installed on each client workstation.
- Office 2000 components will be installable "on-demand," so if a user needs to insert a chart but does not have the Office chart applet installed, the applet can be installed automatically.
- Office 2000 will be "self-repairing"; if a file is damaged or missing, Office 2000 can find and reinstall it. A version of this feature is already available in Office 98 for the Macintosh.

Windows 98 has been released with few, if any of the TCO enhancements that were once anticipated. However, Windows NT 5.0 is promised to have IntelliMirror management technologies that will provide the following:

- Centralized application and operating system maintenance that should dramatically reduce the need for Office administrators to visit individual desktop workstations
- Server mirroring of desktop configurations, allowing users to log onto their own customized desktops from any workstation on the network—and allowing administrators to re-create an individual desktop's data, applications, preferences, and policies on a new PC quickly, after an old PC fails

With capabilities such as these, some organizations are likely to find that waiting for Office 2000 and NT Server 5.0 may be a better TCO strategy than deploying the Zero Administration Kit or Windows NT Terminal Server today. ●

CHAPTER 33

Maximizing Office Security

A key element of managing Office in today's organizations is making sure that business-critical Office documents remain secure, and only get into the hands of people authorized to see them. This means designing a multilayered security strategy that takes advantage of the following:

- Security features built into Office applications, including password protection
- Third-party security solutions, such as up-to-date anti-virus software
- Security built into the network operating system of your choice, such as access controls

This chapter reviews each of these topics, beginning with the precautions built into Office.

Passwords and Encryption in Microsoft Word

Word 97/98 (and Excel 97/98) enable you to protect documents with passwords. When documents are protected with passwords, they are encrypted using a relatively powerful algorithm called RC4. This is a more secure encryption algorithm than was provided in earlier versions of Office.

CAUTION

If you save a password-protected Word 97 document to an older version of Word, such as Word 6/95, password protection is lost, and you will have to reapply it in the older version of Word.

NOTE RC4 password protection is illegal in France. If Regional Settings are set to French in the Windows Control Panel, Word users cannot open password-protected Word 97 documents. If Regional Settings are reset to another locale, the files can be opened.

You can protect entire documents, preventing them from being opened, or permitting them to be opened but not modified.

CAUTION

If you allow a file to be opened but not modified, a user can still save it under another name, change the name in Windows Explorer, and copy the new file over the original file. In other words, this approach is not especially secure.

Word users can also protect the following specific elements of a document:

- Tracked changes (revisions)
- Comments (annotations)
- Forms or sections of forms

Password Protecting an Entire Word Document

To protect an entire document, follow these steps:

1. Choose File, Save As.
2. In the Save As dialog box, click Options. The Save options dialog box opens (see Figure 33.1).
3. If you want to require a password for opening the file, enter the password in the Password to Open text box.

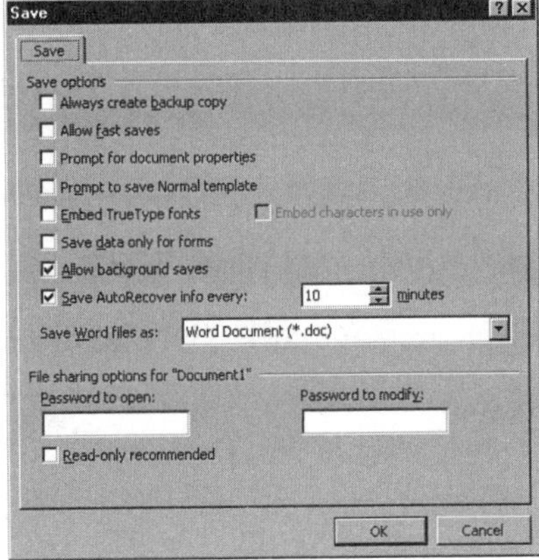

FIGURE 33.1
You can enter passwords to open or modify files in Word's Save dialog box.

4. If you want to require a password for modifying the file, enter the password in the Password to Modify text box.
5. Click OK.
6. Reenter the password or passwords in the confirmation boxes Word displays, and click OK.
7. Click Save to save the file.

CAUTION

If you forget your password, you will not be able to be open your document. Even more serious, if one of your colleagues forgets a password, or leaves the company and does not share the password with someone, you will not be able to open his or her documents. If your workgroup uses passwords, make sure copies of these passwords are stored securely—ideally, in a locked, fireproof, waterproof safe—where the company can access them in an emergency.

Using Word's Read-Only Recommended Option

If you need less security than password protection, but nonetheless want to discourage users from overwriting or changing specific files, use the Read-Only Recommended option in the Save options dialog box. Selecting this option provides very "light" security: when this box is checked, Word displays a dialog box as a file is opened, encouraging the user to open the file as read-only. If the user does so, and then makes edits, the file must be saved under a different name.

Read-Only Recommended can be checked whether or not you have set a password for the document.

Protecting Elements of a Word Document

In some cases, you may want to permit changes to a document, but only within carefully circumscribed parameters. For example, you may want to permit changes for the following:

- Only with the Track Changes feature turned on (that is, so all changes will be tracked)
- Only to permit Comments (annotations), but not to add or remove text from the document
- Only to allow users to fill out electronic forms—or sections of forms—but not make changes to the text, layout, or formatting of the underlying form itself

To set any of these restrictions, choose Tools, Protect Document. The Protect Document dialog box opens (see Figure 33.2). Select the way you want to allow users to edit the document. If you want, enter a password. Click on OK. If you've entered a password, you'll be asked to confirm it; do so and click on OK again.

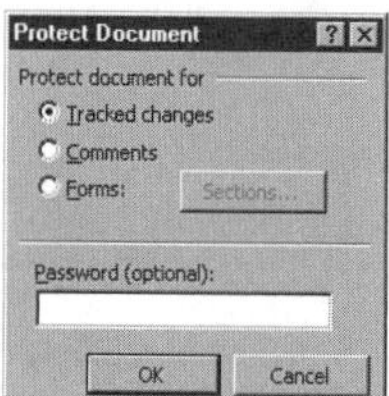

FIGURE 33.2
Choosing how to protect portions of your document.

NOTE When a document is protected in this fashion, the user can open and read it, but not make changes other than those you have permitted. If you don't specify a password, your document will still be protected, but a user can turn off the protection simply by choosing Tools, Unprotect Document, clearing the selected button, and clicking on OK.

If your document has more than one section, and you want to protect it for forms, you can protect only certain sections. Choose the Forms option button, and click on Sections. The Section Protection dialog box appears (see Figure 33.3). Clear the check boxes associated with any sections you do not need to protect.

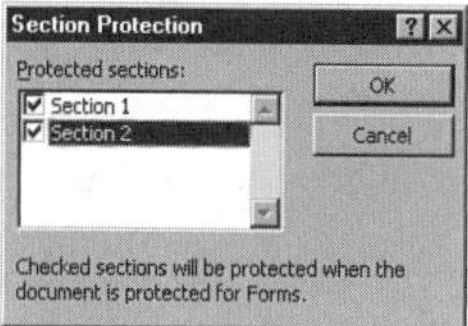

FIGURE 33.3
Protecting only certain sections of a document for forms.

This feature allows you to incorporate a form that cannot be changed into a document that includes other, editable components.

TIP You can use Word's document passwords and protection together. For example, you can specify a password that is required to open a document, and also restrict users to making only tracked changes even after they open the document, unless they present a different password.

Using Excel's Worksheet and Workbook Protection Tools

Like Word, Excel offers two types of password protection, both of which use RC4 encryption (except in France, where it is illegal):

- You can require a password to open a workbook, modify a workbook, or both
- You can either protect a specific worksheet or an entire workbook, or specific elements within a worksheet or workbook

Password Protecting an Entire Excel Workbook

To protect an entire Excel 97/98 workbook, follow these steps:

1. Choose File, Save As.
2. In the Save As dialog box, click Options. The Save options dialog box opens (see Figure 33.4).

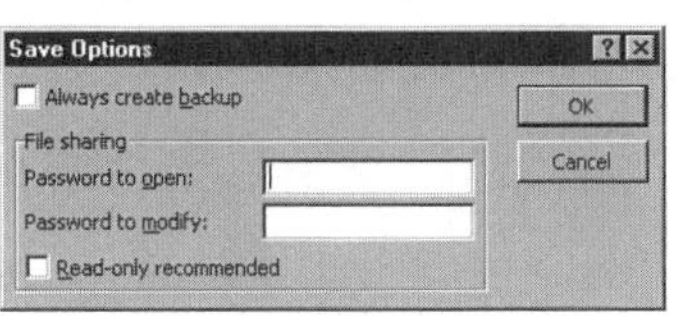

FIGURE 33.4
You can enter passwords required to open or modify Excel workbooks in Excel's Save Options dialog box.

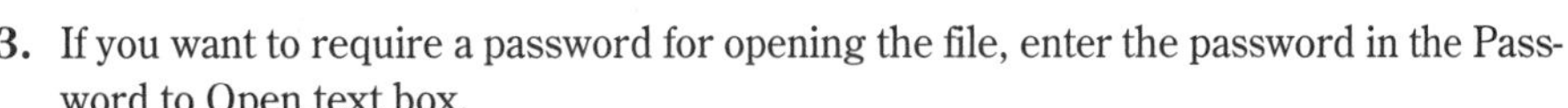

3. If you want to require a password for opening the file, enter the password in the Password to Open text box.
4. If you want to require a password for modifying the file, enter the password in the Password to Modify text box.
5. Click on OK.
6. Reenter the password or passwords in the confirmation boxes Excel displays, and click on OK.
7. Click on Save to save the file.

Protecting Elements of an Excel Workbook

In some cases, you may want to limit changes to an Excel workbook but not prevent them altogether. You might want to permit changes only in a specific worksheet within a workbook, for example, or you may only want to protect certain aspects of your workbook. You might want to prevent others from adding or deleting worksheets. Excel 97 and Excel 98 give you this flexibility.

Password Protecting an Individual Worksheet

To password-protect one worksheet in an Excel 97/98 workbook, perform the following steps:

1. Display the worksheet you want to protect.
2. Choose Tools, Protection, Protect Sheet. The Protect Sheet dialog box opens (see Figure 33.5).
3. Check the boxes associated with the elements you want to protect. (All three boxes are checked by default.)
   - Checking Contents protects the values and text in cells, and the contents and appearance of charts.
   - Checking Objects prevents unauthorized users from moving, editing, deleting, or resizing graphics in a worksheet or a chart.
   - Checking Scenarios prevents unauthorized users from changing the definitions associated with Excel scenarios.
4. If you want, enter a password, and click on OK.
5. If you entered a password, reenter it and click on OK to confirm the password. The document is now protected.

FIGURE 33.5
The Protect Sheet dialog box.

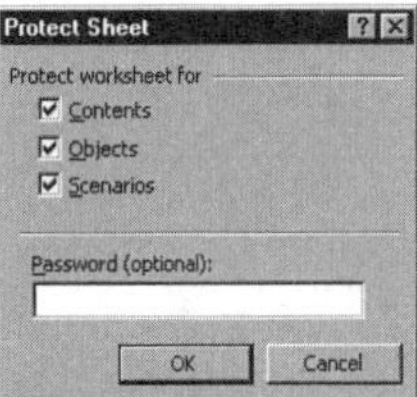

> **CAUTION**
>
> You can't protect a workbook after you've shared it, except by turning off sharing—which deletes all the change histories Excel may have been tracking. You *can*, however, password protect elements of a worksheet or workbook, and *then* share it with the protections intact.

For more information about shared workbooks, refer to Chapter 12.

Protecting Elements of a Workbook

Even if you require a password to open or modify a workbook, you can superimpose a second level of protection for the structure and windows contained in that workbook.

Protecting a workbook's structure prevents individual worksheets from being added, deleted, moved, hidden, unhidden, or renamed. Protecting its windows prevents users from closing, hiding, unhiding, resizing, or moving them. This tactic can be especially helpful if you've used Excel to create an interactive presentation with clickable buttons, where you want the windows to display in a specific way.

To protect the structure or windows in a workbook, or both, perform the following steps:

1. Choose Tools, Protection, Protect Workbook. The Protect Workbook dialog box opens (see Figure 33.6).

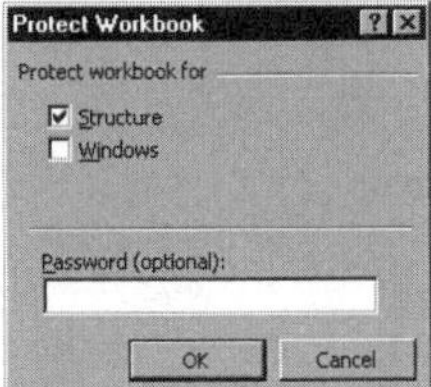

FIGURE 33.6
The Protect Workbook dialog box.

2. Check the Structure and/or Windows check boxes.
3. If you want to use a password, enter it in the Password text box.
4. Click on OK.
5. If you have entered a password, confirm it and click on OK again. The workbook is now protected as you've specified.

Protecting Against Office Macro Viruses

A macro virus is an undesired program that attaches itself to a template or document created in Word, or to a workbook or workbook template created in Excel. In Office 97, macro viruses are written in Visual Basic for Applications, although in earlier versions of Word, they were written in WordBasic, the macro language then provided by Microsoft.

NOTE In most cases, viruses written in WordBasic are disabled when the documents that contain them are opened in Word 97, and the macros are automatically converted to Visual Basic for Applications.

When a user opens the file, the macro is executed and the virus runs, installing itself on the user's system. Typically, the virus runs immediately, because most viruses use one of the names Word sets aside for automatically executing macros, such as AutoOpen. Macro viruses range from the innocuous to the disastrous. By many reports, more than half of all large corporate sites have encountered them. Among the more common symptoms of macro viruses have been the following:

- In Word, you cannot save a file except by saving it as a template
- Odd error messages appear—for example, `STOP ALL FRENCH NUCLEAR TESTING IN THE PACIFIC`
- Odd, unexplained edits appear in your document

Word's and Excel's Macro Warning Dialog Box

Word and Excel 97 provide limited built-in protection against macro viruses. By default, when you open a document or workbook containing macros, a warning lets you know that there are macros in the file (see Figure 33.7). In Word, the dialog box also appears if the document contains customizations, such as specialized toolbars or menus. Neither program can determine whether the macro or customization is actually harmful.

When the dialog box appears, you have four choices:

- **Disable Macros.** Allows the file to open but prevents any macros from running. This protects against virus infection but may also prevent the document or workbook from behaving the way it should.
- **Enable Macros.** Allows macros to load; users can choose this option if they "trust" the document.
- **Do Not Open.** Simply cancels the process of opening the document
- **Tell Me More.** Displays Word or Excel's Help window related to macro viruses

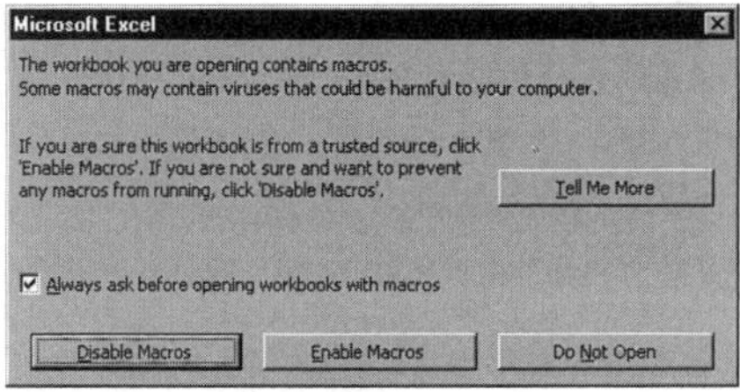

FIGURE 33.7
Word or Excel can warn you of the presence of macros in a file.

If you (or a colleague) aren't expecting to find macros in a file, the appearance of the macro warning dialog box can be a tip-off that the file is actually infected. However, many users are unfamiliar with macros and may not realize when they are supposed to be present. In addition, users who are comfortable with macros may find the dialog box annoying. (You can turn it off by clearing the Always Ask Before Opening Workbooks with Macros check box, or by choosing Tools, Options, clicking on the General tab, and clearing the Macro Virus Protection check box.)

TIP In Word 97, if a document once contained macros but they have been removed, support structures for those macros remain, and these support structures trigger the macro warning dialog box. The only ways to eliminate the warnings are to save the file as an RTF file or copy its contents to a new file.

Using Protection.doc to Protect the Normal Template

In Word 97, many viruses infect the Normal template because once they are present in Normal, they can infect every document Word opens—and propagate easily to other computers as documents are shared. Therefore, one strategy for preventing macro virus infection in Word is to password protect Normal. Microsoft provides a document, Protection.doc, designed to add this password protection.

Protection.doc is available at **www.microsoft.com/office/antivirus/word/normaldot.htm**. After you retrieve it, follow these steps:

1. Open Protection.doc as a Word document.
2. You may see the macro warning dialog box discussed earlier. Click Enable Macros to permit the document's macros to load.
3. Click on Yes.
4. Click on Accept. The AutoProtection dialog box appears.
5. Enter a password in the Enter New Password text box.
6. Confirm the password in the Confirm Password text box.
7. Click on OK. AutoProtection is installed.
8. Restart Windows.

Adding password protection to Normal means that whenever a user wants to record or edit a macro, he or she has to enter the password.

After the password is entered, the Normal template remains unprotected for the remainder of the Word editing session. So if you open a virus-infected document after allowing Normal to be edited, you can still be infected. In addition, if you use Word as your email editor (via the WordMail feature), a portion of Word remains open even after you exit the program. Therefore, when you restart Word, Normal password protection may already be turned off if you manually turned it off in your previous Word session.

One more limitation: when Normal is password protected, it is also encrypted, so no other anti-virus software can disinfect it if it *is* infected.

Using Anti-Virus Software

The hard reality is that the best virus protection is to purchase and install anti-virus software on both individual workstations *and network servers*, and to update it regularly—at least once a month with new virus definition files downloaded from the Web. Table 33.1 lists software packages that protect networks against Word 97 and Excel 97 macro viruses.

Table 33.1 Network Anti-Virus Software

Product Name	Web Site
Computer Associates InocuLAN 4.0	`www.cheyenne.com`
Dr Solomon's Anti-Virus Toolkit	`www.drsolomon.com`
Network Associates NetShield 3.0	`www.nai.com`
Symantec Norton AntiVirus 4.0	`www.symantec.com`

In selecting anti-virus software, obviously your number one concern has to be effectiveness: does the software recognize all or virtually all macro viruses, and is it updated at least once a month to reflect new viruses?

There are, however, other issues to consider as well:

- You will also want a product that allows you to distribute updates to individual workstations from a central location, avoiding the necessity of visiting every workstation to apply updates every month (or even more).
- Network anti-virus software can vary widely in its impact on your server performance, especially in NetWare environments where it is loaded as a NetWare Loadable Module (NLM).
- Some anti-virus software developers, such as Symantec, have begun to charge for updates after a specific number of free updates. Take into account the cost and management effort required to pay for these updates.

Securing Access Databases

Microsoft Access provides several complementary means of limiting access to databases. These include the following:

- Restricting user access through startup options
- Requiring a password in order to open a database
- Protecting the source code in a database by saving it as an MDE file
- Encrypting a database to prevent it from being viewed with a text or disk editor
- Setting user-level security similar to that provided for files and folders in NT Server and other network operating systems

Each of these options is covered briefly in the following text. They represent all the security many organizations will ever need. If database security is truly business-critical to your organization, however, you may want to read the following quote, from a Microsoft-published paper entitled *Microsoft Access for Windows 95 Security*:

> Microsoft Access is designed to be the most secure desktop database management system you can buy. However, it has no security rating with the U.S. government or any other certifying body, and it is not guaranteed by Microsoft to be secure. Skilled hackers with enough time and computing resources, and a desire to break into your database, could crack Microsoft Access security. If you have applications that require absolute security, you should consider using a server database such as Microsoft SQL Server on the Microsoft Windows NT operating system, and a compiled application programming language such as Microsoft Visual C/C++.

Restricting User Access Through Startup Options

If your security needs are not extensive, and you aren't protecting your database against sophisticated users, one option is to use startup options. You can use these to restrict access for the following:

- Default menus
- Toolbars
- The database window
- Special keys

The following procedure assumes that you have created a startup form and custom menu bar that includes the commands to which you *do* want users to have access.

To restrict user access through startup options, follow these steps:

1. Choose Tools, Startup.
2. Choose the startup form you want to use from the Display Form drop-down box.
3. Choose the custom menu bar you want from the Menu Bar drop-down box.
4. Click on the Advanced button.
5. Clear these check boxes:
   - Allow Full Menus
   - Allow Default Shortcut Menus
   - Display Database Window
   - Allow Built-in Toolbars
   - Allow Toolbar/Menu Changes
   - Use Access Special Keys
6. Click on OK.

CAUTION

Users who are familiar with Access can still bypass these settings by pressing Shift as Access loads the database. You can set the database's Visual Basic property AllowBypassKey to False to prevent this.

Requiring a Password to Open an Access Database

Like Word and Excel, Access enables you to password protect a database, thereby preventing users from opening it unless they have the password.

NOTE Unlike Word and Excel, Access's password-protection feature does not control the rights users have to modify a database. This is done with user-level security features, as described later. ■

To password protect a database, perform the following steps:

1. Choose File, Open Database.
2. Check the Exclusive check box to specify that no other user can share access to the database while you have it open.
3. Click on Open. The database opens.
4. Choose Tools, Security, Set Database Password.
5. Enter your password in the Password box, and click on OK.
6. Confirm your password in the Verify box, and click on OK.

CAUTION

Although it is always important that your organization have a secure way to access passwords used by individuals who work there, this is even more critical with Access databases, which almost always store information of critical value to large numbers of people.

Protecting Access Database Source Code

In Access 97, you can save a database as an MDE file that contains all the information but none of the Visual Basic source code you may want to protect. Working in an MDE file, users have access to tables, queries, relationships, and macros, but they cannot view, modify, create, import, or export reports, forms, or modules.

Microsoft points out that creating an MDE file could make it more difficult to keep data consistent; users may be entering different information in MDB and MDE files, which would then have to be reconciled. As a result, Microsoft suggests using MDE files as front-ends to applications where the data is stored in a single database on the back-end database server.

To create an MDE file from an existing database, perform the following steps:

1. Choose File, Close to close the database.
2. Choose Tools, Database Utilities, Make MDE File. The Save As MDE dialog box opens.
3. Browse to and select the database you want to create an MDE file from.
4. Click on the Make MDE button. The Save MDE As dialog box opens.
5. Enter a filename and click on Save.

CAUTION

Because it's likely that you'll need to edit reports, forms, or modules, make sure you keep a current backup of the database.

MDE files are not "runtime files," which is to say they still require the presence of Access 97 in order to run. However, if you want to provide database information to a user who does not have Access 97 installed, such as a user of Microsoft Office Standard Edition or Small Business Edition, you have two ways to do so:

- Using tools in Microsoft Office 97 Professional Edition, you can create a runtime file from an MDE file.
- Using the Access Snapshot Viewer, distribute a static "snapshot" of an Access report containing only the specific data you want to share. The Access Snapshot Viewer is included in Service Release 1 or is downloadable separately at **www.microsoft.com/accessdev/articles/snapshot.htm**.

Encrypting Access Databases

Access databases can be encrypted using the same RC4 encryption algorithm available to other Office applications, except in France where RC4 is illegal. Once encrypted, a text editor or any other utility cannot read Access databases. As with most security precautions, there is a tradeoff; in this case, it's a performance penalty of approximately 15 percent. To encrypt a database, choose Tools, Security, Encrypt/Decrypt Database.

This runs the User-Level Security Wizard, which walks you through the process of encrypting the database. If you choose to save the encrypted database with the same name and in the same location as the original, Access will first proceed through the entire encryption; once encryption has been successful, it will delete the original unencrypted file.

Providing User-Level Security

Access 97 provides both share-level and user-level security. Share-level security assigns passwords to individual databases, as you've already seen. In Access 97, user-level security looks a lot more like the rights and permissions you might expect to use with folders and files on a Windows NT Server (or NetWare)-based network.

As an Office administrator, you can grant specific permissions to individuals or groups of users for specific actions they can take on specific objects. When the user logs onto Access, he or she enters a name and password. Then, every time he or she attempts to perform an action—such as reading data or modifying the database design—Access checks its internal workgroup information file, to see if the user has the right to perform this action. If so, the user can keep working; if not, the user encounters a message box stating that permission is denied. By default, all users have rights to perform all actions on all objects, unless you specify otherwise.

To secure a database with user-level security, perform the following steps:

1. Double-click Wrkgadm.exe in the Windows 95 System folder (or the System32 folder in Windows NT Workstation). The Workgroup Administrator utility runs. You'll be asked to enter Name and Organization data, as well as a workgroup ID number of your choice. Write these down—precisely—and store the information off-premises. You'll need the exact, case-sensitive information to restore your workgroup information file if it's ever damaged.
2. Run the User-Level Security Wizard, which walks you through the process of identifying which objects you want to secure, and then creates a new, secured copy of your database, where only you have permissions to those objects.
3. Log onto your new database, and choose Tools, Security, User and Group Accounts. In the User and Group Accounts dialog box, create user and group accounts and assign specific permissions to them.

Combining Operating System Security with Application Security

You can enhance all the security mechanisms built into specific Office applications by using the security built into your network operating system.

Suppose that you are running Windows NT Server and you have a shared folder containing files to be used by your entire workgroup. One of these files, however, perhaps next year's salary projections, needs to be kept strictly confidential. If the file is stored on a network drive formatted with the NTFS file system (rather than FAT), you can set up file permissions so that only the individuals who *should* access that file can do so.

To limit a file's permissions to a specific user, perform the following steps:

1. Right-click on the file in Windows NT Explorer.
2. Click on Properties. The Properties dialog box opens, listing the properties associated with the file.
3. Click on Security to display the Security tab.
4. Click on Permissions. The File Permissions dialog box opens, showing that everyone currently has permission to access the file. (NT doesn't know about any Word, Excel, or Access passwords that may be built into the file itself.)

5. Make sure the Everyone group is selected, and click on Remove. Now, *nobody* has access to the file.
6. Click on Add. The Add Users and Groups dialog box opens.
7. Click on Show Users to display a list of the users on your network.
8. Select the name of the user you want to have access to the file.
9. Choose Full Control from the Type of Access drop-down box.
10. Click on OK three times.

In NetWare and IntranetWare 4.*x*, you can achieve much the same result by setting file system trustee rights using the NetWare Administrator Windows-based utility.

Integrating Office with Document Management Systems

Yet another way to improve the security of Office documents is to integrate Office with an Open Document Management (ODMA)-compatible Document Management System. Systems like these typically replace the Open and Save dialog boxes in Office applications, providing more sophisticated options, including security features such as the following:

- More control over accessing, moving, or removing documents
- Mechanisms that allow documents to be "checked out" and "returned"
- Locks on documents
- Security mechanisms that follow distributed documents

Suppliers of ODMA-compliant Document Management Systems include the following:

- Documentum, Inc. (telephone 888-362-3367, or on the Web at **www.documentum.com**)
- Novell Groupwise (telephone 801-222-6000, or on the Web at **www.novell.com/groupwise**)
- PC DOCS, Inc. (telephone 800-933-3627, or on the Web at **www.pcdocs.com**)
- Saros (telephone 800-827-2767, or on the Web at **www.saros.com**)

CHAPTER 34

Supporting Office

At first glance, the task of supporting the entire Microsoft Office suite can appear overwhelming. The sheer range of possible problems is too large for any single individual to grasp and manage effectively, and the complexity rises exponentially with the number of supported users.

On closer scrutiny, you can find ways to make the required support a bit easier. After some initial planning, you might take things a step further and incorporate custom help features into your organization. This chapter helps you develop a plan for Office support and exposes you to a variety of tools you might find useful.

The Office Help Desk: A Brief Overview

A help desk exists to serve the needs of technology users. Whether your organization is large or small, you probably have some incarnation of a help desk; perhaps it's one part-time volunteer (who already has a full-time job), or perhaps you have a full-time support department. Your help desk might exist as a phone number for users to call when they are having trouble, or it might include a live person who comes to users' aid. The sole purpose of a help desk is to get the user of technology productive again, as soon as possible.

Who Pays for Support?

To keep things in perspective, remember that a help desk is usually considered overhead in an organization. The cost of maintaining a help desk comes right out of company profits, and businesses typically attempt to minimize such costs. Unfortunately, with the growing complexity of applications such as Microsoft Office, the help desk is needed now more than ever. And this issue is not unique to a particular business—the escalating costs of support are affecting businesses in all industries.

Businesses are complaining to anyone who will listen. One result of business protests to Microsoft about the increasing costs of support is the Zero Administration Kit (ZAK) discussed in Chapter 32.

A help desk must cover a wide range of subjects, from basic hardware to detailed feature levels of program applications. This chapter suggests ways to make Office support and the associated administrative functions a little bit easier.

Common Goals for All Help Desks

The purpose of a help desk is to assist users in resolving difficulties that arise while using their computers. Effective assistance includes good communication, the ability to solve problems, and a system that incorporates the knowledge and experience you have gained from solving past problems. After you have a system of support in place, you'll want to measure its effectiveness; but before you can, you'll need to define your goals.

Common help desk goals include the following:

- *Provide expert coverage of targeted subject material.* Becoming an expert on all features of a given product might not be possible, but the help desk should always be an expert on the products and features required by your organization. Technical reference material should be readily available, and several are recommended later in this chapter, including Microsoft TechNet and the Knowledge Bases.
- *Provide quick problem resolution.* When a problem comes to the attention of the help desk, it should be resolved within set time parameters or guidelines. Tracking tools are usually required to maintain consistency and measure results.
- *Minimize involvement of help desk personnel.* Also known as "call avoidance," this strategy attempts to make all users self-sufficient. Doing so requires training of users in the

required applications, availability of self-help resources, and—often—implementation of policies and procedures.

- *Reduce actual visits of a support technician.* Having a technician walk over and assist a user is usually the most expensive method of support (although the most preferred by users). Software tools are available for controlling the user's computer screen from a remote location, enabling you to "talk them through" a problem without visiting them in person.
- *Build on existing talent and knowledge base.* If your users have previously been trained in WordPerfect, respect that knowledge and encourage them to use the WordPerfect help features in Word. If you notice users developing specialized skills, encourage them to be a resource for peers.

One Size Does Not Fit All

Particular needs of any organization vary, and so will the organization's underlying support structure. The most effective help desk is designed according to business requirements. The amount of staffing might range from a single individual with general knowledge to a fully supervised and managed department of technical specialists.

From a business perspective, the best help desk is lean and mean, with the fewest number of dedicated technicians able to cover the widest range of problems.

Help desks large enough to appear on the company organizational chart usually start with a minimum of one to three generalists, and with three or more, they develop a hierarchy of specialty and supervisory responsibility. Larger organizations often specify minimum support headcount ratios, such as one support person for every 40–50 users, but suggesting a recommended ratio outside the context of your particular business is meaningless. At a minimum, management should observe the effectiveness and potential of the help desk and allocate resources accordingly.

Outsourcing is a method of supplementing, or replacing, your help desk function. When you *outsource*, you pay an external organization to provide technical support to yours. Support implementation might include software tools, telephone numbers to call, or even onsite technicians. Sometimes a company turns to outsourcing when the help desk fails to meet expectations.

Change with the Times

Your help desk should be flexible. Understand your business operations and the nature of tasks performed; try to provide the required training to get the tasks accomplished. After establishing this base knowledge, you can quickly move on to advanced support. Actually, you'll have no choice, because support requirements change as users become more proficient—they start asking more complex questions.

A new installation of Office requires support on basic Office functions such as file creation, saving, and importing of existing information. When the dust settles, users start asking about formatting features, integrating other applications, and so on. Experienced users start demanding more complex training on advanced features, and the help desk is charged with meeting this demand.

Knowing Your Target Audience

To run an effective help desk, you have to know your audience. Understand your users' priorities and what they need from technology. Users don't always have the time for you to ask such questions, but you can observe the tasks they accomplish and determine the role of technology in your organization.

The "80:20 rule" applies well to the help desk. This rule suggests that 80 percent of your time and effort will be spent satisfying 20 percent of your user population. This group will include both your brightest workers and your novices, who stand out because of some particular requirement the majority of your users either never notice or choose to ignore. Come up with a strategy in advance to handle this 20 percent, and you can save yourself lots of headaches.

These are the people who will impact your support efforts the most:

- *Busy people who have no time for training classes but expect personal service at their convenience.* You'll waste time repeating material previously available in class. Strategy: schedule training classes at a variety of times; provide alternative forms of education; give them easy access to self-help tools.
- *Fearful people who tend to avoid technology (fear of breaking something, fear of public display of their ignorance, and so on).* They stick with what they know, avoiding features or methods that might make their lives easier. Strategy: demonstrate tasks with recordings; provide help via remote-control programs; find them a technology mentor; start a support group.
- *Stubborn people who believe they are experts, refuse to listen to others, and in the end do things their own way.* They tend to ignore procedures and policies they don't understand. Strategy: implement System Policies for Office (see Chapter 32); educate them in the value of standardization; convince them they are part of the ultimate solution.
- *People who simply don't care and are probably in the wrong job.* They aren't consistent in how they use technology and don't care about the resulting impact on others. Strategy: suggest that computer skills are valuable for anyone; demonstrate the impact of not following standards in the organization; ask management for assistance with these individuals.

When the Help Desk Fails

If you don't handle these individuals properly, they're likely to have a negative impact on your company. Errant users tend to stray from the imposed standards created for efficiency. For example, one standard might state that Word documents are to be created with consistent styles to foster workgroup productivity and document re-use. If people ignore this simple rule, they nullify any productivity gains from Word features such as the table of contents or authorities in the later stages of document construction, and their work might require hours of cleanup effort. A single poorly constructed document can have a chain-reaction effect that impacts other employees, managers, executives, the secretarial pool, and support staff (even temporary staffing agencies) and might even result in missed deadlines and lost business.

Measuring Help Desk Effectiveness

When an organization invests in an official help desk, it then wants to know if it's getting its money's worth. One way to measure effectiveness is to record the frequency and outcome of a particular activity. A common example is the number of help desk phone calls answered per day. In itself, this number might not hold much information (you don't know the nature of the call, whether the user was actually helped, and so on), so refine your measurements until they align with your intended goals:

- How many calls are related to Word versus Excel or Access?
- How long does it take to solve the average page-formatting problem?
- How many users have called about a troublesome template?
- Is a particular department demanding a disproportionate amount of the help desk resources?
- Are users beginning to ask about a rarely used feature? Perhaps the technology needs of your users have changed. If so, the help desk must adapt accordingly to maintain effectiveness.

A successful help desk continually asks itself these types of questions and acts accordingly. When the help desk is comfortable with providing a guaranteed level of support, it communicates this information to the users in what is known as a service-level agreement.

A service-level agreement is like a contract between the help desk and the users. The help desk agrees, for example, to return all calls within an hour. This simple agreement sets expectations for everyone. Now your users know they can call the help desk, leave a message, and expect a response in a reasonable time period instead of becoming frustrated while waiting in an unknown queue of undisclosed priorities. User satisfaction with the help desk typically increases after you establish minimum service-level agreements. However, a help desk that does not live up to published agreements can quickly become perceived as ineffective. In this example, if the help desk fails to respond within an hour, the users will want to know why they aren't getting the attention they deserve.

Other examples of service-level agreements include

- Designation of supported and nonsupported applications (making it easier for the help desk to say "no")
- Definitions of what is considered an emergency call versus merely high or low priority (removing the politics from assigning call priority)
- Off-hour and weekend support availability
- Guaranteed closure to all calls within a certain time period

Creating a Trouble Ticket Most organizations benefit from maintaining a record of solved help desk problems. One option for doing this is to create a printed help desk ticket, or trouble ticket, for each incident. At a minimum, a trouble ticket should include the time and date, who asked for help, and the problem resolution. If you gather such information, anyone can sort through it to determine how well the help desk is performing.

CAUTION

Unfortunately, the trouble ticket doesn't always provide the whole story. The best measure of a help desk's effectiveness is not the quantity of tickets you process, but the quality of the solutions you provide.

A better system than the printed trouble ticket is a paperless database. A database is easy enough to create, and it provides the obvious benefits of letting you sort, track, and maintain online trouble tickets. Furthermore, you can analyze the data to track trends and measure the effectiveness of the help desk. You can also let users access the database so they can search for solutions on their own.

To start your paperless system, create an online trouble ticket. Depending on your needs and skills, you can design your trouble ticket by using Word, Excel, Access, Outlook (or any combination of these applications) and then save it as a template or form. Here are the key elements typically included:

- Automated data and time field
- User identification from a pop-up list
- Subject category for problem from a pop-up list
- Urgency checklist
- Data-entry fields for problem details
- Data-entry fields for problem tracking and resolution

You don't have to work too hard to create this form; simply choose from among the many types of standard fields and controls that already exist in all Office products, and link to databases that already contain your user list (such as an address book or contact list). Figure 34.1 shows an example of an online trouble ticket. You probably want to create your own custom database of problem categories that apply to your organization and product selection. (See Chapters 11, 14, and 15 for help with standardizing document production, working with Outlook forms, and using Access to streamline data entry.)

After you create your template, store it on a network share available to the help desk staff, and start using it. You'll find that taking advantage of your form's time and date stamp, user information, subject categories, and notes about problem resolution will improve your accuracy and save you a lot of time.

FIGURE 34.1
A simple online form can help you monitor the performance of your help desk.

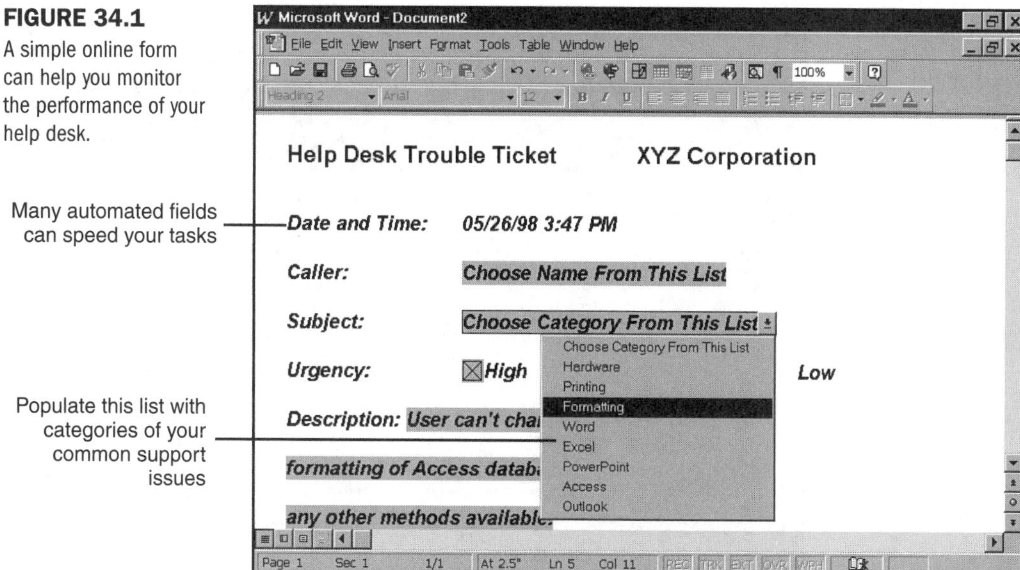

If your users are cooperative, let them fill in and track their own online trouble tickets. They might prefer this option to calling the help desk, especially if you include some sort of automated, immediate response informing them you're receiving and processing their call. Once again, make it as easy as possible to include all necessary information without any hassle.

You can create an Outlook form to gather date, time, and user information automatically, and place a custom button that opens this form on a toolbar. The user can choose the most appropriate problem category from a list in the form and describe the necessary details. The benefit of letting the users fill in the form is that they become more involved in problem resolution. If your form also lets users read about possible solutions to problems, the users might be able to find the information they need without even submitting the ticket. For example, Figure 34.2 shows a collection of trouble tickets stored in Outlook, where viewing and sorting the entire collection is easy, including searches for specific information.

Training Users for an Office Upgrade

Depending on your previous installation of computer applications, a migration to Microsoft Office can be a simple task or a moderately complex one. Okay, a complex one. Most organizations don't take change lightly, and you should never mess with the tools used to create documents, workbooks, presentations, databases, and email without careful planning and understanding.

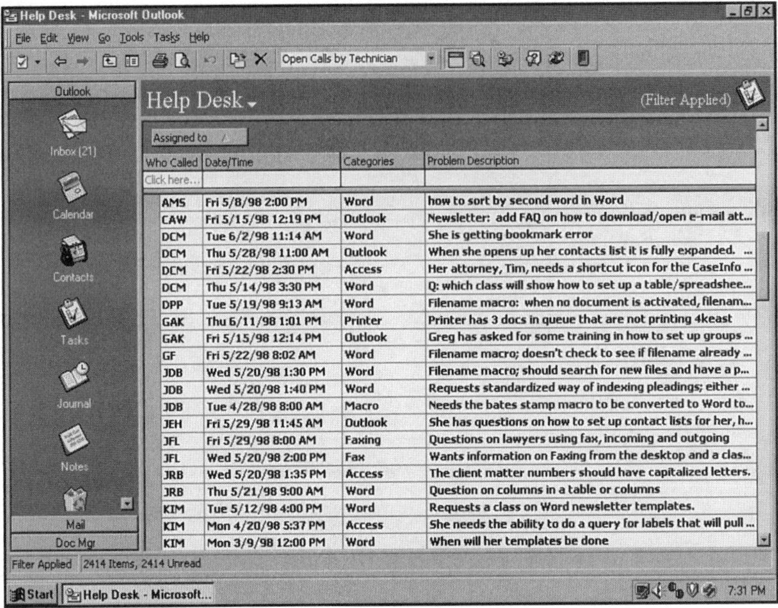

FIGURE 34.2
Outlook can make tracking problems easy.

Understand the Previous Work Environment

If you are migrating from an earlier version of Microsoft Office, most of your work relating to users has already been accomplished. The products have the same look and feel, and any changes the users notice will generally be for the better.

If you are migrating from non-Microsoft office applications such as WordPerfect or mainframe environments, the effects of the change can be significant to your users. Productivity can be significantly impacted by the simplest detail if you fail to plan for it.

Planning begins with understanding the previous work environment. Be sure to allow enough time to do the appropriate research. You'll be much closer to a smooth migration when you can answer these questions for your users:

- Where is our previous work stored? Can we still use it?
- How do we create new work?
- Where should we store things? How can we find our work after we create it?

Soon after the initial panic, users become aware that lots of features exist in the new applications, but they don't know how to use them. Be sure you don't bombard users with all the features of Office at once. Analyze how work was accomplished before Office, and break it down into discrete tasks. Now convert each task into a set of steps that use comparable features in Office. You might need to prepare lots of these new tasks, and different users in your organization might require completely different tasks, but users will be much happier when they have a proven solution to follow.

Demonstrate the New Office Environment

Successful rollouts of Office require careful planning. Getting early feedback from selected users, such as a pilot group, is an effective way to ensure that you are staffed to provide the required training and assistance. The sooner you can expose yourself and your users to the new Office environment, the less likely you are to forget something important, such as required filters, templates, accessible storage locations, and so on. Perhaps you can set up a computer, or a whole training room of computers, with the Office suite to allow users to experience the new environment before it is imposed on them. You can start winning their support and confidence with actions such as these:

- Demonstrate how tasks will be accomplished in Office. Be sure to include any custom toolbar buttons you have designed to make life easier.
- Use language they can relate to, such as "We used to press this key combination; now we click this button."
- After demonstrating a task, do it again, and this time pretend you've forgotten what to do next, so you can demonstrate how to use all the available help to finish the task.
- Start exposing them to new ways of doing things, and ask their opinion on whether various features are valuable. Be sure to include the exciting stuff such as Find and Replace, AutoCorrect, or how to customize the Office bar to clean up a desktop full of shortcuts.

Don't expect your users to love Office immediately. For example, users coming to Word from a WordPerfect background might be terror-stricken when they realize there is no "Reveal Codes." You can, of course, explain the alternatives to Reveal Codes in Word, but this change and some others will require a period of adjustment on the part of your users.

Create a plan for handling bugs and software glitches. Users need to understand the value of the AutoSave feature in Office products, and they need to know how it works. (For example, they need to know that documents that were open when an application crashed will be labeled as Recovered the next time they start the application.) There is always the possibility that documents, workbooks, presentations, and databases will become corrupted and require repair. The ideal repair procedure will be specific to your organization. You should document it and make it available to all users.

Provide Awareness of Available Help

You don't want to be swamped with support issues, so publicize every avenue of technical assistance available to your users. Built-in Office help features should be among the first training items on your agenda. Getting a user to try the help features is more than half the battle. Users typically get the answer they are looking for from the Office Assistant on their first attempt, and if they try to construct their questions to the Office Assistant more carefully, their likelihood of success increases dramatically. If they don't like the Office Assistant, you can customize it to suit their preferences.

Training Support Professionals for an Office Upgrade

As a technical support professional, you want the migration to Microsoft Office to be as smooth as possible. The Office 97 Resource Kit, along with the other Windows Resource Kits, should provide most of the planning documentation you will need. The next three sections discuss the most important upgrade-related issues.

Migrating to Office from Other Systems

If you are migrating to Office from another product, computer system, or mainframe, you need to make sure users can still access the work they created under the old system. You have a few choices for handling this issue:

- *Convert all old work to new Office 97 files before allowing any users to access it.* This requires lots of up-front work, but eliminates most user problems relating to conversion and compatibility.
- *Leave old work where it is and allow users to access it directly using Office 97 products.* You can install Office with the appropriate filters to automatically open and convert most existing formats.
- *Convert as much work as you can, and leave the remainder in the previous format.* For instance, convert everything created in the last year, and leave the rest to be converted on an as-needed basis.

You should try to gather as much information as you can about how users created work on the old system. This will help you decide what features and tools to make available when you roll out Office.

Planning for Office System Policies

If you've ever wanted to "lock down" Office program settings to prevent users from accidentally changing something, you can accomplish this by using System Policies. A *System Policy* is an extension to the Windows registry that controls the way a computer behaves for a particular user. Microsoft provides Policy templates you can modify and implement in your organization. To use System Policies, you create a single file that resides on the server; you don't need to touch the user's computer.

You can use System Policies to establish global default settings users can later customize. To determine which settings can be changed, use the Windows 95 or Windows NT System Policy Editor in conjunction with Office 97 Policy templates.

The Microsoft Office 97 Resource Kit is a great resource for installing, configuring, and supporting Office Policy templates in your organization. It's designed especially for support staff and offers complete coverage of issues relating to Microsoft Office on Windows 95/98, Windows NT Workstation, and the Macintosh.

NOTE You can download the Microsoft Office Resource Kit from Microsoft's Web site at **www.microsoft.com/msoffice/ork/default.htm**. The Office 97 Resource Kit is also available wherever computer books are sold or directly from Microsoft Press (call 800-MS-PRESS in the United States or 800-667-1115 in Canada, or visit the Microsoft Press Web site at **mspress.microsoft.com**).

CAUTION

Apple Macintosh software and earlier versions of Microsoft Windows NT (3.51 or older) do not support System Policies.

To reduce your support workload, consider these suggestions when creating your own System Policies:

- Set the default file format for Office documents. For example, during migration you might want to save Word documents as TXT files.
- Set the File Save locations. Don't let users guess where to store their work; simplify their choices. Storing documents on a network share means you can back up all work each night.
- Set the workgroup template locations. When your users choose File, New in any Office application, they'll see the templates you want them to see. You can store the workgroup templates on the network, making them a whole lot easier to maintain.
- Standardize help settings to guarantee all users are exposed to the same help resources.
- Set the default options in the Tools, Options dialog box for all Office applications. For example, you might want to enable the AutoSave features, which users might forget to implement on their own.
- Choose Word as your default email editor in Outlook.

Implementing System Policies does not prevent you from making future changes. You can revise an existing policy by following the same procedure as when you first created it. In most cases, the change takes effect the next time the user logs on to the network.

Strategies for Supporting Office

Even under the best of circumstances, you're likely to have continuing support issues with an Office installation. Although there are no magic answers, some of these tips might help you minimize problems:

- *Plan your installation carefully.* When rolling out Office to many users, use preset installation parameters to avoid a partial install that is missing components such as filters, graphics, clip art, and templates.

- *Create a feedback mechanism to receive information and complaints from your users.* If you're getting lots of calls on a particular feature or function, publicize the method or solution to everyone. You can post solutions in Outlook folders, or modify training classes to incorporate new information.
- *Get the training required to support your users.* If you can't attend traditional classes, consider alternative education (discussed later in this chapter) such as Web training, videos, or interactive CD-ROM courseware.
- *Communicate with your users.* Try to use as many different ways to get computer know-how into their heads as you can, because different users respond to different methods. Some methods you might use include informal luncheon workshops, published newsletters, internal and external training classes, books, recordings, and videos.
- *Obtain the necessary support tools, whether books, videos, or software.* Several of each are discussed later in this chapter.

NOTE When you understand the needs of your users, customize the Office products yourself. Create simpler toolbars by eliminating buttons that are rarely used, or try creating new toolbars that focus on a custom business process and name them accordingly. For example, you might create a toolbar called Billing that contains custom buttons for choosing templates, inserting AutoText entries, and saving and printing. Users can later learn how to customize and expand their own toolbars as their experience and skills grow.

Promoting Office Self-Help

The sad fact is, most users ignore the built-in help features of most application programs. Microsoft has created an impressive collection of help tools and has done its best to make them interesting enough for users to try. But getting your users to work with the help tools in earnest is up to you.

Maximizing Office Built-in Help Features

Office is loaded with advanced help features that might never see the light of day in your organization, because they don't apply to you. But you might take at least one look at everything to determine if a help feature should be used in your organization. For your evaluation, be sure to install the entire Office suite—including all tools, filters, converters, help files, and ValuPack components—so you can decide which components will play a role in your installation.

The Office help system contains several complementary components, each designed to serve a particular need. Expose your users to all of them, but allow them to choose the tools they like best.

Help Contents and Index Your users should be trained in how to get help the usual way in any Office program. Choose Help, Contents and Index to open the Help Topics dialog box. Click the Contents tab to scroll through a table of contents for the help file. Click the Index tab to search for topics by using an index of help subjects. And click the Find tab to use full-text search and look for specific words or phrases. You can print any help topic by choosing Options, Print Topic.

ScreenTips Most frustrated users can at least point to their computer screen and ask "What's that?" Now you can give them a better tool that will actually answer them. ScreenTips display information about almost any element in any Office window. To see a ScreenTip for a menu command, toolbar button, document text, or screen region, choose Help, What's This?, and then click on the element for which you want information. To display similar ScreenTips for elements in a dialog box, click on the Help button (the question mark) in the upper right corner of the dialog box and then click on the item in question. If you happen to be using a dialog box that doesn't have a Help button, select the option in question and then press Shift+F1. To see the name of a toolbar button at any time, hover the mouse pointer over the button until the name appears. Besides buttons and menus, you can also click on What's This on text, revealing formatting characteristics, as shown in Figure 34.3.

Direct Access to the Web Microsoft provides free and current help information on all Office applications via its Web site. Users might find this resource helpful because they can access it precisely when they need it, without having to leave the Office application in which they are working.

To access Microsoft help on the Web, perform the following steps:

1. From an Office application, choose Help, Microsoft On The Web.
2. Click on any of the Web resources in the submenu that appears. The help files you access are dynamic and might be updated automatically during or after your visit.
3. If you like, you can tile your Web browser and Office application so you can see both of them at the same time.

The Office Assistant The Office Assistant, available in all Office applications, provides a single entrance into all Microsoft help files. You can ask questions in everyday language ("How do I print sideways?"), and the Assistant will lead you to where it thinks you're most likely to find the answers. The Office Assistant is not always perfect, but well over half the time it will point you in the right direction.

And Office Assistant doesn't just answer your questions; it sits quietly observing as you work. Occasionally, the Assistant has a better idea for how to handle a task you've performed. An animation occurs to get your attention; right-click on the Assistant and choose See Tips for on-the-spot training.

The default Office Assistant appears as an animated paper clip, but Microsoft provides many different Assistant personalities so your users won't get bored. Expose your users to these and allow them to choose their own, but be aware that Mother Nature and the Genius require four times more disk space than the others. To try a different personality, right-click on the Office Assistant and click Choose Assistant. The Assistant is shared by all Office programs, so any options you change affect the Assistant in all your Office programs.

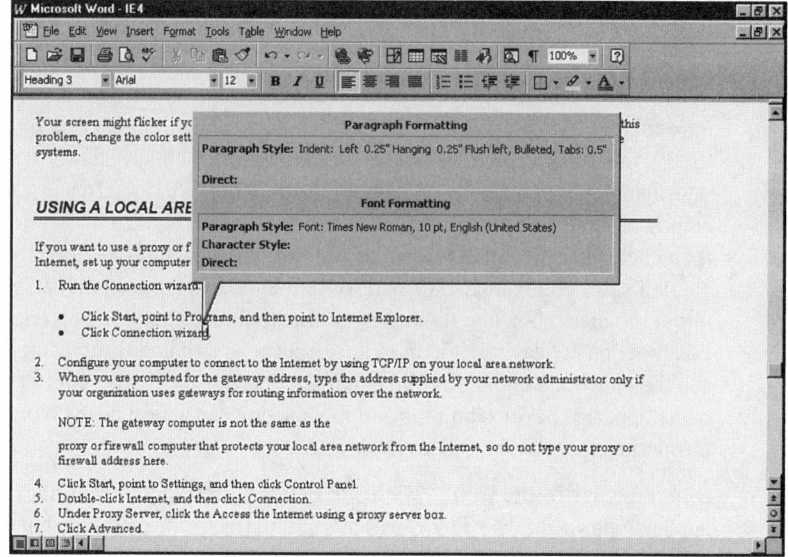

FIGURE 34.3
Debugging corrupted documents is easier with ScreenTips.

Office Assistant Tips The Office Assistant shows tips about the program you are working in, such as how to use the program features or the mouse more effectively or how to use keyboard shortcuts. The Assistant also shows tips based on the way you work, while you work. When a light bulb appears in the Assistant, click on it to see the relevant tip.

Microsoft FastTips is an automated, toll-free service that provides quick answers to your common technical questions 24 hours a day, 7 days a week. In the United States, call 800-936-4100 from a touch-tone telephone. Follow the prompts to hear recorded answers to your technical questions, obtain a catalog of available information, and order items by fax. Outside the United States, contact your local Microsoft subsidiary for information.

Settings that Make the Office Assistant More Effective If your users complain about anything regarding the Assistant, you can show them how to change the settings. Right-click on the Assistant and choose Options to display the Options tab of the Office Assistant dialog box (see Figure 34.4). Here is a sampling of the settings that can make getting help more effective:

- *Guess Help Topics.* This option keeps the help engine running in the background to anticipate the help you might need, based on your actions.
- *Keyboard Shortcuts.* You can display the keyboard equivalents of all tasks onscreen by category (such as formatting), and you have the option to print them out as a quick reference guide you can keep near your computer.
- *Only Show High Priority Tips.* This option displays only the tips that relate to time-saving features.
- *Show the Tip of the Day at Startup.* This is a painless way to slowly and steadily ingest all the features and tips in Office applications.

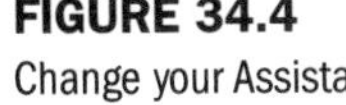

FIGURE 34.4

Change your Assistant to make it more useful.

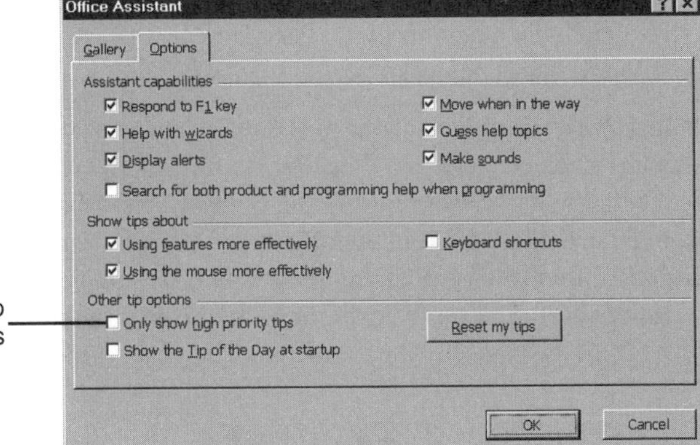

Choose this option to filter the Assistant tips

- *Move When in the Way.* Use this option if you want the Office Assistant to automatically shrink and move to the side after several minutes of not being used.

WordPerfect Help Options If your company is converting from WordPerfect, you might explore some of Word's features designed to make the transition easier for your users. To access these features, double-click on the WPH box on the status bar, or choose Help, WordPerfect Help. The Help for WordPerfect Users dialog box opens.

The Command Keys scroll box includes a list of WordPerfect for DOS command keys. When you select a command key, Word displays a description of how to accomplish the same task in Word 97. If Word offers additional help for any key submenus, the command key is followed by an ellipsis. You can view the additional information by clicking on Help Text. When you've drilled down to the bottom level of information, you can click on Help Text again, and Word displays the help information over your document window so you can view the information and perform the task at the same time.

If your users are coming from a WordPerfect background, they are likely to be more comfortable with keyboard shortcuts than the mouse. And anyone who can speed type usually avoids the mouse at all costs. Publish the keyboard shortcuts for them found on the Help Topics Index tab (search for *shortcut keys*) and click on the Print button. They'll thank you for it.

Word can also provide demonstrations of equivalent features when a user types a recognized WordPerfect for DOS key combination. To see these demos, choose Help, WordPerfect Help. Click on Options to display the Help Options dialog box, and mark the Help for WordPerfect Users check box. Word will now monitor the keyboard, and if it catches you pressing a WordPerfect key combination, it will automatically demonstrate the new way to do it in Word. While this option is selected, the WPH box on the status bar is highlighted.

Depending on the speed of your computer, you might find these feature demonstrations run either too quickly or too slowly. You can change the speed by opening the Help Options dialog box and choosing Fast, Medium, or Slow in the Demo Speed drop-down box.

The Help Options dialog box also contains a Navigation Keys for WordPerfect Users check box. If you mark this option, the functions of the Page Up, Page Down, Home, End, and Esc keys change to their WordPerfect equivalents.

You already know that Word can open WordPerfect documents automatically, but do you know what logic Word applies when converting a WordPerfect document? You can see these details and change them to better suit your needs using the Compatibility tab of Word's Tools, Options dialog box, shown in Figure 34.5. Different option sets are available for each version of WordPerfect, along with other word processing programs. If you don't get the results you expect from your choices here, you can quickly return to the default settings by clicking on Default.

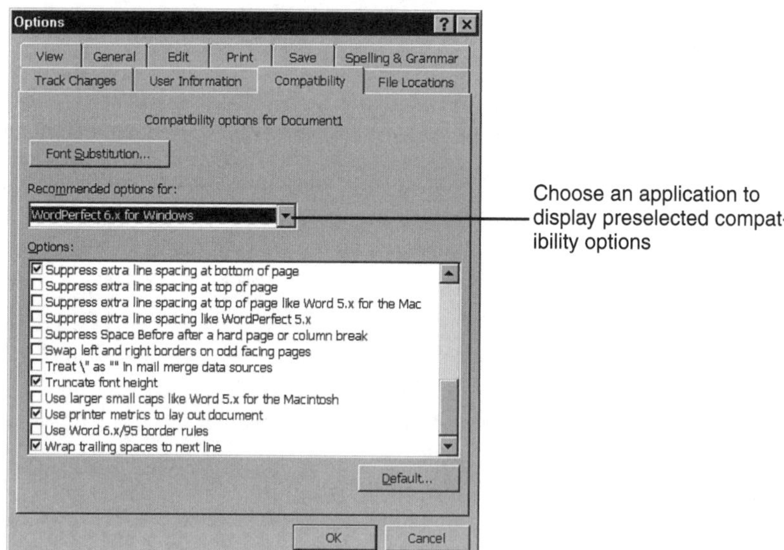

FIGURE 34.5
Support for WordPerfect compatibility can help you through a migration effort.

Just-in-Time Training Techniques

Lots of good advice goes in one ear and out the other, without sticking around in memory. Experts explain that humans don't retain knowledge very efficiently if they can't understand how to apply that knowledge. You've probably attended a technical seminar that had a great teacher and interesting subject matter, but because you had no immediate use for the information, you can hardly remember any of it.

You can help your new Office users avoid similar frustrations by applying some just-in-time training techniques—training solutions that stay unnoticed until they are needed, at which time users receive targeted information to solve the problem at hand. If the training works, the user generally retains the knowledge, which in turn makes your life easier.

Customized Help for Forms If you are developing any custom forms, databases, or applications within your Office environment, put in the extra effort to include custom help files. Word and Excel make two levels of help available for form fields: Status Bar and Help Key. Status Bar help displays a line of context-sensitive guidance (up to 83 characters) in the status bar when the user activates the form field. The Help Key feature displays help text (up to 255 characters) for the active form field when the user presses the F1 key.

To add help to your form fields, follow these steps:

1. Double-click on the desired form field.
2. In the Form Field Options dialog box, click on the Add Help Text button.
3. If you want context-sensitive help to appear on the status bar, click the Status Bar tab.
4. To use an AutoText entry for the help text, click the AutoText Entry option button and select the entry from the drop-down box.
5. To type the help text, click the Type Your Own option button and type the text in the large text area.
6. If you want context-sensitive help to appear when the user presses F1, click the Help Key (F1) tab and follow steps 4 and 5.
7. Click OK when you finish.
8. Lock the form by using the Protect Form button on the Forms toolbar.

You can use both help features together. For example, if you have constructed an expense account form, you might create Status Bar help for a form field that says, "Enter total meal cost—press F1 to list allowable meal expenses by city." You can then create Help Key text for the same form field, listing the allowable meal expenses by city.

Camcorder AVI Files Here's a simple way to communicate good Office techniques, and it's also fun. The Microsoft Camcorder is a free program you can use to record your actions on the computer screen, including mouse movements, menu pull-downs, and so on. You save this recording to a file, and then anyone can play it back and watch the same events replayed. Camcorder movies can include a sound track, so you might include voice narration to describe the actions on screen.

You can use Camcorder to create computer demonstrations or training sessions. Most business functions can be reduced to a simple set of repetitive tasks. Each set of tasks has a right way—and many wrong ways—of being accomplished. You choose the best way, record yourself performing the task as a model, and then distribute the Camcorder file to your users. Make it available so they can view it conveniently when they need it the most. You can save Camcorder movies as AVI or EXE files, although the EXE files are much larger because they include the Camcorder player (this enables you to play the movie on a computer that doesn't have the Camcorder player installed). Figure 34.6 shows the opening screen of a Camcorder movie.

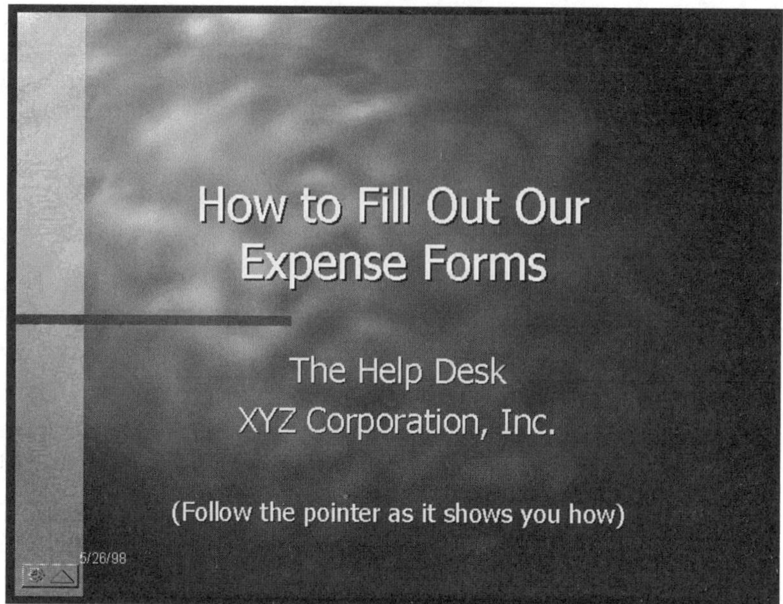

FIGURE 34.6
Camcorder files can show your users the correct way to perform a task.

Start the recording by clicking on the red Record button. You can record mouse movements as well as keystrokes. When you've finished the actions you want to record, press Esc (or the key you've set as the stop key in Camcorder preferences). You can play back the movie by clicking on the Play button. If it meets your satisfaction, save the file by choosing File, Save As or File, Create Standalone Movie. If you need to make basic changes in how Camcorder functions, such as choosing audio settings or an alternative stop key, you'll find them in Camcorder Movie, Preferences (as shown in Figure 34.7).

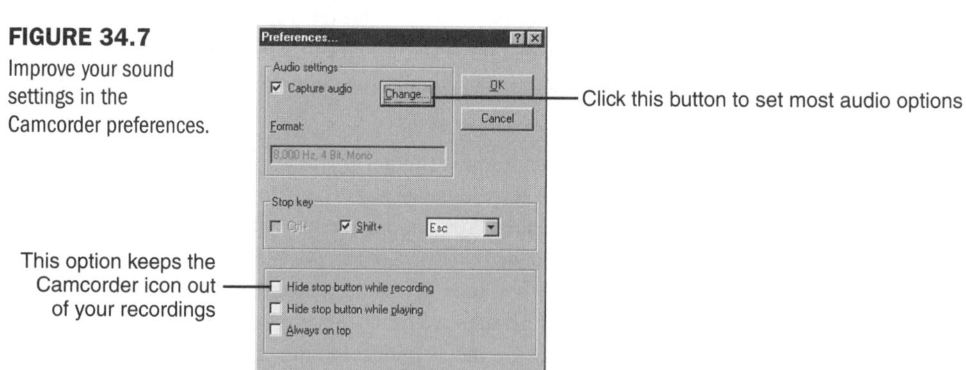

FIGURE 34.7
Improve your sound settings in the Camcorder preferences.

Don't go crazy. These files can get big quickly. Your network could get bogged down if lots of users are accessing long recordings. Camcorder is best for creating short, concise exercises that are available when needed, just in time to prevent a call to the help desk. You can even include suggestions in your recordings about when it's appropriate to call the help desk.

When you have a large selection of your best help desk recordings, you might want to burn a CD-ROM (or several) to store them all. This type of CD-ROM could make a great training tool; you could lend it out as needed, and human resources could make it required material for new employees.

Where can you find Camcorder? It is stored on the Office 97 CD-ROM as a component of the ValuPack. You can also download it from the Microsoft Office Web site at **www.microsoft.com/office/office/enhancements/camcordr.asp**.

Here are tips for creating an award-winning recording:

- Record your movie at the same screen resolution in which you plan to view it. If your audience will have varied resolution settings, record at a lower screen resolution, such as 640×480.
- For the highest quality movie, make sure Camcorder has plenty of memory to draw on. It's a good idea to quit programs you're not using before you record your movie. If you have low or insufficient memory available, Camcorder displays an alert.
- Properly introduce the segment. Provide a title, and perhaps a summary at the end. You can have multiple programs running while you run Camcorder, so why not use PowerPoint to create an impressive title and description, and keep PowerPoint running in the background? During your recording, you can toggle between the PowerPoint slides and the task at hand. If Camcorder disappears during a recording, just press Alt+Tab or click on the Camcorder taskbar button to bring it to the front.
- Rehearse your movie before you record. Practice the steps you want to capture, so your movements will be smooth and natural while recording. Camcorder records six frames per second, so moving your mouse slowly and steadily results in the smoothest playback.
- Camcorder normally displays the Stop button to make stopping the recording easy for you, but you can hide the Stop button if you prefer. Choose Movie, Preferences and mark the Hide Stop Button While Recording check box. You can then specify which keys you want to press to stop a recording.
- Keep it short. Multiple short segments are better than one long recording. You'll be more likely to keep the attention of your audience, and you'll save on storage space as well.

Network and Intranet-Based Training Because all your users are likely to be networked and have a Web browser installed, you've got what's needed for creating and providing Intranet-based education for them. To create your Intranet training site, you can simply gather your support documentation, save the files in HTML format, and store them in a shared folder on the network. You might want to create a title page in Word to organize your site. You might also let users search your help desk database from the site.

You can also purchase training materials you can deliver through your network. With these products, you purchase a license for your site, install them on a server, and allow your users to access them. Here's a brief sampling of products, but you'll also want to explore the Web to find out what's currently available:

- *Que Education and Training* publishes teaching materials for corporate training. To see what's available, visit its Web page at **www.mcp.com/resources/education**.
- *Microsoft Office 97 Professional Essentials* (ISBN 1-57576-787-2), by Laura Acklen, Linda Bird, Robert Ferrett, Donna Matherly, John Preston, Sally Preston, Michele Reader, Rob Tidrow, Thomas Underwood, and Suzanne Weixel, includes data disks and instructor's disks that further develop the written text.
- *Learn On-Demand*, from PTS Learning Systems and Que E&T, provides interactive applications training. For more information, visit **www.mcp.com/learning**.
- *Complete Office 97* (ISBN 1-58076-015-5) and *Complete Office 97 Annotated Instructor's Edition* (ISBN 1-58076-132-1) feature full-semester applications with a business emphasis.
- *MOUS Essentials Series,* by Jane Calabrai and Dorothy Burke. Microsoft has certified this courseware for the Microsoft Office User Specialist (MOUS) program. The included Student Test Preparation Guide provides general exam information, including how and where to register.

For information about authorized training for Office, call 800-SOLPROV (800-765-7768) for a referral to a local Microsoft Solution Provider Authorized Technical Education Center (ATEC), or call the Microsoft Fax Server at 800-727-3351 and request document number 10000256 for the location of the Authorized Academic Training Program (AATP) site nearest you. Microsoft ATECs and Microsoft AATPs offer Microsoft Official Curriculum delivered by Microsoft Certified Trainers to educate computer professionals on Microsoft technology.

Interactive CD-ROM Instructional Products Another good source of training material is interactive CD-ROM courseware. These products require the use of a computer and usually a local CD-ROM drive, although several of the products can also be installed and shared over a network. Most are produced using multimedia and provide excellent graphics and sound accompaniment.

This class of products appeals to the user who needs a quick response to a specific question. Typically, a start menu provides direct access to various topics and then directs the user to specific lessons and objectives. The user can control the pace and the order of the topics. These products are helpful both as primary instruction and as refreshers.

Books (Que and Macmillan Resources) Your help desk should maintain a well-stocked reference library so you can look up answers to everyday problems. Macmillan Computer Publishing is an excellent source of reference materials. Here are a few recent titles relating to Microsoft Office administration:

- *Migrating to Office 95 and Office 97: A Corporate User's Quick Reference,* by Laura Monsen (ISBN 0-7897-1569-4), Que, Feb 1998. Retail Price: $17.99

- *Platinum Edition Using Microsoft Office 97,* by Kathy Ivens et al (ISBN 0-7897-1301-2) Que, Sep 1997. Retail Price: $60.00
- *Special Edition Using Microsoft Office 97 Professional, Best Seller Edition,* by Jim Boyce et al. (ISBN 0-7897-1396-9) Que, Oct 1997. Retail Price: $39.99
- *Special Edition Using Microsoft Office Small Business Edition,* by Rick Winter & Patty Winter (ISBN 0-7897-1356-X) Que, Sep 1997. Retail Price: $34.99
- *Special Edition Using Office 97 with Windows 98,* by Ed Bott (ISBN 0-7897-1661-5) Que, Jun 1998. Retail Price: $39.99
- *Using Microsoft Office 97, 3rd Edition,* by Ed Bott (ISBN 0-7897-1567-8) Que, Apr 1998. Retail Price: $29.99
- *Using Microsoft Office 97 Small Business Edition,* by Tom Barich (ISBN 0-7897-1570-8) Que, May 1998. Retail Price: $29.99
- *Using Microsoft Outlook 98,* by Gordon Padwick (ISBN 0-7897-1516-3) Que, Apr 1998. Retail Price: $29.99

Instructional Video Products

You might want to offer self-study training to users who can't attend a traditional class or who have special needs. Lots of training companies have created literally hundreds of self-study products from which to choose. These products generally fall into two categories: video courseware and interactive computer courseware (or a combination of both).

To provide training that does not require the use of computers, try the large market of video products. In general, these products are recorded instruction sessions taught by an expert and professionally produced.

The range of subject material available in video will boggle your mind, as will the quality. Be sure to do research and check the return policies before you spend company money on a video training session.

Videos, by nature, tend to be a passive experience. The user watches the video and observes instruction. Then, you hope, the user returns to the work environment and applies that knowledge effectively. If some of it sticks, that's good, and you can consider the investment worthwhile. Unfortunately, many users have short attention spans and expect to be entertained, not engaged. Many videos try to accommodate this group by providing lively instructors and interesting instruction.

Most video products are available on VCR, but some Web-accessed streaming video products are starting to emerge. You might find the same titles offered both in video and via the Web. The rules are the same: stick with a reliable company that has provided you with good service in the past.

What are appropriate uses of these products?

- In a company conference room turned into a "learning room"
- As part of a check-out system for employee home use

- As an extension of training or support staff
- As a required part of human resource development for all employees

Video products have a downside (even the very best ones) if they are used incorrectly:

- The students typically have no control over the pace of instruction or the order of material (especially in a group setting). With long exposure, this can become frustrating for all but the most disciplined students.
- If students do not sense that they need this information immediately, they'll have a strong tendency to forget the material quickly.
- Users needing information in a panic might become frustrated if the exact solution is not presented on the particular video.
- These same users might also be in a panic if they have difficulty locating a specific subject by fast-forwarding and rewinding through a tape. The material is linear and is usually intended to be viewed that way.
- The material on the video might describe a procedure or policy not consistent with your own. For instance, a Word video might tell users they can easily modify templates, but your company might restrict access to templates. In this case, the video sends the wrong message, and users might start questioning the appropriateness of other material.

Microsoft Knowledge Base/TechNet Resources

At Microsoft's support site (**support.microsoft.com/support**), you can access a wealth of information about Microsoft products. Each Microsoft product has an associated Knowledge Base (a collection of articles addressing issues raised in actual support calls). If you search these databases, you will often find that someone else has previously asked exactly the same question. The information in the Knowledge Base articles is accurate because it comes from Microsoft's own support desk. Knowledge Base articles are grouped by product, so you start by choosing a product and then typing search words. If you know the article number, you can use that as the search text instead of keywords.

You can retrieve up to five Knowledge Base articles by sending an email message to **mshelp@microsoft.com**. Type the article numbers in the Subject field, separated by commas. You'll receive the articles as email messages.

NOTE You can build an Outlook form for requesting Microsoft Knowledge Base articles so you won't have to remember the address or syntax. Open Outlook and click on the New Mail Message toolbar button. Type `mshelp@microsoft.com` in the To text box, and type `Q######,Q######,Q######` in the Subject text box. Type yourself a reminder in the message body; for example, type `Replace the Q###### with the article number, such as Q118672.` Choose File, Save As to save the message as an Outlook template file, or choose File, Publish Form to save it either in your Personal Forms library or in the Organization Forms Library, where everyone can use it.

TechNet is an annual subscription support service offered by Microsoft. At a cost of about a single Office Professional license, TechNet is a bargain you should not pass up. Each month you get an updated CD-ROM containing all the major support categories found on the Microsoft Web site, including all the Knowledge Bases, online books, planning documents, resource kits, and service packs.

With TechNet installed on your computer, you'll have quick access to the complete support package offered by Microsoft, without having to visit its Web site. The TechNet application window is shown in Figure 34.8.

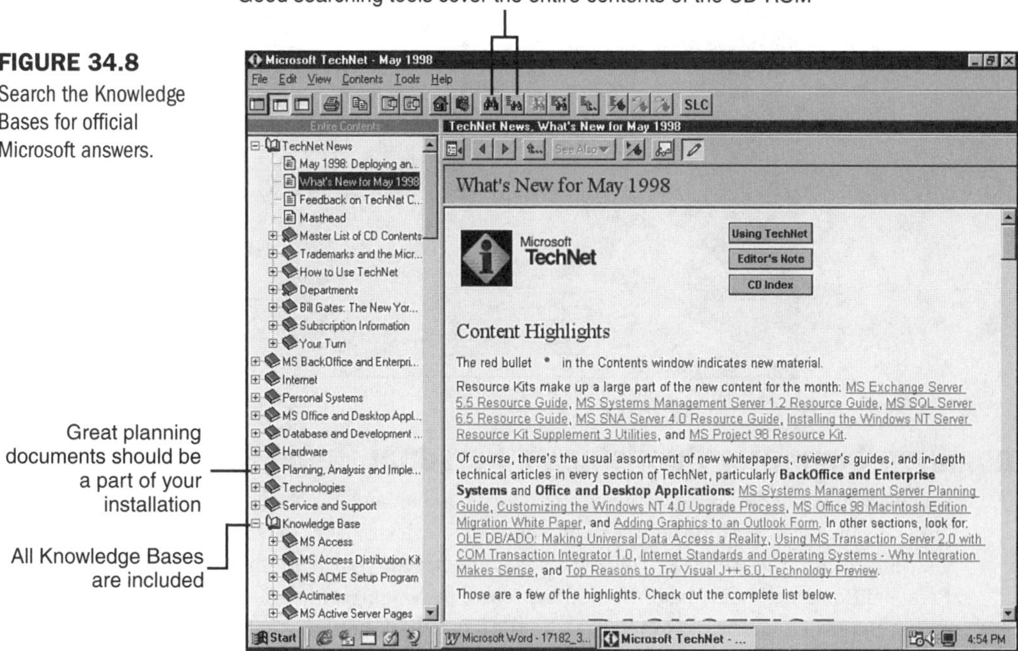
Good searching tools cover the entire contents of the CD-ROM
Great planning documents should be a part of your installation
All Knowledge Bases are included
Microsoft TechNet - May 1998
What's New for May 1998
Content Highlights

FIGURE 34.8
Search the Knowledge Bases for official Microsoft answers.

Web-Based Training

If users in your organization can't afford any time out of the office to take training, suggest one of the many online courses available on the Web. The good ones cost money, but the cost is much less than you'd pay for live instruction and associated travel expenses. Plus, Web-based training is convenient. You schedule and take the classes at the best time for your users.

Search the Web for the latest online training resources. The two resources listed here are established companies that provide excellent training in both Office products and administration topics:

- *Microsoft Online Institute* (**moli.microsoft.com**). MOLI offers online technical Microsoft product training for computer professionals.

- *ZD University* (**www.zdu.com**). ZD Education publishes computer training products and services for users at every level (see Figure 34.9).

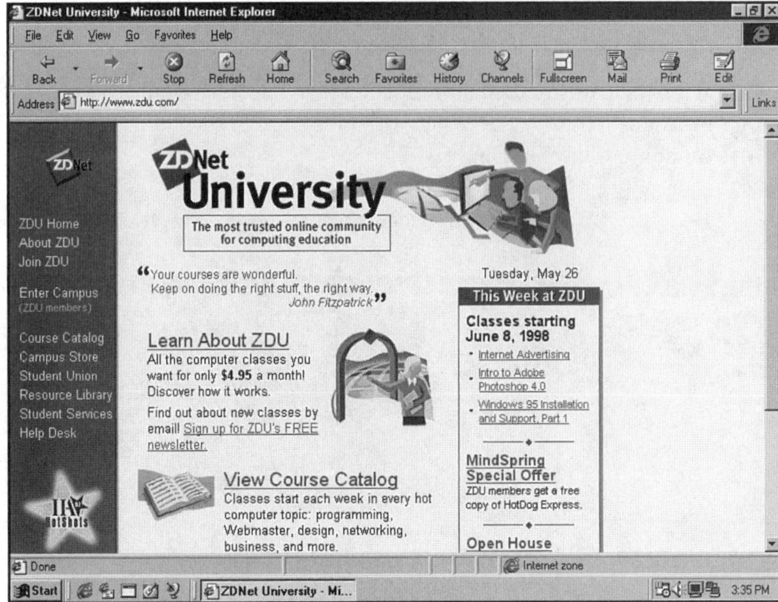

FIGURE 34.9
Save travel time and expense by using your Web browser to experience online education.

Macmillan Computer Publishing's Personal Bookshelf

Customized online libraries are becoming more popular, and Macmillan Computer Publishing offers a valuable one. Hundreds of online books are available for "check-out" after registering your interests at the Web site. To view a book, you access your personal bookshelf via the Personal Bookshelf home page (**www.mcp.com/personal**), enter your email address, click on the Bookshelf button, and then click on the View Book button.

You can review the current Macmillan online book inventory at **www.mcp.com/personal/ebooklist.html**.

Ninety days is the longest time a book can be checked out. After the expiration date, a book loses its View Book button. At that time, you can either check out another book or check out the same book again.

After you gain access to your personal bookshelf, you can change your interest areas by clicking on the Modify Interest Areas button near the top of your personal bookshelf page. Fill out and submit the form that appears, and your new preferences will take effect the next time you visit your personal bookshelf. ●

CHAPTER 35

Managing Mobile Office Users

As more employees begin to take work to their homes, to clients, to suppliers, and even on vacation, the role of the supporting staff becomes more challenging. Employees expect the same productivity from their computers wherever they go. They expect notebook computers to be accommodating. They can afford their own palm computing devices and expect you to integrate the devices with the business needs of your organization. And they don't want to hear excuses about the speed of phone lines, login scripts, or profiles—they just want things to work. When something doesn't work, they call you. This chapter clarifies some of the obstacles to productivity for mobile office users and suggests some creative alternatives.

Conserving Disk Space on Laptops and Notebook PCs

Purchase a laptop today and you're likely to have several gigabytes of available disk space. You'll have no problem installing the entire Microsoft Office suite (you'll even have enough space to copy the entire Bookshelf CD to disk if you like), but you might need to conserve some space for other purposes. You might also have to support older laptops with very little disk space remaining, or newer ones packed full with applications and games.

The Office 97 setup program gives you three installation options. Unless you specify otherwise, setup performs a Typical install. If you are installing to a computing device with limited disk space, you could consider one of the other choices.

- *Typical.* What Microsoft assumes to be the most commonly used components are installed. This is the default type of installation.
- *Custom.* You get to select which components to install. Also use Custom if you want to install all components.
- *Run From CD/Server.* According to Microsoft, only files that are required to be on your computer's hard disk are copied. All other files are stored on the CD-ROM or server and accessed from that location.

Of the three install options, Run From CD/Server does not actually consume the smallest amount of hard disk space. It assumes you might run all the Office applications at some time, so it installs more files than might be necessary. You can achieve a smaller installation by choosing the Custom option, installing only the specific applications you need, and removing all extraneous features and optional components.

What Can You Leave Out?

If Office must consume the absolute minimum amount of disk space possible, use the Custom install option and get rid of as many miscellaneous components as you can during installation. (You can also run the Office setup program at any time after installation to see what components are installed and remove ones that aren't essential.)

See if you can live without Access, Bookshelf Basics, Web Page Authoring, and the converters and filters. Review the components of the Office Tools category to see if you need them. You can save up to 50MB of disk space by not installing these parts of Office.

Decide if you really need the nonessential components of each Office application:

- Excel requires only 7.7MB of disk space if you leave out the help program, Microsoft Map, the sample templates, the add-ins, and the spreadsheet converters.
- Word requires only 8.3MB of disk space if you eliminate the help program, the wizards and templates, the miscellaneous proofing tools, the address book, WordMail, and the text converters.

- PowerPoint requires only 15.5MB of disk space if you leave out the help program, the templates, the animation effects, the presentation translators, and the Genigraphic Wizard.
- Access requires only 12.5MB of disk space if you leave out the help program, the wizards and advanced wizards, the sample databases, the calendar control, and Briefcase Replication.
- Outlook requires only 15.7MB of disk space if you eliminate the help program, Exchange Server support, the Forms Designer, the converters, and the Schedule+ support files.

Other Strategies for Handling Low Disk Space

If you are still hurting for disk space, step back and ask yourself these larger questions:

1. Can you remove any other programs?
2. Have you cleared out all temporary storage folders?
3. Have you run ScanDisk to remove disk errors?
4. Is it practical to compress the hard disk?
5. Can you back up and temporarily remove anything?

Using Viewers Instead of Applications

If your requirements for portability include no more than viewing existing Office documents, you can save lots of disk space by ignoring the programs altogether. Just install the required viewers and copy the documents. Office 97 comes with viewers for Word, Excel, PowerPoint, and Access. The viewers provide enough function to display their respective documents (although Access databases must be prepared for viewing, as described in the section "Using Only Viewers" later in this chapter), and they're all free. The viewers do not require a licensed copy of an Office application, so you can freely distribute them anywhere.

Installing Viewers You'll find viewers on the Office 97 CD-ROM, in the ValuPack folder. Follow these steps to install them:

1. Use the Explorer to navigate to the ValuPack folder on your Office 97 CD-ROM.
2. Open the Valupk8.hlp file.
3. Find the desired viewer in the list of ValuPack components, and follow the links to install it.

You can also find the latest versions of all viewers on the Microsoft Web site. An easy way to get there from an Office program is to choose Help, Microsoft on the Web, Free Stuff.

NOTE The Word viewer's installation program checks to see whether Word is already installed. If it is, it asks you to choose whether to use Word or the Word viewer to open Word documents by default (see Figure 35.1). The setting you choose will be used when you open Word documents via My Computer or Windows Explorer. If you choose the viewer as the default but decide later you need to edit an opened document, you can accomplish this. Choose File, Open For Edit in the viewer, and the full-featured Word appears with the document ready to edit (or simply start Word and then open the document).

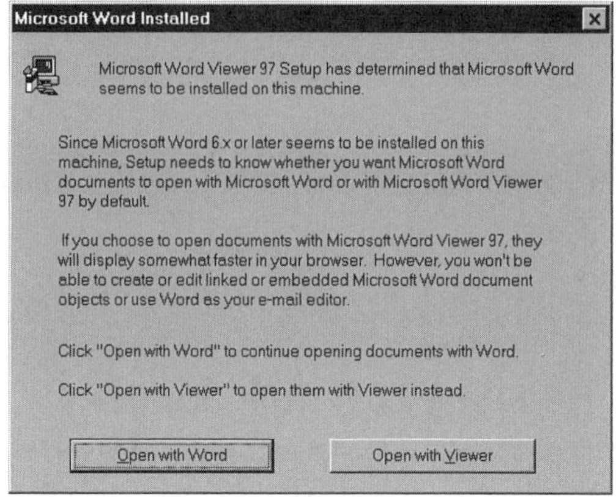

FIGURE 35.1
If the Word viewer's setup program finds Word on your hard disk, it asks you to choose the default method of opening Word documents.

Using Only Viewers When you install the Word, Excel, and PowerPoint viewers, they appear on your Start, Programs menu. The SnapShot viewer for Access appears in its own SnapShot submenu of the Programs menu, along with a help file.

The Word, Excel, and PowerPoint viewers open files in their respective formats so users need only copy their data files onto their laptops. To view an Access database with SnapShot (the Access viewer), you must first use Access to save the database as a SnapShot file.

The viewers share the same features you would expect in any Windows program: they let you cut, copy, and paste portions of the viewed content directly into another application; navigate by using the keyboard and scrollbars (even hyperlinks); and print by using the standard File, Print command. Additionally, viewers can typically open both Windows and Macintosh file formats. As you would expect, the viewers cannot let you edit or save changes directly to the file you are currently viewing.

Microsoft Word Viewer 97 is now optimized for displaying Word documents inside Microsoft Internet Explorer. If you have Netscape Navigator, the Word viewer's setup program installs a plug-in that enables Word Viewer 97 to display documents inside the Navigator window.

The Word viewer includes the same views—Normal, Page Layout, and so on—as standard Word. In the Word viewer window shown in Figure 35.2, the Document Map is displayed. The View tab of the Options dialog box, as shown in Figure 35.3 (to get there, choose File, Options), provides additional viewing options. Important options include the Draft Font and Picture Placeholders, which can significantly speed up viewing large documents. Navigating and printing in the Word viewer are exactly the same as in Word.

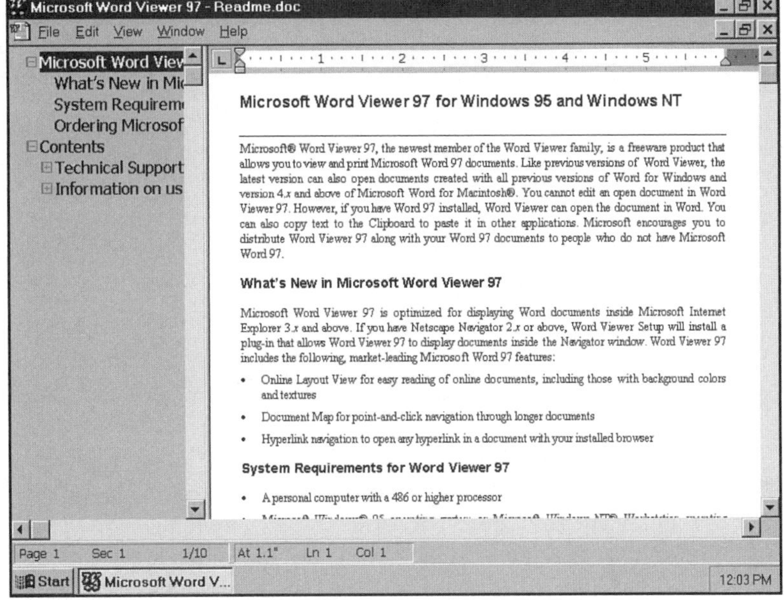

FIGURE 35.2
The Word viewer provides the look and feel of the full-featured Word.

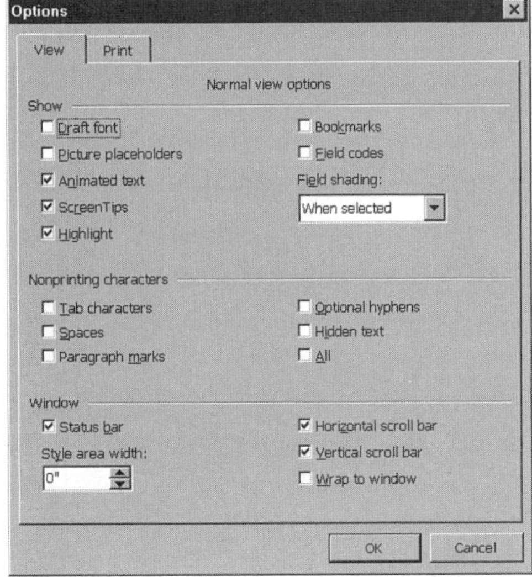

FIGURE 35.3
View Options can improve performance.

Figure 35.4 shows the Excel viewer displaying a simple workbook. You can adjust the columns for more comfortable viewing. The Excel viewer also lets you view macros, templates, and charts.

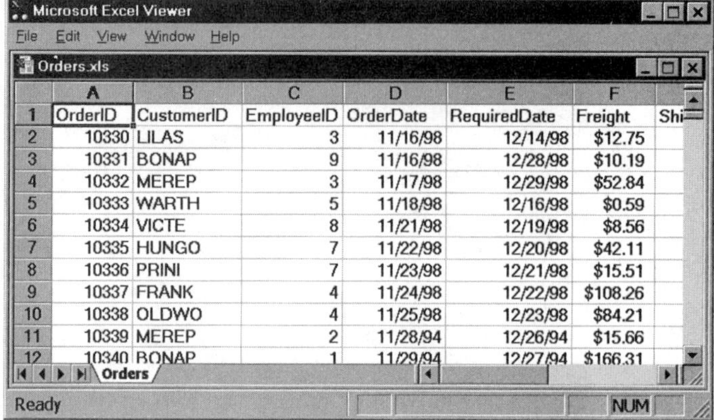

	A	B	C	D	E	F	
1	OrderID	CustomerID	EmployeeID	OrderDate	RequiredDate	Freight	Shi
2	10330	LILAS	3	11/16/98	12/14/98	$12.75	
3	10331	BONAP	9	11/16/98	12/28/98	$10.19	
4	10332	MEREP	3	11/17/98	12/29/98	$52.84	
5	10333	WARTH	5	11/18/98	12/16/98	$0.59	
6	10334	VICTE	8	11/21/98	12/19/98	$8.56	
7	10335	HUNGO	7	11/22/98	12/20/98	$42.11	
8	10336	PRINI	7	11/23/98	12/21/98	$15.51	
9	10337	FRANK	4	11/24/98	12/22/98	$108.26	
10	10338	OLDWO	4	11/25/98	12/23/98	$84.21	
11	10339	MEREP	2	11/28/94	12/26/94	$15.66	
12	10340	BONAP	1	11/29/94	12/27/94	$166.31	

FIGURE 35.4
Workbooks appear in the Excel viewer almost exactly as they do in Excel.

The PowerPoint viewer operates differently than the Word or Excel viewer. When you start the viewer, you are presented with the dialog box displayed in Figure 35.5. Here you can preview the presentations (displayed in the lower right corner of the dialog box) before you run the viewer. You can also specify whether to manually advance slides or use the timings built into the presentation. When you've selected your presentation, click on the Show button to start the viewer.

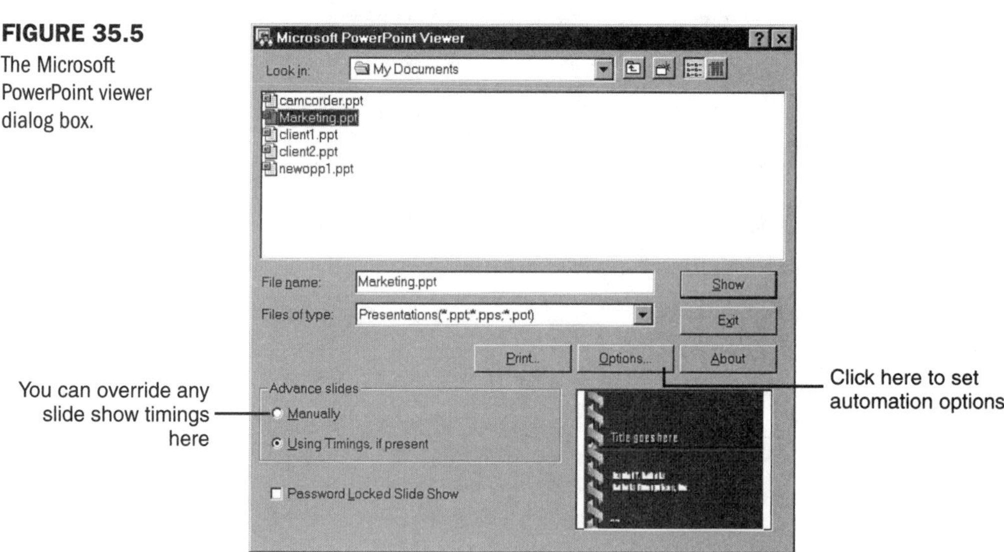

FIGURE 35.5
The Microsoft PowerPoint viewer dialog box.

If you want to view an Access database in the Access SnapShot viewer, you first have to save the database in SnapShot format. Open the database and choose File, Save As. Then select Snapshot Format in the Save As Type drop-down box (see Figure 35.6). After you save the file, you can distribute it to people along with the SnapShot viewer so they can view your database fully on computers that do not have Access installed (see Figure 35.7). The viewer provides fully functioning data controls and scroll bars, and printing is available through the File menu.

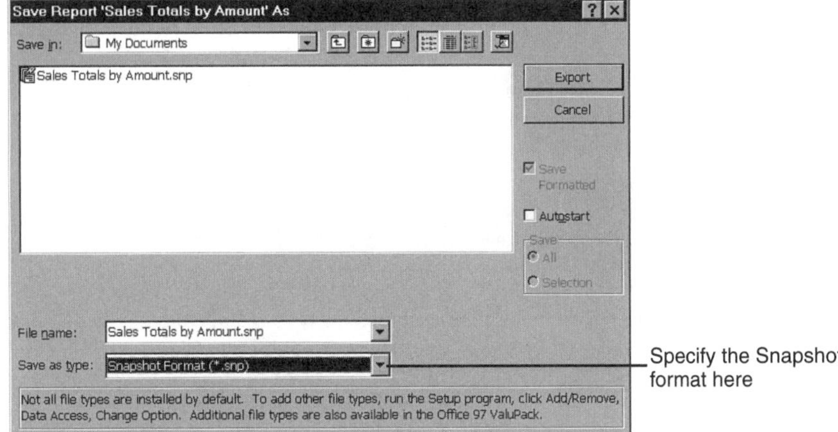

FIGURE 35.6
You have to specify the SnapShot format in Access first.

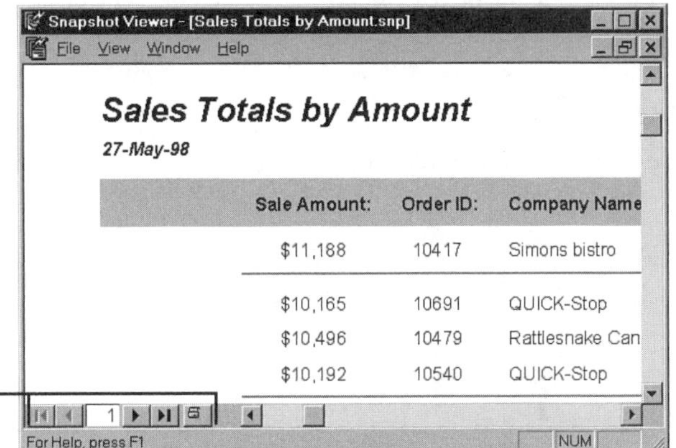

FIGURE 35.7
And then you can view the Access file in SnapShot.

The Quick Viewer for Windows 95/98 and NT does a fine job of displaying most files, and it requires the least amount of disk space. If your needs are minimal, you might be able to use this single viewer for all of your Office applications. If Quick Viewer is installed, you'll see it as an option in the shortcut menu when you right-click on any file. If it's not installed, you can add it through the Add/Remove Programs applet in the Control Panel (click on the Windows Setup tab).

PowerPoint Pack-and-Go for Notebook Presentations

Laptop and notebook computers carry the bulk of the presentations in the world. If your users need to use their portable computers to make PowerPoint presentations, and their presentations are sometimes too large to fit on a single disk, you might consider using PowerPoint's Pack-and-Go feature.

Pack-and-Go gives you an alternative to copying your presentation files to floppy disks when you want to save backup copies or transfer your presentations to a portable computer. It compresses your presentation files onto multiple floppy disks (including all linked documents and multimedia files) and includes an executable file you use to unpack your files on the destination computer.

CAUTION

Pack-and-Go is not able to pack HTTP hyperlinked files in PowerPoint.

Pack-and-Go uses all of the space on each disk and even splits individual files across two or more floppy disks if necessary. The program embeds special commands on the disks to decompress and reunite split files when you unpack your presentation on the destination computer.

When you run Pack-and-Go, you specify one or more files to back up, where to back the files to, and what to include in addition to the presentations. You can back up the presentation you're currently working on, or you can browse and choose one or more presentations stored on your computer or network.

Running Pack-and-Go

Pack-and-Go is installed automatically when you install PowerPoint. To package a presentation, follow these steps:

1. Open any presentation in PowerPoint to make the Pack-and-Go option available.
2. Choose File, Pack And Go to start the Pack-and-Go Wizard.
3. If your presentation is already open and you don't need to add anything else, mark Active Presentation, click on Next, and continue with step 5.
4. To pack a presentation that is not currently open, mark Other Presentation, click on Browse to display the Select a Presentation To Package dialog box, and select your presentation. (If you need to choose multiple presentations, Ctrl+click on each filename.) Click on the Select button, and then click on Next. (Note that you can mark both the Active Presentation and Other Presentation check boxes, as shown in Figure 35.8.)
5. Choose your destination; this is most likely your floppy drive, but you could also copy the presentation to a network drive or to a Jaz or Zip drive. Click on OK to continue.
6. Any linked files in your presentation will already be selected. Choose Embed TrueType Fonts if you've used them in your presentation and aren't sure whether the destination computer will have them. Click on Next.
7. If you'll be giving the presentation on a computer that does not have PowerPoint installed, choose Viewer For Windows 95 or NT. Click on Next.
8. Click on Finish and place your first disk in the drive. Continue swapping disks until Pack-and-Go says it has finished.

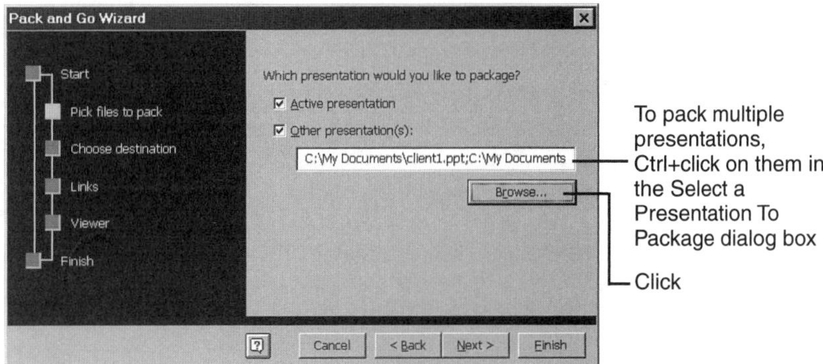

FIGURE 35.8
You can pack more than one presentation.

The PowerPoint viewer is a large file (taking more than a disk itself), so don't include it if it isn't needed.

During the packing, if the wizard can't locate a linked file, it asks you to find and select it. After the wizard has backed up the files on your hard drive, it begins placing them on your destination disk. Be sure to use empty or nearly empty disks for this process, and number the disks as you use them.

After the presentation has been packaged, the first disk contains a file named Pngsetup.exe, a self-executing program that will unpackage your presentation. The other file, named Pres0.ppz, contains the first part of the backup. The subsequent disks contain files named PP1, PP2, and so on, to indicate the order in which the disks should be unpacked.

Unpacking a Presentation onto a Notebook

To unpack the presentation, place the first disk into the destination notebook computer, use Windows Explorer to view it, and double-click on the Pngsetup.exe file.

In the Pack And Go Setup dialog box (shown in Figure 35.9), you specify a destination for the packaged files.

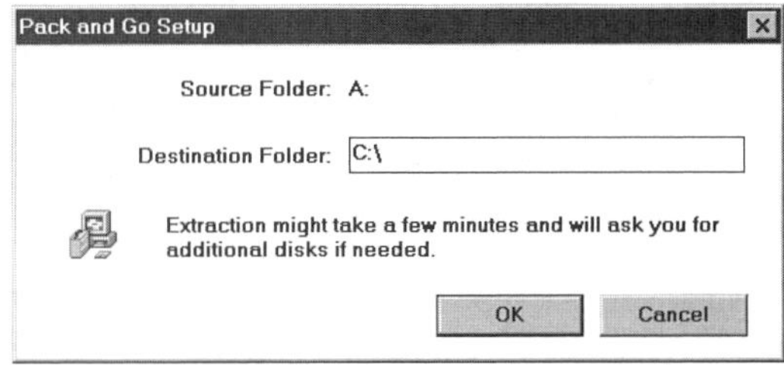

FIGURE 35.9
Your presentation self-extracts on the destination computer.

You should now see the names of the presentation files, linked files, the viewer (if you included it), and a play list. If PowerPoint is installed on the destination computer, you can edit or run the presentation as you normally would. If PowerPoint isn't installed and you included the viewer, you can run any slide show by double-clicking on its presentation filename in Explorer.

NOTE The Pack-and-Go Wizard uses short 8.3 filenames when it packs presentations. If your presentation uses long filenames, including links, it will still be packed; however, the files will have short filenames when they are unpacked. The name changes do not affect the operation of Pack-and-Go, PowerPoint, or the PowerPoint viewer.

Synchronizing Office Files with the Windows Briefcase

A common problem with mobile Office users is finding a way to keep their files synchronized. They might copy files to and from laptops, using floppy disks, but sooner or later they lose track of where the latest file exists, and work gets lost.

Solve this problem before your users experience it by teaching them to use the Windows Briefcase. They drag the files they want to take with them into the Briefcase. They take the Briefcase along as they travel by keeping it on their laptop or dragging it onto a disk. They can make changes either to the files inside the Briefcase or to the original files. When they return, the Briefcase synchronizes the files. During this process, Briefcase checks the time stamps of the files and copies the most recent files over the older ones.

Installing the Windows Briefcase

The Briefcase is not a part of the Typical or Custom default installation in the most recent versions of Windows 95, Windows 98, and Windows NT, but you can select it as an option during installation.

The original Windows 95 setup program (before OSR2) automatically installs Briefcase if you choose the Portable Setup option or if you choose the Custom Setup option and specify that Briefcase should be installed. If you did not install Briefcase during setup, you must reinstall Windows 95.

If your computer is using Windows 95 (OSR2) or later, it is not necessary to reinstall Windows 95 to install Briefcase after setup. To install Briefcase, follow these steps (these same steps apply to installing My Briefcase on Windows 98 and Windows NT):

1. Click on Start, point to Settings, click on Control Panel, and then double-click on Add/Remove Programs.
2. Click on Accessories, and then click on Details.
3. Mark the Briefcase check box, click on OK, and then click on OK again.

If you accidentally remove the Briefcase icon from the Desktop, right-click on the Desktop, point to New, and then click on Briefcase to create a new Briefcase icon.

Using Briefcase to Keep Files Synchronized

Here is the recommended procedure for using the Briefcase to synchronize files. Yes, there are variations on this procedure that might enhance performance and speed, but before experimenting, you should first understand the way Microsoft intended the Briefcase to work. This procedure uses a single Briefcase and a single floppy disk:

1. Decide which files you want to take with you. Copy these files to the Briefcase (you can also right-click on your file and choose Send To, My Briefcase, as shown in Figure 35.10). You can copy an entire folder to the Briefcase if you want to work with all the files in that folder.

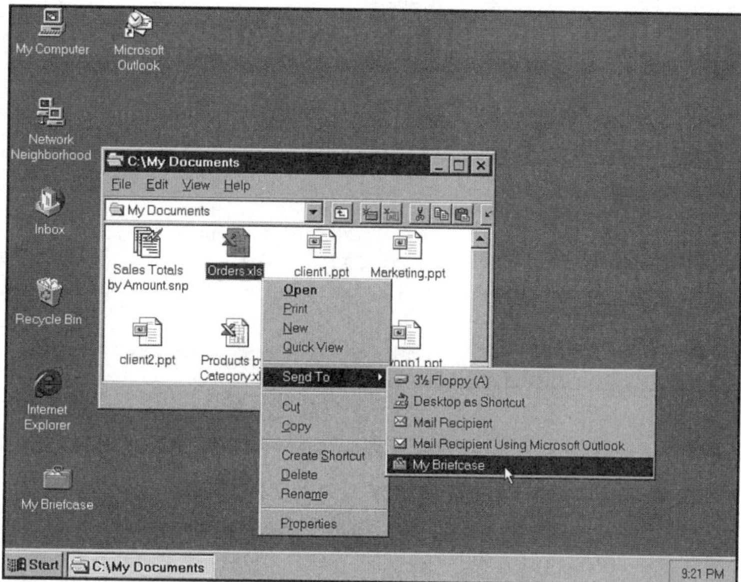

FIGURE 35.10
Select your files and then send them to the Briefcase.

2. Insert a disk into your floppy disk drive.
3. Use Windows Explorer to drag the Briefcase to the floppy disk. The Briefcase and all of its contents are moved to your floppy. (Unlike other files, dragging the Briefcase between drives actually performs a move, not a copy.) The Briefcase temporarily disappears from your Desktop, as shown in Figure 35.11.
4. Take the floppy to your laptop computer (or home computer) and work directly on the files stored on this disk (now playing the role of your "briefcase").
5. When you return to your first computer and are ready to synchronize the files, insert the floppy disk containing Briefcase. Double-click on the My Briefcase icon on the floppy disk.

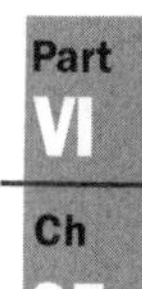

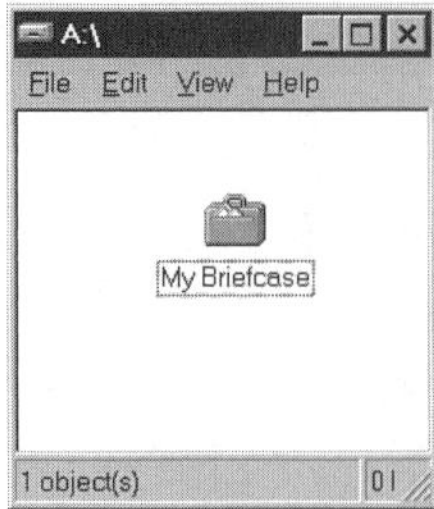

FIGURE 35.11
Drag to move the Briefcase to your floppy disk.

6. Choose Briefcase, Update All. To update only certain files, click on the files you want to update and choose Update Selection from the same menu, as shown in Figure 35.12.

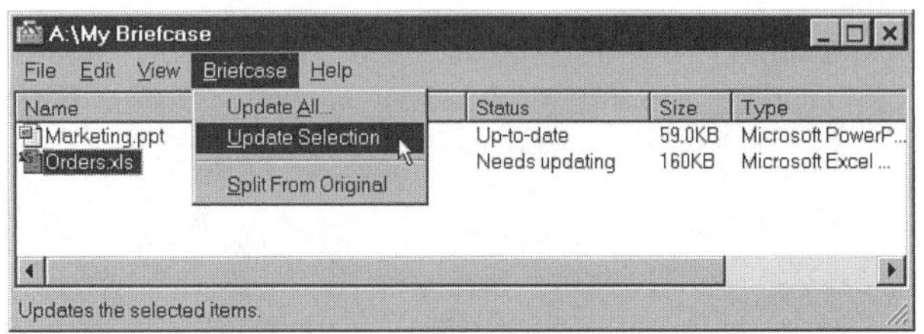

FIGURE 35.12
After editing your files, you can use Briefcase to synchronize them.

7. The Update My Briefcase dialog box appears, asking you to confirm that you want to synchronize the files (see Figure 35.13). Click on the Update button. The status for the selected files in the My Briefcase window changes from Needs Updating to Up-to-Date.

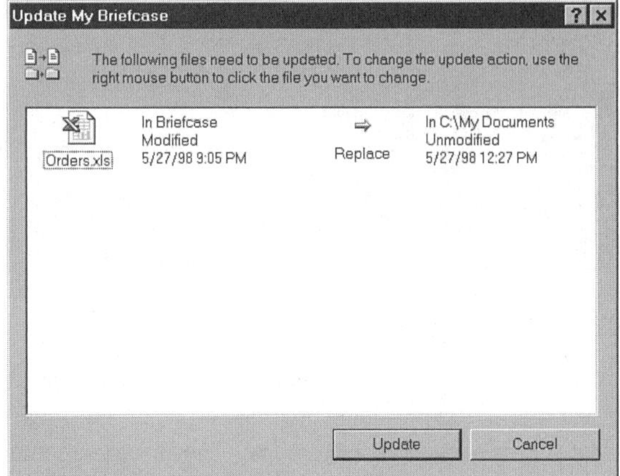

FIGURE 35.13
Briefcase assumes that the modified file should overwrite the unmodified one.

When you synchronize files using a floppy disk, do not perform a copy. When you copy the Briefcase to a floppy disk rather than dragging it, you create multiple copies of Briefcase. If you do this, you might not know which copy of Briefcase to use when you're ready to synchronize your files.

NOTE You can have more than one Briefcase on your Desktop. You might want to use multiple Briefcases when you have so many files that you exceed the capacity of a single disk. You can also use multiple Briefcases to organize files that and folders, keeping similar files grouped together for convenience. You can rename each Briefcase as you would any other file (right-click on it and choose Rename) to help keep them organized.

Checking the Status of Files in the Briefcase

When the Briefcase is opened on your screen, you can choose View, Details to see the synchronization status of each file in the Briefcase (either Up-to-Date or Needs Updating). You can also check the status of a file in the Briefcase by selecting it and then choosing File, Properties. Then click on the Update Status tab in the file's Properties dialog box (see Figure 35.14).

The Update Status tab in the Properties dialog box for a file also contains the Find Original button. Click on this button if you ever need to quickly locate the original file; the folder will be located and opened, with the original file selected.

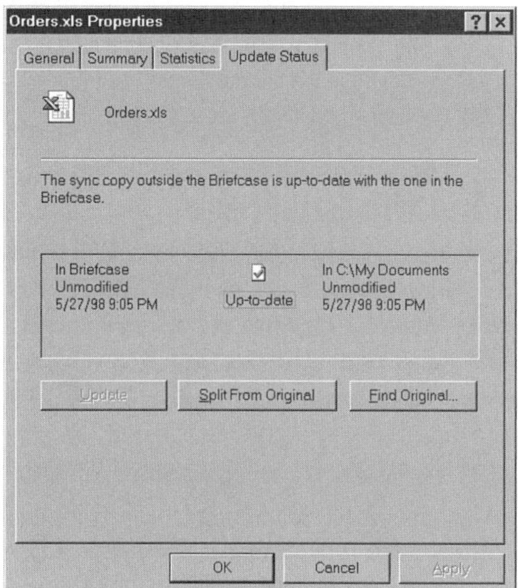

FIGURE 35.14
The Properties dialog box for a file includes an Update Status tab after you've used the file with Briefcase.

Separating Briefcase Files from Originals

If you no longer need a file to be synchronized, you can remove it from the Briefcase to make room for other files. To separate a Briefcase file from its original, click on Split From Original in the Update Status tab of the File, Properties dialog box.

If a file is split from the original, it is labeled an *orphan* and cannot be updated. An orphan file inside Briefcase is not linked to any file outside of Briefcase and will not be synchronized when you update files. You can delete orphans from the Briefcase.

Using Briefcase on Your Network

You can also use the Briefcase on your network. The advantage of using the network is that you can avoid using floppies, so you have unlimited space to work with and it's much faster.

To begin using the Briefcase with a shared network folder, follow these steps:

1. Share a folder that will contain Briefcase files.
2. Copy the original files into the shared folder.
3. From anywhere else on the network, you can now copy files from this share into your local Briefcase.
4. Work on the files in your local Briefcase, as usual. You do not have to be connected to the network at this point.
5. When you have finished updating files and want to synchronize, connect to the network and double-click on My Briefcase. On the Briefcase menu, choose Update All or Update Selection.

NOTE If speed is a concern, you might not want to edit large files directly on your Briefcase floppy. Using Windows Explorer, carefully drag your Briefcase from the floppy to the Desktop of your notebook computer. Now you can edit from the copy of Briefcase on your Desktop. When you are finished, be sure to drag the Briefcase back to the floppy the same way.

Zip Drive Solutions, Using the Briefcase

Although Microsoft suggests that a portable Briefcase should never exceed 1.44MB in size (it assumes you will only use a floppy), creative alternatives exist for synchronizing larger numbers of files. For instance, if you have a Zip drive on both your laptop and your desktop, you can use the huge capacity of a Zip disk as your Briefcase. In fact, you can use most removable media—Iomega's Zip, Jaz, and DittoMax drives, Imation's 120MB SuperDisk, and many others.

Special Synchronization Issues in Microsoft Access Databases

Microsoft Access comes with support for Briefcase that allows for *database replication*. This means users can use the Briefcase to copy a database to their laptop and take it with them. They can edit the database on the road as needed. When they return to the Office and perform the Briefcase synchronization, the database updates the original, and only those records with changes are altered.

Briefcase Replication with Access

When you copy an Access database into the Briefcase, the database replication begins automatically. Special copies (called *replicas*) of a database are created in Access so users at different locations can all work on their own copies at the same time and share, or synchronize, their changes.

If you are using Briefcase to keep your company database and your laptop replica of the database synchronized, the replica set consists of just the Design Master (the file considered to be the master) and one replica. If necessary, several users in your company can make their own replicas, and the resulting replica set will consist of the Design Master and several replicas. (See Chapter 15 for more about database replication.)

Using the Briefcase method, you can drag a Microsoft Access database from a shared folder on the corporate network to My Briefcase on your laptop. The database on the network is converted to a Design Master, and a replica is created in your Briefcase. When you reconnect the laptop to the office network, you can synchronize changes between your laptop replica and the Design Master at the office. Each one will receive changes to data from the other.

To place an Access database into the Briefcase, these steps are required:

1. Place your database in a shared folder so it can be accessed by your laptop.
2. Using your laptop, drag the database to your local Briefcase.
3. Click on Yes to have Access prepare the database for replication. The message box shown in Figure 35.15 describes what is about to happen.

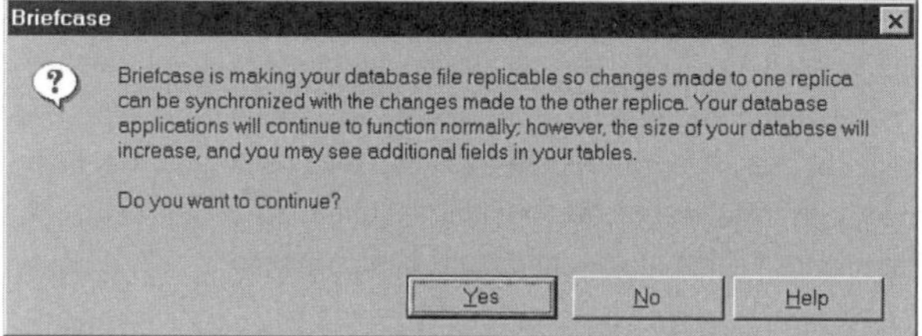

FIGURE 35.15
When you copy a database to Briefcase, the original file becomes a Design Master.

4. Click on Yes to make a backup of your original database, as shown in Figure 35.16.

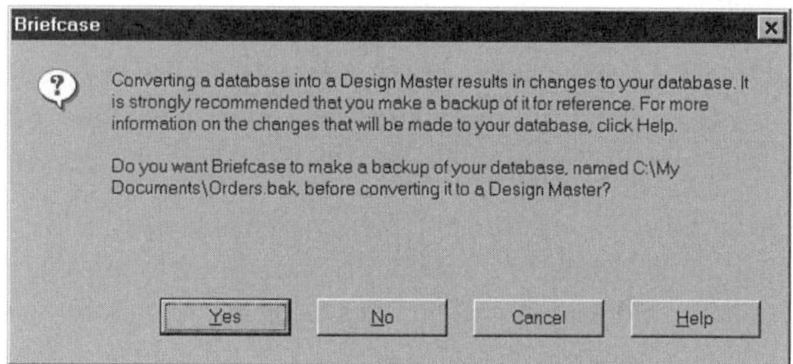

FIGURE 35.16
Always make a backup before attempting replication.

5. Click on Yes to designate your original database as the Design Master, as shown in Figure 35.17.

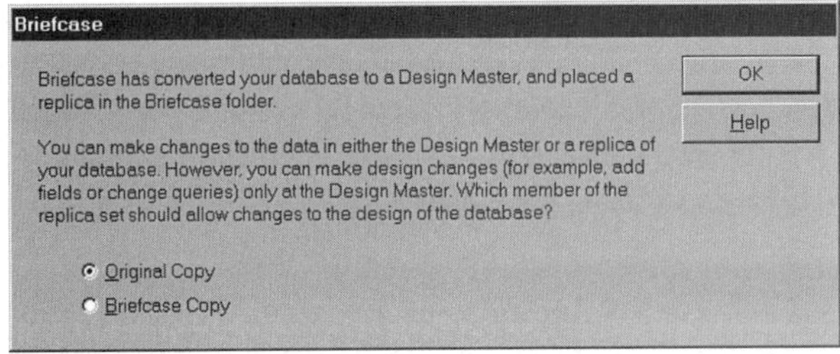

FIGURE 35.17
Designate your original database as the Design Master.

6. Take your laptop with you and work on the database (the replica) as needed. Edit it directly in your Briefcase.
7. When you return to the office, reconnect to the network share, and choose Briefcase, Update All In Briefcase to automatically merge the files on your main computer with the modified files in your Briefcase.

To prevent problems, a good rule is to synchronize the data in your Design Master or replica just before you print a report or just after you make changes to the structure of the Design Master.

NOTE With Microsoft Access 97, you can extend the functionality of the Briefcase to the Internet. By using *Internet Replication*, you can transfer data changes via FTP in either the Design Master or replica databases. This enables users to keep their data current by using the most efficient connection available. Synchronization over the Internet requires the Replication Manager, available in the Office 97 Developer's Edition at **www.microsoft.com/officedev/**.

Copying Outlook Calendars Between Office and Home Systems

Outlook lets your mobile users access their calendars while away from the office. They can even update their calendars while away, and then synchronize their office calendars with the changes when they return. They accomplish this by using their personal folders.

You might need to help your users set up their personal folders so they work correctly. Several of the steps could cause headaches if you aren't careful (such as making sure they synchronize correctly and stop the old calendar when the synchronization is complete).

Creating a Personal Folder for Your Calendar

If you know how Outlook functions, you might be tempted to create a personal folder, stick everything in it, and copy it from one computer to another. One problem with this technique is that the resulting PST file is usually very large; it might be too large to copy to a disk. The size typically results from having lots of email stored in the Inbox and Deleted Items.

A better solution is to create a new personal folder and copy only your calendar into it (or perhaps include your contacts and tasks as well). In most cases, the resulting file fits easily on a single floppy disk.

Start at your office computer, where your existing calendar is stored in Outlook, and follow these steps to create a new personal folder:

1. Open Outlook and choose Tools, Services to display the Services dialog box.
2. Click on Add to display the Add Service To Profile dialog box (shown in Figure 35.18). Then choose Personal Folders and click on OK.

FIGURE 35.18
A personal folder is actually a service in Outlook.

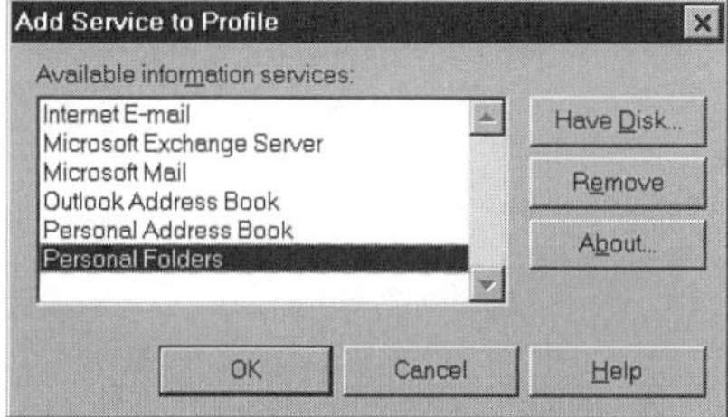

3. In the Create/Open Personal Folders File dialog box, type a unique name for this new folder. To prevent confusion with someone else's personal folder, give your folder your name or initials instead of just calling it Calendar.pst.
4. Click on Open to display the Personal Folders dialog box (see Figure 35.19). Type a name that will be used to display this folder in Outlook; a good name might be `Portable Calendar Folder`. You can also apply a password to this folder to prevent others from viewing it. Click on OK, and then on OK again.

FIGURE 35.19
Remember the filename and your new folder name.

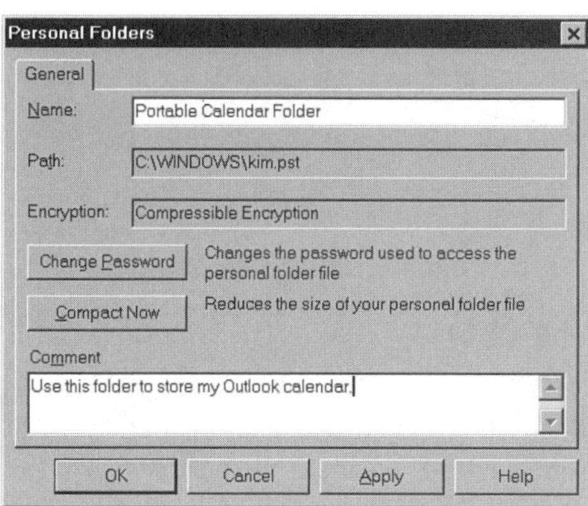

5. Close Outlook by choosing File, Exit and Log Off. The next time you start Outlook, your new folder will appear. Now it's time to copy your calendar into this personal folder, as described in the next section.

Copying the Calendar to Your New Personal Folder

Open Outlook and follow these steps to copy your existing calendar (and perhaps your tasks and contacts) to your new personal folder.

1. Start Outlook. Right-click on your old Calendar folder in the Folder List and then choose Copy "Calendar," as shown in Figure 35.20.

FIGURE 35.20
Copy the original calendar into your new personal folder.

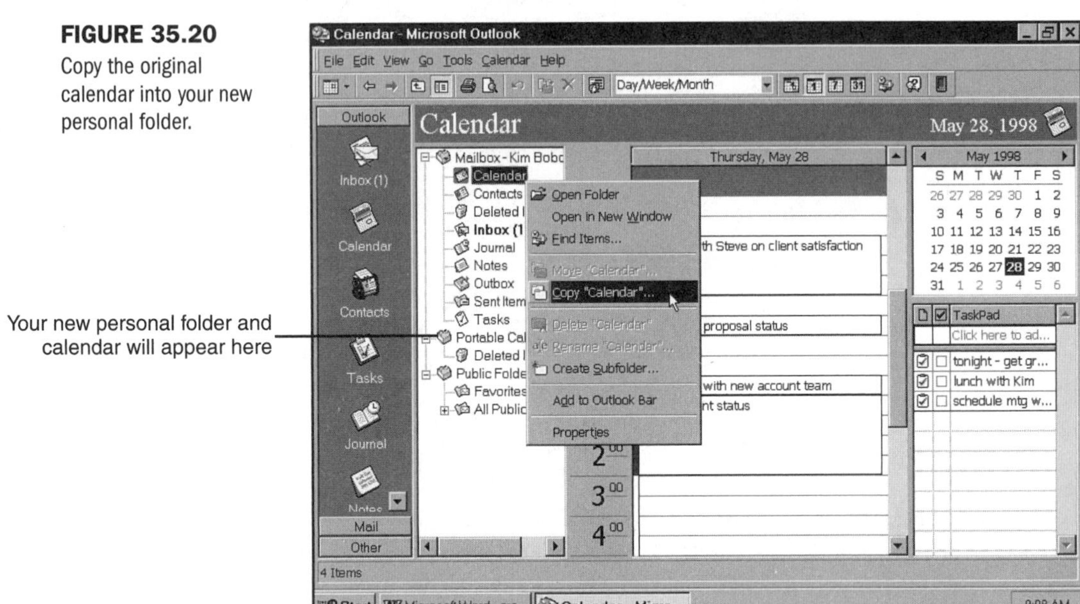

2. In the Copy Folder dialog box, select the personal folder you created earlier (Portable Calendar Folder) and click on OK.

Follow these same steps with your Tasks and Contacts folders if you want to include them in your new personal folder as well.

> **CAUTION**
>
> Verify that your calendar really made it to your new personal folder before you delete the original calendar!

For this brief time, you now have two identical copies of your calendar. After you've confirmed that the copy in your personal folder is identical, the next step is to remove the original calendar to prevent any possible confusion regarding which calendar to use.

Removing the Contents of the Old Calendar

Now you must convince the user to begin using only the calendar in her personal folder, not the original calendar. The best way to do this is to delete the contents of the original calendar. Before doing this, confirm that the calendar you copied to the personal folder is complete and working correctly. Then follow these steps to delete the contents of the original calendar:

1. Display your original Outlook calendar, and choose View, Current View, Active Appointments.
2. Choose Edit, Select All.
3. Right-click on the selected items and click on Delete. The contents of your original calendar are removed.
4. If you've also copied tasks or contacts to your new personal folder, now is the time to delete their original contents as well. Follow steps 1–3 to do so.

Your new Outlook environment should continue to operate as efficiently as it did before. Email is still delivered to your original folder, while the calendar (and possibly your contacts and tasks) is in your new personal folder.

Taking Your Calendar Home with You

Outlook 97 does not let you automatically synchronize a personal folder file between two computers, but you can use the Windows Briefcase to accomplish this task. Use Briefcase to take your personal folder (containing the calendar) to your other computer (the notebook or your computer at home). Briefcase first creates the file on the second computer and then makes sure its contents (in this case, your personal folder, containing your calendar) always stay in sync between the computers.

First close Outlook. Then copy the personal folder containing your calendar to your Briefcase, and drag the Briefcase to your floppy disk. To accomplish this, follow these steps:

1. Click on Start, point to Find, and click on Files Or Folders. Search the C:\Windows directory for the Personal Folder (PST) file containing your calendar.
2. Right-click on your PST file and choose Send To, My Briefcase.
3. Drag your Briefcase to your floppy disk.
4. Take your Briefcase to your notebook computer. Double-click on the Briefcase stored on your floppy.
5. Select your personal folder file and choose File, Properties. Then click on the Update Status tab.
6. Click on Find Original. Briefcase discovers that it doesn't exist on this computer (it shouldn't, anyway) and therefore needs to be updated.
7. Choose Briefcase, Update All. The file does not exist yet, so you should right-click on the Delete action and change it to Create, as shown in Figure 35.21. Then click on Update.

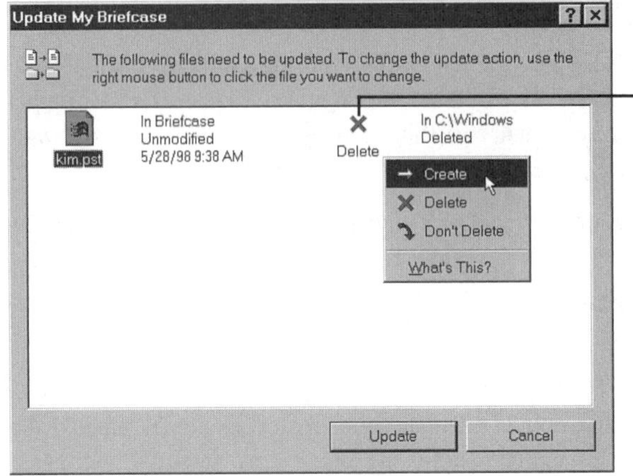

FIGURE 35.21.
Your personal folder file won't yet exist on your second computer, so create it by using the Briefcase.

You can have multiple Briefcases on your desktop. Why not create one called Calendar and use it strictly for synchronizing your Outlook calendar?

Now you've placed an exact copy of your personal folder containing your calendar onto your home computer. The next section describes how to include it in the Outlook profile on your home computer so your calendar appears just as it did on your office computer.

Opening Your Calendar on the Other Computer

Finally, start Outlook on your home or notebook computer. To make your new personal folder appear in Outlook, follow these steps:

1. Choose File, Open Special Folders, and choose Personal Folder.
2. In the Connect to Personal Folders dialog box, locate and open your Briefcase.
3. Click to select your PST file. Then click on OK to load this file into your current Outlook profile.

From now on, before starting Outlook, you must right-click on the Briefcase and choose Update All. When Outlook starts, it will have the latest copy of your calendar.

If you make changes to your calendar, you should also remember to update the Briefcase each time you quit Outlook, so the Personal Folder file stays synchronized.

You can also use one of the large-capacity removable drives to store your personal folder. Most of these are large enough to make it possible to carry all your email in a personal folder.

Integrating Office with Windows CE Systems

The handheld PC (H/PC) and palm-sized PC (P/PC) are designed to use the Windows CE operating system. These devices are made to work in conjunction with your Windows-based computer and are packaged with a miniature Office-like suite of programs. The convenience of the small devices lets you keep your most vital information on hand and then synchronize it with your Windows-based computer so it is always current. An example of a palm-sized PC is shown in Figure 35.22.

FIGURE 35.22
Windows CE runs on handheld and palm-sized computers, and includes scaled-down Office programs.

You will not find Windows CE in retail stores. Windows CE comes preinstalled in read-only memory (ROM) on H/PC and P/PC devices. The Windows CE operating system is not designed to run on a desktop or laptop computer—and certainly not on a third-party personal digital assistant (such as 3Com's PalmPilot). Your desktop computer runs a special program called Windows CE Services that enables it to communicate with your CE device.

Setting Up a Handheld or Palm-Sized PC

To set up a Windows CE device, attach it to your desktop computer, using the serial cable provided. Install Windows CE Services on your desktop computer from the CD-ROM. When Windows CE Services is installed on your desktop computer, it automatically detects when your handheld or palm-sized PC is connected to your desktop and synchronizes data continuously while connected.

The installation process includes creating a "partnership" between your desktop computer and your handheld or palm-sized computer so they can synchronize (update) information during the *ActiveSync* process. During this process, files stored in the Synchronized File folder on each computer are compared, and the most recent version of the files is then stored in both locations.

To view or change your ActiveSync options:

1. At your desktop computer, choose Start, point to Programs, choose Microsoft Windows CE Services, and click on Mobile Devices.
2. Choose Tools, ActiveSync Options (you can perform a manual synchronization at this point by clicking on Synchronize Now).
3. Select the desired ActiveSync option to specify how and when the synchronization will occur. Choose Automatic (always, if the computers are connected), Continuous (only when there's a change and only the file that changes), or Manual.
4. Click on OK and then on Close. Then close the Mobile Devices window.

Built-in IrDA-compatible infrared support enables infrared transfer of information between handheld and palm-sized devices and synchronization with infrared-equipped Windows-based computers. A print job can also be sent to a supported printer over this IrDA connection.

NOTE Windows CE devices support modems and network connections for performing synchronization. Also, if your desktop computer is on a network that has a RAS server, you can use a dial-up connection to connect your mobile device to your desktop computer and perform file synchronization. Open the Mobile Devices folder, display the File menu, and make sure Enable Network Connection is checked.

Moving Files Back and Forth

Now that you've set up a partnership between your handheld or palm-sized computer and your desktop computer, and you've decided how and when to synchronize them, it's time to understand what actually occurs during an ActiveSync.

Here are the events that occur during a typical synchronization process:

- Files located in the My Documents\Synchronized Files folder on your handheld or palm-sized computer are automatically synchronized with files located in the My Documents\Synchronized Files folder on your desktop computer.
- Data in Contacts, Calendar, and Tasks is synchronized with Outlook on your desktop computer.
- Email messages in Microsoft Exchange or Outlook on your desktop computer are synchronized with the Inbox on your handheld or palm-sized computer.

Windows CE Services uses a *partnership profile* to store information about your device connection, backup files, and synchronization. The settings for your partnership are stored in Windows CE Services and appear in the Mobile Devices window under the unique name you give the mobile device when you create the partnership. There's nothing difficult about creating these partnerships, because most of it is automatically created the first time an ActiveSync occurs.

Your desktop computer can create partnerships with many different mobile devices. However, your mobile device might have limitations on how many partnerships it can have with different desktop computers.

To provide security from unauthorized mobile devices trying to connect remotely, you must establish a partnership with your mobile device by using a cable connection before connecting remotely.

NOTE You can create multiple partnerships to synchronize two computers (for instance, your desktop and your home computer) with one Windows CE device. Create a multiple partnership if you plan to use email extensively in both locations. Just remember to give each partnership a unique name that you will recognize, such as *Home* and *Office*.

What's Included in Windows CE?

Microsoft produces the Windows CE operating system (a shell) and a suite of basic programs for the handheld and palm-sized computers, all of which run on hardware designed and produced by other manufacturers. Standard Windows CE programs for these devices include:

- Pocket Word for simple word processing, reviewing, editing, and printing
- Pocket Excel for simple spreadsheet activity
- Pocket PowerPoint for miniature presentation graphics (or an external VGA display)
- Pocket Outlook for managing contacts, calendars, tasks, and email
- Voice Recorder and Note Taker
- Mobile Channels, a browser for viewing Web content offline

The next four sections describe some of the capabilities of this miniature Office suite of programs and some of the integration details you might need to know.

Pocket Word for Windows CE Microsoft Pocket Word is a companion application that contains many of the features from Microsoft Word required for mobile professionals. For proper integration of Pocket Word into your environment, you need to know how to convert files between your desktop computer and the CE device.

To convert a Word document to Pocket Word, start Windows CE Services on your desktop computer and choose File, Open. Open the Word document and save it as a Pocket Word file. Pocket Word files use the PWD extension for documents and PWT for templates. After you convert the file, perform an ActiveSync so you can open the file by using Pocket Word on your mobile device. Depending on the complexity of your document, some formatting and information might be changed or removed. Be sure to test the conversion process with your existing files before promising your users anything.

To convert a Pocket Word document to Word, first run an ActiveSync to move the document to your desktop. Next, open the Pocket Word file in the Windows CE Services window on your desktop computer, and save it as a DOC (Word) or RTF (Rich Text Format) file. After you convert the file, Pocket Word can no longer read it.

NOTE The Pocket Word conversion process uses other converters installed by Microsoft Office. If you receive an error message during file conversion indicating that a particular converter cannot be found, rerun Microsoft Office setup on your desktop computer and install the missing converter.

Pocket Word is missing these key Word 97 features:

- Page setup information (such as paper size and margins)
- Sections
- Styles (except the built-in heading styles)
- Headers and footers
- Footnotes
- Tracked changes (they're visible but cannot be changed)
- Comments

Before you suggest that Pocket Word looks like nothing more than a "pocket notepad," remember that these products are still early in their development. Besides, with such a small display, adding these features would certainly make viewing documents on a handheld or palm-sized computer more challenging.

Templates and sample files for all Pocket programs are located in the My Handheld PC\Programs\Office\Templates folder on both your desktop computer and your handheld or palm-sized computer.

Pocket Excel You can use Windows CE Services to convert a Microsoft Excel workbook (XLS file) or template (XLT) file to a Pocket Excel workbook (PXL) or template (PXT) file and back again. After a file is converted, you can open it by using Pocket Excel on your mobile device. If your worksheets aren't too complicated and contain no macros, you probably won't see much difference in their appearance. File attributes that don't convert are simply stripped out without warning.

Only people with huge workbooks are going to be upset that Pocket Excel supports only 16,384 rows. Rows beyond this are deleted during conversion (as a comparison, Excel 97 supports 65,536 rows). But here are some of the more significant consequences of converting a workbook to Pocket Excel:

- Text boxes, drawing objects, pictures, and controls are removed.
- Pivot table data is converted to values.
- All chart objects are removed.
- Hidden sheets become visible.

Pocket PowerPoint You cannot convert a Pocket PowerPoint file to a PowerPoint file. Also, a presentation copied from your desktop computer to your handheld or palm-sized computer is automatically converted from a PowerPoint file to a Pocket PowerPoint file (the file extension changes from PPT to PPV). This file includes the text, pictures, notes, and layout positions of the original PowerPoint presentation, but little of the glamour.

Here are some of the issues you'll want to consider before implementing Pocket PowerPoint:

- Pocket PowerPoint is much slower than the desktop version you are familiar with. You might be able to reallocate lots of memory on your handheld or palm-sized PC and use it for caching in an attempt to speed up Pocket PowerPoint, but you should still allow ten seconds per slide for your average load time.
- Animation and slide transitions are not available.
- Resolution is less than optimal. Pocket PowerPoint lets you choose compact, 640×480, or 800×600 output, with respective increases in file size and sluggishness.

Pocket Outlook Pocket Outlook includes the Inbox email program, which supports the SMTP, POP3, and IMAP4 protocols (see Figure 35.23). Inbox works with any TCP/IP network, including the Internet. Windows CE Services synchronizes your email, including attachments, with your Windows-based desktop computer.

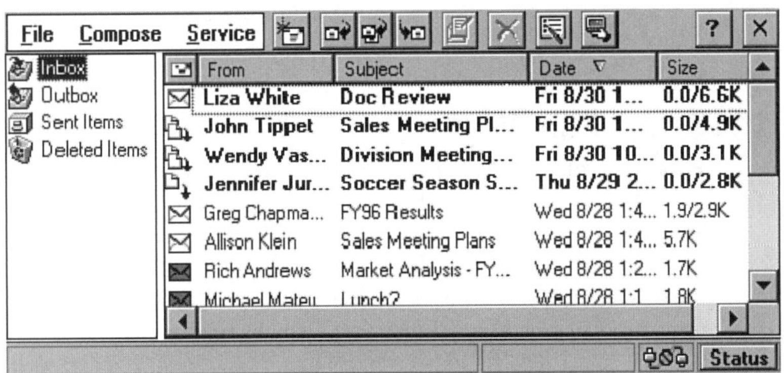

FIGURE 35.23
Pocket Outlook lets you take your email anywhere.

You can work in your Inbox online, which means you can read and respond to messages while connected to the server just as if you were using a LAN-based email program. Messages are sent as soon as you click on Send, which saves space on your handheld or palm-sized PC.

You can also work offline, after downloading your new message headers during an ActiveSync. While you're offline, you can read the headers and mark the messages you want to download later. The next time you connect, Inbox automatically sends composed messages created offline and downloads the messages you've marked for retrieval. To save time and space, you can choose to download message headers only. Choose Services, Properties to change your email preferences.

Pocket Outlook doesn't suffer from performance issues as much as the other suite members, and its function is clearly limited to email services only, so you can safely target Pocket Outlook as one of the first handheld or palm-sized PC applications to implement in your organization.

Integrating the PalmPilot with Outlook

Does it surprise you to know that you can access email from Outlook without using a Windows-based computer? After all, the core of all email is simply the text message, and basic text does not always have to be wrapped up in rich text formatting, logos, and hype. More than one million people now use 3Com's PalmPilot personal digital assistants. This device is appealing because its batteries (standard AAA) last months rather than hours, you can scribble notes within a second of turning on the device, and—most important—it's fast.

Most people want to integrate the PalmPilot with Outlook and Excel, but the PalmPilot has limited support for these applications. Your users will probably want more. PocketMirror, a program that can improve Outlook connectivity, has been designed exclusively for the PalmPilot (see Figure 35.24). You can also modify the default Excel expense templates included on your PalmPilot, but you might want to research the Web for the latest details. Start with the Web site for PalmPilot fans, **www.palm.com**.

The PalmPilot works equally well with both Macintosh and Windows desktops.

Setting Up a PalmPilot

A PalmPilot comes with a cradle and serial cable for connecting to your desktop computer. Each application on your desktop computer can synchronize with the corresponding application on the PalmPilot through a process called *HotSync*, which runs over the necessary *conduit*. To initiate a HotSync, press the HotSync button on the cradle while the PalmPilot is connected. Figure 35.25 shows the most common conduits connecting programs on your desktop computer with their corresponding programs on the PalmPilot.

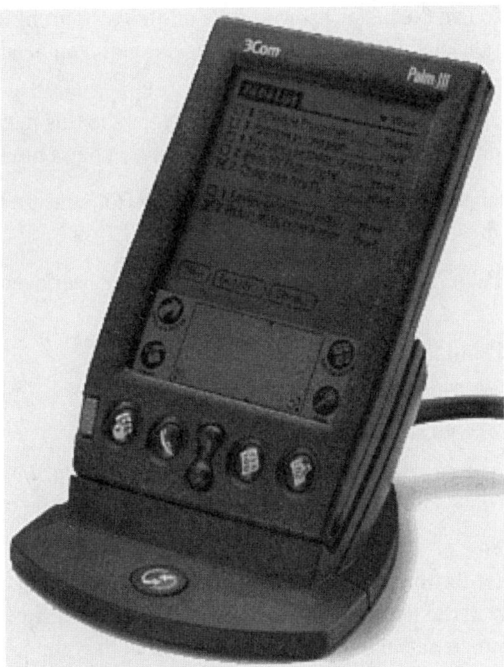

FIGURE 35.24
You can integrate the PalmPilot with Outlook email.

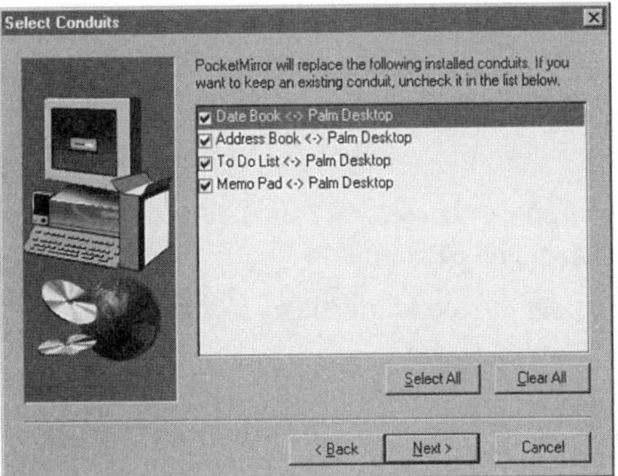

FIGURE 35.25
Conduits are the program connectors to your desktop computer.

Performing a HotSync

You can set up the HotSync program on your desktop computer to listen for the command to execute from the PalmPilot through the serial port, over a modem, or over a network connection running TCP/IP:

- *Serial port.* You use the serial cable that comes with the PalmPilot to connect the cradle to the serial port on your desktop computer. The serial cable stays permanently attached to the cradle.

- *Modem*. You can use the battery-powered PalmModem (purchased separately; it costs about $100) or any standard external modem, although you need to purchase a special cable (for about $20) to connect the modem to your PalmPilot.
- *Network connection and TCP/IP*. The PalmPilot refers to this method as the *Network HotSync*. This option also works in conjunction with either a modem or the serial port.

With any of these connection methods, steps for running HotSync are basically the same. To run HotSync, follow these steps:

1. Connect your PalmPilot, using your desktop computer's serial port, a modem, or your network.
2. Turn on your PalmPilot.
3. Click on the Applications icon.
4. Click on the HotSync application.
5. Depending on your connection, click on either Local Sync or Modem Sync. The average HotSync takes only a few minutes and can download hundreds of email messages in that time.

Changing the HotSync Settings Understanding what occurs during an email synchronization is easy—deleted mail on the desktop computer is deleted on the PalmPilot, and vice versa. New mail and replies are processed and the results appear on both computers. But at times, you need to alter this process. For example, you might prefer to dump email to the PalmPilot for quick browsing and casual deleting, but you don't want to lose anything from your desktop computer's Outlook email during the next HotSync. Or perhaps you want to turn off only email synchronization and leave other components (such as expense account information or address book updates). To view or change the way your PalmPilot synchronizes its files with your desktop computer, follow these steps:

1. On your desktop computer, choose Start and point to Programs. Then choose Palm Desktop, HotSync Manager, Custom.
2. Click on the User box at the top of the dialog box and select the user account for the change in HotSync conduit action.
3. Double-click on the conduit you want to change in the Select Conduits dialog box.
4. Choose the action you prefer for this service, as shown in Figure 35.26. Decide whether the desktop computer or the PalmPilot will be the focus of your synchronization. In most cases, choose Synchronize the Files. If you never want the PalmPilot to modify your desktop's Outlook, choose Desktop Overwrites Handheld. Finally, if you don't want a HotSync to occur with this particular conduit service, choose Do Nothing.
5. Check the Set As Default box if you want this change to become permanent; otherwise, it will occur just this one time. Click on OK to leave the HotSync Manager.

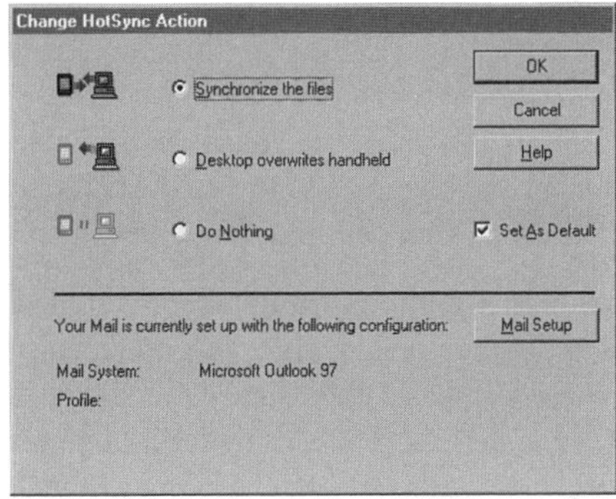

FIGURE 35.26
Choices available for synchronizing email between your desktop computer and the PalmPilot.

NOTE You might experience a problem the first time you try to use email. If you do, you probably forgot to install an email conduit during setup (it's not a default setting). If the Mail component is not installed and you try to send a message, no warning of failure appears on the PalmPilot. To solve this problem, simply install the Mail component.

PocketMirror

PocketMirror contains additional features that can improve PalmPilot's connectivity to Outlook 97/98. PocketMirror was designed exclusively for Outlook. When you install the software, you are given the option of replacing one or more of the existing conduits (Date Book, Address Book, To Do List, and Memo Pad). If you are standardizing on either Outlook 97 or 98, the best idea is to replace all the existing conduits. Table 35.1 lists what you get.

Table 35.1 Updating Your PalmPilot for Integration with Outlook 97/98

New Conduit	Synchronizes with Outlook Feature
Date Book	Default calendar
Address Book	Contacts folder
To Do List	Tasks folder
Memo Pad	Notes folder

The primary advantage of using the new conduits is that all the Outlook features are synchronizing to a consistent location on the PalmPilot. This becomes especially important if you support more than a few PalmPilots; the benefits include fewer hassles, faster training, easier recovery from disaster, and the ability to design quick *sync stations* for your travelling users.

For installation information, go to **www.palm.com** and search for **PalmPilot**.

During a HotSync, the new conduits of PocketMirror synchronize your desktop Outlook with the PalmPilot.

Working with Email on the PalmPilot

After performing a HotSync by using the Outlook Mail conduit, your PalmPilot will be carrying a copy of all the mail in your Outlook Inbox. To see your email, choose Applications, Mail. Your messages appear in date sequence, displaying up to ten on the screen at a time. A check mark designates any messages you've already opened. Here are a few tips to get you started:

- To view a message, click on it, using the writing tool provided with the PalmPilot. To view information stored in the message header, click on Details. To close the message, click on Done. The message now has a check mark to indicate it has been opened. Click on Reply to create a response queued for sending during the next HotSync. New messages can incorporate your Outlook Contacts address folder to simplify entering names.
- If you begin to lose your eyesight, change to a larger screen font. Click on the Menu icon, click on Options, click on Font, and click on a larger font to select it.
- Click on the Menu icon, click on Options, and click on Preferences to add signature text that speeds creation of mail.

Unlike the Windows CE device, the IR beaming used with the PalmPilot is designed to only share information with other PalmPilot organizers. It's not able to share information with other IR devices, such as a printer or laptop.

Remote Access Options for Office Users: An Overview

In the traditional sense, two forms of remote access in an existing computer network are possible:

- *Remote control.* Your computer "takes over" another computer and gives you complete control over it. For example, your home computer could dial up and take over a live computer at work. Your computer then acts as if it is the computer at work.
- *Remote node.* Your computer dials in and actually becomes a node on the network, using real networking protocols. Administrators love it (they can do almost anything), and users hate it (primarily for the lack of speed).

Remote Control

In general, remote control solutions are quickest to implement, because they provide everything the user is likely to need, require the least amount of training, require virtually no configuring on the computer, and are the fastest. You can overcome file-transfer limitations by learning the capabilities of the particular application. Most programs come with commands to invoke a file transfer session.

TIP The most common example of remote control software is Symantec's pcAnywhere. You load it on both computers, and one becomes the host, the other a remote.

Many users request remote access to the email system, and people hate to wait for their email. Without remote control, email connectivity could be a configuration nightmare because of the delays and the many variables to consider, such as where to store mail. With a remote control solution, the user experiences exactly the same office environment at approximately the same speed.

Remote control quickly becomes expensive when users start complaining about busy signals. Incremental growth is expensive because of the dedicated computer resources, cost of the modems, physical space for storing the dedicated computer, and so on. Installing phone lines and incurring these costs can quickly become a major expense as well.

Remote Node

Remote node is the most powerful way of connecting a remote computer. You can tackle any job as if you were on the network, because you really are on the network, but the speed limitations of standard phone lines can make this type of connection impractical. Human resource benefit packages are beginning to include faster connections such as ISDN or fractional T1 to homes or remote facilities as a perk. With these faster connections, anything is possible on a network (including backups).

TIP The most common examples of remote node are Microsoft Windows Dial-Up Networking (DUN) and the solutions provided by Shiva.

Remote node solutions also require more technical expertise on the part of the users. To successfully connect, users must know many more details about the network, including domain names and passwords, protocol support, file server names, drive mappings, and so on. Getting this information to your users in the correct format (including all the variations and configurations they might have) is a major chore. And for users to be productive, they must have at least a cursory knowledge of the difference between transferring 50K of data versus a 2.5MB application.

The best-planned remote node installations limit to a minimum the information travelling over the wire. You can do this by moving as many program files as possible to the remote node's computer, including utilities, programs, help files, and even system files.

Remotely Accessing Office

Given the choices, how do you decide what's best for running Office remotely? It all depends on what your users want to accomplish, and that can change rapidly in ways that are difficult to predict. Many companies have a combination of remote node and remote control access and provide different phone numbers to reach the different services.

You should never try to run any component of Office by using remote node. Even Microsoft recommends not running Office over a dial-up connection, referring to the most common form of remote node—Windows Dial-Up Networking (DUN). This means you shouldn't try to copy the application over a dial-up connection. Make sure all users have the applications installed remotely, and only use the dial-up connection to access folders and documents stored on the network.

Several companies are now successfully using a new-generation solution—the World Wide Web. Microsoft Exchange provides an optional component called Outlook Web Access. Install it in your office, and users can dial into their local ISP from anywhere and connect to your central email system through the Internet. This means they can access just about everything they need (email, public folders, network shared folders, and so on), regardless of where they happen to be and regardless of which type of computer or Web browser they happen to be using. Visit the Microsoft Web site (**www.microsoft.com/msoffice**) for the latest success stories on remote access using Office. ●

CHAPTER 36

Using Office in a Global Organization

According to Microsoft, there are now 36 international versions of Office, each localized to a specific region or language. In addition, two thirds of Office sales are now made outside of the United States. As business grows increasingly global, it's more likely that you'll be called upon to support Office users working in multiple languages and multiple international locations. In this chapter, you'll walk through some of the key issues associated with providing international support for Office, including the following:

- Purchasing international versions of Office
- Purchasing international proofing tools
- Purchasing international fonts
- Working with the global Unicode character set
- Using the new Euro currency symbol
- Sorting in different languages
- Installing support for Chinese, Japanese, and Korean languages

For additional information on Office 97's international features, download the file global.doc from Microsoft's Office Resource Kit Web site (**www.microsoft.com/office/ork/appa/appa.htm**).

Installing Operating System Support for Multiple Languages

Before you can easily create multilingual documents with Office, you may need to prepare the Windows operating system. Here's how to do it in Windows 98:

1. Choose Start, Settings, Control Panel.
2. Double-click Add/Remove Programs.
3. Click the Windows Setup tab (see Figure 36.1).
4. Mark the Multilanguage Support check box.
5. If you want to specify individual character sets and keyboard layouts, click Details. The Multilanguage Support dialog box appears (see Figure 36.2).
6. Clear the language components you do not want to install, and click OK.
7. Insert your Windows 98 CD-ROM and click OK again. Windows installs the new files.
8. When Windows finishes, reboot your computer as Windows requests.

FIGURE 36.1
Checking Multilanguage Support in the Windows Setup tab of the Add/Remove Programs Properties dialog box.

NOTE The process of creating multilingual documents is identical in Windows 95, except that Windows 98 comes with Baltic and Turkish keyboard layouts and Windows 95 does not.

FIGURE 36.2
Choosing character sets to add through the Multilanguage Support dialog box.

TIP Multilanguage support is enabled by default in Windows NT 4.0 and Pan-European versions of Windows 95/98.

Next, if the language that you want to use has a different keyboard layout, activate keyboard switching with that language, as follows:

1. Choose Start, Settings, Control Panel.
2. Double-click Keyboard.
3. Display the Language tab (see Figure 36.3).
4. Click Add. The Add Language dialog box opens (see Figure 36.4).
5. Select the language from the drop-down box and click on OK.
6. Click OK again. Windows copies the appropriate keyboard layouts from the Windows 98 CD-ROM.

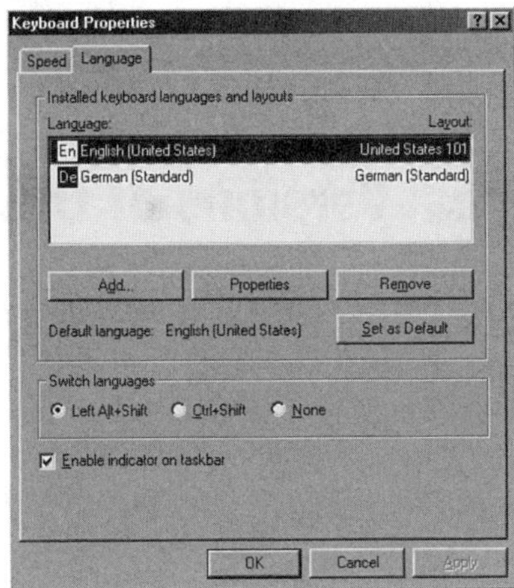

FIGURE 36.3
Displaying the Language tab of the Keyboard Properties dialog box.

FIGURE 36.4
Adding a new keyboard layout.

A square blue indicator now appears on the taskbar, showing which keyboard you're using. You can click on the indicator to switch keyboards, as shown in Figure 36.5.

NOTE If you or your colleagues often find yourself switching languages and keyboards, consider standardizing on the United States-International keyboard layout, which allows you to enter most European-language characters without having to learn new locations for each key. In this keyboard layout, you can get the same foreign-language characters using special keyboard shortcuts that use the right Alt key. To choose this keyboard layout, display the Language tab of Keyboard Properties dialog box, select English (United States), click Properties to display the Language Properties dialog box, and select United States-International in the Keyboard Layout drop-down box.

FIGURE 36.5
Switching keyboards with the Windows 98 taskbar.

Purchasing International Versions of Office 97/98

You can make arrangements to purchase international versions of Office through your Microsoft account executive, or locally from Microsoft divisions in each country.

If you take advantage of the Microsoft Select volume discount plan, international purchases of Office will be counted toward discount commitments and pricing. International versions of Office contain customized user interfaces and proofing tools, and they may also contain additional fonts that reflect the character sets used in their respective regions.

NOTE In some cases, you can use the U.S. version of Office with foreign versions of Windows 95/98, although minor problems can arise and Microsoft does not support the configuration. The reverse scenario—using a foreign language version of Office 97 with U.S. Windows 95/98—is also not supported, and Asian versions of Office do not work with Windows 95/98 at all. (Microsoft says these scenarios will work with the forthcoming Windows NT 5.0, however.)

Some local versions of Office 97, notably the Arabic, Hebrew, and Thai versions, rely on specific features of the Windows operating system customized for their localities, and they cannot run on other international versions of Windows.

Note also that some international versions of Office 97 require their own service packs and cannot be upgraded using the standard Office 97 SR-1 or SR-2 for U.S. markets.

Foreign-language versions of Word ship with corresponding proofing tools, but what if you're working in the United States or Canada and need to prepare and proofread documents for international markets? You can purchase the same proofing tools you would receive if you purchased Office 97 overseas. By agreement with Microsoft, Alki Software, Inc., markets these tools in North America. Table 36.1 lists current availability.

Table 36.1 Foreign-Language Proofing Tools Provided by Alki Software, Inc.

Language	Spelling	Hyphenation	Thesaurus	Grammar
Basque	X	X		
Catalan	X	X	X	
Czech	X	X	X	
Danish	X	X	X	
Dutch	X	X	X	X
English (Aus.)	X	X	X	X
English (UK)	X	X	X	X
Estonian	X	X	X	
Finnish	X	X	X	
French	X	X	X	X
German/Swiss	X	X	X	X
Greek	X	X	X	
Hungarian	X	X	X	X
Italian	X	X	X	X

continues

Table 36.1 Continued

Language	Spelling	Hyphenation	Thesaurus	Grammar
Latvian	X	X		
Lithuanian	X	X		
Norwegian (Bokmål & Nynorsk)	X	X	X	
Polish	X	X	X	
Portuguese (European & Brazilian)	X	X	X	
Romanian	X	X	X	
Russian	X	X	X	X
Slovak	X	X	X	
Spanish	X	X	X	X
Swedish	X	X	X	
Turkish	X	X	X	

Note that foreign-language proofing tools designed for previous versions of Office do not work with Office 97.

Unlike Office 97 for Windows, Office 98 for the Macintosh CD-ROM already contains proofing tools for these languages and dialects:

- Australian (Dictionary and Hyphenation)
- Danish (Dictionary, Hyphenation, Thesaurus)
- Dutch (Dictionary, Hyphenation, Thesaurus)
- French (Dictionary, Hyphenation, Thesaurus)
- German (Dictionary, Hyphenation, Thesaurus)
- Italian (Dictionary, Hyphenation, Thesaurus)
- Norwegian (Dictionary, Hyphenation, Thesaurus)
- Portuguese (Dictionary, Hyphenation, European and Brazilian Portuguese Thesauri)
- Spanish (Dictionary, Hyphenation, Thesaurus)
- Swedish (Dictionary, Hyphenation, Thesaurus)
- UK English (Thesaurus)

A set of Office 97 for Windows German/Swiss proofing tools that can recognize spellings from before and after Germany's recent spelling reform may be downloaded from Microsoft's Germany Web site, **www.microsoft.com/germany/office/word/rechtsch.htm**.

Using the Set Language Feature

You can flag text for proofing in any language you want, even if that language's proofing tools aren't installed.

For example, one of your colleagues might be preparing a document in English that contains sections written in French. If so, your colleague can flag the French paragraphs as French. The English-language proofing tools will skip over that paragraph; but when the document is proof-read on a computer that does have French-language proofing tools, the paragraph will be read and checked.

To select text for proofing in a language other than English, follow these steps:

1. Choose Tools, Language, Set Language. The Language dialog box opens (see Figure 36.6).
2. In the Mark Selected Text As scroll box, choose the language you want (or choose No Proofing, which tells Word not to proof the text at all, regardless of the installed proofing tools).
3. Click OK.

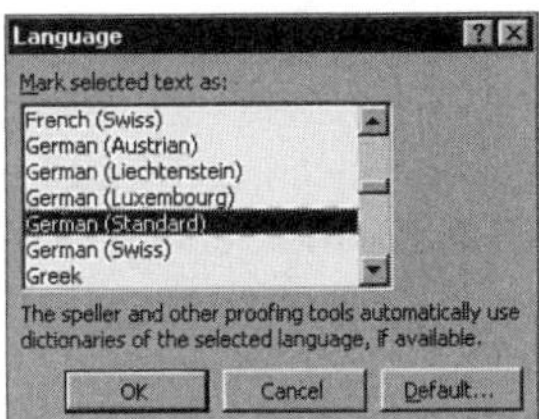

FIGURE 36.6
Specifying text to be proofed in a different language.

Set Language controls more features in Word than just proofing tools. For example, assume that you've selected a block of text and formatted it as German. If you now choose Insert, Date and Time within that block of text, Word displays the date and time formats used in Germany, with DD.MM.YY as the default setting instead of MM/DD/YY.

Alphabetizing Text from Different Languages

Different languages have different sorting rules for alphabetizing text. For example, in Swedish, the characters Å and ä are sorted at the end of the language, rather than between A and B, as is the convention in English. Whether you are running Windows 98, 95, or NT, you can control which language is used for sorting in Excel, Word, and Access.

Excel chooses its sorting algorithm based on the country setting specified in Windows' Regional Settings control panel applet.

Word also defaults to a sorting algorithm that matches Windows' Regional Settings, but you can specify a different sort order for a specific table or text selection, as follows:

1. Select the text that you want to sort.
2. Choose Table, Sort.
3. Click on Options. The Sort Options dialog box appears (see Figure 36.7).
4. Choose the language from the Sorting Language drop-down box.
5. Click on OK twice.

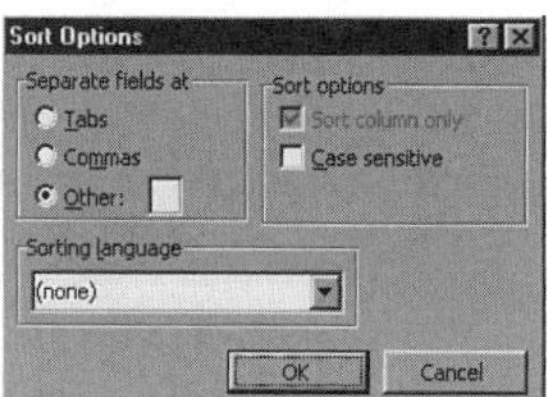

FIGURE 36.7
Specifying which country's sorting algorithm to use when sorting text in Word.

In Access, the sort order is determined by whatever Windows' Regional Settings were when the database was created. You can change these by selecting the desired sorting language from the New Database Sort Order drop-down box in the General tab of the Tools, Options dialog box.

Understanding Unicode 2.0

One key technology for streamlining global communications is Unicode 2.0, which attempts to represent nearly all international language characters in a single character set. Traditional ASCII used one byte (8 bits of data) to represent each character, limiting ASCII character sets to 256 characters. Unicode uses 16 bits, which gives it room to represent over 65,000 characters—ideal for complex, ideographic languages such as Chinese.

Because Unicode uses two bytes per character instead of one, supporting Unicode adds overhead to applications and enlarges file sizes. Office 97 is the first version of Office with substantial Unicode support. Word, Excel, and PowerPoint use Unicode internally. However, Access 97 does not; the MAPI-based email functions in Outlook do not; and there are limitations on Unicode support in Visual Basic for Applications.

CAUTION

Windows 95 does not support Unicode in filenames; use standard ASCII characters instead.

To understand what Unicode support means, compare how Word 95 and Word 97 handle the display of foreign languages. Word 95 displayed multilingual text by applying different fonts to the text depending on the required character set. If you needed a Greek character, Word would look for a Greek font (for example, Times New Roman Greek) and format the character using that font. If you then inadvertently changed the formatting of that character to use a non-Greek font, the character would appear incorrectly.

In Word 97, each character is defined with a specific value from the Unicode character set, and it never changes. Of course, you'll need fonts that include all the Unicode characters you're likely to encounter—typically, all 652 characters used in the Roman, Greek, and Cyrillic language families. Word 97 installs new fonts, called Windows Glyph List 4 (WGL4) fonts, which include all of these characters. On typical systems, the following WGL4 fonts are installed:

- Times New Roman
- Courier New
- Arial
- Arial Narrow
- Arial Black
- Bookman Old Style
- Garamond
- Impact

WGL4 fonts support the following languages: Afrikaans, Albanian, Basque, Breton, Bulgarian, Byelorussian, Catalan, Croat, Czech, Danish, Dutch, English, Esperanto, Estonian, Faeroese, Finnish, Flemish, French, Frisian, Friuli, Gaelic, Galician, German, Greek, Greenlandic, Hungarian, Icelandic, Indonesian, Italian, Latvian, Lithuanian, Livonian, Luxemburgish, Macedonian, Malay, Maltese, Norwegian, Polish, Portuguese, Provençal, Romanian, Rumantsch, Russian, Sami, Serbian, Slovak, Slovenian, Sorbian, Spanish, Swedish, Turkish, Ukrainian, and Welsh.

The Word 97 file format stores text as Unicode. (This is one reason Word 97 files can be significantly larger than Word 6.0/95 files.) Note that when you save a Word 97 file to true Word 6.0/95 format, some Unicode characters may be lost; however, the information is retained if you save a Word 97 file in Rich Text Format (RTF).

NOTE The next version of Office, expected to be named Office 2000, is supposed to have more-thorough Unicode support. Through the use of Unicode (and other internationalization techniques), Microsoft promises that it will have one set of Office programs, with modular language support stored in separate files. This should streamline the compilation and testing of foreign language versions of Office, helping Microsoft to release them more quickly after the U.S. version is released. ■

Troubleshooting Unicode Printing

Sometimes Unicode displays perfectly on screen but causes problems in printing. If you find that Unicode characters are replaced by square boxes in printed documents, chances are your printer driver does not support Unicode. This problem has been reported to occur with the following printers:

- Canon inkjet printers: BubbleJet BJ-C600, 4000, 4200, 4500, 4550, and Multipass 2500 using driver version 3.40
- Epson inkjet printers: Color 500, Stylus Color using driver version 2.x, and Stylus Pro/XL using driver version 2.11BE
- HP laser printers: HP Color LaserJet 5 PCL using driver version F 1.300; HP LaserJet 4 PCL, using driver version 3.78; HP LaserJet 6P laser printer
- HP inkjet printer: DeskJet 1600C, using driver version 4.20
- Okidata laser printer: Okidata 4

The best solution is to see whether your printer manufacturer provides an updated driver. The second best solution is to edit Word's settings in the Windows registry, setting a "print flag" that uses ANSI character layouts instead of Unicode. If you're running Word 97 SR-1 or higher, you can set one print flag for all of your printers, as follows:

1. Choose Start, Run.
2. Type `regedit` and click OK. The Windows Registry Editor opens.
3. Browse to the registry key HKEY_CURRENT_USER\Software\Microsoft\Office\8.0\Word\Options.
4. Double-click on Options.
5. Choose Edit, New, String Value. A new registry key, New Value #1, appears in the right-hand pane.
6. Replace the text *New Value #1* with `NoWideTextPrinting` (do not add spaces between the words).
7. Select NoWideTextPrinting.
8. Choose Edit, Modify.
9. In the Value Data box, type `1` and click OK.
10. Exit the registry.
11. Restart Word.

If you're still running Word 97 without the service release, see Knowledge Base article Q159418 for the correct procedure.

Working with the Euro Currency Symbol

From January 1, 1999 through the year 2002, Europe will gradually introduce its unified currency, the Euro. If you do business in Europe, you'll increasingly need to use the new Euro symbol in financial and other documents. Because the Euro symbol didn't exist until recently, it is not built into Windows 95 or Windows NT 4.0, or even the new Unicode fonts that ship with Office 97. Neither is it listed as one of the currency options in Microsoft Excel's Format, Cells dialog box. However, the Euro symbol is built into Windows 98 and the forthcoming Windows NT 5.0, and Microsoft recently committed to adding Euro character support to Office.

In the meantime, at Microsoft's typography Web site (**www.microsoft.com/typography**) you can download new Windows TrueType fonts (Times New Roman, Arial, Courier New, Tahoma, Comic Sans, and Monotype.com) that do contain the Euro character. In Figure 36.8, you can see how the Euro looks in these and other fonts.

FIGURE 36.8
The new Euro currency symbol in a variety of fonts.

Acquiring Foreign-Language Fonts

Each international version of Windows and Office comes with its own set of local fonts, and the WGL4 fonts that ship with Office 97 can take care of your needs to publish documents in virtually all Roman, Cyrillic, or Greek languages. However, you may occasionally need fonts for other languages not included in the WGL4 character set.

One excellent source for such fonts is Linguist's Software (telephone: 425-775-1130, or on the Web at **www.linguistsoftware.com**), which provides TrueType and PostScript Type 1 fonts for 365 languages, from Acholi to Zuñi.

Linguist's Software even sells fonts for dead languages that only appear on inscriptions in ancient cities.

Using International Currency Formats in Excel

By default in the United States, Excel formats currency references with dollar signs. You can, however, specify a different currency. To do so, follow these steps:

1. Select the cells (or entire worksheet or workbook) you want to change.
2. Choose Format, Cells.
3. Click Currency in the Category scroll box.
4. Choose the currency symbol you want from the Symbol drop-down box (see Figure 36.9), and click OK.

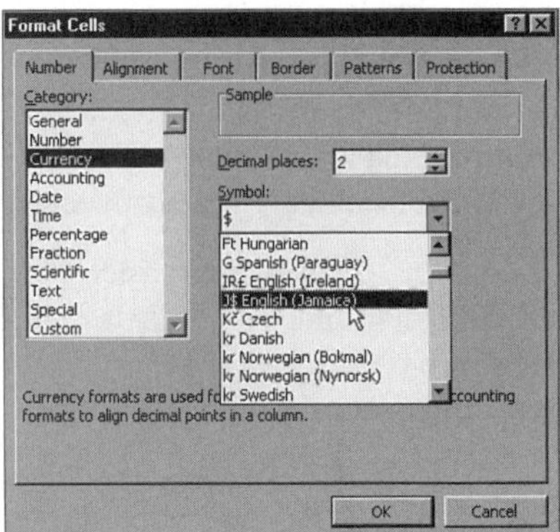

FIGURE 36.9
Formatting Excel cells with a specific currency.

You may want to create templates that include international currency formatting built in, to help ensure that your colleagues work with it properly.

Installing Far East Support in Office 97

If you exchange files with individuals or organizations in China, Korea, or Japan, you may need to adapt Office so that it can read files that were created with Asian versions of Office 97. To do so, install the appropriate Far East support files, which can be found in \Valupack\Fareast on the Office 97 CD-ROM. The files are listed below:

- Chinese (Simplified): Chssupp.exe
- Chinese (Traditional): Chtsupp.exe
- Korean: Korsupp.exe
- Japanese: Jpnsupp.exe

Double-clicking on one of these files installs a font and code page translation table for the Asian language you've chosen. After you've done so, you can

- Properly display Asian characters, which would otherwise appear as boxes.
- Convert and view documents created with Asian versions of Office 95 (7.0), without losing Asian characters in the translation.
- Read and convert Chinese HTML documents in Office 97 and Internet Explorer 3.0 and above.
- Read the properties of a file created with the Asian version of Office 97; without the Asian support files installed, the File, Properties dialog box would appear blank.

Far East support does not permit you to run Asian versions of Office; it only permits you to read the files that they create. ●

CHAPTER 37

Managing Office-Related Year 2000 Compliance Issues

Over the past several months, those responsible for administering desktop PCs have come to the worrisome realization that they are not immune from the Year 2000 crisis: many PCs and software packages are shot through with code that cannot accurately handle dates after December 31, 1999. In this chapter, you'll take a brief look at the fundamentals of PC Year-2000 (Y2K) compliance, and then a somewhat closer look at Year 2000 compliance issues specifically related to Microsoft Office.

Up-to-Date Resources for Year 2000 Compliance

Since you may be reading this book well after its publication date, this section introduces key sources for updated information on PC-based Y2K compliance.

The Microsoft Year 2000 Web Site

Microsoft has posted detailed information about Microsoft Office, Windows, and MS-DOS Y2K compliance at its Year 2000 Web site, **www.microsoft.com/y2k** (see Figure 37.1). The site contains the following types of information:

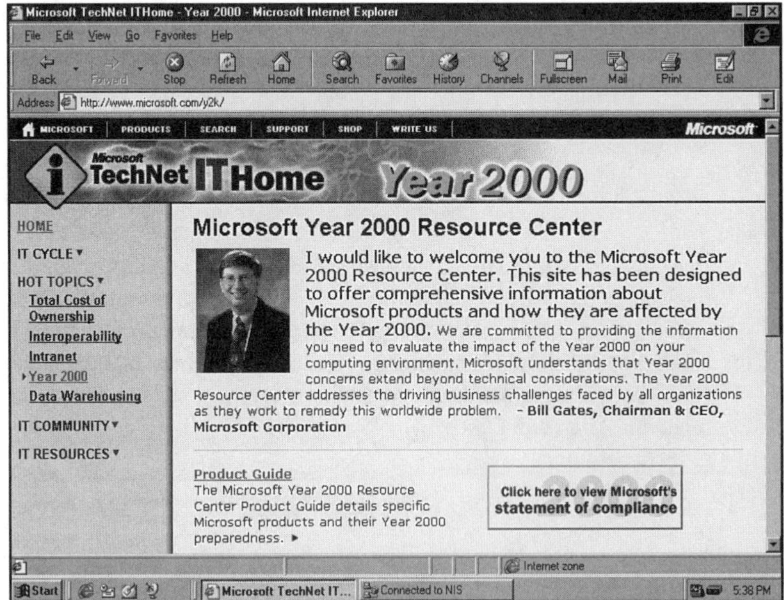

FIGURE 37.1
Microsoft's Y2K Web site.

- Listings of Microsoft products and whether they are Y2K compliant
- Frequently asked questions about Microsoft Y2K compliance
- Listings of third-party tool vendors for desktop and client/server Y2K compliance
- Guidance on how to evaluate and test Y2K compliance on PCs

Other Key Y2K Web Sites

The Web is now full of Y2K resources; there are too many to list. Following are a few, though, that you may find especially valuable:

- The "big daddy" of Y2K sites is **www.year2000.com**, which contains links to a wide range of Y2K resources for desktop, midrange, UNIX, and mainframe computing.

- An excellent white paper on the Year 2000 and Microsoft desktop applications can be found at **www.fmsinc.com/tpapers/year2000/index.html**.
- The search engine Yahoo lists well over 100 important sources for Year 2000 information at **www.yahoo.com/Computers_and_Internet/Year_2000_Problem/**.
- Finally, if you're worried about being sued, visit **www.y2k.com** for a detailed practical briefing on liability, stockholder disclosure, negotiating Y2K outsourcing contracts, and other key legal and management issues.

An Overview of PC Y2K Compliance

Realistically, if your users run into Year 2000 problems in Microsoft Office, they're unlikely to care whether the problems are directly attributable to Office, or to some other software or hardware component on their PCs. If you're responsible for managing Office, it's possible that you are responsible for your users' PCs as well. Therefore, you'll probably benefit from an overview of the Year 2000 problem on PCs in general.

The millennium bug can bite your PC in the following ways:

- At the hardware level (your PC's real-time clock and BIOS)
- At the operating system level (Windows 95/98, Windows 3.1/DOS, or Windows NT)
- At the standard application level (Microsoft Word, Excel, Access, and PowerPoint)
- At the custom application level (custom macros, Visual Basic programs, or client/server applications)

Unfortunately, the interactions between these elements can be complex and sometimes unpredictable. It makes sense to check, and if possible fix, hardware and operating system Y2K compliance prior to addressing applications.

PC Hardware Compatibility

All PCs contain a real-time clock (RTC) that stores the time and date while your computer is turned off. Unfortunately, in many PCs this RTC contains only the last two digits of the year—in other words, 99 or 00.

Each PC also contains a BIOS chip with critical information that your computer needs to operate. This BIOS chip interprets the information in the real-time clock to tell your operating system and software what day and time it is. Some non-compliant BIOSs always append the prefix 19 to the two-digit year, no matter what. The result is that the year 2000 becomes 1900. However, DOS and Windows don't recognize the year 1900—they know they didn't exist then, so that date can't possibly be right. Typically, they display 1980 as the first date that *could* be possible.

Some BIOSs may manifest other Y2K problems. In the simplest case, a BIOS may work properly once the year 2000 arrives, but may not transition properly from 12/31/99 to 1/1/2000. For these BIOSs, resetting the system clock manually once after January 1, 2000 arrives may be all that's needed to solve the problem.

In other cases, the fix may require physically replacing the BIOS with a new chip, or running special software that upgrades it. If a major manufacturer makes your PCs, you may be able to contact them for a BIOS upgrade. If your PCs are no-name clones, you may be able to get the BIOS upgrade from your motherboard's manufacturer, or in rare cases, from the BIOS manufacturer directly.

Some Year 2000-compliant BIOSs use a *windowing* technique that automatically appends 20 instead of 19 whenever they encounter a two-digit year beneath 30 (or some similar number). This solves the BIOS problem—at least until the year 2030 (or thereabouts). It is also possible to build a BIOS that works with a newer RTC to accept an accurate four-digit date, eliminating the need for windowing.

You can avoid some BIOS upgrades by installing Y2KPCPro.Com from RighTime (telephone 305-644-6500, or on the Web at **www.rightime.com**). This is a small program that runs at startup under DOS, OS/2, Windows 3.*x*, Windows for Workgroups, or Windows 95, fixing the Year 2000 date change flaw in the real-time clock of 286 and higher computers. You can download a trial version from RighTime's Web site. (Keep in mind that the program must always load at startup, or Y2K protection will be lost.)

Microsoft Operating Systems Compatibility

Windows NT 4.0 (and 3.51 with Service Pack 5), Windows 98, and the forthcoming Windows NT 5.0 can all compensate for some common BIOS problems by recognizing the year 1900 as an error and substituting the year 2000. Microsoft says, however, that there are many BIOS problems that will not be corrected by these versions of Windows. In some cases, for example, Windows will fix the BIOS date perfectly through the year 2000, but when 2001 arrives and the BIOS reports 1901, Windows will revert back to 1980. A few BIOSs recognize that 1900 is incorrect but substitute another incorrect date, such as 1993. If that date is more recent than 1980, Microsoft's operating system assumes that the BIOS knows what it's talking about, and makes no attempt to correct the date. The bottom line is that even if you are planning to upgrade all your systems to new Microsoft operating systems, you ideally should still test your hardware.

While Microsoft says Windows 98 and Windows NT 5.0 are fully Y2K compliant, previous versions of Microsoft operating systems do have a few Y2K bugs of their own, although mostly minor. For example, if you try to set the DATE from a DOS prompt in the original version of Windows 95, using a two-digit year between 00 and 79 (in other words, between the year 2000 and 2079), Windows reports "Invalid Date." This was fixed in the Windows 95 Service Release 1 and OSR-2 versions. You can also fix this (and a few other equally small Windows 95 Y2K bugs) by downloading and installing the file Win95y2k.exe from Microsoft's FTP site at **ftp.microsoft.com/softlib/mslfiles**.

For Windows NT Workstation 4.0 to be Y2K-compliant, several fixes must be installed, including (as of press time) Service Pack 3, which is available at **backoffice.microsoft.com/downtrial/moreinfo/nt4sp3.asp**, and Windows NT Year 2000 (Y2K) QFE Fixes, at **backoffice.microsoft.com/downtrial/moreinfo/y2kfixes.asp**. Without these fixes, Windows NT manifests a number of Y2K problems, again mostly minor. For example, User

Manager—the NT applet that controls user accounts—doesn't recognize the year 2000 as a leap year, and won't let you expire a user's account on February 29, 2000.

NOTE Although some Macintosh applications may be vulnerable to the Year 2000 bug, the Macintosh hardware and Mac OS operating system is not. It can recognize dates through February 6, 2040, although the Mac OS Date and Time Control Panel can currently only set dates through December 31, 2019. ■

Testing Hardware and Operating System Y2K Compatibility

You can test your computer's ability to handle Y2K manually, or use an automated utility to do so. The simplest way to test a PC manually is as follows:

1. Disconnect the PC from your network. (In some cases, the network may send time information to the PC, invalidating the results of the test.)
2. Set up your PC so that it will not automatically run any software or load any files that could be seriously damaged or confused by Y2K testing, such as scheduling software. (This may involve removing icons from the \Windows\Start Menu\Programs\StartUp folder.)
3. From a DOS prompt, set your PC's date to 12/31/99.
4. From a DOS prompt, set your PC's time to 23:56 (11:56 p.m.).
5. Exit the DOS session.
6. Choose Start, Shut Down to shut down your PC.
7. Physically switch your PC off.
8. Wait at least five minutes, turn the PC back on, and then check the date and time. For the PC to be Y2K compliant, you should see the correct information, with the year specified as 2000 (not 00).
9. Reset the date and time to the correct (current) settings, and then shut down and reboot again.

Software That Automates Hardware and Operating System Testing

Several packages are available to streamline testing of hardware and operating systems. Some of these packages can also help test applications, or at least compare them against a built-in database of compliant and non-compliant software. Following is a sampling of what's available. More specialized tools for testing Excel worksheets and Access databases are discussed later in this chapter.

- Test2000.exe from RighTime (**www.rightime.com**) is a free, simple diagnostic program that tests two key aspects of Y2K hardware compatibility: whether the BIOS can transition to the year 2000 properly, and whether it retains the correct post-2000 date after reboot.
- YMARK2000, a free testing tool from the National Software Testing Laboratories (**www.nstl.com/html/ymark_2000.html**), tests real-time clock compatibility,

accurate transition from 12/31/1999 to 1/1/2000, and recognition and support of leap years from 2000 through 2009.

- Survive 2000 V 2.1 Professional (**www.survive-2000.com**) performs detailed testing and generates a printout with results and recommendations, which can be archived to protect the company against potential litigation. Administrators can run tests across the network from a server, avoiding the need to install the software on each system. Survive 2000 links to an online database containing extensive information on Y2K application compliance as provided by software vendors. It also performs extensive testing on its own; a detailed description of these tests can be found at **www.survive-2000.com/explain.htm**. A free subset of Survive 2000 that tests the RTC, BIOS, and correct operating system bootup is available for downloading.
- Check 2000 PC from Greenwich Mean Time, Inc. (telephone 703-908-6600 or on the Web at **www.gmt-2000.com**) compares your shrink-wrapped software against a compliance knowledge base; identifies data known to be date-sensitive, showing how recently that data was used to help you prioritize; and performs six hardware-level BIOS checks.

CAUTION

Don't assume that you can test only "representative" PCs. Many companies have discovered that even large batches of computers purchased from the same vendor at the same time will respond to the Year 2000 differently. Unfortunately, the best approach is to test them all.

Setting Your PC to Request Four-Digit Dates

One key to making your programs and data Y2K compliant is, wherever possible, to ensure that users enter four-digit year dates rather than two-digit dates. This is slightly more inconvenient, but helps to ensure that the data will be accurate. You can make four-digit date entry Windows' default setting as follows:

1. Choose Start, Settings, Control Panel.
2. Double-click on Regional Settings.
3. Click the Date tab (see Figure 37.2).
4. In the Short Date Style drop-down box, choose M/d/yyyy.
5. Click OK.

Changing this setting solves one more problem: it ensures that Excel will export four-digit year data without eliminating the century digits. If you do not change the setting, when you export to CSV (comma-separated values) and other text output formats, Office will use the Windows default "dd/mm/yy" setting.

CAUTION

Some Office administrators and developers mistakenly believe that changing the Short Date Style setting is all they need to do to guarantee Y2K compliance, and it's true that most commercial software does refer to this setting when asking users to enter year data. In fact, this is only a partial solution, for two reasons. First, most people who write custom macros or VBA procedures do not use this setting. Second, sophisticated users can override it, and may do so because it will save them time in entering data.

Changing this setting can also require you to widen Excel worksheet columns that currently contain two-digit dates. Because this changes the length of the data you enter, it may also confuse custom Visual Basic applications that retrieve text strings, parse out two characters in a specific location within the string, and utilize those characters as dates.

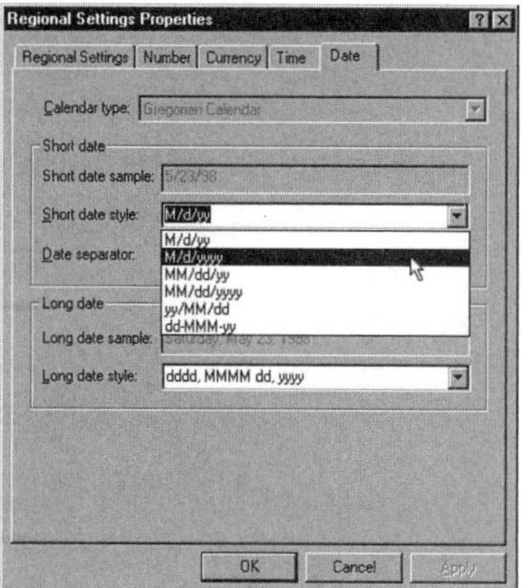

FIGURE 37.2
Setting Windows for four-digit date entry.

An Overview of Office Compliance

Now that you've considered the issue of PC hardware and operating system compliance, this next section looks at Office. Microsoft has published a list of Office (and other) applications it views to be compliant, "compatible with minor issues," and non-compliant. This list is summarized in Table 37.1.

Table 37.1 Office Application Y2K Compliance (Source: Microsoft)

Application	Status
Access 2.0	Not compliant
Access 95 (7.0)	Compliant
Access 97 (8.0)	Compliant
Bookshelf 98	Compliant
Excel 95 (7.0)	Compliant
Excel 97 (8.0)	Compliant

continues

Table 37.1 Continued

Application	Status
Excel 98 (Mac)	Compliant
Excel 5.0	Compliant
Exchange Server 5.5	Compliant
FoxPro v. 2.6	Compliant with minor issues
FrontPage 98	Compliant
Int. Explorer (16-bit, 4.01)	Compliant
Int. Explorer (32-bit, 3.0*x*)	Compliant with minor issues
Int. Explorer (32-bit, 4.0*x*)	Compliant with minor issues
Int. Explorer (Mac, 4.0*x*)	Compliant
Internet Explorer (UNIX, 4.0)	Compliant
Office 98 (Macintosh)	Compliant
Office 4.*x* Standard Edition	Compliant with minor issues
Office 4.3 Professional	Not compliant (Access only)
Office 95 Prof. Edition	Compliant with minor issues
Office 95 Standard Edition	Compliant with minor issues
Office 97 Prof. Edition	Compliant
Office 97 Standard Edition	Compliant
Office 98 (Mac)	Compliant
Outlook 97 (8.0*x*)	Compliant
Outlook 98 (8.5)	Compliant
Outlook Express (Mac, 4.0)	Compliant with minor issues
PowerPoint 98 (Mac)	Compliant
PowerPoint 95 (7.0)	Compliant
PowerPoint 97 (8.0)	Compliant
PowerPoint (4.0)	Compliant with minor issues
Project 98, 98 SR-1	Compliant
SNA Server 4.0	Compliant
SQL Server 6.5	Compliant with minor issues
Systems Mgmt. Server v. 1.2	Compliant

Application	Status
Visual Basic (1.0-5.0)	Compliant with minor issues
Visual C++	Compliant with minor issues
Visual FoxPro (3.0b)	Compliant with minor issues
Visual FoxPro (5.0a)	Compliant
Word 6.0	Compliant with minor issues
Word 95 (7.0)	Compliant with minor issues
Word 97 (8.0)	Compliant
Word 98 for the Macintosh	Compliant
Word for MS-DOS v. 5.0	Not compliant

Following this paragraph is an excerpt from Microsoft's official definition of Year 2000 compliance. While for most purposes it seems quite solid, be aware that it does not address all the issues that have been raised by Y2K consultants. For example, as discussed later, a "compliant" application such as Excel 97 may nevertheless misinterpret dates beyond 2036.

> A Year 2000 Compliant product from Microsoft will not produce errors processing date data in connection with the year change from December 31, 1999 to January 1, 2000 when used with accurate date data in accordance with its documentation and the recommendations and exceptions set forth in the Microsoft Year 2000 Product Guide. That is, provided all other products (for example, other software, firmware, and hardware) used with it properly exchange date data with the Microsoft product. A Year 2000 Compliant product from Microsoft will recognize the Year 2000 as a leap year. Disclaimer: The Statement of Compliance refers to the Microsoft product as delivered by Microsoft. The Compliance Statement does not apply to user customizable features or third party add-on features or products, including items such as macros and custom programming and formatting features…

Excel Compliance Issues

More than most programs, Excel faces the challenge of translating two-digit date entries into four-digit values for use in calculations and reports.

One of the most common ways in which software handles the Year 2000 problem is *date windowing*. In this technique, the software arbitrarily sets a cutoff value. If you enter a two-digit year beneath that value, the software interprets it as being in the 21st century. If you enter a value at or above the window, the date is considered to be part of the 20th century. For example, if the window is 50, and you enter the date 4/1/51, the program treats it as 1951; but if you enter 4/1/49, the program treats it as 2049.

Excel uses windowing extensively, but the way it does so has changed over the years, as described in Table 37.2:

Table 37.2 How Excel Uses Date Windowing

Version	Date Window
Excel 2.*x*	None (All 2-digit dates interpreted as 19xx)
Excel 3.*x*-7.*x*	20 (2-digit dates below 1/1/20 interpreted as 20xx; others interpreted as 19xx)
Excel 97/98	30 (2-digit dates below 1/1/30 interpreted as 20xx; others interpreted as 19xx)

In short, entering the same date in Excel 7 (Excel 95) and Excel 97 may return different values. The problem may even occur without user input, if your worksheets contain the **=DATEVALUE** (text) function, which interprets a text argument as if it was data entered from the keyboard.

To help you assess whether the change in date windowing is a problem in your worksheets, download the Date Migration Wizard for MS Excel 97 (datemig1.e XE) from **http://support.microsoft.com/support/excel/content/utilities/xlutil.asp**, and then install and run it as follows:

1. Double-click on DateMig1.exe to extract its contents, DateScan.xla and ReadMe.txt.
2. Copy these files to the C:\Program Files\Microsoft Office\Office\Library folder.
3. Start Excel.
4. Choose Tools, Add-Ins.
5. In the Add-Ins dialog box, mark the Date Migration Wizard for Windows check box.
6. Click OK. The wizard becomes available.
7. Choose Tools, Date Migration, Date Migration Wizard.
8. Follow the wizard's instructions for choosing which functions and workbooks to scan.

The Date Migration Wizard adds a report to each workbook, listing known problems, potential problems, cells containing multiple affected date functions, and formulas with unaffected functions. You will still need to review the cells it has flagged to make any necessary changes.

In Excel 97 and Excel 98, recorded macros can also encounter the date windowing problem, if recorded with Windows' default Short Date Style setting. Under these circumstances, if you enter a date in a cell as you record a VBA macro, Excel may enter a date precisely 100 years off when you run the macro later. For example, you enter 1/1/2032, but the macro only stores the last two digits (32). Then, when the macro is run, it interprets 32 as 1932, as per Excel 97/98's date windowing rule.

The best solution is to go into the Regional Settings applet in the Control Panel, and change the Short Date Style setting to contain four digits. However, what about any non-compliant macros you (or your colleagues) already have? You can edit these manually.

In the previous example, you would change the VBA line

```
ActiveCell.FormulaR2C2 = "1/1/32"
```

to read as follows:

```
ActiveCell.FormulaR2C2 = "1/1/2032"
```

With all four digits present in the date, Excel will run the macro properly.

NOTE Excel VBA macros follow different date-windowing rules than the rest of Excel. Their rules are similar to those of Microsoft Access 95 and 97, as discussed in the next section of this chapter.

NOTE Excel contains one more date-handling inconsistency that you might want to be aware of. When Excel was first introduced, a decision was made to maximize compatibility with Lotus 1-2-3, then the market leader. With this goal in mind, Excel was (and is) designed to incorrectly treat the year 1900 as a leap year, just as 1-2-3 did.

One systematic software solution for testing Excel macros is OnMark 2000 WorkBench for Excel, from Viasoft (**www.onmark.viasoft.com/index.html**). You can download a trial copy that expires after it is used on 25 files. This program analyzes Excel workbooks to identify potential date problems and other inconsistencies. It highlights data, formulas, and other date-sensitive areas, as well as cells that reference VB application code or external functions, and provides an environment where these issues can be assessed and fixed. You can see OnMark 2000 WorkBench for Excel in Figure 37.3.

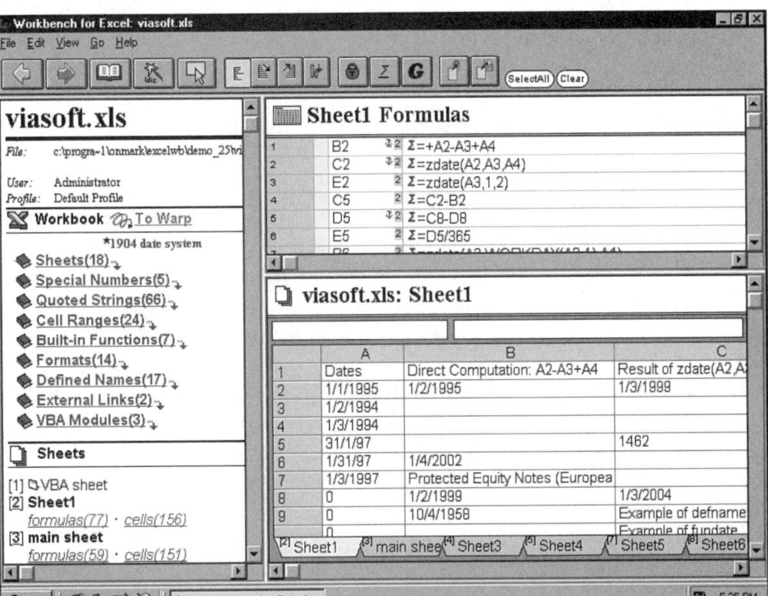

FIGURE 37.3
OnMark 2000 Workbench for Excel, from Viasoft.

Another solution is DateSpy from AMS Group International Distributors, Inc. (telephone 414-352-4896 or on the Web at **www.datespy.com**). DateSpy is available in Standard, Professional, and Enterprise editions, all of which work with Excel 5.*x*, Excel 95 (7.*x*) and Excel 97 (8.*x*) on both standalone PCs and LANs. DateSpy Professional can run in batch mode over a network. It also offers extensive filtering options that can, for example, focus on files that have been used recently, identify only date values newer than a specific date, or scan files with unusual extensions, such as CSV comma-separated values files exported from Excel. DateSpy Enterprise builds on DateSpy Pro, creating a customizable summary of all your Excel worksheets, companywide.

A great source for detailed information about Excel Y2K issues is Patrick O'Beirne's Year 2000 and Spreadsheets site at **http://homepages.iol.ie/~pobeirne/y2ksprds.htm**.

Access Compliance Issues

Date windowing gets even trickier in Microsoft Access. First of all, in Microsoft Access 2.0 and earlier, all two-digit dates are considered part of the 20th century (19xx)—*period*. These versions of Access are Y2K non-compliant.

In most cases, the best move is to update your database to a newer version of Access, but if you prefer not to, see Microsoft Knowledge Base Q132067 for some workarounds that may extend the life of your Access 2.0 databases.

In Access 95 (and Windows 95/NT), Microsoft made two important changes. Whereas the application previously set the date rules, it now defers to a Windows OLE Automation file called Oleaut32.dll. When Access 95 first shipped, Oleaut32.dll used the following simple rules:

1. Check the system clock.
2. If the clock says it's still the 20th century, then assume all two-digit dates are 20th century dates.
3. If the clock says it's the 21st century, assume all two-digit dates are 21st century dates.

You can see that this works only as long as your databases don't include both 20th and 21st century dates. Microsoft quickly noticed the problem and updated Oleaut32.dll to include date windowing, similar to that of Excel 97. Two-digit dates 12/31/29 or earlier are assumed to be 21st century dates; two digit-dates 1/1/30 or higher are assumed to be 20th century dates.

The change was made in Oleaut32.dll version 2.20.4049 and all later versions. To find out which version you're using, right-click on Oleaut32.dll in the C:\Windows\System folder and choose Properties. Click the Version tab, and click Product Version in the Item Name box. The version number appears in the Value box, as shown in Figure 37.4.

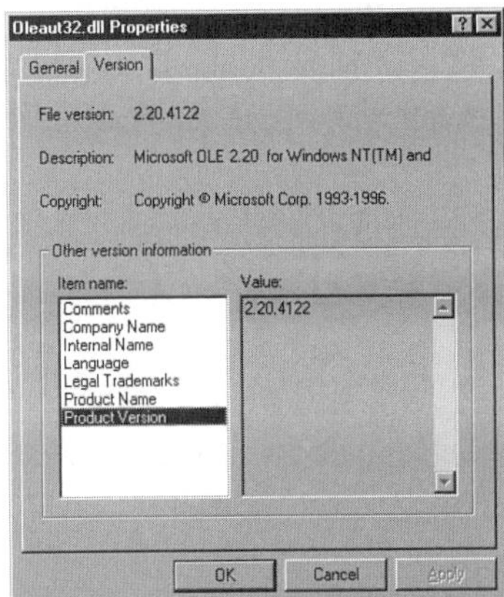

FIGURE 37.4
Checking the version of your Oleaut32.dll file.

The bottom line is as follows:

- If you've installed Office 97, you should have an Oleaut32.dll file that uses the new windowing rules (but it doesn't hurt to check).
- If you are running Access 95, you may be using the old *or* new rules, depending on the version of Oleaut32.dll you have installed. Programs such as Internet Explorer, Visual Basic 5.0, and Microsoft Windows 95 OSR2 install new versions of this file, so you may no longer be using the original version.
- If you are running multiple versions of Access in your organization, the same date information could be stored differently, depending on the version being used.
- Since Office 97 Visual Basic for Applications also looks to Oleaut32.dll for direction, all your new Office macros should reflect the 30-year date window.

Adjusting your Access databases to reflect four-digit years throughout can also require you to make adjustments in module code and to widen the date fields on your forms and reports.

You can find more detailed information about ensuring Y2K compliance in Access databases at Patrick O'Beirne's Year 2000 issues in PC Database Packages site at **http://homepages.iol.ie/~pobeirne/y2kxbase.htm**.

Word Compliance Issues

Microsoft Word is generally compliant, but following are a few issues of which you should be aware:

- Given a choice, always enter, import, or format years as four digits. Especially watch out for data imported into Word from external sources.
- Many users (at Microsoft's suggestion) have used nested fields as a workaround for doing date arithmetic in Word tables. Microsoft now discourages this approach as prone to Year 2000 errors.

- When sorting rows of text based on two-digit dates, the Table, Sort command works differently in Word 97 than in earlier versions. In earlier versions, Word assumed that all dates were in the 20th century, except that 00 was equivalent to the year 2000. Items would sort as shown in the following example:

  2/15/02

  3/27/56

  9/14/98

  3/5/00

  Word 97 uses date windowing, assuming that two-digit dates from 00 to 29 are in the 21st century. So the same set of entries would sort as follows:

  3/27/56

  9/14/98

  3/5/00

  2/15/02
- In Word 6.0 and 95, {QUOTE} fields, form-field date formatting, custom document properties, and WordBasic text-to-date conversions all treat two-digit years as representing dates between 1901 and 2000.
- In Word 6.0 for Windows and the Macintosh, the Find File feature does not work if you search for files with 21st century dates.

PowerPoint Compliance Issues

PowerPoint is generally Y2K compliant, with two significant exceptions.

First, if you save a PowerPoint 95, 97, or 98 file to PowerPoint 4.0, date fields in the year 2000 and beyond will be truncated incorrectly, with the number 1 substituting for 20. For example, the year 2003 will read 103. Microsoft's Pp7trans.dll and Pp8trans.dll translator files are not Y2K-compliant.

Second, starting on January 1, 2000, if you create a presentation in PowerPoint 95 or 97 using two-digit date formats, and you mark the Update Automatically (Insert As Field) check box in the Date and Time dialog box, PowerPoint also truncates the date improperly. The solution is to either use four-digit dates or insert the dates as text, not as fields that can automatically update themselves.

Outlook Compliance Issues

Like other Office applications, Outlook 97 uses a date window, but unlike the other applications, Outlook's date window moves forward as the years progress. For Outlook's Tasks, Events, and Meetings features, the window starts 30 years before the current date and continues 70 years past the current date. If you enter a two-digit year as part of a birthday, however, the window begins 95 years ago and stretches five years beyond the current date. (So if you're entering the birthday of a centenarian, enter it with four digits.)

More seriously, Outlook 97 incorrectly handles two-digit dates whenever you schedule an event that starts in the 20th century and ends in the 21st century. After December 31, 1999, Outlook 97 will treat events in the past (for example, an event that occurred 12/1/1999) as if they were scheduled for the end of the following century (in other words, 12/1/2099). The solution is to download and install version 8.03.5228 (or higher) of the Outllib.dll file, or to upgrade to Outlook 98.

Other Compliance Issues

Don't forget that linkages between Office and external data can be especially troublesome. Pay close attention to make sure accurate four-digit dates are stored and preserved in the following types of data:

- Imported and exported data, both outside *and among* Office applications. (For example, data exported to Word from Access databases uses two-digit year format unless the Four Digit Years option has been checked in Access' Export dialog box.)
- Database queries via ODBC or SQL.
- Links to data stored on other platforms, such as mainframes, minicomputers, or client/server applications on servers.
- Data imported from sources beyond your control via OLE or DDE.
- Formulas imported from other software, such as 1-2-3.

Finally, if you depend on custom applications built with third-party OCX or DLL files, Access MDA library databases, or Visual Basic RES files, you may want to ask the suppliers to confirm that these files are Y2K compliant. ●

PART VII

Troubleshoot and Optimize Office

CHAPTER 38

Troubleshooting and Optimizing Word

Bad things happen to good software, and if that software is Microsoft Word, odds are it's going to be your problem. In this chapter, you'll walk through the key elements of Word troubleshooting: what to do when Word won't start, or won't keep running, or corrupts the documents and templates that your business depends upon. You'll also take a quick look at some settings that can help optimize Word for the systems you're running it on.

Keeping Word Up-to-Date

While Microsoft makes little pretense that its service releases fix *all* the bugs in Word (or any other program), they do fix many of the problems Microsoft has found it easiest to reproduce. Therefore, it usually makes sense to qualify and deploy Word service releases as quickly as possible.

Thus far, Microsoft has issued two Service Releases for Office 97, and each includes fixes that are relevant to Word. Among the most important problems largely solved by service releases are the following:

- Loss of graphics data, with Word displaying a red X in place of graphics (fixed in SR-1)
- Corrupted documents when saving to a hard disk with less than 20MB free space (improved in SR-1, but Word still works more reliably with more free space)
- Problems with headers and footers containing field codes; invalid page faults (IPFs) when saving such documents as RTF files (fixed in SR-1)
- In GroupWise and Document Management System environments, problems with reopening files that are closed after copying large amounts of text (fixed in SR-2)

At this time, there have been no service releases for Word 98 for the Macintosh. Microsoft has, however, posted fixes for two obscure Word 98 problems, one of them potentially dangerous:

- Microsoft's Remove Office 98 Utility is designed to search for the Microsoft Office 98 library and then move the entire folder surrounding it into the trash. Some users have manually moved this library into their System folders. Upon encountering the library there, the Remove Office 98 Utility moves the entire System folder into the trash—potentially rendering the Macintosh inoperable. The new Remove Office 98 utility, available at **www.microsoft.com/macoffice/default.asp**, fixes this problem.
- In the Memo, Resume, Newsletter, Calendar, and Agenda Wizards, when you click Finish, Word 98 quits. You may also get unexpected quits with third-party add-ins. This behavior occurs on G3 Power Macintoshes or other Macintoshes with 512K or larger caches, and on the UMAX S900 Macintosh clone. To solve the problem, download Microsoft's Memo-Resume Wizard Updater 1.0 at the same location.

Troubleshooting Damaged Word 97/98 Documents

What could be worse than going through the trouble of building a complex document, and then finding that document corrupted? When this happens to you—or to a panicked colleague—the first step is to calm down.

NOTE It will be a lot easier to calm down if you know you have a recent backup. Making sure that you have a reliable system for backing up files is one of the most important things you can do as an Office administrator.

The second step is to do some basic troubleshooting, intended to rule out causes that are external to the document:

- Does the problem occur only in this document? (Try opening other documents, especially documents containing similar elements.)
- Is the problem related to the template that is attached to the document? (Try attaching a different template via the Tools, Templates and Add-Ins dialog box.)
- Is the problem specific to this computer? (Try opening the file on another computer.)
- Is the problem specific to Word? (Try running other programs to see if the problem recurs.)
- Does the problem only occur when you are using a specific printer driver? (Try switching printers and printer drivers.)
- Is the problem video-related, in other words, are there unreadable characters on screen? (In Windows, try running Windows with the standard Vga.drv video driver.)

If, after this, it appears that the problem is actually with the document, try the steps discussed in the next section.

Recovering a Damaged Word 97/98 Document

You have the following several options for recovering all or most of the information in a damaged Word document:

- Copy the entire document, except for the last paragraph mark, into a new document. Word stores a great deal of information in paragraph marks, and the last paragraph mark in the document contains even more information, including critical section and style data. If the document corruption is contained there, copying everything else into a new document could solve the problem.
- Save the entire document to another format, such as Word 6.0/95 or RTF. Often, this solves the problem—but you lose document elements that are new to Word 97, and saving to the older format sometimes causes graphics in your document to be resized.
- Copy chunks of your document into a new document, a piece at a time—saving the new document after each copy. You may be able to figure out roughly where in your document the corruption exists, and copy all the other elements before and after the corruption. Often, you'll find that the problem is in a damaged image, which you can then delete and replace. Or, it may be in a specific paragraph; you may then be able to copy the contents of that paragraph, except for the paragraph mark at the end of the paragraph.
- Use Insert, File to insert the damaged file into a new document.
- Try viewing the file in Draft mode. Choose Tools, Options, click the View tab, mark the Draft Font check box, and click OK.

The preceding techniques are intended to preserve both text and formatting. If these fail, you may still be able to preserve most of the text in your document by using one of the following techniques. You'll have to reformat the document, but it's better than losing everything.

- Save the file as Text Only. (Choose File, Save As; choose Text Only in the Save As Type drop-down box; click Save.)
- Open the file using the Recover Text From Any File filter, which strips everything except text from any formatted file. (Choose File, Open. Choose Recover Text from Any File in the Files of Type drop-down box. Browse to and select the file you want to open. Click Open.) If Word's Fast Save feature was turned on when you last saved this file successfully, you may find that the text is out of order. Still, most or all of it should be there—*somewhere.*

NOTE In Word 97, if the Recover Text from Any File filter is not present, run a maintenance install to install it. You'll find this filter in the Converters and Filters/Text Converters category of installation options.

You may be able to mix-and-match these techniques. You could, for example, copy formatted text from your original file wherever possible, and copy unformatted text from a Text Only copy where this is the only text available.

Troubleshooting Word 97 Startup Crashes

If Word 97 has run properly before, but now consistently crashes at startup, chances are your problem is in one of five places:

- A damaged AutoCorrect (.acl) file
- The Normal.dot global template
- Another global template or add-in (.wll) that loads at startup
- The Data key for Word 97 in the Windows registry
- A damaged Tahoma font, which Word 97 uses to display dialog boxes and menus

NOTE Many of the troubleshooting recommendations made throughout the remainder of this chapter can take a significant amount of time to perform. As an Office administrator, you may at times decide that it is a better use of your time to simply uninstall and reinstall Office and/or Windows.

TIP If Word has never started properly, your Office installation may have failed. For more information about fixing failed Office installations, refer to Chapter 5.

NOTE If you've upgraded from Windows 95 or 98 to Windows NT 4.0, remember that you need to reinstall Word 97 and Office 97 in order to place the appropriate registry settings in the Windows NT registry. Otherwise, the programs will not run properly.

When Word crashes, click Details to see where the problem was. If you receive a message that states `WINWORD caused an invalid page fault in module MSO97.DLL at 014f:306c59b`, the ACL file is probably the problem. In general, upgrading to Service Release 1 can solve this problem. If this does not work, rename the ACL files, except Mso97.acl, and try running Word again to generate a new ACL file. You will lose any custom AutoCorrect settings associated with this computer.

Assuming that the ACL file is not the problem, begin troubleshooting by starting Word without the items that normally run at startup. Follow these steps:

1. Choose Start, Run.
2. In the Run dialog box, enter Word's path and filename, along with the /a switch. In a typically installation, the command is:

```
C:\Program Files\Microsoft Office\Microsoft Word /a
```


CAUTION

When you run Word with the /a switch, any changes that you make to Tools, Options settings or to Normal.dot during that session are lost when you exit Word.

If Word starts properly, you know that the problem is in Normal.dot, a global template, or the registry key. To determine if the problem is in Normal.dot, perform the following steps:

1. Exit Word.
2. Rename Normal.dot, typically stored in the C:\Program Files\Microsoft Office\Template folder. (Note that there may be more than one Normal.dot on your computer, especially if you've retained an older copy of Word. Make sure you rename the correct one.)
3. Run Word again (without using the /a switch).

If Word runs properly, the problem is in Normal.dot. Word regenerates a new Normal.dot with no custom settings. You can then use the Organizer to copy all or most macros, toolbars, AutoText entries, and styles from the renamed Normal.dot to the new one.

If Word still does not run normally, check if the problem is with global templates or add-ins that load at startup.

1. Run Windows Explorer and browse to Word's startup folder, typically c:\Program Files\Microsoft Office\Office\Startup.
2. If there are any DOT or WLL files there, move them to another folder outside of the Microsoft Office folder.
3. Run Word again.

If Word runs properly, the problem is in one of the global templates or add-ins. To discover which one, you can restore them one at a time until the problem recurs. If the problem still exists, it may be with the Data key associated with Word in the Windows registry. You may be able to solve the problem by deleting the Data key, using the Registry Editor (regedit.exe).

CAUTION

As always, be extremely careful with the Registry Editor; if you delete or edit the wrong information, you could render your computer inoperable. Be aware that deleting the Word 97 Data key clears a variety of custom settings, notably the settings accessible through the Tools, Options dialog box.

You can delete the Data key as follows:

1. Exit Word (and also exit WordMail, if it is running in connection with your email program).
2. Choose Start, Run.
3. In the Run dialog box, type **regedit** and click OK.
4. Navigate to the following key: HKEY_CURRENT_USER\Software\Microsoft\Office\8.0\Word\Data.
5. Make sure the Data folder is selected in the left-hand pane of the Registry Editor, and press the Delete key.
6. Click Yes to confirm that you want to delete the Data key.
7. Exit the Registry Editor.
8. Run Word (without the /a switch).

If Word runs normally, you've solved the problem, although you may have to re-customize Word's registry settings.

If none of this works, the problem may be with the Tahoma font that Word uses to display dialog boxes and menus; try reinstalling it from the Office 97 CD-ROM.

Troubleshooting Other Word-Related Protection Faults

If you are experiencing an unacceptable number of system crashes (invalid page faults) while working in Word 97, the following troubleshooting steps can help you identify and solve the problem.

When the invalid page fault occurs, click Details to see where it occurred. If you find that a printer or video driver is at fault, concentrate your efforts there. For example, switch from your video driver to Windows' basic Vga.drv video driver, or check your printer or video card vendor's Web site to see if a more recent driver is available for the device in question. It's common for IPFs related to printer or video drivers to occur while you are printing or formatting a document, but they can happen at other times as well.

You can install a printer driver in Windows and select it in Word regardless of whether you actually have the corresponding printer (although of course you will not actually be able to send the print job to be printed). To simulate printing (and therefore see whether Word and the file can actually be printed), install the test print driver to the FILE: port instead of to a parallel port such as LPT1 or LPT2.

NOTE When you change the printer driver, make sure you switch to a printer that does not use the same core mini-driver. Most HP-compatible printers use Unidrv.dll, and most PostScript printers use Pscript.drv. To ensure that you fully test your printer driver, if you've been working with a PostScript printer driver, switch to an HP-compatible printer driver—or vice versa.

NOTE Printer or video drivers may also be at fault if Word hangs on exit. In some cases, a DLL file called Msgsrv32.dll may receive an incomprehensible error message from a Windows driver, leading it to stop responding. In Windows 95/98, press Ctrl+Alt+Del once to display the Close Program list of currently running tasks, and look for the line Msgsrv32.dll (Not responding). If it's there, try swapping print or video drivers. ■

If the module that causes the system crash is a DLL file that is part of Word or Windows, the file may be damaged. If the file is part of Office (see Appendix B), try a maintenance install of Office to replace it with a clean version. In some cases, you can solve the problem by copying a clean version directly off your original Office CD-ROM, but be careful never to copy an older version than the one already running on your system.

If the problem is in Winword.exe, the main Word program file, continue your troubleshooting to see which interactions are actually causing the problem.

Try to figure out whether all of the problem documents have the same element in common. These elements may include the following:

- **The same font.** Create a new document using the same fonts, and systematically reduce the number of fonts in the document one at a time until the problem disappears. If it does disappear, the last font you removed may be damaged, and you should reinstall it from its original disk.
- **The same graphic.** Again, remove graphics one at a time to see if the problem disappears. If you find a damaged graphic, replace it with one that is intact.
- **Links to the same documents.** Check whether there is damage to one of the linked documents that you can fix.
- **The same custom template.** Try attaching the document to a different template.

If none of this works, the problem could be with Word's automatic features or proofing tools. Whenever a user presses the spacebar to end a word, Word's background spelling and proofreading tools go to work, checking your custom dictionaries (DIC files) and AutoCorrect lists (ACL files). If any of these files are damaged, Word may crash with a protection fault. To troubleshoot these files, exit Word, and then rename the files with a different extension. (As mentioned earlier, *do not* rename Mso97.acl.)

Restart Word, and work in a few documents. If the problem disappears, a DIC or ACL file may have caused it. If the problem remains, it may be that your spelling or grammar tools themselves are at fault.

To find out, turn off background spell checking and grammar checking through the Spelling & Grammar tab of the Tools, Options dialog box. If Word now works properly—and especially if you can cause the protection fault by running the spell checker manually—the solution may be to remove and reinstall the proofing tools via a maintenance install of Word or Office. (You must remove them in one maintenance install, and then reinstall them in a second.)

If none of these steps work, and you've already upgraded Office 97 to the latest service release, the problem may be with Windows, or with a damaged Office installation, or you may need to upgrade your hardware:

- Troubleshoot Windows by loading it in Safe Mode (In Windows 95, press F8 at startup, and then choose Safe Mode from the list of options. In Windows 98, press and hold the Ctrl key during startup, and choose Safe Mode). This loads Windows without any unnecessary drivers or options. Run Word and see if the problem goes away. If it does, the problem may be with another Windows driver or optional feature. Try running a maintenance installation of Windows.
- If you have been running Word 97 on a machine with only 16 or 24MB RAM, or with very little hard drive space free, stop running simultaneous programs and clean up your hard drive to create more space. If this does not help, either add memory or hard disk space, and see if this solves the problem.
- Remove Office completely. Start by running the Office setup program's Remove All option. Then, run the Office Upgrade Wizard (Offcln97.exe), which removes components that setup sometimes leaves behind. Then reinstall Office from scratch. You can find this on the Office 97 CD-ROM in the \Valupack\Offclean folder.

Troubleshooting Performance Problems

If you are running Word on a low-powered computer, you may be able to make some adjustments to improve speed. Each of the following adjustments has tradeoffs, which may or may not be acceptable in your environment, but all of them can make Word perform at least a little bit better.

Following is an adjustment you can make to hardware:

- Add memory. Microsoft has said that Word 97 will run in 8MB RAM on Windows 95, or 16MB if you want to work with documents in excess of 50 pages. The practical reality is dramatically different. Expect to require at least 32MB if you're running Windows 95/98, and 64MB if you're running Windows NT 4.0 Workstation.

Following are some adjustments you can make to Windows:

- Defragment your hard drive using Windows 95's built-in Disk Defragmenter (choose Start, Programs, Accessories, System Tools, Disk Defragmenter). If you are running Windows 98, the Disk Defragmenter can relocate Word to the fastest area on your hard drive.
- If your computer has more than one drive, consider adjusting Windows 95's virtual memory settings to place the swap file on a local drive that has more space available, or is significantly faster than your boot drive.

- Use fewer fonts.
- Use lower color depth—in other words, use 16 or 256 colors instead of millions of colors.
- Don't use wallpaper.
- Disable screen savers, especially while printing.

Following are adjustments to where you run Word:

- Install Word locally, not on a network server.
- Run Word and store your documents on uncompressed drives, not drives that use DriveSpace.

Following are adjustments you can make to Word features:

- Turn off Check Spelling As You Type and Check Grammar As You Type in the Spelling & Grammar tab of the Options dialog box.
- Turn off other automatic features, including all the check boxes in the AutoFormat As You Type and AutoCorrect tabs of the AutoCorrect dialog box.
- Use Normal view instead of Page Layout view whenever possible.
- Mark Picture Placeholders (in the View tab of the Options dialog box) to display boxes instead of images whenever possible. And in text-only documents where formatting is not a constant worry, mark Draft Font to display text in Windows' built-in system font.
- When precise formatting doesn't matter, speed printing by using the Draft Output option (in the Print tab of the Options dialog box).
- In documents converted from Word 6.0 or Word 95, where slight changes in page layout are acceptable, improve scrolling speed by clearing the check box labeled Use Printer Metrics to Lay Out Document in the Compatibility tab of the Options dialog box.

Following is an adjustment you can make to Office:

- Turn off the Journal feature in Microsoft Outlook that tracks every Word document when it is closed or saved.

Troubleshooting Word 98 for the Macintosh

If you support Word 98 for the Macintosh, you may be called upon to troubleshoot system errors that occur while Word is running. You can try several things to identify and solve the problem.

Try to Reproduce the Problem

As with all troubleshooting, see if you can reproduce the problem: does it always occur when you perform a specific task, or only on a system configured in a specific way? What message do you get? (For example, does the Macintosh consistently display a Type 1 or Type 3 message?)

Also consider whether the problem happens only (or mostly) in Word. If so, you may have a MacOS system problem or, much less likely, a hardware problem.

NOTE Be aware that errors such as Type 1 and Type 3 are common on the Macintosh. It's likely they will happen occasionally no matter what you do. This troubleshooting process is intended to help when you are getting an unacceptable number of errors, or when they happen consistently at certain times.

As Apple has upgraded the MacOS, it has taken steps to reduce the number of system errors and their severity. Most Macintosh users agree that MacOS 8.1, the current version at the time of this writing, is the most stable version of MacOS. If you are having consistent problems, and your other software is compatible with MacOS 8.1, consider an upgrade. ■

Troubleshoot Macintosh Extensions

Now that you (hopefully) know what kind of problem you have, try to determine whether the cause is a conflict with a specific *extension*—a file loaded into the Macintosh's memory at startup to add specific capabilities to the MacOS.

Shut down the Macintosh and restart it with extensions off. To do this, press the Shift key as you start the Macintosh, and keep it held down until the Macintosh reports that extensions are turned off. Now, run Word and see if the error still occurs. If not, chances are there is a conflict between Word and an extension.

Now you need to start the trial-and-error process of trying to figure out which extension is causing the problem. Double-click on the Extensions Manager in the System folder's Control Panel to display a list of extensions currently running. One at a time, clear an extension, click Restart to restart the Macintosh, load Word, and see if the problem still exists.

In MacOS 8.*x*, you can streamline the process of testing by choosing the MacOS Base set of extensions from the list of extension sets in the Selected Set box. The MacOS Base set represents the minimum number of extensions your Macintosh needs to run properly. If Word runs correctly with the MacOS Base set of extensions, you can begin loading additional extensions one at a time to see which one caused the problem.

You can see that, even under the best of circumstances, troubleshooting extension conflicts can be a lengthy process. Fortunately, a third-party program, Conflict Catcher 4.1 from Casady & Greene (**www.casadyg.com/products/conflictcatcher/default.html**), may be able to help.

Conflict Catcher helps identify and resolve potential conflicts, especially those that occur at startup when all of the Macintosh's extensions and resources first load into memory. It also provides more powerful tools than the built-in Extension Manager for creating extension sets designed to serve particular purposes. (If you know you're planning to work extensively with Word, for example, you can build a set that doesn't include the extensions you don't need, reducing the likelihood of conflicts.)

NOTE Some extensions are necessary to the operation of your Macintosh; you have no choice but to run them. If one of these has caused the conflict, see if Apple or the third party who provided it has updated the extension. In other cases, you may be able to disable an extension permanently and never notice the difference.

Rebuild the Desktop File

The Macintosh contains a hidden desktop database that tracks program locations, icons, file types, comments stored in Get Info windows, and more. Over time, this database can either become corrupted or become disorganized so that it does not run as well. If you are having unexplained problems with Word, try rebuilding it (this process is usually called *rebuilding the desktop*).

Restart the Macintosh while pressing the Command and Option keys. After all extensions load, the Finder asks if you want to build the startup disk (the disk containing the Macintosh's working system folder). Click OK. Depending on the size of your disk, rebuilding the desktop may take several minutes. When MacOS finishes, if you have more than one disk, you'll be asked if you want to rebuild the next one; choose OK. When you're finished, restart the Macintosh again and run Word to see if the problem has disappeared.

Many MacOS experts recommend routinely rebuilding the desktop once a month.

Replace the Word Settings File

In Word 98, a wide variety of settings are stored in the Word Settings (8) file, including many of the settings that would be stored in the registry in Windows 95, 98, or NT. Word Settings files can be damaged, preventing Word for the Macintosh from working properly. The easiest solution is to quit Word, and then drag your settings file out of the System Folder:Preferences folder onto the Macintosh desktop. Now, restart Word. Word looks for its settings file, and not finding one, creates a new copy.

If Word works properly now, you have solved the problem—but you will have to manually re-enter any custom settings in the Tools, Options dialog box.

NOTE Previous versions of Word for the Macintosh have corresponding files, such as Word Settings (6) and Word Settings (5)

Troubleshooting OLE on the Macintosh

When you install Office for the Macintosh, OLE support is also added, allowing OLE-compliant programs to link and embed each other's data. OLE is native to Windows; the approximate Macintosh equivalent is Publish and Subscribe, also supported in Word 98 for the Macintosh. You may occasionally run into trouble with OLE on the Macintosh. When you choose Insert, Object, for example, Word may not display the program containing the data you want to embed or link with. Assuming that the program is also OLE-compliant, try taking these steps:

1. If possible, reinstall the program in question to "re-register" it in the OLE database.
2. If this is impractical, run that application; in most cases, this should re-register it. Note that some OLE applications must be run from within Word or another OLE-compatible program.
3. If neither of the first two methods work, delete the Office Registration Cache file and allow Office to rebuild it.
4. As an absolute last resort, delete the Registration Database and PPC Registration Database files. This eliminates all OLE information on your computer, including information related to non-Office programs such as Adobe PageMaker. It also has some effects within Office. You might, for example, have to re-register the Clip Art Gallery and reset the Custom dictionary.

CHAPTER 39

Troubleshooting and Optimizing Excel

In this chapter, you explore the structure of an Excel workbook and the different types of data files you can create in Excel. You'll also learn how to design the most efficient Excel workbooks and how to solve some of the most common problems that affect workbook performance and accuracy.

Understanding Excel's Architecture

You can create several types of data files with Excel. Understanding the different document types will help you design the most efficient solutions in Excel.

Excel Workbooks

The most common type of document you use in Excel is a workbook. A workbook is stored as a single file and can contain several different components. Some components of a workbook are visible as sheets, like pages in the workbook, which are indicated by tabs along the bottom of the screen. Other components are not represented by visible sheets. A workbook can contain any number of the following components:

- *Worksheets.* The most common type of sheet in a workbook, worksheets are organized as a collection of cells, arranged in rows and columns. Each cell can contain a literal value, such as a number or text, or a formula, which calculates a result. Figure 39.1 shows a workbook with a worksheet as the active sheet.

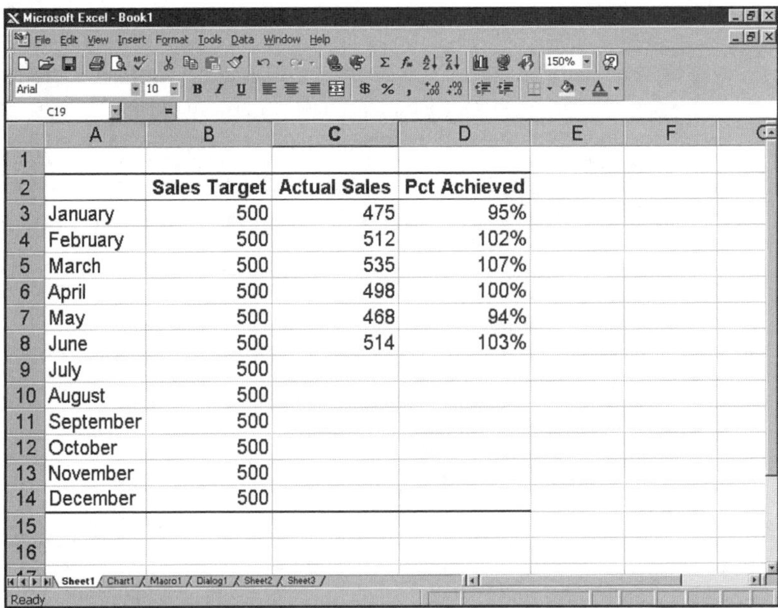

	A	B	C	D
1				
2		Sales Target	Actual Sales	Pct Achieved
3	January	500	475	95%
4	February	500	512	102%
5	March	500	535	107%
6	April	500	498	100%
7	May	500	468	94%
8	June	500	514	103%
9	July	500		
10	August	500		
11	September	500		
12	October	500		
13	November	500		
14	December	500		

FIGURE 39.1
The cells in a worksheet contain text, numbers, and formulas.

- *Charts.* Used to create graphical representations of the data in your Excel workbooks. Excel includes many different chart types—such as line, bar, and pie charts—and lets you combine more than one type of chart into a single chart. You can create a chart as an object embedded in a worksheet, or as a separate chart sheet. In Figure 39.2, a chart sheet is the active sheet.

FIGURE 39.2
A chart sheet contains a graphical representation of the data in the workbook.

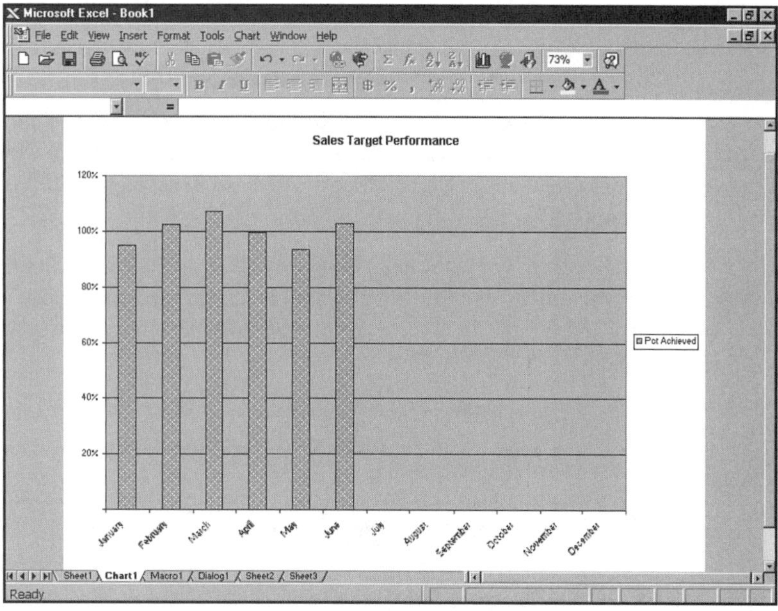

- *Modules.* Used to store Excel macros, written in Visual Basic for Applications (VBA). In Excel 97, modules are not visible as sheets in the workbook but are edited in the Visual Basic Editor (VBE) that is shared by all Office 97 applications. In Excel 5 and 7, modules are stored as sheets in a workbook. Figure 39.3 shows a recorded macro as it is displayed in the VBE.

FIGURE 39.3
The Visual Basic Editor displays the VBA macros in your workbook.

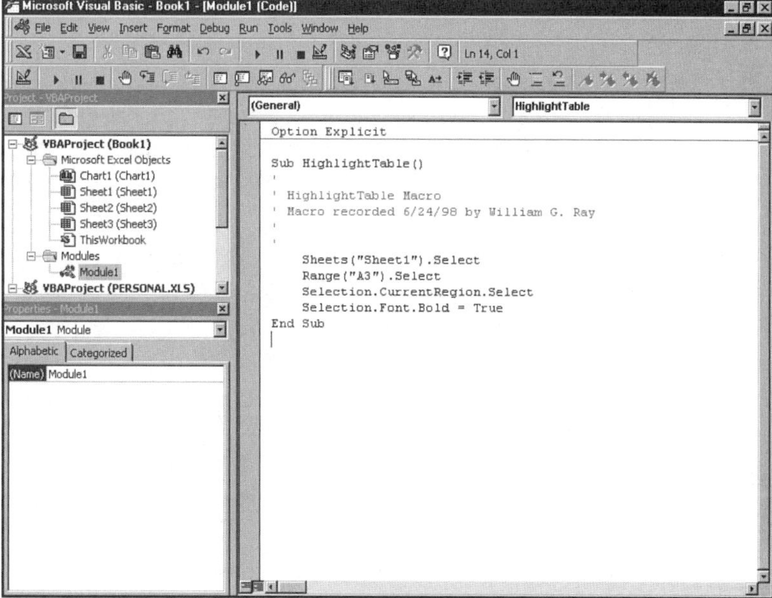

- *Excel 4.0 macro sheets.* These contain macros written in Excel's older, function-style macro language. These macros, sometimes called XLM macros, are retained for compatibility with existing Excel applications.
- *Excel 5.0 dialog boxes.* These contain custom dialog boxes as they were designed for Excel 5 and Excel 7 VBA macros and appear as sheets in the workbook. New dialog boxes designed for Excel 97 are created as UserForms in the Visual Basic Editor and are not visible as sheets in the workbook.

When you create a new workbook, the only visible sheets are worksheets. In Excel 97, a workbook contains three worksheets by default. In Excel 5 and Excel 95, a workbook contains 16 worksheets by default. To control the number of sheets in a new workbook, set the following Excel option:

1. Choose Tools, Options. The Options dialog box appears.
2. Enter a number in the Sheets In New Workbook text box, and click on OK.

Now whenever you create a new workbook it will have the designated number of sheets. You can add sheets or remove them from the workbook later, as well.

NOTE In Excel 4.0, a workbook was a file that contained links to separate worksheet files. The individual worksheets could be opened independent of the Excel 4.0 workbooks.

Beginning in Excel 5.0, Excel stores worksheets in the workbook file, not as separate worksheet files.

Excel Templates

A template is a special type of workbook file used as a model for creating new workbooks. If you often need to create similar workbooks and spreadsheet models, you might want to consider creating a template.

Templates can contain many Excel features; these features characterize any new workbooks based on the template. When you design a template, you can include cell formats, menu and toolbar customizations, macros, page formatting, and the number and type of sheets in a workbook. You can also store row and column styles and worksheet content such as text, numbers, formulas, or graphics.

For example, you might want to create new workbooks that have six worksheets and one Excel 4.0 macro sheet, with a default font of 11 point Arial. You can create a workbook with these features, and then save it as a template.

To create a template:

1. Create a workbook with the features you want in your template.
2. Choose File, Save As. The Save As dialog box appears.
3. Enter the file name in the File Name text box, and select the folder where you want to store the template.
4. Select Template in the Save As Type list and click on Save.

When you open a template, Excel creates a copy of the template, including all the features you saved in the template. Now you can edit and save the new workbook without affecting the original template file.

If you store a template in the Excel startup or alternate startup folder, the new template is automatically available when you choose File, New.

NOTE If you are used to using templates in Word, you should know that the behavior of templates in Excel is a little different. In Excel, the new workbooks you create based on a template do not retain any link or reference to the template; therefore, making a change to an Excel template has no effect on existing workbooks based on that template. Also, because the new workbook inherits all of the template's features, including macros, you don't need to distribute the template if you transfer the new workbook via disk or email. ■

Autotemplates are special templates that determine the features of the new workbooks created by default when you start Excel. If you want to change the characteristics of the default workbook, you can customize the Autotemplate.

To create an Autotemplate, design a workbook with the features you want in your default workbook. Save the workbook in your startup or alternate startup folder, and give it one of the following names:

- Book.xlt for Windows
- Workbook for Macintosh

The next time you start Excel, any new workbooks you create will be based on your new Autotemplate.

Workspace Files

You can open a group of workbooks at the same time by using a workspace file. The workspace file keeps track of the file names, their locations, and the positions of the windows on the screen. A workspace file is really just a list and doesn't actually contain the workbooks. Even if you create a workspace file, you can still open its workbooks individually.

To create a workspace file:

1. Open the workbooks you want to include in the workspace file, and arrange them the way you want them on the screen.
2. Choose File, Save Workspace.
3. Enter a name for the workspace in the File Name text box, or accept the default name of Resume (see Figure 39.4). Click on Save to complete the command.

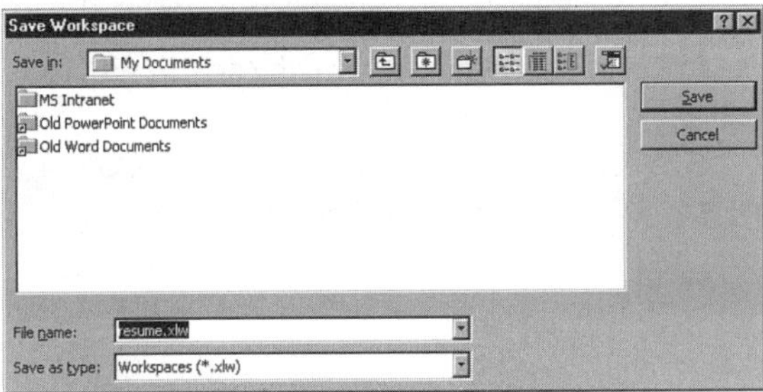

FIGURE 39.4
Enter the workspace name in the Save Workspace dialog box.

You can distribute a workspace file to other users as long as the workbooks in the workspace are stored on a shared network drive. The workspace file does not contain the individual workbooks but is just a list of the workbooks and their locations.

If you place the workspace file in your startup or alternate startup folder, Excel will open it automatically when you start Excel.

CAUTION

If you move or rename the individual workbooks in a workspace, the workspace file won't be able to locate them. Whenever possible, save the workspace file in the same folder as the individual workbooks.

Excel Add-Ins

Add-ins are workbooks that have been saved in a special format, which is used for running macros and custom applications. When an add-in file is opened, it is not visible, but its macros and other customizations are available. The add-in file is opened as a read-only file, so the user can't make any changes, accidental or otherwise. Add-ins are a good way to distribute automated solutions you have created in Excel VBA.

To create an add-in, create a workbook with the features you want. Make sure to save the workbook as a standard Excel workbook in case you ever want to make changes later. (You can't convert an add-in back to a standard workbook, so keeping a copy of the original workbook is very important.) Then choose File, Save As, and select Microsoft Excel Add-in in the Save As Type list box.

Add-ins can also be created by using the C programming language. Many commercial developers create add-ins in this way for high-performance, secure applications.

Excel includes several add-ins you can use to enhance the power of Excel. Installing one of these add-ins makes new commands available on the menus and toolbars and adds new worksheet functions that can be entered in worksheet cells.

Some of the add-ins that come with Excel 97 are:

- *Analysis ToolPak.* Adds engineering and financial functions to Excel.
- *AutoSave add-in.* Enables you to save Excel workbooks automatically.
- *File Conversion Wizard.* Speeds the process of converting files from other formats to Excel.
- *Microsoft Query.* Enables you to retrieve data from database files.
- *Report Manager.* Enables you to print and save reports based on Excel views and scenarios.
- *Template Wizard.* Provides Data Tracking, which assists you in exporting Excel data into database files.
- *Web Form Wizard.* Helps you convert an Excel spreadsheet into an HTML form, the most common type of Internet page.

Storing Information in Worksheet Cells

The information you enter in a worksheet cell is either a literal value or a formula. Literal values are simply text or numeric information that can be used either for display or for calculations.

Formulas are Excel expressions that perform calculations. The calculation might involve the literal values you have entered in other cells, or it could be the result of built-in functions, such as date or time functions.

Formulas can refer to data in other cells by using references. A reference is an expression Excel can interpret to identify one or more cells containing data. You can use three types of references in a formula:

- A1 style references
- R1C1 style references
- Name references

A1 and R1C1 References In Excel, you can identify the rows and columns of your worksheet by either of two systems. In the A1 referencing system, columns are identified by letters and rows are identified by numbers. For example, C10 is the cell at the intersection of the tenth row and third column of a sheet. In the R1C1 referencing system, both rows and columns are identified by numbers. The cell at the intersection of the tenth row and third column of a sheet is R10C3 with this system.

You can choose which referencing system to use. Many spreadsheet users are more familiar with the A1 referencing style, especially because it is the style used by most other spreadsheets, including Lotus 1-2-3; however, some older spreadsheet programs used the R1C1 style.

Neither style has any functional advantage. Some experienced Excel users find that the R1C1 style makes debugging the formulas in a worksheet easier.

To select the spreadsheet referencing style:

1. Choose Tools, Options, and click on the General tab in the Options dialog box.
2. To use the R1C1 style, check the R1C1 Reference Style check box. To use the A1 style, leave the box unchecked.
3. Click on OK.

Using Names in Worksheets

Using names makes your worksheets much easier to read and understand. In Excel, you can assign a name to a cell or group of cells or to embedded objects such as charts, ActiveX controls, or drawing objects. Then you can create formulas that use the name of the object instead of the A1 or R1C1 reference to the object.

For example, you might have a cell that contains the following formula:

```
=SUM(A3:A54)
```

Even though this formula clearly calculates the total of the values stored in a range of cells, it doesn't convey the business meaning of the calculation.

If you create a name for these same cells, you can enter the formula as follows:

```
=SUM(WeeklySales)
```

This formula uses the name "WeeklySales" to make the calculation easier to understand.

To name a cell or other object:

1. Select the cell or object you want to name.
2. Choose Insert, Name, Define. The Define Name dialog box appears.
3. Type the name you want to create, and then click on OK.

Because the names you create in this manner are available through the workbook, you can't have two ranges in a workbook with the same name.

You can make a name local to a worksheet by including the sheet name as part of the name. For example the name Sheet1!Totals is local to Sheet1 and is not available to formulas in other sheets in the workbook.

Formatting and Styles in Excel

Each cell in an Excel workbook contains a collection of formatting attributes. Using the Format, Cells command, you can customize the following types of formatting of individual cells:

- *Number formatting*. Controls the appearance of numeric data, including the results of formulas. You can include currency symbols, decimal points, thousand separators, and many other custom numeric formats.

- *Alignment formatting.* Controls how data is displayed within the cells. The data can be aligned vertically or horizontally, and you can control whether text wraps within a cell.
- *Font formatting.* Controls the font name, size, color, and other font characteristics of the cell.
- *Border formatting.* Lets you place various styles and colors of borders around any of the sides of a cell.
- *Pattern formatting.* Controls the color, shading, and special patterns of the background of a cell.
- *Protection formatting.* Lets you mark cells as *locked* or hide the formulas for the cell. These feature don't take effect until you apply protection by using the Tools, Protection command.

For more information on using worksheet protection, see "Securing a Workbook and its Components," later in this chapter.

Excel lets you format individual cells and ranges directly, but if you want a consistent format in your workbooks, you can use styles to apply formats systematically. A *style* is simply a named collection of the formatting you can apply to one or more cells. After you create a style, you can apply that style to cells and ranges throughout your workbook to achieve quick and consistent formatting, without having to remember or individually apply all the formatting options that make up the style.

To create a style:

1. Apply formatting to one or more cells in the workbook. This will be the formatting in the style you are creating.
2. Select the cells that contain the formatting.
3. Choose Format, Style. The Style dialog box appears.
4. Type a name for the style in the Style name combo box, and click on the Add button.
5. Click on OK to close the dialog box and apply the style to the selected cells.

To apply a style:

1. Select the cells to which you want to apply a style.
2. Choose Format, Style. The Style dialog box appears.
3. Select the name of the style you want to apply from the Style name combo box, and click on OK to close the dialog box and apply the style.

You can also copy styles from one workbook to another, extending the consistency beyond a single workbook.

To copy styles between workbooks:

1. Open the workbook that contains the styles you want to copy.
2. Open the workbook into which you want to copy the styles.

3. With the destination workbook active, choose Format, Style.
4. Click on Merge and, in the Merge Styles dialog box that appears, select the workbook containing the style you want to copy to this workbook.
5. Click on OK to close the Merge Styles dialog box, and click on OK again to close the Styles dialog box.

Storing Charts in Excel

Charts are based on the data in a range of cells in a worksheet. To create a chart, select the data you want to use for the chart, and then choose Insert, Chart. The Chart Wizard appears, providing instructions for selecting the chart type and chart options such as titles, legends, and colors.

The final step of the Chart Wizard shows the Chart Location options. Select As New Sheet to insert a new chart sheet into the workbook. Select As Object In to create the chart as an object embedded in the selected worksheet.

Embedding a chart in a worksheet sometimes makes it easier to show the chart alongside text and numeric data in a worksheet. Storing the chart on a separate sheet makes it easier to display and print the chart independent of other elements of the workbook.

Storing and Distributing Macros

Excel's primary macro language is Visual Basic for Applications (VBA). VBA macros are stored in modules in workbooks, templates, and add-ins. The modules are not visible as sheets in the workbook, but can be viewed and edited in the Visual Basic Editor (VBE), which is integrated into Office 97.

Each worksheet in a workbook contains a module to handle the event procedures for the worksheet. Event procedures execute automatically when certain events occur, such as opening or closing the workbook or activating an individual sheet.

For more information on storing and distributing macros, see Chapter 16.

Securing a Workbook and Its Components

Microsoft Excel provides security for workbooks and for individual worksheets. The security features can be password protected, preventing others from changing the parts of the workbook you have protected. Because security settings are stored with the workbook, you must open the workbook and unprotect before you can change any security settings.

Applying Worksheet Level Protection To apply protection at the worksheet level, choose Tools, Protection, Protect Sheet. The Protect Sheet dialog box appears. You can check any or all of the following protection options:

- *Contents.* Prevents the user from deleting or editing cells in a worksheet or from making changes to chart sheets.

- *Objects.* Prevents the user from editing, moving, resizing, or deleting embedded objects on a sheet, such as drawings, ActiveX controls, or embedded charts.
- *Scenarios.* Prevents the user from changing the definition of scenarios.

You can also type a password to prevent the user from turning off the protection you have enabled. You'll need the password to make any changes to the protection. Users who don't know the password won't be able to turn off the protection.

To remove protection from a sheet, choose Tools, Protection, Unprotect Sheet. If you used a password when you protected the sheet, you must enter the password at this time to unprotect the sheet.

Locking and Unlocking Cells All cells in a worksheet are locked initially, but the locking doesn't take effect until you protect the sheet contents, as just described. To allow data entry in a sheet but protect its text and formulas, you can unlock individual cells before you protect the sheet contents.

To unlock or lock individual cells:

1. Select the cells in which you want to allow data entry, and choose Format, Cells.
2. Click on the Protection tab in the Format Cells dialog box.
3. Uncheck the Locked check box to unlock the cells. Check the Locked check box to lock the cells.

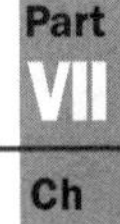

Applying Workbook-Level Protection To apply protection at the workbook level, choose Tools, Protection, Protect Workbook. In the Protect Workbook dialog box, select either or both of the protection options:

- *Structure.* Prevents the user from changing the structure of the workbook by adding, deleting, moving, renaming, hiding, or unhiding any sheets in the workbook.
- *Windows.* Prevents the user from moving, resizing, hiding, unhiding, or closing windows in the workbook.

Type a password to prevent the user from turning off the protection you have enabled. You'll need the password to make any changes to the protection.

To remove protection from a workbook, choose Tools, Protection, Unprotect Workbook. If you used a password when you protected the workbook, you must enter the password at this time to unprotect the workbook.

Passwords are case sensitive. You must remember your password exactly to be able to remove the protection from a worksheet or a workbook.

Storing Custom Toolbars and Lists

You can customize your toolbars and list settings in Excel and make the customizations available to all workbooks. For example, you might add frequently used commands to your toolbars or remove the items you don't ever use. You can customize your toolbars by using the Tools, Customize command or by using VBA code.

With custom lists, you can easily enter a series of items in order by entering the first item and extending the selection horizontally or vertically. Excel comes with some built-in lists, such as months or days of the week, but you can add new lists for your convenience. A list of products, personnel, or offices might be especially useful.

You can create custom lists by choosing Tools, Options and clicking on the Custom Lists tab. You can either type the new list into the List Entries list box or you can enter a cell reference in the Import List From Cells text box to include a list you have already entered into the worksheet.

Toolbar and list customizations are stored in your Windows directory in a file called Username.xlb, where Username is your Windows logon name. Toolbars attached to VBA modules are stored in the workbook file.

The toolbar and list customizations you create can be shared throughout a workgroup, further extending their convenience.

To share your custom toolbars and lists within a workgroup:

1. Create the custom toolbars you want to share in a new workbook.
2. Save the workbook on a network drive shared by your workgroup.
3. When users open the workbook, the custom toolbars are saved to their Username.xlb file.

After you update your custom lists and toolbars, you don't need to open the workbook again, because the customizations are stored separately in the XLB file.

Troubleshooting Inaccurate Calculations

The main function of a spreadsheet is to perform numeric calculations, so accurate calculations are certainly important. To ensure the accuracy of your calculations, you need to understand how Excel stores and displays data.

Displayed Values Versus Stored Values

Numeric data in a cell is stored as a floating-point number, with 15 digits of accuracy. This might differ from the displayed value in the cell, which is controlled by the cell's number formatting. When performing calculations, Excel uses the stored value, not the displayed value, which can create some misleading results if you are not careful.

For example, consider the example shown in Figure 39.5. The cells in this worksheet are displayed in the General number format, the default format for new workbooks. The formulas in column D calculate a net price by subtracting a 33.33% discount from the original unit prices in column B. Cell D5 displays the sum of the net prices, and the answer displayed is the one we would expect. Of course, the results aren't displayed in a common currency format, so the next natural step is to apply some number formatting.

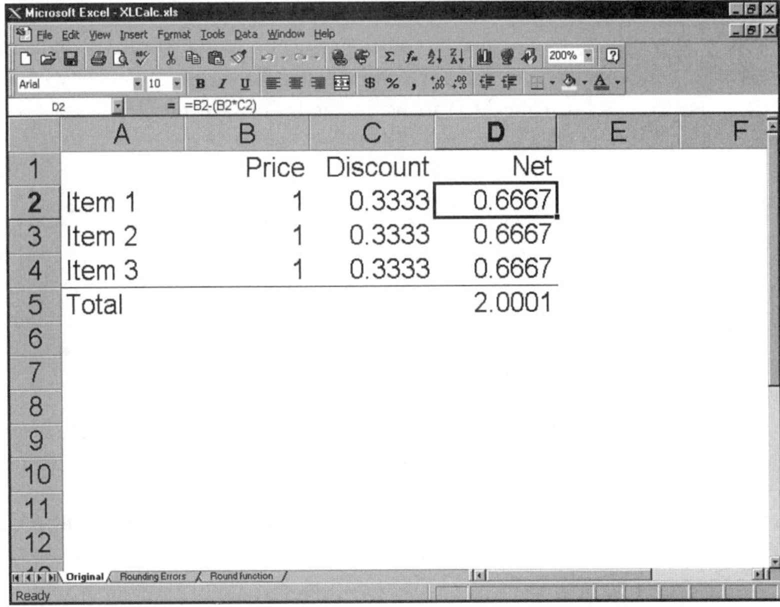

FIGURE 39.5
The numbers and formula results in this worksheet are displayed in the General number format.

Figure 39.6 shows the results of applying 2-digit number formatting to columns B and D. Now a problem seems to appear—0.67 + 0.67 + 0.67 should be 2.01, not 2.00. The apparent error occurs because cells D2 through D4 still contain the true result of the calculations, which is 66 2/3 cents. The sum of 66 2/3 + 66 2/3 + 66 2/3 is $2.00, so the answer is technically correct; however, the visual effect of the sum appears to be an error.

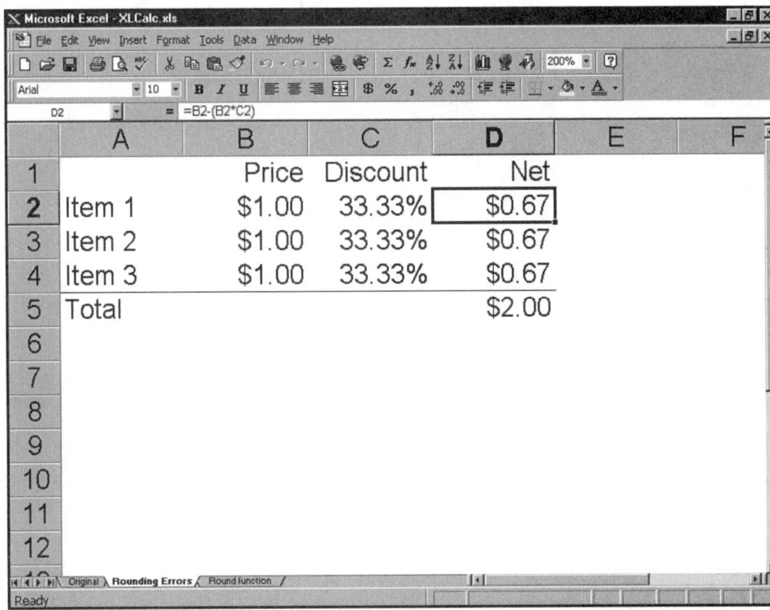

FIGURE 39.6
The Currency formatting in this worksheet causes an apparent error in the total.

Because formatting is often useful to control the appearance of the numbers and calculations in your worksheets, you need to be able to accommodate this type of precision conflict. To resolve the conflict, you can perform rounding at various points in your calculations, or you can use Excel's Precision As Displayed option. The next two sections explain how to use rounding functions and the Precision As Displayed feature in Excel.

Controlling Rounding with Worksheet Functions

A common solution to precision conflicts is to use the ROUND() function or other related Excel worksheet functions to clarify the accuracy of the calculations in your worksheets. In the discount example, the solution is to round the prices to the nearest cent when the individual discount is applied. Then when the net prices are summed, the total displays the expected result.

Figure 39.7 shows the use of the ROUND() function. In cell D2, the net price is calculated to the nearest penny. The ROUND() function requires two arguments, or input values. The first argument is the value that needs to be rounded, in this case, the expression B2–(B2*C2), which calculates the net price. The second argument tells Excel how many digits to round the number to. In the example, the value 2 is used, which rounds the net price to the nearest hundredth, or cent.

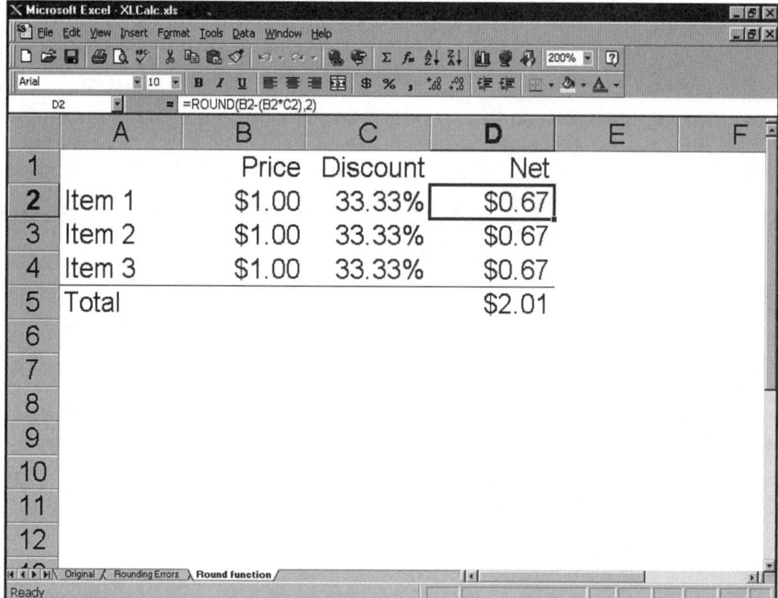

FIGURE 39.7
The ROUND() worksheet function corrects the discount calculations by rounding to the nearest cent.

Number formatting changes the cell's display but not the value used in calculations. When you use the ROUND() function, in contrast, the rounded value is used in all further calculations, so the total now yields the expected value, $2.01.

Several functions perform actions similar to the ROUND() function, depending on your requirements. Some of the ones you might find useful are

- *ROUND()*. Rounds to a specified number of decimal places.
- *ROUNDDOWN()*. Rounds to a specified number of places but always rounds closer to zero. For example, ROUNDDOWN(–1.3333,2) = –1.33.
- *ROUNDUP()*. Rounds a specified number of places, but always rounds away from zero. For example, ROUNDUP(–1.3333,2) = –1.34.
- *INT()*. Rounds a number to the next lower integer. For example, INT(4.8) = 4, and INT(–4.8)=-5.
- *TRUNC()*. Simply truncates a value to a number of decimal places, eliminating any further detail. For example, TRUNC(4.5,0) = 4, and TRUNC(15.875,1) = 15.8.
- *CEILING()*. Adjusts the result up to a number of significance, moving away from zero. For example, to round a price to the next higher nickel, you can use CEILING(0.23, 0.05), which returns 0.25 as a result.
- *FLOOR()*. Adjusts the result down to a number of significance, moving closer to zero. For example, to round a price to the next lower nickel, you can use FLOOR(0.23, 0.05), which returns 0.20 as a result.

By carefully considering the precision requirements of your spreadsheet application, you can select the appropriate rounding function to provide the desired accuracy.

Using Precision As Displayed

Excel provides another solution for controlling numeric precision in calculations—the Precision As Displayed option. This option is turned off by default and can be turned on for an individual workbook. When you turn on Precision As Displayed, Excel uses the formatted precision of cell contents in calculations. In the earlier price discount example, using the Precision As Displayed option would have given the correct answer of $2.01 without requiring any rounding functions.

To activate Precision As Displayed, choose Tools, Options. Then click on the Calculation tab and check the Precision As Displayed check box.

When you turn on the Precision As Displayed option, Excel displays the warning "Data will permanently lose accuracy," with an option for you to cancel. This is a reminder that Excel will no longer store values with a precision beyond the display format of their cells, so precision will be lost.

Although turning on Precision As Displayed is clearly less work than entering the various rounding functions into your formulas, the precision option is less flexible and could be dangerous if you're not careful. If you apply the wrong format to a cell or range, Excel throws away the accuracy of the data and will not recover it when you change the format back. You should only use this option for very simple and uniform applications.

Troubleshooting Performance Problems

Excel is a high-performance analytical application that can perform thousands of calculations on very large amounts of data. As your spreadsheets become larger and more complex, you might notice a decrease in performance. Several strategies are available to maximize your performance.

Optimizing Hardware for Excel

One solution is to upgrade your hardware. The two hardware factors most important to Excel are the processor speed and the amount of memory you have installed.

Because most Excel workbooks perform lots of calculations, the processor speed has a direct bearing on performance. If you are buying a new computer, test a similar model to make sure the processor is fast enough to handle your applications. Many older computers can be upgraded with replacement processors or motherboards.

As memory prices continue to fall to all-time lows, adding more memory to your system is often the most cost-effective upgrade available. Because Excel sometimes needs to keep large amounts of data in memory, increasing this resource can greatly improve Excel's performance. The amount of memory you should install depends on the complexity of your spreadsheet applications. If you have access to other users' computers, try your spreadsheets out on a computer with more memory to see whether this has a significant effect on performance.

Upgrading older video cards can increase Excel's performance, especially if you use lots of charts. In addition, today's larger, high-resolution displays allow you to display significantly more data at one time. You'll see a big difference between Excel's appearance on a 12-inch or 14-inch display and on a 20-inch or larger display.

Most video cards let you use the Display tool in the Windows Control Panel to adjust the screen resolution and the number of colors you can see. Depending on the overall performance of your system, you might be able to improve performance by choosing a lower display resolution and fewer colors.

Installing a larger and faster hard drive in your system generally results in some improvement in overall performance, although this is usually not as crucial to Excel as to database applications. With a faster drive, your workbook loads and saves faster. If you have a large amount of unfragmented free space on your hard drive, you can increase the amount of virtual memory used by Windows, which improves performance somewhat. However, adding more physical memory usually has a greater impact on performance in Excel than adding virtual memory.

Building Faster, More Efficient Workbooks

In addition to upgrading your hardware, you can use several spreadsheet design strategies to maximize Excel's performance. If you get in the habit of employing these strategies, your workbooks will take best advantage of Excel's power on your hardware platform.

Organizing Your Worksheets Efficiently

You can use several strategies to organize your Excel workbooks for best performance. Combine these ideas to create the best overall solutions. Sometimes, improving your workbook's design can have a significant effect on its performance.

- Excel works most efficiently when data is organized in consistent tables in the upper-left corner of the sheet. Many spreadsheet designers are in the habit of storing different tables of unrelated data on a single sheet. This is especially true of older spreadsheets that have been upgraded from earlier applications that only supported the use of one spreadsheet at a time.
- If your spreadsheet has many tables, put each table in a separate sheet in the workbook. You can use formulas to look up the data on any sheet in the workbook.
- If you have large amounts of data that are not referenced often, you can store them in a separate workbook. You can open the second workbook only when needed, speeding up the process by creating a workspace file to open several workbooks at once.
- If possible, formulas should refer to cells above them in the spreadsheet. In this case, Excel performs its calculations from top to bottom, which is most efficient.
- Use the simplest formulas possible to perform your calculations. For example, if you can use a constant number instead of a calculated value, your formulas will calculate faster.
- The Data Table feature can have a large impact on performance. Setting tables to calculate manually instead of automatically improves the overall performance of workbooks with data tables. Choose Tools, Options and click on the Calculation tab. Check the Automatic Except Tables option button to set the manual calculation option for your tables.
- Only cells with equals signs (=) recalculate. You can temporarily suspend the calculation of a range of cells by replacing the equals signs with another unique string. Then restore the equals signs for only those cells you need to recalculate.

Changing the Number of Excel's Undo Levels

You can change the number of undo levels Excel 97 uses by modifying the Windows registry. Excel stores up to 16 levels of Undo actions by default. Setting the undo level to a higher number reserves more memory for undoing operations, which has a negative impact on performance. Setting the undo to a lower level increases performance. Microsoft recommends keeping the undo level at 100 or lower.

Always make a backup copy of your registry files before making any changes to the registry. If you are familiar with the registry editing tools for Windows, you can change the following registry key:

```
Hkey_CURRENT_USER\Software\Microsoft\Office\8.0\Excel\Microsoft Excel
```

Create a new DWORD value in this key named UndoHistory. Set the value to a number from 0 to 100.

Selecting the Best Installation Strategy for Networked Users

Two general strategies can be used for networked installations of Microsoft Office:

- Install Office locally on each computer. This installation option reduces network traffic and still improves overall performance. It also permits users to operate Office applications when the network is not available, although in this situation, data files stored on the network won't be available. The disadvantage is that storage space is required on each local computer.
- Use the Run From Network Server installation. The advantage of this installation is that you need to store just a single copy of the Office program files, on the network server. You can also use Office applications on a diskless workstation with this strategy. The disadvantages include slower performance due to network and server activity. Also, users won't be able to operate Office applications if the network is unavailable.

Make sure your installation strategy is consistent with your organization's licensing agreement for Microsoft Office.

Troubleshooting Application Problems in Excel for Windows

This section covers some Excel problems that might concern Office administrators and users, and describes the solutions to those problems.

The Microsoft Excel 97 for Windows Auto-Recalculation Patch

The Microsoft Excel 97 Service Release 1 (SR-1) introduced a variety of problems concerning automatic recalculation of worksheet values. Microsoft has released a free patch to correct these problems.

To learn more about the problems addressed by the patch, search for the following articles on the Microsoft Knowledge Base:

- Q171339 - XL97, Some Values Not Recalculated When Using Multiple Formulas
- Q154134 - XL97, Functions in Filled Formulas May Not Be Recalculated
- Q182999 - XL97, Chart Data Labels Linked to Formulas Are Not Updated

The Microsoft Excel 97 for Windows Auto-Recalculation Patch is an update for SR-1 only. If you don't have SR-1 installed, you must install it first. The patch is a self-executing file that replaces several files in your Excel 97 installation.

For more information, or to download the patch, visit the Web site **www.microsoft.com/office/excel/enhancements/xl8p1.asp**.

Increased File Sizes After Using the Visual Basic Editor

If you are running the Visual Basic Editor while you have a workbook open, the size of the workbook might increase, even if you don't create any macros. The file size increases because Excel creates a new VBA module for each worksheet and chart sheet in the workbook. Each new module increases the size of the workbook file by about 1,000 to 1,500 bytes.

If you don't intend to use any VBA macros with a particular workbook, you should open it only while the Visual Basic Editor is not running.

NOTE If you have VBA modules or forms in your workbook, you can reduce the file size by deleting any unused worksheets from the workbook. ■

Increased File Sizes for Files Converted to Excel 97 Format

When you open an Excel 5.0 workbook and save it as an Excel 97 workbook, the file size might increase, sometimes significantly, for two reasons:

- More summary information is saved in Excel 97 format than in earlier versions. The impact of this additional information is usually no more than 25–30KB.
- If you save the workbook with a zoom setting of less than 100%, including a preview picture, the file size might increase significantly. To reduce the file size in this case, choose File, Properties and uncheck the Save Preview Picture check box in the workbook's properties. If you want to save the preview picture, do so with the zoom size set to 100% or greater.

Increased File Sizes While Editing VBA Procedures

If you have made many changes to the VBA macros in a workbook, the file size might increase dramatically, because Excel does not automatically recover the space used by variables in deleted code.

To correct this problem, save the Visual Basic module of the workbook to Basic Code (text) format, delete the module from the workbook, and import the text file back into the workbook. The next time you save the workbook, the file size decreases.

Microsoft Office 97 Service Release 2 (SR-2)

Microsoft recently announced that Office Service Release 2 (SR-2) was under development and would be released in the second half of 1998. Until the release of SR-2, some of its individual components are available for downloading and installation from Microsoft's Web site. These items include the Microsoft Excel 97 Auto-Recalculation Patch and the PowerPoint 97 date-correction file.

Office Service Release 2 is an upgrade to Office Service Release 1 (SR-1). If you do not have SR-1 installed, you must download and install it before installing SR-2.

You can download SR-1 at the following Web site:

www.microsoft.com/office/office/enhancements/sr1off97.asp

For more information on updates and enhancements for Microsoft Office, visit the Office Web site at:

www.microsoft.com/office/

CHAPTER 40

Troubleshooting and Optimizing PowerPoint

Understanding how a PowerPoint presentation is structured is the first step in figuring out how presentations are created, edited, printed, and presented successfully. To master your options for working with a PowerPoint presentation's components—graphics, slide layouts, and the problems that can sometimes occur with them—it's important to understand the various troubleshooting methods available to you.

Understanding PowerPoint's Architecture

Slides are the basic building blocks of PowerPoint's structure. Two or more slides create a presentation. A presentation can contain many different elements in its individual slides, including text, clip art, charts, animation, and sound.

Each individual slide has a layout, which is dictated by the AutoLayout you select when you add the slide to the presentation. Most presentations begin with a title slide; you then choose other layouts for the additional slides you insert in the presentation (see Figure 40.1).

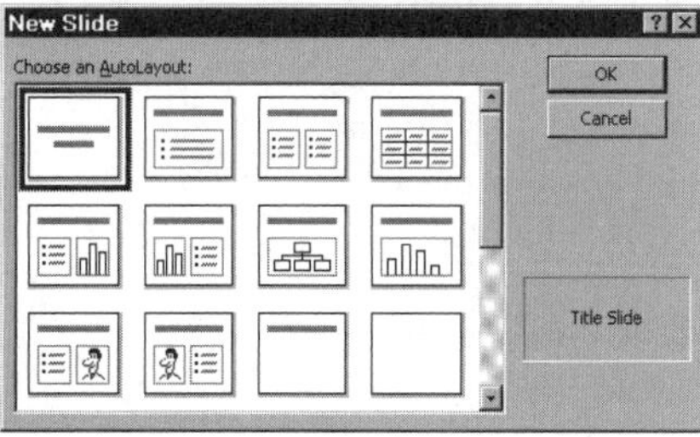

FIGURE 40.1
Users can select from 24 different AutoLayouts for individual slides.

All slides contain the following elements:

- *A background.* Even a blank slide has a background; it's blank. If a slide is created with a presentation template, it has a graphical background, filled with color and often clip art and drawn images.
- *Text boxes.* Title slides have a title text box and a subtitle text box, as shown in Figure 40.2. Other slides, based on different AutoLayouts, may have two or three text boxes.

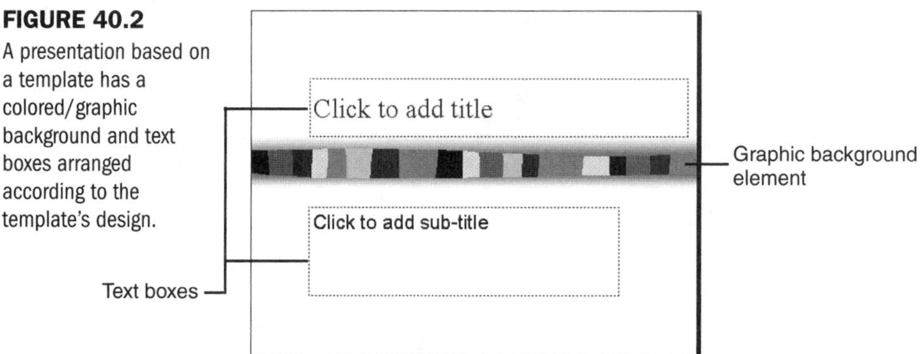

FIGURE 40.2
A presentation based on a template has a colored/graphic background and text boxes arranged according to the template's design.

You can add other elements, either to individual slides or to all the slides at once, by adding them to the Master. The Master is the template for the presentation after it's been started. Following are some of the elements that you can add to individual slides:

- *Text boxes.* If you need to include text that won't fit or isn't appropriate for the existing text boxes, you can add more.

- *Clip art.* You can insert any installed Office image through the Microsoft Clip Gallery. You can also add clip art from a variety of other sources, including the Internet, CD-ROM collections, or other software on your computer. When using clip art or other graphic images found on the Internet, be sure that they are not copyrighted images and that you only use images that are considered public domain. PowerPoint can insert graphic files in most common formats. The number of file formats your installation of PowerPoint can recognize depends on which graphic filters you included when you installed Office 97.
- *Charts.* You can add a variety of graphs and organization chart types to individual slides through Microsoft Graph and Microsoft Organization Chart, programs that run within PowerPoint. When you insert a graph or chart, the program becomes embedded in the slide, displayed as the created chart.
- *Drawn objects.* Using PowerPoint's Drawing toolbar, you can draw simple geometric shapes, elaborate AutoShapes, or lines and arrows. You can then fill these objects with solid colors, patterns, textures, or pictures, and you can apply 3D effects and shadows to them.
- *Word tables and Excel worksheets.* You can embed a table or worksheet in a slide. After you've done this, you can type text and numbers in the cells and format the table or worksheet using the Word or Excel tools that are activated when you select the embedded object.
- *Hyperlinks.* You can insert a hyperlink to link to another presentation, Office document (or a document from any other Windows application), or Web address.

The default color and style of text, drawn objects, and embedded charts in a presentation is based on the template that you used to create the presentation. After you've started the presentation, you use its Master to make global changes, such as changing the font for the title text box or adding a graphic image to every slide. Figure 40.3 shows the Slide Master view.

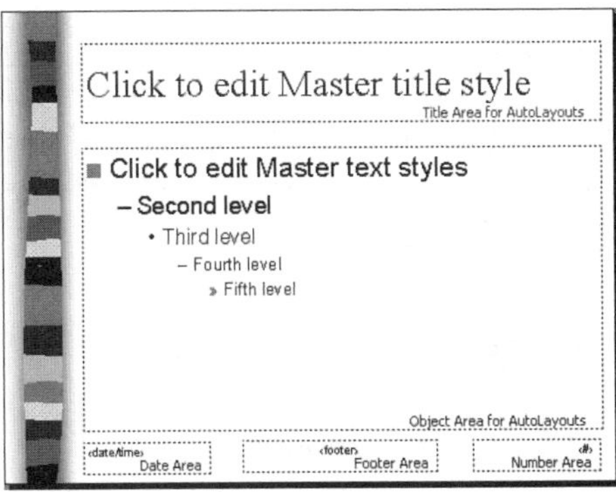

FIGURE 40.3
Use the Master to make global changes to the content and appearance of all the slides currently in and later added to a presentation.

You can print and display presentations in a variety of formats:

- *Slides.* Displayed onscreen in Slide view or as a slide show. Each slide takes up most or all of the screen.

- *Notes pages.* A small version of the slide appears on a portrait-oriented page with a large text box under it for speaker's notes or additional information for the audience beyond the slide's actual text content (see Figure 40.4).

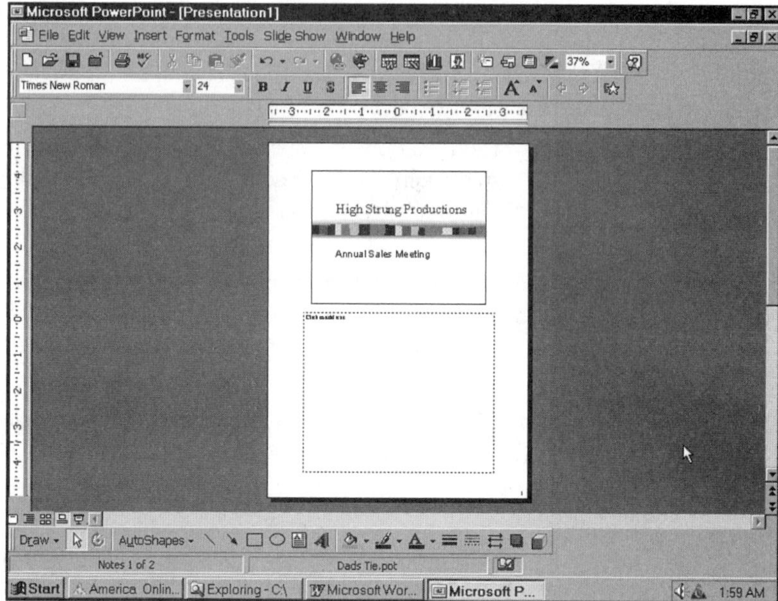

FIGURE 40.4
Notes pages are often used as audience handouts because you can add marketing or training information to the Notes text box.

- *Handouts.* You can print two, three, or six handouts per page. You can't display handouts onscreen.
- *Outline.* You can display or print a presentation as an outline with slide titles serving as the highest level headings in the outline, followed by subtitle and bullet text within each section of the outline (see Figure 40.5). You can import outlines from Word or export them to Word.

You can save PowerPoint presentations in a variety of formats, although the default format is PPT. To use a different file format, choose File, Save As, and select the desired format from the Save As Type drop-down box (see Figure 40.6).

Troubleshooting Graphics and Layout Problems

Graphics problems in PowerPoint normally surface when slides are printed. Incomplete printouts and printer errors often occur when the PowerPoint slides' printable content exceeds the capability of your printer—namely, its memory.

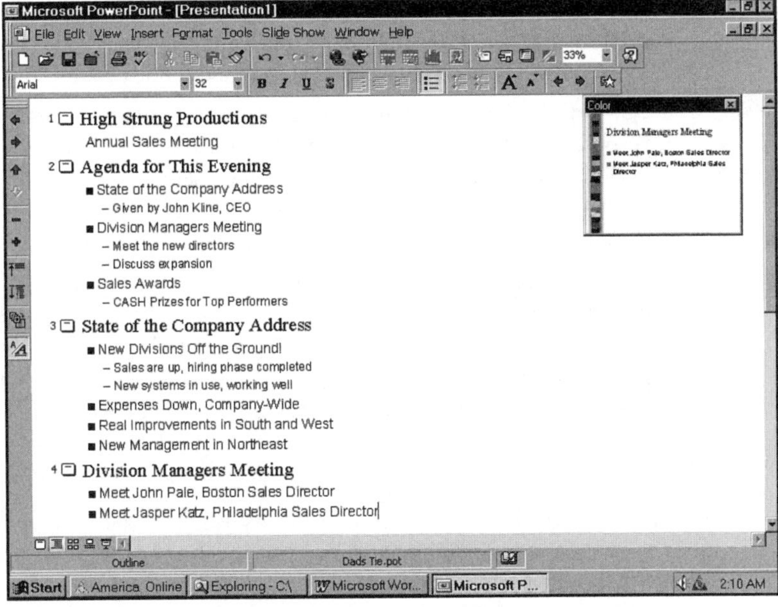

FIGURE 40.5
You can view outlines with or without text formatting, although the formatting is always part of the slide, and thus the presentation file.

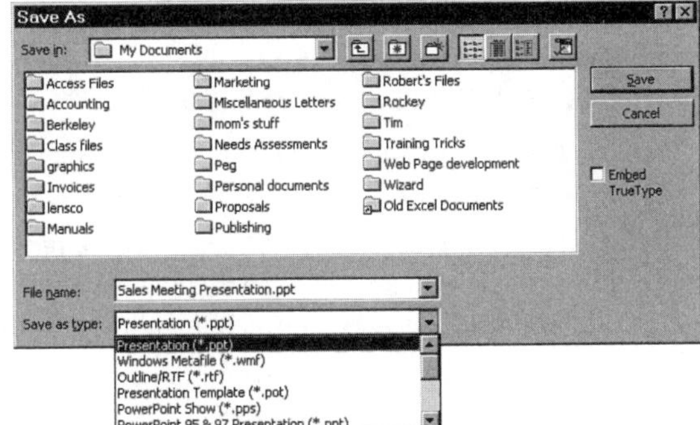

FIGURE 40.6
The file formats that appear in your Save As Type list vary depending on the filters installed with Office at your site.

Following are some additional problems that you may experience:

- *Colors onscreen don't match what's printed.* This, of course, only applies to color printers. Your monitor's display of colors invariably differs from the colors on your printout. If this is a chronic problem, contact your printer manufacturer—it may have a newer printer driver that improves color matching.
- *The printout is missing clip art, charts, or text.* If the missing items have thick lines or borders in or on them, try making them thinner. Many times this change is all it takes to make an item reappear. If this doesn't work, try resetting your printer's spool settings through your printer's Properties dialog box. Open your Printers folder and right-click the printer icon. Choose Properties from the shortcut menu, and click the Details tab.

Click the Spool Settings button, and select an alternate spool data format, if any. Try printing with the new setting. If the problem persists, return to your default setting and try reinserting the missing slide object and printing again.

- *Slow printing.* This normally happens if there are too many demands on your system resources, and you may notice other functions slowing down, too. Try turning off background printing. Background printing enables your print job to spool and then print while you continue to work in PowerPoint or any other program. To turn this feature off, choose Tools, Options, click the Print tab, and clear the Background Printing check box.
- *PowerPoint shuts down during a print job.* If you can determine that the print job was the culprit (by restarting PowerPoint and trying to print again), you probably have a corrupt element in one of your slides, and graphics (clip art, photos) are usually to blame. If one particular slide is the one that doesn't make it through the printer on each of your attempts, try deleting each graphic element on that slide and attempting to print after each deletion. The process of elimination, in most cases, shows you which graphic is corrupt. You can try reinserting it or substituting another graphic file.

Layout problems are normally due to problems with how you've composed your slides. The most common errors are to place too many elements on a slide, add graphics or text to the Master that conflict with existing elements on individual slides, and place elements too close to the edge of the slide (when slides will be printed).

Here are some layout dos and don'ts:

- *Keep text to a minimum.* Don't try to list eight bullet points on one slide. No more than five bullets, each on a single line, is a good rule of thumb.
- *Don't crowd the slide.* Keep your charts and clip art images spare. It's better to have more slides than a few crowded ones.
- *If you want to print your slides, keep the slide elements clear of the slide edges.* To keep elements from getting cut off, you should keep them at least a half-inch away from the edge of the slide. The required distance between the edge of the slide and the paper's edge varies by printer.
- *Be prepared to adjust the Master.* If you've added your company logo or some repeated text or graphic on every slide via the Master, you may find that the item's placement interferes with charts, clip art, or text on some of your slides. Placing the Master item as far out of the main slide area as possible and keeping it small helps to mitigate the problem. Consider placing your logo on the slide as a watermark (a lightly shaded object behind your slide content) instead.

Troubleshooting Other PowerPoint Problems

PowerPoint is notorious for running slowly and crashing on systems without enough memory. If you are often running PowerPoint with other Office or large-scale applications, you may find that PowerPoint "locks up" and ceases to respond, eventually resulting in a message from Windows stating that the program is no longer responding. The following are some warning signs that PowerPoint is about to crash:

- Screen refreshes don't work. When you switch from Slide view to Slide Sorter view, you can see your slide through the mosaic of slides in the sorter window.
- Clicking on and activating embedded objects such as charts, tables, and worksheets takes longer than usual.
- Your fonts change to Courier or some other system font.
- Your graphics don't show.
- Your slide show (onscreen) takes longer than usual, and the transitions between slides are choppy or halting.

When any of these symptoms appear, save your work, and shut down PowerPoint. This avoids an unceremonious crash that results in lost work. After shutting down, consider closing any other applications that you're not using in tandem with PowerPoint. Then restart PowerPoint.

NOTE Do you have more than 200 fonts in your \Fonts folder? If so, you probably won't be able to run Microsoft Organization Chart. When you double-click the organization chart icon on your slide, there will be a long delay, after which PowerPoint will tell you that you don't have enough memory to run Microsoft Organization Chart. This isn't the case. To resolve the problem, copy some of your extra fonts (fancy fonts, fonts that you know were installed with programs other than Office and Windows 95/98) to another folder, one that you create for just this purpose. Then, carefully delete these copied fonts from your \Fonts folder. Try running Microsoft Organization Chart again.

PowerPoint 98 for Macintosh Troubleshooting

PowerPoint 98 for the Macintosh contains many of the features of PowerPoint 97 for Windows, including improved animation tools and an enhanced set of presentation designs.

Memory is rarely an issue on a Macintosh, so problems with this version of PowerPoint are more user-oriented, and you can solve most of them by creating standardized presentations and establishing a default template for your company's slide shows.

None of the known Office 98 for Macintosh problems (VBA macro errors with Word templates and the Remove Office utility failures) directly affect PowerPoint 98 for the Macintosh.

CHAPTER 41

Troubleshooting and Optimizing Access

The power of Access is sometimes offset by its intricacy. For it to run smoothly, the database administrator needs to be aware of the pitfalls of poor logic and inefficient tables (among other easily imagined problems). Because Access is a complex program that uses many resources, it must be well kept and tweaked to run at its fullest potential.

Understanding Access Architecture

Microsoft Access is a relational database tool. The databases you create with it can include several tables, all connected by relationships. You can divide data into multiple tables and link it with common fields. Access also provides queries, forms, reports, macros, and modules.

The database window contains all the objects in your database and organizes them in separate tabs for each type of object (see Figure 41.1).

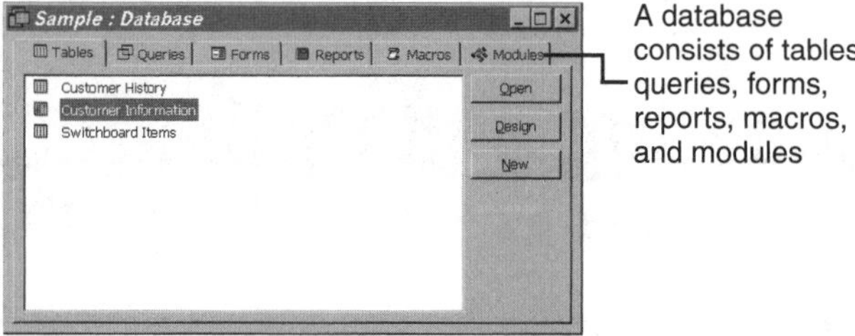

FIGURE 41.1
Click the tabs to see the different objects.

The next six sections describe the function of each type of object.

Tables

Tables are the objects where the data is stored; they are an arrangement of facts and figures on a particular topic. You can link tables within the database so that you can pull data from several different locations.

Creating Table Relationships To create the relationships between tables, choose Tools, Relationships to display the Relationships window. Then choose Relationships, Show Table to display the Show Table dialog box. The Tables tab in this dialog box contains a list of the tables in the database. Select the tables you want to create relationships with (Ctrl+click to select more than one), click on Add, and then click on Close to return to the Relationships window.

Next, click on the related field on one table and drag over to the desired field on another table. This creates a join between the tables. When you create a join, the Relationships dialog box appears (see Figure 41.2). This dialog box lets you choose the type of join you want and set options for referential integrity. You can display the Relationships dialog box at any time by double-clicking on the join that you want to examine.

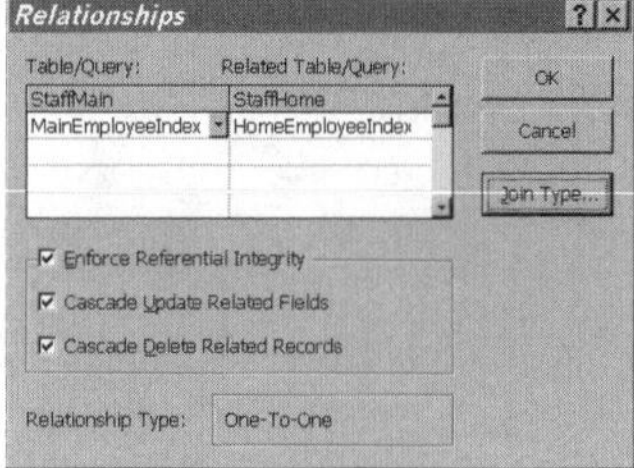

FIGURE 41.2
When you create a join between tables, the Relationships dialog box appears.

Figure 41.3 shows relationships in an employee database. This database contains several tables with different types of information about the employee. The tables are all linked by a Main Index field. StaffMain is the primary table; all employees are in the StaffMain table but not necessarily in the StaffHome, StaffPhone, and StaffSchedule tables. There are seven entries in the StaffMain table, as shown in Figure 41.4.

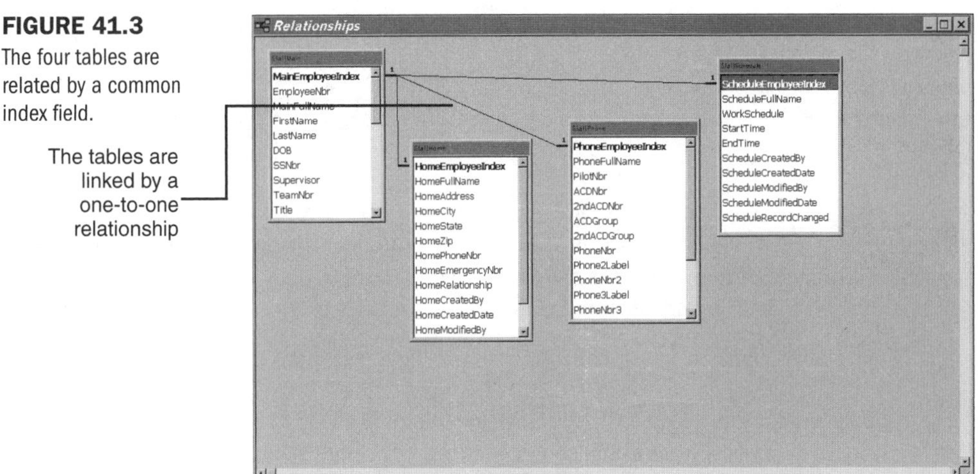

FIGURE 41.3
The four tables are related by a common index field.

The tables are linked by a one-to-one relationship

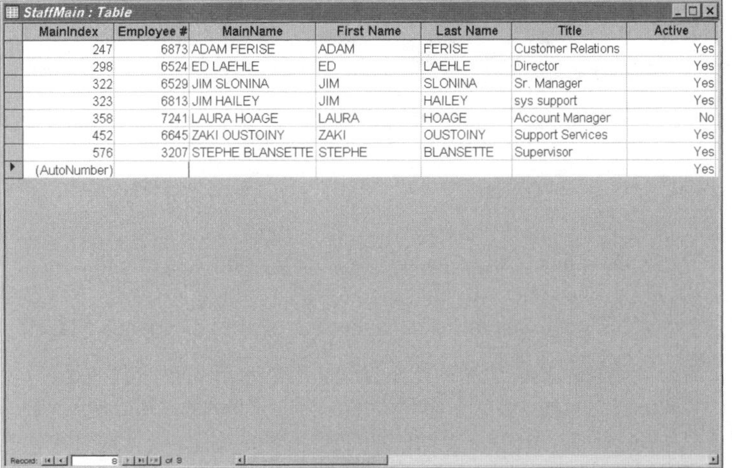
StaffMain : Table

MainIndex	Employee #	MainName	First Name	Last Name	Title	Active
247	6873	ADAM FERISE	ADAM	FERISE	Customer Relations	Yes
298	6524	ED LAEHLE	ED	LAEHLE	Director	Yes
322	6529	JIM SLONINA	JIM	SLONINA	Sr. Manager	Yes
323	6813	JIM HAILEY	JIM	HAILEY	sys support	Yes
358	7241	LAURA HOAGE	LAURA	HOAGE	Account Manager	No
452	6645	ZAKI OUSTOINY	ZAKI	OUSTOINY	Support Services	Yes
576	3207	STEPHE BLANSETTE	STEPHE	BLANSETTE	Supervisor	Yes
(AutoNumber)						Yes

FIGURE 41.4
There are seven entries in the primary table StaffMain.

Types of Joins When creating joins between tables, you will be prompted to choose the type of join. This section introduces the different types of joins and integrity options.

Joins tell Access how the data in your tables are related; the type of join you use affects the results of your queries. In a query with tables that have one-to-one joins, the results include only data from the joined tables where the linked fields are equal.

For example, if the two tables StaffMain and StaffPhone are linked by a one-to-one relationship, only those records in which the employee is in the main table and in the phone table will be included in the result set. Figure 41.5 shows the result set from both tables. Notice that there are only six entries instead of seven. Although Laura was in the StaffMain table, she was not in the StaffPhone table; therefore, no records are shown for her.

FIGURE 41.5
The query result set shows records only for those entries that are in both the StaffMain and StaffPhone tables.

Query1 : Select Query

MainIndex	Employee #	MainName	ACD #
247	6873	ADAM FERISE	5309
298	6524	ED LAEHLE	5425
322	6529	JIM SLONINA	5456
323	6813	JIM HAILEY	5241
452	6645	ZAKI OUSTOINY	5238
576	3207	STEPHE BLANSETTE	5851
(AutoNumber)			

Laura Hoage is not shown because she is not in the StaffPhone table

The other two types of joins—left-outer join and right-outer join—include all the data from one table but only matching records from the other table. A left-outer join includes all the records from the table on the left, and matching records from the table on the right; a right-outer join includes all the records from the table on the right, and matching records from the table on the left.

For example, we can join all records in StaffMain but only those in StaffPhone where the fields are equal. The query result set would show every record in StaffMain even if it is not in the StaffPhone table. However, if the record is not in the StaffPhone table, there will be a null value in any fields from that table, as shown in Figure 41.6.

FIGURE 41.6
The result set of a query with an outer join.

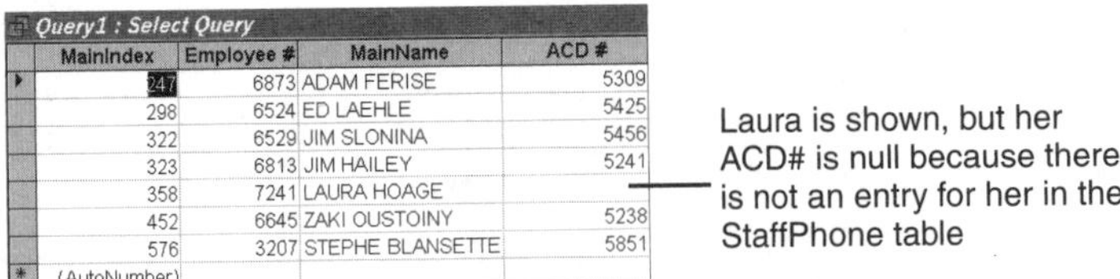

Query1 : Select Query

MainIndex	Employee #	MainName	ACD #
247	6873	ADAM FERISE	5309
298	6524	ED LAEHLE	5425
322	6529	JIM SLONINA	5456
323	6813	JIM HAILEY	5241
358	7241	LAURA HOAGE	
452	6645	ZAKI OUSTOINY	5238
576	3207	STEPHE BLANSETTE	5851
(AutoNumber)			

Laura is shown, but her ACD# is null because there is not an entry for her in the StaffPhone table

You can also link in the opposite way—in the previous example, you could include all records from StaffPhone but only those in StaffMain where the fields are equal. However, in this case such a join would not make sense because StaffMain contains data for all employees.

When you create a join between tables, you can specify three other options for the join: Enforce Referential Integrity, Cascade Update Related Fields, and Cascade Delete Related Fields (refer to Figure 41.2). *Referential integrity* refers to rules that ensure that the relationships between related tables are accurate. This includes making sure that, if you add or delete a field from one table, the related tables are also changed. In order to use referential integrity, the following conditions must be met:

- The related field from the primary table is a primary key or has a unique index.
- The related fields have the same data type.

- The tables reside in the same database. They can be linked tables, but they must be linked to the same location.

If you choose to enforce referential integrity, Access imposes these rules:

- You cannot enter data in a field of a related table that is not in the primary key of the primary table. For example, you could not enter a phone number in the StaffPhone table for a person who is not in the StaffMain table.
- You cannot delete records from a primary table if there are matching records in a related table.
- You cannot change the value of a primary key if there are related records.

You can override the last two rules by marking the Cascade Update Related Fields and Cascade Delete Related Fields check boxes. If these options are activated, you can update or delete from the primary table; the related records in the related tables will also be updated or deleted.

Queries

Queries allow you to view, change, or manipulate data. They can pull information from one or several tables and even calculate new fields.

You might want to use a query as the data source for a form or report. Queries can pull fields from several linked tables or create new fields to be used as a data source. You can also use them to create new tables, update records, and delete records.

Forms

Forms in Microsoft Access provide a user-friendly interface. You can use a form as a switchboard, as a data-entry tool, as a dialog box, or just to display data.

As a switchboard, a form helps the user navigate through a database. See Chapter 9 to learn more about setting up a switchboard form.

As a data-entry tool, a form can provide a comfortable interface for the user. The user does not have to delve through records in tables to enter data; he or she can simply enter the data as prompted by the form. For more on using a form for data entry, see Chapter 15.

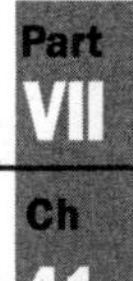

As a dialog box, a form can receive user input. When the user enters parameters in the dialog box, actions are carried out based on the input.

Finally, you can use a form simply to display data. Creating a form lets you display information in a different format than a datasheet, as it appears in a table. However, in most cases, if you just want the user to view (not modify) data, you should create a report (see the next section) instead of a form.

Reports

A report lets you present data in a printed format. The data on a report is for viewing only; it cannot be modified. A report can range from a spreadsheet to a letter. The underlying data behind a report is usually a table or query. You can modify the design of the report to organize and format the data to suit your needs.

Macros

A macro is a group of actions that performs a certain operation. You can use macros to automate many tasks in Access. The macros can include operations that use tables, queries, forms, and reports.

Modules

Modules are similar to macros, but they contain Visual Basic code instead of a series of actions. A module contains declarations and procedures such as functions. Code in Access modules can use fields and records based on tables and queries, and it can incorporate reports and forms.

In summary, the architecture of Access lets you use data from tables and queries in reports and forms, which you can then automate and customize with macros and modules.

Troubleshooting Damaged Databases

Usually, Access can detect that a database is damaged or corrupted. If this happens, Access won't let you open the database, and it will ask if you want to repair the database. If you say yes, Access automatically compacts and repairs the database.

If Access does not indicate that a database is damaged but you suspect that it is, you can repair it on your own. Indications of a damaged database are frequent lockups, extremely slow reactions to commands, or corrupt data. To repair a database, choose Tools, Database Utilities, Repair Database.

NOTE If you repair a database but it still acts suspicious, check to see if tables are attached. If they are, the database where the attached tables reside could be the damaged database. ■

The best way to avoid damaged databases is to be proactive. Watch the size of your database; the larger a database, the more likely it is that it will become corrupted. The maximum size for a database is 1 gigabyte. If your database is approaching this limit, think about options for archiving or splitting the database.

Compact databases often, especially if you frequently delete tables. When you delete tables, the database becomes fragmented and does not use disk space efficiently; compacting the database defragments it and recovers disk space, resulting in a smaller database. Even if you delete objects, the database won't shrink in size unless you compact it.

To compact a database, choose Tools, Database Utilities, Compact Database. You are asked where you want the database to compact from and where you want the database to compact into. These can be the same name, or you can compact to a different database. If you use the same name and location, the new and compacted database replaces the original one.

NOTE Avoid compacting a database if someone has it open. This prevents users from modifying the database while it is being compacted. ■

Troubleshooting Wizard Problems

The most common wizard problem is that the wizard that you want to use is not installed. Some wizards are automatically installed, and others are installed when you select the Wizards or Advanced Wizards component during Access setup. The term wizards as used here refers to builders and add-ins as well.

Wizards that are installed automatically are the Color Builder, Expression Builder, Field Builder, Query Builder, and Subform/Subreport Linker.

If you select Wizards during Access setup, the following wizards will be added: AutoForm, AutoReport, Combo Box, Command Button, Crosstab Query, Database Wizard, Export Text, Form, Import HTML, Import Spreadsheet, Import Text, Label, Link HTML, Link Spreadsheet, Link Text, List Box, Lookup, Microsoft Word Mail Merge, Picture Builder, Pivot Table, Web Publishing, Report, Simple Query, Switchboard Manager, and Table Wizard.

If you select Advanced Wizards during setup, the following wizards will also be added: Add-In Manager, Chart Wizard, Conflict Resolver, Database Splitter, Documenter, Find Duplicates Query, Find Unmatched Query, Input Mask, Linked Table Manager, Macro to Module Converter, ODBC Connection String Builder, Option Group, Performance Analyzer, Subform/Subreport, Table Analyzer, and User Level Security.

To optimize Access's potential, you should install the advanced wizards. If you did not install the wizards and would like to add them, rerun Office 97 setup. Click on Add/Remove, highlight Microsoft Access, click on the Change Options button, and mark the Wizards and Advanced Wizards check boxes.

Troubleshooting Form Problems

Many form problems occur when the underlying object is deleted or renamed. If a form is using a table or query as its data source and that object is renamed, the form does not know where to obtain the data. When a form cannot find the control source, "#Error#" appears in that field in form view. Check the form data source and verify that the name matches an existing table or query. The same thing can happen with fields. If a field is deleted or renamed in an underlying table or query, the field on the form will not know where to find the data.

If you add a field to a table and also want it to appear on a form, add it to the form using Design view. If you add a field for a fax number to a table, for example, but you do not add it to the data entry form, your users will not know that they are supposed to enter this information.

Many other form problems involve the properties of the fields contained in the form. The following sections discuss some problems that users may encounter.

When I Try to Change or Type Data in My Date Field, the Data Does Not Change

Form controls have an Enable property. When this property for a field is set to No, you can't enter data in the field; the field will appear grayed in form view. You usually set Enable to No if the field is automatically calculated—such as in an AutoNumber or date stamp field—and should not be changed.

I Get a Message That the Value That I Entered Is Not Valid for My Field

Data entered in a field must use the same data type as the field. For example, letters cannot be entered into a zip code field because it is a numeric field.

Another cause for this problem could be a validation error. You can set fields to have a validation rule—an expression that is evaluated when data is entered. If the data entered does not match the validation rule, a message appears. The message that is displayed is determined by the validation text, which you specified in the field's properties in the form's Design view.

NOTE You can enter numbers in a text field, but they will be saved as text. Access can't perform calculations on the numbers that are stored as text. ■

My Insertion Point Stops at a Certain Point When Entering Data

The field size determines how many characters can be entered in a field. If you are trying to type in more characters than the field size allows, the insertion point will stop. To fix this problem, switch to the Design view of the underlying table and increase the field size. If you want to enter extensive text in the field, change the field type to memo. A memo field can hold up to 64,000 characters. The problem with memos, however, is that they cannot be sorted or indexed.

There Is No Data on My Form

Make sure the record source has data; the form may be pulling from a blank table. This problem could also be based on a query that does not return any data. If your form is based on a query, check the Design view of the query to ensure that you are pulling the correct information.

Another possibility is that the form is opened in data entry mode. In this mode, the user does not see the other records and can only add new ones.

My Combo Box Displays the Wrong Column

In a combo box, you can choose the widths of each column. These widths are specified in the properties of the combo box and are separated by a comma. For example if the width specified is "0,.33" the first column will not be visible due to its width. To change this, simply increase or decrease the column widths in the properties for the combo box.

Using Performance Analyzer

The performance analyzer looks at the database objects and determines if there is a more efficient way to design your objects. It then gives you recommendations, suggestions, and ideas. If you decide to alter your objects based on its recommendations and suggestions, the performance analyzer can make the changes automatically. However, if you choose to carry out the analyzer's ideas, you must perform the steps yourself.

Choose Tools, Analyze, Performance to display the Performance Analyzer dialog box. You will see tabs for each of the eight available objects that can be analyzed: Table, Query, Form, Report, Macro, Module, Current Database, and All. You can select all the objects by clicking on the Select All button, or you can manually mark the check boxes next to each object that you want to analyze.

Figure 41.7 shows the results of a query that was analyzed. This query pulled information from a table based on a customer number.

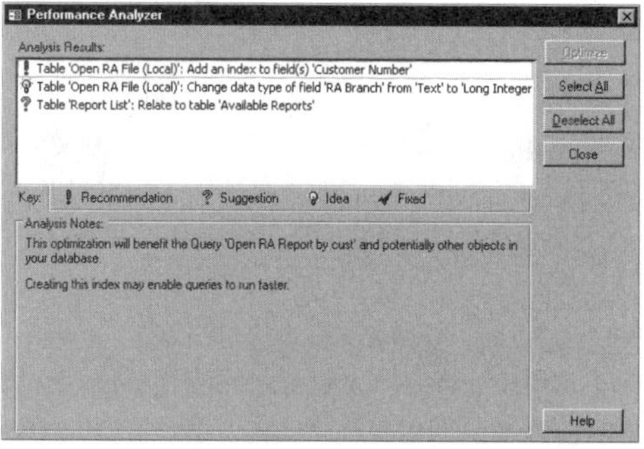

FIGURE 41.7
The performance analyzer displays recommendations, suggestions, and ideas.

The analysis result in Figure 41.7 includes a recommendation, a suggestion, and an idea. The recommendation is to add an index to the Customer Number field, which will speed up searching by the customer number. (See the next section for more about optimizing tables.) Notice in the analysis notes at the bottom of the dialog box that adding an index to this field could also help other queries within the database.

The suggestion in the example is to change the data type of one of the fields from text to long integer. This is only a suggestion, because doing this could cause existing data to be deleted and could affect what data you can add in the future. You should consider the impact of these types of changes before performing them.

If you decide to perform the recommendation or suggestion, select the item and click on Optimize. After you have chosen everything that you want to optimize, click on Close, and Access will perform the changes.

The third item in the Analysis Results in Figure 41.7 is an idea. In this case the idea is to link two of the tables. The performance analyzer can't carry out the idea automatically, but it will tell you the steps necessary to make the change.

The performance analyzer usually offers good ideas regarding indexing, linking, and data types. It's a good idea to use the performance analyzer when your database is complete. Even if you follow the guidelines for optimizing tables and queries in the next two sections, there still may be something that you overlooked.

NOTE After you have made the optimization changes, be sure to compact your database to recover lost disk space and mend fragmentation.

Creating More Efficient Tables

As discussed in the previous section, you can use the performance analyzer to check your tables for efficiency; but it is good to create efficient tables from the start. Creating efficient tables involves using indexes, primary keys, correct data types, and logic.

Using Indexes

An index creates a pointer to the records and thus speeds up searches. Using indexes greatly improves table scans as well as queries. You can double the improvement by indexing both sides of a join. For example, using an earlier example, you could join the StaffMain and StaffPhone tables on the MainEmployeeIndex and the PhoneEmployeeIndex. Indexing both of these fields increases performance when querying the tables.

You can decide whether an index can have duplicates. If a field is set to have no duplicates, Access checks existing data as well as new data to ensure that this condition is met. In the example in the previous paragraph, you would want indexes with no duplicates because you want only one employee index per person. This ensures data integrity for multiple entries for one employee.

Although indexes increase query and search performance, they are not always suitable. Indexes increase the size of your database and reduce the ability for multiple users to update data. Indexes can also decrease performance when updating, adding, or deleting fields. This is because the database has to place a pointer on the record and then find the appropriate spot for it within the database.

You should test different scenarios with and without indexes. Test the search and query speed versus the update and delete speed. Determine which are the most important or appropriate for your database, and then implement indexes accordingly.

Use indexes only on fields that have mostly unique values. Indexes will not help if there are multiple records that have the same value in the indexed field.

You can set indexes in the Design view of a table by choosing the desired option in the Indexes drop-down list. Some combinations of indexed fields may produce better performance than others. You can experiment by turning indexing on and off for individual fields until you figure out what works best. If you change an index from No to Yes (No Duplicates), the table will check for duplicates before updating the fields. If duplicate records are in the field that is to be indexed with no duplicates, the table will not be saved.

Primary Keys

A primary key is a tag that uniquely identifies the record. You can use a primary key only on a field that is indexed with no duplicates. If you assign a primary key to a field, Access automatically indexes the field with no duplicates, including null values.

The primary key is used to identify records in other tables. For example, the primary key in the StaffMain table is the MainEmployeeIndex field. This tells Access which record to look up in the StaffHome or StaffPhone table. You could link the tables without a primary key, but it would slow down data retrieval.

Following are the three types of primary keys:

- *AutoNumber primary keys.* Assign a number to each record as it is entered. Each number is incremental and non-repeating. This is the easiest way to set a primary key. When you create a table using the Table Wizard or you import a table, Access asks if you want to add a primary key. If you answer yes, Access adds an AutoNumber primary key to your table.
- *Single-field primary keys.* Can be set to fields of any data type that do not have duplicate entries or null values. Access will not let you set a primary key on a field that contains duplicates or nulls. The MainEmployeeIndex primary key in the StaffMain table is a single-field primarykey. The data type of this field is long integer.
- *Multiple-field primary key.* If a field used to identify your records contains duplicates, you can use several fields instead—creating a multiple-field primary key. For example, let's say you have a table that has a field for customer numbers and a field for location. Each of these fields can have duplicate values, but there cannot be a duplicate for a customer number and a location together. Customer X can be located in location 1 and 2, as well as another Customer Y in location 1 and 2. The multiple-field primary key would be on the combination of X1, X2, Y1, and Y2. Multiple-field primary keys are sorted based on their order in the Design view of the table.

To set primary keys, go to the Design view of the table. Select the field that you would like to be your primary key and click on the Primary Key toolbar button.

To view the indexes and primary keys on a table, choose View, Indexes. In the Indexes window that appears, you can move the indexes around if you do not like the way they are sorted for a multiple-field primary key.

NOTE If you choose a primary key for a table that already has data, be sure that there are no nulls or duplicates. If there are, you will not be able to save changes to the table.

Correct Data Types

When you choose the data type for your field, select the smallest type and size that will work for your data. Be careful not to set the field size too small, but also do not set a size of 250 for a field that will contain, say, city names. Be sure to use a number field if calculations will be performed, but choose the appropriate number type. Byte is the smallest, whereas double is the largest.

Logic

When designing tables in a database, use logic. Try to create tables with related data that is not redundant. Do not have the same field located in several tables (unless it is a primary key field). For example, do not have a customer's phone number listed in several tables. Have it stored in one table and linked to another main table.

Use the Relationships window (Tools, Relationships) to look at your tables and see if the setup is logical. Check for duplicate fields and make changes if necessary.

The better a database is designed, the better its performance. The Table Analyzer Wizard can check your tables for duplicates and divide a table with duplicate information into different tables where the data is stored only once. To start the Wizard, choose Tools, Analyze, Table. The first two wizard dialog boxes introduce the table analyzer, explain duplicate information in tables, and show examples. The next dialog box lets you select the table that you want to split; this does not alter your original table. You can decide which fields should go into the new tables, or else you can have the wizard decide. If you let the wizard decide, you will be able to make modifications to the proposed changes.

The wizard will ask you to choose names for the new tables (the default names are Table1 and Table2). You also have to verify that the links and primary keys are correct. After Access splits the table, you can still create a query based on your original table. You might want to do this if you want a record set that contains all the fields in the original table. The query based on the original table is a select query that joins the two split tables in order to display fields from both tables. If you create the query, it will acquire the name of your original table, and the original table will be renamed. All forms and reports that were linked to the original table will use the new query as the record source.

Improving Query Speed

You can enhance query performance in several ways. The suggestions for optimizing tables in the previous section also optimize query performance. Use indexes on the fields that will be joined in a query or on the fields that will be based on criteria.

When you run a query, use only the fields that are needed. Do not use all the fields in the table if you do not need them. Including unnecessary fields will only slow down your query.

A nongrouped query performs faster than a grouped query. But when you do need a group, you can do a few things to improve the speed. If you are joining tables, group by the field in the same table that you are calculating. For example, let's say you are joining two tables by a CustomerID and summing the revenue from one of the tables. Place the "group by" on the CustomerID field in the table that has the revenue. Do not use "group by" unnecessarily; using first and last statements instead can increase speed.

If you are specifying criteria, use the Between statement instead of "Greater than x" and "Less than y." For example, if you want to see data from 1/1/98 to 3/1/98, use "Between 1/1/98 and 3/1/98" in the criteria instead of "> 1/1/98 and < 3/1/98".

Also, use the In statement instead of several Ors. If you are looking for the states Indiana, Ohio, and Kentucky, use "IN("Indiana","Ohio","Kentucky")" instead of "Like Indiana or Like Ohio or Like Kentucky". You should also index fields that use these operators.

Use make table queries instead of sub queries. For example, instead of nesting a query within a query that performs an operation, make a table with the information needed from the first query and have the second query use the new table.

Do not use more tables than needed. The more tables in a query, the slower the performance. Make a table using two or three of the tables, and then use that table in another query. This can reduce the number of tables by at least half.

Compact your database frequently. A compacted database reorganizes the records and space. The reduced space will speed up queries that have to scan tables.

Optimizing Virtual Memory

In Windows 95, the most important function of optimizing virtual memory is to ensure that there is enough space and continuous space. Even though the minimum RAM requirement for Microsoft Office 97 is 12MB, it's better to add an additional 16MB.

The default virtual memory settings should be sufficient, but if you still experience problems and you have closed all other unnecessary applications, you can change some of the settings. Try setting the disk space available for virtual memory to at least 25MB minus available RAM.

To change the virtual memory settings, open the System applet in the Control Panel, and click the Performance tab. Click the Virtual Memory button, and then adjust the settings in the Virtual Memory dialog box.

Changing Registry Settings

Microsoft recommends that you do not change the registry settings; but if you choose to do so, use the Registry Editor. You should always back up the current registry settings before making changes.

The registry is a database that stores configuration information. When a system is turned on, it looks at these registry settings to tell it how to run. This information is used by Windows and the application that is running. The registry contains keys that represent branches within the registry hierarchy. For example, the HKEY_LOCAL_MACHINE branch has information regarding hardware and software on the local machine. This is the key where you can make changes for Access.

To use the Registry Editor, choose Start, Run. Type regedit and click OK. Figure 41.8 shows the Registry Editor.

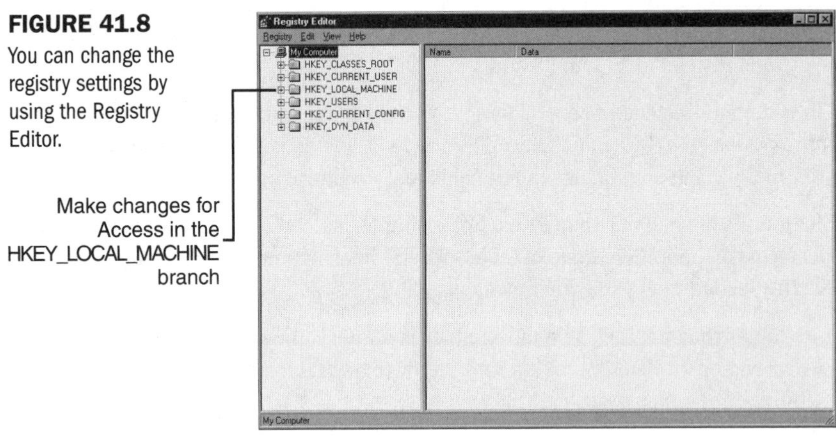

FIGURE 41.8
You can change the registry settings by using the Registry Editor.

These are the two registry keys for Access:

HKEY_LOCAL_MACHINE\SOFTWARE\Microsoft\Office\8.0\Access

HKEY_LOCAL_MACHINE\SOFTWARE\Microsoft\Jet\3.5

These keys control how Access uses memory and resources. Usually, the default settings give you optimal performance, but this can vary from computer to computer depending on available memory and the type and level of activity on the databases.

Click on the plus signs in the left pane of the Registry Editor to navigate down the HKEY_LOCAL_MACHINE branch.

When you select the Access key or the Jet\3.5 key, you will see "Default" in the right pane. Double-click on it to change its value.

To make a backup of the registry, choose Registry, Export Registry File in the Registry Editor window.

NOTE Changes to the Jet\3.5 key affect other Office products, such as Excel. ■

CHAPTER 42

Troubleshooting and Optimizing Outlook

In this chapter, you learn how Outlook organizes its data using items, forms, and profiles. You also learn how to back up your Outlook data using the archiving feature. Finally, you get some tips on troubleshooting problems that might arise in Outlook at startup time, or when you are using Outlook to send and receive mail.

Understanding Outlook's Architecture

Microsoft Outlook enables users to combine electronic mail, calendar, and information management functions into a single application. All these features are provided under a single system of data management, which consists of the following three basic types of information:

- *Item.* A single unit of information, such as an email message, a calendar appointment, a contact entry, or a journal entry. Each type of item has a variety of properties that characterize the information stored in that item.
- *Folder.* Items are stored in folders, and each folder is designed to hold a particular type of item, such as task items, or journal items.
- *View.* You can use views to control how Outlook displays items in a folder. You can define many views for each folder and activate the view with which you want to display items in a sorted order, or filter so that only certain items appear.

Because Outlook is fundamentally an email (or messaging) system, it is designed to comply with MAPI, which is a standard interface for communication between clients and messaging servers such as Microsoft Exchange Server. Outlook uses the MAPI profiles on your computer to define which messaging systems, address books, and personal folders are available on your computer. Profiles enables you to exchange messages and other data with many systems, such as Microsoft Fax, the Microsoft Network, Internet mail, and other email systems.

Understanding Outlook Items

You can store six types of items in Outlook folders:

- *Mail items.* Email messages.
- *Appointment items.* Include meetings, appointments, and events. Appointments can be recurring or nonrecurring.
- *Contact items.* Contain information such as names, addresses, phone, and fax numbers, and much more.
- *Journal items.* Store information that you can use to track the date and times of phone calls, email messages, and many other activities.
- *Note items.* Contain simple text that you can organize any way you like.
- *Task items.* Include to-do information, such as when a task is due, its priority, and who owns the task.

In addition to viewing the contents of Outlook folders, you can also use Outlook to view the contents of filefolders on your computer's disk drives.

Exporting an Outlook Item

You can save an Outlook item as a separate file in one of these formats:

- *Text files.* Can be opened in any text editor, such as Windows Notepad.

- *Rich text (RTF) files* Include common formatting, such as fonts. Many word processors, including Word and Windows WordPad, can open and edit RTF files.
- *Message format* Retains all the properties of the item. If the item is an email message, you can open it in the Microsoft Exchange Client (also known as Windows Messaging). Other item types can only be opened in Outlook.
- *Outlook templates* Can be used to create other Outlook items of the same type.
- *vCard file*. In Outlook 98, you can save a contact item as a vCard file, which you can then send as an attachment to an email message. vCards provide a convenient way to share contact information using email over the Internet.

To export an Outlook item to a file, follow these steps:

1. Select the Outlook item that you want to save in a different format.
2. Choose File, Save As. The Save As dialog box appears (shown in Figure 42.1).

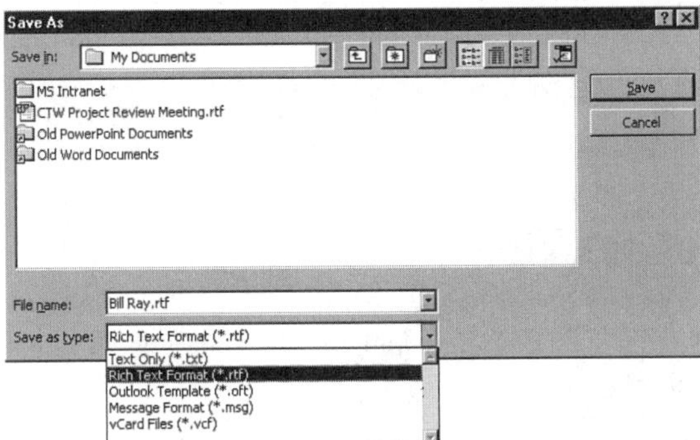

FIGURE 42.1
Use the Save As dialog box to select a name, location, and file type for an exported Outlook item.

3. Type a filename for the item in the File Name text box, and select the file type in the Save as Type drop-down box.
4. Click Save to complete the command.

Understanding Outlook Folders

Outlook provides a standard set of folders that contain the different types of items you can create in Outlook. These folders are created automatically:

- *Calendar folder*. Holds appointment items.
- *Contacts folder*. Holds contact items.
- *Inbox folder*. Holds mail items. By default, Outlook is configured to store all newly received email messages in the Inbox folder.
- *Journal folder*. Holds journal items.
- *Notes folder*. Holds note items.

- *Outbox folder.* Holds mail items. By default, Outlook is configured to store newly created messages in the Outbox folder, until they are sent to your email system. When a message is sent, it is deleted from the Outbox folder.
- *Sent Items folder.* Holds mail items. By default, Outlook stores a copy of the messages you have sent in this folder.
- *Tasks folder.* Holds task items.
- *Deleted Items folder.* Holds items of any type. When you delete an item, it is moved to the Deleted Items folder. You can "undelete" an item by moving it out of the Deleted Items folder. When you empty the Deleted Items folder, you cannot recover the items that were previously stored there.
- *Drafts folder.* New in Outlook 98, this holds mail items. New messages that you have begun composing but have not sent to the Outbox are stored here so that you can edit them later before sending them.

If you are connected to Microsoft Exchange Server, you can also view Exchange public folders using Outlook. Public folders work much like Outlook folders, but their contents are stored centrally on the Exchange Server. The person who creates an Exchange Server public folder can set specific access privileges on the folder, controlling who can view, edit, or create new items in the folder.

Understanding Outlook Views

Outlook provides a variety of views to display the contents of folders. A view determines the appearance of the items in a folder and controls how much data is displayed. All Outlook views are based on five view types:

- *Card views.* Display information much like a card file. The Detailed Address Cards view, shown in Figure 42.2, is an example of a Card view.
- *Day/Week/Month views.* Used with calendar items to arrange appointment items by day, week, or month. Outlook's Day/Week/Month view, shown in Figure 42.3, is an example of the Day/Week/Month type.
- *Icon views.* Use icons to represent items or files. In Figure 42.4, note items are displayed in Icons view.
- *Table views.* Display a folder's information in a grid of rows and columns. The Messages view, shown in Figure 42.5, is an example of a Table view.
- *Timeline views.* Display a horizontal bar indicating the time and duration of an item. The Message Timeline view, shown in Figure 42.6, is an example of a Timeline view.

Each folder has a variety of views associated with it. You can select any existing view at any time, by choosing View, Current View, and selecting from the list of views available.

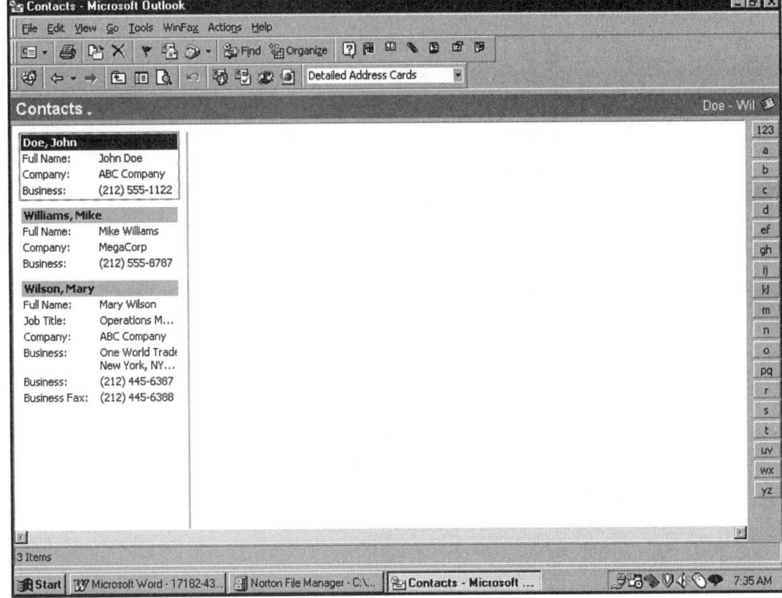

FIGURE 42.2
The Detailed Address Cards view shows Outlook contact information.

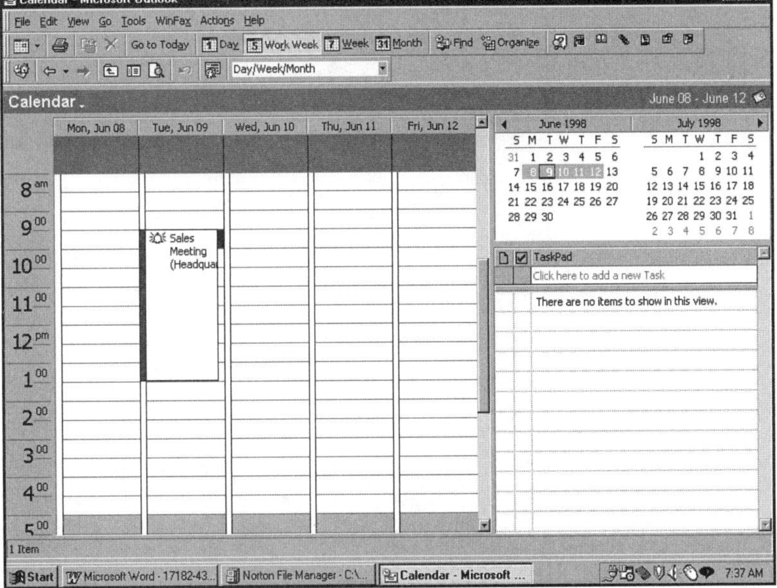

FIGURE 42.3
The Day/Week/Month view shows appointments and meetings in a calendar layout.

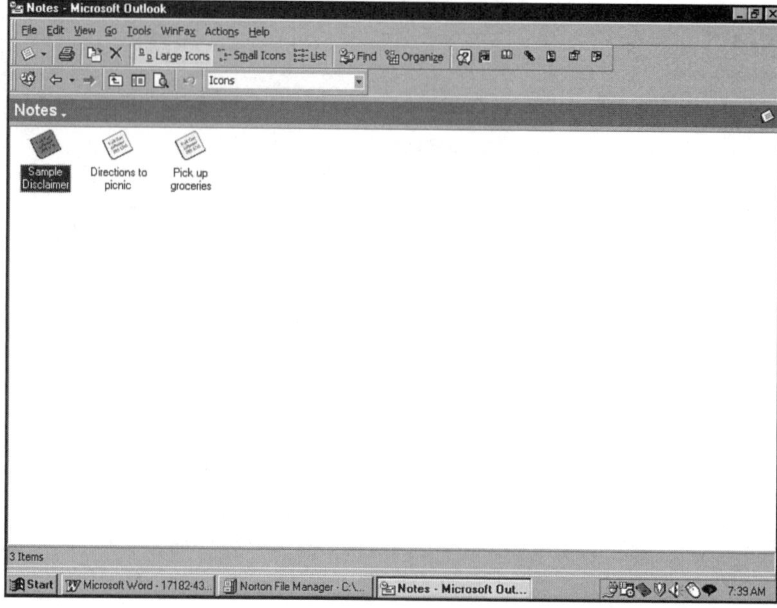

FIGURE 42.4
The Icons view displays Outlook note items as icons.

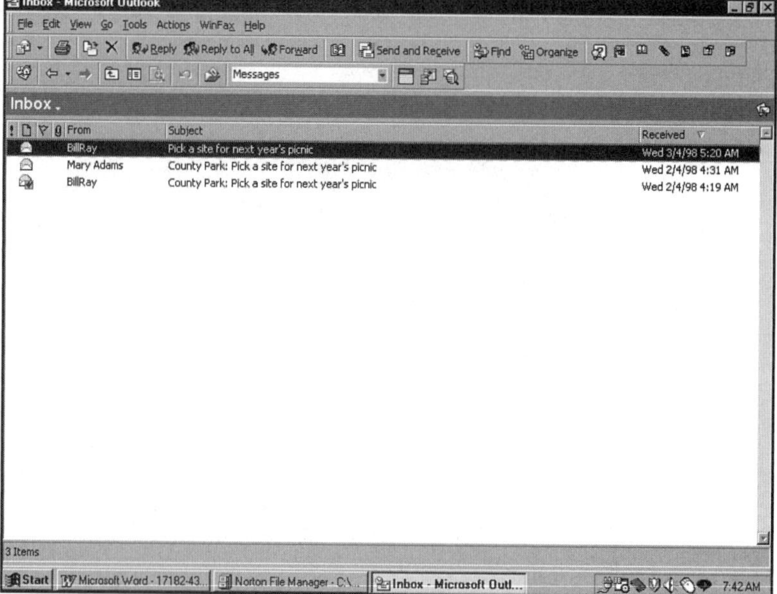

FIGURE 42.5
Messages view displays information in rows and columns.

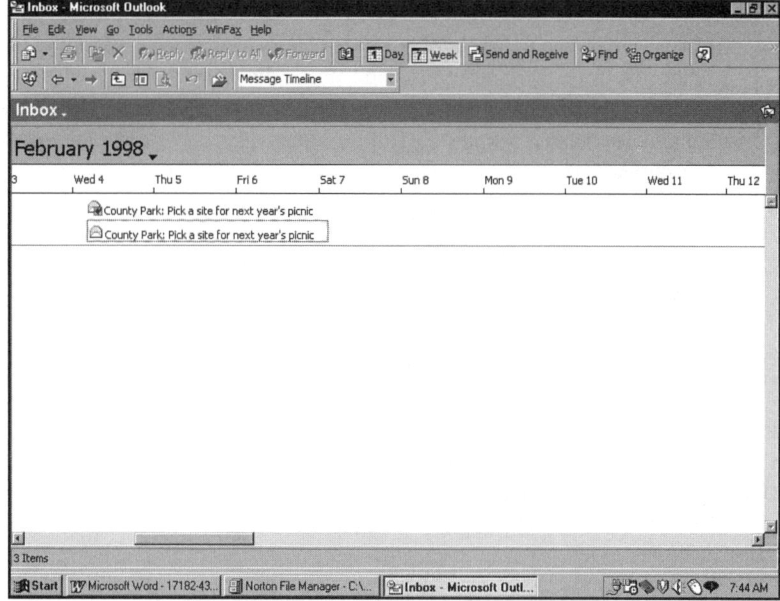

FIGURE 42.6
Message Timeline view displays information in relation to the time it was created or accessed.

Managing Outlook Backups

To back up data in Outlook, you must first understand where Outlook data is stored. Outlook items are stored in folders, but these are not the same kind of folders that you can view in the Windows Explorer. Where the folders are stored depends on how each user is configured.

For users on a network who are directly connected to a messaging system, such as Microsoft Exchange Server or Microsoft Mail, the primary storage location is the message store of the mail system you are using. For example, the items created by Outlook users on an Exchange Server system are stored in the Exchange Server message store. Exchange Server provides utilities that your Exchange administrator can use to back up the message store, and to perform additional maintenance on this data.

Users who work only while connected to the messaging system do not require any additional storage and do not need to back up any files that are on their hard drives or personal storage areas on the network. These networked users may still want to use personal folders, however, so that they can use Outlook even if the network is not available.

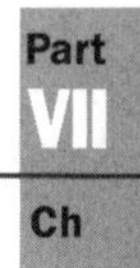

Understanding Personal Folders

You can create personal folders to give yourself more options for storing and organizing your Outlook items. Personal folders are displayed in the folders list, along with Outlook's standard folders. You can further customize your personal folders by creating subfolders within each folder.

Personal folders are stored in a Personal Folders (PST) file, which you can store on your local hard drive or in a network folder. Personal folders provide a method for storing Outlook items when you are not connected to your messaging system. Users who use Outlook only as an information manager, without using any email services, store their Outlook items in personal folders. By default, a single PST file contains all your Outlook folders, so it can grow to be a very large file.

Before you can create personal folders, you have to make sure that the Personal Folders service is installed in your profile. To do so, take these steps:

1. Customize your profile by opening the Mail icon in the Windows Control Panel or by choosing the Tools, Services command in Outlook. In either case, the Services dialog box appears (shown in Figure 42.7).

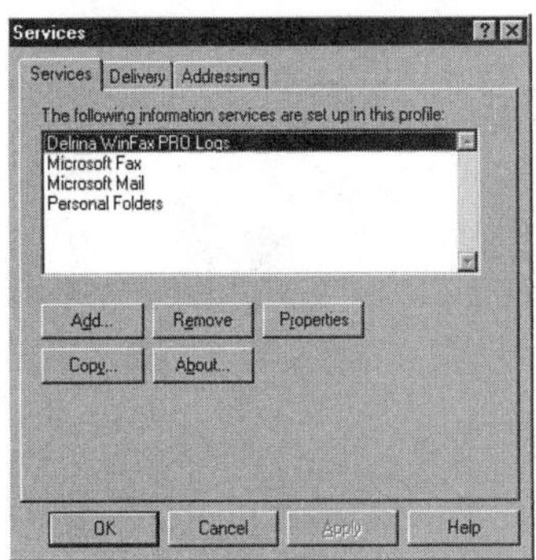

FIGURE 42.7
Use the Services dialog box to install and configure messaging services for use with Outlook.

2. If Personal Folders is not listed, click the Add button to add a service to your profile. The Add Service to Profile dialog box appears (shown in Figure 42.8).

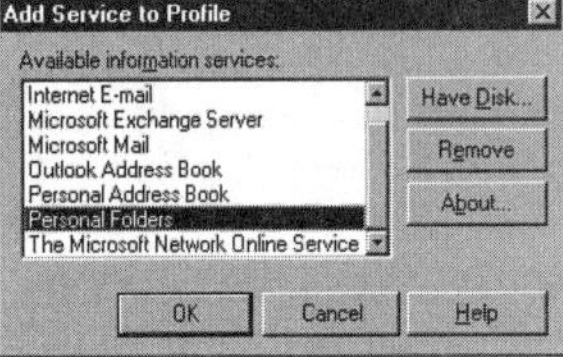

FIGURE 42.8
Select Personal Folders to add the Personal Folders service.

3. Select Personal Folders, and then click OK. The Create/Open Personal Folders File dialog box appears (shown in Figure 42.9).
4. Enter a name and location for the Personal Folders file, and click Open. The Create Microsoft Personal Folders dialog box appears (shown in Figure 42.10).
5. Type a name for the Personal Folders file, and select an encryption setting. You can't change the encryption setting after you have created the Personal Folders file. The compressible encryption setting enables your Personal Folders file to be compressed by compression software that you have installed on your computer.

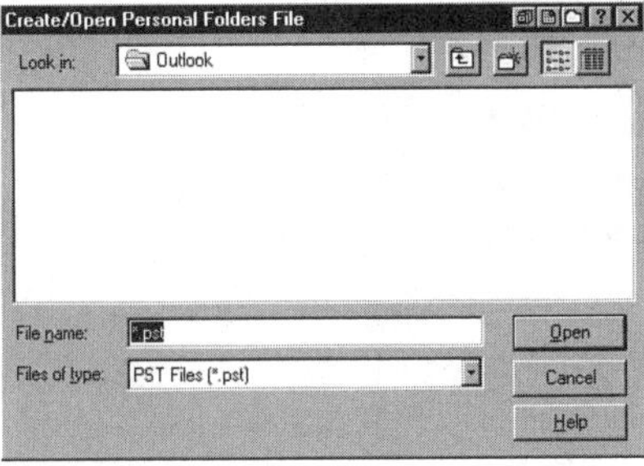

FIGURE 42.9
Enter the name and location of the Personal Folders file.

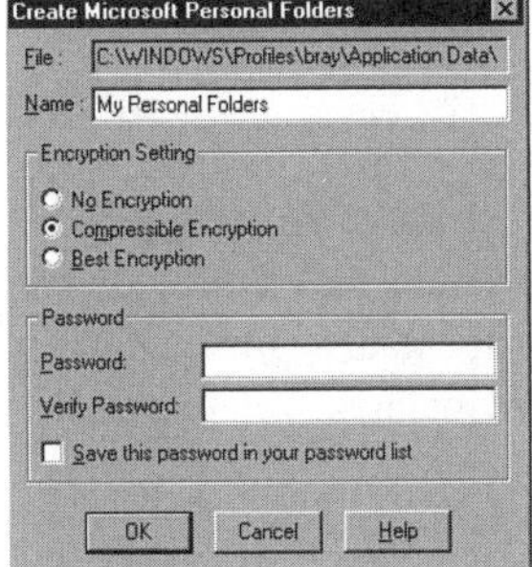

FIGURE 42.10
Use the Create Microsoft Personal Folders dialog box to customize the settings for your new Personal Folders file.

6. Add a password if you want to add a level of security to the use of your personal folders. Outlook prompts you for your password each time you start Outlook or connect to the Personal Folders file, unless you mark the Save This Password in Your Password List check box.
7. Click OK to save the Personal Folders file.

If you have more than one set of personal folders, or more than one messaging system installed, you can designate where to deliver your incoming messages. If you are connected to Microsoft Exchange Server, for example, you can choose to have your messages delivered to your personal folders. Each time you connect to the Exchange Server, the messages in your Exchange Server inbox are moved to your personal folders Inbox. Exchange Server does not keep a copy of the messages. This option is useful for users who work primarily via a laptop computer, and who are responsible for their own backups. Because Exchange Server doesn't keep a copy of the messages, the routine backup procedures of the Exchange administrator do not back up these users' work.

To have your messages delivered to your personal folders, follow these steps:

1. Choose Tools, Services, and the click the Delivery tab in the Services dialog box (shown in Figure 42.11).
2. In the Deliver new Mail to the Following Location list, select the destination for your mail delivery.
3. Click OK.

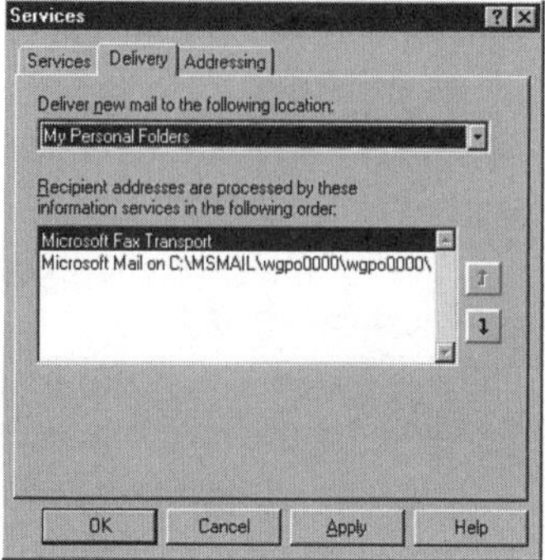

FIGURE 42.11
Select the destination for delivery of your messages. In this example, the user has named his/her personal folder My Personal Folders.

Archiving Outlook Data

Outlook enables you to archive the data in your personal storage files, copying older items to a separate personal storage file. Archiving prevents your primary personal storage file from growing too large, which slows Outlook's performance. You can use archiving with a Personal Folders file, or with your Microsoft Exchange mailbox. You can archive any Outlook folder, and all its subfolders, at any time.

1. Choose File, Archive. The Archive dialog box appears (see Figure 42.12).

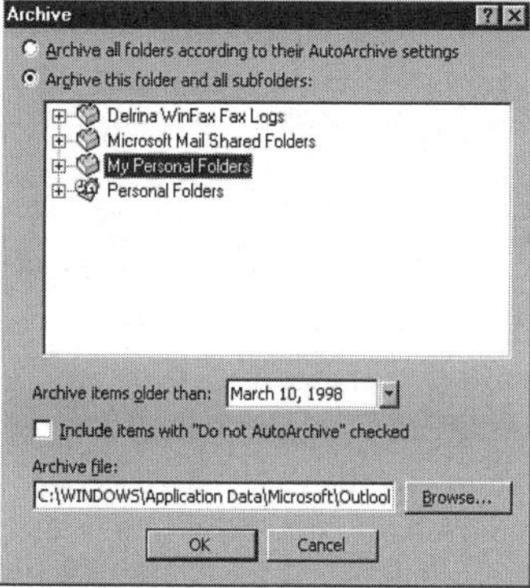

FIGURE 42.12
Select the folder you want to archive in the Archive dialog box.

2. Select a folder to be archived, and adjust the settings for how old items should be before they are archived.
3. Type the name of the archive file you want to use, or click the Browse button to browse the folders on your computer or network. You can also choose to accept the default filename, Archive.pst.
4. Click OK to begin the archiving process.

Archiving can take a long time, depending upon the size of the folder branch you have selected and the speed of your disk drives or network. In Outlook 97, you can't use Outlook until the archiving is complete. Outlook 98 archives in the background, so you can continue using Outlook during the archiving process.

You can configure Outlook to perform archiving on a regular basis, according to your instructions. To do so, follow these steps:

1. Choose Tools, Options, and click the Other tab. The AutoArchive dialog box appears (shown in Figure 42.13).

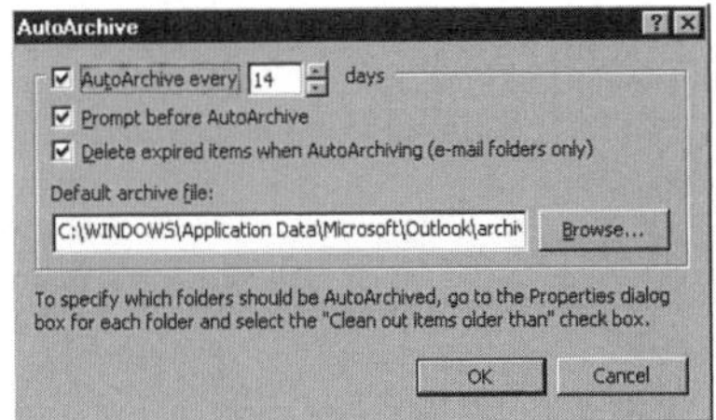

FIGURE 42.13
Use the AutoArchive dialog box to set your archive options.

2. Mark the AutoArchive Every *x* Days check box, and enter the number of days between AutoArchive sessions. Select Prompt Before AutoArchive if you want Outlook to ask for permission to execute the archive according to schedule. Select Delete Expired Items When AutoArchiving (E-mail Folders Only) to move expired email messages from your Inbox folder to the Deleted Items folder.
3. Enter the filename for the AutoArchive file, or click the Browse button to browse the folders on your computer or network.
4. Click OK.

When Outlook performs AutoArchiving, it follows the AutoArchiving properties of each Outlook folder. To view the properties for a folder, select the folder in the Folder List, choose File, Folder, and then select Properties for the folder. Click the AutoArchive tab to view and modify the AutoArchiving settings for the folder. You can choose the age after which items will be archived, and whether to move the items to an archive file, or simply to delete them. AutoArchiving does not affect (the Inbox, Contacts, and Notes folders.)

Exporting and Importing Data with Personal Folder Files

You can export the contents of any Outlook folder and its subfolders to a personal folder file. This provides an easy mechanism for transferring Outlook items between two or more computers because you can also import the contents of a personal folder file into Outlook.

The Outlook Import and Export Wizard helps you through the steps of exporting items to a personal folder file. Take the following steps:

1. Choose File, Import and Export. The Import and Export Wizard appears.
2. Select Export to a File, and click Next.
3. Select Personal Folder File (PST), and click Next.

4. Select the folder from which you want to export. If you want to export items in that folder's subfolders, mark the Include Subfolders check box.
5. To filter the items so that not all items are copied, click the Filter button. Use the options in the Filter dialog box to select items based upon date ranges, names of email recipients, or contents of the items. Click OK in the Filter dialog box to return to the wizard, and click Next.
6. Enter the filename for the personal folder file that you want to create, or click Browse to search your disk drives or network folders. If you are exporting to a personal folder file that already contains items, select the option you prefer for handling duplicate items.
7. Click Finish. Outlook creates the personal folder file or opens the existing file, and copies the selected items to the file.

The Import and Export Wizard also helps with importing Outlook items from a personal folder file.

1. Choose File, Import and Export. The Import and Export Wizard appears.
2. Select Import from Another Program or File, and click Next.
3. Select Personal Folder File (PST), and click Next.
4. Enter the filename for the personal folder file from which you want to import items, or click Browse to search your disk drives or network folders. Select the option you prefer for handling duplicate items, and click Next.
5. Outlook displays the folder structure of the file from which you are importing. Select the folder from which you want to import items, and specify whether to include subfolders.
6. To filter the items so that not all items are copied, click the Filter button. Use the options in the Filter dialog box to select items based upon date ranges, names of email recipients, or contents of the items. Click OK in the Filter dialog box to return to the wizard.
7. Select the destination folder location, and then click Finish to complete the importing operation.

Using Offline Folders with Microsoft Exchange

Remote users who are using Outlook tosend and receive mail through Microsoft Exchange Server can choose to set up *offline folders*. Offline folders contain a copy of the user's Microsoft Exchange folders, so he or she can view items on a remote computer, even when not connected to the Exchange Server. Each time you connect via modem, the offline folders are synchronized with the server folders so that their contents match. Because the offline folders contain only a copy of the server folders, the original items on the server are still backed up according to the operations of the Exchange administrator.

Offline folders are especially convenient for users with both an office and a home computer. Because Exchange Server automatically synchronizes the contents of the folders, these users don't have to worry about messages being on the wrong computer. Offline folders are a feature of Microsoft Exchange Server, and thus are not available to users of other email systems.

Follow these steps to configure Outlook to use offline folders:

1. Choose Tools, Services, and select Microsoft Exchange Server. Click Properties to view and modify settings for Exchange Server.
2. Click the Advanced tab, and mark the Enable Offline Use check box (shown in Figure 42.14).

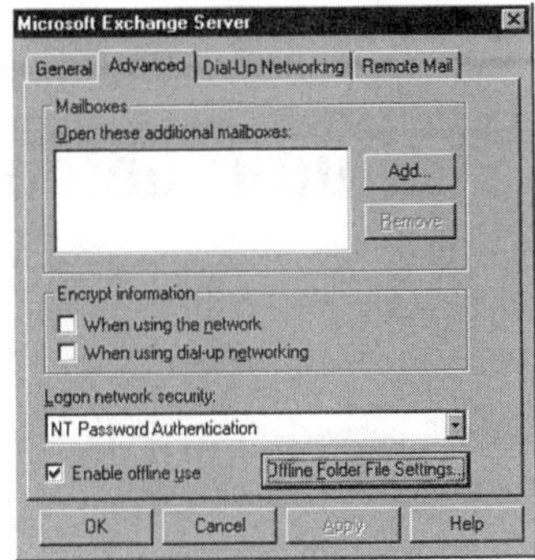

FIGURE 42.14
Use the Advanced tab of the Microsoft Exchange Server dialog box to enable offline use.

3. Click the Offline Folder File Settings button to customize your offline folder file (shown in Figure 42.15).

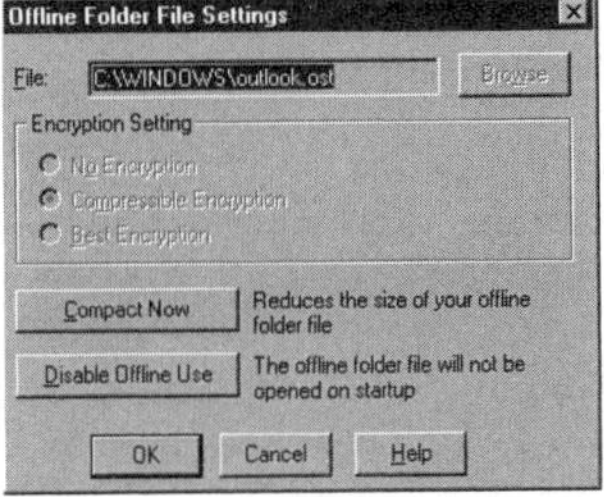

FIGURE 42.15
Use the Offline Folder File Settings dialog box to customize your offline folders.

4. Enter the filename for the offline folder file, or click Browse to browse the folders on your computer. After you have an offline folder file active, you can't change the name or location of the file.
5. Select an encryption setting for the offline folder file. You can't change the encryption setting after you have created the offline folder file. The compressible encryption setting enables your folder file to be compressed by compression software that you have installed on your computer.
6. Click OK.

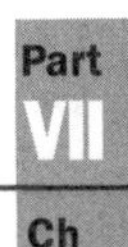

The next time you start Outlook, your offline folders are opened automatically. When you connect to Exchange Server, either via modem or by logging onto the Exchange Server, Outlook synchronizes the contents of your offline folders with your Exchange Server folders.

The following are two other operations you can perform while the Offline Folder File Settings dialog box is open:

- Click Compact Now to reduce the size of your offline folder, recovering the space that was used by items that you have deleted. This operation is usually not necessary, because Outlook and Exchange routinely compact the offline folders during normal use.
- Click Disable Offline Use to turn off the use of offline folders. The next time you start Outlook, the offline folder file is not opened.

Troubleshooting Outlook Startup Problems

When Outlook starts, it loads the default mail profile, or prompts you for which profile to use, and then opens the folders specified by the profile. When the program is loaded and the folders are opened, Outlook displays the folder that you have designated as your startup folder.

For several reasons, the startup may not work properly. This section lists some of the common symptoms, and the solutions to the problems.

Permissions Error Starting Outlook 97

If you are using Outlook 97 for the first time after installing Office 97, you might get the following message:

```
Upload of offline changes could not be completed. You do not have sufficient permission to perform this operation on this object. See the folder contact or your system administrator.
```

The same message might appear if you start the Microsoft Exchange Inbox (Windows Messaging) after installing Office 97.

This message indicates that you didn't install the Microsoft Exchange Server Support option when you installed Office 97. Exchange Server support is not installed by default. You can add this option into your Office 97 installation by running the maintenance setup of Office 97.

1. Exit all programs, including the Office Shortcut Bar.
2. Open the Windows Control Panel, and double-click Add/Remove Programs.
3. Select the Install/Uninstall tab, and select Microsoft Office 97. Click Add/Remove.
4. Setup prompts you for your Office 97 CD-ROM. Insert the CD-ROM and click OK.
5. Select Add/Remove, select Microsoft Outlook, and click Change Option.
6. Mark the Microsoft Exchange Server Support check box, click OK, and Continue to complete the installation.

MAPI Service Error in Gwmspi.dll Starting Outlook

If you have Outlook 97 installed on the same computer as Novell GroupWise, you might get the following message when you try to start Outlook:

```
Unable to open your default mail folders. MAPI was unable to load the information
service GWMSPI.DLL.
```

This message occurs if the messaging services for both GroupWise and Outlook 97 were installed in the same mail profile. If this occurs, use the Windows Control Panel to create two separate Windows Mail profiles (Windows Messaging profiles), one for each service.

Access Violation in Riched20.dll When You Start Outlook

When you start Outlook, the following message may appear:

```
Outlook.exe caused an 'access violation' fault in module Riched20.dll at
014f:4802bc95.
```

This indicates that the file Riched20.dll may be damaged. This error is most likely to occur if you are using Word as your email editor.

Find the file on your hard drive and rename it as Riched20.old. Then search your Office 97 or Outlook CD-ROM for the file Riched20.dll, and copy it to your Windows\System folder. (Refer to Appendix B for a list of file locations on the Office 97 CD-ROM.)

Startup Errors in Outlook 98

One or more of the followingmessages might appear when you try to start Outlook 98:

```
Error in configuration file 'C:\Program Files\Microsoft Office 97\
Office\Addins\<filename>.ecf.'

The extension configuration file 'C:\Program Files\Microsoft Office 97\
Office\Addins\<filename>.ecf.' could not be loaded

Unable to load <filename>.dll. You may be out of memory, out of system resources,
or missing a .dll file.
```

Add-in extensions for Outlook are stored in extension control files (ECF), which are loaded along with any required dynamic link libraries (DLL) required by the add-ins. If any of the required files are damaged or missing, Outlook displays the error message and won't start.

To solve the problem, reinstall the damaged or missing files. Rename them with the extension OLD before copying new versions of the files from your Outlook 98 CD-ROM or running the Outlook 98 Active Setup to reinstall the files.

Troubleshooting Outlook Mail Problems

After you send a mail message, you may receive a message in your Inbox from the system administrator with the following body text:

```
No transport provider was available for delivery to this recipient.
```

The following are several reasons why you might receive this message:

- Your Personal Folder file might be damaged. Remove the Personal Folder from your profile, and create a new one. You can then import the old Outlook items from the old Personal Folder file into the new file.
- You have no mail transport service in your mail profile. Use the Mail and Fax icon in the Control Panel to add the mail transport service you want to install.
- You are using the CompuServe mail transport. See the Microsoft Knowledge Base article Q170694, titled "OL97: Unable to Send Mail Using the CompuServe Mail Service."
- You upgraded your MSN mail to POP3/SMTP format. Change your email type to SMTP by following these steps:
    1. Open a contact, right-click the email address, and then select Properties.
    2. Type **SMTP** in the Email Type box, and click OK.
    3. Click Save and Close.
- The Contact item may be damaged. Delete and recreate the contact.
- You may have an apostrophe in your computer name. Open the Network icon in the Windows Control Panel. On the Identification tab, type a new name for your computer.
- Your offline folders are not configured. Connect to your Microsoft Exchange Server and reestablish your offline folder file.

Troubleshooting Outlook Mail File Attachment Problems

Many users send email messages with attached files created in other applications, such as Word documents, Excel workbooks, graphics, and many other types of files. Although this method of transferring files is extremely convenient and fast, some problems can arise.

Your ISP Disconnects You When You Send Large Attachments

When you send mail with an attachment from Outlook through an ISP, you might be disconnected from the ISP. This can happen if your attachment exceeds the maximum allowable size for attachments supported by the ISP. Contact your ISP to verify the maximum attachment size, and inquire about the availability of alternate mail servers to handle larger attachments.

If you are sending the attached files in their original size, consider using a file compression program to reduce the file size before attaching the files. If you are sending a message with several attached files, you might need to break the message into several messages, one for each attachment.

Your Messages Are Delivered, But the Attachment Isn't Received

If your ISP or mail system appears to be sending the message properly, but some of your recipients are not able to receive the attachments, ask them to check with their ISP or their company's email administrator to verify any limitations on the size and number of attachments.

Double-clicking an Attachment Generates an Error Message

If you receive an email message with an attached file, you might get the following message:

```
The file <file name>, does not have a program associated with it for this action.
To create an association, double-click My Computer on your desktop. On the View
menu, click Options, then click File Types.
```

This message indicates that the attachment doesn't match any entries in your Windows file associations. The attachment may not have an extension, or its extension may not be associated with a program on your computer.

If the file has an extension, and want to register the file type for future use, follow the instructions in the message that was presented.

To prevent sending messages without extensions, follow these steps:

1. Double-click My Computer on the Windows Desktop.
2. Choose View, Options (or Folder Options in Windows 98), and click the View tab.
3. Clear the check box labeled Hide MS-DOS File Extensions for File Types That Are Registered (or Hide File Extensions for Known File Types in Windows 98), and click OK.

Troubleshooting Other Outlook Problems

This section discusses two problems that might occur when you are using Outlook, and how to troubleshoot them.

Outlook Keeps Accessing My Floppy Drive

Outlook might seem to unnecessarily access your floppy drive. The following are reasons Outlook might look to the floppy drive:

- Outlook might be looking for a Personal Folder file. Check the locations for your Personal Folder files by choosing Tools, Services. One at a time, select your Personal Folder files, and click Properties to verify the path to the files.
- Outlook might be attempting to save archive information to the floppy drive. Choose Tools, Options, and select the AutoArchive tab. (In Outlook 98, click the Other tab and then click the AutoArchive button.) Check the path to the default AutoArchive file.

- Reminders might be trying to access a sound file on the floppy drive. Choose Tools, Options, and click the Reminders tab. (In Outlook 98, click the Other tab, and then click Advanced Options and Reminder Options.) Check the path for the Reminder sound.
- WordMail might be searching for a template on the floppy drive. Choose Tools, Options, and click the Email tab. If you have marked Use Microsoft Word As the Email Editor, check the path to the template.

OLE Registration Error When Opening a Message or Contact

After installing Office 97 Service Release 1 (SR-1), you might receive the following message when trying to open an email message or a contact item:

```
Can't open this item. An OLE registration error occurred. The program is not cor-
rectly installed. Run Setup again for the program.
```

The following are two possible causes for this error:

- A security feature of the SR-1 patch might cause the error. Choose Tools, Options, and click the Attachments tab. Change the Security Method to None.
- The OLE registration for Outlook may have an error. Exit Outlook, and insert your Office 97 CD-ROM. Choose Start, Run, and type **`D:\Setup.exe /y`**. Substitute the correct letter for your CD-ROM if it is not `D:`. Click OK to rerun setup, updating the registry entries.

CHAPTER 43

Microsoft and Third-Party Resources for Office Administrators

The Internet is filled with technical and product support for Microsoft Office 97 aimed at network administrators, computer technicians, and individual users. This chapter focuses your efforts squarely at a small number of Internet sites designed for the intermediate, advanced, and expert user or network administrator.

Office Administrators have the ability to take advantage of many different and varied resources available on the Net, in books, with subscription services, and as software on CD-ROM. This chapter will highlight some of the resources available. It will concentrate primarily on Web resources that are Microsoft Office-related and will include a concise list of Internet sites that deal with Microsoft Office. Let the reader beware, however, that changes to millions of commercial and individual Web sites occur daily and are subject to removal at any time. Be cognizant of the fact that the Web sites surveyed are dependent on the constant evolution of the Internet environment. The survey of resource topics in this chapter includes:

- Web Site Resources
- On-Line Office Resource Kit
- TechNet
- ValuPack Resources
- Microsoft Developers Network (MSDN)
- BugNet
- ZDNet
- Webreference
- MagNet

Microsoft Resources for Office Administrators

When you type **Microsoft Office 97** in any search engine on the Internet, it will yield millions of matches. Narrowing the field for reliable and informed support is a time-consuming process. The following sites are not necessarily Microsoft Office-specific, but they do yield plenty of useful information that can be helpful to administrators using Office 97.

The following are nine sites to help jump-start your online search.

Frank Condron's World O'Windows

www.worldowindows.com

This resource site lists a collection of news, resources, and helpful tips about Microsoft versions of Windows, Windows 95, Windows 98, Windows NT, and Windows CE.

The news bites keep you up-to-date on Microsoft's antitrust suit and news releases concerning its latest products.

The sidebar leads you to eight areas: Windows News, Windows 95, Windows 98, Windows NT, Windows CE, Office 97, Frank's Commentary, and Book Reviews.

In the Office 97 area you will find a wealth of information for network administrators and individual users. This area includes the following:

- Discussion Groups: Over 20 different subcategories analyzing Office 97.

NOTE If you are new to newsgroups, Frank explains what they are and how to use them effectively, ensuring ease of use and offering plenty of information.

- Updates and Patches: SR-1 Patch for Office 97 and Excel 97 recalculation patch. SR-2 will be available soon.
- Microsoft Resources: A number of bug patches, office assistants, and the final version of Outlook 98.

What I liked was that World O'Windows provided many opportunities to ask questions and interact.

NOTE This is an example of the type of question and advice given when interacting on World O'Windows.

An inquirer writes: "I work on a site that has over 100 PCs and we are just about to install Office 97 on the majority of these. We have the Office CD on a network server and will be installing from this. Is it at all possible to make a script, batch, or INF file so that I can automatically install Office with selected components? For example, should I install everything apart from Outlook and Photo Editor and then get it to run the SR1 patch and XL8 patch? If there is a way, it could save me a lot of time. Yours in anticipation..."

Bob Buckland, a member of the discussion group, responds: "Yes, you can use the Microsoft Office Network Installation Wizard (NIW v2. 1) to do this. See the online (current) Office 97 Resources Kit (ORK97) at **microsoft.com/office/ork**. You can download the NIW from Appendix A.

"But, you cannot use the SR1 patch on a networked installation. Since, except for the Small Business Edition, the upgrade to the full product replacement Office 97 SR1 (your edition) Edition CD (formerly enterprise update) is free, get that version then do your rollout.

"If you bought Office 97 retail, call Microsoft (800) 370-9272 for the update. If you got it OEM/bundled, call that supplier for the CDs.

"You will need to have SR1 installed to install the SR2 patch. This is due out this summer and that one will work with networked installations." ■

SupportHelp: Your Pipeline to Tech Support

supporthelp.com/

This site provides instant access to computer hardware and software companies. When you need it most, tech support is on hand, fast, and easy. This site will respond to inquiries concerning company information, industry phone numbers, email addresses, and Web links. By typing Microsoft into the search, you have access to product downloads, tech support, and information about all the Office 97 applications.

The Web site menu also offers:

- *Search.* This database separates the search engine into three main areas: company, product, and keyword.
- *Forums.* This is a support area with free access for nonmembers. You will find a variety of discussions concerning the Internet, platforms, and applications, including network management products and technology.
- *Newsgroups.* SupportHelp did much of the work for you by sifting through thousands of newsgroups, and it came up with the following manageable list:
    - Y2K Issues
    - Security Issues
    - Database Structure
    - Hardware/Software Issues
    - Windows NT Issues
    - Microsoft Help Information

WIN95

www.win95mag.com

This site is a good online resource for users of Windows 95, 98, and NT. However, the site layout was a bit confusing at first. One of several menus offered included the following items:

- *Editor's Choice Awards.* These are applications and Web sites reviewed by online magazine editors.
- *The Bookshop.* WIN95 users will appreciate this selection of books and materials designed for all levels of computer expertise.
- *Forums.* They take pains to encourage posting of questions, answers, and opinions.

Shareware.com

www.shareware.com

This search database hosts more than 250,000 files. It is a site that provides direct links organized in two main categories: new files and hot downloads.

NOTE The Shareware.com sidebar includes:

- New Arrivals
- Browsers
- Power Search
- Newsletter
- Help

To access the Office information, type Office 97 in the search section; there is a great deal of information available.

Download.com

www.download.com

This site is a comprehensive database that provides reviews of downloadable software. It is the sister site of Shareware.com.

The menu is organized for quick reference with easy access. The topic areas include:

- *Highlights.*
- *At A Glance.* The list includes categories for Most Popular, Newest Titles, and Top Pick.
- *Quick Search.*
- *Categories.* The list includes Business, Development Tools, Drivers, Education, Games, Home & Personal, Internet, Multimedia & Design, and Utilities.

NOTE The Download.com sidebar includes:

- Free Newsletter
- All Categories
- All Reviews
- Weekly Picks
- Power Search

The EnterSoft Network

www.esn.net/

NOTE The esn.net sidebar includes:

- Search
- News
- Help!
- Business Sites
- Personal Sites
- Community Sites
- WWW Sites
- Kiosk
- Toys

For those computers (and computer users) that are sound-sensitive, be aware: This site opens with a lively sound clip.

If your interest is in Microsoft specifically, go directly to the shareware evaluation area, highlight the Business and Productivity Category, and click on Microsoft Office.

Take a look at this site's subcategories and feast on all the add-ons for Access, Excel, General Office, Outlook, PowerPoint, and Word. Each subheading has its own page full of new releases, downloads, editor's picks, and add-ons.

In addition, this Microsoft Office area offers:

- The top 10 downloads
- Other resources, including download guide and newsletter
- In the spotlight

Benchin

www.benchin.com

NOTE The Benchin sidebar includes:

- Home
- Members
- Store
- Info
- Links
- Help!
- Customize

This site has lots of personality and stores of information. It is well laid out and easy to navigate. The site resources include:

- Over 100,000 product reviews
- Comprehensive product information
- Chat rooms and discussion groups
- A Fast Find database

This site evaluates programs such as Microsoft Office 97 through product ratings and recommendations for professionals, novices, experts, and nonprofessionals. Benchin gives you the opportunity to share your opinion about listed products and hosts discussion groups on a variety of subjects.

Benchin discussion groups are available to members only. A short, online registration form is the only barrier between you and some expert advice for your questions.

Baarns, Your Microsoft Office Resource Center

www.baarns.com/Office-97/

NOTE The Baarns sidebar includes:

- Office 97 Overview
- Excel 97
- Word 97
- Access 97
- PowerPoint 97
- Outlook 97

This is an excellent site providing current information on the benefits and features of Office 97. When you enter individual menu categories on the sidebar, Baarns spells out new features and outlines any current changes. For example, in the Word 97 area you will find over sixty suggestions for updating your Office suite.

There is more. The best feature of the Microsoft Office 97 area is the step-by-step feature explanations, complete with corresponding graphics.

Online Office Resource Kit

www.microsoft.com/office/ork/default.htm

The Office Resource Kit is an invaluable tool for any Office administrator. It contains a great deal of information for cross-application users and for troubleshooting, deploying, and configuring Microsoft Office 97. It is written for administrators, help-desk technicians and Information Systems professionals. It encompasses the use of computers with Windows 95, Windows NT Server, Windows NT Workstations, and Microsoft Office 98 for Macintosh.

This comprehensive Internet site consists of four major sections: an exhaustive index, a Table of Contents that includes 39 chapters and 5 appendixes, a Tools and Utilities section, and the "Top Ten Ways the Office Resource Kit Can Help." The following segments explain the sections in greater detail.

Top Ten Ways the Office Resource Kit Can Help This segment shows the user different ways to make Microsoft Office 97 more convenient and flexible. It offers "how to" tips and also provides links that will help carry them out. For instance, to install a single Office 97 for Windows configuration on a number of user computers, it recommends creating a network installation point, then using the Network Installation Wizard to customize Office Setup. It permits links to the Network Installation Wizard.

Table of Contents The Table of Contents for Microsoft Office Resource Kit is divided into the following six parts:

- Part 1 is the welcome area and generally shows how to use the Office Resource Kit. It also shows what is new in Microsoft Office 97.
- Part 2 deals with deploying Microsoft Office. The guide includes useful information for installing, customizing, training, and troubleshooting.
- Part 3 discusses upgrading from previous versions of Microsoft Office, Access, Excel, Outlook, Word, and PowerPoint.
- Part 4 discusses switching from other applications to their counterparts in Microsoft Office 97.
- Part 5 describes using Microsoft Office throughout your organization. This ranges from supporting multiple versions of Office to Web support in applications. Also included in Part 5 are finding documents on the network, sharing information, and workgroup features of all the Office components.
- Part 6 concerns the Microsoft Office Architecture, as well as Office, Access, Excel, Outlook, PowerPoint, and Word. The appendix at the end is very informative. Its coverage ranges from setup command-line options and file formats to Registry keys and values. A list of installed components is available, as is a link to Tools and Utilities.

Index The index contains massive amounts of information about Microsoft Office. It is easy to use with its alphabetical tabs and a multitude of subheadings.

Tools and Utilities In this section are a variety of client installation tools, PowerPoint and Word converters, and Web and intranet tools. Other tools mentioned are used for extracting and copying files for Office floppy disks. The general tools section covers a variety of useful administrative utilities.

There is also documentation, including Microsoft Technical Helpline for Office. If you purchase a printed version of the Office Resource Kit, it comes with a Tools and Utilities CD. However, be sure to check out the Web site, for it has a substantial amount of information at no charge.

Office 97 Assistance This section features product information and demos, product enhancement tips, and product assistance. It encompasses the entire Microsoft Office 97 suite, including Office, Word, Excel, PowerPoint, Access, Outlook, and Publisher.

NOTE The business resource link for large organizations includes the capability to link to an anti-virus clinic, and an Intranet center. These may be especially helpful sites for administrators. Office 97 Assistance provides features that deal with current issues. There are also tips and suggestions for improving efficiency and troubleshooting. The URL is **www.microsoft.com/msoffice/astoffice.asp**.

TechNet

www.microsoft.com/msvs/product/docs/dtlsht/159_dtl.htm

Microsoft TechNet gives fast and easy access to the complete collection of Microsoft technical information.

The TechNet subscription can help keep an administrator current with the latest technology trends at Microsoft. You can find white papers on trends, case studies, and information on integrating legacy systems with Microsoft products. There is a great deal of data at this site that deals directly with Office 97.

The one-year subscription will give an administrator access to at least two CDs every month (some months might even bring three) with over 150,000 pages of technical information.

The CDs contain the following information:

- Technical notes
- Supplemental drivers and patches
- Application notes
- Microsoft Knowledge Base—the same information used by Microsoft support engineers

Microsoft Knowledge Base contains the following:

- Articles on more than 55,000 topics
- Troubleshooting tips
- Application notes
- Usage and optimization techniques

ValuPack Resources

The Microsoft Office 97 ValuPack is located on the CD-ROM that installs Office 97. It contains 34 additional folders that may be added to the Microsoft Office 97 Suite. The ValuPack 97 components may be installed separately with their own Setup procedures. Some of the add-ons may be opened within a particular Microsoft Office 97 program or from the Start menu. Many add-ons may be opened and installed from the Help Menu in the ValuPack 97 folder. The following is a complete listing of the 37 components, with a brief synopsis of each one.

Additional Help Files

There are four supplementary help files in the ValuPack. These include using Microsoft Outlook and Visual Basic, Microsoft Office Binder Visual Basic, Microsoft Graph VBA, and Microsoft Map Visual Basic. Complete installation instructions are included.

Animated Cursors

Animated cursors are available in the Microsoft Office ValuPack. These cursors can become a printer with pages printing, envelopes when you send mail in Outlook, and more. These whimsical extras add fun and animation to everyday tasks. They may be installed from the Help menu. Be aware that they may slow down your computer considerably, if it is an older model.

Animated Graphics Interchange Format (GIF) Files

The 16 animated pictures in this folder may be added to a World Wide Web page in order to embellish the design and draw attention to specific information. The animation includes pulsating beams of light, a bull's-eye, rotating exclamation points, a file inserted into a folder that closes, and a ringing phone, to name a few. The viewing and installation details are provided on each graphic.

Avery Wizard

The Avery Wizard may be used in conjunction with Avery Dennison products. It can be helpful with mail merges and lining up text correctly on a label. This may be installed from the Help menu.

Building Applications with Microsoft Access 97

This is a developer's guide to managing databases. It is a book designed to help with database solutions. It may be printed out or viewed online. The chapters include:

- Using Forms to Collect, Filter, and Display Information
- Working with Objects and Collections
- Creating Multi-user Applications
- Optimizing Your Application
- Using Active X Controls
- Creating Wizards, Builders, and Menu Add-Ons
- Developing Client/Server Applications
- Working with the Internet

This developer's guide may be installed from the Help menu.

Two files are necessary when maintaining the Setup Wizard: Microsoft Office 97 Developer Edition Service Pack 2 and Updated ODBC 3.0 Driver Manager.

Data Access Pack

The Data Access Pack allows installation of all ODBC drivers and IISAMS (built-in drivers) to access data outside Microsoft Access or Excel. It allows the importing of FoxPro data into Excel. The nine drivers may be installed from the Help menu in ValuPack or as part of the Microsoft Office 97 Setup.

Microsoft Excel Viewer

The Excel Viewer is designed to allow non-Microsoft users access to Excel files. It may be installed from the Help menu.

Internet Help for Microsoft Access

The Internet Help for Microsoft Access folder includes features for the use of Microsoft Access on the Internet. Some of the information you can find includes troubleshooting tips for using Active X Server Page (ASP) files with Access and Web browser control Help files.

Lotus cc: Mail Information Service

This is a Messaging Application Programming Interface (MAPI) service provider that allows you to use Microsoft Outlook as your email client with a Lotus cc: Mail Post Office. When it is installed, you may exchange mail with other users. Special instructions are included for Windows NT users.

Microsoft Active Movie

Active Movie provides digital video technology for Internet and desktop use. Synchronized, sharp, audio, video, and special effects are included. Active Movie can be installed from the Help menu. Some of the features include Internet playback and streaming, and MPEG playback for full-screen, TV-quality video.

Microsoft Camcorder

Create a tutorial and send it to others! Microsoft Camcorder allows you to record actions, sounds, and procedures on your PC. This can be installed from the Help menu.

Microsoft Internet Explorer can be installed from the Help menu.

Kodak Flash Pix/Microsoft Picture It! 1.0 Graphic Import Filter

This option allows the importing of either Kodak Flash Pix or Microsoft Picture It! into Microsoft Office 97 documents. This feature can be installed from the Help menu.

Microsoft Office 97 Sounds

The sounds included in the ValuPack that are available to the individual user are not available on Windows NT Workstation 3.51 or Windows NT Server 3.51.

Microsoft Office 97 Upgrade Wizard

The Office 97 Upgrade Wizard helps you eliminate old versions of Office (4.x and 95) from your hard drive. It can run three phases: remove files that you don't need, remove old Office components of your choice, or remove all previous Office versions. Wizard may be installed from the Help menu.

Microsoft Office 97 Binder Templates

To use these time-saving templates, copy them from the ValuPack Binders Folder into Office templates. Instructions are found in the Help menu.

Microsoft Office 97 Far East Support

The Office 97 Far East Support add-on allows the use of Far East characters and converts documents originating in the Far East. The languages include Japanese, Korean, and simplified and traditional Chinese.

Microsoft Office 97 Templates, Forms, and Wizards

This folder contains a multitude of Word, Excel, and PowerPoint templates, wizards, and forms. An example for Word includes agendas and press releases. Excel has budgets, quotes, and more. There are over 40 new background designs for PowerPoint presentations, and forms for training management and vacation requests in Outlook.

Microsoft Outlook Import/Export Converters

These converters enable you to import and export to and from Outlook journal entries, mail messages, notes, and more. There are six different files.

Microsoft Outlook Rules Wizard

The Outlook Rules Wizard is a client/server messaging manager. It is useful for users receiving high volumes of email. This wizard can be installed from the Help menu.

Microsoft PowerPoint Viewer

The PowerPoint Viewer is similar to the Excel Viewer and allows PowerPoint users to do presentations on PCs without Microsoft PowerPoint installed. You can install this viewer from the Help menu.

Microsoft PowerPoint 97 Translator

The PowerPoint 97 Translator program lets users of PowerPoint 4.0 open files saved in PowerPoint 97 format.

Microsoft PowerPoint Custom Soundtrack

Users may add their own soundtrack to PowerPoint presentations using this program. This program can be installed from the Help menu.

Microsoft Publish to ActiveMovie Stream Format (ASF)

This ASF tool permits you to publish audio/visual PowerPoint presentations on the Internet or intranet. It allows for compression and streaming across a network. This program can be installed from the Help menu.

Microsoft Word 97 True Type Fonts

There are up to 150 additional True Type fonts in the Microsoft Office 97 ValuPack. They may be viewed before installation if you have a GIF file viewer, or you may look in the MSFonts folder. Install as many as you need. Complete installation instructions and guidelines are included.

Microsoft Web Publishing Wizard

Web Wizard enables you to publish World Wide Web pages on the Internet. It automatically helps you copy files from your computer to a Web server. It may be used with a local ISP, the larger national companies (such as AOL or CompuServe), and intranet servers on your LAN. This wizard can be installed from the Help menu.

Microsoft Word 97 Converter

The Word 97 Converter is necessary if you ever share files with different versions of Word. It permits the conversion of Word 97 to Word 95 or Word 6.0 format. This can be installed from the Help menu.

Presentation and World Wide Web Page Textures

Presentation and World Wide Web Page textures are JPEG files that enhance the background with texture or images. They include fifteen files ranging from backgrounds of cotton candy to liquid metal to parchment.

Software Patches

The three patches included are the MSPlus! Themes patch, MSWorks 4.0a patch, and Microsoft Outlook Inbox Icon patch.

Timex Data Link Watch Wizard

To easily import into Outlook appointments, tasks, phone numbers and important dates, select this folder. You can install the Data Link Watch Wizard from the Help menu.

Microsoft Word Viewer

The Word Viewer enables you to view Word documents without the Microsoft Word program. It does not permit editing, but it does allow copying. The Word Viewer can be installed from the Help menu.

Snapshot Viewer

You can record, store, or view a report snapshot with Microsoft Access using the Snapshot Viewer. It creates a snapshot report—a high-fidelity copy of a Microsoft Access report preserving the two-dimensional layout, graphics, and embedded objects.

Third-Party Resources

Many resources are available on the Internet via Microsoft. In addition, there are many other resources that various companies or organizations offer. Several of these resources are highlighted in the following sections.

Microsoft Developers Network: MSDN

www.microsoft.com/msdn/

This is specifically for developers of applications, but there is a variety of tools and tips here for administrators as well. It includes the following main options to choose from:

- *Online.* Delivers developer news and information via the free online newsletter "Buzz"
- *Online Membership.* Includes access to many databases (primarily the MSDN library, which contains technical articles, knowledge base, bug list, and much more), software downloads, and special discounts; and offers an emailed list of tips and tricks
- *Universal Subscription.* Delivers a CD that includes the MSDN library (updated quarterly), phone support, discounts on books, subscription to bimonthly Developer Network News, a complete set of operating systems, BackOffice test platform, Visual Studio 97, Office 97 Developers Edition, FrontPage 97, Team Manager 97, Microsoft Project, and updates and new releases sent throughout the year (some limitations may apply)

BugNet

www.bugnet.com

This site offers a wonderful subscription service to help administrators tackle the awesome task of managing bugs for various software packages. Once upon a time, administrators had to manage bugs by combing through magazines and then newsgroups; today, with the help of

BugNet, the information is brought to you. This Web site is a little difficult to manage and understand, but the information can save bundles of time and money. A subscription to BugNet offers the following:

- *BugNet newsletter.* An online newsletter discussing glitches, bugs, and incompatibilities
- *BugNet database.* An online database with bugs and fixes
- *BugNet yearbook.* Thousands of bugs and fixes for your own system
- *BugNet alert.* Special bulletins for serious problems

ZDNet

www.zdnet.com

The publishers of *PC Computing* and *PC Magazine* offer help and articles on a variety of topics. From news on industry-specific topics to downloadable shareware/freeware, this site is chock full of helpful advice. Another plus: it's easy to get around!

Webreference.com

www.webreference.com/internet/magazines/computers.html

This reference is a listing of magazines related to the computer industry, organized in alphabetical order, and separated into PC and Macintosh.

MagNet

www.cris.com/~milewski/magnet.html

MagNet is another magazine listing related to the computer industry. It is an excellent resource and organized in alphabetical order. ●

PART VIII

Appendixes

CHAPTER A

What's on the CD-ROM

On the accompanying CD-ROM software, we have included products that will be of use to Office Administrators and perhaps to those they serve as well. Most of the software is an evaluation or demo version of the full product. Please try the software that interests you and contact the vendor about acquiring the full version of the product if it meets your needs. Vendor contact information is provided.

The software is arranged on the CD-ROM in the following categories:

- Electronic Books
- Word-Related Software
- Excel-Related Software
- Access-Related Software
- PowerPoint-Related Software
- Internet Software
- General Software

Electronic Books

The following four books are provided on the CD-ROM in PDF format:

- Migrating to Office 95 and Office 97: Professional Reference Edition
- Sams Teach Yourself Microsoft Publisher 98 in 24 Hours
- Windows 95 and NT 4.0 Registry and Customization Handbook
- Sams Teach Yourself Microsoft Project 98 in 24 Hours

These can be viewed using the Adobe Acrobat Reader. A 32-bit, 16-bit, and Macintosh version of the Reader are available on the CD-ROM. You can access the 32-bit and 16-bit versions from the CD-ROM interface, or you can find them in the 3rdparty\General\Acrobat directory in Windows Explorer. The Macintosh version is found in the MacSoftware\Acrobat directory, which is only viewable from a Macintosh computer.

Macmillan Computer Publishing provides these books. To obtain a hard copy of these products, visit our online catalog at **www.mcp.com/online_catalog**.

Also provided is our Windows 98 Knowledgebase. The Que, New Riders, and Sams Publishing imprints have joined forces to bring you this collection of information and excerpts from their best-selling Windows 98 titles. (Requires a Web browser.)

Word-Related Software

The following software products are found in the 3rdparty\Word directory on the CD-ROM. They are also accessible via the CD-ROM interface.

ANT_HTML

The ANT_HTML.DOT template by Jill Swift is designed to work within Word 6.0 (and above) to facilitate the creation of hypertext documents. HTML tags can be inserted into any new or previously prepared Word document or any ASCII document. The "Form Thing" provides 10 tools to simplify and speed the creation of HTML forms.

To Order: Visit the Telacommunications Web site at **www.telacommunications.com/ant/register.htm**.

Doc-To-Help

Doc-To-Help by WexTech Systems, Inc., uses a true single-source approach that enables you to create and maintain Online Help and printed documentation from one source document without having to compromise in either medium. You can format your document and Help independently from a single-source document, and can indicate material as print only, online only, WinHelp only, HTML only, and HTML Help only.

To Order: Call 800-939-8324 or visit the Web site at **www.wextech.com**.

EasyHelp/Web

EasyHelp/Web by Eon Solutions, Ltd., is the easy way to create professional Windows help (WinHelp) and Web pages (HTML) from Microsoft Word.

To Order: Email **sales@easyhelp.com**, or call +44 1625 827037 (tel/fax).

GhostFill

GhostFill by LAWEX, takes up where off-the-shelf word processors made for Windows leaves off, offering true document automation through powerful template building and filling. In short, it enables you to create automated documents easily and rapidly—and you don't need any programming skills to do so! After you've created and saved these document templates, you can run them repeatedly, saving yourself time and effort, increasing your accuracy and boosting your productivity.

To Order: Call LAWEX at 800-377-5844, or visit **www.lawex.com**.

Microsoft Word 97 Viewer

Microsoft's Word 97 Viewer allows users of Windows® 95 or Windows NT® 3.51 or later to open Word 97 documents.

To Order: Free from Microsoft. Visit the Microsoft Web site at **www.microsoft.com**.

Office In Color Templates

The Office In Color Sampler from KMT Software, Inc., is a collection of spectacular color templates for Word, Excel, and PowerPoint. These templates are great productivity tools and help you make a great first impression.

To Order: Call 1-800-KMT-CALC, or send email to **sales@kmt.com.** See the ad in the back of the book for additional details.

Supplemental Text Converters for Microsoft Word

These supplemental text converters from Microsoft allow users of Word 97 to open files created by other applications: Pro 3.x; WordStar 3.3–7.0 for MS-DOS®; WordStar for Windows 1.0-2.0 (import only); and WordStar 4.0 or 7.0 for MS-DOS (export only).

Order: Free from Microsoft. Visit the Microsoft Web site at **www.microsoft.com**.

Virus ALERT for Macros

Virus ALERT for Macros™ by LOOK Software Systems, Inc., detects and cleans known and supplemental text convertersunknown macro viruses. Provides continuous automatic protection. Their state-of-the-art and patent-pending heuristic technology will sniff out and eliminate tomorrow's new macro viruses before they can damage your documents.

To Order: Contact LOOK Software at any of the following: 1-800-678-5511; **sales@look.com**; **www.look.com**; 2750 Fenton Road, Ottawa, Ontario, Canada, K1T-3T7.

Word 6.0/95 Binary Converter for Word 97

Microsoft's Word 6.0/95 Binary Converter for Word 97 allows users of Word 97 to save documents in true Word 6.0/95 format.

To Order: Free from Microsoft. Visit the Microsoft Web site at **www.microsoft.com**.

Word 97 Converter for Word 6.0/95

Microsoft's Word 97 converter allows users of Word for Windows 6.0 or 95 to read Word 97 files.

Order: Free from Microsoft. Visit the Microsoft Web site at **www.microsoft.com**.

Excel-Related Software

The following software products are found in the 3rdparty\Excel directory on the CD-ROM. They are also accessible via the CD-ROM interface.

DecisionTools Suite

The DecisionTools Suite by Palisade Corporation is a suite of five powerful programs running from an Excel platform. The Suite includes @RISK for Excel, PrecisionTree, TopRank for Excel, BestFit, and RISKview. These programs all work together to perform combined risk and decision analyses that are not available from any one package.

To Order: Contact the Palisade Sales Department by phone at 800-432-7475 or 607-277-8000, by fax at 607-277-8001, by email at **sales@palisade.com**, or by visiting their Web site at **www.palisade.com**.

Excel Recovery

Excel Recovery by Concept Data is a Microsoft Excel add-in for recovering data from corrupted Excel files of all modern versions, including Excel 97, Excel 95, and Excel 5.0. Also allows you to "downgrade" file versions: by using Excel Recovery, Excel 97 files can be opened from Excel 95. Very easy to use: adds "Recover…" item right into File menu!

To Order: Visit **www.conceptdata.com/excel/** for purchasing information. Various options are described there, including extra fast online purchasing option (get full commercial copy in minutes).

Microsoft Excel 97 Viewer

Microsoft Excel 97 Viewer is a small, no-charge, freely distributable program that lets people view and print Microsoft Excel for Windows (version 2.0 and greater) and Microsoft Excel for the Macintosh® (versions 2.2a and greater) spreadsheet files. Microsoft Excel Viewer gives users the flexibility to view page layout, copy, zoom, AutoFilter, and control cell sizes. The Microsoft Excel Viewer supports OLE DocObject as well as the ability to view any Microsoft Excel file.

To Order: Free from Microsoft. Visit the Microsoft Web site at **www.microsoft.com**.

Office In Color Templates

The Office In Color Sampler from KMT Software, Inc. is a collection of spectacular color templates for Word, Excel, and PowerPoint. These templates are great productivity tools and help you make a great first impression.

To Order: Call 1-800-KMT-CALC, or send email to **sales@kmt.com**. See the ad in the back of the book for additional details.

Power Utility Pak for Excel 97

Power Utility Pak 97 by JWalk & Associates adds 31 general-purpose utilities, 40 custom worksheet functions, and enhanced shortcut menus to Microsoft Excel 97. The Power Utility Pak is suitable for users of all levels. The complete VBA source code is also available for a nominal fee.

To Order: Register online at **www.j-walk.com/ss/**.

Sound-Proof

Sound-Proof by JWalk & Associates is an Excel 97 add-in that uses a synthesized voice to read the contents of selected cells. It's the perfect proofreading tool for anyone who does data entry in Excel. Choose straight digits or natural language and decide whether you want the cells read in rows or columns. The pause between cells is adjustable. The program recognizes text, but does not read it; it simply says "text" or remains silent. This add-in doesn't require system changes and can be a big help for checking your data on large spreadsheets. The shareware is fully functional but only lets you read a range of 12 cells until registered.

To Order: Register online at **www.j-walk.com/ss/**.

Edwin's Power Tools

Edwin's Power Tools is a sophisticated Excel shareware add-in, fully optimized for Excel 97. It includes tools for 3-D formatting, special selection, text manipulation, spreadsheet management, and more. New features include Spreadsheet Sorter, Matrix Transform, Negativa Reposition, and so on. Version 2.1 also includes a re-designed Number to English utility that is very well done. EPT 2 is designed to run on Excel 7 and 8 for Windows and Excel 5 for Macintosh. (The Macintosh version of the software is located in the Macsoftware\EPT directory. It is visible only from a Macintosh.)

To Order: Use the "Register EPT" program that is a part of the evaluation software or visit the online registration page at **order.kagi.com/?R4**.

Access-Related Software

The following software products are found in the 3rdparty\Access directory on the CD-ROM. They are also accessible via the CD-ROM interface.

Alma Page Generator

Alma Page Generator by Alma Internet Publishing generates HTML pages from templates and Access using active content fields. This program essentially separates design/layout from content, thus making the management of both easier, and greatly reduces site management work.

To Order: Visit the Alma Internet Publishing Web site at **www.alma.co.uk**.

Baccess

Baccess by Redei Enterprises is a powerful backup utility for MSAccess. Baccess, itself, determines what needs to be backed up. It creates a list from all files referenced in the database. The user can delete unwanted files from the list. Baccess allows series backup, it includes a scheduler that allows unattended processing, and it provides its own Restore. Baccess supports LAN and all Windows operating systems. It also supports secured databases.

To Order: Visit the Redei Enterprises Web site at **ourworld.compuserve.com/homepages/p_redei2**.

c:JAM

c:JAM (Central Jet Accounts Manager) by J. Mueller is a powerful security and user accounts management tool for MS Access 2.0–8.0. c:JAM simplifies operation, enhances security, supports large distributed workgroups, and provides a security model for replicated databases.

To Order: Visit J. Mueller's IT Consulting and Development Web site at **ourworld.compuserve.com/homepages/jomdev/**.

Compare '98

Compare '98 by Ashish Computer Systems compares two MS-Access databases and gives you the differences between them. As an Access developer, how many times have you struggled to find and synchronize the differences between the client database (table and queries) and your own? Now you can easily determine the differences by using Compare '98.

To Order: Visit the Ashish Computer Systems Web site at **www.ashishsystems.com**.

DBmaintMS

DBmaintMS by West Coast Systems is a tool for managing Microsoft Access 95 (version 7.0) and Access 97 (version 8.0) databases in Windows 95. It includes backup, restore, compact, repair, move, copy, history, and logging functions. Scripts allow the user to process multiple desktop and even network databases. This utility is also capable of time-deferred backups.

To Order: Visit the West Coast Systems Web site at **www.wcsys.com**.

GetPass '98

GetPass '98 by Ashish Computer Systems recovers and unsets Access database file passwords that you may have forgotten. It also helps you set new passwords without having MS-Access. GetPass '98 helps you by showing the Access Database password so that you can access the database without harming it.

To Order: Visit the Ashish Computer Systems Web site at **www.ashishsystems.com**.

PowerPoint-Related Software

The following software products are found in the 3rdparty\PowerPoint directory on the CD-ROM. They are also accessible via the CD-ROM interface.

Office In Color Templates

The Office In Color Sampler from KMT Software, Inc. is a collection of spectacular color templates for Word, Excel, and PowerPoint. These templates are great productivity tools and help you make a great first impression.

To Order: Call 1-800-KMT-CALC, or send email to **sales@kmt.com**. See the ad in the back of the book for additional details.

Microsoft PowerPoint 97 Batch Converter

PowerPoint 97 automatically converts a presentation from a previous version when you open the file and then save it in PowerPoint 97 format. However, converting presentations one at a time can be tedious if your organization is switching to PowerPoint 97 and you have a large number of presentations in PowerPoint 3.0, 4.0, or 95 format. The PowerPoint 97 batch converter can convert a large number of presentations at once to PowerPoint 97 format.

To Order: Free from Microsoft. Visit the Microsoft Web site at **www.microsoft.com**.

Microsoft PowerPoint 97 Viewer

The Microsoft PowerPoint 97 Viewer allows people who use Microsoft PowerPoint to share their presentations with users who do not have PowerPoint. This product also allows users who want to post full fidelity PowerPoint presentations on the Internet to expand their online audience to people who might not have PowerPoint. The PowerPoint Viewer allows users who do not have Microsoft PowerPoint for Windows to view and print PowerPoint presentations, but it does not allow them to edit PowerPoint presentations.

To Order: Free from Microsoft. Visit the Microsoft Web site at **www.microsoft.com**.

Microsoft PowerPoint Animation Player and Publisher

With Microsoft PowerPoint Animation Player and Publisher, you can create live, interactive animations for HTML pages that play seamlessly in today's standard Web browser environments. Using compressed PPZ files, users can decrease download and rendering time. You can create branches to other Web pages through interactive settings defined for objects or your PowerPoint slides and add continuous sound. You can link RealAudio files to play or narrate continuously throughout the PowerPoint presentation. Sound is streamed in, so download speed is fast. All the sounds, animation, and fills used in the PowerPoint 95 presentation will be displayed and played when using the PowerPoint animation player.

To Order: Free from Microsoft. Visit the Microsoft Web site at **www.microsoft.com**.

Internet Software

The following software products are found in the 3rdparty\Internet directory on the CD-ROM. They are also accessible via the CD-ROM interface. Mac versions of each of these products are also available on the CD-ROM. To access them, insert the CD-ROM into a Mac disk drive and go to the Macsoftware directory.

EarthLink TotalAccess

The EarthLink Network TotalAccess™, our Internet software and registration package, has been hailed by the press and our customers alike for its ease of use. And for good reason! Preconfigured with all the software you need to get on the Internet with one call, it also points to EarthLink's award-winning Web site that leads new customers to hundreds of important online resources and all the information they need to make the most of their EarthLink Network Internet account.

To Order: Visit the EarthLink Web site at **www.earthlink.com/ta/**.

Microsoft Internet Explorer

Microsoft's Internet Explorer 4.0 is an open, integrated suite of Internet software that includes the industry's premier Internet client and basic collaboration solution for end users, IT managers, and developers. Internet Explorer 4.0 expands on the innovation introduced in version 3.0 to achieve Microsoft's vision: complete integration of the Internet and the PC. The end result is a dramatically easier and more personalized way for people to get the most out of the Internet.

To Order: Visit the Microsoft Web site at **www.microsoft.com**.

NetObjects Fusion

The latest version of NetObjects Fusion by NetObjects, Inc. delivers an open Web-site–building environment that provides enhanced flexibility and layout control along with robust site management and cross-browser support. Choose from graphical page layout for pixel-perfect positioning of elements, text editor mode when ultralean HTML is a top priority, or work with an external HTML editor. Allaire HomeSite 3.0 is included free to create part or all of a page. Take advantage of Dynamic Actions, the visual, message-based environment for creating DHTML-based animation and interactivity. This trial version of NetObjects Fusion contains all the features and functionality of the full version, except that you cannot stage or publish the sites you create with it.

To Order: Visit the NetObjects Web site at **www.netobjects.com**.

Netscape Communicator

Netscape Communicator 4.05 is the latest maintenance release of the Internet software suite from Netscape. In addition to the Netscape Navigator browser, Communicator includes a complete set of tools for effective everyday communication. The set includes Messenger and Collabra, which provide email and Usenet capabilities; Netcaster, Netscape's push technology client; and Composer, which offers HTML design and editing functions. Communicator also includes AOL Instant Messenger, which lets you exchange messages over the Internet in real time. Version 4.05 lets users import and export text in Composer, and users can now print without saving in Composer. Netscape has improved stability in the Message Center and has added security enhancements to support the different encryption levels available to users.

To Order: Visit the Netscape Web site at **www.netscape.com**.

General Software

The following software products are found in the 3rdparty\General directory on the CD-ROM. They are also accessible via the CD-ROM interface.

Adobe Acrobat Reader

The free Adobe® Acrobat® Reader allows you to view, navigate, and print PDF files across all major computing platforms. Acrobat Reader is the free viewing companion to Adobe Acrobat 3.0 and to Acrobat Capture® software. (A Macintosh version is also available on CD.)

To Order: Free from Adobe Systems, Inc. Visit the Adobe Web site at **www.adobe.com**.

Anyware Anti-Virus

Anyware Anti-Virus by Anyware Software protects your computer from known viruses and detects the presence of new viruses. Anyware Anti-Virus checks the integrity of all files delivered to your computer via online services or local area networks. It works continuously in the background to protect you from virus attacks. This update includes recognition of the newest viruses.

To Order: Visit the Anyware Web site at **www.helpvirus.com**.

Easy Translator

Easy Translator by Transparent Language is an award-winning translation tool that instantly translates documents, email, Web pages, and more by using the applications you already have on your desktop. Now you can get quick, easy, automatic translations in Spanish, French, German, English, Italian, and Portuguese with a simple click of your mouse.

To Order: Call 800-332-8851.

Multi-Remote Registry Change

Multi-Remote Registry Change by Eytcheson Software is the fastest and easiest way to change the registry on multiple remote computers running Windows NT. It was designed for network administrators working with groups of systems requiring the same change(s).

To Order: Visit the Eytcheson Software Web site at **www54.pair.com/eytch/credit.htm**.

Office Toys 98

Office Toys 98 is an add-in suite for Microsoft Word 97 from Merlot International. Its features include sophisticated file and project management, enhanced formatting, proofing, printing, and viewing tools. The suite introduces novelty concepts such as AutoPilot, Favorite Views, Favorite Fonts, Favorite Print Jobs, and Favorite Symbols. It also adds AutoFractions, AutoCalculate, AutoAccents, and AutoQuotes to Microsoft's IntelliSense™. Office Toys 98 includes SpeedBar and SwitchBar to reduce screen clutter. The trial version limited to 100 documents.

To Order: Follow the links to the secure ordering service on **www.officetoys.com/**.

PassKeeper

PassKeeper by Brad Greenlee is a Windows utility that allows the user to keep a list of accounts with usernames, passwords, and notes. This list is stored encrypted.

To Order: The software is free for non-commercial use. For commercial use, please contact Brad Greenlee at **greenlee@best.com**.

Random Password Generator

Random Password Generator by Tim Hirtle now creates up to one million unique passwords with as many as 25 characters in a single execution. You may select the password criteria using numbers, upper- and lowercase letters, and special characters. Up to 94 different characters are available for selection. Many other features come with this program to help you create uncrackable passwords.

To Order: Visit the Hirtle Software Web site at **ourworld.compuserve.com/homepages/hirtle/**.

Z.E.N.works Starter Pack

The directory-enabled power of Z.E.N.works by Novell improves productivity for users of networked Windows PCs, enhancing reliability, improving Help Desk support, and making it faster and easier to access the full range of applications and resources on the network. In addition, Z.E.N.works empowers network managers and other IT professionals with a range of new software management and distribution and desktop management and maintenance capabilities that simplify and reduce the total cost of maintaining Windows PCs on the network.

To Order: Full Z.E.N.works product can be ordered from Novell distributors and resellers.

ConsulNet Support Log & PC Administrator

ConsulNet Support Log is a comprehensive help desk software tool used to help track and resolve support calls and user inquiries. There has never been an easier way to improve end-user support and reduce support call response times. Improve your ability to track and manage your resources. Justify increased hardware and software expenditures as well as staffing levels. Improve user support and customer service. Running a help desk has never been so easy.

PC Administrator is a comprehensive asset management software tool that manages computer equipment inventory and purchases. It tracks important system information (What hardware and software, down to the component level, do we have? Who has it? Where is it? Is it under a service contract? Is it connected to a network?) and purchasing information (What equipment has been bought? Who was it bought from? How much was paid? Has it been delivered and installed? When was it bought?). Highly customizable, PC Administrator can also be used to track mainframe hardware, software, copiers, and audio/visual equipment.

ConsulNet eReply

Is your Inbox constantly full?

Are you spending too much time generating and responding to email?

Is your corporate web site receiving too much mail to handle?

Is your customer service department repeatedly responding to the same questions from your consumers?

Are you spending a lot of time generating cost quotes and other documents that only change slightly from one customer to the next?

eReply can help in three easy steps!

1. Store commonly used "phrases", addresses, product information, and so on (collectively, these will be referred to as "items").
2. Assemble the above items together with just a few mouse clicks.
3. Create formatted custom messages quickly and easily.

Your customers get the information they need quickly. Messages are complete and accurate. Your staff completes the communication in a fraction of the time. Consistent, quality messages are sent to your clients.

To Order: Contact ConsulNet Computing by calling 416-227-0363, or by visiting their Web site at **www.consulnet.com**. ●

APPENDIX B

Office 97 File List and Reference

In this appendix

This appendix lists all the files that install with the *original* Office 97 Professional Edition release (for Microsoft Windows 95, 98, and NT), along with the following:

- File size information that you can use to determine whether you have the original file, a damaged file, or a more recent file (in other words, a component of Service Release 1 or 2)
- Information about which component of Office each file belongs to; you can use this information to reinstall or add components as part of a maintenance installation
- Where each file installs in a conventional (non-customized) installation; you can use this information to troubleshoot damaged or missing files
- Where to find each file on the Office 97 CD-ROM
- Whether each file is installed as part of a typical installation

Office 97 File List

Component	File Name	File Size	Where It Installs	Where It Is Located on the CD-ROM	Typical? *
Microsoft Access					
Advanced Wizard	Books.gif	11,272	\Program Files\Microsoft Office\Office\Bitmaps\Dbwiz	\office\bitmaps\dbwiz	Y
Advanced Wizard	Contacts.gif	12,085	\Program Files\Microsoft Office\Office\Bitmaps\Dbwiz	\office\bitmaps\dbwiz	Y
Advanced Wizard	Dbmusic.gif	13,648	\Program Files\Microsoft Office\Office\Bitmaps\Dbwiz	\office\bitmaps\dbwiz	Y
Advanced Wizard	Eatdrink.gif	12,979	\Program Files\Microsoft Office\Office\Bitmaps\Dbwiz	\office\bitmaps\dbwiz	Y
Advanced Wizard	Houshold.gif	12,061	\Program Files\Microsoft Office\Office\Bitmaps\Dbwiz	\office\bitmaps\dbwiz	Y
Advanced Wizard	Invntory.gif	11,575	\Program Files\Microsoft Office\Office\Bitmaps\Dbwiz	\office\bitmaps\dbwiz	Y
Advanced Wizard	Members.gif	12,474	\Program Files\Microsoft Office\Office\Bitmaps\Dbwiz	\office\bitmaps\dbwiz	Y
Advanced Wizard	Monytrak.gif	12,249	\Program Files\Microsoft Office\Office\Bitmaps\Dbwiz	\office\bitmaps\dbwiz	Y
Advanced Wizard	Phonordr.gif	12,650	\Program Files\Microsoft Office\Office\Bitmaps\Dbwiz	\office\bitmaps\dbwiz	Y
Advanced Wizard	Photos.gif	12,033	\Program Files\Microsoft Office\Office\Bitmaps\Dbwiz	\office\bitmaps\dbwiz	Y
Advanced Wizard	Resource.gif	11,703	\Program Files\Microsoft Office\Office\Bitmaps\Dbwiz	\office\bitmaps\dbwiz	Y
Advanced Wizard	School.gif	12,138	\Program Files\Microsoft Office\Office\Bitmaps\Dbwiz	\office\bitmaps\dbwiz	Y
Advanced Wizard	Videos.gif	13,320	\Program Files\Microsoft Office\Office\Bitmaps\Dbwiz	\office\bitmaps\dbwiz	Y
Advanced Wizard	Workout.gif	11,846	\Program Files\Microsoft Office\Office\Bitmaps\Dbwiz	\office\bitmaps\dbwiz	Y
Advanced Wizard	Clouds.wmf	42,422	\Program Files\Microsoft Office\Office\Bitmaps\Styles	\office\bitmaps\styles	Y
Advanced Wizard	globe.wmf	27,606	\Program Files\Microsoft Office\Office\Bitmaps\Styles	\office\bitmaps\styles	Y
Advanced Wizard	Sea_dusk.wmf	25,718	\Program Files\Microsoft Office\Office\Bitmaps\Styles	\office\bitmaps\styles	Y
Advanced Wizard	Cnfdntl.bmp	9,446	\Program Files\Microsoft Office\Office\Bitmaps\Styles	\office\bitmaps\styles	Y
Advanced Wizard	Pattern.bmp	9,434	\Program Files\Microsoft Office\Office\Bitmaps\Styles	\office\bitmaps\styles	Y
Advanced Wizard	Stone.bmp	11,822	\Program Files\Microsoft Office\Office\Bitmaps\Styles	\office\bitmaps\styles	Y
Advanced Wizard	Flax.bmp	9,094	\Program Files\Microsoft Office\Office\Bitmaps\Styles	\office\bitmaps\styles	Y
Advanced Wizard	Wzmain 80.mde	3,938,304	\Program Files\Microsoft Office\Office	\office	Y
Advanced Wizard	accwiz.dll	123,392	\Windows\System	\os\system	Y
Advanced Wizard	Wiz.srg	15,794	\Program Files\Microsoft Office\Office	\office	Y
Advanced Wizard	Wzdat80.mdt	1,476,608	\Program Files\Microsoft Office\Office	\office	Y
Advanced Wizard	gifimp32.flt	130,560	\Program Files\Common Files\Microsoft Shared\Grphflt	\os\msapps\grphflt	Y
Advanced Wizard	Ms.gif	1,069	\Program Files\Common Files\Microsoft Shared\Grphflt	\os\msapps\grphflt	Y

Component	File Name	File Size	Where It Installs	Where It Is Located on the CD-ROM	Typical? *
Microsoft Access					
Advanced Wizard	png32.flt	222,720	\Program Files\Common Files\Microsoft Shared\Grphflt	\os\msapps\grphflt	Y
Advanced Wizard	ms.png	1,682	\Program Files\Common Files\Microsoft Shared\Grphflt	\os\msapps\grphflt	Y
Advanced Wizard	Graph8.exe	1,597,200	\Program Files\Microsoft Office\Office	\office	Y
Advanced Wizard	graph8.olb	111,104	\Program Files\Microsoft Office\Office	\office	Y
Advanced Wizard	gr8409.dll	5,120	\Program Files\Microsoft Office\Office	\office	Y
Advanced Wizard	Grintl32.dll	161,792	\Program Files\Microsoft Office\Office	\office	Y
Advanced Wizard	Graph8.srg	5,297	\Program Files\Microsoft Office\Office	\office	Y
Advanced Wizard	gr8galry.gra	186,880	\Program Files\Microsoft Office\Office	\office	Y
Advanced Wizard	vbagrp8.hlp	17,952	\Program Files\Microsoft Office\Office	\office	Y
Advanced Wizard	vbagrp8.cnt	198	\Program Files\Microsoft Office\Office	\office	Y
Advanced Wizard	graph8.hlp	520,680	\Program Files\Microsoft Office\Office	\office	Y
Advanced Wizard	graph8.aw	296,578	\Program Files\Microsoft Office\Office	\office	Y
Advanced Wizard	graph8.cnt	16,761	\Program Files\Microsoft Office\Office	\office	Y
Advanced Wizard	Wztool80.mde	2,639,872	\Program Files\Microsoft Office\Office	\office	
Advanced Wizard	Wzcnf80.mda	186,368	\Program Files\Microsoft Office\Office	\office	
Briefcase Replic.	msrclr35.dll	43,280	\Program Files\Microsoft Office\Office	\office	
Briefcase Replic.	msrecr35.dll	23,824	\Program Files\Microsoft Office\Office	\office	
Briefcase Replic.	rplbrf35.hlp	188,393	\Program Files\Microsoft Office\Office	\office	Y
Briefcase Replic.	rplbrf35.cnt	2,215	\Program Files\Microsoft Office\Office	\office	Y
Calendar Control	msstkprp.dll	47,104	\Windows\System	\os\system	
Calendar Control	mscal.ocx	89,600	\Windows\System	\os\system	
Calendar Control	mscal.dep	390	\Windows\System	\os\system	
Calendar Control Help	mscal.hlp	68,359	\Windows\System	\os\system	
Calendar Control Help	mscal.cnt	3,819	\Windows\System	\os\system	
Product Help	acmain80.hlp	2,273,202	\Program Files\Microsoft Office\Office	\office	Y
Product Help	acmain80.cnt	93,360	\Program Files\Microsoft Office\Office	\office	Y
Product Help	acmain80.aw	430,193	\Program Files\Microsoft Office\Office	\office	Y
Product Help	accore80.aw	271,089	\Program Files\Microsoft Office\Office	\office	Y

Component	File Name	File Size	Where It Installs	Where It Is Located on the CD-ROM	Typical? *
Microsoft Access					
Product Help	rplbrf35.hlp	188,393	\Program Files\Microsoft Office\Office	\office	Y
Product Help	rplbrf35.cnt	2,215	\Program Files\Microsoft Office\Office	\office	Y
Program File	accfil80.ode	6,803	\Program Files\Microsoft Office\Office	\office	Y
Program File	msaccess.exe	2,998,544	\Program Files\Microsoft Office\Office	\office	Y
Program File	msacc8.olb	311,296	\Program Files\Microsoft Office\Office	\office	Y
Program File	comcat.dll	22,288	\Windows\System	\os\system	Y
Program File	msaccess.srg	28,561	\Program Files\Microsoft Office\Office	\office	Y
Program File	wrkgadm.exe	47,104	\Windows\System	\os\system	Y
Program File	msacnv30.dll	236,800	\Program Files\Microsoft Office\Office	\office	Y
Program File	msacnv30.exe	102,400	\Program Files\Microsoft Office\Office	\office	Y
Program File	msaexp30.dll	168,448	\Program Files\Microsoft Office\Office	\office	Y
Program File	utility.mda	319,488	\Program Files\Microsoft Office\Office	\office	Y
Program File	Msain800.dll	500,736	\Program Files\Microsoft Office\Office	\office	Y
Program File	soa800.dll	207,360	\Program Files\Microsoft Office\Office	\office	Y
Program File	acread80.wri	64,768	\Program Files\Microsoft Office\Office	\office	Y
Program File	odbckey.inf	3,010	\Windows\System	\	Y
Program File	odbcstf.dll	22,016	\Windows\System	\	Y
Program File	odbc32.dll	246,544	\Windows\System	\os\system	Y
Program File	odbcad32.exe	10,240	\Windows\System	\os\system	Y
Program File	odbccp32.cpl	8,464	\Windows\System	\os\system	Y
Program File	odbccp32.dll	93,968	\Windows\System	\	Y
Program File	odbccr32.dll	179,200	\Windows\System	\os\system	Y
Program File	odbcinst.hlp	26,340	\Windows\System	\os\system	Y
Program File	odbcinst.cnt	244	\Windows\System	\os\system	Y
Program File	odbcint.dll	63,488	\Windows\System	\	Y
Program File	odbcji32.dll	37,888	\Windows\System	\os\system	Y
Program File	odbcjt32.dll	241,664	\Windows\System	\os\system	Y
Program File	odbctl32.dll	77,824	\Windows\System	\os\system	Y
Program File	odbctrac.dll	142,336	\Windows\System	\os\system	Y
Program File	dao350.dll	582,144	\Program Files\Common Files\Microsoft Shared\DAO	\os\msapps\Dao	Y
Program File	dao2535.tlb	73,184	\Program Files\Common Files\Microsoft Shared\DAO	\os\msapps\Dao	Y

Component	File Name	File Size	Where It Installs	Where It Is Located on the CD-ROM	Typical? *
Microsoft Access					
Program File	msrdo20.dll	368,400	\Windows\System	\os\system	Y
Program File	rdocurs.dll	93,456	\Windows\System	\os\system	Y
Program File	odbc32.dll	246,544	\Windows\System	\os\system	Y
Program File	dao35.hlp	649,868	\Program Files\Common Files\Microsoft Shared\DAO	\os\msapps\Dao	Y
Program File	dao35.cnt	6,117	\Program Files\Common Files\Microsoft Shared\DAO	\os\msapps\Dao	Y
Program File	dao35.aw	177,111	\Program Files\Common Files\Microsoft Shared\DAO	\os\msapps\Dao	Y
Program File	ven2232.olb	37,376	\Windows\System	\os\system	Y
Program File	ASSETS.MDZ	18,432	\Program Files\Microsoft Office\Templates\Databases	\Temp\\Database	Y
Program File	BOOKS.MDZ	13,824	\Program Files\Microsoft Office\Templates\Databases	\Temp\\Database	Y
Program File	CONTACTS.MDZ	18,432	\Program Files\Microsoft Office\Templates\Databases	\Temp\\Database	Y
Program File	DONATION.MDZ	18,432	\Program Files\Microsoft Office\Templates\Databases	\Temp\\Database	Y
Program File	EVTMGMT.MDZ	18,432	\Program Files\Microsoft Office\Templates\Databases	\Temp\\Database	Y
Program File	EXPENSES.MDZ	18,432	\Program Files\Microsoft Office\Templates\Databases	\Temp\\Database	Y
Program File	HINV.MDZ	13,824	\Program Files\Microsoft Office\Templates\Databases	\Temp\\Database	Y
Program File	INVENTRY.MDZ	18,432	\Program Files\Microsoft Office\Templates\Databases	\Temp\\Database	Y
Program File	LEDGER.MDZ	13,824	\Program Files\Microsoft Office\Templates\Databases	\Temp\\Database	Y
Program File	MEMBERS.MDZ	18,432	\Program Files\Microsoft Office\Templates\Databases	\Temp\\Database	Y
Program File	MUSIC.MDZ	13,824	\Program Files\Microsoft Office\Templates\Databases	\Temp\\Database	Y
Program File	ORDPROC.MDZ	18,432	\Program Files\Microsoft Office\Templates\Databases	\Temp\\Database	Y
Program File	PICLIB.MDZ	13,824	\Program Files\Microsoft Office\Templates\Databases	\Temp\\Database	Y
Program File	RECIPES.MDZ	13,824	\Program Files\Microsoft Office\Templates\Databases	\Temp\\Database	Y
Program File	RESOURCE.MDZ	18,432	\Program Files\Microsoft Office\Templates\Databases	\Temp\\Database	Y
Program File	SCHOOL.MDZ	13,824	\Program Files\Microsoft Office\Templates\Databases	\Temp\\Database	Y
Program File	SERVICE.MDZ	18,432	\Program Files\Microsoft Office\Templates\Databases	\Temp\\Database	Y
Program File	TIMEBILL.MDZ	18,432	\Program Files\Microsoft Office\Templates\Databases	\Temp\\Database	Y
Program File	VIDEOS.MDZ	13,824	\Program Files\Microsoft Office\Templates\Databases	\Temp\\Database	Y
Program File	WINELIST.MDZ	13,824	\Program Files\Microsoft Office\Templates\Databases	\Temp\\Database	Y
Program File	WORKOUT.MDZ	13,824	\Program Files\Microsoft Office\Templates\Databases	\Temp\\Database	Y
Program File	ADDBOOK.MDZ	13,824	\Program Files\Microsoft Office\Templates\Databases	\Temp\\Database	Y
Program File	mfcans32.dll	149,504	\Windows\System		Y
Program File	Ctl3d32.dll	27,136	\Windows\System		Y

Component	File Name	File Size	Where It Installs	Where It Is Located on the CD-ROM	Typical? *
Microsoft Access					
Program File	MSVCRT20. DLL	253,952	\Windows\System		Y
Program File	Wzlib80.mde	575,488	\Program Files\Microsoft Office\Office	\office	Y
Program File	msjet35.dll	1,038,848	\Windows\System	\os\system	Y
Program File	msjint35.dll	36,624	\Windows\System	\os\system	Y
Program File	msjter35.dll	24,336	\Windows\System	\os\system	Y
Program File	msrepl35.dll	402,704	\Windows\System	\os\system	Y
Program File	msrd2x35.dll	251,664	\Windows\System	\os\system	Y
Program File	vbajet32.dll	18,192	\Windows\System	\os\system	Y
Program File	100.htm	177	\Program Files\Microsoft Office\Templates\Access	\Templ\Access	Y
Program File	100.jpg	6,685	\Program Files\Microsoft Office\Templates\Access	\Templ\Access	Y
Program File	gray.htm	178	\Program Files\Microsoft Office\Templates\Access	\Templ\Access	Y
Program File	gray.jpg	5,548	\Program Files\Microsoft Office\Templates\Access	\Templ\Access	Y
Program File	grayst.htm	197	\Program Files\Microsoft Office\Templates\Access	\Templ\Access	Y
Program File	grayst.jpg	27,771	\Program Files\Microsoft Office\Templates\Access	\Templ\Access	Y
Program File	mc.htm	176	\Program Files\Microsoft Office\Templates\Access	\Templ\Access	Y
Program File	mc.jpg	7,516	\Program Files\Microsoft Office\Templates\Access	\Templ\Access	Y
Program File	mcst.jpg	16,884	\Program Files\Microsoft Office\Templates\Access	\Templ\Access	Y
Program File	mcst.htm	195	\Program Files\Microsoft Office\Templates\Access	\Templ\Access	Y
Program File	MSAccess.jpg	9,400	\Program Files\Microsoft Office\Templates\Access	\Templ\Access	Y
Program File	sky.jpg	2,778	\Program Files\Microsoft Office\Templates\Access	\Templ\Access	Y
Program File	sky.htm	177	\Program Files\Microsoft Office\Templates\Access	\Templ\Access	Y
Program File	stones.htm	197	\Program Files\Microsoft Office\Templates\Access	\Templ\Access	Y
Program File	stones.jpg	19,820	\Program Files\Microsoft Office\Templates\Access	\Templ\Access	Y
Program File	default.htm	174	\Program Files\Microsoft Office\Templates\Access	\Templ\Access	Y
Program File	tiles.htm	179	\Program Files\Microsoft Office\Templates\Access	\Templ\Access	Y
Program File	tiles.jpg	430	\Program Files\Microsoft Office\Templates\Access	\Templ\Access	Y
Program File	zigzag.htm	180	\Program Files\Microsoft Office\Templates\Access	\Templ\Access	Y
Program File	zigzag.jpg	516	\Program Files\Microsoft Office\Templates\Access	\Templ\Access	Y
Program File	mso97.acl	35,262	\Windows	\os	Y
Programming Help	veenlr3.hlp	1,052,485	\Program Files\Common Files\Microsoft Shared\VBA	\os\msapps\vba	
Programming Help	veena3.aw	209,406	\Program Files\Common Files\Microsoft Shared\VBA	\os\msapps\vba	

Component	File Name	File Size	Where It Installs	Where It Is Located on the CD-ROM	Typical? *
Microsoft Access					
Programming Help	veenlr3.cnt	21,576	\Program Files\Common Files\Microsoft Shared\VBA	\os\msapps\vba	
Programming Help	veencn3.hlp	119,327	\Program Files\Common Files\Microsoft Shared\VBA	\os\msapps\vba	
Programming Help	veencn3.cnt	3,581	\Program Files\Common Files\Microsoft Shared\VBA	\os\msapps\vba	
Programming Help	acvba80.aw	122,592	\Program Files\Microsoft Office\Office	\office	
Programming Help	acspc80.hlp	230,967	\Program Files\Microsoft Office\Office	\office	
Programming Help	acspc80.cnt	692	\Program Files\Microsoft Office\Office	\office	
Programming Help	dao35.hlp	649,868	\Program Files\Common Files\Microsoft Shared\DAO	\os\msapps\Dao	Y
Programming Help	dao35.cnt	6,117	\Program Files\Common Files\Microsoft Shared\DAO	\os\msapps\Dao	Y
Programming Help	dao35.aw	177,111	\Program Files\Common Files\Microsoft Shared\DAO	\os\msapps\Dao	Y
Programming Help	oftip8.hlp	594,164	\Program Files\Microsoft Office\Office	\office	Y
Programming Help	ofnew8.hlp	9,921	\Program Files\Microsoft Office\Office	\office	Y
Programming Help	ofnew8.cnt	782	\Program Files\Microsoft Office\Office	\office	Y
Programming Help	commtb32.hlp	6,885	\Windows\System	\office	Y
Programming Help	hlp95en.dll	31,744	\Windows\System	\office	Y
Programming Help	accore80.aw	271,089	\Program Files\Microsoft Office\Office	\office	Y
Programming Help	jetsql35.hlp	198,576	\Windows\System	\os\system	Y
Programming Help	jetsql35.cnt	2,018	\Windows\System	\os\system	Y
Programming Help	vbaoff8.hlp	320,282	\Program Files\Microsoft Office\Office	\office	
Programming Help	vbaoff8.aw	168,843	\Program Files\Microsoft Office\Office	\office	
Programming Help	vbaoff8.cnt	10,080	\Program Files\Microsoft Office\Office	\office	
Samp. DB: Dev Sols	nwind.mdb	1,546,240	\Program Files\Microsoft Office\Office\Samples	\office\samples	Y
Samp. DB: Dev Sols	nwind80.hlp	49,183	\Program Files\Microsoft Office\Office\Samples	\office\samples	Y
Samp. DB: Dev Sols	nwind80.cnt	1,433	\Program Files\Microsoft Office\Office\Samples	\office\samples	Y
Samp. DB: Dev Sols	cajbkgrn.gif	4,440	\Program Files\Microsoft Office\Office\Samples	\office\samples	Y
Samp. DB: Dev Sols	cajun.htm	4,996	\Program Files\Microsoft Office\Office\Samples	\office\samples	Y
Samp. DB: Dev Sols	cajlogo.gif	6,294	\Program Files\Microsoft Office\Office\Samples	\office\samples	Y
Samp. DB: Dev Sols	forbkgrn.gif	3,208	\Program Files\Microsoft Office\Office\Samples	\office\samples	Y
Samp. DB: Dev Sols	formaggi.htm	6,001	\Program Files\Microsoft Office\Office\Samples	\office\samples	Y
Samp. DB: Dev Sols	forlogo.gif	5,958	\Program Files\Microsoft Office\Office\Samples	\office\samples	Y
Samp. DB: Dev Sols	whatsnew.gif	1,670	\Program Files\Microsoft Office\Office\Samples	\office\samples	Y
Samp. DB: Dev Sols	nwindtem.htm	597	\Program Files\Microsoft Office\Office\Samples	\office\samples	Y
Samp. DB: Dev Sols	nwlogo.gif	2,430	\Program Files\Microsoft Office\Office\Samples	\office\samples	Y

Component	File Name	File Size	Where It Installs	Where It Is Located on the CD-ROM	Typical? *
Microsoft Access					
Samp. DB: Dev Sols	products.doc	12,800	\Program Files\Microsoft Office\Office\Samples	\office\samples	Y
Samp. DB: Dev Sols	msstkprp.dll	47,104	\Windows\System	\os\system	
Samp. DB: Dev Sols	mscal.ocx	89,600	\Windows\System	\os\system	
Samp. DB: Dev Sols	mscal.dep	390	\Windows\System	\os\system	
Samp. DB: Dev Sols	mscal.hlp	68,359	\Windows\System	\os\system	
Samp. DB: Dev Sols	mscal.cnt	3,819	\Windows\System	\os\system	
Samp. DB: Dev Sols	solution.mdb	1,280,000	\Program Files\Microsoft Office\Office\Samples	\office\samples	
Samp. DB: Dev Sols	soltn80.cnt	1,578	\Program Files\Microsoft Office\Office\Samples	\office\samples	
Samp. DB: Dev Sols	soltn80.hlp	247,579	\Program Files\Microsoft Office\Office\Samples	\office\samples	
Samp. DB: Nwind	nwind.mdb	1,546,240	\Program Files\Microsoft Office\Office\Samples	\office\samples	Y
Samp. DB: Nwind	nwind80.hlp	49,183	\Program Files\Microsoft Office\Office\Samples	\office\samples	Y
Samp. DB: Nwind	nwind80.cnt	1,433	\Program Files\Microsoft Office\Office\Samples	\office\samples	Y
Samp. DB: Nwind	cajbkgrn.gif	4,440	\Program Files\Microsoft Office\Office\Samples	\office\samples	Y
Samp. DB: Nwind	cajun.htm	4,996	\Program Files\Microsoft Office\Office\Samples	\office\samples	Y
Samp. DB: Nwind	cajlogo.gif	6,294	\Program Files\Microsoft Office\Office\Samples	\office\samples	Y
Samp. DB: Nwind	forbkgrn.gif	3,208	\Program Files\Microsoft Office\Office\Samples	\office\samples	Y
Samp. DB: Nwind	formaggi.htm	6,001	\Program Files\Microsoft Office\Office\Samples	\office\samples	Y
Samp. DB: Nwind	forlogo.gif	5,958	\Program Files\Microsoft Office\Office\Samples	\office\samples	Y
Samp. DB: Nwind	whatsnew.gif	1,670	\Program Files\Microsoft Office\Office\Samples	\office\samples	Y
Samp. DB: Nwind	nwindtem.htm	597	\Program Files\Microsoft Office\Office\Samples	\office\samples	Y
Samp. DB: Nwind	nwlogo.gif	2,430	\Program Files\Microsoft Office\Office\Samples	\office\samples	Y
Samp. DB: Nwind	products.doc	12,800	\Program Files\Microsoft Office\Office\Samples	\office\samples	Y
Samp. DB: Orders	orders.mdb	903,168	\Program Files\Microsoft Office\Office\Samples	\office\samples	
Samp. DB: Orders	orders80.hlp	27,569	\Program Files\Microsoft Office\Office\Samples	\office\samples	
Samp. DB: Orders	orders80.cnt	465	\Program Files\Microsoft Office\Office\Samples	\office\samples	
Wizard	Books.gif	11,272	\Program Files\Microsoft Office\Office\Bitmaps\Dbwiz	\office\bitmaps\dbwiz	Y

Component	File Name	File Size	Where It Installs	Where It Is Located on the CD-ROM	Typical? *
Microsoft Access					
Wizard	Contacts.gif	12,085	\Program Files\Microsoft Office\Office\Bitmaps\Dbwiz	\office\bitmaps\dbwiz	Y
Wizard	Dbmusic.gif	13,648	\Program Files\Microsoft Office\Office\Bitmaps\Dbwiz	\office\bitmaps\dbwiz	Y
Wizard	Eatdrink.gif	12,979	\Program Files\Microsoft Office\Office\Bitmaps\Dbwiz	\office\bitmaps\dbwiz	Y
Wizard	Houshold.gif	12,061	\Program Files\Microsoft Office\Office\Bitmaps\Dbwiz	\office\bitmaps\dbwiz	Y
Wizard	Invntory.gif	11,575	\Program Files\Microsoft Office\Office\Bitmaps\Dbwiz	\office\bitmaps\dbwiz	Y
Wizard	Members.gif	12,474	\Program Files\Microsoft Office\Office\Bitmaps\Dbwiz	\office\bitmaps\dbwiz	Y
Wizard	Monytrak.gif	12,249	\Program Files\Microsoft Office\Office\Bitmaps\Dbwiz	\office\bitmaps\dbwiz	Y
Wizard	Phonordr.gif	12,650	\Program Files\Microsoft Office\Office\Bitmaps\Dbwiz	\office\bitmaps\dbwiz	Y
Wizard	Photos.gif	12,033	\Program Files\Microsoft Office\Office\Bitmaps\Dbwiz	\office\bitmaps\dbwiz	Y
Wizard	Resource.gif	11,703	\Program Files\Microsoft Office\Office\Bitmaps\Dbwiz	\office\bitmaps\dbwiz	Y
Wizard	School.gif	12,138	\Program Files\Microsoft Office\Office\Bitmaps\Dbwiz	\office\bitmaps\dbwiz	Y
Wizard	Videos.gif	13,320	\Program Files\Microsoft Office\Office\Bitmaps\Dbwiz	\office\bitmaps\dbwiz	Y
Wizard	Workout.gif	11,846	\Program Files\Microsoft Office\Office\Bitmaps\Dbwiz	\office\bitmaps\dbwiz	Y
Wizard	Clouds.wmf	42,422	\Program Files\Microsoft Office\Office\Bitmaps\Styles	\office\bitmaps\styles	Y
Wizard	globe.wmf	27,606	\Program Files\Microsoft Office\Office\Bitmaps\Styles	\office\bitmaps\styles	Y
Wizard	Sea_dusk.wmf	25,718	\Program Files\Microsoft Office\Office\Bitmaps\Styles	\office\bitmaps\styles	Y
Wizard	Cnfdntl.bmp	9,446	\Program Files\Microsoft Office\Office\Bitmaps\Styles	\office\bitmaps\styles	Y
Wizard	Pattern.bmp	9,434	\Program Files\Microsoft Office\Office\Bitmaps\Styles	\office\bitmaps\styles	Y
Wizard	Stone.bmp	11,822	\Program Files\Microsoft Office\Office\Bitmaps\Styles	\office\bitmaps\styles	Y
Wizard	Flax.bmp	9,094	\Program Files\Microsoft Office\Office\Bitmaps\Styles	\office\bitmaps\styles	Y
Wizard	Wzmain 80.mde	3,938,304	\Program Files\Microsoft Office\Office	\office	Y
Wizard	accwiz.dll	123,392	\Windows\System	\os\system	Y
Wizard	Wiz.srg	15,794	\Program Files\Microsoft Office\Office	\office	Y
Wizard	Wzdat80.mdt	1,476,608	\Program Files\Microsoft Office\Office	\office	Y
Wizard	gifimp32.flt	130,560	\Program Files\Common Files\Microsoft Shared\Grphflt	\os\msapps\grphflt	Y
Wizard	Ms.gif	1,069	\Program Files\Common Files\Microsoft Shared\Grphflt	\os\msapps\grphflt	Y
Wizard	png32.flt	222,720	\Program Files\Common Files\Microsoft Shared\Grphflt	\os\msapps\grphflt	Y
Wizard	ms.png	1,682	\Program Files\Common Files\Microsoft Shared\Grphflt	\os\msapps\grphflt	Y
Microsoft Binder					
Program File	vbabdr8.hlp	12,118	\Program Files\Microsoft Office\Office	\office	
Program File	vbabdr8.cnt	270	\Program Files\Microsoft Office\Office	\office	

Component	File Name	File Size	Where It Installs	Where It Is Located on the CD-ROM	Typical? *
Microsoft Binder					
Program File	msbdr8.olb	11,776	\Program Files\Microsoft Office\Office	\office	
Program File	binder.exe	260,096	\Program Files\Microsoft Office\Office	\office	
Program File	bdrec.dll	47,616	\Program Files\Microsoft Office\Office	\office	
Program File	binder.obd	6,144	\Windows\ShellNew	\office	
Program File	bdrintl.dll	110,592	\Program Files\Microsoft Office\Office	\office	
Program File	unbind.dll	26,112	\Program Files\Microsoft Office\Office	\office	
Help	binder8.hlp	103,209	\Program Files\Microsoft Office\Office	\office	
Help	binder8.aw	185,236	\Program Files\Microsoft Office\Office	\office	
Help	binder8.cnt	4,363	\Program Files\Microsoft Office\Office	\office	
Templs	Report.obt	158,720	\Program Files\Microsoft Office\Templates\Binders	\Templ\Binders	
Data Access Files					
DAO for VB	odbckey.inf	3,010	\Windows\System	\	Y
DAO for VB	odbcstf.dll	22,016	\Windows\System	\	Y
DAO for VB	odbc32.dll	246,544	\Windows\System	\os\system	Y
DAO for VB	odbcad32.exe	10,240	\Windows\System	\os\system	Y
DAO for VB	odbccp32.cpl	8,464	\Windows\System	\os\system	Y
DAO for VB	odbccp32.dll	93,968	\Windows\System	\	Y
DAO for VB	odbccr32.dll	179,200	\Windows\System	\os\system	Y
DAO for VB	odbcinst.hlp	26,340	\Windows\System	\os\system	Y
DAO for VB	odbcinst.cnt	244	\Windows\System	\os\system	Y
DAO for VB	odbcint.dll	63,488	\Windows\System	\	Y
DAO for VB	odbcji32.dll	37,888	\Windows\System	\os\system	Y
DAO for VB	odbcjt32.dll	241,664	\Windows\System	\os\system	Y
DAO for VB	odbctl32.dll	77,824	\Windows\System	\os\system	Y
DAO for VB	odbctrac.dll	142,336	\Windows\System	\os\system	Y
DAO for VB	dao350.dll	582,144	\Program Files\Common Files\Microsoft Shared\DAO	\os\msapps\Dao	Y
DAO for VB	dao2535.tlb	73,184	\Program Files\Common Files\Microsoft Shared\DAO	\os\msapps\Dao	Y
DAO for VB	msrdo20.dll	368,400	\Windows\System	\os\system	Y
DAO for VB	rdocurs.dll	93,456	\Windows\System	\os\system	Y
DAO for VB	odbc32.dll	246,544	\Windows\System	\os\system	Y
DAO for VB	dao35.hlp	649,868	\Program Files\Common Files\Microsoft Shared\DAO	\os\msapps\Dao	Y

Component	File Name	File Size	Where It Installs	Where It Is Located on the CD-ROM	Typical? *
Data Access Files					
DAO for VB	dao35.cnt	6,117	\Program Files\Common Files\Microsoft Shared\DAO	\os\msapps\Dao	Y
DAO for VB	dao35.aw	177,111	\Program Files\Common Files\Microsoft Shared\DAO	\os\msapps\Dao	Y
Db Driver Access	odbc32.dll	246,544	\Windows\System	\os\system	Y
Db Driver Access	odbcad32.exe	10,240	\Windows\System	\os\system	Y
Db Driver Access	odbccp32.cpl	8,464	\Windows\System	\os\system	Y
Db Driver Access	odbccp32.dll	93,968	\Windows\System	\	Y
Db Driver Access	odbccr32.dll	179,200	\Windows\System	\os\system	Y
Db Driver Access	odbcinst.hlp	26,340	\Windows\System	\os\system	Y
Db Driver Access	odbcinst.cnt	244	\Windows\System	\os\system	Y
Db Driver Access	odbcint.dll	63,488	\Windows\System	\	Y
Db Driver Access	odbc16gt.dll	26,224	\Windows\System	\os\system	Y
Db Driver Access	odbc32gt.dll	8,192	\Windows\System	\os\system	Y
Db Driver Access	ds16gt.dll	4,656	\Windows\System	\os\system	Y
Db Driver Access	ds32gt.dll	5,632	\Windows\System	\os\system	Y
Db Driver Access	Ctl3d32.dll	27,136	\Windows\System		Y
Db Driver dBASE/FoxPro	msxbse35.dll	290,816	\Windows\System	\os\system	Y
Db Driver Excel	msexcl35.dll	254,976	\Windows\System	\os\system	Y
Db Driver SQL Srvr	sqlsrv32.dll	244,224	\Windows\System	\os\system	
Db Driver SQL Srvr	dbnmpntw.dll	23,552	\Windows\System	\os\system	
Db Driver SQL Srvr	drvssrvr.hlp	87,427	\Windows\System	\os\system	
Db Driver SQL Srvr	mscpxl32.dll	14,848	\Windows\System	\os\system	
Db Driver SQL Srvr	12520437.cpx	2,151	\Windows\System	\os\system	
Db Driver SQL Srvr	12520850.cpx	2,233	\Windows\System	\os\system	
Db Driver Text/HTML	mstext35.dll	166,912	\Windows\System	\os\system	Y
MS Query 8.0	xlodbc32.dll	67,584	\Program Files\Microsoft Office\Office\Library\MSQuery	\office\library\msquery	
MS Query 8.0	xlodbc.xla	50,176	\Program Files\Microsoft Office\Office\Library\MSQuery	\office\library\msquery	

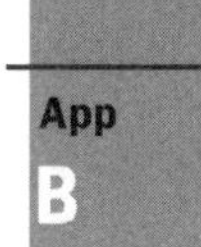

Component	File Name	File Size	Where It Installs	Where It Is Located on the CD-ROM	Typical? *
Data Access Files					
MS Query 8.0	msqry32.exe	760,592	\Program Files\Microsoft Office\Office	\office	
MS Query 8.0	qryint32.dll	93,456	\Program Files\Microsoft Office\Office	\office	
MS Query 8.0	xlquery.xla	71,680	\Program Files\Microsoft Office\Office\Library\MSQuery	\office\library\msquery	
MS Query 8.0	msqry32.hlp	311,595	\Program Files\Microsoft Office\Office	\office	
MS Query 8.0	msqry32.aw	85,868	\Program Files\Microsoft Office\Office	\office	
MS Query 8.0	msqry32.cnt	4,539	\Program Files\Microsoft Office\Office	\office	
MS Query 8.0	customer.dbf	918	\Program Files\Microsoft Office\Office	\office	
MS Query 8.0	employee.dbf	529	\Program Files\Microsoft Office\Office	\office	
MS Query 8.0	orders.dbf	989	\Program Files\Microsoft Office\Office	\office	
Microsoft Excel					
Add-In: Access Links	acclink.xla	228,352	\Program Files\Microsoft Office\Office\Library	\office\library	
Add-In: Analysis ToolPak	analys32.xll	307,712	\Program Files\Microsoft Office\Office\Library\Analysis	\office\library\analysis	Y
Add-In: Analysis ToolPak	atpvbaen.xla	446,976	\Program Files\Microsoft Office\Office\Library\Analysis	\office\library\analysis	Y
Add-In: Analysis ToolPak	funcres.xla	74,240	\Program Files\Microsoft Office\Office\Library\Analysis	\office\library\analysis	Y
Add-In: Analysis ToolPak	procdb.xla	99,840	\Program Files\Microsoft Office\Office\Library\Analysis	\office\library\analysis	Y
Add-In: AutoSave	autosave.xla	68,096	\Program Files\Microsoft Office\Office\Library	\office\library	Y
Add-In: Condit. Sum Wizard	sumif.xla	335,872	\Program Files\Microsoft Office\Office\Library	\office\library	Y
Add-In: File Conv. Wizard	fileconv.xla	322,560	\Program Files\Microsoft Office\Office\Library	\office\library	
Add-In: File Conv. Wizard	lookup.xla	356,864	\Program Files\Microsoft Office\Office\Library	\office\library	Y
Add-In: Report Manager	reports.xla	152,576	\Program Files\Microsoft Office\Office\Library	\office\library	
Add-In: Solver	solver.xla	617,984	\Program Files\Microsoft Office\Office\Library\Solver	\office\library\solver	
Add-In: Solver	solver32.dll	112,640	\Program Files\Microsoft Office\Office\Library\Solver	\office\library\solver	
Add-In: Solver	solvsamp.xls	131,072	\Program Files\Microsoft Office\Office\Examples\Solver	\office\examples\solver	
Add-In: Solver	wztemplt.xla	705,024	\Program Files\Microsoft Office\Office\Library	\office\library	
Converter (Quattro Pro 1-5)	xlqpw.dll	79,872	\Program Files\Microsoft Office\Office	\office	

Component	File Name	File Size	Where It Installs	Where It Is Located on the CD-ROM	Typical? *
Microsoft Excel					
Help/Samp. (Program)	xlmacr8.hlp	19,637	\Program Files\Microsoft Office\Office	\office	Y
Help/Samp. (Program)	xlmain8.hlp	2,660,704	\Program Files\Microsoft Office\Office	\office	Y
Help/Samp. (Program)	xlmain8.aw	1,026,563	\Program Files\Microsoft Office\Office	\office	Y
Help/Samp. (Program)	xlmain8.cnt	114,706	\Program Files\Microsoft Office\Office	\office	Y
Help/Samp. (Program)	xltip8.hlp	402,319	\Program Files\Microsoft Office\Office	\office	Y
Help/Samp. (Program)	workfunc.aw	315,161	\Program Files\Microsoft Office\Office	\office	Y
Help/Samp. (Program)	xlnew8.hlp	79,312	\Program Files\Microsoft Office\Office	\office	Y
Help/Samp. (Program)	xlnew8.cnt	1,497	\Program Files\Microsoft Office\Office	\office	Y
Help/Samp. (Samp.)	samples.xls	145,408	\Program Files\Microsoft Office\Office\Examples	\office\examples	Y
Help/Samp. (VBA)	veenlr3.hlp	1,052,485	\Program Files\Common Files\Microsoft Shared\VBA	\os\msapps\vba	
Help/Samp. (VBA)	veena3.aw	209,406	\Program Files\Common Files\Microsoft Shared\VBA	\os\msapps\vba	
Help/Samp. (VBA)	veenlr3.cnt	21,576	\Program Files\Common Files\Microsoft Shared\VBA	\os\msapps\vba	
Help/Samp. (VBA)	veenui3.hlp	366,147	\Program Files\Common Files\Microsoft Shared\VBA	\os\msapps\vba	
Help/Samp. (VBA)	veen3.aw	210,191	\Program Files\Common Files\Microsoft Shared\VBA	\os\msapps\vba	
Help/Samp. (VBA)	veenui3.cnt	14,472	\Program Files\Common Files\Microsoft Shared\VBA	\os\msapps\vba	
Help/Samp. (VBA)	veenob3.hlp	149,149	\Program Files\Common Files\Microsoft Shared\VBA	\os\msapps\vba	
Help/Samp. (VBA)	veenob3.cnt	5,690	\Program Files\Common Files\Microsoft Shared\VBA	\os\msapps\vba	
Help/Samp. (VBA)	veenmc3.hlp	24,734	\Program Files\Common Files\Microsoft Shared\VBA	\os\msapps\vba	
Help/Samp. (VBA)	veencn3.hlp	119,327	\Program Files\Common Files\Microsoft Shared\VBA	\os\msapps\vba	
Help/Samp. (VBA)	veencn3.cnt	3,581	\Program Files\Common Files\Microsoft Shared\VBA	\os\msapps\vba	
Help/Samp. (VBA)	veenhw3.hlp	55,589	\Program Files\Common Files\Microsoft Shared\VBA	\os\msapps\vba	
Help/Samp. (VBA)	veenhw3.cnt	2,390	\Program Files\Common Files\Microsoft Shared\VBA	\os\msapps\vba	
Help/Samp. (VBA)	veendf3.hlp	76,366	\Program Files\Common Files\Microsoft Shared\VBA	\os\msapps\vba	Y
Help/Samp. (VBA)	vbaxl8.aw	629,575	\Program Files\Microsoft Office\Office	\office	
Help/Samp. (VBA)	vbaxl8.cnt	82,494	\Program Files\Microsoft Office\Office	\office	
Help/Samp. (VBA)	vbaxl8.hlp	1,984,703	\Program Files\Microsoft Office\Office	\office	

App B

Component	File Name	File Size	Where It Installs	Where It Is Located on the CD-ROM	Typical? *
Microsoft Excel					
Help/Samp. (VBA)	fm20enu.dll	25,872	\Windows\System	\os\system	
Help/Samp. (VBA)	fm20.dll	1,123,600	\Windows\System	\os\system	
Help/Samp. (VBA)	asycfilt.dll	119,056	\Windows\System	\os\system	
Help/Samp. (VBA)	vbaoff8.hlp	320,282	\Program Files\Microsoft Office\Office	\office	
Help/Samp. (VBA)	vbaoff8.aw	168,843	\Program Files\Microsoft Office\Office	\office	
Help/Samp. (VBA)	vbaoff8.cnt	10,080	\Program Files\Microsoft Office\Office	\office	
MS Map File	msmap.exe	945,664	\Program Files\Common Files\Microsoft Shared\Datamap	\os\msapps\datamap	Y
MS Map File	msmap.pen	1,522	\Program Files\Common Files\Microsoft Shared\Datamap	\os\msapps\datamap	Y
MS Map File	datainst.exe	292,864	\Program Files\Common Files\Microsoft Shared\Datamap	\os\msapps\datamap	Y
MS Map File	emptymap.wmf	5,302	\Program Files\Common Files\Microsoft Shared\Datamap	\os\msapps\datamap	Y
MS Map File	diintl.dll	43,008	\Program Files\Common Files\Microsoft Shared\Datamap	\os\msapps\datamap	Y
MS Map File	dmtmdl.dll	580,096	\Program Files\Common Files\Microsoft Shared\Datamap	\os\msapps\datamap	Y
MS Map File	dmintl.dll	115,712	\Program Files\Common Files\Microsoft Shared\Datamap	\os\msapps\datamap	Y
MS Map File	dmtmintl.dll	38,912	\Program Files\Common Files\Microsoft Shared\Datamap	\os\msapps\datamap	Y
MS Map File	msmap.tlb	12,751	\Program Files\Common Files\Microsoft Shared\Datamap	\os\msapps\datamap	Y
MS Map File	mapxpres.url	51	\Program Files\Common Files\Microsoft Shared\Datamap	\os\msapps\datamap	Y
MS Map File	miwww.url	58	\Program Files\Common Files\Microsoft Shared\Datamap	\os\msapps\datamap	Y
MS Map File	msmap.srg	3,085	\Program Files\Common Files\Microsoft Shared\Datamap	\os\msapps\datamap	Y
MS Map File	ausairpt.dat	2,208	\Program Files\Common Files\Microsoft Shared\Datamap\Data	\os\msapps\datamap\data	Y
MS Map File	ausairpt.id	168	\Program Files\Common Files\Microsoft Shared\Datamap\Data	\os\msapps\datamap\data	Y
MS Map File	ausairpt.map	2,560	\Program Files\Common Files\Microsoft Shared\Datamap\Data	\os\msapps\datamap\data	Y
MS Map File	ausairpt.tab	178	\Program Files\Common Files\Microsoft Shared\Datamap\Data	\os\msapps\datamap\data	Y
MS Map File	auscitya.dat	298	\Program Files\Common Files\Microsoft Shared\Datamap\Data	\os\msapps\datamap\data	Y
MS Map File	auscitya.id	44	\Program Files\Common Files\Microsoft Shared\Datamap\Data	\os\msapps\datamap\data	Y
MS Map File	auscitya.map	1,536	\Program Files\Common Files\Microsoft Shared\Datamap\Data	\os\msapps\datamap\data	Y
MS Map File	auscitya.tab	179	\Program Files\Common Files\Microsoft Shared\Datamap\Data	\os\msapps\datamap\data	Y
MS Map File	auscityb.dat	2,166	\Program Files\Common Files\Microsoft Shared\Datamap\Data	\os\msapps\datamap\data	Y
MS Map File	auscityb.id	400	\Program Files\Common Files\Microsoft Shared\Datamap\Data	\os\msapps\datamap\data	Y
MS Map File	auscityb.map	3,072	\Program Files\Common Files\Microsoft Shared\Datamap\Data	\os\msapps\datamap\data	Y
MS Map File	auscityb.tab	173	\Program Files\Common Files\Microsoft Shared\Datamap\Data	\os\msapps\datamap\data	Y
MS Map File	aushiway.dat	1,284	\Program Files\Common Files\Microsoft Shared\Datamap\Data	\os\msapps\datamap\data	Y

Component	File Name	File Size	Where It Installs	Where It Is Located on the CD-ROM	Typical? *
Microsoft Excel					
MS Map File	aushiway.id	232	\Program Files\Common Files\Microsoft Shared\Datamap\Data	\os\msapps\datamap\data	Y
MS Map File	aushiway.map	52,736	\Program Files\Common Files\Microsoft Shared\Datamap\Data	\os\msapps\datamap\data	Y
MS Map File	aushiway.tab	178	\Program Files\Common Files\Microsoft Shared\Datamap\Data	\os\msapps\datamap\data	Y
MS Map File	ausstate.dat	315	\Program Files\Common Files\Microsoft Shared\Datamap\Data	\os\msapps\datamap\data	Y
MS Map File	ausstate.id	32	\Program Files\Common Files\Microsoft Shared\Datamap\Data	\os\msapps\datamap\data	Y
MS Map File	ausstate.ind	1,024	\Program Files\Common Files\Microsoft Shared\Datamap\Data	\os\msapps\datamap\data	Y
MS Map File	austrlia.gst	575	\Program Files\Common Files\Microsoft Shared\Datamap\Data	\os\msapps\datamap\data	Y
MS Map File	ausstate.map	86,016	\Program Files\Common Files\Microsoft Shared\Datamap\Data	\os\msapps\datamap\data	Y
MS Map File	ausstate.tab	251	\Program Files\Common Files\Microsoft Shared\Datamap\Data	\os\msapps\datamap\data	Y
MS Map File	can_fsa.dat	5,827	\Program Files\Common Files\Microsoft Shared\Datamap\Data	\os\msapps\datamap\data	Y
MS Map File	can_fsa.id	5,760	\Program Files\Common Files\Microsoft Shared\Datamap\Data	\os\msapps\datamap\data	Y
MS Map File	can_fsa.ind	21,504	\Program Files\Common Files\Microsoft Shared\Datamap\Data	\os\msapps\datamap\data	Y
MS Map File	can_fsa.map	24,576	\Program Files\Common Files\Microsoft Shared\Datamap\Data	\os\msapps\datamap\data	Y
MS Map File	can_fsa.tab	269	\Program Files\Common Files\Microsoft Shared\Datamap\Data	\os\msapps\datamap\data	Y
MS Map File	can_prov.dat	379	\Program Files\Common Files\Microsoft Shared\Datamap\Data	\os\msapps\datamap\data	Y
MS Map File	can_prov.id	48	\Program Files\Common Files\Microsoft Shared\Datamap\Data	\os\msapps\datamap\data	Y
MS Map File	can_prov.ind	1,024	\Program Files\Common Files\Microsoft Shared\Datamap\Data	\os\msapps\datamap\data	Y
MS Map File	can_prov.map	27,648	\Program Files\Common Files\Microsoft Shared\Datamap\Data	\os\msapps\datamap\data	Y
MS Map File	can_prov.tab	251	\Program Files\Common Files\Microsoft Shared\Datamap\Data	\os\msapps\datamap\data	Y
MS Map File	canada.gst	712	\Program Files\Common Files\Microsoft Shared\Datamap\Data	\os\msapps\datamap\data	Y
MS Map File	canairpt.dat	2,639	\Program Files\Common Files\Microsoft Shared\Datamap\Data	\os\msapps\datamap\data	Y
MS Map File	canairpt.id	332	\Program Files\Common Files\Microsoft Shared\Datamap\Data	\os\msapps\datamap\data	Y
MS Map File	canairpt.map	3,072	\Program Files\Common Files\Microsoft Shared\Datamap\Data	\os\msapps\datamap\data	Y
MS Map File	canairpt.tab	175	\Program Files\Common Files\Microsoft Shared\Datamap\Data	\os\msapps\datamap\data	Y
MS Map File	canhiway.dat	934	\Program Files\Common Files\Microsoft Shared\Datamap\Data	\os\msapps\datamap\data	Y
MS Map File	canhiway.id	112	\Program Files\Common Files\Microsoft Shared\Datamap\Data	\os\msapps\datamap\data	Y
MS Map File	canhiway.map	31,232	\Program Files\Common Files\Microsoft Shared\Datamap\Data	\os\msapps\datamap\data	Y
MS Map File	canhiway.tab	175	\Program Files\Common Files\Microsoft Shared\Datamap\Data	\os\msapps\datamap\data	Y
MS Map File	canlakes.dat	275	\Program Files\Common Files\Microsoft Shared\Datamap\Data	\os\msapps\datamap\data	Y
MS Map File	canlakes.id	32	\Program Files\Common Files\Microsoft Shared\Datamap\Data	\os\msapps\datamap\data	Y
MS Map File	canlakes.map	4,608	\Program Files\Common Files\Microsoft Shared\Datamap\Data	\os\msapps\datamap\data	Y
MS Map File	canlakes.tab	169	\Program Files\Common Files\Microsoft Shared\Datamap\Data	\os\msapps\datamap\data	Y

Component	File Name	File Size	Where It Installs	Where It Is Located on the CD-ROM	Typical? *
Microsoft Excel					
MS Map File	cncity_a.dat	768	\Program Files\Common Files\Microsoft Shared\Datamap\Data	\os\msapps\datamap\data	Y
MS Map File	cncity_a.id	108	\Program Files\Common Files\Microsoft Shared\Datamap\Data	\os\msapps\datamap\data	Y
MS Map File	cncity_a.map	1,536	\Program Files\Common Files\Microsoft Shared\Datamap\Data	\os\msapps\datamap\data	Y
MS Map File	cncity_a.tab	176	\Program Files\Common Files\Microsoft Shared\Datamap\Data	\os\msapps\datamap\data	Y
MS Map File	cncity_b.dat	2,328	\Program Files\Common Files\Microsoft Shared\Datamap\Data	\os\msapps\datamap\data	Y
MS Map File	cncity_b.id	348	\Program Files\Common Files\Microsoft Shared\Datamap\Data	\os\msapps\datamap\data	Y
MS Map File	cncity_b.map	4,096	\Program Files\Common Files\Microsoft Shared\Datamap\Data	\os\msapps\datamap\data	Y
MS Map File	cncity_b.tab	170	\Program Files\Common Files\Microsoft Shared\Datamap\Data	\os\msapps\datamap\data	Y
MS Map File	eurairpt.dat	6,849	\Program Files\Common Files\Microsoft Shared\Datamap\Data	\os\msapps\datamap\data	Y
MS Map File	eurairpt.id	532	\Program Files\Common Files\Microsoft Shared\Datamap\Data	\os\msapps\datamap\data	Y
MS Map File	eurairpt.map	3,584	\Program Files\Common Files\Microsoft Shared\Datamap\Data	\os\msapps\datamap\data	Y
MS Map File	eurairpt.tab	175	\Program Files\Common Files\Microsoft Shared\Datamap\Data	\os\msapps\datamap\data	Y
MS Map File	eurcitya.dat	1,678	\Program Files\Common Files\Microsoft Shared\Datamap\Data	\os\msapps\datamap\data	Y
MS Map File	eurcitya.id	248	\Program Files\Common Files\Microsoft Shared\Datamap\Data	\os\msapps\datamap\data	Y
MS Map File	eurcitya.map	2,560	\Program Files\Common Files\Microsoft Shared\Datamap\Data	\os\msapps\datamap\data	Y
MS Map File	eurcitya.tab	176	\Program Files\Common Files\Microsoft Shared\Datamap\Data	\os\msapps\datamap\data	Y
MS Map File	eurcityb.dat	3,732	\Program Files\Common Files\Microsoft Shared\Datamap\Data	\os\msapps\datamap\data	Y
MS Map File	eurcityb.id	568	\Program Files\Common Files\Microsoft Shared\Datamap\Data	\os\msapps\datamap\data	Y
MS Map File	eurcityb.map	4,096	\Program Files\Common Files\Microsoft Shared\Datamap\Data	\os\msapps\datamap\data	Y
MS Map File	eurcityb.tab	170	\Program Files\Common Files\Microsoft Shared\Datamap\Data	\os\msapps\datamap\data	Y
MS Map File	eurhiway.dat	14,994	\Program Files\Common Files\Microsoft Shared\Datamap\Data	\os\msapps\datamap\data	Y
MS Map File	eurhiway.id	3,732	\Program Files\Common Files\Microsoft Shared\Datamap\Data	\os\msapps\datamap\data	Y
MS Map File	eurhiway.map	185,856	\Program Files\Common Files\Microsoft Shared\Datamap\Data	\os\msapps\datamap\data	Y
MS Map File	eurhiway.tab	86	\Program Files\Common Files\Microsoft Shared\Datamap\Data	\os\msapps\datamap\data	Y
MS Map File	europe.dat	1,837	\Program Files\Common Files\Microsoft Shared\Datamap\Data	\os\msapps\datamap\data	Y
MS Map File	europe.gst	566	\Program Files\Common Files\Microsoft Shared\Datamap\Data	\os\msapps\datamap\data	Y
MS Map File	europe.id	188	\Program Files\Common Files\Microsoft Shared\Datamap\Data	\os\msapps\datamap\data	Y
MS Map File	europe.ind	4,608	\Program Files\Common Files\Microsoft Shared\Datamap\Data	\os\msapps\datamap\data	Y
MS Map File	europe.map	243,200	\Program Files\Common Files\Microsoft Shared\Datamap\Data	\os\msapps\datamap\data	Y
MS Map File	europe.tab	356	\Program Files\Common Files\Microsoft Shared\Datamap\Data	\os\msapps\datamap\data	Y
MS Map File	geodict.dct	3,730	\Program Files\Common Files\Microsoft Shared\Datamap\Data	\os\msapps\datamap\data	Y

Component	File Name	File Size	Where It Installs	Where It Is Located on the CD-ROM	Typical? *
Microsoft Excel					
MS Map File	grid15.dat	333	\Program Files\Common Files\Microsoft Shared\Datamap\Data	\os\msapps\datamap\data	Y
MS Map File	grid15.id	152	\Program Files\Common Files\Microsoft Shared\Datamap\Data	\os\msapps\datamap\data	Y
MS Map File	grid15.map	19,968	\Program Files\Common Files\Microsoft Shared\Datamap\Data	\os\msapps\datamap\data	Y
MS Map File	grid15.tab	171	\Program Files\Common Files\Microsoft Shared\Datamap\Data	\os\msapps\datamap\data	Y
MS Map File	grtlakes.dat	353	\Program Files\Common Files\Microsoft Shared\Datamap\Data	\os\msapps\datamap\data	Y
MS Map File	grtlakes.id	44	\Program Files\Common Files\Microsoft Shared\Datamap\Data	\os\msapps\datamap\data	Y
MS Map File	grtlakes.map	6,656	\Program Files\Common Files\Microsoft Shared\Datamap\Data	\os\msapps\datamap\data	Y
MS Map File	grtlakes.tab	168	\Program Files\Common Files\Microsoft Shared\Datamap\Data	\os\msapps\datamap\data	Y
MS Map File	mapstats.xls	223,232	\Program Files\Common Files\Microsoft Shared\Datamap\Data	\os\msapps\datamap\data	Y
MS Map File	mexico.gst	562	\Program Files\Common Files\Microsoft Shared\Datamap\Data	\os\msapps\datamap\data	Y
MS Map File	mx_airpt.dat	1,188	\Program Files\Common Files\Microsoft Shared\Datamap\Data	\os\msapps\datamap\data	Y
MS Map File	mx_airpt.id	88	\Program Files\Common Files\Microsoft Shared\Datamap\Data	\os\msapps\datamap\data	Y
MS Map File	mx_airpt.map	1,536	\Program Files\Common Files\Microsoft Shared\Datamap\Data	\os\msapps\datamap\data	Y
MS Map File	mx_airpt.tab	175	\Program Files\Common Files\Microsoft Shared\Datamap\Data	\os\msapps\datamap\data	Y
MS Map File	mx_hiway.dat	810	\Program Files\Common Files\Microsoft Shared\Datamap\Data	\os\msapps\datamap\data	Y
MS Map File	mx_hiway.id	96	\Program Files\Common Files\Microsoft Shared\Datamap\Data	\os\msapps\datamap\data	Y
MS Map File	mx_hiway.map	16,896	\Program Files\Common Files\Microsoft Shared\Datamap\Data	\os\msapps\datamap\data	Y
MS Map File	mx_hiway.tab	177	\Program Files\Common Files\Microsoft Shared\Datamap\Data	\os\msapps\datamap\data	Y
MS Map File	mx_state.dat	1,154	\Program Files\Common Files\Microsoft Shared\Datamap\Data	\os\msapps\datamap\data	Y
MS Map File	mx_state.id	128	\Program Files\Common Files\Microsoft Shared\Datamap\Data	\os\msapps\datamap\data	Y
MS Map File	mx_state.ind	3,584	\Program Files\Common Files\Microsoft Shared\Datamap\Data	\os\msapps\datamap\data	Y
MS Map File	mx_state.map	64,000	\Program Files\Common Files\Microsoft Shared\Datamap\Data	\os\msapps\datamap\data	Y
MS Map File	mx_state.tab	313	\Program Files\Common Files\Microsoft Shared\Datamap\Data	\os\msapps\datamap\data	Y
MS Map File	mxcity_a.dat	1,366	\Program Files\Common Files\Microsoft Shared\Datamap\Data	\os\msapps\datamap\data	Y
MS Map File	mxcity_a.id	200	\Program Files\Common Files\Microsoft Shared\Datamap\Data	\os\msapps\datamap\data	Y
MS Map File	mxcity_a.map	2,560	\Program Files\Common Files\Microsoft Shared\Datamap\Data	\os\msapps\datamap\data	Y
MS Map File	mxcity_a.tab	176	\Program Files\Common Files\Microsoft Shared\Datamap\Data	\os\msapps\datamap\data	Y
MS Map File	mxcity_b.dat	3,264	\Program Files\Common Files\Microsoft Shared\Datamap\Data	\os\msapps\datamap\data	Y
MS Map File	mxcity_b.id	492	\Program Files\Common Files\Microsoft Shared\Datamap\Data	\os\msapps\datamap\data	Y
MS Map File	mxcity_b.map	3,584	\Program Files\Common Files\Microsoft Shared\Datamap\Data	\os\msapps\datamap\data	Y
MS Map File	mxcity_b.tab	170	\Program Files\Common Files\Microsoft Shared\Datamap\Data	\os\msapps\datamap\data	Y

Component	File Name	File Size	Where It Installs	Where It Is Located on the CD-ROM	Typical? *
Microsoft Excel					
MS Map File	n_amerca.gst	1,171	\Program Files\Common Files\Microsoft Shared\Datamap\Data	\os\msapps\datamap\data	Y
MS Map File	ocean.dat	73	\Program Files\Common Files\Microsoft Shared\Datamap\Data	\os\msapps\datamap\data	Y
MS Map File	ocean.id	4	\Program Files\Common Files\Microsoft Shared\Datamap\Data	\os\msapps\datamap\data	Y
MS Map File	ocean.map	3,584	\Program Files\Common Files\Microsoft Shared\Datamap\Data	\os\msapps\datamap\data	Y
MS Map File	ocean.tab	168	\Program Files\Common Files\Microsoft Shared\Datamap\Data	\os\msapps\datamap\data	Y
MS Map File	uk_2dpc.dat	430	\Program Files\Common Files\Microsoft Shared\Datamap\Data	\os\msapps\datamap\data	Y
MS Map File	uk_2dpc.id	484	\Program Files\Common Files\Microsoft Shared\Datamap\Data	\os\msapps\datamap\data	Y
MS Map File	uk_2dpc.ind	2,048	\Program Files\Common Files\Microsoft Shared\Datamap\Data	\os\msapps\datamap\data	Y
MS Map File	uk_2dpc.map	3,584	\Program Files\Common Files\Microsoft Shared\Datamap\Data	\os\msapps\datamap\data	Y
MS Map File	uk_2dpc.tab	265	\Program Files\Common Files\Microsoft Shared\Datamap\Data	\os\msapps\datamap\data	Y
MS Map File	uk_airpt.dat	1,443	\Program Files\Common Files\Microsoft Shared\Datamap\Data	\os\msapps\datamap\data	Y
MS Map File	uk_airpt.id	108	\Program Files\Common Files\Microsoft Shared\Datamap\Data	\os\msapps\datamap\data	Y
MS Map File	uk_airpt.map	1,536	\Program Files\Common Files\Microsoft Shared\Datamap\Data	\os\msapps\datamap\data	Y
MS Map File	uk_airpt.tab	171	\Program Files\Common Files\Microsoft Shared\Datamap\Data	\os\msapps\datamap\data	Y
MS Map File	uk_hiway.dat	462	\Program Files\Common Files\Microsoft Shared\Datamap\Data	\os\msapps\datamap\data	Y
MS Map File	uk_hiway.id	144	\Program Files\Common Files\Microsoft Shared\Datamap\Data	\os\msapps\datamap\data	Y
MS Map File	uk_hiway.map	12,800	\Program Files\Common Files\Microsoft Shared\Datamap\Data	\os\msapps\datamap\data	Y
MS Map File	uk_hiway.tab	171	\Program Files\Common Files\Microsoft Shared\Datamap\Data	\os\msapps\datamap\data	Y
MS Map File	uk_regns.dat	2,274	\Program Files\Common Files\Microsoft Shared\Datamap\Data	\os\msapps\datamap\data	Y
MS Map File	uk_regns.gst	667	\Program Files\Common Files\Microsoft Shared\Datamap\Data	\os\msapps\datamap\data	Y
MS Map File	uk_regns.id	384	\Program Files\Common Files\Microsoft Shared\Datamap\Data	\os\msapps\datamap\data	Y
MS Map File	uk_regns.ind	4,608	\Program Files\Common Files\Microsoft Shared\Datamap\Data	\os\msapps\datamap\data	Y
MS Map File	uk_regns.map	419,328	\Program Files\Common Files\Microsoft Shared\Datamap\Data	\os\msapps\datamap\data	Y
MS Map File	uk_regns.tab	262	\Program Files\Common Files\Microsoft Shared\Datamap\Data	\os\msapps\datamap\data	Y
MS Map File	ukcity_a.dat	1,288	\Program Files\Common Files\Microsoft Shared\Datamap\Data	\os\msapps\datamap\data	Y
MS Map File	ukcity_a.id	188	\Program Files\Common Files\Microsoft Shared\Datamap\Data	\os\msapps\datamap\data	Y
MS Map File	ukcity_a.map	2,560	\Program Files\Common Files\Microsoft Shared\Datamap\Data	\os\msapps\datamap\data	Y
MS Map File	ukcity_a.tab	172	\Program Files\Common Files\Microsoft Shared\Datamap\Data	\os\msapps\datamap\data	Y
MS Map File	ukcity_b.dat	3,446	\Program Files\Common Files\Microsoft Shared\Datamap\Data	\os\msapps\datamap\data	Y
MS Map File	ukcity_b.id	520	\Program Files\Common Files\Microsoft Shared\Datamap\Data	\os\msapps\datamap\data	Y
MS Map File	ukcity_b.map	3,584	\Program Files\Common Files\Microsoft Shared\Datamap\Data	\os\msapps\datamap\data	Y

Component	File Name	File Size	Where It Installs	Where It Is Located on the CD-ROM	Typical? *
Microsoft Excel					
MS Map File	ukcity_b.tab	166	\Program Files\Common Files\Microsoft Shared\Datamap\Data	\os\msapps\datamap\data	Y
MS Map File	us_airpt.dat	4,197	\Program Files\Common Files\Microsoft Shared\Datamap\Data	\os\msapps\datamap\data	Y
MS Map File	us_airpt.id	324	\Program Files\Common Files\Microsoft Shared\Datamap\Data	\os\msapps\datamap\data	Y
MS Map File	us_airpt.map	3,072	\Program Files\Common Files\Microsoft Shared\Datamap\Data	\os\msapps\datamap\data	Y
MS Map File	us_airpt.tab	185	\Program Files\Common Files\Microsoft Shared\Datamap\Data	\os\msapps\datamap\data	Y
MS Map File	us_hiway.dat	4,184	\Program Files\Common Files\Microsoft Shared\Datamap\Data	\os\msapps\datamap\data	Y
MS Map File	us_hiway.id	568	\Program Files\Common Files\Microsoft Shared\Datamap\Data	\os\msapps\datamap\data	Y
MS Map File	us_hiway.map	76,288	\Program Files\Common Files\Microsoft Shared\Datamap\Data	\os\msapps\datamap\data	Y
MS Map File	us_hiway.tab	171	\Program Files\Common Files\Microsoft Shared\Datamap\Data	\os\msapps\datamap\data	Y
MS Map File	us_nacty.dat	1,366	\Program Files\Common Files\Microsoft Shared\Datamap\Data	\os\msapps\datamap\data	Y
MS Map File	us_nacty.id	200	\Program Files\Common Files\Microsoft Shared\Datamap\Data	\os\msapps\datamap\data	Y
MS Map File	us_nacty.map	2,560	\Program Files\Common Files\Microsoft Shared\Datamap\Data	\os\msapps\datamap\data	Y
MS Map File	us_nacty.tab	172	\Program Files\Common Files\Microsoft Shared\Datamap\Data	\os\msapps\datamap\data	Y
MS Map File	us_state.dat	1,271	\Program Files\Common Files\Microsoft Shared\Datamap\Data	\os\msapps\datamap\data	Y
MS Map File	us_state.id	204	\Program Files\Common Files\Microsoft Shared\Datamap\Data	\os\msapps\datamap\data	Y
MS Map File	us_state.ind	4,096	\Program Files\Common Files\Microsoft Shared\Datamap\Data	\os\msapps\datamap\data	Y
MS Map File	us_state.map	78,336	\Program Files\Common Files\Microsoft Shared\Datamap\Data	\os\msapps\datamap\data	Y
MS Map File	us_state.tab	342	\Program Files\Common Files\Microsoft Shared\Datamap\Data	\os\msapps\datamap\data	Y
MS Map File	usa.dat	1,271	\Program Files\Common Files\Microsoft Shared\Datamap\Data	\os\msapps\datamap\data	Y
MS Map File	usa.id	204	\Program Files\Common Files\Microsoft Shared\Datamap\Data	\os\msapps\datamap\data	Y
MS Map File	usa.ind	4,096	\Program Files\Common Files\Microsoft Shared\Datamap\Data	\os\msapps\datamap\data	Y
MS Map File	usa.map	78,848	\Program Files\Common Files\Microsoft Shared\Datamap\Data	\os\msapps\datamap\data	Y
MS Map File	usa.tab	326	\Program Files\Common Files\Microsoft Shared\Datamap\Data	\os\msapps\datamap\data	Y
MS Map File	uscity_a.dat	1,366	\Program Files\Common Files\Microsoft Shared\Datamap\Data	\os\msapps\datamap\data	Y
MS Map File	uscity_a.id	200	\Program Files\Common Files\Microsoft Shared\Datamap\Data	\os\msapps\datamap\data	Y
MS Map File	uscity_a.map	2,560	\Program Files\Common Files\Microsoft Shared\Datamap\Data	\os\msapps\datamap\data	Y
MS Map File	uscity_a.tab	188	\Program Files\Common Files\Microsoft Shared\Datamap\Data	\os\msapps\datamap\data	Y
MS Map File	uscity_b.dat	2,718	\Program Files\Common Files\Microsoft Shared\Datamap\Data	\os\msapps\datamap\data	Y
MS Map File	uscity_b.id	408	\Program Files\Common Files\Microsoft Shared\Datamap\Data	\os\msapps\datamap\data	Y
MS Map File	uscity_b.map	3,072	\Program Files\Common Files\Microsoft Shared\Datamap\Data	\os\msapps\datamap\data	Y
MS Map File	uscity_b.tab	180	\Program Files\Common Files\Microsoft Shared\Datamap\Data	\os\msapps\datamap\data	Y

Component	File Name	File Size	Where It Installs	Where It Is Located on the CD-ROM	Typical? *
Microsoft Excel					
MS Map File	us.gst	633	\Program Files\Common Files\Microsoft Shared\Datamap\Data	\os\msapps\datamap\data	Y
MS Map File	worldcap.dat	5,084	\Program Files\Common Files\Microsoft Shared\Datamap\Data	\os\msapps\datamap\data	Y
MS Map File	worldcap.id	772	\Program Files\Common Files\Microsoft Shared\Datamap\Data	\os\msapps\datamap\data	Y
MS Map File	worldcap.map	4,608	\Program Files\Common Files\Microsoft Shared\Datamap\Data	\os\msapps\datamap\data	Y
MS Map File	worldcap.tab	174	\Program Files\Common Files\Microsoft Shared\Datamap\Data	\os\msapps\datamap\data	Y
MS Map File	world.gst	481	\Program Files\Common Files\Microsoft Shared\Datamap\Data	\os\msapps\datamap\data	Y
MS Map File	world.dat	14,584	\Program Files\Common Files\Microsoft Shared\Datamap\Data	\os\msapps\datamap\data	Y
MS Map File	world.id	876	\Program Files\Common Files\Microsoft Shared\Datamap\Data	\os\msapps\datamap\data	Y
MS Map File	world.ind	40,448	\Program Files\Common Files\Microsoft Shared\Datamap\Data	\os\msapps\datamap\data	Y
MS Map File	world.map	166,400	\Program Files\Common Files\Microsoft Shared\Datamap\Data	\os\msapps\datamap\data	Y
MS Map File	world.tab	429	\Program Files\Common Files\Microsoft Shared\Datamap\Data	\os\msapps\datamap\data	Y
MS Map File	zipcodes.cpf	400,064	\Program Files\Common Files\Microsoft Shared\Datamap\Data	\os\msapps\datamap\data	Y
MS Map File	zipcodes.tab	187	\Program Files\Common Files\Microsoft Shared\Datamap\Data	\os\msapps\datamap\data	Y
MS Map File	sabnds.dat	382	\Program Files\Common Files\Microsoft Shared\Datamap\Data	\os\msapps\datamap\data	Y
MS Map File	sabnds.gst	471	\Program Files\Common Files\Microsoft Shared\Datamap\Data	\os\msapps\datamap\data	Y
MS Map File	sabnds.id	60	\Program Files\Common Files\Microsoft Shared\Datamap\Data	\os\msapps\datamap\data	Y
MS Map File	sabnds.ind	1,024	\Program Files\Common Files\Microsoft Shared\Datamap\Data	\os\msapps\datamap\data	Y
MS Map File	sabnds.map	54,272	\Program Files\Common Files\Microsoft Shared\Datamap\Data	\os\msapps\datamap\data	Y
MS Map File	sabnds.tab	226	\Program Files\Common Files\Microsoft Shared\Datamap\Data	\os\msapps\datamap\data	Y
MS Map File	samtwns.dat	1,010	\Program Files\Common Files\Microsoft Shared\Datamap\Data	\os\msapps\datamap\data	Y
MS Map File	samtwns.id	236	\Program Files\Common Files\Microsoft Shared\Datamap\Data	\os\msapps\datamap\data	Y
MS Map File	samtwns.ind	3,072	\Program Files\Common Files\Microsoft Shared\Datamap\Data	\os\msapps\datamap\data	Y
MS Map File	samtwns.map	2,560	\Program Files\Common Files\Microsoft Shared\Datamap\Data	\os\msapps\datamap\data	Y
MS Map File	samtwns.tab	205	\Program Files\Common Files\Microsoft Shared\Datamap\Data	\os\msapps\datamap\data	Y
MS Map File	mapsym.ttf	7,360	\Windows\Fonts	\os\fonts	Y
MS Map File	msmap8.hlp	90,321	\Program Files\Common Files\Microsoft Shared\Datamap	\os\msapps\datamap	Y
MS Map File	msmap8.cnt	1,993	\Program Files\Common Files\Microsoft Shared\Datamap	\os\msapps\datamap	Y
MS Map File	mapcat8.hlp	246,336	\Program Files\Common Files\Microsoft Shared\Datamap	\os\msapps\datamap	Y
MS Map File	datains8.hlp	16,386	\Program Files\Common Files\Microsoft Shared\Datamap	\os\msapps\datamap	Y
MS Map File	VBAMAP8.HLP	11,989	\Program Files\Common Files\Microsoft Shared\Datamap	\os\msapps\datamap	Y
MS Map File	VBAMAP8.CNT	190	\Program Files\Common Files\Microsoft Shared\Datamap	\os\msapps\datamap	Y

Component	File Name	File Size	Where It Installs	Where It Is Located on the CD-ROM	Typical? *
Microsoft Excel					
MS Map File	mfcans32.dll	149,504	\Windows\System		Y
Program File	excel.exe	5,599,504	\Program Files\Microsoft Office\Office	\office	Y
Program File	refedit.dll	62,976	\Windows\System	\office	Y
Program File	xl8409.dll	24,064	\Program Files\Microsoft Office\Office	\office	Y
Program File	scanload.dll	12,288	\Program Files\Microsoft Office\Office	\office	Y
Program File	xlrec.dll	31,744	\Windows\System	\office	Y
Program File	recncl.dll	25,600	\Windows\System	\office	Y
Program File	excel8.srg	37,509	\Program Files\Microsoft Office\Office	\office	Y
Program File	xlintl32.dll	556,032	\Program Files\Microsoft Office\Office	\office	Y
Program File	xlread8.txt	30,202	\Program Files\Microsoft Office\Office	\office	Y
Program File	excel8.olb	584,704	\Program Files\Microsoft Office\Office	\office	Y
Program File	xl5en32.olb	228,864	\Program Files\Microsoft Office\Office	\office	Y
Program File	xlcall32.dll	5,120	\Program Files\Microsoft Office\Office	\office	Y
Program File	excel8.xls	13,824	\Windows\ShellNew	\os\shellnew	Y
Program File	msencode.dll	94,208	\Windows\System	\os\msapps\textconv	Y
Program File	xl8galry.xls	178,688	\Program Files\Microsoft Office\Office	\office	Y
Program File	Mswfx95.xls	40,960	\Program Files\Microsoft Office\Office\XLSTART		Y
Program File	vbaen32.olb	24,848	\Windows\System	\os\system	Y
Program File	scp32.dll	15,872	\Windows\System	\os\system	Y
Templ: Expense Report	expense.xlt	337,920	\Program Files\Microsoft Office\Templates\Spreadsheet Solutions	\TempN\Excel	
Templ: Expense Report	expdb.xls	28,672	\Program Files\Microsoft Office\Office\Library	\office\library	
Templ: Invoice	invoice.xlt	303,616	\Program Files\Microsoft Office\Templates\Spreadsheet Solutions	\TempN\Excel	Y
Templ: Invoice	invdb.xls	28,672	\Program Files\Microsoft Office\Office\Library	\office\library	Y
Templ: Purchase Order	purorder.xlt	314,880	\Program Files\Microsoft Office\Templates\Spreadsheet Solutions	\TempN\Excel	
Templ: Purchase Order	podb.xls	28,160	\Program Files\Microsoft Office\Office\Library	\office\library	
Getting Results Book	result97.htm	0	Not installed locally		Y

Component	File Name	File Size	Where It Installs	Where It Is Located on the CD-ROM	Typical? *
Graphics Filters					
BMP Import	Bmpimp32.flt	61,952	\Program Files\Common Files\Microsoft Shared\Grphflt	\os\msapps\grphflt	Y
BMP Import	ms.bmp	2,102	\Program Files\Common Files\Microsoft Shared\Grphflt	\os\msapps\grphflt	Y
CDR Import	cdrimp32.flt	203,264	\Program Files\Common Files\Microsoft Shared\Grphflt	\os\msapps\grphflt	
CDR Import	ms.cdr	15,558	\Program Files\Common Files\Microsoft Shared\Grphflt	\os\msapps\grphflt	
CGM Import	cgmimp32.flt	393,728	\Program Files\Common Files\Microsoft Shared\Grphflt	\os\msapps\grphflt	
CGM Import	Ms.cgm	1,908	\Program Files\Common Files\Microsoft Shared\Grphflt	\os\msapps\grphflt	
CGM Import	Cgmimp32.fnt	606,062	\Program Files\Common Files\Microsoft Shared\Grphflt	\os\msapps\grphflt	
CGM Import	cgmimp32.cfg	6,615	\Program Files\Common Files\Microsoft Shared\Grphflt	\os\msapps\grphflt	
CGM Import	cgmimp32.hlp	31,497	\Program Files\Common Files\Microsoft Shared\Grphflt	\os\msapps\grphflt	
DRW Import	Drwimp32.flt	265,728	\Program Files\Common Files\Microsoft Shared\Grphflt	\os\msapps\grphflt	
DRW Import	Ms.drw	2,989	\Program Files\Common Files\Microsoft Shared\Grphflt	\os\msapps\grphflt	
DXF Import	Dxfimp32.flt	280,576	\Program Files\Common Files\Microsoft Shared\Grphflt	\os\msapps\grphflt	
DXF Import	ms.dxf	17,909	\Program Files\Common Files\Microsoft Shared\Grphflt	\os\msapps\grphflt	
EMF Import	Emfimp32.flt	340,480	\Program Files\Common Files\Microsoft Shared\Grphflt	\os\msapps\grphflt	Y
EMF Import	ms.emf	2,396	\Program Files\Common Files\Microsoft Shared\Grphflt	\os\msapps\grphflt	Y
EPS Import	epsimp32.flt	52,224	\Program Files\Common Files\Microsoft Shared\Grphflt	\os\msapps\grphflt	Y
EPS Import	Ms.eps	15,067	\Program Files\Common Files\Microsoft Shared\Grphflt	\os\msapps\grphflt	Y
GIF Import	gifimp32.flt	130,560	\Program Files\Common Files\Microsoft Shared\Grphflt	\os\msapps\grphflt	Y
GIF Import	Ms.gif	1,069	\Program Files\Common Files\Microsoft Shared\Grphflt	\os\msapps\grphflt	Y
GIF Import	png32.flt	222,720	\Program Files\Common Files\Microsoft Shared\Grphflt	\os\msapps\grphflt	Y
GIF Import	ms.png	1,682	\Program Files\Common Files\Microsoft Shared\Grphflt	\os\msapps\grphflt	Y
JPEG Import	jpegim32.flt	171,520	\Program Files\Common Files\Microsoft Shared\Grphflt	\os\msapps\grphflt	Y
JPEG Import	ms.jpg	1,061	\Program Files\Common Files\Microsoft Shared\Grphflt	\os\msapps\grphflt	Y
Mac PICT Import	pictim32.flt	81,920	\Program Files\Common Files\Microsoft Shared\Grphflt	\os\msapps\grphflt	Y
Mac PICT Import	Ms.pct	3,314	\Program Files\Common Files\Microsoft Shared\Grphflt	\os\msapps\grphflt	Y
PCD Import	pcdimp32.flt	69,120	\Program Files\Common Files\Microsoft Shared\Grphflt	\os\msapps\grphflt	
PCD Import	pcdlib32.dll	212,480	\Windows\System	\os\msapps\grphflt	
PCX Import	Pcximp32.flt	57,344	\Program Files\Common Files\Microsoft Shared\Grphflt	\os\msapps\grphflt	
PCX Import	Ms.pcx	1,359	\Program Files\Common Files\Microsoft Shared\Grphflt	\os\msapps\grphflt	
PNG Import	png32.flt	222,720	\Program Files\Common Files\Microsoft Shared\Grphflt	\os\msapps\grphflt	Y
PNG Import	ms.png	1,682	\Program Files\Common Files\Microsoft Shared\Grphflt	\os\msapps\grphflt	Y

Component	File Name	File Size	Where It Installs	Where It Is Located on the CD-ROM	Typical? *
Graphics Filters					
Targa Import	Tgaimp32.flt	55,808	\Program Files\Common Files\Microsoft Shared\Grphflt	\os\msapps\grphflt	
Targa Import	ms.tga	1,810	\Program Files\Common Files\Microsoft Shared\Grphflt	\os\msapps\grphflt	
TIFF Import	Tiffim32.flt	104,960	\Program Files\Common Files\Microsoft Shared\Grphflt	\os\msapps\grphflt	Y
TIFF Import	Ms.tif	2,650	\Program Files\Common Files\Microsoft Shared\Grphflt	\os\msapps\grphflt	Y
WMF Import	wmfimp32.flt	13,312	\Program Files\Common Files\Microsoft Shared\Grphflt	\os\msapps\grphflt	Y
WMF Import	ms.wmf	3,238	\Program Files\Common Files\Microsoft Shared\Grphflt	\os\msapps\grphflt	Y
WPG Export	Wpgexp32.flt	68,608	\Program Files\Common Files\Microsoft Shared\Grphflt	\os\msapps\grphflt	Y
WPG Import	Wpgimp32.flt	149,504	\Program Files\Common Files\Microsoft Shared\Grphflt	\os\msapps\grphflt	Y
WPG Import	ms.wpg	1,382	\Program Files\Common Files\Microsoft Shared\Grphflt	\os\msapps\grphflt	Y
Office Tools					
Find All Word Forms	mswds_en.lex	444,027	\Program Files\Common Files\Microsoft Shared\Proof	\os\msapps\proof	Y
Find Fast	findfast.exe	111,376	\Program Files\Microsoft Office\Office	\office	Y
Find Fast	findfast.cpl	22,528	\Windows\System	\os\system	Y
Find Fast	ffastlog.txt	43	\Windows\System	\os\system	Y
Find Fast	Findfast.hlp	28,183	\Program Files\Microsoft Office\Office	\office	Y
Find Fast	findfast.cnt	934	\Program Files\Microsoft Office\Office	\office	Y
Find Fast	IFilter.cnv	45,328	\Program Files\Microsoft Office		Y
Find Fast	Ctl3d32.dll	27,136	\Windows\System		Y
Lotus VIM Mail Supp't.	Mapivi32.dll	130,048	\Windows\System		
Lotus VIM Mail Supp't.	Mapivitk.dll	18,944	\Windows\System		
Lotus VIM Mail Supp't.	mvthksvr.exe	11,856	\Windows\System		
MS Clip Gallery	mfcans32.dll	149,504	\Windows\System		Y
MS Clip Gallery	Artgalry.exe	44,032	\Program Files\Common Files\Microsoft Shared\Artgalry	\os\msapps\artgalry	Y
MS Clip Gallery	wmfimp32.flt	13,312	\Program Files\Common Files\Microsoft Shared\Grphflt	\os\msapps\grphflt	Y
MS Clip Gallery	ms.wmf	3,238	\Program Files\Common Files\Microsoft Shared\Grphflt	\os\msapps\grphflt	Y
MS Clip Gallery	Bmpimp32.flt	61,952	\Program Files\Common Files\Microsoft Shared\Grphflt	\os\msapps\grphflt	Y
MS Clip Gallery	ms.bmp	2,102	\Program Files\Common Files\Microsoft Shared\Grphflt	\os\msapps\grphflt	Y

Component	File Name	File Size	Where It Installs	Where It Is Located on the CD-ROM	Typical? *
Office Tools					
MS Clip Gallery	Artgalry.dll	339,968	\Program Files\Common Files\Microsoft Shared\Artgalry	\os\msapps\artgalry	Y
MS Clip Gallery	Artgalry.hlp	49,346	\Program Files\Common Files\Microsoft Shared\Artgalry	\os\msapps\artgalry	Y
MS Clip Gallery	Qartglry.hlp	16,134	\Program Files\Common Files\Microsoft Shared\Artgalry	\os\msapps\artgalry	Y
MS Clip Gallery	Artgalry.cnt	3,592	\Program Files\Common Files\Microsoft Shared\Artgalry	\os\msapps\artgalry	Y
MS Clip Gallery	Artgalry.srg	6,421	\Program Files\Common Files\Microsoft Shared\Artgalry	\os\msapps\artgalry	Y
MS Clip Gallery	www_clip.url	115	\Program Files\Common Files\Microsoft Shared\Artgalry	\os\msapps\artgalry	Y
MS Clip Gallery	Picstore.dll	12,288	\Windows\System	\os\system	Y
MS Clip Gallery	Pubdlg.dll	27,136	\Windows\System	\os\system	Y
MS Clip Gallery	MSVCR T20.DLL	253,952	\Windows\System		Y
MS Clip Gallery	selfreg.dll	32,256	\Windows\System	\	Y
MS Clip Gallery	MFC40.dll	921,872	\Windows\System	\os\system	Y
MS Clip Gallery	mmedia.cag	0	not installed locally		Y
MS Clip Gallery	scrbeans.cag	0	not installed locally		Y
MS Clip Gallery	photos.cag	0	not installed locally		Y
MS Clip Gallery	powerpnt.cag	0	not installed locally		Y
MS Clip Gallery	office.cag	0	not installed locally		Y
MS Clip Gallery	pop97.cag	0	not installed locally	\Clipart\Popular	Y
MS Equation Ed.	eqnedt32.exe	521,216	\Program Files\Common Files\Microsoft Shared\Equation	\os\msapps\Equation	
MS Equation Ed.	eqnedt32.cnt	2,557	\Program Files\Common Files\Microsoft Shared\Equation	\os\msapps\Equation	
MS Equation Ed.	eqnedt32.hlp	147,903	\Program Files\Common Files\Microsoft Shared\Equation	\os\msapps\Equation	
MS Equation Ed.	Eqnedt32.srg	4,402	\Program Files\Common Files\Microsoft Shared\Equation	\os\msapps\Equation	
MS Equation Ed.	Mtextra.ttf	7,656	\Windows\Fonts	\os\fonts	
MS Graph 97	Graph8.exe	1,597,200	\Program Files\Microsoft Office\Office	\office	Y
MS Graph 97	graph8.olb	111,104	\Program Files\Microsoft Office\Office	\office	Y
MS Graph 97	gr8409.dll	5,120	\Program Files\Microsoft Office\Office	\office	Y
MS Graph 97	Grintl32.dll	161,792	\Program Files\Microsoft Office\Office	\office	Y
MS Graph 97	Graph8.srg	5,297	\Program Files\Microsoft Office\Office	\office	Y
MS Graph 97	gr8galry.gra	186,880	\Program Files\Microsoft Office\Office	\office	Y
MS Graph 97	vbagrp8.hlp	17,952	\Program Files\Microsoft Office\Office	\office	Y
MS Graph 97	vbagrp8.cnt	198	\Program Files\Microsoft Office\Office	\office	Y

Component	File Name	File Size	Where It Installs	Where It Is Located on the CD-ROM	Typical? *
Office Tools					
MS Graph 97 Help	graph8.hlp	520,680	\Program Files\Microsoft Office\Office	\office	Y
MS Graph 97 Help	graph8.aw	296,578	\Program Files\Microsoft Office\Office	\office	Y
MS Graph 97 Help	graph8.cnt	16,761	\Program Files\Microsoft Office\Office	\office	Y
MS Info	msinfo32.exe	452,096	\Program Files\Common Files\Microsoft Shared\MSInfo	\os\msapps\msinfo	Y
MS Info	imgwalk.dll	18,432	\Program Files\Common Files\Microsoft Shared\MSInfo	\os\msapps\msinfo	Y
MS Info	msinf16h.exe	16,304	\Program Files\Common Files\Microsoft Shared\MSInfo	\os\msapps\msinfo	Y
MS Info	Msinfo32.hlp	40,815	\Program Files\Common Files\Microsoft Shared\MSInfo	\os\msapps\msinfo	Y
MS Info	MSINFO32.CNT	2,967	\Program Files\Common Files\Microsoft Shared\MSInfo	\os\msapps\msinfo	Y
MS Org. Chart	orgchart.hlp	101,379	\Program Files\Common Files\Microsoft Shared\Orgchart	\os\msapps\orgchart	Y
MS Org. Chart	Templ.mso	2,905	\Program Files\Common Files\Microsoft Shared\Orgchart	\os\msapps\orgchart	Y
MS Org. Chart	orgchart.cnt	3,787	\Program Files\Common Files\Microsoft Shared\Orgchart	\os\msapps\orgchart	Y
MS Org. Chart	Orgchart.srg	4,599	\Program Files\Common Files\Microsoft Shared\Orgchart	\os\msapps\orgchart	Y
MS Org. Chart 2.0	Orgchart.exe	1,420,288	\Program Files\Common Files\Microsoft Shared\Orgchart	\os\msapps\orgchart	Y
MS Photo Editor	photoed.exe	803,844	\Program Files\Common Files\Microsoft Shared\PhotoEd	\os\msapps\Photoed	
MS Photo Editor	ChalkCha.dll	81,920	\Program Files\Common Files\Microsoft Shared\PhotoEd	\os\msapps\Photoed	
MS Photo Editor	Emboss.dll	78,848	\Program Files\Common Files\Microsoft Shared\PhotoEd	\os\msapps\Photoed	
MS Photo Editor	GraphicP.dll	78,848	\Program Files\Common Files\Microsoft Shared\PhotoEd	\os\msapps\Photoed	
MS Photo Editor	NotePape.dll	79,872	\Program Files\Common Files\Microsoft Shared\PhotoEd	\os\msapps\Photoed	
MS Photo Editor	StainedG.dll	92,160	\Program Files\Common Files\Microsoft Shared\PhotoEd	\os\msapps\Photoed	
MS Photo Editor	Stamp.dll	78,336	\Program Files\Common Files\Microsoft Shared\PhotoEd	\os\msapps\Photoed	
MS Photo Editor	Texturiz.dll	160,768	\Program Files\Common Files\Microsoft Shared\PhotoEd	\os\msapps\Photoed	
MS Photo Editor	WaterCol.dll	87,040	\Program Files\Common Files\Microsoft Shared\PhotoEd	\os\msapps\Photoed	
MS Photo Editor	photoed.srg	9,902	\Program Files\Common Files\Microsoft Shared\PhotoEd	\os\msapps\Photoed	
MS Photo Editor	TWAIN.DLL	87,328	\Windows	\os	
MS Photo Editor	TWAIN_32.DLL	77,312	\Windows	\os	
MS Photo Editor	TWUNK_16.EXE	48,560	\Windows	\os	
MS Photo Editor	TWUNK_32.EXE	69,632	\Windows	\os	
MS Photo Editor	MSVCRT20 .DLL	253,952	\Windows\System		Y
MS Photo Editor	Tiffim32.flt	104,960	\Program Files\Common Files\Microsoft Shared\Grphflt	\os\msapps\grphflt	Y
MS Photo Editor	Ms.tif	2,650	\Program Files\Common Files\Microsoft Shared\Grphflt	\os\msapps\grphflt	Y

Component	File Name	File Size	Where It Installs	Where It Is Located on the CD-ROM	Typical? *
Office Tools					
MS Photo Editor	Tgaimp32.flt	55,808	\Program Files\Common Files\Microsoft Shared\Grphflt	\os\msapps\grphflt	
MS Photo Editor	ms.tga	1,810	\Program Files\Common Files\Microsoft Shared\Grphflt	\os\msapps\grphflt	
MS Photo Editor	Pcximp32.flt	57,344	\Program Files\Common Files\Microsoft Shared\Grphflt	\os\msapps\grphflt	
MS Photo Editor	Ms.pcx	1,359	\Program Files\Common Files\Microsoft Shared\Grphflt	\os\msapps\grphflt	
MS Photo Editor	pcdimp32.flt	69,120	\Program Files\Common Files\Microsoft Shared\Grphflt	\os\msapps\grphflt	
MS Photo Editor	pcdlib32.dll	212,480	\Windows\System	\os\msapps\grphflt	
MS Photo Editor	jpegim32.flt	171,520	\Program Files\Common Files\Microsoft Shared\Grphflt	\os\msapps\grphflt	Y
MS Photo Editor	ms.jpg	1,061	\Program Files\Common Files\Microsoft Shared\Grphflt	\os\msapps\grphflt	Y
MS Photo Editor	gifimp32.flt	130,560	\Program Files\Common Files\Microsoft Shared\Grphflt	\os\msapps\grphflt	Y
MS Photo Editor	Ms.gif	1,069	\Program Files\Common Files\Microsoft Shared\Grphflt	\os\msapps\grphflt	Y
MS Photo Editor	png32.flt	222,720	\Program Files\Common Files\Microsoft Shared\Grphflt	\os\msapps\grphflt	Y
MS Photo Editor	ms.png	1,682	\Program Files\Common Files\Microsoft Shared\Grphflt	\os\msapps\grphflt	Y
MS Photo Editor	Bmpimp32.flt	61,952	\Program Files\Common Files\Microsoft Shared\Grphflt	\os\msapps\grphflt	Y
MS Photo Editor	ms.bmp	2,102	\Program Files\Common Files\Microsoft Shared\Grphflt	\os\msapps\grphflt	Y
MS Photo Editor	photoed.hlp	93,529	\Program Files\Common Files\Microsoft Shared\PhotoEd	\os\msapps\Photoed	
MS Photo Editor	photoed.cnt	4,271	\Program Files\Common Files\Microsoft Shared\PhotoEd	\os\msapps\Photoed	
Office Assistant	clippit.act	468,266	\Program Files\Microsoft Office\Office\Actors	\office\actors	Y
Office Assistant	logo.acp	3,200	\Program Files\Microsoft Office\Office\Actors	\office\actors\preview	Y
Office Assistant	genius.acp	81,930	\Program Files\Microsoft Office\Office\Actors	\office\actors\preview	Y
Office Assistant	scribble.acp	38,225	\Program Files\Microsoft Office\Office\Actors	\office\actors\preview	Y
Office Assistant	dot.acp	10,932	\Program Files\Microsoft Office\Office\Actors	\office\actors\preview	Y
Office Assistant	mnature.acp	87,942	\Program Files\Microsoft Office\Office\Actors	\office\actors\preview	Y
Office Assistant	hoverbot.acp	9,387	\Program Files\Microsoft Office\Office\Actors	\office\actors\preview	Y
Office Assistant	will.acp	41,133	\Program Files\Microsoft Office\Office\Actors	\office\actors\preview	Y
Office Assistant	powerpup.acp	23,514	\Program Files\Microsoft Office\Office\Actors	\office\actors\preview	Y
Office Shortcut Bar	msoffice.exe	333,824	\Program Files\Microsoft Office\Office	\office	
Office Shortcut Bar	osbreg.dll	16,384	\Program Files\Microsoft Office\Office	\office	
Office Shortcut Bar	cpanel.lnk	120	\Program Files\Microsoft Office\Office\Shortcut Bar\Office	\office	
Office Shortcut Bar	printers.lnk	120	\Program Files\Microsoft Office\Office\Shortcut Bar\Office	\office	
Office Shortcut Bar	msdos.pif	1,157	\Program Files\Microsoft Office\Office\Shortcut Bar\Office	\office	
Popular Clipart	agree.wmf	26,454	\Program Files\Microsoft Office\Clipart\Popular	\Clipart\Popular	Y

Component	File Name	File Size	Where It Installs	Where It Is Located on the CD-ROM	Typical? *
Office Tools					
Popular Clipart	amconfus.wmf	1,494	\Program Files\Microsoft Office\Clipart\Popular	\Clipart\Popular	Y
Popular Clipart	amdisast.wmf	3,190	\Program Files\Microsoft Office\Clipart\Popular	\Clipart\Popular	Y
Popular Clipart	amhappy.wmf	1,718	\Program Files\Microsoft Office\Clipart\Popular	\Clipart\Popular	Y
Popular Clipart	amidea.wmf	1,622	\Program Files\Microsoft Office\Clipart\Popular	\Clipart\Popular	Y
Popular Clipart	amorgani.wmf	4,342	\Program Files\Microsoft Office\Clipart\Popular	\Clipart\Popular	Y
Popular Clipart	amproble.wmf	2,102	\Program Files\Microsoft Office\Clipart\Popular	\Clipart\Popular	Y
Popular Clipart	amvictor.wmf	1,398	\Program Files\Microsoft Office\Clipart\Popular	\Clipart\Popular	Y
Popular Clipart	amwin.wmf	3,254	\Program Files\Microsoft Office\Clipart\Popular	\Clipart\Popular	Y
Popular Clipart	arrows1.wmf	4,630	\Program Files\Microsoft Office\Clipart\Popular	\Clipart\Popular	Y
Popular Clipart	arrows2.wmf	2,838	\Program Files\Microsoft Office\Clipart\Popular	\Clipart\Popular	Y
Popular Clipart	arrows3.wmf	2,454	\Program Files\Microsoft Office\Clipart\Popular	\Clipart\Popular	Y
Popular Clipart	arrows4.wmf	3,382	\Program Files\Microsoft Office\Clipart\Popular	\Clipart\Popular	Y
Popular Clipart	arrows5.wmf	758	\Program Files\Microsoft Office\Clipart\Popular	\Clipart\Popular	Y
Popular Clipart	arrows6.wmf	2,358	\Program Files\Microsoft Office\Clipart\Popular	\Clipart\Popular	Y
Popular Clipart	arrows7.wmf	1,686	\Program Files\Microsoft Office\Clipart\Popular	\Clipart\Popular	Y
Popular Clipart	arrows8.wmf	982	\Program Files\Microsoft Office\Clipart\Popular	\Clipart\Popular	Y
Popular Clipart	arrowsgn.wmf	1,878	\Program Files\Microsoft Office\Clipart\Popular	\Clipart\Popular	Y
Popular Clipart	bandaid.wmf	9,494	\Program Files\Microsoft Office\Clipart\Popular	\Clipart\Popular	Y
Popular Clipart	beartrap.wmf	4,022	\Program Files\Microsoft Office\Clipart\Popular	\Clipart\Popular	Y
Popular Clipart	bomb.wmf	9,558	\Program Files\Microsoft Office\Clipart\Popular	\Clipart\Popular	Y
Popular Clipart	brick.wmf	9,878	\Program Files\Microsoft Office\Clipart\Popular	\Clipart\Popular	Y
Popular Clipart	building.wmf	10,806	\Program Files\Microsoft Office\Clipart\Popular	\Clipart\Popular	Y
Popular Clipart	car.wmf	7,222	\Program Files\Microsoft Office\Clipart\Popular	\Clipart\Popular	Y
Popular Clipart	champgne.wmf	34,806	\Program Files\Microsoft Office\Clipart\Popular	\Clipart\Popular	Y
Popular Clipart	checkmrk.wmf	758	\Program Files\Microsoft Office\Clipart\Popular	\Clipart\Popular	Y
Popular Clipart	clap.wmf	5,462	\Program Files\Microsoft Office\Clipart\Popular	\Clipart\Popular	Y
Popular Clipart	clock.wmf	10,550	\Program Files\Microsoft Office\Clipart\Popular	\Clipart\Popular	Y
Popular Clipart	coins.wmf	26,358	\Program Files\Microsoft Office\Clipart\Popular	\Clipart\Popular	Y
Popular Clipart	darts.wmf	6,838	\Program Files\Microsoft Office\Clipart\Popular	\Clipart\Popular	Y
Popular Clipart	destryer.wmf	2,198	\Program Files\Microsoft Office\Clipart\Popular	\Clipart\Popular	Y
Popular Clipart	dice.wmf	2,966	\Program Files\Microsoft Office\Clipart\Popular	\Clipart\Popular	Y

Component	File Name	File Size	Where It Installs	Where It Is Located on the CD-ROM	Typical? *
Office Tools					
Popular Clipart	diploma.wmf	3,510	\Program Files\Microsoft Office\Clipart\Popular	\Clipart\Popular	Y
Popular Clipart	dominoes.wmf	6,198	\Program Files\Microsoft Office\Clipart\Popular	\Clipart\Popular	Y
Popular Clipart	donkey.wmf	5,078	\Program Files\Microsoft Office\Clipart\Popular	\Clipart\Popular	Y
Popular Clipart	door.wmf	2,678	\Program Files\Microsoft Office\Clipart\Popular	\Clipart\Popular	Y
Popular Clipart	dove.wmf	4,086	\Program Files\Microsoft Office\Clipart\Popular	\Clipart\Popular	Y
Popular Clipart	dynamite.wmf	15,318	\Program Files\Microsoft Office\Clipart\Popular	\Clipart\Popular	Y
Popular Clipart	examine.wmf	7,542	\Program Files\Microsoft Office\Clipart\Popular	\Clipart\Popular	Y
Popular Clipart	fistslam.wmf	8,758	\Program Files\Microsoft Office\Clipart\Popular	\Clipart\Popular	Y
Popular Clipart	flower.wmf	8,182	\Program Files\Microsoft Office\Clipart\Popular	\Clipart\Popular	Y
Popular Clipart	hammer.wmf	1,814	\Program Files\Microsoft Office\Clipart\Popular	\Clipart\Popular	Y
Popular Clipart	hatecomp.wmf	22,326	\Program Files\Microsoft Office\Clipart\Popular	\Clipart\Popular	Y
Popular Clipart	hndshak1.wmf	3,862	\Program Files\Microsoft Office\Clipart\Popular	\Clipart\Popular	Y
Popular Clipart	hndshak2.wmf	6,038	\Program Files\Microsoft Office\Clipart\Popular	\Clipart\Popular	Y
Popular Clipart	hndshak3.wmf	10,422	\Program Files\Microsoft Office\Clipart\Popular	\Clipart\Popular	Y
Popular Clipart	jetplane.wmf	7,414	\Program Files\Microsoft Office\Clipart\Popular	\Clipart\Popular	Y
Popular Clipart	jigsaw.wmf	4,054	\Program Files\Microsoft Office\Clipart\Popular	\Clipart\Popular	Y
Popular Clipart	key.wmf	3,478	\Program Files\Microsoft Office\Clipart\Popular	\Clipart\Popular	Y
Popular Clipart	light.wmf	5,334	\Program Files\Microsoft Office\Clipart\Popular	\Clipart\Popular	Y
Popular Clipart	lion.wmf	3,606	\Program Files\Microsoft Office\Clipart\Popular	\Clipart\Popular	Y
Popular Clipart	lock.wmf	8,214	\Program Files\Microsoft Office\Clipart\Popular	\Clipart\Popular	Y
Popular Clipart	magichat.wmf	8,534	\Program Files\Microsoft Office\Clipart\Popular	\Clipart\Popular	Y
Popular Clipart	magnify.wmf	6,262	\Program Files\Microsoft Office\Clipart\Popular	\Clipart\Popular	Y
Popular Clipart	meeting.wmf	4,950	\Program Files\Microsoft Office\Clipart\Popular	\Clipart\Popular	Y
Popular Clipart	meeting2.wmf	12,054	\Program Files\Microsoft Office\Clipart\Popular	\Clipart\Popular	Y
Popular Clipart	money.wmf	10,358	\Program Files\Microsoft Office\Clipart\Popular	\Clipart\Popular	Y
Popular Clipart	moneybag.wmf	2,198	\Program Files\Microsoft Office\Clipart\Popular	\Clipart\Popular	Y

Component	File Name	File Size	Where It Installs	Where It Is Located on the CD-ROM	Typical? *
Office Tools					
Popular Clipart	oildrill.wmf	14,422	\Program Files\Microsoft Office\Clipart\Popular	\Clipart\Popular	Y
Popular Clipart	openhand.wmf	5,910	\Program Files\Microsoft Office\Clipart\Popular	\Clipart\Popular	Y
Popular Clipart	ptrup.wmf	3,766	\Program Files\Microsoft Office\Clipart\Popular	\Clipart\Popular	Y
Popular Clipart	rabbit.wmf	7,190	\Program Files\Microsoft Office\Clipart\Popular	\Clipart\Popular	Y
Popular Clipart	ribbon.wmf	2,678	\Program Files\Microsoft Office\Clipart\Popular	\Clipart\Popular	Y
Popular Clipart	runner.wmf	14,230	\Program Files\Microsoft Office\Clipart\Popular	\Clipart\Popular	Y
Popular Clipart	sailboat.wmf	10,422	\Program Files\Microsoft Office\Clipart\Popular	\Clipart\Popular	Y
Popular Clipart	scales.wmf	2,902	\Program Files\Microsoft Office\Clipart\Popular	\Clipart\Popular	Y
Popular Clipart	shark.wmf	4,662	\Program Files\Microsoft Office\Clipart\Popular	\Clipart\Popular	Y
Popular Clipart	soccer.wmf	12,854	\Program Files\Microsoft Office\Clipart\Popular	\Clipart\Popular	Y
Popular Clipart	star.wmf	1,334	\Program Files\Microsoft Office\Clipart\Popular	\Clipart\Popular	Y
Popular Clipart	stop.wmf	2,966	\Program Files\Microsoft Office\Clipart\Popular	\Clipart\Popular	Y
Popular Clipart	stoplght.wmf	6,646	\Program Files\Microsoft Office\Clipart\Popular	\Clipart\Popular	Y
Popular Clipart	tennis.wmf	20,022	\Program Files\Microsoft Office\Clipart\Popular	\Clipart\Popular	Y
Popular Clipart	thumbdn.wmf	5,302	\Program Files\Microsoft Office\Clipart\Popular	\Clipart\Popular	Y
Popular Clipart	triumph.wmf	7,734	\Program Files\Microsoft Office\Clipart\Popular	\Clipart\Popular	Y
Popular Clipart	trophy.wmf	3,862	\Program Files\Microsoft Office\Clipart\Popular	\Clipart\Popular	Y
Popular Clipart	turtle.wmf	6,870	\Program Files\Microsoft Office\Clipart\Popular	\Clipart\Popular	Y
Popular Clipart	wearhat.wmf	16,918	\Program Files\Microsoft Office\Clipart\Popular	\Clipart\Popular	Y
Popular Clipart	whatnow.wmf	11,702	\Program Files\Microsoft Office\Clipart\Popular	\Clipart\Popular	Y
Popular Clipart	yinyang.wmf	1,590	\Program Files\Microsoft Office\Clipart\Popular	\Clipart\Popular	Y
Popular Clipart	pop97.cag	480,768	\Program Files\Microsoft Office\Clipart\Popular	\Clipart\Popular	Y
Spell Check	Custom.dic	20	\Program Files\Microsoft Office\Office	\office	Y
Spell Check	Mssp2_en.lex	252,801	\Program Files\Common Files\Microsoft Shared\Proof	\os\msapps\proof	Y
Spell Check	Mssp232.dll	138,240	\Program Files\Common Files\Microsoft Shared\Proof	\os\msapps\proof	Y

Component	File Name	File Size	Where It Installs	Where It Is Located on the CD-ROM	Typical? *
Office Tools					
Spell Check	Mssp2_ea.lex	327,823	\Program Files\Common Files\Microsoft Shared\Proof		Y
TT Font: Arial Black	Ariblk.ttf	103,992	\Windows\Fonts	\os\fonts	Y
TT Font: Arial Narrow	Arialn.ttf	123,976	\Windows\Fonts	\os\fonts	Y
TT Font: Arial Narrow	Arialni.ttf	130,180	\Windows\Fonts	\os\fonts	Y
TT Font: Arial Narrow	Arialnb.ttf	127,720	\Windows\Fonts	\os\fonts	Y
TT Font: Arial Narrow	Arialnbi.ttf	126,980	\Windows\Fonts	\os\fonts	Y
TT Font: Bookman OS	Bookos.ttf	150,412	\Windows\Fonts	\os\fonts	Y
TT Font: Bookman OS	Bookosbi.ttf	150,900	\Windows\Fonts	\os\fonts	Y
TT Font: Bookman OS	bookosb.ttf	143,368	\Windows\Fonts	\os\fonts	Y
TT Font: Bookman OS	Bookosi.ttf	149,704	\Windows\Fonts	\os\fonts	Y
TT Font: Garamond	Gara.ttf	185,680	\Windows\Fonts	\os\fonts	Y
TT Font: Garamond	Garabd.ttf	186,744	\Windows\Fonts	\os\fonts	Y
TT Font: Garamond	Garait.ttf	176,916	\Windows\Fonts	\os\fonts	Y
TT Font: Impact	Impact.ttf	126,056	\Windows\Fonts	\os\fonts	Y
Microsoft Outlook 97					
Exch. Srvr. Sup.	msriched.vbx	88,240	\Windows\System	\os\system	Y
Exch. Srvr. Sup.	mapifvbx.tlb	4,569	\Windows\System	\os\system	Y
Exch. Srvr. Sup.	comdlg16.ocx	81,104	\Windows\System	\os\system	Y
Exch. Srvr. Sup.	threed16.ocx	177,824	\Windows\System	\os\system	Y
Exch. Srvr. Sup.	efdocx.srg	17,232	\Windows\System	\os\system	Y
Exch. Srvr. Sup.	vaen2.dll	9,136	\Windows\System	\os\system	Y
Exch. Srvr. Sup.	vaen21.olb	35,200	\Windows\System	\os\system	Y
Exch. Srvr. Sup.	vb4en16.dll	19,616	\Windows\System	\os\system	Y
Exch. Srvr. Sup.	wmsui.dll	1,201,312	\Windows\System	\os\system	Y
Exch. Srvr. Sup.	riched.dll	241,072	\Windows\System	\os\system	Y
Exch. Srvr. Sup.	mlctrl.dll	117,792	\Windows\System	\os\system	Y
Exch. Srvr. Sup.	oc25.dll	536,048	\Windows\System	\os\system	Y
Exch. Srvr. Sup.	efdocx.srg	17,232	\Windows\System	\os\system	Y
Exch. Srvr. Sup.	efdform.hlp	60,000	\Program Files\Microsoft Office\Office	\os\system	Y
Exch. Srvr. Sup.	emsabp32.dll	105,744	\Windows\System	\os\system	Y

Component	File Name	File Size	Where It Installs	Where It Is Located on the CD-ROM	Typical? *
Microsoft Outlook 97					
Exch. Srvr. Sup.	emsmdb32.dll	419,600	\Windows\System	\os\system	Y
Exch. Srvr. Sup.	emsui32.dll	111,984	\Windows\System	\os\system	Y
Exch. Srvr. Sup.	ole32.dll	558,704	\Windows\System	\office\WMS\Common	Y
Exch. Srvr. Sup.	olethk32.dll	79,424	\Windows\System	\office\WMS\Common	Y
Exch. Srvr. Sup.	compobj.dll	31,120	\Windows\Sysbckup	\office\WMS\Common	Y
Exch. Srvr. Sup.	compobj.dll	31,120	\Windows\sysbckup	\office\WMS\Common	Y
Exchange Server Supp't.	mapiform.vbx	127,936	\Windows\System	\os\system	Y
Exchange Server Supp't.	vb40016.dll	935,632	\Windows\System	\os\system	Y
Help	outltip.hlp	289,601	\Program Files\Microsoft Office\Office	\office	Y
Help	outlhlp.aw	577,834	\Program Files\Microsoft Office\Office	\office	Y
Help	outlhlp.cnt	53,812	\Program Files\Microsoft Office\Office	\office	Y
Help	outlhlp.hlp	1,297,060	\Program Files\Microsoft Office\Office	\office	Y
Help	outlhlp.dll	14,848	\Program Files\Microsoft Office\Office	\office	Y
Help	outlnew.cnt	2,748	\Program Files\Microsoft Office\Office	\office	Y
Help	outlnew.hlp	130,225	\Program Files\Microsoft Office\Office	\office	Y
Help	vbaoutl.hlp	18,679	\Program Files\Microsoft Office\Office	\office	Y
Help	vbaoutl.cnt	197	\Program Files\Microsoft Office\Office	\office	Y
Holidays/Forms	outlook.txt	214,625	\Program Files\Microsoft Office\Office	\office	Y
Holidays/Forms	welcome.msg	366,592	\Program Files\Microsoft Office\Office	\office	Y
Holidays/Forms	Whileout.oft	81,408	\Program Files\Microsoft Office\Templates\Outlook	\Templ\Outlook	Y
Holidays/Forms	Appt.oft	14,848	\Program Files\Microsoft Office\Templates\Outlook	\Templ\Outlook	Y
Holidays/Forms	Contact.oft	17,408	\Program Files\Microsoft Office\Templates\Outlook	\Templ\Outlook	Y
Holidays/Forms	Mail.oft	12,288	\Program Files\Microsoft Office\Templates\Outlook	\Templ\Outlook	Y
Holidays/Forms	Post.oft	12,800	\Program Files\Microsoft Office\Templates\Outlook	\Templ\Outlook	Y
Holidays/Forms	Task.oft	13,824	\Program Files\Microsoft Office\Templates\Outlook	\Templ\Outlook	Y
Lotus Org. Conv.	org10.tlb	9,492	\Windows\System	\os\system	
Lotus Org. Conv.	org11svr.exe	40,896	\Windows\System	\os\system	
Lotus Org. Conv.	org21.tlb	13,364	\Windows\System	\os\system	
Lotus Org. Conv.	org21svr.exe	55,760	\Windows\System	\os\system	
Lotus Org. Conv.	orgapi.dll	30,944	\Windows\System	\os\system	

Component	File Name	File Size	Where It Installs	Where It Is Located on the CD-ROM	Typical? *
Microsoft Outlook 97					
Lotus Org. Conv.	orgcsw10.tlb	163,570	\Windows\System	\os\system	
Lotus Org. Conv.	org11.sam	202,752	\Program Files\Microsoft Office\Office\Convert	\office\convert	
Lotus Org. Conv.	org21.sam	221,696	\Program Files\Microsoft Office\Office\Convert	\office\convert	
Program File	mfcans32.dll	149,504	\Windows\System		Y
Program File	contab32.dll	92,784	\Windows\System	\os\system	Y
Program File	emsuix32.dll	506,128	\Windows\System	\os\system	Y
Program File	etexch32.dll	301,392	\Windows\System	\os\system	Y
Program File	vbscript.dll	206,848	\Windows\System	\os\system	Y
Program File	cnfnot32.exe	150,048	\Windows\System	\os\system	Y
Program File	outlook.ttf	6,272	\Windows\Fonts	\os\fonts	Y
Program File	comic.ttf	63,040	\Windows\Fonts	\os\fonts	Y
Program File	comicbd.ttf	55,892	\Windows\Fonts	\os\fonts	Y
Program File	msjet35.dll	1,038,848	\Windows\System	\os\system	Y
Program File	msjint35.dll	36,624	\Windows\System	\os\system	Y
Program File	msjter35.dll	24,336	\Windows\System	\os\system	Y
Program File	msrepl35.dll	402,704	\Windows\System	\os\system	Y
Program File	msrd2x35.dll	251,664	\Windows\System	\os\system	Y
Program File	vbajet32.dll	18,192	\Windows\System	\os\system	Y
Program File	outform.dat	45,568	\Program Files\Microsoft Office\Office	\office	Y
Program File	outlvbs.dll	39,808	\Program Files\Microsoft Office\Office	\office	Y
Program File	reminder.wav	25,816	\Windows\Media\Office97	\sounds	Y
Program File	outlook.exe	25,872	\Program Files\Microsoft Office\Office	\office	Y
Program File	outllib.dll	4,355,344	\Program Files\Microsoft Office\Office	\office	Y
Program File	finder.exe	16,144	\Program Files\Microsoft Office\Office	\office	Y
Program File	outlrpc.dll	50,448	\Program Files\Microsoft Office\Office	\office	Y
Program File	olkfstub.dll	35,264	\Program Files\Microsoft Office\Office	\office	Y
Program File	sendfile.exe	15,120	\Program Files\Microsoft Office\Office	\office	Y
Program File	outlook.prf	791	\Windows	\office	Y
Program File	msoutl8.olb	117,760	\Program Files\Microsoft Office\Office	\office	Y
Program File	dlgsetp.dll	83,328	\Program Files\Microsoft Office\Office	\office	Y

Component	File Name	File Size	Where It Installs	Where It Is Located on the CD-ROM	Typical? *
Microsoft Outlook 97					
Program File	recall.dll	20,848	\Program Files\Microsoft Office\Office	\office	Y
Program File	outlook.srg	39,779	\Program Files\Microsoft Office\Office	\office	Y
Program File	fatns.srg	6,001	\Program Files\Microsoft Office\Office	\office	Y
Program File	dlgsetp.ecf	719	\Program Files\Microsoft Office\Office\Addins	\office\addins	Y
Program File	cserve.ecf	671	\Program Files\Microsoft Office\Office\Addins	\office\addins	Y
Program File	msn.ecf	714	\Program Files\Microsoft Office\Office\Addins	\office\addins	Y
Program File	EMSUIX.ECF	4,479	\Program Files\Microsoft Office\Office\Addins	\office\addins	Y
Program File	ETEXCH.ECF	3,120	\Program Files\Microsoft Office\Office\Addins	\office\addins	Y
Program File	MAIL3.ECF	845	\Program Files\Microsoft Office\Office\Addins	\office\addins	Y
Program File	MSFSMENU.ECF	1,737	\Program Files\Microsoft Office\Office\Addins	\office\addins	Y
Program File	MSFSPROP.ECF	599	\Program Files\Microsoft Office\Office\Addins	\office\addins	Y
Program File	ccmxp.ecf	1,683	\Program Files\Microsoft Office\Office\Addins	\office\addins	Y
Program File	minet.ecf	953	\Program Files\Microsoft Office\Office\Addins	\office\addins	Y
Program File	msspc.ecf	710	\Program Files\Microsoft Office\Office\Addins	\office\addins	Y
Program File	awfext.ecf	2,364	\Program Files\Microsoft Office\Office\Addins	\office\addins	Y
Program File	forward.usa	476	\Program Files\Microsoft Office\Office\Headers	\office\headers	Y
Program File	reply.usa	461	\Program Files\Microsoft Office\Office\Headers	\office\headers	Y
Program File	post.usa	497	\Program Files\Microsoft Office\Office\Headers	\office\headers	Y
Program File	taskhdr.usa	746	\Program Files\Microsoft Office\Office\Headers	\office\headers	Y
Program File	appthdr.usa	534	\Program Files\Microsoft Office\Office\Headers	\office\headers	Y
Program File	forward.rtf	476	\Program Files\Microsoft Office\Office\Headers	\office\headers	Y
Program File	reply.rtf	461	\Program Files\Microsoft Office\Office\Headers	\office\headers	Y
Program File	post.rtf	497	\Program Files\Microsoft Office\Office\Headers	\office\headers	Y
Program File	taskhdr.rtf	746	\Program Files\Microsoft Office\Office\Headers	\office\headers	Y
Program File	appthdr.rtf	534	\Program Files\Microsoft Office\Office\Headers	\office\headers	Y
Program File	localdv.dll	34,304	\Program Files\Microsoft Office\Office\Convert	\office\convert	Y
Program File	rm.dll	171,008	\Program Files\Microsoft Office\Office\Convert	\office\convert	Y
Program File	transmgr.dll	128,000	\Program Files\Microsoft Office\Office\Convert	\office\convert	Y
Program File	delimwin.fae	30,720	\Program Files\Microsoft Office\Office\Convert	\office\convert	Y
Program File	delimdos.fae	30,720	\Program Files\Microsoft Office\Office\Convert	\office\convert	Y
Program File	oladd.fae	104,960	\Program Files\Microsoft Office\Office\Convert	\office\convert	Y

Component	File Name	File Size	Where It Installs	Where It Is Located on the CD-ROM	Typical? *
Microsoft Outlook 97					
Program File	olappt.fae	104,448	\Program Files\Microsoft Office\Office\Convert	\office\convert	Y
Program File	oltask.fae	100,352	\Program Files\Microsoft Office\Office\Convert	\office\convert	Y
Program File	pab.sam	52,736	\Program Files\Microsoft Office\Office\Convert	\office\convert	Y
Program File	odbc.sam	75,264	\Program Files\Microsoft Office\Office\Convert	\office\convert	Y
Program File	ol.sam	24,064	\Program Files\Microsoft Office\Office\Convert	\office\convert	Y
Program File	desksam.sam	21,504	\Program Files\Microsoft Office\Office\Convert	\office\convert	Y
Program File	olreadme.txt	41,408	\Program Files\Microsoft Office\Office	\office	Y
Program File	newprof.exe	40,064	\Program Files\Windows Messaging	\office\WMS\Win95	Y
Program File	scanpst.exe	295,008	\Program Files\Windows Messaging	\office\WMS\Win95	Y
Program File	mapirpc.reg	11,886	\Program Files\Windows Messaging	\office\WMS\Common	Y
Program File	mlshext.dll	11,136	\Program Files\Windows Messaging	\office\WMS\Common	Y
Program File	exchng32.exe	83,776	\Program Files\Windows Messaging	\office\WMS\Common	Y
Program File	mapif0.cfg	797	\Windows\forms\configs	\office\WMS\Common	Y
Program File	mapif0l.ico	766	\Windows\forms\configs	\office\WMS\Common	Y
Program File	mapif0s.ico	766	\Windows\forms\configs	\office\WMS\Common	Y
Program File	mapif1.cfg	799	\Windows\forms\configs	\office\wordmail	Y
Program File	mapif1l.ico	766	\Windows\forms\configs	\office\wordmail	Y
Program File	mapif1s.ico	766	\Windows\forms\configs	\office\wordmail	Y
Program File	mapif2.cfg	3,868	\Windows\forms\configs	\office\WMS\Common	Y
Program File	mapif2l.ico	766	\Windows\forms\configs	\office\WMS\Common	Y
Program File	mapif2s.ico	766	\Windows\forms\configs	\office\WMS\Common	Y
Program File	mapif3.cfg	795	\Windows\forms\configs	\office\WMS\Common	Y
Program File	mapif3l.ico	766	\Windows\forms\configs	\office\WMS\Common	Y
Program File	mapif3s.ico	766	\Windows\forms\configs	\office\WMS\Common	Y
Program File	mapif4.cfg	789	\Windows\forms\configs	\office\WMS\Common	Y
Program File	mapif4l.ico	766	\Windows\forms\configs	\office\WMS\Common	Y
Program File	mapif4s.ico	766	\Windows\forms\configs	\office\WMS\Common	Y
Program File	mapif5.cfg	907	\Windows\forms\configs	\office\WMS\Common	Y
Program File	mapif5l.ico	766	\Windows\forms\configs	\office\WMS\Common	Y
Program File	mapif5s.ico	766	\Windows\forms\configs	\office\WMS\Common	Y
Program File	mapi32.dll	725,136	\Windows\System	\office\WMS\Win95	Y

Component	File Name	File Size	Where It Installs	Where It Is Located on the CD-ROM	Typical? *
Microsoft Outlook 97					
Program File	mapisrvr.exe	40,112	\Windows\System	\office\WMS\Win95	Y
Program File	mdisp32.exe	98,112	\Windows\System	\office\WMS\Win95	Y
Program File	mdisp32.tlb	18,270	\Windows\System	\office\WMS\Win95	Y
Program File	mspst32.dll	498,288	\Windows\System	\office\WMS\Win95	Y
Program File	cmc.dll	6,624	\Windows\System	\office\WMS\Win95	Y
Program File	mapi.dll	494,688	\Windows\System	\office\WMS\Win95	Y
Program File	mapisp32.exe	24,880	\Windows\System	\office\WMS\Common	Y
Program File	ml3xec16.exe	7,904	\Windows\System	\office\WMS\Common	Y
Program File	mdisp32.reg	3,061	\Windows\System	\office\WMS\Common	Y
Program File	mdisp.tlb	18,122	\Windows\System	\office\WMS\Common	Y
Program File	mlcfg32.cpl	45,984	\Windows\System	\office\WMS\Common	Y
Program File	appxec32.dll	7,440	\Windows\System	\office\WMS\Common	Y
Program File	wmsui32.dll	1,038,608	\Windows\System	\office\WMS\Common	Y
Program File	scanpst.hlp	9,785	\Windows\Help	\office\WMS\Win95	Y
Program File	exchng.hlp	106,850	\Windows\Help	\office\WMS\Common	Y
Program File	exchng.cnt	93	\Windows\Help	\office\WMS\Common	Y
Program File	msfs.hlp	39,343	\Windows\Help	\office\WMS\Common	Y
Program File	msfs.cnt	1,204	\Windows\Help	\office\WMS\Common	Y
Program File	int-mail.cnt	1,255	\Windows\Help	0	Y
Program File	int-mail.hlp	36,853	\Windows\Help	0	Y
Program File	newprof.exe	42,320	\Program Files\Windows Messaging	\office\WMS\Win95	Y
Program File	scanpst.exe	295,488	\Program Files\Windows Messaging	\office\WMS\Win95	Y
Program File	mapirpc.reg	11,886	\Program Files\Windows Messaging	\office\WMS\Common	Y
Program File	mlshext.dll	11,136	\Program Files\Windows Messaging	\office\WMS\Common	Y
Program File	exchng32.exe	83,776	\Program Files\Windows Messaging	\office\WMS\Common	Y
Program File	mapif0.cfg	797	\Windows\forms\configs	\office\WMS\Common	Y
Program File	mapif0l.ico	766	\Windows\forms\configs	\office\WMS\Common	Y
Program File	mapif0s.ico	766	\Windows\forms\configs	\office\WMS\Common	Y
Program File	mapif1.cfg	799	\Windows\forms\configs	\office\wordmail	Y
Program File	mapif1l.ico	766	\Windows\forms\configs	\office\wordmail	Y
Program File	mapif1s.ico	766	\Windows\forms\configs	\office\wordmail	Y

App B

Component	File Name	File Size	Where It Installs	Where It Is Located on the CD-ROM	Typical? *
Microsoft Outlook 97					
Program File	mapif2.cfg	3,868	\Windows\forms\configs	\office\WMS\Common	Y
Program File	mapif2l.ico	766	\Windows\forms\configs	\office\WMS\Common	Y
Program File	mapif2s.ico	766	\Windows\forms\configs	\office\WMS\Common	Y
Program File	mapif3.cfg	795	\Windows\forms\configs	\office\WMS\Common	Y
Program File	mapif3l.ico	766	\Windows\forms\configs	\office\WMS\Common	Y
Program File	mapif3s.ico	766	\Windows\forms\configs	\office\WMS\Common	Y
Program File	mapif4.cfg	789	\Windows\forms\configs	\office\WMS\Common	Y
Program File	mapif4l.ico	766	\Windows\forms\configs	\office\WMS\Common	Y
Program File	mapif4s.ico	766	\Windows\forms\configs	\office\WMS\Common	Y
Program File	mapif5.cfg	907	\Windows\forms\configs	\office\WMS\Common	Y
Program File	mapif5l.ico	766	\Windows\forms\configs	\office\WMS\Common	Y
Program File	mapif5s.ico	766	\Windows\forms\configs	\office\WMS\Common	Y
Program File	mapi32.dll	730,384	\Windows\System	\office\WMS\Win95	Y
Program File	mapisrvr.exe	40,128	\Windows\System	\office\WMS\Win95	Y
Program File	mdisp32.exe	96,528	\Windows\System	\office\WMS\Win95	Y
Program File	mdisp32.tlb	18,274	\Windows\System	\office\WMS\Win95	Y
Program File	mspst32.dll	505,104	\Windows\System	\office\WMS\Win95	Y
Program File	cmc.dll	6,624	\Windows\System	\office\WMS\Win95	Y
Program File	mapi.dll	494,688	\Windows\System	\office\WMS\Win95	Y
Program File	mapisp32.exe	24,880	\Windows\System	\office\WMS\Common	Y
Program File	ml3xec16.exe	7,904	\Windows\System	\office\WMS\Common	Y
Program File	mdisp32.reg	3,061	\Windows\System	\office\WMS\Common	Y
Program File	mdisp.tlb	18,122	\Windows\System	\office\WMS\Common	Y
Program File	mlcfg32.cpl	45,984	\Windows\System	\office\WMS\Common	Y
Program File	appxec32.dll	7,440	\Windows\System	\office\WMS\Common	Y
Program File	wmsui32.dll	1,038,608	\Windows\System	\office\WMS\Common	Y
Program File	exchng.cnt	93	\Windows\Help	\office\WMS\Common	Y
Program File	msfs.hlp	39,343	\Windows\Help	\office\WMS\Common	Y
Program File	msfs.cnt	1,204	\Windows\Help	\office\WMS\Common	Y
Program File	scanpst.hlp	10,104	\Windows\Help	\office\WMS\Win95	Y
Program File	exchng.hlp	106,850	\Windows\Help	\office\WMS\Common	Y

Component	File Name	File Size	Where It Installs	Where It Is Located on the CD-ROM	Typical? *
Microsoft Outlook 97					
Program File	int-mail.cnt	1,255	\Windows\Help	0	Y
Program File	int-mail.hlp	36,853	\Windows\Help	0	Y
Sched+ Supp't.	msscd32.dll	164,112	\Program Files\Microsoft Office\Office	\office	Y
Sched+ Supp't.	mscal32.dll	169,744	\Program Files\Microsoft Office\Office	\office	Y
Sched+ Supp't.	msspc32.dll	1,526,032	\Program Files\Microsoft Office\Office	\office	Y
Sched+ Supp't.	mstre32.dll	33,072	\Program Files\Microsoft Office\Office	\office	Y
Sched+ Supp't.	schdpl32.exe	93,040	\Program Files\Microsoft Office\Office	\office	Y
Sched+ Supp't.	schdpls.srg	2,641	\Program Files\Microsoft Office\Office	\office	Y
Sched+ Supp't.	schplus.sam	234,496	\Program Files\Microsoft Office\Office\Convert	\office\convert	Y
Vis./Forms Design	activity.cfg	968	\Program Files\Microsoft Office\Office\Forms	\office\forms	Y
Vis./Forms Design	appt.cfg	789	\Program Files\Microsoft Office\Office\Forms	\office\forms	Y
Vis./Forms Design	contact.cfg	770	\Program Files\Microsoft Office\Office\Forms	\office\forms	Y
Vis./Forms Design	doc.cfg	765	\Program Files\Microsoft Office\Office\Forms	\office\forms	Y
Vis./Forms Design	exitem.cfg	838	\Program Files\Microsoft Office\Office\Forms	\office\forms	Y
Vis./Forms Design	ipm.cfg	795	\Program Files\Microsoft Office\Office\Forms	\office\forms	Y
Vis./Forms Design	note.cfg	781	\Program Files\Microsoft Office\Office\Forms	\office\forms	Y
Vis./Forms Design	ooftmpl.cfg	830	\Program Files\Microsoft Office\Office\Forms	\office\forms	Y
Vis./Forms Design	post.cfg	777	\Program Files\Microsoft Office\Office\Forms	\office\forms	Y
Vis./Forms Design	postit.cfg	777	\Program Files\Microsoft Office\Office\Forms	\office\forms	Y
Vis./Forms Design	remote.cfg	779	\Program Files\Microsoft Office\Office\Forms	\office\forms	Y
Vis./Forms Design	report.cfg	781	\Program Files\Microsoft Office\Office\Forms	\office\forms	Y
Vis./Forms Design	resend.cfg	779	\Program Files\Microsoft Office\Office\Forms	\office\forms	Y
Vis./Forms Design	task.cfg	768	\Program Files\Microsoft Office\Office\Forms	\office\forms	Y
Vis./Forms Design	repltmpl.cfg	826	\Program Files\Microsoft Office\Office\Forms	\office\forms	Y
Vis./Forms Design	taskreq.cfg	797	\Program Files\Microsoft Office\Office\Forms	\office\forms	Y
Vis./Forms Design	secure.cfg	862	\Program Files\Microsoft Office\Office\Forms	\office\forms	Y
Vis./Forms Design	sign.cfg	879	\Program Files\Microsoft Office\Office\Forms	\office\forms	Y
Vis./Forms Design	taskdec.cfg	807	\Program Files\Microsoft Office\Office\Forms	\office\forms	Y
Vis./Forms Design	taskupd.cfg	806	\Program Files\Microsoft Office\Office\Forms	\office\forms	Y
Vis./Forms Design	taskacc.cfg	804	\Program Files\Microsoft Office\Office\Forms	\office\forms	Y
Vis./Forms Design	cnfnot.cfg	320	\Program Files\Microsoft Office\Office\Forms	\office\forms	Y

Component	File Name	File Size	Where It Installs	Where It Is Located on the CD-ROM	Typical? *
Microsoft Outlook 97					
Vis./Forms Design	cnfres.cfg	338	\Program Files\Microsoft Office\Office\Forms	\office\forms	Y
Vis./Forms Design	recall.cfg	1,623	\Program Files\Microsoft Office\Office\Forms	\office\forms	Y
Vis./Forms Design	rclrpt.cfg	808	\Program Files\Microsoft Office\Office\Forms	\office\forms	Y
Vis./Forms Design	activitL.ico	1,078	\Program Files\Microsoft Office\Office\Forms	\office\forms	Y
Vis./Forms Design	activitS.ico	766	\Program Files\Microsoft Office\Office\Forms	\office\forms	Y
Vis./Forms Design	apptL.ico	1,078	\Program Files\Microsoft Office\Office\Forms	\office\forms	Y
Vis./Forms Design	apptS.ico	766	\Program Files\Microsoft Office\Office\Forms	\office\forms	Y
Vis./Forms Design	contactL.ico	1,078	\Program Files\Microsoft Office\Office\Forms	\office\forms	Y
Vis./Forms Design	contactS.ico	766	\Program Files\Microsoft Office\Office\Forms	\office\forms	Y
Vis./Forms Design	docL.ico	1,078	\Program Files\Microsoft Office\Office\Forms	\office\forms	Y
Vis./Forms Design	docS.ico	766	\Program Files\Microsoft Office\Office\Forms	\office\forms	Y
Vis./Forms Design	exitemL.ico	1,078	\Program Files\Microsoft Office\Office\Forms	\office\forms	Y
Vis./Forms Design	exitemS.ico	766	\Program Files\Microsoft Office\Office\Forms	\office\forms	Y
Vis./Forms Design	ipmL.ico	1,078	\Program Files\Microsoft Office\Office\Forms	\office\forms	Y
Vis./Forms Design	ipmS.ico	766	\Program Files\Microsoft Office\Office\Forms	\office\forms	Y
Vis./Forms Design	noteL.ico	1,078	\Program Files\Microsoft Office\Office\Forms	\office\forms	Y
Vis./Forms Design	noteS.ico	766	\Program Files\Microsoft Office\Office\Forms	\office\forms	Y
Vis./Forms Design	postitL.ico	1,078	\Program Files\Microsoft Office\Office\Forms	\office\forms	Y
Vis./Forms Design	postitS.ico	766	\Program Files\Microsoft Office\Office\Forms	\office\forms	Y
Vis./Forms Design	remoteL.ico	1,078	\Program Files\Microsoft Office\Office\Forms	\office\forms	Y
Vis./Forms Design	remoteS.ico	766	\Program Files\Microsoft Office\Office\Forms	\office\forms	Y
Vis./Forms Design	reportL.ico	1,078	\Program Files\Microsoft Office\Office\Forms	\office\forms	Y
Vis./Forms Design	reportS.ico	766	\Program Files\Microsoft Office\Office\Forms	\office\forms	Y
Vis./Forms Design	resendL.ico	1,078	\Program Files\Microsoft Office\Office\Forms	\office\forms	Y
Vis./Forms Design	resendS.ico	766	\Program Files\Microsoft Office\Office\Forms	\office\forms	Y
Vis./Forms Design	cnfnot.ico	766	\Program Files\Microsoft Office\Office\Forms	\office\forms	Y
Vis./Forms Design	conflict.ico	766	\Program Files\Microsoft Office\Office\Forms	\office\forms	Y
Vis./Forms Design	securl.ico	1,078	\Program Files\Microsoft Office\Office\Forms	\office\forms	Y
Vis./Forms Design	securs.ico	766	\Program Files\Microsoft Office\Office\Forms	\office\forms	Y
Vis./Forms Design	taskL.ico	1,078	\Program Files\Microsoft Office\Office\Forms	\office\forms	Y
Vis./Forms Design	taskS.ico	766	\Program Files\Microsoft Office\Office\Forms	\office\forms	Y

Component	File Name	File Size	Where It Installs	Where It Is Located on the CD-ROM	Typical? *
Microsoft Outlook 97					
Vis./Forms Design	taskreqL.ico	1,078	\Program Files\Microsoft Office\Office\Forms	\office\forms	Y
Vis./Forms Design	taskreqS.ico	766	\Program Files\Microsoft Office\Office\Forms	\office\forms	Y
Vis./Forms Design	oofL.ico	1,078	\Program Files\Microsoft Office\Office\Forms	\office\forms	Y
Vis./Forms Design	oofs.ico	766	\Program Files\Microsoft Office\Office\Forms	\office\forms	Y
Vis./Forms Design	signl.ico	1,078	\Program Files\Microsoft Office\Office\Forms	\office\forms	Y
Vis./Forms Design	signs.ico	766	\Program Files\Microsoft Office\Office\Forms	\office\forms	Y
Vis./Forms Design	taskaccl.ico	1,078	\Program Files\Microsoft Office\Office\Forms	\office\forms	Y
Vis./Forms Design	taskaccs.ico	766	\Program Files\Microsoft Office\Office\Forms	\office\forms	Y
Vis./Forms Design	taskdecl.ico	1,078	\Program Files\Microsoft Office\Office\Forms	\office\forms	Y
Vis./Forms Design	taskdecs.ico	766	\Program Files\Microsoft Office\Office\Forms	\office\forms	Y
Vis./Forms Design	recallL.ico	1,078	\Program Files\Microsoft Office\Office\Forms	\office\forms	Y
Vis./Forms Design	recallS.ico	766	\Program Files\Microsoft Office\Office\Forms	\office\forms	Y
Microsoft PowerPoint					
Anim. (Sounds)	CarBrake.wav	14,076	\Windows\Media\Office97	\sounds	
Anim. (Sounds)	Chimes.wav	74,546	\Windows\Media\Office97	\sounds	
Anim. (Sounds)	Clap.wav	64,200	\Windows\Media\Office97	\sounds	
Anim. (Sounds)	CashReg.wav	7,551	\Windows\Media\Office97	\sounds	
Anim. (Sounds)	Applause.wav	77,260	\Windows\Media\Office97	\sounds	
Anim. (Sounds)	DrumRoll.wav	19,426	\Windows\Media\Office97	\sounds	
Anim. (Sounds)	Explode.wav	23,584	\Windows\Media\Office97	\sounds	
Anim. (Sounds)	Glass.wav	11,532	\Windows\Media\Office97	\sounds	
Anim. (Sounds)	GunShot.wav	4,423	\Windows\Media\Office97	\sounds	
Anim. (Sounds)	Projctor.wav	10,398	\Windows\Media\Office97	\sounds	
Anim. (Sounds)	Ricochet.wav	8,903	\Windows\Media\Office97	\sounds	
Anim. (Sounds)	CashReg.wav	7,551	\Windows\Media\Office97	\sounds	
Anim. (Sounds)	CarBrake.wav	14,076	\Windows\Media\Office97	\sounds	
Anim. (Sounds)	Chimes.wav	74,546	\Windows\Media\Office97	\sounds	
Anim. (Sounds)	Clap.wav	64,200	\Windows\Media\Office97	\sounds	
Cont. Templ: Add'l.	buspln_o.pot	76,288	\Program Files\Microsoft Office\Templates\Presentations	\Templ\Cont.	
Cont. Templ: Add'l.	buspln_s.pot	61,440	\Program Files\Microsoft Office\Templates\Presentations	\Templ\Cont.	
Cont. Templ: Add'l.	cohome_o.pot	100,352	\Program Files\Microsoft Office\Templates\Presentations	\Templ\Cont.	

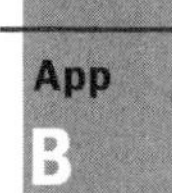

Component	File Name	File Size	Where It Installs	Where It Is Located on the CD-ROM	Typical? *
Microsoft PowerPoint					
Cont. Templ: Add'l.	cohome_s.pot	95,744	\Program Files\Microsoft Office\Templates\Presentations	\Templ\Cont.	
Cont. Templ: Add'l.	prog_o.pot	38,400	\Program Files\Microsoft Office\Templates\Presentations	\Templ\Cont.	
Cont. Templ: Add'l.	prog_s.pot	26,624	\Program Files\Microsoft Office\Templates\Presentations	\Templ\Cont.	
Cont. Templ: Add'l.	acallsht.srg	2,691	\Program Files\Microsoft Office\Templ		
Cont. Templ: Add'l.	acalllng.srg	3,039	\Program Files\Microsoft Office\Templates	\Templ	
Cont. Templ: Typical	comtg_o.pot	33,792	\Program Files\Microsoft Office\Templates\Presentations	\Templ\Cont.	Y
Cont. Templ: Typical	comtg_s.pot	31,744	\Program Files\Microsoft Office\Templates\Presentations	\Templ\Cont.	Y
Cont. Templ: Typical	dcttha_s.pot	37,888	\Program Files\Microsoft Office\Templates\Presentations	\Templ\Cont.	Y
Cont. Templ: Typical	dctmot_s.pot	43,520	\Program Files\Microsoft Office\Templates\Presentations	\Templ\Cont.	Y
Cont. Templ: Typical	dctsel_s.pot	41,984	\Program Files\Microsoft Office\Templates\Presentations	\Templ\Cont.	Y
Cont. Templ: Typical	dctgui_s.pot	49,664	\Program Files\Microsoft Office\Templates\Presentations	\Templ\Cont.	Y
Cont. Templ: Typical	dctman_s.pot	45,568	\Program Files\Microsoft Office\Templates\Presentations	\Templ\Cont.	Y
Cont. Templ: Typical	dctint_s.pot	40,448	\Program Files\Microsoft Office\Templates\Presentations	\Templ\Cont.	Y
Cont. Templ: Typical	dctfac_s.pot	43,520	\Program Files\Microsoft Office\Templates\Presentations	\Templ\Cont.	Y
Cont. Templ: Typical	dcttec_s.pot	41,472	\Program Files\Microsoft Office\Templates\Presentations	\Templ\Cont.	Y
Cont. Templ: Typical	flyer_o.pot	102,400	\Program Files\Microsoft Office\Templates\Presentations	\Templ\Cont.	Y
Cont. Templ: Typical	flyer_s.pot	20,992	\Program Files\Microsoft Office\Templates\Presentations	\Templ\Cont.	Y
Cont. Templ: Typical	hrksk_o.pot	120,832	\Program Files\Microsoft Office\Templates\Presentations	\Templ\Cont.	Y
Cont. Templ: Typical	hrksk_s.pot	60,928	\Program Files\Microsoft Office\Templates\Presentations	\Templ\Cont.	Y
Cont. Templ: Typical	mktpln_o.pot	101,888	\Program Files\Microsoft Office\Templates\Presentations	\Templ\Cont.	Y
Cont. Templ: Typical	mktpln_s.pot	68,096	\Program Files\Microsoft Office\Templates\Presentations	\Templ\Cont.	Y
Cont. Templ: Typical	status_o.pot	84,480	\Program Files\Microsoft Office\Templates\Presentations	\Templ\Cont.	Y
Cont. Templ: Typical	status_s.pot	77,824	\Program Files\Microsoft Office\Templates\Presentations	\Templ\Cont.	Y
Cont. Templ: Typical	stratg_o.pot	48,640	\Program Files\Microsoft Office\Templates\Presentations	\Templ\Cont.	Y
Cont. Templ: Typical	stratg_s.pot	47,616	\Program Files\Microsoft Office\Templates\Presentations	\Templ\Cont.	Y
Cont. Templ: Typical	smpbanr1.pot	174,080	\Program Files\Microsoft Office\Templates\Web Pages	\Templ\Webpages	Y
Cont. Templ: Typical	smpbanr2.pot	33,280	\Program Files\Microsoft Office\Templates\Web Pages	\Templ\Webpages	Y
Cont. Templ: Typical	actypsht.srg	5,603	\Program Files\Microsoft Office\Templates		Y
Cont. Templ: Typical	actyplng.srg	6,863	\Program Files\Microsoft Office\Templates	\Templ	Y
Design Templ	Angles.pot	12,800	\Program Files\Microsoft Office\Templates\Presentation Designs	\Templ\Designs	Y

Component	File Name	File Size	Where It Installs	Where It Is Located on the CD-ROM	Typical? *
Microsoft PowerPoint					
Design Templ	Dadstie.pot	32,768	\Program Files\Microsoft Office\Templates\Presentation Designs	\Temp\Designs	Y
Design Templ	Meadow.pot	133,120	\Program Files\Microsoft Office\Templates\Presentation Designs	\Temp\Designs	Y
Design Templ	Zesty.pot	14,336	\Program Files\Microsoft Office\Templates\Presentation Designs	\Temp\Designs	Y
Design Templ	Serene.pot	125,440	\Program Files\Microsoft Office\Templates\Presentation Designs	\Temp\Designs	Y
Design Templ	Portnote.pot	69,120	\Program Files\Microsoft Office\Templates\Presentation Designs	\Temp\Designs	Y
Design Templ	highvolt.pot	64,512	\Program Files\Microsoft Office\Templates\Presentation Designs	\Temp\Designs	Y
Design Templ	Pulse.pot	50,688	\Program Files\Microsoft Office\Templates\Presentation Designs	\Temp\Designs	Y
Design Templ	Fans.pot	36,352	\Program Files\Microsoft Office\Templates\Presentation Designs	\Temp\Designs	Y
Design Templ	Whrlpool.pot	72,704	\Program Files\Microsoft Office\Templates\Presentation Designs	\Temp\Designs	Y
Design Templ	Ribbons.pot	54,272	\Program Files\Microsoft Office\Templates\Presentation Designs	\Temp\Designs	Y
Design Templ	Blush.pot	83,456	\Program Files\Microsoft Office\Templates\Presentation Designs	\Temp\Designs	Y
Design Templ	contport.pot	38,912	\Program Files\Microsoft Office\Templates\Presentation Designs	\Temp\Designs	Y
Design Templ	Notebook.pot	65,024	\Program Files\Microsoft Office\Templates\Presentation Designs	\Temp\Designs	Y
Design Templ	fireball.pot	31,232	\Program Files\Microsoft Office\Templates\Presentation Designs	\Temp\Designs	Y
Genigraphics Wizard	Pptgeni.hlp	86,684	\Program Files\Microsoft Office\Office	\office	
Genigraphics Wizard	Geniwiz.ppa	772,096	\Program Files\Microsoft Office\Office	\office	
Genigraphics Wizard	Geniwiz.dll	14,848	\Program Files\Microsoft Office\Office	\office	
Genigraphics Wizard	Graflink.exe	344,576	\Program Files\Microsoft Office\Office	\office	
Help (Program)	ppnew8.cnt	717	\Program Files\Microsoft Office\Office	\office	Y
Help (Program)	ppnew8.hlp	78,543	\Program Files\Microsoft Office\Office	\office	Y
Help (Program)	ppmain8.cnt	40,143	\Program Files\Microsoft Office\Office	\office	Y
Help (Program)	ppmain8.hlp	904,147	\Program Files\Microsoft Office\Office	\office	Y

Component	File Name	File Size	Where It Installs	Where It Is Located on the CD-ROM	Typical? *
Microsoft PowerPoint					
Help (Program)	ppmain8.aw	545,143	\Program Files\Microsoft Office\Office	\office	Y
Help (Program)	ppread8.txt	29,086	\Program Files\Microsoft Office\Office	\office	Y
Help (Program)	pptip8.hlp	190,548	\Program Files\Microsoft Office\Office	\office	Y
Help (Program)	oftip8.hlp	594,164	\Program Files\Microsoft Office\Office	\office	Y
Help (Program)	ofnew8.hlp	9,921	\Program Files\Microsoft Office\Office	\office	Y
Help (Program)	ofnew8.cnt	782	\Program Files\Microsoft Office\Office	\office	Y
Help (Program)	commtb32.hlp	6,885	\Windows\System	\office	Y
Help (Program)	hlp95en.dll	31,744	\Windows\System	\office	Y
Help (VBA)	veenlr3.hlp	1,052,485	\Program Files\Common Files\Microsoft Shared\VBA	\os\msapps\vba	
Help (VBA)	veena3.aw	209,406	\Program Files\Common Files\Microsoft Shared\VBA	\os\msapps\vba	
Help (VBA)	veenlr3.cnt	21,576	\Program Files\Common Files\Microsoft Shared\VBA	\os\msapps\vba	
Help (VBA)	veenui3.hlp	366,147	\Program Files\Common Files\Microsoft Shared\VBA	\os\msapps\vba	
Help (VBA)	veen3.aw	210,191	\Program Files\Common Files\Microsoft Shared\VBA	\os\msapps\vba	
Help (VBA)	veenui3.cnt	14,472	\Program Files\Common Files\Microsoft Shared\VBA	\os\msapps\vba	
Help (VBA)	veenob3.hlp	149,149	\Program Files\Common Files\Microsoft Shared\VBA	\os\msapps\vba	
Help (VBA)	veenob3.cnt	5,690	\Program Files\Common Files\Microsoft Shared\VBA	\os\msapps\vba	
Help (VBA)	veenmc3.hlp	24,734	\Program Files\Common Files\Microsoft Shared\VBA	\os\msapps\vba	
Help (VBA)	veencn3.hlp	119,327	\Program Files\Common Files\Microsoft Shared\VBA	\os\msapps\vba	
Help (VBA)	veencn3.cnt	3,581	\Program Files\Common Files\Microsoft Shared\VBA	\os\msapps\vba	
Help (VBA)	veenhw3.hlp	55,589	\Program Files\Common Files\Microsoft Shared\VBA	\os\msapps\vba	
Help (VBA)	veenhw3.cnt	2,390	\Program Files\Common Files\Microsoft Shared\VBA	\os\msapps\vba	
Help (VBA)	veendf3.hlp	76,366	\Program Files\Common Files\Microsoft Shared\VBA	\os\msapps\vba	Y
Help (VBA)	vbappt8.hlp	808,832	\Program Files\Microsoft Office\Office	\office	
Help (VBA)	vbappt8.cnt	34,357	\Program Files\Microsoft Office\Office	\office	
Help (VBA)	vbappt8.aw	225,053	\Program Files\Microsoft Office\Office	\office	
Help (VBA)	vbaoff8.hlp	320,282	\Program Files\Microsoft Office\Office	\office	
Help (VBA)	vbaoff8.aw	168,843	\Program Files\Microsoft Office\Office	\office	
Help (VBA)	vbaoff8.cnt	10,080	\Program Files\Microsoft Office\Office	\office	
Program File	Powerpnt.exe	3,492,112	\Program Files\Microsoft Office\Office	\office	Y
Program File	Pp7trans.dll	103,424	\Program Files\Microsoft Office\Office\xlators	\office\xlators	Y
Program File	Pp4x322.dll	585,728	\Program Files\Microsoft Office\Office\xlators	\office\xlators	Y

Component	File Name	File Size	Where It Installs	Where It Is Located on the CD-ROM	Typical? *
Microsoft PowerPoint					
Program File	Pp7x32.dll	175,104	\Program Files\Microsoft Office\Office\xlators	\office\xlators	Y
Program File	Pp7trans.dll	103,424	\Program Files\Microsoft Office\Office\xlators	\office\xlators	Y
Program File	Pptview.dll	1,657,216	\Program Files\Microsoft Office\Office\xlators	\office\xlators	Y
Program File	Ppttools.ppa	1,537,024	\Program Files\Microsoft Office\Office	\office	Y
Program File	packngo.dll	62,464	\Program Files\Microsoft Office\Office	\office	Y
Program File	pngsetup.exe	55,376	\Program Files\Microsoft Office\Office	\office	Y
Program File	Powerpnt.exe	3,492,112	\Program Files\Microsoft Office\Office	\office	Y
Program File	Msppt8.olb	164,352	\Program Files\Microsoft Office\Office	\office	Y
Program File	Ppintl.dll	440,832	\Program Files\Microsoft Office\Office	\office	Y
Program File	Pp8.srg	33,197	\Program Files\Microsoft Office\Office	\office	Y
Program File	Ppttools.dll	448,512	\Program Files\Microsoft Office\Office	\office	Y
Program File	Presconf.dll	54,272	\Program Files\Microsoft Office\Office	\office	Y
Program File	autoclip.dll	142,336	\Program Files\Microsoft Office\Office	\office	Y
Program File	wd95ppt.tlb	6,957	\Program Files\Microsoft Office\Office	\office	Y
Program File	ppcentrl.pps	485,888	\Program Files\Microsoft Office\Office	\office	Y
Program File	brochr_o.pot	74,240	\Program Files\Microsoft Office\Templates\Presentations	\Templ\Cont.	Y
Program File	brochr_s.pot	56,832	\Program Files\Microsoft Office\Templates\Presentations	\Templ\Cont.	Y
Program File	financ_o.pot	145,920	\Program Files\Microsoft Office\Templates\Presentations	\Templ\Cont.	Y
Program File	financ_s.pot	158,720	\Program Files\Microsoft Office\Templates\Presentations	\Templ\Cont.	Y
Program File	genric_o.pot	25,088	\Program Files\Microsoft Office\Templates\Presentations	\Templ\Cont.	Y
Program File	genric_s.pot	23,040	\Program Files\Microsoft Office\Templates\Presentations	\Templ\Cont.	Y
Program File	orgn_o.pot	89,600	\Program Files\Microsoft Office\Templates\Presentations	\Templ\Cont.	Y
Program File	orgn_s.pot	86,016	\Program Files\Microsoft Office\Templates\Presentations	\Templ\Cont.	Y
Program File	phome_o.pot	52,224	\Program Files\Microsoft Office\Templates\Presentations	\Templ\Cont.	Y
Program File	phome_s.pot	45,056	\Program Files\Microsoft Office\Templates\Presentations	\Templ\Cont.	Y
Program File	prjovr_o.pot	71,168	\Program Files\Microsoft Office\Templates\Presentations	\Templ\Cont.	Y
Program File	prjovr_s.pot	32,256	\Program Files\Microsoft Office\Templates\Presentations	\Templ\Cont.	Y
Program File	acwiz.pwz	225,792	\Program Files\Microsoft Office\Templates\Presentations	\Templ\Cont.	Y
Program File	ppcentrl.pps	485,888	\Program Files\Microsoft Office\Office	\office	Y
Program File	Profess.pot	60,928	\Program Files\Microsoft Office\Templates\Presentation Designs	\Templ\Designs	Y

App B

Component	File Name	File Size	Where It Installs	Where It Is Located on the CD-ROM	Typical? *
Microsoft PowerPoint					
Program File	Contemp.pot	20,992	\Program Files\Microsoft Office\Templates\Presentation Designs	\Templ\Designs	Y
Program File	msimrt16.dll	10,544	\Windows\System	\os\system	Y
Program File	msimrt32.dll	22,016	\Windows\System	\os\system	Y
Program File	msimusic.dll	120,320	\Windows\System	\os\system	Y
Program File	msimrt.dll	14,336	\Windows\System	\os\system	Y
Program File	Blank.pot	9,728	\Program Files\Microsoft Office\Templates	\Templ	Y
Program File	Pp8.srg	33,197	\Program Files\Microsoft Office\Office	\office	Y
Program File	acminsht.srg	5,273	\Program Files\Microsoft Office\Templates		Y
Program File	acminlng.srg	5,605	\Program Files\Microsoft Office\Templates	\Templ	Y
Program File	Ctl3d32.dll	27,136	\Windows\System		Y
Program File	Custom.dic	20	\Program Files\Microsoft Office\Office	\office	Y
Program File	vbaen32.olb	24,848	\Windows\System	\os\system	Y
Program File	scp32.dll	15,872	\Windows\System	\os\system	Y
Program File	msroute.dll	70,656	\Program Files\Microsoft Office\Office	\office	Y
Transl: Freelance 1-2.1/Win	Fl21win.pdi	324,096	\Program Files\Microsoft Office\Office\Xlators	\office\xlators	
Transl: Freelance 4.0/DOS	Fl40dos.pdi	234,496	\Program Files\Microsoft Office\Office\Xlators	\office\xlators	
Transl: Harvard 2.3/DOS	Hg23dos.pdi	246,272	\Program Files\Microsoft Office\Office\Xlators	\office\xlators	
Transl: Harvard 3.0/DOS	Hg30dos.pdi	302,592	\Program Files\Microsoft Office\Office\Xlators	\office\xlators	
Text Converters					
Text Conv. Wd./ Mac 4.0-5.1	macwrd32.cnv	181,248	\Program Files\Common Files\Microsoft Shared\Textconv	\os\msapps\textconv	
Text Conv. Wd./ Mac 4.0-5.1	Rtf_mw5.txt	2,212	\Program Files\Common Files\Microsoft Shared\Textconv	\os\msapps\textconv	
Text Conv. Wd./ Mac 4.0-5.1	msconv97.dll	125,440	\Program Files\Common Files\Microsoft Shared\Textconv	\os\msapps\textconv	Y
Excel	excel32.cnv	136,192	\Program Files\Common Files\Microsoft Shared\Textconv	\os\msapps\textconv	Y
Excel	msconv97.dll	125,440	\Program Files\Common Files\Microsoft Shared\Textconv	\os\msapps\textconv	Y
HTML	html32.cnv	377,344	\Program Files\Common Files\Microsoft Shared\Textconv	\os\msapps\textconv	Y
HTML	gifimp32.flt	130,560	\Program Files\Common Files\Microsoft Shared\Grphflt	\os\msapps\grphflt	Y

Component	File Name	File Size	Where It Installs	Where It Is Located on the CD-ROM	Typical? *
Text Converters					
HTML	Ms.gif	1,069	\Program Files\Common Files\Microsoft Shared\Grphflt	\os\msapps\grphflt	Y
HTML	png32.flt	222,720	\Program Files\Common Files\Microsoft Shared\Grphflt	\os\msapps\grphflt	Y
HTML	ms.png	1,682	\Program Files\Common Files\Microsoft Shared\Grphflt	\os\msapps\grphflt	Y
HTML	msencode.dll	94,208	\Windows\System	\os\msapps\textconv	Y
HTML	msconv97.dll	125,440	\Program Files\Common Files\Microsoft Shared\Textconv	\os\msapps\textconv	Y
Lotus 1-2-3	Lotus32.cnv	109,568	\Program Files\Common Files\Microsoft Shared\Textconv	\os\msapps\textconv	
Lotus Notes	mscthunk.dll	10,240	\Program Files\Common Files\Microsoft Shared\Textconv		Y
Lotus Notes	nims32.dll	26,112	\Program Files\Common Files\Microsoft Shared\Textconv		Y
Lotus Notes	excel32.cnv	136,192	\Program Files\Common Files\Microsoft Shared\Textconv	\os\msapps\textconv	Y
Lotus Notes	msconv97.dll	125,440	\Program Files\Common Files\Microsoft Shared\Textconv	\os\msapps\textconv	Y
Lotus Notes	mswrd632.cnv	135,680	\Program Files\Common Files\Microsoft Shared\Textconv	\os\msapps\textconv	Y
Recover Text	recovr32.cnv	38,912	\Program Files\Common Files\Microsoft Shared\Textconv	\os\msapps\textconv	Y
Recover Text	msconv97.dll	125,440	\Program Files\Common Files\Microsoft Shared\Textconv	\os\msapps\textconv	Y
Wd 6/95	mswrd632.cnv	135,680	\Program Files\Common Files\Microsoft Shared\Textconv	\os\msapps\textconv	Y
Wd 6/95	msconv97.dll	125,440	\Program Files\Common Files\Microsoft Shared\Textconv	\os\msapps\textconv	Y
Wd 6/95 Export	wrd6ex32.cnv	19,456	\Program Files\Common Files\Microsoft Shared\Textconv	\os\msapps\textconv	Y
Wd 97/98 Wn/Mc	mswrd832.cnv	259,072	\Program Files\Common Files\Microsoft Shared\Textconv	\os\msapps\textconv	Y
Wd 97/98 Wn/Mc	Emfimp32.flt	340,480	\Program Files\Common Files\Microsoft Shared\Grphflt	\os\msapps\grphflt	Y
Wd 97/98 Wn/Mc	ms.emf	2,396	\Program Files\Common Files\Microsoft Shared\Grphflt	\os\msapps\grphflt	Y
Wd 97/98 Wn/Mc	jpegim32.flt	171,520	\Program Files\Common Files\Microsoft Shared\Grphflt	\os\msapps\grphflt	Y
Wd 97/98 Wn/Mc	ms.jpg	1,061	\Program Files\Common Files\Microsoft Shared\Grphflt	\os\msapps\grphflt	Y
Wd 97/98 Wn/Mc	png32.flt	222,720	\Program Files\Common Files\Microsoft Shared\Grphflt	\os\msapps\grphflt	Y
Wd 97/98 Wn/Mc	ms.png	1,682	\Program Files\Common Files\Microsoft Shared\Grphflt	\os\msapps\grphflt	Y
Wd 97/98 Wn/Mc	msconv97.dll	125,440	\Program Files\Common Files\Microsoft Shared\Textconv	\os\msapps\textconv	Y
Wd for Win 2.0	Wnwrd232.cnv	183,808	\Program Files\Common Files\Microsoft Shared\Textconv	\os\msapps\textconv	
Works/Win 3.0	works332.cnv	118,272	\Program Files\Common Files\Microsoft Shared\Textconv	\os\msapps\textconv	
Works/Win 4.0	works432.cnv	260,096	\Program Files\Common Files\Microsoft Shared\Textconv	\os\msapps\textconv	
WP 5.x	Wpequ532.dll	108,544	\Program Files\Common Files\Microsoft Shared\Textconv	\os\msapps\textconv	Y
WP 5.x	Wpgimp32.flt	149,504	\Program Files\Common Files\Microsoft Shared\Grphflt	\os\msapps\grphflt	Y
WP 5.x	ms.wpg	1,382	\Program Files\Common Files\Microsoft Shared\Grphflt	\os\msapps\grphflt	Y
WP 5.x	Wpgexp32.flt	68,608	\Program Files\Common Files\Microsoft Shared\Grphflt	\os\msapps\grphflt	Y

Component	File Name	File Size	Where It Installs	Where It Is Located on the CD-ROM	Typical? *
Text Converters					
WP 5.x	Wpft532.cnv	340,480	\Program Files\Common Files\Microsoft Shared\Textconv	\os\msapps\textconv	Y
WP 5.x	Wpequ532.dll	108,544	\Program Files\Common Files\Microsoft Shared\Textconv	\os\msapps\textconv	Y
WP 5.x	rtf_wp5.txt	5,528	\Program Files\Common Files\Microsoft Shared\Textconv	\os\msapps\textconv	Y
WP 5.x	msconv97.dll	125,440	\Program Files\Common Files\Microsoft Shared\Textconv	\os\msapps\textconv	Y
WP 6.x	Wpequ532.dll	108,544	\Program Files\Common Files\Microsoft Shared\Textconv	\os\msapps\textconv	Y
WP 6.x	Wpgimp32.flt	149,504	\Program Files\Common Files\Microsoft Shared\Grphflt	\os\msapps\grphflt	Y
WP 6.x	ms.wpg	1,382	\Program Files\Common Files\Microsoft Shared\Grphflt	\os\msapps\grphflt	Y
WP 6.x	Wpgexp32.flt	68,608	\Program Files\Common Files\Microsoft Shared\Grphflt	\os\msapps\grphflt	Y
WP 6.x	wpft632.cnv	252,928	\Program Files\Common Files\Microsoft Shared\Textconv	\os\msapps\textconv	Y
WP 6.x	msconv97.dll	125,440	\Program Files\Common Files\Microsoft Shared\Textconv	\os\msapps\textconv	Y
Web Page Authoring					
Web Page Auth. (HTML)	html.xla	582,144	\Program Files\Microsoft Office\Office\Library	\office\library	Y
Web Page Auth. (HTML)	xlhtml.dll	29,696	\Program Files\Microsoft Office\Office	\office	Y
Web Page Auth. (HTML)	webform.xla	564,736	\Program Files\Microsoft Office\Office\Library	\office\library	Y
Web Page Auth. (HTML)	ppt2html.srg	2,359	\Program Files\Microsoft Office\Office	\office	Y
Web Page Auth. (HTML)	text.tpl	1,085	\Program Files\Microsoft Office\Office	\office	Y
Web Page Auth. (HTML)	outline.tpl	555	\Program Files\Microsoft Office\Office	\office	Y
Web Page Auth. (HTML)	image.tpl	621	\Program Files\Microsoft Office\Office	\office	Y
Web Page Auth. (HTML)	standard.tpl	769	\Program Files\Microsoft Office\Office	\office	Y
Web Page Auth. (HTML)	Ppt2html.dll	439,808	\Program Files\Microsoft Office\Office	\office	Y
Web Page Auth. (HTML)	note.tpl	705	\Program Files\Microsoft Office\Office	\office	Y
Web Page Auth. (HTML)	index.tpl	1,199	\Program Files\Microsoft Office\Office	\office	Y
Web Page Auth. (HTML)	frame.tpl	4,742	\Program Files\Microsoft Office\Office	\office	Y

Component	File Name	File Size	Where It Installs	Where It Is Located on the CD-ROM	Typical? *
Web Page Authoring					
Web Page Auth. (HTML)	Ppt2html.ppa	401,920	\Program Files\Microsoft Office\Office	\office	Y
Web Page Auth. (HTML)	ppt2html.srg	2,359	\Program Files\Microsoft Office\Office	\office	Y
Web Page Auth. (HTML)	jpegim32.flt	171,520	\Program Files\Common Files\Microsoft Shared\Grphflt	\os\msapps\grphflt	Y
Web Page Auth. (HTML)	ms.jpg	1,061	\Program Files\Common Files\Microsoft Shared\Grphflt	\os\msapps\grphflt	Y
Web Page Auth. (HTML)	gifimp32.flt	130,560	\Program Files\Common Files\Microsoft Shared\Grphflt	\os\msapps\grphflt	Y
Web Page Auth. (HTML)	Ms.gif	1,069	\Program Files\Common Files\Microsoft Shared\Grphflt	\os\msapps\grphflt	Y
Web Page Auth. (HTML)	png32.flt	222,720	\Program Files\Common Files\Microsoft Shared\Grphflt	\os\msapps\grphflt	Y
Web Page Auth. (HTML)	ms.png	1,682	\Program Files\Common Files\Microsoft Shared\Grphflt	\os\msapps\grphflt	Y
Web Page Auth. (HTML)	html32.cnv	377,344	\Program Files\Common Files\Microsoft Shared\Textconv	\os\msapps\textconv	Y
Web Page Auth. (HTML)	msencode.dll	94,208	\Windows\System	\os\msapps\textconv	Y
Web Page Auth. (HTML)	msconv97.dll	125,440	\Program Files\Common Files\Microsoft Shared\Textconv	\os\msapps\textconv	Y
Web Page Auth. (HTML)	communty.dot	26,112	\Program Files\Microsoft Office\Office\Web Page Templates\Styles	\office\webtmpl\styles	Y
Web Page Auth. (HTML)	contmpry.dot	24,576	\Program Files\Microsoft Office\Office\Web Page Templates\Styles	\office\webtmpl\styles	Y
Web Page Auth. (HTML)	Elegant.dot	24,576	\Program Files\Microsoft Office\Office\Web Page Templates\Styles	\office\webtmpl\styles	Y
Web Page Auth. (HTML)	festive.dot	27,648	\Program Files\Microsoft Office\Office\Web Page Templates\Styles	\office\webtmpl\styles	Y
Web Page Auth. (HTML)	harvest.dot	28,672	\Program Files\Microsoft Office\Office\Web Page Templates\Styles	\office\webtmpl\styles	Y
Web Page Auth. (HTML)	jazzy.dot	25,088	\Program Files\Microsoft Office\Office\Web Page Templates\Styles	\office\webtmpl\styles	Y
Web Page Auth. (HTML)	outdoors.dot	27,648	\Program Files\Microsoft Office\Office\Web Page Templates\Styles	\office\webtmpl\styles	Y
Web Page Auth. (HTML)	profesnl.dot	27,136	\Program Files\Microsoft Office\Office\Web Page Templates\Styles	\office\webtmpl\styles	Y

Component	File Name	File Size	Where It Installs	Where It Is Located on the CD-ROM	Typical? *
Web Page Authoring					
Web Page Auth. (HTML)	register.doc	63,488	\Program Files\Microsoft Office\Office\Web Page Templates\Content	\office\webtmpl\Cont.	Y
Web Page Auth. (HTML)	survey.doc	51,200	\Program Files\Microsoft Office\Office\Web Page Templates\Content	\office\webtmpl\Cont.	Y
Web Page Auth. (HTML)	feedback.doc	49,152	\Program Files\Microsoft Office\Office\Web Page Templates\Content	\office\webtmpl\Cont.	Y
Web Page Auth. (HTML)	simple.doc	22,016	\Program Files\Microsoft Office\Office\Web Page Templates\Content	\office\webtmpl\Cont.	Y
Web Page Auth. (HTML)	personal.doc	29,184	\Program Files\Microsoft Office\Office\Web Page Templates\Content	\office\webtmpl\Cont.	Y
Web Page Auth. (HTML)	centered.doc	22,016	\Program Files\Microsoft Office\Office\Web Page Templates\Content	\office\webtmpl\Cont.	Y
Web Page Auth. (HTML)	2column.doc	26,624	\Program Files\Microsoft Office\Office\Web Page Templates\Content	\office\webtmpl\Cont.	Y
Web Page Auth. (HTML)	3column.doc	22,528	\Program Files\Microsoft Office\Office\Web Page Templates\Content	\office\webtmpl\Cont.	Y
Web Page Auth. (HTML)	calendar.doc	22,016	\Program Files\Microsoft Office\Office\Web Page Templates\Content	\office\webtmpl\Cont.	Y
Web Page Auth. (HTML)	toc.doc	22,016	\Program Files\Microsoft Office\Office\Web Page Templates\Content	\office\webtmpl\Cont.	Y
Web Page Auth. (HTML)	commbkgd.gif	26,810	\Program Files\Microsoft Office\Office\Web Page Templates\Styles	\office\webtmpl\styles	Y
Web Page Auth. (HTML)	contbkgd.gif	7,160	\Program Files\Microsoft Office\Office\Web Page Templates\Styles	\office\webtmpl\styles	Y
Web Page Auth. (HTML)	elegbkgd.gif	5,166	\Program Files\Microsoft Office\Office\Web Page Templates\Styles	\office\webtmpl\styles	Y
Web Page Auth. (HTML)	festbkgd.gif	3,572	\Program Files\Microsoft Office\Office\Web Page Templates\Styles	\office\webtmpl\styles	Y
Web Page Auth. (HTML)	harvbkgd.gif	962	\Program Files\Microsoft Office\Office\Web Page Templates\Styles	\office\webtmpl\styles	Y
Web Page Auth. (HTML)	jazzbkgd.gif	4,127	\Program Files\Microsoft Office\Office\Web Page Templates\Styles	\office\webtmpl\styles	Y
Web Page Auth. (HTML)	outdbkgd.gif	10,362	\Program Files\Microsoft Office\Office\Web Page Templates\Styles	\office\webtmpl\styles	Y
Web Page Auth. (HTML)	profbkgd.gif	23,498	\Program Files\Microsoft Office\Office\Web Page Templates\Styles	\office\webtmpl\styles	Y
Web Page Auth. (HTML)	commbull.gif	285	\Program Files\Microsoft Office\Clipart\Bullets	\Clipart\Bullets	Y

Component	File Name	File Size	Where It Installs	Where It Is Located on the CD-ROM	Typical? *
Web Page Authoring					
Web Page Auth. (HTML)	contbull.gif	591	\Program Files\Microsoft Office\Clipart\Bullets	\Clipart\Bullets	Y
Web Page Auth. (HTML)	elegbull.gif	591	\Program Files\Microsoft Office\Clipart\Bullets	\Clipart\Bullets	Y
Web Page Auth. (HTML)	festbull.gif	983	\Program Files\Microsoft Office\Clipart\Bullets	\Clipart\Bullets	Y
Web Page Auth. (HTML)	harvbull.gif	257	\Program Files\Microsoft Office\Clipart\Bullets	\Clipart\Bullets	Y
Web Page Auth. (HTML)	jazzbull.gif	275	\Program Files\Microsoft Office\Clipart\Bullets	\Clipart\Bullets	Y
Web Page Auth. (HTML)	outdbull.gif	1,120	\Program Files\Microsoft Office\Clipart\Bullets	\Clipart\Bullets	Y
Web Page Auth. (HTML)	profbull.gif	971	\Program Files\Microsoft Office\Clipart\Bullets	\Clipart\Bullets	Y
Web Page Auth. (HTML)	commline.gif	2,820	\Program Files\Microsoft Office\Clipart\Lines	\Clipart\Lines	Y
Web Page Auth. (HTML)	contline.gif	1,558	\Program Files\Microsoft Office\Clipart\Lines	\Clipart\Lines	Y
Web Page Auth. (HTML)	elegline.gif	808	\Program Files\Microsoft Office\Clipart\Lines	\Clipart\Lines	Y
Web Page Auth. (HTML)	festline.gif	3,357	\Program Files\Microsoft Office\Clipart\Lines	\Clipart\Lines	Y
Web Page Auth. (HTML)	harvline.gif	6,677	\Program Files\Microsoft Office\Clipart\Lines	\Clipart\Lines	Y
Web Page Auth. (HTML)	jazzline.gif	1,692	\Program Files\Microsoft Office\Clipart\Lines	\Clipart\Lines	Y
Web Page Auth. (HTML)	outdline.gif	8,081	\Program Files\Microsoft Office\Clipart\Lines	\Clipart\Lines	Y
Web Page Auth. (HTML)	profline.gif	2,795	\Program Files\Microsoft Office\Clipart\Lines	\Clipart\Lines	Y
Web Page Auth. (HTML)	moreweb.dot	88,064	\Program Files\Microsoft Office\Templates\Web Pages	\Templ\Webpages	Y
Web Page Auth. (HTML)	webpage.wiz	37,888	\Program Files\Microsoft Office\Templates\Web Pages	\Templ\Webpages	Y
Web Page Auth. (HTML)	html.wll	563,200	\Program Files\Microsoft Office\Office\HTML	\office\html	Y
Web Page Auth. (HTML)	htmlview.dot	36,352	\Program Files\Microsoft Office\Office\HTML	\office\html	Y

Component	File Name	File Size	Where It Installs	Where It Is Located on the CD-ROM	Typical? *
Web Page Authoring					
Web Page Auth. (HTML)	htmlmarq.ocx	82,944	\Program Files\Microsoft Office\Office\HTML	\office\html	Y
Web Page Auth. (HTML)	htmlmm.ocx	91,648	\Program Files\Microsoft Office\Office\HTML	\office\html	Y
Web Page Auth. (HTML)	wdhtml8.cnt	4,018	\Program Files\Microsoft Office\Office\HTML	\office\html	Y
Web Page Auth. (HTML)	wdhtml8.hlp	97,390	\Program Files\Microsoft Office\Office\HTML	\office\html	Y
Web Page Auth. (HTML)	wdhtml8.aw	156,697	\Program Files\Microsoft Office\Office\HTML	\office\html	Y
Web Page Auth. (HTML)	html32.cnv	377,344	\Program Files\Common Files\Microsoft Shared\Textconv	\os\msapps\textconv	Y
Web Page Auth. (HTML)	gifimp32.flt	130,560	\Program Files\Common Files\Microsoft Shared\Grphflt	\os\msapps\grphflt	Y
Web Page Auth. (HTML)	Ms.gif	1,069	\Program Files\Common Files\Microsoft Shared\Grphflt	\os\msapps\grphflt	Y
Web Page Auth. (HTML)	png32.flt	222,720	\Program Files\Common Files\Microsoft Shared\Grphflt	\os\msapps\grphflt	Y
Web Page Auth. (HTML)	ms.png	1,682	\Program Files\Common Files\Microsoft Shared\Grphflt	\os\msapps\grphflt	Y
Web Page Auth. (HTML)	msencode.dll	94,208	\Windows\System	\os\msapps\textconv	Y
Web Page Auth. (HTML)	msconv97.dll	125,440	\Program Files\Common Files\Microsoft Shared\Textconv	\os\msapps\textconv	Y
Web Page Auth. (HTML)	bullet1.gif	122	\Program Files\Microsoft Office\Office\HTML\Dialogs	\office\html\dialogs	Y
Web Page Auth. (HTML)	bullet2.gif	150	\Program Files\Microsoft Office\Office\HTML\Dialogs	\office\html\dialogs	Y
Web Page Auth. (HTML)	bullet3.gif	148	\Program Files\Microsoft Office\Office\HTML\Dialogs	\office\html\dialogs	Y
Web Page Auth. (HTML)	bullet4.gif	880	\Program Files\Microsoft Office\Office\HTML\Dialogs	\office\html\dialogs	Y
Web Page Auth. (HTML)	bullet5.gif	101	\Program Files\Microsoft Office\Office\HTML\Dialogs	\office\html\dialogs	Y
Web Page Auth. (HTML)	bullet6.gif	79	\Program Files\Microsoft Office\Office\HTML\Dialogs	\office\html\dialogs	Y
Web Page Auth. (HTML)	bullet7.gif	140	\Program Files\Microsoft Office\Office\HTML\Dialogs	\office\html\dialogs	Y

Component	File Name	File Size	Where It Installs	Where It Is Located on the CD-ROM	Typical? *
Web Page Authoring					
Web Page Auth. (HTML)	bullet8.gif	204	\Program Files\Microsoft Office\Office\HTML\Dialogs	\office\html\dialogs	Y
Web Page Auth. (HTML)	line1.gif	286	\Program Files\Microsoft Office\Office\HTML\Dialogs	\office\html\dialogs	Y
Web Page Auth. (HTML)	Line2.gif	403	\Program Files\Microsoft Office\Office\HTML\Dialogs	\office\html\dialogs	Y
Web Page Auth. (HTML)	Line3.gif	1,636	\Program Files\Microsoft Office\Office\HTML\Dialogs	\office\html\dialogs	Y
Web Page Auth. (HTML)	line4.gif	2,501	\Program Files\Microsoft Office\Office\HTML\Dialogs	\office\html\dialogs	Y
Web Page Auth. (HTML)	line5.gif	1,235	\Program Files\Microsoft Office\Office\HTML\Dialogs	\office\html\dialogs	Y
Web Page Auth. (HTML)	line6.gif	917	\Program Files\Microsoft Office\Office\HTML\Dialogs	\office\html\dialogs	Y
Web Page Auth. (HTML)	line7.gif	917	\Program Files\Microsoft Office\Office\HTML\Dialogs	\office\html\dialogs	Y
Web Page Auth. (HTML)	line8.gif	1,504	\Program Files\Microsoft Office\Office\HTML\Dialogs	\office\html\dialogs	Y
Web Page Auth. (HTML)	line9.gif	1,785	\Program Files\Microsoft Office\Office\HTML\Dialogs	\office\html\dialogs	Y
Web Page Auth. (HTML)	html.dot	94,720	\Program Files\Microsoft Office\Office	\office	Y
Web Page Auth. (HTML)	MFC40.dll	921,872	\Windows\System	\os\system	Y
Microsoft Word					
Address Book	Schdmapi.dll	187,392	\Program Files\Microsoft Office\Office	\office	Y
Address Book	wwpab.cnv	40,960	\Program Files\Microsoft Office\Office	\office	Y
Help (Program)	wdmain8.hlp	1,968,249	\Program Files\Microsoft Office\Office	\office	Y
Help (Program)	wdmain8.cnt	81,391	\Program Files\Microsoft Office\Office	\office	Y
Help (Program)	wdtip8.hlp	404,638	\Program Files\Microsoft Office\Office	\office	Y
Help (Program)	wdmain8.aw	691,757	\Program Files\Microsoft Office\Office	\office	Y
Help (Program)	wdnew8.hlp	74,713	\Program Files\Microsoft Office\Office	\office	Y
Help (Program)	wdnew8.cnt	1,713	\Program Files\Microsoft Office\Office	\office	Y
Help (VBA)	veenlr3.hlp	1,052,485	\Program Files\Common Files\Microsoft Shared\VBA	\os\msapps\vba	
Help (VBA)	veena3.aw	209,406	\Program Files\Common Files\Microsoft Shared\VBA	\os\msapps\vba	

App B

Component	File Name	File Size	Where It Installs	Where It Is Located on the CD-ROM	Typical? *
Microsoft Word					
Help (VBA)	veenlr3.cnt	21,576	\Program Files\Common Files\Microsoft Shared\VBA	\os\msapps\vba	
Help (VBA)	veenui3.hlp	366,147	\Program Files\Common Files\Microsoft Shared\VBA	\os\msapps\vba	
Help (VBA)	veen3.aw	210,191	\Program Files\Common Files\Microsoft Shared\VBA	\os\msapps\vba	
Help (VBA)	veenui3.cnt	14,472	\Program Files\Common Files\Microsoft Shared\VBA	\os\msapps\vba	
Help (VBA)	veenob3.hlp	149,149	\Program Files\Common Files\Microsoft Shared\VBA	\os\msapps\vba	
Help (VBA)	veenob3.cnt	5,690	\Program Files\Common Files\Microsoft Shared\VBA	\os\msapps\vba	
Help (VBA)	veenmc3.hlp	24,734	\Program Files\Common Files\Microsoft Shared\VBA	\os\msapps\vba	
Help (VBA)	veencn3.hlp	119,327	\Program Files\Common Files\Microsoft Shared\VBA	\os\msapps\vba	
Help (VBA)	veencn3.cnt	3,581	\Program Files\Common Files\Microsoft Shared\VBA	\os\msapps\vba	
Help (VBA)	veenhw3.hlp	55,589	\Program Files\Common Files\Microsoft Shared\VBA	\os\msapps\vba	
Help (VBA)	veenhw3.cnt	2,390	\Program Files\Common Files\Microsoft Shared\VBA	\os\msapps\vba	
Help (VBA)	veendf3.hlp	76,366	\Program Files\Common Files\Microsoft Shared\VBA	\os\msapps\vba	Y
Help (VBA)	vbaoff8.hlp	320,282	\Program Files\Microsoft Office\Office	\office	
Help (VBA)	vbaoff8.aw	168,843	\Program Files\Microsoft Office\Office	\office	
Help (VBA)	vbaoff8.cnt	10,080	\Program Files\Microsoft Office\Office	\office	
Help (VBA)	vbawrd8.hlp	2,519,191	\Program Files\Microsoft Office\Office	\office	
Help (VBA)	vbawrd8.cnt	94,994	\Program Files\Microsoft Office\Office	\office	
Help (VBA)	vbawrd8.aw	508,710	\Program Files\Microsoft Office\Office	\office	
Help (WordPerfect)	wdwph8.hlp	165,735	\Program Files\Microsoft Office\Office	\office	
Program File	winword.exe	5,317,904	\Program Files\Microsoft Office\Office	\office	Y
Program File	MSWord8.olb	459,776	\Program Files\Microsoft Office\Office	\office	Y
Program File	winword8.srg	26,907	\Program Files\Microsoft Office\Office	\office	Y
Program File	winword8.doc	10,752	\Windows\ShellNew	\os\shellnew	Y
Program File	MSART14.BDR	51,388	\Program Files\Microsoft Office\Office\Borders	\office\borders	Y
Program File	Msart15.bdr	27,412	\Program Files\Microsoft Office\Office\Borders	\office\borders	Y
Program File	Msart3.bdr	57,646	\Program Files\Microsoft Office\Office\Borders	\office\borders	Y
Program File	Msart4.bdr	14,594	\Program Files\Microsoft Office\Office\Borders	\office\borders	Y
Program File	Msart2.bdr	47,188	\Program Files\Microsoft Office\Office\Borders	\office\borders	Y
Program File	Msart5.bdr	15,788	\Program Files\Microsoft Office\Office\Borders	\office\borders	Y
Program File	Msart6.bdr	55,222	\Program Files\Microsoft Office\Office\Borders	\office\borders	Y
Program File	Msart7.bdr	3,876	\Program Files\Microsoft Office\Office\Borders	\office\borders	Y

Component	File Name	File Size	Where It Installs	Where It Is Located on the CD-ROM	Typical? *
Microsoft Word					
Program File	Msart8.bdr	49,098	\Program Files\Microsoft Office\Office\Borders	\office\borders	Y
Program File	Msart9.bdr	50,838	\Program Files\Microsoft Office\Office\Borders	\office\borders	Y
Program File	Msart10.bdr	9,292	\Program Files\Microsoft Office\Office\Borders	\office\borders	Y
Program File	Msart1.bdr	32,246	\Program Files\Microsoft Office\Office\Borders	\office\borders	Y
Program File	Msart11.bdr	30,920	\Program Files\Microsoft Office\Office\Borders	\office\borders	Y
Program File	Msart12.bdr	58,756	\Program Files\Microsoft Office\Office\Borders	\office\borders	Y
Program File	Msart13.bdr	28,368	\Program Files\Microsoft Office\Office\Borders	\office\borders	Y
Program File	wwintl32.dll	1,157,904	\Program Files\Microsoft Office\Office	\office	Y
Program File	wdread8.txt	29,613	\Program Files\Microsoft Office\Office	\office	Y
Program File	commtb32.dll	57,344	\Windows\System	\os\system	Y
Program File	Email.dot	49,152	\Program Files\Microsoft Office\Office	\office	Y
Program File	hightech.dot	49,152	\Program Files\Microsoft Office\Office	\office	Y
Program File	flame.dot	49,664	\Program Files\Microsoft Office\Office	\office	Y
Program File	urgent.dot	47,616	\Program Files\Microsoft Office\Office	\office	Y
Program File	ocean.dot	48,128	\Program Files\Microsoft Office\Office	\office	Y
Program File	rain.dot	53,760	\Program Files\Microsoft Office\Office	\office	Y
Program File	midnight.dot	50,688	\Program Files\Microsoft Office\Office	\office	Y
Program File	Email.oft	12,288	\Program Files\Microsoft Office\Templates\Outlook	\Templ\Outlook	Y
Program File	hightech.oft	12,288	\Program Files\Microsoft Office\Templates\Outlook	\Templ\Outlook	Y
Program File	flame.oft	12,288	\Program Files\Microsoft Office\Templates\Outlook	\Templ\Outlook	Y
Program File	urgent.oft	12,288	\Program Files\Microsoft Office\Templates\Outlook	\Templ\Outlook	Y
Program File	ocean.oft	14,848	\Program Files\Microsoft Office\Templates\Outlook	\Templ\Outlook	Y
Program File	rain.oft	12,288	\Program Files\Microsoft Office\Templates\Outlook	\Templ\Outlook	Y
Program File	midnight.oft	12,288	\Program Files\Microsoft Office\Templates\Outlook	\Templ\Outlook	Y
Proof Tools: Grammar	msgr_en.lex	1,672,698	\Program Files\Common Files\Microsoft Shared\Proof	\os\msapps\proof	Y
Proof Tools: Grammar	msgren32.dll	1,531,152	\Program Files\Common Files\Microsoft Shared\Proof	\os\msapps\proof	Y
Proof Tools: Hyphenation	mshy32.dll	29,696	\Program Files\Common Files\Microsoft Shared\Proof	\os\msapps\proof	Y
Proof Tools: Hyphenation	mshy_en.lex	134,144	\Program Files\Common Files\Microsoft Shared\Proof	\os\msapps\proof	Y

App B

Component	File Name	File Size	Where It Installs	Where It Is Located on the CD-ROM	Typical? *
Microsoft Word					
Proof Tools: Thesaurus	Msth_am.lex	669,695	\Program Files\Common Files\Microsoft Shared\Proof	\os\msapps\proof	Y
Proof Tools: Thesaurus	Msth_br.lex	354,113	\Program Files\Common Files\Microsoft Shared\Proof	\os\msapps\proof	Y
Proof Tools: Thesaurus	Msth32.dll	19,456	\Program Files\Common Files\Microsoft Shared\Proof	\os\msapps\proof	Y
Text Conv: Text w/Layout	Txtlyt32.cnv	189,440	\Program Files\Common Files\Microsoft Shared\Textconv	\os\msapps\textconv	
Wizard/Templ: Faxes	contfax.dot	61,952	\Program Files\Microsoft Office\Templates\Letters & Faxes	\Templ\Letters	Y
Wizard/Templ: Faxes	elegfax.dot	48,640	\Program Files\Microsoft Office\Templates\Letters & Faxes	\Templ\Letters	Y
Wizard/Templ: Faxes	proffax.dot	49,152	\Program Files\Microsoft Office\Templates\Letters & Faxes	\Templ\Letters	Y
Wizard/Templ: Faxes	Fax.wiz	477,184	\Program Files\Microsoft Office\Templates\Letters & Faxes	\Templ\Letters	Y
Wizard/Templ: Letters	contltr.dot	53,248	\Program Files\Microsoft Office\Templates\Letters & Faxes	\Templ\Letters	Y
Wizard/Templ: Letters	elegltr.dot	47,104	\Program Files\Microsoft Office\Templates\Letters & Faxes	\Templ\Letters	Y
Wizard/Templ: Letters	profltr.dot	47,104	\Program Files\Microsoft Office\Templates\Letters & Faxes	\Templ\Letters	Y
Wizard/Templ: Letters	letter.wiz	63,488	\Program Files\Microsoft Office\Templates\Letters & Faxes	\Templ\Letters	Y
Wizard/Templ: Letters	label.wiz	54,784	\Program Files\Microsoft Office\Templates\Letters & Faxes	\Templ\Letters	Y
Wizard/Templ: Letters	envelope.wiz	49,152	\Program Files\Microsoft Office\Templates\Letters & Faxes	\Templ\Letters	Y
Wizard/Templ: Macros	Convert8.dll	22,528	\Program Files\Microsoft Office\Office	\office	
Wizard/Templ: Macros	Convert8.wiz	240,128	\Program Files\Microsoft Office\Office\Macros	\office\macros	
Wizard/Templ: Macros	Support8.dot	177,152	\Program Files\Microsoft Office\Office\Macros	\office\macros	
Wizard/Templ: Macros	Macros8.dot	585,216	\Program Files\Microsoft Office\Office\Macros	\office\macros	
Wizard/Templ: Memos	contmemo.dot	47,616	\Program Files\Microsoft Office\Templates\Memos	\Templ\Memos	Y
Wizard/Templ: Memos	elegmemo.dot	41,984	\Program Files\Microsoft Office\Templates\Memos	\Templ\Memos	Y

Component	File Name	File Size	Where It Installs	Where It Is Located on the CD-ROM	Typical? *
Microsoft Word					
Wizard/Templ: Memos	profmemo.dot	41,984	\Program Files\Microsoft Office\Templates\Memos	\Templ\Memos	Y
Wizard/Templ: Memos	Memo.wiz	415,744	\Program Files\Microsoft Office\Templates\Memos	\Templ\Memos	Y
Wizard/Templ: Newsletter Wizard	Newslttr.wiz	424,448	\Program Files\Microsoft Office\Templates\Publications	\Templ\Pub	
Wizard/Templ: Pleading Wizard	Pleading.wiz	680,960	\Program Files\Microsoft Office\Templates\Legal Pleadings	\Templ\Legal	
Wizard/Templ: Reports	contrepo.dot	89,600	\Program Files\Microsoft Office\Templates\Reports	\Templ\Reports	
Wizard/Templ: Reports	elegrepo.dot	57,856	\Program Files\Microsoft Office\Templates\Reports	\Templ\Reports	
Wizard/Templ: Reports	profrepo.dot	60,416	\Program Files\Microsoft Office\Templates\Reports	\Templ\Reports	
Wizard/Templ: Resumes	Resume.wiz	428,544	\Program Files\Microsoft Office\Templates\Other Documents	\Templ\Other	Y
Wizard/Templ: Resumes	contresu.dot	53,248	\Program Files\Microsoft Office\Templates\Other Documents	\Templ\Other	Y
Wizard/Templ: Resumes	elegresu.dot	54,784	\Program Files\Microsoft Office\Templates\Other Documents	\Templ\Other	Y
Wizard/Templ: Resumes	profresu.dot	44,544	\Program Files\Microsoft Office\Templates\Other Documents	\Templ\Other	Y
WordMail/ Exchange	mfcans32.dll	149,504	\Windows\System		Y
WordMail/ Exchange	Wordmail.dll	420,272	\Program Files\Microsoft Office\Office\WordMail		Y
WordMail/ Exchange	wordmail.reg	2,286	\Program Files\Microsoft Office\Office\WordMail		Y
WordMail/ Exchange	Wordfls.ico	766	\Program Files\Microsoft Office\Office\WordMail		Y
WordMail/ Exchange	Wordfll.ico	766	\Program Files\Microsoft Office\Office\WordMail		Y
WordMail/ Exchange	Wordfl.cfg	726	\Program Files\Microsoft Office\Office\WordMail		Y
WordMail/ Exchange	mfcuiw32.dll	118,752	\Windows\System		Y

Component	File Name	File Size	Where It Installs	Where It Is Located on the CD-ROM	Typical? *
Microsoft PowerPoint					
WordMail/ Exchange	Mapif1.cfg	799	\Program Files\Microsoft Office\Office\WordMail	\office\wordmail	Y
WordMail/ Exchange	Mapif1L.ico	766	\Program Files\Microsoft Office\Office\WordMail	\office\wordmail	Y
WordMail/ Exchange	Mapif1S.ico	766	\Program Files\Microsoft Office\Office\WordMail	\office\wordmail	Y
WordMail/ Exchange	Station.dll	43,888	\Program Files\Microsoft Office\Office		Y
Assorted					
Other Essential Files	msreftl.dll	160,768	\Program Files\Common Files\Microsoft Shared\ Reference Titles	\aamsstp\app	Y
Other Essential Files	vba332.dll	1,597,200	\Program Files\Common Files\Microsoft Shared\VBA	\os\system	Y
Other Essential Files	vbacv10.dll	439,808	\Program Files\Common Files\Microsoft Shared\VBA	\os\system	Y
Other Essential Files	vbe.dll	746,256	\Program Files\Common Files\Microsoft Shared\VBA	\os\system	Y
Other Essential Files	acdef80.cnt	187	\Program Files\Microsoft Office\Office	\office	Y
Other Essential Files	acdef80.hlp	292,711	\Program Files\Microsoft Office\Office	\office	Y
Other Essential Files	acnew80.cnt	1,613	\Program Files\Microsoft Office\Office	\office	Y
Other Essential Files	acnew80.hlp	108,897	\Program Files\Microsoft Office\Office	\office	Y
Other Essential Files	actip80.cnt	103	\Program Files\Microsoft Office\Office	\office	Y
Other Essential Files	actip80.hlp	340,520	\Program Files\Microsoft Office\Office	\office	Y
Other Essential Files	acvba80.cnt	68,304	\Program Files\Microsoft Office\Office	\office	Y
Other Essential Files	acvba80.hlp	2,060,712	\Program Files\Microsoft Office\Office	\office	Y
Other Essential Files	bsh32.wll	69,120	\Program Files\Microsoft Office\Office	\office	Y
Other Essential Files	bshppt97.ppa	58,368	\Program Files\Microsoft Office\Office	\office	Y
Other Essential Files	Eula8.cnt	268	\Program Files\Microsoft Office\Office	\office	Y
Other Essential Files	eula8.cnt	288	\Program Files\Microsoft Office\Office	\office	Y
Other Essential Files	Eula8.hlp	33,074	\Program Files\Microsoft Office\Office	\office	Y
Other Essential Files	eula8.hlp	39,427	\Program Files\Microsoft Office\Office	\office	Y
Other Essential Files	mso7enu.dll	487,184	\Program Files\Microsoft Office\Office	\office	Y
Other Essential Files	mso97.dll	3,782,416	\Program Files\Microsoft Office\Office	\office	Y
Other Essential Files	msoc.dll	86,016	\Program Files\Microsoft Office\Office	\office	Y
Other Essential Files	Pss8.cnt	162	\Program Files\Microsoft Office\Office	\office	Y

Component	File Name	File Size	Where It Installs	Where It Is Located on the CD-ROM	Typical? *
Assorted					
Other Essential Files	pss8.cnt	690	\Program Files\Microsoft Office\Office	\office	Y
Other Essential Files	Pss8.hlp	15,896	\Program Files\Microsoft Office\Office	\office	Y
Other Essential Files	pss8.hlp	35,904	\Program Files\Microsoft Office\Office	\office	Y
Other Essential Files	xltmpl8.hlp	17,717	\Program Files\Microsoft Office\Office	\office	Y
Other Essential Files	postL.ico	1,078	\Program Files\Microsoft Office\Office\Forms	\office\forms	Y
Other Essential Files	postS.ico	766	\Program Files\Microsoft Office\Office\Forms	\office\forms	Y
Other Essential Files	scdcnclL.ico	1,078	\Program Files\Microsoft Office\Office\Forms	\office\forms	Y
Other Essential Files	scdcnclS.ico	766	\Program Files\Microsoft Office\Office\Forms	\office\forms	Y
Other Essential Files	scdreqL.ico	1,078	\Program Files\Microsoft Office\Office\Forms	\office\forms	Y
Other Essential Files	scdreqS.ico	766	\Program Files\Microsoft Office\Office\Forms	\office\forms	Y
Other Essential Files	scdresnL.ico	1,078	\Program Files\Microsoft Office\Office\Forms	\office\forms	Y
Other Essential Files	scdresnS.ico	766	\Program Files\Microsoft Office\Office\Forms	\office\forms	Y
Other Essential Files	scdrespL.ico	1,078	\Program Files\Microsoft Office\Office\Forms	\office\forms	Y
Other Essential Files	scdrespS.ico	766	\Program Files\Microsoft Office\Office\Forms	\office\forms	Y
Other Essential Files	scdrestL.ico	1,078	\Program Files\Microsoft Office\Office\Forms	\office\forms	Y
Other Essential Files	scdrestS.ico	766	\Program Files\Microsoft Office\Office\Forms	\office\forms	Y
Other Essential Files	schdcncl.cfg	821	\Program Files\Microsoft Office\Office\Forms	\office\forms	Y
Other Essential Files	schdreq.cfg	1,034	\Program Files\Microsoft Office\Office\Forms	\office\forms	Y
Other Essential Files	schdresn.cfg	835	\Program Files\Microsoft Office\Office\Forms	\office\forms	Y
Other Essential Files	schdresp.cfg	833	\Program Files\Microsoft Office\Office\Forms	\office\forms	Y
Other Essential Files	schdrest.cfg	840	\Program Files\Microsoft Office\Office\Forms	\office\forms	Y
Other Essential Files	bshxl.xla	96,768	\Program Files\Microsoft Office\Office\Library	\office\library	Y
Other Essential Files	common.xls	14,336	\Program Files\Microsoft Office\Office\Library	\office\library	Y
Other Essential Files	tmpltnum.xla	47,616	\Program Files\Microsoft Office\Office\Library	\office\library	Y
Other Essential Files	updtlink.xla	25,088	\Program Files\Microsoft Office\Office\Library	\office\library	Y
Other Essential Files	msxl.iqy	59	\Program Files\Microsoft Office\Queries	\queries	Y
Other Essential Files	pqtdet.iqy	127	\Program Files\Microsoft Office\Queries	\queries	Y
Other Essential Files	pqtdj.iqy	70	\Program Files\Microsoft Office\Queries	\queries	Y
Other Essential Files	pqtmul.iqy	123	\Program Files\Microsoft Office\Queries	\queries	Y
Other Essential Files	village.xlt	56,832	\Program Files\Microsoft Office\Templates\ Spreadsheet Solutions	\Temp\\Excel	Y

Component	File Name	File Size	Where It Installs	Where It Is Located on the CD-ROM	Typical? *
Assorted					
Other Essential Files	hatten.ttf	41,408	\Windows\Fonts	\os\fonts	Y
Other Essential Files	Mtsorts.ttf	76,920	\Windows\Fonts	\os\fonts	Y
Other Essential Files	tahoma.ttf	105,312	\Windows\Fonts	\os\fonts	Y
Other Essential Files	tahomabd.ttf	101,336	\Windows\Fonts	\os\fonts	Y
Other Essential Files	Camera.wav	5,524	\Windows\Media\Office97	\sounds	Y
Other Essential Files	DriveBy.wav	12,479	\Windows\Media\Office97	\sounds	Y
Other Essential Files	Laser.wav	1,837	\Windows\Media\Office97	\sounds	Y
Other Essential Files	Type.wav	9,200	\Windows\Media\Office97	\sounds	Y
Other Essential Files	Whoosh.wav	1,758	\Windows\Media\Office97	\sounds	Y
Other Essential Files	awfaxp32.dll	116,736	\Windows\System		Y
Other Essential Files	awlinz32.dll	32,256	\Windows\System		Y
Other Essential Files	awsnto32.exe	35,328	\Windows\System		Y
Other Essential Files	convdsn.exe	7,680	\Windows\System	\os\system	Y
Other Essential Files	iso88591.trn	601	\Windows\System	\office\WMS\Common	Y
Other Essential Files	jetdef35.hlp	86,101	\Windows\System	\os\system	Y
Other Essential Files	jeterr35.cnt	337	\Windows\System	\os\system	Y
Other Essential Files	jeterr35.hlp	384,399	\Windows\System	\os\system	Y
Other Essential Files	mapiu.dll	5,440	\Windows\System	\office\WMS\Common	Y
Other Essential Files	mapix.dll	4,544	\Windows\System	\office\WMS\Common	Y
Other Essential Files	minet32.dll	224,528	\Windows\System	\office\WMS\Common	Y
Other Essential Files	mmfmig32.dll	294,736	\Windows\System	\office\WMS\Win95	Y
Other Essential Files	msfs32.dll	490,864	\Windows\System	\office\WMS\Common	Y
Other Essential Files	msvcrt.dll	266,240	\Windows\System	\office\WMS\Common	Y
Other Essential Files	norweg.trn	601	\Windows\System	\office\WMS\Common	Y
Other Essential Files	odbcjet.cnt	6,931	\Windows\System	\os\system	Y
Other Essential Files	odbcjet.hlp	163,384	\Windows\System	\os\system	Y
Other Essential Files	odbcjtnw.cnt	3,176	\Windows\System	\os\system	Y

Component	File Name	File Size	Where It Installs	Where It Is Located on the CD-ROM	Typical? *
Assorted					
Other Essential Files	odbcjtnw.hlp	61,269	\Windows\System	\os\system	Y
Other Essential Files	riched32.dll	174,352	\Windows\System	\office\WMS\Common	Y
Other Essential Files	swedish.trn	601	\Windows\System	\office\WMS\Common	Y
Other Essential Files	t2embed.dll	222,720	\Windows\System	\os\system	Y
Other Essential Files	usascii.trn	601	\Windows\System	\office\WMS\Common	Y

APPENDIX C

Office 98 File List and Reference

In this chapter

This appendix lists all the files that install with the original Office 98 for the Macintosh, along with

- File size information that you can use to determine whether you have the original file, a damaged file, or a more recent file (in other words, a component of a service release)
- Information about which component of Office each file belongs to; you can use this information to reinstall or add components as part of a maintenance installation
- Where each file installs in a conventional (non-customized) installation; you can use this information to troubleshoot damaged or missing files
- Where to find each file on the Office 98 CD-ROM
- Whether each file is installed as part of an Easy Install installation

Office 98 File List

Component	File Name	Where It Installs	Size	Where It Is Located on the Office 98 CD-ROM	Easy Install?
Address Book					
Address Book	Address Book Converter	Microsoft Office 98:Office	30,941	Microsoft Office 98:Office	Y
Address Book	Address Book Library	Microsoft Office 98:Office	215,842	Microsoft Office 98:Office	Y
Address Book	OE Address Book Lib	Microsoft Office 98:Office	112,851	Microsoft Office 98:Office	Y
Clip Art					
Popular	Agree	Microsoft Office 98:Clipart:Popular	18,370	Microsoft Office 98:Clipart:Popular	Y
Popular	Arrows 1	Microsoft Office 98:Clipart:Popular	3,604	Microsoft Office 98:Clipart:Popular	Y
Popular	Arrows 2	Microsoft Office 98:Clipart:Popular	2,072	Microsoft Office 98:Clipart:Popular	Y
Popular	Arrows 3	Microsoft Office 98:Clipart:Popular	2,224	Microsoft Office 98:Clipart:Popular	Y
Popular	Arrows 4	Microsoft Office 98:Clipart:Popular	4,624	Microsoft Office 98:Clipart:Popular	Y
Popular	Arrows 5	Microsoft Office 98:Clipart:Popular	776	Microsoft Office 98:Clipart:Popular	Y
Popular	Arrows 6	Microsoft Office 98:Clipart:Popular	1,796	Microsoft Office 98:Clipart:Popular	Y
Popular	Arrows 7	Microsoft Office 98:Clipart:Popular	1,300	Microsoft Office 98:Clipart:Popular	Y
Popular	Arrows 8	Microsoft Office 98:Clipart:Popular	1,124	Microsoft Office 98:Clipart:Popular	Y
Popular	Bandaid	Microsoft Office 98:Clipart:Popular	2,258	Microsoft Office 98:Clipart:Popular	Y
Popular	Bear Trap	Microsoft Office 98:Clipart:Popular	2,504	Microsoft Office 98:Clipart:Popular	Y
Popular	Bomb	Microsoft Office 98:Clipart:Popular	5,686	Microsoft Office 98:Clipart:Popular	Y
Popular	Brick	Microsoft Office 98:Clipart:Popular	3,754	Microsoft Office 98:Clipart:Popular	Y
Popular	Building	Microsoft Office 98:Clipart:Popular	4,336	Microsoft Office 98:Clipart:Popular	Y
Popular	Car	Microsoft Office 98:Clipart:Popular	11,182	Microsoft Office 98:Clipart:Popular	Y
Popular	Champagne	Microsoft Office 98:Clipart:Popular	9,746	Microsoft Office 98:Clipart:Popular	Y
Popular	Check Mark	Microsoft Office 98:Clipart:Popular	650	Microsoft Office 98:Clipart:Popular	Y
Popular	Clap	Microsoft Office 98:Clipart:Popular	3,806	Microsoft Office 98:Clipart:Popular	Y
Popular	Clock	Microsoft Office 98:Clipart:Popular	4,368	Microsoft Office 98:Clipart:Popular	Y
Popular	Coins	Microsoft Office 98:Clipart:Popular	51,342	Microsoft Office 98:Clipart:Popular	Y
Popular	Confused	Microsoft Office 98:Clipart:Popular	1,548	Microsoft Office 98:Clipart:Popular	Y
Popular	Darts	Microsoft Office 98:Clipart:Popular	3,538	Microsoft Office 98:Clipart:Popular	Y
Popular	Destroyer	Microsoft Office 98:Clipart:Popular	2,254	Microsoft Office 98:Clipart:Popular	Y
Popular	Dice	Microsoft Office 98:Clipart:Popular	1,150	Microsoft Office 98:Clipart:Popular	Y

Component	File Name	Where It Installs	Size	Where It Is Located on the Office 98 CD-ROM	Easy Install?
Address Book					
Popular	Diploma	Microsoft Office 98:Clipart:Popular	3,836	Microsoft Office 98:Clipart:Popular	Y
Popular	Disaster	Microsoft Office 98:Clipart:Popular	3,226	Microsoft Office 98:Clipart:Popular	Y
Popular	Dominoes	Microsoft Office 98:Clipart:Popular	3,666	Microsoft Office 98:Clipart:Popular	Y
Popular	Donkey	Microsoft Office 98:Clipart:Popular	4,448	Microsoft Office 98:Clipart:Popular	Y
Popular	Door	Microsoft Office 98:Clipart:Popular	1,242	Microsoft Office 98:Clipart:Popular	Y
Popular	Dove	Microsoft Office 98:Clipart:Popular	12,138	Microsoft Office 98:Clipart:Popular	Y
Popular	Dynamite	Microsoft Office 98:Clipart:Popular	18,344	Microsoft Office 98:Clipart:Popular	Y
Popular	Examine	Microsoft Office 98:Clipart:Popular	7,898	Microsoft Office 98:Clipart:Popular	Y
Popular	Fist Slam	Microsoft Office 98:Clipart:Popular	10,418	Microsoft Office 98:Clipart:Popular	Y
Popular	Flower	Microsoft Office 98:Clipart:Popular	9,876	Microsoft Office 98:Clipart:Popular	Y
Popular	Hammer	Microsoft Office 98:Clipart:Popular	1,284	Microsoft Office 98:Clipart:Popular	Y
Popular	Handshake 1	Microsoft Office 98:Clipart:Popular	3,046	Microsoft Office 98:Clipart:Popular	Y
Popular	Handshake 2	Microsoft Office 98:Clipart:Popular	5,868	Microsoft Office 98:Clipart:Popular	Y
Popular	Handshake 3	Microsoft Office 98:Clipart:Popular	7,296	Microsoft Office 98:Clipart:Popular	Y
Popular	Happy	Microsoft Office 98:Clipart:Popular	1,764	Microsoft Office 98:Clipart:Popular	Y
Popular	Hate Computers	Microsoft Office 98:Clipart:Popular	11,682	Microsoft Office 98:Clipart:Popular	Y
Popular	Idea	Microsoft Office 98:Clipart:Popular	1,720	Microsoft Office 98:Clipart:Popular	Y
Popular	Jet Plane	Microsoft Office 98:Clipart:Popular	3,880	Microsoft Office 98:Clipart:Popular	Y
Popular	Jigsaw	Microsoft Office 98:Clipart:Popular	6,584	Microsoft Office 98:Clipart:Popular	Y
Popular	Key	Microsoft Office 98:Clipart:Popular	1,448	Microsoft Office 98:Clipart:Popular	Y
Popular	Light	Microsoft Office 98:Clipart:Popular	4,346	Microsoft Office 98:Clipart:Popular	Y
Popular	Lion	Microsoft Office 98:Clipart:Popular	3,702	Microsoft Office 98:Clipart:Popular	Y
Popular	Lock	Microsoft Office 98:Clipart:Popular	5,228	Microsoft Office 98:Clipart:Popular	Y
Popular	Magic Hat	Microsoft Office 98:Clipart:Popular	18,322	Microsoft Office 98:Clipart:Popular	Y
Popular	Magnify	Microsoft Office 98:Clipart:Popular	6,354	Microsoft Office 98:Clipart:Popular	Y
Popular	Meeting 1	Microsoft Office 98:Clipart:Popular	1,742	Microsoft Office 98:Clipart:Popular	Y
Popular	Meeting 2	Microsoft Office 98:Clipart:Popular	8,880	Microsoft Office 98:Clipart:Popular	Y
Popular	Money	Microsoft Office 98:Clipart:Popular	12,830	Microsoft Office 98:Clipart:Popular	Y
Popular	Moneybag	Microsoft Office 98:Clipart:Popular	1,762	Microsoft Office 98:Clipart:Popular	Y
Popular	Oil Drill	Microsoft Office 98:Clipart:Popular	8,494	Microsoft Office 98:Clipart:Popular	Y
Popular	Open Hand	Microsoft Office 98:Clipart:Popular	3,880	Microsoft Office 98:Clipart:Popular	Y

Component	File Name	Where It Installs	Size	Where It Is Located on the Office 98 CD-ROM	Easy Install?
Address Book					
Popular	Organized	Microsoft Office 98:Clipart:Popular	3,904	Microsoft Office 98:Clipart:Popular	Y
Popular	Point Up	Microsoft Office 98:Clipart:Popular	2,876	Microsoft Office 98:Clipart:Popular	Y
Popular	Problem Solver	Microsoft Office 98:Clipart:Popular	2,160	Microsoft Office 98:Clipart:Popular	Y
Popular	Rabbit	Microsoft Office 98:Clipart:Popular	5,180	Microsoft Office 98:Clipart:Popular	Y
Popular	Ribbon	Microsoft Office 98:Clipart:Popular	9,850	Microsoft Office 98:Clipart:Popular	Y
Popular	Runner	Microsoft Office 98:Clipart:Popular	13,392	Microsoft Office 98:Clipart:Popular	Y
Popular	Sailboat	Microsoft Office 98:Clipart:Popular	6,242	Microsoft Office 98:Clipart:Popular	Y
Popular	Scales	Microsoft Office 98:Clipart:Popular	3,906	Microsoft Office 98:Clipart:Popular	Y
Popular	Shark	Microsoft Office 98:Clipart:Popular	4,546	Microsoft Office 98:Clipart:Popular	Y
Popular	Signpost	Microsoft Office 98:Clipart:Popular	1,998	Microsoft Office 98:Clipart:Popular	Y
Popular	Soccer	Microsoft Office 98:Clipart:Popular	7,742	Microsoft Office 98:Clipart:Popular	Y
Popular	Star	Microsoft Office 98:Clipart:Popular	1,080	Microsoft Office 98:Clipart:Popular	Y
Popular	Stop	Microsoft Office 98:Clipart:Popular	1,730	Microsoft Office 98:Clipart:Popular	Y
Popular	Stoplight	Microsoft Office 98:Clipart:Popular	6,452	Microsoft Office 98:Clipart:Popular	Y
Popular	Tennis	Microsoft Office 98:Clipart:Popular	13,538	Microsoft Office 98:Clipart:Popular	Y
Popular	Thumbs Down	Microsoft Office 98:Clipart:Popular	3,476	Microsoft Office 98:Clipart:Popular	Y
Popular	Triumph	Microsoft Office 98:Clipart:Popular	7,988	Microsoft Office 98:Clipart:Popular	Y
Popular	Trophy	Microsoft Office 98:Clipart:Popular	5,752	Microsoft Office 98:Clipart:Popular	Y
Popular	Turtle	Microsoft Office 98:Clipart:Popular	6,702	Microsoft Office 98:Clipart:Popular	Y
Popular	Victory	Microsoft Office 98:Clipart:Popular	1,540	Microsoft Office 98:Clipart:Popular	Y
Popular	Wear Many Hats	Microsoft Office 98:Clipart:Popular	13,232	Microsoft Office 98:Clipart:Popular	Y
Popular	What Now	Microsoft Office 98:Clipart:Popular	12,228	Microsoft Office 98:Clipart:Popular	Y
Popular	Winners	Microsoft Office 98:Clipart:Popular	3,282	Microsoft Office 98:Clipart:Popular	Y
Popular	Yin & Yang	Microsoft Office 98:Clipart:Popular	2,318	Microsoft Office 98:Clipart:Popular	Y
Popular	Popular Clip Package	Microsoft Office 98:Clipart:Popular	492,032	Microsoft Office 98:Clipart:Popular	Y
Clip Gallery					
Clip Gallery	Microsoft C Runtime Library	Microsoft Office 98:Office	324,045	Microsoft Office 98:Office	Y
Clip Gallery	Microsoft Clip Gallery	Microsoft Office 98:Office	1,310,406	Microsoft Office 98:Office	Y
Clip Gallery	MS Clip Gallery Help	Microsoft Office 98:Office:Help	45,317	Microsoft Office 98:Office:Help	Y

Component	File Name	Where It Installs	Size	Where It Is Located on the Office 98 CD-ROM	Easy Install?
Equation Ed.					
Equation Ed.	Equation Editor	Microsoft Office 98:Shared Applications:Equation Editor	545,767	Microsoft Office 98:Shared Applications:Equation Editor	
Equation Ed.	MT Extra	:System Folder:Fonts	18,781	Office Custom Install:Installer Files	
Equation Ed. Help	MS Equation Editor Help	Microsoft Office 98:Shared Applications:Equation Editor	154,359	Microsoft Office 98:Shared Applications:Equation Editor	
Microsoft Excel					
Program File	Excel 409 Lexicon	Microsoft Office 98:Office	11,688	Microsoft Office 98:Office	Y
Program File	Excel Chart Gallery (8)	:System Folder:Preferences	143,360	Office Custom Install:Installer Files	Y
Program File	Excel Macro Scanner	Microsoft Office 98:Office	5,505	Microsoft Office 98:Office	Y
Program File	Microsoft Excel	:Microsoft Office 98	5,662,751	Microsoft Office 98	Y
Add-ins	Analysis Toolpak	Microsoft Office 98:Office:Excel Add-Ins:Analysis Tools	342,542	Microsoft Office 98:Office:Excel Add-Ins:Analysis Tools	Y
Add-ins	Auto Save	Microsoft Office 98:Office:Excel Add-Ins	73,390	Microsoft Office 98:Office:Excel Add-Ins	Y
Add-ins	Conditional Sum Wizard	Microsoft Office 98:Office:Excel Add-Ins	286,720	Microsoft Office 98:Office:Excel Add-Ins	Y
Add-ins	FuncRes	Microsoft Office 98:Office:Excel Add-Ins:Analysis Tools	69,120	Microsoft Office 98:Office:Excel Add-Ins:Analysis Tools	Y
Add-ins	Internet Assistant Wizard	Microsoft Office 98:Office:Excel Add-Ins	726,528	Microsoft Office 98:Office:Excel Add-Ins	Y
Add-ins	Lookup Wizard	Microsoft Office 98:Office:Excel Add-Ins	321,024	Microsoft Office 98:Office:Excel Add-Ins	Y
Add-ins	ProcDBRes	Microsoft Office 98:Office:Excel Add-Ins:Analysis Tools	96,256	Microsoft Office 98:Office:Excel Add-Ins:Analysis Tools	Y
Add-ins	Update Add-In Links	Microsoft Office 98:Office:Excel Add-Ins	54,784	Microsoft Office 98:Office:Excel Add-Ins	Y
Add-ins	File Conversion Wizard	Microsoft Office 98:Office:Excel Add-Ins	330,240	Microsoft Office 98:Office:Excel Add-Ins	Y
Add-ins	Report Manager	Microsoft Office 98:Office:Excel Add-Ins	155,136	Microsoft Office 98:Office:Excel Add-Ins	Y
Add-ins	Solver	Microsoft Office 98:Office:Excel Add-Ins:Solver	735,264	Microsoft Office 98:Office:Excel Add-Ins	Y
Add-ins	Solver Samples	Microsoft Office 98:Office: Examples:Solver	96,768	Microsoft Office 98:Office:Examples:Solver	Y
Add-ins	Template Wizard	Microsoft Office 98:Office:Excel Add-Ins	712,704	Microsoft Office 98:Office:Excel Add-Ins	Y
Help	MS Excel AW	Microsoft Office 98:Office:Help	852,447	Microsoft Office 98:Office:Help	Y

Component	File Name	Where It Installs	Size	Where It Is Located on the Office 98 CD-ROM	Easy Install?
Microsoft Excel					
Help	MS Excel Functions AW	Microsoft Office 98:Office:Help	281,028	Microsoft Office 98:Office:Help	Y
Help	MS Excel 4 Macro Help	Microsoft Office 98:Office:Help	19,738	Microsoft Office 98:Office:Help	Y
Help	MS Excel Balloon Help	Microsoft Office 98:Office:Help	347,752	Microsoft Office 98:Office:Help	Y
Help	MS Excel Help	Microsoft Office 98:Office:Help	2,301,664	Microsoft Office 98:Office:Help	Y
Help	MS Excel Readme	Microsoft Office 98:ReadMe	29	Microsoft Office 98:ReadMe	Y
Help	MS Excel Solutions Help	Microsoft Office 98:Office:Help	23,017	Microsoft Office 98:Office:Help	Y
Help	MS Excel Upgrade Help	Microsoft Office 98:Office:Help	94,134	Microsoft Office 98:Office:Help	Y
Help	MS Excel VBA AW	Microsoft Office 98:Office:Help	592,074	Microsoft Office 98:Office:Help	
Help	MS Excel VBA Help	Microsoft Office 98:Office:Help	2,098,662	Microsoft Office 98:Office:Help	
Templates	Employee Information	Microsoft Office 98:Office:Excel Add-Ins	15,872	Microsoft Office 98:Office:Excel Add-Ins	Y
Templates	Invoice	Microsoft Office 98:Templates: Spreadsheet Solutions	206,848	Microsoft Office 98:Templates: Spreadsheet Solutions	Y
Templates	Invoice Database	Microsoft Office 98:Office:Excel Add-Ins	15,872	Microsoft Office 98:Office:Excel Add-Ins	Y
Templates	Template Utilities	Microsoft Office 98:Office:Excel Add-Ins	35,840	Microsoft Office 98:Office:Excel Add-Ins	Y
Templates	Village Software	Microsoft Office 98:Templates: Spreadsheet Solutions	49,152	Microsoft Office 98:Templates: Spreadsheet Solutions	Y
Templates	Expense Database	Microsoft Office 98:Office:Excel Add-Ins	15,360	Microsoft Office 98:Office:Excel Add-Ins	
Templates	Expense Statement	Microsoft Office 98:Templates: Spreadsheet Solutions	246,272	Microsoft Office 98:Templates: Spreadsheet Solutions	
Templates	Purchase Order	Microsoft Office 98:Templates: Spreadsheet Solutions	233,984	Microsoft Office 98:Templates: Spreadsheet Solutions	
Templates	Purchase Order Database	Microsoft Office 98:Office:Excel Add-Ins	15,360	Microsoft Office 98:Office:Excel Add-Ins	
Fonts					
TT Font	Monotype Sorts	:System Folder:Fonts	78,474	Office Custom Install:Installer Files	Y
TT Font	Arial	:System Folder:Fonts	292,046	Office Custom Install:Installer Files	Y
TT Font	Arial Black	:System Folder:Fonts	50,746	Office Custom Install:Installer Files	Y
TT Font	Impact	:System Folder:Fonts	60,014	Office Custom Install:Installer Files	Y
TT Font	Symbol	:System Folder:Fonts	65,626	Office Custom Install:Installer Files	Y
TT Font	Times New Roman	:System Folder:Fonts	354,222	Office Custom Install:Installer Files	Y
TT Font	Wingdings	:System Folder:Fonts	72,107	Office Custom Install:Installer Files	Y

Component	File Name	Where It Installs	Size	Where It Is Located on the Office 98 CD-ROM	Easy Install?
Forms					
Forms3 Help	MS Forms AW	Microsoft Office 98:Office:Help	153,290	Microsoft Office 98:Office:Help	
Forms3 Help	MS Forms Help	Microsoft Office 98:Office:Help	491,875	Microsoft Office 98:Office:Help	
Genigraphics Wizard					
Genigraphics Wizard	GraphicsLink	Microsoft Office 98:Office	1,018,180	Microsoft Office 98:Office	
Genigraphics Wizard Help	Genigraphics Help	Microsoft Office 98:Office	70,479	Microsoft Office 98:Office	
Graph					
Graph	Graph 409 Lexicon	Microsoft Office 98:Office	2,174	Microsoft Office 98:Office	Y
Graph	Graph Chart Gallery (8)	:System Folder:Preferences	186,880	Office Custom Install:Installer Files	Y
Graph	Microsoft Graph	Microsoft Office 98:Office	1,730,866	Microsoft Office 98:Office	Y
Graph Help	MS Graph AW	Microsoft Office 98:Office:Help	273,328	Microsoft Office 98:Office:Help	Y
Graph Help	MS Graph Help	Microsoft Office 98:Office:Help	473,480	Microsoft Office 98:Office:Help	Y
Graph Help	MS Graph VBA Help	Microsoft Office 98:Office:Help	13,899	Microsoft Office 98:Office:Help	Y
Graphics Filters					
Graphics Filter	EPS Import	Microsoft Office 98:Shared Applications:Graphic Filters	91,910	Microsoft Office 98:Shared Applications:Graphic Filters	Y
Graphics Filter	GIF Import & Export	Microsoft Office 98:Shared Applications:Graphic Filters	246,102	Microsoft Office 98:Shared Applications:Graphic Filters	Y
Graphics Filter	JPEG Import & Export	Microsoft Office 98:Shared Applications:Graphic Filters	227,379	Microsoft Office 98:Shared Applications:Graphic Filters	Y
Graphics Filter	Metafile Import	Microsoft Office 98:Shared Applications:Graphic Filters	259,428	Microsoft Office 98:Shared Applications:Graphic Filters	Y
Graphics Filter	PNG Import & Export	Microsoft Office 98:Shared Applications:Graphic Filters	166,894	Microsoft Office 98:Shared Applications:Graphic Filters	Y
Graphics Filter	TIFF Import	Microsoft Office 98:Shared Applications:Graphic Filters	105,028	Microsoft Office 98:Shared Applications:Graphic Filters	Y
Help Files					
Help	Microsoft Help	Microsoft Office 98:Office	267,211	Microsoft Office 98:Office	Y
Help	Microsoft Help Bookmarks	Microsoft Office 98:Office	63	Microsoft Office 98:Office	Y
Help	License Agreement	Microsoft Office 98:Office:Help	36,073	Microsoft Office 98:Office:Help	Y
Help	MS Help on Help	Microsoft Office 98:Office	26,316	Microsoft Office 98:Office:Help	Y
Help	MS License Agreement	Microsoft Office 98:Office:Help	37,162	Microsoft Office 98:Office:Help	Y
Help	MS MTS Help	Microsoft Office 98:Office:Help	32,257	Microsoft Office 98:Office:Help	Y

Component	File Name	Where It Installs	Size	Where It Is Located on the Office 98 CD-ROM	Easy Install?
Help Files					
Help	MS Office Administrator Readme	Microsoft Office 98:ReadMe	44	Microsoft Office 98:ReadMe	Y
Help	MS Office Balloon Help	Microsoft Office 98:Office:Help	540,711	Microsoft Office 98:Office:Help	Y
Internet Files					
Internet	Advanced Networking	:System Folder:MS Preference Panels	67,027	System Files:MS Preference Panels	Y
Internet	Configuration Manager	:System Folder:Control Panels	29,523	Office Custom Install:Installer Files	Y
Internet	Cookies	:System Folder:MS Preference Panels	115,403	System Files:MS Preference Panels	Y
Internet	Favorites	Microsoft Office 98:Office	326,916	Microsoft Office 98:Office	Y
Internet	File Helpers	:System Folder:MS Preference Panels	127,223	System Files:MS Preference Panels	Y
Internet	General E-mail	:System Folder:MS Preference Panels	55,309	System Files:MS Preference Panels	Y
Internet	Home/Search Panel	:System Folder:MS Preference Panels	38,469	System Files:MS Preference Panels	Y
Internet	Internet Config Extension	:System Folder:Extensions	23,956	Office Custom Install:Installer Files	Y
Internet	Internet Preferences	:System Folder:Preferences	34,246	Office Custom Install:Installer Files	Y
Internet	Microsoft Hyperlink Library	:System Folder:Extensions	251,291	Office Custom Install:Installer Files	Y
Internet	MS C++ Library (PPC)	:System Folder:Extensions: MS Library Folder	111,851	System Files:MS Library Folder	Y
Internet	MS Configuration Lib PPC	:System Folder:Extensions: MS Library Folder	93,884	System Files:MS Library Folder	Y
Internet	MS Container Lib (PPC)	:System Folder:Extensions: MS Library Folder	192,463	System Files:MS Library Folder	Y
Internet	MS Favorites Library (PPC)	:System Folder:Extensions: MS Library Folder	120,463	System Files:MS Library Folder	Y
Internet	MS Internet Library (PPC)	:System Folder:Extensions: MS Library Folder	603,110	System Files:MS Library Folder	Y
Internet	MS Parser Library (PPC)	:System Folder:Extensions: MS Library Folder	37,440	System Files:MS Library Folder	Y
Internet	MS Preferences Library PPC	:System Folder:Extensions: MS Library Folder	147,743	System Files:MS Library Folder	Y
Internet	MS Variant Lib (PPC)	:System Folder:Extensions: MS Library Folder	33,922	System Files:MS Library Folder	Y
Internet	Password Dialogs	:System Folder:MS Preference Panels	21,430	System Files:MS Preference Panels	Y
Internet	Protocol Helpers	:System Folder:MS Preference Panels	100,938	System Files:MS Preference Panels	Y
Internet	Proxies	:System Folder:MS Preference Panels	51,000	System Files:MS Preference Panels	Y
Internet	Ratings	:System Folder:MS Preference Panels	166,734	System Files:MS Preference Panels	Y

Component	File Name	Where It Installs	Size	Where It Is Located on the Office 98 CD-ROM	Easy Install?
Internet Files					
Internet	Security	:System Folder:MS Preference Panels	74,914	System Files:MS Preference Panels	Y
Internet	User Passwords	:System Folder:MS Preference Panels	98,367	System Files:MS Preference Panels	Y
MS Info					
MS Info	Microsoft System Information	Microsoft Office 98:Office	9,573	Microsoft Office 98:Office	Y
MS Info	MSInfo	Microsoft Office 98:Office	19,051	Microsoft Office 98:Office	Y
Office Assistant					
Office Assistant	Clippit	Microsoft Office 98:Office:Assistants	677,641	Microsoft Office 98:Office:Actors	Y
Office Assistant	Genius	Microsoft Office 98:Office: Assistants	2,667,395	Microsoft Office 98:Office:Actors	Y
Office Assistant	Rocky	Microsoft Office 98:Office: Assistants	3,122,917	Microsoft Office 98:Office:Actors	Y
Office AutoCorrect List	Default MS Office ACL (8)	Microsoft Office 98:Office	35,262	Microsoft Office 98:Office	Y
Office Library	Microsoft Office 98	Microsoft Office 98:Office	5,385,883	Microsoft Office 98:Office	Y
Office Manager	Microsoft Office Manager	:System Folder:Control Panels	135,592	Office Custom Install:Installer Files	Y
OLE Files					
OLE	Microsoft Component Library	:System Folder:Extensions	55,902	Office Custom Install:Installer Files	Y
OLE	Microsoft OLE Automation	:System Folder:Extensions	640,217	Office Custom Install:Installer Files	Y
OLE	Microsoft OLE Library	:System Folder:Extensions	658,616	Office Custom Install:Installer Files	Y
OLE	Microsoft RPC Runtime Library	:System Folder:Extensions	254,457	Office Custom Install:Installer Files	Y
OLE	Microsoft Structured Storage	:System Folder:Extensions	601,186	Office Custom Install:Installer Files	Y
OLE TypeLib	Standard OLE Types (PowerMac)	:System Folder:Extensions:Type Libraries	4,762	System Files:Type Libraries	Y
OLE TypeLib	Standard OLE Types 2	:System Folder:Extensions:Type Libraries	13,821	System Files:Type Libraries	Y
Online Help					
Online Help	Black.gif	Microsoft Office 98:Office:Help:Images	799	Microsoft Office 98:Office:Help:Images	Y
Online Help	MacEdition.gif	Microsoft Office 98:Office:Help:Images	2,612	Microsoft Office 98:Office:Help:Images	Y
Online Help	MOffLogo.gif	Microsoft Office 98:Office:Help:Images	6,960	Microsoft Office 98:Office:Help:Images	Y
Online Help	Register.htm	Microsoft Office 98:Office:Help	2,862	Microsoft Office 98:Office:Help	Y
Online Help	TileOf.gif	Microsoft Office 98:Office:Help:Images	4,689	Microsoft Office 98:Office:Help:Images	Y
Online Help	WebHelp.htm	Microsoft Office 98:Office:Help	2,687	Microsoft Office 98:Office:Help	Y

Component	File Name	Where It Installs	Size	Where It Is Located on the Office 98 CD-ROM	Easy Install?
MS Organization Chart					
Org Chart	Microsoft Help Runtime	Microsoft Office 98:Office	11,193	Microsoft Office 98:Office	Y
Org Chart	MS Organization Chart 2.0	Microsoft Office 98:Office	1,982,773	Microsoft Office 98:Office	Y
Org Chart	MS Organization Chart Template	Microsoft Office 98:Office	3,088	Microsoft Office 98:Office	Y
Org Chart Help	MS Organization Chart 2.0 Help	Microsoft Office 98:Office	106,052	Microsoft Office 98:Office	Y
PowerPoint					
Program File	Blank Presentation	Microsoft Office 98:Templates	18,432	Microsoft Office 98:Templates	Y
Program File	Contemporary	Microsoft Office 98:Templates: Presentation Designs	26,112	Microsoft Office 98:Templates: Presentation Designs	Y
Program File	Generic (Online)	Microsoft Office 98:Templates: Presentations	29,696	Microsoft Office 98:Templates: Presentations	Y
Program File	Generic (Standard)	Microsoft Office 98:Templates: Presentations	30,208	Microsoft Office 98:Templates: Presentations	Y
Program File	Microsoft PowerPoint	:Microsoft Office 98	5,487,527	Microsoft Office 98	Y
Program File	PP Translator 4-8	Microsoft Office 98:Office: Translators	979,586	Microsoft Office 98:Office:Translators	Y
Program File	PP Translator 7-8	Microsoft Office 98:Office: Translators	309,124	Microsoft Office 98:Office:Translators	Y
Program File	PP Translator 8-4	Microsoft Office 98:Office: Translators	2,434,384	Microsoft Office 98:Office:Translators	Y
Program File	Professional	Microsoft Office 98:Templates: Presentation Designs	54,784	Microsoft Office 98:Templates: Presentation Designs	Y
Program File	Recommend Strategy (Online)	Microsoft Office 98:Templates: Presentations	43,520	Microsoft Office 98:Templates: Presentations	Y Y
Program File	Recommend Strategy (Standard)	Microsoft Office 98:Templates: Presentations	41,984	Microsoft Office 98:Templates: Presentations	Y Y
Program File	Reporting Progress (Online)	Microsoft Office 98:Templates: Presentations	33,792	Microsoft Office 98:Templates:Presentations	Y
Program File	Reporting Progress (Standard)	Microsoft Office 98:Templates: Presentations	30,720	Microsoft Office 98:Templates:Presentations	Y
Help	MS PowerPoint AW	Microsoft Office 98:Office:Help	448,199	Microsoft Office 98:Office:Help	Y
Help	MS PowerPoint Balloon Help	Microsoft Office 98:Office:Help	127,467	Microsoft Office 98:Office:Help	Y
Help	MS PowerPoint Help	Microsoft Office 98:Office:Help	680,897	Microsoft Office 98:Office:Help	Y
Help	MS PowerPoint Readme	Microsoft Office 98:ReadMe	34	Microsoft Office 98:ReadMe	Y
Help	MS PowerPoint Upgrade Help	Microsoft Office 98:Office:Help	46,975	Microsoft Office 98:Office:Help	Y

Component	File Name	Where It Installs	Size	Where It Is Located on the Office 98 CD-ROM	Easy Install?
PowerPoint					
Help	MS PowerPoint VBA AW	Microsoft Office 98:Office:Help	199,095	Microsoft Office 98:Office:Help	
Help	MS PowerPoint VBA Help	Microsoft Office 98:Office:Help	883,569	Microsoft Office 98:Office:Help	
Sounds	Camera	Microsoft Office 98:Sounds	6,056	Microsoft Office 98:Office:Sounds	Y
Sounds	Clapping	Microsoft Office 98:Sounds	64,772	Microsoft Office 98:Office:Sounds	Y
Sounds	Drive By	Microsoft Office 98:Sounds	13,009	Microsoft Office 98:Office:Sounds	Y
Sounds	Laser	Microsoft Office 98:Sounds	2,364	Microsoft Office 98:Office:Sounds	Y
Sounds	Typewriter	Microsoft Office 98:Sounds	9,774	Microsoft Office 98:Office:Sounds	Y
Sounds	Whoosh	Microsoft Office 98:Sounds	2,290	Microsoft Office 98:Office:Sounds	Y
Sounds	Applause	Microsoft Office 98:Sounds	77,836	Microsoft Office 98:Office:Sounds	
Sounds	Breaking Glass	Microsoft Office 98:Sounds	12,068	Microsoft Office 98:Office:Sounds	
Sounds	Cash Register	Microsoft Office 98:Sounds	8,086	Microsoft Office 98:Office:Sounds	
Sounds	Chimes	Microsoft Office 98:Sounds	75,120	Microsoft Office 98:Office:Sounds	
Sounds	Drum Roll	Microsoft Office 98:Sounds	19,957	Microsoft Office 98:Office:Sounds	
Sounds	Explosion	Microsoft Office 98:Sounds	24,115	Microsoft Office 98:Office:Sounds	
Sounds	Gunshot	Microsoft Office 98:Sounds	4,952	Microsoft Office 98:Office:Sounds	
Sounds	Ricochet	Microsoft Office 98:Sounds	9,433	Microsoft Office 98:Office:Sounds	
Sounds	Screeching Brake	Microsoft Office 98:Sounds	14,614	Microsoft Office 98:Office:Sounds	
Sounds	Slide Projector	Microsoft Office 98:Sounds	10,935	Microsoft Office 98:Office:Sounds	
Content Templts	Business Plan (Online)	Microsoft Office 98:Templates: Presentations	70,656	Microsoft Office 98:Templates: Presentations	Y
Content Templts	Business Plan (Standard)	Microsoft Office 98:Templates: Presentations	49,152	Microsoft Office 98:Templates:Presentations	Y
Content Templts	Company Meeting (Online)	Microsoft Office 98:Templates: Presentations	32,768	Microsoft Office 98:Templates:Presentations	Y
Content Templts	Company Meeting (Standard)	Microsoft Office 98:Templates: Presentations	30,208	Microsoft Office 98:Templates:Presentations	Y
Content Templts	Corp Financial Info (Online)	Microsoft Office 98:Templates: Presentations	127,488	Microsoft Office 98:Templates:Presentations	Y
Content Templts	Corp Financial Info (Standard)	Microsoft Office 98:Templates: Presentations	145,408	Microsoft Office 98:Templates:Presentations	Y
Content Templts	Corp Home Page (Online)	Microsoft Office 98:Templates: Presentations	96,256	Microsoft Office 98:Templates:Presentations	Y
Content Templts	Corp Home Page (Standard)	Microsoft Office 98:Templates: Presentations	96,256	Microsoft Office 98:Templates:Presentations	Y

Component	File Name	Where It Installs	Size	Where It Is Located on the Office 98 CD-ROM	Easy Install?
PowerPoint					
Content Templts	Facilitate a Meeting (Standard)	Microsoft Office 98:Templates: Presentations	36,352	Microsoft Office 98:Templates:Presentations	Y
Content Templts	Flyer (Online)	Microsoft Office 98:Templates: Presentations	108,032	Microsoft Office 98:Templates:Presentations	Y
Content Templts	Flyer (Standard)	Microsoft Office 98:Templates: Presentations	26,624	Microsoft Office 98:Templates:Presentations	Y
Content Templts	Generic (Online)	Microsoft Office 98:Templates: Presentations	29,696	Microsoft Office 98:Templates:Presentations	Y
Content Templts	Generic (Standard)	Microsoft Office 98:Templates: Presentations	30,208	Microsoft Office 98:Templates:Presentations	Y
Content Templts	H.R. Info Kiosk (Online)	Microsoft Office 98:Templates: Presentations	109,056	Microsoft Office 98:Templates:Presentations	Y
Content Templts	H.R. Info Kiosk (Standard)	Microsoft Office 98:Templates: Presentations	48,640	Microsoft Office 98:Templates:Presentations	Y
Content Templts	H.R.'s Changing Role (Standard)	Microsoft Office 98:Templates: Presentations	39,424	Microsoft Office 98:Templates:Presentations	Y
Content Templts	Introducing Speaker (Standard)	Microsoft Office 98:Templates: Presentations	33,280	Microsoft Office 98:Templates:Presentations	Y
Content Templts	Marketing Plan (Online)	Microsoft Office 98:Templates: Presentations	84,992	Microsoft Office 98:Templates:Presentations	Y
Content Templts	Marketing Plan (Standard)	Microsoft Office 98:Templates: Presentations	48,640	Microsoft Office 98:Templates:Presentations	Y
Content Templts	Motivating a Team (Standard)	Microsoft Office 98:Templates: Presentations	34,816	Microsoft Office 98:Templates:Presentations	Y
Content Templts	Org Overview (Online)	Microsoft Office 98:Templates: Presentations	101,376	Microsoft Office 98:Templates:Presentations	Y
Content Templts	Org Overview (Standard)	Microsoft Office 98:Templates: Presentations	98,304	Microsoft Office 98:Templates:Presentations	Y
Content Templts	Personal Home Page (Online)	Microsoft Office 98:Templates: Presentations	36,352	Microsoft Office 98:Templates:Presentations	Y
Content Templts	Personal Home Page (Standard)	Microsoft Office 98:Templates: Presentations	34,816	Microsoft Office 98:Templates:Presentations	Y
Content Templts	Presentation Guidelines	Microsoft Office 98:Templates: Presentations	41,472	Microsoft Office 98:Templates:Presentations	Y
Content Templts	Product Overview (Online)	Microsoft Office 98:Templates: Presentations	52,736	Microsoft Office 98:Templates:Presentations	Y
Content Templts	Product Overview (Standard)	Microsoft Office 98:Templates: Presentations	44,032	Microsoft Office 98:Templates:Presentations	Y

Component	File Name	Where It Installs	Size	Where It Is Located on the Office 98 CD-ROM	Easy Install?
PowerPoint					
Content Templts	Project Overview (Online)	Microsoft Office 98:Templates: Presentations	58,880	Microsoft Office 98:Templates:Presentations	Y
Content Templts	Project Overview (Standard)	Microsoft Office 98:Templates: Presentations	34,304	Microsoft Office 98:Templates:Presentations	Y
Content Templts	Project Status (Online)	Microsoft Office 98:Templates: Presentations	65,536	Microsoft Office 98:Templates:Presentations	Y
Content Templts	Project Status (Standard)	Microsoft Office 98:Templates: Presentations	60,928	Microsoft Office 98:Templates:Presentations	Y
Content Templts	Recommend Strategy (Online)	Microsoft Office 98:Templates: Presentations	43,520	Microsoft Office 98:Templates:Presentations	Y
Content Templts	Recommend Strategy (Standard)	Microsoft Office 98:Templates: Presentations	41,984	Microsoft Office 98:Templates:Presentations	Y
Content Templts	Reporting Progress (Online)	Microsoft Office 98:Templates: Presentations	33,792	Microsoft Office 98:Templates:Presentations	Y
Content Templts	Reporting Progress (Standard)	Microsoft Office 98:Templates: Presentations	30,720	Microsoft Office 98:Templates:Presentations	Y
Content Templts	Sample Banner 1	Microsoft Office 98:Templates: Presentations	175,104	Microsoft Office 98:Templates:Presentations	Y
Content Templts	Sample Banner 2	Microsoft Office 98:Templates: Presentations	26,112	Microsoft Office 98:Templates:Presentations	Y
Content Templts	Selling Your Ideas (Standard)	Microsoft Office 98:Templates: Presentations	35,840	Microsoft Office 98:Templates:Presentations	Y
Content Templts	Technical Report (Standard)	Microsoft Office 98:Templates: Presentations	31,744	Microsoft Office 98:Templates:Presentations	Y
Content Templts	Thanking a Speaker (Standard)	Microsoft Office 98:Templates: Presentations	29,696	Microsoft Office 98:Templates:Presentations	Y
Design Templts	Angles	Microsoft Office 98:Templates: Presentation Designs	19,456	Microsoft Office 98:Templates:Presentation Designs	Y
Design Templts	Blush	Microsoft Office 98:Templates: Presentation Designs	41,472	Microsoft Office 98:Templates:Presentation Designs	Y
Design Templts	Contemporary	Microsoft Office 98:Templates: Presentation Designs	26,112	Microsoft Office 98:Templates:Presentation Designs	Y
Design Templts	Contemporary Portrait	Microsoft Office 98:Templates: Presentation Designs	23,040	Microsoft Office 98:Templates:Presentation Designs	Y
Design Templts	Dad's Tie	Microsoft Office 98:Templates: Presentation Designs	34,304	Microsoft Office 98:Templates:Presentation Designs	Y
Design Templts	Fans	Microsoft Office 98:Templates: Presentation Designs	36,352	Microsoft Office 98:Templates:Presentation Designs	Y

Component	File Name	Where It Installs	Size	Where It Is Located on the Office 98 CD-ROM	Easy Install?
PowerPoint					
Design Templts	Fireball	Microsoft Office 98:Templates: Presentation Designs	20,992	Microsoft Office 98:Templates:Presentation Designs	Y
Design Templts	High Voltage	Microsoft Office 98:Templates: Presentation Designs	43,520	Microsoft Office 98:Templates:Presentation Designs	Y
Design Templts	Meadow	Microsoft Office 98:Templates: Presentation Designs	104,448	Microsoft Office 98:Templates:Presentation Designs	Y
Design Templts	Notebook	Microsoft Office 98:Templates: Presentation Designs	31,744	Microsoft Office 98:Templates:Presentation Designs	Y
Design Templts	Portrait Notebook	Microsoft Office 98:Templates: Presentation Designs	35,840	Microsoft Office 98:Templates:Presentation Designs	Y
Design Templts	Professional	Microsoft Office 98:Templates: Presentation Designs	54,784	Microsoft Office 98:Templates:Presentation Designs	Y
Design Templts	Pulse	Microsoft Office 98:Templates: Presentation Designs	41,472	Microsoft Office 98:Templates:Presentation Designs	Y
Design Templts	Ribbons	Microsoft Office 98:Templates: Presentation Designs	41,472	Microsoft Office 98:Templates:Presentation Designs	Y
Design Templts	Serene	Microsoft Office 98:Templates: Presentation Designs	99,840	Microsoft Office 98:Templates:Presentation Designs	Y
Design Templts	Whirlpool	Microsoft Office 98:Templates: Presentation Designs	64,512	Microsoft Office 98:Templates:Presentation Designs	Y
Design Templts	Zesty	Microsoft Office 98:Templates: Presentation Designs	19,968	Microsoft Office 98:Templates:Presentation Designs	Y
Web Pub. Tools	activem.gif	Microsoft Office 98:Office: HTML:Fancy Buttons	2,474	Microsoft Office 98:Office:HTML:Fancy Buttons	Y
Web Pub. Tools	activem.gif	Microsoft Office 98:Office:HTML: Classic Buttons	2,430	Microsoft Office 98:Office:HTML:Classic Buttons	Y
Web Pub. Tools	activem.gif	Microsoft Office 98:Office:HTML: Regular Buttons	2,402	Microsoft Office 98:Office:HTML:Regular Buttons	Y
Web Pub. Tools	activep.gif	Microsoft Office 98:Office:HTML: Classic Buttons	2,442	Microsoft Office 98:Office:HTML:Classic Buttons	Y
Web Pub. Tools	activep.gif	Microsoft Office 98:Office:HTML: Fancy Buttons	2,478	Microsoft Office 98:Office:HTML:Fancy Buttons	Y
Web Pub. Tools	activep.gif	Microsoft Office 98:Office:HTML: Regular Buttons	2,413	Microsoft Office 98:Office:HTML:Regular Buttons	Y

Component	File Name	Where It Installs	Size	Where It Is Located on the Office 98 CD-ROM	Easy Install?
PowerPoint					
Web Pub. Tools	collapse.gif	Microsoft Office 98:Office:HTML:Classic Buttons	2,440	Microsoft Office 98:Office:HTML:Classic Buttons	Y
Web Pub. Tools	collapse.gif	Microsoft Office 98:Office:HTML:Regular Buttons	2,407	Microsoft Office 98:Office:HTML:Regular Buttons	Y
Web Pub. Tools	collapse.gif	Microsoft Office 98:Office:HTML:Fancy Buttons	2,479	Microsoft Office 98:Office:HTML:Fancy Buttons	Y
Web Pub. Tools	expand.gif	Microsoft Office 98:Office:HTML:Regular Buttons	2,414	Microsoft Office 98:Office:HTML:Regular Buttons	Y
Web Pub. Tools	expand.gif	Microsoft Office 98:Office:HTML:Classic Buttons	2,441	Microsoft Office 98:Office:HTML:Classic Buttons	Y
Web Pub. Tools	expand.gif	Microsoft Office 98:Office:HTML:Fancy Buttons	2,480	Microsoft Office 98:Office:HTML:Fancy Buttons	Y
Web Pub. Tools	first.gif	Microsoft Office 98:Office:HTML:Fancy Buttons	2,481	Microsoft Office 98:Office:HTML:Fancy Buttons	Y
Web Pub. Tools	first.gif	Microsoft Office 98:Office:HTML:Regular Buttons	2,409	Microsoft Office 98:Office:HTML:Regular Buttons	Y
Web Pub. Tools	first.gif	Microsoft Office 98:Office:HTML:Classic Buttons	2,438	Microsoft Office 98:Office:HTML:Classic Buttons	Y
Web Pub. Tools	Frame HTML Template	Microsoft Office 98:Office:HTML	5,117	Microsoft Office 98:Office:HTML	Y
Web Pub. Tools	home.gif	Microsoft Office 98:Office:HTML:Classic Buttons	2,444	Microsoft Office 98:Office:HTML:Classic Buttons	Y
Web Pub. Tools	home.gif	Microsoft Office 98:Office:HTML:Fancy Buttons	2,484	Microsoft Office 98:Office:HTML:Fancy Buttons	Y
Web Pub. Tools	home.gif	Microsoft Office 98:Office:HTML:Regular Buttons	2,410	Microsoft Office 98:Office:HTML:Regular Buttons	Y
Web Pub. Tools	ielogo.gif	Microsoft Office 98:Office:HTML:Common Components	3,329	Microsoft Office 98:Office:HTML: Common Components	Y
Web Pub. Tools	Image HTML Template	Microsoft Office 98:Office:HTML	907	Microsoft Office 98:Office:HTML	Y
Web Pub. Tools	Index HTML Template	Microsoft Office 98:Office:HTML	1,485	Microsoft Office 98:Office:HTML	Y
Web Pub. Tools	info.gif	Microsoft Office 98:Office:HTML:Classic Buttons	2,439	Microsoft Office 98:Office:HTML:Classic Buttons	Y
Web Pub. Tools	info.gif	Microsoft Office 98:Office:HTML:Regular Buttons	2,412	Microsoft Office 98:Office:HTML:Regular Buttons	Y
Web Pub. Tools	info.gif	Microsoft Office 98:Office:HTML:Fancy Buttons	2,482	Microsoft Office 98:Office:HTML:Fancy Buttons	Y

Component	File Name	Where It Installs	Size	Where It Is Located on the Office 98 CD-ROM	Easy Install?
PowerPoint					
Web Pub. Tools	last.gif	Microsoft Office 98:Office:HTML:Fancy Buttons	2,481	Microsoft Office 98:Office:HTML:Fancy Buttons	Y
Web Pub. Tools	last.gif	Microsoft Office 98:Office:HTML:Classic Buttons	2,442	Microsoft Office 98:Office:HTML:Classic Buttons	Y
Web Pub. Tools	last.gif	Microsoft Office 98:Office:HTML:Regular Buttons	2,412	Microsoft Office 98:Office:HTML:Regular Buttons	Y
Web Pub. Tools	next.gif	Microsoft Office 98:Office:HTML:Fancy Buttons	2,463	Microsoft Office 98:Office:HTML:Fancy Buttons	Y
Web Pub. Tools	next.gif	Microsoft Office 98:Office:HTML:Classic Buttons	2,423	Microsoft Office 98:Office:HTML:Classic Buttons	Y
Web Pub. Tools	next.gif	Microsoft Office 98:Office:HTML:Regular Buttons	2,396	Microsoft Office 98:Office:HTML:Regular Buttons	Y
Web Pub. Tools	Note HTML Template	Microsoft Office 98:Office:HTML	991	Microsoft Office 98:Office:HTML	Y
Web Pub. Tools	pptani.gif	Microsoft Office 98:Office:HTML:Common Components	3,780	Microsoft Office 98:Office:HTML:Common Components	Y
Web Pub. Tools	prev.gif	Microsoft Office 98:Office:HTML:Fancy Buttons	2,456	Microsoft Office 98:Office:HTML:Fancy Buttons	Y
Web Pub. Tools	prev.gif	Microsoft Office 98:Office:HTML:Classic Buttons	2,423	Microsoft Office 98:Office:HTML:Classic Buttons	Y
Web Pub. Tools	prev.gif	Microsoft Office 98:Office:HTML:Regular Buttons	2,392	Microsoft Office 98:Office:HTML:Regular Buttons	Y
Web Pub. Tools	space.gif	Microsoft Office 98:Office:HTML:Common Components	2,300	Microsoft Office 98:Office:HTML:Common Components	Y
Web Pub. Tools	Standard HTML Template	Microsoft Office 98:Office:HTML	1,055	Microsoft Office 98:Office:HTML	Y
Web Pub. Tools	Text html Template	Microsoft Office 98:Office:HTML	1,371	Microsoft Office 98:Office:HTML	Y
Web Pub. Tools	text.gif	Microsoft Office 98:Office:HTML:Classic Buttons	2,435	Microsoft Office 98:Office:HTML:Classic Buttons	Y
Web Pub. Tools	text.gif	Microsoft Office 98:Office:HTML:Regular Buttons	2,408	Microsoft Office 98:Office:HTML:Regular Buttons	Y
Web Pub. Tools	text.gif	Microsoft Office 98:Office:HTML:Fancy Buttons	2,476	Microsoft Office 98:Office:HTML:Fancy Buttons	Y

Component	File Name	Where It Installs	Size	Where It Is Located on the Office 98 CD-ROM	Easy Install?
Proofing Tools					
Grammar	MS English Grammar Dictionary	Microsoft Office 98:Shared Applications:Proofing Tools	1,672,063	Microsoft Office 98:Shared Applications:Proofing Tools	Y
Grammar	MS Grammar	Microsoft Office 98:Shared Applications:Proofing Tools	1,436,450	Microsoft Office 98:Shared Applications:Proofing Tools	Y
Hyphenation	Australian Hyphenation	Microsoft Office 98:Shared Applications:Proofing Tools	164,153	Microsoft Office 98:Shared Applications:Proofing Tools	Y
Hyphenation	English Hyphenation	Microsoft Office 98:Shared Applications:Proofing Tools	164,157	Microsoft Office 98:Shared Applications:Proofing Tools	Y
Hyphenation	Hyphenation	Microsoft Office 98:Shared Applications:Proofing Tools	21,127	Microsoft Office 98:Shared Applications:Proofing Tools	Y
Spelling	Australian Dictionary	Microsoft Office 98:Shared Applications:Proofing Tools	330,289	Microsoft Office 98:Shared Applications:Proofing Tools	Y
Spelling	English Dictionary	Microsoft Office 98:Shared Applications:Proofing Tools	255,191	Microsoft Office 98:Shared Applications:Proofing Tools	Y
Spelling	MS Spelling 2	Microsoft Office 98:Shared Applications:Proofing Tools	166,983	Microsoft Office 98:Shared Applications:Proofing Tools	Y
Thesaurus	MS Thesaurus	Microsoft Office 98:Shared Applications:Proofing Tools	23,601	Microsoft Office 98:Shared Applications:Proofing Tools	Y
Thesaurus	UK English Thesaurus	Microsoft Office 98:Shared Applications:Proofing Tools	354,428	Microsoft Office 98:Shared Applications:Proofing Tools	Y
Thesaurus	US English Thesaurus	Microsoft Office 98:Shared Applications:Proofing Tools	670,008	Microsoft Office 98:Shared Applications:Proofing Tools	Y
Setup	Microsoft Office First Run	Microsoft Office 98:Office	3,717,237	Microsoft Office 98:Office	Y
Text Converters					
Text Conv.	Microsoft Conversion Library	Microsoft Office 98:Office	160,376	Microsoft Office 98:Office	Y
Text Conv.	Microsoft Excel 2.x-8.0	Microsoft Office 98:Shared Applications:Text Converters	147,883	Microsoft Office 98:Shared Applications:Text Converters	Y
Text Conv.	Recover Text Converter	Microsoft Office 98:Shared Applications:Text Converters	26,429	Microsoft Office 98:Shared Applications:Text Converters	Y
Text Conv.	Word 4.x-5.x for the Macintosh	Microsoft Office 98:Shared Applications:Text Converters	181,628	Microsoft Office 98:Shared Applications:Text Converters	Y
Text Conv.	Word 6.0/95 Export	Microsoft Office 98:Shared Applications:Text Converters	2,163,755	Microsoft Office 98:Shared Applications:Text Converters	Y
Text Conv.	Word 6.0/95 Import	Microsoft Office 98:Shared Applications:Text Converters	133,371	Microsoft Office 98:Shared Applications:Text Converters	Y

Component	File Name	Where It Installs	Size	Where It Is Located on the Office 98 CD-ROM	Easy Install?
Text Converters					
Text Conv.	Word 97-98 Import	Microsoft Office 98:Shared Applications:Text Converters	276,969	Microsoft Office 98:Shared Applications:Text Converters	Y
Text Encodings	Arabic Encodings	:System Folder:Text Encodings	27,058	System Files:Text Encodings	Y
Text Encodings	Central European Encodings	:System Folder:Text Encodings	11,493	System Files:Text Encodings	Y
Text Encodings	Chinese Encodings	:System Folder:Text Encodings	251,457	System Files:Text Encodings	Y
Text Encodings	Chinese Encodings	:System Folder:Text Encodings Supplement	127,979	System Files:Text Encodings	Y
Text Encodings	Cyrillic Encodings	:System Folder:Text Encodings	9,857	System Files:Text Encodings	Y
Text Encodings	Greek Encodings	:System Folder:Text Encodings	6,459	System Files:Text Encodings	Y
Text Encodings	Hebrew Encodings	:System Folder:Text Encodings	11,448	System Files:Text Encodings	Y
Text Encodings	Indic Encodings	:System Folder:Text Encodings	16,799	System Files:Text Encodings	Y
Text Encodings	Japanese Encodings	:System Folder:Text Encodings	87,246	System Files:Text Encodings	Y
Text Encodings	Korean Encodings	:System Folder:Text Encodings	100,342	System Files:Text Encodings	Y
Text Encodings	Symbol Encodings	:System Folder:Text Encodings	6,984	System Files:Text Encodings	Y
Text Encodings	Text Encoding Converter	:System Folder:Extensions	178,807	Office Custom Install:Installer Files	
Text Encodings	Thai Encodings	:System Folder:Text Encodings	4,063	System Files:Text Encodings	
Text Encodings	Turkish Encodings	:System Folder:Text Encodings	6,659	System Files:Text Encodings	
Text Encodings	Unicode Encodings	:System Folder:Text Encodings	38,448	System Files:Text Encodings	
Text Encodings	Western Language Encodings	:System Folder:Text Encodings	24,001	System Files:Text Encodings	
Visual Basic for Applications Files					
VBA	VBA Converter (1.0)	Microsoft Office 98:Office	560,944	Microsoft Office 98:Office	Y
VBA	vba en olb (PowerMac) Type Libraries	:System Folder:Extensions:	20,865	System Files:Type Libraries	Y
VBA	VBA Extensibility Library (1)	Microsoft Office 98:Office	29,288	Microsoft Office 98:Office	Y
VBA	VBA Localization Library (1)	Microsoft Office 98:Office	68,853	Microsoft Office 98:Office	Y
VBA	VBA Object Library (1)	Microsoft Office 98:Office	43,372	Microsoft Office 98:Office	Y
VBA	Visual Basic for Applications	Microsoft Office 98:Office	4,323,436	Microsoft Office 98:Office	Y
VBA Help	MS Office VBA AW	Microsoft Office 98:Office:Help	108,463	Microsoft Office 98:Office:Help	
VBA Help	MS Office VBA Editor AW	Microsoft Office 98:Office:Help	112,861	Microsoft Office 98:Office:Help	
VBA Help	MS Office VBA Ref AW	Microsoft Office 98:Office:Help	166,818	Microsoft Office 98:Office:Help	
VBA Help	MS Office VBA Add-in Help	Microsoft Office 98:Office:Help	181,714	Microsoft Office 98:Office:Help	

Component	File Name	Where It Installs	Size	Where It Is Located on the Office 98 CD-ROM	Easy Install?
Visual Basic for Applications Files					
VBA Help	MS Office VBA Core Help	Microsoft Office 98:Office:Help	1,043,048	Microsoft Office 98:Office:Help	
VBA Help	MS Office VBA Definitions Help	Microsoft Office 98:Office:Help	59,315	Microsoft Office 98:Office:Help	
VBA Help	MS Office VBA Editor Help	Microsoft Office 98:Office:Help	234,668	Microsoft Office 98:Office:Help	
VBA Help	MS Office VBA Editor Ref Help	Microsoft Office 98:Office:Help	107,169	Microsoft Office 98:Office:Help	
VBA Help	MS Office VBA Help	Microsoft Office 98:Office:Help	313,477	Microsoft Office 98:Office:Help	
VBA Help	MS Office VBA Ref Help	Microsoft Office 98:Office:Help	46,310	Microsoft Office 98:Office:Help	
Web Queries					
Web Queries	Get More Web Queries	Microsoft Office 98:Office:Queries	94	Microsoft Office 98:Office:Queries	Y
Web Queries	Microsoft Investor Currencies	Microsoft Office 98:Office:Queries	103	Microsoft Office 98:Office:Queries	Y
Web Queries	Microsoft Investor Dow 30	Microsoft Office 98:Office:Queries	171	Microsoft Office 98:Office:Queries	Y
Web Queries	Microsoft Investor Indices	Microsoft Office 98:Office:Queries	115	Microsoft Office 98:Office:Queries	Y
Web Queries	Microsoft Investor Mutual Fund	Microsoft Office 98:Office:Queries	104	Microsoft Office 98:Office:Queries	Y
Web Queries	Microsoft Investor Options	Microsoft Office 98:Office:Queries	95	Microsoft Office 98:Office:Queries	Y
Web Queries	Microsoft Investor Stock Quote	Microsoft Office 98:Office:Queries	123	Microsoft Office 98:Office:Queries	Y
Word					
Program File	Microsoft Word	Microsoft Office 98	5,385,261	Microsoft Office 98	Y
Program File	MS Font Embed Library (PPC)	:System Folder:Extensions	230,559	Office Custom Install:Installer Files	Y
Program File	Word Font Substitutes	:System Folder:Preferences	2,677	Office Custom Install:Installer Files	Y
Border Art	MS Border Art Gallery 1	Microsoft Office 98:Office:Borders	30,006	Microsoft Office 98:Office:Border Art	Y
Border Art	MS Border Art Gallery 10	Microsoft Office 98:Office:Borders	10,721	Microsoft Office 98:Office:Border Art	Y
Border Art	MS Border Art Gallery 11	Microsoft Office 98:Office:Borders	24,256	Microsoft Office 98:Office:Border Art	Y
Border Art	MS Border Art Gallery 12	Microsoft Office 98:Office:Borders	47,840	Microsoft Office 98:Office:Border Art	Y
Border Art	MS Border Art Gallery 13	Microsoft Office 98:Office:Borders	19,217	Microsoft Office 98:Office:Border Art	Y
Border Art	MS Border Art Gallery 14	Microsoft Office 98:Office:Borders	80,256	Microsoft Office 98:Office:Border Art	Y
Border Art	MS Border Art Gallery 15	Microsoft Office 98:Office:Borders	20,534	Microsoft Office 98:Office:Border Art	Y
Border Art	MS Border Art Gallery 2	Microsoft Office 98:Office:Borders	177,985	Microsoft Office 98:Office:Border Art	Y
Border Art	MS Border Art Gallery 3	Microsoft Office 98:Office:Borders	345,691	Microsoft Office 98:Office:Border Art	Y
Border Art	MS Border Art Gallery 4	Microsoft Office 98:Office:Borders	10,117	Microsoft Office 98:Office:Border Art	Y

Component	File Name	Where It Installs	Size	Where It Is Located on the Office 98 CD-ROM	Easy Install?
Word					
Border Art	MS Border Art Gallery 5	Microsoft Office 98:Office:Borders	12,238	Microsoft Office 98:Office:Border Art	Y
Border Art	MS Border Art Gallery 6	Microsoft Office 98:Office:Borders	314,981	Microsoft Office 98:Office:Border Art	Y
Border Art	MS Border Art Gallery 7	Microsoft Office 98:Office:Borders	2,875	Microsoft Office 98:Office:Border Art	Y
Border Art	MS Border Art Gallery 8	Microsoft Office 98:Office:Borders	46,489	Microsoft Office 98:Office:Border Art	Y
Border Art	MS Border Art Gallery 9	Microsoft Office 98:Office:Borders	61,942	Microsoft Office 98:Office:Border Art	Y
Forms Dictionary	English (US) Word Forms	Microsoft Office 98:Shared Applications:Proofing Tools	444,313	Microsoft Office 98:Shared Applications:Proofing Tools	Y
Help	MS Word AW	Microsoft Office 98:Office:Help	605,236	Microsoft Office 98:Office:Help	Y
Help	MS Word Balloon Help	Microsoft Office 98:Office:Help	391,573	Microsoft Office 98:Office:Help	Y
Help	MS Word Help	Microsoft Office 98:Office:Help	1,590,578	Microsoft Office 98:Office:Help	Y
Help	MS Word Readme	Microsoft Office 98:ReadMe	28	Microsoft Office 98:ReadMe	Y
Help	MS Word Upgrade Help	Microsoft Office 98:Office:Help	70,547	Microsoft Office 98:Office:Help	Y
Help	MS Word VBA AW	Microsoft Office 98:Office:Help	468,632	Microsoft Office 98:Office:Help	
Help	MS Word VBA Help	Microsoft Office 98:Office:Help	2,617,779	Microsoft Office 98:Office:Help	
Internet	Blank Web Page	Microsoft Office 98:Templates: Web Pages	98,304	Microsoft Office 98:Templates:Web Pages	Y
Internet	HTML Converter	Microsoft Office 98:Shared Applications:Text Converters	439,965	Microsoft Office 98:Shared Applications: Text Converters	Y
Internet	HTML Library	Microsoft Office 98:Office	774,343	Microsoft Office 98:Office	Y
Internet	More Cool Stuff	Microsoft Office 98:Templates: Web Pages	88,350	Microsoft Office 98:Templates:Web Pages	Y
Internet	View HTML Source	Microsoft Office 98:Office:HTML	37,888	Microsoft Office 98:Office	Y
Internet	Web Page Wizard	Microsoft Office 98:Templates: Web Pages	40,262	Microsoft Office 98:Templates:Web Pages	Y
Internet Bullets	3D Diamond	Microsoft Office 98:Clipart:Bullets	3,261	Microsoft Office 98:Clipart:Bullets	Y
Internet Bullets	Black Dash	Microsoft Office 98:Clipart:Bullets	2,945	Microsoft Office 98:Clipart:Bullets	Y
Internet Bullets	Bullet 1	Microsoft Office 98:Clipart:Bullets	2,792	Microsoft Office 98:Clipart:Bullets	Y
Internet Bullets	Bullet 2	Microsoft Office 98:Clipart:Bullets	2,820	Microsoft Office 98:Clipart:Bullets	Y
Internet Bullets	Bullet 3	Microsoft Office 98:Clipart:Bullets	2,818	Microsoft Office 98:Clipart:Bullets	Y
Internet Bullets	Bullet 4	Microsoft Office 98:Clipart:Bullets	3,550	Microsoft Office 98:Clipart:Bullets	Y
Internet Bullets	Bullet 5	Microsoft Office 98:Clipart:Bullets	2,771	Microsoft Office 98:Clipart:Bullets	Y
Internet Bullets	Bullet 6	Microsoft Office 98:Clipart:Bullets	2,749	Microsoft Office 98:Clipart:Bullets	Y
Internet Bullets	Bullet 7	Microsoft Office 98:Clipart:Bullets	2,810	Microsoft Office 98:Clipart:Bullets	Y

Component	File Name	Where It Installs	Size	Where It Is Located on the Office 98 CD-ROM	Easy Install?
Word					
Internet Bullets	Bullet 8	Microsoft Office 98:Clipart:Bullets	2,874	Microsoft Office 98:Clipart:Bullets	Y
Internet Bullets	Festive	Microsoft Office 98:Clipart:Bullets	3,653	Microsoft Office 98:Clipart:Bullets	Y
Internet Bullets	Green and Black Diamond	Microsoft Office 98:Clipart:Bullets	3,261	Microsoft Office 98:Clipart:Bullets	Y
Internet Bullets	Green Ball	Microsoft Office 98:Clipart:Bullets	2,927	Microsoft Office 98:Clipart:Bullets	Y
Internet Bullets	Metallic Orb	Microsoft Office 98:Clipart:Bullets	3,641	Microsoft Office 98:Clipart:Bullets	Y
Internet Bullets	Pebble	Microsoft Office 98:Clipart:Bullets	3,790	Microsoft Office 98:Clipart:Bullets	Y
Internet Bullets	Red Swirl	Microsoft Office 98:Clipart:Bullets	2,955	Microsoft Office 98:Clipart:Bullets	Y
Internet Bullets	Stained Glass Ball	Microsoft Office 98:Clipart:Bullets	3,653	Microsoft Office 98:Clipart:Bullets	Y
Internet Content	2-Column Layout	Microsoft Office 98:Office:Web Page Templates:Content	26,910	Microsoft Office 98:Office:Web Page Templates:Content	Y
Internet Content	3-Column Layout	Microsoft Office 98:Office:Web Page Templates:Content	22,814	Microsoft Office 98:Office:Web Page Templates:Content	Y
Internet Content	Calendar	Microsoft Office 98:Office:Web Page Templates:Content	27,422	Microsoft Office 98:Office:Web Page Templates:Content	Y
Internet Content	Centered Layout	Microsoft Office 98:Office:Web Page Templates:Content	22,302	Microsoft Office 98:Office:Web Page Templates:Content	Y
Internet Content	Form - Feedback	Microsoft Office 98:Office:Web Page Templates:Content	49,438	Microsoft Office 98:Office:Web Page Templates:Content	Y
Internet Content	Form - Registration	Microsoft Office 98:Office:Web Page Templates:Content	63,774	Microsoft Office 98:Office:Web Page Templates:Content	Y
Internet Content	Form - Survey	Microsoft Office 98:Office:Web Page Templates:Content	51,486	Microsoft Office 98:Office:Web Page Templates:Content	Y
Internet Content	Personal Home Page	Microsoft Office 98:Office:Web Page Templates:Content	29,470	Microsoft Office 98:Office:Web Page Templates:Content	Y
Internet Content	Simple Layout	Microsoft Office 98:Office:Web Page Templates:Content	22,302	Microsoft Office 98:Office:Web Page Templates:Content	Y
Internet Content	Table of Contents	Microsoft Office 98:Office:Web Page Templates:Content	22,302	Microsoft Office 98:Office:Web Page Templates:Content	Y
Internet Help	MS Word HTML AW	Microsoft Office 98:Office:Help	113,130	Microsoft Office 98:Office:Help	Y
Internet Help	MS Word HTML Help	Microsoft Office 98:Office:Help	82,984	Microsoft Office 98:Office:Help	Y
Internet Lines	Autumn Leaves	Microsoft Office 98:Clipart:Lines	9,347	Microsoft Office 98:Clipart:Lines	Y
Internet Lines	Colorful Stone Stripe	Microsoft Office 98:Clipart:Lines	5,465	Microsoft Office 98:Clipart:Lines	Y
Internet Lines	Etched Double Line	Microsoft Office 98:Clipart:Lines	3,478	Microsoft Office 98:Clipart:Lines	Y
Internet Lines	Festive	Microsoft Office 98:Clipart:Lines	6,027	Microsoft Office 98:Clipart:Lines	Y
Internet Lines	Green and Black Stripe	Microsoft Office 98:Clipart:Lines	4,228	Microsoft Office 98:Clipart:Lines	Y

Component	File Name	Where It Installs	Size	Where It Is Located on the Office 98 CD-ROM	Easy Install?
Word					
Internet Lines	Line 1	Microsoft Office 98:Clipart:Lines	2,956	Microsoft Office 98:Clipart:Lines	Y
Internet Lines	Line 2	Microsoft Office 98:Clipart:Lines	3,073	Microsoft Office 98:Clipart:Lines	Y
Internet Lines	Line 3	Microsoft Office 98:Clipart:Lines	4,306	Microsoft Office 98:Clipart:Lines	Y
Internet Lines	Line 4	Microsoft Office 98:Clipart:Lines	5,171	Microsoft Office 98:Clipart:Lines	Y
Internet Lines	Line 5	Microsoft Office 98:Clipart:Lines	3,905	Microsoft Office 98:Clipart:Lines	Y
Internet Lines	Line 6	Microsoft Office 98:Clipart:Lines	3,587	Microsoft Office 98:Clipart:Lines	Y
Internet Lines	Line 7	Microsoft Office 98:Clipart:Lines	3,587	Microsoft Office 98:Clipart:Lines	Y
Internet Lines	Line 8	Microsoft Office 98:Clipart:Lines	4,174	Microsoft Office 98:Clipart:Lines	Y
Internet Lines	Line 9	Microsoft Office 98:Clipart:Lines	4,455	Microsoft Office 98:Clipart:Lines	Y
Internet Lines	Neighborhood	Microsoft Office 98:Clipart:Lines	5,490	Microsoft Office 98:Clipart:Lines	Y
Internet Lines	Orange Spheres	Microsoft Office 98:Clipart:Lines	3,587	Microsoft Office 98:Clipart:Lines	Y
Internet Lines	Over Under	Microsoft Office 98:Clipart:Lines	4,362	Microsoft Office 98:Clipart:Lines	Y
Internet Lines	Row of Pebbles	Microsoft Office 98:Clipart:Lines	10,751	Microsoft Office 98:Clipart:Lines	Y
Internet Lines	Stained Glass Line	Microsoft Office 98:Clipart:Lines	6,027	Microsoft Office 98:Clipart:Lines	Y
Internet Styles	Brick Wall	Microsoft Office 98:Office:Web Page Templates:Styles	29,480	Microsoft Office 98:Office:Web Page Templates:Styles	Y
Internet Styles	Club Deco	Microsoft Office 98:Office:Web Page Templates:Styles	6,797	Microsoft Office 98:Office:Web Page Templates:Styles	Y
Internet Styles	Community	Microsoft Office 98:Office:Web Page Templates:Styles	26,112	Microsoft Office 98:Office:Web Page Templates:Styles	Y
Internet Styles	Contemporary	Microsoft Office 98:Office:Web Page Templates:Styles	24,576	Microsoft Office 98:Office:Web Page Templates:Styles	Y
Internet Styles	Elegant	Microsoft Office 98:Office:Web Page Templates:Styles	24,576	Microsoft Office 98:Office:Web Page Templates:Styles	Y
Internet Styles	Fancy Green Patterns	Microsoft Office 98:Office:Web Page Templates:Styles	9,830	Microsoft Office 98:Office:Web Page Templates:Styles	Y
Internet Styles	Festive	Microsoft Office 98:Office:Web Page Templates:Styles	27,648	Microsoft Office 98:Office:Web Page Templates:Styles	Y
Internet Styles	Granite Edifice	Microsoft Office 98:Office:Web Page Templates:Styles	26,168	Microsoft Office 98:Office:Web Page Templates:Styles	Y
Internet Styles	Harvest	Microsoft Office 98:Office:Web Page Templates:Styles	28,672	Microsoft Office 98:Office:Web Page Templates:Styles	Y
Internet Styles	Jazzy	Microsoft Office 98:Office:Web Page Templates:Styles	25,088	Microsoft Office 98:Office:Web Page Templates:Styles	Y
Internet Styles	Leaves on the Side	Microsoft Office 98:Office:Web Page Templates:Styles	13,032	Microsoft Office 98:Office:Web Page Templates:Styles	Y

Component	File Name	Where It Installs	Size	Where It Is Located on the Office 98 CD-ROM	Easy Install?
Word					
Internet Styles	Off Yellow Bookcover	Microsoft Office 98:Office:Web Page Templates:Styles	7,836	Microsoft Office 98:Office:Web Page Templates:Styles	Y
Internet Styles	Outdoors	Microsoft Office 98:Office:Web Page Templates:Styles	27,648	Microsoft Office 98:Office:Web Page Templates:Styles	Y
Internet Styles	Professional	Microsoft Office 98:Office:Web Page Templates:Styles	27,136	Microsoft Office 98:Office:Web Page Templates:Styles	Y
Internet Styles	Stained Glass on Side	Microsoft Office 98:Office:Web Page Templates:Styles	6,242	Microsoft Office 98:Office:Web Page Templates:Styles	Y
Internet Styles	Wheat	Microsoft Office 98:Office:Web Page Templates:Styles	3,632	Microsoft Office 98:Office:Web Page Templates:Styles	Y
Templs: Faxes	Contemporary Fax	Microsoft Office 98:Templates: Letters & Faxes	57,630	Microsoft Office 98:Templates: Letters & Faxes	Y
Templs: Faxes	Elegant Fax	Microsoft Office 98:Templates: Letters & Faxes	57,630	Microsoft Office 98:Templates: Text	Y
Templs: Faxes	Fax Wizard	Microsoft Office 98:Templates: Letters & Faxes	663,838	Microsoft Office 98:Templates: Letters & Faxes	Y
Templs: Faxes	Professional Fax	Microsoft Office 98:Templates: Letters & Faxes	54,558	Microsoft Office 98:Templates: Letters & Faxes	Y
Templs: Letters	Contemporary Letter	Microsoft Office 98:Templates: Letters & Faxes	70,430	Microsoft Office 98:Templates: Letters & Faxes	Y
Templs: Letters	Elegant Letter	Microsoft Office 98:Templates: Letters & Faxes	56,094	Microsoft Office 98:Templates: Letters & Faxes	Y
Templs: Letters	Letter Wizard	Microsoft Office 98:Templates: Letters & Faxes	80,670	Microsoft Office 98:Templates:Letters & Faxes	Y
Templs: Letters	Professional Letter	Microsoft Office 98:Templates: Letters & Faxes	55,070	Microsoft Office 98:Templates:Letters & Faxes	Y
Templs: Memos	Contemporary Memo	Microsoft Office 98:Templates: Memos	45,854	Microsoft Office 98:Templates:Memos	Y
Templs: Memos	Elegant Memo	Microsoft Office 98:Templates: Memos	49,950	Microsoft Office 98:Templates:Memos	Y
Templs: Memos	Memo Wizard	Microsoft Office 98:Templates: Memos	450,334	Microsoft Office 98:Templates:Memos	Y
Templs: Memos	Professional Memo	Microsoft Office 98:Templates: Memos	47,902	Microsoft Office 98:Templates:Memos	Y
Templs: More Wizards	Envelope Wizard	Microsoft Office 98:Templates: Letters & Faxes	71,454	Microsoft Office 98:Templates:Letters & Faxes	Y

App C

Component	File Name	Where It Installs	Size	Where It Is Located on the Office 98 CD-ROM	Easy Install?
Word					
Templs: More Wizards	Mailing Label Wizard	Microsoft Office 98:Templates: Letters & Faxes	72,478	Microsoft Office 98:Templates: Letters & Faxes	Y
Templs: More Wizards	More Wizards and Templates	Microsoft Office 98:Templates: Other Documents	89,886	Microsoft Office 98:Templates:Other Documents	Y
Templs: More Wizards	Legal Pleading Wizard	Microsoft Office 98:Templates: Legal Pleadings	740,638	Microsoft Office 98:Templates: Legal Pleadings	Y
Templs: Newsletters	Newsletter Wizard	Microsoft Office 98:Templates: Publications	531,230	Microsoft Office 98:Templates: Publications	Y
Templs: Reports	Contemporary Report	Microsoft Office 98:Templates: Other Documents	83,230	Microsoft Office 98:Templates:Other Documents	Y
Templs: Resumes	Contemporary Resume	Microsoft Office 98:Templates: Other Documents	57,630	Microsoft Office 98:Templates:Other Documents	Y
Templs: Resumes	Elegant Resume	Microsoft Office 98:Templates: Other Documents	52,510	Microsoft Office 98:Templates:Other Documents	Y
Templs: Resumes	Professional Resume	Microsoft Office 98:Templates: Other Documents	53,534	Microsoft Office 98:Templates:Other Documents	Y
Templs: Resumes	Resume Wizard	Microsoft Office 98:Templates: Other Documents	562,974	Microsoft Office 98:Templates:Other Documents	Y

Index

A

D

E

G

I

J-K

L

M

O

P

Q

R

S

T

U

V

W

X-Y

Z

Use the refinancing calculator to see if refinancing makes sense	Compute monthly payments and final payment for balloon mortgage
Amortize a loan; calculate a biweekly mortgage; determine housing affordability	Understand your personal safety debt ratio

The Ultimate Financial Calculator is $59.95 and is available for both Excel 95 and Excel 97. As a Macmillan reader the product is available for $49.95. Check out the KMT bonus pack for even greater savings!.

Personal Financial Primer

Use the power of Microsoft Excel to better maximize your personal financial goals. The Personal Financial Primer guides you each step of the way. Select a topic like Personal Net Worth, Retirement Planning, 401 K Planning, or College Savings, and the Primer defines each topic for you clearly -- you just enter the data in the predefined area. The Personal Financial Primer prepares summary worksheets based on your data entry and charts your financial progress. With the primer, you will be able to plan your financial future by better understanding the following:

- Personal Data and Goals
- Personal Financial Statements
- Cash Flow Plan
- Retirement Plan
- 401 K Analysis
- Invested Asset Allocation
- Life Insurance Needs
- Disability Insurance Needs
- College Funding Needs

Valued at $39.95 . . . . . Special Price for Macmillan readers $29.95. Check out the KMT bonus pack for even greater savings!

Special Order Form for Additional KMT Products

To order additional KMT products directly from KMT Software, Inc., print out this form, fill it in and:

Fax it to 978-287-0132
Mail it to KMT Software, Inc., 71 Lee Dr., Concord, MA 01742.
E-mail to sales@kmt.com
To order by phone call 1-800-KMT-CALC (568-2252) (Orders only). International call 1-978-287-4125

Name __________

Address __________

City, State, Zip __________

Telephone __________

Email __________

Office 97 ☐ Office 2000 ☐ Other __________

Credit Card ☐ Visa ☐ MasterCard ☐ Check Enclosed ☐

Credit Card # __________ Expiration Date __________

Product Name and Description	Regular List	Book Special	Quantity	Total
Special Office in Color Template Collections				
Office in Color Platinum Edition *(Over 650 templates)*	$99.95	$49.95		
Task Based Applications				
Winning Business Plans in Color	$129.95	$79.95		
Ultimate Financial Calculator	$59.95	$49.95		
Personal Financial Primer	$39.95	$29.95		
KMT Bonus Pack: special price on the 3 above products	$229.95	$99.95		
Microsoft Excel 97 Template Master Toolkit (call for info)	$149.95	$129.95		

Mail in Your Order:	**KMT Software, Inc.**	**Subtotal**	
	71 Lee Drive,	5% Sales tax (MA only)	
	Concord, MA 01742	*Add an additional $5.00 for FedEx shipping*	
Fax in Your Order:	978-287-0132	Shipping ($12 outside USA)........	$7.00
Call in Your Order:	**800-568-2252**. 978-371-2052, Outside USA	**TOTAL in $US**	
KMT on the Web:	http://www.kmt.com		

Unconditional Money back guarantee

Don't forget to ask about how our expert consulting on Microsoft Office can help your organization!

The demo is found on the CD-ROM in the 3rdParty\VirusAlt directory.

Special Rebate Offer
$ 5.00 US

Highlighted Features

1. *Real time macro virus protection*
2. *Cleaning (Automatic)*
3. *Scan documents & files on opening*
4. *Scan documents & files by association*
5. *Scan documents & files on demand*
6. *Scan Network drives*
7. *Generate Log Reports*
8. *Embedded in Microsoft Word*
9. *Heuristic Scanning (unknown macro viruses)*
10. *FREE signature file updates for registered users*

LOOK Software Systems Inc.
http://www.look.com
sales@look.com

Virus ALERT for Macros

(Microsoft Office97 Edition)

What is a Macro Virus?

A macro virus is a type of destructive 'program' that infects Microsoft® Word® documents and templates. Their effects vary from minor inconvenience to major system damage and data loss. Macro viruses are very difficult to detect and safely remove. Competitive anti virus software's are designed to use standard virus detection and removal techniques which are not effective against non-standard viruses like the macro virus family - their unique nature demands a unique solution.

The *first* Word in Macro Virus Detection

VIRUS ALERT *for* Macros™ has been designed to address the unique nature of Microsoft Word macro viruses in an innovative way which allows it to achieve levels of detection accuracy, cleaning and user friendliness that cannot be matched by standard anti-virus utilities.

The Key - Integration

VIRUS ALERT *for* Macros™ achieves its' superior results by installing completely and seamlessly *into* Microsoft® Word 97. *Effectively* VIRUS ALERT *for* Macros™ becomes part of Microsoft® Word®. This results in truly accurate macro virus protection during normal Word operation.

Documents and templates are automatically scanned when opened. No manual commands are required - *it protects as you use* Microsoft® Word®.

Remove the Virus Keep the Document

VIRUS ALERT *for* Macros™ uses a *safe macro virus cleaning* technique which removes only the viral macros from an infected file, without corrupting the file or removing legitimate macros. VIRUS ALERT *for* Macros™ leaves the document, text and all other contents fully intact - as if they were never infected.

FREE Signature Upgrades and Technical Support

All registered users of VIRUS ALERT™ products receive ***FREE*** virus signature updates, down-loadable from our World Wide Web site at 'www.look.com', as well as ***FREE*** technical support via our toll free number, email and website. * *some restrictions may apply.*

Pricing

Single User	$ 29.95 US
Corp 5 Pack	$ 89.00 US
Corp10 Pack	$189.00 US
Corp25 Pack	$297.50 US

License Agreement

This package contains one CD-ROM that includes some of the software described in this book, as well as a number of other related software products. See the CD-ROM for a description of these programs.

By opening this package you agree to be bound by the following:

This software is copyrighted and all rights are reserved by the publisher and its licensers. You are licensed to use this software on a single computer. You may copy the software for backup or archival purposes only. Making copies of the software for any other purpose is a violation of United States copyright laws. THIS SOFTWARE IS SOLD AS IS, WITHOUT WARRANTY OF ANY KIND, EITHER EXPRESS OR IMPLIED, INCLUDING BUT NOT LIMITED TO THE IMPLIED WARRANTIES OF MERCHANTABILITY AND FITNESS FOR A PARTICULAR PURPOSE. Neither the publisher nor its licensers, dealers, or distributors assumes any liability for any alleged or actual damages arising from the use of this software. (Some states do not allow exclusion of implied warranties, so the exclusion may not apply to you.)

The entire contents of this disc and the compilation of the software are copyrighted and protected by United States copyright laws. The individual programs on this disc are copyrighted by the authors or owners of each program. Each program has its own use permissions and limitations. To use each program, you must follow the individual requirements and restrictions detailed for each. Do not use a program if you do not agree to follow its licensing agreement.